INSIDE COVERS ABBREVIATIONS AND SYMBOLS
English, French, German, Italian, Spanish

4 DISCOUNT SCHEME

5 FOREW
A letter from

10 PREF

16 PERCENTA
The AA introduces a new syste

24 BEST NEWCOMER
Featuring the best of the rece
and restaurants

35 BRITAIN'S TOP HOTELS
A complete list of hotels which have been awarded red stars

41 HOW WE CLASSIFY HOTELS
An explanation of the AA's classification and awards system

45 SOME POINTS TO REMEMBER
Helpful advice on reservations, licensing laws, complaints, etc.

49 BRITAIN'S TOP RESTAURANTS
A complete list of restaurants with Rosette awards

52 HOW TO USE THIS GUIDE
An explanation of a sample gazetteer entry

55 GAZETTEER OF HOTELS AND RESTAURANTS
A – Z directory, by location, of hotels and restaurants

407 LONDON HOTELS AND RESTAURANTS
including an alphabetical index of establishments and street plans

735 COUNTRY HOUSE HOTELS
Hotels offering a friendly, peaceful atmosphere, usually, but not always, in a rural location

738 AA LODGES
Hotels near motorways and major roads offering reliable, reasonably priced rooms

741 HOTEL GROUPS
A key to abbreviations used in the gazetteer, and a list of central reservation telephone numbers

742 OVERSEAS OFFICES OF THE BRITISH TOURIST AUTHORITY

743 INDEX OF TOWN PLANS
Street maps of major towns and cities showing locations

793 LOCATION ATLAS

Owners of the 1990 edition of the Hotel and Restaurant Guide may claim a 10 per cent discount off their room bill at more than 900 of the hotels listed in the gazetteer. The hotels which have agreed to participate in this scheme display the (£) symbol at the end of their gazetteer entry.

In order to take advantage of the discount, guests *must* remember to present their copy of the 1990 Hotel and Restaurant Guide at reception when *checking in*. If you do not do so, the hotel may legitimately refuse to give you the discount when you come to check out. This is very important, because many hotel accounts are now computerised and it may cause difficulties and delays if the account has to be adjusted at the last minute.

The discount only applies to the full-tariff room rate, and does *not* apply if you are already benefitting from any other form of discount or a special bargain rate.

The discount is off the room rate and may not be claimed for restaurant or bar meals or drinks. In the case of a joint booking for a group of individuals, the discount would only apply to the person who presents the guide on checking in, *not* to the entire party.

If two persons are sharing a double room, however, at the full tariff rate, the discount would apply to the double room.

Please note that the discount may *only* be claimed at the hotels which display the (£) symbol at the end of their gazetteer entry, and that the bill must be settled before you leave the hotel. The discount is not applicable to company accounts.

THE AA/SHELL GUIDE TO HOTELS AND RESTAURANTS

An introduction from
Roy Reynolds, Managing Director, Shell UK Oil.

I am pleased to be able to join with the Automobile Association in sponsoring the AA/Shell Guide to Hotels and Restaurants.

Both our organisations have long associations with motoring.

It seems there has always been a time when the highways and by-ways of Britain have featured AA services and that Shell service stations could be relied upon to be around nearly every corner.

But more than this. Both Shell and the AA have also been successful in promoting the variety and excellence of the British landscape, its towns and villages, its houses, its curiosities, its wildlife and its people. We like to think that by encouraging the motorist to look around him, we have also raised an appreciation of the freedom and the pleasures that motoring can bring.

It is a heritage of which we, in particular, are proud. And it goes back a long way. The first Shell guides to the regions of Britain were edited by John Betjeman and made their appearance in 1934. We have been producing them ever since.

It seems therefore the most natural thing in the world that we and the AA should find ourselves touching shoulders in this popular guide to all that is good in living and eating away from home.

For both our organisations, it continues to show our total commitment to you the motorist and your needs.

Roy Reynolds

THE SHELL GU

1948

1955

1961

1971

1930

1904

1900

SHELL started business as the Shell Transport and Trading Company, dealing with Victorian bric-a-brac, antiques and shells.

Then the company began transporting kerosene as a replacement for whale oil, and later petrol from Romania and Indonesia.

(An interesting illustrated booklet on the history of the Royal Dutch Shell group of companies is available from Marketing Communications UOMC/O, Shell UK Oil, Shell-Mex House, Strand, London WC2.)

Marcus Samuel Junior

Shell has marketed fuels and oils in Britain since the turn of the century, but the most well-known Shell company, Shell-Mex & BP, was formed in 1931.

It established offices in the Strand next to the Savoy on the site of the Cecil Hotel. These offices, Shell-Mex House, are now the headquarters of Shell UK. The "Mex" in the name comes from the Mexican Eagle Oil Company, which Shell began to manage in 1919.

Y O U   C A N   B E   S

DE TO SHELL.

Shell-Mex House is a striking example of 1930s Art Deco, with statues carved by Eric Gill on either side of the largest clock face in London.

Shell and BP formed a joint marketing operation to compete with the new American companies such as Rockefeller's Standard Oil Company (Esso). This continued until 1975.

A striking feature of this partnership was its focus on the pleasures of motoring. Posters and lorry bills were commissioned from some of the up and coming artistic talent of the day, including the young Graham Sutherland, Rex Whistler, Tristam Hillier and many more.

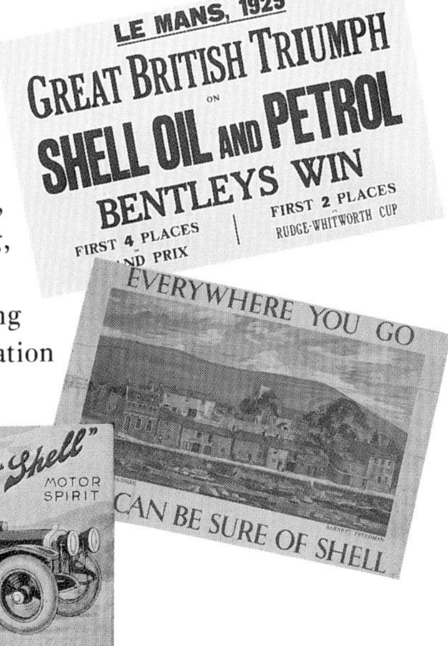

It was at this time that one of the most famous advertising slogans in history was born. "Everywhere you go, you can be sure of Shell" is still in use today.

Back in the Britain of the 1930s, motoring journeys were seen as exciting, pleasurable and liberating.

Shell played its part with a growing network of "garages," encouraging the exploration of the towns and countryside of Britain.

The first Shell Guides produced by John Betjeman were designed to widen the horizons of the new motorist.

E OF SHELL

(First editions are becoming collectors' items, so keep a look out in second-hand bookshops.)

Title after title followed. Some, such as "The Shell Pilot's Guides to the English Channel," are now in their 51st year and are an essential feature of nearly every Channel sailor's chart locker.

As oil consumption grew so did Shell's UK operations. In the 1960s Shell found gas in the southern North Sea, and, a few years later, oil in the waters off Dundee. In the 1970s more oil was discovered in the inhospitable waters to the north of the Shetlands.

Here Shell UK runs 13 platforms, each nearly 1000 feet high and designed to withstand 100 foot waves.

Oil fields in these cold deep waters, often more than 200 miles from land, now produce the equivalent of Britain's total oil demand.

There's an oilman's saying that oil is where you find it: from the North Sea seabed to the deserts of Saudi Arabia. Oil is therefore an international commodity, bought and sold in dollars on the world's markets.

A country's exchange rate affects the price, but it is mainly determined by international supply and demand.

Not surprisingly, transport fuels always attract the attention of the taxman.

Our Chancellor is no exception. His tax take on Shell fuels in 1988 was £1·4 billion (and that does not include the VAT.)

Today's cars are more demanding. So the technology behind Shell's leading oil, Gemini, is tested under the most arduous conditions – the World Champion Formula One Marlboro Honda McLaren racing cars.

Petrol is changing too. Shell's Advanced petrols (both leaded and unleaded) contain detergents that clean the fuel inlet systems of the car, maintaining performance and helping

YOU CAN BE S

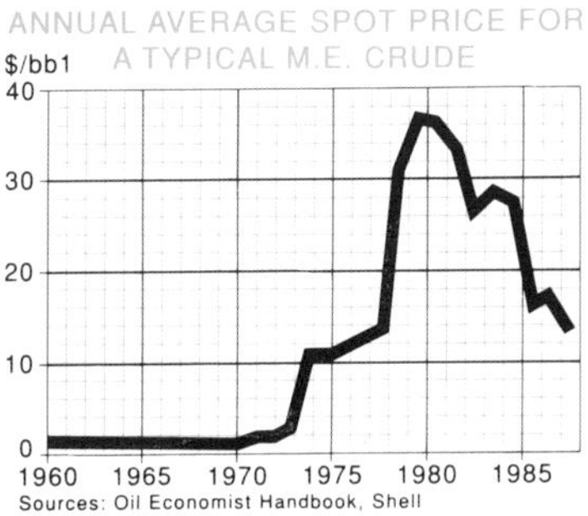

to reduce carbon monoxide emissions. Shell Advanced diesel has similar properties.

We even add a perfume to improve the smell of diesel, together with an anti-foaming agent that helps stop splash-back when filling up.

You can always be sure that the products you use are indeed Shell products.

ANNUAL AVERAGE SPOT PRICE FOR A TYPICAL M.E. CRUDE

$/bb1

Y axis	0, 10, 20, 30, 40
X axis	1960, 1965, 1970, 1975, 1980, 1985

Sources: Oil Economist Handbook, Shell

You see, although the oil industry has exchanged raw petrol for many years, Shell petrol is different. The compounds that keep Shell fuels out in front are only added at Shell's own terminals. So only Shell petrols and diesels are Advanced.

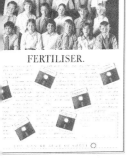

)R BUDDING SCIENTISTS,

Oil and petrol will continue to be the major fuels of the world's transport systems for years to come.

But as environmental concerns loom larger, we will change to unleaded fuel, employ catalytic converters to reduce exhaust emissions, use smaller more efficient engines to cut down on carbon dioxide and develop new petrols to improve performance in today's engines.

Caring for the motorist will always be of the utmost importance to Shell.

Our network of stations throughout Britain is continually being improved.

Shell Traveller's Checks feature telephones, clean loos, hot drinks, snacks and many basic chemists' goods.

''Everywhere you go you can be sure of Shell'' is as demanding a commitment today as it was nearly 60 years ago.

E OF SHELL

PREFACE

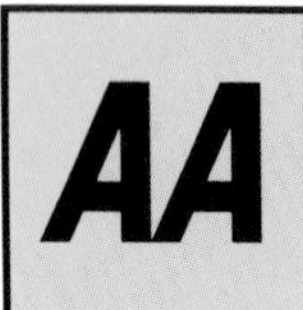

The AA's system of classifying hotels using the now famous star ratings is the most widely known and most often used by UK hotel guests when selecting a hotel to stay in.

It was first introduced in 1909 when there was little information available to the travelling motorist. Over the years the scheme has been modified, developed and refined to ensure that hotels appointed provide the facilities and services required by today's travellers.

The purpose of this guide is to provide comprehensive and accurate information on more than 4,000 hotels and restaurants that are currently recognised by the AA. You can expect to find the usual meticulous research associated with an AA publication and you can be assured that the establishments featured have undergone rigorous inspections to ensure that they meet our exacting standards.

This year we have introduced a major change in the way we present information about each hotel that we are confident will be of great benefit to our readers. You will find that each 3, 4 and 5 Star hotel featured has been given a percentage score shown alongside the star classification awarded. This score is designed to help you choose the right hotel by enabling you to compare the relative merits of hotels within the same star classification level.

Stars are, of course, a guarantee that the hotel concerned is meeting the minimum level of services, facilities, and hospitality expected. However, on their own they do not tell you if there is any significant difference in the overall quality of operation at one hotel compared with another in the same star classification. Regular hotel users will appreciate that even within star levels, standards do vary. All will meet the minimum requirements for classification but whilst some will provide modest, simple and functional levels of facilities and services others will offer higher standards and perhaps a more extensive range of facilities and services. We feel it is essential that we reflect this variance.

The new percentage score, combined with the existing AA star classification, gives you more information upon which to base your choice of hotel. You can, for example, expect a hotel scoring more than 70% to provide a significantly higher standard of services and facilities than a hotel of the same star rating scoring 55%. You should remember, however, that the hotel with the lower percentage is not a sub standard hotel. Though certainly more modest, it still offers acceptable standards.

We believe that as well as enabling a comparison of standards, the percentage system, when considered with price, offers the opportunity to make a 'value-for-money' judgement. Taking the previous example you may well prefer to stay in the modest 55% hotel if the tariff charged is substantially less than that of the 70% hotel.

Additionally, percentage scores may well offer guidance in choosing between two hotels of different star ratings. A 3 Star 79% hotel could, in this case, be considered preferable to a 4 Star 57% hotel.

In practice you will find there are no hotels featured with a percentage score of less than 50%. Our method of arriving at the appropriate score is very detailed and hotels scoring less than half marks are generally not of sufficient standard to be classified and awarded a star rating. Equally, hotels scoring in excess of 80% will be considered for the AA's ultimate accolade of being awarded Red Stars. In this guide Red Star hotels are shown as a boxed entry and in such cases, because they are the best in their category, percentages are not shown.

Applying percentage scores to 3, 4 and 5 Star hotels is just the first step and in future years we intend to ensure that all AA appointed hotels are given a percentage assessment.

It was market research that highlighted the need to provide more extensive information on the standards offered by hotels, and the same research has been instrumental in identifying changes needed in the criteria used to assess star rating. We consider it essential to establish what guests expect from hotels at each star level, and we see our role as representing AA members and consumers when encouraging the hotel industry. We also believe this to be in the wider interest of tourism generally.

During the first six months of 1989 we had extensive discussion with the British Hotels, Restaurants, and Caterers Association to agree to a new set of criteria for the 1990s. Details of our new requirements were announced to the industry in July 1989 and implementation in full should be complete by 1 January 1992.

I mentioned earlier 'value for money' in the context of the percentage scores awarded to hotels. It is a concept we constantly seek to apply to this guide and accordingly we have this year introduced a discount scheme in which we are glad to report over 800 of our hotels are participating. Ensure that you carry your copy of this guide with you when staying at one of our hotels – it could mean a 10% reduction in your room tariff. Further details on the operation of the scheme are given in full on page 4.

Over the past year we have again paid close attention to the award of our prestigious Red Stars and Rosettes. It is not always appreciated that these accolades are awarded annually and that they automatically lapse when there is a change of ownership or, in the case of rosettes, when the chef who achieved the award leaves. Our view is that the new proprietor or chef must themselves prove worthy of such an award, it cannot be inherited or bought with the establishment.

According to Dr Samuel Johnson, 'a characteristic of an English Inn was the welcome it accorded to its guests – the more noise they made, the more trouble they gave and the more good things they called for, the more welcome they were'. Though AA appointed hotels of today are a far cry from the coaching inns of centuries past, the emphasis remains on hospitality. Clean accommodation, good food and drink are of course fundamental, but it is the combination of quality, personal service and attention to detail that are the hallmarks of a fine hotel.

Only the very best hotels qualify for AA appointment. The criteria we set for classification are strict and our inspections are thorough. We place emphasis on quality and are therefore confident that the establishments featured in this guide will meet your requirements. Should this not be the case we would be pleased to hear from you.

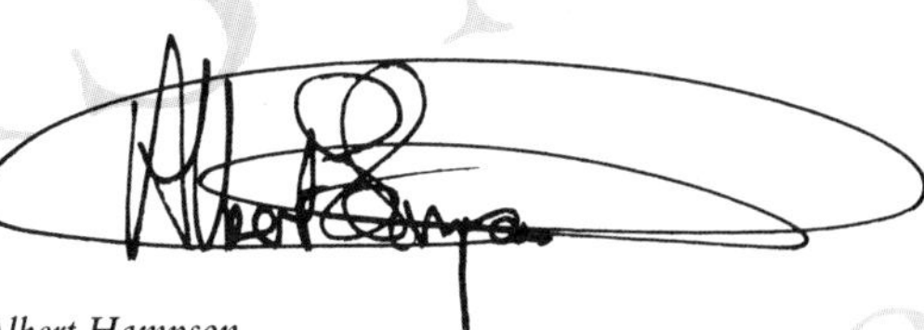

Albert Hampson
Manager, Hotel Services

THE WESTBURY, LONDON.

Ringed by Mayfair's quality jewellers, boutiques and art galleries, the Westbury has strong sporting links, particularly in the world of polo and tennis.

The original Westbury Hotel on Madison Avenue was named after the Long Island polo ground.

The Polo Restaurant is in the inspirational hands of the Trusthouse Forte Hotels Chef of the Year.

Not surprisingly, the depth of the wine list is matched by the width and imagination of the modern French menu.

Previously a 15th-century Manor House, now renovated with tact and care. The Shires Restaurant is in a fully restored 17th century barn with a wealth of exposed beams and Minstrel gallery: a superb setting to enjoy the best of cuisine.

Alongside the Stour, in some of Kent's most picturesque countryside, Ashford is the perfect location for meetings, just by the M20.

THE POST HOUSE, ASHFORD

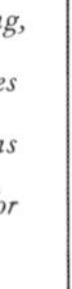

This elegant Georgian building, noted for its fine architecture, dates from the days when the town was a fashionable resort famous for its medical spas.

Originally six private residences dating from 1723, The Francis has retained all the splendour of that gracious era within its spacious well-proportioned rooms decorated in the classical manner to reflect the luxurious style of the 18th century. The hotel makes an ideal touring base for business in Somerset.

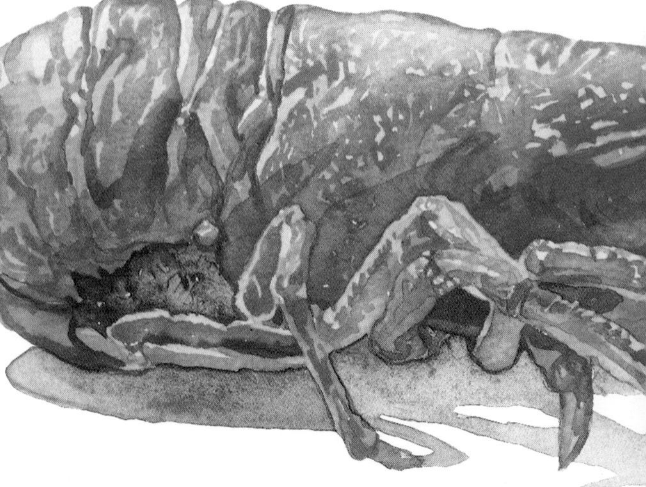

THE FRANCIS, BATH.

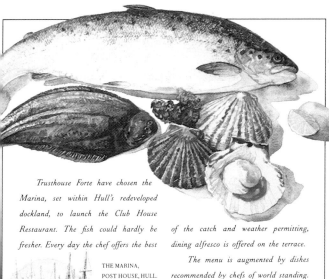

AILY
2½d
SKETCH
TUESDAY, NOVEMBER 17, 1959
The paper that looks after you
TOP COPS
PICTURES PAGE 8
SLAM M1
New Motorway One
"unsatisfactory"
say 5 police chiefs.
The people who read US
Figures released to-day by the Institute of Practitioners in Advertising showing who reads which newspapers, reveal that the Daily Sketch has again increased its readership. It shows that there are over 4½ million people now reading the Daily Sketch. The big increase has been with young people—a leap of 205,000.
With 40.7% of its readers under 34, the Daily Sketch now has a higher proportion of its readers in the young age group than any other national morning paper.
BRITAIN'S new high speed London to Birmingham road has been slammed as a disgrace by FIVE constables whose forces cover its route.
By NICK PRIMMER
Lucky dog! Five flavoured mixed ovals
NEW PET SHOP SCANDAL
SEE PAGE 6

Percentage Rating

%

In this edition of the Hotel and Restaurant Guide the AA introduces a new assessment scheme. Hotels are awarded a percentage score, within their particular star classification, based on *quality*. For this year, the quality assessment has been applied to all three, four and five star hotels; after 1990 it will also apply to all one and two star hotels. The percentage scores, printed in red immediately after the stars, are an indication of where each hotel stands in comparison to others within the same star classification. Hotels have been assessed for quality under a number of broad headings: hospitality, cleanliness, services, food, bedrooms, overall impression and the Inspector's personal view. Marks are awarded in each of these categories in order to arrive at a percentage score. All hotels recognised by the AA may be expected to score at least 50 per cent, and a score of around 61 per cent is considered to be the average benchmark.

Castle and Ball, Marlborough

Users of the Guide can now compare all the three, or four or five star hotels we list in any given town, to see which scores the highest percentage: for example there could be four three-star hotels of which Hotel A may have 69 per cent, Hotel B, 63 percent, Hotel C, 59 per cent and Hotel D, 72 per cent.

Hotel B (63 per cent) will be a sound three-star hotel, where the bedrooms will be well equipped, most, if not all, with en-suite bathrooms, the public areas well furnished, and the restaurant will offer a full meals service.

Mansion House, Poole

Hotel C (59 per cent) will meet all the basic requirements for three stars, but standards of decor, service or comfort may not be quite as high, or perhaps it is impersonal and offers no extra little touches. On the other hand, Hotels A (69 per cent) and D (72 per cent) will have many extra touches, above what is normally required of an AA three-star hotel. The standard of hospitality is likely to be high, bedrooms may be prettier or more comfortable (or both), the bathrooms could have quality fixtures and fittings, public areas are likely to be especially pleasant and comfortable, and the cuisine better than average. In other words, Hotels A and D will show the signs of personal attention to their guests' well-being that lift them out of the ordinary.

Castle and Ball, Marlborough

Mansion House, Poole

Castle and Ball, Marlborough

Mansion House, Poole

Please remember that a high percentage score within a star classification does *not* necessarily mean that there are more facilities and services than at another hotel with a lower score. What it does mean however is that the standard of services and facilities it offers is better. In short the overall standard and quality of the hotel will be higher as the percentage awarded increases.

It may be that Hotels B (63 per cent) and C (59 per cent) are less expensive than Hotels A (69 per cent) and D (72 per cent); so if price is a consideration these may be preferable; on the other hand, Hotels B and C may in fact be more expensive than A or D, in which case, the percentage rating is a clear guide to value for money.

A small number of hotels have reached such a standard of excellence that they have been awarded *red stars* – the AA's highest accolade – and no percentages are given for this select category as they are judged to be the *very best* in their star classification, and therefore outside the scope of the percentage scheme. For a full list of the *red-star* hotels, see page 35.

A straightforward comparison of two hotels, the Castle and Ball at Marlborough, rated 64 per cent and the Mansion House at Poole, rated 75 per cent, will show the differences one might expect to find in the three-star range. The difference in price, incidentally, for dinner, bed and breakfast, was insignificant.

Both hotels are old buildings of considerable character and charm, both at the centre of small towns. The Castle and Ball is an old coaching inn and stands in Marlborough's attractive High Street; the Mansion House is in a quiet street off Poole's old harbour.

My letter to the Castle and Ball was answered by a telephone call asking me to confirm that I would indeed be arriving that day The Mansion House wrote a welcoming letter of confirmation of all the details. Reception at both hotels was efficient and correct. At the Castle and Ball no help was offered with luggage (though if I had asked, it would probably have have been forthcoming) and I found my own way to the bedroom; at the Mansion House I was taken up to the room and everything was explained. Both bedrooms were of good size and both were fully equipped, with a good range of toiletries in the bathroom, a shower over the bath (better at the Castle and Ball than at the Mansion House). At the Castle and Ball amenities included a hairdryer and trouser press, radio and television, tea and coffee-making facilities; at the Mansion House, where a cup of tea or other refreshment was also offered when I was shown to my room, there were a sewing kit, clothes brush, fresh fruit, sweets, iced water and a complementary glass of sherry.

The furnishings at the Castle and Ball were generally good, but the single easy chair was not comfortable, and there was no chair at the desk/ dressing-table. At the Mansion House, the room was furnished in keeping with the 18th-century period of the building, there were two comfortable easy chairs, a writing table and chair and an occasional table. The beds at both hotels were very comfortable and the rooms at both were well-kept and clean.

I had booked a table for dinner at both hotels. At the Castle and Ball there is a public bar and a lounge bar for residents, but drinks must be fetched from the public bar. I asked for a menu and took it into the lounge bar where several couples were also studying menus. Here I think I must make a small criticism of the otherwise efficient Castle and Ball. Although restaurant staff came in to take orders for dinner, I, as a single woman, was ignored until I went into reception to complain. Thereafter, service was prompt and efficient, rather than friendly. The food in the restaurant was well served, but the end of the meal was slightly spoilt as all around

Castle and Ball, Marlborough

me the staff were making ready tables for breakfast as I drank my coffee. At the Mansion House the dining room is very elegant and the staff courteous and welcoming. They give the impression of knowing who you are and making you feel comfortable. The food, also, is far above average and dinner quite an occasion. If guests, however, prefer simpler meals, these are available in a separate bar.

In the evenings the atmosphere at the Mansion House is rather formal and restrained, whereas at the Castle and Ball it is lively, with much coming and going of residents and locals in the bar. It is a matter of personal choice which atmosphere you prefer – both have their merits.

My overall impression was that both hotels were comfortable and well run. Both had similar facilities but both furnishings and food were of a better standard at the Mansion House, where you are welcomed as an individual guest, and services are offered without having to be requested; at the Castle and Ball you feel rather anonymous and you must ask for what you want rather than expect that anything extra will be volunteered. If you do ask, however, help is forthcoming. For the 64 per cent rating, therefore, you can expect a basically comfortable, well equipped and well run hotel; for the 75 per cent rating you can expect, over and above all this, a personal welcome and service, something more individual in the way of furnishings in the bedroom, and a notable standard of cooking.

The percentage ratings act as a quality gauge within each star classification, and can also be used across the star classification bands, to help you decide, for example, whether to stay at a very good three-star hotel, or at an average four-star hotel. For example the Mansion House, with its 75 per cent rating for quality, might suit you better than a four-star hotel scoring 61 per cent. Such a four-star hotel would have a greater range of facilities, and a more extensive range of services but would not necessarily pay the individual attention to its guests that many appreciate and prefer.

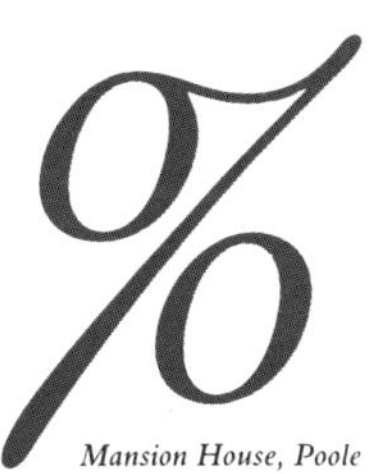

Mansion House, Poole

HOTELS

All the hotels selected for the award of 'Best Newcomer' hotel share the same physical attributes. They have all been furnished and equipped to the highest standards of comfort and elegance, all offer very good service, and all serve excellent food. The larger hotels may have more facilities, but in terms of quality, there is little to choose objectively between any of our six candidates. The choice rests therefore on something which it is difficult to define on paper, but which you can sense immediately on arrival at an hotel, and that is the atmosphere of personal welcome that makes guests feel instantly at home. We felt that this was that extra 'something' that distinguished Halmpstone Manor, in North Devon, near Barnstaple, owned and run by Mr and Mrs Stanbury. It is especially pleasing to be able to make the award to Halmpstone, as the owners, who are also farmers, have developed the hotel from a high-quality bed-and-breakfast operation, started first as a sideline to the farm, then as its popularity increased, concentrating on building up the restaurant, until they have finally transformed their attractive old manor house into an excellent country-house hotel of red-star standard.

NATIONAL WINNER

& REGIONAL WINNER · WEST OF ENGLAND

HALMPSTONE MANOR

BARNSTAPLE, DEVON

Halmpstone Manor is not only a delightful and exceptionally welcoming hotel, it is also, and this must be a unique combination for a red-star hotel, a working farm, with cows grazing the fields around the gardens.

Charles Stanbury, whose family have lived at Halmpstone for generations, both runs the farm and ably and enthusiastically shares with his wife, Jane, the running of this superb hotel. Friendly and informal in atmosphere, it also offers the highest standards of comfort and hospitality, with the owners and their small team of helpers making sure that every guest feels welcome and at ease. On arrival you are greeted with offers of refreshment before being shown to a beautifully furnished and decorated room, where a decanter of sherry, mineral water, fruit and chocolate await you as well as all the usual accoutrements of a first-class hotel room. The sitting room is light and airy, with comfortable chairs and sofas, many of them family pieces, and there are fresh flowers everywhere. Dinner is served in an intimate dining room, where the fine panelling has been restored to its original beauty after having been hidden for years under many coats of paint. The food is excellent, the kitchens being supervised by Jane Stanbury. When they decided to open Halmpstone as an hotel, Jane wrote to Albert Roux at Le Gavroche, to ask if she could spend some time in his kitchens to observe their methods.

As well as this invaluable experience, Jane also has an excellent local butcher and fishmonger to supply the best raw materials for her skills. Dishes may include crevettes grilled with garlic and served with aïoli, langoustines in filo pastry, or lightly poached oysters served on a bed of spinach with a champagne sauce, to be followed by noisettes of venison with pear and cinammon, or the house speciality of three fillets of meats (veal, lamb, beef) each with its own sauce. Puddings are delicious and there is an excellent selection of cheeses. The service is unfussy, but correct and attentive, and Mr and Mrs Stanbury find time to talk to their guests as well as maintaining the service. They have deliberately kept the hotel to a size that they can manage without losing the personal touch. Halmpstone Manor has grown in reputation rather than in size – there are only five bedrooms – and what makes it an outstanding hotel and a clear choice as the Best Newcomer for this year is the comment from our Inspector, that 'warmth and hospitality come naturally to Charles and Jane Stanbury.'

REGIONAL WINNER · SOUTH OF ENGLAND

AMBERLEY CASTLE

AMBERLEY, WEST SUSSEX

Imagine yourself standing in front of a massive crenellated gatehouse, its portcullis raised to welcome you inside. on either side, great curtain walls that have stood for centuries stretch out, enclosing the place in which you will be guest. It would be an unromantic person indeed who could fail to be excited by the prospect of a stay at this very special new hotel.

For 900 years Amberley Castle has stood in the lee of the South Downs, concealed from public view. Then, in 1988 (400 years after Queen Elizabeth 1 held its lease) Joy and Martin Cummings bought the castle and undertook the fulfilment of their dream to transform such a building into a fine hotel and restaurant. It is to their great credit that this has been achieved without detriment to this wonderful historic building. Inside, the character has been preserved too – you will find no modern reception desk in its lovely old hall, and the three lounges contain fine old pieces of furniture and what no castle should be without – suits of armour and old weaponry on the thick stone walls. Great studded oak doors and leaded windows complete the scene. One of the glories of the castle is the Queen's Room restaurant on the first floor. At one end is a magnificent restored mural depicting Charles II and Catherine of Braganza hunting at Arundel Park during their visit to Amberley Castle.

Here guests can enjoy the excellent French cuisine created by head Chef Christophe Durlait, formerly at

Chewton Glen, and his team of five French chefs.

The bedrooms are luxurious, each named after a Sussex castle and individually styled, using first class fabrics and furnishings. Bathrooms are of a comparable standard, with spa baths, bidets, large washbasins and brass fittings. One of the bathrooms has an extra oak door, behind which an ancient stone spiral stairway leads up to the battlements! Within the castle walls are 1½ acres of lawns and ornamental gardens in which guests are free to roam, and to climb the battlements (taking due care, of course) to enjoy the wonderful views across the Sussex countryside. The Cummings family, who also live at the castle, will not be installing a mass of leisure facilities here. They believe that the castle itself – and the standard of accommodation provided – is the only attraction they need.

We visited Amberley Castle in its very early stages of operation, but we were most impressed by the charming Manager, Jonathon Critchard. Willingly helping out wherever needed, he had obviously infected his team with same enthusiasm and pride in the hotel. We have high hopes for the future of Amberley Castle.

REGIONAL WINNER · MIDLANDS

RIVERSIDE COUNTRY HOUSE HOTEL
ASHFORD-IN-THE-WATER, DERBYSHIRE

Over the past eight years or so, Roger and Sue Taylor have transformed this ivy-clad Georgian house into a hotel of immense charm. At the heart of one of Derbyshire's most picturesque villages, it is, nevertheless, in a very peaceful situation, tucked away behind high stone walls with its acre of lawns and gardens bordering the lovely River Wye.

The Riverside first opened as a restaurant, and that side of the business is still extremely popular with non-residents, some of whom travel a considerable distance to sample the cooking of chef Jeremy Buckingham. Trained at The Cavendish in Baslow, he produces interesting menus of British and French dishes, with some adventurous combinations of flavour. Nouvelle cuisine is the main influence, and excellent presentation, combined with sensible portions, make for a very satisfying meal. Breakfasts, too, are very good – our inspector reported 'the best black pudding ever'.

The two dining rooms are furnished with gleaming antique tables, and one still has a magnificent cast-iron range set into its rare, Ashford-marble fireplace. There are also two lounges, one with a bar, the other very elegant, with long windows looking out over the garden.

The bedrooms are delightful, each individual in style and décor. Sue Taylor is responsible for the lovely colour schemes and quality fabrics used, and her skills as a needlewoman are much in evidence, from the lace-trimmed drapes on the four-poster beds, to the hand-made cushions and sewing kits which add such charm to the rooms.

The team of staff at the Riverside is relatively small, but they are all friendly and helpful, and their enthusiasm reflects the personal involvement and commitment of the owners. The Taylors have created a very welcoming, rather special small hotel, and their emphasis remains firmly on providing quality in all areas.

REGIONAL WINNER · NORTH OF ENGLAND

BILBROUGH MANOR

BILBROUGH, NORTH YORKSHIRE

Although it looks much older – and has a history dating back to the 13th century – the present Bilbrough manor was in fact built in 1901 by Guy Thomas Fairfax, a member of one of the great noble families of Yorkshire. Subsequently it was divided into four separate private houses and remained so until 1986 when Colin and Susan Bell saw it as the ideal place for a really gracious country-house hotel and set about the task of restoration. So sympathetically has the work been carried out that there remains no hint of the manor's changing fortunes, and from the moment you are greeted at the door by the impeccably dressed butler you will find no jarring note.

The reception hall immediately evokes the country-house atmosphere, with its superbly comfortable sofas and roomy armchairs, and leading off from this the drawing room has an air of ease and elegance, its windows overlooking well-tended gardens, and the panelled dining room offers an intimate setting for the delicate and imaginative dinners created by chef Idris Caldora, 1986 winner of the 'Young Chef of the Year' award. Dishes such as a salad of smoked duck with pink grapefruit in a caramel ginger vinaigrette, medallions of wild salmon in a cream and chive sauce, or loin of lamb seasoned with herbs and encased in filo pastry, served with a sauce périgourdine have given the hotel's cuisine an excellent reputation in the area.

All the bedrooms are luxuriously and individually furnished, and provided with every comfort. All enjoy views over the extensive grounds, which may one day be the basis of the hotel's own golf course. Mr. and Mrs. Bell and their staff are justly proud of their achievement, and we are sure guests would endorse the comment made by one of our Inspectors that Bilbrough Manor is 'the best hotel I have stayed in for a long time'.

REGIONAL WINNER · WALES

SEIONT MANOR HOTEL

LLANRUG, GWYNEDD

As you follow the long drive which leads to this hotel, you might assume that your destination is a converted manor house, but what you actually find is much more interesting. The hotel has been created from the original farmstead of the manor, and old buildings have been cleverly linked together by new additions, retaining the appearance of the farm with low buildings of stone and slate.

The interior, however, is far from rustic and no expense has been spared on its furnishings and décor. The bar and library have hand-made oak panelling and the lofty ceilings

show the original beams. An end section of the library bookshelves is also the 'secret' door into the residents' sitting room – a real hideaway, with deep, comfortable seating and an open fire.

The restaurant, converted from an old cottage has four separate, but interconnected rooms, and each is light and airy with heavy rattan chairs and crisp table linen. Chef Richard Treble, formerly at Le Manoir aux Quat' Saisons, is gaining a good reputation for his mainly French classical cooking and good local produce is used including salmon, Arctic char, Welsh beef and, of course, lamb.

The bedrooms are in two wings and each is spacious and individual in style. The furniture includes antiques and hand-crafted pieces from around the world, including a magnificent carved rosewood suite from China, interesting white rattan from the Philippines and locally-made oak furniture.

Leisure facilities include a lovely indoor swimming pool, housed in a lofty brick-built replica of a Welsh chapel, with large arched windows. Adjacent to this are the sauna, spa bath and mini-gym, where the resident aromatherapist is in attendance. For those who prefer to take their exercise out of doors, the grounds include a jogging track. Eighty acres of grounds surround the hotel, much of it used as grazing for sheep and cattle; the River Seiont flows along the boundary and there is a stream which feeds the mill pond beside the hotel. The hotel's gardener is also a keen conservationist and he has planned the grounds with a view to nurturing its wild flowers in a natural environment. This is a most interesting hotel, and a welcome addition to our guide.

REGIONAL WINNER · SCOTLAND

MURRAYSHALL COUNTRY HOUSE HOTEL

NEW SCONE, PERTHSHIRE

Superb parkland and its own golfcourse surround this exceptionally pleasant and welcoming country-house hotel two miles from the ancient city of Perth. Murrayshall is essentially a Victorian baronial mansion, but with a modern extension.

Comfort and hospitality are the keynotes, and if some of the bedrooms are not over-large, they are all nicely furnished and equipped with good quality toiletries and towels. All the staff, ably supervised by General Manager Tony Heath, are friendly and eager to please, and the hotel is justly proud of the reputation of its Old Masters' Restaurant, which in 1988 won the 'Taste of Scotland Restaurant of the Year' Award, and consolidated its high reputation in 1989 when their Chef Bruce Sangster became 'Scottish Chef of the Year.'

His menus are well chosen, offering a choice of dishes at every course. Dinners may start with a salad of mixed leaves in walnut oil, crowned with thin slices of Perthshire pigeon, a soup of prawns lightly perfumed with curry, followed by a roast loin of venison served on a bed of wild mushrooms and green lentils with a red wine sauce or a mille feuille of scallops with a spinach and tomato fondue presented with a coulis of fresh langoustine. Service in the restaurant and throughout the hotel is attentive and in keeping with the best traditions of Scottish hospitality.

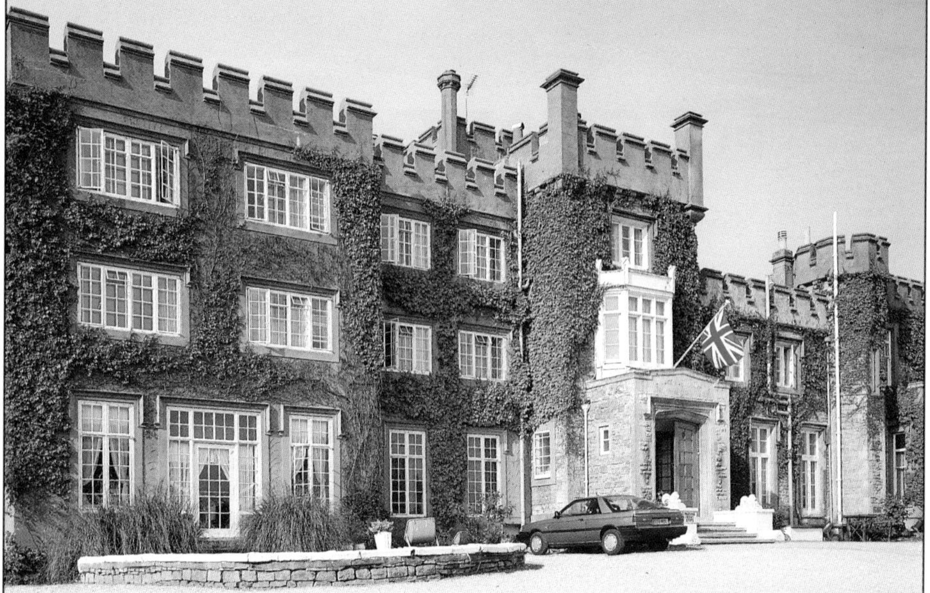

Best Newcomer Restaurants

Among the many new restaurants that the Inspectors visit every year a small number stand out in their memory as having offered an exceptionally enjoyable experience, and these Best Newcomers to the Guide are described in mouthwatering detail in the pages which follow. **Adlard's** recently moved from the small market town of Wymondham to larger premises in Norwich; the **Bay Horse Inn** in Ulverston is the first independent venture by Robert Lyons, chef for many years at John Tovey's famous Lake District Hotel, Miller Howe; **Le Cassoulet** at Cardiff offers an authentic taste of the French countryside in the heart of Wales; **Clos du Roy**, for several years a tiny but immensely popular restaurant in Bath has now moved to a historic Georgian mansion on the edge of Box, a little village between Bath and Chippenham; the **Mansion House** at Dartmouth is a second independent venture for chef Richard Cranfield who until recently owned another very popular local restaurant, Bistro 33.

The Mansion House
Dartmouth, Devon

Marsden & Batley Photographers, Torquay

The elegant Mansion House, once owned in the 18th century by a mayor of Dartmouth, situated on a side street near the quay in historic Dartmouth, has recently been refurbished, providing a ground-floor, bistro-style wine bar, with a sweeping staircase leading up to the former ballroom which has now been converted to a spacious and elegant restaurant. Decorative alcoves and the ornate plaster ceiling have been highlighted to good effect, and there is an atmosphere of warmth and quality – the ideal surroundings in which to enjoy the delicate dishes produced by chef Richard Cranfield, until recently the chef/patron of the popular Bistro 33.

In keeping with the area, fresh fish features strongly on the menus: seabass hot-smoked over fennel with stuffed peppers and garlic and rosemary butter; charcoal-grilled turbot steak with parsley-scented veal stock; cervelas of salmon, halibut and prawns on a bed of creamed leeks; honey-glazed squab on a wedge of egg noodle cake with basil. The desserts are particularly good at the Mansion House, and offerings can include roast almond bavarois, muscat and raisin tart with vanilla ice cream, and poppyseed cream with pears in red wine. Our inspector revelled in the crême brulée, and reported 'I need write nothing other than that this was as near perfect as I can remember'.

A friendly welcome and relaxed hospitality and warmth complement the memorable experience of a meal at the Mansion House.

CLOS DU ROY
BOX, WILTSHIRE

Chef Philippe Roy and his wife Emma, formerly proprietors of the tiny and very popular Clos du Roy in the city of Bath, have now moved their restaurant from the city to a Grade II listed Georgian mansion on the edge of the village of Box, set in seven acres of well-kept gardens amid the rolling countryside outside Bath. The interior of the house has been completely refurbished, and three elegant, spacious and attractively decorated rooms are available for dining.

The 'menu surprise' offers good value for money, with unusual and imaginative combinations, and the delicate sauces which are Philippe Roy's forte. The seasonal à la carte menu may offer items such as feuilletté d'asperges – a wonderfully flavoured hot starter, ragôut du marin, noisettes d'agneau aux St Jacques, suprême de poulade du loue au vin jaune, crisply cooked vegetables – full of colour and flavour – served in filo pastry, tarte aux pommes moderne, and vert galant Charlotte. The highest quality produce is used, and many of the vegetables and unusual herbs come from the Box house's own carefully tended and well-stocked kitchen garden.

The proprietors' friendly welcome and attention, and the correct and professional service by smartly-dressed staff complement the meal here. Our inspector says that 'Guests will, I'm sure, be very happy with Clos du Roy at Box'.

ADLARD'S
NORWICH, NORFOLK

At the end of 1988 David and Mary Adlard came from their previous establishment in Wymondham to these new larger premises in Norwich. The interior of the restaurant is richly decorated, with green baize-like walls in strikingly effective contrast to the sparkling white tablecloths. Tables are candlelit, and a lovely collection of original watercolours and oils on the walls are subtly illuminated, creating the most wonderful sumptuous and restful atmosphere for relaxing dining.

Our inspector had a most enjoyable meal here, from the lovely little freshly-made rolls with creamy butter at the beginning, to the good strong pot of filter coffee and delightful petits fours at the end. The menu offers mainly British dishes – usually a choice of four items for each course, which David Adlard prepares with immaculate care from choice ingredients, with sauces of delicate lightness; flavours, textures, presentation are all wonderful. The wine list here is particularly notable and very extensive.

When our inspector visited, he sampled a perfectly poached fresh supreme of salmon with a lovely chive butter sauce, four tiny trimmed spring lamb cutlets cooked to perfection with a crust of green herbs and rock salt on a garnish of Oyster mushrooms; a large dish of mixed vegetables – lightly cooked, buttery and full of flavour; followed by a super dessert of caramelised apple between ultra-thin flakes of pastry with a fluffy flavourful calvados sabayon.

Mary Adlard is a most welcoming and charming hostess, and friendly and courteous staff make an enjoyable meal here complete. Our inspector marked Adlard's as 'One of the most pleasant restaurants I've visited for some time'.

BAY HORSE INN AND BISTRO
ULVERSTON, CUMBRIA

'Such an enjoyable experience', said our inspector, after a meal at the Bay Horse Inn and Bistro near Ulverston, a new venture for Robert Lyons who was chef at John Tovey's Miller Howe hotel for many years. The exterior of the inn belies the character within – oak beams, brasses, beaten copper table, dried flowers and two open fires create a good initial impression; the bar is very popular with the locals. The restaurant here is in the newly built conservatory – a light and airy place to enjoy a peaceful meal with beautiful expansive views overlooking the tranquil sands and waters of the Leven estuary.

Although Robert Lyons was at Miller Howe for 17 years, he has created his own style at the Bay Horse. The à la carte menu, changed weekly, offers five choices at each course plus daily specials, all straightforwardly described in English and sounding most appetising. The main course presentation is on one plate, the generous portions all looking – and tasting – very good. When our inspector visited, main courses included escalope of Scottish salmon lightly breadcrumbed, fried in butter and served with a fresh tomato and basil sauce; strips of fillet steak cooked in sour cream, brandy and paprika and served on a bed of tagliatelle; breast of chicken poached with fresh asparagus served on diced leeks and waterchestnuts with a lemon and rosemary cream sauce. Our inspector's choice comes highly recommended: medallions of venison pan-fried with strips of bacon, garlic and chestnuts with a rich red-wine sauce. Everything, of course, is carefully prepared from the best fresh ingredients to a consistently high standard. Desserts are irresistible and quite delicious.

The service is friendly and informal but professional, and a meal here offers the pleasant prospect of a happy blend of style and quality amid wonderful surroundings.

LE CASSOULET
CARDIFF, SOUTH GLAMORGAN

Step out of the streets of Cardiff, straight into the heart of France, where Gilbert and Claire Viader have created this delightfully simple restaurant offering a wonderful sampling of robust French country cooking. The owners are from Toulouse, and the restaurant takes its name from the cassoulet de Toulouse, a renowned dish that by itself forms a substantial and satisfying meal. Many of the dishes of this serious little restaurant come from the area around Toulouse, and feature strong, rich flavours and marvellous colours – all skilfully and authentically prepared in the best traditions of French family cooking.

On a lunchtime visit, our inspector particularly enjoyed saucisse de Toulouse, a wonderful peppery coarse pork sausage made to the Viaders' own recipe by a local butcher, grilled to perfection and accompanied by a fresh and carefully prepared assortment of seasonal vegetables.

The service here is impeccably courteous – the professional yet relaxing manner perfectly complements a meal here, and staff are always happy to explain anything on the menu. The wine list has a good selection of French wines at very moderate prices, and, again, staff are very happy to offer advice and explanations. According to our inspector, 'This little place was a delight . . . so very French and certainly a must for our guide'.

BRITAIN'S TOP HOTELS

The award of Red Stars to an hotel is the AA's highest accolade for excellence and means that our Inspectors have judged the hotels listed below (63 out of the 3,000 or more we inspect and classify every year) to be the very best in their star classification and therefore the best hotels in Britain. For 1990 we welcome seven newcomers to the list: Halmpstone Manor at Barnstaple (winner of the Best Newcomer Award), Bilbrough Manor near York (best newcomer in the North of England), Hintlesham Hall at Hintlesham, Lower Slaughter Manor at Lower Slaughter and Wood Hall at Wetherby all gain Red Stars for the first time. Ardanaiseig at Kilchrenan and Eastwell Manor at Ashford regain their Red Star awards under their new management.

Twelve hotels have unfortunately lost their Red Stars, three of them – Lovelady Shield at Alston, Breamish House at Powburn, and Hunstrete House at Hunstrete – on change of ownership, and it is hoped that they will shortly return to the list.

ENGLAND

AVON

FRESHFORD ❀ ★★★ Homewood Park
A charming Victorian house, where the attentiveness of the staff reflects the close involvement of owners Stephen and Penny Ross. Darren McGrath's subtle cuisine is a notable feature.

HUNSTRETE Hunstrete House
This long-established West-Country hotel has recently changed hands and, in accordance with AA policy, Red Stars have, we hope temporarily, been withdrawn.

THORNBURY ★★★ Thornbury Castle
With its vineyard and walled garden, this authentic old castle makes a beautiful and evocative setting for a stay.

BUCKINGHAMSHIRE

ASTON CLINTON ❀ ★★★ Bell Inn
The Harrises create a relaxing and welcoming atmosphere at this attractive old coaching inn, noted for its fine wines. The bedrooms are attractively set around a courtyard.

CHANNEL ISLANDS, JERSEY

ST SAVIOUR ❀ ★★★★ Longueville Manor
A handsome and historic manor house, providing luxurious accommodation in unique, atmospheric surroundings.

CHESHIRE

CHESTER ★★★★ Chester Grosvenor
Friendly and attentive service is an outstanding feature of this stylish hotel which has just completed a £10-million refurbishment.

CORNWALL

LISKEARD ❀ ★★ Well House
Owner Nick Wainsford seems to spare no effort in providing for guests' comfort at this charming Victorian house. Chef David Pope's cuisine, complemented by a well-chosen wine list, is equally memorable.

CUMBRIA

ALSTON Lovelady Shield Country House
This charming hotel has recently changed hands, and Red Stars have been withdrawn, in accordance with AA policy, pending a re-inspection.

BRAMPTON ❀ ★★ Farlam Hall
Over the last 15 years the Quinion and Stevenson families have turned this 17th-century house into a very welcoming hotel. Barry Quinion is the skilful chef.

GRASMERE ❀ ★★★ Michael's Nook
Lakeland scenery and outstanding cooking ensure a memorable stay at this Victorian hotel. It is beautifully furnished with antiques.

GRASMERE ❀ ★ White Moss House
A most appealing lakeland hotel set in pleasant grounds, and immaculately kept by Susan and Peter Dixon.

HOWTOWN ❀❀ ★★★ Sharrow Bay
Very much the creation of Brian Sack and Frances Coulson. For over 40 years they have lavished care on this hotel and made it deservedly famous. Delicious and very fattening food.

WATERMILLOCK ★★ Old Church
Kevin and Maureen Whitemore have created a particularly warm and welcoming atmosphere at this delightful hotel beside Lake Ullswater.

WINDERMERE ★★ Miller Howe
A combination of caring service and excellent cuisine in a wonderful setting have made John Tovey's hotel world-famous. It remains unique, especially the theatrical dinners.

WITHERSLACK ★ Old Vicarage
A place to put stress behind you and enjoy wonderful family hospitality in charming surroundings.

Derbyshire

BASLOW ★★★ Cavendish
This attractively furnished hotel is set in the heart of the Peak District and enjoys fine views of the Chatsworth Estate. A new conservatory has greatly added to its appeal and comfort.

Devon

BARNSTAPLE ★ Halmpstone Manor
The only red-star hotel which is also a working farm, Halmpstone Manor is delightfully informal and friendly. Mr and Mrs Stanbury are charming hosts.

CHAGFORD ★★★ Gidleigh Park
Shaun Hill's cooking, together with Paul and Kay Henderson's insistence on high standards of comfort and service, continue to please all those who come to this beautifully situated hotel on the edge of Dartmoor.

NORTH HUISH ★★ Brookdale
Home-made biscuits and fresh flowers are among the touches which make guests feel welcome at Charles and Carol Trevor-Roper's tucked-away hotel. The always- reliable cuisine is reaching new heights under the regime of Trevor Rich.

Dorset

GILLINGHAM ★★ Stock Hill House
Chef/patron Peter Hauser's comfortable Victorian manor house is definitely a place to unwind. A swimming pool and jacuzzi are among the luxuries available in this tranquil setting.

East Sussex

BATTLE ★★★ Netherfield Place
The close involvement of chef patron Michael Collier and wife Helen is reflected in the impeccable service at this relaxed country house. Michael Collier's cuisine makes good use of home-grown produce.

UCKFIELD ★★★ Horsted Place
A superb Victorian country house in the grand manner, now a luxurious hotel, with dignified yet caring service and fine drawing rooms.

Essex

DEDHAM ★★★ Maison Talbooth
Recent improvements have further enhanced this hotel, which already had a good reputation for comfort and tranquility. Chef Stephen Blake has also brought new vigour to its celebrated nearby restaurant, Le Talbooth.

Gloucestershire

BUCKLAND ★★★ Buckland Manor
An utterly relaxing atmosphere awaits guests at this beautiful Cotswolds manor, which Adrienne and Barry Berman have turned into an outstanding hotel.

CHELTENHAM ★★★ Greenway
Views of the Cotswolds and a setting in delightful parkland combine with caring service to make this a very welcoming hotel.

LOWER SLAUGHTER
★★★ Lower Slaughter Manor
Lovely gardens surround this interesting 17th-century house. Its friendly service and high standards of comfort have resulted in the well-deserved award of Red Stars.

TETBURY ★★★ Calcot Manor
A mellow-stone Cotswolds house is the setting for the warm hospitality offered by the Ball family. Chef Ramon Farthing's cooking has earned praise for some time and remains a delight.

Hampshire

NEW MILTON ★★★★ Chewton Glen
An acclaimed and beautifully appointed hotel whose welcoming grounds include a golf course.

Hereford & Worcester

BROADWAY ★★★★ Lygon Arms
Standing in the centre of this lovely Cotswolds village, the Lygon Arms combines old world atmosphere with high standards of comfort.

KENT

ASHFORD ★★★★ Eastwell Manor
Extensive parkland surrounds this luxurious country house hotel, which has regained its Red Star awards following a change of ownership in 1988.

LEICESTERSHIRE

OAKHAM ❀★★★ Hambleton Hall
An elegant and luxurious hotel overlooking Rutland Water, and celebrated for its high standard of cuisine.

LONDON

SW1 ★★★★★ Berkeley Hotel
Formal, discreet and extensive service in the traditional manner is the hallmark of this hotel, which also enjoys the luxury of a heated swimming pool.

SW1 ★★★★ Goring Hotel
A hotel with a very special character created by generations of the Goring family. This is a particular favourite with our inspectors, who pay tribute to its caring hospitality and high standards.

SW1 ★ Ebury Court
There is nowhere else quite like this small and delightful hotel run by the Topham family. Making few concessions to modern tastes for gadgetry, Ebury Court has an old-fashioned charm which ensures the loyalty of both staff and guests.

SW3 ❀ ★★★★ The Capital
A modern hotel of high quality and great charm. Proprietor David Levin and Managing Director Keith Williams lead the way in ensuring a good atmosphere, and the restaurant is deservedly popular.

W1 ★★★★★ Claridges
A stay at this splendid Mayfair hotel has always been a memorable experience. In recent years extensive improvements have further enhanced the traditional luxury which has made Claridges the favourite of a very distinguished clientele.

W1 ❀❀★★★★★ The Connaught
Celebrated hotel which shuns publicity and rests its excellent reputation on exquisite standards. The Connaught was judged to be 'the best hotel in Europe' in a recent AA survey

W1 The Dorchester
This impressive hotel is currently undergoing a £70 million refurbishment and has therefore been temporarily withdrawn from the guide.

W1 ★★★★ The Athenaeum
Views over Green Park and a particularly pleasant attitude among the staff combine to set this 15-year-old hotel in a class apart.

W1 ★★★★ Browns
One of London's oldest hotels, cherished as a place of character and a certain club-like atmosphere.

WC2 ❀★★★★★ The Savoy
Always outstanding, the Savoy has acquired a new vitality in recent years. Highlights include the traditional luxury of the rooms, and dancing in the celebrated restaurant which overlooks the River Thames.

NORFOLK

GRIMSTON
❀★★★ Congham Hall Country House
Beautiful parkland and numerous thoughtful touches ensure guests' well-being at this handsome country-house hotel.

NORTHUMBERLAND

POWBURN Breamish House
Due to a change of hands, the Red Star award has, in accordance with AA policy, been withdrawn pending re-inspection.

NORTH YORKSHIRE

BILBROUGH ★★★ Bilbrough Manor
This fine stone-built manor house has been transformed by owners Mr and Mrs Bell into a truly distinguished country-house hotel. Elegance and good service are its hallmarks.

WETHERBY ★★★ Wood Hall Hotel
Parkland walks can be enjoyed in the spacious grounds of this peaceful Georgian country-house hotel. A sense of well-being is enhanced by Andrew Mitchell's excellent cooking. Some fine bedrooms and caring staff make this a welcome newcomer to the Red Star list.

OXFORDSHIRE

GREAT MILTON
❀❀❀ ★★★ Le Manoir aux Quat' Saisons
Le Manoir's own kitchen garden provides many of the fine ingredients for Raymond Blanc's celebrated culinary skills. They are all the more memorable in the elegant setting of this beautiful Cotswolds manor, which stands in spacious parkland

SOMERSET

DULVERTON ★★ Ashwick House
This relaxing, away-from-it all hotel is beautifully run by the Sherwood family. It stands on the edge of Exmoor, with fine views of the River Barle.

STON EASTON ★★★ Ston Easton Park
This Palladian country house combines splendid surroundings with a notably welcoming atmosphere.

Eastwell Manor, Ashford, Kent

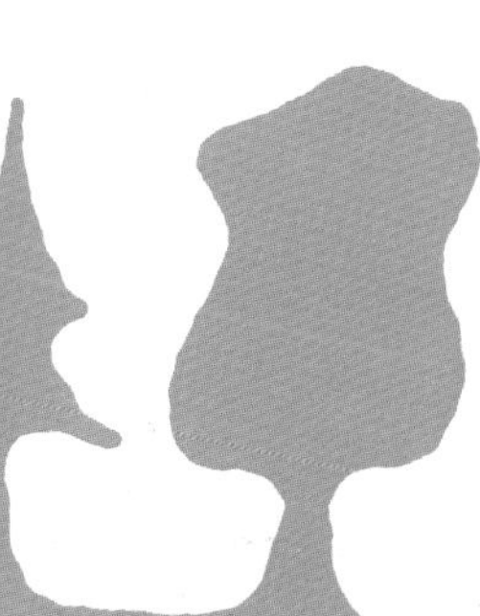

WIVELISCOMBE ❀ ★ Langley House
Set in attractive gardens with fine views of the Brendon Hills, this is a charming small hotel with a most friendly atmosphere.

SUFFOLK

HINTLESHAM ❀ ★★★ Hintlesham Hall
Long famed as a place to enjoy fine food in an elegant setting, Hintlesham Hall receives the Red Stars award for the first time this year.

WARWICKSHIRE

LEAMINGTON SPA
❀ ★★★ Mallory Court
A luxurious country house where guests can revel in delicious cooking and beautiful gardens.

LEAMINGTON SPA ★ The Lansdowne
A much loved little Regency hotel, run with great charm by Gillian and David Allen.

WEST SUSSEX

EAST GRINSTEAD
❀ ★★★ Gravetye Manor
Luxurious comfort in the tranquil setting of a beautiful Tudor house is the great attraction of this renowned hotel.

WALES

GWYNEDD

LLANDUDNO ★★★ Bodysgallen Hall
This 17th-century house combines the traditional and modern in relaxing luxury for guests. Local produce features prominently in the menus.

LLANDUDNO ❀ ★★ St Tudno
Martin and Janette Bland have created something quite out of the ordinary at this very welcoming little hotel. Guests are cosseted throughout, and a memorable stay is virtually guaranteed.

TAL-Y-LLYN ★ Minfordd
The tradition of friendly and informal service by the Pickles family continues at this former drovers' inn, whose character and charm will appeal to many.

SCOTLAND

Ardanaiseig, Kilchrenan, Strathclyde

CENTRAL

DUNBLANE ❀ ★★★ Cromlix House
The hurly-burly of modern life seems far away from this welcoming hotel, built in spacious Victorian and Edwardian style. Chef Mark Salter makes skilful use of game from the surrounding estate.

DUMFRIES & GALLOWAY

PORTPATRICK
❀❀ ★★ Knockinaam Lodge
Memories of spectacular views over the Irish Sea are treasured by guests at Marcel and Corinna Frichot's delightful hotel. Daniel Galmiche's remarkable cuisine is as impressive as the hotel's beautiful setting.

GRAMPIAN

BANCHORY ★★★ Banchory Lodge
The warm hospitality of Dugald and Maggie Jaffray has earned this hotel a reputation for its very special atmosphere. A stunning setting on the banks of the River Dee is another attraction.

HIGHLAND

ARISAIG ★★★ Arisaig House
A country-house hotel that offers a real country house welcome. Run by the Smithers family, it stands in some of the Highlands' most magnificent scenery.

FORT WILLIAM
❀❀ ★★★★ Inverlochy Castle
Views of Ben Nevis await guests at Grete Hobbs's baronial hotel, where traditional splendour is combined with 20th-century comfort. The attentive staff ensure guests' well-being throughout, whilst the honesty and quality of the food are a special joy.

FORT WILLIAM ★ The Factor's House
Peter Hobbs makes guests feel very must at home in this comfortable and hospitable small hotel, where fine views and good cooking combine to make a delightful visit.

WHITEBRIDGE ★★ Knockie Lodge
A former hunting lodge magnificently positioned high above Loch Ness, Knockie Lodge maintains its reputation for traditional Scottish hospitality.

STRATHCLYDE

ERISKA ★★★ Isle of Eriska
Peacefully situated on its own private island the hotel is in the traditional country-house style, and offers good food based on home-grown and local produce.

KILCHRENAN ❀ ★★★ Ardanaiseig
This lovely mansion house on the shores of Loch Awe is now personally run by owners Jonathan and Jane Brown. We are delighted to restore them to the Red Star list for 1990.

PORT APPIN ❀ ★★ Airds
Local produce is a notable feature of the sound cooking at this idyllic little hotel. Run with great charm by Betty and Eric Allen, it also enjoys views of Loch Linnhe.

TAYSIDE

AUCHTERARDER ★★★★★ Gleneagles
A self-contained resort of luxury, with four acclaimed golf courses and an equestrian centre among its numerous facilities.

This guide aims to provide, in an easily understood form, as much up-to-date information as possible about AA-inspected hotels and restaurants in Britain. Classifications are decided on a purely objective basis, as distinct from accolades such as red stars and rosettes which reflect personal opinions. In this edition of the Guide, the AA introduces a new system of quality assessment, awarding a percentage rating to all three, four and five star hotels. For a full explanation, see pages 16-23. The AA system of appointing hotels began in 1909. Over the years standards have been adapted to take into account current trends in hotel construction and operation, and the changing requirements of AA members.

The Hotel and Restaurant Inspectors

Much of the inspectors' work consists of regular and detailed examination of premises, furniture, equipment and facilities. Inspectors either have a background in the hotel and catering industries or have gained wide experience within the Association. This creates a balance between qualified men and women with specialised knowledge of the industry on the one hand, and those with an expert appreciation of AA members' needs on the other. Regular courses serve to keep their knowledge abreast of the times, and consultants are available in each region to assist the inspectors in providing informed and unbiased reports upon which the Committees can base their decisions to grant and withhold recognition. Additional information from AA members – who themselves form a nation-wide inspectorate – is also greatly valued.

Hotels

When an hotel applies to the AA for recognition and appointment, the following procedure is adopted. An inspector visits the hotel unannounced, stays overnight and takes every opportunity of testing as many services as possible. Having settled the bill in the morning, the inspector introduces himself or herself and makes a thorough inspection of the entire premises. At subsequent discussion with the management the inspector will draw attention to any points which may affect the classification. Once granted recognition and given a rating, the hotel is subject to annual inspection to ensure that standards are maintained. If the hotel changes hands, it is automatically deleted until the new proprietor applies for recognition and the hotel has been reassessed. Current applications and possible reclassifications or deletions are considered regularly by the Hotel Appointment Committee. This Committee also keeps the Association's general policy of classification under review. A fee is levied for both registration and appointment.

Basic requirements for appointed hotels are: bedrooms with hot and cold water; adequate bath and lavatory arrangements; service of all meals (with a choice of main dishes) to residents. Full details of the principal requirements for each classification are printed in the leaflet HH5 'AA-Appointed Hotels,' available from Hotel Services, Fanum House, Basingstoke, Hants RG21 2EA. All classifications shown in this edition of the Hotel and Restaurant Guide reflect an establishment's AA status as at June 1989.

What Classifications Indicate

The star classification of hotels by the AA, in addition to providing an indication of the type of hotel, may be regarded as a universally accepted standard, ranging from the simplest to the most luxurious hotel.

The majority of hotels are classified with black stars, the method introduced and used by the AA since 1912. A new classification, the AA Lodge, denotes a motel-style establishment. Lodges cater for overnight stops and offer good, functional, reasonably priced rooms in a block adjacent to a restaurant.

⇧ Lodge with bedroom accommodation only. At least two-star standard, all rooms with private facilities with adjacent motorway or roadside restaurant.

★	Hotels generally of small scale with good facilities and furnishings. Adequate bath and lavatory arrangements. Meals provided for residents but availability to non-residents may be limited. The AA now accepts private hotels at one and two star level, where the requirements for ready public access and full lunch service may be relaxed.
★★	Hotels offering a higher standard of accommodation and some bedrooms with private facilities. The AA now accepts private hotels at one and two star level, where the requirements for ready public access and full lunch service may be relaxed.
★★★	Well-appointed hotels with more spacious accommodation, the majority of bedrooms having a private bath/shower room with lavatory. Fuller meal facilities are provided.
★★★★	Exceptionally well-appointed hotels offering a high standard of comfort and service, and all bedrooms providing a private bath/shower room with lavatory.
★★★★★	Luxury hotels offering the highest international standard.
[Country House symbol]	This denotes an AA Country House hotel where a relaxed, informal atmosphere and personal welcome prevail. Some of the facilities may differ, however, from those found in urban hotels of the same classification. Country House hotels are often secluded and, though not always rurally situated, are quiet. Hotels attracting frequent conferences or functions are not normally granted this symbol. See list on page 735.
○	Hotels due to open during the currency of this annual guide which have not been inspected or classified at the time of going to press.
NOTE:	Hotels often satisfy some of the requirements for a higher classification than that awarded.

RED STAR HOTELS

Red stars are the AA's highest accolade and were introduced in 1975. They are awarded only to hotels that AA inspectors consider to offer the very best quality of accommodation, services and food within their classification. In each of them it is hoped you will find a warm welcome and a high standard of hospitality. Red stars are awarded only after a great deal of consideration, and a change of management or ownership is likely to result in the award being carefully reviewed. In the whole of Great Britain there are only 63 Red-Star hotels (see list on page 35). They are highlighted in the gazetteer by a special panel containing a detailed description and a photograph, as well as the standard information. Look out for red stars and the words 'A RED STAR HOTEL' on those familiar, yellow AA hotel signs.

RESTAURANTS

Restaurants are assessed differently from hotels. For the most part, the approach is made by the Association rather than the proprietor. AA inspectors seek out new restaurants and visit them anonymously. Subsequently they report to the Restaurant Committee who, if they consider the cuisine to be of a high enough standard, award 'crossed knives and forks' to denote the amenities.

The basic requirements for recommendation are a high standard of cuisine, prompt and courteous service, pleasant atmosphere and value for money.

✕	Modest but good restaurant.
✕✕	Restaurant offering a higher standard of comfort than above.
✕✕✕	Well-appointed restaurant.
✕✕✕✕	Exeptionally well-appointed restaurant.
✕✕✕✕✕	Luxury restaurant.
N.B.	Any accommodation available at classified restaurants must not be assumed to be of a standard suitable for hotel appointment.

ROSETTES

Very few restaurants are considered worthy of rosettes. This is the AA's highest award for quality of food and service in a restaurant. First introduced in 1955, rosettes are still awarded to only 133 establishments. See page 49 for rosette awards.

❀	Food is of a higher standard than expected for its classification.
❀❀	Excellent food and service.
❀❀❀	Outstanding food and service, equal to the highest international standards.

Booking

Book as early as possible, particularly if accommodation is required during a holiday period (beginning of June to end of September, public holidays and, in some parts of Scotland, during the skiing season). Some hotels ask for a deposit, and some also ask for full payment in advance, especially for one-night bookings taken from chance callers. Not all hotels take advance bookings for bed and breakfast for overnight or short stays, and some will not accept reservations from mid-week.

Cancellation

Once the booking has been confirmed, notify the hotel straight away if you are in any doubt about whether you can keep to your arrangements. If the hotel cannot re-let your accommodation, you may be liable to pay about two-thirds of the price you would have paid had you stayed there (your deposit will count towards this payment).

In Britain it is accepted that a legally binding contract has been made as soon as an intending guest accepts an offer of accommodation, either in writing or on the telephone. Illness is not accepted as a release from this contract. For these reasons you are advised to effect insurance cover, e.g. AA Travelsure, against a possible cancellation.

Complaints

Members who wish to complain about food, services or facilities are urged to do so promptly and on the spot. This should provide an opportunity for the hotelier or restaurateur to correct matters. If a personal approach fails, members should inform AA Hotel Services, Fanum House, Basingstoke, Hampshire RG21 2EA.

Fire Precautions

As far as we can discover, every hotel in Great Britain listed in this book has applied for, and not been refused, a fire certificate. The Fire Precautions Act does not apply to the Channel Islands, or the Isle of Man, which exercise their own rules regarding fire precautions for hotels.

License To Sell Alcohol

Hotels and Restaurants. All establishments in this guide are licensed unless otherwise stated. Basically, hotel residents can obtain alcoholic drinks at all times, if the owner is prepared to serve them. Restaurant customers can obtain drinks with their meals.

The sale of alcoholic drinks is controlled by separate licensing laws in England, Wales, Scotland, Isle of Man, the Isles of Scilly and each of the islands forming the Channel Islands.

Licensing hours in public houses are generally from mid morning to early afternoon and from mid evening to an hour or two before midnight. Some will remain open throughout the afternoon.

Club Licence. Drinks can be served only to club members, but an interval of 48 hours must elapse after joining.

Children under 14 (18 in Scotland) may be excluded from bars, except areas intended for the service of food. Those under 18 may not be allowed to purchase or consume alcoholic drinks.

Meals

Unless otherwise stated, the terms quoted in the gazetteer section of this book include full cooked breakfast.

In some parts of Britain, particularly in Scotland, *high teas* (i.e. a savoury dish followed by bread and butter, scones, cakes, etc) is sometimes served instead of dinner, which may, however, be available on request. The last time at which high tea or dinner may be ordered on weekdays is shown, but this may be varied at weekends.

On Sundays, some hotels serve the main meal at midday, and provide only a cold supper in the evening.

PAYMENT

Most hotels will only accept cheques in payment of accounts if notice is given and some form of identification (usually a cheque card) is produced. Travellers' cheques issued by the leading banks and agencies are accepted by many hotels but not all. If a hotel accepts leading credit or cheque cards, this is shown in the gazetteer entry (see page 41 for details).

PRICES

The Hotel Industry Voluntary Code of Booking Practice was revised in 1986, and the AA encourages its use in appropriate establishments. Its prime object is to ensure that the customer is clear about the precise services and facilities he is buying, and what price he will have to pay, before he commits himself to a contractually binding agreement. If the price has not been previously confirmed in writing, the guest should be handed a card at the time of registration, stipulating the total obligatory charge.

The Tourism (Sleeping Accommodation Price Display) Order 1977 compels hotels, motels, guesthouses, farmhouses, inns and self-catering accommodation with four or more letting bedrooms to display in entrance halls the minimum and maximum prices charged for each category of room. This order complements the voluntary Code of Booking Practice.

The tariffs quoted in the gazetteer of this book may be affected by inflation, variations in the rate of VAT and many other factors. You should always ascertain the current prices before making a booking. Those given in this book have been provided by hoteliers and restaurateurs in good faith and must be accepted as indications rather than firm quotations. Where information about 1990 prices is not given, you are requested to make enquiries direct.

Prices quoted show minimum and maximum for one or two persons and include a full breakfast unless otherwise stated. Where a Continental breakfast is included in the price, this is stated in the gazetteer. However, some prices may vary for the following reasons:

a) weekday/weekend terms offered

b) season of the year

c) if double room is used for single occupancy

d) dinner is normally charged for separately, but in some areas an inclusive dinner, bed and breakfast option may be offered at a cheaper rate.

Some hotels charge for bed, breakfast and dinner, whether dinner is taken or not. Many hotels, particularly in short-season holiday areas, accept booking only at full board rate.

For main meals served in hotels and restaurants, minimum and maximum *table d'hôte* (set menu) prices are given. Where an *à la carte* menu is available, the price of a three-course dinner and lunch is shown. Where establishments offer both types of menu, *table d'hôte* prices are the only ones shown but the abbreviation (& alc) is used to indicate that an *à la carte* menu is also available.

VAT is payable, in the United Kingdom and in the Isle of Man, on both basic prices and any service. VAT does not apply in the Channel Islands. With this exception, prices quoted in this guide are inclusive of VAT (and service where this is included on the bill.)

BRITAIN'S TOP RESTAURANTS

The AA's rosette awards are given to restaurants where the cooking is of an exceptionally high standard, and where presentation of the dishes and service reach the same level of excellence. Rosette awards are a recognition of a chef's ability and are based on the subjective assessment of the AA's most experienced Inspectors.

The highest award is three rosettes, and this supreme distinction has been given to only three restaurants in the whole country; Chez Nico, owned by Nico Ladenis, gains this supreme accolade for the first time; Le Gavroche, owned by Albert Roux, and Le Manoir aux Quat' Saisons, owned by Raymond Blanc, retain their three rosettes.

Harvey's, owned by Marco Pierre White, and Inverlochy Castle, where Chef Newbold presides over the cooking, have been awarded two rosettes this year.

New one-rosette awards have been made to 17 restaurants:

Kildonan, **Barrhill**
Billesley Manor, **Billesley**
Redmonds at Malvern View, **Cleeve Hill**
Morton's House, **Corfe Castle**
Mansion House, **Dartmouth**
Le Talbooth, **Dedham**
Lewtrenchard Manor, **Lewdown**
The Lake, **Llangammarch Wells**
Alastair Little, **London W1**
Murrayshall Country House Hotel, **New Scone**
Adlards, **Norwich**
Longueville Manor, **St Saviour (Jersey)**
Glenview Inn, **Skye, Isle of, Culnacnoc**
New Hall, **Sutton Coldfield**
Table Restaurant, **Torquay**
Bay Horse, **Ulverston**
Lords of the Manor, **Upper Slaughter**

Thirty-eight restaurants have lost their rosettes, either because the management or chef has changed, because they have closed, or because they no longer meet the standards the AA sets for its rosette awards. Altogether only 132 restaurants (including hotel restaurants) have been awarded rosettes.

Please consult the gazetteer for full details of the establishments listed below. Some restaurants have been awarded rosettes for their dinner menu only.

ENGLAND

AVON

Bath★★★★ ❀ Royal Crescent Hotel
Freshford★★★ ❀ Homewood Park Hotel

BERKSHIRE

Bray ❀❀ ✕✕✕✕ Waterside Restaurant
Maidenhead★★★★ ❀ Fredrick's Hotel
Shinfield ❀ ✕✕✕ L'Ortolan

BUCKINGHAMSHIRE

Aston Clinton★★★ ❀ The Bell Inn

CAMBRIDGESHIRE

Ely ❀✕ The Old Fire Engine House

CHANNEL ISLANDS

St Saviour, Jersey
★★★★ ❀ Longueville Manor Hotel

CHESHIRE

Wilmslow★★★ ❀ Stanneylands Hotel

CORNWALL

Liskeard★★ ❀ Well House Hotel
Padstow ❀ ✕✕ Seafood Restaurant

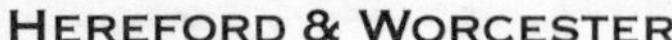

CUMBRIA

Brampton★★ ❀ Farlam Hall Hotel
Cartmel ❀ ✕✕ Uplands
Grasmere★★★ ❀ Michael's Nook Hotel
★ ❀ White Moss House Hotel
Howtown ❀❀ ★★★Sharrow Bay Hotel
Ulverston ❀ ✕ Bay Horse Inn
Watermillock★★ ❀ Rampsbeck Hotel
Windermere★★ ❀ Miller Howe Hotel
❀ ✕ Porthole Eating House

DEVON

Chagford★★★❀ Gidleigh Park Hotel
★★★❀ Teignworthy Hotel
Dartmouth ❀ ✕✕ Carved Angel
❀✕✕ Mansion House
Lewdown★★ ❀ Lewtrenchard Manor
Plymouth ❀ ✕ Chez Nous
Torquay ❀ ✕✕ Table Restaurant

DORSET

Corfe Castle★★ ❀ Morton's House Hotel
Sturminster Newton❀✕✕Plumber Manor

EAST SUSSEX

Hastings ❀ ✕ Roser's

ESSEX

Broxted★★★ ❀ Whitehall Hotel
Dedham ❀✕✕✕ Le Talbooth

GLOUCESTERSHIRE

Buckland★★★ ❀ Buckland Manor Hotel
Cheltenham★★★ ❀ Greenway Hotel
Cleeve Hill❀✕✕ Redmonds at Malvern View
Stroud ❀ ✕ Oakes
Tetbury★★★ ❀ Calcot Manor Hotel
Upper Slaughter★★★❀ Lords of the Manor Hotel

GREATER MANCHESTER

Manchester ❀✕✕Moss Nook

HAMPSHIRE

Brockenhurst ❀ ✕✕Le Poussin
Fordingbridge❀ ✕ Three Lions
Grayshott ❀ ✕ Woods
Hordle ❀✕✕ Le Provence
New Milton★★★★ ❀ Chewton Glen Hotel
Romsey ❀ ✕✕ Old Manor House
Southampton ❀ ✕ Golden Palace
❀✕✕ Kuti's
Wickham★★ ❀ Old House Hotel
Winchester★★★ ❀ Lainston House Hotel

HEREFORD & WORCESTER

Ledbury★★ ❀ Hope End Hotel
Malvern ❀ ✕✕Croque en Bouche

ISLE OF WIGHT

Seaview★★ ❀ Seaview Hotel

KENT

Faversham ❀ ✕✕ Read's
Tunbridge Wells ❀ ✕✕ Thackeray's House

LANCASHIRE

Wrightington ❀ ✕✕High Moor

LEICESTERSHIRE

Oakham★★★ ❀ Hambleton Hall Hotel

LONDON

EC2❀ ✕✕✕ Le Poulbot
SW1 ❀ ✕ Ciboure
❀ ✕✕ Ken Lo's Memories of China
❀ ✕✕ Le Mazarin
❀ ✕✕ Salloos
SW3❀ ✕✕ Bibendum
★★★★ ❀ Capital Hotel
❀❀ ✕✕ Tante Claire
❀ ✕✕ Turners
SW7 ❀✕✕ Hilaire
SW8 ❀✕✕ Cavaliers
❀✕✕ L'Arlequin
SW17❀❀ ✕✕ Harvey's
W1 ❀ ✕ Alastair Little
❀ ✕✕ Au Jardin des Gourmets
❀❀❀ ✕✕ Chez Nico
★★★★★ ❀❀ Connaught Hotel
W1★★★★★❀ Inter-Continental Hotel (Le Soufflé)
❀❀❀✕✕✕✕ Le Gavroche
★★★★★ ❀ Le Meridien Hotel (Oak Room)
❀✕✕✕✕✕Ninety Park Lane
❀ ✕✕ Odin's
❀✕✕✕ Rue St Jacques
❀ ✕✕ Sutherlands
W8 ❀✕✕ La Ruelle
WC2 ❀✕✕✕ Boulestin
★★★★★ ❀ Savoy Hotel (Savoy Restaurant)

NORFOLK

Grimston★★★ ❀ Congham Hall Hotel
Norwich ❀ ✕✕ Adlard's

NORTHAMPTONSHIRE

Horton ❀ ✕✕ French Partridge

OXFORDSHIRE

Great Milton★★★❀❀❀ Le Manoir aux Quat' Saisons
Horton-cum-Studley★★★❀ Studley Priory
Stonor❀ ✕✕ Stonor Arms

SOMERSET

Williton★★❀ White House Hotel
Wiveliscombe★ ❀ Langley House Hotel

STAFFORDSHIRE

Waterhouses ❀✕✕Old Beams

SUFFOLK

Hintlesham★★★ ❀ Hintlesham Hall Hotel
Long Melford❀✕✕ Chimneys

SURREY

Haslemere❀ ✕✕ Morel's

WARWICKSHIRE

Billesley★★★❀ Billesley Manor Hotel
Leamington Spa★★★ ❀ Mallory Court Hotel

WEST MIDLANDS

Birmingham❀ ✕✕✕Sloan's
Hockley Heath★★★❀ Nuthurst Grange Hotel
Solihull ❀✕✕Liaison
Sutton Coldfield★★★❀ New Hall

WEST SUSSEX

East Grinstead★★★❀ Gravetye Manor Hotel
Pulborough❀ ✕Stane Street Hollow
Storrington ❀✕✕✕Manleys
Thakeham★★★ ❀ Abingworth Hall Hotel

WEST YORKSHIRE

Pool❀❀ ✕✕✕Pool Court
Ilkley❀✕✕✕The Box Tree

WALES

GWENT

Llanddewi Skyrrid ❀✕ Walnut Tree

GWYNEDD

Llandudno★★ ❀ St Tudno Hotel

POWYS

Llangammarch Wells★★★ ❀ Lake Hotel
Three Cocks★★ ❀ Three Cocks Hotel

SOUTH GLAMORGAN

Cardiff ❀ ✕La Chaumière

SCOTLAND

CENTRAL

Dunblane★★★ ❀ Cromlix House Hotel

DUMFRIES & GALLOWAY

Portpatrick★★ ❀❀ Knockinaam Lodge Hotel

FIFE

Austruther❀ ✕✕The Cellar
Cupar ❀✕ Ostler's Close
Peat Inn ❀ ✕✕Peat Inn

HIGHLAND

Ardelve★ ❀ Loch Duich Hotel
Drumnadrochit★★❀ Polmaily House Hotel
Fort William★★★★ ❀❀ Inverlochy Castle Hotel
Kentallen★★ ❀ Ardsheal House
Kingussie ❀ The Cross
Skye, Isle of; Culnacnoc ★❀ Glenview Inn
Isle Ornsay★★ ❀ Kinloch Lodge
Ullapool ❀ ✕✕ Altnaharrie Inn

LOTHIAN

Gullane ❀ ✕La Potinière

STRATHCLYDE

Barrhill★★★ ❀ Kildonan Hotel
Glasgow ❀ ✕✕ Colonial
Kilchrenan★★★ ❀ Ardanaiseig Hotel
Langbank★★★ ❀ Gleddoch House Hotel
Port Appin★★ ❀ Airds Hotel

TAYSIDE

New Scone★★★ ❀ Murrayshall Country House Hotel

SAMPLE ENTRY The entry is fictitious

BEESTON Derbyshire Map **15** NJ90	**1. Town name**
★★★ 65% **Red Lion** The Square AB00 XY1 (GB Hotels) ☎(0685) 8276 Telex no 739619	**2. Hotel name**
RS Nov–Mar	**3. Restricted service**
Attractive old coaching inn with comfortable, pretty bedrooms. 19rm(14🛁5🚿) Annexe5rm(8fb) CTV in all bedrooms ® ✈ T sB&B🛁🚿£16.50-£24.50 dB&B🛁🚿£31-£49 B	**4. Accommodation details**
Lift ☾ CTV 100P 3🚗 CFA ♫ nc 3yrs	**5. Hotel facilities**
English & French V Lunch £3-£4.50 Tea 85p-£1.40 High Tea £2.75-£6 Dinner £8.25-£11 &alc Last dinner 9pm	**6. Meals**
Credit Cards [1] [2] [3] [4] [5] (£)	**7. Payment details**

1. Town name listed in gazetteer in strict alphabetical order. This is followed by the county or region, which is the administrative county or region, and not necessarily part of the correct postal address. Towns on islands (not connected to the mainland by a bridge) are listed under the island name. Scottish regions or islands are followed by the old county name in italics. The **map reference** which follows denotes the map-page number and grid reference. Read 1st figure across, 2nd figure vertically, within the appropriate square.

2. Hotel name, address (including postcode) and telephone number with classification and percentage (see pp 16–23 for details). When establishments' names are shown in ***italics*** the particulars have not been confirmed by the management. Within towns the order is red stars, then black by alphabetical listing, each classification in descending star order. Hotels precede restaurants. London hotels are listed under London postal districts. **Company owned hotels** and marketing consortia are shown using abbreviations (key on page 741). Before its name is shown in the guide a company must own at least five AA-appointed hotels, or a hotel must be affiliated to one of the following marketing consortia: Best Western, Consort, Exec Hotels, Guestaccom, Inter-Hotels, Minotel, Prestige, Relais et Châteaux and Pride of Britain. The **telephone exchange** is that of the town heading, unless the name of the exchange is given after the ☎ symbol and before the dialling code and number. In some areas, numbers are likely to be changed during the currency of this book. In case of difficulty check with the operator. When making a reservation by **telex** it is advisable to specify which hotel you wish to book with as some hotels (particularly those in groups) use a central telex service.

3. Restricted service. Some hotels, while remaining open, operate a restricted service during the less busy months. This may take the form of a reduction in meals served, accommodation or facilities available, or in some cases both.

4. Accommodation details. The first figure shows the number of letting bedrooms. Where rooms have *en suite* bath or shower and WC, the number precedes the appropriate symbol.

Annexe — bedrooms available in an annexe are noted only if they are at least of the same standard as those in the rest of the hotel. Facilities may not be the same as in the main building however, and it is advisable to check the nature of the accommodation and the tariff before making a reservation. In some hotels, accommodation is available only in an annexe.

🚭 — number of bedrooms and/or area of the restaurant set aside for non-smokers.

fb — family bedrooms.

CTV/TV — can mean colour or black and white television in lounge or available in bedrooms. Check when making reservations.

🐕 — no dogs allowed into bedrooms. Some hotels may restrict the type of dogs permitted and the rooms into which they may be taken. Hotels which do not normally accept dogs may accept guide dogs. Generally dogs are not allowed in the dining room. Check when booking the conditions under which pets are accepted.

T — automatic direct-dial telephone facilities available from bedrooms. Many hotels impose a surcharge for calls made from bedrooms, so check before making the call. A public telephone is usually available in the hotel hallway or foyer.

Prices — prices given have been provided by hoteliers and restaurateurs in good faith and are indications rather than firm quotations. Unless otherwise stated, they include full cooked breakfast. Check current prices before booking. See also page 46.

5. Hotel facilities. For key to symbols see inside front cover.

☾ — All hotels employing a night porter are shown thus except 4 and 5 star hotels, all of which have night porters on duty.

🚌 — No coaches. This information is published in good faith from information supplied by the establishments concerned. Inns, however, have well-defined legal obligations towards travellers, and it is for the customer to take up any queries with the proprietor or the local licensing authority.

♫ — Live entertainment should be available at least once a week throughout the year. Some hotels without this symbol will provide entertainment during high season or at certain other specified times only. You are advised to check this information before booking.

nc — No children. Where this abbreviation does not appear, the hotels listed will accommodate children, but may not provide any special facilities. A minimum age (e.g. nc4yrs — no children under four years old) may be specified. For very young children, check before booking about such provisions as cots and high chairs and any reductions made.

🏠 — establishments with special facilities for children, which will include baby-sitting service or baby intercom system, playroom or playground, laundry facilities, drying and ironing facilities, cots, high chairs and special meals. Some hotels offer free accommodation to children provided they share the parents' room.

CFA — hotels with conference facilities available, selected within the following guidelines. Each hotel has a minimum of 20 rooms with *en suite* facilities, one or more conference rooms seating a minimum of 40 people, and a separate dining room or dining area for delegates.

Suitable for the disabled — Full details for disabled people will be found in AA *Guide for the Disabled Traveller* available from AA offices, free to members, £2.95 to non-members. Intending guests with any form of disability should notify proprietors so that arrangements can be made to minimise difficulties, particularly in the event of an emergency.

6. Meals. Details of the style of food served, last dinner orders and likely price ranges are given. Where the *table d'hôte* prices are given, the abbreviation "& alc" indicates that there is also an *à la carte* menu, which may be considerably dearer than the set menu.

V — a choice of vegetarian dishes available (but check before booking).

☕ — morning coffee or afternoon tea are served to chance callers. All 4 and 5 star hotels serve morning coffee and, normally, afternoon tea to residents.

Prices — See page 46.

7. Payment details (but check current position when booking)

1 — Access/Euro/Mastercard
2 — American Express
3 —Barclaycard/Visa
4 — Carte Blanche
5 — Diners
(£) — Hotel may offer a discount. See p. 4 for details.

ABBERLEY Hereford & Worcester Map **07** SO76

★★★[red star]77% Elms WR6 6AT (on A443) (Norfolk Capital)(Prestige)

☎Great Witley (0299)896666
Telex no 337105
FAX (0299) 896804

An attractive avenue of limes leads to this lovely Queen Anne house. Early last year the hotel was completely restored and refurbished to a very high standard; all the bedrooms have lovely views over the Teme Valley or over the hotel's formal gardens. A very British menu is prepared in the modern style using top-quality, well-chosen produce, and generous portions are attactively presented.

16⇔Annexe9⇔1[four-poster] CTV in all bedrooms **T** [no dogs] (ex guide dogs) ✱ S10% sB&B⇔£75-£80 dB&B⇔£95-£125 [menu]
(60P 2[garage] ✲ [tennis] (hard) croquet putting [riding] *xmas*
[restaurant] English & French **V** ♔ [coffee] S10% Lunch fr£12.95 Dinner fr£19 Last dinner 9.30pm
Credit Cards [1] [2] [3] [4] [5] Ⓔ

★★Manor Arms at Abberley WR6 6BN
☎Great Witley(0299)896507 Telex no 335672
FAX (0562) 747488
A pleasant village inn, some 300 years old, with well-equipped bedrooms.
7⇔Annexe3⇔ CTV in all bedrooms ® **T** ✱ sB&B⇔fr£32 dB&B⇔fr£42 [menu]
40P ✲
V ♔ [coffee] Lunch £5.20-£6.75alc Dinner £12.50 Last dinner 9.30pm
Credit Cards [1] [3]

ABBOTSBURY Dorset Map **03** SY58

★★Ilchester Arms Market St DT3 4JR ☎(0305)871243
8rm(6[shower])Annexe2⇔(2fb) CTV in all bedrooms ® ✱ sB&B£30-£34 sB&B⇔[shower]£30-£34 dB&B£40 dB&B⇔[shower]£40 [menu]
40P *xmas*
[restaurant] English & Continental **V** ♔ [coffee] [no smoking] Lunch £2.95-£7.95 High tea £1-£1.75 Dinner £2.95-£7.95 Last dinner 9pm
Credit Cards [1] [3]

ABERDARON Gwynedd Map **06** SH12

★★Ty Newydd LL53 8BE ☎(075886)207
RS Dec-Jan
A personally-run hotel and bar with direct access to the beach stands at the centre of the village, next to its Norman church.
17rm(8⇔1[shower])(3fb) CTV in 12bedrooms TV in 5bedrooms [no dogs] (ex guide dogs) sB&Bfr£18 sB&B⇔[shower]fr£21.25 dB&Bfr£36 dB&B⇔[shower]fr£40.50
CTV
[restaurant] Mainly grills **V** ♔ Bar Lunch £8.50-£8.75alc Dinner £8.50-£8.75alc Last dinner 9.30pm
Credit Cards [1] [3] Ⓔ

All AA-appointed establishments are inspected regularly to ensure that required standards are maintained.

ABERDEEN Grampian *Aberdeenshire* Map **15** NJ90

See **Town Plan Section**
See also **Aberdeen Airport & Westhill**

★★★★60% Bucksburn Moat House Old Meldrum Rd, Bucksburn AB9 2LN (3m N A947) (Queens Moat)
☎(0224)713911 Telex no 73108 FAX (0224) 714020
Close to the airport, this modern hotel has spacious bedrooms and a good standard of room service The cuisine in the Maritime restaurant offers good value for money and friendly service.
98⇔[shower](20fb)[no smoking]in 11 bedrooms CTV in all bedrooms ® **T** ✱ sB⇔[shower]£64.40 dB⇔[shower]£73.60 (room only) [menu]
Lift (180P CFA [indoor pool](heated) gymnasium ♫ *xmas*
[restaurant] Scottish & French **V** ♔ [coffee] Lunch £12 Dinner £13 Last dinner 10.30pm
Credit Cards [1] [2] [3] [4] [5] Ⓔ

★★★★51% *Skean Dhu Altens* Souter Head Rd, Altens AB1 4LF (3m S off A956) (Mount Charlotte) ☎(0224)877000
Telex no 739631
RS Xmas wk
A spacious hotel standing on the main route to Aberdeen Harbour. Some bedrooms have views across the city towards the coast.
221⇔[shower](70fb)[no smoking]in 10 bedrooms CTV in all bedrooms ® **T**
Lift (⊞ CTV 450P ✲ CFA [outdoor pool](heated) Games room
[restaurant] Scottish & International **V** ♔ [coffee]
Credit Cards [1] [2] [3] [4] [5]

★★★64% Amatola 448 Great Western Rd AB1 6NP
☎(0224)318724 Telex no 739743 FAX (0224) 312716
This business hotel has been extended and modernised to provide well-appointed public rooms and good parking facilities.
53rm(41⇔12[shower]) CTV in all bedrooms ® **T** ✱ S8% sB⇔[shower]£30-£49.50 dB⇔[shower]£60-£66 (room only) [menu]
(250P *xmas*
[restaurant] Scottish & Continental **V** ♔ [coffee] S8% Lunch £8.35 Dinner £10.35&alc Last dinner 9.30pm
Credit Cards [1] [2] [3] [5]

See advertisement on page 57

★★★70% Caledonian Thistle 10 Union Ter AB9 1HE (Thistle)
☎(0224)640233 Telex no 73758 FAX (0224) 641627
This particularly well-managed hotel is ideally set in the heart of Aberdeen. There is a choice of either well-equipped, generally compact 'club' bedrooms, or larger 'executive club' rooms and suites. Public areas include a café-bar, attractive restaurant, cocktail lounge and a smart function room.
80rm(72⇔8[shower])(4fb)2[four-poster][no smoking]in 2 bedrooms CTV in all bedrooms ® **T** ✱ sB⇔[shower]£65-£85 dB⇔[shower]£76-£97 (room only) [menu]
Lift (25P sauna solarium ♫
[restaurant] International ♔ [coffee] [no smoking] Lunch fr£9&alc Dinner fr£14.95&alc Last dinner 10pm
Credit Cards [1] [2] [3] [4] [5]

See advertisement on page 57

★★★71% Copthorne Hotel 122 Huntly St AB1 1SU (Best Western) ☎(0224)630404 Telex no 739707 FAX (0224) 640573
66⇔[no smoking]in 12 bedrooms CTV in all bedrooms ® **T** ✱ sB⇔£74 dB⇔£84 (room only) [menu]
Lift (20[garage] ♫ *xmas*
[restaurant] Scottish French **V** ♔ [coffee] Lunch £17.50-£21alc Dinner £17.50-£21alc Last dinner 10pm
Credit Cards [1] [2] [3] [4] [5]

★★★69% New Marcliffe 51-53 Queen's Rd AB9 2PE
☎(0224)321371 Telex no 73225 FAX (0224) 311162
Tasteful conversion of two granite buildings has created a small, elegant hotel with an almost club-like atmosphere. The bedrooms are attractive and well-equipped.
27⇔[shower](3fb) CTV in all bedrooms ® **T** [no dogs] ✱ sB&B⇔[shower]£30-£52 dB&B⇔[shower]£36-£60 [menu]
(74P [snooker] *xmas*

▶

♡ Scottish & French V ♔ ⊡ Lunch £9.50-£15.50alc High tea £4.50 Dinner £15.50&alc Last dinner 10pm
Credit Cards 1 2 3 5 £

★★★ 66% **Stakis Treetops** 161 Springfield Rd AB1 7SA (Stakis) ☎(0224)313377 Telex no 73794 FAX (0224) 312028
This modern hotel is nicely situated in attractive landscaped grounds in the western residential area of the city.
113⇌♪(28fb)1⊟⊬in 50 bedrooms CTV in all bedrooms ® T sB⇌♪£50-£90 dB⇌♪£60-£100 (room only) ⊟
Lift (CTV 300P ✲ CFA ⊡(heated) ℘ (hard) sauna solarium gymnasium ♫ *xmas*
♡ Scottish & Continental V ♔ ⊡ ⊬ Lunch £7.25-£8.50&alc Dinner £12.50-£14.50&alc Last dinner 10pm
Credit Cards 1 2 3 5

★★★ 62% **Swallow Imperial** Stirling St AB1 2ND (Swallow) ☎(0224)589101 Telex no 73365 FAX (0224) 574288
Conveniently situated close to the station and city centre shops, this Victorian hotel offers neatly-appointed accommodation, the public rooms and fifty-four of the bedrooms having been refurbished to a high standard.
108rm(36⇌70♪)(6fb) CTV in all bedrooms ® T ✱ sB&B⇌♪£45-£58 dB&B⇌♪£60-£70 ⊟
Lift (CTV ₽
V ♔ ⊡ ⊬ S% Lunch fr£5.80 Dinner fr£12.30 Last dinner 9.30pm
Credit Cards 1 2 3 5

✕ **Atlantis** 16/17 Bonaccord Crescent AB1 2DE ☎(0224)591403
An attractive seafood restaurant where dishes are artistically presented in the modern style.
Closed Sun , Xmas & New Year
Lunch not served Sat
V 34 seats Last lunch 2pm Last dinner 10pm 10P
Credit Cards 1 2 3 4 5

ABERDEEN AIRPORT Grampian *Aberdeenshire* Map **15** NJ81

★★★★ 61% **Holiday Inn** Riverview Dr, Dyce AB2 0AZ (Holiday Inns) ☎Aberdeen(0224)770011 Telex no 739651 FAX (0224) 722347
Accomodation at this hotel includes very spacious and well-equipped bedrooms, and some king-size 'Leisure' and 'Club Europe' rooms. The combined coffee shop/restaurant features well-cooked dishes inventive and visually appealing.
154⇌♪(71fb)⊬in 9 bedrooms CTV in all bedrooms T ✱ sB⇌♪fr£76 dB⇌♪fr£82 (room only) ⊟
(⊞ 300P CFA ⊡(heated) sauna solarium gymnasium jacuzzi ⌂ *xmas*
♡ International V ♔ ⊡ Lunch fr£13.95 Dinner fr£14.50&alc Last dinner 10.30pm
Credit Cards 1 2 3 4 5 £

★★★★ 57% ***Skean Dhu*** Argyll Rd AB2 0DU (adjacent to main entrance 1m N of A96) (Mount Charlotte) ☎Aberdeen(0224)725252 Telex no 739239 FAX (0224) 723745
A purpose built hotel by the air terminal. Bedrooms are arranged around a central garden area with an open air swimming pool.
148⇌♪(6fb)⊬in 6 bedrooms CTV in all bedrooms ® T
(⊞ 450P ✲ CFA ⌂(heated) ⌂
♡ Scottish & French V ♔ ⊡ Last dinner 10.45pm
Credit Cards 1 2 3 5

★★★ 63% ***Skean Dhu Dyce*** Farburn Terrace, Dyce AB2 0DW (off A947) (Mount Charlotte) ☎Aberdeen(0224)723101 Telex no 73473
A friendly and well-managed hotel with modern bedrooms, a coffee shop, restaurant, and very good conference facilities.
Annexe220⇌♪(75fb)⊬in 6 bedrooms CTV in all bedrooms ® T
(250P CFA squash sauna solarium gymnasium pool table tennis
♡ Scottish & French V ♔ ⊡
Credit Cards 1 2 3 4 5

ABERDOUR Fife Map **11** NT18

★★ ***Woodside*** High St KY3 0SW ☎(0383)860328 Telex no 72165
The public areas of this beautifully renovated hotel feature woodwork from the Mauretania and the ornately decorated captain's cabin from RMS Orontes. Bedrooms are all attractive and well equipped, though some are on the small side. Attentive service is provided by the hotel staff.
21rm(16⇌5♪)1⊟ CTV in all bedrooms ® T
(50P ✲ sauna ♫
♔ ⊡
Credit Cards 1 2 3 4 5

★ **Fairways** 17 Manse St KY3 0TT ☎(0383)860478
Reasonably priced meals are available at this homely little hotel, which offers fine views across the Firth of Forth.
10rm(2⇌)(2fb) CTV in all bedrooms ® ✱ sB&B£18.50-£22 sB&B⇌£27.50-£32 dB&B£24.50-£32.50 dB&B⇌£36.50-£43 ⊟
CTV 12P ⌂ ⌂
♔ ⊡ Bar Lunch £1.50-£3.95 Dinner £4.50-£7.50 Last dinner 8.45pm
Credit Cards 1 3 £

ABERDOVEY Gwynedd Map **06** SN69

★★★ 64% **Hotel Plas Penhelig** LL35 0NA (Inter)
☎(065472)676
FAX (065472) 7783
Closed Jan & Feb
A splendid Edwardian country house set in its own extensive grounds overlooking the Dovey Estuary. The house is delightfully furnished; there is an imposing oak panelled hall and lounge; and bedrooms have all modern facilities. David Richardson and his staff are always on hand to look after their guests.
12rm(11⇌1♪)(3fb) CTV in 11bedrooms T ✈ ✱ sB&B⇌♪£48-£51.75 dB&B⇌♪£81-£98.50 (incl dinner) ⊟
48P ⌂ ✲ ℘ (hard) Croquet lawn putting green
♡ English & French V ♔ ⊡ Sunday Lunch fr£8.50alc Dinner fr£13.95alc Last dinner 8.45pm
Credit Cards 1 2 3 5

★★★ 65% **Trefeddian** LL35 0SB ☎(065472)213
Closed 3 Jan – 29 Mar
Occupying an unrivalled position overlooking the sea, this is a well furnished, comfortable hotel with efficient and friendly staff.
46rm(37⇌5♪)(4fb) CTV in all bedrooms ® T sB&B⇌♪£31-£40 dB&B⇌♪£62-£80 (incl dinner) ⊟
Lift CTV 50P 18⌂ (75p per night) ⌂ ✲ ⊡(heated) ℘ (hard) solarium pool table tennis badminton pitch & putt ⌂ *xmas*
♡ English & French ♔ ⊡ ⊬ Lunch fr£6.50 Dinner fr£11.75 Last dinner 8.45pm
Credit Cards 1 3

See advertisement on page 59

★★*Harbour* 17 Glandovey Ter LL35 0EB ☎(065472)7792 & 250
This comfortable hotel is pleasantly furnished. The bedrooms are well designed and the food is of a good standard.
16rm(3⇨5♠)(4fb)2⊟ CTV in 14 bedrooms ®
CTV ₱
English & French V ♁ ⊡ ⊬ Last dinner 10pm
Credit Cards [1] [2] [3] [5]

★★Penhelig Arms LL35 0LT ☎(065472)215 FAX (065472) 7761
Closed Xmas
Set between the hills and the sea, this small hotel provides very comfortable accommodation and good food.
11rm(4⇨7♠) ® T sB&B⇨♠£27 dB&B⇨♠£45-£58 ⊟
CTV 12P ⇼
V ♁ ⊡ Bar Lunch £1.20-£4.95alc Dinner fr£13.50 Last dinner 9.30pm
Credit Cards [1] [3] Ⓔ

★Maybank LL35 0PT ☎(065472)500
Closed 10 Jan-9 Feb RS Nov-Apr
A delightful small hotel and restaurant overlooking the Dovey estuary. There are attractive bedrooms with lots of extras provided, a small bar and a charming lounge in Victorian style, all of which add to the appeal of the house. Service is friendly and attentive and cooking is commendable.
5rm(1⇨4♠)(1fb) CTV in all bedrooms ®
sB&B⇨♠£22.45-£31.95 dB&B⇨♠£30-£43.90 ⊟
CTV ₱ ⇼ ✲
English & French Lunch £6.95-£7.95 Dinner £10.95-£22.85 Last dinner 10pm
Credit Cards [1] [3]

ABERFELDY Tayside *Perthshire* Map **14** NN84

★★Weem Weem PH15 2LD (1m NW B846) ☎(0887)20381
A friendly roadside inn, full of character and with an interesting history.
14rm(9⇨5♠)(4fb)⊬in 4 bedrooms CTV in all bedrooms ® T ✱ sB&B⇨♠£20-£23 dB&B⇨♠£40-£46 ⊟
20P ✲ ⌡ shooting *xmas*
European V ♁ ⊡ ⊬ Lunch £4-£15alc High tea £4-£6alc Dinner £10-£15&alc Last dinner 8.30pm
Credit Cards [2] [3] [5] Ⓔ

ABERFOYLE Central *Perthshire* Map **11** NN50

✕✕Braeval Mill Braeval FK8 3UY ☎(08772)711
This old mill has been most effectively restored to create an attractive restaurant, the original wheel being retained externally, while the stone walls of the interior are decked with interesting hangings. The proprietor prepares the carefully presented, modern-style food, the intensity of flavour in his sauces being particularly noteworthy, and his wife acts as a charming and attentive hostess.
Closed Mon, 3 wks Feb, 1 wk May & 1 wk Nov
Lunch not served Tue-Sat
Scottish & French 32 seats Sunday Lunch £10.95 Dinner £14.50-£20alc Last lunch 1.30pm Last dinner 9.30pm 18P nc10yrs ⊬
Credit Cards [1] [2] [3]

ABERGAVENNY Gwent Map **03** SO21

★★★60% The Angel Cross St NP7 5EW (Trusthouse Forte) ☎(0873)7121 FAX (0873) 78059
Former coaching inn, situated in the town centre, with well-equipped bedrooms.
29⇨(1fb)1⊟⊬in 2 bedrooms CTV in all bedrooms ® T sB⇨£49-£56 dB⇨£59-£69 (room only) ⊟
27P *xmas*
V ♁ ⊡ ⊬ Lunch £7.95-£13.50&alc Dinner £11.50-£13.50&alc Last dinner 9.30pm
Credit Cards [1] [2] [3] [4] [5]

★★Llanwenarth Arms Brecon Rd NP8 1EP
☎Crickhowell(0873)810550 FAX (0873) 811880
Two-and-a-half miles west of Abergavenny, on the A40, the hotel stands perched on the bank of the River Usk, commanding spectacular views. Its main building dates back to the 16th century, but a complex of very comfortable modern bedrooms stands adjacent. There are two welcoming bars and a modern restaurant.
18⇨♠ CTV in all bedrooms ® T ✕ ✱ sB&B⇨♠£40 dB&B⇨♠£48 ⊟
60P ⇼ ⌡
International V ♁ Lunch £10-£18alc Dinner £10-£18alc Last dinner 10pm
Credit Cards [1] [2] [3] [5]

✕Bagan Tandoori 35 Frogmore St NP7 5AN ☎(0873)4790
Authentically cooked food, well marinated in quality spices and efficiently served by friendly staff, is the hallmark of this ornately decorated town-centre restaurant.
Closed Xmas day & Boxing day
Indian V 36 seats ✱ Lunch fr£10 Dinner fr£10 Last lunch 2.30pm Last dinner 11.30pm P nc5yrs
Credit Cards [1] [2] [3] [5]

ABERGELE Clwyd Map **06** SH97

★★Kinmel Manor St Georges Rd LL22 9AS ☎(0745)832014
Detached Georgian hotel, with modern extension, set in its own grounds.
25rm(21⇨4♠)(3fb) CTV in all bedrooms ® T sB&B⇨♠£38 dB&B⇨♠£55 ⊟
CTV 120P ✲ ⊡(heated) sauna solarium gymnasium spa bath *xmas*
English & French V ♁ ⊡ ⊬ Lunch £7.50&alc High tea £2.50-£4.50 Dinner £12.50&alc Last dinner 9.30pm
Credit Cards [1] [2] [3] [4] [5] Ⓔ

ABERLADY Lothian *East Lothian* Map **12** NT47

★★Greencraig Country House EH32 0PY (1m NE on A198)
☎(08757)301

This family-run country hotel is situated in a quiet coastal setting and is a popular base for golfers. A relaxed atmosphere prevails in the public rooms. Bedrooms are modest but well-equipped.
8rm(5⇨) CTV in all bedrooms ® T ✕ (ex guide dogs) ✱ sB£25.50-£28 sB⇨£29.50-£33 dB⇨£41-£45 (room only)
20P ⇼ ✲ CFA
Scottish & French V ♁ Bar Lunch £1.95-£6.30alc Dinner £14.95-£16.95 Last dinner 9pm
Credit Cards [1] [3] Ⓔ

★★Kilspindie House Main St EH32 0RE ☎(08757)682
A traditional hotel with recently refurbished bedrooms. Popular with business clients and golfers.
26rm(18⇨8♠)1⊟ CTV in all bedrooms ® T sB&B⇨♠£25-£32 dB&B⇨♠£43-£46 ⊟
30P ⇼
V ♁ ⊡ Lunch fr£6.75 High tea fr£5.50 Dinner fr£9.90&alc Last dinner 8.30pm
Credit Cards [1] [3] Ⓔ

A

ABERLOUR Grampian *Banffshire* Map **15** NJ24

★★**Aberlour** High St AB3 9QB ☎(03405)287 & 218
Friendly, homely hotel situated in the centre of this Speyside village.
19rm(14⇨1↱)(1fb) Ⓡ sB&Bfr£20.50 sB&B⇨↱fr£22.60 dB&B⇨↱fr£38.50
CTV 29P 4🚗
V ♔ ☕ Lunch fr£4&alc High tea £3.95-£9 Dinner fr£10.60&alc Last dinner 9pm

★**Lour** The Square AB3 9QB ☎(03405)224
Traditional stone Victorian hotel in the centre of this busy Speyside village.
9rm Ⓡ ✱ sB&B£13.65-£18.65 dB&B£24.50-£29.50
CTV 8P 8🚗 ♪
♔ ✂ Bar Lunch £1.85-£3 High tea £3.30-£4 Dinner £6.50-£8.75 Last dinner 8pm

ABERPORTH Dyfed Map **02** SN25

★★★56% **Hotel Penrallt** SA43 2BS ☎(0239)810227
FAX (0239) 811375
Closed 23-31 Dec
Much improved, and set in very pleasant park and woodland, the hotel provides comfortable accommodation which includes a self-catering complex and leisure centre.
16rm(12⇨4↱)(2fb) CTV in all bedrooms Ⓡ sB&B⇨↱£38 dB&B⇨↱£56 ▤
100P ⛟ ✲ ⛆(heated) ⚲ (hard) sauna solarium gymnasium pitch & putt ♧
♔ ☕ Lunch fr£6.95 High tea fr£3.50 Dinner fr£12&alc Last dinner 9pm
Credit Cards [1] [2] [3] [5] Ⓔ

★★**Highcliffe** SA43 2DA ☎(0239)810534
Small proprietor-run hotel in an elevated position, 200 yards from two sandy beaches.
9rm(5⇨)Annexe6⇨(4fb) CTV in all bedrooms Ⓡ **T**
sB&B£25.75-£37 sB&B⇨£25.75-£37 dB&B£44.80-£64 dB&B⇨£44.80-£64 ▤
CTV 18P *xmas*
☊ International **V** ♔ ☕ Lunch £2.95-£6 Dinner £10-£11.50&alc Last dinner 9.30pm
Credit Cards [1] [2] [3] Ⓔ

★★**Penbontbren Farm** Glynarthen SA44 6PE (3.5m SE off A487)
☎(0239)810248
Annexe10rm(8⇨2↱)(6fb) CTV in all bedrooms Ⓡ ✱
sB&B⇨↱£18-£21 dB&B⇨↱£36-£42 ▤
35P ⛟ ✲ ♪
V ♔ ☕
Credit Cards [1] [3] Ⓔ

★**Glandwr Manor** Tresaith SA43 2JH ☎(0239)810197
Closed Nov-Feb
A secluded, small hotel, reputedly designed by John Nash, offers comfortable accommodation, good food and friendly service.
7rm(2⇨3↱)(2fb) ✗ sB&B£15.50-£17.50
sB&B⇨↱£16.50-£18.50 dB&B£31-£35 dB&B⇨↱£33-£37 ▤
CTV 14P ⛟ ✲
♔ ☕

ABERSOCH Gwynedd Map **06** SH32

★★★63% **Abersoch Harbour** LL53 7HR ☎(075881)2406 & 2523
Prominent detached holiday hotel with small garden.
9rm(5⇨1↱)1▣ CTV in all bedrooms Ⓡ **T**
50P
☊ English & French **V** ♔ ☕ ✂ Last dinner 9.30pm
Credit Cards [1] [2] [3]

★★★🏅68% Porth Tocyn
Bwlch Tocyn LL53 7BU
☎(075881)2966
Closed mid Nov-mid Mar

This delightfully situated hotel stands in 25 acres of farmland with superb views over Cardigan Bay. Owned by the same family since the 1940's it offers a relaxing informal atmosphere in the excellent lounges and dining room. The cuisine has a good reputation and bedrooms are attractively furnished.

17⇌↿(1fb) CTV in all bedrooms **T** ✱ sB&B⇌↿£33-£42 dB&B⇌↿£51.50-£78 ⊟
CTV 50P ⊞ ✼ ⇌(heated) 🎾 (hard) windsurfing
⚘ ⊻ Lunch £5-£20alc High tea £5.50 Dinner £13.50-£19 Last dinner 9.30pm
Credit Cards [1]

★★★68% Riverside LL53 7HW ☎(075881)2419 & 2818
Closed Dec-Feb
A comfortable hotel on the banks of the River Soch with attractive bedrooms and delightful lounges. The restaurant provides well-prepared dishes using the best ingredients.
12rm(11⇌1↿)(4fb) CTV in all bedrooms ® **T** ✗ ✱ sB&B⇌↿fr£30 dB&B⇌↿fr£60 ⊟
25P ⊞ ✼ ⊡(heated) sailing windsurfing
☋ Cosmopolitan ⚘ ⊻ Bar Lunch fr£2 High tea fr£3.50 Dinner fr£15.95 Last dinner 9pm
Credit Cards [1] [3]

★★Deucoch LL53 7LD ☎(075881)2680
This pleasant, bright hotel overlooks Cardigan Bay, the bedrooms are well appointed and food is good
10rm(3⇌6↿)(2fb) CTV in all bedrooms ® sB&B£20-£22 dB&B£40-£44 ⊟
CTV 50P ✼ ⌂ *xmas*
☋ Welsh, English & French **V** ⚘ ⊻ Bar Lunch £3.75-£3.50 High tea fr£3 Dinner fr£10 Last dinner 9pm
Credit Cards [1] [2] [3] [5]

★★Neigwl Lon Sarn Bach LL53 7DY ☎(075881)2363
Resident owners provide high standards of caring hospitality, offering warm, comfortable rooms and serving good, home-cooked meals in a delightful restaurant with fine sea views.
7rm(1⇌4↿)Annexe2⇌(2fb) CTV in 7bedrooms ® ✗ (ex guide dogs) sB&Bfr£30 sB&B⇌↿fr£30 dB&Bfr£48 dB&B⇌↿fr£48 ⊟
CTV 30P ⊞ ✼ ⌂ *xmas*
⚘ ⊻ Lunch fr£8 Dinner fr£13 Last dinner 9pm
Credit Cards [1] [2] [3] [5]

All hotels awarded three or more stars are now also given a percentage grading for the quality of their facilities. Please see p 16 for a detailed explanation.

ABERYSTWYTH Dyfed Map 06 SN58

★★★🏅61% *Conrah*
Ffosrhydygaled, Chancery
SY23 4DF
☎(0970)617941
Telex no 35892
Closed 24-31 Dec

A country mansion in Georgian style, set in pleasant lawns and gardens just south of the town. Public areas are elegant and comfortable and the restaurant has earned a good local reputation for the quality of its food.
13rm(11⇌)Annexe9rm(3⇌6↿)(1fb) CTV in all bedrooms ® **T** ✗
Lift 60P ⊞ ✼ ⊡(heated) sauna table tennis croquet nc5yrs
☋ International **V** ⚘ ⊻ Last dinner 9.30pm
Credit Cards [1] [2] [3] [5]

★★Belle Vue Royal Marine Ter SY23 2BA ☎(0970)617558
FAX (0970) 612190
RS 24-26 Dec
An impressive Victorian hotel on the promenade, offering friendly service from owners and local staff alike; recent upgrading of public rooms has not marred their traditional charm.
42rm(16⇌8↿)(6fb) CTV in all bedrooms ® **T** ✗ (ex guide dogs) sB&B£24-£25 sB&B⇌↿£29-£31 dB&B£40-£44 dB&B⇌↿£45-£49 ⊟
☾ CTV 6P 9🚗
V ⚘ ⊻ Lunch fr£6.95&alc Dinner fr£9.50&alc Last dinner 9pm
Credit Cards [1] [2] [3] [5] £

★★Cambrian Alexandra Rd SY23 1LG ☎(0970)612446
Closed 25 Dec
A small, mock-Tudor hotel standing opposite the railway station provides accommodation in compact bedrooms; its popular bars and the first-floor Saddlers Restaurant have recently been restyled.
12rm(2⇌5↿)(3fb) CTV in all bedrooms ® sB&B£23 sB&B⇌↿£26 dB&B£42 dB&B⇌↿£46 ⊟
☋ Welsh, English & Continental **V** ⚘ ⊻ Lunch fr£6.50&alc High tea fr£4 Dinner fr£8.50&alc Last dinner 9.30 pm
Credit Cards [1] [3] £

★★Court Royale Eastgate SY23 2AR ☎(0970)611722
Positioned in the heart of the town yet close to the beach, this small, friendly hotel has recently been totally refurbished and offers a high standard of bedroom accommodation.
10rm(6⇌4↿)(3fb) CTV in all bedrooms ® **T** ✱ sB&B⇌↿£28-£32 dB&B⇌↿£42-£46 ⊟
⊞ CTV Ᵽ ⊞
V ⚘ ⊻ Sunday Lunch £5.25-£5.95 Dinner £5-£10alc Last dinner 10pm
Credit Cards [1] [2] [3]

★★*Four Seasons* 50-54 Portland St SY23 2DX ☎(0970)612120
Closed 24 Dec-3 Jan
Centrally situated, this small, family-run hotel offers comfortable accommodation and good food.
15rm(7⇌)(1fb) CTV in all bedrooms ® **T**
CTV 10P ⌂
☋ English & Continental **V** ⚘ ⊻ Last dinner 8.30pm
Credit Cards [1] [3]

A

★★Groves 42-46 North Pde SY23 2NF (Minotels)
☎(0970)617623
Closed Xmas
A comfortable, friendly hotel set in the heart of the town and close to beaches. Owned and run by a conscientious family, it promotes commendable home cooking with imaginative menus. The bright, cosy bedrooms offer modern facilities and appointments.
12rm(6⇨6🚿)(1fb) CTV in all bedrooms ® **T** ✗ (ex guide dogs) sB&B⇨🚿fr£26 dB&B⇨🚿fr£44 ⊟
8P 🚗 nc3yrs
🍷 Welsh & International **V** ✪ ⊕ Lunch fr£1alc Dinner £8.50-£11.50alc Last dinner 8.30pm
Credit Cards [1] [2] [3] [5] (£)

★★Queensbridge Promenade, Victoria Ter SY23 2BX
☎(0970)612343 & 615025
Closed 1wk Xmas
Situated on the promenade almost at the foot of Constitution Hill, this small hotel with a basement dining room and a cosy lounge bar is ideal for both businessmen and holidaymakers.
15rm(8⇨7🚿)(6fb) CTV in all bedrooms ® **T**
sB&B⇨🚿£26-£28 dB&B⇨🚿£38-£40 ⊟
Lift CTV P̸
✪ Bar Lunch £3-£6.50alc Dinner £9 Last dinner 8pm
Credit Cards [1] [3] (£)

★★*Seabank* Victoria Ter SY23 2DH ☎(0970)617617
The small, family hotel is situated at the northern end of Cardigan Bay.
22rm(12⇨4🚿)(4fb) CTV in all bedrooms ® ✗
Lift P̸ 🚗
🍷 French ✪ ⊕ Last dinner 8pm
Credit Cards [1] [2] [3] [5]

ABINGDON Oxfordshire Map **04** SU49

★★★60% Abingdon Lodge Marcham Rd OX14 1TZ (Consort)
☎(0235)553456 Telex no 837750 FAX (0235) 554117
Closed 25-26 Dec
Conveniently situated at the junction of the A34/A415 and designed for the popular business market, this new, purpose-built hotel offers comfortable bedrooms with a good range of facilities and equipment, though public rooms are a little restrictive.
63⇨ CTV in all bedrooms ® **T** ✗ (ex guide dogs) S10% sB&B⇨£40-£68 dB&B⇨£45-£75 Continental breakfast ⊟
☾ 85P
🍷 English & French **V** ✪ ⊕ S10% Lunch £7.95-£9.50&alc Dinner £9.95&alc Last dinner 10pm
Credit Cards [1] [2] [3] [5] (£)

★★★61% Upper Reaches Thames St OX14 3JA (Trusthouse Forte) ☎(0235)22311 FAX (0235) 555182
The hotel overlooks the River Thames on one side and an old mill stream on the other, enjoying one of the most attractive locations in the historic town of Abingdon. The original building was an abbey cornmill, now converted to provide cosy public rooms, including the Mill Wheel Restaurant, and comfortable bedrooms. There is a private mooring beside the hotel and attractive garden terraces prove popular in the summer.
26⇨🚭in 2 bedrooms CTV in all bedrooms ® **T** ✳ S%
sB⇨£62 dB⇨£78 (room only) ⊟
90P ✿ *xmas*
V ✪ ⊕ 🚭 Lunch £10.50-£10.95 Dinner £14.95 Last dinner 9.30pm
Credit Cards [1] [2] [3] [4] [5]

★★Crown & Thistle Hotel Bridge St OX14 3HS (Berni/Chef & Brewer) ☎(0235)22556
A small, friendly hotel with a popular Berni grill restaurant operation and well-equipped bedrooms. Popular with both commercial and private guests.
21⇨🚿 CTV in all bedrooms ® **T** ✗ (ex guide dogs)
sB&B⇨🚿£37.50-£43 dB&B⇨🚿fr£66.50 ⊟
☾ 36P *xmas*
🍷 Mainly grills **V** ✪ ⊕ 🚭 Lunch fr£8alc Dinner fr£9alc Last dinner 10.30pm
Credit Cards [1] [2] [3] [5]

ABOYNE Grampian *Aberdeenshire* Map **15** NO59

★★Balnacoil House Rhu-Na-Haven Rd AB3 5JD
☎(03398)86806
Large neat hotel standing in its own grounds on the banks of the River Dee, popular with fishermen.
11rm(4⇨7🚿)(2fb) CTV in all bedrooms ® **T** ✗ (ex guide dogs) ✳ sB&B⇨🚿fr£27.50 dB&B⇨🚿fr£46 ⊟
CTV 40P 🚗 ✿
🍷 Mainly grills **V** ✪ ⊕ Lunch £5.50-£9.50 Dinner £12.75-£16 Last dinner 9.30pm
Credit Cards [1] [2] [3] [5]

★★Huntley Arms Charlestown Rd AB3 5HS (Consort)
☎(03398)86101 Telex no 57515 ATT 99
Friendly, traditional hotel close to the field where the Aboyne Games are played.
30rm(22⇨4🚿)(2fb)🚭in 1 bedroom ® **T** sB&B£17-£20.50 sB&B⇨🚿£31-£36 dB&B£41-£46 dB&B⇨🚿£45-£55 ⊟
☾ CTV 200P 4🚗 (charged) ✿ snooker sauna gymnasium
V ✪ ⊕ 🚭 Lunch fr£8.50 Dinner fr£14.50&alc Last dinner 9.30pm
Credit Cards [1] [2] [3] [5]

ABRIDGE Essex Map **05** TQ49

✗✗*Roding* Market Pl RM4 1UA ☎Theydon Bois(037881)3030
Within a beamed building of the 15th century, this restaurant is tastefully appointed and now enhanced by a new lounge area. Caring service and a good selection of reasonably priced wines, though the Chinatown-style menu is perhaps too extensive.
Closed Mon & 26 Dec-early Jan
Lunch not served Sat
Dinner not served Sun
🍷 Chinese 55 seats Last dinner 10pm 20P
Credit Cards [1] [2] [3] [5]

ACCRINGTON Lancashire Map **07** SD72

★★★61% Dunkenhalgh Blackburn Rd, Clayton le Moors BB5 5JP (adj to M65, junct 7) (Associated Leisure)
☎Blackburn(0254)398021 Telex no 63282 FAX (0254) 872230
An impressive country house with modern bedrooms, attractive public rooms and extensive leisure facilities.
35rm(31⇨4🚿)Annexe28⇨🚿(12fb)1⊞ CTV in all bedrooms ® **T** ✳ sB&B⇨🚿£58-£62 dB&B⇨🚿£68-£72 ⊟
☾ CTV 400P 10🚗 ✿ ⊡(heated) snooker sauna solarium gymnasium ♫ *xmas*
🍷 International **V** ✪ ⊕ Lunch £8.25&alc Dinner £12-£13.95&alc Last dinner 9.45pm
Credit Cards [1] [2] [3] [5]

Entries for rosetted restaurants, red-star and country-house hotels are highlighted by a tinted panel. For a full list of these establishments, consult the Contents page.

A

ACHNASHEEN Highland *Ross & Cromarty* Map **14** NH15

★★Ledgowan Lodge
IV22 2EJ (Best Western)
☎(044588)252
Telex no 75431
Closed 31 Oct-12 Apr

Traditional Highland tourist hotel, formerly a shooting lodge, offering friendly, attentive, service and good wholesome country cooking.

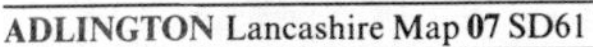

15rm(13⇌)(4fb) CTV in all bedrooms ® **T**
sB&B£27.50-£29.50 sB&B⇌£32.50-£37.50
dB&B£39.50-£44 dB&B⇌£50-£60 ⊟
25P ✻
V ♡ ☕ Lunch £7.50-£15 High tea £2.50-£10alc Dinner £15-£20 Last dinner 9pm
Credit Cards [1] [2] [3] [5] £

ADLINGTON Lancashire Map **07** SD61

★★Gladmar Railway Rd PR6 9RG (Best Western)
☎(0257)480398 FAX (0257) 482681
Closed Xmas Day & New Years Day
A peaceful, tranquil atmosphere pervades this friendly little hotel, set in a walled garden and managed by the resident proprietor.
20rm(7⇌13↑)(1fb)⊬in 2 bedrooms CTV in all bedrooms ® **T**
✕ (ex guide dogs) sB&B⇌↑fr£35 dB&B⇌↑fr£45 ⊟
CTV 30P ✻
V ♡ ☕ ⊬
Credit Cards [1] [3]

AIRDRIE Strathclyde *Lanarkshire* Map **11** NS76

★★Tudor Alexander St ML6 OPA ☎(0236)64144
A commercial hotel located by the main road and providing extensive parking. Bedrooms are neatly appointed with en suite facilities; bars and dining room are wood panelled and are pleasantly furnished.
19rm(17⇌2↑) CTV in all bedrooms ® **T**
sB&B⇌↑£36.50-£45 dB&B⇌↑fr£54.50 ⊟
☾ 60P
☋ European ♡ Lunch fr£9.95&alc Dinner fr£9.95&alc Last dinner 9.30pm
Credit Cards [1] [2] [3] [5] £

ALCESTER Warwickshire Map **04** SP05

★★Arrow Mill Arrow B49 5NL (On A435 S of town)
☎(0789)762419 Telex no 312522 FAX (0789) 765170
An historic building set in a tranquil location amidst 55 acres of rural Warwickshire. Now a family managed hotel, it still retains its charm and character – an attractive example being the original water wheel, driven by the stream, in the Miller's Bar.
18rm(17⇌1↑)(4fb) CTV in all bedrooms ® **T** sB&B£48-£56 dB&B⇌↑£56-£72 ⊟
250P 6🚗 (£10) ✻ ♩ archery clay pigeon shooting
☋ English & French V ♡ ☕ Lunch £8.25-£14&alc High tea fr£2.45 Dinner fr£14&alc Last dinner 9.30pm
Credit Cards [1] [2] [3] [5] £

★★Cherrytrees Stratford Rd B49 6LN ☎(0789)762505
Closed 25 & 26 Dec
Modern motel with cedar wood chalets, popular restaurant and conference facilities.
Annexe22rm(18⇌4↑)(2fb)1⊞ CTV in all bedrooms ® **T** ✻
sB&B⇌↑fr£33 dB&B⇌↑fr£45 ⊟
CTV 80P ✻
☋ International V ♡ S% Lunch fr£5.95
Credit Cards [1] [2] [3]

ALCONBURY Cambridgeshire Map **05** TL17

★★*Alconbury Hill* Alconbury Weston PE17 5JG (1.5m N on A1)
☎Huntingdon(0480)890807
Conveniently situated on the northbound carriageway of the A1, 6 miles from Huntingdon, this hotel caters for both businessmen and tourists. There is an adjacent sports complex.
24↑(2fb) CTV in all bedrooms ® **T**
80P ✻ squash snooker sauna solarium
♡ ☕
Credit Cards [1] [2] [3]

ALDBOURNE Wiltshire Map **04** SU27

✕✕Raffles The Green SN8 2BW ☎Marlborough(0672)40700
Attractive cottage-style restaurant offering interesting food and attentive, friendly service.
Closed Sun, last 2 wks Aug & 25-30 Dec
Lunch not served Mon & Sat
☋ French 36 seats Lunch £12.55-£19.05alc Dinner £12.55-£19.05alc Last lunch 2.15pm Last dinner 10.30pm nc3yrs
Credit Cards [1] [2] [3] [5]

ALDEBURGH Suffolk Map **05** TM45

★★★61% Brudenell The Parade IP15 5BU (Trusthouse Forte)
☎(0728)452071
Restaurant and lounge both take advantage of the magnificent views over beach and sea which this hotel enjoys from its fine position on the front, whilst the comfort of its pleasantly furnished ▶

and well-equipped bedrooms also contributes to guests' enjoyment of a relaxing break.
47⇌(3fb)⚟in 4 bedrooms CTV in all bedrooms ® **T** ✱ S%
sB⇌£48-£52 dB⇌£64-£70 (room only) ⊟
Lift ☾ 14P 6🚗 *xmas*
V ♧ ⊡ ⚟ S% Lunch £5.95-£6.95 Dinner £11.95&alc Last dinner 9pm
Credit Cards 1 2 3 4 5

★★★63% Wentworth Wentworth Rd IP15 5BD (Consort)
☎(0728)452312
Closed 28 Dec-12 Jan
Behind the rather plain exterior of this Victorian building facing the sea lies a comfortable, well-furnished hotel. Bedrooms are attractive with co-ordinating fabrics whilst framed prints, antiques and open fires provide warmth and elegance in the comfortable lounges, small bar and smart dining room.
31rm(24⇌4↱) CTV in all bedrooms **T** sB&B£29.75-£35.50 sB&B⇌↱£33.50-£42.50 dB&B⇌↱£60-£85.25 ⊟
16P ⛟ *xmas*
♉ English & French **V** ♧ ⊡ Lunch £10-£14&alc Dinner £13-£17&alc Last dinner 9pm
Credit Cards 1 2 3 5

★★★71% White Lion Market Cross Place IP15 5BL (Best Western) ☎(0728)452720 FAX (0728) 453909
The White Lion is in an attractive position on the sea front. It dates from 1563 and is Aldeburgh's oldest hotel. All bedrooms have been recently refurbished and there are some very attractive four-poster bedrooms. There are two elegant lounges, one of which is non-smoking, a popular restaurant which serves fresh, well-prepared food in a relaxed, candle-lit atmosphere, and the Buttery Bar for snacks/light meals.
38⇌(1fb)2⊠ CTV in all bedrooms ® **T** ✱ sB&B⇌£40-£45 dB&B⇌£55-£75 ⊟
16P ⛟ ⌂ *xmas*
♉ English & French **V** ♧ ⊡ Sunday lunch £7.95-£8.50 Dinner £12.95-£13.50&alc Last dinner 9pm
Credit Cards 1 2 3 5

★★Uplands Victoria Rd IP15 5DX ☎(0728)452420
Closed 22-29 Dec
Two storey period house with its own grounds, on main approach road.
12rm(9⇌)Annexe8rm(7⇌1↱)(2fb) CTV in 16bedrooms TV in 4bedrooms ® **T** sB&B£24-£35 sB&B⇌↱fr£35 dB&B£50 dB&B⇌↱£50 ⊟
CTV 22P ⛟ nc12yrs
V Dinner fr£11&alc Last dinner 8.30pm
Credit Cards 1 2 3 5

ALDERMINSTER Warwickshire Map 04 SP24

★★★★64% Ettington Park CV37 8BS (Select) ☎Stratford-upon-Avon(0789)740740 Telex no 311825 FAX (0789) 87472
A Victorian mansion in Gothic style, glimpsed through the mature trees of forty acres of parkland, now offers standards of comfort unprecedented in the many years that it has operated as an hotel. The new wing's modern accommodation, though plainer and more uniform than the spacious, ornate and individually styled bedrooms of the main house, is equally comfortable; the restaurant enjoys a well-earned reputation for good food. A small but attractive leisure centre is available for guests' use.
48⇌1⊠ CTV in all bedrooms **T** ✗ sB&B⇌£85-£95 dB&B⇌£115-£125 ⊟
Lift ☾ 85P ✲ ⊡(heated) ℘ (hard) ⤶ ∪ sauna solarium croquet clay pigeon shooting & archery ♫ nc7yrs *xmas*
♉ English & French **V** ♧ ⊡ Lunch £15-£20&alc Dinner £25-£30&alc Last dinner 9.30pm
Credit Cards 1 2 3 5 £

See advertisement under STRATFORD-UPON-AVON

ALDERNEY

See **Channel Islands**

ALFORD Lincolnshire Map 09 TF47

★White Horse 29 West St LN13 9DG
☎(05212)2218 due to change to (0507) 462218
This small, comfortable inn offers a welcoming and friendly atmosphere, with the new owners working hard to meet guests' needs. Bedrooms vary in size but all are delightfully decorated with co-ordinating fabrics and wallpaper.
9rm(7⇌)(2fb) CTV in all bedrooms ® ✱ sB&B£20 sB&B⇌£24 dB&B£30 dB&B⇌£34
10P 3🚗
♉ English & Continental ♧ Lunch £5-£15alc
Credit Cards 1 3

ALFRETON Derbyshire Map 08 SK45

○***Granada Lodge*** A38/A61 DE55 1JH (junc A38/A61) (Granada)
☎(0773)520040
Due to have opened Sep 1989
61⇌

ALFRISTON East Sussex Map 05 TQ50

★★★59% *Deans Place* BN26 5TW ☎(0323)870248
Looking across woodland from its peaceful setting on the edge of the village, close to the River Cuckmere, an hotel dating back to Tudor times stands in the seclusion of a well-kept walled garden. Bedrooms are all equipped with modern facilities, though they vary in size, and the comfortable lounge accommodation is warmed by log fires in winter.
40⇌(4fb)1⊠ CTV in all bedrooms ® **T** ✗
☾ 100P ⛟ ✲ ⌓(heated) ℘ (hard) snooker
V ♧ ⊡ ⚟ Last dinner 9pm
Credit Cards 1 2 3

★★★50% Star Inn BN26 5TA (Trusthouse Forte)
☎(0323)870495 FAX (0323) 870922
This is one of England's oldest inns, the present fabric dating from about 1450 and replacing an original 13th-century building. The beamed interior of the main part retains an old world atmosphere enhanced by the log fires that warm it, while a new wing provides modern bedroom accommodation. Standards of service are acceptable throughout.
35⇌⚟in 4 bedrooms CTV in all bedrooms ® **T** S%
sB⇌£56-£60 dB⇌£76-£80 (room only) ⊟
36P *xmas*
V ♧ ⊡ ⚟ S% Lunch £10.25-£11&alc Dinner £12.50&alc Last dinner 9pm
Credit Cards 1 2 3 4 5

✕Moonraker's High St BN26 5TD ☎(0323)870472
Delightful small 14th-century cottage restaurant featuring inglenook log fire and a homely lounge. Chef Elaine Wilkinson's cooking is very reliable, wholesome and interesting. A good wine selection is available, particularly Estate and Domaine bottled wines. All is complemented by friendly supervision and service.
Closed Sun, Mon & 10 Jan-13 Feb
Lunch not served
♉ French **V** 32 seats ✱ Dinner £17.40 Last dinner 9.15pm
Ᵽ nc5yrs

All AA-appointed establishments are inspected regularly to ensure that required standards are maintained.

ALLENDALE Northumberland Map **12** NY85

★★ **Bishopfield Country House Hotel** NE47 9EJ
☎(0434)683248
FAX (0434) 683830
Closed 24-26 Dec

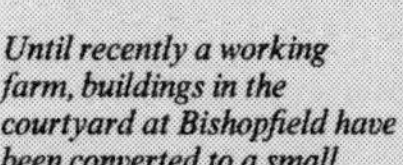

Until recently a working farm, buildings in the courtyard at Bishopfield have been converted to a small country-house hotel. The bedrooms are modern and well equipped, and there are two comfortable lounges. The dinner menu offers honest country cooking.
11rm(5⇌6↱)(3fb) CTV in all bedrooms ® T
sB&B⇌↱£30-£35 dB&B⇌↱£50-£60
20P snooker
English & French V Dinner £12-£15 Last dinner 8.30pm
Credit Cards 1 5

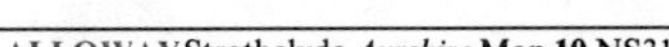

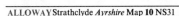

ALLOWAY Strathclyde *Ayrshire* Map **10** NS31

✕**Burns Byre** Mount Oliphant Farm KA6 6BU ☎(0292)43644
40 seats ✱ Lunch £5.50-£11alc Dinner £8.50-£20alc Last lunch 2pm Last dinner 9.30pm 20P
Credit Cards 1 2 3 5

ALNWICK Northumberland Map **12** NU11

★★★ 57% **White Swan** Bondgate Within NE66 1TD (Swallow)
☎(0665)602109
Comfortable hotel in the centre of town with character public rooms and good bedrooms.
43⇌↱(2fb) in 4 bedrooms CTV in all bedrooms ® T ✱
sB&B⇌↱fr£52 dB&B⇌↱fr£70
☾ 30P *xmas*
English & French V Lunch fr£7.50&alc High tea fr£6.50 Dinner fr£13.50&alc Last dinner 9pm
Credit Cards 1 2 3 5

★★ ***Hotspur*** Bondgate Without NE66 1PR ☎(0665)602924
Closed 24-26 Dec & 1 Jan
Historic coaching inn with good comfortable restaurant.
28rm(17⇌11↱)(2fb) CTV in all bedrooms ® T
CTV 25P
V Last dinner 9pm
Credit Cards 1 3

★★ ***The Oaks*** South Rd NE66 2PN ☎(0665)510014
4rm(2⇌2↱)Annexe4⇌↱(1fb) CTV in all bedrooms ® T
32P
English V Last dinner 9pm
Credit Cards 1 3

ALRESFORD Hampshire Map **04** SU53

✕***Old School House*** 60 West St SO24 9AU ☎(096273)2134
This restaurant could justifiably claim to serve the best school dinners in Hampshire. Meals of excellent quality, selected from two fixed-price menus, are based on good-quality ingredients, well seasoned and individually cooked; there is a separate pudding menu and a popular wine list. Service is efficient, attentive and friendly.
Lunch not served Tue-Sat
Dinner not served Sun
English & French 36 seats Last dinner 10pm

ALREWAS Staffordshire Map **07** SK11

○ ***Travelodge*** A38 Rykneld St(Trusthouse Forte)
☎Central reservations 01-567 3444
Due to open winter 1989
32⇌
P

ALSAGER Cheshire Map **07** SJ75

★★★ 60% **Manor House** Audley Rd ST7 2QQ
☎Crewe(0270)878013 FAX (0270) 882483
Situated on the edge of town, about 3 miles from junction 16 of the M6. The hotel is conveniently placed for business people visiting nearby towns or holidaymakers wishing to break their journey. The hotel was originally a farmhouse and oak beams remain in the restaurant and bars. Bedrooms are compact but very well equipped.
27rm(14⇌13↱)(1fb)1 CTV in all bedrooms ® T
sB&B⇌↱£42.50-£52.50 dB&B⇌↱£57.50-£67.50
☾ CTV 178P
French & English V Lunch £7.75-£9.95 Dinner £11.25-£15.25&alc Last dinner 9.30pm
Credit Cards 1 2 3 5 £

See advertisement under CREWE

See the preliminary section 'Hotel and Restaurant Classification' for an explanation of the AA's appointment and award scheme.

ALSTON Cumbria Map **12** NY74

Alston telephone numbers are due to change during the currency of this guide.

★★Lovelady Shield
CA9 3LF

☎(0498)81203 due to change to (0434) 381203

Closed 3 Jan-21 Feb

This attractive country-house hotel, set in well-kept gardens amid the high Pennine fells 2.5 miles east of Alston, has recently changed hands. The new owners, Mr and Mrs Lyons have taken over what has for many years been one of the AA's best-known red-star hotels, and the withdrawal of this award for the time being does not imply any criticism of the owners, but is in accordance with AA policy on change of hands. On a recent visit, our inspector commented very favourably on the five-course dinner with its excellent selection of local cheeses, and on the friendliness of the owners and their staff.

12rm(8⇨4♠)(1fb)1 CTV in all bedrooms **T**
sB&B⇨♠£46 dB&B⇨♠£90-£112 (incl dinner)

20P ✲ (hard) *xmas*

English & French Sunday Lunch £10-£15alc Dinner £18 Last dinner 8.30pm

Credit Cards [2] [5] (£)

★★Lowbyer Manor Country CA9 3JX ☎(0498)81230
This interesting period house on the A686, 1 mile north of the town centre, has a cosy bar, attractive dining room and comfortable lounge.
7rm(3⇨4♠)Annexe4⇨ ® sB&B⇨♠£27.50
dB&B⇨♠£47
CTV 14P ✲ *xmas*
English & Continental **V** Bar Lunch £3.85-£9.85alc Dinner £11.65-£27.25alc Last dinner 8.30pm
Credit Cards [1] [2] [3] [5] (£)

★Hillcrest CA9 3RA ☎(0498)81250 due to change to (0434) 381251
Closed 1-28 Feb
A small, friendly hotel under the personal supervision of the resident proprietors.
11rm(1fb) ® sB£19 dB£33 (room only)
CTV 16P 3 (£1) ✲
Dinner £10.50-£15alc Last dinner 9pm
Credit Cards [1] [3] (£)

ALTHORPE Humberside Map **08** SE81

See **Scunthorpe** for details of other hotels.

★★*Lansdowne House* Main St DN17 3HJ ☎(0724)783369
A tastefully converted Victorian country house managed by friendly proprietors. The restaurant offers interesting, good value dishes.
6rm(5⇨)Annexe1⇨(5fb) CTV in all bedrooms ® **T**
CTV 40P 4 ✲
English & French **V**
Credit Cards [1] [2] [3] [5]

The AA's star-rating scheme is the market leader in hotel classification.

ALTON **Hampshire** Map **04** SU73

★★Alton House Normandy St GU34 1DW ☎(0420)80033 FAX (0420) 89222
A comfortable Regency-style hotel with well-equipped modern bedrooms and good leisure facilities.
38rm(35⇨3♠)(2fb)1 CTV in all bedrooms ® **T**
sB&B⇨♠£28-£41 dB&B⇨♠£38-£51
80P 6 ✲ (heated) (hard) snooker
English & Continental **V** Lunch £5-£12alc Dinner fr£8.25&alc Last dinner 9.45pm
Credit Cards [1] [2] [3]

★★Grange 17 London Rd, Holybourne GU34 4EG ☎(0420)86565
Closed Xmas-New Year
A personally-run hotel on the outskirts of Alton. The en suite bedrooms are modern and well equipped. The table d'hôte and à la carte menus are soundly cooked.
9rm(6⇨3♠)Annexe6rm(3⇨2♠)(1fb)1 CTV in all bedrooms ® **T** ✱ sB&B⇨♠£39.50-£44
dB&B⇨♠£49.50-£59.50
CTV 40P ✲ (heated) croquet putting nc3yrs
English & French **V** Lunch £5.25-£7.50&alc Dinner £9.95&alc Last dinner 9pm
Credit Cards [1] [2] [3] [5]

ALTON **Staffordshire** Map **07** SK04

★★Bull's Head Inn High St ST10 4AQ ☎(0538)702307
Situated in Alton village centre, close to Alton Towers, the small 18th-century inn provides a friendly, informal atmosphere and well-equipped accommodation.
6rm(3♠)(2fb) CTV in all bedrooms ® sB&B£25-£35
sB&B♠£25-£35 dB&B£30-£40 dB&B♠£30-£40
CTV 15P
V Lunch £7.50-£13.50&alc Dinner £7.50-£13.50&alc Last dinner 9.45pm
Credit Cards [1] [3]

ALTRINCHAM Greater Manchester Map **07** SJ78

★★★55% **Ashley** Ashley Rd, Hale WA15 9SF (De Vere) ☎061-928 3794 Telex no 669406 FAX 061-926 9046
Closed 26 Dec RS 27-31 Dec
Purpose built commercial hotel, forming part of a shopping precinct, with compact public areas. There are no lounge facilities.
49⇨♠ CTV in all bedrooms ® **T** ✱ S10% sB&B⇨♠£25-£58
dB&B⇨♠£50-£70
Lift CTV 100P CFA bowling green
English & French **V** S10% Lunch £6-£11&alc Dinner £6-£11&alc Last dinner 9.45pm
Credit Cards [1] [2] [3] [5] (£)

★★★63% **Bowdon** Langham Rd, Bowdon WA14 2HT ☎061-928 7121 Telex no 668208 FAX 061-927 7560
RS 25 & 26 Dec
An hotel well placed for access to Manchester, the airport and the M56 motorway offers the ideal centre for business meetings and conferences. Modernisation has provided bedrooms of a high standard, well appointed and having en-suite facilities, whilst retaining many traditional features.
82⇨(1fb) CTV in all bedrooms ® **T** ✱ sB&B⇨£30-£54
dB&B⇨£42-£62
168P ♫
English & French **V** Lunch £11.50&alc Dinner £11.50&alc Last dinner 8pm
Credit Cards [1] [2] [3] [5]

Book as early as possible for busy holiday periods.

★★★61% **Cresta Court** Church St WA14 4DP (Best Western)
☎061-927 7272 Telex no 667242 FAX 061-926 9194
A modern hotel with amenities to cater for most needs. There are three bars, two restaurants and a wide range of suites suitable for conferences or social functions. Bedrooms are very well equipped, all with en suite facilities.
139⇨↱(5fb) CTV in all bedrooms ® T S% sB&B⇨↱£28-£50 dB&B⇨↱£36.50-£61 ⊟
Lift ☾ 200P CFA
♈ English & French V ♈ ☕
Credit Cards 1 2 3 5

★★★61% **The Swan Hotel** WA16 6RD (De Vere)
☎Bucklow Hill(0565)830295 Telex no 666911
FAX (0565) 830614
(For full entry see Bucklow Hill)

★★★60% **Woodland Park** Wellington Rd WA15 7RG (Inter)
☎061-928 8631 Telex no 635091 FAX 061-941 2821
A family-owned hotel situated in a quiet residential area. A high standard of accommodation is provided and extensive facilities for functions and conferences are available. The lounge and bar contain antique furniture and gas lamps to create an aura of Victorian elegance.
44rm(32⇨12↱)(6fb)5⊟ CTV in all bedrooms ® T ✗ (ex guide dogs) ✱ sB&B⇨↱£36-£58 dB&B⇨↱£52-£80 ⊟
☾ 150P 1🚗 (charged)
♈ International V ♈ ☕ Lunch fr£15&alc Dinner fr£15&alc
Last dinner 9.45pm
Credit Cards 1 2 3 5 £
See advertisement under MANCHESTER AIRPORT

Red-star hotels offer the highest standards of hospitality, comfort and food.

★★

17 London Road,
Holybourne, ALTON,
Hampshire GU34 4EG
Telephone: Alton (0420) 86565

A warm and friendly country house hotel. Set in beautiful grounds with 9-hole putting green and croquet lawn. All bedrooms are en-suite with colour TV, tea/coffee making & direct-dial phones. Dine by candlelight in the excellent gourmet restaurant, recommended by Egon Ronay. Log fires in winter. Open all year round except Christmas.

★★

NENTHEAD ROAD, NEAR ALSTON,
CUMBRIA CA9 3LF
Tel: Alston (0434) 381203

The hotel nestles in beautiful countryside between a wooded hill and the river Nent high in the Pennines. The most tranquil spot you could possibly imagine. An extremely comfortable Georgian style hotel with a warm and friendly atmosphere. Bedrooms are tastefully furnished and decorated to a high standard, most have superb views. The drawing room and library have open fires which invite guests to relax in style. The restaurant maintains the feeling of gracious living. Five course dinners offer an interesting choice of traditional and innovative dishes. Freshly squeezed orange juice and home made marmalades make breakfast memorable too. Nothing is too much trouble here and the tariff represents real value for money. **Please write or telephone for a brochure.**

★★**George & Dragon** Manchester Rd WA14 4PH (De Vere) ☎061-928 9933 Telex no 665051
A comfortable hotel with well-appointed modern bedrooms, thoughtfully planned bar areas and a congenial restaurant conveniently situated on the A56 approach to Manchester.
47rm(38⇌9⇌)(2fb) CTV in all bedrooms ® T ✻ sB&B£15-£53.50 sB&B⇌⇌£53.50 dB&B£69 dB&B⇌⇌£30-£69 ⊟
Lift ☾ 80P
English & Continental V Lunch £8.25 Dinner £10.95&alc Last dinner 9.45pm
Credit Cards 1 2 3 5 £

★★**Grove Park** Park Rd, Bowdon WA14 3JE ☎061-928 6191
Standing in a suburban area within easy reach of the M56 motorway and Manchester Airport, the hotel features popular restaurants which are open for both lunch and dinner.
13rm(11⇌2⇌) CTV in all bedrooms ® T ✻
sB&B⇌⇌fr£43 dB&B⇌⇌fr£53 ⊟
☾ CTV 28P
International V Lunch fr£5.95 High tea fr£5.95 Dinner fr£10 Last dinner 11.30pm
Credit Cards 1 3

★★**Pelican Inn & Motel** Manchester Rd WA14 5NH ☎061-962 7414 Telex no 668014
Situated on the busy Manchester-Altrincham road, this mock Tudor building has similarly styled motel bedrooms, and is popular with both locals and visitors alike.
50⇌ CTV in all bedrooms ® T sB&B⇌fr£49 dB&B⇌fr£66 ⊟
☾ 150P
English & French V Lunch £3.75-£15 Dinner £4.50-£15 Last dinner 10pm
Credit Cards 1 2 3 5

ALVELEY Shropshire Map **07** SO78

○***Mill Hotel*** Birds Green WV15 6HL ☎(0746)780437
Due to have opened July 1989
21⇌

ALVESTON Avon Map **03** ST68

★★★71% **Alveston House** BS12 2LJ ☎Thornbury(0454)415050 Telex no 449212 FAX (0454) 415425
This popular and very pleasant hotel, conveniently situated for easy access to Bristol and the M4/M5 motorways, appeals to both tourists and business people with its comfortable, well-equipped bedrooms and friendly service, whilst the new conference centre provides an additional attraction.
30⇌ CTV in all bedrooms ® T sB&B⇌£59.50-£63.50 dB&B⇌£71.50-£85 ⊟
CTV 75P ✽ CFA
English & French V Lunch fr£11.75&alc Dinner fr£13.95&alc Last dinner 9.30pm
Credit Cards 1 2 3 5 £

See advertisement under BRISTOL

★★★64% **Post House** Thornbury Rd BS12 2LL (Trusthouse Forte) ☎Thornbury(0454)412521 Telex no 444753 FAX (0454) 413920
Conveniently situated for the M4/M5. Public areas of this hotel are situated in the original Tudor inn whilst a modern wing provides generally spacious bedroom accomodation with good facilities.
75⇌(13fb)⊬in 7 bedrooms CTV in all bedrooms ® T S% sB⇌fr£65 dB⇌fr£78 (room only) ⊟
☾ 100P ✽ CFA (heated) mini golf pitch & putt *xmas*
English & French V ⊬ Lunch £8.95-£9&alc High tea £7 Dinner £11.75&alc Last dinner 10pm
Credit Cards 1 2 3 4 5

ALWALTON Cambridgeshire Map **04** TL19

★★★★58% **Swallow** PE2 0GB (Swallow) ☎Peterborough(0733)371111 Telex no 32422 FAX (0733) 236725
Opened in summer 1988, this hotel exemplifies both the ever-improving quality of Swallow hotels, and the modern, expansive spirit of Peterborough. The hotel faces the East of England Showground and is designed for business use, but offers useful leisure facilities too.
163⇌(10fb)⊬in 56 bedrooms CTV in all bedrooms ® T sB&B⇌£56-£70 dB&B⇌£75-£90 ⊟
☾ CTV 200P ✽ (heated) sauna solarium gymnasium Steam room spa bath beauty therapist ♫ *xmas*
V ⊬ Lunch £8.50-£17.50&alc Dinner £12.50-£17.50&alc Last dinner 10.30pm
Credit Cards 1 2 3 4 5

ALYTH Tayside *Perthshire* Map **15** NO24

★★**Lands of Loyal** Loyal Rd PH11 8JQ
☎(08283)3151

Victorian red sandstone mansion in eight acres of gardens and grounds overlooking the town and the Sidlaw Hills. Bedrooms vary in style from traditional to modern whilst the public rooms retain much of the original character of the house. Service is personal and friendly.
11⇌(2fb)1 CTV in 3bedrooms ® T sB&B⇌£22.50 dB&B⇌£40 ⊟
CTV 20P 6 ✽ snooker shooting *xmas*
Scottish & Continental V Lunch £4.30-£10.10alc Dinner £12.50 Last dinner 10pm
Credit Cards 1 2 3 £

AMBERLEY Gloucestershire Map **03** SO80

★★**Amberley Inn** GL5 5AF (Best Western) ☎(0453)872565 Telex no 9401224
A warm and comfortable inn offering a superb view and situation.
10rm(9⇌)Annexe4⇌(1fb) CTV in all bedrooms ® S% sB&B⇌£48-£56 dB&B⇌£60-£66 ⊟
30P *xmas*
S% Lunch £6.75-£7.50&alc Dinner £12.50-£14&alc Last dinner 9.30pm
Credit Cards 1 2 3

AMBERLEY West Sussex Map **04** TQ01

★★★ 79% **Amberley Castle Country House Hotel** BN18 9ND
☎Bury(0798)831992 FAX (0798) 831998

A private home for 900 years, this fine old castle has been lovingly converted by Joy and Martin Cummings into a hotel of character, comfort and considerable style. The 3

lounges are adorned with fine paintings, and, with their open fires in colder months, are very relaxing. Bedrooms are equally well designed with individual schemes, and each has a spa bath among the en suite facilities. The Queen's Room restaurant would be memorable enough for its restored mural depicting Charles II and Catherine of Braganza, but chef Christophe Durlait is determined that Amberley Castle will enjoy a culinary reputation to match its other splendours. His chicken mosaic and medallions of lamb encased in puff pastry with tomato fondue are particularly notable, and the extensive wine list has a depth and age not normally associated with a new venture.

12 2 CTV in all bedrooms ® **T** (ex guide dogs) sB £85-£100 dB £130-£175 (room only)

50P (grass) *xmas*

French **V** Lunch fr£19.50&alc Dinner fr£19.50&alc Last dinner 10.30pm

Credit Cards 1 2 3 5

✕ ***Quins*** Houghton Bridge BN18 9LR (Close to Amberley Station 1m S of village) ☎Bury (West Sussex)(0798)831790

Attractively situated beside the River Arun on the medieval Houghton Bridge (B2139), and named after the Harlequins rugby football team, this friendly restaurant is personally run by George and Marion Walker.

Closed Mon, Tue & 1 wk end Apr & 1st 2 wks Oct

Dinner not served Sun

English, French & Swiss **V** 40 seats Last lunch 2.15pm Last dinner 9.30pm 20P nc5yrs

Credit Cards 1 3 5

AMBLESIDE Cumbria Map **07** NY30

See also **Elterwater**

★★★ 61% **Regent** Waterhead Bay LA22 0ES (1m S A591) ☎(05394)32254

This comfortable hotel adjacent to Lake Windermere provides modern bedrooms, some in a purpose-built block situated across a paved courtyard. The short table d'hôte menu served at dinner in the George IV restaurant is accompanied by an extensive wine list. Happy, young staff are supervised by the Hewitt family.

21rm(18 3)(2fb)3 CTV in all bedrooms ® **T** ✱ sB&B fr£35.50 dB&B fr£59

30P (heated) *xmas*

English & French Bar Lunch fr£5.50alc Dinner fr£15.50 Last dinner 9pm

Credit Cards 1 3

★★★ 73% **Rothay Manor** Rothay Bridge LA22 0EH ☎(05394)33605

Closed 2 Jan-8 Feb

An elegant, Regency house on the southern approach to the town is personally run by the proprietors to retain the relaxed atmosphere of a country residence. Comfortable, attractively decorated bedrooms with many thoughtful touches are particularly well appointed, whilst the high standards of maintenance and housekeeping are matched by attentive service.

15 Annexe3 (8fb) CTV in all bedrooms **T** (ex guide dogs) sB&B £52-£58 dB&B £72-£94

30P croquet *xmas*

English & Continental **V** Lunch £11.50-£13 High tea £3-£5 Dinner £16-£21 Last dinner 9pm

Credit Cards 1 2 3 5

★★★ 55% **Waterhead** Lake Rd LA22 0ER (Best Western) ☎(05394)32566 Telex no 65273 FAX (05394) 34072

A resort hotel at the southern end of town with views over the lake. Bedrooms are mainly compact and functional though some are more spacious and comfortable.

29rm(14 15)(6fb) CTV in all bedrooms ® **T** ✱ sB&B £39-£52 dB&B £58-£74

▶

50P ✲ ♫ *xmas*
English & French V ✿ ☐ ⚡ S% Sunday Lunch £8.50 High tea £5-£7.50 Dinner £14.50&alc Last dinner 8.30pm
Credit Cards 1 2 3 5

★★Borrans Park Borrans Rd LA22 0EN ☎(05394)33454
Closed 3 days Xmas
This fine Georgian house is set in its own landscaped gardens on the southern outskirts of the town. It has been extended to provide comfortable public rooms and some very attractive bedrooms. A 4 course dinner is served at about 7pm and breakfasts, too, are enjoyable. The hotel offers good value for money and pleasantly relaxed service.
14rm(9⇌4♠)(2fb)7⊞ CTV in 13bedrooms ® T ✗ S%
sB&B£24 dB&B⇌♠£48-£58 ₱
20P ⊞ ✲ nc7yrs
V ⚡ Bar Lunch fr£5 Dinner £12 Last dinner 8pm

★★Crow How Hotel
Rydal Rd LA22 9PN
☎(05394)32193
RS 10 Nov-8 Apr

Beautifully located in attractive gardens three-quarters of a mile north of Ambleside, the hotel provides comfortable, well decorated bedrooms, a relaxing lounge and a cosy bar.
9rm(7⇌1♠)(2fb) CTV in all bedrooms ®
sB&B£16.50-£19.25 sB&B⇌♠£35-£41 dB&B£33-£38.50 dB&B⇌♠£40-£46.20 ₱
9P ⊞ ✲
English & French V ✿ ☐ Dinner £10 Last dinner 7.30pm

★★Elder Grove Lake Rd LA22 0DB (on A591 .5m S)
☎(05394)32504
Closed Nov-Feb
Resident proprietors provide a warm, friendly atmosphere in this comfortable hotel.
12rm(11⇌1♠)(1fb)1⊞ CTV in all bedrooms ® sB&B⇌♠£20 dB&B⇌♠£40 ₱
CTV 12P ⊞
V ✿ ☐ ⚡ Bar Lunch £1-£2.50alc Dinner £12.50 Last dinner 7.30pm
Credit Cards 1 3 £

★★Fisherbeck Old Lake Rd LA22 0DH ☎(05394)33215
Closed Jan
The proprietors are constantly improving this cheerful family-run hotel which is set in attractive gardens away from the road.
20rm(3⇌14♠)(3fb) CTV in all bedrooms ® ✗
CTV 24P ⊞
V ✿ ☐ Last dinner 7.30pm
Credit Cards 1 3

★★Glen Rothay Rydal LA22 9LR ☎(05394)32524
A quaint, historical hotel, close to the road yet set back in the rockside and surrounded by its own gardens. Bedrooms vary considerably in size.
11rm(4⇌7♠)(2fb)3⊞ ® sB&B⇌♠£22-£25 dB&B⇌♠£44-£60 ₱
CTV 45P ⊞ ✲ ♩ *xmas*
V ✿ ⚡ Bar Lunch £7.50-£9.50 Dinner £12.95-£14.50 Last dinner 7.45pm
Credit Cards 1 3

★★Kirkstone Foot Country Kirkstone Pass Rd LA22 9EH
☎(05394)32232
Closed 3-22 Dec & 3 Jan-8 Feb
A converted 17th-century manor house located in an attractive elevated position above the town with well-kept grounds in which the popular self catering cottages and apartments are situated. Lounges are comfortable and spacious, and provide guests with lots of books relating to local information. Emphasis is on traditional English food. A 5-course dinner, with no choice until pudding, is served at 8pm. Bedrooms are very pretty with all necessary facilities.
15rm(13⇌2♠)(2fb) CTV in all bedrooms ® T ✗ ✳
sB&B⇌♠£30-£41 dB&B⇌♠£60-£82 (incl dinner) ₱
35P ⊞ ✲ *xmas*
V ✿ ☐ ⚡ High tea £2.50-£5 Dinner £16 Last dinner 8pm
Credit Cards 1 2 3 5

★★Nanny Brow Country House Clappersgate
LA22 9NF
☎(05394)32036
Telex no 265871
Closed mid Dec-Jan

This attractive Edwardian country house sits in its own grounds high above the A593, 2 miles from the town. A stylish and comfortable lounge, together with other more traditional rooms of the original house, are complemented by a garden wing of suites and studio bedrooms. The 6-course dinner is predominantly a set menu.
19rm(16⇌1♠)(3fb)4⊞ CTV in all bedrooms ® T
sB&B⇌♠£29-£43 dB&B⇌♠£58-£86 ₱
20P ⊞ ✲ ♩ snooker solarium croquet spa bath
English & French V ✿ ☐ ⚡ High tea £2.50 Dinner fr£15 Last dinner 8pm
Credit Cards 1 2 3

★★Riverside Hotel Under Loughrigg, Rothay Bridge LA22 9LJ
☎(05394)32395
Closed Dec-Jan
A delightfully warm and friendly riverside hotel providing very comfortable accommodation and home cooked five course dinners. The lodge 200 yards away is particularly pleasant.
10rm(7⇌3♠)(2fb)1⊞ CTV in all bedrooms ® T ✗ (ex guide dogs) sB&B⇌♠£35-£40 dB&B⇌♠£60-£68 (incl dinner) ₱
CTV 20P ⊞ ✲ ♩
Continental V ✿ ☐ ⚡ Bar Lunch £3-£6 High tea £6-£10 Dinner £12&alc Last dinner 8pm
Credit Cards 1 3 £

★★Skelwith Bridge Skelwith Bridge LA22 9NJ (2.5m W A593)
☎(05394)32115
This pleasantly up-dated Lakeland inn dates from the seventeenth century and has retained some original features. It offers well-proportioned bedrooms, an interesting Georgian lounge with separate TV room and a fashionable restaurant.
18rm(13⇌5♠)Annexe6rm(5⇌1♠)(3fb) CTV in all bedrooms ® sB&B⇌♠£20-£35 dB&B⇌♠£35-£60 ₱
60P ⊞ ♩ *xmas*
English & French V ✿ ☐ ⚡ Lunch fr£7 Dinner fr£14.75 Last dinner 9pm
Credit Cards 1 3 £

For key to symbols see the inside front cover.

A

★★*Vale View* Lake Rd LA22 0BH (Minotels) ☎(05394)33192
Closed 6 Nov-11 Mar
An old established hotel, being refurbished, yet retaining the original character.
20rm(9⇌4♪)(3fb) CTV in 13bedrooms ® ✗
CTV 11P ▦ games room pool & table tennis
✿ ⚡ Last dinner 7.45pm
Credit Cards [1] [2] [3] [5]

★★**Wateredge** Borrans Rd, Waterhead LA22 0EP
☎(05394)32332
Closed mid Dec-1 Feb
Two 17th-century fisherman's cottages form the heart of this skilfully extended and remarkably comfortable hotel on the edge of Windermere. From the lounges there are lovely views of the lake, and the hotel's garden extends to the water's edge. Dinner in the oak-beamed dining room is very much a special occasion, with six courses of predominantly home-cooked English fare and a good selection of wines. The young staff provide friendly and helpful service.
18rm(13⇌5♪)Annexe5⇌(1fb) CTV in all bedrooms ® T ✱
sB&B⇌♪£38.50-£50.50 dB&B⇌♪£74-£114 (incl dinner) ⊟
CTV 25P ▦ ✲ rowing boat nc7yrs
✿ ☕ Bar Lunch £5.50-£10.50alc Dinner £17.50 Last dinner 8.30pm
Credit Cards [1] [2] [3]

AMERSHAM Buckinghamshire Map 04 SU99

★★**The Crown** High St HP7 0DH (Trusthouse Forte)
☎(0494)721541
This Elizabethan inn with a handsome Georgian façade retains many of its original features and embodies the charm of history. The comfortable accommodation has been tastefully arranged to suit the building. A varied menu of good, imaginative cooking is offered.
25rm(13⇌1♪) CTV in all bedrooms ® T S% sBfr£56
sB⇌♪fr£67 dBfr£70 dB⇌♪fr£83 (room only) ⊟
51P *xmas*
V ✿ ☕ ⚡ S% Lunch £8.50-£16.95&alc Dinner £13-£16.95&alc Last dinner 9.30pm
Credit Cards [1] [2] [3] [4] [5]

AMESBURY Wiltshire Map 04 SU14

★★**Antrobus Arms** Church St SP4 7EY (Inter) ☎(0980)623163
Closed Xmas afternoon & evening
This older-style town-centre hotel is notable for its pleasant atmosphere and helpful staff. There is an attractive restaurant and a garden at the rear.
20rm(12⇌)(1fb) CTV in all bedrooms ® T
80P ✲
♉ English & French V ✿ ☕
Credit Cards [1] [2] [3] [4] [5]

○ ***Travelodge*** A303(Trusthouse Forte)
☎Central reservations 01-567 3444
Due to have opened summer 1989
32⇌
P

AMLWCH Gwynedd Map 06 SH49

★★**Trecastell** Bull Bay LL68 9SA (Frederic Robinson)
☎(0407)830651
A warm and friendly hotel overlooking impressive Bull Bay.
12rm(8⇌3♪)(3fb) CTV in 10bedrooms ® sB&B⇌♪£18-£20
dB&B⇌♪£30-£32 ⊟
CTV 60P ▦ ✲
✿ Bar Lunch £1-£5 Dinner fr£7.95&alc Last dinner 8.30pm
Credit Cards [1] [2] [3]

AMMANFORD Dyfed Map 02 SN61

★★**Mill at Glynhir** Glyn-Hir, Llandybie SA18 2TE (3m NE off A483) (Exec Hotel) ☎(0269)850672
RS 24-28 Dec
A former 17th-century mill converted into a unique small comfortable, family run hotel. Offers extensive views over the River Loughor Valley.
9rm(6⇌3♪)Annexe2rm(1⇌1♪) CTV in all bedrooms ® T
sB&B⇌♪£27 dB&B⇌♪£54 ⊟
20P ▦ ✲ ▭(heated) ⚑ 18 ⤴ nc11yrs
♉ Welsh & French V ✿ Dinner £12&alc Last dinner 8.30pm
Credit Cards [1] [3]

AMPFIELD Hampshire Map 04 SU32

★★★62% **Potters Heron** SO51 9ZF (Lansbury)
☎Southampton(0703)266611 Telex no 47459
Standing on the site of the original 'Potters Horn' – the name reflecting an industry based on the local Blue Clay and Bagshot Sand – a charming, thatched hotel of great character and warmth offers accommodation in comfortable, well-equipped bedrooms with modern facilities. The Pantry is very popular for light meals, while the à la carte restaurant offers a wider choice and a more formal setting.
60⇌♪(3fb)1▣⚡in 12 bedrooms CTV in all bedrooms ® T ✗
sB&B⇌♪£33-£65 dB&B⇌♪£66-£75 ⊟
Lift ☾ 200P CFA sauna gymnasium *xmas*
♉ English & French V ✿ ☕ Lunch fr£8.50 Dinner fr£12.50 Last dinner 10pm
Credit Cards [1] [2] [3] [5]

AMULREE Tayside *Perthshire* Map 11 NN83

★★**Amulree** PH8 0EF ☎(03505)218
12rm(5⇌3♪)(1fb) CTV in all bedrooms ® sB&B fr£19.50
sB&B⇌♪£22.50 dB&B£39 dB&B⇌♪£45
CTV 100P 2🚘 ✲ ⤴ *xmas*
♉ International V ✿ ☕ Lunch £6.95&alc Dinner £10&alc Last dinner 9pm
Credit Cards [1] [2] [3] [5] [£]

ANDOVER Hampshire Map 04 SU34

★★***Danebury*** High St SP10 1NX ☎(0264)23332 Telex no 47587
Here, late 16th-century origins blend with tasteful modern furnishings to create a high standard of comfort. Service is extensive, well managed and friendly.
24⇌1▣ CTV in all bedrooms ® T ✗ (ex guide dogs)
☾ CTV 40P ▦
♉ European V ✿ ☕ ⚡ Last dinner 10.30pm
Credit Cards [1] [2] [3] [5]

ANNAN Dumfries & Galloway *Dumfriesshire* Map 11 NY16

★★***Queensberry Arms Toby*** ☎(04612)2024
New owners are refurbishing this town centre, commercial hotel which offers comfortable and well-equipped bedrooms.
27rm(8⇌16♪)(4fb) CTV in all bedrooms ® T
25P 6🚘 ✲
V ✿ ☕ Last dinner 9.30pm
Credit Cards [1] [2] [3] [5]

★★**Warmanbie** DG12 5LL ☎(04612)4015
A modernised country house on the outskirts of town which is informally run. Bedrooms are well-appointed and reflect some thoughtful touches.
7rm(5⇌2♪)(1fb) CTV in all bedrooms ® T
sB&B⇌♪£31.75-£36.25 dB&B⇌♪£44-£55.90 ⊟
25P 1🚘 ✲ ⤴ clay pigeon shooting *xmas*
V ✿ ☕ Bar lunch fr£4 Dinner £12.25&alc Last dinner 9.30pm
Credit Cards [1] [2] [3]

★*Corner House* High St DG12 6DL (Mount Charlotte)
☎(04612)2754
Situated in the centre of town this hotel provides friendly, helpful service at competitive prices, and will appeal to the business traveller and tourist alike.
31rm(1⇌)(3fb) ®
CTV 40P
Mainly grills
Credit Cards [1] [2] [3] [5]

ANSTRUTHER Fife Map **12** NO50

★★★60% *Craws Nest* Bankwell Rd KY10 3DA ☎(0333)310691
Telex no 727049
Popular with tourists, golfers and business people this hotel has a superior annexed wing of spacious and comfortable bedrooms.
31rm(30⇌1♠)Annexe19rm(3⇌16♠)(4fb)2 CTV in all bedrooms ® **T** (ex guide dogs)
CTV 150P ✲ solarium games room ♫
V Last dinner 9pm
Credit Cards [1] [2] [3] [4] [5]

★★**Smugglers Inn** High St KY10 3DQ ☎(0333)310506
A former inn, set in the main street but having views of the Firth of Forth to the rear, offers accommodation in bedrooms that are for the most part compact.
8rm(2⇌6♠) CTV in all bedrooms ✱ sB&B⇌♠£21-£22 dB&B⇌♠£42-£44
CTV 12P
Scottish, French & Italian **V** Bar lunch £4-£6.50 Dinner £10.50-£12.50&alc Last dinner 9.30pm
Credit Cards [1] [2] [3] [5]

A

XX Cellar 24 East Green KY10 3AA
☎(0333)310378

Located in one of the narrow streeets of this small fishing port, this period restaurant possesses a lot of character and charm. It specialises in seafood which comes fresh from various sources in Scotland. The cooking is skilled, presentation is imaginative and service, by both owner and staff, is friendly. The carefully chosen wine list offers a good quality range.

Closed Sun, 24 Dec-4 Jan & 1 wk May

Lunch not served Mon

French 32 seats * Lunch £7.50-£14alc Dinner £17.95-£25 Last lunch 1.30pm Last dinner 9.30pm nc5yrs

Credit Cards 1 2 3

ANSTY Warwickshire Map **04** SP38

★★★ 70% **Ansty Hall** CV7 9HZ ☎Coventry(0203)612222 FAX (0203)602155
Set in 8 acres of garden and parkland, this mellow red-brick Caroline house has been carefully and sympathetically furnished. The hotel is spacious and comfortable, and the bedrooms are particularly well-equipped.
13⇌(3fb) in 7 bedrooms CTV in all bedrooms T (ex guide dogs) * sB⇌£65 dB⇌£85-£95 (room only)
xmas
V Lunch £15&alc High tea £4-£15 Dinner £15&alc Last dinner 9.30pm
Credit Cards 1 2 3 5

APPIN Strathclyde *Argyllshire* Map **14** NM94

★★ ***Invercreran Country House*** Glen Creran PA38 4BJ
☎(063173)414 & 456

Built in the late 1960's and surrounded by 15 acres of grounds, this unique building overlooks glens and mountains from its hillside position. Impressive, spacious bedrooms are in process of upgrading, skilfully prepared and attractively served meals make good use of local produce, and the private-house atmosphere is enhanced by the constant, friendly service offered by the owner's family.
7rm(4⇌2)(3fb) in 1 bedroom T
CTV 18P sauna games room
V Last dinner 8pm
Credit Cards 3

APPLEBY-IN-WESTMORLAND Cumbria Map **12** NY62

★★★ 65% **Appleby Manor** Roman Rd CA16 6JD (Best Western)

☎Appleby(07683)51571
Telex no 9401297

Closed 24-26 Dec

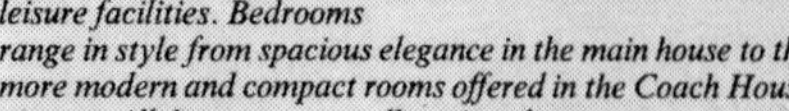

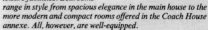

This fine country mansion, set high above the town, is now a popular hotel with extensive leisure facilities. Bedrooms range in style from spacious elegance in the main house to the more modern and compact rooms offered in the Coach House annexe. All, however, are well-equipped.
11rm(10⇌1)Annexe7⇌(6fb)2 CTV in all bedrooms ® T S% sB&B⇌£38-£48.50 dB&B⇌£56-£77
40P 3 (£1) (heated) sauna solarium gymnasium croquet jacuzzi pool table steam room
V S% Lunch £11.50-£12.25&alc Dinner £11.50-£12.25&alc Last dinner 9pm
Credit Cards 1 2 3 5

★★ ***Royal Oak Inn*** Bongate CA16 6UN ☎Appleby(07683)51463
This traditional coaching inn, dating back to the 15th century, has attractive bedrooms and serves very good food.
6rm(1⇌2) CTV in all bedrooms ®
International
Credit Cards 1 2 3

★★ **White Hart** Boroughgate CA16 6XG
☎Appleby(07683)51598
This 18th-century, small, modernised hotel is situated in the town centre.
15rm(7⇌3)(4fb) in all bedrooms CTV in all bedrooms ® * sB&B£15-£25.50 sB&B⇌£18-£30 dB&B£30-£34 dB&B⇌£36-£40
6P hairdresser beauty consultant
International V Lunch fr£8.75&alc Dinner fr£8.75&alc Last dinner 9.30pm
Credit Cards 1 2 3 £

★ **Courtfield** Bongate CA16 6UP ☎Appleby(07683)51394
A small homely establishment, set in three acres of garden on the outskirts of town.
6rm(2⇌2)Annexe5rm(1⇌)(1fb) CTV in 6bedrooms TV in 2bedrooms ® * sB£15-£15.50 sB⇌£20 dB£30-£31 dB⇌£40 (room only)
CTV 20P 2
V Lunch fr£5.50 High tea fr£5.50 Dinner £9-£9.50 Last dinner 8pm
£

All AA-appointed establishments are inspected regularly to ensure that required standards are maintained.

See the preliminary section 'Hotel and Restaurant Classification' for an explanation of the AA's appointment and award scheme.

APPLETON-LE-MOORS North Yorkshire Map **08** SE78

★★ Dweldapilton Hall
YO6 6TF
☏Lastingham
(07515)227 & 452
FAX (07515) 540
Closed Jan

The early Regency/Victorian house stands in attractively landscaped grounds at the centre of a moorland village. The public rooms are furnished in the style of the period and the comfortable bedrooms have been upgraded and restored. The atmosphere is relaxing.

12rm(10⇌2↱) CTV in all bedrooms ® S%
sB&B⇌↱fr£38.50 dB&B⇌↱fr£77 ⊟
Lift CTV 30P ✿ croquet nc16yrs *xmas*
English & Continental V S% Lunch fr£11.95
Dinner £16.50 Last dinner 8.15pm
Credit Cards 1 2 3 £

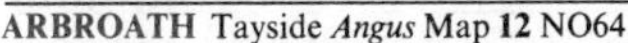

ARBROATH Tayside *Angus* Map **12** NO64

★★★66% ***Letham Grange*** Colliston DD11 4RL (Best Western)
☏Gowanbank(024189)373 FAX (024189) 414
Originally a Victorian mansion house, this hotel stands in 200 acres of wooded grounds, has its own championship golf course and a splendid 4 sheet curling rink. Elegant public rooms feature ornate ceilings, beautiful oak panelling and intricate carving around the fireplaces. Bedrooms, which vary in size, have been individually designed and are comfortable and well-equipped.

▶

A

International cuisine is served in the stylish Rosehaugh Restaurant.
19⇨(4fb)1⊟ CTV in all bedrooms ® T ✗ (ex guide dogs)
☾ 100P ⛟ ⚑ 18 ℘ (hard & grass) ∪ croquet putting pool tables
♡ International V ♡ ☕ Last dinner 9.30pm
Credit Cards [1] [2] [3] [5] £

★★*Hotel Seaforth* Dundee Rd DD11 1QF ☎(0241)72232
This commercial hotel, close to the seafront on the south side of the town, has a snooker club on the premises.
21rm(18⇨)(2fb) CTV in all bedrooms ®
80P 6⛟ (£10 per night) ✲ ⊟(heated) snooker sauna solarium gymnasium
♡ French V ♡ ☕ Last dinner 9pm
Credit Cards [1] [2] [3] [5]

★★Windmill Millgate Loan DD11 1QG ☎(0241)72278
Standing in its own grounds, with coastal and harbour views from its elevated site, this converted private mansion dates from 1824.
15rm(8⇨1↱)(3fb) CTV in all bedrooms ® T ✱ sB&B£18 sB&B⇨↱£23 dB&B£32 dB&B⇨↱£38 ⊟
CTV 70P ✲
V ♡ ☕ Lunch £5.50-£7.50 High tea £4.95-£5.95 Dinner £9.50-£10.50&alc Last dinner 9pm
Credit Cards [1] [2] [3]

✕✕Carriage Room Meadow Bank Inn, Montrose Rd DD11 5RA ☎(0241)75755
This small, friendly and well-appointed restaurant stands beside the A92, forming part of a complex on the northern fringe of the town. The à la carte menu offers a range of imaginative French and Scottish dishes with game in season and a selection of fresh, local sea food which is particularly recommended. Also worthy of mention is the delicious bread and butter pudding with a yoghurt sauce.
Closed Sun, Mon & 1st wk Jan
Lunch not served Sat
♡ Scottish & French V 54 seats Lunch £7.25-£9&alc Dinner £15-£17.50&alc Last lunch 2pm Last dinner 9.30pm 200P ⊁
Credit Cards [1] [2] [3] [5]

ARCHIRONDEL

See **Jersey under Channel Islands**

ARDELVE Highland *Ross & Cromarty* Map **14** NG82

❀★*Loch Duich* IV40 8DY (Minotels)
☎Dornie(059985)213
Closed Oct-Etr
(Rosette awarded for dinner only)
Rod and Geraldine Stenson and their friendly staff ensure a warm, homely atmosphere at this hotel, which is renowned for hospitality and good food. The latter might best be described as first-class home cooking, but this does not begin to do justice to the skill and imagination which goes into presenting dishes bursting with flavour and freshness. The seafood and game enjoyed by one of our inspectors surpassed anything experienced at more renowned gastronomic establishments, and the puddings should also be much appreciated. The hotel is set well back from the road, and gives magnificent views of Loch Duich, Eilean Donan Castle and the surrounding mountains.
18rm⊁in 2 bedrooms
CTV 40P 1⛟ ⛟ ✲ shooting
V ♡ ☕ Last dinner 9pm
Credit Cards [1] [3]

ARDEN Strathclyde *Dunbartonshire* Map **10** NS38

★★★ 50% Lomond Castle G83 8RB (Inter) ☎(038985)681
Telex no 777203 FAX (038985) 257
This hotel, which forms part of a chalet and leisure complex on the shores of Loch Lomond, is now undergoing refurbishment.
21rm(16⇨5↱)(4fb) CTV in all bedrooms ® T
sB&B⇨↱£38-£45 dB&B£49.50-£65 ⊟
☾ 200P ✲ ⊟(heated) ℘ (hard) ♪ snooker sauna solarium gymnasium spa bath *xmas*
♡ Scottish & French V ♡ ☕ ⊁ Lunch £2.75-£15 Dinner £14&alc Last dinner 9.30pm
Credit Cards [1] [2] [3] [5]

ARDENTINNY Strathclyde *Argyllshire* Map **10** NS18

★★*Ardentinny* PA23 8TR (Inter) ☎(036981)209 & 275
Closed 3 Nov-13 Mar RS Nov-Dec
Friendly roadside inn full of character and delightfully situated with gardens leading down to the sea. Popular with yachtsmen and those who enjoy good food.
11rm(5⇨5↱)(1fb) CTV in all bedrooms ®
CTV 30P ✲ boating
♡ Scottish, French & German V ♡ ☕ ⊁ Last dinner 9.30pm
Credit Cards [1] [2] [3] [5]

ARDEONAIG Central *Perthshire* Map **11** NN63

★★Ardeonaig South Loch Tayside FK21 8SU
☎Killin(05672)400
Closed 15 Nov-14 Jan
Relaxed informal roadside inn, in quiet rural location.
12rm(7⇨5↱)(2fb) ® sB&B⇨↱£24-£26
dB&B⇨↱£48-£52 ⊟
CTV 40P ⛟ ✲ ♪ clay pigeon shooting canoeing
♡ Scottish, English & Continental ♡ ☕ Bar Lunch £3.75-£7.50 Dinner £13.50-£15 Last dinner 9pm
Credit Cards [1] [2] [3] [5] £

ARDUAINE Strathclyde *Argyllshire* Map **10** NM80

★★★ 61% Loch Melfort PA34 4XG ☎Kilmelford(08522)233
FAX (08522) 214
Closed mid Oct-Etr
Spectacular views are a feature of this popular hotel with its chalet extension.
6rm(3⇨)Annexe20⇨ CTV in 3bedrooms ® ✱ sB&B⇨fr£34 dB&B⇨fr£68 ⊟
CTV 40P ✲
V ♡ ☕ Bar Lunch £3-£8alc Dinner £17.50&alc Last dinner 8.30pm
Credit Cards [1]

ARDVASAR

See **Skye, Isle of**

ARISAIG Highland *Inverness-shire* Map **13** NM68

★★★ ARISAIG HOUSE
Beasdale PH39 4NR (Relais et Châteaux) ☎(06875)622
Telex no 777279
Closed Nov-8 Apr

A family-run, country house hotel that stands in the

stunning Highlands scenery on the celebrated Road to the Isles – and lives up to its setting. Much of the atmosphere of the original Victorian house survives, though it was rebuilt in the 1930s. The drawing room, with its Italian vaulted ceiling has a log fire and notably luxurious sofas and armchairs which invite one to sit and gaze at gardens beyond, and the smaller morning room is equally comfortable. A magnificent carved staircase leads up from the inner hall, and the bar has window seats looking onto the beautiful rose garden. Outside there are also croquet lawns, and woodland and meadow walks down to the loch. Bedrooms are stocked with flasks of iced water, fresh fruit and flowers, and all are individually styled in warm, welcoming schemes with the master bedrooms being particularly spacious. The hospitable owners are Ruth and John Smithers, who run the hotel with the help of their children, Andrew and Alison. Son-in-law, David Wilkinson, is the chef, and he provides a commendable set menu of 5 courses with alternatives, making good use of fresh, local produce (some of it from the walled kitchen garden). Meals in the panelled dining room are complemented by a well-chosen wine list that ranges from worthy clarets to French country wines.

14rm(13⇌) CTV in all bedrooms T ✗ (ex guide dogs) sB&B⇌fr£72.50 dB&B⇌£165-£220 (incl dinner) ⊟

16P ⇌ ✲ snooker croquet nc10yrs

☋ British & French ✧ ⊻ ⊁ Bar Lunch £6-£17.50alc Dinner £27.50 Last dinner 8.30pm

Credit Cards 1 3

★★Arisaig PH39 4NH ☎(06875)210

A roadside hotel with commanding views of the island of Eigg. Highland hospitality is provided by the Stewart family and includes good, honest food using local produce, particularly seafood.

15rm(6⇌)(4fb) ® T sB&B£19.50-£27 dB&B£39-£54 dB&B⇌£47-£65 ⊟

CTV 60P ⇌ ♫

V ✧ ⊻ Lunch £2-£12alc High tea £2.50-£10alc Dinner £18.50 Last dinner 8.30pm

ARNCLIFFE North Yorkshire Map **07** SD97

★★⚜Amerdale House
BD23 5QE
☎(075677)250
Closed mid Nov-mid Mar

A very friendly atmosphere, really comfortable lounge and superb meals are features of this delightfully located hotel.

10rm(6⇌4⚐)(2fb)1⊞ CTV in all bedrooms ® ✗ (ex guide dogs) ✱ sB&B£37-£39 sB&B⇌⚐£39-£44 dB&B£64-£68 dB&B⇌⚐£72-£78 (incl dinner) ⊟

30P ⇌ ✲

V ⊁ Dinner £15 Last dinner 8.30pm

Credit Cards 1 3

A rosette is the AA's highest award for quality of food and service in a restaurant.

ARRAN, ISLE OF Strathclyde *Bute* Map **10**

LAGG Map **10** NR92

★★**Lagg** KA27 8PQ ☎Sliddery(077087)255
15rm(9⇌6⋔)(3fb) ® sB&B⇌⋔£25-£45
dB&B⇌⋔£50-£90 (incl dinner)
CTV 40P ⊕ ✽ ♩ *xmas*
☊ Scottish & French V ♧ ⚘ Lunch £4.50-£20alc High tea £2.50-£18alc Dinner £13-£18alc Last dinner 9pm

ARUNDEL West Sussex Map **04** TQ00

★★★66% **Norfolk Arms** High St BN18 9AD (Forestdale) ☎(0903)882101 Telex no 878436 FAX (0903) 884275
A gracious Georgian coaching inn built two centuries ago by the 10th Duke of Norfolk. It still has that atmosphere of traditional permanence, but it has been tastefully furnished and well equipped to satisfy the most discerning guest. Modern annexe bedrooms combine with the original and there are two bars, a restaurant, a breakfast room and a comfortable lounge.
21⇌Annexe13⇌(1fb)6⊟⊬in 3 bedrooms CTV in all bedrooms ® T ✻ sB&B⇌£42.50-£49.50 dB&B⇌£60-£66 ⊨
☾ 15P 15⌂ *xmas*
☊ International V ♧ ⚘ ⊬ Lunch £8.95-£10.45&alc Dinner £12.95-£18.95alc Last dinner 10pm
Credit Cards 1 2 3 4 5

★★**Howards** Crossbush BN18 9PQ ☎(0903)882655
Guests staying at this very popular hotel have a choice of two restaurants, the Carvery and the Café des Amis Basement Rendezvous; well-equipped bedrooms are furnished in the modern style and levels of comfort are generally acceptable.
10⇌(1fb) CTV in all bedrooms ® T ✗ ✻ sB&B⇌fr£38
dB&B⇌fr£48 ⊨
150P ⊕ ✽ ♫
☊ English & French ♧ Lunch £9.25-£11.80 Dinner £10.25-£12.80 Last dinner 10pm
Credit Cards 1 2 3 5

★♣**Burpham Country** Old Down, Burpham BN18 9RJ (3m NE off A27)
☎(0903)882160
Peacefully set overlooking the South Downs, this small, privately-run hotel offers attractive and comfortable bedrooms, good home cooking and a warm welcome.
10rm(8⇌1⋔) CTV in all bedrooms ® ✗
sB&B⇌⋔£38-£40 dB&B⇌⋔£50-£60 ⊨
12P ⊕ ✽ nc12yrs *xmas*
V ♧ ⚘ ⊬ Lunch fr£9 Dinner fr£11 Last dinner 8pm
Credit Cards 1

ASCOT Berkshire Map **04** SU96

★★★★50% **Berystede** Bagshot Rd, Sunninghill SL5 9JH (Trusthouse Forte) ☎(0990)23311 due to change to (0344) 23311 Telex no 847707 FAX (0990) 872301
Set in attractive grounds, this smart, well-appointed hotel continues to upgrade its bedrooms. It is popular with both conferences and private guests.
91rm(90⇌1⋔)(6fb)2⊟⊬in 14 bedrooms CTV in all bedrooms ® T S% sB⇌⋔£81-£125 dB⇌⋔£96-£150 (room only) ⊨
Lift ☾ 240P ✽ ⌓(heated) games room ♫ *xmas*
☊ English & French V ♧ ⚘ S% Lunch £14-£14.75&alc Dinner £17.50-£22.50&alc Last dinner 9.45pm
Credit Cards 1 2 3 4 5

★★★★58% **The Royal Berkshire** London Rd, Sunninghill SL5 0PP (Hilton) ☎(0990)23322 Telex no 847280
FAX (0990) 27100
A handsome, Queen Anne mansion, dating from 1705 and delightfully set in mature parkland, offers guests a choice of renovated bedrooms ranging through courtyard rooms and the new wing to the splendour of the Polo Suite. The Stateroom Restaurant features an interesting and creative menu complemented by a well-chosen wine list, while leisure facilities for all seasons include an indoor swimming pool.
64rm(63⇌1⋔)Annexe18⇌(2fb)2⊟ CTV in all bedrooms ® T ✻ sB⇌⋔£69-£90 dB⇌⋔£94-£326 (room only) ⊨
☾ 150P ✽ ⌓(heated) ♇ (hard) squash sauna croquet *xmas*
☊ English V ♧ ⚘ S12.5% Lunch £18-£22&alc Dinner £22.50-£27&alc Last dinner 9.30pm
Credit Cards 1 2 3

ASHBOURNE Derbyshire Map **07** SK14

★★♣**Callow Hall**
Mappleton Rd DE6 2AA
☎(0335)43403 & 43164
FAX (0335) 43624
Closed 25-26 Dec & 2 wks Feb
A stone-built hotel, set in its own grounds and surrounded by farmland, is personally run by the family whose efforts over the last few years have converted it from their family home to the high-quality, country house establishment that it is today. Patron David Spencer, a master baker, is rapidly gaining a good local reputation as a chef.
9⇌1⊟ CTV in all bedrooms ® T ✗ (ex guide dogs)
sB&B⇌£50.50-£58 dB&B⇌£73-£103 ⊨
20P 1⌂ ⊕ ✽ ♩
☊ English & French Dinner fr£19.50&alc Last dinner 9.15pm
Credit Cards 1 2 3 5 £

○*Ashbourne Lodge* Derby Rd DE6 1XH ☎(0335)46666
Due to have opened July 1989
51⇌

ASHBURTON Devon Map **03** SX77

★★**Dartmoor Motel** Peartree Cross TQ13 7JW (Exec Hotel) ☎(0364)52232
RS 25 & 26 Dec
Privately owned and run touring and business motel, conveniently situated just off the A38, on the B3357 Ashburton road. Offers friendly services, character bar, dining room, and bedrooms which continue to be upgraded to a very attractive and good standard.
30rm(24⇌6⋔)(6fb)2⊟ CTV in all bedrooms ® T
sB&B⇌⋔£29.85-£37.85 dB&B⇌⋔£41.85-£66.85 ⊨
Lift 50P 2⌂ (£1.50) ✽
☊ English & French V ♧ ⚘ ⊬ Lunch £5.50-£7.50&alc High tea fr£2.50 Dinner £6.50-£8.50&alc Last dinner 9.30 pm
Credit Cards 1 2 3 5 £

Book as early as possible for busy holiday periods.

★★ Holne Chase TQ13 7NS (Inter)

Poundsgate(03643)471
FAX (03643) 453

An attractive period house in a magnificent setting with most impressive views.

12rm(9 2)1 CTV in all bedrooms ® T
sB&B fr£50 dB&B £65-£95
30P croquet putting *xmas*
English & French V Lunch fr£9.75&alc Dinner fr£16.50&alc Last dinner 9pm
Credit Cards 1 2 3 5 £

See advertisement on page 81

★★Tugela House 68-70 East St TQ13 7AX (0364)52206
Comfortable family-run hotel in this moorland town, offering attractive bedrooms and public areas, good home cooking and friendly services.
7rm(3 2) CTV in all bedrooms sB&B£25-£30 sB&B £27.50-£32 dB&B£35-£37 dB&B £37-£40
6P 2
English & French V Lunch fr£9 Dinner fr£10.50 Last dinner 9pm
£

ASHBY-DE-LA-ZOUCH Leicestershire Map **08** SK31

★★★60% **Royal Osprey** Station Rd LE6 5GP (Toby)
☎(0530)412833 Telex no 341629
RS 24 Dec-1 Jan
Situated on the A453 close to the town centre this Georgian building provides quite well equipped accomodation and caters mainly for commercial guests. Extensive refurbishment during 1989 should greatly improve the quality and comfort throughout.
31rm(25⇨6↱)(3fb)⊁in 3 bedrooms CTV in all bedrooms ® T ✳ sB&B⇨↱£18.50-£44 dB&B⇨↱£31-£54 ⊟
☾ 100P ✲ ♫
♉ English & French V ♧ ⊒ ⊁ Lunch £8.35&alc Dinner £11.95&alc Last dinner 9.45pm
Credit Cards 1 2 3 4 5

ASHFORD Kent Map **05** TR04

★★★★⚑
EASTWELL MANOR

Eastwell Park TN25 4HR
(Norfolk Capital)(Prestige)
☎(0233)635751
Telex no 966281
FAX (0233) 35530

This grand manor house may appear rather imposing, but it has a great deal of charm and guests will find the staff to be formal and courteous yet, at the same time, pleasant and attentive. A stay here is certainly a very enjoyable experience. The setting is delightful and, with over 3, 000 acres of private parkland surrounding the hotel, tranquility is assured. There are quite outstanding views from the bedrooms, all of which have been refurbished to provide both quality and comfort. Bathrooms are, in general, spacious and are particularly well equipped. the large public areas, too, have been receiving a great deal of attention and the oak panelling in the bar lounge is now looking at its very best. Throughout, the public areas are well appointed and comfortable, with large open fires promoting a relaxing atmosphere. We are very pleased to welcome Eastwell Manor back into our select band of Red Star hotels.

23⇨ CTV in all bedrooms **T** ✗ (ex guide dogs)
sB&B⇨£80-£105 dB&B⇨£95-£200 ⊟
Lift ☾ 70P 20⛍ ✲ ℘ (hard) snooker croquet *xmas*
V ♧ ⊒ Lunch £12-£15&alc Dinner £22.50-£26&alc Last dinner 9.30pm
Credit Cards 1 2 3 5 £

★★★66% **Ashford Post House** Canterbury Rd TN24 8QQ (Trusthouse Forte) ☎(0233)625790 Telex no 966685
FAX (0233) 43176
A high degree of modern comfort has been incorporated into the well-equipped bedrooms of this purpose-built hotel. An effective contrast in style is provided by the restaurant, a restored, oak-framed, 17th-century barn with minstrels' gallery, where table d'hôte and à la carte menus are complemented by a fairly extensive wine list that should suit most tastes.
60⇨⊁in 10 bedrooms CTV in all bedrooms ® **T** ✳
sB⇨£70-£86 dB⇨£81-£95 (room only) ⊟
☾ 95P ✲ ♫ *xmas*
V ♧ ⊒ ⊁ S% Lunch £9.50-£12&alc Dinner £14.95-£15.95&alc Last dinner 10pm
Credit Cards 1 2 3 4 5

★★★57% **Spearpoint** Canterbury Rd, Kennington TN24 9QR (Best Western) ☎(0233)36863 Telex no 965978
FAX (0233) 610119
A pleasant hotel set in five acres of delightful grounds offers functional bedrooms (some in a new wing) and a restaurant that operates as a carvery at lunchtime. The ground level bar/lounge is supplemented by a small lounge on the first floor.
36rm(32⇨4↱)(1fb) CTV in all bedrooms ® **T** ✳
sB&B⇨↱£58-£60 dB&B⇨↱£75-£77 ⊟
60P ✲
♉ International **V** ♧ ⊒ Lunch £1-£4alc Dinner £13-£26alc Last dinner 9.45pm
Credit Cards 1 2 3 5 £

ASHFORD Surrey London plan **5** *A2* (Page 412)

✕✕**Terrazza** 45 Church St TW15 2TY
☎(0784)244887 & 241732
Closed Sun & BH's
Lunch not served Sat
♉ Continental **V** 70 seats Lunch £16.50&alc Dinner £16.50&alc Last lunch 2.15pm Last dinner 10.30pm ⊅
Credit Cards 1 2 3 5

ASHFORD-IN-THE-WATER Derbyshire Map **08** SK17

★★⚑**Riverside Country House Hotel** Fennel St
DE4 1QF
☎Bakewell(0629)814275

At the heart of this picturesque Derbyshire village, this hotel is, indeed, by the river, with lawns and gardens leading to its banks. The Georgian building has been carefully improved by owners, Sue and Roger Taylor, to provide individually styled bedrooms with co-ordinated décor, and each has its own beautifully equipped bathroom. Lots of extras in the bedrooms make guests feel at home, but the pleasant, friendly and obliging staff are also on hand to provide that personal service so often missing in larger hotels. The restaurant is very popular with non-residents and chef Jeremy Buckingham produces British and French food with some adventurous combinations of flavour, excellently presented with sensible portions.

7rm(5⇨2↱)2⊞ CTV in all bedrooms ® **T** ✳
sB&B⇨↱£59-£69 dB&B⇨↱£69-£73 ⊟
CTV 30P ⊞ ✲ ♩ ∪ *xmas*
♉ English & French **V** ♧ ⊒ ⊁ Lunch £11.50 Dinner £20-£25 Last dinner 9.30pm
Credit Cards 1 2 3

ASHINGTON West Sussex Map **04** TQ11

★★**Mill House** Mill Ln RH20 3BZ ☎(0903)892426
FAX (0903) 892855
A tastefully furnished 18th-century farm millhouse, quietly situated off the north carriageway of the A29. The agreeable olde worlde atmosphere is enhanced by friendly personal service. There is a popular restaurant, a comfortable lounge, a small bar and a new conference room.
11rm(7⇨2↱)2⊞ CTV in all bedrooms ® **T** ✳ sB&Bfr£35
sB&B⇨↱fr£38.50 dB&Bfr£55 dB&B⇨↱£62.50-£70 ⊟
12P ⊞ ✲ ⌂ *xmas*

♀ English & French V ✿ ☕ S10% Lunch fr£8.95&alc High tea £2.50-£6.50 Dinner fr£11.55&alc Last dinner 9.30pm
Credit Cards 1 2 3 4 5 £

See advertisement on page 83

✕✕**Ashington Court** London Rd RH20 3JR ☎(0903)892575
This elegant, beamed farmhouse-style restaurant has a bar lounge and log fires, and is personally run by Mr Andrew James. A good value à la carte menu features fresh fish, local produce, and a daily special; all desserts are home made. The service is particularly efficient and helpful.
Closed Mon, 2 wks Feb & 2 wks Sep
Dinner not served Sun
♀ English & French V 30 seats ✱ Lunch fr£11.95&alc Dinner £15-£25alc Last lunch 1.30pm Last dinner 9.30pm 25P
Credit Cards 1 2 3 5

ASHLEY HEATH Dorset Map 04 SU10

★★**Struan** Horton Rd BH24 2EG
☎Ringwood(0425)473553 & 473029 FAX (0425) 480529
This attractive, white-rendered hotel stands in a quiet, wooded, residential area on the edge of the New Forest. A good range of carefully prepared and cheerfully served food is available in its popular restaurant and Bush Bar.
10rm(2♠)(2fb) ® sB&B♠£28-£35 dB&B♠£48-£55
CTV 75P ✲ solarium ♫
♀ English & French V ✿ ☕ Lunch £2.50-£9.50&alc Dinner £15-£19.50alc Last dinner 9.30pm
Credit Cards 1 2 3 5

ASHTON-UNDER-LYNE Greater Manchester Map 07 SJ99

★★**York House** York Place, Richmond St OL6 7TT ☎061-330 5899 FAX 061-343 1613
Closed Bank Hols
You are assured of both a warm welcome and professional standards of service at this family-run hotel which stands among recently planted gardens in a quiet cul de sac just off the Manchester approach to the town. Bedrooms are extemely well-appointed, and an excellent restaurant offers a high standard of cuisine, combining classical dishes with a range of its own delicious creations which make full use of seasonal produce.
24rm(18⇔5♠)Annexe10⇔(2fb)1⊞ CTV in all bedrooms ® T S10% sB&B⇔♠£39.50-£45 dB&B⇔♠£52-£57 ⊟
☾ 34P ✲
♀ English & French V ✿ ☕
Credit Cards 1 2 3 4 5

See advertisement on page 83

ASKRIGG North Yorkshire Map 07 SD99

★★**King's Arms** Market Place DL8 3HQ (Minotels)
☎Wensleydale(0969)50258
18th-century coaching inn of great character and warmth and location for the 'Herriot' TV series. The comfortable, modernised bedrooms are furnished in period style.
10rm(3⇔6♠)(1fb)6⊞ CTV in all bedrooms ® T
sB&B⇔♠£25-£35 dB&B⇔♠£40-£55 ⊟
14P *xmas*
♀ English & French V ✿ Lunch fr£6.95 Dinner fr£13.75&alc Last dinner 9pm
Credit Cards 1 2 3 5 £

ASPLEY GUISE Bedfordshire Map 04 SP93

★★★70% **Moore Place Hotel** The Square MK17 8DW (Select)
☎Milton Keynes(0908)282000 FAX (0908) 281888
RS 26-28 Dec
This Georgian building has been refurbished to a high standard to provide tastefully appointed and well-equipped bedrooms - some are in the main building whilst others form a courtyard overlooking a very pleasant rock garden. The attractive restaurant, with a ▶

A

Victorian-style conservatory, serves interesting French and English dishes using good fresh produce.
39⇌Annexe15⇌ CTV in all bedrooms ® T ✻
sB&B⇌£75-£100 dB&B⇌£90-£115 ⊟
☾60P ✼ ℛ
V ♆ ☕
Credit Cards 1 2 3 5

ASTON CLINTON Buckinghamshire Map **04** SP81

❀★★★ **BELL INN**
HP22 5HP (Relais et Châteaux)
☎Aylesbury(0296)630252
Telex no 83252
FAX (0296) 631250
RS Sun eve & Mon

The fresh flowers that fill this beautiful old coaching house raise expectation of friendly hospitality which are handsomely fulfilled by the owners, Michael and Patsy Harris. Here one can relax and enjoy the charm of the old courtyard also full of flowers and the stone-flagged bar. Most of the comfortable, spacious bedrooms are set apart from the main building, in the inn's former malthouses and stables, and some are furnished with fine antiques. A scheme of small sections within the spacious restaurant makes for intimacy, and young chef Kevin Cape uses the best fresh produce with innovative skill, producing such dishes as a light Ravioli filled with wild mushrooms, and superb fillets of Dover Sole stuffed with spring vegetables with a fluffy herb mousse. A particularly well-chosen wine list continues to excite the most fastidious of wine lovers. the greatest compliment that one can pay this famous long-established inn is its remarkable consistency. The faces may change, but it is to the eternal credit ofthe Harris family that standards remain so uniformly high.
21⇌⌐2⊟ CTV in all bedrooms T ✻ sB&B⇌⌐£76-£82 dB&B⇌⌐£90-£110 Continental breakfast
150P ✼ croquet *xmas*
♅ English & French V ♆ ☕ Lunch fr£15.50&alc Dinner fr£16.50&alc Last dinner 9.45pm
Credit Cards 1 3

ATTLEBOROUGH Norfolk Map **05** TM09

★★***Sherbourne Country House*** Norwich Rd NR17 2JX
☎(0953)454363
This small family hotel, set on the outskirts of Attleborough aims to provide personal service in keeping with its country atmosphere.
8rm(4⇌1⌐)3⊟ CTV in all bedrooms ® T
50P 1⌂ ✼
♅ International ♆ ☕ ⚔ Last dinner 9pm
Credit Cards 1 2 3

All hotels awarded three or more stars are now also given a percentage grading for the quality of their facilities. Please see p 16 for a detailed explanation.

AUCHENCAIRN Dumfries & Galloway *Kirkcudbright* Map **11** NX75

★★★♚ **69% Balcary Bay**
DG7 1QZ
☎(055664)217 & 311
Closed Nov-Feb

A delightful hotel, in a charming coastal situation, whose grounds run down to the waters edge. Bedrooms are bright and airy and public areas comfortable and tastefully appointed.
13rm(11⇌1⌐)(1fb) CTV in all bedrooms ® T
sB&B⇌⌐£32-£35 dB&B£45-£50 dB&B⇌⌐£55-£65 ⊟
50P ⌂ ✼ snooker
♅ English & French V ♆ ☕ Lunch £13-£17alc Dinner £13&alc Last dinner 9pm
Credit Cards 1 3 £

AUCHTERARDER Tayside *Perthshire* Map **11** NN91

★★★★★ **THE GLENEAGLES**
PH3 1NF ☎(0764)62231
Telex no 76105
FAX (0764) 62134

Set amidst the rugged grandeur of Perthshire, this celebrated hotel offers a dazzling array of recreational facilities in its 610-acre estate. Four championship 18-hole golf courses, the Mark Phillips Equestrian Centre and the Jackie Stewart Shooting School are perhaps the jewels in a crown which also includes tennis, squash, bowling, pitch-and-putt, a fully-equipped gymnasium anda semi-tropical country club with landscaped pool, jacuzzi and solarium. Guests may also promenade through the arcade of shops or indulge themselves in a range of health and beauty treatments. High standards prevail in all departments here. The bedrooms and suites have 24-hour room service and are lavishly equipped. Splendid public rooms include a new champagne bar where a pianist plays in the evening, and an elegant drawing room where light refreshments are served all day, with traditional tea in the afternoon and dancing every night. The four restaurants include the relaxed Dormy House and Grill, and the poolside restaurant for light meals and a bar menu. More formal are the Conservatory and the Strathearn, which has magnificent views towards the Ochil Hills. There is also an air-conditioned conference centre; and last, but by no means least, this hotel is renowned for its hospitable atmosphere.
241⇌10⊟⚔in 18 bedrooms CTV in all bedrooms T ✻
sB⇌£75-£85 dB⇌£125-£155 (room only) ⊟
Lift ☾200P 6⌂ ✼ CFA ⊡(heated) ⚑18 ℛ (hard & grass) ♪ squash ∪ snooker sauna solarium gymnasium croquet bowls putting shooting school ♫ *xmas*
♅ International V ♆ ☕ ⚔ Lunch fr£19 Dinner fr£24 Last dinner 10pm
Credit Cards 1 2 3 4 5

★★★ 69% **Auchterarder House** PH3 1DZ (Prestige)

☎(0764)63646 & 63647
FAX (0764)62939

12⇌ CTV in all bedrooms T ✱ sB&B⇌£70-£90 dB&B⇌£95-£135

(40P ✿ croquet lawn pitch & putting green *xmas*

Scottish & French V Lunch £21.50 Dinner £27.50&alc Last dinner 10pm

Credit Cards 1 2 3 4 5 £

All hotels awarded three or more stars are now also given a percentage grading for the quality of their facilities. Please see p 11 for a detailed explanation.

A

AUCHTERHOUSE Tayside *Forfarshire* Map **11** NO33

★★★ 68% Old Mansion House DD3 0QN
☎(082626)366
FAX (082626) 400
Closed 25 Dec-3 Jan

A baronial home, dating back to the sixteenth-century and set in ten acres of attractive garden and woodland, provides accommodation in bedrooms that are comfortably furnished, well decorated and thoughtfully equipped. Dinner in the elegant restaurant is a civilised and enjoyable experience, service being attentive but relaxed and the atmosphere friendly throughout the hotel.
6rm(5⇌1♮)(2fb)1 CTV in all bedrooms ® T ✱
sB&B⇌♮£55-£60 dB&B⇌♮£60-£80
50P 1 ✲ (heated) (grass) squash croquet
Scottish & French V Lunch £12.95-£13.95&alc Dinner £20-£25 Last dinner 9.30pm
Credit Cards 1 2 3 5

AULTBEA Highland *Ross & Cromarty* Map **14** NG88

★★Aultbea IV22 2HX ☎(044582)201
Small, friendly family run hotel, delightfully set on the shore of Loch Ewe.
8rm(7⇌)(1fb) CTV in all bedrooms ® T sB&B⇌£16-£25.50 dB&B⇌£32-£51
CTV 40P ✲ pool table xmas
International V Lunch £6.50 High tea £4-£10 Dinner £13&alc Last dinner 9.30pm
Credit Cards 1 3

★★*Drumchork Lodge* IV22 2HU ☎(044582)242
RS Nov-Feb
This family-run hotel enjoys a fine elevated position overlooking the village, harbour and Loch Ewe.
11rm(6⇌3♮)Annexe3⇌(4fb) CTV in all bedrooms ®
CTV 50P ✲ snooker sauna solarium
Scottish & Continental Last dinner 8.00pm
Credit Cards 1 2 3 5

AUST MOTORWAY SERVICE AREA (M4) Avon Map **03** ST58

○***Rank Motor Lodge*** M4 Motorway (junc 21) BS12 3BJ (Rank)
☎Pilning(04545)3789 due to change to 3313
Due to open Dec 1989
50⇌♮

AUSTWICK North Yorkshire Map **07** SD76

★*The Traddock* LA2 8BY ☎Clapham(04685)224
Closed Oct-Etr
A Georgian country house of stone construction in its own grounds.
12rm(3⇌7♮)(4fb) CTV in 3bedrooms ®
CTV 12P ✲ nc5yrs
Last dinner 5.30pm

See the preliminary section 'Hotel and Restaurant Classification' for an explanation of the AA's appointment and award scheme.

AVIEMORE Highland *Inverness-shire* Map **14** NH81

★★★★64% Stakis Four Seasons Aviemore Centre PH22 1PF (Stakis) ☎(0479)810681 Telex no 75213 FAX (0479) 810862
Extensive refurbishment has much improved this popular holiday and conference hotel which is located in the Aviemore Centre. Bedrooms are tastefully furnished and well-equipped while the new Coffee Lounge and Leisure Club add to the appeal of the hotel's public areas.
88⇌♮(3fb)⅟in 54 bedrooms CTV in all bedrooms ® T ✱
sB&B⇌♮£49-£68 dB&B⇌♮£41-£101 (incl dinner)
Lift ☾ 100P ✲ (heated) sauna solarium gymnasium Turkish bath & whirlpool ♫ xmas
Scottish, English & French
Credit Cards 1 2 3 5

★★★59% Post House Aviemore Centre PH22 1PJ (Trusthouse Forte) ☎(0479)810771 Telex no 75597 FAX (0479) 811473
This modern hotel is set in the Aviemore Complex with a splendid backdrop of hills and pine forest. It provides pleasant, well-appointed bedrooms, a restaurant and coffee shop, two bars and open plan lounges. There is also a supervised nursery and laundry. Mussels and venison are specialities on a mainly Scottish menu.
103⇌(34fb)⅟in 27 bedrooms CTV in all bedrooms ® T ✱
sB⇌fr£53 dB⇌fr£69 (room only)
Lift ☾ 140P solarium games room xmas
V S% Bar Lunch fr£5alc Dinner £11-£12&alc Last dinner 9.30pm
Credit Cards 1 2 3 4 5

★★★63% *Red McGregor* Main Rd PH22 1RH ☎(0479)810256 FAX (0479) 810685
A modern tourist hotel of Swedish design has recently been refurbished to provide thoughtfully appointed bedrooms, attractive public areas which include a coffee shop specialising in home baked bread, croissants and pastries, and a well equipped leisure complex.
30⇌(8fb) CTV in all bedrooms ® T
☾ CTV 65P ✲ (heated) sauna solarium gymnasium
Mainly grills Last dinner 10pm
Credit Cards 1 2 3 5

AVON Hampshire Map **04** SZ19

★★Tyrrells Ford Country House BH23 7BH (4m S of Ringwood on B3347) ☎Bransgore(0425)72646 FAX (0425) 72262
Pheasants and rabbits wander freely through the ten acres of garden and woodland surrounding this Georgian hotel on the edge of the New Forest. Recent refurbishment has provided comfortable, well-equipped and restfully decorated bedrooms, there is an unusual galleried lounge, and the restaurant's carefully prepared meals make it popular locally.
16rm(10⇌6♮) CTV in all bedrooms ® T ✗ (ex guide dogs)
sB&B⇌♮£35-£50 dB&B£55-£70 dB&B⇌♮£55-£70
100P ✲ xmas
English & French V Lunch £8.95-£10.95&alc Dinner £12.95-£14.95&alc Last dinner 10pm
Credit Cards 1 3

AXBRIDGE Somerset Map **03** ST45

★★*Oak House* The Square BS24 2AP ☎(0934)732444
Set in the town square, the Oak House provides relaxing accommodation in pleasantly appointed bedrooms, whilst a good à la carte selection of well-prepared dishes is available in the comfortable restaurant.
9rm(7⇌)(1fb) CTV in all bedrooms ® T ✗
1P
English & French V
Credit Cards 1 2 3 5

See advertisement under CHEDDAR

AXMINSTER Devon Map **03** SY29

★★***George Hotel*** Trinity Square EX13 5DW (Minotels)
☎(0297)32209 FAX (0297) 34234
A Georgian coaching inn in the centre of the town, featuring one of the country's few remaining 'Adam' fireplaces. It is personally run by Mr and Mrs Andrews who offer a warm welcome. All bedrooms have good facilities. There are two busy bars and a small restaurant with an à la carte menu.
11rm(8⇔3↱)(5fb)1⊞ CTV in all bedrooms ® **T**
CTV 20P
☋ English & French **V** ♡ ☕ Last dinner 9pm
Credit Cards 1 2 3 5

★★**Woodbury Park Country House** Woodbury Cross EX13 5TL
☎(0297)33010
Standing in 5.5 acre grounds with magnificent views across the Axe Valley, the small, family-run hotel offers tranquility combined with discreet twentieth-century comforts.
8rm(5⇔1↱)(1fb) CTV in all bedrooms ® ✱ sB&B£20-£24 sB&B⇔↱£22-£26 dB&B£34-£40 dB&B⇔↱£36-£42 ⊟
CTV 30P ⊞ ✻ ⛆(heated) sauna
V ♡ ☕ Lunch £7.95 Dinner £7.95&alc Last dinner 9pm
Credit Cards 1 2 3 5 £

AYLESBURY Buckinghamshire Map **04** SP81

★★★★**68% Forte Hotel** Aston Clinton Rd HP22 5AA (Trusthouse Forte) ☎(0296)393388 Telex no 838820 FAX (0296) 392211
A modern commercial/conference hotel with a spacious lounge, well-equipped bedrooms and good leisure facilities.
100⇔↱(8fb)⊬in 22 bedrooms CTV in all bedrooms ® **T** S% sB⇔↱£74.50-£91 dB⇔↱£90.50-£162 (room only) ⊟
☾ 150P ✻ ⛆(heated) sauna solarium gymnasium *xmas*
V ♡ ☕ ⊬ S% Lunch £11.95-£13 Dinner £14.50-£16&alc Last dinner 10pm
Credit Cards 1 2 3 4 5

★★**Bell** Market Square HP20 1TX (Trusthouse Forte)
☎(0296)89835
Comfortable and friendly old coaching house with sound cooking and excellent breakfasts.
17rm(16⇔1↱) CTV in all bedrooms ® sB⇔↱£56-£60 dB⇔↱£68-£74 (room only) ⊟
Ꝑ ⊞ *xmas*
V ♡ ☕ ⊬ Lunch £7.50-£9.95 Dinner £11.30-£15.80alc Last dinner 9.30pm
Credit Cards 1 2 3 5

○***Hartwell House*** Oxford Rd HP17 8NL ☎(0296)747444
Due to have opened July 1989
30⇔

✕**Pebbles** 1 Pebbles Ln ☎(0296)86622
In the friendly atmosphere of this small, intimate restaurant you can enjoy a choice of dishes from both fixed price and à la carte menus, both featuring a range of interesting dishes that illustrate the chef's skill and imagination; an impressive wine list includes some reasonably priced offers, and friendly staff provide efficient service.
Closed Mon Dinner not served Sun
☋ French English **V** 32 seats ✱ Lunch £12.50-£18.50&alc Dinner fr£22alc Last lunch 2.15pm Last dinner 10pm Ꝑ
Credit Cards 1 2 3 5

AYR Strathclyde *Ayrshire* Map **10** NS32

★★★**53% Belleisle House** Belleisle Park KA7 4DU
☎(0292)42331
A mansion set in parkland overlooking the golf course features an interesting foyer and restaurant complemented by modern-style bedrooms with up-to-date facilities.
17rm(9⇔5↱)4⊞ CTV in all bedrooms ® **T**
☾ 50P ✻ ⚑
☋ French **V** ♡ ☕
Credit Cards 1 2 3 5

★★★**56% Caledonian** Dalblair Rd KA7 1UG (Embassy)
☎(0292)269331 Telex no 776611 FAX (0292) 610722
The bright, spacious public areas of this centrally-located, modern hotel include a terrace café which is open from 7am to 11pm. Many of the comfortable bedrooms have sea views and all are attractively presented, with pastel décor and light wood furniture.
114⇔(12fb)⊬in 22 bedrooms CTV in all bedrooms ® **T** S10% sB⇔£20.50-£53 dB⇔£41-£69 (room only) ⊟
Lift ☾ 70P CFA ⛆(heated) snooker sauna solarium gymnasium jacuzzi ♫ *xmas*
☋ Scottish & French **V** ♡ ☕ ⊬ S10% Lunch fr£7.95&alc High tea fr£4.75 Dinner fr£12.50&alc Last dinner 10pm
Credit Cards 1 2 3 5

★★★**58% Pickwick** 19 Racecourse Rd KA7 2TD
☎(0292)260111
Friendly, personally-run hotel in a Victorian mansion with good parking facilities. Bedrooms are comfortably furnished and equipped whilst public areas are wood panelled with lots of Victorian prints.
15rm(10⇔5↱)(3fb)1⊞ CTV in all bedrooms ® **T** ✈ S10% sB&B⇔↱£35-£40 dB&B⇔↱£55-£63 ⊟
☾ 100P ⊞ ✻ ⛳ putting green ⌂ *xmas*
☋ Scottish & French **V** ♡ ☕ S10% Lunch £7.50-£8.50 High tea £5-£6.50 Dinner £12.50-£13.50&alc Last dinner 9.45pm
Credit Cards 1 2 3 5

★★★**53% Savoy Park** 16 Racecourse Rd KA7 2UT
☎(0292)266112
Red-sandstone building standing in two acres of grounds, and located to the south of the town centre.
16rm(13⇔3↱)(4fb) CTV in all bedrooms ® **T**
sB&B⇔↱£30-£45 dB&B⇔↱£45-£65 ⊟

▶

A

☾ CTV 80P ✲ *xmas*
☋ Scottish & French V ♈ ♊ Lunch fr£6.50 High tea £4.50-£6 Dinner £15 Last dinner 9pm
Credit Cards 1 2 3 £

★★Ayrshire & Galloway 1 Killoch Place KA7 2EA
☎(0292)262626
RS Xmas & New Year
Commercial hotel overlooking Burns Statue Square, with attractive bars and comfortable, simple rooms.
25rm(8⇌)(3fb) CTV in 8bedrooms ✗ ✳ sB&B£15-£20 sB&B⇌£20-£25 dB&B£30-£35 dB&B⇌£35-£40
☾ CTV 20P ♫
♈ Bar Lunch £2.50-£7.50alc High tea £5-£7.50alc Last high tea 7.30pm
Credit Cards 1 3

★★Carrick Lodge 46 Carrick Rd KA7 2RE ☎(0292)262846
Well-maintained throughout, this small friendly hotel offers reasonably spacious accomodation in bright and clean bedrooms. There are two comfortable lounge bars and an attractive, popular restaurant.
8rm(1⇌7♠)(2fb) CTV in all bedrooms ® T ✗ ✳ sB&B⇌♠£30 dB&B⇌♠£45 ⊟
☾ 25P
V ♈ ♊ Lunch fr£5.25 High tea £4.75-£7.50 Dinner fr£10.50&alc Last dinner 9.45pm
Credit Cards 1 2 3

★★Elms Court 21 Miller Rd KA7 2AX
☎(0292)264191 & 282332 FAX (0292) 610254
Centrally situated between the town and seafront, this is a family run hotel with modest accommodation. Enjoyable bar meals are served in the recently refurbished lounge bar, which is popular with locals at lunchtime.
20rm(12⇌8♠)(4fb) CTV in all bedrooms ® T sB&B⇌♠fr£23.50 dB&B⇌♠fr£47
☾ 40P *xmas*
☋ Scottish & French V ♈ ♊ Lunch fr£5.75 High tea fr£3.50 Dinner fr£10 Last dinner 9.30pm
Credit Cards 1 2 3

★Aftongrange 37 Carrick Rd KA7 2RD ☎(0292)265679
This small, family-run hotel has a relaxed, informal atmosphere.
8rm(1⇌4♠)(2fb) CTV in all bedrooms ® T sB&B£18.50 sB&B⇌♠£20 dB&B£30 dB&B⇌♠£36 ⊟
30P pool table
V ♈ ♊ Lunch £4.75-£9.45 High tea £4.50-£6.75 Dinner £8-£9.50 Last dinner 9pm
£

AYTON, GREAT North Yorkshire Map **08** NZ51

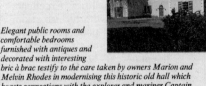

★★★ 70% Ayton Hall
Low Green TS9 6BW
☎Middlesborough (0642)723595

Elegant public rooms and comfortable bedrooms furnished with antiques and decorated with interesting bric à brac testify to the care taken by owners Marion and Melvin Rhodes in modernising this historic old hall which boasts connections with the explorer and mariner Captain James Cook. The kitchens are Melvin's domain and here he creates unusual dishes for the menu, using all his considerable flair and enthusiasm for cooking.

9rm(7⇌2♠)(2fb)3⊞ CTV in all bedrooms T ✗ ✳ sB&B⇌♠£65-£79 dB&B£89-£99 dB&B⇌♠£89-£99 ⊟
☾ 35P ✠ ✲ ♪ (hard) croquet archery ♫ nc11 yrs *xmas*
☋ International V ♈ ♊ ⅟ Lunch fr£12.95&alc Dinner fr£18.95&alc Last dinner 9.45pm
Credit Cards 1 2 3

BABBACOMBE
See **Torquay**

BADMINTON
See **Petty France**

BAGINTON Warwickshire Map **04** SP37

★★Old Mill Mill Hill CV8 2BS (Berni/Chef & Brewer)
☎Coventry(0203)303588
On the banks of the River Soure, conveniently situated for access to major motorways, stands an old mill that has been converted to provide well-equipped and comfortable bedrooms, all with en suite facilities. Many of the building's original features have been preserved, the restaurant featuring the original 18-foot mill wheel.
20⇌(4fb)1⊞ CTV in all bedrooms ® T ✗ (ex guide dogs) sB&B⇌fr£48.50 dB&B⇌fr£59 ⊟
☾ CTV 200P ✲ U
V ♈ ♊ ⅟ Lunch fr£8 Dinner fr£9 Last dinner 9.30pm
Credit Cards 1 2 3 5

BAGSHOT Surrey Map **04** SU96

★★★★ 69% Pennyhill Park College Ride GU19 5ET
(Prestige)
☎(0276)71774
Telex no 858841
FAX (0276) 73217

Surrounded by acres of garden and parkland – including its own golf course – this impressive,
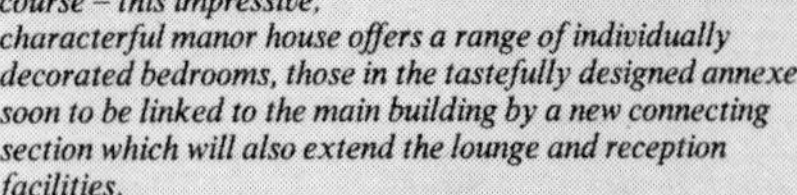
characterful manor house offers a range of individually decorated bedrooms, those in the tastefully designed annexe soon to be linked to the main building by a new connecting section which will also extend the lounge and reception facilities.
17⇌Annexe30⇌ CTV in all bedrooms T ✗ (ex guide dogs)
☾ 250P ✲ ⇌(heated) ▶9 ♪ (hard) ↲ U sauna clay pigeon shooting
☋ English & French V ♈ ♊ Last dinner 10.30pm
Credit Cards 1 2 3 4 5

★★*Cricketers* London Rd GU19 5 ☎(0276)73196
Closed 25 Dec
A popular inn, with the local cricket ground at the rear.
21rm(6⇌11♠)Annexe8⇌(11fb) CTV in all bedrooms ® T ✗ (ex guide dogs)
☾ 85P ✲
☋ Mainly grills V ♈ ♊ ⅟
Credit Cards 1 2 3 4 5

For key to symbols see the inside front cover.

BAINBRIDGE North Yorkshire Map **07** SD99

★★**Rose & Crown** Village Green DL8 3EE
☎Wensleydale(0969)50225
Original 15th-century inn, featuring an open fireplace and many old beams.
12rm(3⇔9♠)(1fb)3⊠ CTV in all bedrooms ® sB&B⇔♠£28 dB&B⇔♠£50 ⊟
65P ✲ ♪
V ♦ ☕ Lunch £5.85-£10.60alc Dinner £10.20-£13.50alc Last dinner 9pm
Credit Cards [1] [3]

BAKEWELL Derbyshire Map **08** SK26

★★★**60%** ***Rutland Arms*** The Square DE4 1BT (Best Western)
☎(062981)2812 Telex no 377077
A traditional-style hotel set in the heart of the Peak District, that is busy with both business people and tourists. The restaurant has a good reputation for the quality of food prepared by chef John Brunner, who maintains and enhances natural flavours.
19⇔Annexe17⇔(2fb) CTV in all bedrooms ® **T** ✈
25P 2🚗
☕ English & French **V** ♦ ☕ Last dinner 9.30pm
Credit Cards [1] [2] [3] [5]

Places with AA hotels and restaurants are identified on the location atlas at the back of the book.

B

★★Croft Country House
Great Longstone DE4 1TF
☎Great Longstone (062987)278
Closed 22-28 Dec RS Jan & Feb
A steep, winding drive out of the village leads to a secluded hotel which combines spacious accommodation with an intimate atmosphere, offering standards of personal service that ensure a relaxed stay for guests.
9rm(4⇌3♠) CTV in all bedrooms ® ✗ (ex guide dogs) ✱ sB&B⇌♠£37-£40 dB&B£45-£51 dB&B⇌♠£53-£59 ⊟
Lift CTV 30P ⚘ ✲
English & French ⊬ Dinner £13.25 Last dinner 7.30pm
Credit Cards 1 3

★★Milford House Mill St DE4 1DA ☎(0629)812130
Closed Jan & Feb RS Nov Dec & Mar
Secluded rear gardens are an attractive feature of this traditional English hotel, located conveniently close to the town centre and run by the same family for many years.
12rm(8⇌4♠) CTV in all bedrooms ® ✗ ✱ sB&B⇌♠£25-£27 dB&B⇌♠£46-£55
10P 7⌂ ⚘ ✲ nc10yrs
V Lunch £9.80 Dinner £10.35 Last dinner 7.30pm

BALA Gwynedd Map **06** SH93

★★Bala Lake LL23 7YF (1m S on B4403) ☎(0678)520344
Regency hunting lodge with motel block at the rear, situated 1m from Bala.
1⇌Annexe12♠(2fb) CTV in all bedrooms ® T
40P 10⌂ ⚘ ⌂(heated) ▶9
⚘ ⊒ Last dinner 8.30pm
Credit Cards 1 3 5

★★Plas Coch High St LL23 7AB ☎(0678)520309
Closed Xmas day
Originally built as a coaching inn in about 1780, this is now a comfortable and friendly hotel situated in the town centre, close to Bala Lake.
10rm(3⇌7♠)(4fb) CTV in all bedrooms ® sB&B⇌♠£27-£37 dB&B⇌♠£43 ⊟
20P ⚘ windsurfing canoeing sailing
V ⚘ ⊒ ⊬ Lunch fr£5.25 Dinner fr£8.50&alc Last dinner 8.30pm
Credit Cards 1 2 3 5 £

★★White Lion Royal Hotel 61 High St LL23 7AE (Consort) ☎(0678)520314
Closed 25 Dec RS 26 Dec
The old coaching inn has well-equipped bedrooms and a friendly staff who offer a warm welcome to guests.
22rm(20⇌2♠)(3fb) CTV in all bedrooms ® T ✱ sB&B⇌♠£29.50-£32 dB&B⇌♠£42-£49 ⊟
CTV 30P
V ⚘ ⊒ Lunch £6.75-£7.25 Dinner £8.75-£9.25 Last dinner 8.30pm
Credit Cards 1 2 3 5 £

The AA's star-rating scheme is the market leader in hotel classification.

BALDOCK Hertfordshire Map **04** TL23

○ ***Travelodge*** A1 Great North Rd, Hinxworth SG7 5EX (Trusthouse Forte) ☎Hinxworth(0462)835329
40⇌
P

BALLACHULISH Highland *Argyllshire* Map **14** NN05

See also **North Ballachulish**
★★★ 60% Ballachulish PA39 4JY (Inter) ☎(08552)606 Telex no 9401369 6 FAX (08552) 629
A Scottish baronial-style hotel with good views of Loch Linnhe and the surrounding mountain scenery. It has attractive, well-equipped bedrooms and comfortable public areas with service provided by a team of friendly, young staff.
30rm(21⇌9♠)(2fb)1⊟ CTV in all bedrooms ® T sB&B⇌♠£36.50-£45 dB&B⇌♠£49-£74 ⊟
☾ 50P 4⌂ ✲ ♫ ⌂ *xmas*
International V ⚘ ⊒ ⊬ S10% Lunch £1.20-£10alc High tea £2.75-£7.50alc Dinner £14.50&alc Last dinner 10pm
Credit Cards 1 3 £

BALLASALLA

See **Man, Isle of**

BALLATER Grampian *Aberdeenshire* Map **15** NO39

★★★★ 64% *Craigendarroch Hotel & Country Club* Braemar Rd AB3 5XA ☎(0338)55858 Telex no 739952 FAX (0338) 55447
A splendid country house with its superb setting overlooking the seaside. It now provides comfortable accommodation with especially good bedrooms. There are 3 restaurants with different types of menus to suit all tastes. The facilities for children make it an ideal family hotel. An excellent leisure complex is available free to all hotel guests.
29⇌♠(2fb)1⊟ CTV in all bedrooms ® T ✗
Lift ☾ 100P ✲ ⌂(heated) ♪ squash snooker sauna solarium gymnasium games room beauty salon ⌂
V ⚘ ⊒ ⊬ Last dinner 10pm
Credit Cards 1 2 3 5

★★Darroch Learg AB3 5UX ☎(03397)55443
Closed Nov-Jan
Set in landscaped gardens with magnificent views over the River Dee, this hotel has a relaxed, friendly atmosphere and individually decorated bedrooms. Good, wholesome food is served in the dining room.
15rm(13⇌2♠)Annexe8rm(3⇌2♠)(2fb) CTV in all bedrooms ® T sB&B£21 sB&B⇌♠£27 dB&B£42 dB&B⇌♠£46-£60 ⊟
25P ⚘ ✲
V ⚘ ⊒ Lunch £4-£6 Dinner £14 Last dinner 8.30pm
Credit Cards 1 3

★★Glen Lui Invercauld Rd AB3 5RP ☎(03397)55402 FAX (03397) 55545
Closed Nov
The hotel is quietly situated in 2 acres of grounds next to Ballater Golf Club. There is a choice of well-equipped bedrooms, including 2 suites, most of which have lovely views of Loch Nager. Public rooms have been tastefully furnished and the restaurant makes good use of fresh local produce. Service is well-managed, informal and helpful.
10rm(2⇌8♠)(1fb) CTV in all bedrooms ® T ✱ sB&B⇌♠£25 dB&B⇌♠£40-£60 ⊟
CTV 12P ✲ ⌂ *xmas*
V ⚘ ⊒ Sunday Lunch £7.50 Dinner £14-£15 Last dinner 10pm
Credit Cards 1 2 3

Book as early as possible for busy holiday periods.

B

★★**Invercauld Arms** 5 Bridge Square AB3 5QJ (Inter)
☎(03397)55417 Telex no 9401597 3
This 19th-century hotel has been extensively modernised and facilities include a good lounge, a spacious bar and a popular restaurant. The bedrooms are well equipped and several overlook the River Dee. Local fishing and golf can be arranged. From early 1990 the hotel is expected to change its name to Monaltrie Lodge.
23rm(18⇌3♠)(3fb)1▣ CTV in all bedrooms ® T S%
sB&B⇌♠£25-£32 dB&B⇌♠£40-£54 ▤
45P ✻ ♫ *xmas*
V ♧ ☕ ⅟ Bar Lunch £2.95-£7.95 High tea £3.95 Dinner £14
Last dinner 8.30pm
Credit Cards 1 2 3 5 £

See advertisement on page 91

BALMACARA Highland *Ross & Cromarty* Map **14** NG82

★★**Balmacara** IV40 8DH ☎(059986)283
A comfortable holiday hotel attractively situated on the shores of Loch Alsh with mainly modern and well-equipped bedrooms and traditional lounges.
29rm(25⇌4♠)(3fb)1▣ CTV in all bedrooms ® T ✻ S%
sB&B£29.50 sB&B⇌♠£29.50 dB&B£47-£50
dB&B⇌♠£47-£50 ▤
CTV 50P fishing trips watersports ⌂ *xmas*
☋ Scottish & French V ♧ ☕ S% Bar Lunch £1.50-£6 Dinner £12.50 Last dinner 8.45pm
Credit Cards 1 2 3 5

Places with AA hotels and restaurants are identified on the location atlas at the back of the book.

B

BALSALL COMMON West Midlands Map **04** SP27

★★**Haigs** Kenilworth Rd CV7 7EL ☎Berkswell(0676)33004 FAX (0676) 34572
Closed 26 Dec-3 Jan
Family run hotel with high standard of cooking and informal atmosphere. Near NEC and airport.
14rm(11↱) CTV in all bedrooms ® T sB&B£22.50-£28 sB&B↱£26.50-£39.50 dB&B↱£36.50-£52
CTV 22P ✿ nc4yrs
French V Lunch £8.25-£8.80 Dinner £10.85-£12.40&alc Last dinner 9pm
Credit Cards 1 2 3 5 £

See advertisement under BIRMINGHAM (NATIONAL EXHIBITION CENTRE)

BAMBURGH Northumberland Map **12** NU13

★★**Lord Crewe Arms** Front St NE69 7BL ☎(06684)243
Closed Dec-Mar
Comfortable, proprietor-run hotel with peaceful atmosphere.
25rm(14⇌6↱)(1fb) CTV in all bedrooms ® sB&B£28-£30 sB&B⇌↱£36-£38 dB&B£38-£40 dB&B⇌↱£48-£50
34P nc5yrs
English & French Bar Lunch £4.50-£7.50alc Dinner £13-£14.50 Last dinner 9pm
Credit Cards 1 3

★★**Victoria** Front St NE69 7BP ☎(06684)431
Family-run hotel, recently refurbished to offer modern bedrooms and character public rooms.
23rm(15⇌1↱)(3fb)1 CTV in all bedrooms ® T sB&B£20.30-£26.55 sB&B⇌↱£24.25-£30.45 dB&B£34.60-£43.30 dB&B⇌↱£41.60-£53.10
CTV 7P games room *xmas*
V Sunday Lunch £5-£7.50 Dinner fr£14 Last dinner 7.45pm
Credit Cards 1 2 3 5 £

★***Sunningdale*** NE69 7BS ☎(06684)334
Closed Nov-Mar
Friendly, informal hotel with comfortable accomodation and offering good value dinners.
18rm(6⇌)(3fb) in 2 bedrooms
CTV 16P games room
V

BAMFORD Derbyshire Map **08** SK28

★★***Marquis of Granby*** Hathersage Rd S30 2BH ☎Hope Valley(0433)51206
Standing in one of Derbyshire's most attractive Peak District valleys and recently converted from a roadside inn, the hotel offers spacious, well-equipped bedrooms of character and historic public rooms. A cosy 'village' bar and smart lounge adjoin the attractive restaurant, which looks out on a lawned garden.
7rm(5⇌2↱)(2fb)1 CTV in all bedrooms ®
CTV 100P ✿
V
Credit Cards 1 2 3 5

★★**Rising Sun** Castleton Rd S30 2AL (on main A625 Road) ☎Hope Valley(0433)51323
Charming roadside inn in the Hope Valley with modern comfortable accommodation and Tudor-style atmosphere.
13rm(9⇌4↱)(1fb)1 CTV in all bedrooms ® T ✱ sB&B⇌↱£32-£42 dB&B⇌↱£44-£52
80P 2 ✿ ♫ *xmas*
V Lunch £4.50-£5.50&alc Dinner fr£5.25&alc Last dinner 9.30pm
Credit Cards 1 2 3

BAMPTON Devon Map **03** SS92

★★**Bark House** Oakford Bridge EX16 9HZ (2.5m W A396) ☎Oakford(03985)236
Closed 21 Dec-Apr
Situated beside the A396 in the hamlet of Oakford Bridge near the River Exe. The hotel is a stone building, formerly a tannery. The well-kept garden is terraced on the hillside of this Devonshire valley to picturesque effect. The bedrooms are comfortable and well-decorated, and the public rooms promote a cottage atmosphere. A warm welcome and good home cooking are offered.
6rm(2⇌2↱)(1fb) CTV in 5bedrooms S% sB&B£16 sB&B⇌↱£24-£27 dB&B⇌↱£38-£44 Continental breakfast
12P 2 (£1) ✿ nc5yrs
English, French & American Lunch £7.50 Dinner £11.50 Last dinner 8.30pm
Credit Cards 1 2 3 5

BANAVIE Highland *Inverness-shire* Map **14** NN17

★★**Moorings** PH33 7LY (3m from Fort William on A830) (Exec Hotel) ☎Corpach(03977)797 FAX (03977) 441
Standing in its own grounds beside the Caledonian Canal's 'Neptune's Staircase', this family-run hotel has long been known for its warmth and friendliness. However, the French chef Laurent Bienfait, adds another dimension to the hotel's reputation. He has created an appealing à la carte 'Taste of Scotland' menu to complement the interesting 5-course table d'hôte dinner menus. Both use only best quality local fresh produce and the chef's acknowledged skills are much in evidence, while meals also represent good value for money.
21rm(17⇌4↱)Annexe3↱1 CTV in all bedrooms ® T (ex guide dogs) sB&B⇌↱£40-£55 dB&B⇌↱£48-£68
60P ✿ ♫ nc10yrs
Scottish & French V Lunch £9.50-£14.50&alc Dinner £16&alc Last dinner 9.30pm
Credit Cards 1 2 3 5

See advertisement under FORT WILLIAM

BANBURY Oxfordshire Map **04** SP44

★★★**60% Banbury Moat House** 27-29 Oxford Rd OX16 9AH (Queens Moat) ☎(0295)59361 Telex no 838967 FAX (0295) 270954
This hotel features modern well-equipped bedrooms, with spacious bathrooms and more traditonal public rooms.
52rm(50⇌2↱)(2fb)1 CTV in 50bedrooms ® T sB&B⇌↱£59 dB&B⇌↱£69
48P CFA
International V Lunch £9.50&alc Dinner £10.50&alc Last dinner 9.45pm
Credit Cards 1 2 3 5

★★★**71% Whately Hall** Banbury Cross OX16 0AN (Trusthouse Forte) ☎(0295)3451 due to change t o 263451 Telex no 837149 FAX (0295) 271736
The hotel – called the Three Tuns until it was renamed in honour of William Whately, a famous vicar of the town – stands beside Banbury Cross in pleasant, secluded gardens, set back from the road. It successfully combines the charm of its 17th-century origins with the provision of modern comforts in public areas and well-equipped bedrooms alike.
74rm(69⇌5↱) in 30 bedrooms CTV in all bedrooms ® T ✱ sB⇌↱£66-£79 dB⇌↱£85-£130 (room only)
Lift 60P 20 ✿ CFA croquet *xmas*
V Lunch £6.95-£9.95&alc Dinner £6.95-£13.50&alc Last dinner 9.15pm
Credit Cards 1 2 3 4 5

For key to symbols see the inside front cover.

★★Cromwell Lodge North Bar OX16 OTB ☎(0295)59781
Telex no 83343
Closed 1 wk Xmas & New Year
Pleasant, professionally run hotel with pleasant staff. Modern, well-equipped bedrooms and attractive restaurant.
32rm(29⇌3♪)(1fb) CTV in all bedrooms ® T
sB&B⇌♪fr£53 dB&B⇌♪fr£65
☾ CTV 25P
International V Sunday Lunch £10-£12 Dinner £12-£13&alc Last dinner 9.30pm
Credit Cards 1 2 3 4 5

See advertisement under STRATFORD-UPON-AVON

★★*Lismore Hotel & Restaurant* 61 Oxford Rd OX16 9AJ (Minotels) ☎(0295)67661
Closed 24Dec-3Jan
Homely hotel offering comfortable accommodation and good food.
14rm(9⇌2♪)(3fb)1 CTV in all bedrooms ® T
15P 1
V Last dinner 9.30pm
Credit Cards 1 3

Places with AA hotels and restaurants are identified on the location atlas at the back of the book.

BANCHORY Grampian *Kincardineshire* Map **15** NO69

★★★★♚71% Invery House Bridge of Feugh
AB3 3NJ (Prestige)
☎(03302)4782
Telex no 73737
FAX (03302) 4712

A lovely half-mile drive, through silver birches and beech trees and by the side of the River Feugh, leads to this elegant and luxurious Deeside mansion. With fishing rights on the river and shooting parties organised, it is popular with sportsmen and those simply seeking peace and quiet. A stone-flagged hall leads to a large foyer-lounge with a lovely drawing room beyond. Quality furnishings abound, and bedrooms are spacious and well-appointed. Food is ably cooked by chef Ken McPhee and the friendly staff ensure that one's stay is enjoyable.

14⇌↱1⊟ CTV in all bedrooms **T** ✗ (ex guide dogs) sB&B⇌↱£80-£115 dB&B⇌↱£95-£150 ⊟

☾20P 3⌂ ⊞ ✲ ℘ (grass) ♩ snooker croquet lawn putting green nc8yrs *xmas*

♡ Scottish & French ♔ ⊒ Lunch £15.50 Dinner £26.50 Last dinner 9.45pm

Credit Cards 1 2 3 5 £

★★★♚ BANCHORY LODGE
AB3 3HS ☎(03302)2625
Closed 13 Dec-Jan

With the River Dee running through the 12-acre grounds, this welcoming house enjoys a wonderful setting. The river is overlooked by many of the bedrooms, some of which are being refurbished. There is a choice of four-poster beds, and antique furniture throughout helps to make Banchory Lodge a pleasant place to stay. An oak-panelled breakfast room and elegant lounges add to the charm. The principal attraction, though, remains as it has been for many years the relaxing atmosphere created by the owners, Dugald and Maggie Jaffray. Their involvement is evident in the abundance of fresh flower decorations, the splendour and character of the furnishings and the agreeable, traditional courtesy of the staff. Appropriately in this classic salmon fishing area, the cooking has a strong emphasis on local fish and game, with meals suited to the appetites of hungry sportsmen, and guests will cherish memories of evenings in the warm, inviting bar for a long time to come.

23rm(22⇌1↱)(11fb)2⊟ CTV in all bedrooms ® **T** ✳ sB&B£39-£45 sB&B⇌↱£39-£45 dB&B£65-£75 dB&B⇌↱£65-£75

CTV 50P ⊞ ✲ ♩ sauna pool table

♡ English & French **V** ♔ ⊒ Lunch fr£7.50 High tea fr£7.50 Dinner fr£18.50 Last dinner 9.30pm

Credit Cards 1 2 3 4 5

★★★♚75% Raemoir
AB3 4ED
☎(03302)4884
Telex no
73315 CHACOM G
FAX (03302) 2171

Magnificently set in 3, 500 acres, this elegant 18th-century mansion is furnished throughout with antiques, many of them unusual. The panelled morning room dates from 1817 and all the bedrooms have been individually furnished to preserve the character of the house. The young chef makes good use of fresh local ingredients to produce an interesting menu. The friendly service is complemented by the personal involvement of owner, Kit Sabin, and her daughter Judy Ollis.

17⇌Annexe6rm(4⇌2↱)(1fb)1⊟ CTV in all bedrooms ® **T** sB&B⇌↱£45-£50 dB&B⇌↱£80-£90 ⊟

CTV 200P 2⌂ (£1) ⊞ ✲ ▶9 ℘ (hard) ♩ sauna solarium gymnasium croquet mini golf shooting stalking ♘ *xmas*

♡ International **V** ♔ ⊒ ⚡ Lunch £10.50 Dinner £18.50&alc Last dinner 9pm

Credit Cards 1 2 3 5 £

★★★60% Tor-na-Coille AB3 4AB ☎(03302)2242
FAX (03302) 4012
Comfortable tourist/business hotel in its own grounds.
24rm(17⇌7↱)(4fb) CTV in all bedrooms ® **T** ✳ sB&B⇌↱£34.50-£60 dB&B⇌↱£55-£80 ⊟
Lift 130P ✲ squash croquet lawn ♘ *xmas*
♡ Scottish & French **V** ♔ ⊒ ⚡ Lunch £9.50 Dinner £13.50&alc Last dinner 9.30pm
Credit Cards 1 2 3 5 £

★★Burnett Arms 25 High St AB3 3TD (Consort) ☎(03302)4944
Telex no 739925 FAX (0224) 744354
This old coaching inn has been completely modernised and provides a lounge, 2 popular bars, a dining room and bedrooms which are well equipped and functional. Service is well managed and friendly and there is a self-contained function suite offering good facilities for both private and business purposes.
18rm(4⇌12↱)(5fb) CTV in all bedrooms ® **T** sB&Bfr£21 sB&B⇌↱fr£22 dB&B⇌↱fr£34 ⊟
40P ♫ *xmas*
V ♔ ⊒ Lunch fr£4.50&alc High tea £3-£7alc Dinner fr£10 Last dinner 9.30pm
Credit Cards 1 2 3 5 £

BANFF Grampian *Banffshire* Map **15** NJ66

★★★56% Banff Springs Golden Knowes Rd AB4 2JE (Consort) ☎(02612)2881 FAX (02612) 5546
This purpose-built hotel, situated to the west of the town enjoys fine views over the Moray Firth to the Sutherland mountains and is a popular venue for local weddings and large functions.
30rm(25⇌5↱)(4fb) CTV in all bedrooms ® **T** ✳ sB&B⇌↱fr£30 dB&B⇌↱fr£40 ⊟
☾120P *xmas*
♡ French **V** ♔ ⊒ Lunch fr£7.50 Dinner fr£10.50&alc Last dinner 9pm
Credit Cards 1 2 3 4 5

★★County 32 High St AB4 1AE (Guestaccom) ☎(02612)5353
A charming Georgian house in the town centre with bedrooms and public rooms in period style. Throughout the hotel the ambience of a town house in former days is retained, enhanced by the personal involvement of the owners.

7rm(5⇌)(2fb)2⊞ CTV in all bedrooms ® **T** ✖ (ex guide dogs)
sB&B£25-£30 sB&B⇌£25-£30 dB&B£38-£42
dB&B⇌£38-£42 ⊟
7P ✲ ♩ ⌂ *xmas*
V ♔ ⊥ ⊬ Lunch £3-£6 High tea £2-£5 Dinner £7-£8.50&alc
Last dinner 9pm
Credit Cards [1] [2] [3] [5] £

BANGOR Gwynedd Map **06** SH57

★★**Menai Court** Craig y Don Rd LL57 2BG ☎(0248)354200
Closed 26 Dec-7 Jan
This delightful, well-furnished hotel offers well-equipped, comfortable bedrooms, good food and friendly service.
12rm(7⇌5↱)(2fb) CTV in all bedrooms ® **T** ✳
sB&B⇌↱£40-£48.50 dB&B⇌↱£69 ⊟
22P ⊞ ♫ *xmas*
♕ British & French **V** ♔ Lunch £9.50-£12alc Dinner £9.50-£18.50alc Last dinner 9.30pm
Credit Cards [1] [3] £

★★***Telford*** Holyhead Rd LL57 2HX ☎(0248)352543
Friendly, resident owners create a home-like atmosphere at an hotel which enjoys fine views of Telford's suspension bridge from its position on the Menai Straits.
10rm(4↱)(2fb)⊬in 2 bedrooms CTV in 9bedrooms TV in 1bedroom ✖ (ex guide dogs)
☾ ⊞ CTV 15P ✲ ♩
V ♔ ⊥ ⊬
Credit Cards [1] [3]

★★**Ty Uchaf** Tal-y-Bont LL57 3UR ☎(0248)352219
Closed 24 Dec-2 Jan
This modern, comfortable hotel, within easy reach of main line train services, prides itself on the quality of food served.
9⇌↱ CTV in all bedrooms ® ✖ (ex guide dogs)
sB&B⇌↱£20-£28 dB&B⇌↱£35-£45 ⊟
40P ✲ nc10yrs
V ♔ ⊥ Lunch £5-£7.50 High tea £4-£6.50 Dinner £7.50-£10.50&alc Last dinner 8.30pm
Credit Cards [1] [3] £

BARDON MILL Northumberland Map **12** NY76

★**Vallum Lodge** Military Rd, Twice Brewed NE47 7AN
☎(04984)248 changing to Haltwhistle (0434) 344248
Closed Nov-Mar
Standing on earthworks which were once part of Hadrian's Wall and next to the military road (B6318) that runs alongside it, this small hotel offers bright, comfortable accommodation in a friendly informal atmosphere.
7rm(2fb) ® sB&Bfr£16 dB&Bfr£30 ⊟
CTV 30P ⊞ ✲
♕ Mainly grills **V** ♔ ⊥ ⊬ Bar Lunch £5.50-£6.50alc Dinner £7.50-£8.50 Last dinner 8pm

BARFORD Warwickshire Map **04** SP26

★★★**54% Glebe** Church St CV35 8BS ☎Warwick(0926)624218
Telex no 312440 FAX (0926) 624625
Tempting menus, agreeable accommodation and convivial, peaceful surroundings are offered by the Glebe Hotel, a Georgian house adjacent to the village church.
15rm(7⇌6↱) CTV in all bedrooms ® **T** ✖ ✳ sB&B£42-£48
sB&B⇌↱£42-£48 dB&B£60-£62 dB&B⇌↱£60-£62 ⊟
☾ 45P ⊞ ✲ ⌂ *xmas*
♕ English & Continental **V** ♔ ⊥ Lunch £6-£12&alc Dinner £17.50&alc Last dinner 9.30pm
Credit Cards [1] [2] [3] [5] £

B

BAR HILL Cambridgeshire Map **05** TL36

★★★63% **Cambridgeshire Moat House** CB3 8EU (Queens Moat) ☎Crafts Hill(0954)80555 Telex no 817141 FAX (0954) 80010
Situated just 5.5 miles from the centre of the city, this modern, well-managed hotel features a sporting theme. Its 134 acres offer extensive leisure facilities which include tennis and squash courts, an 18-hole championship golf course, swimming pool, multigym, steam room and solarium. The hotel also boasts two bars – The Gallery and the aptly named Sportsman's Bar overlooking the golf course.
100⇌(8fb) CTV in all bedrooms ® **T** sB&B⇌fr£65 dB&B⇌fr£82 ⊟
(200P ❊ CFA ⊡(heated) ▸ 18 ℘ (hard) squash sauna solarium gymnasium putting green *xmas*
♡ English & French **V** ♡ ⊅ Lunch fr£13.50 High tea fr£3 Dinner fr£13.50&alc Last dinner 10pm
Credit Cards 1 2 3 4 5

BARKSTON Lincolnshire Map **08** SK94

✕✕**Barkston House** NG32 2NH ☎Loveden(0400)50555
Sound British dishes with fresh produce treated in a light, modern style, from the basis of the short but imaginative menu here, where the quality of food is matched by charming attentive service. The dining room – originally the kitchen of the pleasant eighteenth-century house – has stripped beams, complete with servants' bells, and open fireplace. The warm, country atmosphere carries through to an attractive sitting room and a large, comfortable bar. Two fine bedrooms are available for overnight guests.
Closed Sun, 25-30 Dec & 2 wks Jun
Lunch not served Sat & Mon
28 seats Lunch fr£7.75 Dinner fr£14.25alc Last lunch 1.30pm Last dinner 9.15pm 16P 2 bedrooms available
Credit Cards 1 2 3 5

BARMOUTH Gwynedd Map **06** SH61

★★**Ty'r Graig** Llanaber Rd LL42 1YN ☎(0341)280470
Closed Nov-Feb
An impressive Victorian mock castle with an array of stained glass, wood panelling and decorated ceilings. Family owned and run, it offers comfortable bedrooms, well-furnished lounges and a bar/conservatory which has lovely views over Barmouth Bay. Good home cooking is served in the restaurant.
12rm(4⇌8↱)2⊟ CTV in all bedrooms ® **T** ✗
sB&B⇌↱fr£30 dB&B⇌↱fr£50 ⊟
15P ⇏ ❊ windsurfing yachting sea fishing
♡ Welsh, English & French **V** ♡ ⊅ ⚡ Lunch fr£7.50 Dinner fr£10.50&alc Last dinner 8.30pm
Credit Cards 1 3

★**Bryn Melyn** Panorama Rd LL42 1DQ ☎(0341)280556 FAX (0341) 280990
Closed Dec-Feb
This family-run hotel provides comfortable accommodation and occupies a commanding position over the Mawddach Estuary.
10rm(8↱)(2fb) CTV in all bedrooms ® sB&B↱£23 dB&B↱fr£38 ⊟
10P ⇏ ❊
V ♡ Bar Lunch fr£3 Dinner fr£10 Last dinner 8.30pm
Credit Cards 1

★**Marwyn** 21 Marine Pde LL42 1NA ☎(0341)280185
A small family owned and run hotel on the seafront, with well-furnished bedrooms and friendly service.
7rm(3⇌4↱)(1fb)1⊟ CTV in all bedrooms ®
dB&B⇌↱£31-£39 ⊟
CTV ⇏ nc7yrs
V ♡ ⊅ Bar Lunch £4.90-£6&alc Dinner fr£9.50&alc Last dinner 11pm
Credit Cards 1 3 £

BARNBY MOOR Nottinghamshire Map **08** SK68

★★★66% **Ye Olde Bell** DN22 8QS (Trusthouse Forte) ☎Retford(0777)705121 FAX (0777) 860424
An original 17th-century posting house whose guests have included Queen Victoria and Queen Maud of Norway.
55rm(54⇌1↱)2⊟⚡in 8 bedrooms CTV in all bedrooms ® **T** sB⇌↱fr£54 dB⇌↱fr£64 (room only) ⊟
(250P ❊ *xmas*
V ♡ ⊅ ⚡ Lunch £9.95&alc Dinner £12.95&alc Last dinner 9.45pm
Credit Cards 1 2 3 4 5

BARNHAM BROOM Norfolk Map **05** TG00

★★★62% **Barnham Broom Hotel Conference & Leisure Centre** NR9 4DD (Best Western) ☎(060545)393 Telex no 975711 FAX (060545) 8224
A modern hotel set in extensive grounds close to the A47 west of Norwich. There are comfortable bedrooms, two cosy bars and a well-managed restaurant. But the hotel's particular attraction is its extensive sports and leisure facilities – notably the championship standard golf course. The purpose-built conference centre is also much in demand.
52⇌(12fb) CTV in all bedrooms ® **T** ✗ (ex guide dogs) S% sB&B⇌£60-£70 dB&B⇌£80-£90 ⊟
(200P CFA ⊡(heated) ▸ 36 ℘ (hard) squash sauna solarium gymnasium hairdressing salon beautician *xmas*
V ♡ ⊅ ⚡ S% Lunch £7.50-£10 High tea £2.50-£3.50 Dinner £12-£14&alc Last dinner 9.30pm
Credit Cards 1 2 3 5

See advertisement under NORWICH

BARNSDALE BAR South Yorkshire Map **08** SE51

○ ***Travelodge*** A1 Wentbridge WS8 3JB (Trusthouse Forte) ☎Pontefract(0977)620711 Telex no 557457
Situated on an A1 service area midway between London and Edinburgh, the hotel offers modern bedrooms.
72⇌⚡in 7 bedrooms CTV in all bedrooms ® **T**
(120P ⇏
♡ Mainly grills **V** ♡ ⊅ ⚡
Credit Cards 1 2 3 4 5

BARNSLEY South Yorkshire Map **08** SE30

★★★65% **Ardsley Moat House** Doncaster Rd, Ardsley S71 5EH (Queens Moat) ☎(0226)289401 Telex no 547762 FAX (0226) 205374
Closed Xmas day
Comfortable and well-appointed, the hotel offers friendly service and some very interesting restaurant menus.
73⇌↱(3fb)3⊟ CTV in all bedrooms ® **T** ✱ sB⇌↱£47-£52 dB⇌↱£59 (room only) ⊟
(300P ❊ snooker ♫
♡ English & French **V** ♡ ⊅ Lunch £9.50&alc High tea fr75p Dinner £11.50&alc Last dinner 10.30pm
Credit Cards 1 2 3 5

★***Royal*** Church St S70 2AD ☎(0226)203658
Closed Xmas day RS Bank Hols
Comfortable, well-appointed hotel with spacious lounge bars and restaurant featuring local dishes.
17rm(1⇌)(1fb) CTV in all bedrooms ®
CTV 2🚗
V ♡ ⊅ ⚡ Last dinner 9.30pm
Credit Cards 1 2 3 4 5

Red-star hotels offer the highest standards of hospitality, comfort and food.

BARNSTAPLE Devon Map **02** SS53

★★★66% **Imperial** Taw Vale Pde EX32 8NB (Trusthouse Forte)
☎(0271)45861
Good facilities are provided for both commercial guests and holiday makers at this busy, town centre hotel. Comfortable bedrooms are complemented by welcoming public area, both table d'hôte and à la carte menus are available in the spacious restaurant, and staff are pleasant and friendly.
56rm(55⇌1♠)(3fb)⊁in 22 bedrooms CTV in all bedrooms ® T ✳ sB⇌♠£56-£60 dB⇌♠£72-£78 (room only) ⊟
Lift ☾ 80P *xmas*
V ♘ ⊻ ⊁ Sunday Lunch £10.25 Dinner £13.75&alc Last dinner 9pm
Credit Cards 1 2 3 4 5

★★★57% **North Devon Motel** Taw Vale EX32 8NJ (Brend)
☎(0271)72166 Telex no 42551 FAX (0271) 78558
A small hotel with modern amenities, and a restaurant on the first floor.
25rm(24⇌1♠)Annexe17rm(16⇌1♠)(7fb) CTV in all bedrooms ® T sB&B⇌♠£35-£40 dB&B⇌♠£50-£60 ⊟
☾ 80P ♫ *xmas*
♔ English & French **V** ♘ ⊻ Lunch £5.75-£6.50 Dinner £9-£10&alc Last dinner 9pm
Credit Cards 1 2 3 5

★★★⚑57% ***Roborough House*** EX31 4JG (Exec Hotel)
☎(0271)72354
Closed 26 Dec-17 Jan
Extended Georgian house on the edge of the town has a panoramic view over the Taw Valley. It has well furnished rooms and its restaurant is popular with local people.
9rm(6⇌3♠)Annexe17rm2⊞ CTV in 9bedrooms **T**
40P ⊞ ✲
♔ English & French **V**
Credit Cards 1 2 3 5

★★⚑**Downrew House**
Bishops Tawton EX32 0DY
☎(0271)42497 & 46673
Closed Jan & Feb

This delightful little country house stands just a few miles south-east of the town in extensive grounds which boast an 18-hole golf course and an outdoor swimming pool that is kept heated throughout the year. Its compact but attractively-appointed public areas offer cosy comfort, while bedrooms are for the most part charming, though those in the adjoining lodge tend to be a little more functional. Meals are straightforward but enjoyable, and service is closely supervised by the proprietors.
6⇌Annexe6⇌(2fb) CTV in all bedrooms **T** ✳
sB&B⇌£47-£65 dB&B⇌£79-£99 (incl dinner) ⊟
12P ⊞ ✲ ⇌(heated) ℘ (hard) snooker solarium golf, 15 hole approach nc7yrs *xmas*
▸

B

English & French V Last high tea 5.30pm
Credit Cards 1 3

★★Royal & Fortescue Boutport St EX31 1HG (Brend) ☎(0271)42289 Telex no 42551 FAX (0271) 78558
Named after 'Royal' King Edward VII, the then Prince of Wales, who was a guest here.
62rm(33⇌2⌐)(4fb) CTV in all bedrooms ® T sB&B£29 sB&B⇌⌐£38 dB&B£48 dB&B⇌⌐£55 ⊟
Lift ☾ CTV 20P 6 ♫ *xmas*
English & French V Lunch £5&alc Dinner £9-£10&alc Last dinner 9pm
Credit Cards 1 2 3 5

★HALMPSTONE MANOR,
Bishops Tawton EX32 0EA
☎Swimbridge (0271)830321
Fax (0271)830826

Our Best Newcomer hotel (see special feature). Charles and Jane Stanbury have created this delightful hotel from what began as a bed-and-breakfast sideline to their farm. The farming continues, with cows grazing the fields around the garden, and this lends a rural charm to the hotel. The manor was mentioned in the Domesday Book, and parts of the present building date back to the 12th and 13th centuries. It is beautifully furnished with antiques and lovely fabrics, and the informal reception bar and elegant lounge are very relaxing. In the wood-panelled dining room, guests can enjoy skilfully prepared dishes from table d'hôte and à la carte menus and, as the restaurant is very popular locally, booking is advisable.
5⇌ 2 ® CTV in all bedrooms T dB&B£80-£100
12P nc10yrs
English & French ✱ Lunch £18.50alc Dinner £13.50&alc Last dinner 9.30pm
Credit Cards 1 2 3 4 5

XXXLynwood House Bishops Tawton Rd EX32 9DZ ☎(0271)43695 FAX (0271) 79340
A detached Victorian residence on the edge of town where the Roberts family have been maintaining their service and facilities for two decades. There is now only one dining room, which is open for both lunch and dinner, the same menu being used for both meals. Only fresh foods are used, especially seafood, and are carefully cooked. Three comfortable bedrooms are also now available.
V 50 seats ✱ Lunch £12.85-£28.50alc Dinner £12.85-£28.50alc Last lunch 2pm Last dinner 9.30pm 25P 3 bedrooms available
Credit Cards 1 3

BARRA, ISLE OF Western Isles *Inverness-shire* Map **13**

TANGUSDALE Map **13** NF60

★★Isle of Barra Tangusdale Beach, Castlebay PA80 5XW (Consort) ☎Castlebay(08714)383 FAX (08714) 385
Closed Nov-Mar RS Apr
A modern hotel occupying a delightful position beside one of the island's most beautiful sandy beaches. Accommodation is practical, warm and comfortable, though rooms are compact. The local staff are friendly and seafood is a regular item on the menu.
36⇌(5fb) CTV in all bedrooms ® S% sB&B⇌£27.50-£39 dB&B⇌£47-£55 ⊟
CTV
V Lunch fr£6.50 High tea fr£5.50 Dinner fr£11.50 Last dinner 8.30pm
Credit Cards 1 2 3 5 £

BARR, GREAT West Midlands Map **07** SP09

★★★58% *Great Barr Hotel & Conference Centre* Pear Tree Dr, off Newton Rd B43 6HS (1m W of junc A34/A4041) ☎021-357 1141 Telex no 336406 FAX 021-357 7557
Ideally sited for access to Birmingham and the M6, the hotel offers a range of extensive conference facilities and bedrooms designed for the business guest, all having modern facilities, though some are rather compact.
114⇌⌐(1fb) CTV in all bedrooms ® T (ex guide dogs)
☾ 175P ♫
English & Continental V Last dinner 9.45pm
Credit Cards 1 2 3 4 5

★★★59% Post House Chapel Ln B43 7BG (at junction M6/A34) (Trusthouse Forte) ☎021-357 7444 Telex no 338497 FAX 021-357 7503
Conveniently situated for the M6 and access to both Birmingham and Walsall, this large, modern hotel provides pleasant accommodation in well-equipped bedrooms and has comfortable lounges. The hotel offers a choice of dining styles as well as the use of a health and fitness centre.
204⇌(42fb) CTV in all bedrooms ® T sB⇌fr£69 dB⇌fr£80 (room only) ⊟
☾ 300P CFA (heated) sauna solarium gymnasium ♫ *xmas*
V Lunch fr£9.25 Dinner fr£14&alc Last dinner 10pm
Credit Cards 1 2 3 4 5

B

BARRHEAD Strathclyde *Renfrewshire* Map **11** NS45

★★**Dalmeny Park** Lochlibo Rd G78 1LG ☎041-881 9211
19th-century house with gardens, on the edge of town, with open fires and Georgian-style function suite.
18rm(3⇨10♠)(2fb) CTV in all bedrooms ® sB&B£25-£35.50 sB&B⇨♠£28-£42 dB&B£40-£50 dB&B⇨♠£44-£57 ⊟
☾150P ✽
V ✧ ☕ Lunch £4-£5.50 Dinner £14.50&alc Last dinner 9.30pm
Credit Cards 1 2 3 4 5

BARRHILL Strathclyde *Lanarkshire* Map **10** NX28

❀★★★ 77% **Kildonan**
KA26 0PU (Consort)
☎(046582)360
FAX (046582) 292

31rm(29⇨2♠)(7fb)1⊟ CTV in all bedrooms ® T ✱
sB&B⇨♠£52.50 dB&B⇨♠£105-£135 ⊟
☾60P ✽ ✽ ⊡(heated) ▶9 ♩ squash snooker sauna solarium gymnasium badminton beautician hairdressing ♔ *xmas*
☋ English, French & Swiss V ✧ ☕ ✂ Lunch £13.50&alc Dinner £18.95&alc Last dinner 9.30pm
Credit Cards 1 2 3 5

BARRINGTONS, THE Gloucestershire Map **04** SP21

(Near Burford)
★★★ 63% ***Inn For All Seasons*** The Barringtons OX8 4TN (3m W of Burford on A40) ☎Windrush(04514)324
Retaining much of the original character and charm, with old stone walls and exposed beams, the former coaching inn provides well-furnished bedrooms and good standards of food.
9⇨(1fb) CTV in all bedrooms ® T ✗
30P ✽ Shooting nc10yrs
V ✧ ☕ Last dinner 9.30pm
Credit Cards 1 2 3 5

See advertisement under BURFORD

BARROW-IN-FURNESS Cumbria Map **07** SD16

★★★ 53% ***Victoria Park*** Victoria Rd LA14 5JS (Consort)
☎(0229)21159
An extensively-modernised Victorian building situated just off the A590.
40rm(24⇨10♠)(3fb) CTV in all bedrooms ® T
☾60P crown bowling green pool table
☋ English & French V ✧ ☕ Last dinner 9.30pm
Credit Cards 1 2 3

★★**Lisdoonie** 307/309 Abbey Rd LA14 5LF ☎(0229)27312
Closed Xmas & New Year
A compact and homely hotel on the main road.
12rm(7⇨5♠)(2fb) CTV in all bedrooms ® T
sB&B⇨♠£20-£35 dB&B⇨♠£30-£45 ⊟
CTV 30P
☋ English & French ✧ ☕ Dinner £12&alc Last dinner 7.30pm
Credit Cards 1 2 3 £

★**White House** Abbey Rd LA13 9AE ☎(0229)27303
A commercial hotel on the main road to the town centre, the White House has lively bars and offers neat and well-equipped bedroom accommodation.
29rm(3⇨) TV available ® T ✱ sB&Bfr£19.50 sB&B⇨fr£34.50 dB&Bfr£30 dB&B⇨fr£42.50 ⊟
☾CTV 60P 20⌂ (£1.50)
☋ English & French V ✧ ☕ Lunch fr£6&alc Dinner £9.50&alc Last dinner 9.30pm
Credit Cards 1 2 3 5

BARRY South Glamorgan Map **03** ST16

★★★ 53% **Mount Sorrell** Porthkerry Rd CF6 8AY (Consort)
☎(0446)740069 Telex no 497819 FAX (0446) 746600
Commanding fine views of the town and Bristol Channel from its elevated position, and conveniently situated for Cardiff Airport, this hotel has undergone major refurbishment, to provide new bedrooms, conference facilities and a leisure centre.
48rm(31⇨17♠)Annexe4⇨(4fb) CTV in all bedrooms ® T
sB&B⇨♠£42-£48 dB&B⇨♠£55-£67.50 ⊟
☾17P ⊡(heated) sauna solarium gymnasium *xmas*
☋ Continental V ✧ Lunch £3.50-£6.50&alc Dinner £11-£12.50&alc Last dinner 10pm
Credit Cards 1 2 3 4 5

BARTLE Lancashire Map **07** SD43

★★★ 50% **Bartle Hall** Lea Ln PR4 0HA ☎Preston(0772)690506
An hotel in country house style offers imaginative, good-value menus in both its restaurants and the less formal Kissing Gate Bistro.
12rm(7⇨5♠)(1fb)3⊟ CTV in all bedrooms ® T ✗
sB&B⇨♠fr£49 dB&B⇨♠fr£55
☾CTV 150P ✽ ✽ ⛵ ℛ (hard)
☋ English & French V
Credit Cards 1 2 3 5

BARTON Lancashire Map **07** SD43

★★★ 62% **Barton Grange** Garstang Rd PR3 5AA (Best Western) ☎Broughton(0772)862551 Telex no 67392
FAX (0722) 861267
Closed 23-29 Dec
An extended and modernised hotel set in a garden centre complex.
56⇨Annexe10⇨(10fb)1⊟ CTV in all bedrooms ® T ✗ (ex guide dogs) ✱ sB&B⇨£38-£58 dB&B⇨£45-£75 ⊟
Lift ☾CTV 250P ✽ CFA ⊡(heated) (Apr-Oct only)
☋ English & French V ✧ ☕ Lunch fr£7.25 Dinner £12.50-£15.50 Last dinner 10pm
Credit Cards 1 2 3 5

BARTON MILLS Suffolk Map **05** TL77

○ ***Travelodge*** A11 IP28 6AE (Trusthouse Forte) ☎(0638)717675
32⇨
P

BARTON STACEY Hampshire Map **04** SU44

⌂**TraveLodge** SO21 3NP (on A303) (Trusthouse Forte)
☎Andover(0264)72260
One of the chain which is run in conjunction with standard Little Chef restaurants. Accommodation is flexible to your needs and well equipped, with all bedrooms at ground floor level. Service is friendly and efficient.
Annexe20⇨♠(20fb) CTV in all bedrooms ® sB⇨♠£21.50 dB⇨♠£27 (room only)
☾20P ✽
☋ Mainly grills
Credit Cards 1 2 3

BARTON UNDER NEEDWOOD Staffordshire
Map **07** SK11

⌂ **TraveLodge** DE13 0ED (on A38) (Trusthouse Forte)
☎ Barton-under-Needwood(028371)6343
A busy lodge on the A38 dual carriageway; easy access if you are travelling northbound, but ask lodge for directions if southbound, which will be via Barton-Under-Needwood village.
20⇔↱(20fb) CTV in all bedrooms Ⓡ sB⇔↱£21.50
dB⇔↱£27 (room only)
☾ 20P
Mainly grills
Credit Cards [1] [2] [3]

BASILDON Essex Map **05** TQ78

★★★61% **Crest** Cranes Farm Rd SS14 3DG (Crest)
☎(0268)533955 Telex no 995141 FAX (0268) 530119
Modern hotel with plain but good quality bedrooms, some of which have been refurbished recently. General facilities now include various meeting rooms and conference facilities for up to 150 people. Recreation is not overlooked with a games room and pitch and putt. Fat Sam's cocktail bar is complete with lights and music.
110⇔↱ in 25 bedrooms CTV in all bedrooms Ⓡ **T** ✱
sB⇔↱£69 dB⇔↱£80 (room only)
Lift ☾ 200P ✱ CFA snooker snooker room putting green ♫
International **V** Lunch £8.50&alc Dinner fr£11.95&alc Last dinner 9.45pm
Credit Cards [1] [2] [3] [5] (£)

⌂ **Campanile** Miles Grey Rd, Pipps Hill Industrial Estate, Southend Arterial Rd SS14 3AE (A127) (Campanile)
☎(0268)530810 Telex no 995068
Annexe98⇔↱(4fb) CTV in 47bedrooms Ⓡ **T**
sB⇔↱fr£29 (room only)
63P
English & French Lunch £3.75-£5 Dinner £6.80-£8.90 Last dinner 10pm
Credit Cards [1] [3]

⌂ **Watermill Travel Inn** Felmores, East Mayne SS13 1BW
☎(0268)522227 FAX (0268) 530092
Closed 25 & 26 Dec
Situated next to the popular Watermill Steak House, this establishment offers a new style of comfortable, modern, well-equipped accommodation and convenient parking.
Annexe32⇔ in 5 bedrooms CTV in all bedrooms Ⓡ (ex guide dogs) ✱ sB⇔£24.50 dB⇔£27.50 (room only)
160P
Mainly grills **V**
Credit Cards [1] [2] [3] [5]

BASINGSTOKE Hampshire Map **04** SU65

See also **Odiham**
★★★★79% **Tylney Hall** RG27 9AJ (Prestige)
☎Hook(0256)764881 Telex no 859864 FAX (0256) 768141
(For full entry see Rotherwick)

★★★61% **Crest** Grove Rd RG21 3EE (Crest) ☎(0256)468181
Telex no 858501 FAX (0256) 840081
Bright modern hotel, conveniently situated on the southern outskirts of the town. Bedrooms have been equipped to suit the needs of the business person. A limited lounge area is provided, together with a choice of two bars and a popular restaurant.
85⇔↱ in 21 bedrooms CTV in all bedrooms Ⓡ **T** ✱
sB⇔↱fr£74 dB⇔↱fr£88 (room only)
☾ 150P CFA snooker pool table *xmas*
English & French **V** Lunch £7.95-£9.50 High tea 85p-£1 Dinner £12.95-£15 Last dinner 10pm
Credit Cards [1] [2] [3] [4] [5]
See advertisement on page 101

★★★55% **Hilton Lodge** Old Common Rd, Black Dam RG21 3PR (Hilton) ☎(0256)460460 Telex no 859038 FAX (0256) 840441

The hotel is modern and well-managed, its good bedrooms equipped to a high standard. The fixed price buffet in the Hillside Restaurant represents good value for money, and service is both helpful and unpretentious.

144⇨♠(17fb)⚡in 54 bedrooms CTV in all bedrooms ® T ✱ sB⇨♠£73-£88 dB⇨♠£83-£98 (room only) ⊟

☾ ⊞ 100P ✲ ⊡(heated) sauna gymnasium fitness trail *xmas*

♀ International V ♢ ♀ ⚡ Lunch fr£11.50 Dinner fr£13.50&alc Last dinner 10pm

Credit Cards 1 2 3 4 5

★★★55% **Hilton National** Popley Way, Aldermaston Roundabout, Ringway North (A339) RG24 9NV (Hilton) ☎(0256)20212 Telex no 858223 FAX (0256)842835

Palms piano bar and eating house create a lively atmosphere. Bedrooms are well equipped and there are good leisure facilities..

138⇨♠(10fb)⚡in 26 bedrooms CTV in all bedrooms ® T ✱ sB⇨♠fr£70 dB⇨♠fr£85 (room only) ⊟

Lift ☾ 160P CFA ⊡(heated) sauna gymnasium ♫ *xmas*

♀ English & American V ♢ ♀ Lunch fr£8.50&alc Dinner £10-£25alc Last dinner 11pm

Credit Cards 1 2 3 5

★★**Red Lion** 24 London St RG21 1NY (Trusthouse Forte) ☎(0256)28525 FAX (0256) 844056

In a central position with good car parking. Bedrooms are of various standards. The Pavillion Restaurant serves à la carte and Best of British table d'hôte menus. There is no lounge as such.

62rm(32⇨30♠)(2fb)⚡in 18 bedrooms CTV in all bedrooms ® T

Lift ☾ 50P

V ♢ ♀ ⚡ Last dinner 9.30pm

Credit Cards 1 2 3 4 5

★★**Wheatsheaf Hotel** RG25 2BB (Lansbury) ☎Dummer(0256)758282 due to change to (0256) 398282 Telex no 859775 FAX (0256) 398253

(For full entry see North Waltham)

○***Audleys Wood Thistle*** Alton Rd RG25 2JP (Thistle) ☎(0256)817555

Due to have opened Oct 1989

71⇨

○***Travelodge*** Stag and Hounds, Winchester Rd RG22 6HN (Trusthouse Forte) ☎(0256)843566

Due to have opened July 1989

32⇨

P

BASLOW Derbyshire Map **08** SK27

★★★ CAVENDISH

DE4 1SP ☎(024688)2311 Telex no 547150

Much of the bedroom furniture at the Cavendish has been made by craftsmen in the workshops of Chatsworth House, and several rooms enjoy wonderful views of the Chatsworth estate. Once a simple 18th-century inn, the Cavendish has been rebuilt and extended quite recently to become an elegantly furnished and comfortable hotel. The choice of the antique furnishings and pictures which provide so much of its character reflect the interest of the Duchess of Devonshire, who has played an important part in the hotel's transformation. A closely knit team of attentive staff and the skills of chef Nick Buckingham, combine with a wonderful Peak District setting to make a visit memorable. Eric Marsh is the well-known proprietor and he remains actively involved, to the extent that he tries to greet each new guest personally. Not all his staff respond as naturally and enthusiastically as he, but the overall experience of staying here remains a considerable delight.

24⇨♠1⊟ CTV in all bedrooms ® T ✗ (ex guide dogs) ✱ sB⇨♠fr£55 dB⇨♠fr£65 (room only) ⊟

☾ 50P ⊞ ✲ ♩ putting green *xmas*

V ♢ ♀ ⚡ Lunch fr£18 Dinner fr£18 Last dinner 11pm

Credit Cards 1 2 3 5

BASSENTHWAITE Cumbria Map **11** NY23

★★★★♣51%
Armathwaite Hall CA12 4RE

☎Bassenthwaite Lake (059681)551 Telex no 64319 FAX (059681) 220

Historic building in large park with woodland, near Bassenthwaite Lake.

42rm(35⇨7♠)(4fb)2⊟ CTV in all bedrooms ® T ✱ sB&B⇨♠£45-£85 dB&B⇨♠£92-£160 ⊟

Lift ☾ 100P ✲ ⊡(heated) ♪ (hard) ♩ ∪ snooker sauna solarium gymnasium croquet games room pitch & putt *xmas*

♀ English & French V ♢ ♀ Lunch fr£9.95 High tea fr£5 Dinner fr£22 Last dinner 9.30pm

Credit Cards 1 2 3 5 £

See advertisement under KESWICK

★★★53% ***Castle Inn*** CA12 4RG ☎Bassenthwaite Lake(059681)401

Closed mid 2wks Nov & Xmas

Situated at the junction of the A591 and the B5291, this leisure hotel features attractive, formal gardens.

22rm(18⇨1♠)(2fb)1⊟ CTV in all bedrooms T

100P ✲ ⊡(heated) ♪ (grass) sauna solarium ♫

V ♢ ♀ Last dinner 8.30pm

Credit Cards 1 2 3 4 5

★★♣**Overwater Hall** Ireby CA5 1HH

☎Bassenthwaite Lake (059681)566

Closed 24 Dec-23 Feb

Set in splendid seclusion near Overwater, north of Bassenthwaite, this family-run hotel is popular locally for its dinners. Bedrooms are furnished comfortably and most have unspoilt views over local countryside. There are good lounges – with some fine pieces of china and porcelain on

B

display. In the cocktail bar a grand piano is used as the bar counter.
13rm(10⇨3↱)(4fb)3⊞ CTV in all bedrooms ®
sB&B⇨↱fr£28 dB&B⇨↱fr£46 ⊟
25P ⊞ ✲
☋ English & French ♔ ⊻ Dinner fr£13.50 Last dinner 8.30pm
Credit Cards [1] [3]

★★**Pheasant Inn** CA13 9YE ☎Bassenthwaite Lake(059681)234 due to change to (07687) 76234
Closed Xmas Day
A charming and very popular inn, the Pheasant combines abundant character with a pleasant atmosphere and good food.
17rm(16⇨1↱)Annexe3rm(2⇨1↱) ® ✗ ✻ S10%
sB&B⇨↱£38 dB&B⇨↱£68 ⊟
80P ⊞ ✲
V ♔ ⊻ ⚡ S10% Lunch £3.50-£10.50alc Dinner £16.50 Last dinner 8.30pm

See advertisement on page 103

BATH Avon Map **03** ST76

See **Town Plan Section.**
See also Colerne
★★★★ 50% **Francis** Queen Square BA1 2HH (Trusthouse Forte)
•☎(0225)24257 Telex no 449162 FAX (0225) 319715
Comfortable accommodation and an elegant restaurant are found in this Georgian-style hotel.
94⇨⚡in 9 bedrooms CTV in all bedrooms ® T S%
sB⇨£70-£75 dB⇨£97-£102 (room only) ⊟
Lift ☾ 30P CFA *xmas*

▶

English & French V S% Lunch fr£11.95&alc Dinner fr£16.15&alc Last dinner 10pm
Credit Cards 1 2 3 4 5

B

★★★★70% **Royal Crescent** 16 Royal Crescent BA1 2LS (Norfolk Capital)(Prestige)
(0225)319090 Telex no 444251 FAX (0225) 339401
A finer setting for a hotel could hardly be imagined. It stands in the centre of Bath's great architectural showpiece, the magnificent terrace of grand houses built by John Woods in the 18th century. One drawback is the difficulty of finding somewhere to park, but thoughtful and helpful staff are always on hand to assist. Bedrooms range from comfortable doubles to sumptuous suites, each individually decorated in fitting style. Behind the hotel is a delightful garden, and the main restaurant is in the Dower House which has a further selection of splendid bedrooms, with more suites in the Pavilion.
28rm(26⇌)Annexe17⇌(8fb)4 CTV in all bedrooms T S10% sB⇌£89 dB⇌£110-£250 (room only)
Lift 14 (£4 per night) croquet boules *xmas*
English & French V Lunch £19-£23&alc Dinner £33&alc Last dinner 9.30pm
Credit Cards 1 2 3 5

★★★63% ***Bath*** Widcombe Basin BA2 4JB (Best Western)
(0225)338855 Telex no 445876 FAX (0225) 28941
Enjoying picturesque, waterside views from an attractive position where the Kennet and Avon Canal joins the River Avon – yet only a few moments' walk from the city centre – this large, purpose-built hotel offers ninety-six comfortable bedrooms with en suite facilities, equipped to cater for business and leisure guests alike, and a restaurant and bar overlooking the terrace.
96rm(95⇌1)(4fb) CTV in all bedrooms ® T
Lift 102P
V
Credit Cards 1 2 3 4 5

★★★68% **Lansdown Grove** Lansdown Rd BA1 5EH (Best Western) (0225)315891 Telex no 444850 FAX (0225)448092
Comfortable amenities and attentive, friendly service provided by a traditionally-run hotel which commands magnificent views of the city beyond its small, well-kept garden area.
45rm(41⇌4)(3fb) in 9 bedrooms CTV in all bedrooms ® T sB&B⇌£50-£60 dB&B⇌£72-£90
Lift 38P 6 CFA
English & French V Lunch £8.25-£9.75 Dinner £14.50-£16&alc Last dinner 9.30pm
Credit Cards 1 2 3 4 5 £

★★★61% ***Pratts*** South Pde BA2 4AB (Forestdale)
(0225)60441 Telex no 444827
Once the home of Sir Walter Scott, this classically designed and beautifully preserved Georgian building offers well-equipped and comfortable accommodation; its convenient situation, close to both city centre and railway station, make it popular with tourists and business people alike.
46rm(45⇌1)(6fb)1 in 2 bedrooms CTV in all bedrooms ® T
Lift
English & French V Last dinner 10pm
Credit Cards 1 2 3 5

★★★78% **The Priory** Weston Rd BA1 2XT (Select)
(0225)331922 Telex no 44612 FAX (0225) 448276
An early 19th-century house, standing in a peaceful postion in a residential area not far from the city centre, that has been converted into a particularly comfortable hotel. Bedrooms vary widely in size but all have furniture and soft furnishings of high quality and good large beds. Food is very good indeed, and an interesting menu with occasional 'special' dishes. There is a general atmosphere of friendliness with staff eager to see that you are always fully satisfied. All in all, it is not surprising that many guests return again and again.
21rm(20⇌1)1 CTV in all bedrooms T (ex guide dogs) S% sB&B⇌£80-£85 dB&B⇌£110-£160
24P 1 (heated) croquet *xmas*
French V Lunch £15-£18&alc Dinner £25-£28&alc Last dinner 9.15pm
Credit Cards 1 2 3 4 5 £

★★★50% ***Redcar*** Henrietta St BA2 6LR (Mount Charlotte)
(0225)69151 Telex no 444842
A city-centre hotel forming part of a Georgian terrace.
31rm(22⇌)(2fb) CTV in all bedrooms ® T
18P CFA
International V Last dinner 11.30pm
Credit Cards 1 2 3 4 5

★★**Duke's** Great Pulteney St BA2 4DN (0225)463512
Telex no 449227
A charming, historic hotel (built in 1780) offering well-furnished bedrooms with good facilities. Comfortable public areas include a small, relaxing bar and guests are assured of warm service and hospitality from the resident owners.
22rm(18⇌2)(4fb) CTV in all bedrooms ® T sB&Bfr£35 sB&B⇌£40-£50 dB&Bfr£55 dB&B⇌£55-£85
V Lunch fr£12.50alc Dinner fr£12.50alc Last dinner 8.30pm
Credit Cards 1 2 3

Book as early as possible for busy holiday periods.

The Lansdown Grove Hotel

Centenary 1888-1988

AA★★★

BATH

Best Western

□ Situated in a charming position overlooking the fine Georgian City of Bath, the Lansdown Grove Hotel has a distinctly relaxed and individual style. □ Bedrooms are, of course, centrally heated with telephone, radio and colour television, mini bar, hairdryers and trouser press. □ The Lansdown Restaurant offers a delicious range of English and Continental cuisine together with a select choice of wines and liquers. □ Take in the beauty of Bath – the Royal Crescent, the Pump Rooms and the Abbey – during your stay. For your evenings' entertainment there is always the historic Theatre Royal. □ Please contact us for an illustrated brochure and any further information you require – we are always at your service.

Telephone Bath (0225) 315891

The Pheasant Inn ★★

Bassenthwaite Lake, Near Cockermouth, CUMBRIA

Tel: Bassenthwaite Lake (07687) 76234

Just off road A66
8 miles NW of Keswick

An old country inn in quiet surroundings near the lake and Thornthwaite Forest. Modernized to suit the present but retaining the traditional atmosphere. Good food and cellar, friendly service. 20 bedrooms all with private facilities. Open all the year except Christmas Day. Ideal for a Lakeland holiday, a passing meal or a private party. Excellent self-catering accommodation also available nearby.

A British Tourist Authority commended hotel and restaurant

B

★★Haringtons Queen St BA1 1HE ☎(0225)461728
A comfortable, small hotel and restaurant at the centre of the city in a quiet, cobbled street. Bedrooms are well-furnished and friendly, family attention is always provided.
12rm(1⇨4♠) CTV in all bedrooms ® ✈ (ex guide dogs) ✱ sB&B£20 sB&B⇨♠£26 dB&B£30 dB&B⇨♠£36 ⊟
P
English French Dinner fr£10alc Last dinner 10pm
Credit Cards 1 2 3

★Berni Royal Manvers St BA1 1JP (Berni/Chef & Brewer)
☎(0225)63134
This hotel is situated in the town centre, close to the railway station. Well-furnished bedrooms are available here together with a popular Berni grill restaurant.
30rm(4⇨26♠)(4fb) CTV in all bedrooms ® T ✈ (ex guide dogs) sB&B⇨♠fr£41.50 dB&B⇨♠fr£50.50 ⊟
Lift (P
Mainly grills V Lunch fr£8 Dinner fr£8 Last dinner 10.30pm
Credit Cards 1 2 3 5

★Gainsborough Weston Ln BA1 4AB ☎(0225)311380
Closed Xmas & first 2 wks Jan
Attractive, detached stone house in good sized grounds, in a quiet location to the west of the city centre. Rooms are simply furnished. There is a small à la carte menu and wine list at modest prices.
16rm(12⇨4♠)(2fb)1 CTV in all bedrooms ® T ✈
sB&B⇨♠£25-£31 dB&B⇨♠£49-£57 ⊟
17P
V Dinner £8.50 Last dinner 8.30pm
Credit Cards 1 2 3

○*Bath Spa Hotel* Sidney Rd BA2 6JF (Trusthouse Forte)
☎(0225)444424
Due to have opened autumn 1989, this luxury hotel is set in its own landscaped gardens.
105⇨

✕✕✕Popjoys Beau Nash House, Sawclose BA1 1EU
☎(0225)460494 FAX (0225) 446319
In the heart of the city, close to the Theatre Royal, the house was built in 1720 by Beau Nash and the restaurant is named after his mistress, Juliana Popjoy. The menu is restricted to a small but interesting selection of West Country produce and dishes. Seafood, game, poultry and meats are cooked to retain their flavour and presented in the modern way by the skilled chef Anton Edwards and his team. There is a smaller, more international menu available at lunchtime which allows just one course but is popular.
Closed Sun & Mon
Lunch not served Sat
French V 32 seats ✱ Lunch £15 Dinner £22.50 Last lunch 2pm Last dinner 10.30pm P nc6yrs
Credit Cards 1 2 3 4

✕✕*Hole In The Wall* 16 George St BA1 2EN ☎(0225)25242
An established restaurant in a Georgian terraced building in the centre of Bath. Aperitifs served in the spacious lounge will whet your appetite for the traditional continental cuisine served in the dining room.
Lunch not served Sun
French V 45 seats Last dinner 10pm P
Credit Cards 1 2 3 5

✕✕Rajpoot Tandoori Rajpoot House, 4 Argyle St BA2 4BA
☎(0225)466833 & 464758 FAX (0225) 442462
A popular well-appointed Indian-style restaurant near the city centre offering Tandoori and Biriani specialities and some vegetarian dishes. The food is well-cooked and service prompt and polite.
North Indian V 110 seats S12% Lunch £10-£25&alc Dinner £11.95-£19.95&alc Last lunch 2.30pm Last dinner 11pm P
Credit Cards 1 2 3 5

✕*Flowers* 27 Monmouth St BA1 2AP ☎(0225)313774
This small, popular restaurant, its bright, attractive interior hung with many pictures stands in a row of Georgian buildings near the city centre. A short menu of French style cuisine features some interesting dishes accompanied by fresh vegetables, and the wine list is strong in clarets. Service is pleasant and leisurely.
Closed Sun, Mon & 2 wks Xmas
V 30 seats Last dinner 10.30pm P
Credit Cards 1 3 5

✕Garlands 7 Edgar Buildings, George St BA1 2EH
☎(0225)442283
A new partnership has taken over these premises in central Bath. The small restaurant offers an intimate and relaxing atmosphere together with enthusiastic service. Dishes are well presented in the modern French style and include Duck Terrine layered with its own livers, Oyster Mushrooms and hazlenuts and some appetizing desserts.
Closed Mon & 2 Jan for 3 wks
Lunch not served Sun
V 30 seats ✱ Lunch £9.25-£10.95&alc Last lunch 2.15p, Last dinner 10.30pm P
Credit Cards 1 3

BATLEY West Yorkshire Map 07 SE22

★★Alder House Towngate Rd, off Healey Ln WF17 7HR
☎(0924)444777
Maintaining a comfortable, country house style, though set in a built-up area, the hotel complements well-appointed accommodation with good home cooking.
14rm(6⇨6♠)(1fb) CTV in all bedrooms ® T sB&Bfr£30.25 sB&B⇨♠fr£41.25 dB&B⇨♠fr£55.30 ⊟
CTV 20P 2

▶

English & Continental **V** Lunch £7 Dinner £10.50-£13.50 Last dinner 9.30pm
Credit Cards 1 2 3

BATTLE East Sussex Map **05** TQ71

★★★ NETHERFIELD PLACE

Netherfield TN33 9PP (3m NW B2096) ☎(04246)4455
Telex no 95284
FAX (04246) 4024
Closed 2 wks Xmas & New Year

Set in 30 acres of lovely grounds, this peaceful Georgian-style hotel now attracts quite an international set of travellers who clearly appreciate the discreet and professional style of service provided by the Colliers. Michael Collier is responsible for the sound and inspired nouvelle cuisine served in the elegant wood-panelled dining room. Making good use of the hotel's own fruit and vegetables, he combines a good value table d'hôte dinner with an imaginative à la carte menu. Among the choice of main courses are fresh boned quail, filled with chicken mousse, wrapped in filo pastry and served with a port wine sauce; breast of duck wrapped in pastry, baked and coated with fresh ginger and honey sauce sharpened with lemon, or saddle of Sussex lamb, roasted and served with a rich Brouilly wine sauce. The wine list has over 300 bins. Michael's wife, Helen, is totally involved with ensuring that guests feel welcome, and a relaxed country house atmosphere prevails, whilst still maintaining a degree of formality. All of the bedrooms are individually furnished, some with marble-tiled bathrooms, and the best of them enjoy lovely views over the gardens. Lots of thoughtful little extras are provided and improvements are continually being made at this excellent hotel which reflects such quiet good taste.

14(1fb)1 CTV in all bedrooms **T** (ex guide dogs)
sB&B£45 dB&B£70-£95
30P 2 (hard) croquet
French **V** Lunch £12.50-£13.95 Dinner £16.95&alc Last dinner 9.30pm
Credit Cards 1 2 3 5 £

See advertisement under HASTINGS & ST LEONARDS

★★The George 23 High St TN33 0EA ☎(04246)4466
An old coaching inn set in the centre of this busy historic town. Bedrooms are well-equipped, if functional, and public areas are cosy. There is a range of menus at both lunch and dinner, while service is provided by pleasant young staff supervised by the owner.
21rm(192)(4fb)1 CTV in all bedrooms ®
sB&B£30-£33
dB&B£38-£40 Continental breakfast
CTV 22P *xmas*
English & Continental **V** Lunch £5-£7.50&alc Dinner £11-£12 Last dinner 9.30pm
Credit Cards 1 2 3 5

★★La Vieille Auberge 27 High St TN33 0EA ☎(04246)5171
FAX (04246) 4014
This small auberge with the ambience of a French provincial hotel offers individually furnished, well equipped bedrooms, a choice of quality menus based on good, fresh, local produce, a fine wine list, and warm personal service.
7rm(5)(1fb)1 CTV in all bedrooms ® **T** (ex guide dogs) sB&B£24.50 sB&B£29.50-£39.50 dB&B£39.50-£49.50 dB&B£39.50-£49.50
xmas
French **V** Lunch £14.50-£18.50&alc High tea 95p-£3.50 Dinner £14.50-£18.50&alc Last dinner 10pm
Credit Cards 1 2 3 5

BAWTRY South Yorkshire Map **08** SK69

★★★66% Crown Hotel & Posting House High St DN10 6JW (Trusthouse Forte) ☎Doncaster(0302)710341 Telex no 547089
FAX (0302) 711798
An interesting old coaching inn, now modernised, and standing in the old Market Place on the Great North Road.
571in 12 bedrooms CTV in all bedrooms ® **T**
sB£56-£66 dB£66-£100 (room only)
40P CFA *xmas*
V Lunch £7.75-£8&alc Dinner £14&alc Last dinner 9.30pm
Credit Cards 1 2 3 4 5

BEACONSFIELD Buckinghamshire Map **04** SU99

★★★60% Bellhouse Oxford Rd HP9 2XE (2m E A40) (De Vere) ☎Gerrards Cross(0753)887211 Telex no 848719
FAX (0753) 888231
This popular commercial hotel has been extensively upgraded to provide its already comfortable accommodation with additional amenities, notably a new leisure complex. Well equipped bedrooms have been thoughtfully furnished and decorated, while a well appointed restaurant offers a comprehensive menu of skilfully prepared dishes served by friendly, helpful staff.
136(5fb)in 18 bedrooms CTV in all bedrooms ® **T**
S10% sB&B£35-£78 dB&B£70-£94
Lift 405P CFA pool table tennis *xmas*
English & Continental **V** S10% Lunch fr£12.75&alc Dinner fr£13.75&alc Last dinner 10pm
Credit Cards 1 2 3 4 5

★★*White Hart Toby* Aylesbury End HP9 1LW (Toby) ☎(0494)671211 Telex no 837882
A 16th-century inn with a friendly, relaxing atmosphere, and a modern annexe of well-equipped bedrooms.
6Annexe281in 5 bedrooms CTV in all bedrooms ® **T**
80P
V
Credit Cards 1 2 3 5

BEAMINSTER Dorset Map **03** ST40

✕✕Bridge House Hotel Restaurant DT8 3AY ☎(0308)862200
Lunch not served Mon
Dinner not served Sun
International **V** 36 seats Lunch £8.75-£11.25&alc Last lunch 2pm Last dinner 9pm 30P nc4yrs 8 bedrooms available
Credit Cards 1 3

BEARSDEN Strathclyde *Dunbartonshire* Map **11** NS57

✕✕La Bavarde 19 New Kirk Rd G61 3SJ ☎041-942 2202
Small restaurant run by friendly proprietors.
Closed Sun, Mon, 2 wks Xmas/New Year & last 3 wks Jul
V 50 seats Lunch £3.75-£5.50 Dinner £10.75-£15.90alc Last lunch 2pm Last dinner 9.30pm
Credit Cards 1 2 3 4 5

✕✕Octobers Restaurant 128 Drymen Rd G61 3RB ☎041-942 7272
A complete transformation of the interior of this originally simple restaurant has created an elegant, sophisticated environment in which guests can sample such delights as onion and tarragon soup, cheese soufflé or mussels with garlic from the interesting range of dishes on a well-balanced menu. Service is friendly and unpretentious, the small selection of wines represents most of the growing areas and a short, value-for-money menu is available at lunchtime.

Closed Sun, BH's, 1 wk Etr & 1st 2 wks Aug
☋ International **V** 48 seats Lunch £8.75&alc Last lunch 2pm Last dinner 10pm
Credit Cards [1] [3]

BEATTOCK Dumfries & Galloway *Dumfriesshire* Map **11** NT00

See also **Moffat**

★★★63% Auchen Castle DG10 9SH (Inter) ☎(06833)407
Closed 20 Dec-8 Jan
Set in 50 acres of grounds and gardens a mile north of the village, and offering direct access to the A74, this splendid, Victorian country house provides comfortable, individually styled bedrooms, relaxing public rooms, and helpful and friendly service from enthusiastic staff.
15rm(13⇌2↱)Annexe10↱(11fb) CTV in all bedrooms ® **T**
sB&B⇌↱£36 dB&B⇌↱£39-£57 ⊟
35P ✻ ♪
V ♡ ☕ Bar Lunch £6-£8alc Dinner £11-£14alc Last dinner 9pm
Credit Cards [1] [2] [3] [4] [5] £

★★Beattock House DG10 9QB ☎(06833)403 & 402
A friendly, family-run hotel offering traditional services. It stands in 6 acres of grounds well back from the A74, with extensive lawns to front and rear. The hotel keeps rabbits, deer and chickens which are especially popular with younger guests.
7rm(3↱)(2fb) CTV in 3bedrooms TV in 1bedroom ®
sB&Bfr£22.50 sB&B↱fr£25 dB&Bfr£42 dB&B↱fr£45 ⊟
CTV 30P ✻ ♪ putting
V ♡ ☕ Lunch fr£6.95 High tea fr£4.75 Dinner fr£12.75 Last dinner 9.30pm
Credit Cards [2] [3] [5]

BEAULIEU Hampshire Map **04** SU30

★★★64% Beaulieu Hotel SO4 7YQ ☎Ashurst(042129)3344
FAX (0421) 283719
A coaching inn during the 19th-century, this hotel is adjacent to Beaulieu Road Railway Station. The majority of bedrooms within this hotel are en suite and are well equipped. There is a choice of places to eat – the Beaulieu Road Pub, which serves an extensive array of hot and cold bar food, and the attractive Conservatory Restaurant.
10⇌↱(2fb) CTV in all bedrooms ® ✱ S% sB&B⇌↱£45-£59 dB&B⇌↱£65-£85 ⊟
Lift ⊞ 100P ✻ ⩦(heated) ∪ ♫ ⌂ *xmas*
☋ English & French **V** ♡ ☕ ⚡ Lunch £3.50-£7&alc Last dinner 9.45pm
Credit Cards [1] [2] [3]

★★★72% Montagu Arms SO42 7ZL ☎(0590)612324
Telex no 47276
Individually furnished and decorated bedrooms are complemented here by terraced gardens, fine cuisine and a discerning wine cellar; the Wine Press Bar serves real ale and wines from its own list (several of them being available by the glass), while the spacious restaurant is particularly well managed.
25⇌↱(4fb)5⊠ CTV in all bedrooms **T** ✗ (ex guide dogs)
sB&B⇌↱£54-£60 dB&B⇌↱£77-£98 ⊟
☾80P 6⌂ ✻ *xmas*
V ♡ ☕ ⚡ Lunch £7.50-£15&alc Dinner £22-£29.50&alc Last dinner 9.30pm
Credit Cards [1] [2] [3] [5]

BEAULY Highland *Inverness-shire* Map **14** NH54

★★Priory The Square IV4 7BX (Inter) ☎(0463)782309
FAX (0463) 782531
Modernised hotel set in the town square.
11rm(5⇌6↱)(1fb) CTV in all bedrooms ® **T** ✱
sB&B⇌↱£23.95-£25.95 dB&B⇌↱£39.50 ⊟
⊬ ♫
V ♡ ☕ Lunch £3.50-£8.25alc High tea £3.95-£7.50alc Dinner £6-£16.50alc Last dinner 9pm
Credit Cards [1] [2] [3] [5] £

BEAUMARIS Gwynedd Map **06** SH67

★★Bishopsgate House 54 Castle St LL58 8AB ☎(0248)810302
Closed Xmas-Jan
An elegant Georgian town house situated in the centre of the town just 50 yards from the shores of the Menai Straits. It is family owned and run, and service is warm and friendly. The hotel retains a magnificent Chinese Chippendale staircase and is furnished in the style of that period. Bedrooms are comfortable and well-equipped. A good standard of food is served in the attractive restaurant.
10rm(4⇌6↱)1⊠ CTV in all bedrooms ® **T**
sB&B⇌↱£20-£26 dB&B⇌↱£40-£45 ⊟
10P ⊯ nc5yrs
☋ English & French **V** ♡ Lunch £7-£7.50 Dinner £9.50-£10.50&alc Last dinner 9pm
Credit Cards [1] [3] £

BEAUMONT

See **Jersey under Channel Islands**

BEBINGTON Merseyside Map **07** SJ38

★★*Bridge Inn* Bolton Rd, Port Sunlight L62 4UQ ☎051-645 8441
This popular inn, standing close to the church in the unique setting of Port Sunlight Village, provides comfortable accommodation in well-equipped bedrooms.
16rm(11⇌)(2fb)1⊠ CTV in all bedrooms ® **T** ✗

▶

50P
🍷 English & Continental V ♔ ☕ Last dinner 10.30pm
Credit Cards 1 2 3 5

B

TraveLodge New Chester Rd L62 9AQ (A41/M53 junc 5) (Trusthouse Forte) ☎051-327 2489
Situated on the A41 to Liverpool Road at Eastham off juntion 5 of the M53. The lodge is set with car park frontage and flower beds around the building. It maintains a good degree of comfort and cleanliness, safety and security and provides excellent value for money.
31⇌♨(31fb) CTV in all bedrooms ® sB⇌♨£21.50 dB⇌♨£27 (room only)
☾31P
🍷 Mainly grills
Credit Cards 1 2 3

BECCLES Suffolk Map 05 TM49

★★**Kings Head** New Market NR34 9HA (Berni/Chef & Brewer) ☎(0502)712147
Conveniently situated in the town centre, a hotel dating back to the 16th century boasts attractively furnished rooms with a range of modern facilities and a restaurant offering a choice of popular dishes.
12rm(8⇌3♨) CTV in all bedrooms ® T ✗ (ex guide dogs) sB&B⇌♨fr£36 dB&B⇌♨fr£48
18P
V ♔ ☕ ⚡ Lunch fr£8 Dinner fr£9 Last dinner 9.30pm
Credit Cards 1 2 3 5

★★***Waveney House*** Puddingmoor NR34 9PL ☎(0502)712270
Standing on the banks of the River Waveney, this old hotel dates back to the 16th century yet offers modern facilities in its comfortable rooms. The bar, made busy in summer by the custom of passing river traffic, serves food both at lunchtimes and in the evenings.
13⇌♨(2fb)1 CTV in all bedrooms ® T
CTV 100P ✲ ♩
🍷 English & French V ♔ ☕ Last dinner 9.30pm
Credit Cards 1 2 3 4 5

BECKINGHAM Lincolnshire Map 08 SK85

✕✕**Black Swan** Hillside LN5 0RF
☎Fenton Claypole(063684)474
Situated in a peaceful corner of the country on the banks of the River Witham. Dinner is a 6 course experience at an inclusive price and certainly represents value for money. Anton Indans, previously with Peter Kromberg at the Intercontinental, cooks in the fashionable light style. Portions are small, but that is compensated for by the quality and number of courses. Soufflés are a predominant element on the menu, whether as a first course or as a lovely light pudding. The staff are discreet and professional yet friendly.
Closed Mon, 2 wks Jan/Feb & 2 wks Aug
Lunch not served (ex by reservation)
Dinner not served Sun
🍷 English & French 28 seats ✻ Dinner fr£12.90 Last lunch 2pm Last dinner 10pm 9P
Credit Cards 1 3

BEDALE North Yorkshire Map 08 SE28

★★***Motel Leeming*** DL8 1DT (1m NE junc A1/A684)
☎(0677)23611
Part of service area complex, motel offers simple, modern accomodation.
40⇌ CTV in all bedrooms ® T
☾100P 14🚗 (charged) ✲
🍷 English & Continental V ♔ ☕ ⚡
Credit Cards 1 2 3 5

BEDDGELERT Gwynedd Map 06 SH54

★★★ 57% **Royal Goat** LL55 4YE ☎(076686)224 & 343
A well-furnished, family-run hotel in the village centre, lying amidst spectacular scenery.
31⇌♨(4fb)1 ⚡in 5 bedrooms CTV in all bedrooms ® T sB&B⇌♨£35-£66.50 dB&B⇌♨£60-£70
Lift ☾ 150P ♩ games room *xmas*
🍷 Welsh & French V ♔ ☕ ⚡ Lunch £8.50-£10&alc High tea £3-£6&alc Dinner £15&alc Last dinner 10pm
Credit Cards 1 2 3 5 £

★ **Bryn Eglwys Country House** LL55 4NB
☎(076686)210

A former Georgian country house in its own grounds, standing in mountainous splendour on the edge of the village, now provides well-furnished accomodation comprising bedrooms with good facilities, comfortable lounges and a delightful restaurant which offers a wide choice of well-prepared dishes.
16rm(12⇌)(3fb) CTV in 12bedrooms ® T ✻ S% sB&B£33 sB&B⇌£45 dB&B£58 dB&B⇌£78 (incl dinner)
30P ✲ *xmas*
🍷 English & French V ♔ ☕ ⚡ Lunch £7.50-£9 High tea £4.50 Dinner £11.50&alc Last dinner 9pm
Credit Cards 1 3 5

★**Tanronen** LL55 4YB (Frederic Robinson) ☎(076686)347
A two-storey tourist hotel, in the centre of the village.
8rm CTV in all bedrooms ® ✗ sB&B£15 dB&B£30
CTV 12P 3🚗 *xmas*
V ♔ ☕ Lunch £5.50 Dinner £10.50 Last dinner 9pm
Credit Cards 1 3 5

BEDFORD Bedfordshire Map 04 TL04

★★★ 71% **Bedford Moat House** 2 Saint Mary's St MK42 0AR (Queens Moat) ☎(0234)55131 Telex no 825243
FAX (0234) 40447
RS Bank hols
Upgrading has provided this modern, commercial hotel with well-equipped bedrooms and an attractive new restaurant while you can enjoy an interesting range of skilfully prepared dishes; a well-managed staff successfully combines friendliness with efficient service.
100⇌♨(20fb) CTV in all bedrooms ® T ✗ (ex guide dogs) sB&B⇌♨fr£59 dB&B⇌♨fr£79
Lift ☾ CTV 72P sauna jacuzzi mini-gym
🍷 English & Continental ♔ ☕ Lunch fr£9.25 High tea fr£1.40 Dinner fr£12.50 Last dinner 9.45pm
Credit Cards 1 2 3 5

★★★ 78% **Woodlands Manor** Green Ln, Clapham MK41 6EP (2m N A6) ☎(0234)63281 Telex no 825007
FAX (0234) 272390
A privately-run Victorian manor house, set in wooded grounds and garden, offers a choice of well-appointed bedrooms, an elegant restaurant and a drawing room. Chef Kevin Bull shows skill and flair in the production of the well-seasoned, attractively presented dishes that make up an attractive à la carte menu.

26rm(22⇨4⌐)Annexe3⇨ CTV in all bedrooms T ✕ ✳
sB&B⇨⌐£45-£69
dB&B⇨⌐£59.50-£77 Continental breakfast
☾100P ✲ nc7yrs
English & French V Lunch £11.95-£14.95&alc Dinner £23.50&alc Last dinner 9.45pm
Credit Cards 1 2 3

★★Bedford Swan The Embankment MK40 1RW ☎(0234)46565
Telex no 827779
A popular commercial hotel has been upgraded to provide refurbished bedrooms which are equipped to a high standard, comfortable, well appointed public areas and new leisure facilities; friendly staff offer unobtrusively efficient service throughout.
115⇨(4fb)1 CTV in all bedrooms ® T sB&B⇨£54-£59
dB&B⇨fr£64
Lift ☾ 70P CFA (heated) *xmas*
English & French V Lunch fr£9.75&alc Dinner fr£9.75&alc Last dinner 9.30pm
Credit Cards 1 2 3 5

BEER Devon Map **03** SY28

★★*Anchor Inn* EX12 3ET ☎Seaton(0297)20386
Closed 1 wk Xmas
Facing the 'slip way' to the beach, this small, traditional-looking hostelry retains the character which makes it so popular, despite complete refurbishment of the interior. Wholesome fare based on local produce is available in the dining room amd a varied selection of snacks is served in the bar.
9rm(2⇨2⌐)(1fb) CTV in all bedrooms ® ✕
CTV nc10yrs

Credit Cards 1 3

B

BEETHAM Cumbria Map **07** SD47

★**Wheatsheaf** LA7 7AL ☎Milnthorpe(04482)2123
An attractive village inn, with oak beams, close to lakeland.
7rm(5⇌)(1fb) CTV in all bedrooms ® ✱ sB&Bfr£18 sB&B⇌fr£20.50 dB&Bfr£26.50 dB&B⇌fr£32
CTV 50P
Lunch £3-£6.50 Dinner £6.75 Last dinner 8.30pm
Credit Cards 1

BELFORD Northumberland Map **12** NU13

★★**Blue Bell** Market Place NE70 7NE (Consort) ☎(06683)543
RS 13 Jan-21 Feb
This comfortable stone-built village inn offers friendly service and good value bar meals and dinners.
15rm(12⇌3)(1fb)1 CTV in all bedrooms ® T ✱
sB&B⇌£32-£38 dB&B⇌£56-£80
10P 2 (£3 per night) putting green *xmas*
V Lunch £3-£5&alc Dinner fr£13.50&alc Last dinner 8.45pm
Credit Cards 1 2 3 5

★★**Waren House** Waren Mill NE70 7EE
☎Bamburgh(06684)211
FAX (06684) 484

A delightful country house set in 6 acres of wooded grounds on the west corner of Budle Bay and only 2 miles from the A1. Service is courteous and friendly, bedrooms comfortable and the restaurant offers freshly prepared dishes at good value.
6⇌1 in 1 bedroom CTV in all bedrooms ® T ✱
sB&B⇌£30-£55 dB&B⇌£50-£65
20P nc
Lunch £5.50-£6.50 Dinner £15-£17.50&alc Last dinner 8.30pm
Credit Cards 1 2 3 5

BELLINGHAM Northumberland Map **12** NY88

★★**Riverdale Hall** NE48 2JT (Exec Hotel) ☎(0660)20254
Just outside the village, the hotel overlooks its own cricket pitch and the River Tyne. Additional bedrooms and a new lounge have recently been added, signs of the constant imporovement here. Friendly and attentive service is assured from the resident proprietors and their experienced staff.
20rm(19⇌1)(6fb)3 CTV in all bedrooms ® T
sB&B⇌£26-£29 dB&B⇌£46-£51
CTV 60P (heated) sauna solarium cricket field *xmas*
English & Danish V Lunch £5.95-£6.95&alc High tea £4-£6 Dinner £12-£13&alc Last dinner 9.30pm
Credit Cards 1 2 3 5 £

BELPER Derbyshire Map **08** SK34

✕✕**Rémy's Restaurant Français** 84 Bridge St DE5 1AZ
☎(0773)822246
This small first-floor restaurant, situated on the A6, offers mainly French cuisine, prepared from good fresh ingredients. Orders are taken in the small aperitif bar before proceeding to the modestly furnished restaurant, which encourages a non-smoking clientele. There is a good wine list, with items to suit all tastes. Chef/proprietor, Martin Smee, will usually leave the kitchen at some point to converse with his customers.
Closed Sun, 1st wk Jan & 2 wks Jul
Lunch not served Sat
French 28 seats Lunch £10-£12 Dinner £13.95-£16.50 Last lunch 1.30pm Last dinner 9.30pm nc10yrs
Credit Cards 1 2 3 5

BEMBRIDGE

See Wight, Isle of

BENLLECH BAY Gwynedd Map **06** SH58

★★***Bay Court*** Beach Rd LL74 8SW ☎Tynygongl(0248)852573
A modern hotel only 200 yards from the beach.
18rm(2⇌1)Annexe4⇌(9fb) CTV in 14bedrooms ®
CTV 65P
English & French V
Credit Cards 1 2 3 5

BERKELEY Gloucestershire Map **03** ST69

★★**Berkeley Arms** Canonbury St GL13 9BG
☎Dursley(0453)810291
This hotel, extensively refurbished, has retained the cosy and relaxed atmosphere of the original coaching inn whilst extending and improving the bedrooms. A good range of bar meals is offered in addition to the lunch time buffet and evening set-price menus.
10⇌ CTV in all bedrooms ® ✱ sB&B⇌£31-£39 dB&B⇌£42-£59
50P
English & French V Lunch fr£8.95 Dinner fr£8.95 Last dinner 9.30pm
Credit Cards 1 2 3

★★***Old Schoolhouse Hotel*** Canonbury St GL13 9BG
☎Dursley(0453)811711
A small hotel offers friendly, personal service, complementing distinctive public areas with comfortable bedrooms which include all modern facilities.
7rm(3⇌4) CTV in all bedrooms ® T
15P
International V Last dinner 8.45pm
Credit Cards 1 3

BERKELEY ROAD Gloucestershire Map **03** SO70

★★**Prince of Wales** Berkeley Rd GL13 9HD
☎Dursley(0453)810474 Telex no 437464
Recent improvements by the new owners of this hotel have resulted in bright, comfortable, modern accommodation and good facilities which are complemented by attentive, friendly service. Its pleasant location near the historic village of Berkeley, yet only a few miles from the business centres of Bristol, Cheltenham and Gloucester, makes it attractive to both tourist and businessman.
8rm(7⇌1)(1fb) CTV in all bedrooms ® T
150P
English & French V Last dinner 9pm
Credit Cards 1 2 3

BERWICK-UPON-TWEED Northumberland Map **12** NT95

★★★53% **Turret House** Etal Rd, Tweedmouth TD15 2EG (Inter) ☎(0289)330808 FAX (0289) 330467
Elegant hotel in its own grounds with tastefully decorated open-plan bar, dining room and lounge.
13rm(8⇌5)(1fb) CTV in all bedrooms ® T
sB&B⇌£37.50-£44 dB&B⇌£54-£59
100P
V Bar Lunch £3-£8alc Dinner £6.75-£14alc Last dinner 9.30pm
Credit Cards 1 2 3 5 £

★**Queens Head** Sandgate TD15 1EP ☎(0289)307852
Charming character hotel with cosy lounge and bar, and large bedrooms.
6rm(5fb) CTV in all bedrooms ® T
P
Mainly grills **V** Last dinner 8.30pm
Credit Cards 1 3 £

BETWS-Y-COED Gwynedd Map **06** SH75

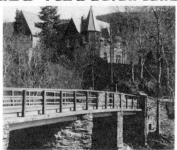

★★★ **66% Plas Hall**
Pont-y-Pant, Dolwyddelan LL25 0PJ (3m SW A470) (Minotels)
☎Dolwyddelan(06906)206
Telex no 61155

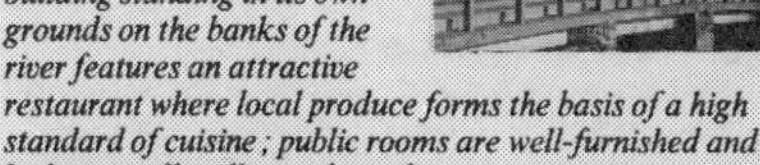

A delightful welsh stone building standing in its own grounds on the banks of the river features an attractive restaurant where local produce forms the basis of a high standard of cuisine; public rooms are well-furnished and bedrooms offer all-round comfort.
16rm(15⇌1♠)(3fb)2 CTV in all bedrooms ® T
dB&B⇌♠£55-£74
36P xmas
Welsh & French **V** Lunch £6.95-£15&alc Dinner fr£10.25&alc Last dinner 8.30pm
Credit Cards 1 2 3 4 5 £

★★★**64%** ***Royal Oak*** Holyhead Rd LL24 0AY ☎(06902)219
Closed 25-26 Dec
A choice of eating styles and a range of well-equipped bedrooms are available at this nicely appointed hotel in the centre of the village.
27⇌♠(5fb) CTV in all bedrooms **T**
60P
English, French & Italian **V** Last dinner 9.30pm
Credit Cards 1 2 3 5

★★★**64% Waterloo** LL24 0AR (Consort) ☎(06902)411
A well-furnished hotel and motel set amidst spacious grounds, backed by the Gwydyr Forest and close to the village centre. The attractive Garden Room serves good food.
9⇌Annexe19⇌(2fb) CTV in all bedrooms ® T
sB&B⇌£33-£39.75 dB&B⇌£51.50-£61.50
200P (heated) sauna solarium *xmas*
International **V** Lunch £6.95-£7.50 Dinner £10.85-£11.50&alc Last dinner 9.30pm
Credit Cards 1 2 3 5 £

See advertisement on page 113

★★***Park Hill*** Llanrwst Rd LL24 0HD ☎(06902)540
Set in an acre of well-kept garden, with views across the River Conwy to the mountains beyond, this charming house, furnished to a high standard, provides a warm welcome and good hospitality.
11rm(6⇌3♠)(1fb) CTV in all bedrooms ®
14P (heated) sauna nc6yrs
Welsh, English & French **V**
Credit Cards 1 2 3 5

See advertisement on page 113

★★**Ty Gwyn** LL24 0SG (Best Western) ☎(06902)383 & 787
Overlooking the River Conwy from its fine setting in spectacular scenery on the edge of the village, this centuries-old coaching inn is well-furnished throughout, with particularly delightful bedrooms. Food is of a high standard, whilst hospitality is warm and friendly. ▶

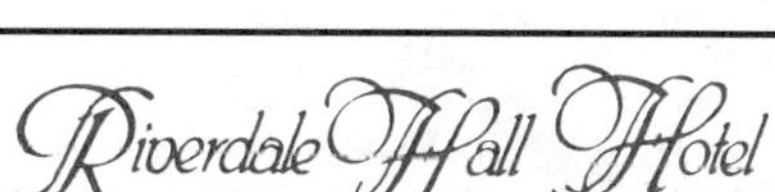

13rm(2⇌7↱)(1fb)4⊟ CTV in 5bedrooms ® ✱ sB&B£16 dB&Bfr£32 dB&B⇌↱£40-£60 ⊟
CTV 12P *xmas*
☋ English & French V ♈ Lunch fr£7.50&alc Dinner fr£10.75&alc Last dinner 9.30pm
Credit Cards 1 3 £

★**Fairy Glen** LL24 0SH ☎(06902)269
Closed Dec & Jan
17th century hotel by the river near Fairy Glen beauty spot. It is family run with a homely atmosphere.
10rm(5⇌2↱)(3fb) CTV in all bedrooms ® sB&B£13-£15 dB&B£26-£30 dB&B⇌↱£30-£34 ⊟
☾ CTV 10P ✿ ❊
V ♈ ☐ ⅟ Lunch fr£5 Dinner fr£8.50 Last dinner 7.30pm
Credit Cards 1 3 5

BEVERLEY Humberside Map **08** TA03

★★★**59% Beverley Arms** North Bar Within HU17 8DD (Trusthouse Forte) ☎Hull(0482)869241 Telex no 597568 FAX (0482) 870907
A modernised coaching inn offers sound accommodation in functional, up-to-date bedrooms complemented by public areas whose traditional features have been highlighted to good effect.
57⇌(4fb) CTV in all bedrooms ® **T** sB⇌£56-£64 dB⇌£67-£74 (room only) ⊟
Lift ☾ 70P ♫ *xmas*
V ♈ ☐ ⅟ Lunch £6.95-£8.95&alc Dinner £11.95&alc Last dinner 9.45pm
Credit Cards 1 2 3 4 5

★★★**68% Tickton Grange** Tickton HU17 9SH (3m NE on A1035) ☎Hornsea(0964)543666 Telex no 527254
RS 25-29 Dec
A peaceful country house just off the A1079 provides comfortable accomodation, interesting menus and friendly service.
17rm(10⇌7↱)(1fb)1⊟ CTV in all bedrooms ® **T** ✱ sB&B⇌↱£52 dB&B⇌↱£62 ⊟
65P ❊
V ♈ ☐ Dinner £10.95-£19.95alc Last dinner 9.30pm
Credit Cards 1 2 3 5 £

★★***Lairgate*** 30-34 Lairgate HU17 8EP ☎Hull(0482)882141
The restaurant of this town centre hotel offers particularly interesting menus and courteous, friendly service.
25rm(9⇌8↱)(2fb)1⊟ CTV in all bedrooms ® **T**
☾ CTV 18P
☋ English & Continental V ♈ ☐ Last dinner 9.30pm
Credit Cards 1 3

BEWDLEY Hereford & Worcester Map **07** SO77

★★**Black Boy** Kidderminster Rd DY12 1AG ☎(0299)402119
Closed 25 Dec
An eighteenth-century inn, standing on the A456 close to both the River Severn and the centre of this lovely old town, offers accomodation that is equally suitable for business people and tourists, with simple but comfortable bedrooms, pleasent bar facilities and a small, cosy restaurant.
17rm(5⇌)Annexe8rm(2⇌)(4fb) CTV in 15bedrooms ® **T** sB&Bfr£24.50 sB&B⇌£28.60-£38.50 dB&Bfr£38.50 dB&B⇌£42.90-£53.90 ⊟
CTV 28P ✿ ❊
V ♈ Lunch £1-£7 Dinner fr£9.50 Last dinner 8.45pm
Credit Cards 1 2 3

BEXHILL-ON-SEA East Sussex Map **05** TV70

See also **Cooden Beach**

★★★**64% Granville** Sea Rd TN40 1EE ☎Bexhill(0424)215437 FAX (0424) 225028
A friendly hotel, with a pervading sense of charm and peace. The hotel has been refurbished and modernised to provide comfortable bedrooms that have been decorated attractively, a pleasant lounge and popular bar. Staff are helpful and are led by the personal involvement of the proprietors.
50⇌(1fb) CTV in all bedrooms ® **T** sB&B⇌£29.50 dB&B⇌£49.50 ⊟
Lift ☾ ✿ *xmas*
♈ ☐ Lunch £6.95&alc Dinner £9.95&alc Last dinner 9pm
Credit Cards 1 2 3 5

BEXLEY Greater London Map **05** TQ47

★★★**69% Crest** Black Prince Interchange, Southwold Rd DA5 1ND (Crest) ☎(0322)526900 Telex no 8956539 FAX (0322) 526113
This efficiently-managed commercial hotel offers a good standard of well-equipped accomodation – and the new bedroom wing will add executive studies, rooms for lady executives and spa rooms. Attractive public areas include a seperate lounge bar for residents and a business centre.
106⇌↱⅟in 16 bedrooms CTV in all bedrooms ® **T** S% sB⇌↱fr£77 dB⇌↱fr£85 (room only) ⊟
Lift ☾ 180P ❊ games room ⌂ *xmas*
☋ English & French V ♈ ☐ ⅟ Lunch fr£12 Dinner fr£15 Last dinner 9.45pm
Credit Cards 1 2 3 4 5

The Lairgate Hotel is a building of considerable character situated in the centre of Beverley. It is privately owned and prides itself on the relaxed happy atmosphere that is generated by a friendly and conscientious staff with a little help from the proprietor. A residential and table licence only is held which assists the management to create an intimate environment for our guests.

The Bechstein restaurant, which is open to non - residents, sets standards of cuisine and service which are envied in the area and is at your disposal every day and evening. Care and thought are given to both menus and an extensive wine list, with value for money being of prime importance.

Every effort will be made to meet your requirements.

The Lairgate Hotel, Lairgate, Beverley HU17 8EP

Tel. 0482 882141 

★★ *Park Hill Hotel*

BETWS-Y-COED, GWYNNED LL24 0HD

Tel: 06902 540

Nestling in more than an acre of gardens overlooking Betws-y-Coed Village and Golf Course and with breath taking views along the Conwy and Llugwy Valleys our Ashley Courtenay Recommended Country House Hotel is ideally situated to help you enjoy the pleasures of Snowdonia National Park. Our magnificent indoor heated swimming pool, Jacuzzi and Sauna Complex is free and for the exclusive use of our guests. All rooms Colour TV and Tea/Coffee Trays. Children over six welcome. New Four Poster Ensuite Bedroom.

Waterloo Hotel

AND MOTEL, BETWS-Y-COED

GWYNEDD LL24 0AR

The leading hotel in Snowdonia, ideally situated for touring the mountains, coastline and attractions of North Wales.

All rooms en suite with colour T.V., direct telephone, tea/coffee tray.

Beautiful Garden Room Restaurant offering table d'hote and à la carte menus along with well balanced wine list. Excellent bar meals menu.

'Now open indoor pool, gym & leisure complex'

Three well stocked bars with games room — snooker, pool, darts, real ale. Weekend and Midweek Breaks available.

Brochure & Tariff D.A. Nesbitt **Tel: 06902-411**

B

BIBURY Gloucestershire Map **04** SP10

★★★64% **Swan** GL7 4NW ☎(028574)204 & 277
Telex no 437360
Set beside the River Coln, deep in the Cotswolds, a creeper-clad former coaching inn retains much of its original character in comfortable lounges, and the stylish traditionally furnished restaurant. Individually decorated bedrooms in the cottage style vary in size but are all well equipped with modern facilities. Standards of cuisine are high, good use is made of quality ingredients in the creation of imaginative dishes, and friendly service is provided in all areas.
24rm(23⇌1↱)(2fb)1⊞ CTV in all bedrooms **T**
sB&B⇌↱fr£38.50 dB&B⇌↱£68.50-£82.50 ⊟
20P 4🚗 ⊞ ✻ ♩ *xmas*
☋ English & French **V** ♡ ☕ Lunch fr£12.50 Dinner £16.50
Last dinner 8.30pm
Credit Cards [1] [3]

★★♜**Bibury Court** GL7 5NT
☎(028574)337
Closed 24-30 Dec

Friendly staff provide relaxed, informal service which perfectly complements the quiet, country house atmosphere of this delightful hotel in its beautiful gardens.
17⇌(1fb)10⊞ CTV in all bedrooms **T** sB&B⇌£36–£48
dB&B⇌£52-£58 Continental breakfast ⊟
CTV 100P ⊞ ✻ ♩
☋ English & French ♡ ☕ Bar Lunch £2-£4.50alc Dinner £14.50-£15alc Last dinner 9pm
Credit Cards [1] [3]

BIDEFORD Devon Map **02** SS42

See also **Fairy Cross, Landcross & Westward Ho**

★★★62% ***Durrant House*** Heywood Rd, Northam EX39 3QB
(Consort) ☎(02372)72361 Telex no 46740
Attractive building with 30 new comfortable bedrooms in a top floor extension. The public areas are attractively decorated and offer a friendly atmosphere to both commercial and holiday trade. The restaurant offers adequate menus, and steaks and bar meals are available in the Bridge steak bar.
79⇌↱(6fb)3⊞ CTV in all bedrooms ® **T**
Lift 150P ✻ CFA ⛆ sauna solarium
☋ English & French Last dinner 9.30pm
Credit Cards [1] [2] [3] [5]

★★★67% **Royal** Barnstaple St EX39 4AE (Brend)
☎(02372)72005 due to change to (0237) 472005 Telex no 42551
FAX (0271) 78558
Older style hotel, situated at the eastern end of the bridge.
30rm(28⇌2↱)(3fb) CTV in all bedrooms ® **T**
sB&B⇌↱£41-£46 dB&B⇌↱£70-£80 ⊟
☾ CTV 70P ♫ *xmas*
☋ English & French **V** ♡ ☕ Lunch £6.50-£7.50&alc Dinner £9-£10&alc Last dinner 9pm
Credit Cards [1] [2] [3] [5]

★★***Orchard Hill Hotel & Restaurant*** Orchard Hill, Northam
EX39 2QY ☎(02372)72872
Set in its own grounds, with views across the river, this small personally-run hotel offers simply-appointed bedrooms and attractive public areas; guests can relax in its friendly atmosphere and enjoy well-cooked meals chosen from a good menu.
9rm(8⇌1↱) CTV in all bedrooms ® ✗ (ex guide dogs)
15P ⊞ ✻ nc6 yrs
V ♡ ☕ Last dinner 9.30pm
Credit Cards [1] [3]

★★**Riversford** Limers Ln EX39 2RG (Inter) ☎(02372)74239 due to change to (0237)474239
This peacefully-situated, comfortable hotel has extensive views over the Torridge River. The owner and his family provide friendly service and honest cooking.
16rm(14⇌1↱)(3fb)2⊞ CTV in all bedrooms ® **T**
sB&B£22-£39 sB&B⇌↱£39-£42 dB&B⇌↱£58-£68 ⊟
☾ CTV 20P 2🚗 ✻ solarium badminton putting ⌂ *xmas*
☋ English & Continental **V** ♡ ☕ ⚟ Lunch £7.30 High tea £4.95 Dinner £16&alc Last dinner 8.30pm
Credit Cards [1] [2] [3] [5] ⓔ

★★***Sonnenheim*** Heywood Rd EX39 2QA ☎(02372)74989
The personally-run country-house-style hotel provides pleasant bedrooms, comfortable public areas, and a friendly atmosphere throughout. A table d'hôte menu of honest cooking, using fresh garden produce whenever possible, offers an interesting choice of dishes.
9rm(6⇌2↱)(1fb) CTV in all bedrooms ® ✗ (ex guide dogs)
10P ⊞ ✻
☋ English & Continental **V** ♡ ☕ Last dinner 8pm
Credit Cards [1] [3]

★★♜***Yeoldon House***
Durrant Ln, Northam
EX39 2RL
☎(02372)74400 & 76618
Telex no 46410
FAX (02372) 21489

A hotel in country house style commands an expansive view over the River Torridge – to which its lawns slope down – and across woodland to the village beyond. Bedrooms are well-equipped, and public areas include a comfortable lounge, pleasant dining room and cosy residents' bar.
10rm(8⇌2↱)(2fb)1⊞ CTV in all bedrooms ® **T**
20P ✻ sauna solarium gymnasium shooting
☋ English & Continental **V** ♡ ☕ ⚟ Last dinner 8.30pm
Credit Cards [1] [2] [3] [4] [5]

See advertisement on page 117

BIDFORD-ON-AVON Warwickshire Map **04** SP05

★★**White Lion** High St B50 4BQ ☎(0789)773309 & 773218
FAX (0789)490058
Fully modernised old riverside hotel offering guests a warm welcome.
10⇌↱1⊞ CTV in all bedrooms ® **T** sB&B⇌↱£28-£35
dB&B⇌↱£58-£78 ⊟
18P ♩ *xmas*
☋ English & French ♡ ☕ ⚟ Lunch £13&alc Dinner £13&alc
Last dinner 9.30pm
Credit Cards [1] [2] [3] [5] ⓔ

See advertisement on page 117

BIGBURY-ON-SEA Devon Map **03** SX64

★**Henley** TQ7 4AR (Minotels) ☎(0548)810240
Commanding beautiful views of both coast and countryside from its elevated position, and having a private cliff path to beach and gardens, the hotel promotes a cottage atmosphere in its thoughtfully decorated lounge and well equipped bedrooms. An attractive dining room offers home-cooked food prepared from ▶

B

fresh produce, varying the table d'hôte menu daily; service is friendly, and a 'no smoking' policy is applied.
9rm(4⇌1♠)(1fb)⊬in all bedrooms CTV in all bedrooms ®
sB&B£16.50-£18.90 sB&B⇌♠£18.50-£20.90 dB&B£31-£37.80
dB&B⇌♠£37-£41.80 ⊟
9P ⛟ ✲ *xmas*
☋ English & French ♔ ⚑ ⊬ Lunch £6.50 High tea £3.50&alc Dinner £9.75&alc Last dinner 7.30pm
Credit Cards 1 3

BILBROOK Somerset Map **03** ST04

★★Dragon House TA24 6HQ ☏Washford(0984)40215
Set in 2.5 acres of beautiful gardens beside the A39, this 17th-century character property stands only six miles from Minehead, providing an excellent centre from which to tour the Exmoor National Park. Beauty and technology combine in attractive, comprehensively equipped bedrooms with extensive en suite facilities, whilst pleasant public areas feature open fires, beams and exposed stonework. Table d'hôte and à la carte menus offer an interesting range of dishes, based exclusively on top-quality fresh produce and complemented by personal service from resident proprietors.
8rm(5⇌3♠)Annexe2⇌(1fb)1⊞ CTV in all bedrooms ® **T** ✳
sB&B⇌♠£38-£48 dB&B⇌♠£76-£96 (incl dinner) ⊟
25P ⛟ ✲ *xmas*
☋ English & French **V** ♔ ⚑ Lunch £11.50&alc High tea £1.50-£7alc Dinner £11.50&alc Last dinner 9pm
Credit Cards 1 2 3 5

★Bilbrook Lawns TA24 6HE ☏Washford(0984)40331
Closed Nov
This comfortable, well-appointed Georgian house offers a friendly atmosphere and good food.
7rm(1⇌3♠)(1fb) CTV in 2bedrooms TV in 5bedrooms ®
sB&Bfr£17.50 sB&B⇌♠£20-£22.50 dB&Bfr£30
dB&B⇌♠£35-£40 ⊟
8P ⛟ ✲
☋ English & French **V** ♔ ⚑ ⊬ Lunch £7.50 Dinner £9.50 Last dinner 7.30pm

BILBROUGH North Yorkshire Map **08** SE54

★★★♛ BILBROUGH MANOR COUNTRY HOUSE
YO2 3PH
☏Tadcaster(0937)834002
FAX (0937) 834724

Although very much a newcomer to the quality hotels sector, Bilbrough Manor has a long and distinguished history going back to around 1285. Since 1986, it has been carefully restored by the present owners, Colin and Susan Bell, to reflect the best of both hotel and private house – the presence of a Butler certainly adds to the country house atmosphere. Bedrooms are individually decorated and have all the thoughtful touches one would associate with this kind of hotel. The public rooms abound with interesting features and of particular note is the oak-panelled dining room, presided over by restaurant manager, Antonio Esteve. Our inspectors have, without exception, praised the innovative creations of Idris Caldora – 1986 Young Chef of the Year. Salade de poulet marinée, gratinée d'homard et tomate au parfum d'estragon, medaillon de chevreuil sauce orange, and maquise de chocolat have been singled out for a mention. In addition to the basic 2, 3 or 4 courses, various little treats appear from the kitchen between courses. Breakfasts are no less an occasion, choices including scrambled egg with smoked salmon and chive cream. kedgeree and omelette Arnold Bennet.
12rm(11⇌1♠)1⊞ CTV in all bedrooms **T** ✗
☾CTV 50P ⛟ ✲ croquet nc12yrs
☋ French **V** ♔ ⚑ Last dinner 9.30pm
Credit Cards 1 2 3 5

See advertisement under YORK

BILLESLEY Warwickshire Map **04** SP15

⊛★★★♛ 76%Billesley Manor B49 6NF (3m W off A422) (Norfolk Capital)(Prestige)
☏Stratford-upon-Avon(0789)400888
Telex no 312599
FAX (0789) 764145

Originally an Elizabethan manor house, the Great Hall is now an impressive panelled bar complete with gallery and some of the older bedrooms are also panelled and furnished in period style, whilst more recent bedrooms are spacious and equipped to provide many comforts. The lovely garden is a quiet haven in the extensive grounds, while a tiny church occupies another peaceful corner. There is also tennis and an indoor swimming-pool. Service is good throughout, but especially in the restaurant where the cooking of chef Mark Naylor is very commendable in its use of good produce and truly honest flavours.
41⇌(6fb)3⊞ CTV in all bedrooms **T** ✗ sB&B⇌£75-£120
dB&B⇌£85-£180 ⊟
☾200P ✲ ⊡(heated) ♩ (hard) croquet shooting pitch & putt ⛳ *xmas*
☋ English & French **V** ♔ ⚑ Lunch fr£15&alc High tea £6 Dinner fr£21&alc Last dinner 9.30pm
Credit Cards 1 2 3 5

BILLINGHAM
See **Stockton-on-Tees**

BINGLEY West Yorkshire Map **07** SE13

★★★ 64% Bankfield Bradford Rd BD16 1TU (Embassy)
☏Bradford(0274)567123 FAX (0274) 551331
This modernised country house offers comfortable, well-appointed bedrooms and friendly service.
103rm(101⇌2♠)(5fb)⊬in 6 bedrooms CTV in 101bedrooms ® **T**
Lift ☾250P ✲ CFA pool table tennis ♫
♔ ⚑ ⊬
Credit Cards 1 2 3 5

★★★ 64% Oakwood Hall Lady Ln BD16 4AW
☏Bradford(0274)564123 & 563569
Closed 25-28 Dec
An attractive country house type hotel in a quiet residential area. Lounges, dining room and bedrooms have been tastefully decorated and furnished to be in keeping with the style of the house.
16rm(9⇌7♠)(1fb)1⊞ CTV in all bedrooms ® **T** ✳
sB&B⇌♠£50-£60 dB&B⇌♠£50-£60
☾100P ✲
▶

V ♔ Lunch £10-£15&alc Dinner £10-£15&alc Last dinner 9.30pm
Credit Cards [1] [2] [3] [4] [5] £

BIRCHGROVE West Glamorgan Map **03** SS79

★★**Oak Tree Parc** SA7 9JR (300yds from M4 junc 44)
☎Skewen(0792)817781
Closed 25-31 Dec
A small, family-run hotel, standing adjacent to junction 44 of the M4 and convenient for businessmen or tourists, offers well-equipped bedrooms and a good standard of cuisine which owes much to the use of fresh, home-grown produce.
10rm(3⇨7↱)(2fb) CTV in all bedrooms ® **T**
☾ 40P ✼
☋ Welsh, English, French & Italian **V** ♔ ☖ ⊁ Last high tea 6.30pm
Credit Cards [1] [2] [3] [5]

BIRCH MOTORWAY SERVICE AREA (M62) Greater Manchester Map **07** SD80

⌂**Granada Lodge** M62 Service Area OL10 2HQ (Granada)
☎061-655 3403 FAX 061-653 1005
37⇨(5fb)⊁in 5 bedrooms CTV in all bedrooms ® ✗ (ex guide dogs) S% sB⇨£23-£26 dB⇨£26-£28 (room only)
200P ⛟
Credit Cards [1] [2] [3] [5]

See advertisement under MANCHESTER

BIRDLIP Gloucestershire Map **03** SO91

★★★59% **Royal George** GL4 8JH (Lansbury)
☎Gloucester(0452)862506 Telex no 437238
FAX (0452) 862277
The hotel stands in rural surroundings on the edge of the village, and guests can expect to enjoy a much more peaceful stay now that the completed bypass has diverted the majority of the traffic. For a drink in surroundings full of atmosphere, visit the Applecart Pub, converted from a 17th-century chapel.
34rm(24⇨)Annexe2⇨(4fb)1⊟⊁in 6 bedrooms CTV in all bedrooms ® **T** ✗ (ex guide dogs) sB&B⇨fr£55
dB&B⇨fr£65 ⊟
☾ 120P ✼ sauna solarium 9 hole putting green *xmas*
V ♔ ☖ Lunch £5.45-£9.75alc High tea £3.50 Dinner £5.45-£9.75alc Last dinner 10pm
Credit Cards [1] [2] [3] [5]

✕**Kingshead House** GL4 8JH ☎Gloucester(0452)862299
An 18th-century house that was originally a coaching inn is now a popular restaurant. Poultry and game are prominent in the selection of dishes on the menu, with at least one vegetarian dish on offer. Desserts have strong flavours and the chocolate mousse is especially good. The wine list is well chosen and includes a good variety of half bottles.
Lunch not served Sat
Dinner not served Sun
V 30 seats ✻ Lunch £10-£12 Dinner £16.50 Last lunch 2pm Last dinner 9.45pm 10P
Credit Cards [1] [2] [3] [5]

BIRKENHEAD Merseyside Map **07** SJ38

★★★61% **Bowler Hat** 2 Talbot Rd, Oxton L43 2HH ☎051-652 4931 Telex no 628761
Peacefully situated in a residential area, this period house with neat, well-tended lawns and gardens offers sound accommodation in both its original building and the modern wing to the rear.
29rm(27⇨2↱) CTV in all bedrooms ® **T** ✻
sB&B⇨↱£31-£49.50
dB&B⇨↱£48-£64 Continental breakfast
☾ 40P ✼
☋ English, French & Italian **V** ♔ ☖ Lunch £9-£15 High tea £3.50-£6.50 Dinner £12.75-£18 Last dinner 10pm
Credit Cards [1] [2] [3] [5] £

★★**Riverhill** Talbot Rd, Oxton L43 2HJ ☎051-653 3773
The restaurant is an attractive feature of this hotel, being recently refurbished in elegant, Victorian style and providing a choice of dishes spanning Bistecchina Casanova on the Anglo-Italian menu to Lamb Noisettes Soubise or Duckling aux Grand Marnier from the more classical range. Resident proprietors create a convivial atmosphere throughout the hotel, and accommodation is in well-appointed bedrooms.
16⇨↱(1fb)2⊟ CTV in 10bedrooms ® **T** ✗ ✻
sB&B⇨↱£27.50-£36.50 dB&B⇨↱£38.50-£46.50
30P ⛟ ✼
☋ English, French & Italian **V** Lunch £8&alc Dinner £11&alc Last dinner 9.30pm
Credit Cards [1] [2] [3] [5]

BIRMINGHAM West Midlands Map **07** SP08

See **Town Plan Section**
See also **Birmingham Airport and Birmingham (National Exhibition Centre).**

★★★★51% **Albany** Smallbrook Queensway B5 4EW (Trusthouse Forte) ☎021-643 8171 Telex no 337031 FAX 021-631 2528
An impressive, modern, thirteen-storey building with extensive views over the city.
254⇨⊁in 25 bedrooms CTV in all bedrooms ® **T**
sB⇨£72-£79 dB⇨£89-£98 (room only) ⊟
Lift ☾ ⊞ ℙ CFA ⊡(heated) squash sauna solarium gymnasium health & fitness club
☋ European **V** ♔ ☖ ⊁ Lunch £10.50-£15&alc Dinner £12.50-£17.50&alc Last dinner 11pm
Credit Cards [1] [2] [3] [4] [5]

★★★★50% **Holiday Inn** Holliday St B1 1HH ☎021-631 2000 Telex no 337272 FAX 021-643 9018
International standard hotel reached from Suffolk Street Queensway before junction with Paradise Circus.
290⇨(210fb)⊁in 64 bedrooms CTV in all bedrooms ® **T**
Lift ☾ ⊞ 300🚗 ⊡(heated) sauna solarium gymnasium
☋ International **V** ♔ ☖
Credit Cards [1] [2] [3] [4] [5] £

★★★★66% **Plough & Harrow** Hagley Rd, Edgbaston B16 8LS (Crest) ☎021-454 4111 Telex no 338074 FAX 021-454 1868
Prestigious hotel with individual style and modern bedrooms. The restaurant serves interesting food.
44⇨↱⊁in 9 bedrooms CTV in all bedrooms **T** ✻
sB⇨↱£91-£95 dB⇨↱£103-£108 (room only) ⊟
Lift ☾ 80P ⛟ sauna
V ♔ ☖ Lunch fr£18&alc Dinner fr£27.50&alc Last dinner 10.30pm
Credit Cards [1] [2] [3] [4] [5]

★★★55% ***Apollo*** 243-247 Hagley Road, Edgbaston B16 9RA (Mount Charlotte) ☎021-455 0271 Telex no 336759
Modern, purpose-built hotel offering guests comfortable bedrooms and a choice of two restaurants.
128⇨↱(8fb)⊁in 6 bedrooms CTV in all bedrooms ® **T**
Lift ☾ CTV 130P CFA
☋ English & French **V** ♔ ☖
Credit Cards [1] [2] [3] [5]

★★★56% **Grand** Colmore Row B3 2DA (Queens Moat) ☎021-236 7951 Telex no 338174 FAX 021-233 1465
Closed 4 days Xmas
Set in the heart of the city centre, this large, traditional hotel provides bedrooms with good facilities and a choice of dining styles.
173⇨↱(7fb) CTV in all bedrooms ® **T** sB&B⇨↱£70
dB&B⇨↱£85 ⊟

Lift ☾ ⁄P CFA
☋ English & French V ✿ ⅅ S% Lunch £10.50&alc Dinner £10.50&alc Last dinner 9.45pm
Credit Cards [1] [2] [3] [5] £

★★★58% *Great Barr Hotel & Conference Centre* Pear Tree Dr, off Newton Rd B43 6HS ☎021-357 1141 Telex no 336406 FAX 021-357 7557
(For full entry see Barr, Great)

★★★59% Post House Hotel Chapel Ln B43 7BG (Trusthouse Forte) ☎021-357 7444 Telex no 338497 FAX 021-357 7503
(For full entry see Barr, Great)

★★★64% Royal Angus Thistle St Chads, Queensway B4 6HY (Thistle) ☎021-236 4211 Telex no 336889 FAX 021-233 2195
A modern city centre hotel with adjacent NCP offers comfortable public areas, extensive conference amenities and rooms equipped with all the facilities a business person would expect.
135⇨⌐(4fb)⁄in 8 bedrooms CTV in all bedrooms ® T ✳
sB⇨⌐£65-£85 dB⇨⌐£72-£92 (room only) ⊟
Lift ☾ 600🚗 (charged) CFA
☋ International ✿ ⅅ ⁄ Lunch fr£10.25&alc Dinner fr£13.50&alc Last dinner 10pm
Credit Cards [1] [2] [3] [4] [5]

★★★66% Strathallan Thistle 225 Hagley Rd, Edgbaston B16 9RY (Thistle) ☎021-455 9777 Telex no 336680 FAX 021-454 9432
A striking circular building on the main thoroughfare into the city.
167⇨⌐(5fb)⁄in 18 bedrooms CTV in all bedrooms ® T ✳
sB⇨⌐£65-£75 dB⇨⌐£72-£82 (room only) ⊟
Lift ☾ ⊞ 250P 150🚗 CFA ♫
☋ International ✿ ⅅ ⁄ Lunch fr£15alc Dinner fr£15alc Last dinner 10pm
Credit Cards [1] [2] [3] [4] [5]

B

★★★63% **Westmead Hotel & Restaurant** Redditch Rd, Hopwood B48 7AL (Lansbury) ☎021-445 1202 Telex no 335956 FAX 021-445 6163
Situated in a peaceful rural area, yet conveniently placed only 8 miles south of the city centre and close to junction 2 of the M42, with Birmingham International Airport and the National Exhibition Centre within easy reach. The accommodation is spacious, modern, comfortable and well-equipped. The hotel also has good facilities for conferences and social functions.
60⇌(4fb)2⊞⚟in 4 bedrooms CTV in all bedrooms ® T sB⇌fr£60 dB⇌fr£70 (room only) ⊟
(250P ✲
English & French V ✿ ⊡ Lunch £7.95-£12.50&alc High tea £1.25-£5 Dinner £12.50&alc Last dinner 10pm
Credit Cards 1 2 3 5

★★ ***Beechwood hotel*** 201 Bristol Rd, Edgbaston B5 7UB ☎021-440-2133 FAX 021-446 4549
A well-furnished and friendly hotel to the south of the city features extensive rear gardens with a well-stocked trout lake.
18rm(6⇌10♠)(4fb) CTV in all bedrooms ® T
⊞ CTV 30P ✲ Trout lake ⌂
V ✿ ⊡ Last dinner 10pm
Credit Cards 1 3 5

★★ ***Bristol Court*** 250 Bristol Road, Edgbaston BS5 7SL ☎021-472 0413
Closed 25 & 26 Dec
Set in the suburbs, yet with easy access to the city centre, this small hotel offers value-for-money accommodation.
26rm(10⇌10♠)(4fb) CTV in all bedrooms ®
(CTV 28P 6⌂ ✲ badminton ⌂
Mainly grills ✿ ⊡
Credit Cards 1 2 3 5

★★**Cobden** 166 Hagley Rd, Edgbaston B16 9NZ (Consort) ☎021-454 6621 Telex no 333851 FAX 021-454 1910
Conveniently located on the A456 close to the centre of Birmingham, the original hotel has been extended considerably. Some rooms have been refurbished to a high standard, while the others tend to be more compact and basic. The hotel has its own leisure centre that includes solarium, sauna, swimming pool and gymnasium. The restaurant choice is somewhat limited but the daily carvery joints are popular.
241rm(103⇌112♠)(8fb)2⊞⚟in 40 bedrooms CTV in all bedrooms ® T sB&B⇌♠£46.50-£54 dB&B⇌♠£55.50-£62.50 Continental breakfast ⊟
Lift (200P ✲ ⊡(heated) sauna solarium gymnasium jacuzzi *xmas*
English & French V ✿ ⊡ ⚟ Lunch £9.25-£10.50&alc Dinner £10.50-£11.75&alc Last dinner 9.45pm
Credit Cards 1 2 3 5 £

★★**Copperfield House** 60 Upland Rd, Selly Park B29 7JS ☎021-472 8344
Closed 24 Dec-2 Jan RS 30 Jul & 14 Aug
A well-furnished, comfortable hotel which is personally owned and managed. Situated in a quiet residential area to the south of the city. Good home cooking is served.
14⇌(1fb) CTV in all bedrooms ® T ✱ sB&B⇌£25-£32.50 dB&B⇌£42.50-£47.50
12P ⌂
V ⚟ Lunch £8.95-£10.95 Dinner £8.95 Last dinner 7.30pm
Credit Cards 1 3 £

★★**Norfolk** 257/267 Hagley Rd, Edgbaston B16 9NA (Consort) ☎021-454 8071 Telex no 339715 FAX 021-454 1910
Closed 24 Dec-2 Jan
Large hotel, recently modernised, on busy main road offering value for money accommodation.
175rm(32⇌56♠)⚟in 15 bedrooms CTV in all bedrooms ® T sB&B⇌♠fr£46.50
dB&B⇌♠fr£55.50 Continental breakfast ⊟
Lift (CTV 130P ✲ putting green
V ✿ ⊡ ⚟ Lunch £9.25-£10.50&alc Dinner £10.50-£11.75&alc Last dinner 9.45pm
Credit Cards 1 2 3 5 £

★★**Portland** 313 Hagley Rd, Edgbaston B16 9LQ ☎021-455 0535 Telex no 334200 FAX 021-456 1841
This modernised hotel is in a prominent position just west of the city centre on the A456. The clientèle tends to be commercial for the most part. Staff are very pleasant. Recent extensions have added some larger rooms with better facilities together with new conference amenities. Meanwhile, work is progressing to bring the older rooms up to the same high standard.
64rm(57⇌7♠)(2fb) CTV in all bedrooms ® T ✗ (ex guide dogs) sB&B⇌♠£37-£44 dB&B⇌♠£55-£62 ⊟
Lift (CTV 80P
English & French V ⊡ Lunch £8.95-£10.75 Dinner £8.95-£11.25&alc Last dinner 10pm
Credit Cards 1 2 3 5

★★**Sheriden House** 82 Handsworth Wood Rd, Handsworth Wood B20 2PL ☎021-554 2185 & 021-523 5960 FAX 021-551 4761
A small, popular hotel situated in the suburbs of Birmingham and quite close to junction 7 of the M6. The hotel offers a variety of bedrooms, a cosy bar and a small lounge. The restaurant offers limited table d'hôte and à la carte menus.
12rm(7♠)(2fb)1⊞ CTV in all bedrooms ® ✱ sB&B£24-£25 sB&B♠£36-£37 dB&B£38-£39 dB&B♠£50-£53 ⊟
(CTV 30P
English & French V ✿ ⊡ S% Lunch £9-£10.50 Dinner £9.66-£11&alc Last dinner 9.30pm
Credit Cards 1 2 3 £

★★**Westbourne Lodge Hotel** 27/29 Fountain Rd, Edgbaston B17 8NJ ☎021-429 1003 & 021-429-7436
The comfortable, well-furnished hotel, set in a quiet area just off the Hagley Road and personally supervised by the owners, offers good value for money.
20rm(12⇌8♠)(4fb) CTV in all bedrooms ® T sB&B⇌♠£33-£42 dB&B⇌♠£50-£50
CTV 12P
English, French & Italian V ✿ ⊡ Lunch £7.50-£10.20 High tea £3.45-£4.60 Dinner £7.50-£12.20 Last dinner 7.45pm
Credit Cards 1 3

★★**Wheatsheaf** Coventry Rd, Sheldon B26 3EH (Porterhouse) ☎021-742 6201 021-743 2021 FAX 021-722 2703
Conveniently situated on the A45 three miles from the NEC and airport, this well-run hotel offers good service by a helpful team of staff, pleasantly decorated rooms with excellent facilities, a well appointed restaurant and three bars.
86rm(4⇌82♠)⚟in 10 bedrooms CTV in all bedrooms ® T ✗ (ex guide dogs) sB&B⇌♠fr£46 dB&B⇌♠fr£56 ⊟
(100P *xmas*
English, French & Italian V ⚟ Lunch £8-£10&alc Dinner £10-£12&alc Last dinner 10pm
Credit Cards 1 2 3 5 £

⌂**Campanile** 55 Irving St, Lee Bank B1 1DH (Campanile) ☎021-622 4925 Telex no 333701
Annexe48⇌♠ CTV in all bedrooms ® T sB⇌♠fr£29 dB⇌♠fr£29 (room only) ⊟
50P *xmas*
English & French Lunch £3.75-£8.90 Dinner £6.80-£8.90 Last dinner 10pm
Credit Cards 1 3

○ ***Norton Place*** 180 Lifford Ln, Kings Norton B30 3NT ☎021-433-5656
Due to open Apr 1990
10⇌

✻✕✕✕Sloan's 27-29 Chad Square, Hawthorne Rd, Edgbaston B15 3TQ
☎021-455 6697

Unusually located in a small square of shops to the west of the city centre, this chic, split-level restaurant offers an imaginative menu of dishes in the light French style, making good use of fresh seasonal produce, and complementingits cuisine with a fine wine list and friendly, professional service.

Closed 25 Dec-1 Jan & BH's

Lunch not served Sat

Dinner not served Sun

French **V** 60 seats Lunch fr£13.50&alc Dinner £16.50-£21.50alc Last lunch 2pm Last dinner 9.45pm 40P

Credit Cards [1] [2] [3] [5]

✕✕✕The Lombard Room 180 Lifford Ln, Kings Norton B30 3NT ☎021-451 3991

About 10 minutes drive south of the city centre and convenient from the M42 is the famous Patrick Collection motor museum. Within the beautiful grounds is the complex that contains the Lombard Room, an elegant restaurant with a large conservatory which holds the lounge and bar – all furnishings and décor are of very good quality. A short, imaginative à la carte menu offers a selection of tempting dishes. The quality of the food is complemented by professional, attentive service and a magnificent selection of wines.

Lunch not served Sat – open from 1990

Dinner not served Sun – open from 1990

V 45 seats ✻ Lunch £13.80&alc Last lunch 2.00pm Last dinner 9.30pm 300P ♫

Credit Cards [1] [2] [3] [5]

B

✕✕Biarritz 148/9 Bromsgrove St B5 6RG ☎021-622 1989
An Italian owner and an English chef combine to produce the soundest French cuisine for many miles, the quality of fresh ingredients used reflecting the proximity of Birmingham's fish and vegetable markets.
Closed Sun & 24 Dec-2 Jan
Lunch not served Sat
French 50 seats Lunch £7.50&alc Dinner £21&alc Last lunch 2pm Last dinner 10.30pm
Credit Cards 1 2 3 5

✕✕Chung Ying 16-18 Wrottesley St B5 4TR ☎021-622 5669
In a prominent central location, this Cantonese restaurant continues to provide some of the most interesting food to be found in Birmingham. Fresh ingredients from nearby markets feature in the food, which includes excellent hot and sour soup, fried squid, various offal dishes and the unusual braised ducks' web. The truly adventurous diner should ask for a translation of the Chinese daily special menu.
Cantonese **V** 200 seats Last dinner 11.45pm 10P
Credit Cards 1 2 3 5

✕✕Henry's 27 St Pauls Square B3 1RB ☎021-200 1136
Closed Sun, BH's & 1 wk Aug
Cantonese **V** 90 seats ✱ Lunch fr£11&alc Dinner fr£11&alc Last lunch 2pm Last dinner 11pm
Credit Cards 1 2 3 5

✕✕Rajdoot 12-22 Albert St B4 7UD ☎021-643 8805 & 021-643 8749
Birmingham's premier Indian restaurant, it has maintained its elegance, along with its standard of service and its authentic cuisine, for many years. Recent additions to the menu include tandoori and massalla quail and pheasant.
Closed 25-26 Dec
Lunch not served Sun & BH's
North Indian **V** 74 seats ✱ S12.5% Lunch fr£6.75&alc Dinner £11.50-£14.50&alc Last lunch 2.15pm Last dinner 11.30pm
Credit Cards 1 2 3 4 5

✕Franzl's 151 Milcote Rd B67 5BN ☎021-429 7920 FAX 021-429 1615
Set in a quiet, residential area, this popular small restaurant features a menu offering well-prepared and attractively presented Austrian specialities served by ladies in national dress; the wine list features mainly Austrian types and the décor of both the dining room and its little basement bar echo the theme, making this an interesting and unique place in which to dine.
Closed Sun, Mon, 1-22 Aug & 25-29 Dec
Lunch not served
Austrian **V** 40 seats ✱ Dinner £10.50-£14.95alc Last dinner 10.30pm
Credit Cards 1 3

✕Henry Wong 283 High St, Harborne B17 9QH ☎021-427 9799
Housed in a converted bank in the High Street, this authentic Cantonese restaurant offers a good range of dishes, the set meals providing particularly excellent value. Bright, fresh décor combines with friendly, attentive service to create a pleasant atmosphere.
Closed Sun, Bank hols & last wk Aug
Cantonese 140 seats ✱ Lunch fr£11&alc Dinner fr£11&alc Last lunch 2pm Last dinner 11pm
Credit Cards 1 2 3 5

✕J Jays Restaurant 1347 Stratford Rd, Hall Green B28 9HW ☎021-777 3185
Just a short drive from the city centre, J Jays is an attractive and tastefully appointed Indian restaurant. Tender meats are used in carefully spiced dishes, and there is a selection of imaginative vegetarian dishes. Staff enthusiastically explain the intricacies of the cuisine. The restaurant is very popular and good value: it is essential to book in the evening.
Closed Sun & Xmas Day
Northern Indian **V** 78 seats ✱ Lunch fr£4.95 Dinner fr£8.95 Last lunch 2.30pm Last dinner 10.30pm ♫
Credit Cards 1 2 3 5

BIRMINGHAM AIRPORT West Midlands Map **07** SP18

★★★50% Excelsior Coventry Rd, Elmdon B26 3QW (Trusthouse Forte) ☎021-782 8141 Telex no 338005 FAX 021-782 2476
Set on the A45 beside Birmingham Airport, this well-renovated, 1930s-style hotel offers convenient access to both the motorway network and the city; it is also popular as a conference venue or as a base from which to visit the nearby NEC.
141(3fb) in 9 bedrooms CTV in all bedrooms ® **T** S% sB£75-£81 dB£81-£90 (room only)
200P CFA *xmas*
V S% Lunch £9 High tea £4.75 Dinner £14&alc Last dinner 10.15pm
Credit Cards 1 2 3 4 5

BIRMINGHAM (NATIONAL EXHIBITION CENTRE) West Midlands Map **07** SP18

★★★57% Arden Hotel & Leisure Club Coventry Rd, Bickenhill Village B92 0EH (A45) ☎Hampton-in-Arden(06755)3221 Telex no 334913
Located by the A45, in front of the NEC complex, and convenient for rail and air travel, this busy hotel features a leisure complex comprising swimming pool, jacuzzi, solarium and gymnasium.
76(4fb) CTV in all bedrooms ® **T** sB£62-£68 dB£68 (room only)
Lift 150P CFA (heated) snooker sauna solarium gymnasium jacuzzi ♫
French **V** Lunch £9.50&alc High tea £3-£6 Dinner £9.50&alc Last dinner 10pm
Credit Cards 1 2 3 5

BISHOP AUCKLAND Co Durham Map **08** NZ22

★★Park Head New Coundon DL14 8QT (1m N on A688) ☎(0388)661727
Bedrooms in both main building and annexe extenension of this modernised roadside hotel are comfortable, well-decorated and equipped to a high standard. Lounge areas are very limited, but there is an attractive lounge bar with an open fire, and guests can choose between à la carte restaurant and popular carvery for their meals.
8rm(7 1)Annexe7(3fb)1 CTV in all bedrooms ® **T** ✱ sB&B£22-£32 dB&B£30-£42
96P ♫ *xmas*
English, French & Italian **V** Lunch £5.95-£6.50&alc High tea £3.25-£4.75 Dinner £7.95-£8.75&alc Last dinner 9.45pm
Credit Cards 1 2 3 4 5 £

★★The Postchaise 36 Market Pl DL14 7NX ☎(0388)661296
A rambling former coaching inn overlooking the market square.
12rm(10 2)(1fb)2 CTV in all bedrooms ® S10% sB&B£17-£27.50 dB&B£32-£37
♫
Lunch £4.50&alc Dinner £4-£9alc Last dinner 9pm
Credit Cards 1 3 5 £

★★*Queens Head* Market Place DL14 7NX ☎(0388)603477
Old fashioned hotel in market place with excellent value carvery.
13rm(4 1)(4fb) CTV in all bedrooms ®
30P pool table
English & French **V**
Credit Cards 1 2 3 5

For key to symbols see the inside front cover.

B

BISHOP'S CASTLE Shropshire Map **07** SO38

★***Castle*** SY9 5DG ☎Bishop's Castle(0588)638403
Built in 1719 on the site of the old castle keep, this rambling, family-run hotel provides good accommodation with an abundance of panelled walls, beamed ceilings and open fires; an extensive choice of meals is served in its restaurant.
8rm(1⬚)(2fb) CTV in 1bedroom ®
CTV 40P
Credit Cards [1] [2] [5]

BISHOP'S STORTFORD Hertfordshire Map **05** TL42

✕✕ ***The Mill*** Hallingbury Mill, Old Mill Lane, Gaston Green, Little Hallingbury CM22 7QS ☎(0279)726554
Hallingbury Mill, dating back to 1874, was converted by the present owners to house 2 restaurants. Keen to preserve the atmosphere of the Mill, the proprietors have retained much of the machinery, which diners can watch turning as they sip their aperitifs. Those that come for the peaceful surroundings will not be disappointed, and for those in search of gastronomic satisfaction the Mill's well-served choice of food should prove rewarding.
English & Continental 45 seats Last dinner 10pm 50P
Credit Cards [1] [2] [3]

BISHOPSTEIGNTON Devon Map **03** SX87

★★***Cockhaven Manor*** Cockhaven Rd TQ14 9RF ☎Teignmouth(0626)775252
Closed 25 Dec
From its hillside position at the foot of Haldon Moor, the Manor has looked out over the Teign Estuary since the sixteenth century. Now tastefully and completely modernised, its quiet location off the A381 makes it particularly attractive to the tourist. ▶

13rm(3⇨4♠)(3fb)4⊟ CTV in all bedrooms ®
50P ⊟ ♫
Credit Cards 1 3

BLACKBURN Lancashire Map **07** SD62

See also **Langho**

★★★ 64% ***Blackburn Moat House*** Preston New Rd BB2 7BE (Queens Moat) ☎(0254)64441 Telex no 63271
FAX (0254) 682435
A functional modern hotel with comfortable, well-appointed bedrooms.
98⇨♠(2fb)⊬in 12 bedrooms CTV in all bedrooms ® **T**
Lift ☾ CTV 350P ✲ CFA pool table
☋ English & French **V** ♦ ⊻ Last dinner 10pm
Credit Cards 1 2 3 4 5

★★**Millstone** Church Ln, Mellor BB10 7JR (3m NW) (Shire)
☎Mellor(025481)3333 Telex no 635309
This stone-built hotel in the centre of Mellor village offers well-furnished bedrooms and a good restaurant.
19rm(9⇨10♠)(1fb)⊬in 2 bedrooms CTV in all bedrooms ® **T**
✳ sB&B⇨♠fr£42.50 dB&B⇨♠fr£59 ⊟
40P
☋ English & French **V** ♦ ⊻ Lunch £7.95&alc High tea fr£1.50 Dinner £14.50-£16.95&alc Last dinner 9.45pm
Credit Cards 1 2 3 5

BLACKPOOL Lancashire Map **07** SD33

★★★★ 50% **Imperial** North Promenade FY1 2HB (Trusthouse Forte) ☎(0253)23971 Telex no 677376 FAX (0253) 751784
Imposing Victorian building overlooking sea with spacious public areas and elegant modern Palm Court restaurant.
183rm(169⇨14♠)(9fb)1⊟⊬in 21 bedrooms CTV in all bedrooms ® **T** S% sB⇨♠£59-£65
dB⇨♠£79-£87 (room only) ⊟
Lift ☾ 200P ⊡(heated) sauna solarium gymnasium *xmas*
V ♦ ⊻ ⊬ Lunch £7-£8.50&alc Dinner £11.50-£13.50&alc Last dinner 10.30pm
Credit Cards 1 2 3 4 5

★★★★ 67% **Pembroke** North Promenade FY1 2JQ
☎(0253)23434 Telex no 677469 FAX (0253) 27864
A large, impressive seafront hotel provides comfortable lounges, well appointed bedrooms, extensive leisure facilities and attentive, friendly service.
206⇨(12fb) CTV in all bedrooms ® **T** sB&B⇨£75-£85
dB&B⇨£95 ⊟
Lift ☾ ⊞ 300P ✲ ⊡(heated) sauna solarium games room ♫
xmas
☋ English & French **V** ♦ ⊻ ⊬ Lunch £10 Dinner £11&alc
Last dinner 10.30pm
Credit Cards 1 2 3 4 5

★★★ 69% **New Clifton** Talbot Square FY1 1ND ☎(0253)21481
Telex no 67570
Centrally sited and overlooking the sea, the hotel has well-furnished bedrooms and public areas.
80⇨♠(6fb) CTV in all bedrooms ® **T** sB&B⇨♠£30-£60
dB&B⇨♠£40-£80 ⊟
Lift ☾ CTV ⊁ ♫ *xmas*
☋ English, French & Italian **V** ♦ ⊻ Lunch 90p-£4 High tea £3.50-£9 Dinner fr£9&alc Last dinner 10pm
Credit Cards 1 2 3 5

★★**Brabyns** Shaftesbury Av, North Shore FY2 9QQ (Exec Hotel) ☎(0253)54263
A well-furnished, friendly hotel, situated just off the North Promenade, offers good value for money.
22rm(19⇨3♠)Annexe3rm(1⇨2♠)(10fb) CTV in all bedrooms ® **T** sB&B⇨♠£25.50-£28 dB&B⇨♠£45-£53 ⊟
CTV 12P *xmas*
V ♦ ⊻ Lunch £4.75-£5.50 Dinner fr£7.50 Last dinner 7.30pm
Credit Cards 1 3 5

★★***Carlton*** North Prom FY1 2EZ ☎(0253)28966
Sea front hotel with a gabled roof.
57rm(36⇨7♠)(6fb) CTV in all bedrooms ®
Lift ☾ 50P ♫
☋ English & French ♦ Last dinner 8.45pm
Credit Cards 1 2 3 5

★★**Claremont** 270 North Prom FY1 1SA ☎(0253)293122
FAX (0253) 752409
A comfortable sea-front hotel provides accommodation in well-appointed bedrooms; dinner represents particularly good value for money and service is very friendly.
143⇨♠Annexe25⇨(51fb) CTV in all bedrooms ® **T** S%
sB&B⇨♠£21-£45 dB&B⇨♠£42-£70 ⊟
Lift ☾ 60P CFA ♫ *xmas*
♦ ⊻ ⊬ Lunch £4-£7.95 High tea £4-£7.95 Dinner £8.50-£9.50
Last dinner 8.30pm
Credit Cards 1 2 3 ⓔ

★★**Cliffs** Queens Promenade FY2 9SG ☎(0253)52388
Telex no 67191 FAX (0253) 500394
Quietly situated on the seafront, yet within easy reach of all amenities, the hotel offers bedrooms in the modern style, though lounge and dining room remain comfortably 'old fashioned'.
160⇨(30fb) CTV in all bedrooms ® **T** sB&B⇨£24-£50
dB&B⇨£48-£90 ⊟
Lift ☾ 70P ⊡(heated) squash snooker sauna gymnasium jacuzzi ♫ *xmas*
☋ English & French ♦ ⊻ ⊬ Lunch £5-£5.50 High tea £5-£8.50alc Dinner £9-£10 Last dinner 8.30pm
Credit Cards 1 2 3

B

★★**Headlands** 611-613 South Prom FY4 1NJ ☎(0253)41179
Closed 2-13 Jan
A pleasant family hotel, situated on south shore sea front.
44rm(36⇌8♠)(12fb) CTV in all bedrooms ®
sB&B⇌♠£16.50-£31 dB&B⇌♠£33-£57.60 ⊟
Lift CTV 40P 8🚗 snooker solarium pool table tennis ♫ *xmas*
V ♡ ☕ ⚡ Lunch £7.15 Dinner £10.75 Last dinner 7.30pm
Credit Cards 1 3 £

★★**Revill's** 190-4 North Promenade FY1 1RJ
☎(0253)25768 & 24736
A tall sea-front hotel close to the town centre.
50rm(23⇌5♠)(11fb) CTV in all bedrooms ® T ✈
sB&B£17.32-£20.62 sB&B⇌♠£19.52-£21 dB&B£31.25-£33.55
dB&B⇌♠£34.65-£37.95
Lift ☾ CTV 21P snooker *xmas*
V ♡ ☕
Credit Cards 1 3

★★**Hotel Sheraton** 54-58 Queens Promenade FY2 9RP
☎(0253)52723
The friendly, well-run hotel, overlooking the sea on the north shore, offers good all-round value and is ideal for family holidays.
66rm(14⇌52♠)(25fb) CTV in all bedrooms ®
sB&B⇌♠£24-£27 dB&B⇌♠£44-£54 ⊟
Lift ☾ ₱ ▭(heated) sauna solarium ♫ *xmas*
V ♡ ☕
Credit Cards 1 3

★★**Warwick** 603-609 New South Promenade FY4 1NG (Best Western) ☎(0253)42192 Telex no 677334 FAX (0253) 52346
This delightful hotel overlooks the sea from a crescent off the main promenade; it provides comfortably furnished bedrooms and lounges, leisure facilities and friendly, courteous service.
52rm(47⇌5♠)(10fb) CTV in all bedrooms ® T
sB&B⇌♠£26.50-£32.25 dB&B⇌♠£45.50-£57 ⊟
☾ 30P ▭(heated) solarium ♫ *xmas*
V ♡ ☕ Bar Lunch £1.50-£4alc Dinner £9.95-£10.95 Last dinner 8.30pm
Credit Cards 1 2 3 5

★**Kimberley** New South Promenade FY4 1NQ ☎(0253)41184
Closed 3-13 Jan
A family hotel with modern furnishings, located on the sea front.
51rm(36⇌6♠)(8fb) CTV in all bedrooms ® sB&Bfr£18
sB&B⇌♠fr£20.30 dB&Bfr£34 dB&B⇌♠fr£38.60 ⊟
Lift ☾ CTV 26P ⊞ table tennis ♫ *xmas*
♡ ☕ Lunch fr£4.95 Dinner fr£8.50 Last dinner 7.30pm
Credit Cards 1 3 £

✕✕**White Tower** Blackpool Pleasure Beach, Promenade/Balmoral Rd FY4 1EZ ☎(0253)46710 & 41036 Telex no 67251 FAX (0253) 401098
Located in Blackpool's Pleasure Beach complex, the restaurant overlooks sea and promenade. Food is of a very good standard, and is served in well-furnished surroundings by professional but friendly staff.
Closed Jan
Lunch not served Tue-Sat
Dinner not served Sun & Mon
🍷 English & French V 70 seats Lunch £6.75-£7 Dinner £11.75-£13&alc Last dinner 10.45pm 500P ♫
Credit Cards 1 2 3 5

BLACKWATER Cornwall & Isles of Scilly Map **02** SW74

✕ ***Blackbird Cottage*** TR4 8EY ☎St Day(0209)820347
It is easy to forget the traffic rumbling past as you enjoy your meal in this period cottage on the A30. Surroundings are simple, the atmosphere relaxing and the cuisine from the short à la carte menu and fish menu is light in style. Of particular delight are Mr Peter's own bresoala and the boned quail stuffed with mushrooms and cashew nuts. The small carefully-chosen wine list represents excellent value for money.
Closed Sun
🍷 French & German 20 seats Last lunch 2pm Last dinner 9.30pm 10P
Credit Cards 1 2 3

BLACKWOOD Gwent Map **03** ST19

★★★51% **Maes Manor** NP2 0AG ☎(0495)224551 & 220011
This carefully restored 19th-century manor is set in 9 acres of secluded woodland and provides good facilities for visiting business people.
10rm(8⇌1♠)Annexe14⇌(2fb)1⊟ CTV in all bedrooms ® T
sB&B⇌♠fr£40 dB&B⇌♠fr£55
☾ 100P ✲
🍷 Welsh, English & French V ♡ ☕ Lunch £12-£20alc High tea £3-£5alc Dinner £12-£20alc Last dinner 9.30pm
Credit Cards 1 2 3 5

BLAIR ATHOLL Tayside *Perthshire* Map **14** NN86

★★***Atholl Arms*** PH18 5SG ☎Blairatholl(079681)205
A large baronial hall, complete with minstrel's gallery, provides the dining room of this sizeable, traditional hotel in its attractive Highland village setting.
30rm(28⇌2♠)1⊟ CTV in all bedrooms ®
CTV 100P 3🚗 ✲ ⌡ rough shooting
V ♡ ☕
Credit Cards 1 3

All the information in the guide is annually updated, but details of prices and facilities may change during the currency of this guide.

BLAIR DRUMMOND Central *Stirlingshire* Map **11** NS79

✕**Broughton's Restaurant** Burnbank Cottages FK9 4XE (1m W on A873) ☎Doune(0786)841897

This delightful country cottage restaurant offers a warm welcome and cosy atmosphere, while a dedicated chef ensures that a consistently high standard of cuisine is maintained so that its reputation continues to grow. Such seasonal game specialities as venison, rabbit, pigeon and pheasant are particularly enjoyable, but all meals are of excellent quality and based on fresh ingredients, the good-value light lunches being increasingly popular.

Closed Sun, Mon & 2-3 wks Feb

International **V** 42 seats Lunch £2.50-£9.50 Dinner £16.25-£17 Last lunch 2.30pm Last dinner 10pm 22P ⚟

Credit Cards 1 3

BLAIRGOWRIE Tayside *Perthshire* Map **15** NO14

★★★ 71% **Kinloch House** PH10 6SG (3m W of Blairgowrie on A923)

☎Essendy(025084)237 FAX (025084) 333

Closed 7-28 Dec

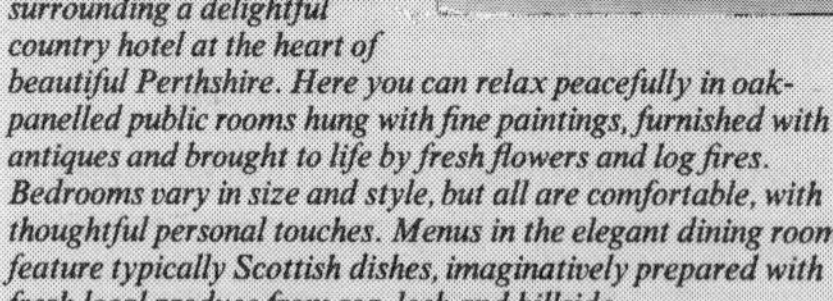

Highland cattle graze freely in the 20 acres of grounds surrounding a delightful country hotel at the heart of beautiful Perthshire. Here you can relax peacefully in oak-panelled public rooms hung with fine paintings, furnished with antiques and brought to life by fresh flowers and log fires. Bedrooms vary in size and style, but all are comfortable, with thoughtful personal touches. Menus in the elegant dining room feature typically Scottish dishes, imaginatively prepared with fresh local produce from sea, loch and hillside.

21rm(16⇔4↱)(1fb)5⊞ CTV in 13bedrooms ® T sB&B⇔↱£38.50 dB&B⇔↱£60-£88

CTV 40P ⊞ ❊

V ⚟ Lunch £10.50 Dinner £17.50 Last dinner 9.15pm

Credit Cards 1 2 3 5

★★ **Altamount House** Coupar Angus Rd PH10 6JN

☎(0250)3512 & 3814

Closed 4 Jan-14 Feb

Built as a private residence in 1806, this Georgian manor has been converted by its proprietors into a comfortable hotel standing in its own gardens.

7rm(4⇔3↱)(2fb) CTV in all bedrooms ® T sB&B⇔↱£30 dB&B⇔↱£55

40P 3🚗 ❊

Lunch fr£8.95 High tea fr£6.50 Dinner fr£14.50 Last dinner 9pm

Credit Cards 1 2 3 5

Book as early as possible for busy holiday periods.

★★**Angus** 46 Wellmeadow PH10 6NQ (Consort) ☎(0250)2838 Telex no 76526 FAX (0250) 5289

Busy town centre hotel with its own sporting facilities.

85rm(68⇔17↱)(4fb) CTV in all bedrooms ® T sB&B⇔↱£21.50-£27.50 dB&B⇔↱£43-£55

Lift 60P CFA ⊡(heated) squash snooker sauna solarium ♫ *xmas*

British & French **V** Bar Lunch fr£2.75alc High tea £3.40-£5alc Dinner fr£10.50&alc Last dinner 8.30pm

Credit Cards 1 2 3 £

★★**Rosemount Golf** Golf Course Rd, Rosemount PH10 6LJ ☎(0250)2604

Popular with golfers, this family-run hotel stands in its own spacious, well-maintained grounds not far from the town's Rosemount Course. A relaxed atmosphere prevails in the comfortable public rooms. Bedrooms are compact but furnished with practical fitted units.

8rm(7⇔1↱)Annexe4↱(2fb) CTV in all bedrooms ® ✈ (ex guide dogs) sB&B⇔↱£24-£27 dB&B⇔↱£40

70P ⊞ ❊

V S% Bar Lunch £3.50-£9alc High tea £3.70-£7.50alc Dinner £10-£12alc Last dinner 9pm

Credit Cards 1 3 £

BLAKENEY Norfolk Map **09** TG04

★★★65% **Blakeney** The Quay NR25 7NE ☎Cley(0263)740797 FAX (0263) 740795

Standing in fine, south-facing, enclosed gardens on the quayside, with good views of Blakeney Point, this traditional-style hotel features a hairdressing salon, games room and large ballroom, with the helpful services of friendly staff throughout.

39rm(37⇔2↱)Annexe13⇔(4fb)1⊞ CTV in all bedrooms ® T sB&B⇔↱£33-£54 dB&B⇔↱£66-£104

☾ CTV 100P ⊞ ❊ CFA ⊡(heated) sauna solarium *xmas*

V Lunch £5-£12alc Dinner £12-£15 Last dinner 9.30pm

Credit Cards 1 2 3 5

★★**Manor** NR25 7ND ☎Cley(0263)740376

Closed 4-28 Dec

Former manor house with sheltered, secluded gardens.

8⇔Annexe27rm(25⇔2↱)(6fb)1⊞ CTV in all bedrooms ® S10% sB&B⇔↱£24-£28 dB&B⇔↱£46-£66

60P ❊ bowling green

English & Continental **V** ⚟ S10% Bar Lunch £3-£4.20 Dinner fr£10.75&alc Last dinner 8.30pm

BLANCHLAND Northumberland Map **12** NY95

★★**Lord Crewe Arms** DH8 9SP ☎(043475)251 FAX (043475) 337

An interesting hotel at the heart of the village near the abbey, retaining the charm of bygone days in its flagstone floors, original stonework and the vaulted ceilings that survive in some public areas. Bedrooms continue the period theme but are thoughtfully equipped to meet the needs of the modern traveller, some annexe rooms being contained in an original building across the square.

8rm(6⇔2↱)Annexe7⇔(2fb)1⊞ CTV in all bedrooms ® T sB&B⇔↱£54 dB&B⇔↱£76

CTV ❊ *xmas*

V Lunch £8.50-£9.50 Dinner fr£13.50&alc Last dinner 9.15pm

Credit Cards 1 2 3 5

BLANDFORD FORUM Dorset Map **03** ST80

★★★54% **Crown** 1 West St DT11 7AJ (Consort) ☎(0258)456626 Telex no 418292 FAX (0258) 451084

Standing in the town centre, yet with rural views, this Georgian hotel offers spacious public rooms, full of character and charm, and bedrooms which are well equipped though slightly in need of updating.

29rm(28⇨1↱)(1fb)1⊠ CTV in all bedrooms ® T
sB&B⇨↱£48 dB&B⇨↱£58 ⊟
80P 4⌂ (£2.50) ✲ ♩ croquet lawn ⌂
♡ English & French V ♧ ⊈ Lunch fr£6.50&alc Dinner £9&alc
Last dinner 9.15pm
Credit Cards 1 2 3 5

✕✕La Belle Alliance Portman Lodge, Whitecliff Mill St
DT11 7BP ☎(0258)452842 FAX (0258) 480054
This charming 'restaurant with rooms' stands on the edge of town. The short fixed price menu offers interesting dishes which are freshly-cooked with skill and flair and presented in the modern style with well-made sauces. Our inspectors have reported a good fish mousseline with tomato flavoured butter sauce, breast of French duck with pineapple sauce and some good flavoursome desserts. A well-chosen wine list is available and the service and hospitality is good.
Closed Sun (ex BH's) & 1st 3 wks Jan
Lunch not served (ex by arrangement only)
♡ British & French 28 seats Dinner £18.50-£21.50 Last dinner 9.30pm 9P 5 bedrooms available ⊁
Credit Cards 1 2 3

BLAWITH Cumbria Map **07** SD28

★★⌂Highfield Country
LA12 8EG
☎Lowick Bridge (022985)238
Closed 1-17 Jan
This period country house sits in its own grounds overlooking Crake Valley, on the outskirts of the village. Bedrooms are spacious and comfortable – stables have been attractively converted to house 8 of them, accessible by French windows through the lounge and dining room or from outside. Fresh ingredients are used to provide country cooking of a high standard. The public rooms, although compact, are cosy and appealing. The whole house is decorated with lovely paintings and pictures.
12⇨↱(1fb) CTV in all bedrooms ® ✱ sB&B⇨↱£25-£35
dB&B⇨↱£40-£50 ⊟
CTV 30P ⌂ ✲ ♩
♡ English, French & Italian V ♧ Lunch £6.95-£8.95
Dinner fr£11.50&alc Last dinner 8.30pm
Credit Cards 1 3

BLOCKLEY Gloucestershire Map **04** SP13

★★★61% Crown Inn High St GL56 9EX ☎(0386)700245
FAX (0386) 700247
At this old Cotswold-stone inn you are assured of genuine hospitality and a relaxed, informal atmosphere; parts of the building date back to the 16th century, but modern improvements – particularly the attractive dining room – blend in well.
7⇨↱Annexe8⇨↱(2fb) CTV in all bedrooms ® T
sB&B⇨↱£49.50 dB&B⇨↱£62.50-£78.50 ⊟
50P *xmas*
♡ English & Continental V ♧ ⊈ Lunch £11.95 Dinner £15.95
Last dinner 9.30pm
Credit Cards 1 2 3

For key to symbols see the inside front cover.

★★Lower Brook House GL56 9DS ☎(0386)700286
Closed Jan
Set in a delightful unspoiled village, this hotel, which dates back to the 17th century, boasts an oak-beamed lounge with a vast inglenook fireplace. Guests are offered good food with cheerful service in the stone-flagged dining room.
8rm(6⇨2↱)(1fb) CTV in all bedrooms ®
12P ⌂ ✲ Horse riding, golf
V ♧ ⊈ Last dinner 9.30pm
Credit Cards 1 5

BLOXHAM Oxfordshire Map **04** SP43

★★Olde School Church St OX15 4ET (Inter)
☎Banbury(0295)720369 Telex no 838070
RS New Years Day
One-time village school with small, well-equipped bedrooms and professional restaurant.
11rm(6⇨5↱)1⊠ CTV in all bedrooms ® T ✗ (ex guide dogs)
✱ sB&B£44-£55 sB&B⇨↱£49-£59 dB&B£55-£75
dB&B⇨↱£65-£85 Continental breakfast ⊟
50P squash
♡ English & French V ♧ ⊈ ⊁ Lunch £9.50&alc Dinner
£13.50&alc Last dinner 10pm
Credit Cards 1 2 3 5 ⓔ

BLUE ANCHOR Somerset Map **03** ST04

★Langbury TA24 6LB ☎Dunster(0643)821375
Closed Nov-Feb
An attractive, comfortable hotel offering attentive service and with pretty bedrooms and a well tended garden.
9rm(1⇨4↱)(3fb) CTV in all bedrooms ® sB&B£14.50-£16
sB&B⇨↱£19.50-£21 dB&B£29-£31 dB&B⇨↱£31-£33 ⊟
10P ⌂ ✲ ⌒
♧ ⊁ Bar Lunch £2.50-£5 Dinner £8.75 Last dinner 7pm

BLUNDELLSANDS Merseyside Map **07** SJ39

★★★59% Blundellsands Serpentine L23 6TN (Lansbury) ☎051-924 6515 Telex no 626270 FAX 051-931 5364
An Edwardian red brick building situated in a suburb of Crosby. Bedrooms are well equipped, and there are comfortable bars, a wide range of facilities for conferences or social events and the ornate Mauretania restaurant which is designed in the style of the dining room of that famous ocean liner.
39rm(31⇨8↱)(4fb)⊁in 7 bedrooms CTV in all bedrooms ® T
sB&B⇨↱fr£52 dB&B⇨↱fr£62 ⊟
Lift ☾ CTV 350P
♡ English & French V ♧ ⊈ Lunch fr£7.50&alc High tea £2.50
Dinner fr£10.50&alc Last dinner 9.30pm
Credit Cards 1 2 3 5

BLYTH Nottinghamshire Map **08** SK68

★★★59% Charnwood Sheffield Rd S81 8HF ☎(090976)610 due to change to (0909) 591610
A well-furnished, modern hotel and restaurant offers good bedrooms and skilfully prepared food.
8⇨(1fb) CTV in all bedrooms ® T ✗ sB&B⇨£38-£50
dB&B⇨£44-£58 Continental breakfast ⊟
70P ⌂ ✲
♡ English & French V Lunch £7.25-£7.85&alc Dinner
£11.95&alc Last dinner 9.45pm
Credit Cards 1 2 3 5

See advertisement on page 131

⌂Granada Lodge Hilltop Roundabout S81 8HG (junct. A1M/ A614) (Granada) ☎(090976)836 FAX (0909) 76831
37⇨(6fb)⊁in 8 bedrooms CTV in all bedrooms ® ✗ (ex guide dogs) sB⇨£23-£26 dB⇨£26-£28 (room only)

▶

☾100P
International V ✧ ⊥ ⊬
Credit Cards 1 2 3 5

B

BOAT OF GARTEN Highland *Inverness-shire* Map **14** NH91

★★★63% **Boat** PH24 3BH (Best Western) ☎(047983)258
Telex no 94013436 FAX (047983) 414
A friendly, family-run tourist hotel just two minutes' drive from the golf course features a comfortable tasteful lounge and a privileged position overlooking the station which is the home of the preserved Strathspey Steam Railway.
32rm(25⇌7♠)(1fb) CTV in all bedrooms ® T
sB&B⇌♠£30-£40 dB&B⇌♠£56-£66 ⊟
36P ⛟ ❊ CFA ⌂ *xmas*
Scottish, English & French V ✧ ⊥ ⊬ Lunch £8.50-£12.50alc High tea £5-£7 Dinner £13-£14.50&alc Last dinner 9pm
Credit Cards 1 2 3 5 £

★★**Craigard Country House** Kinchurdy Rd PH24 3BP
☎(047983)206
This former shooting lodge is now a friendly, family-run hotel, standing in 2.5 acres of wooded grounds. Attractive lounges make for easy relaxation; some bedrooms are compact, but all have an extensive range of facilities. Fresh local produce, including salmon, venison and Angus beef, is served in the smart restaurant.
20rm(7⇌13♠)(2fb) CTV in all bedrooms ® sB&B⇌♠fr£28
dB&B⇌♠fr£56 ⊟
20P 6🚗 (£2.00) ❊ Clay pigeon shooting nc10 yrs *xmas*
Scottish & French V ✧ ⊥ ⊬ Lunch fr£10 High tea fr£6 Dinner fr£15 Last dinner 9pm
Credit Cards 1 2 3

BODINNICK Cornwall & Isles of Scilly Map **02** SX15

★**Old Ferry Inn** PL23 1LX ☎Polruan(072687)237
RS Nov-Feb
A delightful, 400-year-old inn, overlooking the centuries-old Bodinnick/Fowey Ferry, offers comfortable accommodation, a relaxed atmosphere and good food.
13rm(6⇌1♠)(1fb)1⊟ CTV in 10bedrooms sB&B£24-£31
sB&B⇌♠£27.50-£31 dB&B£28-£62 dB&B⇌♠£55-£62
CTV 8P 2🚗 ⛟
English & French ✧ Dinner £16.50 Last dinner 8.30pm
Credit Cards 1 3

BODMIN Cornwall & Isles of Scilly Map **02** SX06

★★**Hotel Allegro** 50 Higher Bore St PL31 1JW ☎(0208)73480
Set on the edge of the main road, the Allegro is a small commercial hotel built around a courtyard.
12rm(3⇌1♠)(1fb) CTV available ✗ ✱ sB&B£18.50-£20
sB&B⇌♠£27.50 dB&B£32-£34 dB&B⇌♠£36
20P
V ✧ Lunch £5.25&alc Dinner £5.25&alc Last dinner 9pm
Credit Cards 1 2 3 5 £

★★**Westberry** Rhind St PL31 2EL ☎(0208)72772
Closed 5 days Xmas/New Year
A busy hotel, popular for local functions, and sited conveniently near to the town centre. The hotel has been modernised and now offers very well-equipped bedrooms, a spacious lounge bar and restaurant.
15rm(5⇌4♠)Annexe8rm(4⇌4♠)(3fb) CTV in 20bedrooms
® T ✱ sB&B£19.50-£29.50 sB&B⇌♠£29.50
dB&B£28.50-£38.50 dB&B⇌♠£38.50 ⊟
CTV 30P ⛟ snooker sauna gymnasium
V ✧ ⊥ Sunday Lunch £4.90 Dinner £8&alc Last dinner 8.45pm
Credit Cards 1 3 5

BOGNOR REGIS West Sussex Map **04** SZ99

★**Black Mill House** Princess Av, Aldwick PO21 2QU (Minotels)
☎(0243)821945 & 865596 FAX (0243) 821316
This long-established, family-run and fully licensed hotel on the west side of the town provides comfortable lounge and bar facilities with an old-fashioned atmosphere which is complemented by friendly service.
22rm(10⇌8♠)Annexe4rm(6fb) CTV in all bedrooms ® T
sB&B£26-£33 sB&B⇌♠£28-£35 dB&B£46-£60
dB&B⇌♠£50-£64 ⊟
CTV 13P ⛟ table tennis putting ⌂ *xmas*
English & French V ✧ ⊥ ⊬ Lunch fr£6.50 Dinner fr£8 Last dinner 8pm
Credit Cards 1 2 3 5 £

BOLDON Tyne & Wear Map **12** NZ36

○***Friendly Lodge*** Boldon Business Park
☎Central reservation 0800-591910
Due to open Apr 1990
84⇌

BOLLINGTON Cheshire Map **07** SJ97

★★★57% **Lukic-Belgrade** Jackson Ln, Kerridge SK10 5BG
☎(0625)73246 Telex no 667554 FAX (0625) 74791
Standing in its own grounds high above the village, this Victorian house with modern bedroom wing has recently undergone further improvements.
54♠ CTV in all bedrooms ® T ✗ (ex guide dogs)
sB&B♠fr£55 dB&B♠fr£66
☾200P ❊ CFA *xmas*
English & French V ✧ ⊥ Lunch £9&alc Dinner fr£11.75&alc Last dinner 9.45pm
Credit Cards 1 2 3 5 £

✕✕**Mauro's** 88 Palmerston St SK10 5PW ☎(0625)73898
In this attractive little Italian restaurant you can watch the chef/proprietor at work through a glazed arch, while he and his wife may well wait on you, too, both being very actively involved in the running of the establishment. Pasta is home-made, menus feature a fresh fish each day and you can enjoy all the traditional Italian specialities – accompanied by a reasonably-priced bottle of Italian wine – in a warm, convivial atmosphere.
Closed Sun, Mon, 25-26 Dec & 2-3 wks Jul/Aug
Italian V 50 seats Lunch £5.50-£19.50alc Dinner £6.80-£20alc Last lunch 2pm Last dinner 10pm P
Credit Cards 1 2 3

BOLNEY West Sussex Map **04** TQ22

★★***Hickstead Resort*** Jobs Ln RH17 5PA
☎Burgess Hill(0444)248023 Telex no 877247
FAX (0444) 245280
A popular conference venue, this hotel in peaceful surroundings offers modern purpose-built bedrooms with good facilities and an indoor pool with spa bath.
49⇌ CTV in all bedrooms ® T
☾150P ⛟ ▭(heated) sauna solarium gymnasium massage room spa bath
English & Continental ✧ ⊥ Last dinner 9.15pm
Credit Cards 1 2 3 4 5 £

BOLTON Greater Manchester Map **07** SD70

★★★62% **Crest** Beaumont Rd BL3 4TA (Crest) ☎(0204)651511
Telex no 635527 FAX (0204) 61064
The hotel – conveniently situated on the A58, close to junction 5 of the M61 motorway – features attractive, well-appointed bedrooms and a pleasant restaurant where à la carte and fixed price menus offer a wide choice of dishes.
100⇌♠(10fb)⊬in 26 bedrooms CTV in all bedrooms ® T ✱
sB⇌♠£71.50 dB⇌♠£83.50 (room only) ⊟

(CTV 150P ❋ CFA games room pool table
♀ English & French V ♈ ☐ ⚡ Lunch £9.50-£10.50 Dinner £14.50-£15.50&alc Last dinner 9.45pm
Credit Cards [1] [2] [3] [4] [5] (£)

★★★63% ***Egerton House*** Blackburn Rd, Egerton BL7 9PL (3m N A666) (Associated Leisure) ☎(0204)57171 Telex no 635322
Secluded, in 4·5 acres of grounds and gardens, this comfortable hotel provides accommodation in attractive, well-appointed bedrooms, friendly service, and facilities for banquetting and conferences in a recently converted barn.
29⇌♠(7fb) CTV in all bedrooms ® T
(CTV 100P ❋ ♧
♀ International V ♈ ☐ Last dinner 9.30pm
Credit Cards [1] [2] [3] [5]

★★★67% **Last Drop** Hospital Rd, Bromley Cross BL7 9PZ (3m N off B6472) (Associated Leisure) ☎(0204)591131 Telex no 635322 FAX (0204) 54122
This unique hotel, together with tea room, craft shop and public house, forms part of a village created in 1964 from derelict farm buildings and now one of the north-west's popular tourist attractions. The accommodation on offer has been considerably developed in recent years to comprise very well appointed bedrooms, comprehensive conference and banqueting facilities and an outstanding leisure complex comprising indoor heated swimming pool, solarium, large gymnasium, snooker room and squash court. The old shippon has been converted into a charming restaurant which preserves some of the cattle stalls and associated antique items.
73⇌♠Annexe10⇌♠(35fb)4⊟ CTV in all bedrooms ® T ✻ sB&B⇌♠£45-£67 dB&B⇌♠£55-£80 ⊟
(400P ❋ CFA ▭(heated) squash snooker sauna solarium gymnasium *xmas*

▶

International **V** Lunch fr£8.75&alc Dinner £9.95-£11.95&alc Last dinner 10.30pm
Credit Cards 1 2 3 5

B

★★★ 61% **Pack Horse** Bradshawgate, Nelson Square BL1 1DP (De Vere) (0204)27261 Telex no 635168 FAX (0204) 364352
In a town centre position, yet within easy reach of the national motorway network, stands a traditional hotel with an attractive Georgian façade.
74rm(68 3)(4fb) in 14 bedrooms CTV in all bedrooms ® **T** ✱ S% sB&B fr£58 dB&B fr£70
Lift CFA *xmas*
English & French **V** S% Lunch fr£7.25&alc Dinner fr£10.25&alc Last dinner 10pm
Credit Cards 1 2 3 5

★**Broomfield Hotel** 33-35 Wigan Rd, Deane BL3 5PX (0204)61570
16rm(5 11)(1fb) CTV in 15bedrooms ® (ex guide dogs) ✱ sB fr£25 dB fr£34 (room only)
CTV 20P
Credit Cards 1 3

BOLTON ABBEY North Yorkshire Map **07** SE05

★★★ 71% **Devonshire Arms Country House** BD23 6AJ (Best Western) (075671)441 Telex no 51218 FAX (075671)564
Beautifully located within the Yorkshire Dales National Park, alongside historic Bolton Abbey, this hotel has been part of the Duke of Devonshire's estate for more than 200 years. Well run by a hospitable host and courteous young staff, it offers comfortable accommodation ranging from individually designed bedrooms, furnished in traditional style with antiques, to the lighter rooms of the more modern wing. Fine public areas include a wealth of modern lounges and a handsome, stone-flagged reception hall with open log fire, many of the furnishings and pictures on view coming from Chatsworth.
40 6 in 5 bedrooms CTV in all bedrooms ® **T** ✱ sB&B £63-£68 dB&B £75-£85
CTV 150P clay pigeon shooting *xmas*
French **V** S10% Lunch £10.95&alc Dinner £19.50&alc Last dinner 10pm
Credit Cards 1 2 3 5 £

BONAR BRIDGE Highland *Sutherland* Map **14** NH69

★★ ***Bridge*** IV24 3EB (Exec Hotel) Ardgay(08632)204 & 685 FAX (08632) 686
Closed 1 & 2 Jan
Two-storey stone house situated on the main road, with views of Kyle of Sutherland.
16rm(5 5)(3fb) CTV in all bedrooms ® **T**
20P
Scottish & French **V** Last dinner 10pm
Credit Cards 1 2 3 5

BONCHURCH

See **Wight, Isle of**

BONTDDU Gwynedd Map **06** SH61

★★★ 65% **Bontddu Hall** LL40 2SU (034149)661
FAX (0341) 49284
Closed Jan-Etr RS Nov-Dec
Standing in two acres of lovely grounds with superb views over the Mawddach estuary to the mountains beyond, this charming, delightfully furnished hotel in the style of a Victorian country house offers well-equipped bedrooms and excellent public areas; service is friendly and professional.
16rm(13 3)Annexe6 (6fb)1 CTV in all bedrooms ® **T** sB&B £37.50-£42.50 dB&B £59-£65
50P putting nc3yrs
V Lunch £6.95 Dinner £16.50&alc Last dinner 9.30pm
Credit Cards 1 2 3 5

BOOTLE Merseyside Map **07** SJ39

★★★ 57% **Park** Park Ln West, Netherton L30 3SU (De Vere) 051-525 7555 Telex no 629772 FAX 051-525 2481
Situated on the A5036 close to the M57 and M58 motorways, this business and conference hotel stands only 15 minutes' drive from Liverpool city centre. Aintree Racecourse is also nearby, as reflected by a themed bar at the hotel.
58rm(23 35) CTV in all bedrooms ® **T** sB&B £49.50 dB&B £62
Lift 250P 2 CFA
English & French **V** Lunch £8-£12&alc High tea £2-£5 Dinner £8-£12&alc Last dinner 9pm
Credit Cards 1 2 3 4 5

BOREHAM STREET East Sussex Map **05** TQ61

★★★ 60% **White Friars** BN27 4SE (Best Western) Herstmonceux(0323)832355 Telex no 877440 FAX (0323) 32072
Closed Jan-Feb
This 18th-century hotel, set amid the Sussex Weald, provides a homely atmosphere with its beamed lounges and a good professional standard of cooking. The gardens are well-tended and inside, the family owners are always looking to improve their hotel.
10 Annexe8 (2fb)2 CTV in all bedrooms ® **T** (ex guide dogs) sB&B £42-£48 dB&B £80-£90
180P croquet *xmas*
V Lunch £8.25-£15.95&alc Dinner £12.95-£15.95&alc Last dinner 10pm
Credit Cards 1 2 3

BOROUGHBRIDGE North Yorkshire Map **08** SE36

★★★ 63% **Crown** Horsefair YO5 9LB (Best Western) Harrogate(0423)322328 Telex no 57906
Once a very busy coaching inn, this town-centre hotel is still popular with modern-day coach parties touring the area. The well-equipped bedrooms are equally suitable for both tourists and business travellers.
42rm(41 1)(6fb) CTV in all bedrooms ® **T** ✱ sB £36 dB £55-£110 (room only)
Lift 60P
French & Italian **V** Lunch £5.75-£9&alc High tea £4.75-£7.50 Dinner £14.50&alc Last dinner 9.15pm
Credit Cards 1 2 3 5

★★★ 59% **Three Arrows** Horsefair YO5 9LL (Embassy) Harrogate(0423)322245
Closed 27-30 Dec
A Victorian country mansion set in extensive and attractive grounds. There is a large drawing room, pleasant restaurant and bar lounge.
17rm(16 1)(4fb) CTV in all bedrooms ® ✱ sB £45 dB £50 (room only)
50P *xmas*
V Lunch £7 Dinner £13 Last dinner 9pm
Credit Cards 1 2 3 5

✕✕ **Fountain House** St James Square YO5 9AR Harrogate(0423)322241
Closed Mon
Dinner not served Sun
International **V** 40 seats Last lunch 2pm Last dinner 9.30pm
6P
Credit Cards 1 2 3

BORROWDALE Cumbria Map **11** NY21

See also **Grange (in-Borrowdale), Keswick & Rosthwaite**

★★★★ **73% Lodore Swiss** CA12 5UX (Stakis) ☎(059684)285 Telex no 64305 FAX (054684) 343
Closed 4 Jan-14 Feb

A delightfully located hotel at the head of the Borrowdale valley, the Lodore Swiss offers an excellent range of leisure facilities, efficient and friendly service and comfortable accomodation.

70rm(68⇌2↱)(13fb) CTV in all bedrooms ® **T** ✈ sB&B⇌↱£40-£65 dB&B⇌↱£80-£130 (incl dinner) ⊟
Lift ☾ 55P 24⛟ (£2.5) ⛳ ✲ ▭(heated) ⌂(heated) ♀ (hard) squash sauna solarium gymnasium ♫ ⌂ *xmas*
☋ British, French & Swiss **V** ♥ ⚐ ✂ Lunch £5-£16alc Dinner £20&alc Last dinner 9.30pm
Credit Cards 1 2 3 5

See advertisement under KESWICK

★★★ **69% Borrowdale** CA12 5UY ☎(07687 84)224

A welcoming and relaxing hotel, originally built as a coaching inn, has been carefully modernised to provide guests with comfortable, well-equipped bedrooms, two lounges where log fires blaze in cooler weather and an attractive restaurant. Well-supervised young staff give friendly, efficient service.

34rm(29⇌5↱)(8fb)6⊟ CTV in all bedrooms ® **T** ✱ sB&B⇌↱£35-£47 dB&B⇌↱£70-£95 (incl dinner) ⊟
100P ⛳ ✲ ⌂ *xmas*
☋ English & Continental **V** ♥ ⚐ Lunch £8.50&alc Dinner £15 Last dinner 9.15pm
Credit Cards 1 3

BOSCASTLE Cornwall & Isles of Scilly Map **02** SX09

★★ **Bottreaux House** PL35 0BG ☎(08405)231
Closed Dec-Feb

Standing on a hill overlooking the picturesque harbour village, the personally-run hotel offers a friendly atmosphere and accommodation in bright, clean bedrooms equipped to modern standards. There is a pleasant lounge (with separate bar) and also an attractive dining room providing a good choice of imaginative dishes.

7rm(4⇌3↱) CTV in all bedrooms ® sB&B⇌↱£21.50 dB&B⇌↱£40 ⊟
10P ⛳ nc10 yrs
☋ English, French & Italian **V** ♥ ✂ Bar Lunch £1.85-£6.50 Dinner £8.50-£11.50alc Last dinner 9.30pm
Credit Cards 1 3 £

★★ ***Wellington Hotel*** The Harbour PL35 0AQ ☎(08405)202

Some parts of this charming hotel date back to the 16th century, but the majority is the result of extension in the 1850s. Its Georgian restaurant, La Belle Alliance, serves French and English cuisine of a good standard, and there is a busy free house with an attractive bar.

21rm 4⊟

See advertisement on page 135

BOSHAM West Sussex Map **04** SU80

★★ **The Millstream** Bosham Ln PO18 8HL (Best Western) ☎(0243)573234 FAX (0243) 573459

This former millhouse and cottage in picturesque village setting offers attractive bedrooms, comfortable public areas and a very popular restaurant, acceptably served by an eager, if unevenly managed, staff.

29⇌↱(2fb)1⊟ CTV in all bedrooms ® **T** sB&B⇌↱£43-£50 dB&B⇌↱£57-£75 ⊟
☾ CTV 40P ✲ *xmas*
☋ English & French ♥ ⚐ Lunch £7.50-£13.50 Dinner £14-£16&alc Last dinner 9.30pm
Credit Cards 1 2 3 5

B

✕✕Wishing Well Tandoori Main Rd PO18 8
☎Chichester(0243)572234 & 575016
Helpful and courteous waiters offer a menu of mainly north Indian cuisine at this modern cottage-style restaurant.
Closed 25 & 26 Dec
Indian **V** 80 seats ✱ Lunch £8-£13 Dinner fr£9 Last lunch 2pm Last dinner 11pm 45P
Credit Cards 1 2 3 5

BOSTON Lincolnshire Map **08** TF34

★★New England 49 Wide Bargate PE21 6SH (Trusthouse Forte)
☎(0205)65255 FAX (0205) 310597
This three-storey Victorian building, with its attractive public areas and comfortable, well-equipped bedrooms, is conveniently situated near to the town centre and is popular with both commercial customers and tourists.
25⇌in 5 bedrooms CTV in all bedrooms ® **T** ✱
sB⇌£49-£55 dB⇌£60 (room only)
xmas
Mainly grills **V** Lunch £9.50&alc Dinner £7.50-£15alc Last dinner 10pm
Credit Cards 1 2 3 4 5

★★White Hart 1-5 High St, Bridge Foot PE21 8SH (Berni/Chef & Brewer) ☎(0205)64877
An impressive, Regency-style building, the White Hart stands on the bank of the River Witham near the town centre, opposite the famous St Botolph's Church (the Stump). It has been tastefully modernised to provide comfortable bedrooms and pleasant public areas which include a choice of restaurants, each with its own bar.
23rm(8⇌10)(2fb) CTV in all bedrooms ® **T** (ex guide dogs) sB&B⇌£30-£37.50 dB&B⇌£43-£53
35P
Mainly grills **V** Lunch £8 Dinner £9 Last dinner 10.30pm
Credit Cards 1 2 3 5

BOTALLACK Cornwall & Isles of Scilly Map **02** SW33

✕✕Count House TR19 7QQ ☎Penzance(0736)788588
This lofty restaurant is set amidst ruined mine workings in the heart of 'Penmarric' country. The short à la carte menu is prepared with a degree of nouvelle cuisine and is good value for money.
Closed Mon
Lunch not served Tue
Dinner not served Sun & Tue in winter
English & French **V** 50 seats Lunch £2.85-£5.95alc Dinner £15-£22alc Last lunch 2pm Last dinner 10pm 50P
Credit Cards 1 2 3 5

BOTHWELL Strathclyde *Lanarkshire* Map **11** NS75

★★★60% Bothwell Bridge 89 Main St G71 8LN ☎(0698)852246
Telex no 776838
A modernised Victorian mansion with a new extension, standing in its own grounds. It offers pleasant bedrooms and an attractive restaurant featuring menus and a wine list with a strong Italian influence.
41rm(32⇌9)(5fb)1 CTV in all bedrooms ® **T** (ex guide dogs) ✱ sB&B⇌£38-£45 dB&B⇌£48-£55
90P ♫ *xmas*
Continental **V** S10% Lunch £5.50-£6.60 Dinner £11-£13.75 Last dinner 10.30pm
Credit Cards 1 2 3 5 £

★★Silvertrees Silverwells Crescent G71 8DP ☎(0698)852311
This large sandstone house stands in spacious grounds in a quiet residential area. Many of the bedrooms are located in well-furnished annexes within the grounds. The hotel caters for all types of functions with an attractive, totally self-contained suite to accommodate large groups.
7⇌Annexe19⇌(1fb)1 CTV in all bedrooms ® **T**
sB&B⇌£50 dB&B⇌£55
100P 4
V Lunch £7.50-£8.25&alc High tea £6.50 Dinner £10.50&alc Last dinner 8.45pm Credit Cards 1 2 3 5

BOTHWELL MOTORWAY SERVICE AREA (M74)

○ **Road Chef Lodge** G71 8BG (M74 southbound)
☎(0693)854123
Opening summer 1990.

BOTLEY Hampshire Map **04** SU51

✕✕Cobbett's 15 The Square SO3 2EA
☎(04892)2068 due to change t o 782068
A 16th-century cottage restaurant, enhanced by colourful country floral arrangements, where service is friendly and relaxed. Mme Lucie Skipworth, who comes from St Emilion, and her young kitchen team use good ingredients to prepare enterprising French regional dishes. Delightful parfait de volaille, sorbets, opera au chocolat et cáfe are among the dishes on offer.
Closed Sun, 2 wks summer & BH's
Lunch not served Sat & Mon
French **V** 45 seats ✱ Lunch £9-£12&alc Dinner £16.50-£25alc Last lunch 1.45pm Last dinner 9.45pm 20P nc11yrs Credit Cards 1 2 3

BOURNE Lincolnshire Map **08** TF02

★★*Angel* Market Place PE10 9AE ☎(0778)422346
Comfortable 16th-century town centre inn with well-equipped accomodation.
13rm(4⇌6)(1fb)2 CTV in all bedrooms ® **T** (ex guide dogs)
♫
French **V** Credit Cards 1 3

BOURNEMOUTH Dorset Map **04** SZ09

See **Town Plan Section**
See also **Christchurch, Longham & Poole**

★★★★★65% Royal Bath Bath Rd BH1 2EW (De Vere)
☎(0202)25555 Telex no 41375 FAX (0202) 24158
Now 150 years old, this spaciously elegant hotel, attractively set in a commanding position overlooking the sea, has undergone major refurbishment to bring standards to an even higher level of excellence with a new leisure complex and exceptionally good conference facilities which make it particularly popular with the business fraternity. Lively dinner dances take place in the main restaurant on Saturday evenings, 'Oscar's' offering more formal cuisine in a separate, well-appointed room.
131⇌2 CTV in all bedrooms **T** (ex guide dogs)
sB&B⇌£70-£75 dB&B⇌£110-£150
Lift 120 (£3.50 per day) CFA (heated) sauna solarium gymnasium beauty salon putting green croquet lawn ♫ *xmas*
French **V** S% Lunch fr£15 High tea fr£4.50 Dinner fr£21 Last dinner 10.30pm
Credit Cards 1 2 3 4 5 £

★★★★59% Highcliff St Michaels Rd, West Cliff BH2 5DU (Best Western) ☎(0202)27702 Telex no 417153
FAX (0202) 21233
This hotel is situated on top of a cliff overlooking the sea. Bedrooms are spacious with good décor and fittings; there are a few bedrooms in the converted coastguard cottages which are reached by a covered walkway. Leisure facilities are also available. Service is friendly and efficient.
146rm(136⇌10)Annexe14⇌(30fb) CTV in all bedrooms ® **T** (ex guide dogs) sB⇌£50-£70
dB⇌£86-£120 (room only)
Lift 150P CFA (heated) (hard) snooker sauna solarium putting & croquet lawn *xmas*

▶

Activity..Leisure..and Pleasure await you at..

DE VERE HOTELS

AA ★★★★

THE DORMY

NEW ROAD, FERNDOWN,
NR BOURNEMOUTH
TEL. BOURNEMOUTH (0202) 872121
FAX: (0202) 895388

Set in 10 acres of scenic grounds, adjacent to the Ferndown Golf Course and located near Bournemouth and the New Forest. All guests have free use of the fully fitted exclusive Leisure Club, featuring indoor pool and squash courts. A la Carte and Table D'Hôte restaurant plus snack bar in addition to the 3 bars. Friday night Barbecue/Dance (Summer Months) and Dinner Dance every Saturday. 134 De Luxe en suite bedrooms. Special Leisure Breaks all year and summer specials (July/August). Please telephone for brochure and tariff.

Bothwell Bridge Hotel ★★★

Main Street, Bothwell G71 8LN
TEL. 0698 852246/TELEX: 776838

At the Bothwell Bridge Hotel we bid you a welcome to a world of friendly hospitality in the peaceful surroundings of an elegant country house

ITALIAN RESTAURANT
SUITABLE FOR ALL OCCASIONS
DINNER DANCE MOST EVENINGS

Fully Licensed
Weddings – Functions – Meetings – Conferences – Large Car Park – Country View
Conveniently situated 1½ miles from M74

BOSCASTLE

A delightful, historic, listed c. 16th century Coaching Inn of real character offering charm, comfort and excellent cuisine.

Set in glorious National Trust Countryside by Boscastle's famous Elizabethan Harbour the magic of North Cornwall is literally on your doorstep.

Very comfortable with full central heating, 21 bedrooms, colour TV's, tea/coffee making etc. We even have a 4 Poster bed.

Our excellent Anglo French Georgian restaurant is famed for its fine food with an English and French flavour. We also have a FREEHOUSE with Real Ales and a buffet.

Lots of atmosphere, log fires, beams, and real hospitality. Antiques and Wellingtonia on display throughout the hotel and pets are always welcome.

★★

The Wellington Hotel

Solange and Victor Tobutt.

The Harbour, Boscastle, Cornwall PL35 0AQ (08405) 202

V ✿ ☐ ⅟ S% Lunch £8.50-£12.50&alc High tea £3-£5.50 Dinner £13.50-£15&alc Last dinner 9.30pm
Credit Cards [1] [2] [3] [5]

★★★★70% Norfolk Royale Hotel Richmond Hill BH2 6EN ☎(0202)21521 Telex no 418474
An Edwardian hotel in the town centre that has undergone extensive renovation but manages to retain its original character. It has distinctive, ornate iron balconies, a good à la carte restaurant, and the Orangery buffet restaurant housed in a twin atrium beside a swimming pool. The management are efficient and the staff are friendly.
95⇌(9fb)⅟in 14 bedrooms CTV in all bedrooms ® T ✗ (ex guide dogs) ✱ sB&B⇌£72.50-£82.50 dB&B⇌£100-£110 ⊟
Lift ☾ 85⌂ ✲ ⊡(heated) sauna steamroom whirlpool ♫
☋ English & French V ✿ ☐ Lunch £9-£12.75&alc Dinner £12.50&alc Last dinner 10.30pm
Credit Cards [1] [2] [3] [4] [5] ⓔ

★★★58% Belvedere Bath Rd BH1 2EU ☎(0202)21080 FAX (0202) 294699
Comfortable public rooms are matched by neat modern bedrooms, some with sea views. The young, informal staff provide cheerful service. Cuisine is modest.
35rm(24⇌11↱)(5fb)1⊞ CTV in all bedrooms ® T sB&B⇌↱£35-£39 dB&B⇌↱£60-£68 ⊟
Lift ☾ 26P nc6yrs *xmas*
☋ English & Continental V ✿ Lunch £7.50 Dinner £8.50 Last dinner 8.30pm
Credit Cards [1] [2] [3] [5]

★★★55% Burley Court Bath Rd BH1 2NP ☎(0202)22824
Closed Xmas
The public areas of this holiday hotel include a large lounge and games room, together with a newly-decorated dining room, and guests enjoy individual attention from the friendly, helpful staff.
39rm(30⇌3↱)(8fb)1⊞ CTV in 33bedrooms TV in 6bedrooms ® sB&B⇌↱£23-£35 dB&B⇌↱£45-£69 ⊟
Lift ☾ CTV 35P ⛟ ≏(heated) solarium games room
☋ English & French ✿ ☐ S5% Lunch fr£6.50 Dinner fr£9 Last dinner 8.30pm
Credit Cards [1] [3]

★★★61% Hotel Cecil Bath Rd BH1 2HJ ☎(0202)293336 FAX (0202) 294699
A modern hotel, conveniently situated for the town centre, offers value for money in its comfortable bedrooms and bright, attractive public areas.
27rm(21⇌6↱)(3fb) CTV in all bedrooms ® T sB&B⇌↱£35-£39 dB&B⇌↱£60-£68 ⊟
Lift 27P ♫ *xmas*
☋ English & French V ✿ ☐ Lunch £7.50 Dinner £8.50 Last dinner 9pm
Credit Cards [1] [2] [3] [5]

★★★61% Chesterwood East Overcliff Dr BH1 3AR ☎(0202)28057 FAX (0202) 293457
A detached hotel on the East Cliff with unrestricted views to sea. The resident proprietors manage their hotel well, with genuine friendliness.
49rm(40⇌9↱)Annexe3⇌(13fb) CTV in all bedrooms ® T ✗ (ex guide dogs) S% sB&B⇌↱£34.50-£45.50 dB&B⇌↱£65-£86 (incl dinner) ⊟
Lift ☾ 39P 8⌂ ✲ ≏(heated) games room ♫ ♔ *xmas*
V ✿ ☐ ⅟ S% Sunday Lunch £5.50-£6.50 Dinner £11-£12.50 Last dinner 8.30pm
Credit Cards [1] [2] [3] [5] ⓔ

★★★66% Chine Hotel Boscombe Spa Rd BH5 1AX ☎(0202)36234 Telex no 41338 FAX (0202) 391737
There are spacious public rooms here, including a comfortable lounge, while bedrooms are modern and provide good facilities. This is one of four hotels in Bournemouth with both indoor and outdoor swimming pools.
97rm(92⇌5↱)(15fb) CTV in all bedrooms ® T ✗ (ex guide dogs) ✱ sB&B⇌↱£25-£35 dB&B⇌↱£50-£70 ⊟
Lift ☾ 40P ✲ ⊡(heated) ≏(heated) sauna solarium gymnasium use of Haven Sports & Leisure Centre ♫ *xmas*
V ✿ ☐ Lunch fr£8.50 High tea £2.10-£4.10 Dinner £11 Last dinner 8.30pm
Credit Cards [1] [2] [3] [5] ⓔ

★★★52% *Cliffeside* East Overcliff Dr BH1 3AQ ☎(0202)25724 Telex no 418297
The smart restaurant here overlooks the pool and sun terrace, whilst other public rooms have panoramic sea views.
61rm(47⇌14↱)(10fb) CTV in all bedrooms ® T
Lift ☾ CTV 45P ⛟ CFA ≏(heated) snooker table tennis ♫
☋ French & Italian ✿ ☐ Last dinner 8.30pm
Credit Cards [1] [3]

★★★62% Hotel Courtlands 16 Boscombe Spa Rd, East Cliff BH5 1BB (Best Western) ☎(0202)302442 Telex no 41344 FAX (0202) 309880
An efficient and friendly hotel in a peaceful location, suitable for both business and leisure use. There are some smart new bedrooms and a pleasant garden.
60rm(52⇌8↱)(15fb) CTV in all bedrooms ® T sB&B⇌↱£33-£38.50 dB&B⇌↱£61.50-£68.50 ⊟
Lift ☾ 50P ⛟ ✲ CFA ≏(heated) sauna solarium spa bath ♫ *xmas*
☋ English & French V ✿ ☐ Lunch fr£8.30 Dinner £12.50-£15 Last dinner 8.30pm
Credit Cards [1] [2] [3] [5]

★★★65% Crest Lansdowne BH1 2PR (Crest) ☎(0202)23262 Telex no 41232 FAX (0202) 27698
A modern, purpose-built hotel of an interesting circular design.
102⇌↱(78fb)⅟in 34 bedrooms CTV in all bedrooms ® T ✱ sB⇌↱fr£64 dB⇌↱fr£78 (room only) ⊟
Lift ☾ CTV 50⌂ snooker table tennis darts games room skittles *xmas*
☋ English & French V ✿ ☐ ⅟ Lunch £5.95-£8.50 Dinner fr£12.80&alc Last dinner 9.45pm
Credit Cards [1] [2] [3] [4] [5] ⓔ

★★★67% Cumberland East Overcliff Dr BH1 3AF ☎(0202)290722 Telex no 418297 FAX (0202) 294810
Helpful staff create a friendly atmosphere at this comfortable hotel overlooking the sea; a pleasantly furnished lounge is complemented by bedrooms which are all well equipped, though those at the front of the building tend to be larger than those at the rear.
102⇌↱(6fb)3⊞ CTV in all bedrooms ® T ✗ (ex guide dogs) ✱ S% sB&B⇌↱£28-£34 dB&B⇌↱£56-£86 ⊟
Lift ☾ CTV 65P ≏(heated) solarium games room table tennis pool ♫ ♔ *xmas*
☋ British & Continental V ✿ ☐ Lunch £6.95 High tea £4.25 Dinner £12.95 Last dinner 8.30pm
Credit Cards [1] [3] ⓔ

★★★56% Durley Hall Durley Chine Rd, West Cliff BH2 5JS (Consort) ☎(0202)766886 FAX (0202) 762236
This recently extended hotel offers bedrooms both in executive style and more modest. A formal dining room is augmented by a coffee shop, and there are new indoor sports facilities and a sun lounge.
70rm(50⇌18↱)Annexe11⇌↱(22fb)1⊞ CTV in all bedrooms ® T sB&B⇌↱£42-£60 dB&B⇌↱£65-£98 ⊟
Lift ☾ 150P ✲ CFA ⊡(heated) ≏(heated) sauna solarium gymnasium jacuzzi steam cabinet hairdresser ♫ ♔ *xmas*
☋ English & Continental V ✿ ☐ Sunday Lunch fr£6.75 Dinner fr£13.50&alc Last dinner 8.45pm
Credit Cards [1] [2] [3] [5]

★★★52% **Durlston Court** Gervis Rd, East Cliff BH1 3DD
☎(0202)291488 FAX (0202) 299615
Friendly hotel, catering mainly for holiday makers, with a spacious lounge and bar. Some of the bedrooms have been smartly refurbished.
54rm(48⇌6↱)Annexe6rm(5⇌1↱)(16fb) CTV in all bedrooms ® **T** sB&B⇌↱£46-£50 dB&B⇌↱£74-£80 ⊟
Lift ☾ 50P CFA ⇌(heated) solarium ♫ *xmas*
☋ English & French **V** ♈ ♉ Lunch £7.50&alc High tea £3.50&alc Dinner £9 Last dinner 8.30pm
Credit Cards 1 2 3 5 £

★★★66% **East Anglia** 6 Poole Rd BH2 5QX ☎(0202)765163
FAX (0202) 752949
Owned and run by the same family for over 30 years, this hotel is conveniently situated for the town centre and beaches. Public rooms have been recently refurbished and the staff are friendly and professional. The French chef – another member of the family – produces good, tasty dishes.
49rm(39⇌10↱)Annexe24rm(20⇌4↱)(19fb) CTV in all bedrooms ® **T** ✗ (ex guide dogs) sB&B⇌↱£30.50-£34.50 dB&B⇌↱£55-£69 ⊟
Lift ☾ 73P CFA ⇌(heated) sauna solarium gymnasium jacuzzi games room ♫ *xmas*
☋ English & French ♈ ♉ ⚡ Lunch fr£6.50 Dinner fr£11 Last dinner 8.30pm
Credit Cards 1 2 3 5

★★★58% **Elstead** 12-14 Knyveton Rd BH1 3QP
☎(0202)293071 FAX (0202) 293827
Closed Oct-Mar
This hotel, in a quiet situation, has undergone complete renovation. Facilities include two bedrooms designed specifically for disabled guests, extensive conference rooms and full-size snooker table and pool table.

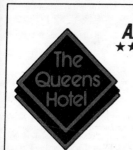

▶

51rm(39⇌7⛆)(4fb)⚟in 5 bedrooms CTV in all bedrooms ® T sB&B£20-£21.50 sB&B⇌⛆£24-£26 dB&B£40-£43 dB&B⇌⛆£48-£52
Lift ☾ 40P 6🚗 (£1.50 per night) snooker ♫
Lunch fr£5 Dinner fr£7.50&alc Last dinner 8.30pm
Credit Cards 1 3

★★★58% *Embassy* Meyrick Rd, Boscombe BH1 3DW ☎(0202)290751
Quietly located in a tree-lined avenue convenient for the town and the East Cliff, this friendly hotel offers garden annexe bedrooms of a good standard and comfortable lounge areas.
39rm(38⇌1⛆)(6fb)1⊞ CTV in all bedrooms ® T
Lift ☾ CTV 48P CFA ⛆(heated)
French Last dinner 8.30pm
Credit Cards 1 2 3 5

★★★56% Grosvenor Bath Rd, East Cliff BH1 2EX ☎(0202)28858 Telex no 417200
This hotel is personally managed by the proprietor, aided by a capable, friendly staff, and it now offers new leisure facilities as well as many refurbished bedrooms.
38rm(33⇌5⛆)(10fb)2⊞ CTV in all bedrooms ® T sB&B⇌⛆£29-£33 dB&B⇌⛆£58-£67
Lift ☾ CTV 40P ⛆(heated) sauna solarium gymnasium spa exercise area ♫ *xmas*
English & French V ⚟ Lunch £5.95-£8.95 High tea £1-£4 Dinner £9.75-£13.25&alc Last dinner 8.45pm
Credit Cards 1 3

★★★61% Heathlands 12 Grove Rd, East Cliff BH1 3AY ☎(0202)23336 Telex no 8954665 FAX (0202) 25937
Quietly situated near East Cliff, a large, modern hotel provides well co-ordinated public areas which include good conference and banqueting facilities. Coffee shop type lunches are available, as well as the well-balanced table d'hôte menus available in the evening, and service is provided by smartly-uniformed, professional staff.
116rm(111⇌5⛆)(17fb) CTV in all bedrooms ® T sB&B⇌⛆£46.50-£49 dB&B⇌⛆£74-£78
Lift ☾ 80P ✲ CFA ⛆(heated) sauna solarium gymnasium croquet boules games room health club *xmas*
English & French V Lunch £7.50-£9 Dinner £11-£13 Last dinner 8.30pm
Credit Cards 1 2 3 5 £

★★★64% Langtry Manor 26 Derby Rd, East Cliff BH1 3QB (Consort) ☎(0202)23887 FAX (0202) 290115
Built in 1877 by King Edward VII for his mistress Lillie Langtry, it is now an appealing hotel with a romantic atmosphere. Well-equipped bedrooms vary in size and style and there are some suites complete with four poster beds. Edwardian dinner parties are held in the elegant Dining Hall on Saturdays.
17rm(14⇌3⛆)4⊞ CTV in all bedrooms ® T sB&B⇌⛆£39.50-£49.50 dB&B⇌⛆£70-£87
30P ✲ nc5yrs *xmas*
International V ⚟ Bar Lunch £5-£12 Dinner £15.75-£17&alc Last dinner 9pm
Credit Cards 1 2 3 5 £

★★★64% Marsham Court Russell Cotes Rd BH1 3AB ☎(0202)22111 Telex no 41420 FAX (0202) 294744
This large, professionally-run seafront hotel specialises in business functions, having several conference and syndicate rooms. Public areas and the majority of the bedrooms have been stylishly and imaginatively refurbished.
86rm(81⇌5⛆)(16fb) CTV in all bedrooms ® T (ex guide dogs) sB&B⇌⛆£43-£46 dB&B⇌⛆£76-£82
Lift ☾ 55P 36🚗 ⛆(heated) snooker ♫ *xmas*
English & French V Lunch £6.50-£9 High tea £4 Dinner £12.50-£13.50&alc Last dinner 9pm
Credit Cards 1 2 3 5 £

★★★59% Melford Hall St Peters Rd BH1 2LS ☎(0202)21516
Quietly yet centrally situated, the large, traditional holiday hotel offers excellent value for money, with good parking facilities and substantial meals. The unusual fibre-optic displays in the public areas are worthy of note.
60rm(54⇌1⛆)(16fb) CTV in all bedrooms ® T S10% sB&B£22-£28 sB&B⇌⛆£24-£32 dB&B⇌⛆£48-£64
Lift ☾ 55P ✲ ♫ *xmas*
English & French V S10% Lunch £7-£7.50 Dinner £9.50-£9.70 Last dinner 8.30pm
Credit Cards 1 3

★★★50% *Miramar Hotel* Grove Rd BH1 3AL ☎(0202)26581
Warm, comfortable hotel where many rooms have fine sea views.
42rm(30⇌5⛆)(4fb) CTV in all bedrooms T (ex guide dogs)
Lift ☾ CTV 40P 4🚗 (charged) ✲ putting green
V Last dinner 8.30pm
Credit Cards 1 2 3

★★★65% New Durley Dean Westcliff Rd BH2 5HE ☎(0202)27711 FAX (0202) 292815
An elegant Victorian red-brick hotel that has been recently refurbished and reopened. Leisure facilities include an indoor pool with whirlpool spa, a turkish steam room and a well-equipped "trymnasium". the Green Room Restuarant offers a buffet style breakfast, a carvery at lunchtime and full service at dinner. Bedrooms are comfortable and well-designed.
110rm(102⇌8⛆)(25fb)5⊞ CTV in all bedrooms ® T (ex guide dogs) ✱ sB&B⇌⛆£22.50-£31.50 dB&B⇌⛆£45-£63
Lift ☾ 40P ⛆(heated) snooker sauna solarium gymnasium Turkish steam room whirlpool spa ♫ *xmas*
English & Continental V ⚟ Lunch £6.50-£8.50 High tea £3-£5 Dinner £11-£12.50 Last dinner 8.30pm
Credit Cards 1 2 3

★★★67% Pavilion 22 Bath Rd BH1 2NS ☎(0202)291266 Telex no 418253
The bedrooms of this well-appointed, centrally situated hotel are all attractively co-ordinated, though a few are rather compact. New conference facilities are available, and the restaurant features a short à la carte choice of dishes as well as its well-balanced table d'hôte menu, while service – under the personal supervision of the owner – is unfailingly attentive.
44rm(35⇌9⛆)(2fb)2⊞ CTV in all bedrooms ® T S% sB&B⇌⛆£33.50-£37 dB&B⇌⛆£50-£55
Lift ☾ 35P ♫ *xmas*
English ⚟ S% Lunch £6-£8.50 High tea £3.50-£4.50 Dinner £10.50-£12.50&alc Last dinner 8.30pm
Credit Cards 1 2 3 5

★★★66% Picadilly Bath Rd BH1 2NN ☎(0202)22559 FAX (0202) 298235
Centrally situated hotel with friendly staff. Bedrooms have all been upgraded recently. A table d'hôte dinner menu is on offer in The Fountain Restaurant. Conference facilities are also available.
45rm(44⇌1⛆)(2fb)1⊞ CTV in all bedrooms ® T (ex guide dogs) ✱ sB&B⇌⛆£30-£38 dB&B⇌⛆£40-£56
Lift ☾ 30P ♫ *xmas*
English & French V ⚟ Lunch fr£6.95&alc Dinner fr£9.75&alc Last dinner 9pm
Credit Cards 1 2 3 5

★★★61% Queens Meyrick Rd, East Cliff BH1 3DL ☎(0202)24415 Telex no 418297 FAX (0202) 294810
Large modern hotel in a quiet location, catering for both conferences and holidaymakers. Dinner is well-cooked and offers a good choice.
114rm(104⇌10⛆)(15fb)1⊞ CTV in all bedrooms ® T sB&B⇌⛆£34-£38 dB&B⇌⛆£68-£76
Lift ☾ 80P 12🚗 (£1.50) ✲ snooker ♫ *xmas*
English & French V Lunch fr£7.50 Dinner fr£13.95 Last dinner 9pm
Credit Cards 1 3 £

B

★★★55% **Trouville** Priory Rd BH2 5DH ☎(0202)22262 FAX (0202) 294810
Closed Dec- Jan
In a central position, convenient for Bournemouth International Centre and the Winter Gardens, this hotel has been owned for more than 40 years by the same family.
75rm(68⇌6🚿)(21fb) CTV in 73bedrooms ® T ✳ sB&B⇌🚿£28-£37 dB&B⇌🚿£56-£72 (incl dinner) 🅱
Lift ☾ 55P 4🚗 (£2.50 per night) sauna solarium gymnasium jacuzzi ♫
🍷 English & French V ♡ ☕ Dinner £10-£13.50 Last dinner 8.30pm
Credit Cards 1 3 £

★★★67% **Wessex** West Cliff Rd BH2 5EU (Forestdale) ☎(0202)21911 due to change to 551911 FAX (0202) 297354
Situated on the West Cliffs, this large, well maintained Victorian hotel offers well equipped, recently upgraded, modern bedrooms and a good range of public rooms, including a spacious, tastefully appointed lounge and two restaurants, all areas enjoying prompt attentive service. A small leisure and recreational complex has recently been added.
84rm(77⇌7🚿)(15fb)⚟in 3 bedrooms CTV in all bedrooms ® T sB&B⇌🚿£54.50-£59.50 dB&B⇌🚿£74-£79 🅱
Lift ☾ 250P CFA ▭(heated) ⛱(heated) snooker sauna solarium gymnasium table tennis ♫ *xmas*
🍷 International V ♡ ☕ ⚟ Bar Lunch £2.50-£6.50alc High tea fr£4alc Dinner £13-£15alc Last dinner 9.15pm
Credit Cards 1 2 3 5 £

★★★67% **Hermitage** Exeter Rd BH2 5AH ☎(0202)27363 Telex no 418316
A large, sea-facing hotel provides excellent facilities for either holidaymaker or commercial travellers; guests are assured of a warm welcome, friendly service, and a good choice of meals from the table d'hôte and à la carte menus featured in its wood-panelled restaurant.

▶

B

85rm(65⇌12🚿)(17fb) CTV in all bedrooms ® T sB&B⇌🚿£37.50-£50 dB&B⇌🚿£61-£85 ⊟
Lift ☾ CTV 58P CFA sauna solarium *xmas*
🍷 English & French V ☆ ☑ ⚡ Lunch £4.50-£15alc Dinner fr£10.50&alc Last dinner 8.30pm
Credit Cards [1] [3] [4]

★★Arlington Exeter Park Rd BH2 5BD ☎(0202)22879 & 23012
RS Jan-Mar
Centrally situated and offering direct access to the lower pleasure gardens, this friendly, family-run hotel provides modern, well-equipped bedrooms and a caring atmosphere which makes it easy to relax.
28⇌🚿Annexe1🚿(6fb) CTV in 28bedrooms ® T ✗ ✻ sB&B⇌🚿£25.50-£31.50 dB&B⇌🚿£51-£63 (incl dinner) ⊟
Lift CTV 21P ✿ nc2yrs *xmas*
🍷 English & French V ☆ ☑ ⚡ Lunch £5.25 Dinner £8.75 Last dinner 8pm
Credit Cards [1] [3] £

★★Chinehead 31 Alumhurst Rd, Westbourne BH4 8EN ☎(0202)752777
Guests, whether holiday-makers or business people, receive individual consideration at this small, proprietor-run hotel with its clean, fresh bedrooms and comfortable bar lounge.
21rm(12⇌3🚿)(2fb) CTV in 24bedrooms ® T ✗ (ex guide dogs) ✻ sB&B£19.25-£22.75 sB&B⇌🚿£22.25-£25.75 dB&B⇌🚿£44.50-£51.50 ⊟
20P ⛟ hairdressing salon *xmas*
V ☆ ☑ ⚡ Lunch £4.50-£14&alc Dinner £5.25-£14&alc Last dinner 8.30pm
Credit Cards [1] [3]

★★Chinehurst 18-20 Studland Rd, Westbourne BH4 8JA ☎(0202)764583
A small, family-run hotel which provides comfortable accommodation in bedrooms with modern facilities and offers pleasant views over Alum Chine.
31⇌🚿(4fb)1⊟ CTV in all bedrooms ® T sB&B⇌🚿£24-£44 dB&B⇌🚿£48-£68 ⊟
14P 2🚘(£2.50 per night) games room *xmas*
🍷 Continental V ☆ ☑ ⚡ Lunch fr£5.50&alc Dinner fr£9.50&alc Last dinner 9pm
Credit Cards [1] [2] [3] [5]

See advertisement under POOLE

★★Connaught West Hill Rd, West Cliff BH2 5PH ☎(0202)298020
Here tastefully furnished and very well equipped modern bedrooms are complemented by public areas including a small television lounge, restaurant, bar and patio. Service is friendly and helpful, and the hotel is set amid sheltered lawns and gardens.
60rm(53⇌7🚿)(15fb)2⊟⚡in 12 bedrooms CTV in all bedrooms ® T sB&B⇌🚿£30-£38 dB&B⇌🚿£60-£76 ⊟
Lift ☾ 45P ✿ ⊡(heated) ⩯(heated) snooker sauna solarium gymnasium pool table table tennis games room ⌂ *xmas*
🍷 English & French V ☆ ☑ ⚡ Lunch £6.75-£12.95 Dinner £14.50-£18&alc Last dinner 8.45pm
Credit Cards [1] [2] [3] [5]

★★Cottonwood Grove Rd, East Cliff BH1 3AP (Minotels) ☎(0202)23183
A colour-washed brick building, surrounded by well-kept lawns and gardens, overlooking the sea.
32rm(25⇌7🚿)(8fb) CTV in all bedrooms ® T ✗ (ex guide dogs) ✻ sB&B⇌🚿£21.50-£26 dB&B⇌🚿£43-£52 (incl dinner) ⊟
Lift 50P ✿ snooker ♫ *xmas*
🍷 English & French V ☆ ☑ ⚡ Bar Lunch 85p-£3.50 Dinner £8 Last dinner 8pm
Credit Cards [1] [2] [3] [5] £

★★County Westover Rd BH1 2BT ☎(0202)22385
In a good central location, this hotel caters for those on holiday and for business people. Bedrooms have modern facilities and there is a disco bar in addition to the more traditional lounges and dining room.
52rm(37⇌9🚿)(11fb) CTV in all bedrooms ® T sB&B£20 sB&B⇌🚿£30 dB&B£40 dB&B⇌🚿£50 ⊟
Lift ☾ 𝑃 *xmas*
☆ ☑ Bar Lunch £2-£5alc Dinner £8 Last dinner 8pm
Credit Cards [1] [2] [3] £

★★Durley Chine Chine Crescent, West Cliff BH2 5LB ☎(0202)21926
Set in the quiet surroundings of its own grounds, the tastefully furnished hotel creates a comfortable, relaxing atmosphere. A choice of particularly well furnished bedrooms is complemented by public areas which include a pleasant lounge, separate bar and basement dining room.
22rm(8⇌9🚿)Annexe14rm(8⇌2🚿)(9fb) CTV in 22bedrooms ® T sB&B⇌🚿£21.75-£28 dB&B⇌🚿£43.50-£56 ⊟
40P ✿ ♫ nc3yrs *xmas*
🍷 English & Continental ☆ ☑ Lunch £5.95 Dinner £8.95 Last dinner 7.30pm
Credit Cards [1] [3] £

★★Durley Grange 6 Durley Rd, West Cliff BH2 5JL ☎(0202)24473
Closed Dec-Feb (ex Xmas & New Year)
Within short distance of Durley Chine this hotel is also near the town centre.
50rm(36⇌14🚿)(6fb) CTV in all bedrooms ® T sB&B⇌🚿£22-£25 dB&B⇌🚿£44-£50
Lift ☾ CTV 25P ♫ *xmas*
☆ ⚡ Lunch £2.50-£7 Dinner £12 Last dinner 8pm
Credit Cards [1] [3] £

★★Fircroft 4 Owls Rd, Boscombe BH5 1AE ☎(0202)309771
A large Victorian building with modern extensions, set in its own grounds.
49rm(43⇌6🚿)(18fb) CTV in all bedrooms ® T sB&B⇌🚿£18-£23 dB&B⇌🚿£36-£46 ⊟
Lift ☾ CTV 50P squash ♫ *xmas*
☆ ☑ Bar Lunch £2.50-£6.50 Dinner fr£10 Last dinner 8pm
Credit Cards [1] [3] £

★★*Gresham Court* 4 Grove Rd, East Cliff BH1 3AX ☎(0202)21732
Pleasant, friendly hotel with comfortable, soundly appointed bedrooms.
34rm(15⇌19🚿)(12fb) CTV in all bedrooms ® T
Lift CTV 35P ✿ ♫
☆ ☑ Last dinner 7.30pm
Credit Cards [1] [2] [3] [5]

★★Hinton Firs Manor Rd, East Cliff BH1 3HB (Exec Hotel) ☎(0202)25409 FAX (0202) 299607
Attentive service and well furnished lounges makes this an attractive hotel.
46rm(42⇌4🚿)Annexe6⇌(19fb) CTV in all bedrooms ® T ✗ ✻ sB&B⇌🚿£31.50-£42.90 dB&B⇌🚿£53-£75.80 (incl dinner) ⊟
Lift ☾ CTV 40P ⛟ ⊡(heated) ⩯(heated) sauna solarium games room ♫ *xmas*
🍷 English & French ☆ ☑ ⚡ Lunch £5.75 Dinner £8.25 Last dinner 8pm
Credit Cards [1] [3]

★★Manor House Manor Rd, East Cliff BH1 3EZ ☎(0202)36669
Mar-Oct
Attractive hotel with pleasant garden and personal attention by resident owner.
27rm(8⇌3🚿)(10fb) CTV in all bedrooms ® ✗

CTV 27P ♫
V Last dinner 7.30pm
Credit Cards [1] [3] £

★★Mansfield West Cliff Gardens BH2 5HL ☎(0202)22659
Closed 28 Dec-18 Jan
The hotel stands in a quiet road at West Cliff, an easy walk from cliff top and beach. Friendly, attentive resident owners provide personal service, and the bedrooms are very comfortable.
30rm(18⇔12↱)(7fb)1 CTV in all bedrooms ® T
sB&B⇔↱£18-£24 dB&B⇔↱£36-£48
12P ♫ *xmas*
English & French Lunch £6-£7 Dinner £7-£8 Last dinner 8pm
Credit Cards [1] [3]

See advertisement on page 143

★★Overcliff Overcliff Dr, Southbourne BH6 3JA
☎(0202)428300
Closed 3-30 Jan
There are views out to the bay from the restaurant and some of the bedrooms – those with balconies also have colour TV. There is a well-balanced table d'hôte menu for dinner and an extensive range of bar meals are available at lunchtime. The friendly owners commit themselves totally to the running of their hotel.
26rm(17⇔4↱)(10fb) CTV in 4bedrooms ® (ex guide dogs)
✱ sB&B£20-£30 sB&B⇔↱£22.50-£32.50 dB&B£40-£60 dB&B⇔↱£45-£65 (incl dinner)
CTV 22P ♫ *xmas*
V Sunday Lunch fr£5.50 Dinner fr£8 Last dinner 8pm
Credit Cards [1] [3]

For key to symbols see the inside front cover.

VISA Access

Hinton Firs (HF11),
Manor Road,
East Cliff,
Bournemouth
BH1 3HB
Tel: (0202) 25409

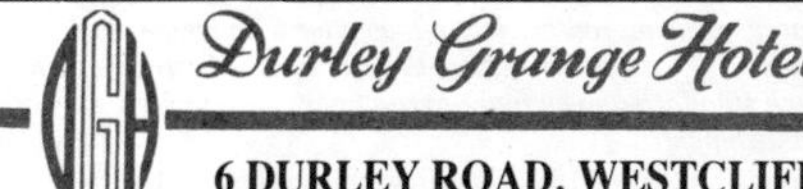

6 DURLEY ROAD, WESTCLIFF
BOURNEMOUTH BH2 5JL ★★

Modern family managed hotel situated in the heart of Bournemouth.

50 en-suite bedrooms all with colour TV, radio, telephone and tea maker. Excellent food served in our spacious dining room. Superb Lounge Bar, where Bar Lunches are available March – November. Entertainment twice weekly during season. Lift. Central Heating. Car Park. Sun Patio.

LET'S GO Bargain Breaks. October – May. Any Two Days Dinner, Room and Breakfast from £50.00 inclusive of VAT.
EASTER, CHRISTMAS AND NEW YEAR PROGRAMME.

Reductions for Parties. Conference delegates and Children over 5 very welcome. Extra Special Terms when sharing with 2 Adults, September – June excluding Bank Holidays.

Telephone: Reception 0202 554473

"Probably the most central hotel in the whole of Bournemouth"

Arlington stands in an unsurpassed central position 100 metres level walk to the Beach, Square, Bournemouth International Centre, and Premier shops. 28 bedrooms, all with bath/shower and toilet en suite, colour TVs with satellite channels, direct dial telephones, tea and coffee making facilities, radios and central heating. Passenger lift. Free Brochure, Tariff, and sample Menu's sent on request. Xmas & New Year programme.

·THE ARLINGTON HOTEL·

Exeter Park Road, Bournemouth BH2 5BD
Telephone (0202) 23012 also 22879 AA ★★

★★Pinehurst West Cliff Gardens BH2 5HR ☎(0202)26218
A large, pleasant red-brick hotel, popular with holidaymakers, stands on West Cliff. Top floor bedrooms have been refurbished to a high standard and similar upgrading is continuing throughout the establishment.
75rm(46⇨26↱)(11fb) CTV in all bedrooms ® T sB&B⇨↱£22-£26.50 dB&B⇨↱£44-£53 ₿
Lift ☾ 48P solarium ♫ *xmas*
Lunch fr£6 Dinner fr£9.50 Last dinner 8pm
Credit Cards 1 2 3 £

★★Riviera Burnaby Rd, Alum Chine BH4 8JF ☎(0202)763653
Telex no 41363 FAX (0202) 299182
Closed 4-31 Jan
White painted hotel with good facilities.
70rm(52⇨10↱)Annexe9rm(3⇨6↱)(24fb) CTV in all bedrooms ® T sB&B⇨↱£27-£38 dB&B⇨↱£54-£76 (incl dinner) ₿
Lift 79P ▭(heated) ⌓(heated) snooker sauna solarium 2 games rooms ♫ *xmas*
☋ French & English V ✿ ☐ S% Lunch £4.95-£7.50 Dinner £12-£14 Last dinner 8.30pm
Credit Cards 1 3

★★Hotel Riviera West Cliff Gardens BH2 5HL ☎(0202)22845
Closed Jan-Mar & 6 Nov-Dec
The terrace and some bedrooms of this modern hotel have sea views.
34rm(29⇨5↱)(5fb) CTV in all bedrooms ® ✗ sB&B⇨↱£20-£40 dB&B⇨↱£40-£50 ₿
Lift ☾ 24P ⌗ ♫ ⌂ *xmas*
✿ ☐ Sunday Lunch £4.95-£6 Dinner £6-£7 Last dinner 7.30pm
Credit Cards 1 2 3

★★Royal Exeter Exeter Rd BH2 5AG (Berni/Chef & Brewer) ☎(0202)290566 & 290567
This large, popular hotel, ideally situated for all local amenities, offers particularly well-equipped bedrooms furnished in modern style. Public areas include the Steak Bar Restaurant, a separate Disco and Carvery opening in the summer, and bars.
36rm(12↱)(10fb) CTV in all bedrooms ® T ✗ (ex guide dogs) sB&B↱£29-£40 dB&B↱£45-£54.50 ₿
Lift ☾ 50P *xmas*
☋ Mainly grills V ✿ ☐ ⚡ Lunch £8 Dinner £9 Last dinner 10pm
Credit Cards 1 2 3 5

★★Russell Court Bath Rd BH1 2EP ☎(0202)295819
This hotel, in its central location, is suitable as a base for holidays or business. It provides personal friendly service, attractive public areas and well-equipped bedrooms, some with a view to sea.
62rm(54⇨4↱) CTV in all bedrooms ® ✗ (ex guide dogs) ✱ sB&B£15-£24 sB&B⇨↱£15-£32 dB&B⇨↱£30-£60 ₿
60P *xmas*
V ✿ ☐ Lunch fr£2.50 Dinner £6-£6.95 Last dinner 8pm
Credit Cards 1 2 3 5

★★St George West Cliff Gardens BH2 5HL ☎(0202)26075
Closed 12 Nov-Feb
Peacefully situated on the West Cliff, overlooking the bay and only ten minutes walk from the town centre and pier.
21rm(14⇨7↱)(5fb) CTV in all bedrooms ® T sB&B⇨↱£23-£28 (incl dinner) ₿
Lift 10P ⌗ nc5yrs
✿ ☐ Bar Lunch £1-£4 Dinner £12-£14 Last dinner 7.30pm

★★Sun Court West Hill Rd BH2 5PH ☎(0202)21343
Holidaymakers and commercial guests alike are attracted to this attractively presented modern hotel; well-equipped bedrooms continue to be upgraded, and there is a pleasant Piano Bar.
36rm(20⇨16↱)(4fb) CTV in all bedrooms ® T sB&B⇨↱£21.25-£35 dB&B⇨↱£42.50-£70 (incl dinner) ₿
Lift ☾ CTV 50P 1⌂ ⌓(heated) solarium gymnasium *xmas*
☋ English & Italian ✿ ☐ Lunch £5.50 Dinner £11&alc Last dinner 8pm
Credit Cards 1 2 3 5

★★Ullswater West Cliff Gardens BH2 5HW ☎(0202)25181
In a quiet position near Clifftop, this red-brick hotel has undergone complete refurbishment, service is relaxed and friendly, and meals are simple. The establishment caters for both holiday and commercial guests.
42rm(12⇨30↱)(7fb) CTV in all bedrooms ® T ✗ (ex guide dogs) ✱ sB&B⇨↱£19.50-£26.50 dB&B⇨↱£39-£53 (incl dinner) ₿
Lift 10P ♫ *xmas*
☋ English & French ✿ ☐ Bar Lunch £1-£3.50alc High tea £1-£3.50alc Dinner £7 Last dinner 8pm
Credit Cards 1 3

★★West Cliff Hall 14 Priory Rd BH2 5DN (Best Western) ☎(0202)299715
An hotel in a central location used mostly by holiday makers. Bedrooms have good colour schemes and are well equipped. A stay here provides good value for money.
49rm(28⇨21↱)(9fb) CTV in all bedrooms ® T S% sB&B⇨↱£18-£32 dB&B⇨↱£36-£64 (incl dinner) ₿
Lift CTV 36P ♫ *xmas*
V ✿ ☐ S% Lunch £4-£4.95 High tea £3-£5 Dinner £4-£5 Last dinner 8pm
Credit Cards 1 2 3 5 £

See advertisement on page 145

★★Whitehall Exeter Park Rd BH2 5AX ☎(0202)24682
Closed 6 Nov-Feb
A quiet holiday hotel in an elevated position overlooking the central gardens to the rear and close to the town centre.
49⇨↱(5fb) CTV in all bedrooms ® T ✱ sB&B⇨↱£20-£24 dB&B£36-£44 dB&B⇨↱£38-£46 ₿

▸

B

St.George Hotel

West Cliff Gardens, Bournemouth.

Peacefully situated on the West Cliff, overlooking Bournemouth Bay.

Ten minutes' walk to the Town and Conference Centre.

A spacious hotel, offering a high degree of comfort, personal service and an exceptionally high standard of food. All rooms en suite with tea & coffee facilities, telephone, radio intercom and colour T/V – lift to all floors. You will be tempted to return again and again to the relaxed atmosphere of our hotel.

Colour brochure and tariff sent on request.

Telephone: 0202-26075 AA ★★

The Royal Exeter Hotel

★★

- ★ Recently Refurbished
- ★ All rooms 'en-suite'
- ★ All rooms with remote TV
- ★ Berni Restaurant
- ★ Full central heating
- ★ Car Park
- ★ Full licence
- ★ Open all year
- ★ All major credit cards
- ★ Night Porter
- ★ Passenger lift
- ★ 200 mtrs to Bournemouth Beach
- ★ 30 mtrs to B.I.C.
- ★ 30 mtrs to heated indoor pool with wave machine and aqua slide
- ★ Bar snacks
- ★ Special Weekend Rates available
- ★ Special Summer 7- & 5-day breaks
- ★ Tea & coffee facilities in every room
- ★ Conference accommodation rates available

Exeter Road, Bournemouth (opposite the BIC)
Telephone: 290566

AA★★

Mansfield Hotel

West Cliff Gardens, Bournemouth, BH2 5HL
Telephone: (0202) 22659

A family run Hotel in a convenient but quiet location on the West Cliff, which has recently been re-decorated and refurbished to a very high standard. All the bedrooms have private bathrooms or shower rooms en-suite, colour T.V., central heating and tea making facilities. An excellent choice of traditionally cooked food is available in the Victorian styled restaurant.

Lift ☾ 25P ❖
♡ ♖ Bar Lunch £1-£3 Dinner £8 Last dinner 8pm
Credit Cards [1] [2] [3] [5]

★★Winterbourne Priory Rd BH2 5DJ ☎(0202)296366
Closed 1-9 Jan
In an elevated position, with good views.
41rm(34⇨7↱)(12fb) CTV in all bedrooms ® T
sB&B⇨↱£26.50-£33.50 dB&B⇨↱£46-£54 ⛿
Lift 32P 1⌂ ❖ ⇨(heated) ⌂ *xmas*
V ♡ ♖ Bar Lunch £1.25-£6 Dinner fr£9 Last dinner 8pm
Credit Cards [1] [3] £

★★*Woodcroft Tower* Gervis Rd, East Cliff BH1 3DE
☎(0202)28202 & 21807
Standing in its own grounds, a convenient walking distance from shops, pier and the seafront.
43rm(18⇨14↱)(4fb) CTV in 40bedrooms ® T ✗ (ex guide dogs)
Lift ☾ 60P (charged) ❖
♔ English & French ♡ ♖ Last dinner 8.30pm
Credit Cards [1] [2] [3] [5]

★*Commodore* Overcliff Dr, Southbourne BH6 3TD
☎(0202)423150 & 427127
14rm(3⇨7↱)(1fb) CTV in all bedrooms ®
Lift 14P ⛟
♡
Credit Cards [1] [2] [3] [5]

★Hartford Court Hotel 48 Christchurch Rd BH1 3PE
☎(0202)21712 & 293682
30rm(7⇨17↱)(3fb)⊬in 2 bedrooms CTV in all bedrooms ® T
S5% sB&B⇨↱£20-£24 dB&B⇨↱£40-£48 ⛿
Lift CTV 25P ⛟ nc10yrs *xmas*
♡ ♖ S5% Bar Lunch £2-£3 Dinner £5-£6 Last dinner 7pm
Credit Cards [1] [3] £

★*Lynden Court* 8 Durley Rd, West Cliff BH2 5JL ☎(0202)23894
Closed Nov-Mar (ex Xmas & New Year)
A pleasant holiday hotel, with garden at rear and bungalow annexe, features attractive public rooms and offers a good range of facilities.
24rm(18⇨6↱)Annexe7rm(7fb) CTV in all bedrooms ®
Lift 20P ♫
Last dinner 7.15pm
Credit Cards [1] [2] [3] [5]

★New Dorchester 64 Lansdowne Rd BH1 1RS ☎(0202)21271
Closed 24 Dec-3 Jan
An attractive Victorian villa with a homely atmosphere provides a well furnished lounge and bedrooms in the modern style. Facilities include a residents' bar with television and a secluded, south-facing garden.
11rm(5⇨) CTV in all bedrooms ® ✗ sB&B£15-£17
sB&B⇨£23-£26 dB&B£28-£32 dB&B⇨£30-£37
11P ⛟ nc12yrs
♡ Bar Lunch £3-£4 Dinner £8-£9 Last dinner 7pm
Credit Cards [1] [2] [3] [5]

★Silver How West Cliff Gardens, West Cliff BH2 5HN
☎(0202)21537
Closed Jan
This small, family-managed hotel is quietly situated, yet convenient for the town centre. It offers pleasant public rooms, well-equipped bedrooms, simple home cooking, friendly staff and a relaxed atmosphere.
22rm(9⇨9↱)(11fb) CTV in all bedrooms ® ✱ S%
sB&B£17-£24 sB&B⇨↱£19-£22 dB&B⇨↱£38-£44 ⛿
12P solarium *xmas*
S% Dinner £5-£8 Last dinner 7pm
Credit Cards [1] [3] £

★Taurus Park 16 Knyveton Rd BH1 3QN ☎(0202)27374
The hotel stands in a quiet, tree-lined avenue. It is run by a friendly Spanish family, who involve themselves totally with the welfare of their guests. Most bedrooms have been refurbished, the food is simple but wholesome and there is evening entertainment on several nights each week during the holiday season. All in all, good value for money.
47rm(9⇨14↱)(4fb) CTV in 23bedrooms ® ✗ ✱
sB&B£17-£22 sB&B⇨↱£19.50-£24.50 dB&B£34-£44
dB&B⇨↱£39-£49 (incl dinner)
Lift CTV 30P games room nc3yrs *xmas*

✕✕Sophisticats 43 Charminster Rd BH8 8UE ☎(0202)291019
In a street of shops about 1.5 miles from the centre of Bournemouth. Booth seating and friendly service create an intimate atmosphere. The à la carte menu has sensibly been extended and is supplemented by daily additions. Local fish and game are delicious, as are some imaginative dishes from the Far East. The menu includes pheasant in red wine with bacon and chipolata, grilled halibut with tarragon and chervil hollandaise and Javanese fillet steak. The vegetables are cooked al dente *to retain their colour and flavour.*
Closed Sun & Mon, 1st 2 wks Jan & last 2 wks Oct
Lunch not served
♔ International V 34 seats Dinner £14-£18alc Last dinner 10pm ⊁

BOURTON-ON-THE-WATER Gloucestershire Map 04 SP12

★★*Chester House Hotel & Motel* Victoria St GL54 2BS (Minotels) ☎Cotswold(0451)20286 FAX (0451) 20471
Closed mid Nov-mid Feb
Some of the rooms are in a converted row of Cotswold stone cottages, the rest are in the main hotel building.
12rm(8⇨4↱)(5fb)1⊞ CTV in all bedrooms ® T
23P
V ♡ Last dinner 9.30pm
Credit Cards [1] [2] [3] [4] [5]

★★Old New Inn High St GL54 2AF ☎Cotswold(0451)20467
Closed 25 Dec
Part 18th-century building with intriguing model village in the garden.
17rm(6⇨1↱)1⊞ CTV in 9bedrooms S10% sB&B£23-£28
sB&B⇨↱fr£28 dB&B£46-£40 dB&B⇨↱£54-£56 ⛿
CTV 25P 6⌂ (£1) ⛟ ❖
V ♡ S10% Lunch £6-£8 Dinner fr£12 Last dinner 8.30pm
Credit Cards [1] [3]

BOVEY TRACEY Devon Map 03 SX87

★★Coombe Cross Coombe Cross TQ13 9EY (Inter)
☎(0626)832476
Comfortable and well appointed traditional country hotel, personally run.
26rm(23⇨1↱)(2fb) CTV in all bedrooms ® T ✱ sB&B£25.95
sB&B⇨↱£29.95 dB&B⇨↱£49 ⛿
☾ CTV 26P ❖
V ♡ ♖ ⊬ Bar Lunch fr£4.95 High tea fr£5 Dinner fr£13.95
Last dinner 8pm
Credit Cards [1] [2] [3] [5]

★★*Edgemoor* Haytor Rd TQ13 9LE ☎(0626)832466
Family-run rural hotel with spacious reception rooms and open fires.
18rm(10⇨)(3fb) CTV in all bedrooms
CTV 45P (charged) ⛟ ❖
♔ French V ♡ ♖ Last dinner 8pm
Credit Cards [1] [2] [3] [5]

BOWMORE

See **Islay, Isle of**

COOMBE CROSS HOTEL AA ★★

Bovey Tracey, South Devon TQ13 9EY
Tel Bovey Tracey (0626) 832476

Ashley Courtenay Recommended
Inter Hotel

A beautiful country house with spectacular views of Dartmoor. Quietly situated on the edge of town yet only 3 minutes from the A38 Exeter to Plymouth road. 23 delightful bedrooms with private bathroom, colour television, direct dial telephones and tea-making facilities. Fully centrally heated, luxuriously furnished and set in its own splendid gardens with many rare and interesting plants and shrubs. Coombe Cross offers the discerning guest every comfort. For those business guests wishing an early departure breakfast served by arrangement. There is also an excellent function room suitable for business meetings and receptions.

★★

Bourton-on-the-Water, Cheltenham, Gloucestershire, GL54 2BU
Telephone: Cotswold (0451) 20286
Fax: 0451 20471

Under personal supervision of the proprietor, Mr Julian Davies. 22 rooms, 21 with private bath or shower, Central heating, Colour TV, Telephone, Radio, Intercom, Tea & Coffee Making facilities in all rooms. Comfortable Lounge and Dining Room. Parking for 25 cars.

Ideal centre for touring picturesque Cotswold villages. Dogs are accepted at the discretion of the management. Licensed restaurant open daily to residents and non-residents.

West Cliff Hall —HOTEL— AA★★

- ★ 46 bedrooms, all with private bath/shower and toilet, colour television, tea-making, direct dial telephone and radio
- ★ Central heating throughout
- ★ Cocktail bar where you can relax and make new friends
- ★ Wide choice of menu with plenty of fresh produce and generous portions
- ★ Dancing to live music three times weekly during the season, and at other popular times
- ★ Free parking, with additional large car park at rear
- ★ Lift
- ★ Families welcome – reduced rates for children
- ★ 100 metres to the Bournemouth International Centre
- ★ Full 4-day Christmas programme

The West Cliff Hall Hotel is a friendly, family-run 2-star hotel in the town centre. With its own car park and central location you are within easy walking distance of the beach, entertainments, shops and Conference Centre.

WEST CLIFF HALL HOTEL
14 Priory Road, Bournemouth, BH2 5DN. Tel: (0202) 299715

BOWNESS ON WINDERMERE

See Windermere

BOX Wiltshire Map 03 ST86

✕✕✕Clos du Roy Box House SN14 9NR ☎Bath(0225)744447 Telex no 831476 FAX (0225) 743971

Chef Philippe Roy and his wife Emma have transplanted their immensely popular restaurant from its tiny premises in Bath to a spacious Georgian mansion on the outskirts of Box, a tiny village lying between Bath and Chippenham. The mansion, completely refurbished, now offers a choice of three dining rooms in which to sample Philippe Roy's imaginative dishes with their delicate sauces. The 'menu surprise' offers good value for money, and the à la carte menu takes full advantage of seasonal ingredients. Dishes such as feuilleté d'asperges, ragôut du marin or noisettes d'agneau au St Jacques are typical of the specialities and many of the herbs and vegetables come from their own kitchen garden.

French **V** 55 seats Last lunch 2.30pm Last dinner 10pm 35P
Credit Cards 1 2 3 4 5

BRACKLESHAM West Sussex Map 04 SZ89

✕Cliffords Cottage Bracklesham Ln PO20 8JA ☎(0243)670250

Small 17th-century cottage restaurant with a cosy atmosphere, serving good, honest cooking of a very good standard.

Closed Tue winter only
Lunch Sun only
Dinner not served Tue & Sun
French **V** 28 seats Bar Lunch £9 Dinner £14&alc Last dinner 9pm 16P nc3yrs
Credit Cards 1 2 3 5

BRACKLEY Northamptonshire Map 04 SP53

★Crown Market Square NN13 5DP (Berni/Chef & Brewer) ☎(0280)702210

Dating back to the 13th century, and originally a private house, this town-centre hotel was for many years a coaching inn. Much of its original character has been retained whilst providing pleasant public areas and modern, well-equipped, comfortable bedrooms.

14⇌ CTV in all bedrooms ® **T** (ex guide dogs) sB&B⇌fr£38.50 dB&B⇌fr£54.50
CTV 20P
Mainly grills **V** Lunch fr£8 Dinner fr£9 Last dinner 10pm
Credit Cards 1 2 3 5

BRADFORD West Yorkshire Map 07 SE31

★★★★61% ***Stakis Norfolk Gardens*** Hall Ings BD1 5SH (Stakis) ☎(0274)734734 Telex no 517573 FAX (0274) 306146

RS 1 Jan

This large, modern hotel stands in the city centre adjoining a multi-storey car park. Accommodation has been updated to a high standard and wedding receptions are a speciality.

126⇌(9fb) in 24 bedrooms CTV in all bedrooms ® **T**
Lift P
V Last dinner 10pm
Credit Cards 1 2 3 5

★★★56% **Novotel Bradford** Merrydale Rd BD4 6SA (3m S adjacent to M606) (Novotel) ☎(0274)683683 Telex no 517312 FAX (0274) 651342

Conveniently situated just off the A606 and only minutes from the M62, this functional modern hotel offers basic but clean accommodation.

132⇌(132fb) CTV in all bedrooms ® **T** ✱ sB⇌£46 dB⇌£46 (room only)
Lift 180P (heated)
English & French **V** Lunch £9.95&alc Dinner £9.95&alc Last dinner mdnt
Credit Cards 1 2 3 4 5

★★★53% **The Victoria** Bridge St BD1 1JX (Trusthouse Forte) ☎(0274)728706 Telex no 517456 FAX (0274) 736358

A typically English hotel adjacent to St George's Hall in the heart of the city. There are spacious public rooms, a fixed price carvery restaurant and friendly staff to serve you.

59rm(53⇌6)(1fb) in 10 bedrooms CTV in all bedrooms ® **T** S% sB⇌£60-£72 dB⇌£79-£85 (room only)
Lift 40P
Mainly grills **V** S% Lunch fr£8.25 Dinner fr£10.75 Last dinner 10pm
Credit Cards 1 2 3 4 5

★★***Dubrovnik*** 3 Oak Av, Manningham BD8 7AQ ☎(0274)543511

A friendly hotel managed by the resident proprietor providing comfortable bedrooms and pleasant service.

20⇌(6fb) CTV in all bedrooms ®
60P
English & Yugoslavian **V** Last dinner 9.30pm
Credit Cards 1 3

✕✕Restaurant Nineteen 19 North Park Rd, Heaton BD9 4NT ☎(0274)492559

An elegant restaurant offering comfort, genteel service and an interesting 4-course menu. Imagination and skill are very evident in the dishes produced – starters include chicken breast stuffed with asparagus, smoked trout mousse with yogurt sauce and home made soup. Main courses may include spring lamb with asparagus mousse, breast of duck, sea bass and veal, while a tempting array of desserts, such as cherry and almond pudding, home-made ice cream and rich chocolate cake, make for a difficult choice.

Closed Sun, Mon, 1 wk after Xmas, 1 wk Jun & 2 wks Aug/Sep
Lunch not served (ex by arrangement only)
English & French 40 seats ✱ Dinner £23-£25 Last dinner 9.30pm 15P nc8yrs
Credit Cards 2 3 5

BRADFORD ON AVON Wiltshire Map 03 ST86

★★★73% **Woolley Grange** Woolley Green BA15 1TX ☎(02216)4705 4773 FAX (02216) 4059

This delightful, 17th-century Cotswold stone house was recently opened as an hotel and is run by the Chapman family with their friendly staff. The house stands in well-kept grounds with open country views that encompass a one-acre kitchen garden that provides vegetables and fruit for the restaurant. Anand Sastry leads the small team in the kitchen producing modern British cuisine; the food is accompanied by a good selection of wines at reasonable prices. Public areas are comfortable and are furnished in a Victorian style whilst bedrooms vary in size and facilities. There is a play area for older children that includes a juke box and table tennis. It adjoins a small nursery with a nanny available from 10am-6pm.

14rm(12⇌2)Annexe1⇌ CTV in all bedrooms **T** ✱ sB&B⇌£67.50-£121.50 dB&B⇌£75-£135
40P (heated) (grass) croquet nc *xmas*

V ✥ ⌂ Lunch £14.50 High tea £5 Dinner £19.50&alc Last dinner 9.30pm
Credit Cards 1 2 3 5

BRAE

See Shetland

BRAEMAR Grampian *Aberdeenshire* Map **15** NO19

★★Braemar Lodge Glenshee Rd AB3 5YQ ☎(03397)41627
Closed Nov & Apr
A granite-built lodge, enjoying splendid Highland views from its two-acre grounds, has been tastefully converted to provide well-appointed bedrooms and delightful public rooms warmed by log fires. The food is worthy of note, and service throughout the hotel is willing and friendly.
8rm(6⌐) CTV in all bedrooms ® ✗ S% sB&B£15-£21.50 dB&B£30-£43 dB&B⌐£37-£55 ⊟
20P 1⌂ ⌗ ❖
V ✥ ⌂ ⊁ Dinner £12.50 Last dinner 8.30pm
Credit Cards 1 3

BRAINTREE Essex Map **05** TL72

★★White Hart Bocking End CM7 6AB (Lansbury)
☎(0376)21401 Telex no 988835 FAX (0376) 552628
This popular inn, a focal point of the town since the 15th century, has recently been refurbished without loss of character or charm. Well-appointed bedrooms are tastefully decorated in Laura Ashley designs, the Beefeater Steakhouse restaurant offers a range of popular dishes, and guests are assured of a warm welcome and friendly atmosphere.
35rm(34⇨1⌐)(4fb)1⊟⊁in 5 bedrooms CTV in all bedrooms ® **T** ✗ (ex guide dogs) sB&B⇨⌐fr£47 dB&B⇨⌐fr£57 ⊟
☾ 40P
☋ Mainly grills **V** ✥ Lunch fr£6alc Dinner fr£9alc Last dinner 10.30pm
Credit Cards 1 2 3 5

BRAITHWAITE Cumbria Map **11** NY22

★★Ivy House CA12 5SY ☎(059682)338
Closed Jan
Nestling in the centre of the village, a charming little hotel, parts of which date back to the 17th century, maintains the character of bygone days in its delightful lounge and in the homely dining room which is reached by open stairs. Run almost in the style of a country house, the hotel offers Cordon Bleu cuisine to complement the fine accommodation.
9rm(7⇨1⌐)2⊟ CTV in all bedrooms ® **T** ✱ sB&B⇨⌐fr£33 dB&B⇨⌐fr£60 (incl dinner)
9P ⌗ nc *xmas*
✥ ⊁ Dinner £12.75 Last dinner 7.30pm
Credit Cards 1 2 3 5

See advertisement on page 149

★★*Middle Ruddings* CA12 5RY ☎(059682)436 Telex no 934999
Closed Jan & Feb
After extensive refurbishment, this is now a very comfortable and well-appointed hotel, quality being the keynote throughout.
13rm(8⇨2⌐)1⊟ CTV in 12bedrooms ® **T** ✗
20P 2⌂ (£1) ⌗ ❖ bowls nc14yrs
☋ English & French ✥ ⌂ ⊁ Last dinner 8.45pm
Credit Cards 1 2 3 5

A rosette is the AA's highest award for quality of food and service in a restaurant.

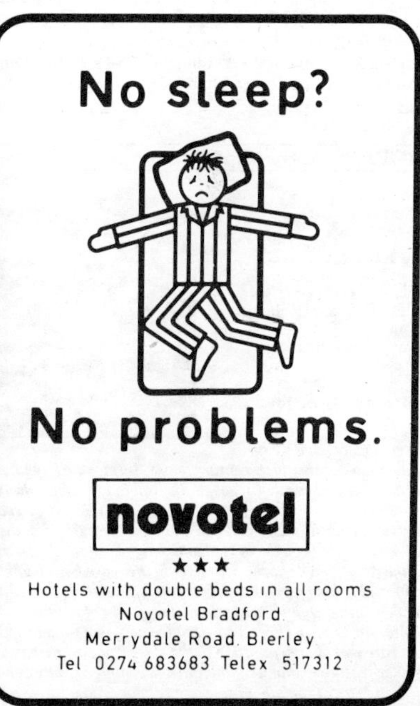

BRAMHALL Greater Manchester Map **07** SJ88

★★★**62% Bramhall Moat House** SK7 2EB (Queens Moat)
☎061-439 8116 Telex no 668464 FAX 061-440 8071
A recently extended and refurbished hotel with well-appointed bedrooms, catering mainly for a business clientele. Very convenient for the city of Manchester and only a short distance from Manchester International Airport.
65⇔↱(3fb) CTV in all bedrooms ® **T** ✗ (ex guide dogs)
sB&B⇔↱£35-£65 dB&B⇔↱£48-£80 ⊟
Lift ☾ 132P sauna gymnasium
♉ English & French **V** ♢ ☐ Lunch £7.50-£9.80&alc Dinner £12.95&alc Last dinner 9.45pm
Credit Cards [1][2][3][5]

BRAMHOPE West Yorkshire Map **08** SE24

★★★**70% Post House** Otley Rd LS16 9JJ (Trusthouse Forte)
☎Leeds(0532)842911 Telex no 556367 FAX (0532) 843451
Comfortable accommodation is complemented by interesting menus in an hotel which enjoys an attractive rural setting whilst still being within easy reach of Leeds and the airport.
130⇔⊁in 30 bedrooms CTV in all bedrooms ® **T** S%
sB⇔£67-£88 dB⇔£91-£99 (room only) ⊟
Lift ☾ 220P ✿ CFA ▭(heated) sauna solarium gymnasium Health and fitness club ♫ *xmas*
♉ French **V** ♢ ☐ ⊁ Lunch fr£10.95&alc Dinner £14.50-£18.95&alc Last dinner 10.15pm
Credit Cards [1][2][3][4][5]

BRAMPTON Cambridgeshire Map **04** TL27

★★**Grange** 115 High St PE18 8TG ☎Huntingdon(0480)59516
This 18th-century property, situated conveniently close to Huntingdon, offers thoughtfully equipped accommodation, some of the rooms being rather compact, but all receiving attentive service from both the committed management and the friendly staff.
9rm(1⇔6↱)(1fb) CTV in all bedrooms ® **T** ✗ ✳ sB&B£25
sB&B⇔↱£32.50-£37.50 dB&B⇔↱£42.50-£49.50
CTV 40P ✿
♉ English & Continental **V** ♢ Lunch £6.95-£8.75&alc Dinner £8.65-£19.15alc Last dinner 10pm
Credit Cards [1][3]

BRAMPTON Cumbria Map **12** NY56

❀★★♔ **FARLAM HALL**

Hallbankgate CA8 2NG (2.75 miles SE A689) (Relais et Châteaux) ☎Hallbankgate (06976)234 & 357
Closed Feb
(Rosette awarded for dinner only)
Do not be deterred by the austere look of this 17th-century house. Inside, the keynotes are comfort and the warm hospitality offered (unobtrusively) by the Quinion and Stevenson families. Over the last 15 years they have transformed the hotel, and many of the bedrooms in particular have been decorated to the highest standards, while all the rooms have charm. Downstairs there are two elegant, comfortable lounges where guests can relax – and place orders for chef Barry Quinion's excellent and good-value table d'hôte. An English cheeseboard, coffee and home-made petits fours are included in addition to the three courses. Fish is a regular feature and among the starters commended by our inspectors are a roulade of sole and salmon with a tarragon dressing, and poached brill en croute. The chief attraction of Farlam Hall, however, remains its honest hospitality, which has few equals and ensures that guests receive friendly, caring attention without intrusion.
13rm(11⇔2↱)1⊟ CTV in all bedrooms **T**
sB&B⇔↱£65-£80 dB&B⇔↱£60-£80 (incl dinner) ⊟
35P ⛟ ✿ croquet nc5yrs
V ♢ ☐ Dinner £20-£21.50 Last dinner 8.30pm
Credit Cards [1][2][3]

★★**Tarn End** Talkin Tarn CA8 1LS (2m S off B6413)
☎(06977)2340
Closed Feb RS Oct-Jan
This friendly, peaceful, family-run hotel on the banks of Talkin Tarn is justifiably proud of the standard of its French haute cuisine, offering à la carte and table d'hôte menus at lunch and dinner. Breakfasts also deserve commendation, and lunchtime bar snacks are available.
6rm(5⇔1↱)(1fb) CTV in all bedrooms ® ✗ (ex guide dogs) ✳
sB&B⇔↱£29 dB&B⇔↱£50 ⊟
70P ⛟ ✿ ♩ rowing *xmas*
♉ French **V** ♢ ☐ Dinner £15.50-£26.40alc Last dinner 9pm
Credit Cards [1][2][3][5] Ⓔ

BRANDON Suffolk Map **05** TL78

★★★**64% Brandon House** High St IP27 0AX
☎Thetford(0842)810171
Combining the beauty of a Grade II listed building with modern facilities, this personally-run small hotel provides comfortable accommodation in spacious rooms and personal attention from a warm and dedicated staff. The good restaurant offers an à la carte menu with some unusual German dishes supplementing the daily table d'hôte selection.
15⇔ CTV in all bedrooms ® **T** ✳ sB&B⇔£42.50
dB&B⇔£56.50 ⊟
☾ 60P ⛟ ✿ nc7yrs
♉ English, French & German **V** ♢ Lunch £10.95&alc Dinner £10.95&alc Last dinner 9.15pm
Credit Cards [1][2][3][5]

★★★**65% Brandon Park Hotel** Brandon Country Park IP27 0SU
☎Thetford(0842)812400 FAX (0842) 813213
This grand hotel, perfectly situated in the beautiful location of Brandon Country Park, offers excellent accommodation in both the original early 17th-century house and in a modern wing. Whether bedrooms are traditional or modern, however, all are extremely well equipped and comfortable. Public areas include an elegant restaurant, a lounge and bar cosily furnished with leather chesterfields, and a good leisure centre with swimming pool.
32⇔↱ CTV in all bedrooms ® **T** ✗ (ex guide dogs) ✳
sB⇔↱£49.50 dB⇔↱£62.50 (room only) ⊟
☾ 60P ✿ ▭(heated) ♪ (hard) sauna solarium gymnasium *xmas*
♉ English, French **V** ♢ ☐ Lunch fr£12.50 Dinner fr£12.50
Credit Cards [1][2][3]

BRANDON Warwickshire Map **04** SP47

★★★ **61% Brandon Hall** Main St CV8 3FW (Trusthouse Forte)
☎Coventry(0203)542571 Telex no 31472 FAX (0203) 544909
Standing in its own wooded grounds in a quaint village, this company hotel has recently been refurbished to offer comfortable accommodation and a range of well-equipped facilities, the most popular among them being squash, snooker and pitch and putt.
60⇔⊁in 6 bedrooms CTV in all bedrooms ® **T** ✳
sB⇔£71-£102 dB⇔£91-£113 (room only) ⊟
☾ 250P ✿ squash snooker pitch & putt ♫ *xmas*
V ♢ ☐ ⊁ Lunch £8.90-£10.95 Dinner £13.50&alc Last dinner 9.30pm
Credit Cards [1][2][3][4][5]

B

BRANKSOME

See Poole

BRANSCOMBE Devon Map **03** SY18

✕✕**Mason's Arms** EX12 3DJ ☎(029780)300 & 301 FAX (029780) 500

The fourteenth-century thatched inn nestles in a valley not far from the sea. The bar, with its slate floor and exposed beams, is built around a central fireplace. Fine food and wine are served in pleasant surroundings by friendly staff.

Lunch not served Mon-Sat

English & French V 45 seats Sunday Lunch £8.50 Dinner £12.50-£28alc Last lunch 2pm Last dinner 9.30pm 45P 22 bedrooms available

Credit Cards [1] [3]

BRANSTON Lincolnshire Map **08** TF06

★★★52% **Moor Lodge** LN4 1HU (Consort)

☎Lincoln(0522)791366 Telex no 56396 FAX (0522) 510720

An interesting hotel offers a variety of accommodation, its newly refurbished bedrooms providing modern facilities and the older ones being more functional. The Parisian theme of the unusually appointed Arnheim Restaurant helps to create a warm and pleasant atmosphere in which to enjoy some fine cooking.

25rm(22⇌3⌐)(3fb) CTV in all bedrooms ® T sB&B⇌⌐£47.50-£54.50 dB&B⇌⌐£62.50-£72.50

CTV 150P ♫ *xmas*

English & French V Lunch fr£10.25&alc High tea fr£6.50 Dinner fr£12.15&alc Last dinner 9.30pm

Credit Cards [1] [2] [3] [4] [5] £

BRAUNTON Devon Map **02** SS43

★★***Poyers Hotel & Restaurant*** Wrafton EX33 2DV ☎(0271)812149

Closed 2 wks Jan

An attractive thatched house standing in its own grounds near the A361 features annexed bedrooms set round a cobbled courtyard; public rooms in the main building include a cosy restaurant offering an à la carte menu of interesting dishes which make good use of fresh produce, and the whole hotel runs smoothly under the personal supervision of a resident proprietor.

Annexe10rm(6⇌4⌐) CTV in all bedrooms ®

20P

English, French, German & Italian

Credit Cards [1] [2] [3]

See advertisement under BARNSTAPLE

BRAY Berkshire Map **04** SU97

✕✕✕✕ **WATERSIDE** Ferry Rd SL6 2AT (Relais et Châteaux)

☎Maidenhead(0628)20691 & 22941 FAX (0628) 784710

Michel Roux's fine restaurant in its wonderful riverside setting continues to provide the highest standards of cuisine. His young chef, Mark Dodson, adheres to the established principles of Roux's French cooking, and although our inspectors have experienced some inconsistencies, there have been flashes of pure brilliance to even the score. The menu and the dishes therein are well balanced, satisfying, and refreshingly understated. A petit flan d'escargots frais en habit vert, with its delicious tarragon soufflé, and a sparkling cassolette d'écrevisses aux tagliatelles sauce Nantua, garnished with tiny, delicate quenelles of chicken, have been particular favourites among the starters, and might be followed by a tender panache d'agneau de lait aux petits legumes à la fleur de thym, or a more robust duo de cotelettes et noisettes de chevreuil with a silky, intense sauce Grand Veneur. A fine French wine list, including clarets from the 1920s, complements the cuisine. Service is attentive and meticulous throughout, from the hot canapés with the pre-dinner drinks to the hand-made chocolates proffered with the coffee.

Closed Mon & 7 wks fr 26 Dec

Lunch not served Tue

Dinner not served Sun (Oct-Etr)

French V 70 seats Last lunch 2pm Last dinner 10pm 25P nc6yrs

Credit Cards [1] [2] [3] [4] [5]

BRECHIN Tayside *Angus* Map **15** NO56

★★**Northern** Clerk St DD9 6AE ☎(03562)2156

RS 1 & 2 Jan

Homely, commercial town centre hotel in 1890 listed building.

17rm(4⇌11⌐) CTV in all bedrooms ® sB&B£19-£28 sB&B⇌⌐£28 dB&B£30 dB&B⇌⌐£36

20P

V Lunch £4.50-£6 High tea £5 Dinner £9.25-£12alc Last dinner 9.30pm

Credit Cards [1] [2] [3] £

BRECON Powys Map **03** SO02

★★**Castle of Brecon** Castle Square LD3 9DB (Consort)

☎(0874)4611 Telex no 57515 Attn 137

Near the town centre with views across the Usk Valley towards the Brecon Beacons. A traditional coaching inn with modern, bedrooms and comfortable public areas. As far as food is concerned, there is an à la carte menu and a good range of meals from the bar.

34⇌⌐Annexe12⌐(3fb)1 CTV in all bedrooms ® T sB&B⇌⌐£32-£35 dB&B⇌⌐£50

▶

30P ❊ *xmas*
V ♈ S10% Lunch £6.50 Dinner £9.50-£15alc Last dinner 9pm
Credit Cards [1] [2] [3] [4] [5] [£]

★★***Nant Ddu Lodge Country House*** Cwm Taf CF48 2HY (Minotels) ☎Merthyr Tydfil(0685)79111 FAX (0685) 89136
(For full entry see Nant-Ddu)

★★**Wellington** The Bulwark LD3 7AD (Inter) ☎(0874)5225
This Georgian hotel in the centre of the town has been totally renovated to provide very comfortable bedrooms, pleasant public rooms and the attractive Dukes coffee shop, bar and bistro. The cobbled courtyard contains a few tempting shops and an intimate wine and food bar.
21⇌(1fb) CTV in all bedrooms ® T ✈ (ex guide dogs) sB&B⇌£30-£35 dB&B⇌£50-£56 ⊟
⊞ ₽ *xmas*
♉ Welsh, English & French V ♈ ♊ ⅟ Lunch £4-£14alc High tea £4-£8alc Dinner £7.50-£10.50&alc Last dinner 10.30pm
Credit Cards [1] [2] [3] [5]

★***Lansdowne*** 39 The Watton LD3 7EG ☎(0874)3321
This small, personally-run hotel combines character with charm and friendly service. Recent upgrading has provided comfortable bedrooms with modern private facilities.
11rm(1⇌5🚿)(2fb) CTV in all bedrooms ®
CTV 10P ⛟ ❊ pony trekking
♉ English & French V ♈ ♊ ⅟ Last dinner 9.30pm
Credit Cards [1] [2] [3] [5]

BRENDON Devon Map 03 SS74

★★***Stag Hunters Inn*** EX35 6PS (Minotels) ☎(05987)222
Closed Jan-mid Mar
Pleasant, privately owned inn, in this valley village in the heart of Exmoor.
20rm(7⇌2🚿)(2fb)2⊠ CTV in 9bedrooms ®
CTV 50P ⛟ ❊
♈ ♊ Last dinner 8pm
Credit Cards [1] [2] [3] [5]

BRENT KNOLL Somerset Map 03 ST35

★★**Battleborough Grange Country** Bristol Rd TA9 4HJ (Exec Hotel) ☎(0278)760208
This attractive, detached hotel is set in its own grounds overlooking the Somerset countryside. Décor is pleasant throughout and the hotel provides modern bedrooms and attentive service.
18rm(8⇌6🚿)4⊠ CTV in all bedrooms ® T ✈ sB&B£25-£30 sB&B⇌🚿£36-£38 dB&B£32-£36 dB&B⇌🚿£38-£54 ⊟
CTV 60P ❊ nc8yrs *xmas*
♉ English & French V ♈ ♊ Lunch £7.50-£26alc Dinner £7.50-£26alc Last dinner 9pm
Credit Cards [1] [2] [3] [5] [£]

BRENTWOOD Essex Map 05 TQ59

★★★67% **Post House** Brook St CM14 5NF (Trusthouse Forte) ☎(0277)260260 Telex no 995379 FAX (0277) 264264
Parts of this hotel, once the home of Catherine of Aragon, date from 1520, the panelled lounge and raftered dining room being particularly impressive. The chef prepares imaginative dishes for various set-price and à la carte menus. Bedrooms, mostly in the modern, chalet style, are set around a garden.
120⇌⅟in 30 bedrooms CTV in all bedrooms ® T S% sB⇌£74-£80 dB⇌£84-£90 (room only) ⊟
Lift ☾ 148P ❊ CFA ⊡(heated) sauna solarium gymnasium health & fitness club *xmas*
♉ International V ♈ ♊ ⅟ S% Lunch £9.75-£12.50&alc Dinner £15.50&alc Last dinner 10pm
Credit Cards [1] [2] [3] [4] [5]

BRETBY Derbyshire Map 07 SK22

★★★64% **Stanhope Arms** Ashby Rd East DE15 0PU ☎Burton upon Trent(0283)217954 FAX (0283) 226199
The hotel stands by the busy A50 road, but peace can be found at the back of the hotel where there are well-maintained, terraced gardens for guests to relax in. The bedrooms are warm and comfortable, the bar is friendly and the restaurant has been elegantly furnished.
28rm(27⇌1🚿)1⊠⅟in 5 bedrooms CTV in all bedrooms ® T ✈ ✳ sB&B⇌🚿£22-£50 dB&B⇌🚿£44-£65 ⊟
☾ 220P ❊ sauna solarium gymnasium *xmas*
♉ Continental V ♈ ♊ Lunch £5.95-£6.95&alc Dinner £12.25&alc Last dinner 10pm
Credit Cards [1] [2] [3] [5]

BRIDGEND Mid Glamorgan Map 03 SS97

★★★67% **Coed-y-Mwstwr** Coychurch CF35 6AF ☎(0656)860621 FAX (0656) 863122
Set in seven acres of beautiful woodland, this Victorian mansion has been carefully modernised to provide comfortable facilities throughout. Bedrooms are all pleasantly furnished, well equipped and attractively decorated, whilst the popular, oak-panelled dining room offers a good choice of skilfully prepared dishes on its four-course menu.
28rm(27⇌1🚿) CTV in all bedrooms T ✈ (ex guide dogs) sB&B⇌🚿£70-£140
dB&B⇌🚿£90-£140 Continental breakfast ⊟
Lift ☾ 60P ❊ ⛆(heated) ℘ (hard) snooker ♫ nc7yrs
♉ French V ♈ ♊ Lunch £12.95-£15.95 Dinner £18.95-£21.95 Last dinner 10pm
Credit Cards [1] [2] [3] [5] [£]

★★★60% **Heronston** Ewenny CF35 5AW (2m S B4265) ☎(0656)68811 Telex no 498232 FAX (0656) 767391
Modern popular businessman's hotel with comfortable bedrooms, friendly service and good leisure facilities.
76⇌🚿(4fb) CTV in all bedrooms ® T ✳ sB&B⇌🚿£46-£62 dB&B⇌🚿£58-£77 ⊟
Lift ☾ CTV 175P CFA ⊡(heated) ⛆(heated) snooker sauna solarium turkish bath jacuzzi
♉ Welsh & French V ♈ ♊ S10% Lunch £10-£15&alc Dinner £10&alc Last dinner 10pm
Credit Cards [1] [2] [3] [4] [5] [£]

★★**Court Colman** Pen-y-Fai CF31 4NG ☎Aberkenfig(0656)720212
This imposing house, originally a gentleman's country residence, is set amidst woodland and lawns. Inside, there are panelled walls and several beautiful fireplaces. Bedrooms are spacious, public rooms are comfortable and elegant.
26rm(14⇌12🚿)(7fb)2⊠ CTV in all bedrooms ® T ✳ sB&B⇌🚿£34-£39 dB&B⇌🚿£46-£48 ⊟
150P ❊ solarium
♈ ♊ Lunch fr£9.45&alc High tea fr£1.95 Dinner fr£9.45&alc Last dinner 9.45pm
Credit Cards [1] [2] [3] [5]

★★**Wyndham** Dunraven Place CF31 1JE ☎(0656)652080 & 57431 FAX (0656) 766438
Brightly decorated, well-equipped bedrooms, a pleasant restaurant and busy bars are among the attractions of this town-centre hotel, parts of which date back to the 17th century.
28rm(25⇌)1⊠ CTV in all bedrooms ® T ✳ sB&B⇌£32.70 dB&B£39 dB&B⇌£48.50 ⊟
☾ CTV ₽
♉ English & French V ♈ ⅟ Lunch £4-£10&alc Dinner £4-£10alc Last dinner 10pm
Credit Cards [1] [2] [3] [5] [£]

⌂**TraveLodge** CF32 9RW (Trusthouse Forte) ☎(0656)59218
(For full entry see Sarn Park Motorway Service Area)

BRIDGE OF ALLAN Central *Stirlingshire* Map **11** NS79

★★★58% **Royal** Henderson St FK9 4HG ☎(0786)832284
FAX 0786 834377
A commercial and tourist hotel right at the centre of town. The general improvement programme is making good progress: the bedrooms and smart restaurant, where work is completed, are evidence of the high standards the proprietors aim to acheive throughout the hotel.
32rm(28⇔4♠)(2fb) CTV in all bedrooms ® T ✱ sB&B⇔♠£41-£45 dB&B⇔♠£65-£75 ⊟
Lift ☾ 60P *xmas*
♀ Scottish & French V ♦ ☕ Lunch £5.95-£9.95&alc High tea £4.95-£7.50 Dinner £12.50-£13.95&alc Last dinner 9.30pm
Credit Cards 1 2 3 5

See advertisement under STIRLING

✕✕**Kipling's Restaurant** Mine Rd FK9 4DT
☎Stirling(0786)833617
Closed Sun, Mon, 24 Dec-3 Jan & 1st 2 wks Aug
V 68 seats ✱ Lunch £7.50-£8&alc Last lunch 2pm Last dinner 9.30pm 20P
Credit Cards 1 2 3

BRIDGE OF CALLY Tayside *Perthshire* Map **15** NO15

★**Bridge of Cally** PH10 7JJ ☎(025086)231
Closed Nov
This small hotel stands on the banks of the River Ardle and enjoys good views of the Perthshire countryside. Bedrooms and public rooms offer relaxed comfort and the dining room is low-ceilinged and attractive.
9rm(3⇔3♠) ✗ (ex guide dogs) ✱ sB&B£21-£23.50 sB&B⇔♠£21-£23.50 dB&B£37-£41 dB&B⇔♠£39-£43 ⊟
CTV 40P ⊞ ✿ ♩
V ♦ ☕
Credit Cards 1 3 5

BRIDGNORTH Shropshire Map **07** SO79

★★**Falcon** St John St, Lowtown WV15 6AG ☎(07462)3134
FAX (0746) 765401
Old coaching inn in Lowtown, close to River Severn.
15rm(5⇔7♠)(3fb) CTV in all bedrooms ® T ✱ sB&Bfr£25 sB&B⇔♠£32-£37 dB&B£37-£39 dB&B⇔♠£42-£45 ⊟
CTV 200P
♀ English & French V ♦ ☕ Lunch £6.50-£12.50alc Dinner £11.50&alc Last dinner 9.30pm
Credit Cards 1 2 3 4 5 £

See advertisement on page 153

★★**Parlors Hall Hotel** Mill St WV15 5AL ☎(0746)761931
FAX (0746) 767058
Parts of this fine, mainly Georgian building date from the 15th century, when it was owned by Richard Parlor, whose name it still bears. Set on the one-way system in Lower Town, a short walk from the riverside park and bridge, it offers well-equpped bedrooms and public areas, the latter having some fine fireplaces and excellent carved panelling; the restaurant enjoys a particularly pleasant outlook over an enclosed garden, dominated by a large willow tree, and the food served here is sound, although not particularly adventurous.
16rm(10⇔2♠)(1fb)2⊞ CTV in all bedrooms ® T ✗ (ex guide dogs) sB&B£20 sB&B⇔♠£40 dB&B⇔♠£45
24P ♫ *xmas*
♀ European V ♦ ☕ Lunch £6.50&alc Dinner £7.25&alc Last dinner 10pm
Credit Cards 1 3

Book as early as possible for busy holiday periods.

B

★Croft St Mary's St WV16 6DW ☎(0746)767155
A well-run family hotel has been fully extended and modernised to provide bedrooms with up-to-date facilities and an intimate dining room which still retains its character; menus feature a good range of dishes, making full use of seasonal vegetables.
12rm(4⇨6↱)(3fb) CTV in all bedrooms **T** sB&B£18-£20 sB&B⇨↱£24-£34 dB&B⇨↱£39-£42 ⊟
CTV 🅿̸ ⛟ ⌂
V ♁ ☕ Dinner fr£9.95&alc Last dinner 9pm
Credit Cards [1] [2] [3]

★Whitburn Grange 35 Salop St WV16 5BH ☎(0746)766786
A small Victorian coaching inn close to the city centre. The bedrooms are comfortable and well-equipped, while substantial home-cooked meals are available in the attractive restaurant.
9rm(2⇨2↱)Annexe6rm(1⇨)(3fb)1⊞ CTV in all bedrooms ® **T** sB&Bfr£17 sB&B⇨↱fr£26 dB&Bfr£32 dB&B⇨↱fr£38
CTV 9P
♁ ☕
Credit Cards [1] [2] [3]

BRIDGWATER Somerset Map **03** ST33

★★★66% Walnut Tree Inn North Petherton TA6 6QA (North Petherton, 3m S A38) (Best Western)
☎North Petherton(0278)662255 Telex no 46529
FAX (0278) 663946
A warm welcome and cosy atmosphere are the hallmarks of this busy, commercial High Street hotel. Once a coaching inn, it has now been extended to offer a range of bedrooms that includes those in the luxury class as well as less elaborate chalet accommodation. Similarly, guests can choose between the formal à la carte menus of the dining room, simpler meals served in the Cottage Restaurant, and bar snacks.
28⇨(2fb)1⊞ CTV in all bedrooms ® **T** ⚔ (ex guide dogs) sB&B⇨£40-£65 dB&B⇨£55-£85 ⊟
☾ 70P solarium ⌂
☋ Mainly grills **V** ♁ ☕ Lunch £6.50-£12alc Dinner £6.50-£12alc Last dinner 10pm
Credit Cards [1] [2] [3] [5] (£)

★★Friarn Court 37 St Mary St TA6 3LX ☎(0278)452859
FAX (0278) 452988
Close to the town centre and recently converted to provide quality bedrooms with modern facilities – all is new and in good order, though the public rooms are small. The proprietor runs the hotel personally with warm hospitality. An all day menu is served in the restaurant.
12⇨(2fb)1⊞ CTV in all bedrooms ® **T** ⚔ ✱
sB&B⇨£32.50-£53.50
dB&B⇨£45.50-£59.50 Continental breakfast ⊟
☾ 12P ♫ ⌂ *xmas*
☋ English & French **V** ♁ Lunch £5.30-£6.70&alc Dinner £7.50&alc Last dinner 9.30pm
Credit Cards [1] [2] [3] [5]

BRIDLINGTON Humberside Map **08** TA16

★★★66% Expanse North Marine Dr YO15 2LS ☎(0262)675347
FAX (0262) 604928
Comfortable, well-appointed bedrooms, a wealth of cosy lounges and particularly friendly service are the attractions of this large sea-front hotel.
48rm(43⇨2↱)(4fb) CTV in all bedrooms ® **T** ⚔ (ex guide dogs) sB&B£24 sB&B⇨↱£35-£37.50 dB&B£48 dB&B⇨↱£56-£61 ⊟
Lift ☾ 15P 15🚗(£1) ⛟ *xmas*
☋ English & French **V** ♁ ☕ Lunch fr£5.75 Dinner £9.50-£13&alc Last dinner 9pm
Credit Cards [1] [2] [3] [5]

★★Monarch South Marine Dr YO15 3JJ (Consort)
☎(0262)674447 Telex no 57515 FAX (0262) 604928
Closed 18 Dec-7 Jan
The multi-storey building overlooking South Bay provides smartly attractive public rooms and spacious, well-fitted bedrooms.
40rm(33⇨)(5fb) CTV in all bedrooms ® **T** sB&Bfr£27.50 sB&B⇨fr£35 dB&Bfr£42 dB&B⇨fr£55 ⊟
Lift ☾ CTV 10P ⌂
☋ English & French **V** ♁ ⚔ Lunch £5.75-£12 Dinner £9.50-£16.50&alc Last dinner 8.30pm
Credit Cards [1] [2] [3] [5]

★★New Revelstoke 1-3 Flamborough Rd YO15 2HY
☎(0262)672362
A hotel of pleasing proportions close to the town's facilities and North Sands. It is managed by the resident proprietors who are assisted by their family and the keen, young staff. Bedrooms are well-appointed and generally spacious.
25rm(17⇨6↱)(5fb) CTV in all bedrooms ® **T** ⚔ ✱ S%
sB&B£30-£35 sB&B⇨↱£30-£35 dB&B£43-£50
dB&B⇨↱£43-£50 ⊟
9P
☋ English & French **V** ♁ ☕ Lunch £3.75-£6.95&alc Dinner £8.50-£10&alc Last dinner 8.30pm
Credit Cards [1] [2] [3] [5] (£)

See advertisement on page 155

BRIDPORT Dorset Map **03** SY49

★★★61% Haddon House West Bay DT6 4EL (2m S off B3157 Weymouth rd) ☎(0308)23626 & 25323
The atmosphere is relaxed and informal at this Regency-style hotel with its comfortable lounge and spacious, simply furnished but well equipped bedrooms. An attractive dining room with panelled walls and a large fireplace offers a varied menu of dishes which make skilfull use of good produce, local fish being a speciality.
▶

13rm(11⇌2♠)(2fb) CTV in all bedrooms ® T ✱
sB&B⇌♠£32 dB&B⇌♠£37-£50 ⊟
CTV 70P 4⌂ ✲ *xmas*
♔ Lunch £6.50-£8.95 High tea fr£1.50 Dinner £13.95 Last dinner 9pm
Credit Cards 1 2 3 5

★★*Bull* 34 East St DT6 3LF ☎(0308)22878
Closed 24-26 Dec
A 16th-century coaching inn, family-run to provide a friendly, informal atmosphere and personal attention. Accommodation is simple but comfortable.
22rm(5⇌3♠)(1fb) CTV in 16bedrooms ® ✈
40P 2⌂ snooker
French ♔
Credit Cards 1 3

★★**Eype's Mouth Country** Eype DT6 6AL (2m SW)
☎(0308)23300
Standing just 5 minutes from the beach and coastal footpath, this well cared for quality hotel offers spotlessly clean, well equipped bedrooms and a ballroom, dining room and grill room overlooking the sea. Pleasant staff create a friendly, informal atmosphere throughout.
18rm(8⇌9♠)1⊞ CTV in all bedrooms ® T ✈
sB&B⇌♠fr£43.50 dB&B⇌♠fr£62.50 (incl dinner) ⊟
55P ♫
English & French V ♔ ♕ Lunch £6.25&alc Dinner £8.50 Last dinner 9pm
Credit Cards 1 3 £

★★**Roundham House** Roundham Gardens, West Bay Rd DT6 4BD (Exec Hotel) ☎(0308)22753 Telex no 417182 FAX (0308) 421145
Closed Dec-Jan RS Nov
Commanding views of the river valley and the coast beyond from its elevated position, this solidly built Edwardian stone house has been upgraded to provide comfortable accommodation. Its restaurant offers a good value 5-course dinner based on local produce, which is complemented by friendly service.
8rm(4⇌3♠)(2fb) CTV in all bedrooms ® T ✈ ✱
sB&B⇌♠£25-£29 dB&B⇌♠£35-£42.50 ⊟
12P ✲
European ♔ ♕ ⅀ Lunch £3.95-£5.50 Dinner £9.75-£11.25 Last dinner 8.30pm
Credit Cards 1 2 3 5 £

★**Bridport Arms** West Bay DT6 4EN (2m S off B3157 Weymouth rd) ☎(0308)22994
This old, thatched hotel is pervaded by a warm, friendly atmosphere which makes it a pleasant place to stay, although the accommodation is very simple and the services limited. The dining room specialises in grills.
8rm(1⇌5♠)(2fb) ® sB&B£19.50-£25 sB&B⇌♠£20.50-£26 dB&B£35-£50 dB&B⇌♠£38-£52 ⊟
CTV 10P 4⌂
V ♔ Lunch £5.95-£7.50 Dinner £8.50-£12alc Last dinner 8.45pm
Credit Cards 1 3 £

BRIGHOUSE West Yorkshire Map **07** SE12

★★★★62% **Forte Hotel** Clifton Village HD6 4HW (Trusthouse Forte) ☎(0484)400400 Telex no 518204 FAX (0484) 400068
A new hotel built of York stone to blend in with the environment. It lies in an elevated position just off the A644 close to Junction 25 of the M62. Bedrooms are comfortable and well-appointed. There are extensive conference facilities as well as a health and fitness club. The hotel is in a good position for both business people and tourists.
94⇌♠(30fb)⅀in 23 bedrooms CTV in all bedrooms ® T ✱
S% sB⇌♠fr£63 dB⇌♠fr£78 (room only) ⊟
☾ 155P ✲ ⊡(heated) sauna solarium gymnasium croquet *xmas*
British & French V ♔ ♕ ⅀ S% Lunch £8.50-£18&alc High tea £5.50 Dinner £14.50-£18.75&alc Last dinner 10pm
Credit Cards 1 2 3 4 5

BRIGHTON & HOVE East Sussex Map **04** TQ30

See **Town Plan Section**
See also **Rottingdean**

★★★61% **Courtlands** 19-27 The Drive BN3 3JE
☎(0273)731055 Telex no 87574 FAX (0273) 28295
Accommodation is currently being refurbished and upgraded to provide bright, well-equipped bedrooms, a covered swimming pool with terrace, and conference rooms, but with no loss of old-fashioned excellence of service.
53rm(45⇌8♠)Annexe5⇌(3fb) CTV in all bedrooms ® T ✱
sB&B⇌♠£49.50-£69 dB&B⇌♠£69-£85 ⊟
Lift ☾ CTV 26P ✲ CFA ⊡(heated) solarium ♧ *xmas*
International V ♔ ♕ ⅀ Lunch £10.50-£12.50&alc Dinner £12.50-£14.50 Last dinner 9.30pm
Credit Cards 1 2 3 5 £

★★**Alexandra** 42 Brunswick Ter BN3 1HA (Minotels)
☎Brighton(0273)202722 Telex no 877579 FAX (0273) 204018
This popular, terraced hotel on the sea front offers a choice of modern, well-equipped bedrooms, a spacious bar and a small basement restaurant; facilities include a conference room and health club.
63rm(61⇌2♠)(6fb) CTV in all bedrooms ® T S10%
sB&B⇌♠£49.50-£55 dB&B⇌♠£68-£75 ⊟
Lift ☾ ₽ CFA sauna solarium spa bath *xmas*
English & French V ♔ ♕ S10% Lunch £8.50-£10&alc Dinner £10.75-£12&alc Last dinner 9.30pm
Credit Cards 1 2 3 5 £

★★**St Catherines Lodge** Seafront, Kingsway BN3 2RZ (Inter)
☎Brighton(0273)778181 Telex no 877073 FAX (0273) 774949
The hotel has generous and comfortable public rooms and provides extensive and friendly service. Bedrooms vary, but some are furnished particularly tastefully.
51rm(40⇌)(3fb)2⊞ CTV in all bedrooms ® T ✱ sB&B£40 sB&B⇌£55 dB&B£60 dB&B⇌fr£80 ⊟
Lift ☾ CTV 5P 4⌂ (£4) CFA games room *xmas*
European V ♔ ♕ Lunch £3.90-£6.95alc Dinner £13.50&alc Last dinner 9pm
Credit Cards 1 2 3 5 £

See advertisement on page 157

★★**Whitehaven** 34 Wilbury Rd BN3 3JP
☎Brighton(0273)778355 Telex no 877159 FAX (0273) 731177
Conveniently situated in the commercial centre, this hotel has been tastefully modernised to provide spacious, well-equipped bedrooms, quality public areas and a restaurant serving well-cooked, imaginative dishes, all areas being attentively served by friendly staff.
17rm(11⇌6♠)(2fb)1⊞ CTV in all bedrooms ® T ✈
sB&B⇌♠£45-£49 dB&B⇌♠£62-£65 ⊟
₽ solarium nc8yrs
French V ♔ ♕ Lunch £11.50-£14.50 Dinner £12.50-£14.50 Last dinner 9.30pm
Credit Cards 1 2 3 5 £

✕✕✕**Eaton Garden** Eaton Gardens BN3 3TN ☎(0273)738921 Telex no 877247 FAX (0273) 779075
A well appointed restaurant, conveniently situated in the commercial centre of Hove, maintains sound traditional values, offering skilled, attentive service; John Stevens – chef here for the past 22 years – prepares an enjoyable range of English and the more familiar Continental dishes, their flavours enhanced with robust sauces.
Dinner not served Sun
Lunch by arrangement

International **V** 100 seats Lunch fr£12&alc Dinner £15-£17&alc Last lunch 2.15pm Last dinner 9.45pm 40P
Credit Cards 1 2 3 5

✕Le Grandgousier 15 Western St BN1 2PG ☎Brighton(0273)772005

A small but well-established French restaurant, run by Lewis Harris. The 6 course fixed price menu, which includes a half bottle of French table wine, is especially good value, and you can eat as little or as much as you like.

Closed Sun & 23 Dec-3 Jan
Lunch not served Sat
French 36 seats S15% Lunch fr£12 Dinner fr£12 Last lunch 1.30pm Last dinner 9.30pm ~~P~~ nc5yrs
Credit Cards 1 2 3

✕Haywards 51/52 North St BN1 1RN ☎(0273)24261
Closed Sun
English & Continental 70 seats Last dinner 11pm
Credit Cards 1 2 3

✕*Orchard* 33 Western St BN1 2PG ☎Brighton(0273)776618

Chef patron Ian, and Jane Whyte co-ordinate their skills in personally running this small, cosy and attractively furnished restaurant. It features a chef's Fish of the Day as well as a choice of prix fix courses which might include scallops in white wine au gratin, coarse duck liver paté, roast rack of lamb with cassis, supreme of wild salmon and a good selection of desserts and cheeses. Service is particularly attentive and helpful, under the supervision of Jane Whyte. Some interesting wines are available to accompany a meal which represents good value for money.

Closed Sun, Mon & 23-27 Dec
Lunch not served
English & French 24 seats Last dinner 10pm ~~P~~
Credit Cards 1 2 3 4 5

B

BRIMFIELD Hereford & Worcester Map **07** SO56

✕Poppies Roebuck Inn SY8 4LN ☏(058472)230

Carole Evans' cooking has increased and improved in its range, quality and presentation. Fish and local meats continue to be favourites here, while vegetarian dishes like Spinich soufflé and Lentil and mushroom paté have earned themselves a regular place on the menu. The wine list has also increased in range, although prices remain modest.

Closed Mon, 1 wk Oct & 2 wks Feb
Dinner not served Sun
V 40 seats Lunch £15-£24alc Dinner £7.50-£12.50alc Last lunch 2pm Last dinner 10pm 30P ⚡
Credit Cards 1 3

BRISTOL Avon Map **03** ST57

See **Town Plan Section**

★★★★57% Holiday Inn Lower Castle St BS1 3AD (Holiday Inns) ☏(0272)294281 Telex no 449720 FAX (0272) 225838

A large, busy hotel close to the city centre complements spacious, well-equippedaccommodation by extensive conference and function facilities. Guests can relax in a heated swimming pool, solarium or gymnasium.

284⇨↱(138fb)⚡in 78 bedrooms CTV in all bedrooms **T** ✳
sB&B⇨↱£79-£85 dB&B⇨↱£94-£100 ⊟
Lift ☾ ⊞ 20⌂ CFA ⊡(heated) sauna solarium gymnasium
xmas
♉ International **V** ✿ ⊥ ⚡ Lunch £14.95-£15.65 High tea £4.75-£5.25 Dinner £15.65-£16.25&alc Last dinner 10.45pm
Credit Cards 1 2 3 4 5

★★★68% *Avon Gorge* Sion Hill, Clifton BS8 4LD (Mount Charlotte) ☏(0272)738955 Telex no 444237

A large, comfortable hotel situated close to the Clifton Suspension Bridge commands fine views of the Avon Gorge to its rear; recently refurbished bedrooms provide modern, well-equipped accommodation.

76⇨(6fb)2⊞⚡in 2 bedrooms CTV in all bedrooms ® **T**
Lift ☾ P ⊞ ✲ CFA ♫
♉ English & French **V** ✿ ⊥ Last dinner 10.30pm
Credit Cards 1 2 3 5

★★★64% Crest Filton Rd, Hambrook BS16 1QX (6m NE off A4174) (Crest) ☏(0272)564242 Telex no 449376 FAX (0272) 569735

Set in sixteen acres, with easy access to the M4, M5 and M32 motorways, the modern hotel offers comfortable, well-equipped accommodation which includes a new wing of upgraded executive rooms. Among its facilities are the Crest Business Centre, an all-day coffee shop, a leisure club and a well-appointed restaurant serving a wide choice of skilfully-prepared dishes – all complementedby genuine, caring hospitality on the part of the staff.

197⇨↱(6fb)⚡in 43 bedrooms CTV in all bedrooms ® **T**
sB⇨↱£81-£96 dB⇨↱£93-£108 (room only) ⊟
Lift ☾ 400P ✲ CFA ⊡(heated) sauna solarium gymnasium ♫
xmas
V ✿ ⊥ ⚡ Lunch £12.95-£14.95&alc Dinner fr£15.95&alc Last dinner 10pm
Credit Cards 1 2 3 5

★★★68% Henbury Lodge Station Road, Henbury BS10 7QQ (4.5m NW of City centre off B4055) ☏(0272)502615

Built in 1706 and situated in what is now a residential suburb of Bristol, this lovely old hotel provides comfortable, well-equipped accommodation, being family-run in an informally friendly and relaxing manner in keeping with the country house hotel tradition. Its position makes it ideal for business people and tourists alike, providing easy access to both the M5 motorway and the city centre.

10rm(3⇨7↱)Annexe6rm(2⇨4↱)(4fb)⚡in 6 bedrooms CTV in all bedrooms ® **T** sB&B⇨↱£54.50-£62.50 dB&B⇨↱£64.50-£72.50 ⊟

▶

Forget City Centre Problems

ALVESTON HOUSE HOTEL ★★★

15 Minutes Bristol City Centre.
Easy, Quick Access M4/M5/M32.
Attractive, well appointed rooms all en suite.
Recommended Restaurant.
Conference Centre 100.
Ample Car Parking.
Inclusive Short Break Packages.
Please request our Brochure

ALVESTON HOUSE HOTEL
Alveston, Thornbury, Bristol BS12 2LJ
Tel: 0454 415050 Telex: 449212 Fax: 0454 415425

AHHA

St. Catherine's Lodge Hotel

Visit Royal Pavilion, Lanes Antique Shops, Devils Dyke, Arundel Castle, Bluebell Railway, Goodwood House.

AN INTER HOTEL

Kingsway, Hove, Sussex BN3 2RZ
Brighton (0273) 778181
Telex: 877073
Fax: (0273) 774949

Well established seafront hotel with fine regency features. 52 rooms most with private bathroom all with direct dial telephone and colour TV. Four-poster beds and family rooms.
Excellent Restaurant, cocktail bar and games room.
Opposite King Alfred Leisure Centre with water slides, swimming pools and ten pin bowling.
AA★★ ETB

B

24P ✽ sauna solarium gymnasium *xmas*
☋ English & Continental V ♈ ☐ ⊬ Lunch £3.30-£14.20alc
Credit Cards [1] [2] [3] [5]

★★★66% **Redwood Lodge & Country Club** Beggar Bush Ln, Failand BS8 3TG (2m W of Clifton Bridge on B3129)
☎(0272)393901 Telex no 444348 FAX (0272) 392104
Set in its own grounds on the B3129 one mile west of the Clifton Suspension Bridge, this large, popular hotel provides easy access both to the city and to the motorway network. Well-equipped accommodation, combined with extensive function/conference facilities and a vast sports and leisure complex, attracts a wide range of customers from business and private sector alike.
112⇨(4fb) CTV in all bedrooms ® T ✖ (ex guide dogs)
sB&B⇨£80-£85 dB&B⇨£90-£95 ☰
(1000P ✽ CFA ▭(heated) ⛱ ℘ (hard) squash snooker sauna solarium gymnasium badminton cinema (wknds only) ♫ ⌂
xmas
☋ English & French V ♈ ☐ ⊬ Lunch £11-£13 High tea £2.50-£4 Dinner £15-£17.50&alc Last dinner 10pm
Credit Cards [1] [2] [3] [5] (£)

★★★60% **St Vincent Rocks** Sion Hill, Clifton BS8 4BB (Trusthouse Forte) ☎(0272)739251 Telex no 444932
FAX (0272) 238139
Housed in a fine example of Regency architecture, this comfortable, friendly hotel looks directly onto Brunel's famous Suspension Bridge and the convivial Bridge Restaurant itself makes a pleasant location for lunch or dinner.
46rm(39⇨7♪)⊬in 7 bedrooms CTV in all bedrooms ® T S%
sB⇨♪£67-£81 dB⇨♪£78-£90 (room only) ☰
(CTV 18P CFA *xmas*
V ♈ ☐ ⊬ Lunch £8.50-£10.95&alc Dinner £13-£16.95&alc Last dinner 9.30pm
Credit Cards [1] [2] [3] [4] [5]

★★★71% **Stakis Leisure Lodge** Woodlands Ln, Patchway BS12 4JF (Stakis) ☎Almondsbury(0454)201144 Telex no 445774
FAX (0454) 612022
Opened in the summer of 1988, this was one of the first of a chain of Leisure Lodges to be built in England by the company. Its convenient siting, close to junction 16 of the M5, makes it popular with guests engaged on both business andpleasure – as do also its good-sized, well-equipped bedrooms and leisure facilities.
112⇨(35fb)⊬in 28 bedrooms CTV in all bedrooms ® T
sB⇨£67-£73 dB⇨£84-£87 (room only) ☰
(⊞ 132P ▭(heated) sauna solarium gymnasium ♫ *xmas*
V ♈ ☐ ⊬ Lunch £8.50-£9.50 Dinner £12.50-£13.50 Last dinner 10pm
Credit Cards [1] [2] [3] [5] (£)

★★★52% **Unicorn** Prince St BS1 4QF (Rank) ☎(0272)230333
Telex no 44315 FAX (0272) 230300
Modern city centre hotel with its own muli-storey car park.
194⇨♪(29fb) CTV in all bedrooms ® T ✱ sB⇨♪£45-£58
dB⇨♪£65 (room only) ☰
Lift (400⌂ CFA *xmas*
☋ International V ♈ ☐ Lunch £9.50&alc Dinner £12.75&alc Last dinner 10pm
Credit Cards [1] [2] [3] [4] [5]

★★**Clifton** St Pauls Rd, Clifton BS8 1LX ☎(0272)736882
Telex no 449075 FAX (0272) 211594
This busy and popular hotel is situated conveniently close to the city centre and University. It provides well-equipped accommodation suitable for both commercial and tourist visitors. 'Racks' restaurant serves imaginative dishes in 1930s-style surroundings. There is also an appealing cellar wine bar.
64rm(4⇨36♪)(5fb)⊬in 8 bedrooms CTV in all bedrooms ® T
✱ sB&B£26.50 sB&B⇨♪£38.50 dB&B£37.50
dB&B⇨♪£57 ☰
Lift (12P
☋ English & French V ♈ ☐ Lunch £9-£15alc Dinner £9-£15alc Last dinner 10.30pm
Credit Cards [1] [2] [3] [5] (£)

★★***Parkside*** 470 Bath Rd, Brislington BS4 3HQ ☎(0272)711461
FAX 715507
30rm(9⇨1♪)1⊟ CTV in all bedrooms ® T
(⊞ 250P ✽ snooker
V ♈ ☐ Last dinner 10.30pm
Credit Cards [1] [3]

See advertisement on page 161

★★**Rodney Hotel** Rodney Place, Clifton BS8 4HY
☎(0272)735422 Telex no 449075 FAX (0272) 211594
Standing close to the famous Suspension Bridge, with good access to the city centre, this stone-built terraced property has recently been restored to a high standard. Bedrooms are of good quality, modern and well equipped, whilst the pleasant public areas, though restricted in size, are equally sound. A short, but imaginative à la carte menu provides a choice of well-cooked dishes based onfresh produce, and an enthusiastic young staff gives good service.
31⇨♪⊬in 2 bedrooms CTV in all bedrooms ® T
sB&B⇨♪£49-£53 dB&B⇨♪£68-£72 ☰
(P
V ♈ ☐ Lunch £9.75 Dinner £11.25&alc Last dinner 10pm
Credit Cards [1] [2] [3] [5]

See advertisement on page 161

✕✕***Barbizon*** 43-45 Corn St BS1 9HT ☎(0272)262658
This stylish addition to Bristol's restaurants stands at the heart of the city and provides classical surrounds with its marble floor, scrolled ceilings and quality appointments. Imaginative menus are matched by friendly, conscientious service.
Closed Sun & 3 wks Aug
Lunch not served Sat

▶

The Cross Hands Hotel

Old Sodbury, Bristol BS17 6RJ ★★
Telephone: Chipping Sodbury (0454) 313000

Charming old posting house set in extensive gardens. Only 1½ miles from Junction 18 M4 and within 15 minutes of Bristol Centre. 24 rooms with en suite bath/shower, CTV, telephone, radio, hairdryer, trouser press and tea/coffee making facilities. Two large restaurants provide à la carte and Grill cuisine along with extensive wine lists. Two inviting bars and three lounges. Intimate meeting room available for up to 20 people. Parking for 200 cars.

Thornbury Castle ★★★

This beautiful 16th century Castle, built by Edward Stafford, 3rd Duke of Buckingham, was once owned by Henry VIII, and is, in fact, the only Tudor castle in England to be operated as an hotel.
Over the years we have won many accolades due to the luxurious standard of accommodations offered to our guests, together with our award-winning restaurant, our vineyard, and Tudor garden.

Thornbury, Avon, BS12 1HH
Telephone: (0454) 418511
Telex: 449986 Castle G. Fax: (0454) 416188
A Pride of Britain Hotel

Redwood Lodge ★★★
Hotel & Country Club

Beggar Bush Lane, Failand, Bristol BS8 3TG.
Tel: Bristol (0272) 393901 Telex: 444348 Fax: (0272) 392104

112 first class bedrooms, all with private bathroom, direct-dial telephone, remote control colour television, free in-house video, tea/coffee making facilities, trouser press and hairdryer. Most rooms overlook the extensive landscaped grounds.

Situated just 3 miles from Bristol on the edge of the Ashton Park Estate, Redwood Lodge is set in beautiful wooded countryside close to the famous Clifton Suspension Bridge. Easy access from the motorway with Junction 19 of the M5 just 4 miles away.

An impressive Leisure Club is one of the most comprehensive in the UK. The Conference Centre and function suites can accommodate up to 300 for a meeting and 250 for banquets.

7 Tennis Courts

17 Snooker Tables

Sauna

6 Badminton Courts

Multi-Gym

Table Tennis

Cinema

Indoor Pool

2 Outdoor Pools

Solarium

12 Squash Courts

French **V** 80 seats Last lunch 2.15pm Last dinner 10.30pm
nc10 yrs
Credit Cards 1 2 3 5

✕✕Restaurant Danton 2 Upper Byron Place, The Triangle, Clifton BS8 1JY ☎(0272)268314
A restaurant in the intimate tradition, the Danton provides attentive yet unobtrusive service and a French cuisine based on fresh ingredients of the best quality.
Closed Sun, Etr wk & 25-31 Dec
Lunch not served Sat
Dinner not served Tue
French **V** 32 seats ✱ Lunch £15-£18.50alc Dinner £15-£18.50alc Last lunch 2pm Last dinner 11pm
Credit Cards 1 2 3 5

✕✕Orient Rendezvous 95 Queens Rd, Clifton BS8 1LW ☎(0272)745202 & 745231
A most attractive and comfortable Chinese restaurant specialising in authentic Cantonese and Pekinese dishes. The menu is complemented by a well-chosen wine list.
Closed 25-26 Dec
Chinese **V** 150 seats Last lunch 2.25pm Last dinner 11.30pm 25P
Credit Cards 1 2 3 5

✕✕Restaurant Lettonie 9 Druid Hill, Stoke Bishop BS9 1EW (2m NW) ☎(0272)686456
Martin and Sian Blunos are the new owners of this small pleasant restaurant. Both are involved in the kitchen, whilst the front of the house is well looked after by the smartly dressed, attentive and helpful french waiter. The restaurant continues to produce interesting dishes which can be chosen from the short but well balanced price menu. The cooking is of the modern French style, using excellent raw ingredients, with light sauces, with good overall presentation. Try the Raviolis d'Aiglefin Fume A La Crème de Sauternes, Mousse de Carrots au Fumet de Truffles, Noisette d'Agneau aux Grosses d'Ail, Pave aux deux Chocolates or Sauce Caramel. There is also a small selection of well kept french cheeses, excellent coffee with home-made petits fours, and a well balanced wine list which we understand is to be upgraded.
Closed Sun, Mon, Xmas, BH's & last 2 wks Aug
French 24 seats ✱ Lunch £11.50-£17.95 Dinner £17.95 Last lunch 2pm Last dinner 10pm
Credit Cards 1 2 3

✕Bistro Twenty One 21 Cotham Rd South, Kingsdown BS6 5TZ ☎(0272)421744
This popular, crowded bistro, its tables covered with oilcloth, stands in a Victorian residential district. Cuisine is French in style, and interesting dishes are accompanied by good fresh vegetables and complimented by a selective wine list, all served in an informal atmosphere.
Closed Sun & Xmas-New Year
Lunch not served Sat
French **V** 40 seats ✱ Lunch £8-£10.50alc Dinner £8-£10.50alc Last lunch 2.30pm Last dinner 11.30pm
Credit Cards 1 3

✕Boubolina's Restaurant 9 Portland St, Clifton BS8 4JA ☎(0272)731192 & 742833
Closed Sun
Greek **V** 60 seats ✱ Lunch £9.70-£14alc Dinner £9.70-£14alc Last lunch 2.30pm Last dinner 11.30pm
Credit Cards 1 2 3

✕Howard's 1A-2A Avon Crescent, Hotwells BS1 6XQ ☎(0272)262921
Eating is an enjoyable experience in this simple but genial reataurant, located by the floating harbour in the city centre. There is a quality menu supplemented by daily specials. The food is very well cooked and presented, making use of fresh ingredients; the wine list is small but adequate. Staff are friendly and helpful and the owner is always close at hand.
Closed Sun, 1 wk Xmas & 2 wks summer
Lunch not served
English & French **V** 65 seats Dinner £13-£17alc Last dinner 11pm
Credit Cards 1 3

✕*Raj Tandoori* 35 King St BS1 4DZ ☎(0272)291132
Cosily tucked away under Bristol's famous King Street and adjacent to the Old Vic Theatre, this cellar restaurant promotes interesting Indian cuisine and in particular caters for the ethnic vegetarian.
Closed 25 Dec
English & Indian **V** 85 seats Last dinner mdnt
Credit Cards 1 2 3 5

BRIXHAM Devon Map 03 SX95

★★★61% Quayside King St TQ5 9TJ (Inter) ☎(08045)55751 Telex no 336682 FAX (0803) 882733
Closed Xmas & New Year
A beautifully-situated hotel, overlooking the harbour and commanding views across the bay to Torquay, offers compact bedrooms with good facilities and charming public areas; interesting menus make good use of the local fish supply. Car parking is available five hundred yards from the hotel.
30rm(27⇌3♪)2 CTV in all bedrooms ® **T** sB&B⇌♪fr£32 dB&B⇌♪fr£61
37P sailing shooting
English & French **V** Lunch fr£6.75 High tea fr£2.50 Dinner fr£12.50&alc Last dinner 9.45pm
Credit Cards 1 2 3 5

★Smugglers Haunt Church St TQ5 8HH ☎(08045)3050 & 59416
Located near the harbour, this 400-year-old, stone-built inn provides comfortable bedrooms, friendly public areas and extensive menus featuring the best local fish available.
14rm(4⇌)Annexe2rm(2fb) ® ✱ sB&B£23 sB&B⇌£28 dB&B£35 dB&B⇌£39
CTV *xmas*
English & French **V** Lunch £3.65-£6&alc Dinner £6.50-£16.50alc Last dinner 10pm
Credit Cards 1 2 3 5

✕*Elizabethan* 8 Middle St TQ5 8ER ☎(08045)3722
Near the harbour the bow windows and continental awning of the Elizabethan make it stand out from the surrounding shops. The cosy interior in the Tudor style and the menu offers traditional dishes based on local produce; the service is friendly and attentive.
Closed Mon
30 seats Last dinner 10pm nc10 yrs

BROADFORD

See Skye, Isle of

BROADSTAIRS Kent Map 05 TR36

★★★65% Castle Keep Joss Gap Rd, Kingsgate CT10 3PQ (Best Western) ☎Thanet(0843)65222 FAX (0843) 65225
This hotel occupies an impressive site, with good coastal views from the cliff top on which it stands. There is a choice of modern bedrooms and mini-suites, while public areas are open plan with pretty décor. The patio and swimming pool to the rear of the hotel present the opportunity for pleasant relaxation in good weather.
29rm(26⇌3♪)(3fb) CTV in all bedrooms ® **T** ✱ sB&B⇌♪fr£55 dB&B⇌♪fr£74
CTV 100P (heated) *xmas*
English, French & Italian Lunch £12&alc Dinner £16&alc Last dinner 10pm
Credit Cards 1 2 3 4 5

See advertisement on page 163

B

★★Castlemere Western Esplanade CT10 1TD 1683
☎Thanet(0843)61566
This comfortable, well-maintained hotel stands in quiet surroundings facing the sea. Some bedrooms have been redecorated to offer pretty décor and co-ordinating fabrics. Others are plainer, but all provide good facilities, andthroughout the hotel the atmosphere is friendly and pleasant.
37rm(24⇒6↱)(5fb)2⊞ CTV in all bedrooms ® T S%
sB&B£25-£28 sB&B⇒↱£29-£32 dB&B£46-£58
dB&B⇒↱£54-£66 ⊟
☾CTV 30P ⊞ ✲ *xmas*
♀ English & French ✧ ⊈ S% Bar Lunch £1.15-£2.15 Dinner fr£10.50 Last dinner 7.45pm
Credit Cards 1 3

★★Royal Albion Albion St CT10 1LO (Consort)
☎Thanet(0843)68071 Telex no 965761 FAX (0843) 61509
A cosy family-run hotel with well equipped accomodation and friendly service. Many rooms overlook the harbour and bay.
19rm(17⇒2↱)(3fb) CTV in all bedrooms ® T ✗ (ex guide dogs) ✳ sB&B⇒↱£45-£50 dB&B⇒↱£55-£65 ⊟
☾CTV 20P 2⌂ ⌂ *xmas*
♀ French V ✧ ⊈ S10% Lunch fr£9.50&alc Dinner fr£12.75&alc Last dinner 9.30pm
Credit Cards 1 2 3 5 £

BROADWAY Hereford & Worcester Map **04** SP03

See also **Buckland**

★★★★LYGON ARMS

WR12 7DU (Prestige)
☎(0386)852255
Telex no 338260
FAX (0386) 858611

Improvements are continuing at this lovely old Cotswolds inn, so that even more luxury is provided to meet the demands of a particularly international clientele. Bedrooms have been carefully modernised and nearly all now have excellent fabrics and soft furnishings of extremely high quality. The large majority of rooms are spacious, whether in the old part of the building, with its heavy timbers, exposed stone and open fireplaces, or in the more modern wings with their enclosed gardens. Business interests are also catered for, withexcellent conference facilities created from former garages, but careful management ensures that no disruption is caused to guests looking for peace and tranquility. That is assured, even though the inn is at the centre of one of the busiest Cotswolds towns. Our inspectors have reported a greater stability in the restaurant, where manager Isy Salcedo and chef Clive Howe have put together a team of mostly young staff, who are caring and attentive at all times. That attitude is a feature throughout the hotel, under the dedicated management of Kirk Ritchie.
61⇒5⊞ CTV in all bedrooms T sB&B⇒£80-£105
dB&B⇒£122-£175 Continental breakfast ⊟
☾CTV 100P 4⌂ (£7.50 per night) ⊞ ✲ CFA ℘ (hard) *xmas*
♀ International ✧ ⊈ Lunch £14.75-£37.50 Dinner £22.50-£37.50 Last dinner 9.45pm
Credit Cards 1 2 3 5

For key to symbols see the inside front cover.

★★★60% Broadway The Green WR12 7AB ☎(0386)852401
Set on The Green in the centre of the village this sixteenth century coaching house boasting lovely gardens, a courtyard and a putting green offers a warm welcome from a competent team of friendly staff.
13rm(10⇒1↱)Annexe11rm(9⇒2↱)(2fb)1⊞ CTV in all bedrooms ® T ✗ S5% sB&B£28-£32 sB&B⇒↱£33-£35
dB&B£56-£60 dB&B⇒↱£60-£66 ⊟
30P ⊞ ✲ putting green *xmas*
♀ English & French V ✧ ⊈ S5% Lunch £10.50 Dinner £13.95&alc Last dinner 9.25pm
Credit Cards 1 2 3 5 £

★★★65% Dormy House Willersey Hill WR12 7LF (2m E off A44 in Gloucestershire) ☎(0386)852711 Telex no 338275 FAX (0386) 858636
Closed 25 & 26 Dec
This charming house sits high above the vale, on the outskirts of Broadway, surrounded by beautiful scenery. In its conversion to a hotel, the old house has lost none of its charm and character, which are supplemented by fairly traditional service and good food.
26rm(16⇒10↱)Annexe23⇒(3fb)2⊞ CTV in all bedrooms ® T sB&B⇒↱£49-£65 dB&B⇒↱£98-£115 ⊟
☾80P ⊞ CFA
♀ English & French V ✧ ⊈ Lunch fr£16&alc Dinner fr£24&alc Last dinner 10pm
Credit Cards 1 2 3 5

★★ Collin House Collin Ln WR12 7PB
☎(0386)858354 & 852544
Closed 24-27 Dec

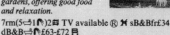

Small, well-restored 16th-century hotel in spacious gardens, offering good food and relaxation.
7rm(5⇒1↱)2⊞ TV available ® ✗ sB&Bfr£34
dB&B⇒↱£63-£72 ⊟
CTV 35P ⊞ ✲ ⌂ croquet *xmas*
V Lunch £13-£15 Dinner £14-£16alc Last dinner 9pm
Credit Cards 1 3

✕✕✕Hunter's Lodge High St WR12 7DT ☎(0386)853247
A typical, Cotswold-stone town house with an attractive rear garden is set back from the High Street and almost hidden by a stone wall. The restaurant's wholesome cuisine enhances rather than masks the flavours of the good fresh produce on which it is based, and guests can relax either in the comfortable lounge with its big, open fire, or in the compact but well-equipped beamed bar. Service is friendly throughout the hotel.
Closed Mon, 1st 2 wks Feb & 1st 2 wks Aug
Dinner not served Sun
♀ English & French V 50 seats ✳ Lunch fr£10&alc Dinner £18-£25alc Last lunch 2pm Last dinner 9.45pm 20P nc8yrs
Credit Cards 1 2 3 5

BROCKENHURST Hampshire Map **04** SU20

★★★68% Carey's Manor Lyndhurst Rd SO4 7RH
☎Lymington(0590)23551 FAX (0590) 22799
Modern bedrooms in a skilfully extended wing of this hotel contrast with the traditional style of those in the 'main' house; lounge and restaurant facilitie are good, whilst provision for leisure includes a supervised gym and the attention of a resident physiotherapist. Service is friendly and helpful throughout.

80⇨4⊟⊬in 22 bedrooms CTV in all bedrooms ® T S%
sB&B⇨£69-£79 dB&B⇨£89-£109 ⊟
☾180P ⊞ ✲ ⊡(heated) sauna solarium gymnasium jacuzzi steam room beauty therapist ♫ *xmas*
♉ English & French V ♉ ⊬ S% Lunch £10-£15&alc Dinner £20-£30&alc Last dinner 10pm
Credit Cards 1 2 3 5

★★★60% Forest Park Rhinefield Rd SO4 7ZG (Forestdale)
☎Lymington(0590)22844 Telex no 47572 FAX (0590) 23948
A pretty roadside hotel on the outskirts of Brockenhurst. Most bedrooms have recently been refurbished and are ideally equipped to suit both leisure and business guests. Cuisine is straightforward and the service is relaxed.
38rm(37⇨1♠)(5fb)3⊟⊬in 3 bedrooms CTV in all bedrooms ® T ✳ sB&B⇨♠fr£52.50 dB&B⇨♠fr£60 ⊟
☾80P ✲ ⩯(heated) ♁ (hard) U sauna solarium pool table ♫ *xmas*
♉ English & French V ♉ ⊻ ⊬ Lunch £6.45 High tea £3.45 Dinner £7.75-£19.65alc Last dinner 10pm
Credit Cards 1 2 3 4 5

★★★59% Balmer Lawn Lyndhurst Rd SO42 7ZB (Hilton)
☎Lymington(0590)23116 Telex no 477649 FAX (0590) 23864
This former hunting lodge, well set back from the busy main road, is now a popular conference hotel offering accommodation in a variety of styles (including some Gold Star rooms) and extensive indoor and outdoor leisure facilities.
58⇨(3fb)⊬in 18 bedrooms CTV in all bedrooms ® T ✳
sB&B⇨£70-£85 dB&B⇨£95-£115 ⊟
Lift ☾90P ✲ CFA ⊡(heated) ⩯(heated) ♁ (hard) squash sauna gymnasium *xmas*
V ♉ ⊻ ⊬ Lunch fr£10&alc High tea fr£5 Dinner fr£15&alc Last dinner 8.45pm
Credit Cards 1 2 3 4 5

B

★★The Cottage Hotel Sway Rd SO42 7SH
☎Lymington(0590)22296
A cosy cottage hotel run personally by the resident proprietors. There is a small restaurant, a beamed open-plan lounge and a choice of modern bedrooms, some of which have excellent bathrooms. Service is friendly and helpful and there is good car parking.
6rm(4⇨2♠) CTV in all bedrooms ® ✱ ✳ sB&B⇨♠£36-£40 dB&B⇨♠£52-£56 ⊟
11P ✲ nc16yrs *xmas*
🍷 English & French **V** ♡ ☕ Lunch £3.50-£7alc High tea £2-£4alc Dinner £10-£16alc Last dinner 9.30pm
Credit Cards 1 3

★★Watersplash The Rise SO42 7ZP ☎Lymington(0590)22344
Standing in its own well-tended gardens, a Victorian house has been extended to create a happy and relaxed family-run hotel with upgraded bar and bedrooms, most popular with holidaymakers.
23rm(20⇨3♠)(6fb)1⊞ CTV in all bedrooms ® ✳ sB&B⇨♠£37-£39 dB&B⇨♠£52-£56 ⊟
CTV 25P 4🚗 (£1.50 per night) ✲ ⛆(heated) *xmas*
🍷 English & Continental **V** ♡ ☕ ⚟ Lunch £10-£15 High tea £2-£4 Dinner £13.95-£15.95 Last dinner 8pm
Credit Cards 1 3 £

★★Whitley Ridge Restaurant Country House
Beaulieu Rd SO4 7QL
☎Lymington (0590)22354 & 22463

You can quite often see a small herd of fallow deer in the area of the New Forest surrounding an eighteenth century Royal hunting Lodge which today offers individually styled, well-equipped bedrooms and a restaurant whose cuisine exhibits a skill and flair that makes it popular with residents and locals alike.
11rm(7⇨4♠)1⊞ CTV in all bedrooms ® **T** S%
sB&B⇨♠£44-£50 dB&B⇨♠£61-£69 ⊟
CTV 30P ✲ 🎾 (hard)
🍷 English & French **V** ♡ ☕ Lunch £8.50-£9 Dinner £14.50-£15&alc Last dinner 9pm
Credit Cards 1 3

★*Cloud* Meerut Rd SO4 7DJ ☎Lymington(0590)22165 & 22254
Closed 29 Dec-14 Jan
A pleasant, old-fashioned, family-run hotel with good lounge accommodation, comfortable bedrooms and good home cooking.
19rm(5fb)
CTV 20P 2🚗 (£1.25 per night) ⊞
V ♡ ☕ Last dinner 8pm

⊛✕✕Le Poussin 57-59 Brookley Rd SO42 7RB
☎Lymington(0590)23063
(Rosette awarded for dinner only)
Hidden behind double-fronted shop windows at the heart of a New Forest village, this pretty restaurant offers a haven of peace in which you can relax to enjoy delicious food efficiently served by professional French waiters. Simple table d'hote lunches represent good value for money, while a short a la carte dinner menu includes a set 'gastronomique' and features such delicacies as Timbale of Smoked Salmon, Roast Monkfish with Tomatoes and Herbs, Crepinette of Veal and Le Grand Dessert du Poisson (a collection of five small portions to experience).
Closed Mon (ex private parties), 3 wks Jan & 1 wk Jun
Dinner not served Sun (ex BH's)
🍷 British & French **V** 35 seats Last lunch 1.45pm Last dinner 9.45pm 2P 2 bedrooms available ⚟
Credit Cards 1 3 4

BRODICK Strathclyde Map **10** NS03

★★Auchrannie Country House KA27 8BZ ☎(0770)2234 & 2235
A modernised and extended Victorian sandstone mansion – former home of the Dowager Duchess of Hamilton – that stands in 10 acres of tree-studded grounds. A good array of facilities in the bedrooms ensures comfort, and the public rooms retain much of their original charm. The Garden Restaurant boasts varied menus, with an emphasis on local produce, and seafood features strongly.
12⇨(1fb) CTV in all bedrooms ® **T** ✱ sB&B⇨£18.50-£44.50 dB&B⇨£37-£75 ⊟
30P ⊞ ✲ *xmas*
🍷 Scottish & French **V** ♡ ☕ Lunch £6.25-£9.50alc High tea fr£4.50alc Dinner £12-£14.50&alc Last dinner 10pm
Credit Cards 1 3 £

BROMBOROUGH Merseyside Map **07** SJ38

★★★62% Cromwell High St L62 7HZ (Lansbury) ☎051-334 2917 Telex no 628225 FAX 051-346 1175
Situated in the town centre, this hotel offers particularly well-appointed bedrooms and good food in its Cromwell restaurant. Service is friendly.
31⇨(3fb)1⊞ CTV in all bedrooms ® **T** sB&B⇨fr£52 dB&B⇨fr£62 ⊟
☾ 110P sauna solarium gymnasium
🍷 English, French & Italian **V** ♡ ☕ Lunch £6.95-£7.50&alc Dinner £12.50-£13.75&alc Last dinner 10pm
Credit Cards 1 2 3 5

BROME Suffolk Map **05** TM17

★★Brome Grange IP23 8AP (on A140) ☎Eye(0379)870456 FAX (0379) 870921
Public areas of this hotel are situated in a roadside inn and include a small cosy bar and restaurant. The chalet-style annexe bedrooms to the rear offer basic accommodation.
Annexe22⇨♠ CTV in all bedrooms ® **T** ✳
sB&B⇨♠£35-£40 dB&B⇨♠£48-£53
CTV 100P ✲ *xmas*
🍷 English & French **V** ♡ ☕ Lunch fr£10.50 Dinner fr£10.50 Last dinner 9.30pm
Credit Cards 1 2 3 5

★★*Oaksmere* IP23 8AJ
☎Eye(0379)870326

Enchanting Tudor/Victorian country house in 20 acres of parkland with fine gardens.

5rm(1⇨4♠)1⊞ CTV in all bedrooms ®
100P ✲

V ♆ Last dinner 9.30pm
Credit Cards [1] [2] [3] [5]

BROMLEY Greater London

See **LONDON plan 5***F2*(page 413)**Telephone codes are due to change on 6th May 1990. See page 421.**

★★★ 54% **Bromley Court** Bromley Hill BR1 4JD (Consort)
☎01-464 5011 Telex no 896310 FAX 01-460 0899
Modernised commercial hotel with informal atmosphere and good lounges.
122⇌(5fb) CTV in all bedrooms ® T ✗ (ex guide dogs) ✱
sB&B⇌fr£64 dB&B⇌fr£86
Lift ☾ ▦ CTV 100P ✿ CFA ♫ *xmas*
English & French V ♆ ✂
Credit Cards [1] [2] [3] [5]

BROMPTON-BY-SAWDON North Yorkshire Map **08** SE98

✕**Brompton Forge** YO13 9DP
☎Scarborough(0723)85409
On the A170 a few miles west of Scarborough, stands a pleasant small restaurant where the table d'hôte menu offers memorable value for money, particularly since the portions are so generous – though varying from it can increase the cost significantly. Good use is made of east coast seafoods in the tantalising choice of starters and main courses, whilst the sticky toffee pudding is particularly worthy of note among the desserts.
Closed Mon & 2 wks Feb

▶

B

Lunch not served Tue, Fri & Sat
Dinner not served Sun
English & French V 70 seats ✱ Lunch fr£8&alc Dinner fr£15&alc Last lunch 1.15pm Last dinner 9pm 20P

BROMSGROVE Hereford & Worcester Map **07** SO97

★★★58% Perry Hall Kidderminster Rd B61 7JN (Embassy)
☎(0527)579976 Telex no 8813387 FAX (0527)575998
A former home of poet A E Houseman, the hotel has added modern extensions. It is popular with businessmen.
55⇌♠ CTV in all bedrooms ® T sB&B⇌♠£55-£65 dB&B⇌♠£65-£85
120P ✼ CFA *xmas*
English & French V Lunch fr£9.75&alc Dinner fr£9.75&alc Last dinner 9.45pm
Credit Cards 1 2 3 4 5

✕✕✕Grafton Manor Grafton Ln B61 7HA ☎(0527)579007 FAX (0527) 575221
A long private drive leads to this grand and historic manor house, now owned and run by the Morris family. John Morris produces an imaginative 4-course menu, which changes frequently and makes full use of home-grown herbs. The cooking is in French country style, while the good cheese selection is English. The wine list is extensive and well chosen, and service is polite and attentive.
Lunch not served Sat
V 45 seats ✱ Lunch £10.50-£17.90 Dinner £24.50 Last lunch 1.45pm Last dinner 9pm 50P nc7yrs 9 bedrooms available
Credit Cards 1 2 3 5

BROOK (near Cadnam) Hampshire Map **04** SU21

★★*Bell Inn* SO43 7HE ☎Southampton(0703)812214
Closed 9 Jan-25 Feb
A pleasant inn on the edge of the New Forest. It is run in conjunction with one of the two adjacent golf courses, and free use of this course is offered to residents. A la carte and table d'hôte menus are served in the restaurant, but the bar features a central servery where you can choose from a good variety of bar meals.
12rm(8⇌)(3fb) CTV in all bedrooms ®
150P ✼ 18
English & French Last dinner 9.30pm
Credit Cards 1 2 3 5

BRORA Highland *Sutherland* Map **14** NC90

★★★58% Links Golf Rd KW9 6QS (Best Western)
☎(0408)21225 Telex no 75242
Standing beside the golf course and enjoying fine sea views, the holiday hotel provides relaxing public rooms and bedrooms with traditional comforts.
22⇌(2fb) CTV in all bedrooms ® T sB&B⇌£35-£39 dB&B⇌£65-£72
55P ✼ 18 *xmas*
International V Lunch £7-£12alc High tea £5-£10alc Dinner £13.50-£13.75 Last dinner 9pm
Credit Cards 1 2 3 4 5 £

★★*Royal Marine* Golf Rd KW9 6QS ☎(0408)21252
Telex no 76165
The public rooms of this hotel still retain the atmosphere of its days as a stately home.
11rm(9⇌1♠)(1fb)1 CTV in all bedrooms ® T
CTV 30P 6 ✼ (heated) 18 snooker ice curling rink in season
Last dinner 9pm
Credit Cards 1 2 3 5

BROUGH Cumbria Map **12** NY71

★★*Castle* Main St CA7 4AX ☎(09304)252
This hotel has recently undergone refurbishment, and offers a good standard of accommodation with well-equipped bedrooms and comfortable public areas.
7⇌ CTV in all bedrooms ® T
CTV 60P
Mainly grills Last dinner 9.30pm
Credit Cards 1 3

BROUGHTON-IN-FURNESS Cumbria Map **07** SD28

★★Eccle Riggs Foxfield Rd LA20 6BN
☎Broughton in Furness(0229)716398 & 716780
This Victorian mansion sits in parkland 1 mile south of the village. Popular with commercial and business travellers it has very well-equipped bedrooms of varying size and standard.
13rm(10⇌)(5fb) CTV in all bedrooms ® sB&B£31-£33 sB&B⇌£36-£38 dB&B£48-£55 dB&B⇌£58-£62
120P ✼ (heated) 9 sauna solarium clay pigeon shooting *xmas*
English & French V Bar Lunch £5-£10alc Dinner £9-£10&alc Last dinner 9pm
Credit Cards 1 2 3 5 £

★*Old King's Head* Station Rd LA20 6HJ
☎Broughton in Furness(06576)293
Old white-washed village inn.
5rm(1♠)(1fb) CTV in all bedrooms ®
50P ✼
Last dinner 9pm

BROXTED Essex Map **05** TL52

❀★★★79% Whitehall Church End CM6 2BZ (Pride of Britain)
☎Bishops Stortford(0279)850603 FAX (0279) 850385
Closed 26-30 Dec
(Rosette awarded for dinner only)
The accent is on informality and comfort at this beautiful old manor house, which stands in well-tended gardens. A place of character, it is charmingly decorated and furnished throughout, from the beamed dining room and restful drawing room to the very well-equipped bedrooms. Owners, Mr & Mrs Keane create a most relaxing atmosphere in which to put aside the stresses of everyday life, and the skilfuul chef is their daughter, Paula, who produces fresh, English cuisine of a high quality.
11⇌ CTV in all bedrooms T (ex guide dogs) ✱ sB&B⇌£60-£75 dB&B⇌£80-£95
35P 2 ✼ (hard) nc5yrs
French V Lunch £16.50 Dinner £27.50 Last dinner 9.30pm
Credit Cards 1 2 3 5

BROXTON Cheshire Map **07** SJ45

★★Broxton Hall Country House CH3 9JS ☎(082925)321
A seventeenth-century black and white building is now a well-furnished and comfortable hotel run by the resident owners.
10⇌(1fb)1 in 1 bedroom CTV in all bedrooms ® T ✱ sB&B⇌£35-£45 dB&B⇌£55-£75
50P ✼ nc12yrs
International V Lunch £12-£14 Dinner £14-£16 Last dinner 9.30pm
Credit Cards 1 3 £

B

BRUTON Somerset Map **03** ST63

✕✕**Clair de Lune** 2-4 High St BA10 0EQ ☎(0749)813395

An attractive restaurant on the corner of the main street in Bruton with hanging baskets and tubs of flowers outside. There is an elegant bar lounge to enjoy a pre-dinner drink whilst choosing from the imaginative menu which includes chicken supreme on a bed of spinach with nutmeg and pine kernels, Scotch fillet of beef with a wild mushroom water ice, all carefully prepared by chef/proprietor Thomas Stewart while his wife and her small team of staff provide attentive service in the beamed restaurant.

Closed Mon, Xmas/New Year
Lunch not served Tues-Sat
Dinner not served Sun
French, English 35 seats ✱ Sunday Lunch £10 Dinner £15.75 Last dinner 9.45pm
Credit Cards 1

✕**Truffles** 95 High St BA10 0AR ☎(0749)812255

A small, quality restaurant run by a husband and wife team features a stone-walled dining room with a fine fireplace, warm-coloured soft furnishings and well-dressed tables. The fixed price menu offers five choices, dishes being skilfully prepared from a variety of top-quality ingredients, and polite – though unhurried – service is provided by cheerful staff. You are advised to make a reservation, as the establishment has a strong local following.

Closed Mon, 1 wk Jan & 1st 2 wks Sep
Lunch not served Tue
Dinner not served Sun
French V 20 seats Lunch £10.50 Dinner £15.95 Last lunch 2pm Last dinner 10.30pm nc5yrs

For key to symbols see the inside front cover.

B

BUCKDEN North Yorkshire Map **07** SD97

★***Buck Inn*** BD23 5JA ☎Kettlewell(075676)227
Charming Dales inn set amid beautiful scenery offering a warm, friendly welcome.
11⌐(2fb) CTV in all bedrooms ® **T**
CTV 36P
Last dinner 9pm
Credit Cards 1 3 £

BUCKHURST HILL Essex London plan 5 F5 (page)

★★**The Roebuck** North End IG9 5QY (Trusthouse Forte) ☎01-505 4636 FAX 01-504 7826
Standing beside Epping Forest, the hotel contains small, elegant public rooms and well-equipped bedrooms.
29⇌in 5 bedrooms CTV in all bedrooms ® **T** S%
sB⇌£64-£67 dB⇌£70-£86 (room only)
45P *xmas*
V S% Lunch £11-£11.75&alc Dinner £13.50&alc Last dinner 9.30pm
Credit Cards 1 2 3 4 5

BUCKIE Grampian *Banffshire* Map **15** NJ46

★★**Cluny** 2 High St AB5 1AL ☎(0542)32922
Closed 1-2 Jan
Situated on a corner site in the town centre, this Victorian commercial hotel offers simple accommodation in clean well-equipped bedrooms and smartly decorated public areas which include a first-floor lounge bar with views out to sea.
10rm(8⇌2⌐)Annexe4rm(1fb) CTV in 10bedrooms ® **T**
sB&B⇌⌐£16-£21 dB&B⇌⌐£32-£36
16P
Scottish & French Lunch £4-£5 High tea £4.25-£7.50 Dinner £7-£13alc Last dinner 8pm
Credit Cards 1 2 3 5 £

BUCKINGHAM Buckinghamshire Map **04** SP63

★★**White Hart** Market Square MK18 1NL (Trusthouse Forte) ☎(0280)815151 FAX (0280) 822215
18th century traditional hotel with comfortable modernised bedrooms.
19rm(18⇌1⌐)(1fb)in 2 bedrooms CTV in all bedrooms ® **T**
✱ sB⇌⌐£52-£58 dB⇌⌐£59-£65 (room only)
30P *xmas*
V S% Lunch £7.50-£12.95 High tea £1.50-£7.50 Dinner £11.50-£14.95&alc Last dinner 9.30pm
Credit Cards 1 2 3 4 5

BUCKLAND (near Broadway) Gloucestershire Map **04** SP03

★★★ **BUCKLAND MANOR**

WR12 7LY
☎Broadway(0386)852626
Closed mid Jan-early Feb

This is a beautiful old manor house in mellow Cotswold stone, which has been turned into an outstanding hotel by totally dedicated hoteliers. The influence of Adrienne and Barry Berman can be felt everywhere here, not least in the welcome provided by the young, attentive staff. The house lies at the end of a narrowing valley, with a backdrop of splendid lawns and flower beds, and a paddock beyond leading up to woods. Inside, lovingly polished antique tables and chairs, masses of fresh flowers and pot plants, comfortable armchairs, sofas and open log fires all create a wonderfully relaxing atmosphere, especially after a meal in the award-winning restaurant. Chef Martin Pearn has a delicate touch and an eye for attractive presentation that further enhances the good use he makes of local produce from the Vale of Evesham. The service by the young staff in the dining room is equally commendable, and the outstanding wine list is additional evidence of Barry Bermans' enthusiasm.

11⇌2 CTV in all bedrooms **T** sB&B⇌£115-£170 dB&B⇌£125-£180
30P (heated) (hard) croquet lawn putting green nc12yrs *xmas*
International **V** Lunch £17.65-£25.50alc Dinner £17.65-£25.50alc Last dinner 8.45pm
Credit Cards 1 3

BUCKLERS HARD Hampshire Map **04** SU40

★★**Master Builders House** SO4 7XB ☎(0590)616253 FAX (0590) 612624
Former home of the 18th century shipbuilder, Henry Adams, this hotel overlooking the river offers warm hospitality and good home cooking.
6⇌⌐Annexe17⇌(9fb)3 CTV in all bedrooms ® **T** ✱
sB&B⇌⌐fr£49 dB&B⇌⌐£66-£75
80P clay pigeon shooting boating *xmas*
English & French **V** Lunch £8.95-£9.95 Dinner fr£9.95&alc Last dinner 9.45pm
Credit Cards 1 2 3 5

BUCKLOW HILL Cheshire Map **07** SJ78

★★★61% **The Swan** WA16 6RD (De Vere) ☎(0565)830295 Telex no 666911 FAX (0565) 830614
Cavaliers and Roundheads once sought sanctuary in this historic hotel where darkened oak beams still add character to both the recently refurbished public areas in the main building and the bedrooms in an adjoining stable block.
70rm(44⇌26⌐)(11fb)3 CTV in all bedrooms ® **T** S%
sB&B⇌⌐£30-£67 dB&B⇌⌐£60-£79
200P
French & English **V** S% Lunch £12.75&alc Dinner £12.75&alc Last dinner 10pm
Credit Cards 1 2 3 5 £

BUDE Cornwall & Isles of Scilly Map **02** SS20

★★★64% **Hartland** Hartland Ter EX23 8JY (Exec Hotel) ☎(0288)55661
Closed mid Nov-Mar
This family-run hotel, with splendid views over the surrounding countryside and sandy beaches, is popular with both tourists and business clientele. The good value table d'hôte menus include a lovely sweet trolley.
29rm(23⇌6⌐)(2fb)3 CTV in all bedrooms **T**
sB&B⇌⌐£28.75-£32.20 dB&B⇌⌐£48.30-£55.20
Lift 30P (heated) ♫ *xmas*
International Lunch £11.50-£14.95 Dinner £13.80-£16.10 Last dinner 8.30pm

★★**Bude Haven** Flexbury Av EX23 8NS ☎(0288)2305
Comfortable, privately owned hotel within walking distance of Crooklets Beach.
13rm(5⇌8⌐)(1fb) CTV in all bedrooms ® sB&B⇌⌐£16-£17 dB&B⇌⌐£32-£34
CTV 8P
V Bar Lunch £2-£4.50 Dinner £6-£7 Last dinner 7.30pm
Credit Cards 1 3 £

★★Camelot Downs View Rd EX23 8RE ☎(0288)2361
FAX (0288) 55470
Situated near the golf course, the privately owned and personally run hotel even provides a Caddies' Room. Bedroom accommodation is comfortable, the pleasant, well-furnished lounge has a separate bar, and in the friendly atmosphere of an attractive dining room guests can enjoy a good range of dishes from both à la carte and table d'hôte menus.
20rm(8⇌12↱)(3fb) CTV in all bedrooms ® T ✗ (ex guide dogs) ✱ sB&B⇌↱£20 dB&B⇌↱£40 ⊟
20P solarium
V ⊁ Dinner fr£10&alc Last dinner 8.30pm
Credit Cards [1] [3]

★★Florida 17-18 Summerleaze Crescent EX23 8HJ
☎(0288)2451
Closed Nov-Feb
Personally run, offering a friendly atmosphere and well-organised activity holidays, the hotel stands in a row of terraced houses near Summerleaze beach and the town centre. It offers accommodation in bright, pleasantly furnished bedrooms, and public areas include three lounges, a bar and an attractive dining room where guests can enjoy the unusual dishes featured on a short table d'hôte menu.
21rm(11↱)(4fb) CTV in all bedrooms ® ✗
sB&B£21.25-£22.90 dB&B↱£46.86-£50 (incl dinner) ⊟
10P games room
V ✿ Bar Lunch 80p-£2.25 Dinner £7.50 Last dinner 7.30pm

★★Penarvor Crooklets Beach EX23 8NE
☎(0288)2036 due to change t o 352036
Closed Nov-Feb
A family-run hotel, standing on a quiet situation, offers friendly, attentive service and good food. Attractively furnished, well-equipped bedrooms are complemented by comfortable public rooms.
15rm(10⇌5↱)(5fb) CTV in all bedrooms ® T
sB&B⇌↱£18.50-£19.50 dB&B⇌↱£37-£39 ⊟
25P ✲ solarium gymnasium pool table games room
☋ English & French ⊁ Bar Lunch £1.50-£4 Dinner £8.50-£9.50&alc Last dinner 7.30pm
Credit Cards [1] [3] £

★★St Margaret's Killerton Rd EX23 8EN ☎(0288)2252 & 2401
FAX (0409) 254351
Small, comfortable hotel near town centre.
10rm(6⇌4↱)(3fb) CTV in all bedrooms ® T
sB&B⇌↱£18-£30 dB&B⇌↱£36-£58
CTV 6P ⊞ ✲ games room *xmas*
☋ English & Continental V ✿ ☕ Lunch £5.50&alc Dinner £6&alc Last dinner 8.30pm
Credit Cards [1] [3] £

★Edgcumbe Summerleaze Crescent EX23 8HJ ☎(0288)3846 due to change to (0288) 353846
Closed Nov-Feb
Personally run hotel specialising in family holidays.
15rm(8↱)(5fb) CTV in all bedrooms ® sB&B£12.50
sB&B↱£14.75 dB&B£25 dB&B↱£29.50 ⊟
CTV 7P pool table *xmas*
V ✿ ☕ Bar Lunch £1.80-£3alc Dinner fr£6 Last dinner 7.30pm
Credit Cards [1] [3]

★Maer Lodge Crooklets Beach EX23 8NG ☎(0288)3306
Closed 14 Oct-1 Dec
Detached, family holiday hotel close to Crooklets Beach with fine views.
20rm(8⇌7↱)(7fb) CTV in all bedrooms ® S% sB&B£22-£24
sB&B⇌↱£24-£26 dB&B£44-£48
dB&B⇌↱£48-£52 (incl dinner) ⊟
CTV 20P ✲ pool mini-golf ♫ ⌂ *xmas*
☋ English & French ✿ ☕ ⊁ Lunch £5.75 Dinner £7.50 Last dinner 7.30pm
Credit Cards [1] [2] [3] [5] £

★Meva Gwin Upton EX23 OLY ☎(0288)2347
Closed 7 Oct-3 Mar
Family holiday hotel set midway between Bude and Widemouth Bay has glorious views of countryside and coast.
13rm(4⇌6↱)(4fb) CTV in all bedrooms ® ✗ ✱ sB&B£12-£16
sB&B⇌↱£14-£16 dB&B£24-£33 dB&B⇌↱£28-£32
CTV 44P ✲ ⌂
✿ ☕ ⊁ Lunch 75p-£5.50 Dinner £6.50 Last dinner 7.30pm

★*Stamford Hill Hotel* EX23 9AY ☎(0288)2709
(For full entry see Stratton)

BUILTH WELLS Powys Map **03** SO05

★★Lion 2 Broad St LD2 3DT ☎(0982)553670
Historic inn in the centre of town, overlooking River Wye.
19rm(9⇌2↱)(4fb) CTV in all bedrooms ® T ✱ sB&Bfr£22
sB&B⇌↱fr£27 dB&Bfr£34 dB&B⇌↱fr£44 ⊟
12P *xmas*
☋ English & French V ✿ ☕ Lunch £6.25-£8 Dinner £8 Last dinner 9pm
Credit Cards [1] [3]

★★Pencerrig Country House Hotel LD2 3TF (Consort)
☎(0982)553226 FAX (0982) 552347
20rm(12⇌8↱)(1fb)1⊠ CTV in all bedrooms ® T ✱
sB&B⇌↱fr£36 dB&B⇌↱£59-£64 ⊟
☾ 40P ✲ ⌂ *xmas*
☋ English & French V ✿ ☕ Lunch fr£6.50 Dinner fr£13.50 Last dinner 9.30pm
Credit Cards [1] [2] [3] [5] £

BUNGAY Suffolk Map **05** TM38

★*King's Head* Market Place NR35 1AF ☎(0986)3583
13rm(3⇌1↱)1⊠ CTV in 5bedrooms ®
CTV 28P ⊞ ♫
V ✿ ☕
Credit Cards [1] [2] [3]

BUNWELL Norfolk Map **05** TM19

★★Bunwell Manor
Bunwell St NR16 1QU
☎(095389)8304

Occupying a secluded position in the heart of the Norfolk countryside south of Norwich and dating back to the sixteenth-century, this family-run hotel offers a real chance to relax. Individually furnished and well-equipped character bedrooms enjoy lovely rural views and there are two comfortable lounges, one with log fire.
10rm(6⇌4↱)(2fb) CTV in all bedrooms ® T
30P ✲
V ✿ ☕ Last dinner 9.30pm
Credit Cards [1] [3] £

Book as early as possible for busy holiday periods.

BURBAGE Wiltshire Map **04** SU26

★★Savernake Forest Savernake SN8 3AY (1m NE off A346)
☎Marlborough(0672)810206
Pleasant, informal hotel in a rural setting. The restaurant serves an interesting choice of dishes and service is by cheerful, young staff.
10rm(9⇌1↱)Annexe6rm(5⇌1↱)(2fb)1⊞ CTV in all bedrooms ® T sB&B⇌↱fr£38 dB&B⇌↱fr£65 ⊟
CTV 80P ❁ ♪ *xmas*
♉ English & French V ♉ Lunch fr£8.50 Dinner fr£12.50&alc
Last dinner 9.15pm
Credit Cards 1 2 3 5 £
See advertisement under MARLBOROUGH

BURFORD Oxfordshire Map **04** SP21

★★Cotswold Gateway Cheltenham Rd OX8 4HX
☎(099382)2695 & 3345
After recent renovation, the hotel now offers modern bedrooms, a smart bar and dining room as well as a coffee shop that is open all day.
13⇌Annexe4⇌(5fb) CTV in all bedrooms ® T ✱
sB&B⇌fr£38.50 dB&B⇌fr£58.50 ⊟
☾60P *xmas*
V ♉ ⊥ Lunch £6.95-£12.50&alc High tea £60-£1.85 Dinner £7.95-£12.50&alc Last dinner 9.45pm
Credit Cards 1 2 3 5

★★Golden Pheasant High St OX8 4RJ ☎(099382)3223
Telex no 849041
In the heart of this attractive Cotswolds town, the Golden Pheasant is a small, family-owned hotel which has recently been renovated. Many of the original beams and stonework have been exposed and large fireplaces provide a cosy atmosphere. Cottage-style bedrooms combine character with a good range of modern facilities and a particularly charming room in the roof space has a 17th-century 4-poster bed. Worthy standards of food place the emphasis on the imaginative use of fresh produce.
12rm(7⇌5↱)(2fb)2⊞ CTV in all bedrooms ® T S15%
sB&B⇌↱£43-£53 dB&B⇌↱£55.50-£75.50 ⊟
☾CTV 18P ⊞ *xmas*
♉ French V ♉ ⊥ ⊁ S15% Lunch £10.95-£14.95&alc High tea £3-£6 Dinner £14.95&alc Last dinner 9.30pm
Credit Cards 1 3 £

★*Highway* High St OX8 4RG (Minotels) ☎(099382)2136
Telex no 838736
An ancient inn on Burford's historic High Street, the hotel is run by the proprietor and provides friendly and concerned service. Some rooms are small, but they are all charming and comfortable.
10rm(6⇌2↱)(2fb)1⊞ CTV in all bedrooms ® T
P ⊞ ❁
V ♉ ⊥ Last dinner 9.30pm
Credit Cards 1 2 3 5

BURGH HEATH Surrey Map **04** TQ25

★★Heathside Brighton Rd KT20 6BW ☎(0737)353355
Telex no 929908 FAX (0737) 370857
This hotel offers modern accommodation. The staff are cheerful, and a cosy atmosphere pervades the compact Milly's bar and restaurant. Additionally, there is a Happy Eater restaurant where breakfast is available.
44⇌↱(19fb) CTV in all bedrooms ® T sB⇌↱fr£52
dB⇌↱fr£64 (room only) ⊟
☾180P ❁ CFA *xmas*
♉ English & French ♉ ⊥ ⊁ Lunch £6-£9.50&alc High tea £3-£5.50 Dinner £6.50-£9.50&alc Last dinner 10pm
Credit Cards 1 2 3 5

For key to symbols see the inside front cover.

BURLEY Hampshire Map **04** SU20

★★★64% Moorhill House BH24 4AG ☎Ringwood(0425)33285
Situated on the edge of the forest in three acres of gardens and lawns, refurbishment has been recently completed: bedrooms are relaxing with good colour coordination, there is an elegant restaurant, a bar that has been extended with views of the indoor pool and plush lounges with leather upholstery.
23rm(17⇌6↱)(7fb)4⊞ CTV in all bedrooms ® T ✱
sB&B⇌↱£45-£59 dB&B⇌↱£65-£110
30P ⊞ ❁ ⊡(heated) sauna ⌂ *xmas*
Last high tea 6.30pm
Credit Cards 1 2 3 5

BURNHAM Buckinghamshire Map **04** SU98

★★★67% Burnham Beeches Grove Rd SL1 8DP (Queens Moat)
☎(0628)603333 FAX (0628) 603994
A former hunting lodge, peacefully set in 600 acres of forest, has been upgraded to meet modern standards of comfort. Lounges are elegant and well-appointed, an attractive dining room offers interesting, skilfully-prepared dishes complemented by a good wine list, and there are excellent leisure facilities. Friendly staff provide efficiently unobtrusive service.
75⇌2⊞ CTV in all bedrooms ® T sB⇌£76-£80
dB⇌£91-£95 (room only) ⊟
Lift ☾150P ❁ ⊡(heated) ♇ (hard) sauna solarium gymnasium putting croquet ⌂ *xmas*
♉ French V ♉ ⊥ Lunch fr£15.50&alc Dinner fr£18.50&alc
Last dinner 10pm
Credit Cards 1 2 3 4 5

★★Grovefield Taplow Common Rd SL1 8LP (Best Western)
☎(06286)3131 Telex no 846873
Closed 1 wk Xmas
Once a Victorian country house, this tastefully modernised hotel sits in 7.5 acres of gardens and parkland overlooking unspoilt countryside. Accommodation is in comfortable, well-equipped bedrooms, and a restaurant decorated in pastel shades offers interesting international cuisine.
42⇌↱ CTV in all bedrooms ® T ✱ S% sB&B⇌↱£75-£100
dB&B⇌↱£85-£120 ⊟
Lift ☾100P ⊠ ⊞ ❁ ⌂ *xmas*
♉ International V ♉ S% Lunch fr£12.50 Dinner fr£15.50 Last dinner 10.30pm
Credit Cards 1 2 3 4 5

BURNHAM-ON-CROUCH Essex Map **05** TQ99

★Ye Olde White Harte The Quay CM0 8AS
☎Maldon(0621)782106
RS 25-26 Dec
Welcoming old coaching inn with comfortable bedrooms overlooking estuary.
11rm(5⇌6↱)(2fb) CTV in all bedrooms ✱ S10%
sB&Bfr£18.18 sB&B⇌↱£26.40-£28.60 dB&Bfr£31.90
dB&B⇌↱£44-£47.30
CTV 15P
V ♉ Lunch £6.95-£7.50&alc Dinner fr£7.50&alc Last dinner 9pm
£

BURNHAM-ON-SEA Somerset Map **03** ST34

★★Dunstan House 8-10 Love Ln TA8 1EU ☎(0278)784343
Attractive Georgian house with additions. The hotel is family run with friendly atmosphere and good food.
10rm(2⇌2↱)(1fb) CTV in all bedrooms ® T ✱ sB&B£19-£22
sB&B⇌↱£28-£30 dB&B£30-£32 dB&B⇌↱£38-£40
CTV 40P (charged) 1⊠ ❁ *xmas*

English & French V Lunch £5-£12&alc Dinner £5-£12&alc Last dinner 9.30pm
Credit Cards [1] [2] [3] [5]

See advertisement under BRIDGWATER

★★Royal Clarence 31 The Esplanade TA8 1BQ (Minotels)
☎Burnham on Sea(0278)783138
An inexpensive seaside and commercial hotel with helpful staff. There are 2 bars, one with a games area, and 3 lounges, one of which overlooks the Bristol Channel towards Wales. Bedrooms are well-equipped and of modest quality.
15rm(5⇨8↱)(2fb) CTV in all bedrooms ® T sB&B⇨↱fr£22 dB&B⇨↱fr£36
CTV 20P xmas
Lunch £4.95 High tea £1.50-£7.50 Dinner £7.95&alc Last dinner 8.30pm
Credit Cards [1] [2] [3] [5] £

See advertisement under BRIDGWATER

★Pine Grange Berrow Rd TA8 2EY
☎Burnham on sea(0278)784214
Neat, well-equipped bedrooms and an extensive choice from table d'hôte and à la carte dinner menus are provided by this cosy, proprietor-run hotel which occupies a red-brick corner property only 200 yards from the beach.
7rm(1⇨5↱) CTV in all bedrooms ® T sB&B£20-£28 sB&B⇨↱£28 dB&B£42 dB&B⇨↱£42
CTV 10P 1 solarium
English & French Lunch £3.50-£6.20 High tea £2.50-£3.50 Dinner fr£9.50&alc Last dinner 8.30pm
Credit Cards [1] [3] £

BURNLEY Lancashire Map **07** SD83

★★★63% Keirby Keirby Walk BB11 2DH ☎(0282)27611
Telex no 63119 FAX (0282) 36370
Closed 24-26 Dec
Tall, modern hotel with well proportioned bedrooms and good facilities.
49⇨↱ in 12 bedrooms CTV in all bedrooms ® T
sB&B⇨↱£46.50-£54
dB&B⇨↱£55.50-£62.50 Continental breakfast
Lift CTV 100P 20
English & French V Lunch £9.25-£10.50&alc Dinner £10.50-£11.75&alc Last dinner 10pm
Credit Cards [1] [2] [3] [5] £

★★★71% Oaks Colne Rd, Reedley BB10 2LF (Shire)
☎(0282)414141 Telex no 635309 FAX (0282) 33401
A country house has been sympathetically converted to offer comfortable, tastefully modernised bedrooms and fine public rooms which retain its original character.
59⇨↱(7fb)2 in 30 bedrooms CTV in all bedrooms ® T ✱
sB&B⇨↱£58 dB&B⇨↱£70
CTV 110P (heated) (hard) squash snooker sauna solarium gymnasium xmas
English & French V Lunch £7.35&alc Dinner £12-£16&alc Last dinner 9.45pm
Credit Cards [1] [2] [3] [4] [5]

★★Rosehill House Rosehill Av B11 2PW ☎(0282)53931
RS 25 Dec-1 Jan
A tastefully converted country house offers comfortable accommodation and interesting menus.
20rm(9⇨11↱)(1fb) CTV in all bedrooms ® T ✱
sB&B⇨↱£18-£36 dB&B⇨↱£36-£50
60P 2
V Lunch £10.25&alc Dinner £10.25&alc Last dinner 9.30pm
Credit Cards [1] [2] [3] £

B

○ ***Travelodge*** Cavalry Barracks, Barracks Rd BB11 4AS (Trusthouse Forte) ☎(0282)416039
32⇨
P

BURNSALL North Yorkshire Map **07** SE06

★★*Fell* BD23 6BT ☎(075672)209
An attractive stone building stands in a elevated position overlooking the valley, offering comfortable accommodation and friendly service.
14rm(10⇨1♠)(4fb) ®
CTV 60P ✽ ⌂
V ♅ ⅅ
Credit Cards 1 2 3

★★Red Lion BD23 6BU ☎(075672)204
An old-world stone built inn on the banks of the River Wharfe in the centre of the village.
8rm(1⇨)Annexe4rm(2⇨2♠)(2fb) CTV in 2bedrooms ® ✗
S10% sB&Bfr£25 sB&B⇨♠fr£33 dB&Bfr£33 dB&B⇨♠fr£44
CTV 40P ♩
🍷 English S10% Lunch fr£6.50 Dinner fr£8.80 Last dinner 9pm

BURNTISLAND Fife Map **11** NT28

★★Inchview Hotel 69 Kinghorn Rd KY3 9EB
☎Kirkcaldy(0592)872239
The interior of this comfortable, friendly hotel features a lot of attractive stone and wood, with welcoming open fires.
11rm(6⇨5♠)(5fb) CTV in all bedrooms ® **T**
sB&B⇨♠£25-£29 dB&B⇨♠£35-£42 ⊟
15P *xmas*
🍷 International **V** ♅ ⅅ Lunch £6.50-£10.50&alc High tea £3.50-£6.50 Dinner £10.50-£12.50&alc Last dinner 9.45pm
Credit Cards 1 2 3 £

BURNT YATES North Yorkshire Map **08** SE26

★★Bay Horse Inn & Motel HG3 3EJ ☎Harrogate(0423)770230
Comfortable, ivy-clad, 18th-century coaching inn, with new motel unit and well fitted bedrooms.
5♠Annexe10♠ CTV in all bedrooms ® **T** sB&B♠£29
dB&B♠£39 ⊟
100P *xmas*
🍷 French **V** ♅ ⅅ Sunday Lunch £6.95 Dinner £9.95&alc Last dinner 9.30pm
Credit Cards 1 2 3 £

BURRINGTON Devon Map **02** SS61

★★★⚑67% Northcote Manor EX37 9LZ (2m NW of village towards Station & A377) (Best Western)
☎High Bickington (0769)60501
Closed Nov-Feb
Set peacefully in its own grounds, surrounded by open countryside, a charming hotel offers comfortable bedrooms, an attractive lounge bar and drawing room, and an elegant split level dining room serving a simple table d'hôte menu.
12⇨ CTV in all bedrooms ® **T** sB&B⇨£45-£65
dB&B⇨£90-£120 (incl dinner) ⊟
20P ⛟ ✽ croquet nc7yrs
🍷 English & French ♅ ⅅ ✗ Lunch £10-£15.50 Dinner £15.50-£20 Last dinner 8.15pm
Credit Cards 1 2 3 5

BURTON-UPON-TRENT Staffordshire Map **08** SK22

★★★63% Riverside Inn Riverside Dr, Branston DE14 3EP
☎Burton upon Trent(0283)511234 FAX (0283) 511441
Closed 30 Dec RS 24-26 & 31 Dec
A small hotel by the river, reached via a suburban route. Service is efficient and friendly, while the Garden Room Restaurant is becoming increasingly popular in the area.
21⇨ CTV in all bedrooms ® **T** ✻ sB&B⇨£21-£42
dB&B⇨£32-£53 ⊟
☾ 130P ✽ ♩
V ♅ ⅅ Lunch £5.95-£9.95&alc Dinner £9.95&alc Last dinner 10pm
Credit Cards 1 2 3

BURY Greater Manchester Map **07** SD81

★★★70% Normandie Elbut Ln, Birtle BL9 6UT ☎061-764 3869 & 061-764 1170 Telex no 635091 FAX 061-764 4866
Closed 26 Dec-8 Jan RS Sun
Situated on the B6222 between Bury and Rochdale, this hillside hotel offers comfortable accommodation, some in luxurious new bedrooms with every modern facility. A delightful restaurant, under the direction of a French chef who has introduced the classical dishes of his country to the menus, enjoys a well deserved reputation for excellence ; here a guest might enjoy medallions of hare wrapped in smoked pork and served with a delicious, peppery sauce, followed, perhaps, by a delectable hot chocolate soufflé baked in a sweet shortcrust case and accompanied by a Cointreau sauce. Service throughout is warm and caring.
21rm(15⇨6♠)Annexe3rm(1⇨2♠) CTV in all bedrooms ® **T**
✗ (ex guide dogs) ✻ sB&B⇨♠£49-£59
dB&B⇨♠£59-£69 Continental breakfast
Lift ☾ 60P ⛟ ✽
🍷 French **V** ✗ Lunch £18.40-£30.15alc Dinner fr£16&alc Last dinner 9.30pm
Credit Cards 1 2 3 5

★★Bolholt Walshaw Rd BL8 1PU ☎061-764 5239 & 061-764 3888 FAX 061-763 1789
Set in semi-rural surroundings, with well-tended gardens at its rear and small lakes in front, this hotel is particularly popular with business people – a fact reflected in the furnishing of most of the bedrooms, though these do include two honeymoon suites. A gymnasium is provided for guests' use.
38rm(28⇨8♠)(2fb)2⊟ CTV in all bedrooms ® **T** ✻
sB&B£29-£39 sB&B⇨♠£29-£39 dB&B£45-£50
dB&B⇨♠£45-£50
CTV 200P ✽ ⚲ (hard) ♩ sauna gymnasium bowling ♫
🍷 International **V** ♅ ⅅ Lunch £8-£12 High tea £6-£8 Dinner £9-£13 Last dinner 9pm
Credit Cards 1 3

★Woolfield House Wash Ln BL9 6BJ ☎061-797 9775
A generally well-appointed hotel, conveniently situated just a short distance from the town centre, caters mainly for business people, providing accommodation in cheerfully bright, modern bedrooms.
16rm(3⇨7♠)1⊟ CTV in 10bedrooms TV in 6bedrooms ® **T**
✗ (ex guide dogs) ✻ sB&Bfr£18 sB&B⇨♠£25-£27
dB&Bfr£30 dB&B⇨♠£36-£37
40P nc
♅ ⅅ Lunch fr£4.25 Dinner fr£7.95alc Last dinner 8pm
Credit Cards 1 3

Book as early as possible for busy holiday periods.

B

BURY ST EDMUNDS Suffolk Map **05** TL86

★★★77% **Angel** Angel Hill IP33 1LT ☎(0284)753926
Telex no 81630 FAX (0284) 750092
Steeped in history, and a resting place for Charles Dickens on two occasions, this splendid hotel continues its programme of improvements. Accommodation is comfortable, the mixture of contemporary and traditional rooms, all being well furnished and thoughtfully equipped. The relaxing public area provides an ideal setting for a delightfully served afternoon tea, and there are two restaurants with individual styles. Hospitable, friendly staff work hard to ensure that each guest's stay here is an enjoyable experience.
41rm(40⇌1♠)4⊞ CTV in all bedrooms **T**
☾ 50P 12♠ CFA ♫
♉ English & French **V** ♡ ☕ Last dinner 9.45pm
Credit Cards 1 2 3 5 £

★★★65% **Butterfly** Symonds Rd, Moreton Hall(A45) IP32 7BW (Consort) ☎(0284)760884 Telex no 818360 FAX (0284) 755476
Conveniently situated next to the A45 and close to the town centre, this purpose-built modern hotel provides good value accommodation in comfortable bedrooms. The open-plan bar and restaurants are attractively furnished in characterful country pine, the menu in the latter displaying a good range of roasts and dishes of the day, with a self-service array of starters.
50⇌♠(2fb) CTV in all bedrooms ® **T** ✗ sB&B⇌♠£53-£55 dB&B⇌♠£57.50-£60 ⊟
☾ 80P
♉ British & European **V** ♡ ☕ Lunch £6.75-£8.75&alc Dinner £6.75-£8.75&alc Last dinner 10pm
Credit Cards 1 2 3 5

★★★♛75% **Ravenwood Hall** Rougham IP30 9JA (3m E off A45)
☎Beyton(0359)70345
The elegant country house hotel, surrounded by seven acres of woodland, traces its history back to the reign of Henry VIII. Comfortable bedroom accommodation and good meals play their part in making a stay here an enjoyable experience.
7⇌1⊞ CTV in all bedrooms ® **T** ✱ sB&B⇌£50 dB&B⇌£70-£75 ⊟
100P 3♠ ✿ ✲ ⇌(heated) ♪ (hard) U croquet shooting parties arranged *xmas*
V ♡ ☕ Lunch £13.50 High tea £4.50 Last high tea 9.30pm
Credit Cards 1 2 3 5

★★**The Suffolk** 38 The Buttermarket IP33 1DC (Trusthouse Forte) ☎(0284)753995 FAX (0284) 750973
Reconstructed ancient inn close to the 12th century Abbey.
33⇌⅟in 15 bedrooms CTV in all bedrooms ® **T** sB⇌£56-£62 dB⇌£67-£74 (room only) ⊟
☾ 20P 16♠ *xmas*
V ♡ ☕ ⅟ Lunch £7.45-£9.85&alc Dinner fr£13.50&alc Last dinner 9.30pm
Credit Cards 1 2 3 4 5

For key to symbols see the inside front cover.

B

✕Mortimer's Seafood 31 Churchgate IP33 1RG ☎(0284)60623
Closed Sun, BH's & following Tue & 23 Dec-3 Jan
Lunch not served Sat
British & French 60 seats Lunch £3.25-£15alc Dinner £5.20-£15alc Last lunch 2pm Last dinner 9pm
Credit Cards 1 2 3 5

BUSBY Strathclyde *Lanarkshire* Map **11** NS55

★★Busby 1 Field Rd G76 8RX ☎041-644 2661
Closed 25 Dec-1 Jan
Attractively situated hotel in conservation area with popular bar and function trade.
14rm(7⇌7)(1fb)1 CTV in all bedrooms ® T
sB&B⇌£29.50-£37 dB&B⇌£36-£45
Lift ☾ 60P
V Lunch £5.95-£7.60 Dinner £8.95&alc Last dinner 9pm
Credit Cards 1 2 3 5

BUSHEY Hertfordshire Map **04** TQ19

★★★56% Hilton National Elton Way WD2 8HA (Hilton)
☎Watford(0923)35881 Telex no 923422 FAX (0923) 220836
This large, modern hotel with good bedrooms has mainly self-service meals from hot and cold buffets.
170⇌(1fb)1 in 5 bedrooms CTV in all bedrooms ® T ✳
S% sB⇌£72-£87 dB⇌£88-£98 (room only)
Lift ☾ 350P CFA Leisure Centre due to open Nov 1989 ♫
International V Lunch fr£11.90&alc High tea fr£1.25 Dinner £14-£16.90&alc Last dinner 9.45pm
Credit Cards 1 2 3 5

BUTE, ISLE OF Strathclyde *Buteshire* Map **10**

ROTHESAY Map **10** NS06

★St Ebba 37 Mountstuart Rd, Craigmore PA20 9EB
☎(0700)2683
12rm(1⇌10)(3fb) CTV in 11bedrooms ® ✳ sB&B£19
sB&B⇌£19 dB&B⇌£38
CTV 5P
V

BUTTERMERE Cumbria Map **11** NY11

★★Bridge CA13 9UZ ☎(059685)252
Typical lakeland inn in beautiful countryside, offering congenial atmosphere.
22⇌ ® T ✳ sB&B⇌£31.50-£39
dB&B⇌£31.50-£44 (incl dinner)
36P *xmas*
English & French V Bar Lunch £2.75-£6.95alc

BUXTON Derbyshire Map **07** SK07

★★★63% Leewood 13 Manchester Rd SK17 6TQ (Best Western) ☎(0298)23002 Telex no 669848 FAX (0298) 23228
Closed 24-29 Dec
A traditional-style hotel set in terraced gardens near the town centre has considerably improved its public areas by the addition of The Garden Room – a large, elegant conservatory dining room – but its warm, family atmosphere and standards of hospitable service remain unchanged.
38rm(35⇌3)(2fb) CTV in all bedrooms ® T
sB&B⇌£48-£54 dB&B⇌£58-£64
Lift ☾ 50P CFA
English & French V Lunch £8.50 Dinner £13.95&alc Last dinner 9.30pm
Credit Cards 1 2 3 5 £

★★★50% *Palace* Palace Rd SK17 6AG (Trusthouse Forte)
☎(0298)2001 Telex no 668169 FAX (0298) 72131
This impressive Victorian building overlooking the spa town provides recently upgraded bedrooms and elegant public areas. Guests can also enjoy the gymnasium, swimming pool and well laid out gardens.
122⇌(12fb) in 10 bedrooms CTV in all bedrooms ® T
Lift ☾ 200P CFA (heated) snooker sauna solarium gymnasium hair-salon pool
English & French Last dinner 9.30pm
Credit Cards 1 2 3 5

★★*Buckingham* 1 Burlington Rd SK17 9AS (Consort)
☎(0298)70481 Telex no 57515
Two large, stone-built, Victorian houses have been combined to provide spacious public rooms and facilities suitable for small in-house conferences. The hotel is situated only a short walk from the town centre.
30rm(15⇌15)(6fb) CTV in all bedrooms ® T (ex guide dogs)
Lift CTV 24P snooker
International V Last dinner 9.30pm
Credit Cards 1 2 3 5

★★*Grove* Grove Pde SK17 6AJ ☎(0298)3804
Former coaching inn above row of shops, with attractive lounges displaying many old features, and smart restaurant featuring local and international dishes.
21rm(4⇌3)(3fb) CTV in 16bedrooms TV in 5bedrooms ®
CTV 10P
English & French V
Credit Cards 1 2 3 5

★★Portland 32 St John's Rd SK17 6XQ (Consort)
☎(0298)2462 & 71493
Situated close to the town centre, this long established family-run hotel has undergone major improvements which have upgraded facilities without detracting from the convivial atmosphere.
25rm(5⇌20)(4fb)2 in 1 bedroom CTV in all bedrooms ® T sB&B⇌fr£35 dB&B⇌fr£50
18P
English & French V Lunch fr£7.25 High tea fr£3.95 Dinner fr£11&alc Last dinner 9pm
Credit Cards 1 2 3 5 £

★Hartington 18 Broad Walk SK17 6JR ☎(0298)22638
Closed 23 Dec-3 Jan RS Nov-Apr
Stone-built house overlooking the Pavilion gardens and a small lake.
17rm(3⇌4)(3fb) CTV in 7bedrooms ® (ex guide dogs)
sB&B£18-£25 sB&B⇌£30 dB&B£35 dB&B⇌£42
CTV 15P
Dinner fr£8 Last dinner 8pm
Credit Cards 1 3 £

CADNAM Hampshire Map **04** SU21

★★★63% Bartley Lodge Lyndhurst Rd SO4 2NR
☎Southampton(0703)812248
This listed, red-brick, Georgian manor house in a tranquil New Forest setting enjoys its reputation as flagship of the Care Leisure group of hotels. Accommodation is of a high standard, with attractively co-ordinated bedrooms which vary in size but not in quality, a galleried, oak-panelled foyer lounge, and conference/function facilities.
19⇌1 CTV in all bedrooms ® T ✳ sB&B⇌£45-£79
dB&B⇌£65-£110
50P (heated) *xmas*
Lunch fr£10&alc High tea fr£5 Dinner fr£15&alc Last dinner 10pm
Credit Cards 1 2 3

B

CAERNARFON Gwynedd Map **06** SH46

★★★63% Stables LL54 5SD (Inter)
☎Llanwnda(0286)830711 & 830935 FAX (0286) 830413
(For full entry see Llanwnda)

★Menai Bank North Rd LL55 1BD ☎(0286)673297
A pleasantly comfortable hotel, family owned and run, enjoys views across the Menai Straits.
15rm(4⇌5♠)(3fb) CTV in all bedrooms ® sB&B£15 sB&B⇌♠£18-£20 dB&B£24-£30 dB&B⇌♠£30-£36 ⊟
CTV 10P pool table
♈ Dinner £8.50&alc Last dinner 7.30pm
Credit Cards 1 3

CAERPHILLY Mid Glamorgan Map **03** ST18

★★Griffin Inn Motel Rudry CF8 3EA ☎(0222)869735
Closed Xmas
The small, friendly, character inn has a rural setting and is personally owned and managed. A combination of modern, well-equipped bedrooms, good bars and a convivial restaurant make it popular with businessmen.
Annexe20⇌(2fb) CTV in all bedrooms ® **T** ✖ (ex guide dogs) sB&B⇌£32-£45 dB&B⇌£45-£58
☾ 100P ⛟ ❉ ⛆(heated)
♉ English & French **V** Sunday Lunch £6.25 Dinner £8.85&alc
Last dinner 10pm
Credit Cards 1 2 3 5

All AA-appointed establishments are inspected regularly to ensure that required standards are maintained.

CALLANDER Central *Perthshire* Map **11** NN60

★★★♔ 68% Roman Camp
FK17 8BG
☎(0877)30003
FAX (0764) 62939

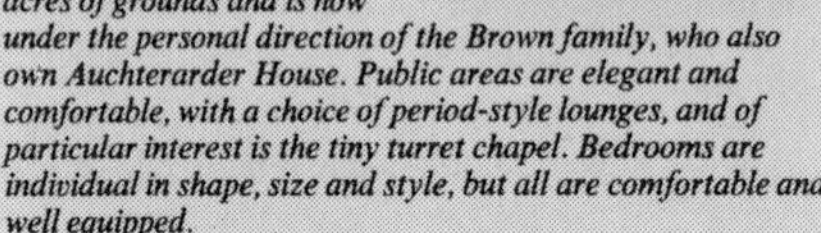

Reminiscent of a small French château, this delightful hotel is set in 20 acres of grounds and is now under the personal direction of the Brown family, who also own Auchterarder House. Public areas are elegant and comfortable, with a choice of period-style lounges, and of particular interest is the tiny turret chapel. Bedrooms are individual in shape, size and style, but all are comfortable and well equipped.
14⇨↾(3fb)1♛ CTV in all bedrooms ® T
sB&B⇨↾£55-£85 dB&B⇨↾£65-£125 ⊟
30P ✲ ♩ *xmas*
♡ Scottish & French ♁ ☐ ⊁ Lunch £11-£15 Dinner £22-£28 Last dinner 9pm
Credit Cards 1 2 3 5

★★*Dalgair House Hotel* 113-115 Main St FK17 8BQ
☎(0877)30283
A converted and modernised Victorian building of considerable character offers comfortable, well-appointed bedrooms and features a cellar wine bar and restaurant where a good range of 'Taste of Scotland' dishes provide quality and interest.
9rm(8⇨1↾)(1fb) CTV in all bedrooms ® ✈
CTV 30P
♁ ☐ Last dinner 10.30pm
Credit Cards 1 2 3 5

★Bridgend House Bridgend FK17 8AH ☎(0877)30130
A personally-run hotel in a quiet location close to the town centre.
7rm(3⇨2↾)(1fb)2♛ CTV in all bedrooms ® T ✳
sB&B£17-£17 sB&B⇨↾£30-£30 dB&B£28-£28
dB&B⇨↾£48-£48
30P ✲ *xmas*
♡ English & Continental V ♁ Bar Lunch £3-£7 Dinner £12-£18alc Last dinner 9.30pm
Credit Cards 1 2 3 5

★Lubnaig Leny Feus FK17 8AS (off A84) ☎(0877)30376
Closed Nov-Etr
Personally supervised hotel set amongst pine trees, with tastefully appointed bedrooms and public rooms. Interesting and varied meals are served in the dining room.
6↾Annexe4↾(2fb) ® dB&B↾£60.50-£66 (incl dinner) ⊟
CTV 14P 2⌂(£2 per night) ⚘ ✲ croquet nc7yrs
⊁

★Pinewood Leny Rd FK17 8AP ☎(0877)30111
FAX (0877) 31337
This family-run holiday hotel is set in its own grounds beside the main road on the edge of town. It offers a friendly atmosphere, comfortable public rooms and functional bedrooms.
16rm(2⇨6↾)(3fb) ® T sB&Bfr£16.50 sB&B⇨↾fr£18 dB&Bfr£30 dB&B⇨↾£33-£30 ⊟
CTV 30P ✲ *xmas*
V ♁ ☐ ⊁ Lunch fr£5 High tea £3.50-£5 Dinner £10-£17.50 Last dinner 8.45pm
Credit Cards 2 3 £

CALNE Wiltshire Map **03** ST97

★★Lansdowne Strand The Strand SN11 0JR ☎(0249)812488
Dating back to the sixteenth century, when it was a coaching inn, the hotel retains many original features, the medieval brewhouse being of particular interest. En suite bedrooms are well equipped and supplied with thoughtful extras, each of the bars has its individual ambience, and an interesting range of dishes is served in the restaurant.
21⇨↾Annexe5⇨(2fb)1♛ CTV in all bedrooms ® T
sB&B⇨↾£40 dB&B⇨↾£52 ⊟
21P
♡ English & French V ♁ ☐ Lunch £7.50-£9.50&alc Dinner £9.50&alc Last dinner 9.15pm
Credit Cards 1 2 3 5 £

CAMBERLEY Surrey Map **04** SU86

★★★ 62% Frimley Hall Portsmouth Rd GU15 2BG (Trusthouse Forte) ☎(0276)28321 Telex no 858446 FAX (0276) 691253
Set in 4 acres of well-kept grounds, this charming Victorian house offers comfortable, modern accommodation whilst retaining its original character. The restaurant is spacious and elegant and there is an adjoining lounge.
66⇨⊁in 10 bedrooms CTV in all bedrooms ® T ✳
sB⇨£69-£79 dB⇨£96-£106 (room only) ⊟
☾200P ✲ CFA *xmas*
V ♁ ☐ ⊁ Lunch £10.50-£17.75&alc Dinner £13.75-£18.75&alc Last dinner 9.45pm
Credit Cards 1 2 3 4 5

CAMBRIDGE Cambridgeshire Map **05** TL45

★★★★ 58% Garden House Granta Place, Mill Ln CB2 1RT (Queens Moat)(Best Western) ☎(0223)63421 Telex no 81463 FAX (0223) 316605
Approached via Trumpington Street, this modern-style hotel, situated in 3 acres of attractive gardens on the banks of the River Cam, is undergoing a lengthy programme of refurbishment. Bedrooms are spacious and comfortable.
118⇨↾ CTV in all bedrooms ® T ✈ (ex guide dogs)
Lift ☾180P ✲ CFA ♩ punting ♫
♡ English & French V ♁ ☐ Last dinner 9.30pm
Credit Cards 1 2 3 5 £

★★★★ 50% Post House Lakeview, Bridge Rd, Impington CB4 4PH (2.5m N, on N side of rdbt jct A45/B1049) (Trusthouse Forte) ☎(0223)237000 Telex no 817123 FAX (0223) 233426
Situated on the north side of the A45 as it bypasses Cambridge, with access from the B1049 Impington road, this hotel has become a popular venue for businessmen during the week and families at weekends. Its spacious rooms have recently undergone extensive improvement, and it features a good health and fitness club.
120⇨(14fb)⊁in 16 bedrooms CTV in all bedrooms ® T ✳
sB⇨£81-£92 dB⇨£97-£105 (room only) ⊟
☾250P ✲ ⊡(heated) sauna solarium gymnasium *xmas*
♡ International V ♁ ☐ ⊁ Lunch fr£13.25&alc High tea £6.25-£7.50 Dinner fr£16&alc Last dinner 10.30pm
Credit Cards 1 2 3 4 5

★★★★ 57% University Arms Regent St CB2 1AD (De Vere)
☎(0223)351241 Telex no 817311 FAX (0223) 315256
115⇨(7fb) CTV in all bedrooms ® T
Lift ☾80P CFA
♡ English & French V ♁ ☐ Last dinner 9.45pm
Credit Cards 1 2 3 5

★★★ 63% Cambridgeshire Moat House CB3 8EU (Queens Moat) ☎Crafts Hill(0954)80555 Telex no 817141
FAX (0954) 80010
(For full entry see Bar Hill)

★★★61% Gonville Gonville Place CB1 1LY ☎(0223)66611
Closed 4 days at Xmas
Conventional hotel overlooking Parker's Piece.
62⇨(6fb) CTV in all bedrooms ® **T** S% sB&B⇨£53 dB&B⇨£70 ▤
Lift ☾ CTV 100P CFA
V ♥ ☕ S10% Lunch fr£7.45&alc Dinner fr£9.50&alc Last dinner 9pm
Credit Cards [1] [2] [3] [4]

★★Arundel House 53 Chesterton Rd CB4 3AN ☎(0223)67701
Closed 25-26 Dec
Friendly, caring staff, good food plus continually improving facilities make this a very popular, busy hotel. Converted from a row of Victorian houses, it overlooks the River Cam and Jesus Green Park and also has good parking facilities.
66rm(20⇨33↱)Annexe22rm(19⇨3↱)(7fb) CTV in all bedrooms ® **T** ✈ sB&B£25-£31.50 sB&B⇨↱£31.50-£42.50 dB&B£37-£49 dB&B⇨↱£42-£58 Continental breakfast ▤
☾ 70P
♀ English, French & Italian V ♥ ☕ ⚔ Lunch £6.25-£7.50&alc High tea £1.25-£5alc Dinner £10.50&alc Last dinner 9.30pm
Credit Cards [1] [2] [3] [5]

★★Cambridge Lodge Huntingdon Rd CB3 0DQ ☎(0223)352833
FAX (0223) 355166
RS Sat
Just a mile from Cambridge, this Edwardian building provides a small, comfortable lounge area with a bar and a well-appointed restaurant, where a good choice of interesting dishes is served. Bedrooms are individually decorated and have modern facilities.
11rm(2⇨9↱) CTV in all bedrooms ® **T** S%
sB&B⇨↱£39-£48 dB&B⇨↱£55-£75 ▤
20P ⊞ ❊

▶

♀ English & Continental **V** S% Lunch £12.95-£14.95&alc Dinner £17.95-£19.95&alc Last dinner 9.30pm
Credit Cards 1 2 3 5

★**Quy Mill Hotel** CB5 9AG ☎(0223)853383 FAX (0223) 853770 (For full entry see Stow Cum Quy)

✕✕**Midsummer House** Midsummer Common CB4 1HA ☎(0223)69299
This stylish and attractive restaurant is situated on the edge of Midsummer Common – a little difficult to find, but staff are well versed in giving directions on the telephone. A number of small dining areas include a conservatory overlooking the pleasant garden. Chef Hans Schweitzer makes skilful use of fresh ingredients to produce such dishes as salmon and cucumber tart with dill sauce and duck with raspberry sauce and green peppercorns.
Closed Mon
Lunch not served Sat
Dinner not served Sun
♀ International 55 seats ✱ Lunch £10.80-£26.50 Dinner £18.50-£26.50 Last lunch 2pm Last dinner 9.30pm ₽
Credit Cards 1 3 5

CAMPBELTOWN Strathclyde *Argyllshire* Map **10** NR72

★★**Royal** Main St PA28 6AG ☎(0586)52017
Popular with both commercial trade and holiday makers, the hotel has fine views.
16rm(8⇌4↱)(2fb) CTV in all bedrooms ® **T** ✱ sB&B£17.95 sB&B⇌↱£22.50 dB&B£31.75 dB&B⇌↱£38 ⊟
Lift CTV 4P ♫
♀ English & French ♆ ♀ ⚟ Lunch £3.50-£5.50alc High tea £3.50-£6.95 Dinner £10&alc Last dinner 9pm
Credit Cards 1 3

★**Seafield** Kilkerran Rd PA28 6JL ☎(0586)54385
3↱Annexe6↱ CTV in all bedrooms ® **T** ✱
sB&B↱£23.50-£25 dB&B↱£39.50-£41.50 ⊟
11P
♆ ♀ Lunch fr£6.50 High tea fr£4.95 Dinner fr£9.75 Last dinner 9pm
Credit Cards 1 3

CANNICH Highland *Inverness-shire* Map **14** NH33

★★**Cozac Lodge** Glen Cannich IV4 7LX (8m W on unclass Glen Cannich rd)
☎(04565)263
Closed Nov-Mar

In a spectacular Highland setting this charming country house offers comfortable accommodation and genuine hospitality. The style of cooking is adventurous and some dishes have an international flavour.

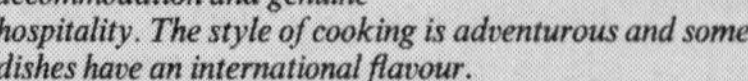

7rm(3⇌4↱)(1fb) CTV in all bedrooms ® ✱
sB&B⇌↱£37-£39 dB&B⇌↱£50-£60 ⊟
CTV 12P ✿ ❀ ⚲
♀ International ♆ ♀
Credit Cards 1 2 3

Red-star hotels offer the highest standards of hospitality, comfort and food.

CANNOCK Staffordshire Map **07** SJ91

★★★60% ***Roman Way*** Watling St, Hatherton WS11 1SH (on A5) (Crown & Raven) ☎(05435)72121
A modern hotel with good standards that meets the needs of business and tourist guests. It lies on the A5 close to junctions 11 and 12 of the M6. Bedrooms have good facilities and there is a choice of bars.
Annexe24rm(20⇌4↱)(6fb) CTV in all bedrooms ® **T**
☾ 200P
♀ English & French **V** ♆ ♀
Credit Cards 1 2 3 5

⌂***Longford House Travel Inn*** Watling St, Longford ☎(05435)72721
A modern bedroom complex situated at the rear of a Georgian house on the A5, close to junction 12 of the M6.
38rm

CANONBIE Dumfries & Galloway *Dumfriesshire* Map **11** NY37

★**Riverside Inn** DG14 0UX ☎(03873)71295 & 71512
Closed 1-15 Nov, Xmas & 2 wks Feb
The proprietors ensure that their guests have a relaxing stay at this charming inn close to the banks of the River Esk. The bedrooms have been individually decorated and furnished and contain many thoughtful touches and there are two cosy lounge areas and a lounge bar with an inviting fire where you can have a bar lunch. In the evening Mr Phillips carefully prepares local produce to provide guests with a most enjoyable dinner complemented by a good variety of wines while Mrs Phillips and the young local staff provide service.
4rm(2⇌2↱)Annexe2⇌1⊞ CTV in all bedrooms ® ✗ (ex guide dogs) sB&B⇌↱£40-£46 dB&B£54 dB&B⇌↱£60 ⊟
25P ✿
♆ ⚟ Bar Lunch £4.50-£7alc Dinner £17.50 Last dinner 8.30pm
Credit Cards 1 3

CANTERBURY Kent Map **05** TR15

★★★63% **The Chaucer** Ivy Ln CT1 1TT (Trusthouse Forte) ☎(0227)464427 Telex no 965096 FAX (0227) 450397
Largely rebuilt after the Second World War, this comfortable hotel has newly-refurbished bedrooms, well-equipped and with private facilities, and a nicely appointed restaurant, where the cooking is sound and the service friendly.
45⇌⚟in 10 bedrooms CTV in all bedrooms ® **T** ✱ sB⇌£64 dB⇌£85 (room only) ⊟
☾ 45P CFA *xmas*
♀ English & French **V** ♆ ♀ ⚟ Lunch £10 Dinner £12.50&alc Last dinner 9.45pm
Credit Cards 1 2 3 4 5

★★★52% **Falstaff** St Dunstans St CT2 8AF (Lansbury) ☎(0227)462138 Telex no 96394 FAX (0227) 463525
This hotel has been accommodating travellers since the 15th century. Standing close to the city's Westgate Tower, it offers a cosy lounge, small bar and beamed restaurant. While bedrooms have most facilities, they, too, retain much of their past character.
25rm(21⇌3↱)(2fb)2⊞⚟in 6 bedrooms CTV in all bedrooms ® **T** ✗ (ex guide dogs) sB&B⇌↱£58 dB&B⇌↱£68 ⊟
☾ 40P *xmas*
♀ English & Continental **V** ♆ ♀ Lunch fr£8.50 Dinner fr£12.50 Last dinner 10pm
Credit Cards 1 2 3 5

★★**Canterbury** 71 New Dover Rd CT1 3DZ ☎(0227)450551 Telex no 965809 FAX (0227) 450873
Elegant Georgian style hotel with good standard of personal service.
27rm(12⇌15↱)(4fb) CTV in all bedrooms ® **T** ✱
sB&B⇌↱£42 dB&B⇌↱£52 ⊟
Lift CTV 40P

☋ English & French ♇ ☐ Lunch fr£6 Dinner fr£10.50 Last dinner 10pm
Credit Cards [1] [2] [3] [5] (£)

✕✕Michael's Restaurant 74 Wincheap CT1 3RS
☎(0227)767411
As you enter this tastefully decorated establishment, there is a cosy sitting area in which you can enjoy a drink before your meal or coffee after it. The atmosphere throughout the restaurant is intimate and friendly, and the standard of food, influenced by nouvelle cuisine, is high.
Closed Sun, 26-30 Dec, 1 wk Etr & BH'S
Lunch not served Sat
☋ British & French **V** 34 seats ✻ Lunch fr£12&alc Dinner fr£18&alc Last lunch 2.30pm Last dinner 9.30pm 10P ⚟
Credit Cards [1] [3]

✕Ristorante Tuo e Mio 16 The Borough CT1 2DR
☎(0227)61471
An appealing restaurant with a comprehensive Italian menu which includes seafood specialities and dishes of the day. Décor is clean and bright with a certain charm and elegance and the staff are pleasant and helpful.
Closed Mon, last 2 wks Aug & 1st wk Sep
Lunch not served Tue
☋ Italian **V** 40 seats ✻ Lunch £15-£20alc Last dinner 10.45pm
P
Credit Cards [1] [2] [3] [5]

CARBIS BAY
See **St Ives**

CARDIFF South Glamorgan Map **03** ST17
See **Town Plan Section**

★★★★66% Holiday Inn Mill Ln CF1 1EZ (Holiday Inns)
☎(0222)399944 Telex no 497365 FAX (0222) 395578
An impressive, modern hotel near the city centre and railway station with well appointed bedrooms and open plan public areas. Good conference and leisure facilities.
182⇌↱(78fb)⚟in 36 bedrooms CTV in all bedrooms ® **T** ✻
sB⇌↱£73-£98 dB⇌↱£78-£86 (room only) ⛿
Lift ☾ ⊞ 90P ▭(heated) squash sauna solarium gymnasium turkish bath ♫ *xmas*
☋ English & French **V** ♇ ⚟ Lunch £10.95-£12.95 Dinner fr£12.95&alc Last dinner 11.30pm
Credit Cards [1] [2] [3] [4] [5]

★★★★63% *Park* Park Place CF1 3UD (Mount Charlotte)
☎(0222)383471 Telex no 497195
The bedrooms and public areas have undergone some exciting transformations during 1989. With its choice of restaurants and bars and its central location, the hotel attracts many businessmen as well as locals.
108⇌(6fb)⚟in 30 bedrooms CTV in all bedrooms ® **T**
Lift ☾ 80P CFA
☋ English & French **V** ♇ ☐
Credit Cards [1] [2] [3] [5]

★★★62% *Crest* Castle St C71 2XB (Crest) ☎(0222)388681
Telex no 497258 FAX (0222) 371495
The modern, company-owned hotel stands adjacent to the National Stadium and overlooks Cardiff Castle. Its popular bars and well equipped bedrooms attract a firm business following.
159⇌↱(24fb)⚟in 20 bedrooms CTV in all bedrooms ® **T**
Lift ☾ 120P CFA ♫
☋ French **V** ♇ ☐ ⚟ Last dinner 9.45pm
Credit Cards [1] [2] [3] [5]

See advertisement on page 181

Book as early as possible for busy holiday periods.

★★★56% Post House Pentwyn Rd, Pentwyn CF2 7XA (Trusthouse Forte) ☎(0222)731212 Telex no 497633
FAX (0222) 549147
Situated alongside the city's Eastern Avenue bypass, this busy hotel caters mainly for business clientele. Bedrooms are well equipped, there are good leisure and conference facilities, an à la carte restaurant and a coffee shop.
150⇌(50fb)⚟in 30 bedrooms CTV in all bedrooms ® **T** ✻
sB⇌fr£67 dB⇌fr£78 (room only) ⛿
Lift ☾ 210P ❃ CFA ▭(heated) sauna solarium gymnasium *xmas*
V ♇ ☐ ⚟ Lunch £7.50&alc High tea £2.55-£8.05alc Dinner £11.95&alc Last dinner 10pm
Credit Cards [1] [2] [3] [4] [5]

★★★52% Royal Saint Mary's St CF1 1LL (Embassy)
☎(0222)383321 Telex no 498062 FAX (0222) 222238
Typical Victorian hotel in the city centre.
63rm(39⇌8↱)(3fb)⚟in 6 bedrooms CTV in all bedrooms ® **T** ✻ S% sBfr£32 sB⇌↱fr£48 dBfr£42
dB⇌↱fr£58 (room only) ⛿
Lift ☾ CTV **P** CFA snooker ♫ *xmas*
☋ British & French **V** ♇ ☐ S% Lunch £9.50&alc Dinner £9.50&alc Last dinner 10pm
Credit Cards [1] [2] [3] [4] [5]

★★*Lincoln* 118 Cathedral Rd CF1 9LQ ☎(0222)395558
Telex no 497492
This small, comfortable hotel, standing only a mile from the city centre, offers a high standard of food and accommodation.
18rm(7⇌11↱)(1fb) CTV in all bedrooms ® **T** ✗ (ex guide dogs)
☾ 18P
V ♇ ☐ Last dinner 9.30pm
Credit Cards [1] [2] [3] [5]

Cardiff

C

★★The Phoenix 199 Fidlas Rd, Llanishen CF4 5NA ☎(0222)764615
24rm(4⇌16🚿)(2fb) CTV in all bedrooms ® T ✱ sB&B⇌🚿£25-£32.95 dB&B£30-£35 dB&B⇌🚿£35-£42.50
Lift ☾ CTV 30P
🍷 English & French V ♿ 🍷 Lunch £6.50&alc High tea £2.25-£2.50 Dinner £6.50&alc Last dinner 10.30pm
Credit Cards 1 3 4

Campanile Caxton Place, Pentwyn CF2 7HA (Campanile) ☎(0222)549044 Telex no 497553
Annexe47⇌🚿 CTV in all bedrooms ® T sB⇌🚿fr£29 dB⇌🚿fr£29 (room only)
50P *xmas*
🍷 English & French Lunch £3.75-£8.90 Dinner £6.80-£8.90 Last dinner 10pm
Credit Cards 1 3

○***Rank Motor Lodge*** Cardiff West, M4 Motorway, Jct 33, Pontyclun CF7 8SB (Rank) ☎(0222)892255
Due to open Apr 1990
50⇌🚿

❀✕**La Chaumière** Cardiff Rd, Llandaff CF5 2DS ☎(0222)555319
Just behind the Maltsters public house and only a short walk from the cathedral stands a delightful little restaurant offering a small, carefully selected menu with a strong French influence. A main course such as succulent chicken or calves' tongues could be preceded by leek tart or stuffed mushrooms, and a mouthwatering range of sweet dishes is always available. Food is skilfully prepared, most attractively presented, and served by friendly staff; the premises have no bar but drinks are served at your table.
Closed Mon & 1st 2 wks Jan
Lunch not served Sat
Dinner not served Sun
🍷 French V 40 seats ✱ Lunch fr£18.50alc Last lunch 2pm Last dinner 9.30pm 20P
Credit Cards 1 2 3 5

✕***Gibsons*** Romilly Crescent CF1 9 ☎(0222)341264
Set away from the city centre, this modest little split-level restaurant offers homely comfort and a convivial atmosphere. Its emphasis is on the presentation of imaginative, quality dishes, and it often promotes keenly-priced regional French evenings. Friendly and informative service is provided by a young staff.
Closed Boxing Day & BH
Dinner not served Sun
🍷 French V 38 seats Last lunch 2.15pm Last dinner 10pm 5P
Credit Cards 1 2 3 5

✕**Le Cassoulet** 5 Romilly Crescent, Canton CF1 9NP ☎(0222)221905
Claire and Gilbert Viader have created a taste of the French countryside in this charming little restaurant in the heart of Cardiff. Both of them come from Toulouse and the rich, strong flavours of the region feature largely on their menus – the restaurant taking its name from one of Toulouse's most famous specialities. The cooking is authentic and maintains the best traditions of French family cooking. The wine list has a good selection of well chosen French wines at very moderate prices; the staff are knowledgeable and happy to explain or advise.
Closed Sun & Mon 4 weeks in summer. Ring for details
Lunch not served Sat
🍷 French 36 seats ✱ Lunch fr£13alc Dinner fr£13alc Last lunch 2pm Last dinner 10pm ₱
Credit Cards 1 2 5

✕**Polydores Fish** 89 City Rd, Roath CF2 4BN ☎(0222)481319
Cardiff's connection with the sea is manifested by this fish restaurant with its wealth of unusual dishes. The sole, skate, red mullet and other fish are available during their best seasons, but there is also fresh tuna, marlin or barracuda amongst others rare to these shores. Alternatively there is a choice of various steaks, poultry of even alligator meat.
Lunch not served Sat
Dinner not served Sun & Mon
🍷 fish dishes of all kinds V 40 seats ✱ Lunch £9&alc Dinner fr£12.50alc Last lunch 2.30pm Last dinner 10.30pm ₱
Credit Cards 1 2 3 5

✕**Riverside** 44 Tudor St CF1 8RH ☎(0222)372163
A Cantonese restaurant, among the best of its kind in Wales.
Closed 24-25 Dec
🍷 Cantonese V 140 seats ✱ Lunch £11-£16&alc Dinner £11-£16&alc Last dinner 11.45pm ₱
Credit Cards 1 2 3 5

The AA's star-rating scheme is the market leader in hotel classification.

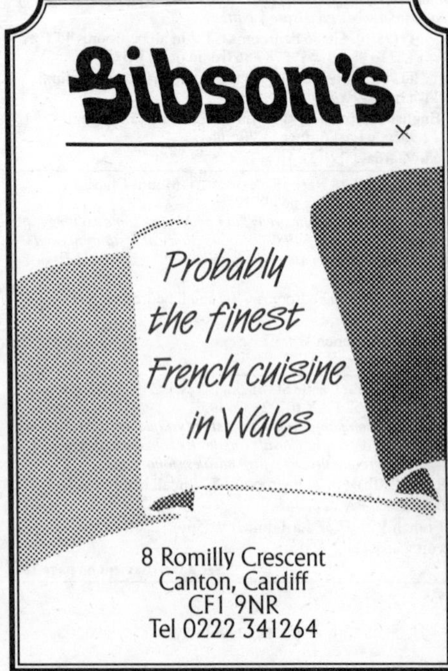

C

CARFRAEMILL Borders *Berwickshire* Map **12** NT55

★★Carfraemill TD2 6RA ☎Oxton(05785)200 Telex no 336587
A roadside hotel, just off the A68.
11rm(2⇔)(2fb) CTV in all bedrooms ® **T** sB&B£30-£40 sB&B⇔£32.50-£50 dB&B£50 dB&B⇔£60 ≡
100P 3⌂
☉ International **V** ⚘ ⌘ Lunch £6.75-£9 High tea £5-£7.50 Dinner £11.25-£12.25&alc Last dinner 9pm
Credit Cards [1] [2] [3] [5]

CARLISLE Cumbria Map **12** NY45

See also **Hayton**

★★★63% Central Victoria Viaduct CA3 8AL (Inter) ☎(0228)20256
Recently refurbished city centre hotel with a comfortable lounge bar.
70rm(22⇔13↱)(6fb) CTV in all bedrooms ® **T** sB&B⇔↱£39.50-£46.50 dB&B⇔↱£55-£65 ≡
Lift ☾ CTV 20⌂ pool *xmas*
☉ English & French **V** ⚘ ⌘ Lunch £3.90-£5.50 High tea £5.50 Dinner £10&alc Last dinner 9pm
Credit Cards [1] [2] [3] [5]

★★★61% Crest Parkhouse Rd, Kingstown CA4 0HR (junc 44/ M6) (Crest) ☎(0228)31201 Telex no 64201 FAX (0228) 43178
Purpose-built hotel, just south of junction 44 of the M6/A74/A7 on the northern outskirts of the town, popular with business clientele.
94⇔↱(12fb)⊁in 23 bedrooms CTV in all bedrooms ® **T** ✱ S% sB⇔↱£40-£64.50 dB⇔↱£50-£76.50 (room only) ≡
☾ CTV 200P CFA snooker ♫ *xmas*
☉ International **V** ⚘ ⌘ ⊁ Lunch £7.50 High tea £7.50 Dinner £12.50-£14.30&alc Last dinner 9.45pm
Credit Cards [1] [2] [3] [4] [5]

★★★*Cumbrian* Court Square CA1 1QY ☎(0228)31951 Telex no 64287 FAX (0228) 47799
Spacious, comfortable hotel with modern bedrooms near railway station.
70⇔↱(6fb)4⊞⊁in 4 bedrooms CTV in all bedrooms ® **T**
Lift ☾ 15P 30⌂ CFA
☉ Continental **V** ⚘ ⌘ ⊁ Last dinner 10pm
Credit Cards [1] [2] [3] [5]

★★★62% Swallow Hilltop London Rd CA1 2PQ (Swallow) ☎(0228)29255 Telex no 64292 FAX (0228) 25238
Large modern hotel with very good facilities and new leisure complex.
97rm(92⇔5↱)(10fb)⊁in 13 bedrooms CTV in all bedrooms ® **T** sB&B⇔↱fr£52 dB&B⇔↱fr£66 ≡
Lift ☾ CTV 350P 1⌂ ✲ CFA ▭(heated) ⚑ sauna solarium gymnasium table tennis massage & beauty ♫ ⚘ *xmas*
☉ English & French **V** ⚘ Lunch fr£7.50&alc Dinner fr£12.95&alc Last dinner 9.45pm
Credit Cards [1] [2] [3] [5]

★★Pinegrove 262 London Rd CA1 2QS ☎(0228)24828
Closed 25 & 31 Dec
Comfortable hotel with hospitable proprietor.
28rm(9⇔13↱)(8fb) CTV in all bedrooms ® **T** ✱ sB&Bfr£22 sB&B⇔↱fr£32 dB&Bfr£34 dB&B⇔↱fr£44
CTV 30P ✲
V ⚘ ⌘ Bar Lunch 65p-£6.25 Dinner £9.50-£12.50 Last dinner 8.30pm
Credit Cards [1] [3]

★★*Woodlands* 264/266 London Rd CA1 2QS ☎(0228)45643
Closed 24 Dec-8 Jan
Small, family-run commercial hotel on the main road, 2 miles south of the city centre.
15rm(7⇔1↱)(1fb) CTV in all bedrooms ®
20P ⊠
☉ English **V** Wine £4.75 Last dinner 9pm
Credit Cards [1] [2] [3] [5] £

★Vallum House Burgh Rd CA2 7NB ☎(0228)21860
Closed 25 & 26 Dec
Small and friendly commercial hotel on the western edge of the city.
9rm(1⇔4↱)(1fb) CTV in 6bedrooms TV in 3bedrooms ® **T** sB&B£25-£30 sB&B⇔↱£30-£35 dB&B⇔↱£40-£45
CTV 30P ✲
☉ English & French **V** ⚘ ⌘ Lunch £6-£10&alc High tea £3.95-£4.50&alc Dinner £8-£11&alc Last dinner 9pm
Credit Cards [1] £

CARMARTHEN Dyfed Map **02** SN42

★★★56% Ivy Bush Royal Spilman St SA31 1LG (Trusthouse Forte) ☎(0267)235111 Telex no 48520 FAX (0267) 234914
Large and popular, the hotel is ideally situated for touring West Wales and also offers good conference facilities. Many bedrooms are now a little dated – though upgrading is planned – but public areas are pleasant and relaxing.
79rm(71⇔8↱)(3fb)⊁in 8 bedrooms CTV in all bedrooms ® **T** sB⇔↱fr£50 dB⇔↱fr£60 (room only) ≡
Lift ☾ 75P 3⌂ ✲ CFA sauna *xmas*
V ⚘ ⌘ ⊁ Lunch fr£7.50 Dinner fr£10.75 Last dinner 9.30pm
Credit Cards [1] [2] [3] [4] [5]

CARNFORTH Lancashire Map **07** SD47

★★Royal Station Market St LA5 9BT ☎(0524)732033 & 733636
A comfortable hotel situated in the town centre provides a noteworthy standard of friendly, courteous service.
12rm(5⇔4↱)(1fb) CTV in all bedrooms ® **T** sB&Bfr£19.50 sB&B⇔↱fr£23 dB&Bfr£35 dB&B⇔↱fr£40 ≡
8P 10⌂
☉ English, French & Italian **V** ⚘ ⌘ Bar Lunch £5-£8alc Dinner £8-£11.25alc Last dinner 8.30pm
Credit Cards [1] [2] [3] [5] £

CARNOUSTIE Tayside *Angus* Map **12** NO53

★★*Carlogie House* Carlogie Rd DD7 6LD ☎(0241)53185
Closed 1-3 Jan
Small, well decorated, family-run hotel set within its own grounds.
11rm(1⇔10↱)(1fb) CTV in all bedrooms ® **T** ✗ (ex guide dogs)
CTV 150P 4⌂ ✲
☉ Scottish & French **V** ⚘ ⌘ Last dinner 9pm
Credit Cards [1] [2] [3] [5]

★★Glencoe Links Pde DD7 7JF ☎(0241)53273
Closed 1 Jan
Homely, family hotel overlooking golf course, offering very good value meals.
11rm(3⇔5↱)(2fb) CTV in all bedrooms **T** S10% sB&B£18.50 dB&B⇔↱£41
CTV 10P ⊠
☉ Scottish & French **V** ⚘ ⌘ S10% Bar Lunch £1-£5alc Dinner £9.50-£15 Last dinner 9pm
Credit Cards [1] [2] [3] [5]

C

★Brax Links Pde DD7 7JF ☎(0241)53032
Small, homely family-run hotel, with modern bedrooms, overlooking the golf course.
6rm(3fl) CTV in all bedrooms ® sB&Bfr£14 sB&Bflfr£19 dB&Bfr£30 dB&Bflfr£38
12P *xmas*
Mainly grills Bar Lunch fr£4alc High tea fr£5.50alc Dinner fr£10alc Last dinner 8.30pm
Credit Cards 1 2 3 £

★Station DD7 6AR ☎(0241)52447
Small, friendly, town centre hotel next to the station and near the beach.
9rm(3fl)(1fb) CTV in 3bedrooms ®
CTV 10P pool ♫
V Last dinner 9pm
Credit Cards 1 3

CARPERBY North Yorkshire Map **07** SE08

★★Wheatsheaf DL8 4DF (Best Western) ☎Aysgarth(09693)216
A quaint country inn whose claim to fame is that James Herriott spent his honeymoon here. Whilst there have been many improvements since then, the charming atmosphere has been retained. Dinner can be especially recommended.
8rm(2⇌6fl)(1fb)2 CTV in all bedrooms ® ✱
sB&B⇌fl£22.50-£25 dB&B⇌fl£45-£55
50P ✼ nc12yrs
V Lunch £4.50-£7.50 High tea £4-£5.50 Dinner £9.50-£11.50&alc Last dinner 9.30pm
Credit Cards 1 2 3 5 £

For key to symbols see the inside front cover.

C

CARRADALE Strathclyde *Argyllshire* Map **10** NR83

★★Carradale PA28 6QQ ☎(05833)223
Standing in its own grounds overlooking Kilbrannan Sound and the Isle of Arran, this pleasant holiday hotel offers modest bedrooms and public rooms and a small leisure centre. The golf course is conveniently situated next to the hotel.
14rm(4⇌3↱)Annexe6rm(1⇌3↱)(2fb) Ⓡ sB&B£20-£28 sB&B⇌↱£20-£28 dB&B£40-£56 dB&B⇌↱£40-£56 ⊟
CTV 20P ✱ squash sauna solarium
V ✿ ☐ Lunch £4.50-£7 High tea £4.50-£8.50 Dinner £12.50-£16.50 Last dinner 8.45pm
Credit Cards 1 3 £

CARRBRIDGE Highland *Inverness-shire* Map **14** NH92

★★Dalrachney Lodge PH23 3AT ☎(047984)252
FAX (047984) 382
This former shooting lodge is now a fine country house hotel, with spacious, lofty bedrooms, a delightful lounge and an elegant dining room. Service is extremely attentive and the artistically presented food features the best of Scottish beef, game and fish. The lodge lies just east of the village, close to the River Durnain.
11rm(8⇌)(2fb) CTV in all bedrooms Ⓡ **T** ✱ sB&B£18-£25 sB&B⇌£18-£25 dB&B⇌£36-£50 ⊟
P ✱ ♩
☐ Scottish, French **V** ✿ ☐ ✗ Lunch £5.50 Dinner £12.50&alc Last dinner 9pm
Credit Cards 1 2 3

CARRUTHERSTOWN Dumfries & Galloway *Dumfriesshire* Map **11** NY17

★★★61% Hetland Hall DG1 4JX (Best Western)
☎Dumfries(0387)84201 Telex no 776819 FAX (0387) 84211
Surrounded by extensive parkland, this converted mansion with its functional modern wing has now been upgraded to provide comfortable and well-equipped bedrooms, whilst the proprietors and their young staff continue to offer friendly, relaxed service.
27rm(15⇌12↱)(3fb)✗in 3 bedrooms CTV in all bedrooms Ⓡ **T** ✱ S% sB&B⇌↱£35-£45 dB&B⇌↱£54-£68 ⊟
☾ CTV 60P ✱ ♩ snooker sauna solarium gymnasium indoor badminton *xmas*
☐ International **V** ✿ ☐ Lunch £6.50-£11.50 High tea £4.50-£11.50 Dinner £11.50-£20&alc Last dinner 9.30pm
Credit Cards 1 2 3 5 £

See advertisement under DUMFRIES

CARTMEL Cumbria Map **07** SD37

★★Aynsome Manor LA11 6HH 1m N on unclass rd
☎(05395)36653
Closed 2-26 Jan
This lovely old manor house features open fires in its comfortable lounges and serves a freshly-prepared five-course dinner of a very high standard.
11rm(9⇌1↱)Annexe2⇌(2fb)1⊟ CTV in all bedrooms Ⓡ **T** ✱ sB&B⇌↱£36.50-£38.50 dB&B£68-£72 dB&B⇌↱£73-£77 (incl dinner) ⊟
20P ✱ ✱ *xmas*
☐ English & French **V** ✿ ✗ Lunch £7.50 Dinner £15-£16.50 Last dinner 8.15pm
Credit Cards 1 2 3

★★*Priory* The Square LA11 6QB ☎(05395)36267
Delightful small hotel, family owned and run with a charming restaurant, popular coffee shop and a comfortable lounge.
9rm(5⇌1↱)(2fb)1⊟ CTV in all bedrooms Ⓡ
8P
☐ English French & Italian **V** ✿ ☐ ✗ Last dinner 8.45pm
Credit Cards 1 3

✿✕✕Uplands Hotel Haggs Ln LA11 6HD
☎(05395)36248
(Rosette awarded for dinner only)
This delightful small hotel sits on a hillside between Cartmel and Grange, with lovely views across open countryside to Morecambe Bay. Whilst acknowledging 'the Miller Howe manner', Tom and Di Peter have adopted their very own style. There is a bright, comfortable lounge, and in the dining room an interesting 5-course menu offers a choice of starters such as fresh scallops in a bacon shallot with white sauce. The soup course, with individual tureens left on the table, is followed by a choice of 3 main course dishes – our inspector enjoyed marinaded hare with oyster mushrooms. Puddings include both traditional and more innovative options. As one would expect, chef/patron Tom makes the fullest use of fresh local produce. Four pleasant bedrooms are also available.
Closed Mon & 2 Jan-25 Feb
30 seats ✱ Lunch £12 Dinner £18.50 Last lunch 1pm Last dinner 8pm 14P nc10yrs 4 bedrooms available ✗
Credit Cards 1 2

CASTERTON Cumbria Map **07** SD67

★★Pheasant Inn LA6 2RX ☎Kirkby Lonsdale(05242)71230
Comfortable village inn, popular for its restaurant dinners and bar lunches. Annexe bedrooms are contained in a modernised coach house.
10rm(9⇌1↱)(1fb)1⊟ CTV in all bedrooms Ⓡ **T** sB&B⇌↱fr£35 dB&B⇌↱fr£50 ⊟
CTV 60P ✱ *xmas*
V ✿ ☐ ✗ Lunch fr£7.50 Dinner fr£12.50 Last dinner 9pm
Credit Cards 1 3

CASTLE ASHBY Northamptonshire Map **04** SP85

★★Falcon ☎Yardley Hastings(060129)200 FAX (060129) 673
6rm(5⇌)Annexe8rm(7⇌1↱)2⊟ CTV in all bedrooms Ⓡ **T** ✗ (ex guide dogs) sB&B⇌↱£40-£50 dB&B⇌↱£50-£60 ⊟
CTV 75P ✱
✿ ☐ Lunch £8-£25alc Dinner £16-£25alc Last dinner 9.30pm
Credit Cards 1 2 3

CASTLE COMBE Wiltshire Map **03** ST87

★★★ 75% Manor House
SN14 7HR
☎(0249)782206
Telex no 449931
FAX (0249) 782159

In a pretty village setting, this attractive hotel is, under new ownership, undergoing considerable change and refurbishment. Splendid, capacious bedrooms in the main house, together with the more functional cottage rooms, are all well equipped and individual in style. Afternoon teas are served in the comfortable lounges and, in the large dining room, chef Evenden's interesting and carefully prepared food is served by pleasant staff.
12⇌↱Annexe20⇌↱6⊟ CTV in all bedrooms **T** ✱ sB⇌↱£75-£95 dB⇌↱£95-£250 (room only) ⊟
☾ 100P ✱ ⇒(heated) ♪ (hard) ♩ croquet lawn jogging track *xmas*

English & French V Lunch £14.50-£18.50&alc High tea £5.95-£10.95 Dinner £21.50-£25&alc Last dinner 10.00pm
Credit Cards 1 2 3 5

CASTLE DONINGTON Leicestershire Map **08** SK42

★★★ 63% **Donington Manor** High St DE7 2PP
Derby(0332)810253 Telex no 934999 FAX (0332) 850330
Closed 27-30 Dec
A family owned and run hotel at the edge of the village, conveniently situated for access to the East Midland Airport, offers good value for money in its well furnished, comfortable accommodation and interesting menus.
35rm(33)Annexe3rm(1)(3fb)5 CTV in all bedrooms ® T (ex guide dogs) * S% sB&B£31-£33 sB&B£44-£51 dB&B£41.50-£44.50 dB&B£45-£60
60P
English & French Lunch fr£5.55 Dinner fr£7.30 Last dinner 9.30pm
Credit Cards 1 2 3 5

★★★ 64% **Donington Thistle** East Midlands Airport DE7 2SH (Thistle) Derby(0332)850700 Telex no 377632
FAX (0332) 850823
A modern purpose-built hotel at the perimeter of the East Midlands Airport with a leisure club and conference facilities. The bedrooms are large and well-equipped and there is 24-hour room service.
110(12fb) in 12 bedrooms CTV in all bedrooms ® T *
sB£63-£66 dB£78 (room only)
180P (heated) sauna solarium gymnasium
International V Lunch fr£9.75&alc Dinner £10.50-£12.95&alc
Credit Cards 1 2 3 5

CASTLE DOUGLAS Dumfries & Galloway
Kirkcudbrightshire Map **11** NX76

★★**Imperial** King St DG7 1AA (0556)2086 & 3009
RS 26 Dec & 1-2 Jan
Neat, homely hotel in main street.
13rm(3 5) in 2 bedrooms CTV in all bedrooms ® T
sB&B£16.50-£17.50 sB&B£21.50-£22.50 dB&B£32-£35 dB&B£38.50-£39.50
20P 9 sailing water-skiing
V Bar Lunch £4.75-£5.75&alc High tea £4.50-£5.50alc Dinner £7.75&alc Last dinner 8pm
Credit Cards 1 3 £

CASTLETOWN

See **Man, Isle of**

CATEL (CASTEL)

See **Guernsey under Channel Islands**

CATTERICK BRIDGE North Yorkshire Map **08** SE29

★★**Bridge House** DL10 7PE Richmond(0748)818331
Old coaching inn with character bars, impressive dining room and homely bedrooms.
17rm(4 3)(2fb)1 CTV in all bedrooms ® T
sB&B£18.50-£20 sB&B£28-£30 dB&B£30-£35 dB&B£38-£45
CTV 70P
English & French V Lunch £6.25-£7.50 Dinner £9.50-£10.50 Last dinner 9.30pm
Credit Cards 1 2 3 5 £

CERRIG-Y-DRUDION Clwyd Map **06** SH94

★★***Saracens Head*** LL21 9SY (049082)684
This 300-year-old coaching house has been completely modernised and extended to provide well-furnished, spacious bedrooms and good bar and restaurant areas (though no lounge facilities exist). A motel-type of operation ensures value-for-money.
15rm(6)Annexe9(4fb) CTV in 15bedrooms ® T
50P

Credit Cards 1 2 3 4

CHADDESLEY CORBETT Hereford & Worcester
Map **07** SO87

★★★ 74% **Brockencote Hall Country House**
DY10 4PY
(056283)876
Telex no 333431
Closed 26 Dec-3rd wk Jan

Since taking over this former private home in 1986, Alison and Joseph Petitjean have painstakingly restored both the magnificent house and the 70 acres of grounds. Although young, they have a great deal of experience in the hotel industry and are personally involved in the running of the hotel in a relaxed but professional manner. Comfortable and elegant throughout, the hotel has spacious and well-equipped bedrooms. The mainly French menu is imaginative and the standard of cuisine very high.

9rm(8⇨1↱)(2fb)1⊞ CTV in all bedrooms **T** ✈ ✳ sB&B⇨↱£58 dB&B⇨↱£72-£95 ⊟
45P ⊕ ✲
☊ French ✧ ⊡ Lunch £14.50&alc Dinner £25&alc Last dinner 9.30pm
Credit Cards 1 2 3 5

CHADLINGTON Oxfordshire Map **04** SP32

★★Chadlington House OX7 3LZ Y ☎(060876)437
Telex no 83138
Closed Jan & Feb
In a rural location, this delightful hotel, with attractive secluded gardens and grounds, offers a welcoming atmosphere, homely accommodation and good cooking standards.
10rm(5⇨5↱)(1fb)1⊞ CTV in all bedrooms ® ✈ (ex guide dogs) ✳ sB&B⇨↱£29.50-£37.50 dB&B⇨↱£42-£70 ⊟
CTV 20P 2⌂ ✲ nc8
☊ English & French **V** ✧ ⊡ ⊬ Lunch £10.50-£12.50 Dinner £15&alc Last dinner 8.30pm
Credit Cards 1 3 £

★★♜The Manor OX7 3LX
☎(060876)711

David Grant has created a comfortable country house of international standard in this small Cotswold stone building behind the village church. Bedrooms are attractively decorated and furnished with antiques, while the public areas are elegant and welcoming. Chris Grant produces a 4-course dinner of fresh English fare.
7⇨ CTV in all bedrooms **T** ✈ (ex guide dogs) ✳ S% sB&B⇨£50-£70 dB&B⇨£80-£100
20P ⊕ ✲ *xmas*
S% Lunch fr£19.50 Dinner fr£19.50 Last dinner 9pm
Credit Cards 2 3

CHAGFORD Devon Map **03** SX78

❀★★★♜ GIDLEIGH PARK
TQ13 8HH (Relais et Châteaux)
☎(0647)32367 & 32225
Telex no 42643
FAX (06473) 2574

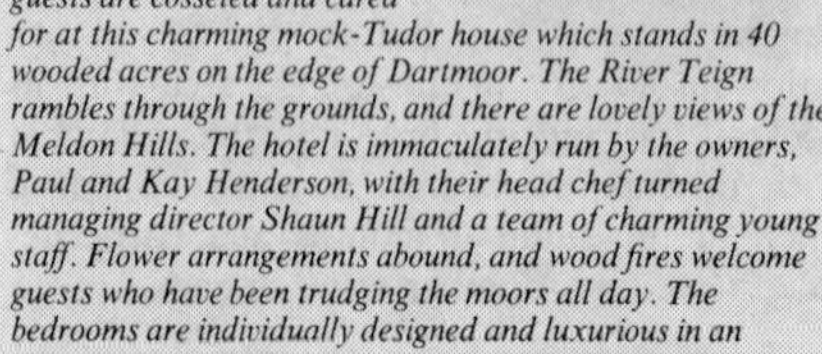

From arrival to departure guests are cosseted and cared for at this charming mock-Tudor house which stands in 40 wooded acres on the edge of Dartmoor. The River Teign rambles through the grounds, and there are lovely views of the Meldon Hills. The hotel is immaculately run by the owners, Paul and Kay Henderson, with their head chef turned managing director Shaun Hill and a team of charming young staff. Flower arrangements abound, and wood fires welcome guests who have been trudging the moors all day. The bedrooms are individually designed and luxurious in an understated way, with antique furniture set off by chintz fabrics. Many have been improved recently and soon all will reach the same high standards. Regular guests will be delighted to know that, despite his promotion, Shaun Hill will – to quote Paul Henderson – 'manage from the cooker'. His splendid cuisine is refreshingly simple – a sausage of salmon with chives and ginger butter sauce was exactly that, and a fillet of beef with morels and celeriac was similarly uncomplicated, honest and full of flavour. Dishes are complemented by an interesting wine list that includes a good selection of North American wines – Paul Henderson is from that continent – and no shortage of rarities and classical vintages.
12⇨Annexe2⇨ CTV in all bedrooms **T** S% sB&B⇨£132-£224
dB&B⇨£161-£253 Continental breakfast (incl dinner) ⊟
25P ⊕ ✲ ♙ (hard) ⅃ croquet
✧ ⊡ S% Lunch £27.50-£37 Dinner £37-£46 Last dinner 9pm
Credit Cards 1 3

★★★♜75% Mill End
Sandy Park TQ13 8JN (2m N on A382)
☎(06473)2282
Closed 13-23 Dec & 12-22 Jan RS Nov-12 Dec & 23 Jan-Mar
A former flour mill, dating back to the seventeenth century and converted into an hotel in 1929, stands beside the River Teign in its own well-kept gardens just one-and-a-half miles from the stannary town of Chagford. Interesting features include the waterwheel, retained to enhance the public rooms, comfortable bedrooms offer every facility for both business client and holiday-maker. Varied and interesting menus are complemented by personal service, and the excellence of the food – all freshly prepared on the day that it is to be eaten – ensures that guests return again and again.
17⇨↱(2fb) CTV in all bedrooms **T** sB£27.50-£37.50 sB⇨↱£45-£65 dB£45 dB⇨↱£50-£65 (room only) ⊟
CTV 17P 4⌂ (£1.50) ⊕ ✲ ⅃ *xmas*
☊ English & French **V** ✧ ⊡ Lunch £14-£17 Dinner £14-£20 Last dinner 9pm
Credit Cards 1 2 3 5

❀★★★♜75%
Teignworthy Frenchbeer
TG13 8EX 2m S on unclass rd to Thornworthy
☎(0647)33355

A granite and slate country hotel, tucked away in an elevated position and commanding views across Dartmoor, provides personal service and a tranquil atmosphere. Cosy public rooms and attractively furnished bedrooms alike – both in the main building and the adjacent cottage – are generously supplied with books, magazines,

flowers and chocolates. The restaurant's table d'hôte menu changes daily and makes full use of seasonal produce and locally grown ingredients in its imaginative dishes, so that you might enjoy pheasant pâté in filo pastry followed by noisettes of Devon lamb cooked in their own juices, with a blackcurrent soufflé to conclude the meal – all complemented by wines chosen from a well balanced list.
6⇌Annexe3⇌1⊞ CTV in all bedrooms **T** ✗
sB&B⇌£59.50 dB&B⇌£100 Continental breakfast ⊟
20P 2⊞ ⊞ ✲ (grass) ♩ sauna solarium nc10yrs *xmas*
V ♧ ⊡ ⊁ Lunch £10-£25alc Dinner £29.50-£35 Last dinner 9.30pm
Credit Cards 1 3 £

★★*Easton Court* Easton Cross TQ13 8JL (1.5m E A382) ☎(06473)3469
This part thatched hotel is run in a friendly and informal manner by owners Peggy Uttley and Joyce Lee. Public areas are cosy, with open fires during the cooler months, and bedrooms offer a variety of styles. Evelyn Waugh's 'Brideshead Revisited' was written here.
8rm(3⇌5↱)2⊞ CTV in all bedrooms ®
CTV 20P ⊞ nc14yrs
V ♧ ⊡ Last dinner 8.30pm
Credit Cards 1 2 3 5

CHALE

See **Wight, Isle of**

CHALFORD Gloucestershire Map **03** SO80

★★*Springfield House Hotel & Restaurant* London Rd GL6 8NW (on A419) ☎Brimscombe(0453)883555
A comfortable small hotel offering personal service and well prepared meals.
7⇌↱2⊞ CTV in all bedrooms ® **T**
20P ✲ croquet
♧ English & French **V** ♧ ⊡ ⊁ Last dinner 9.30pm
Credit Cards 1 2 3 5 £

CHANNEL ISLANDS Map **16**

ALDERNEY

★★Inchalla St Anne ☎(048182)3220
The hotel is small and modern, bright and comfortably appointed. À la carte and table d'hôte menus are available, the food being well cooked and presented.
11rm(8⇌)(2fb) CTV in all bedrooms ® **T** ✗ sB&B£22.20-£27 sB&B⇌£28.20-£48 dB&B⇌£44.40-£56 ⊟
8P ⊞ ✲ sauna solarium jacuzzi
♧ English & French **V** ♧ ⊡ Sunday Lunch fr£8 Dinner fr£9.50&alc Last dinner 8.30pm
Credit Cards 2 3

GUERNSEY

CATEL (CASTEL)

★★Hotel Hougue du Pommier Hougue Du Pommier Rd ☎Guernsey(0481)56531 Telex no 4191664 FAX (0481) 37594
This attractive and well-managed hotel is set in 10 acres of grounds which includes a 6-acre pitch and putt course. Chef Fergus Mackay has won many local awards for his cooking, which can be enjoyed in the candle-lit restaurant.
39rm(18⇌21↱)(12fb) CTV in all bedrooms ® **T** ✗ (ex guide dogs) ✱ sB&B⇌↱£19.50-£33
dB&B⇌↱£39-£66 (incl dinner) ⊟
☾ CTV 87P ✲ ⇌(heated) ▶ 18 solarium gymnasium ♫
♧ English & Continental **V** ♧ ⊡ Lunch £6.80 Dinner £6.80 Last dinner 9.45pm
Credit Cards 1 2 3 4

See advertisement on page 189

FERMAIN BAY

★★★64% Le Chalet (Consort) ☎Guernsey(0481)35716 Telex no 4191342
Closed end Oct-mid Apr
In one of the finest positions on the island, Le Chalet is on a quiet road leading to the bay and has its own extensive woodland. Most of the bedrooms have been refurbished and the bright, attractive restaurant, lounge and bar have commanding sea and woodland views. Friendly and attentive service is provided by British and Austrian staff, many of whom wear national costume.
48rm(40⇌5↱) CTV in all bedrooms ® **T** S%
sB&B⇌↱£25-£27 dB&B⇌↱£43-£52
35P ⊞ ✲
♧ English, Austrian & French **V** ♧ ⊡ S% Lunch £5.50-£10alc Dinner £9.95-£12.95&alc Last dinner 9.30pm
Credit Cards 1 2 3 4 5

★★La Favorita ☎Guernsey(0481)35666 Telex no 94016631 FAX (0481) 35413
Closed 21 Dec-7 Feb RS 1-20 Dec & 8-28 Feb
This modern hotel has a superb location on a quiet road leading to Fermain Bay. The comfortable, well-equipped bedrooms are varied in style and the good public areas include an attractive cocktail bar with panoramic views and an elegant lounge.
29rm(27⇌2↱) CTV in all bedrooms ® **T** ✗
sB&B⇌↱£31-£60 dB&B⇌↱£47-£70 (incl dinner) ⊟
40P ⊞
V ♧ ⊡ ⊁ Lunch £7.75 Dinner £9-£13.50 Last dinner 9pm
Credit Cards 1 3

C

PERELLE

★★★ 66% L'Atlantique Perelle Bay ☎Guernsey(0481)64056
Situated on the coast road and overlooking the bay, this modern hotel stands in well-tended gardens and offers bright, well-equipped bedrooms and tastefully decorated public areas. A wide choice of eating options includes good table d'hôte and à la carte menus and a carvery.
21⇌(3fb) CTV in all bedrooms ® **T** ✗ (ex guide dogs) ✱
sB&B⇌£16-£27.50 dB&B⇌£32-£55 ⊟
80P ✿ ⩍(heated) *xmas*
♉ International **V** ♡ Lunch £1.50-£6.50 High tea fr£1.50 Dinner fr£7.25&alc Last dinner 9.30pm
Credit Cards 1 2 3 5 £

ST MARTIN

★★★ 65% Hotel Bella Luce La Fosse ☎Guernsey(0481)38764
Situated in the quiet rural and residential area of La Fosse, this hotel is set in large mature landscaped gardens. The building dates back to Norman times and the public areas offer both character and comfort. Bedrooms vary in style but all are comfortable and well equipped. The restaurant provides a good table d'hôte and an extensive à la carte menu and service is attentive and friendly.
31rm(27⇌4♪)(9fb) CTV in all bedrooms **T** ✱
sB&B⇌♪£19-£32 dB&B⇌♪£30-£61
☾ 50P ⛟ ✿ ⩍(heated) sauna solarium croquet putting *xmas*
♉ English & Continental **V** ♡ ☕ Lunch £6.45-£10.45&alc High tea £1.50-£4.50&alc Dinner £6-£9.25&alc Last dinner 10pm

★★★ 72% Green Acres Les Hubits ☎Guernsey(0481)35711 FAX (0481) 35978
Peacefully set on the outskirts of the town in beautiful gardens that feature a south-facing patio and a heated swimming pool, the hotel offers well-equipped bedrooms with private facilities, a professionally supervised restaurant where both menu and wine list represent good value for money, and the services of a smart friendly staff.
48rm(44⇌4♪)(3fb) CTV in all bedrooms ® **T** ✗
dB&B⇌♪£46-£70 (incl dinner)
75P ⛟ ✿ ⩍(heated) solarium *xmas*
♉ English & French **V** ♡ ☕ ⚡ Bar Lunch £2.50-£6 Dinner £9&alc Last dinner 8.30pm
Credit Cards 1 3

★★★ 58% *St Margaret's Lodge* Forest Rd ☎Guernsey(0481)35757
Conveniently located for the airport, and set in beautifully laid out gardens in the rural parish of St. Martin, the hotel offers well-equipped bedrooms with private facilities and, in some cases, with balconies overlooking the grounds. A good table d'hôte menu is available in the air conditioned 'Anniversary' restaurant with its well-appointed bar lounge, whilst the tastefully furnished à la carte dining room and cocktail bar are open to non-residents.
47⇌ CTV in 43bedrooms ® **T** ✗
Lift ☾ 100P ⛟ ✿ CFA ⩍(heated) sauna solarium ♫
♉ English & French **V** ♡ ☕ Last dinner 9.30pm
Credit Cards 1 2 3

★★★ 50% St Martin's Country Les Merriennes ☎Guernsey(0481)35644
Closed Nov-Feb
Quietly set in 15 acres of grounds, this hotel offers bedrooms of many shapes and sizes, but all are furnished in the modern style with varying degrees of comfort.
60⇌(24fb) CTV in all bedrooms **T** sB&B⇌£16-£29.50 dB&B⇌£32-£59 ⊟
Lift ☾ CTV 250P 1🚗 ✿ CFA ⩍(heated) 🎾 (hard) putting green croquet table tennis ♫ ⌂
♉ English & French **V** ♡ ☕ ⚡ Lunch £5.75 Dinner fr£7.25 Last dinner 9pm
Credit Cards 1 2 3 4 5 £

★★ Windmill La Rue Poudreuse ☎Guernsey(0481)35383
Closed Nov-Mar
18rm(11⇌7♪)(6fb) CTV in all bedrooms ® **T** ✱
sB&B⇌♪£18-£22 dB&B⇌♪£36-£44 ⊟
CTV 18P ⛟ ✿ ⩍(heated) pool table nc3yrs ⌂
♉ International ♡ ☕ ⚡ Lunch £8 Dinner £8 Last dinner 7.30pm
Credit Cards 1 2 3 5

ST PETER PORT

★★★★ 54% Old Government House Ann's Place ☎Guernsey(0481)24921 Telex no 4191144 FAX (0481) 24429
Long established, modernised hotel with swimming pool, basement disco and comfortable lounge. There are good views over the harbour.
74⇌(8fb) CTV in all bedrooms **T** ✱ sB&B⇌£31-£51 dB&B⇌£62-£102
Lift ☾ 20P CFA ⩍(heated) solarium ♫ ⌂ *xmas*
♉ English, French & Italian **V** ♡ ☕ Lunch fr£7&alc Dinner fr£10&alc Last dinner 9.15pm
Credit Cards 1 2 3 5 £

★★★★ 72% *St Pierre Park* Rohais ☎Guernsey(0481)28282 Telex no 4191146 FAX (0481) 712041
Set in 40 acres of parkland with an ornamental lake and fountain, this modern and elegantly furnished hotel combines excellent facilities with professional service and good management. There are two quality restaurants and a brasserie, complemented by 24-hour room service. Indoor facilities include hairdressing and beauty salons, shopping arcade and snooker, while the grounds include a 9-hole golf course.
135⇌♪(1fb) CTV in all bedrooms ® **T** ✗ (ex guide dogs)
Lift ☾ 350P ✿ ⊡(heated) ▶9 🎾 (hard) sauna solarium gymnasium croquet games room ♫ ⌂
♉ English & French **V** ♡ ☕ Last dinner 10pm
Credit Cards 1 2 3 5

★★★ 68% Hotel De Havelet Havelet(Consort) ☎Guernsey(0481)22199 Telex no 4191445 FAX (0481) 714057
Originally built in the 16th century, but now of a Georgian appearance, this hotel is set on a hillside in 1.5 acres of gardens and enjoys lovely views over Castle Cornet. A choice of restaurants, converted from the stables and coach house, adjoins the main building and chef Hans Herrmann produces reliable standards of cooking. Service is well managed, attentive and very friendly.
32⇌(4fb) CTV in all bedrooms ® **T** ✗ S%
sB&B⇌£22.50-£29.70 dB&B⇌£35.50-£57.20 ⊟
40P ⛟ ✿ *xmas*
♉ English, Austrian & French **V** ♡ ☕ Lunch £8.90-£9.90 Dinner £9.95-£10.95&alc Last dinner 9.30pm
Credit Cards 1 2 3 4 5

★★★ 60% La Collinette St Jacques ☎Guernsey(0481)710331 FAX (0481) 713516
A friendly, informal hotel under the personal supervision of the owner provides modestly furnished, well-equipped bedrooms and attentive service.
27rm(25⇌2♪) CTV in all bedrooms ® **T** ✗ (ex guide dogs)
CTV 25P ⛟ ✿ ⩍(heated) sauna solarium spa bath ⌂
♉ English & Continental **V** ♡ ☕ Last dinner 8.30pm
Credit Cards 1 2 3 5

★★★ 70% La Fregate Les Cotils ☎Guernsey(0481)24624
This delightful 18th-century manor house is tucked away on a garden hillside overlooking the harbour. Bedrooms are in the modern style and are well equipped – 6 have balconies and all but 2 have stunning views. The restaurant has acquired a reputation for fresh seafood and home-grown vegetables and chef Oswald Steindsdorfer continues to produce reliable and professional standards of cooking. Service is very attentive and is particularly well managed by Roberto Chiappa.

13⇌↱ CTV in all bedrooms ® T ✗ ✱ sB⇌↱£30-£40 dB⇌↱£55-£80 (room only)
25P ⛟ ⁂ nc14yrs
☋ Continental **V** Lunch £12-£14&alc Dinner fr£16&alc Last dinner 9.30pm
Credit Cards 1 2 3 4 5

See advertisement on page 191

★★★ **64% Moore's** Pollet(Consort) ☎Guernsey(0481)24452 Telex no 4191342 FAX (0481) 714057

Situated on the attractive shopping street of Le Pollet, this Georgian building has undergone extensive refurbishment. It offers bright, well-equipped bedrooms and an attractive verandah restaurant and coffee shop.

44rm(39⇌)Annexe6rm(3⇌)(8fb) CTV in all bedrooms ® **T** S% sB&B⇌£20-£30 dB&B⇌£38-£56 ⊟
Lift ☾ ₱ ⛟ *xmas*
☋ English & French **V** ♉ ⊻ Lunch £7.50-£10&alc Dinner £9.50-£12.50&alc Last dinner 9pm
Credit Cards 1 2 3 4 5

✕✕✕ **Le Nautique** Quay Steps ☎Guernsey(0481)21714

This first-floor restaurant with a Côte d'Azur ambience is very popular with an international clientele for its friendly atmosphere, imaginative daily menus which make a particular feature of fresh fish, and carefully chosen wine list.

Closed Sun & 1st 2 wks Jan
☋ French **V** 68 seats ✱ S10% Lunch £13-£17alc Dinner £13-£17alc Last lunch 2pm Last dinner 10pm ₱ nc5yrs
Credit Cards 1 2 3 5

✕✕ **La Piazza Ristorante** Under the Arch, Trinity Square ☎Guernsey(0481)25085

Situated opposite Holy Trinity Church, this comfortable, intimate restaurant, in shades of pink and grey, spills onto its attractive walled courtyard in warmer months. The cooking style is very Italian, but great use is made of local fish -nine varieties at the time

►

of our visit – and other fresh produce. Of particular note are the Scallops Brettona and the Veal Marsala, accompanied by an imaginative selection of vegetables. It is also a pleasure to find an Italian restaurant which will prepare a Zabaione for one. The small wine list is carefully balanced and offers good value.
Closed Sun & 24 Dec-23 Jan
♉ French & Italian 55 seats ✱ Lunch £15-£20alc Dinner £15-£20alc Last lunch 2pm Last dinner 10pm ♇ nc6yrs
Credit Cards [1] [2] [3]

VALE

★★★65% *Novotel Guernsey* Les Dicqs(Novotel)
☎Guernsey(0481)48400 Telex no 4191306 FAX (0481) 48706
Purpose-built, and overlooking the bay from its own grounds, the hotel is run with the needs of families in mind. Spacious bedrooms are well-equipped, and the dining room offers meals from noon until midnight (with set menus at lunch and dinner), while leisure facilities include a sun terrace, open-air swimming pool with adjacent children's pool and a gymnasium.
99⇌(99fb) CTV in all bedrooms **T**
Lift 120P ✲ ≃(heated) gymnasium ⌂
♉ English & Continental **V** ✧ ⚲ Last dinner mdnt
Credit Cards [1] [2] [3] [4] [5]

HERM

★★White House ☎Guernsey(0481)22159 FAX (0481) 710066
Closed Oct-Mar
The only hotel on the island, the White House is reached via a 5-minute walk along the cliff path from the boat, while guests' luggage is transported by tractor. Colonial in style, the hotel has nearby cottages which are used as an annexe in the summer. The lounges are attractive and comfortable, with open log fires, and there is a separate bar lounge. In the split-level restaurant guests can choose from interesting set menus or à la carte, and there is an adjacent carvery. Bedrooms are simply appointed, but all have en suite facilities and some have balconies with delightful views.
10⇌ ® ✖ ✱ sB&B⇌£28-£36
dB&B⇌£56-£86 (incl dinner) ⊟
♇ ⊞ ✲ ≃ ℘ (hard)
♉ English & French **V** ✧ ⚲ ⚡ Lunch fr£6.50 Dinner £10.75-£11.50 Last dinner 9pm
Credit Cards [1] [3]

JERSEY

ARCHIRONDEL

★★Les Arches Archirondel Bay ☎Jersey(0534)53839
Telex no 4192085 FAX (0534) 56660
Modernised holiday hotel in a rural area overlooking the sea. The bedrooms, some with balconies, are bright and well equipped. There is a large disco and a Victorian style bar.
54rm(35⇌19↰) CTV in all bedrooms ® **T** S%
sB&B⇌↰£23-£35 dB&B⇌↰£46-£70 ⊟
☾ CTV 120P ⊞ ✲ ≃(heated) ℘ (hard) sauna gymnasium ⌂ *xmas*
♉ English & Continental **V** ✧ ⚲ Lunch £8.25-£15 Dinner £10.50-£20 Last dinner 8.45pm
Credit Cards [1] [3] [4] Ⓔ

BEAUMONT

★★Hotel L'Hermitage ☎Jersey(0534)33314 Telex no 4192170
Closed Nov-mid Mar
An attractive hotel with pleasant, well-kept gardens. The hotel offers good leisure facilities including an indoor and outdoor pool. Accommodation is modest with most rooms located away from the main building arrayed 'chalet style' around the pool. The hotel is popular with holidaymakers and is within easy reach of the airport.
109rm(96⇌13↰) CTV in all bedrooms ® ✖ ✱
sB&B⇌↰£16.70-£26.50 dB&B⇌↰£31.40-£51
☾ 100P ⊞ ✲ ⊡(heated) ≃(heated) sauna solarium spa bath ♫ nc
♉ French & English ✧ ⚲ Lunch £4.50 Dinner £6 Last dinner 8pm

CORBIERE

✕✕✕Sea Crest Hotel Petit Port
☎Jersey(0534)46353 & 46356
Commanding a fine cliff-side position, this popular hotel restaurant has a well-established reputation on the island. Fresh fish is a speciality here and the à la carte menu also offers a good selection of other well-prepared European dishes. Service is pleasant and courteous.
Closed Mon (Nov-Mar) & 5 Jan-10 Feb
Dinner not served Sun (Nov-Mar)
♉ English, French & Italian **V** 60 seats ✱ Lunch £7.50&alc Dinner £5-£25alc Last lunch 2pm Last dinner 10pm 30P
Credit Cards [1] [2] [3] [4]

GOREY

★★★62% Old Court House ☎Jersey(0534)54444
Telex no 4192032
Closed Nov-Feb
Situated in its own grounds on the edge of Gorey and opposite the beach, the Old Court House has modern, well-equipped bedrooms, many with balconies overlooking the garden and pool. Recent refurbishment has upgraded the cocktail bar and lounge, and the restaurant has been extended, while preserving the original 15th-century section.
58⇌↰(4fb) CTV in all bedrooms **T** ✖ sB&B⇌↰£29-£41.50 dB&B⇌↰£58-£88 (incl dinner)

▶

C

Lift ☾ 40P ⛟ ⛆(heated) sauna solarium ♫
♀ English, French & Italian ♆ ♁
Credit Cards [1] [2] [3] [5] (£)

★★**The Moorings** Gorey Pier ☎Jersey(0534)53633
FAX (0534) 56660
16rm(12⇨4♠) CTV in all bedrooms ® **T** S%
sB&B⇨♠£27.50-£36.50 dB&B⇨♠£55-£73 ⊟
☾ CTV ⛟ *xmas*
♀ English & Continental **V** ♆ S% Lunch £8.25-£20 Dinner £11.50-£25 Last dinner 10.15pm
Credit Cards [1] [2] [3] [4] (£)

L'ETACQ

★★★69% **Lobster Pot Hotel & Restaurant**
☎Jersey(0534)82888 Telex no 4192605 FAX (0534) 81574
Closed 4 Jan-2 Feb
Remotely situated on a rocky coastline, very close to St. Ouen's Bay, the hotel provides accommodation in spacious, modern bedrooms that are well furnished and particularly well equipped. Its long-established restaurant is popular and lively, the Coach House Bar is open all day, and service throughout is well-managed but friendly.
13⇨ CTV in all bedrooms ® **T** ✗ (ex guide dogs)
sB&B⇨£32-£48.50 dB&B⇨£64-£97
☾ 90P ✲ ♫ nc14yrs
♀ English & Continental **V** ♆ ♁ Lunch fr£8.75 Dinner fr£12.75&alc Last dinner 10.15pm
Credit Cards [1] [2] [3] [5]

ROZEL BAY

★★★♛76% **Château La Chaire** Rozel Valley
☎Jersey(0534)63354
Telex no 437334
FAX (0534) 65137

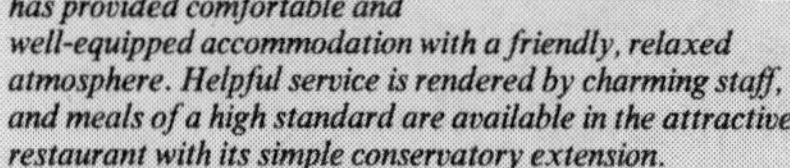

Tasteful refurbishment of an attractive country house in peaceful rural surroundings has provided comfortable and well-equipped accommodation with a friendly, relaxed atmosphere. Helpful service is rendered by charming staff, and meals of a high standard are available in the attractive restaurant with its simple conservatory extension.
13⇨♠(1fb)1⊟ CTV in all bedrooms **T** ✗ (ex guide dogs)
sB&B⇨♠£45-£88 dB&B⇨♠£65-£95 ⊟
☾ 30P ✲ nc7yrs *xmas*
♀ French **V** ♆ ♁ ⚟ Lunch £8.50-£10.75&alc Dinner £18-£24alc Last dinner 10pm
Credit Cards [1] [2] [3] [5]

ST BRELADE

★★★★62% ***Atlantic*** La Moye(Best Western)
☎Jersey(0534)44101 Telex no 4192405
Closed Jan-4 Mar
This pleasant family-run hotel has a beautiful location overlooking the bay and is set in well-kept grounds adjacent to a golf course. Garden wing bedrooms are spacious and overlook the outdoor pool and, although more compact, the rest of the bedrooms all have balconies and have been refurbished to a high standard. The restaurant offers a good standard of professional service and there is a new indoor leisure complex.
50⇨♠ CTV in all bedrooms **T** ✗ (ex guide dogs)
Lift ☾ 60P ⛟ ✲ CFA ⛆(heated) ♈ (hard)
♀ International ♆ ♁ Last dinner 9.15pm
Credit Cards [1] [2] [3] [5]

★★★★71% **Hotel L'Horizon** St Brelade's Bay(Prestige)
☎Jersey(0534)43101 Telex no 4192281 FAX (0534) 46269
A well-appointed holiday hotel with good leisure facilities and a pleasant setting on the seafront offers comfortable, well-equipped bedrooms and public areas; comprehensive menus and a good wine list make its two restaurants popular.
104⇨♠(7fb)1⊟ CTV in all bedrooms **T** ✗ (ex guide dogs)
sB&B⇨♠£50-£60 dB&B⇨♠£130-£150 ⊟
Lift ☾ 125P ⛟ CFA ⛆(heated) sauna gymnasium windsurfing/water skiing spa steam baths ♫ ⛭ *xmas*
♀ English, French & Italian **V** ♆ ♁ Lunch fr£10.50 Dinner fr£19.50 Last dinner 10.45pm
Credit Cards [1] [3]

★★★66% **Chateau Valeuse** Rue de Valeuse, St Brelade's Bay
☎Jersey(0534)46281
Closed Jan-Mar
This friendly hotel has modern, nicely appointed bedrooms, many of which have balconies with lovely views. An outdoor swimming pool is set amongst well-kept gardens and the beach is only a few minutes' walk away. There is a pleasant lounge and bar as well as a small sun terrace.
33rm(25⇨8♠)(1fb) CTV in all bedrooms **T** ✗ ✱
sB&B⇨♠£28-£33 dB&B⇨♠£56-£66 ⊟
☾ 50P ⛟ ✲ ⛆(heated) nc5yrs *xmas*
♀ French **V** ♆ ♁ S10% Lunch £7.50&alc Dinner £9&alc Last dinner 9.15pm
Credit Cards [1] [3]

C

★★★63% **St Brelade's Bay** ☎Jersey(0534)46141
Telex no 4192519
Closed 17 Oct-21 Apr RS 22-30 Apr & 7-16 Oct
72⇌(2fb) CTV in all bedrooms **T** (ex guide dogs) ✱
sB&B⇌£42-£72 dB&B⇌£68-£144
Lift ☾ CTV (heated) (hard) snooker sauna solarium croquet putting green petanque ♫
V Lunch £8 Dinner £14 Last dinner 9pm
Credit Cards 1 2 3 5

★★ ***Beau Rivage*** St Brelades Bay ☎Jersey(0534)45983
Telex no 4192341 FAX (0534) 68330
Closed Dec-Feb
27⇌(9fb) CTV in all bedrooms (ex guide dogs)
Lift ☾ 14P
English, French & Italian **V** Last dinner 7.30pm
Credit Cards 1 2 3

ST HELIER

★★★★56% **The Grand** The Esplanade(De Vere)(Consort)
☎Jersey(0534)22301 Telex no 4192104 FAX (0534) 37815
The hotel stands facing the sea, offering comfortable public areas and bedrooms in a variety of styles which continue to be upgraded. As well as the main dining room, Victoria's Restaurant provides a pleasant atmosphere and a good selection of interesting dishes which makes it popular with local residents.
115⇌ CTV in all bedrooms **T**
Lift ☾ 15P 25 CFA (heated) snooker sauna solarium gymnasium spa bath hairdresser massage parlour ♫
English, French & Italian **V** Last dinner 10.30pm
Credit Cards 1 2 3 5

★★★62% **Apollo** St Saviours Rd ☎Jersey(0534)25441
Telex no 4192086 FAX (0534) 22120
Situated right in the heart of St Helier, but built around its own quiet courtyard, the Apollo has recently been significantly renovated. Bedrooms are bright and comfortable and their modern facilities include satellite TV and teletext. Public rooms have been tastefully decorated, with lounges and a cocktail bar in modern style. The attractive indoor leisure centre includes a stylish coffee shop terrace which in the evening takes on a bistro atmosphere amid the soft-lit waters of the adjacent pool.
85⇌(5fb)1 CTV in all bedrooms ® **T** ✱ sB&B⇌£36-£54 dB&B⇌£64.50-£76.50
Lift ☾ 50P (heated) sauna solarium gymnasium jacuzzi, spa bath *xmas*
English & French **V** Sunday Lunch fr£7.50 High tea fr£2.50 Dinner fr£9 Last dinner 8.45pm
Credit Cards 1 2 3 5

★★★63% **Beaufort** Green St ☎Jersey(0534)32471
Telex no 4192160 FAX (0534) 22120
The provision of a good range of de luxe bedrooms is just part of the upgrading which is in evidence throughout this centrally-situated hotel. An indoor swimming pool and whirlpool spa is another new addition and there are plans to further increase leisure facilities. Nicely decorated throughout, the hotel has comfortable public rooms and staff are efficient and friendly.
54⇌(2fb)1 CTV in all bedrooms ® **T** ✱
sB&B⇌£40-£60.25 dB&B⇌£64.50-£80.50
Lift ☾ 40P (heated) jacuzzi spa bath ♫ *xmas*
English & French **V** Lunch fr£5 High tea fr£2.50 Dinner fr£10 Last dinner 8.45pm
Credit Cards 1 2 3 5

★★★63% **Pomme D'Or** The Esplanade ☎Jersey(0534)78644
Telex no 4192309 FAX (0534) 37781
Central, modernised hotel facing harbour, and having extensive public rooms, coffee shop and carvery. Popular with businessmen.
150⇌(3fb) CTV in all bedrooms ® **T** (ex guide dogs) ✱
sB&B⇌£40-£50 dB&B⇌£60-£73
Lift ☾ ♫ *xmas*
International **V** S10% Lunch £5.70&alc Dinner fr£10.95&alc Last dinner 9pm
Credit Cards 1 2 3 5

★★★60% **Hotel Savoy** Rouge Bouillon ☎Jersey(0534)27521
FAX (0534) 37162
Closed Jan-14 Apr & 22 Oct-Dec
A traditional, bright and spotlessly clean holiday hotel with attractive lounges and well-maintained bedrooms.
61rm(53⇌8)(1fb) CTV in all bedrooms **T**
sB&B⇌£20.50-£27 dB&B⇌£41-£54
Lift ☾ 55P (heated) pool table ♫ nc00
English, French, Italian & Spanish **V** Lunch £5.50-£5.50 Dinner £8.25-£8.25 Last dinner 8.30pm
Credit Cards 1

★★**Mountview** St John's Rd ☎Jersey(0534)78887
FAX (0534) 39763
Closed mid Nov – Mar
An attractive, bright holiday hotel within easy reach of the town centre. There are some self catering flats available.
35rm(15⇌20)(2fb) CTV in all bedrooms **T** ✱ S%
sB&B⇌£21.50-£31.50 dB&B⇌£33-£57
Lift ☾ 12P
English & French S10% Lunch fr£5.50 Dinner fr£8&alc Last dinner 8pm
Credit Cards 1 3 £

★★ ***Royal Yacht*** The Weighbridge ☎Jersey(0534)20511
Telex no 4192642
Though bedrooms have been modernised and well-equipped to meet today's expectation of comfort, the hotel retains much of its original Victorian style and ambience, reflecting the theme in its choice of Victorian dining rooms, carvery and bars.
45rm(18⇌27) CTV in all bedrooms ® **T**
Lift ☾ CTV
English, French & Italian Last dinner 8.30pm
Credit Cards 1 2 3 4

★★ ***Sarum Hotel*** 19-21 New St John's Rd ☎Jersey(0534)58163
Closed Nov-mid Mar
56rm(23⇌12)(1fb) CTV in all bedrooms
Lift ☾ CTV
Last dinner 7.30pm
Credit Cards 3

✕ ***O'Fado*** 20 Esplanade ☎Jersey(0534)71920
A charming little Portuguese restaurant – named after the popular songs of that country – compensates for any lack of luxury by its cheerful atmosphere and the friendly attentiveness of its waiters. Fixed price menus represent good value for money, generally offering fish specialities and a Portuguese dish of the day such as pork cooked with clams, potatoes and herbs.
Closed Sun
International 50 seats Last dinner 10.30pm
Credit Cards 1 2 3 5

ST LAWRENCE

★★★67% **Little Grove** Rue De Haut ☎Jersey(0534)25321
FAX (0534) 25325
Built of pink granite, this delightful hotel is run very much in the country house style, with attractive cosy lounges and bar and an elegant restaurant. Bedroom upgrading continues and some are now splendid. Interesting and enjoyable food is served in the restaurant and throughout the hotel staff are polite and attentive.
13rm(11⇌2) CTV in all bedrooms **T**
sB&B⇌£69.50-£91 dB&B⇌£99-£162
☾ 30P (heated) croquet ♫ nc12yrs *xmas*
English & French **V** Lunch £12.50-£14.50&alc Dinner £19.50&alc Last dinner 9.30pm
Credit Cards 1 2 3 5 £

ST PETER

★★★60% Mermaid ☎Jersey(0543)41255 Telex no 4192249 FAX (0534) 73545

Eighteen acres of grounds and gardens surround this hotel, and many of its bedrooms have balconies overlooking a natural lake. Leisure facilities comprise an 18-hole golf course, putting green, all-weather tennis courts, a gym and a 45-metre-long indoor swimming pool. A small grill room augments the more formal restaurant and there is an historic public bar. Standards of service are formal and reasonably efficient in all areas.

68⇌1 CTV in all bedrooms **T** (ex guide dogs) ✳
sB&B⇌£33.50-£53 dB&B⇌£59-£82
250P ✲ (heated) 9 (hard) sauna solarium gymnasium jacuzzi ♫ *xmas*
English & French **V** Lunch fr£9.50 High tea fr£3 Dinner fr£11 Last dinner 9.30pm
Credit Cards 1 2 3 5

ST SAVIOUR

★★★★ LONGUEVILLE MANOR

off St Helier/Grouville Rd A3 (Relais et Châteaux)
☎Jersey(0534)25501
Telex no 4192306
FAX (0534) 31613
(Rosette awarded for dinner only)

An imposing entrance and attractive gardens tempt the arriving guest to the delights to be found within this magnificent hotel, parts of which date back to the 13th century. It has been sympathetically extended over the years by the present owners, the Lewis and Dufty families, and provides an extensive bar, a fine drawing room with a splendid fireplace, and a pretty lounge – all adorned with fresh flowers, objets d'art and antique furnishings. Individually styled bedooms reflect the good taste expressed throughout the hotel and are not without a slight French influence, with fine French linen, quality towels, mineral water and good toiletries. Even the smallest rooms have charm and the larger ones have useful little lounge areas. In the splendid antique wood-panelled dining room, with a bright annexe, guests can enjoy the fine cuisine of chef Barry Foster and savour such dishes as an excellent terrine of venison with onion marmalade and a rich millefeuille of duck and turnip with griddled foie gras. Service throughout is highly professional and refreshingly hospitable, maintaining the hotel's justifiable reputation as the best on the island.

33⇌1 CTV in all bedrooms **T** S10% sB&B⇌£60-£71 dB&B⇌£93-£146
Lift 40P ✲ (heated) nc7yrs *xmas*
V S10% Lunch £14.75&alc Dinner £21.50&alc Last dinner 9.30pm
Credit Cards 1 2 3 5

TRINITY

✕Granite Corner Rozel Harbour ☎Jersey(0534)63590

The French chef and proprietor Jean-Luc Robin with his wife Louise offer regional French dishes at their delightful little restaurant perched right at the water's edge in Rozel. Some ingredients are specially imported to prepare dishes that include home made terrine of goose foie gras, and ballotine of canard. Sweets are deliciously fresh and brightly presented, there is cinnamon parfait on fresh strawberry coulis or walnut gateau amongst others. Lunch is a more simple affair with a fixed-price menu. The restaurant has a keen following, so booking is essential.

Closed Mon & Dec-Feb
Lunch not served
Dinner not served Sun
French 24 seats ✳ S10% Dinner £17-£25alc Last dinner 9pm nc12yrs
Credit Cards 1 2 3 5

CHAPELTOWN South Yorkshire Map 08 SK39

★★★64% Staindrop Lodge S30 4UH ☎Sheffield(0742)846727
Closed 25 & 26 Dec

A nineteenth-century building of some architectural interest, standing in its own grounds in a quiet area of Sheffield, has been suitably converted into an up-to-date hotel where the interesting international menu and good value wine list are complemented by friendly family service.

13rm(11⇌2)(1fb) CTV in all bedrooms ® **T**
sB&B⇌£48-£55 dB&B⇌£62-£70
60P ✲
English & French **V** Lunch £8.50-£10&alc Dinner £15-£17&alc Last dinner 9.30pm
Credit Cards 1 2 3 5

CHARDSTOCK Devon Map 03 SY30

★★Tytherleigh Cot EX13 7BN ☎South Chard(0460)21170 FAX (0460) 21291

Set in this small village on the Devon/Somerset/Dorset borders, a charming listed building dating from the 14th century offers bedrooms in carefully converted stables and barns, all providing high standards of comfort and excellent facilities. The elegant, air-conditioned restaurant is housed in a Victorian-style conservatory that overlooks an ornamental pond. Guests can enjoy a wide range of imaginative dishes – timbale des champignons forestiere, for example, perhaps being followed by escalope de saumon braisée dorai, and the meal ending with an apple mousse swan on an apricot base.

3⇌Annexe16⇌6 CTV in all bedrooms ® **T** S%
sB&B⇌£39-£45 dB&B⇌£51.50-£98
25P ✲ (heated) sauna solarium nc12yrs *xmas*
V Lunch £7.95-£8.50&alc Dinner £13.95-£14.95&alc Last dinner 9.30pm
Credit Cards 1 3 £

CHARINGWORTH Gloucestershire Map 04 SP13

★★★ 80% Charingworth Manor GL55 6NS (on B4035 3m E of Chipping Campden)
☎Paxford(038678)555
Telex no 333444
FAX (038678) 353
Closed end Jan-mid Feb

This hotel was awarded Best Newcomer in the 1989 Guide, and the splendid care and attention of the Gregory Brothers and their young staff continues to win them favour. It is an ancient manor house sitting high on a hill overlooking its 54 acres that is reached by a long winding driveway off the B4035 Shipston Road just east of Chipping Campden. The bedrooms are all uniquely designed: many have old beams and all are furnished with antiques, but they also incorporate modern comforts. There are lovely old-fashioned gardens with previous outbuildings that have been restored and converted into more bedrooms and a small boardroom style meeting room, all linked to the main house. The excellent food and

commendable wine selection are in themselves a great attraction for discerning diners.
19⇌2⊞ CTV in all bedrooms T ✈ (ex guide dogs) ✱ sB&B⇌£70-£145 dB&B⇌£85-£160 ⛿
☾ 50P ⊕ ✲ croquet clay pigeon shooting nc12yrs *xmas*
V ♆ ☕ Lunch £15.50&alc High tea £2-£6.75alc Dinner £21&alc Last dinner 9.30pm
Credit Cards [1] [2] [3] [5]

CHARLBURY Oxfordshire Map **04** SP31

★★The Bell Hotel Church St OX7 3AP (Best Western) ☎(0608)810278 Telex no 837883 SPEND G FAX (0608) 811447
Situated in the heart of Charlbury, The Bell has the genial atmosphere of a popular village inn. Built of Cotswold stone, it offers pretty, well-equipped bedrooms and sound standards of food.
14rm(9⇌5♠)(1fb) CTV in all bedrooms ® T ✱ sB&B⇌♠£40-£45 dB&B⇌♠£60-£65 ⛿
CTV 50P ✲ clay pigeon shooting fishing riding *xmas*
V ♆ ☕ Lunch £11.50-£21.50alc High tea £2.50-£5alc Dinner £17-£18&alc Last dinner 9.30pm
Credit Cards [1] [2] [3]

CHARLECOTE Warwickshire Map **04** SP25

★★★ 61% Charlecote Pheasant Country CV35 9EW (Queens Moat) ☎Stratford-upon-Avon(0789)470333 Telex no 31688
This hotel complex has a variety of annexe bedrooms converted from former farm buildings. They offer many modern facilites, though some are compact and simply decorated.
Annexe60⇌(1fb)8⊞ CTV in all bedrooms ® T sB&B⇌fr£54 dB&B⇌£67-£60 ⛿
☾ 120P ✲ ⛆(heated) ♪ (hard) sauna solarium gymnasium
♕ English & French V ♆ ☕ Lunch fr£8.50&alc Dinner fr£10.50&alc Last dinner 10pm
Credit Cards [1] [2] [3] [5] £

CHARMOUTH Dorset Map **03** SY39

★★*Charmouth House* The Street DT6 6PH ☎(0297)60319
A charming, sixteenth-century building with a friendly, informal atmosphere offers basic bedroom accommodation, a large, popular lounge bar and an interesting, panelled dining room where guests can choose from a short menu of simple dishes.
12rm(7⇌1♠)(2fb) CTV in all bedrooms ®
23P ✲ ⛆(heated) sauna
V ♆ Last dinner 9pm
Credit Cards [1] [3]

★★Queen's Armes The Street DT6 6QF ☎(0297)60339
Closed 2nd wk Nov-2nd wk Feb
11rm(5⇌5♠)(1fb)1⊞ CTV in all bedrooms ® ✱ sB&B⇌♠£21.50-£24.50 dB&B⇌♠£43-£48 ⛿
CTV 20P ⊕ ✲ nc5yrs
♕ English & French V ♆ ⊁ Bar Lunch £2.50-£5alc Dinner £9-£13.50alc Last dinner 8.30pm
Credit Cards [1] [3]

★★White House 2 Hillside, The Street DT6 6PJ ☎(0297)60411
Closed Dec-Feb
This small, attractive, white-painted hotel has a well appointed interior and a restaurant which provides well prepared meals.
7rm(6⇌) CTV in all bedrooms ® T sB&B⇌£28-£33 dB&B⇌£56-£66 ⛿
15P ⊕ nc14yrs
♆ ☕ Lunch £8.50-£12.50alc Dinner £15&alc Last dinner 9pm
Credit Cards [1] [3]

C

CHARNOCK RICHARD Lancashire Map **07** SD52

★★★64% **Park Hall Hotel, Leisure & Conference Centre** PR7 5LP (off A49 W of village) ☎Eccleston(0257)452090 Telex no 677604 FAX (0257) 451838

This modern hotel, adjacent to the Camelot Theme Park, forms part of a complex of new clubs, shops and exhibition halls not far from the Lake and Spanish Village.

55⇌♠(2fb)1⊠⅟in 13 bedrooms CTV in all bedrooms ® T ✈ sB⇌♠£47-£50 dB⇌♠£58-£60 (room only) ₿

Lift ☾ ⊞ CTV 2500P ⊡(heated) squash snooker sauna solarium gymnasium ♫ *xmas*

♉ English & French V ✿ ℒ Lunch £6.95-£10&alc High tea £6.50 Dinner £6.95-£10&alc Last dinner 10pm

Credit Cards 1 2 3 5 £

See advertisement under PRESTON

CHARNOCK RICHARD MOTORWAY SERVICE AREA (M6) Lancashire Map **07** SD51

★★ ***Welcome Lodge*** Mill Ln PR7 5LR (Trusthouse Forte) ☎Coppull(0257)791746 Telex no 67315

This motorway hotel provides accommodation in modern, well-equipped bedrooms.

103⇌⅟in 10 bedrooms CTV in all bedrooms ®

☾ CTV 120P ⛟

♉ Mainly grills V ✿ ℒ ⅟

Credit Cards 1 2 3 4 5

CHEDDAR Somerset Map **03** ST45

★**Gordons** Cliff St BS27 3PT ☎(0934)742497

Closed 23 Dec-Jan

This small, friendly, owner-run hotel with simple bedrooms is conveniently situated near the Cheddar Gorge.

11rm(2⇌1♠)Annexe2rm(1⇌1♠)(2fb) CTV in 4bedrooms TV in 9bedrooms ® sB&B£15-£17.50 sB&B⇌♠£20-£30 dB&B£27.50-£30 dB&B⇌♠£35-£40

CTV 10P ✿ ⊡(heated) ⛱(heated)

V ✿ ℒ Lunch fr£3.50alc High tea fr£2.50alc Dinner fr£5.50alc Last dinner 9pm

Credit Cards 1 5 £

CHELFORD Cheshire Map **07** SJ87

★★ ***Dixon Arms*** Knutsford Rd SK11 9AS ☎Macclesfield(0625)861313

Closed 24 Dec-1 Jan

Situated in an area famed for its livestock markets – a circumstance reflected in the character of its public bars – this village hotel complements well-appointed bedrooms with a comfortable and attractive lounge.

11♠(2fb) CTV in all bedrooms ® T

100P ✿ CFA bowling

♉ English & French ✿ Last dinner 10pm

Credit Cards 1 2 3 4 5

CHELMSFORD Essex Map **05** TL70

★★★74% **Pontlands Park Country** West Hanningfield Rd, Great Baddow CM2 8HR ☎(0245)76444 Telex no 995256 FAX (0245) 478393

Closed 27-30 Dec, 1st week Jan, all BH (ex Xmas) RS Sat, Sun & Mon

Although it dates back to the mid 16th century, Pontlands Park was rebuilt as a Victorian mansion and subsequently converted into a country house hotel. It has a tastefully appointed lounge and an elegant restaurant offering interesting menus and a good wine list. Individually furnished bedrooms and suites are spacious and well equipped. Within the beautiful grounds is 'Trimmers' health and leisure centre.

17⇌(1fb)3⊠⅟in 6 bedrooms CTV in all bedrooms T ✈ (ex guide dogs) S% sB⇌£60-£70 dB⇌£70-£85 (room only) ₿

☾ 60P ⛟ ✿ ⊡(heated) ⛱(heated) sauna solarium gymnasium jacuzzi

♉ English & French V ✿ ℒ Lunch £22.50-£28.50&alc High tea £3-£12&alc Dinner £22.50-£28.50&alc Last dinner 9.45pm

Credit Cards 1 2 3 5

★★★59% **South Lodge** 196 New London Rd CM2 0AR ☎(0245)264564 Telex no 99452 FAX (0245) 492827

Situated in pleasant grounds just outside the town centre, this hotel has compact bedrooms with facilities to suit visiting business people. The sun lounge room is ideal for small functions and the restaurant offers both table d'hôte and à la carte menus.

24rm(20⇌4♠)Annexe17⇌(3fb) CTV in all bedrooms ® T ✱ sB&B⇌♠£42-£50 dB&B⇌♠£56-£65 Continental breakfast

☾ 50P ⛟

♉ International V ✿ ℒ ⅟ S10% Lunch £11.20&alc Dinner £14&alc Last dinner 9.30pm

Credit Cards 1 2 3 5

★★ ***County*** Rainsford Rd CM1 2QA ☎(0245)491911 FAX (0245) 492762

Closed 27-30 Dec

Busy commercial hotel with modern bedrooms.

30rm(24⇌4♠)Annexe23rm(7⇌)(1fb) CTV in all bedrooms ® T

☾ 80P

♉ English & French V ✿ ℒ

Credit Cards 1 2 3 5

CHELTENHAM Gloucestershire Map **03** SO92

See also **Cleeve Hill**

★★★★56% **Golden Valley Thistle** Gloucester Rd GL51 0TS (Thistle) ☎(0242)232691 Telex no 43410 FAX (0242) 221846

Modern well-appointed hotel with extensive conference facilities.

97⇌♠(24fb)⅟in 9 bedrooms CTV in all bedrooms ® T ✱ sB⇌♠£62-£80 dB⇌♠£73-£115 (room only) ₿

Lift ☾ 275P ✿ CFA ⊡(heated) sauna solarium gymnasium hairdresser ⌂

♉ International ✿ ℒ ⅟ Lunch fr£11.50&alc Dinner fr£14.50&alc Last dinner 10pm

Credit Cards 1 2 3 4 5

★★★★54% **The Queen's** Promenade GL50 1NN (Trusthouse Forte) ☎(0242)514724 Telex no 43381 FAX (0242) 224145

A large, traditional-style hotel with spacious public areas stands in a central position overlooking the town gardens. A programme of refurbishment is at present in progress.

77⇌(8fb)⅟in 7 bedrooms CTV in all bedrooms ® ✱ sB⇌£70-£82 dB⇌£90-£100 (room only) ₿

Lift ☾ 32P CFA *xmas*

V ✿ ℒ ⅟ Lunch fr£13.50&alc Dinner fr£17&alc Last dinner 9.45pm

Credit Cards 1 2 3 4 5

★★★59% **Carlton** Parabola Rd GL50 3AQ ☎(0242)514453 Telex no 43310 FAX (0242)226487

Convenient for the town centre, this popular commercially styled hotel is under family management. New bedrooms have been added and the existing ones upgraded so that all are well equipped.

68rm(67⇌1♠)(2fb)3⊠ CTV in all bedrooms ® T sB&B⇌♠£50 dB&B⇌♠£65-£80 ₿

Lift ☾ 35P CFA *xmas*

Lunch fr£8.50&alc Dinner fr£10.50&alc Last dinner 9pm

Credit Cards 1 2 3 5 £

See the preliminary section 'Hotel and Restaurant Classification' for an explanation of the AA's appointment and award scheme.

C

⊛★★★♛ GREENWAY

Shurdington GL51 5UG
(Pride of Britain)
☎(0242)862352
Telex no 437216
FAX (0242) 862780

Closed 28 Dec-13 Jan RS Sat & BH Mon

A warm and welcoming atmosphere awaits at this charming hotel amidst formal gardens, manicured lawns and parkland, all set against a backdrop of picturesque Cotswold Hills. Tony Elliott is the enthusiastic proprietor and he heads a team of polite and caring staff. The elegant main rooms of the house are of individual character, all furnished to a high standard with many antiques, original paintings and prints – in the superb comfort of the drawing room guests can relax to the sound of the resident pianist. The bedrooms, both in the main house and in the remarkably well-restored coach house, are for the most part very generous, charmingly decorated and furnished with every comfort in mind, and each has a delightful view. The Greenway has a reputation for fine food and wine – chef Tony Robson-Burrell and his team skilfully produce imaginative dishes which taste as good as they look.

11⇌Annexe8⇌1⊟ CTV in all bedrooms **T** ✗
sB&B⇌£75 dB&B⇌£95-£170 ⊟

50P ⊞ ✲ croquet nc7yrs *xmas*

V Lunch £9-£15alc Dinner fr£23alc Last dinner 9.30pm

Credit Cards 1 2 3 4 5

★★★ 58% Hotel De La Bere Southam GL52 3NH (3m NE A46) (Trusthouse Forte) ☎(0242)37771 Telex no 43232 FAX (0242)36016

Well modernised historic hotel with good restaurants and nicely furnished bedrooms.

32rm(30⇌2♠)Annexe25⇌(1fb)6⊟⊁in 6 bedrooms CTV in all bedrooms ® **T** ✱ sB⇌♠fr£64 dB⇌♠fr£91 (room only) ⊟

☾ 150P ✲ CFA ⌂(heated) ♀ (hard) squash snooker sauna solarium badminton courts *xmas*

♀ English & French **V** ✿ ⊁ Lunch fr£8.50 Dinner fr£15.25 Last dinner 10pm

Credit Cards 1 2 3 4 5

★★★ 60% *Wyastone* Parabola Rd GL50 3BG ☎(0242)516654 Telex no 437277

A comfortable, small proprietor-run hotel.

13rm(5⇌8♠)(2fb)1⊟ CTV in all bedrooms ® **T** ✗

17P ⊞

♀ English & Continental **V** ✿ ⊒ ⊁ Last dinner 9pm

Credit Cards 1 2 3 5

★★ *Hayden Court* Gloucester Rd, Staverton GL51 0ST (3m W off B4063) ☎Churchdown(0452)713226

The pleasant, modern hotel stands in the Staverton area, a few miles from the city centre. Accommodation is comfortable, and there is a popular grill restaurant.

48⇌♠(4fb)2⊟ CTV in all bedrooms ® **T**

220P ♫

✿ ⊒ Last dinner 10pm

Credit Cards 1 2 3 5

★★ Lansdown Lansdown Rd GL50 2LB (Berni/Chef & Brewer) ☎(0242)522700

14⇌♠(1fb) CTV in all bedrooms ® **T** ✗ (ex guide dogs)
sB&B⇌♠£43.50 dB&B⇌♠£54.50 ⊟

☾ CTV 25P ✲ *xmas*

♀ Mainly grills **V** ✿ ⊒ ⊁ Lunch £8 Dinner £9 Last dinner 10pm

Credit Cards 1 2 3 5

★★ Prestbury House The Burgage, Prestbury GL52 3DN (2m NE A46) ☎(0242)529533 & 30106 FAX (0242) 227076

Peacefully situated, personally-run period house with pleasant en-suite bedrooms and gracious restaurant offering good food and service.

9⇌♠(3fb)⊁in 8 bedrooms CTV in all bedrooms ® **T** ✱
sB&B⇌♠£30-£40 dB&B⇌♠£40-£50 ⊟

80P ✲ ♫ ♔ *xmas*

♀ English, French & Italian **V** ✿ ⊒ Lunch £12.50-£16.50&alc Dinner £12.50-£16.50&alc Last dinner 9.30pm

Credit Cards 1 3 £

★ Wellesley Court Clarence Square, Pittville GL50 4JR (Minotels) ☎(0242)580411 Telex no 67596 FAX (0242) 224609

Located in a Georgian square near to the well-known Promenade, this elegant Regency hotel is under the personal direction of its owners, who have created a warm, friendly atmosphere. All the bedrooms have modern accessories, whilst a characterful restaurant offers quality meals and attentive service.

20rm(4⇌6♠)(5fb) CTV in all bedrooms ® **T** S%
sB&B£22.50-£28 sB&B⇌♠£33.50-£40 dB&B£33-£40
dB&B⇌♠£53-£60 ⊟

Lift CTV 14P nc6yrs

♀ International **V** ✿ ⊒ S% Lunch £6.95-£10.95&alc Dinner £8.95-£10.95&alc Last dinner 9.30pm

Credit Cards 1 2 3 5 £

✕✕ Le Champignon Sauvage 24 Suffolk Rd GL50 2AQ ☎(0242)573449

This French restaurant, recently refurbished in a striking peach and grey colour scheme, is under the personal management of David and Helen Everitt-Matthaias – she acting as a gracious and caring hostess while he presides over a kitchen which produces imaginative and beautifully presented food. The wine list, though young, offers good value and provides a pleasant accompaniment to the meal.

Closed Sun, 2 wks in Jun, BH's & Xmas-New Year

Lunch not served Sat

♀ French **V** 32 seats Lunch £12.45-£18.50 Dinner £18.50 Last lunch 1.30pm Last dinner 9.30pm ⁄P

Credit Cards 1 2 3

✕✕ Cleeveway House Bishops Cleeve GL52 4SA (3m N A435) ☎Bishop's Cleeve(024267)2585

This well appointed country house restaurant makes commendable use of game, fish and raw materials in season.

Closed 1 wk Xmas & 2 wks annual hols

Lunch not served Sun (ex by reservation) & Mon

Dinner not served Sun

♀ English & French **V** 38 seats ✱ Lunch £12.05-£20alc Dinner £12.05-£20alc Last lunch 1.45pm Last dinner 9.45pm 30P

Credit Cards 1

✕ Mayflower Chinese 32 Clarence St GL50 3NX ☎(0242)522426

This small, personally-run, Chinese Restaurant is served by a helpful and friendly staff. The menu offers a good choice of authentic Cantonese-style dishes, cooked with care and well presented.

Closed 25-28 Dec

Lunch not served Sun

♀ Cantonese **V** 45 seats Lunch £4.50-£5.50&alc Dinner £9.50-£14.50alc Last lunch 1.30pm Last dinner 10.30pm ⁄P

Credit Cards 2 5

See advertisement on page 203

A rosette is the AA's highest award for quality of food and service in a restaurant.

C

CHELWOOD Avon Map **03** ST66

★★**Chelwood House** BS18 4NH ☎Compton Dando(07618)730 Telex no 44830
RS 24 Dec-15 Jan
A seventeenth-century property set in one-and-a-half acres has been sympathetically restored to provide a small, country house hotel with charming, individual guest rooms.
8rm(6⇨2♪)3⊞ CTV in all bedrooms ® T ✕ ✻ S%
sB&B⇨♪£52-£55 dB&B⇨♪£65-£90 ⊟
15P ✽ croquet nc10yrs
♕ English & German ✲ ✕ S% Lunch £12-£12.50 Dinner £15.50-£20alc Last dinner 9pm
Credit Cards 1 2 3 5

CHENIES Buckinghamshire Map **04** TQ09

★★★**63% Bedford Arms Thistle** WD3 6EQ (Thistle) ☎Chorleywood(09278)3301 Telex no 893939
FAX (09278) 4825
Set in a small, peaceful village, this attractive country hotel offers comfortable well-equipped bedrooms and good hospitality. The intimate oak-panelled restaurant has a comprehensive menu of well-prepared dishes.
10⇨♪(4fb)✕in 1 bedroom CTV in all bedrooms T ✻
sB⇨♪£65-£75 dB⇨♪£80-£85 (room only) ⊟
(120P
♕ International ✲ ⊻ ✕ Lunch fr£15alc Dinner fr£15alc Last dinner 10pm
Credit Cards 1 2 3 4 5

CHEPSTOW Gwent Map **03** ST59

★★★**68% St Pierre Hotel, Golf & Country Club** St Pierre Park NP6 6YA (2.5m W off A48) ☎(0291)625261 Telex no 497562
FAX (02912) 79975
Set in 400 acres of parkland, with two 18-hole golf courses and an 11-acre lake, this beautifully preserved 14th-century mansion – complete with its own Norman church – provides well equipped, modern bedroom accommodation in a purpose-built annexe and slightly smaller rooms in an old stable block. The extensive sports and leisure facilities available include tennis, badminton, squash, snooker, and swimming in an indoor pool.
150⇨♪(7fb)1⊞ CTV in all bedrooms ® T
(350P ✽ ⊡(heated) ▶ 18 ♪ (hard) squash snooker sauna solarium gymnasium jacuzzi table tennis croquet badminton
♕ International V ✲ ⊻ Last dinner 9.30pm
Credit Cards 1 2 3 4 5

★★**Beaufort** Beaufort Square, Saint Mary St NP6 5EP (Inter) ☎(0291)625074 & 622497 Telex no 498280
Welcoming 16th-century hotel with warm, modern bedrooms, attractive intimate dining rooms and popular bars.
18rm(10⇨3♪)(2fb) CTV in all bedrooms ® T ✻ sB&Bfr£30
sB&B⇨♪£35-£40 dB&Bfr£45 dB&B⇨♪fr£50 ⊟
12P ✽
♕ International V ✲ ✕ Lunch £6.95-£8.95alc Dinner £14-£18alc Last dinner 9.30pm
Credit Cards 1 2 3

★★**Castle View** 16 Bridge St NP6 5EZ ☎(02912)70349
Telex no 498280 FAX (0291) 625614
Personally owned and managed, this friendly hotel is housed in an 18th-century building which looks directly onto Chepstow Castle. The modern bedrooms are compact but comfortable, and imaginative meals featuring fine home cooking are served in the character dining room, once the kitchen.
9rm(8⇨1♪)Annexe2⇨(5fb) CTV in all bedrooms ® T
sB&B⇨♪£37-£39 dB&B⇨♪£52-£56 ⊟
✽ ✽
V ✲ ✕ Lunch £7.50&alc Dinner £10.20&alc Last dinner 9pm
Credit Cards 1 2 3 5

★★***First Hurdle*** 9/10 Upper Church St NP6 5EX ☎(02912)2189
Tastefully appointed hotel in the centre of town under the personal supervision of the owner. Freshly prepared meals are served in the Beeches Restaurant.
11rm(6♪)✕in 3 bedrooms CTV in all bedrooms T
CTV ✗
♕ English & French V ✲ ⊻ ✕ Last dinner 9.30pm
Credit Cards 1 2 3

★★**The George** Moor St NP6 5DB (Trusthouse Forte)
☎(0291)625363
Small friendly hotel with comfortable bedrooms.
15rm(14⇨1♪)✕in 1 bedroom CTV in all bedrooms ®
sB⇨♪£56-£68 dB⇨♪£67-£78 (room only) ⊟
25P *xmas*
V ✲ ⊻ ✕ Lunch fr£10.25&alc Dinner £9.75-£15alc Last dinner 9.30pm
Credit Cards 1 2 3 4 5

CHESTER Cheshire Map **07** SJ46

★★★★**THE CHESTER GROSVENOR**

Eastgate St CH1 1LT
(Prestige) ☎(0244)324024
Telex no 61240
FAX (0244) 313246
Closed 25-26 Dec

This well-established county town hotel has recently undergone a major refurbishment, and can now claim to be one of the finest hotels of its type in the country. One advantage is that a nucleus of the original staff has been retained and ensures that traditional values of service continue. No requirement seems too much trouble for the friendly and attentive staff, who are always on hand. On the debit side, the most attractive library bar has limited seating and fills up very quickly before meals, and the attractive first-floor lounge can easily be dominated by a single group of people. That said, the bedrooms are spacious and comfortable, and a great deal of thought thas clearly gone into providing them with everything today's traveller might need. Executive chef Paul Reed is building a good local reputation for his delicate and innovative cuisine in the elegant Arkle restaurant, where menus change weekly, and for the popular 'La Brasserie', which serves food all day. Managing director Jonathon Slater is dedicated to the pursuit of excellence, and we are confident that this popular hotel will continue to go from strength to strength.
86⇨♪2⊞ CTV in all bedrooms T ✕ (ex guide dogs)
sB⇨♪fr£95 dB⇨♪fr£140 (room only) ⊟
Lift (⊞ ☗ CFA sauna solarium gymnasium ♫
♕ British & French V ✲ ⊻ ✕ Lunch £10.50-£18.75&alc Dinner £15-£38.50&alc Last dinner 11pm
Credit Cards 1 2 3 4 5

★★★★**69% Mollington Banastre** Parkgate Rd CH1 6NN (A540) (Best Western) ☎(0244)851471 Telex no 61686
FAX (0244)851165
The converted Victorian mansion stands in its own grounds some three miles from Chester. Bedrooms are modern and comfortable, the public areas pleasantly proportioned and elegantly decorated, and the overall atmosphere is one of friendliness and hospitality. There is also a good sports/leisure centre with a swimming pool.
64⇨(6fb)1⊞✕in 5 bedrooms CTV in all bedrooms ® T ✻
sB&B⇨£68-£78 dB&B⇨£85-£95 ⊟

▶

Castle View Hotel

★★

Bridge Street, Chepstow, Gwent NP6 5EZ
Tel: Chepstow (02912) 70349
Telex: 498280 (Quote CVH) Fax: (02912) 625614

- All rooms with private bathroom, colour TV, radio, telephone, movies, mini bar and tea making facilities.
- Commended restaurant and bar food.
- Short breaks and holiday terms.
- Family rooms available.
- Facing Chepstow Castle and car park.

"Our aim is to provide comfort, good food and personal attention in surroundings which retain the charm of the 18th century."

Chelwood House

Hotel & Restaurant

AA★★

A Charles II house of charm & character situated in an area of outstanding beauty with easy accessibility. BATH (10m), BRISTOL (8m), WELLS (13m). Personally run by the owners. Chef-proprietor. Very good cuisine. Excellent breakfasts. Tasteful décor and furnishings. Individually designed bedrooms. 4-posters of different styles and draped beds. Pretty walled garden and croquet lawn.

Chelwood House
Chelwood, Nr. Bristol, BS18 4NH
Tel: (07618) 730

Beaufort Hotel ★★

Beaufort Square, Chepstow, Gwent, NP6 5EP
Telephone: (0291) 625074 (Reception)
622497 (Visitors)
Proprietors R & A Wallace

Privately owned family run Hotel in town centre. 18 bedrooms, majority en suite. All with colour TV, telephone, coffee and tea making facilities. Centrally heated throughout.
Traditional restaurant offering comprehensive menu. Emphasis on fresh produce and home cooking. Comfortable furnished bar. Small conference facilities with private car parking. Weekend breaks October to April.

MAYFLOWER RESTAURANT ×

Fully Licensed
Authentic Chinese Cuisine

Booking Advisable

---

32 Clarence Street
Cheltenham
Tel: (0242) 522426

Lift ☾ 300P ⛟ ✲ CFA ▭(heated) ♀ (hard & grass) squash U sauna solarium gymnasium hairdressing health & beauty salon *xmas*
♉ English & French V ♉ ☐ ⁄ Lunch £9.50-£15&alc High tea fr£5 Dinner £15-£18&alc Last dinner 10.30pm
Credit Cards 1 2 3 5

C

★★★61% Abbots Well Whitchurch Rd, Christleton CH3 5QL (Embassy) ☎(0244)332121 Telex no 61561 FAX (0244) 335287
In spacious grounds beside the southern bypass stands a modern hotel catering for both business clients and tourists; conference and banqueting facilities are available, and a well-equipped leisure centre has recently been opened.
127rm(63⇌64↑)(5fb)⁄in 6 bedrooms CTV in all bedrooms ® T S% sB&B⇌↑£60-£69 dB&B⇌↑£73-£86 ⊟
☾ 200P ✲ CFA ▭(heated) sauna solarium gymnasium jacuzzi pool ♫ *xmas*
♉ English & French V ♉ ☐ Lunch £7.95&alc High tea fr90p
Credit Cards 1 2 3 5 £

★★★61% Blossoms Saint John St CH1 1HL (Trusthouse Forte) ☎(0244)323186 Telex no 61113 FAX (0244) 46433
An original coaching house made of timber and brick that dates back to the 17th-century. It stands in the city centre in a good position for the tourist, while its facilities and attractiveness would also appeal to business people. There are elegant public rooms where you can rest to the accompaniment of soft piano music. The bedrooms have been furnished and decorated to a high standard.
69⇌↑1⛟ CTV in all bedrooms ® T sB⇌↑fr£64 dB⇌↑£82-£93 (room only) ⊟
Lift ☾ ⁄P CFA *xmas*
♉ English & French V ♉ ☐ ⁄ Lunch fr£11&alc Dinner £14&alc Last dinner 9.30pm
Credit Cards 1 2 3 5

★★★ 71% Crabwall Manor Parkgate Rd, Mollington CH1 6NE (Prestige)
☎(0244)851666
Telex no 61220
FAX (0244) 851400

Just outside Chester, but within view of the historic city, Crabwall Manor is set in spacious leafy grounds. The beautifully furnished and comfortable bedrooms and bathrooms are a major attraction, and there are several pretty lounges for drinks before dinner. Word about Crabwall is spreading, and during the week it is increasingly used by business people, who find that the hotel's discreet meeting and seminar facilities more than fulfil their needs. Shortly before going to print, we learnt of a change of management and we shall view developments with particular interest.
48⇌↑1⛟⁄in 2 bedrooms CTV in all bedrooms T ✗ (ex guide dogs) ✱ sB⇌↑£70-£85 dB⇌↑£90-£110 (room only) ⊟
☾ 100P ✲ snooker croquet lawn nc5yrs *xmas*
♉ English & French V ♉ ☐ ⁄ Lunch £10-£12.95&alc Dinner £21&alc Last dinner 9.45pm
Credit Cards 1 2 3 5

★★★64% *Hoole Hall* Warrington Rd, Hoole Village CH2 4EX (Crown & Raven) ☎(0244)350011 Telex no 61292
This impressive Georgian and Victorian mansion is set in 5 acres of parkland, just 2 miles from the city centre. It offers attractive public areas, comfortable modern bedrooms and good conference and function facilities.
99⇌(3fb)⁄in 16 bedrooms CTV in all bedrooms ® T
Lift ☾ ⊞ 200P ✲ ⌂
V ♉ ☐ ⁄ Last dinner 9.45pm
Credit Cards 1 2 3 4 5

★★★57% Plantation Quality Inn Liverpool Rd CH2 1AG ☎(0244)374100 Telex no 61263 FAX (0244) 319262
Closed Xmas
This business and conference hotel is functional with limited lounge facilities, but its bedrooms are well equipped.
93⇌↑(4fb) CTV in all bedrooms ® T sB⇌↑£50-£56 dB⇌↑£65-£79 (room only) ⊟
Lift ☾ ⊞ 150P sauna solarium gymnasium ♫
♉ Continental V ♉ ☐ Lunch £3-£7.50 Dinner £9.95-£11.50&alc Last dinner 10.30pm
Credit Cards 1 2 3 4 5 £

★★★61% Post House Wrexham Rd CH4 9DL (Trusthouse Forte) ☎(0244)680111 Telex no 61450 FAX (0244) 674100
Modern hotel with spacious, well appointed bedrooms.
106⇌⁄in 3 bedrooms CTV in all bedrooms ® T ✱ S10%
☾ 250P CFA ▭(heated) sauna solarium gymnasium spa pool
V ♉ ☐ ⁄ Lunch £6.95&alc Dinner £12.95&alc Last dinner 10pm
Credit Cards 1 2 3 4 5

★★★58% Queen City Rd CH1 3AH ☎(0244)350100 Telex no 617101 FAX (0244) 318483
Situated opposite the railway station, this traditional hotel is housed in an elegant Victorian building with a porticoed entrance. It has a secluded, well-tended garden.
91⇌(10fb) CTV in all bedrooms ® T sB⇌£59-£62 dB⇌£70-£100 (room only) ⊟
Lift ☾ 80P ✲
♉ Traditional & French V ♉ ☐ ⁄ Lunch £7.25-£8 Dinner £11.25-£12.25&alc Last dinner 9.30pm
Credit Cards 1 2 3 5

★★★60% Rowton Hall Whitchurch Road, Rowton CH3 6AD (2m SE A41) (Consort) ☎(0244)335262 Telex no 61172 FAX (0244) 335464
Closed 25-26 Dec
Improvements are continually being made at this one-time Georgian country house, now a popular conference and function venue. Several of the bedrooms have been refurbished to a high standard and the spacious public areas include a comfortable lounge and smart new leisure complex.
42⇌↑(2fb)3⛟ CTV in all bedrooms ® T ✱ sB&B⇌↑£58-£60 dB&B⇌↑£72-£75 ⊟
☾ CTV 120P 3⌂ ✲ ▭(heated) sauna solarium gymnasium
♉ French V ♉ ☐ Lunch £9-£10&alc Dinner £11-£12.50 Last dinner 9.30pm
Credit Cards 1 2 3 5 £

★★Curzon 54 Hough Green CH4 8JQ (Queens Moat) ☎(0244)678581
Closed 25 Dec-1 Jan
A Victorian building set on the A549 one mile from the city centre offers well-appointed accommodation with a relaxed, friendly atmosphere.
16rm(7⇌9↑)(4fb)1⛟ CTV in all bedrooms ® T sB&B⇌↑fr£34 dB&B⇌↑fr£44 ⊟
30P
♉ French ♉ ☐ Dinner £6.70-£13.25alc Last dinner 9.45pm
Credit Cards 1 2 3 5

★★Dene Hoole Rd CH2 3ND ☎(0244)321165
Good parking facilities, well-equipped bedrooms and a traditional atmosphere are provided by this family-run hotel, situated on the A56 about a mile from the city centre and appealing to both business travellers and holidaymakers.
41rm(28⇌11↑)(3fb) CTV in all bedrooms ® T sB&B£23-£25 sB&B⇌↑£33-£35 dB&B⇌↑£44-£46 ⊟
CTV 55P ✲

▶

V ☺ ⊁ High tea £5-£7&alc Dinner £7.50-£8.50&alc Last dinner 8pm
Credit Cards [1] [3] [£]

★★Green Bough 60 Hoole Rd CH2 3NL ☎(0244)326241
Closed 21-28 Dec RS 29-6 Jan
A small, warm and friendly hotel under the personal supervision of the resident proprietors. Accommodation is comfortable and well furnished and the cooking, using fresh local produce, is of a high standard.
11rm(2⇌7↱)(2fb)1⊠ CTV in all bedrooms ® T sB&B£23-£28 sB&B⇌↱£32.50-£36 dB&B£33-£36 dB&B⇌↱£42-£45 ⊟
CTV 11P
V Lunch £5-£6 Dinner fr£9 Last dinner 7.30pm
Credit Cards [1] [3] [£]

★★Royal Oak Warrington Rd, Mickle Trafford CH2 4EX (3m NE A56) (Toby) ☎(0244)301391 Telex no 61536
A well-furnished hotel with good accommodation and attractive carvery-style restaurant.
36⇌↱(10fb) CTV in all bedrooms ® T ✱ sB&B⇌↱fr£41.50 dB&B⇌↱fr£51.50 ⊟
☾ 150P ❊
V ☺ ⊻
Credit Cards [1] [2] [3] [5]

CHESTERFIELD Derbyshire Map 08 SK37

★★★61% Chesterfield Malkin St S41 7UA (Best Western) ☎(0246)271141 Telex no 547492 FAX (0246) 220719
A fully modernised hotel decorated in the elegant style of the 1920's. Situated close to the station, it has facilities for conferences and private functions.
61⇌↱(8fb) CTV in all bedrooms ® T ✱ sB&B⇌↱£32-£55 dB&B⇌↱£48-£65 ⊟
Lift ☾ 100P ♫ *xmas*
♡ International V ☺ ⊻ Lunch £5.25-£7.45&alc Dinner £9.95&alc Last dinner 10pm
Credit Cards [1] [2] [3] [£]

★★Portland West Bars S40 1AY ☎(0246)234502 & 234211
A comfortable, friendly, city centre hotel offers guests a lunchtime choice between the Fountain Restaurant's à la carte or carvery meals and the bistro-style bar meals of the Pantry.
27rm(15⇌1↱)(4fb) CTV in all bedrooms ® T ✗ (ex guide dogs) sB&B£25-£29 sB&B⇌↱£29-£39.50 dB&B⇌↱£39.50-£52 ⊟
☾ CTV 30P ⊞
♡ Mainly grills V ☺ Lunch £5.45-£7.90alc Dinner £6.50-£10.30alc Last dinner 10pm
Credit Cards [1] [2] [3] [5]

CHESTERFORD, GREAT Essex Map 05 TL54

★★The Crown House CB10 1NY ☎Saffron Walden(0799)30515
A small historic building, that also offers well-equipped, modern annexe accommodation.
8⇌Annexe10rm(4⇌6↱)4⊠ CTV in all bedrooms ® T ✗ ✱ sB&B⇌↱£24-£65 dB&B⇌↱£48-£85 ⊟
CTV 30P ⊞ ♫ *xmas*
♡ English & French V ☺ ⊻ Lunch £11.50-£16.50 Dinner £11.50-£16.50&alc Last dinner 9.45pm
Credit Cards [1] [3]

CHESTER-LE-STREET Co Durham Map 12 NZ25

★★★68% Lumley Castle Lumley Castle DH3 4NX ☎091-389 1111 Telex no 537433 FAX 091-387 1437
Closed 25-26 Dec & 1 Jan
Impressive 13th-century castle sympathetically converted to hotel with charming bedrooms.
24rm(11⇌3↱)Annexe41rm(33⇌6↱)(3fb)7⊠⊁in 3 bedrooms CTV in all bedrooms ® T ✗ sB&B⇌↱£45-£88 dB&B⇌↱£59-£148 ⊟
☾ 150P ❊ CFA snooker ♫ *xmas*
♡ English & French V ☺ ⊻ Lunch fr£9.75 Dinner fr£15.50 Last dinner 9.45pm
Credit Cards [1] [2] [3] [5] [£]

CHICHESTER West Sussex Map 04 SU80

★★★54% The Dolphin & Anchor West St PO19 1QE (Trusthouse Forte) ☎(0243)785121 FAX (0243) 533408
This hotel opposite the cathedral combines two ancient inns. Public areas include a coffee shop, bar lounge and restaurant. Car parking can be very difficult.
51rm(49⇌2↱)(5fb)⊁in 22 bedrooms CTV in all bedrooms ® sB⇌↱£60-£75 dB⇌↱£77-£89 (room only) ⊟
☾ 6P 20🚗 CFA *xmas*
♡ English & French V ☺ ⊻ ⊁ Lunch £10.25-£11.35&alc High tea £3.50-£10 Dinner £13-£14.65&alc Last dinner 9.30pm
Credit Cards [1] [2] [3] [4] [5]

★★★72% Goodwood Park Hotel PO18 0QB ☎(0243)775537 Telex no 869173 FAX (0243) 533802
(For full entry see Goodwood)

✕✕Comme Ça 149 St Pancras PO19 1SH ☎(0243)788724
This small, cottage-style restaurant specialises in traditional French cuisine, a comprehensive range of popular regional dishes being prepared from totally fresh ingredients. Basic sauces are particularly good, and guests' enjoyment of the meal is further enhanced by an excellent selection of good-value Burgundy wines and efficient service.
Closed Mon, 25 Dec, 1 Jan & BH's
Lunch not served Sat
Dinner not served Sun
♡ French V 39 seats ✱ Lunch £11.50&alc Dinner £15-£20alc Last lunch 1.45pm Last dinner 10.45pm P̸
Credit Cards [1] [2] [3] [5]

CHILGROVE West Sussex Map 04 SU81

✕✕White Horse Inn PO18 9HX ☎East Marden(024359)219
This small, wisteria-clad free house at the foot of the South Downs has a softly-lit dining room where friendly staff, led by a very able manager, create a warm atmosphere. A fixed price menu is prepared from local produce, including fresh fish, and though dishes tend to be simple, flavours are good and clear. The wine list is possibly the longest and richest in rare vintages in the country.
Closed Mon & 3 wks Feb
Dinner not served Sun
♡ English & French V 60 seats S12.5% Lunch £12.95 Dinner £17.95 Last lunch 1.45pm Last dinner 9.30pm 200P
Credit Cards [1] [3] [4] [5]

CHILLINGTON Devon Map 03 SX74

★★Oddicombe House TQ7 2JD ☎Frogmore(0548)531234
Closed Nov-Etr
Family-run hotel featuring comfortable bedrooms, good home cooking and an extensive garden with a swimming pool. The atmosphere is relaxed and informal and the hotel is well situated for touring the South Hams.
8rm(6⇌)Annexe2rm(1⇌)(3fb) ® sB&B£21-£23 sB&B⇌£25-£27 dB&B£42-£48 dB&B⇌£46-£50
CTV 15P ⊞ ❊ ⩠
♡ European ☺ ⊻ ⊁ Dinner fr£11 Last dinner 8.15pm

★White House TQ7 2JX ☎Kingsbridge(0548)580580
Closed Nov-Etr (ex Xmas)
A charming Georgian house set in mature lawned and terraced gardens, with cosy bedrooms and an elegant dining room. Ideally situated between the Salcombe Estuary and Dartmouth.

8rm(3⇌3⌐)(1fb) CTV in all bedrooms ® dB&B£37-£41 dB&B⇌⌐£42-£53 ⊟
CTV 8P ✿ croquet badminton nc5yrs *xmas*
☺ English, French & Italian ✓ ☐ ⁄ Bar Lunch 75p-£3.95 Dinner £8.50 Last dinner 8.15pm

CHIPPENHAM Wiltshire Map **03** ST97

See also **Sutton Benger**

★The Bear 12 Market Place SN15 3HJ ☎(0249)653272
Closed 25 Dec
This small, friendly hotel, under the personal supervision of the proprietors, features two lively bars and a first-floor restaurant; considerable improvements have been made, and sound, simple standards of service prevail.
9rm(2⇌)(1fb) CTV in all bedrooms ® ✱ sB&B£16-£22 sB&B⇌£22-£30 dB&Bfr£32 dB&B⇌£40
6P
☺ Mainly grills **V** ✓
Credit Cards 1 3

CHIPPERFIELD Hertfordshire Map **04** TL00

★★The Two Brewers Inn The Common WD4 9BS (Trusthouse Forte) ☎King's Langley(09277)65266 FAX (09277) 61884
Overlooking the village green, this charming 17th-century inn has a cosy atmosphere, exposed beams and open fires. Buffet-style lunches are served in the comfortable lounge and the restaurant offers a choice of menus. There is a popular bar and bedrooms are modern and well equipped.
20⇌⁄in 2 bedrooms CTV in all bedrooms ® **T** ✱ S% sB⇌fr£76 dB⇌fr£81 (room only) ⊟
25P ✿ *xmas*
☺ French **V** ✓ ☐ ⁄ Lunch £11.25-£12.50&alc Dinner fr£14.50&alc Last dinner 10pm
Credit Cards 1 2 3 4 5

C

CHIPPING CAMPDEN Gloucestershire Map **04** SP13

★★★ **75% Cotswold House** The Square GL55 6AN
☎Evesham(0386)840330 FAX (0386) 840310
Closed 25-27 Dec
This Regency town house has recently been restored to its former elegance and splendour. The bedrooms are individually designed and fitted and the spacious lounges are comfortable. Well presented imaginative cuisine is served in the charming dining room.
15rm(14⇌1♠) CTV in all bedrooms T ✱ ✳
sB&B⇌♠£45-£52.50 dB&B⇌♠£77-£99 ☰
12P ✇ ✲ croquet nc8yrs
V ♉ ☕ ⚡ Lunch £12.50-£13.50 High tea £2.50-£3.95 Dinner £16.50-£19.50alc Last dinner 9.30pm
Credit Cards 1 2 3 5

★★**Noel Arms** GL55 6AT (Exec Hotel) ☎Evesham(0386)840317
The 600-year-old hotel has been updated to provide guests with modern facilities, but it retains such attractive traditional features as the open fire in the bar, antique furnishings and a fine collection of muskets and armour.
18rm(15⇌3♠)2☐ CTV in all bedrooms ® T ✱ (ex guide dogs) sB&B⇌♠£39.50-£42.50 dB&B⇌♠£52.50-£65 ☰
40P bowling green *xmas*
☋ English & French V ♉ ☕ Sunday Lunch £8.50-£10.50 Dinner £13.95-£14.95&alc Last dinner 9.30pm
Credit Cards 1 2 3

✕✕**Bagatelle** Island House, High St GL55 6AL
☎Evesham(0386)840598
Even though it is alongside the High Street, this lovely stone-built house retains an intimate, restful atmosphere. Owner Joel Coleau and his wife, together with their young staff, are attentive and extremely polite. Fresh local produce is selected with care, supplemented with French ingredients when necessary. Puff pastry cases contain the day's seafood with a lobster bisque sauce, or scrambled eggs and Roquefort; top quality fish includes monkfish with a mustard sauce or plait of Dover Sole with scallop coral sauce, accompanied by lightly cooked vegetables with lovely fresh flavours. The wine list is totally French, extending to around 70 items with some modest prices. The choice of menus here is still novel to English restaurants and the 'Menu Touristique' is very good value.
Closed Mon & 2-3 wks Jan
☋ French 30 seats ✳ Lunch £7.85-£9.10 Dinner £13.45-£20.85alc Last lunch 2pm Last dinner 10pm
Credit Cards 1 3

CHIPPING NORTON Oxfordshire Map **04** SP23

✕**Vittles** 7 Horsefair OX7 5AL ☎(0608)44490
The new owners of this cosy cottage restaurant, Ian and Eve Chapman, have instigated significent refurbishment to give the place a simple yet quality, classical appearance. Ian's cuisine bears evidence of some originality, whilst Eve leads the hospitable and conscientious service in the restaurant.
Dinner not served Sun
V 35 seats Bar Lunch £3.50-£5alc Last lunch 2pm Last dinner 11pm ⚡ nc3yrs
Credit Cards 1 3

CHIPPING SODBURY Avon Map **03** ST78

✕**Sultan** Melbourne House, 29 Horse St BS17 6DA
☎(0454)323510
An Indian restaurant with a difference, the Sultan serves well cooked and authentic regional dishes in the comfortable and relaxed atmosphere of a traditionally-furnished Georgian house typical of this charming Cotswold market town.
☋ Indian V 44 seats Lunch £7.50-£10.50&alc Dinner £7.50-£11.50&alc Last lunch 1.45pm Last dinner 11pm ⚡
Credit Cards 1 2 3

CHITTLEHAMHOLT Devon Map **02** SS62

★★★ **74% Highbullen**
EX37 9HD
☎(07694)561
FAX (07694)492

Standing on high ground between the Mole and Taw valleys, this hotel is in 60 acres of wooded parkland, which includes a 9-hole golf course and a large herd of Manchurian sika deer. Bedrooms are located in the main building and various annexes and all are centrally heated, with private facilities. A varied menu makes good use of local fish, meat, game and vegetables and the standard of cuisine is high. Sports and leisure facilities are excellent.
12⇌Annexe23⇌ CTV in all bedrooms ® T ✱ ✳
sB&B⇌£40-£50
dB&B⇌£85-£100 Continental breakfast (incl dinner)
60P ✇ ✲ ☐(heated) ⛱(heated) ⚑9 ♪ (hard) ♩ squash snooker sauna solarium gymnasium croquet putting billiards table tennis nc10yrs
☋ International V ⚡ Bar Lunch £2-£5alc

CHOLLERFORD Northumberland Map **12** NY97

★★★ **65% George** Humshaugh NE46 4EW (Swallow)
☎Humshaugh(043481)611 FAX (043481) 727
Set on the banks of the River North Tyne, this tourist and business hotel offers a mixture of modern and traditional bedrooms.
54⇌(5fb)1☐ CTV in all bedrooms ® T ✳ sB&B⇌fr£57 dB&B⇌fr£80 ☰
(70P ✲ ☐(heated) ♩ sauna solarium putting *xmas*
☋ International V ♉ ☕ S% Lunch £10.50 Dinner £14.95&alc Last dinner 9.30pm
Credit Cards 1 2 3 5

CHORLEY Lancashire Map **07** SD51

★★★ **64% Park Hall Hotel, Leisure & Conference Centre** PR7 5LP (SW off A49) ☎Eccleston(0257)452090
Telex no 677604 FAX (0257) 451838
(For full entry see Charnock Richard)

★★★ **67% Shaw Hill Hotel Golf & Country** Preston Rd, Whittle-le-Woods PR6 7RP (2m N A6) ☎(02572)69221
FAX (02572) 61223
This comfortably-converted country house is situated on a golf course and has a very good restaurant.
22rm(21⇌1♠)(1fb)1☐ CTV in 18bedrooms ® ✳
sB&B⇌♠£47.50-£52.50 dB&B⇌♠£67.50-£74.50 ☰
(CTV 200P ✲ ⚑18 ♩ snooker sauna solarium *xmas*
☋ International V ♉ ☕ Lunch fr£10.50&alc Dinner fr£14.50&alc Last dinner 9.45pm
Credit Cards 1 2 3 5

★★**Hartwood Hall** Preston Rd PR6 7AX ☎(02572)69966
FAX (02572) 41678
Closed 25-30 Dec
Conveniently situated on the A6 north of the town, near the M61 junction, the hotel offers well-appointed bedrooms, value-for-money menus and friendly service throughout.
12rm(4⇌4♠)Annexe10rm(2⇌8♠)(3fb) CTV in all bedrooms ® T S% sB&B£32-£42 sB&B⇌♠£37-£42 dB&Bfr£44 dB&B⇌♠£48-£55 ☰
CTV 150P ✇

▶

Continental V S% Lunch fr£7&alc High tea fr£7&alc Dinner fr£11&alc Last dinner 9pm
Credit Cards 1 2 3 5 £

CHRISTCHURCH Dorset Map **04** SZ19

C

See also **Avon**

★★★59% **The Avonmouth** Mudeford BH23 3NT (2m E off B3059) (Trusthouse Forte) ☎(0202)483434
Well-equipped bedrooms and attractive, comfortable public rooms are provided by this resort hotel, which enjoys an excellent location alongside Christchurch Harbour.
27⇌Annexe14⇌(3fb) in 4 bedrooms CTV in all bedrooms ® S% sB⇌£60-£70 dB⇌£86-£96 (room only)
(66P (heated) *xmas*
English & French V S% Lunch £5.50-£10 Dinner £12.95&alc Last dinner 9pm
Credit Cards 1 2 3 4 5

★★★70% **Waterford Lodge** 87 Bure Ln, Friars Cliff, Mudeford BH23 4DN (2m E off B3059) (Best Western) ☎Highcliffe(0425)272948 & 278801 Telex no 41588 FAX (0425) 279130
A privately owned hotel under the personal supervision of the proprietors who ensure that their guests have an enjoyable stay. The hotel has been tastefully modernised and has some exceptionally good bedrooms.
20⇌(10fb)1 CTV in all bedrooms ® T sB&B⇌£42-£47 dB&B⇌£64-£74
41P *xmas*
English & French V Lunch £7.60-£13.25&alc Dinner £12-£13.90&alc Last dinner 8.30pm
Credit Cards 1 2 3 5

★★**Fisherman's Haunt** Salisbury Rd, Winkton BH23 7AS (2.5m N on B3347) ☎(0202)477283 & 484071
Closed 25 Dec
This busy hotel, attractively creeper-clad and set in its own grounds near the River Avon, provides an ideal base for fishermen, offering comfortable bedrooms and public bars.
4rm(1⇌2)Annexe15rm(13⇌)(4fb)2 CTV in all bedrooms ® T S10% sB&B£23-£31 dB&B£45 dB&B⇌£48-£52
100P
V Lunch fr£7 Dinner fr£15.20 Last dinner 10pm
Credit Cards 1 2 3 5

CHURCH STRETTON Shropshire Map **07** SO49

★★★58% ***Stretton Hall*** All Stretton SY6 6HE ☎(0694)723224
This 18th-century country house with its spacious grounds provides comfortable accommodation and a relaxed atmosphere.
13rm(10⇌3)(1fb) CTV in all bedrooms ®
CTV 60P
English & French Last dinner 9pm
Credit Cards 1 2 3 5

★★**Mynd House** Little Stretton SY6 6RB (2m S B4370) (Exec Hotel) ☎(0694)722212 FAX (0299)270662
Closed Jan
Set high in pleasant gardens, a large Edwardian house in the peaceful and picturesque village of Little Stretton enjoys good views of the valley and hills opposite; it offers modern, well-equipped accommodation and a warm welcome from the proprietors.
9⇌1 CTV in all bedrooms ® T sB&B⇌£23-£27.50 dB&B⇌£40-£55
16P *xmas*
English & French V Bar Lunch £2.50-£5alc Dinner £11-£11.50&alc Last dinner 9.15pm
Credit Cards 1 3

CHURT Surrey Map **04** SU83

★★★50% **Frensham Pond** GU10 2QB ☎Frensham(025125)3175 Telex no 858610
Spacious bedrooms combined with garden chalet bedrooms provide a varied choice of accommodation here. There is a small cocktail bar and the well-managed Fountain restaurant provides good standards of service and an above average wine list. A new addition is 'Fathoms' leisure centre.
7⇌Annexe12⇌ CTV in all bedrooms ® T
(100P (heated) squash sauna solarium gymnasium jacuzzi
English & French V
Credit Cards 1 2 3 4 5

CIRENCESTER Gloucestershire Map **04** SP00

See also **Ewen**

★★★65% **The Crown of Crucis** Ampney Crucis GL7 5RS ☎Poulton(028585)403

★★★68% **Fleece** Market Place GL7 2NZ (Best Western) ☎(0285)68507 Telex no 437287 FAX (0285) 651017
This Tudor inn in the town centre offers a high standard of bedroom accommodation and a comfortable lounge. The dining room serves new English dishes and a new wine bar will offer char-grilled food. Staff are friendly and courteous.
25⇌(4fb)2 CTV in all bedrooms ® T
12P
English & French V Last dinner 10.30pm
Credit Cards 1 2 3 5

★★★64% **King's Head** Market Place GL7 2NR (Best Western) ☎(0285)653322 Telex no 43470 FAX (0285) 655103
Closed 27-30 Dec
This historic town-centre hotel, dating back to the 14th century, is full of character and traditional in style. The comfortable public rooms, linked by rambling corridors, include an atmospheric cocktail bar and a stylish, intimate restaurant. Here, an extensive range of dishes is produced from quality fresh ingredients. The well-equipped bedrooms are in the process of refurbishment, but retain the style of the building.
70rm(66⇌4)(4fb)2 CTV in all bedrooms ® T S% sB&B⇌£42-£44 dB&B⇌£70-£75
Lift (25P pool skittle alley *xmas*
V S% Lunch fr£9.25 Dinner fr£12.25 Last dinner 9pm
Credit Cards 1 2 3 4 5 £

★★★65% **Stratton House** Gloucester Rd GL7 2LE ☎(0285)651761 FAX (0285) 640024
Set in an attractive walled garden on the outskirts of town, Stratton House dates from Jacobean times with later additions of mellow Cotswold stone. Run on country house lines, it has welcoming log fires in the cooler months in the flagstoned entrance hall, the elegant lounge and the timbered bar.
26rm(22⇌3)(3fb) CTV in all bedrooms ® T sB&B£39 sB&B⇌£43.50 dB&B£50 dB&B⇌£56
CTV 100P 2 croquet *xmas*
English & French V S% Lunch £8.95 High tea £2-£3.50 Dinner £12.50-£13.50 Last dinner 9.45pm
Credit Cards 1 2 3 5

★★**Corinium Court** Gloucester St GL7 2DG ☎(0285)659711 FAX (0285) 885807
Originally a wool merchant's house, dating from 1595, this family-run hotel is in the historic part of the town. Cosy bedrooms of varying shapes and sizes are well equipped with modern facilities. The restaurant, converted from the old barn and wagon shed, overlooks the garden, while the character courtyard bar opens out onto a patio.
16rm(10⇌6)(1fb) CTV in all bedrooms T
sB&B⇌£42-£48 dB&B⇌£45-£60

►

STRATTON HOUSE HOTEL

CIRENCESTER

Tel: (0285) 651761

The hotel is ¾ mile from the Town centre on the Gloucester Road (A417)

Elegant hotel and restaurant with excellent cuisine and fine wine. Buildings part 17th century in lovely setting attractive walled garden bright with flowers, terrace, croquet lawn and ample car parking. Country house atmosphere with comfortable bar and lounges, spacious bedrooms all with telephone, colour television and most with private bathroom en suite. Enjoy a carefree visit to this pleasant hotel where you will find a genuine welcome and courteous friendly service. Colour brochure available.

AA ★★★

The Kings Head Hotel

CIRENCESTER

AA ★★★ Best Western

This historic hotel in the heart of the Cotswolds was formerly a Coaching Inn. It now combines old world charm with every modern comfort. The Hotel is privately owned and offers excellent food and wines. The Management are proud of the reputation the hotel has gained for cheerful, courteous and efficient service provided by the staff, to which tribute is constantly being paid.

Phone 0285 653322 Fax (0285) 655103 Telex 43470

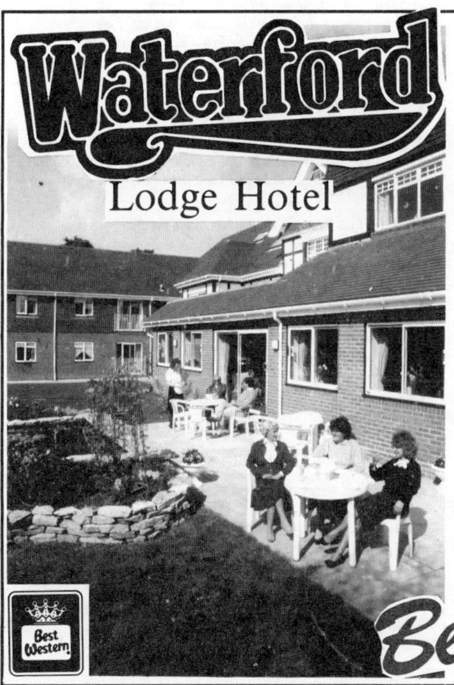

THE WATERFORD LODGE HOTEL

87 Bure Lane
Friars Cliff
Christchurch
Dorset BH23 4DN
Telephone:
Highcliffe
(0425) 272948
Fax: (0425) 279130

Getaway and relax in our friendly hotel with its comfortable bedrooms and fresh restaurant reflecting the beauty of our colourful Garden.

The Waterford Lodge is peacefully situated, two miles east of historic Christchurch and is close to Mudeford Harbour, Avon Beach and the New Forest.

Be our guest

AA ★★★

40P ⛟
V ♆ ☕
Credit Cards 1 2 3 5

CLACHAN-SEIL Strathclyde *Argyllshire* Map **10** NM71

★**Willowburn** Isle of Seil, (via Atlantic Bridge) PA34 4TJ (Guestaccom) ☎Balvicar(08523)276
Closed Nov-mid Mar
6rm(2⇨4♠) CTV in all bedrooms ® sB&B⇨♠£21.50-£23 dB&B⇨♠£37-£39 ⊟
36P ⛟ ❁
♆ ☕ Bar Lunch £3.50-£10alc Dinner fr£10&alc Last dinner 8.30pm
Credit Cards 1 3

CLACTON-ON-SEA Essex Map **05** TM11

★★**King's Cliff** King's Pde, Holland on Sea CO15 5JB ☎(0255)812343 Telex no 817589 FAX (0284) 706502
This imposing sea-front hotel has comfortable bedrooms and the public areas have, for the most part, been refurbished to a good standard. The popular lounge bar includes a food counter which offers good hot and cold snacks at lunchtime, whilst for the more discerning guest there is a new cocktail bar adjacent to the formal restaurant.
15rm(9⇨6♠)(5fb)1⊞ CTV in all bedrooms ® T ⋈ ✱ sB&B⇨♠fr£38.50 dB&B⇨♠fr£54.45 ⊟
☾CTV 80P 5🚘 (£1 per night) ❁ *xmas*
♕ European V ♆ ☕ ⊬ Lunch £4.95&alc High tea £1-£4 Dinner £4.95&alc Last dinner 9pm
Credit Cards 1 2 3 £

CLANFIELD Oxfordshire Map **04** SP20

✕✕✕**Plough at Clanfield** Bourton Rd OX8 2RB ☎(036781)222 & 494 Telex no 449848 FAX (036781) 596
Tranquil surroundings and attentive service combine with imaginative cuisine of a high order at this colourful restaurant, whose setting is an Elizabethan manor at the heart of an Oxfordshire village. The restaurant has a pleasant air of intimacy, and serves fixed-price lunch and dinner menus showing flair and imagination in dishes such as quenelles of chicken parfait in a rich redcurrant sauce, and noisettes of lamb with a rosemary and sorrel sauce. Sweets are of equal quality, and traditional puddings are offered. The Plough also has a choice of good bedrooms.
♕ English & French V 45 seats ✱ Lunch fr£11.95&alc Dinner fr£21&alc Last lunch 2pm Last dinner 10pm 30P nc7yrs 6 bedrooms available ⊬
Credit Cards 1 2 3 5

CLARE Suffolk Map **05** TL74

★★**Bell** Market Hill CO10 8NN (Minotels) ☎(0787)277741 FAX (0787) 278474
The Miles family have continued to improve this hotel, which has individually decorated bedrooms with excellent facilities. There are two restaurants – one traditional and the other the more informal 'Leggers' – and genuine warmth and hospitality are extended to guests.
10rm(3⇨4♠)Annexe11⇨(2fb)4⊞ CTV in all bedrooms ® T sB&B£32.50 sB&B⇨♠£41.25-£55 dB&B£49.50 dB&B⇨♠£54.50-£82.50 ⊟
15P *xmas*
♕ English, French & Italian ♆ ☕ Lunch fr£9.50&alc Dinner fr£11&alc Last dinner 9.30pm
Credit Cards 1 2 3 5

CLAWTON Devon Map **02** SX39

★★🏠**Court Barn Country House** EX22 6PS (Exec Hotel)
☎North Tamerton (040927)219
Closed 1-14 Jan

Dating back to around the 14th-century and re-built in 1853, this hotel stands in 5 acres of grounds and gardens. Personally run, it offers cosy public rooms with a choice of lounges and comfortable, spotlessly clean bedrooms, each individually furnished and decorated with William Morris wallpapers and fabrics. Many also have good views over the countryside. Plentiful home cooking is based on quality produce and complemented by an extensive wine list and a comprehensive selection of teas.
8rm(4⇨3♠)(3fb)1⊞⊬in all bedrooms TV available ® sB&B£26-£29 sB&B⇨♠£26-£29 dB&Bfr£46 dB&B⇨♠fr£50 ⊟
CTV 16P 2🚘 ❁ U solarium gymnasium croquet putting outdoor badminton ⌂ *xmas*
♕ English & French V ♆ ☕ ⊬ Lunch £7.95 High tea £4 Dinner £15.50 Last dinner 9.15pm
Credit Cards 1 2 3 5 £

CLAYGATE Surrey

See **LONDON plan 5*B1***(page 412)

✕✕**Les Alouettes** High St KT10 0JW ☎Esher(0372)64882
This attractive restaurant offers French-style cuisine with an extensive choice of dishes on the menu. This is supplemented by daily specials which are described to diners by the restaurant manager. Carré d'agneau roti aux celeris fondants et son jus parfumé à l'Estragon is an example. Staff are well presented and provide attentive, courteous service.
Closed Sun, 1-12 Jan, 12-29 Aug & BH's
Lunch not served Sat
♕ French 70 seats ✱ Lunch £18-£24alc Dinner £23-£29alc Wine £7.95 Last lunch 2.15pm Last dinner 9.30pm ⁄P
Credit Cards 1 2 3 5

✕***Read's*** 4 The Parade KT10 0NU ☎Esher(0372)65105
A charming little family-run restaurant with a relaxed, welcoming atmosphere and heirloom-adorned walls offers a short – but thoughtfully composed and seasonally appropriate – menu of wholesome dishes based on good-quality ingredients which represent excellent value for money. As food is prepared to order there may be some delay, but the proprietor makes it his business to ensure that every guest's visit is enjoyable.
Lunch not served Sat
28 seats Last lunch 1.45pm Last dinner 9.30pm ⁄P
Credit Cards 1 2 3 5

CLEARWELL Gloucestershire Map **03** SO50

★★**Wyndham Arms** GL16 8JT ☎Dean(0584)33666 FAX (0594) 36450
A family-owned village inn dating back to the 14th-century with modern facilities installed. The staff are helpful and friendly and the good food is popular with the local community as well as hotel guests.
5⇨Annexe12⇨(3fb) CTV in all bedrooms ® T ✱ S10% sB&B⇨£36.50-£43.50 dB&B⇨£40-£50 ⊟
52P 2🚘 ⛟ *xmas*

⊞ International **V** ♆ Lunch £7-£7&alc Dinner £12.75-£12.75&alc Last dinner 9.30pm
Credit Cards [1] [2] [3] [4]

CLEETHORPES Humberside Map **08** TA30

★★Kingsway Kingsway DN35 0AE ☎(0472)601122
Telex no 527920
Closed 25-26 Dec
This traditional hotel is managed by the owning family who, along with their staff, provide warm courteous service. Bedrooms are comfortable and well appointed and public rooms are tasteful.
53⇌↱(1fb) CTV in all bedrooms **T** ✗ sB&B⇌↱£49-£53 dB&B⇌↱£70-£75 ⊟
Lift ◖ 30P 20⌂ (£1.50) ⊞ nc5yrs
⊞ English & French **V** ♆ Lunch £10&alc Dinner £12.75&alc Last dinner 9pm
Credit Cards [1] [2] [3] [5]

★★Wellow Kings Rd DN35 0AQ ☎(0472)695589
A bright, comfortable hotel with modern well-appointed bedrooms and a restaurant which offers interesting, good value dishes.
10⇌↱(4fb) CTV in all bedrooms ® **T** sB&B⇌↱£25-£35 dB&B⇌↱£35-£48 ⊟
60P *xmas*
⊞ English & Continental **V** ♆ ⊥ Lunch fr£6.50&alc Dinner £5-£10alc Last dinner 10pm
Credit Cards [1] [3]

Places with AA hotels and restaurants are identified on the location atlas at the back of the book.

C

CLEEVE HILL Gloucestershire Map **03** SO92

★★★58% **Rising Sun** GL52 3PX (Lansbury)
☎Bishops Cleeve(0242)676281 Telex no 437410
FAX (0242) 673069
Set in an elevated position between the Cotswolds and the Malvern hills, this small and cosy commercial hotel provides compact but well-equipped bedrooms. Small conferences can be accommodated.
24⇌(3fb)1⊟ ⊬in 6 bedrooms CTV in all bedrooms ® T sB&B⇌fr£55 dB&B⇌fr£65 ⊟
(56P ✲ sauna *xmas*
English V ♧ ⊒ Lunch £7.75&alc High tea £3.50 Dinner £5.45-£9.75alc Last dinner 10.30pm
Credit Cards 1 2 3 5

❀ ✕✕**Redmond's at Malvern View** GL52 3PR
☎Bishops Cleeve(0242)672017
(Rosette awarded for dinner only)
Closed Mon & 1st wk Jan
Lunch not served Sat
Dinner not served Sun
32 seats Lunch £14 Dinner £23 Last lunch 1.45pm Last dinner 10pm 16P nc5yrs ⊬
Credit Cards 1 3

CLEISH Tayside *Kinross-shire* Map **11** NT09

★★★68% **Nivingston House** KY13 7LS
☎Cleish Hills(05775)216
FAX (05775) 238

Nestling quietly below the Cleish Hills in 12 acres of landscaped grounds, this delightful country house continues to enjoy a sound reputation under the ownership of Pat and Allan Deeson. Public rooms are warm and welcoming and the bedrooms have been decorated tastefully and furnished well. Food is served in the candle-lit dining room: it is predominantly Scottish with excellent use of fresh local produce which is imaginatively prepared and presented.
17rm(15⇌2↱)(2fb)1⊟ CTV in all bedrooms ® T sB&B⇌↱£50-£60 dB&B⇌↱£70-£90 ⊟
50P ⊞ ✲ croquet putting golf driving range *xmas*
International V ♧ ⊒ Lunch £13.50 Dinner £20 Last dinner 9pm
Credit Cards 1 2 3

CLEOBURY MORTIMER Shropshire Map **07** SO67

★★**Redfern** DY14 8AA (Minotels) ☎(0299)270395
Telex no 335176 FAX (0299) 271011
A small, comfortable hotel, personally run by the Redfern family, providing warm and well-equipped bedrooms. The restaurant has a varied menu and serves ample portions.
5rm(2⇌3↱)Annexe6rm(5⇌1↱)(4fb)1⊟ CTV in all bedrooms ® T S% sB&B⇌↱£35-£45 dB&B⇌↱£50.50-£62 ⊟
20P ⊞ clay pigeon shooting pheasant shooting *xmas*
English & French V ♧ S% Lunch £8 Dinner £12.50 Last dinner 9.30pm
Credit Cards 1 2 3 5 £

★★**Talbot** High St DY14 8DQ ☎(0299)270036 270205
A 15th-century coaching inn of charming appearance. Service is friendly and informal. All the bedrooms have been well-equipped and are maintained efficiently, most of them are 'en suite'.
8rm(2⇌4↱)(1fb)3⊟ CTV in all bedrooms ® T ✗ (ex guide dogs) ✻ sB&B£25 sB&B⇌↱£29 dB&B£39 dB&B⇌↱£45 ⊟
CTV *xmas*
V ♧ ⊒ ⊬ Lunch £2-£10alc High tea £2-£7alc Dinner £3.50-£13alc Last dinner 10pm
Credit Cards 1 3

CLIFTONVILLE

See **Margate**

CLIMPING West Sussex Map **04** TQ00

★★★72% **Bailiffscourt** BN17 5RW
☎Littlehampton (0903)723511
Telex no 877870
FAX (0903) 723107

Situated in rural tranquility and built only 50 years ago, this replica of a 13th-century courthouse has been furnished with sturdy antiques. Several bedrooms have open fireplaces and the thatched house can be reached by an underground passage. Chef Jonas Tester continues to impress with a menu which changes weekly and the levels of service can be extensive particularly during the summer months.
18⇌Annexe2⇌↱(3fb)9⊟ CTV in all bedrooms T sB&B⇌↱£60-£175 dB&B⇌↱£95-£175 ⊟
50P ✲ ⌂ ℛ (hard) ∪ croquet nc 8yrs *xmas*
French V ♧ ⊒ Lunch fr£15.50 High tea fr£6 Dinner fr£19.50&alc Last dinner 10pm
Credit Cards 1 2 3 5

CLOVELLY

See **Horn's Cross**

CLUN Shropshire Map **07** SO38

✕**Old Post Office** 9 The Square SY7 8JA ☎(05884)687
This small village restaurant has recently been extended to provide an extra dining room and a wooden balcony where customers can sit on warm summer days. The varied menu offers 4 choices for each course, including vegetarian dishes, and the extensive cheeseboard boasts over 15 varieties, all well kept and served with celery, nuts and salad. Friendly unhurried service completes the relaxed atmosphere here.
Closed Mon, Tue, Feb-Mar, 29 Aug-6 Sep & 23 Dec-3 Jan
V 30 seats ✻ Lunch £12.50-£18.75alc Dinner £18-£20 Last lunch 1.15pm Last dinner 9.30pm nc10yrs 2 bedrooms available
Credit Cards 1 3

CLYRO Powys Map **03** SO24

★★**Baskerville Arms** HR3 5RZ ☎Hay-On-Wye(0497)820670
FAX (0497) 821224
Set in the heart of Baskerville country and run personally by the Harmsworth Family, this small hotel offers good accommodation and food in a relaxing atmosphere.
12rm(6⇌)(4fb)⊬in 3 bedrooms CTV in all bedrooms ® T ✻ sB&B£19.50-£23.50 sB&B⇌fr£23.50 dB&B£38 dB&B⇌£44 ⊟
P ✲ ♫ *xmas*

V ♔ ☕ ⁄ Lunch fr£1.50alc High tea 60p-£1.95alc Dinner £7.95&alc Last dinner 10.30pm
Credit Cards [1] [3]

COCKERMOUTH Cumbria Map 11 NY13

★★★61% **Broughton Craggs** Great Broughton CA13 0XP ☎(0900)824400
A small country hotel and restaurant that is favoured by business clientele. It sits in its own gardens beside a vicarage 2 miles west of Cockermouth. To reach it you should turn off the A66 at the signpost for Great Broughton, cross a bridge and then bear right uphill towards Keith.
10⇌(1fb)1⊟ CTV in all bedrooms ® T ✗ (ex guide dogs) ✱ sB&B⇌£38-£40 dB&B⇌£50-£60 ⊟
60P ⊞ ✲ ♪ *xmas*
☺ English & Continental V ♔ ☕ ⁄ Lunch £10-£12.75&alc Dinner £12.75-£14&alc Last dinner 9.30pm
Credit Cards [1] [2] [3] [5]

★★★62% **The Trout** Crown St CA13 0EJ ☎(0900)823591
Closed 25 Dec
This historic building with its grounds leading down to the River Derwent retains much of its period character while meeting the needs of the modern business traveller.
22rm(18⇌4♪)(1fb) CTV in all bedrooms ® T ✱ sB&B⇌♪£35 dB&B⇌♪£48 ⊟
(80P ✲ ♪
☺ English, French & Italian V ♔ Lunch £8&alc Dinner £13&alc Last dinner 9.30pm
Credit Cards [1] [3]

★★*Allerdale Court* Market Square CA13 9NQ ☎(0900)823654
Closed Xmas day RS Sun
Dating from the early 18th century and notable for its fine oak beams and panelling, an hotel of character offers an attractive restaurant and tasteful bar areas. Bedrooms vary in size but are generally well decorated and equipped, one particularly comfortable room containing an impressive four-poster bed.
25rm(14⇌6♪)(1fb)2⊟ CTV in all bedrooms ® T
CTV P̸
☺ English, French & Italian V Last dinner 9.30pm
Credit Cards [1] [2] [3]

★★**Globe** Main St CA13 9LE (Consort) ☎(0900)822126
Telex no 57515 FAX (0900) 823705
This hotel is situated close to the lakes and forms an ideal touring base.
30rm(17⇌)(3fb) CTV in all bedrooms ® T sB&Bfr£29 sB&B⇌fr£33 dB&Bfr£39 dB&B⇌£42-£45 ⊟
CTV 12⌂ ♫ *xmas*
V ♔ ☕ ⁄ Lunch £1.85-£7.95 High tea £1.75-£3 Dinner £13&alc Last dinner 9.30pm
Credit Cards [1] [2] [3] [5] £

★★**Wordsworth** Main St CA13 9JS (Consort) ☎(0900)822757
Formerly a coaching inn, dating back to the early 17th century.
18rm(6⇌6♪)(1fb) CTV in all bedrooms ® ✱ sB&B£18-£22 sB&B⇌♪fr£29 dB&Bfr£32 dB&B⇌♪fr£39 ⊟
CTV 20P
☺ English & Continental ♔ Bar Lunch £3.95-£8.50 Dinner £9.50-£12 Last dinner 9pm
Credit Cards [1] [2] [3] [4] [5] £

COGGESHALL Essex Map 05 TL82

★★★61% **White Hart** Market End CO6 1NH (Select) ☎(0376)61654 FAX (0376) 61789
An old hostelry of great character with magnificent roof timbers and a beamed bar lounge with copper tables and log fires in winter. The hotel has been tastefully restored and incorporates many original features. Bar snacks and room service supplement the well-appointed restaurant, which also has a dance floor. The young staff are friendly.
18rm(13⇌5♪) CTV in all bedrooms T ✗ (ex guide dogs) ✱ sB&B⇌♪£50-£65 dB&B⇌♪£70-£85 ⊟
30P ⊞ ✲
V ♔ ☕ Lunch £15-£30&alc Dinner £12-£40alc Last dinner 9pm
Credit Cards [1] [2] [3] [5] £

COLBOST

See Skye, Isle of

COLCHESTER Essex Map 05 TL92

★★★63% **George** 116 High St CO1 0NJ (Queens Moat) ☎(0206)578494 FAX (0206) 761732
A town centre coaching inn featuring a choice of bars, a carvery restaurant, cosy public areas and well equipped bedrooms. There is also a fitness room. Good car parking can be found at the rear of the hotel.
47⇌♪(3fb) CTV in all bedrooms ® T sB&B⇌♪£50-£55 dB&B⇌♪£60-£65 ⊟
(50P sauna solarium gymnasium
♔ ☕ ⁄ Lunch £9.75-£10 Dinner £9.75-£10 Last dinner 10pm
Credit Cards [1] [2] [3] [5]

★★★50% **Marks Tey Hotel** London Rd CO6 1DU ☎(0206)210001 Telex no 987176
(For full entry see Marks Tey)

★★★63% **Red Lion** High St CO1 1DJ (Best Western) ☎(0206)577986 Telex no 987185 ref 186 FAX (0206) 578206
Among the many historic attractions of this Grade 1 listed building are the carefully preserved walls of wattle and daub. Bedrooms are cosy, with antique or Victorian pine furnishings, and there is a small lounge. In the beamed dining room, head chef Trevor Colchester provides innovative menus using good, fresh ingredients.
24rm(22⇌2♪)1⊟ CTV in all bedrooms ® T ✱ sB&B⇌♪£26-£49 dB&B⇌♪£45-£62 ⊟
(20P ⊞
V ♔ ☕ Lunch fr£10.80&alc Dinner fr£13.75&alc Last dinner 9.30pm
Credit Cards [1] [2] [3] [5]

★★**Kings Ford Park** Layer Rd, Layer De La Haye CO2 0HS (2.5m S B1026) ☎(0206)34301 Telex no 987562 FAX (0206) 34512
RS Sun
Comfortable Regency house in woodland park with some modernised bedrooms.
13rm(12⇌1♪)(2fb)1⊟ CTV in all bedrooms ® T ✱ sB&B⇌♪£52 dB&B⇌♪£65 ⊟
CTV 200P ✲ pitch & putt ♫ *xmas*
☺ International V ♔ ☕ Lunch £11.75&alc Dinner £20-£25alc Last dinner 9.30pm
Credit Cards [1] [2] [3] [5] £

COLDSTREAM Borders *Berwickshire* Map 12 NT83

★*Victoria* 71 High St TD12 4AH ☎(0890)2112
Converted sandstone house dating from 1860, close to the River Tweed.
8rm(2♪)(1fb)⁄in 1 bedroom CTV in all bedrooms ®
8P snooker ♫
♔ ☕ Last dinner 9pm

COLEFORD Gloucestershire Map 03 SO51

★★**The Speech House** Forest of Dean GL16 7EL (Trusthouse Forte) ☎Dean(0594)22607
Comfortable, friendly hotel built in 1676 as a court house for the Verderers of the Forest of Dean.
14rm(3⇌)(2fb)3⊟⁄in 1 bedroom CTV in all bedrooms ® T sB£52 sB⇌£65 dB£57-£62 dB⇌£67-£72 (room only) ⊟
▶

40P ✲ *xmas*
V ♉ ⊡ ⁄ S% Lunch £8.50-£10.50&alc High tea £3.45 Dinner £12.50-£17.95&alc Last dinner 9pm
Credit Cards 1 2 3 4 5

★Lambsquay House GL16 8QB ☎Dean(0594)33127
Peacefully situated, attractive Georgian house, offering high quality, home produced cooking.
9rm(8⇨1⌐)(1fb) CTV in all bedrooms ® T
sB&B⇨⌐£24.50-£40.50 dB&B⇨⌐£38-£60 ⊟
30P ✲ ✲ *xmas*
♉ English & Continental ♉ ⊡ Lunch £7-£9 Dinner £9&alc Last dinner 7.30pm
Credit Cards 1 3 5

COLERNE Wiltshire Map **03** ST87

★★★★ 75% Lucknam Park SN14 8AZ (Prestige)
☎(0225)742777 Telex no 445648 FAX (0225) 743536
This magnificent country-house hotel offers a very high standard of comfort, service and cuisine. The main house, set in extensive parkland of 280 acres and approached down a mile-long, tree-lined drive, has 39 bedrooms (including nine suites). The Georgian house has been sympathetically restored to offer gracious and beautifully furnished public rooms, including a spacious drawing room and panelled library with a fine selection of books. The bedrooms are all of comfortable size and well-appointed and some of the larger suites are furnished with a delicate sense of historical context. Near to the house, the former mews have been converted as a bedroom wing. Other facilities at Lucknam Park include a board room with adjacent dining room overlooking the quiet courtyard, plus an excellent leisure spa with large indoor swimming pool, steam room, sauna, jacuzzi, solarium, beauty parlour and hairdressing salon. There are also a snooker room with an antique snooker table and two outdoor tennis courts.
39⇨5⊟ CTV in all bedrooms **T** ✗ (ex guide dogs) ✱
sB&B⇨fr£85 dB&B⇨£110-£185 ⊟
☾ 90P ✲ ✲ ⊡ ⊡ ℘ (hard) snooker sauna solarium gymnasium jacuzzi croquet beauty salon ♫ *xmas*
V ♉ ⊡ ⁄ Lunch fr£16 Dinner £29.50-£34 Last dinner 10pm
Credit Cards 1 2 3 5

COLESHILL Warwickshire Map **04** SP28

★★★ 51% Coleshill 152 High St B46 3BG (Lansbury)
☎(0675)65527 Telex no 333868 FAX (0675) 64013
Situated close to Junction 4 of the M6. The comfortable modern hotel looks much older than it is, for materials from old buildings were cleverly used in its construction in 1982.
15rm(13⇨2⌐)2⊟⁄in 8 bedrooms CTV in all bedrooms ® **T**
✗ (ex guide dogs) sB&Bfr£50 dB&Bfr£60 ⊟
☾ 48P
♉ English & French **V** ♉ Lunch fr£7.95&alc Dinner fr£12.25&alc Last dinner 9.30pm
Credit Cards 1 2 3 5

★★★ 62% Grimstock Country House Gilson Rd, Gilson B46 1BW (off A446 W of Coleshill) ☎(0675)62369 & 62121
Telex no 334256 FAX (0675)467646
This attractive house with a modern extension stands in well-kept gardens, conveniently situated for the NEC and the M42 and M6 motorways. Its comfortable, well furnished bedrooms are complemented by a pleasant restaurant offering an à la carte menu, friendly service being provided by the resident owner and his young staff.
35rm(32⇨3⌐) CTV in all bedrooms ® **T** sB&B⇨⌐fr£44
dB&B⇨⌐fr£54 ⊟
☾ 60P ✲ ✲
♉ English & French ♉ ⊡ Lunch £4-£6alc Dinner £7-£10&alc Last dinner 9.15pm
Credit Cards 1 2 3 5

★★Swan High St B46 3BL (Porterhouse) ☎(0675)64107
FAX (0675) 467493
Fully modernised hotel popular with business people.
32rm(8⇨24⌐) CTV in all bedrooms ® **T** ✗ ✱ sB&B⇨⌐£38
dB&B⇨⌐£48 ⊟
☾ ⊞ 80P 20⊡
V ♉ ⊡ Lunch £8.50-£8.95&alc Dinner £8.50-£8.95&alc Last dinner 10pm
Credit Cards 1 2 3 5 £

COLONSAY, ISLE OF Strathclyde *Argyllshire* Map **10**

SCALASAIG Map **10** NR30

★Colonsay PA61 7YP
☎Colonsay(09512)316 Prestel MBX 109512316
FAX (09512) 353
Closed 6 Nov-28 Feb ex 28 Dec-11 Jan
Kevin Byrne, the owner of this delightful island hotel has a warm welcome for guests, and meets them personally from the ferry. For those who find walking or using the hotel bicycles too strenuous, transport is willingly provided. Accommodation is comfortable, rooms are prettily furnished and the good home cooking, based on local produce, is very enjoyable. Mr Byrne is also extremely knowledgeable about island flora and fauna.
10rm(1⇨7⌐)(1fb) TV in 6bedrooms ® sB&B£24.75-£39.35
dB&B⇨⌐£49.50-£78.70 ⊟
32P ✲ ✲
♉ European ♉ ⊡ ⁄ Bar Lunch £1-£3alc High tea £6.95-£7.45 Dinner £13.25-£14.25 Last dinner 7.30pm
Credit Cards 1 2 3 5 £

COLSTERWORTH Lincolnshire Map **08** SK92

○***Granada Lodge*** A1 NG33 5JR (Granada)
☎Grantham(0476)860686
Due to have opened Sep 1989
38⇨

○***Travelodge*** A1 New Fox, South Witham LE15 8AU
(Trusthouse Forte) ☎Thistleton(057283)586
32⇨

COLVEND Dumfries & Galloway *Kirkcudbrightshire* Map **11** NX85

★★Clonyard House DG5 4QW ☎Rockcliffe(055663)372
This friendly, family-run hotel is on the Solway Coastal Route, close to the picturesque village of Kippford. The house has a modern bedroom extension and is a popular venue for bar meals. There are picnic benches and a children's play area within the 7 acres of grounds.
10rm(5⇨2⌐)(2fb) CTV in all bedrooms ® **T** sB&Bfr£17
sB&B⇨⌐£28 dB&B£32 dB&B⇨⌐£44 ⊟
CTV 40P ✲ ✲ ⊡
♉ British & French **V** ♉ ⊡ Sunday Lunch £5.50&alc Dinner £12&alc Last dinner 9pm
Credit Cards 1 3

COLWYN BAY Clwyd Map **06** SH87

★★★ 68% Norfolk House Princes Dr LL29 8PF ☎(0492)531757
Telex no 61155 FAX (0492) 70009
Professionally run and friendly, the family hotel provides accommodation which is popular with both tourist and businessmen throughout the year, comprising well-equipped bedrooms and a choice of lounge areas in which to relax.
24rm(11⇨13⌐)(4fb) CTV in all bedrooms ®
sB&B⇨⌐£37.50 dB&B⇨⌐£55 ⊟
Lift ☾ 35P ✲
♉ English & French **V** ♉ ⊡ ⁄ Bar Lunch £2-£7alc High tea £3.50-£7alc Dinner £9-£15alc Last dinner 9pm
Credit Cards 1 2 3 4 5

★★★ 66% **Hotel 70 Degrees** Penmaenhead LL29 9LD (2m E A547) (Best Western) ☎(0492)516555 Telex no 61362 FAX (0492) 515565
A low-rise, modern hotel enjoying panoramic views across Colwyn Bay from its lounge, bar and restaurant. All the bedrooms have sea views and provide comfortable accommodation at realistic prices.
41⇨⋔(7fb)1⊟ CTV in all bedrooms ® T ✱ sB&B⇨⋔£45 dB&B⇨⋔£65 ⊟
☾ 200P CFA ♫ *xmas*
International V ✿ ☕ Lunch £10&alc Dinner £14&alc Last dinner 9.30pm
Credit Cards 1 2 3 4 5 £

★★ ***Ashmount*** 18 College Av, Rhos-on-Sea LL28 4NT (Minotels) ☎(0492)45479 & 44582
A well-run seaside hotel, close to all of the amenities at Rhos-on-Sea. Bedrooms are well equipped and service is friendly and attentive.
18rm(5⇨13⋔)(4fb) CTV in all bedrooms ® T
10P
✿ ☕ ⅟ Last dinner 7.30pm
Credit Cards 1 2 3 5

★★ **Edelweiss** Lawson Rd LL29 8HD (Consort) ☎(0492)532314
Detached Victorian house set in its own grounds, half a mile from the beach.
25rm(21⇨4⋔)(3fb)1⊟ CTV in all bedrooms ® T sB&B⇨⋔fr£30 dB&B⇨⋔fr£50 ⊟
CTV 25P ✲ sauna solarium children's play area ⌂ *xmas*
Welsh, English, French & Italian V ✿ ☕ ⅟ Bar Lunch fr£2.75 Dinner fr£10.50&alc Last dinner 8.30pm
Credit Cards 1 2 3 5 £

Book as early as possible for busy holiday periods.

★★Hopeside Princes Dr, West End LL29 8PW ☎(0492)533244
Telex no 61254
An hospitable hotel, situated in a residential area yet close to beach and shops, offers well-equipped bedrooms with improving standards.
19rm(14⇌5♪)(2fb) CTV in all bedrooms ® T
sB&B⇌♪£29.50-£35 dB&B£39 dB&B⇌♪£38-£50 ₽
(CTV 25P solarium nc5yrs
French V Lunch £4.50-£12.50&alc High tea £1.50-£5&alc Dinner £12.50-£12.50&alc Last dinner 9pm
Credit Cards 1 2 3 5

★★*Lyndale* 410 Abergele Rd, Old Colwyn LL29 9AB (Guestaccom) ☎(0492)515429
Modern, relaxing hotel where the Welsh chef provides imaginative, enjoyable food.
14rm(7⇌7♪)(3fb)1 CTV in all bedrooms ® T
CTV 20P
European V Last dinner 8.30pm
Credit Cards 1 2 3

★★St Enoch's Promenade LL28 4BL ☎(0492)532031
Set almost on the promenade, and fronted by a well-maintained, terraced garden, this hotel of character offers genuine hospitality and a warm, friendly atmosphere.
21rm(7⇌2♪)(8fb)1 CTV in 12bedrooms TV in 1bedroom ®
CTV 6P
V Last dinner 7.45pm
Credit Cards 1 2 3

★*Marine* West Promenade LL28 4BP ☎(0492)530295
Closed Nov-Feb
Personally-run holiday hotel overlooking the sea with colourful terraced garden.
14rm(9♪)(4fb) TV available ®
CTV 11P
English V Last dinner 7.30pm
Credit Cards 2 5

★Stanton House Whitehall Rd, Rhos-on-Sea LL28 4ET ☎(0492)44363
Quiet family-run hotel with homely atmosphere and good home cooking.
11rm(3⇌)(3fb) in 2 bedrooms CTV in 4bedrooms TV in 1bedroom ® sB&B£14.50-£16.50 sB&B⇌£17-£19 dB&B£29-£33 dB&B⇌£34-£38 ₽
CTV 8P
S% Lunch £2.50-£3.50 High tea £3-£3.50 Dinner £6-£6.50 Last dinner 7.30pm
Credit Cards 1 3 £

★West Point 102 Conway Rd LL29 7LE ☎(0492)530331
Closed last 2 wks Dec & 1st 2 wks Jan
Large Edwardian house offering good standards at the west end of Colwyn Bay.
10rm(2⇌3♪)(4fb) CTV in 3bedrooms ® sB&B£13.75-£14.75 dB&B£27.50 dB&B⇌♪£31.50 ₽
CTV 8P
English & French V Lunch £4.50-£6.50 Dinner £4.50-£8.50 Last dinner 7pm
Credit Cards 1 3

★*Whitehall* Cayley Prom, Rhos-on-Sea LL28 4EP ☎(0492)47296
Closed Oct-Mar
Bright, family-run hotel overlooking sea.
14rm(6♪)(3fb) CTV in 7bedrooms ®
CTV 5P
Last dinner 7pm

For key to symbols see the inside front cover.

COLYTON Devon Map 03 SY29

★★White Cottage Dolphin St EX13 6NA ☎(0297)52401
Closed 2wks Xmas
The White Cottage is a Grade II listed building on the edge of a historic, East Devon village. The bedrooms, while retaining some original features, provide comfort and good facilities. There is a friendly atmosphere in the lounge and bar and an interesting choice of dishes is available in the charming dining room.
6rm(4⇌2♪)(1fb)1 CTV in all bedrooms ® ✱
sB&B⇌♪£20.50-£23 dB&B⇌♪£41-£50 ₽
15P
International Lunch £5-£8alc Dinner £11-£17alc Last dinner 9.15pm
Credit Cards 1 3

COMBE MARTIN Devon Map 02 SS54

★★*Rone House* King St EX34 0AD ☎(027188)3428
Closed Nov-Feb (ex 23-27 Dec)
Small, family-run hotel in the centre of Combe Martin, providing comfortable accommodation, simple menus and a friendly atmosphere.
11rm(4⇌4♪)(4fb) TV in all bedrooms ®
CTV 15P (heated)
Last dinner 6.30pm
Credit Cards 1

COMRIE Tayside *Perthshire* Map 11 NN72

★★Comrie Drummond St PH6 2DY ☎(0764)70239
RS Nov-Etr
A privately owned and managed ivy clad hotel.
9rm(1⇌5♪)Annexe2⇌ CTV in all bedrooms ® S10%
sB&B£17.50 sB&B⇌♪£22 dB&B£35 dB&B⇌♪£44
24P nc5yrs
Lunch £7.50&alc Dinner £11 Last dinner 9pm
Credit Cards 1 £

★★Royal Melville Square PH6 2DN ☎(0764)70200
Telex no 76277
RS Oct-Mar
Originally a famed hostelry with royal and historic connections. Traditional hospitality, courteous service and comfortable accommodation can now be found here, in the village centre and close to the River Earn. Bedrooms are well furnished and bathrooms are particularly well appointed.
9rm(8⇌)Annexe3⇌(1fb)1 CTV in all bedrooms ® T
sB&B£22-£24 sB&B⇌£22-£24 dB&B£44-£48
dB&B⇌£44-£48 ₽
30P 2 snooker *xmas*
Scottish & French V Lunch £3-£11.40alc Dinner £14&alc Last dinner 9.30pm
Credit Cards 1 2 3 5 £

CONISTON Cumbria Map 07 SD39

★★Coniston Sun LA21 8HQ ☎(05394)41248
Closed Jan & Feb
The beautifully-situated hotel is tastefully decorated and furnished throughout. The elegantly comfortable lounge and dining room, together with many of the bedrooms, have spectacular views.
10rm(7⇌3♪)2 CTV in all bedrooms ® T (ex guide dogs)
✱ sB&B⇌♪£26.50-£45.50 dB&B⇌♪£60-£90 ₽
30P
English & French V Bar Lunch £4.95 Dinner £15.50-£20 Last dinner 8.30pm
Credit Cards 1 3

Book as early as possible for busy holiday periods.

★Black Bull Yewdale Rd LA21 8DU ☎(05394)41335
Old world village inn dating from 16th century.
8rm(4⇔3↱)(3fb)⊘in 1 bedroom CTV in all bedrooms Ⓡ ✱
sB&B⇔↱fr£26.45 dB&B⇔↱fr£40.25 ⊞
CTV 12P 3🚗 ✿ pony trekking sailing ♫ *xmas*
⚘ English & French **V** ❀ ☕ Lunch fr£5.50alc High tea fr£4.50alc Dinner fr£6.75alc Last dinner 9pm
Credit Cards 1

★Yewdale Yewdale Rd LA21 8LU ☎(05394)41280
A charming little village-centre hotel dating back to 1896 has recently been redecorated to provide extremely attractive, simply furnished bedrooms, a small but comfortable lounge and an attractive bar; guests are assured of a warm welcome from the resident proprietors.
12rm(2⇔8↱)(4fb) CTV in all bedrooms Ⓡ ✱ S%
sB&B£15.95-£24.70 sB&B⇔↱£19.50-£28.25 dB&B£31.90 dB&B⇔↱£39-£44 ⊞
6P
V ❀ ☕ ⊘ S% Lunch £2.95-£6.95alc High tea £2.95-£6.95alc Dinner £9.50-£12.50&alc Last dinner 8.45pm
Credit Cards 1 3 £

CONNEL Strathclyde *Argyllshire* Map **10** NM93

★★Falls of Lora PA37 1PB (Exec Hotel) ☎(063171)483
RS Xmas & New Year
A friendly, relaxing hotel with comfortable bedrooms, a tasteful lounge and a popular Bistro Bar. Pleasantly situated overlooking Loch Etive.
30rm(27⇔)(4fb)1⊟ CTV in 3bedrooms **T**
sB&B⇔£24.50-£46.50 dB&B£31-£47 dB&B⇔£35-£89 ⊞
CTV 40P 9🚗 ⛱ ✿
⚘ Scottish & French **V** ❀ ☕ ⊘ Bar Lunch £4.50-£13.50alc High tea £5-£6.50alc Dinner fr£13.50 Last dinner 8pm
Credit Cards 1 2 3 5 £

CONSETT Co Durham Map **12** NZ15

○The Royal Derwent Hole Row, Allensford, Castleside DH8 9BB ☎(0207)592000 Telex no 537238
43⇔

CONSTANTINE BAY Cornwall & Isles of Scilly Map **02** SW87

★★★76% Treglos PL28 8JH (Consort) ☎Padstow(0841)520727 Telex no 45795 FAX (0841) 521163
Closed 4 Nov-7 Mar
A country house-style hotel with views over rocky coastline. The restaurant serves imaginative food, well-cooked and presented. Golfing facilities adjacent.
44⇔↱(12fb) CTV in all bedrooms **T** sB&B⇔↱£44-£52 dB&B⇔↱£84-£104 (incl dinner)
Lift ☾ 50P 8🚗 (90p) ⛱ ✿ CFA ⛱(heated) snooker croquet jacuzzi
⚘ English & French **V** ❀ ☕ ⊘ Lunch £8.50 Dinner fr£15&alc Last dinner 9.30pm
Credit Cards 1

See advertisement under PADSTOW

CONTIN Highland *Ross & Cromarty* Map **14** NH45

★★*Craigdarroch Lodge* Craigdarroch Dr IV14 9EH ☎Strathpeffer(0997)21265
Closed 25 Dec
Situated in twelve acres of woodland, this former shooting lodge and clan dower house has been extended to offer pleasantly appointed bedroom accommodation which blends the modern with the traditional, and simply furnished but comfortable public rooms. Fishing and shooting can be arranged.
13rm(8⇔2↱)(1fb) Ⓡ
CTV 30P ⛱ ✿ nc16yrs
❀ ☕ ⊘ Last dinner 8.30pm

CONWY Gwynedd Map **06** SH77

See also **Rowen**

★★★64% Sychnant Pass Sychnant Pass Rd LL32 8BJ ☎(0492)596868 & 596869 Telex no 61155 FAX (0492) 70009
Delightfully located at the foot of the Sychnant Pass, this personally run hotel offers comfortable, well-furnished accommodation.
13rm(10⇔3↱)(2fb) CTV in all bedrooms Ⓡ **T**
sB&B⇔↱£25-£39 dB&B⇔↱£40-£59 ⊞
CTV 30P ✿ sauna solarium *xmas*
⚘ British & French ❀ ☕ Lunch £7.95 High tea £6 Dinner £13.95-£16.95 Last dinner 9.30pm
Credit Cards 1 2 3 5 £

See advertisement on page 221

★★Berthlwyd Hall Llechwedd LL32 8DQ ☎(0492)592409
6rm(4⇔)(2fb) CTV in all bedrooms Ⓡ (ex guide dogs) ✱
sB&B⇔fr£25 dB&B⇔£35-£52 ⊞
40P ⛱ ✿ (heated)
⚘ French **V** ❀ ☕ Lunch £7.50 Dinner £8.50&alc Last dinner 9.30pm
Credit Cards 1 2 3

★★The Castle High St LL32 8DB (Trusthouse Forte) ☎Aberconwy(0492)592324
An important 19th century coaching house featuring a unique collection of the Victorian artist, JD Watson. The lounge has been refurbished and the bedrooms have been upgraded.
29rm(28⇔1↱)(1fb)1⊟⊘in 2 bedrooms CTV in all bedrooms Ⓡ **T** ✱ S% sB⇔↱fr£50 dB⇔↱fr£65 (room only) ⊞
30P *xmas*

▶

V ♡ ⚡ Sunday Lunch fr£7.50 Dinner fr£11.50&alc Last dinner 9pm
Credit Cards 1 2 3 4 5

★★Castle Bank Mount Pleasant LL32 8NY
☎Aberconwy(0492)593888
Closed Jan RS Dec & Feb
Victorian stone house standing in its own gardens, next to the castle walls.
9rm(8↱)(3fb) CTV in all bedrooms ® ✗ sB&Bfr£21 sB&B↱fr£25.50 dB&B↱fr£42 ⊟
CTV 12P ⇄
♀ International **V** Lunch fr£7.75 Dinner fr£12 Last dinner 8pm
Credit Cards 1 3 £

★★The Park Hall Bangor Rd LL32 8DP ☎(0492)592279
9rm(7⇌2↱)(2fb) CTV in all bedrooms ®
sB&B⇌↱£19.50-£22.50 dB&B⇌↱£35-£40
40P ⇄ ✲ ⌂ *xmas*
♀ English, French & Italian **V** ♡ Lunch £4.75-£5.75alc Dinner fr£9&alc Last dinner 9.30pm
Credit Cards 1 2 3 5 £

COODEN BEACH East Sussex Map 05 TQ70

★★★68% Cooden Resort Cooden Sea Rd TN39 4TT
☎Cooden(04243)2281 FAX (04243) 6142
Situated on the beach and commanding magnificent sea views, this hotel has been extensively modernised and offers well-equipped bedrooms, foyer lounge, two bars and a formal restaurant. There are also good leisure facilities and a health club. Service is extensive and particularly well supervised.
36rm(31⇌5↱)(6fb) CTV in all bedrooms ® **T** ✱
sB&B⇌↱fr£48 dB&B⇌↱fr£70 ⊟
(60P ✲ ▭(heated) ≈(heated) sauna solarium jacuzzi hair salon ♫ *xmas*
♀ English & French **V** ♡ ⊻ Lunch £10&alc Dinner £14.50&alc Last dinner 9.30pm
Credit Cards 1 2 3 5

See advertisement under BEXHILL-ON-SEA

COOKHAM Berkshire Map 04 SU88

✕✕Cookham Tandoori High St SL6 9
☎Bourne End(06285)22584 FAX (0628) 770520
The furnishings and décor of this smart Indian restaurant are more subdued than many. Division into three sections gives an intimate atmosphere, and a selection of well-cooked dishes from the north regions of India are reasonably priced, though more expensive specialities are obtainable by giving 24 hours' notice.
Closed 25 & 26 Dec
♀ Indian **V** 70 seats Last lunch 2pm Last dinner 10.30pm
₱ nc7yrs ⚡
Credit Cards 1 2 3 5

COPTHORNE

See **Gatwick Airport**

CORBIERE

See **Jersey under Channel Islands**

CORBRIDGE Northumberland Map 12 NY96

★★*Angel Inn* Main St NE45 5LA ☎(043471)2119
Attractive old coaching inn with comfortable bedrooms and a wealth of mahogany panelling.
5⇌↱ CTV in all bedrooms ® ✗
5P
♀ English, French & Italian **V** ♡ Last dinner 10pm
Credit Cards 1 2 3 5

★*Riverside* Main St NE45 5LE (Guestaccom) ☎(043471)2942 due to change to (0434) 632942
Closed Xmas & Jan
Small, comfortable hotel with neat accomodation and friendly service.
11rm(3⇌4↱)(1fb) CTV in all bedrooms ®
10P ⇄
♀ English & French Last dinner 8pm

✕✕Ramblers Country House Farnley NE45 5RN (1m SE on A695) ☎(043471)2424
The elegant, country-house restaurant has charming dining rooms, a very comfortable coffee lounge with log fire and a cheerful cocktail bar. An interesting selection of German dishes is offered, and the staff are very happy to give advice on both the menu and the wine list.
Lunch not served (by arrangement only)
♀ Continental **V** 80 seats ✱ Dinner £15-£19alc Last dinner 10pm 25P
Credit Cards 1 2 3 5

CORBY

See **Cottingham**

CORFE CASTLE Dorset Map 03 SY98

⊛★★Mortons House East St BH20 5EE (Exec Hotel)
☎(0929)480988
A charming listed Elizabethan manor house in the midst of this much visited, picturesque village. It has been extended in keeping with the original building and provides delightful well-equipped bedrooms. Head Chef, Tim Hughes, previously at Harveys with Marco Pierre White, creates food in the modern British style, carefully cooked to retain natural flavours and with original ideas. Pan-fried langoustine and monkfish is served with a herb salad and a lime butter sauce; noisette of lamb with a chicken and tarragon mousse. The wine list is well chosen and comprehensive.
7⇌↱1⊞ CTV in all bedrooms T ✱ sB&B⇌↱£40-£80 dB&B⇌↱£60-£140 ⊟
40P ⇄ ✲ *xmas*
V ♡ ⊻ ⚡
Credit Cards 1 3

CORNHILL-ON-TWEED Northumberland Map 12 NT83

★★★⚜58% Tillmouth Park TD12 4UU
☎Coldstream(0890)2255

Set in extensive grounds, 3 miles north-east of the village, this Victorian mansion, which retains its traditional character, has long been popular with the fishing fraternity. The bedrooms, some of which are massive, have all modern amenities.
12rm(11⇌1↱)Annexe1⇌(1fb)1⊞ CTV in all bedrooms ® T ✱ sB&B⇌↱£45 dB&B⇌↱£70 ⊟
50P ✲ ⌡

☺ International V ✿ ☕ Lunch £4-£10alc Dinner £13.95 Last dinner 9.30pm
Credit Cards [1] [2] [3] [4] [5]

See advertisement on page 223

CORSE LAWN Hereford & Worcester Map **03** SO83

★★★69% Corse Lawn House GL19 4LZ
☎Tirley(045278)479 & 771 Telex no 437348
FAX (045278) 840
This fine Queen Anne house was once a posting house and the original coach wash is now an ornamental pond. The Hine family have been at Corse Lawn for several years now, originally running it as a restaurant with a few letting bedrooms, and as such it soon obtained a high reputation. The addition of a new bedroom wing has created an hotel which is equally popular.
10⇨2⊞ CTV in all bedrooms ® T sB&B⇨fr£50 dB&B⇨fr£65
50P ⊞ ✲ ♪ (hard) croquet lawn putting green *xmas*
☺ English & French V ✿ ☕ Lunch fr£13.50&alc Dinner fr£19.75&alc Last dinner 10pm
Credit Cards [1] [2] [3] [5]

CORSHAM Wiltshire Map **03** ST86

★★★68% Rudloe Park Leafy Ln SN13 0PA
☎Bath(0225)810555 FAX (0225) 811412
The continued refurbishment of this Victorian hotel has resulted in very well-appointed bedrooms, though lounge facilities, which are still rather limited, can prove inadequate when conferences are in progress. Sound standards of service are matched by the quality of the meals, and a superb wine list details over 500 different bottles.
11⇨(1fb)1⊞ CTV in all bedrooms ® T S10%
sB&B⇨£52.25-£60.50 dB&B⇨£77-£93.50 ⊟
70P ✲ croquet lawn nc10yrs *xmas*
☺ International V ✿ ☕ ⚡ S10% Lunch £12.65&alc Dinner £15.13&alc Last dinner 9.30pm
Credit Cards [1] [2] [3] [4] [5]

See advertisement under BATH

★★Methuen Arms High St SN13 0HB (Exec Hotel)
☎(0249)714867
RS Sun
Large oak beams, ancient stonework and mullioned windows survive in this hotel—relics of a nunnery built in the early 15th century. Today it offers modern bedrooms, comfortably furnished and well equipped. Guests who do not wish to eat formally in the candle-lit dining room can enjoy a lighter meal in one of the licensed bars – perhaps the interesting Long Bar, so called because it extends for 100ft, which has housed a skittle alley for more than a century.
19rm(17⇨1↱)Annexe6rm(3⇨3↱)(2fb) CTV in all bedrooms ® T ✗ sB&B⇨↱£34-£39 dB&B⇨↱£46-£53 ⊟
60P ✲ skittle-alley
☺ English & French V ✿ Lunch £13-£23alc Dinner £13-£23alc Last dinner 9.30pm
Credit Cards [1] [3]

See advertisement under BATH

✕✕*Copperfields* 1 High St SN13 0ES ☎(0249)713982
This attractive, first-floor restaurant in the town centre offers friendly, attentive service and a good menu selection of well prepared, imaginative dishes.
Lunch not served Tue-Sat
Dinner not served Sun
☺ French V 34 seats Last dinner 9.30pm ⁄P nc5yrs
Credit Cards [1] [3]

For key to symbols see the inside front cover.

C

COTTINGHAM Northamptonshire Map **04** SP89

★★**Hunting Lodge** High St LE16 8XN
☎Rockingham(0536)771370
RS 25-26 Dec & 1 Jan
Restaurant and bar facilities are in a 16th-century building with a wealth of exposed beams and stone walls. The modern, well-equipped bedrooms are housed in 2 purpose-built annexes.
Annexe23rm(15⇌8♠)(3fb)⅟in 3 bedrooms CTV in all bedrooms ® **T** ✱ sB&B⇌♠£25-£37.50 dB&B⇌♠£30-£47.50 ⊟
CTV 120P ✲ ♫
♡ English & French **V** ♡ ⊡ Lunch £6.50-£14alc High tea £2.75-£4 Dinner £6.50-£14alc Last dinner 10.30pm
Credit Cards 1 3 5 £

See advertisement under CORBY

COVENTRY West Midlands Map **04** SP37

★★★★52% **De Vere** Cathedral Square CV1 5RP (De Vere)
☎(0203)633733 Telex no 31380 FAX (0203) 225299
Modern hotel with choice of bars and restaurants and large conference/banqueting facilities.
190⇌♠(9fb) CTV in all bedrooms ® **T** S%
sB&B⇌♠£69.50-£118.50 dB&B⇌♠£87.50-£136.50 ⊟
Lift ☾ 130⊜ CFA ♫ *xmas*
♡ International **V** ♡ ⊡ ⅟ Lunch fr£10.50&alc Dinner fr£12.50&alc Last dinner 10.15pm
Credit Cards 1 2 3 4 5 £

★★★57% ***Allesley*** Birmingham Rd, Allesley Village CV5 9GP
☎(0203)403272 Telex no 311446
Well suited for business guests, this hotel has the best of both worlds – a village location that is convenient for the city, the NEC and the M6. Bedrooms are generally spacious and equipped with modern facilities, and guests have a choice of 2 bars and the Sovereign restaurant.
73rm(40⇌26♠)Annexe15rm(3⇌12♠)⅟in 17 bedrooms CTV in all bedrooms ® **T**
Lift ☾ 500P
♡ English & French **V** ♡ ⊡
Credit Cards 1 2 3 5

★★★61% **Chace Crest** London Rd, Willenhall CV3 4EQ (Crest)
☎(0203)303398 Telex no 311993 FAX (0203) 301816
A large Victorian building, set in its own grounds beside the A423 and convenient for both the city centre and the NEC, offers modern bedrooms with good facilities in an extension to the rear of the main building.
68rm(66⇌2♠)(2fb)1⊟⅟in 10 bedrooms CTV in all bedrooms ® **T** sB⇌♠£32.50-£74 dB⇌♠£65-£95 (room only) ⊟
☾ 80P ✲ pool table ♫ *xmas*
♡ English & French **V** ♡ ⊡ ⅟
Credit Cards 1 2 3 4 5

★★★62% **Crest** Hinckley Rd, Walsgrave CV2 2HP (Crest)
☎(0203)613261 Telex no 311292 FAX (0203) 621736
RS Xmas
Modern, well-furnished and equipped with extensive conference and leisure facilities, this large hotel stands beside the A46, close to the M6 motorway.
147⇌♠(6fb)⅟in 30 bedrooms CTV in all bedrooms ® **T** sB⇌♠fr£74 dB⇌♠fr£90 (room only) ⊟
Lift ☾ 450P ✲ CFA ⊡(heated) sauna solarium gymnasium pool tables ♫ ⌂ *xmas*
♡ French **V** ♡ ⊡ ⅟ S% Lunch £9.25-£11.95&alc Dinner fr£15.50&alc Last dinner 9.45pm
Credit Cards 1 2 3 4 5

Book as early as possible for busy holiday periods.

★★★55% **Hylands** Warwick Rd CV3 6AU (Best Western)
☎(0203)501600 Telex no 312388 FAX (0203) 501027
Closed 24-26 Dec
This hotel's proximity to the city centre and its popular carvery restaurant make it an ideal choice for businessmen.
55rm(54⇌)(4fb) CTV in all bedrooms ® **T** ✱
sB&B⇌£54-£59.50 dB&B⇌£63-£72 ⊟
☾ CTV 60P pool table
♡ English & Continental **V** ♡ ⊡ ⅟
Credit Cards 1 2 3 5

★★★60% ***Novotel Coventry*** Wilsons Ln CV6 6HL (Novotel)
☎(0203)365000 Telex no 31545
On the north side of the city, just off the M6 motorway at junction 3, a large hotel provides modern bedrooms with a good range of facilities and a restaurant that is open from 6 am until midnight seven days a week.
100⇌♠(100fb) CTV in all bedrooms ® **T**
Lift ☾ ⊞ 160P ✲ CFA ⌒(heated) squash sauna solarium gymnasium pool table petanque putting table tennis ⌂
♡ British & French **V** ♡ ⊡
Credit Cards 1 2 3 4 5

★★★56% **Post House** Rye Hill, Allesley CV5 9PH (Trusthouse Forte) ☎(0203)402151 Telex no 31427 FAX (0203) 402235
This large, well-run hotel has recently extended and upgraded its bedrooms to provide comfortable, modern accommodation; a wide range of food is available, and there are good conference facilities.
184⇌⅟in 19 bedrooms CTV in all bedrooms ® **T** S%
sB⇌£67-£78 dB⇌£78-£89 (room only) ⊟
Lift ☾ ⊞ 177P 120⊜ CFA *xmas*
V ♡ ⊡ ⅟ S% Lunch £9.20-£9.70&alc Dinner fr£13.50&alc Last dinner 10pm
Credit Cards 1 2 3 4 5

★★★61% **Royal Court** Tamworth Rd, Keresley CV7 8JG (3m NW on B4098) ☎(0203)334171 Telex no 312549
FAX (0203) 333478
A busy hotel set in 11 acres of wooded grounds and garden approximately 3 miles from Coventry city centre. The existing modern facilities are to be extended and improved with a building programme due for completion in early 1990.
18rm(17⇌1♠)Annexe80rm(68⇌12♠) CTV in all bedrooms ® **T** sB&B⇌♠£56.50-£76 dB&B⇌♠£69-£89 ⊟
Lift ☾ 500P ✲ *xmas*
♡ English & French **V** ♡ ⊡ Lunch £9.80&alc Dinner £11.80&alc Last dinner 10.30pm
Credit Cards 1 2 3 5 £

★★**Beechwood** Sandpits Ln, Keresley CV6 2FR (3m NW on B4098) (Best Western) ☎(0203)338662 FAX (0203) 337080
Set in a rural area, to the north of the city, this well furnished family-run hotel offers a good standard of accommodation and a grill-type menu.
24⇌(1fb) CTV in all bedrooms ® **T** sB&B⇌£36
dB&B⇌£49 ⊟
☾ 62P ✲
V ♡ ⊡ Lunch £5-£15alc Dinner £5-£15alc Last dinner 9.30pm
Credit Cards 1 2 3 5

See advertisement on page 225

★★**Old Mill Hotel** Mill Hill CV8 2BS (Berni/Chef & Brewer)
☎(0203)303588
(For full entry see Baginton)

⌂**Campanile** 4 Wigston Road/Hinkley Rd, Walsgrave CV2 2NE (Campanile) ☎(0203)622311 Telex no 317454
Annexe47⇌♠ CTV in all bedrooms ® **T** sB⇌♠fr£29
dB⇌♠fr£29 (room only) ⊟
50P ✲ *xmas*
♡ English & French Lunch £3.75-£8.90 Dinner £6.80-£8.90 Last dinner 10pm
Credit Cards 1 3

See advertisement on page 225

○*Campanile Hotel* (Coventry South), Abbey Rd(Campanile)
☎Central reservations 01-569 5757
Due to have opened September 1989
50🛁

○*Travelodge* (A444) Bedworth(Trusthouse Forte)
☎Central reservations 01-567 3444
Due to have opened summer 1989
40🛁
P

COWES

See **Wight, Isle of**

CRACKINGTON HAVEN Cornwall & Isles of Scilly Map **02** SX19

★★Coombe Barton EX23 0JG ☎St Gennys(08403)345
Closed Oct-Feb
Comfortable residence, part 18th century, set by the sea.
7rm(3🛁)(1fb) CTV in 3bedrooms ® sB&B£16.50-£18 dB&B£31-£33 dB&B🛁£36-£40
CTV 35P nc2yrs
Lunch £3.85-£14alc Dinner £3.85-£14alc Last dinner 9.45pm

CRAIGHOUSE

See **Jura, Isle of**

CRAIGNURE

See **Mull, Isle of**

CRAIL Fife Map **12** NO60

★Croma Nethergate KY10 3TU ☎(0333)50239
Closed Nov-Mar
Small, well-maintained, family hotel with a garden at the rear, situated in a quiet residential area.
9rm(5🛁)(2fb) ✳ sB&B£15-£17 sB&B🛁£15-£17 dB&B£25-£30 dB&B🛁£30-£32
CTV 10P ✿
V Dinner £10-£10.50 Last dinner 10pm

CRANBROOK Kent Map **05** TQ73

★★*Kennel Holt*
Goudhurst Rd TN17 2PT
☎(0580)712032
FAX (0580) 712931

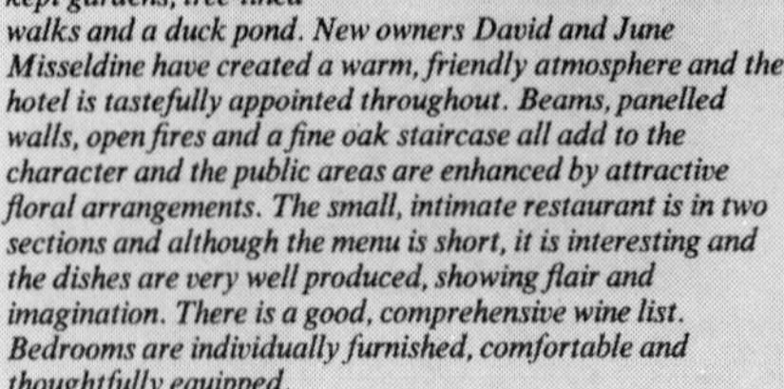

This charming Elizabethan house is in a peaceful, secluded setting with well-kept gardens, tree-lined walks and a duck pond. New owners David and June Misseldine have created a warm, friendly atmosphere and the hotel is tastefully appointed throughout. Beams, panelled walls, open fires and a fine oak staircase all add to the character and the public areas are enhanced by attractive floral arrangements. The small, intimate restaurant is in two sections and although the menu is short, it is interesting and the dishes are very well produced, showing flair and imagination. There is a good, comprehensive wine list. Bedrooms are individually furnished, comfortable and thoughtfully equipped.
9rm(7🛁2🚿)2 CTV in all bedrooms ® T
CTV 35P ✿ croquet 9 hole mini golf putting green nc6yrs
English & French Last dinner 9pm
Credit Cards [1] [3] £

CRANTOCK Cornwall & Isles of Scilly Map **02** SW76

★★Crantock Bay West Pentire TR8 5SE (Minotels)
☎(0637)830229
Closed Dec-Feb
Beautifully situated to overlook Crantock Bay, this owner-run hotel offers good facilities.
36rm(35🛁1🚿)(4fb) CTV in all bedrooms ®
sB&B🛁🚿£20-£35 dB&B🛁🚿£40-£76 (incl dinner)
CTV 35P ✿ (heated) (hard) sauna gymnasium putting croquet
Bar Lunch £2-£4.50 Dinner £8.50-£9.75 Last dinner 8pm
Credit Cards [1] [2] [3] [5] £

★★*Fairbank* West Pentire Rd TR8 5SA ☎(0637)830424
Closed mid Oct-Etr
Small friendly family hotel in a quiet village, commanding views over the nearby coastline.
29rm(4🛁15🚿)(2fb)2 CTV in 5bedrooms
CTV 40P ✿ putting green table tennis
Credit Cards [1] [3] [5]

CRATHORNE North Yorkshire Map **08** NZ40

★★★★ 57% *Crathorne Hall* TS15 0AR
☎Stokesley(0642)700398
Situated in extensive grounds with pleasant views, this large, elegant Edwardian country house has spacious public rooms. Its well-equipped bedrooms and conference and function facilities make is suitable for a wide variety of customers.
39🛁2 CTV in all bedrooms ® T (ex guide dogs)
CTV 100P ✿ snooker pool table
French V Last dinner 10pm
Credit Cards [1] [2] [3] [5]

CRAWLEY West Sussex. Other hotels are listed under **Gatwick Airport**

★★★70% Crest Hotel, Gatwick Langley Drive, Crawley RH11 7SX (Crest) ☎(0293)29991 Telex no 877311
FAX 0293 515913
Recently refurbished throughout, with major new features including the Crest Sensations Leisure Club and indoor pool, the prestigious Colonnade restaurant, La Brasserie, a cocktail lounge and a business centre. Function rooms are nearly complete, and the choice of compact bedrooms includes Lady Crest and Executive. Service is well-managed and helpful.
225🛁🚿(9fb) in 45 bedrooms CTV in all bedrooms ® T ✳
S% sB🛁🚿£76 dB🛁🚿£89 (room only)
Lift 150P (heated) snooker sauna solarium gymnasium jacuzzi steam rooms *xmas*

V ✿ ☕ ⚟ S% Lunch £8.45-£11.50 Dinner fr£14.50&alc Last dinner 9.45pm
Credit Cards 1 2 3 4 5

CREWE Cheshire Map **07** SJ75

★★★ 61% Crewe Arms Nantwich Rd CW1 1DW (Embassy)
☎(0270)213204 FAX (0270) 588615
Elegant Victorian building, adjacent to the main railway station, offering comfortable, well-appointed accommodation, including some very high standard executive rooms.
53rm(50⇨3♠)(3fb)⚟in 7 bedrooms CTV in all bedrooms ® T S% sB⇨♠£45-£57 dB⇨♠£57-£65 (room only) ⛿
☾ 250P CFA games room *xmas*
☋ English & French V ✿ ☕ ⚟ S10% Lunch fr£9.95&alc High tea £7.50-£15 Dinner £10.50&alc Last dinner 9.30pm
Credit Cards 1 2 3 4 5

★★ *White Lion* Weston CW2 5NA (2m S A5020)
☎(0270)587011 & 500303
Closed Xmas & New Year
Once a Tudor farmhouse, the hotel features olde-worlde public areas that are reminiscent of its origins, a restaurant renowned for its high standard of international cuisine, and modern, well-equipped bedrooms. It enjoys a village location two miles outside Crewe and four miles from junction 16 of the M6 motorway.
16rm(8⇨8♠)(2fb)⚟in 2 bedrooms CTV in all bedrooms ® T
☾ 100P ❈ crown green bowling
☋ English & French V ✿ ☕ Last dinner 9.30pm
Credit Cards 1 2 3 4 5

The AA's star-rating scheme is the market leader in hotel classification.

C

CREWKERNE Somerset Map **03** ST40

★★**Old Parsonage** Barn St TA18 8BP (Exec Hotel) ☎(0460)73516
An old stone house on the edge of the town. There is a cosy lounge bar and a dining room with candlelight. Bedrooms vary from large rooms in the main building to the more compact ones in the annexe. The hotel is managed by the friendly proprietors and is popular with business people and holiday makers.
4rm(3⇌1♠)Annexe6rm(4⇌2♠) CTV in all bedrooms ® ✱ sB&B⇌♠£39.50 dB&B⇌♠£58
12P *xmas*
British & French **V** Lunch £11.95&alc Dinner £11.95&alc Last dinner 9pm
Credit Cards 1 2 3 5

CRICCIETH Gwynedd Map **06** SH43

★★★ 69% ***Bron Eifion***
LL52 0SA (Inter)
☎(0766)522385

Standing on a wooded hillside just west of the town, this delightfully tranquil country-house hotel enjoys extensive views over Cardigan Bay. Well-furnished bedrooms are complemented by peaceful lounges with log fires, the resident proprietors taking great pride in both the quality of accommodation and the standard of service offered; a very capable chef produces some excellent dishes which are served in a lovely dining room overlooking the garden.
19rm(13⇌5♠)(1fb) CTV in all bedrooms ® **T**
CTV 50P ✲ putting croquet
English & Continental **V**
Credit Cards 1 3

★★***George IV*** (Consort) ☎(0766)522168
Late-Victorian, holiday/tourist hotel in Criccieth main street.
34rm(28⇌6♠)(6fb) CTV in all bedrooms ®
Lift CTV 60P ✲
V
Credit Cards 1 3

★★**Gwyndy** Llanystumdwy LL52 0SP ☎(076671)2720
Closed Dec & Jan
Converted 17th century farmhouse, retaining some original features, but with most bedrooms in modern annexe.
Annexe10⇌(5fb) CTV in all bedrooms ® ✱ sB&B⇌£23-£25 dB&B⇌£36-£40
CTV 20P
British & French Lunch fr£5.50 Dinner fr£8.95 Last dinner 9pm

★★**Lion** Y Maes LL52 0AA ☎(0766)522460
RS Nov-Mar
Comfortable and friendly hotel, about 450 yards from the sea front.
39rm(14⇌5♠)(4fb) CTV in 40bedrooms ® ✱ sB&Bfr£17.50 sB&B⇌♠fr£20 dB&Bfr£34 dB&B⇌♠fr£38
Lift 20P 12 *xmas*
Welsh & French **V** Lunch £5.67-£9.57 High tea £2.70-£3.50 Dinner fr£10.50 Last dinner 8.15pm
Credit Cards 1 2 3 5 £

★★**Parciau Mawr** High St LL52 0RP ☎(0766)522368
Closed Nov-Feb
A delightful stone-built hotel standing in its own grounds with views over the bay. Family owned and run, it offers good service, well furnished accommodation and good food.
7rm(4⇌1♠)Annexe6♠(1fb) CTV in all bedrooms ® ✱ sB&Bfr£18 sB&B⇌♠fr£21.50 dB&Bfr£36 dB&B⇌♠fr£40
30P ✲ nc5yrs
English & French Dinner fr£7.50 Last dinner 8pm
Credit Cards 1 3

★★***Plas Gwyn*** Pentrefelin LL52 0PT (1m NE A497) ☎(076671)2559
A pleasantly furnished and comfortable hotel, standing beside the A497 one mile east of the town, maintains good standards in both accommodation and food.
14rm(4⇌9♠)(6fb) CTV in all bedrooms ® **T**
CTV 50P
English, French & Italian **V** Last dinner 9pm
Credit Cards 1 2 3 5

★★**Plas Isa** Porthmadog Rd LL52 0HP ☎(0766)522443
The enthusiastic young owners extend a warm welcome to their guests at this comfortable hotel with good sea views.
12⇌(2fb) CTV in all bedrooms ® **T** sB&B£22.50-£25 sB&B⇌£22.50-£25 dB&B£38-£40 dB&B⇌£38-£40
CTV 14P water sports
Chinese, French, Indian & Italian **V** Sunday Lunch £5.95-£6.50 Dinner £9.50-£11&alc Last dinner 9pm
Credit Cards 1 3 5

★**Abereistedd** West Pde LL52 0EN ☎(0766)522710
Closed 30 Oct-25 Feb
Detached Victorian hotel in corner position at end of promenade, half a mile from shops.
12rm(8♠)(2fb) CTV in all bedrooms ® sB&B£14-£15.50 sB&B♠£16-£17.50 dB&B£28-£31 dB&B♠£32-£35
12P
English & French **V** Bar Lunch £2.55-£3.90 Dinner £7 Last dinner 7.30pm
Credit Cards 1 £

★**Caerwylan** LL52 0HW ☎(0766)522547
Closed Nov-Etr
Semi-detached, Victorian sea-front hotel.
26rm(15⇌1♠) CTV in all bedrooms ® ✱ sB&Bfr£13.75 sB&B⇌♠fr£16
Lift CTV 8P 8 (55p) ✲
Lunch fr£4.70 Dinner fr£5.85 Last dinner 7.30pm
£

★**Henfaes** Porthmadog Rd LL52 0HP ☎(0766)522396
Closed Nov-Mar
There are excellent views of sea and mountain from this large, detached hotel which provides spacious bedrooms and caring service by resident proprietors.
10⇌ CTV in all bedrooms ® sB&B⇌£17.50 dB&B⇌£35
7P 3 nc5yrs
Bar Lunch £1.75-£2.50 Dinner £8 Last dinner 7.30pm

CRICK Northamptonshire Map **04** SP57

★★★ 63% **Post House** NN6 7XR (Trusthouse Forte)
☎(0788)822101 Telex no 311107 FAX (0788) 823955
Well-equipped modern hotel close to M1 junction 18.
96⇌♠ in 20 bedrooms CTV in all bedrooms ® **T** sB⇌♠£70-£80 dB⇌♠£80-£90 (room only)
150P ✲ CFA (heated) sauna solarium gymnasium *xmas*
V Lunch £7.75-£9.75&alc Dinner £13-£16.95&alc Last dinner 10pm
Credit Cards 1 2 3 4 5

C

CRICKHOWELL Powys Map **03** SO21

★★**Bear** NP8 1BW ☎(0873)810408 FAX (0873) 811696
The charmingly old-fashioned inn-style hotel has cheerful character bars and an intimate restaurant serving imaginative and commendably cooked food. Bedrooms are compact, but cosy and provided with modern facilities.
14rm(7⇨6♠)Annexe13⇨(6fb)1⊟ CTV in all bedrooms ® T sB&B⇨♠£30-£45 dB&B⇨♠£40-£58
CTV 38P ⛟
♉ English & French V ♡ Lunch £14-£20alc Dinner £14-£20alc
Last dinner 9.30pm
Credit Cards [1] [2] [3]

★★♛**Gliffaes Country House** NP8 1RH
☎Bwlch(0874)730371
FAX (0874) 730463
Closed Jan-9 Mar

Set amid rare trees and shrubs in 30 acres of magnificent grounds, the distinctive hotel commands fine views of the River Usk and its wooded valley. An informal, friendly atmosphere prevails and the standard of the good home cooking is consistent. Elegant lounges and character bedrooms are well-equipped with modern facilities.
19rm(15⇨3♠)Annexe3rm(1⇨2♠)(3fb) CTV in 3bedrooms ® T S10% sB&B⇨♠£24-£48.50 dB&B⇨♠£48-£64 ⊟

▶

CTV 34P ✽ (hard) snooker painting croquet putting

European V S10% Lunch £8.25 Dinner £13&alc Last dinner 9.30pm
Credit Cards 1 2 3 5

✕Glan-y-Dwr Brecon Rd NP8 1 ☎(0873)810756
A well-maintained and attractive restaurant on the main road in the centre of town commended for the cooking and hospitality of the Belgian owner. He displays his skill and versatality through his international menu and by holding regular gourmet evenings that offer food from China, Italy, France and, of course, Belgium. There are also four good bedrooms, two of which have 'en suite' facilities.
Closed Mon, 2nd & 3rd wks Jan
Dinner not served Sun
French **V** 30 seats Sunday Lunch £15-£35alc Dinner £15-£35alc Last lunch 1pm Last dinner 9pm 12P 2 bedrooms available
Credit Cards 1 3

CRICKLADE Wiltshire Map **04** SU09

✕✕*Whites* 93 High St SN6 6DF ☎Swindon(0793)751110
The ambience of this cottage-style restaurant is enhanced by a warm welcome and simple, friendly service. The chef/patron brings skill and dedication to bear in the preparation of appetisers, fish dishes and such meat specialities as pot-cooked beef, his sauces being particularly tasty. A limited choice of sweets includes some delicious home-made options.
Closed Sun, 2 wks Aug & 1wk Jan/Feb
Lunch not served Mon
English, French & Italian **V** 32 seats Last lunch 2pm Last dinner 9.30pm
Credit Cards 1 3

CRIEFF Tayside *Perthshire* Map **11** NN82

★★Crieff 47-49 East High St PH7 3JA ☎(0764)2632
Telex no 779980 FAX (0786)50034
Small, family-run hotel near the town centre with comfortable, though compact, modern bedrooms, a nicely appointed restaurant and a range of health, beauty and fitness facilities. Special shooting, golfing and fishing packages are available.
11rm(2⇌6)(2fb) CTV in 9bedrooms ® **T** S%
sB&B⇌£22.50-£23.50 dB&B⇌£44-£46
CTV 12P 2 sauna solarium gymnasium hairdressing salon
V S% Bar Lunch £4.80-£5.75 Dinner £7.50&alc Last dinner 9.30pm
Credit Cards 1 2 3 5 £

★★Cultoquhey House
PH7 3NE
☎(0764)3253 & 4535
Closed Feb & Mar

A homely, family-run mansion, the hotel offers sincere, friendly service and very good country house cooking.
12rm(5⇌5)(3fb)3 CTV in all bedrooms ® **T**
sB&Bfr£29 sB&B⇌fr£32 dB&Bfr£46
dB&B⇌£56-£72
50P ✽ (hard) snooker game & clay pigeon shooting croquet *xmas*

V Lunch £7-£9 Dinner £14.75-£15.75 Last dinner 9pm
Credit Cards 1 2 3 5 £

★★Murray Park Connaught Ter PH7 3DJ (Inter) ☎(0764)3731
FAX (0764) 5311
Genuine hospitality, together with consistently good and imaginative food, add to the appeal of this welcoming family-run hotel. Comfortable public rooms invite easy relaxation and the smart bedrooms are well equipped.
14rm(13⇌)(1fb) CTV in all bedrooms ® **T** ✻ sB&B£22
sB&B⇌£33.50 dB&B⇌£51
50P ✽ shooting stalking
Scottish & French **V** Lunch fr£7.50 Dinner fr£13.95&alc Last dinner 9.30pm
Credit Cards 1 2 3 5 £

★*George* King St PH7 3HB ☎(0764)2089
Town centre family-run hotel, the George offers a neat, modest standard in bedroom accomodation and lounges.
29rm(10⇌)(2fb) ®
CTV 15P
V Last dinner 9pm
£

★Gwydyr House Comrie Rd PH7 4BP ☎(0764)3277
Closed Nov-Mar
Former private mansion, overlooking MacRosty Park on the west side of Crieff.
10rm(4fb) CTV in all bedrooms ® sB&B£11.50-£13.50
dB&B£23-£27
CTV 15P ✽
British & Continental **V** Bar Lunch £4-£10.80alc Dinner £8.15&alc Last dinner 8pm
£

★*Keppoch House* Perth Rd PH7 3EQ ☎(0764)4341
6rm(5)CTV in all bedrooms ®
20P
Scottish, French & Italian **V** Last dinner 9.30pm
Credit Cards 1 3

★*Lockes Acre* Comrie Rd PH7 4BP ☎(0764)2526
RS Nov-Mar
This attractive little tourist hotel on the edge of the village overlooks the Ochil Hills. It offers a friendly atmosphere and comfortable, modern bedrooms, though some are limited in size.
7rm(4)(1fb) CTV in all bedrooms ®
20P
Last dinner 9pm
Credit Cards 1 3

CRINAN Strathclyde *Argyllshire* Map **10** NR79

★★★65% *Crinan* PA31 8SR ☎(054683)261 FAX (054683) 281
Closed Nov-mid Mar (ex New Year)
In a magnificent setting at the western end of the Crinan Canal, the hotel overlooks the canal locks and sea lochs to Jura and Scarba. Bedrooms are individually decorated and the lounges are relaxing. The hotel provides a choice of restaurants in which to enjoy good cooking, The Roof Top specialising in seafood at its freshest and Scottish views at their finest.
22rm(20⇌2)(1fb) **T**
Lift CTV 100P ✽ water sports boat trips
Last dinner 9pm
Credit Cards 1 3

For key to symbols see the inside front cover.

CROCKETFORD Dumfries & Galloway *Kirkcudbrightshire* Map **11** NX87

★*Lochview Motel* Crocketford Rd DG2 8RF ☎(055669)281
Closed 26 Dec & 1 Jan
This simple roadside motel offers compact, but clean and freshly decorated bedrooms. Public areas are rather limited, but there is a popular lounge bar/restaurant with views of Loch Auchenreoch.
7 CTV in all bedrooms ®
80P ♫
Credit Cards 1 3

CROFT-ON-TEES North Yorkshire Map **08** NZ20

★★★52% **Croft Spa** DL2 2ST ☎Darlington(0325)720319
Large, pleasantly furnished hotel beside River Tees. Was TV setting for All Creatures Great and Small.
34rm(11⇌23)(3fb)2 CTV in all bedrooms ® **T** ✻
sB&B⇌£32.50-£42.50 dB&B⇌£45-£59
CTV 200P snooker sauna solarium gymnasium ♫ *xmas*
English & Continental **V** Lunch £7.50 Dinner £11.50
Last dinner 10.30pm
Credit Cards 1 2 3 £

CROMARTY Highland *Ross & Cromarty* Map **14** NH76

★★*Royal* Marine Ter IV11 8YN (Exec Hotel) ☎(03817)217
A homely hotel with inviting log fires, and cheerful service.
10rm(5⇌2)(2fb) CTV in all bedrooms ®
CTV 20P 3 games room
V Last dinner 8pm
Credit Cards 2 3

✕**Le Chardon** Church St IV11 8XA ☎(03817)471
A pretty little restaurant is sited in a quiet street of this former seaport on the Black Isle. Food is innovative and well cooked.
Lunch not served (by arrangement only)
French **V** 30 seats Lunch £8.50-£10 Dinner £14-£20 Last lunch 2pm Last dinner 9.30pm 3P nc8yrs
Credit Cards 1 2 3

CROMER Norfolk Map **09** TG24

★★*Cliff House* Overstrand Rd NR27 0AL ☎(0263)514094
Closed Jan
22rm(13⇌7)(1fb) CTV in all bedrooms ® **T**
30P
V Last dinner 8.30pm
Credit Cards 1 2 3

★★**Cliftonville** Runton Rd NR27 9AS ☎(0263)512543
Imposing, Victorian building with spacious lounges overlooking the sea.
42rm(12⇌6)(3fb) CTV in 39bedrooms ® **T** ✻
sB&B£20.50-£22.50 sB&B⇌£33.50 dB&B£39-£43
dB&B⇌£56
Lift CTV 20P 2 snooker *xmas*
V Lunch fr£7.50 Dinner fr£10.75 Last dinner 8.45pm
Credit Cards 1 2 3 5 £

CROOKLANDS Cumbria Map **07** SD58

★★★61% **Crooklands** LA7 7NW (Best Western) ☎(04487)432
Telex no 94017303
This 400-year-old inn has modern bedrooms and its restaurant forms part of a converted barn.
15⇌ CTV in all bedrooms ® **T** ✻ S% sB&B⇌£49-£60
dB&B⇌£65-£80
150P ♫ *xmas*
French **V** S% Lunch fr£8.50 Dinner £14.50-£16.50&alc
Last dinner 9.30pm
Credit Cards 1 2 3 5

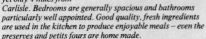

CROSBY-ON-EDEN Cumbria Map **12** NY45

★★★69% Crosby Lodge Country House CA6 4QZ
☎(022873)618
FAX (022873) 428
Closed 24 Dec-mid Jan RS Sun

Antiques abound throughout this relaxing country house, situated in rural surroundings yet only 4 miles from Carlisle. Bedrooms are generally spacious and bathrooms particularly well appointed. Good quality, fresh ingredients are used in the kitchen to produce enjoyable meals – even the preserves and petits fours are home made.

9rm(8⇌1↖)Annexe2⇌(2fb)2 CTV in all bedrooms T sB&B⇌↖£51-£55 dB&B⇌↖£72-£78
40P ✲
English & French V Lunch £12.75-£15.75&alc Dinner £18.75-£21.75&alc Last dinner 9pm
Credit Cards 2 3 5

★★★55% Newby Grange CA6 4RA ☎(022873)645
Closed last 2 days Dec-early Jan
Set in 5 acres of grounds, this hotel has been modernised to provide well-equipped bedrooms, some of them spacious and newly decorated. Service is relaxed and the hotel is popular for functions and weddings.
20rm(18⇌2↖)(4fb) CTV in all bedrooms ® T sB&B⇌↖£38.50 dB&B⇌↖£50
CTV 200P ✲ *xmas*
International V Lunch £6.50&alc Dinner £9.25-£9.95&alc Last dinner 10.30pm
Credit Cards 1 3

CROSS HANDS Dyfed Map **02** SN51

○ ***Travelodge*** A48(Trusthouse Forte) ☎(0269)845700
32⇌
P

CROSSMICHAEL Dumfries & Galloway *Kirkcudbrightshire* Map **11** NX76

★★Culgruff House
DG7 3BB
☎(055667)230
RS Oct-Etr

Genuine warmth and hospitality are foremost in this baronial mansion, furnished with many antiques. Overlooking the village and the Ken Valley, it is set in 35 acres of grounds in which peacocks roam. The lounges with log fires are particularly comfortable and electric blankets are provided on the beds.
16rm(4⇌)(8fb) CTV in 7bedrooms TV in 1bedroom sB&B£10.50-£14 sB&B⇌£16.50-£16.50 dB&B£20-£28 dB&B⇌£33
CTV 50P 8 (60p) ✲
V Lunch £5.75&alc High tea £4.60-£5 Dinner £9.20-£9.20 Last dinner 7.30pm
Credit Cards 1 2 3 5 £

CROSSWAY GREEN Hereford & Worcester Map **07** SO86

★***Mitre Oak*** DY13 9SG ☎Hartlebury(0299)250352
Roadside hotel offering reasonably priced meals and accommodation.
8rm(3fb) ®
CTV 150P ✲
English & French V Last dinner 9.15pm
Credit Cards 1 3

CROWTHORNE Berkshire Map **04** SU86

★★★55% Waterloo Duke's Ride RG11 7NW (Trusthouse Forte)
☎(0344)777711 Telex no 848139 FAX (0344) 778913
Modern facilities and friendly service are found in this basically Victorian building.
58rm(35⇌23↖)1 in 10 bedrooms CTV in all bedrooms ® T ✱ sB⇌↖£75-£85 dB⇌↖£85-£105 (room only)
120P *xmas*
V Lunch £8.95-£12&alc Dinner £12-£15&alc Last dinner 10pm
Credit Cards 1 2 3 4 5

CROYDE Devon Map **02** SS43

★★Croyde Bay House Moor Ln, Croyde Bay EX33 1PA
☎(0271)890270
Closed 22 Nov-Feb
Family-run establishment in an elevated position overlooking Croyde Bay. The hotel has a cottagey atmosphere and personal service is provided by the friendly proprietors.
8rm(3⇌4↖)(2fb) CTV in all bedrooms ® ✱
sB&B⇌↖£21-£31 dB&B⇌↖£42-£46
8P
English Dinner £13.50 Last dinner 8pm
Credit Cards 1 3

★★Kittiwell House St Mary's Rd EX33 1PG (Minotels)
☎(0271)890247
Closed mid Jan-mid Feb
This thatched longhouse stands on the edge of the village, within walking distance of the excellent surfing beaches. All its bedrooms now offer en suite facilities, whilst characterful public areas have enormous charm and the heavily beamed restaurant offers a choice of table d'hôte or à la carte menus.
12rm(7⇌5↖)(2fb)3 in 4 bedrooms CTV in all bedrooms ® sB&B⇌↖£37-£44 dB&B⇌↖£64-£78 (incl dinner)
CTV 14P ✲ *xmas*
English & French V Lunch fr£7.50 Dinner fr£12&alc Last dinner 9.30pm
Credit Cards 1 2 3 5

CROYDON Greater London

See **LONDON plan 5*D1*** (page 413) **Telephone codes are due to change on 6th May 1990. See page 421.**

★★★★62% Selsdon Park Sanderstead CR2 8YA (3m SE off A2022) (Best Western) ☎01-657 8811 Telex no 945003 FAX 01-651 6171
A mansion set in beautiful gardens amid 200-acre grounds has been sympathetically upgraded to retain most of its original character. An impressive entrance lobby features fine carved woodwork and some good pieces of furniture, while the spacious restaurant's light, airy surroundings provide an ideal setting in which to enjoy your choice of dishes from table d'hôte or à la carte menus. Most of the bedrooms have been refurbished to a high standard and are well equipped. New conference facilities are

available, and good leisure amenities are provided both indoors and out.
170⇌🚿(7fb)3⊟ CTV in all bedrooms ® **T** S%
sB&B⇌🚿£83-£109 dB&B⇌🚿£116-£140 ⊟
Lift ☾ 250P 15🚗 (£1.50) ✲ CFA ⊟(heated) ⊟(heated) ▶ 18
℘ (hard & grass) squash snooker sauna solarium gymnasium croquet jacuzzi jogging track putting ♫ *xmas*
☋ International ⚡ S% Lunch £15.50&alc Dinner £16.50-£24&alc Last dinner 9.30pm
Credit Cards 1 2 3 5

See advertisement on page 233

★★★58% *Holiday Inn* 7 Altyre Rd CR9 5AA ☎01-680 9200 Telex no 8956268 FAX 01-760 0426
Modern commercial hotel with good sized, well-equipped bedrooms and good leisure facilities. A bright, spacious restaurant offers a good buffet and an à la cart e menu, and the chef demonstrates his skill in well-prepared dishes using good fresh produce.
214⇌🚿(40fb)⚡in 26 bedrooms CTV in all bedrooms **T**
Lift ☾ ⊞ 118P ⊟(heated) squash sauna solarium gymnasium whirlpool bath
☋ International **V** ♦ ⊡ ⚡ Last dinner 10pm
Credit Cards 1 2 3 4 5

★★★62% Post House Purley Way CR9 4LT (Trusthouse Forte) ☎01-688 5185 Telex no 893814 FAX 01-681 6438
Located at a distance from the town centre, this modern hotel features an attractive split-level restaurant and comfortable bar areas. Bedrooms have recently been upgraded to a good standard, offering most modern facilities, and helpful service is provided by pleasant staff.
86rm(85⇌1🚿)⚡in 8 bedrooms CTV in all bedrooms ® **T** ✱
sB⇌🚿fr£74 dB⇌🚿fr£84 (room only) ⊟
☾ 70P CFA *xmas*
☋ English & French **V** ♦ ⊡ ⚡ S% Lunch £8.50-£10.50 High tea fr£5.25 Dinner fr£15.50 Last dinner 10pm
Credit Cards 1 2 3 5

★★Briarley 8 Outram Rd CR0 6XE ☎01-654 1000 FAX 01-656 6084
Converted from two Victorian houses, but with annexe of very good bedrooms, the family-run hotel is warmly welcoming.
18rm(10⇌8🚿)Annexe10⇌(3fb)1⊟ CTV in all bedrooms ® **T**
sB&B⇌🚿fr£49.50 dB&B⇌🚿fr£59.50 ⊟
CTV 15P
☋ Mainly grills **V** ⚡ Lunch fr£10 Dinner fr£10&alc Last dinner 10pm
Credit Cards 1 2 3 5 £

★Central 3-5 South Park Hill Rd, South Croydon CR2 7DY ☎01-688 0840 & 01-688 5644 FAX 01-760 0861
Warm, compact and simply-appointed bedrooms are complemented by a cosy dining room serving wholesome, freshly-cooked food.
23rm(7⇌13🚿)(1fb)1⊟ CTV in all bedrooms ® **T** ✗ (ex guide dogs) sB&Bfr£39 sB&B⇌🚿fr£49 dB&B⇌🚿fr£62 ⊟
☾ CTV 15P
V ♦ ⊡ S%
Credit Cards 1 3 £

See advertisement on page 232

✗Le Saint Jacques 1123 Whitgift Centre CR0 1UZ ☎01-760 0881
This cosy little French restaurant, situated in a modern shopping centre, is well frequented and particularly popular at lunchtime. The concise menu offers a good selection of well-prepared dishes such as an enjoyable Magret de Caneton au Coulis de Pêche, and a competent Creme Brulée. Service is charming and attentive.
Closed Sun & 24 Dec-4 Jan & BH's
Lunch not served Sat
Dinner not served Mon-Wed
▶

French 36 seats * Lunch £10-£14alc Dinner £14 Last lunch 2.45pm Last dinner 10pm nc8yrs
Credit Cards 1 2 3 4 5

X *Tung Kum* 205/207 High St CR0 1QR 01-688 0748
Closed 25 & 26 Dec & BH Mon's
Cantonese 100 seats Last dinner 11.15pm
Credit Cards 1 2 3 5

CRUDWELL Wiltshire Map **03** ST99

★★Crudwell Court SN16 9EP (06667)7194 & 7195
FAX (06667) 7853
This charming hotel, a 17th-century vicarage, stands in three acres of walled gardens which are enhanced by a lily pond and a heated swimming pool. Its tastefully designed bedrooms all provide good, modern facilities, and the panelled dining room offers a delightful setting in which to enjoy freshly prepared food complemented by an extensive wine list.
15(3fb) CTV in all bedrooms ® **T** sB&Bfr£40 dB&B£70-£90
20P (heated) *xmas*
Lunch fr£12 High tea fr£2.50alc Dinner fr£15 Last dinner 9.30pm
Credit Cards 1 2 3 5

★★Mayfield House SN16 9EW (06667)409 & 7198
A country house hotel, standing in a quiet village and personally run by resident proprietors, offers well equipped bedrooms of good size.
20rm(12 8)(1fb) CTV in all bedrooms ® **T** *
sB&B£39 dB&B£49
CTV 50P
English & French Last high tea 6pm
Credit Cards 1 2 3 £

See advertisement under MALMESBURY

CRUGYBAR Dyfed Map **02** SN63

★★Glanrannell Park
SA19 8SA
Talley(0558)685230
Closed Dec-Mar
Delightful country house in large grounds overlooking a small lake, offering genuine hospitality and quality home cooking.
8rm(5)(2fb) ® sB&B£21-£29 sB&B£25-£33
dB&B£36-£42 dB&B£42-£50
CTV 30P 3(£2)
Bar Lunch £1.50-£7 High tea £3-£5 Dinner £11-£15 Last dinner 8pm

CUCKFIELD West Sussex Map **04** TQ32

★★★69% Ockenden Manor Ockenden Ln RH17 5LD (Best Western) Haywards Heath(0444)416111 FAX (0444)415549
An attractive manor house dating from 1520, providing wood-panelled public rooms and individually furnished and named bedrooms which, in addition to every modern amenity, retain much of their original character and charm. The restaurant offers a prix fix menu, cooking in the modern English style being complemented by an outstanding wine list and attentive service.
14rm(13 1)2 CTV in all bedrooms ® **T** *
sB&B£48-£65
dB&B£70-£100 Continental breakfast
30P *xmas*
V Lunch fr£13.50 Dinner £19.50-£26.50 Last dinner 9.15pm
Credit Cards 1 2 3 5

★★Hilton Park RH17 5EG
Haywards Heath (0444)454555
Peacefully set in 3 acres of grounds and enjoying excellent views of the South Downs, this charming hotel with a residential licence offers a traditional lounge, comfortable, old fashioned bedrooms and a limited range of services.
14rm(10)(5fb) CTV in all bedrooms ® **T** * sB&Bfr£41 sB&Bfr£44 dB&Bfr£55 dB&Bfr£60
CTV 50P 2
English & French Bar Lunch fr£5 Dinner fr£14 Last dinner 8pm
Credit Cards 1 2 3 5

X *Jeremy's at the Kings Head* South St RH17 5JY
Haywards Heath(0444)440386
Jeremy's – named after its chef/patron – retains all the charm of a country town inn in its simple, cosy dining room. A short menu, changed daily, offers a range of flavoursome English dishes, excellently prepared from fresh, quality produce and served by attentive but informal staff.

C

Dinner not served Mon
V 38 seats 10P
Credit Cards 1 2 3 5

CULLEN Grampian *Banffshire* Map **15** NJ56

★★★54% **Seafield Arms** Seafield St AB5 5SG ☎(0542)40791
Originally built by the Earl of Seafield as a coaching inn, this hotel was modernised in the early 70s to provide individually designed, comfortable bedrooms and is now gradually being refurbished. One of the features here is a lovely carved wooden fireplace in the spacious Findlater bar. Service is friendly and informal.
22⇌↱(2fb) CTV in all bedrooms ® T ✻ sB&B⇌↱fr£25 dB&B⇌↱fr£45 ⊟
CTV 28P *xmas*
V ✿ ⊥ Lunch £6-£12alc Dinner £11&alc Last dinner 9.30pm
Credit Cards 1 2 3 5

CULLERCOATS Tyne & Wear Map **12** NZ37

★★**Bay** Front St NE30 4QB ☎091-252 3150
Improvements are gradually being made to this seafront hotel which now has a smart first-floor dining room, cocktail bar and residents' lounge, all of which overlook Cullercoats Bay. There are extensive and popular bars and a separate carvery. Bedroom accommodation remains rather modest.
19rm(4⇌4↱)(2fb)1⊟ CTV in all bedrooms ® T ✗ (ex guide dogs) sB&B£15-£19 sB&B⇌↱£19-£20 dB&B£28-£34 dB&B⇌↱£34-£36
CTV 9P sailing sea fishing *xmas*
♀ English & French ✿ ⊥ Lunch £5-£8 High tea £4-£5.50 Dinner £5-£5.50&alc Last dinner 9pm
Credit Cards 1 2 3 4 5

See advertisement under WHITLEY BAY

CULNACNOC

See Skye, Isle of

CUMNOCK Strathclyde *Ayrshire* Map **11** NS51

★★**Royal** 1 Glaisnock St KA18 1BP ☎(0290)20822
Situated in the town centre, this efficiently managed traditional hotel offers simple but clean accommodation, complemented by honest, well flavoured home cooking.
11rm(2⇌1↱)(1fb) CTV in 4bedrooms TV in 1bedroom ® sB&B£18-£20 dB&B£34-£36 dB&B⇌↱£40-£42
CTV 10P
V ✿ ⊥ Lunch £5-£6.50 High tea £4.80-£6.50 Dinner £9.50-£11 Last dinner 9pm
Credit Cards 1 3 £

CUPAR Fife Map **11** NO31

❀ ✕ **Ostlers Close** Bonnygate KY15 4BU
☎(0334)55574
This cosy, cottage-style restaurant continues to attract praise. As one half of the young family partnership, chef/proprietor, Jimmy Graham, brings together the influence of French provincial cooking and Scotland's best meat, game and seafood. Flavours are honest and refreshingly unambiguous. Fresh scallops in a vermouth sauce, avocado and leek terrine wrapped in smoked salmon and served with a herb vinaigrette, fillet of roast beef with Paris mushrooms served in its own juices and flavoured with sieved fresh horseradish, and local seafood in a crayfish butter sauce are typical dishes. Puddings include chocolate mousse on a champagne sauce and pear and almond tart served with sauce Anglaise. Wife, Amanda, looks after the restaurant and her friendly, effervescent manner creates a convivial atmosphere.
Closed Sun, Mon & 2 wks Jun
♀ French & Swiss 28 seats Lunch £6-£13alc Dinner £14-£22alc Last lunch 2pm Last dinner 9.30pm ⊁ nc6yrs
Credit Cards 1 3

DALKEITH Lothian Map **11** NT36

★★***Eskbank Motel*** 29 Dalhousie Rd EH22 3AT ☎031-663 3234
Situated beside the A7 on the outskirst of Edinburgh, this motel has been substantially refurbished. The main building offers a TV lounge, a small panelled restaurant and a smart lounge bar with an all-day licence. The modern, compact well-equipped bedrooms are located in the chalet block.
16⇌ CTV in all bedrooms ® T
CTV 40P 6⌂ ⊞ ✿
V ✿ ⊥
Credit Cards 1 2 3 5

See advertisement under EDINBURGH

DALRY Dumfries & Galloway *Kirkcudbrightshire* Map **11** NX68

★★***Lochinvar*** Main St DG7 3UP ☎(06443)210
A warm welcome and well prepared food will be found at this personally-run hotel. Bedrooms are comfortable and furnished in traditional style.
16rm(3⇌)(1fb)⊁in 2 bedrooms CTV in 5bedrooms
☾ CTV 50P 4⌂
♀ French V ✿ ⊥ ⊁ Last dinner 10pm
Credit Cards 1 2 3

DALWHINNIE Highland *Inverness-shire* Map **14** NN68

★★**Loch Ericht** PH19 1AF ☎(05282)257 FAX (0463) 782531
Closed Nov-26 Dec RS Jan-Mar
Situated in the Highlands' highest village, amid splendid scenery, this hotel has modern, functional bedrooms and an open plan bar and restaurant of unusual design. Meals are available throughout the day and portions are generous.
27rm(18⇌9↱)(4fb) ® sB&B⇌↱£19.75-£23.95 dB&B⇌↱£35-£40.50 ⊟
CTV 50P ✿ ⌡ shooting ski-ing *xmas*
V ✿ ⊥ Bar Lunch fr£2.75alc High tea £3.25-£7.50alc Dinner £4.90-£12.90alc Last dinner 9pm
Credit Cards 1 2 3 5 £

DARESBURY Cheshire Map **07** SJ58

★★★67% **Lord Daresbury** Chester Rd WA4 4BB (De Vere)
☎Warrington(0925)67331 Telex no 629330 FAX (0925) 65615
This large and popular modern hotel is set in open countryside close to junction11 of the M56. It has a very good leisure centre and comprehensive conference facilities and, of the two restaurants, The Terrace sets the more formal style.
141⇌↱(7fb)⊁in 27 bedrooms CTV in all bedrooms ® T sB&B⇌↱£55-£98 dB&B⇌↱£82-£125 ⊟
Lift ☾ 400P CFA ⊡(heated) squash snooker sauna solarium gymnasium jacuzzi
♀ English & French V ✿ ⊥ ⊁ Lunch £11.50&alc Dinner £14-£19&alc Last dinner 10.30pm
Credit Cards 1 2 3 5

DARLINGTON Co Durham Map **08** NZ21

See also **Neasham & Tee-side Airport**
★★★★62% **Blackwell Grange Moat House** Blackwell Grange DL3 8QH (Queens Moat) ☎(0325)380888 Telex no 587272 FAX (0325) 380899
An impressive, spacious country house on the outskirts of the city. Bedrooms are attractive and comfortable. New leisure facilities are due for completion in early 1990.

98⇨🚿(11fb)3⊟⚟in 14 bedrooms CTV in all bedrooms ® T sB&B⇨🚿£66-£92.50 dB&B⇨🚿£80-£120 ⊟
Lift ☾ ⊞ 250P 3🚗 ✲ CFA ⊠(heated) ▶ 18 ⚲ sauna solarium gymnasium ♫ ⌂ *xmas*
☋ International V ♈ ⊡ ⚟ Lunch £7.50-£12.25&alc High tea £5.25 Dinner £12.25-£14.75&alc Last dinner 9.45
Credit Cards 1 2 3 5

★★★65% Kings Head Priestgate DL1 1NW (Swallow) ☎(0325)380222 Telex no 587112 FAX (0325) 382006
Victorian four-storey town centre hotel.
86⇨🚿(1fb) CTV in all bedrooms ® T ✻ sB&B⇨🚿£27-£54 dB&B⇨🚿£38-£75 ⊟
Lift ☾ 25P CFA ♫ *xmas*
V ♈ ⊡ Lunch £7.50-£9&alc Dinner £10.75-£11.50&alc Last dinner 9.30pm
Credit Cards 1 2 3 5

★★★63% Stakis White Horse Harrowgate Hill DL1 3AD (Stakis) ☎(0325)382121 Telex no 778704 FAX (0325) 355953
Situated on the A167, in the northern suburbs, this Tudor-style building has been extended to make a modern commercial hotel. Although lounge facilities are minimal, bedrooms are comfortable and well equipped. There is also a choice of bars and a steakhouse restaurant.
40⇨🚿(6fb)⚟in 20 bedrooms CTV in all bedrooms ® T ✻ sB⇨🚿fr£55 dB⇨🚿fr£68 (room only) ⊟
Lift ☾ ⊞ 120P *xmas*
V ♈ ⊡ ⚟ Lunch fr£5.95 High tea fr£3.50 Dinner fr£8 Last dinner 10pm
Credit Cards 1 2 3 5 £

✕✕ *Bishop's House* 38 Coniscliffe Rd DL3 7RG ☎(0325)286666
Built round a small, attractive courtyard, this elegant, town-centre restaurant is both comfortable and intimate. The fixed-price menu for both lunch and dinner offer interesting home-made dishes, the delicious puddings being particularly notable.
Lunch not served Sat
☋ English & French V 35 seats Last lunch 2pm Last dinner 9.30pm ⅊
Credit Cards 1 2 3

✕Victor's 84 Victoria Rd DL1 5JW ☎(0325)480818
In this simple little restaurant, just off the city centre, Jayne and Peter Robinson serve honest British cooking, prepared with style and of a quality that represents excellent value. Our inspector enjoyed a lunch of pork with paprika, followed by a first class bread and butter pudding. Evening menus include such items as guinea fowl.
V 20 seats ✻ Lunch fr£5.50 Dinner fr£14.50 Last lunch 2.30pm Last dinner 10.30pm ⅊
Credit Cards 1 2 3 5

DARTMOUTH Devon Map **03** SX85

★★★60% Dart Marina Sandquay TQ6 9PH (Trusthouse Forte) ☎(08043)2580
This hotel is beautifully situated beside the estuary and its first-floor lounge has superb views. Most of the bedrooms have recently been refurbished and offer facilities which are ideal for both business and holiday guests. A table d'hôte menu of interesting dishes is served in the intimate dining room. There is ample car parking and the hotel is within walking distance of the town centre.
31⇨(4fb)⚟in 3 bedrooms CTV in all bedrooms ® T S% sB⇨£59-£75 dB⇨£84-£108 (room only) ⊟
75P ⛟ *xmas*
V ♈ ⊡ ⚟ S% Lunch £6.25-£15alc Dinner £14-£19 Last dinner 9.15pm
Credit Cards 1 2 3 4 5

★★★ 69% **Royal Castle** 11 The Quay TQ6 9PS ☎(08043)4004 FAX (08043) 5445
This 4-storey Regency-fronted Tudor building is beautifully situated alongside the inner harbour with views across the river to Kingswear. There are public bars on the ground floor, while the first floor houses the residents' lounge, the hotel library and an elegant restaurant where interesting table d'hôte menus make good use of local fish and other produce. The bedrooms are individually decorated and have good facilities.
25rm(21⇌4↱)6⊟ CTV in all bedrooms ® T
sB&B⇌↱£29-£35 dB&B⇌↱£58-£70
(7⌂ (£1.50) ♫ *xmas*
V ♉ ⚲ Lunch £7.25-£8.95alc Dinner £11.45-£14.95 Last dinner 9.45pm
Credit Cards 1 3

★★★ 60% **Stoke Lodge** Cinders Lane, Stoke Fleming TQ6 0RA (2m S A379) ☎Stoke Fleming(0803)770523
In an elevated position with some sea views, this family-run hotel has a new leisure complex with a sauna, solarium, mini gym and indoor swimming pool. Bedrooms are comfortable and the bars are busy.
24rm(20⇌4↱)(5fb)1⊟ CTV in all bedrooms ® T
sB&B⇌↱£30-£33 dB&B⇌↱£49-£58 ⊟
50P 4⌂ (£2.50) ⊭ ❊ ⊡(heated) ⌂(heated) ⚲ (hard) sauna solarium gymnasium jacuzzi putting *xmas*
☊ English & Continental V ♉ ⚲ Lunch £6.95-£8.95&alc Dinner £11.25-£11.95&alc Last dinner 9.00pm

★★**Royle House** Mount Boone TQ6 9HZ ☎(08043)3649
RS Dec-Feb
Family-run hotel in its own gardens, approximately 5 minutes walk from the town centre and the river.
10⇌ CTV in all bedrooms ® ✱ sB&B⇌£39-£43
dB&B⇌£52-£66 ⊟
CTV 15P ⊭ ❊ ⊡(heated) sauna solarium
V ♉ ⅟ Bar Lunch fr£3.50 Dinner fr£11.50&alc Last dinner 8pm
Credit Cards 1 3

⊛✕✕**Carved Angel** 2 South Embankment TQ6 9BB ☎(08043)2465
Local fishermen deliver buckets of freshly landed prawn and crab throughout the day to this renowned quayside restaurant. They are used, with other mainly home-grown produce, on a menu which excels in its complete lack of pretentiousness. Joyce Molyneux and her staff prepare well-constructed, satisfying dishes, packed with real flavour, such as a superb twice-baked lobster soufflé, followed, perhaps, by a traditionally roast Gressingham duck with apple and sweet potato. Desserts, too, are most enjoyable – an irresistable iced ginger meringue, for instance. Our inspector found the service a little erratic, but stressed that this should not deter anyone from visiting this fine restaurant.
Closed Mon, Xmas & Jan
Dinner not served Sun
☊ International 34 seats ✱ Lunch £17.50-£22.50&alc Dinner £27.50-£32 Last lunch 1.45pm Last dinner 9.30pm ⚲

⊛✕✕**The Mansion House** TQ6 9AG
☎(08043)5474
Chef/patron Richard Cranfield has recently opened this elegant and attractive restaurant near to the quay after selling his popular Bistro 33. The Mansion House, formerly the home of a Mayor of Dartmouth in the 18th-century, has enabled Mr. Cranfield to open a bistro-style wine bar on the ground floor and a formal restaurant in the former ballroom on the first floor. Seafood is a speciality of the menu, with dishes such as sea bass, hot-smoked over fennel, or charcoal-grilled turbot served with a parsley-scented veal stock. Desserts are especially delectable and our Inspector described his 'Creme bruleé as 'as near perfect as I can remember'.
Closed Mon
Lunch not served Sat Dinner not served Sun
☊ French 44 seats Dinner £19.50-£24alc Last lunch 1.30pm Last dinner 10pm ⚲ ⅟

DARWEN Lancashire Map **07** SD62

★★★ 56% **Whitehall** Springbank, Whitehall BB3 2JU ☎(0254)701595
Closed 25 & 26 Dec
A country house style hotel, managed by the resident proprietors who offer informal, friendly service.
18rm(14⇌) CTV in all bedrooms ® T sB&B⇌£40-£47.50 dB&B⇌£57.50 ⊟
60P ❊ ⊡(heated) snooker sauna solarium
☊ English & French V ♉ ⚲ Lunch £7.50 Dinner £10 Last dinner 10pm
Credit Cards 1 2 3 4 5 £

DATCHET Berkshire Map **04** SU97

★★**The Manor** The Village Green SL3 9EA (Consort) ☎Slough(0753)43442 Telex no 41363 FAX (0202) 299182
Pleasant hotel overlooking village green, with comfortable bedrooms and two bars.
30rm(26⇌4↱)(2fb)1⊟ CTV in all bedrooms ® T ✱
sB&B⇌↱£31-£62 dB&B⇌↱£62-£72 ⊟
(20P *xmas*
☊ English, French, Italian & Spanish V ♉ ⚲ Lunch £9-£13.50&alc Dinner £9-£14.50&alc Last dinner 10pm
Credit Cards 1 2 3 5

See advertisement under WINDSOR

DAVENTRY Northamptonshire Map **04** SP56

○***Staverton Park*** Staverton NN11 6JT ☎(0327)705911
Due to have opened autumn 1989
52⇌

DAWLISH Devon Map **03** SX97

★★★ 58% **Langstone Cliff** Dawlish Warren EX7 0NA (1.5m NE off A379 Exeter rd) (Consort) ☎(0626)865155 Telex no 57515 FAX (0626) 867166
Good leisure facilities and comfortable bedrooms are features of this family hotel, set in its own grounds. There are some sea views.
64⇌↱(52fb) CTV in all bedrooms ® T sB&B⇌↱£34-£38 dB&B⇌↱£58-£66
Lift (CTV 200P ❊ CFA ⊡(heated) ⌂(heated) ⚲ (hard) snooker solarium table-tennis ♫ ⌂ *xmas*
V ♉ ⚲ Lunch £8-£8.50 High tea fr£5 Dinner £9.50-£10.50 Last dinner 8.30pm
Credit Cards 1 2 3 5 £

DEDDINGTON Oxfordshire Map **04** SP43

★★**Holcombe Hotel & Restaurant** High St OX5 4SL (Best Western) ☎(0869)38274 FAX (0869) 37146
Comfortable bedrooms and an upgraded restaurant are provided by this small hotel.
14rm(11⇌3↱)(1fb) CTV in all bedrooms ® T ✱
sB&B⇌↱£47.50-£54.50 dB&B⇌↱£59.50-£63 ⊟
CTV 60P ⌂ *xmas*
☊ English & French V ♉ ⚲ ⅟ S% Lunch £15.50&alc High tea fr£2.25 Dinner £15.50&alc Last dinner 9.30pm
Credit Cards 1 2 3 5 £

DEDHAM Essex Map **05** TM03

★★★ MAISON TALBOOTH

Stratford Rd CO7 6HN (Pride of Britain)
☎Colchester(0206)322367
Telex no 987083
FAX (0206) 322752

Improvements continue at this peaceful hotel, with a change of colour outside, further landscaping of the pleasant grounds, and gradual upgrading of the bedrooms, some of which had become a little shabby. Each bedroom is named after a famous poet, and all are individually designed and well provided with extras. An attractive drawing room with an open fire overlooks the lawns, and is elegantly furnished with a grand piano and fine paintings, set off by pretty flower arrangements and bowls of fresh fruit. Main meals are taken at Le Talbooth restaurant, just over three quarters of a mile away, to which the very pleasant hotel staff will provide transport. Lighter meals and breakfasts are served in the privacy and comfort of the bedrooms.

10⇌(1fb) CTV in all bedrooms **T** ✱ S%
sB&B⇌£70-£95 dB&B⇌£75-£115 Continental breakfast
12P ✿ croquet
English & French **V** Lunch £15-£16&alc Dinner £25.75-£31.25alc Last dinner 9.30pm
Credit Cards [1] [3]

✕✕✕Le Talbooth CO7 6HP
☎Colchester(0206)323150 Telex no 987083
FAX (0206) 322752

Since joining the Talbooth team in January 1988 from Le Meridien in Piccadilly, chef Stephen Blake has put this fine restaurant back on the rails with his fine cuisine. The timber-framed house has undergone change too, and a sympathetic extension now runs along the bank of the River Stour. The menu features both tried and tested dishes and some innovative ideas, with a leaning towards flavours from the Far East. Vegetables have been disappointing, but sauces are generally good. A sherry vinegar sauce with a pithvier of sweetbreads was excellent, and canon of lamb with truffle-juice sauce also impressed. Among the fine desserts, the dish of three chocolate mousses should not be missed. The cellar is comprehensive and service is efficient and polite.

English & French **V** 70 seats ✱ Lunch £15&alc Dinner £25.75-£31.25alc Last lunch 2pm Last dinner 9.30pm 40P
Credit Cards [1] [3]

DEGANWY Gwynedd Map **06** SH77

★★Bryn Cregin Garden Ty Mawr Rd LL31 9UR (Exec Hotel)
☎(0492)85266
The exceptionally comfortable public rooms of the hotel have attractive views across its own grounds to the Conwy Estuary and Castle.
16rm(12⇌4♠)1 CTV in all bedrooms ® **T**
sB&B⇌♠£45-£66 dB&B⇌♠£56-£72
30P ✿
International **V**
Credit Cards [1] [3] £

★★*Deganwy Castle* Station Rd LL31 9DA ☎(0492)8355 85121
Telex no 61155
This large hotel has lovely views across the Conwy estuary. At the time of our inspection, extensive improvements were being carried out.
25rm(21⇌)(3fb)2 CTV in all bedrooms ® **T**
CTV 70P ✿
Credit Cards [1] [2] [3] [5]

See advertisement under LLANDUDNO

DENBIGH Clwyd Map **06** SJ06

★★Bull Hall Square LL16 3NU ☎(074571)2582 & 2072
The former coaching inn is a tourist and commercial hotel in the centre of town.
13rm(7⇌)(4fb) CTV in all bedrooms **T** (ex guide dogs) ✱
sB&Bfr£15 sB&B⇌fr£17 dB&Bfr£29 dB&B⇌fr£31
12P ♫
V Lunch £5.95-£7.20alc Dinner fr£7.20alc Last dinner 9pm
Credit Cards [1] [2] [3] [5] £

DERBY Derbyshire Map **08** SK33

★★★65% Crest Pasture Hill, Littleover DE3 7BA (Crest)
☎(0332)514933 Telex no 377081 FAX (0332) 518668
Situated on the southern edge of the town, this hotel is deceptively large. The modern bedroom extension to the rear overlooks fields and a golf course and there are 2 suites in the cottage annexe.
66⇌ in 21 bedrooms CTV in all bedrooms ® **T** ✱
sB⇌£62-£74 dB⇌£74-£86 (room only)
(250P
International **V** Lunch fr£4.95 Dinner fr£14.30 Last dinner 9.45pm
Credit Cards [1] [2] [3] [4] [5]

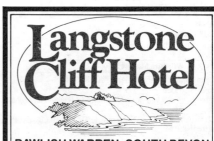

D

★★★63% International Burton Rd (A5250) DE3 6AD (Consort) ☎(0332)369321 Telex no 377759 FAX (0332) 294430
This is a lively hotel on the edge of the town, reached via the A5250. There are well-equipped bedrooms and an extensive menu. Speciality nights are a feature here.
41rm(39⇌2♪)Annexe10⇌(2fb) CTV in 71bedrooms ® **T** sB⇌♪£21-£50.50 dB⇌♪£35-£70 (room only) ⊟
Lift ☾ 70P gymnasium ♫
☋ International **V** ♈ ☕ Lunch £5.25-£7.50 Dinner £11&alc Last dinner 10.30pm
Credit Cards 1 2 3 5

★★★61% Midland Midland Rd DE1 2SQ ☎(0332)45894 Telex no 378373 FAX (0332) 293522
Closed 25-26 Dec & 1 Jan
This busy commercial hotel is located next to the railway station and has conference rooms of various sizes. To the rear is a garden with mature trees and a patio area.
60⇌1⊟ CTV in all bedrooms ® **T** sB&Bfr£31 sB&B⇌£43.50-£66 dB&Bfr£42 dB&B⇌£54.50-£77
☾ 95P 15🚗 CFA ♫
☋ English & French **V** ♈ ☕ Lunch fr£7&alc Dinner fr£9.50&alc Last dinner 10pm
Credit Cards 1 2 3 5

★★Clarendon Midland Rd DE1 2SL ☎(0332)365235
Closed 25-26 Dec & 1 Jan
Late-Victorian, predominantly commercial hotel, close to the railway station.
48rm(13⇌6♪)(1fb) CTV in 22bedrooms ® sB&Bfr£19.50 sB&B⇌♪£28.50-£34 dB&Bfr£30.25 dB&B⇌♪fr£45 ⊟
☾ CTV 80P Petanque (French Boules) ♫
☋ English & French **V** ♈ ☕ Lunch £4.50-£6.95 Dinner £7-£9&alc Last dinner 10pm
Credit Cards 1 2 3 5

★★*Kedleston* Kedleston Rd, Quarndon DE6 4JD (3m NW) ☎(0332)559202 & 556507
15rm(13⇌2♪)1⊟ CTV in all bedrooms ® ✗
120P ⊞
V ♈ ☕ Last dinner 9.15pm
Credit Cards 1 2 3 4 5

DEVIZES Wiltshire Map **04** SU06

★★Bear Market Place SN10 1HS ☎(0380)2444
Closed 25-26 Dec
A 16th-cenury coaching hotel with traditional comfort and good menu.
24⇌(5fb)3⊟ CTV in all bedrooms ® **T** ✱ S% sB&B⇌fr£45 dB&B⇌fr£60 ⊟
CTV 25P (50p) 🚗(£1)
V ♈ ☕ ⚟ Lunch fr£10&alc Dinner fr£12&alc Last dinner 11pm
Credit Cards 1 3

DINAS MAWDDWY Gwynedd Map **06** SH81

★★Buckley Pines SY20 9LP ☎(06504)261
Closed Nov-Jan
The family-run hotel provides comfortable accommodation and specialises in vegetarian dishes. Its setting in the Dovey Valley is particularly picturesque.
12rm(3⇌2♪)(1fb) CTV in all bedrooms ® sB&B£19.50 sB&B⇌♪£23 dB&B£36 dB&B⇌♪£42
40P ⊞ ✲ ⌐
Sunday Lunch £5 Dinner £8&alc Last dinner 9pm
Credit Cards 1 3

Book as early as possible for busy holiday periods.

DINGWALL Highland *Ross & Cromarty* Map **14** NH55

★★*Royal* High St IV15 9HL ☎(0349)62130
Recently renovated commercial hotel on a corner site in the town centre.
22rm(13⇌3♪)(1fb)1⊟ ⚟in 2 bedrooms CTV in all bedrooms ® **T**
☾ 60P ⌂
V ♈ ☕ Last dinner 9pm
Credit Cards 1 2 3 5

DINNINGTON South Yorkshire Map **08** SK58

★★★67% Dinnington Hall Falcon Way S31 3NY ☎Worksop(0909)569661 FAX (0909)563411
A 17th-century building of architectural and historical interest, Dinnington Hall is located in a quiet residential area. Run in country house style, it is distinguished by its interesting restaurant menu.
10rm(7⇌3♪)(2fb)1⊟ CTV in all bedrooms ® **T** ✱ sB⇌♪£38-£55 dB⇌♪£45-£65 (room only) ⊟
☾ 60P ⊞ ✲ *xmas*
☋ French ♈ ☕ ⚟ Last high tea 4pm
Credit Cards 1 2 3

DIRLETON Lothian *East Lothian* Map **12** NT58

★★★66% *Open Arms* EH39 5EG ☎(062085)241 Telex no 727887
This character hotel by the village green has comfortable public areas and bedrooms which are gradually being upgraded. Guests are well looked after by polite staff.
7rm(6⇌1♪) CTV in all bedrooms **T**
CTV 50P ⊞ ✲
☋ Scottish & French **V** ♈ ☕ Last dinner 10pm
Credit Cards 1 2 3 5

DISLEY Cheshire Map **07** SJ98

★★★59% Moorside Mudhurst Ln, Higher Disley SK12 2AP (Best Western) ☎(0663)64151 Telex no 665170 FAX (0663) 62794
Although situated on open moorland, this hotel is within easy reach of the motorway network. Modern bedrooms, comfortable lounges, a wide range of conference facilities and a 9-hole golf course are all available here.
65rm(64⇌1♪)(2fb)1⊟ CTV in all bedrooms ® **T** ✱ sB⇌♪£65-£85 dB⇌♪£75-£95 (room only) ⊟
☾ 250P ✲ CFA ⚑9 ♫
☋ English & French **V** ♈ ☕ Lunch £9.20-£12.20&alc High tea £1.75-£7 Dinner £14.70-£18.70&alc Last dinner 10pm
Credit Cards 1 2 3 5 £

DISS Norfolk Map **05** TM18

★★Park 29 Denmark St IP22 3LE (Berni/Chef & Brewer) ☎(0379)642244
Situated in pleasant gardens close to Diss town centre, the Park Hotel has a popular restaurant serving both à la carte and carvery meals. Accommodation is available in the main building of the hotel and also in an attractive annexe which was originally a double-fronted Georgian residence. the staff are young and friendly.
17⇌ CTV in all bedrooms ® **T** ✗ (ex guide dogs) ✱ S% sB&B⇌£33.50 dB&B⇌£44.50 ⊟
60P ✲ *xmas*
V ♈ ☕ Lunch £4.95 Dinner £9 Last dinner 10pm
Credit Cards 1 2 3 5

For key to symbols see the inside front cover.

✕✕Salisbury House 84 Victoria Rd IP22 3JG ☎(0379)644738
In an attractively refurbished Victorian house, Barry and Sue Davies offer well-cooked food in the light, modern style with the imaginative use of fresh ingredients. In addition to the elegant dining room there are two comfortable lounges. Two attractive bedrooms with en suite facilities are also available.
Closed Sun & Mon, 1wk Xmas & 2wks Summer
Lunch not served Sat
British & French 34 seats ✱ Lunch fr£10.50&alc Dinner £18-£24.60alc Last lunch 1.45pm Last dinner 9.15pm 10P nc8yrs 2 bedrooms available
Credit Cards [1] [3]

DOLGELLAU Gwynedd Map **06** SH71

★★Dolserau Hall Hotel LL40 2AG ☎(0341)422522
Standing in its own delightful grounds, this recently refurbished Victorian building is surrounded by beautiful Welsh countryside.
13rm(9⇌1♠)(7fb) CTV in all bedrooms ® T ✱ sB&B£25 sB&B⇌♠£25 dB&B£44 dB&B⇌♠£50
Lift 70P ✲ ♫ *xmas*
V Lunch £6 Dinner £9.25 Last dinner 9pm
Credit Cards [1] [3]

See advertisement on page 241

★★Royal Ship Queens Square LL40 1AR (Frederic Robinson) ☎(0341)422209
A very attractive building in the centre of the town, with good public areas and a well-furnished restaurant offering a good standard of food.
24rm(13⇌3♠) CTV in 25bedrooms ® ✱ sB&B£15 sB&B⇌♠£24 dB&B£30 dB&B⇌♠£48
Lift CTV 8P 3 *xmas*
V Lunch £6 Dinner £10.50 Last dinner 9pm
Credit Cards [1] [3] [5]

See advertisement on page 241

D

★Clifton House Hotel Smithfield Square LL40 1ES
☎(0341)422554
The basement à la carte restaurant of this town-centre Georgian hotel was the county gaol in the 18th century. Present-day inmates enjoy much improved fare.
7rm(1⇨2♠)(1fb) CTV in all bedrooms ® ✗ sB&B£15-£20 sB&B⇨♠£20-£25 dB&B£26-£32 dB&B⇨♠£34-£40 ⊟
CTV 3P
V ♢ ☕ Lunch £5-£10alc Dinner £8-£12.50alc Last dinner 9.30pm
Credit Cards 1 3 £

DOLPHINTON Strathclyde *Lanarkshire* Map **11** NT14

★★★ 64% Dolphinton House EH46 7AB
☎(0968)82286
FAX (0899) 20456

Standing in 186 acres of parkland and woods, this 19th-century sandstone house has been carefully converted to provide up to date facilities while retaining many of its original Victorian features. Bedrooms and bathrooms are generally spacious and well equipped and the lounge is relaxing. The small bar boasts an extensive range of malt whiskies. A small team of staff provide informal but attentive service.
12rm(10⇨2♠)(2fb)2⊟ CTV in all bedrooms ® T sB&B⇨♠£41.50-£45 dB&B⇨♠£70-£89 ⊟
40P ✲ croquet *xmas*
♢ ☕ ⁄ Lunch £9-£12 Dinner £19.75-£21 Last dinner 9.30pm
Credit Cards 1 2 3 4 5

DOLWYDDELAN Gwynedd Map **06** SH75

★★Elen's Castle LL25 0EJ (Guestaccom) ☎(06906)207
Closed Oct-Mar
A small, attractive creeper-clad hotel in the village centre, with comfortable bedrooms and lounges. Good English and Welsh cooking is served in the two dining rooms and the charming resident owners are most hospitable.
10rm(3⇨4♠)(1fb)1⊟ ⁄in 1 bedroom ® sB&B£16.70-£19.70 sB&B⇨♠£21.70-£24.70 dB&B£33.40-£37.40 dB&B⇨♠£37.40-£41.40
CTV 40P 3♠(£1) ✲ ♩ sauna
♡ Welsh & English V ♢ ☕ ⁄ Bar Lunch fr£2 Dinner fr£7 Last dinner 7pm

DONCASTER South Yorkshire Map **08** SE50

★★★ 58% Danum Swallow High St DN1 1DN (Swallow)
☎(0302)342261 Telex no 547533 FAX (0302) 329034
Located in the town centre, this friendly hotel provides modern bedrooms, with some suites available. The lounge has recently been refurbished to offer peace and comfort, and here light snacks and beverages are served. The first-floor restaurant offers both à la carte and table d'hôte menus.
66rm(57⇨9♠)(2fb)1⊟ ⁄in 20 bedrooms CTV in all bedrooms ® T ✱ sB&B⇨♠£52 dB&B⇨♠£70 ⊟
Lift ☾ 60P 25♠ CFA *xmas*
V ♢ ☕ Lunch £7.25-£7.95 Dinner £10.95 Last dinner 9.45pm
Credit Cards 1 2 3 4 5

★★★ 69% *Doncaster Moat House* Warmsworth DN4 9UX (2.5m SW on A630 at junc with A1) (Queens Moat) ☎(0302)310331 Telex no 547963 FAX (0302) 310197
Situated at Warmsworth on the A630 with easy access to the A1(M) and the M18. The hotel is attractively decorated and management provide food, service and hospitality of a high standard. There is ample car parking space and comfortable accommodation. The hotel also has extensive banquet facilities, both in the main building and in the adjoining Warmsworth Hall.
70♠ ⁄in 10 bedrooms CTV in all bedrooms ® T
☾ 200P ✲
♡ French V ♢ ☕ ⁄ Last dinner 10pm
Credit Cards 1 2 3 4 5

★★Mount Pleasant Great North Rd DN11 0HP (On A638 1.5m E of Rossington) ☎(0302)868696 & 868219
FAX (0302) 865130
(For full entry see Rossington)

★★Regent Regent Square DN1 2DS ☎(0302)364180 & 364336 Telex no 54480
Closed 25 Dec & 1 Jan RS Bank Hols
A comfortable and relaxing atmosphere can be found at this city-centre hotel which offers a good range of menus in the restaurant.
34rm(11⇨23♠)(2fb)2⊟ CTV in all bedrooms ® T ✱ sB&B⇨♠£31.50-£43.50 dB&B⇨♠£38.50-£53.50 ⊟
Lift ☾ 20P 1♠ sauna
♡ English & French V ♢ ☕ Lunch £3.50-£5.95&alc High tea £5&alc Dinner £8&alc Last dinner 10pm
Credit Cards 1 2 3 4 5 £

○*Campanile* Doncaster Leisure Park, Bawtry Rd(Campanile)
☎(0302)370770 Telex no 929956
50⇨

DONNINGTON

See **Telford**

DORCHESTER Dorset Map **03** SY69

★★★ 72% *King's Arms* DT1 1HF (Exec Hotel) ☎(0305)65353 FAX (0305) 60269
An 18th-century coaching inn which has been thoughtfully upgraded to provide well-appointed accommodation, good public areas and a choice of two restaurants. Staff are friendly and helpful and provide efficient service in an informal atmosphere.
31⇨(1fb) CTV in all bedrooms ® T
Lift 36P
♢ ☕ ⁄ Last dinner 8.30pm
Credit Cards 1 2 3

See advertisement on page 243

DORCHESTER-ON-THAMES Oxfordshire Map **04** SU59

★★★ 67% White Hart High St OX9 8HN
☎Oxford(0865)340074 FAX (0865) 341082
This well-established and personally-run 17th-century coaching inn has particularly well furnished and individually styled bedrooms offering a high standard of comfort. The cosy, intimate public rooms are also comfortable, and tempting, well prepared food is available in the two restaurants.
20rm(19⇨1♠)(2fb)2⊟ CTV in all bedrooms ® T ✗ (ex guide dogs) ✱ sB&B⇨♠fr£57.20 dB&B⇨♠fr£79.20 ⊟
CTV 25P *xmas*
♡ English & French V ♢ ⁄ Lunch £11-£15&alc Dinner £15-£18&alc Last dinner 9.30pm
Credit Cards 1 2 3 5

See advertisement on page 243

Book as early as possible for busy holiday periods.

D

★★**George** High St OX9 8HH ☎Oxford(0865)340404 Telex no 83147
Closed 1 wk Xmas
A charming coaching inn with a warm and friendly atmosphere offers comfortable, well-appointed bedrooms which retain much of its original character. The restaurant – slightly more modern in style – offers a range of imaginative dishes from both fixed price and à la carte menus, the excellence of the cheese board alone vouching for the interest the hotel has in the quality of its food.
9⇌♪Annexe8⇌♪2 CTV in all bedrooms ® ✱ sB&B⇌♪£49-£55 dB&B⇌♪£68-£90
CTV 60P ✲
English & French V Lunch fr£13.50 Dinner fr£16&alc Last dinner 9.45pm
Credit Cards [1] [2] [3] [5]

DORKING Surrey Map **04** TQ14

★★★★65% ***The Burford Bridge*** Burford Bridge, Box Hill RH5 6BX (2m NE A24) (Trusthouse Forte) ☎(0306)884561 Telex no 859507 FAX (0306) 880386
Set amidst beautiful gardens on the banks of the River Mole, this hotel was a fashionable rendezvous for country weekends as far back as the 18th century. It continues to offer a warm welcome and comfortable accommodation in well-equipped bedrooms, many of which have been refurbished. Service is well executed by pleasant, courteous and friendly staff.
48⇌3 in 4 bedrooms CTV in all bedrooms ® T
(100P ✲ CFA (heated)
V
Credit Cards [1] [2] [3] [4] [5]

★★★57% **The White Horse** High St RH4 1BE (Trusthouse Forte) ☎(0306)881138 FAX (0306) 887241
Comfortable traditional coaching inn with well-appointed bedrooms in modern extension.
36rm(33⇌3♪)Annexe32⇌(1fb)1 in 12 bedrooms CTV in all bedrooms ® T ✱ sB⇌♪£64-£80 dB⇌♪£75-£89 (room only)
(73P (heated) *xmas*
V Lunch £10&alc Dinner £14-£18alc Last dinner 9.30pm
Credit Cards [1] [2] [3] [4] [5]

○ ***TraveLodge*** Reigate Rd RH4 1QB (on A25) (Trusthouse Forte) ☎(0306)740251
29⇌

DORNOCH Highland *Sutherland* Map **14** NH78

★★★**Royal Golf** Grange Rd IV25 3LG ☎(0862)810283 Telex no 75300
23 Mar-26 Oct
The secluded hotel is set in its own grounds and overlooks the Royal Dornoch Golf Course.
23⇌♪Annexe8⇌(2fb) CTV in all bedrooms ® T (ex guide dogs) ✱ sB&B⇌♪£47-£54 dB&B⇌♪£72-£87
(30P ✲ ♫
Credit Cards [1] [2] [3] [5] £

★★**Dornoch Castle** Castle St IV25 3SD (Inter) ☎(0862)810216
Closed Nov-mid Apr
This hotel is located in the town centre and is popular as a base for golfers and tourists. It has lounges with comfortable furnishings and an appealing cocktail bar. The best bedrooms are in the older part of the castle, those in the wing being modern and practical in style.
19⇌♪(3fb) CTV in 4bedrooms ® T sB&B⇌♪£27-£29 dB&B£37-£43 dB&B⇌♪£47-£64
Lift CTV 20P ✲
Scottish & Continental Sunday Lunch £6.50-£6 Dinner fr£13.50 Last dinner 8.30pm
Credit Cards [1] [2] [3]

DORRIDGE West Midlands Map **07** SP17

★★***Forest*** Station Approach B93 8JA ☎Knowle(05645)2120
A well run private hotel.
12⇌(1fb) CTV in all bedrooms ® T
120P
English & French V Last dinner 9pm
Credit Cards [1] [2] [5]

DORRINGTON Shropshire Map **07** SJ40

✕✕**Country Friends Restaurants** SY5 7JD ☎(074373)707
A restored, half-timbered building in the centre of the village, with the atmosphere of a relaxing country house restaurant. Staff welcome you warmly on arrival and escort you through to the relaxing lounge bar area, where you can study the menus. The à la carte and set menus both make good use of fresh local produce and there is always an interesting selection of vegetables available, such as carrot purée and deep fried cauliflower. Delicious sweets are offered from a hand-written menu, one of the most popular dishes being Queen of Puddings, served with gin and lime home-made ice cream. If a formal meal is not required, bar snacks are available at lunchtime.
Closed Sun & Mon, 5 Days Xmas, 2 wks end Jul & 2 wks Oct
40 seats ✱ Lunch £13.50&alc Dinner £13.50&alc Last lunch 2pm Last dinner 9pm 30P 3 bedrooms available
Credit Cards [1] [2] [3] [5]

DOUGLAS

See **Man, Isle of**

DOVER Kent Map **05** TR34

★★★68% **Crest** Singledge Ln, Whitfield CT16 3LF (3m NW junc A2/A256) (Crest) ☎(0304)821222 Telex no 965866 FAX (0304) 825576
RS 23-27 Dec
Sound service, large, well-equipped bedrooms and a choice of restaurants which include a conservatory-style cocktail bar are features of this well appointed motel.
67⇌♪(15fb) in 13 bedrooms CTV in all bedrooms ® T (ex guide dogs) ✱ sB⇌♪£59.90-£69.90 dB⇌♪£69.90-£79.90 (room only)
(75P ✲
International V Lunch fr£7.25 Dinner fr£12.95 Last dinner 10.30pm
Credit Cards [1] [2] [3] [4] [5]

See advertisement on page 245

★★★59% **White Cliffs** Marine Pde CT17 9BW ☎(0304)203633 Telex no 965422 FAX (0304) 216320
Closed 24-26 Dec
An imposing building on the sea front and within close proximity to the Eastern and Western Docks. The hotel has a slightly old-fashioned air and offers clean and mostly spacious bedroom accommodation, equipped with modern facilities. There is a small terrace where drinks and snacks may be served in summer.
54rm(45⇌9♪)(6fb) CTV in all bedrooms ® T sB&B⇌♪£38 dB&B⇌♪£60
Lift (CTV 25 (£1 per night)
Lunch £6.85-£13 Dinner £6.85-£13 Last dinner 9.30pm
Credit Cards [1] [2] [3] [4] [5] £

See advertisement on page 245

For key to symbols see the inside front cover.

ROYAL GOLF HOTEL

DORNOCH

Standing on the famous Royal Dornoch Golf Course ranked among the leading ten courses in the world. Well-appointed rooms with Colour TV and Direct-Dial telephone, etc. An excellent restuarant and a cordial welcome in superb highland scenery await you. *Inclusive Midweek & Weekend Golf Holidays available. Parties welcome.*

For reservations and further details please phone: *AA****

Tel: (0862) 810283
Telex: 75300

The White Hart Hotel and Restaurant ★★★

DORCHESTER ON THAMES
OXFORD

Tel: Oxford (0865) 340074
Fax: Oxford (0865) 341082

17th C Coaching Inn in Thames side village offering every facility in its tastefully restored luxury suites and bedrooms.

500 YEARS OF HISTORY

The George Hotel

★★

Dorchester-on-Thames, Oxon
Telephone: (0865) 340404

Where you will be welcomed with: Cosy comforts; Old fashioned hospitality; Exceptional food and fine wines; Antiques; Log fires; Four poster beds.

A BRITISH TOURIST AUTHORITY COMMENDED HOTEL

8 MILES FROM OXFORD

The King's Arms

★★★ *Hotel and Restaurant*

DORCHESTER DORSET Telephone: (0305) 65353

5 Day Breaks

In the heart of Dorset, this Famous Coaching Inn is ideally situated for walking, riding, fishing, golfing and touring the magnificent coastline, thatched villages and rural landscape of this unspoilt part of the world. Established for over 300 years, we still retain a first class reputation for comfort, Good English Food and Personal Service. We offer two and three day breaks, anniversary breaks in a four poster bedroom and traditional ale weekends.

★★**Cliffe Court** 25-26 Marine Pde CT16 1LU ☎(0304)211001
A friendly and well mananged hotel adjacent to the Eastern Docks.
25rm(6⇌9↱)(4fb) CTV in all bedrooms **T**
☾ CTV 20P
☋ Continental **V** ♡ ☕ Last dinner 9.30pm
Credit Cards 1 2 3 5 £

DOWNHAM MARKET Norfolk Map **05** TF60

★★**Castle** High St PE38 9HF ☎(0366)384311 Telex no 817787 FAX (0366) 384770
This 300-year-old coaching inn in the town centre provides well-equipped comfortable bedrooms, a busy bar and a relaxing lounge. Well-prepared food is served by friendly staff.
14rm(4⇌6↱)2⊞ CTV in all bedrooms ® **T** ✱ S% sB&B£25.50 sB&B⇌↱£32.50 dB&B£35 dB&B⇌↱£40.50 ⊟
☾ 30P 1⌂ *xmas*
☋ English & Continental **V** ♡ ☕ ⚡ Lunch fr£7.95&alc Dinner fr£9.50&alc Last dinner 9pm
Credit Cards 1 2 3 5

★***Crown*** Bridge St PE38 9DH ☎(0366)382322
This hotel, located in the town centre, dates back to the 17th-century. There are good facilities in the bedrooms and well-prepared food and real ales can be enjoyed here.
10rm(5⇌2↱) CTV in 7bedrooms ® **T**
CTV 50P ⊞
☋ Mainly grills **V** ♡ ☕ Last dinner 10pm
Credit Cards 1 2 3 5

DOWN THOMAS Devon Map **02** SX55

★★**Langdon Court** PL9 0DY ☎(0752)862358
Modernised Elizabethan mansion on an unclassified road between Wembury and Down Thomas.
15⇌(3fb) CTV in all bedrooms ® **T** sB&B⇌£25-£40 dB&B⇌£45-£55
100P ✿ pool room nc5yrs
☋ French **V** ♡ ☕ Lunch fr£7.50 Dinner £12 Last dinner 9.30pm
Credit Cards 1 2 3 5

DRAYCOTT Derbyshire Map **08** SK43

★★★ 56% **Tudor Court** Gypsy Ln DE7 3PB (Best Western) ☎(03317)4581 Telex no 377313 FAX (03317) 3133
Standing in 8 acres of grounds, this modern hotel, built in traditional style, offers good conference facilities. There is also a popular night club within the complex.
30⇌↱(8fb) CTV in all bedrooms ® sB⇌↱£24.75-£49.50 dB⇌↱£49.50-£62 (room only) ⊟
☾ 300P ✿
☋ English & French **V** ♡ ☕ Lunch fr£6 Dinner £10.50-£11.50 Last dinner 10pm
Credit Cards 1 2 3 5 £

DRIFFIELD, GREAT Humberside Map **08** TA05

★★★ 67% **Bell** 46 Market Place YO25 7AP (Best Western) ☎Driffield(0377)46661 Telex no 52341 FAX (0377) 87698
The Bell Hotel is a coaching inn that has been carefully modernised to preserve the historic character and atmosphere. Accommodation is comfortable with appealing décor.
14⇌2⊞ CTV in all bedrooms ® **T** ✗ (ex guide dogs) sB&B⇌£52-£54 dB&B⇌£71.50-£75 ⊟
☾ 50P ✿ ⊡(heated) squash snooker sauna solarium gymnasium nc12yrs *xmas*
V ♡ ☕ ⚡ Lunch £7.60 Dinner £12.10-£16.50alc Last dinner 9.30pm
Credit Cards 1 2 3 5

★★♛Wold House Country
Nafferton YO25 0LD (3m E A166)
☎Driffield(0377)44242
Closed 24-27 Dec

Georgian-style country house with rural views.

13rm(3⇌4↱)(4fb) CTV in 2bedrooms ® sB&B£25-£30 sB&B⇌↱£27-£30 dB&B⇌↱£40-£45
CTV 40P ✿ ⌒(heated) snooker putting table tennis
V ♡ Lunch £6.25-£6.75 Dinner £10-£15 Last dinner 8.30pm
Credit Cards 1 3 £

See advertisement on page 247

DROITWICH Hereford & Worcester Map **03** SO86

★★★★ 70% ***Château Impney*** WR9 0BN ☎(0905)774411 Telex no 336673 FAX (0905) 772371
Closed Xmas
In the style of a French château, this beautiful and elegant hotel was built as a private house in the mid-19th century and stands in extensive landscaped parkland. Popular with a wide variety of guests, it offers good attentive service, well-equipped bedrooms and many other attributes. It also offers arguably the best conference, function and exhibition facilities in the country, certainly in the Midlands.
67⇌↱(2fb)1⊞ CTV in all bedrooms **T**
▶

Bridge Street, Downham Market, Norfolk PE38 9DH
Telephone: Downham Market (0366) 382322

The Crown Hotel offers an interesting and comfortable base from which to explore the historic county of Norfolk. The Hotel itself has an interesting history, dating back to early 17th century and is listed as a 'Building of Historic and Architectural Interest' by the Department of the Environment. The rooms are tastefully modernized with most having en suite facilities and television. A wide selection of real ales can be sampled in the cosy oak beamed bar which is warmed in the winter by a log fire. Weddings, parties and celebration dinners all catered for.

White Cliffs Hotel

Sea Front, Dover ♛♛♛♛ AA ★★★
Telephone Dover (0304) 203633
Telex 965422 Fax (0304) 216320

This renowned hotel, situated on the Sea Front in quiet location, close to Eastern and Western Docks, Hoverport and Jetfoil, offers first-class service and true comfort. Fully Licensed with Bar and Restaurant overlooking Harbour. Well-appointed bedrooms, all with private bathrooms, are fitted with colour television, radios, direct dial telephone and tea and coffee-making facilities. Charges are reasonable and the hotel is admirably suited to the needs of cross Channel travellers and for those wishing to explore the many tourist attractions in this part of south east England. A warm welcome awaits you at the White Cliffs Hotel.

Cliffe Court Hotel

25/26 Marine Parade, Dover, Kent ★★
Telephone: 0304 211001/206000

Stopping in Dover?
Visit our elegant Regency hotel in Dover's most convenient position on the historic seafront opposite the car ferry entrance. Spacious modern single, double and family rooms – all with radio, and telephone, colour TV. Private parking.
The Rendezvous Restaurant on the first floor serves a discerning clientele and offers magnificent seaviews.
Special package offer: *all the year round – any two nights with dinner, bed and breakfast and a free day trip to France from £59 inclusive. Please ask for details. Also conference and group facilities.*
Contact Mr. Villatoro

The Crest Hotel Dover

Located on the A2/M2 London Road, a five minute drive from the Ferry Terminal.
67 comfortable bedrooms, all with private bathroom, colour TV, radio, telephone, trouser press and hospitality tray.
Ample free car parking.

Inclusive short break packages available.
Please request our Welcome Breaks brochure.

Whitfield, Dover ★★★
Kent CT16 3LF
Tel: (0304) 821222
Telex: 965866. Fax: (0304) 825576

Lift ☾ CTV 600P ✽ CFA ℘ (hard)
☋ English & French V ♦ ☡ Last dinner 10pm
Credit Cards 1 2 3 5

★★★★ ***Raven*** Saint Andrews St WR9 8DU ☎(0905)772224 Telex no 336673 FAX (0905) 772371
Closed Xmas
This traditionally styled hotel in the centre of the town specialises in functions, though improvement work continues in other areas.
55⇌(2fb) CTV in all bedrooms **T**
Lift ☾ CTV 250P ✽ CFA
☋ English & French ♦ ☡ Last dinner 10pm
Credit Cards 1 2 3 5

○**TraveLodge** Rashwood Hill WR9 8DA (on A38) (Trusthouse Forte) ☎Wychbold(052786)545
Open
32⇌

D

DRONFIELD Derbyshire Map 08 SK37

★★ ***Manor*** 10 High St S18 6PY ☎(0246)413971
RS Sun
A stone-built, 16th-and 18th-century building has been tastefully converted into an attractive hotel. Modernised bedrooms still reflect the period atmosphere, the beamed lounge-bar is full of character, and there is a good, stylish restaurant.
10rm(1⇌9♠)(1fb) CTV in all bedrooms ®
30P
☋ English & French V ♦ ☡ Last dinner 10pm
Credit Cards 1 2 3

DRUMNADROCHIT Highland *Inverness-shire* Map 14 NH53

❀ ★★ **Polmaily House** Milton IV3 6XT
☎(04562)343
Closed mid Oct-Mar
(Rosette awarded for dinner only)
This cosy little hotel offers personal attention by the proprietors and their friendly, willing staff. The homely bedrooms are thoughtfully equipped and there are plenty of books to read by the log fire in the drawing room. It is the food, however, which has again found particular praise, with the varied and imaginative dinner menu offering first class cooking using the best of Scottish produce.
9rm(7⇌)(1fb)1 ✈ (ex guide dogs) sB&B£35 sB&B⇌£50-£65 dB&B⇌£75
CTV 25P ✽ ℘ (hard) croquet
⅟ Bar Lunch fr£2.50 High tea £4-£5 Dinner £15-£22 Last dinner 9.30pm
Credit Cards 1 3

DRYBRIDGE Grampian *Banffshire* Map 15 NJ46

✕✕ **The Old Monastery** AB5 2JB (1m E off Deskford Rd) ☎Buckie(0542)32660
The name of this country restaurant is self-explanatory, and the dining room retains an appropriately simple style. Meals feature local seafood and game, making good use of fresh produce, and guests can enjoy fine views of the Moray coast.
Closed Sun, Mon, 2 wks Nov, 3 days Xmas & 3 wks Jan
☋ Scottish & French 40 seats Lunch £7.80-£15alc Dinner £12.85-£20alc Last lunch 2pm Last dinner 9pm 20P nc8yrs ⅟
Credit Cards 1 2 3 5

DRYBURGH Borders *Berwickshire* Map 12 NT53

★★★ 56% ***Dryburgh Abbey Hotel*** Newton St Boswells TD6 0RQ
☎St Boswells(0835)22261 Telex no 727201

Adjacent to the famous Abbey ruins, this lovely old red sandstone house is set in beautiful grounds and offers comfortable accommodation in a relaxing situation.
29rm(21⇌)3 CTV in all bedrooms ® **T**
☾ CTV 150P ✽
☋ English & French ♦ ☡ Last dinner 8.30pm
Credit Cards 1 2 3 5

DRYMEN Central *Stirlingshire* Map 11 NS48

★★★ 60% **Buchanan Highland** G63 0BQ (Scottish Highland)(Consort) ☎(0360)60588 Telex no 778215 FAX (0360)60943
Originally a coaching inn, this village hotel has tastefully refurbished modern bedrooms, while the public rooms have a more traditional style of comfort and character.
51rm(50⇌1♠)(3fb)2 CTV in all bedrooms ® **T**
sB&B⇌♠£45-£50 dB&B⇌♠£72-£80.50
☾ 150P ✽ (heated) squash sauna solarium gymnasium bowling green *xmas*
☋ Scottish & French V ♦ ☡ Lunch £7.50-£8.95&alc Dinner £14.50-£20&alc Last dinner 9.30pm
Credit Cards 1 2 3 4 5

DUDLEY West Midlands Map 07 SO99

See also Himley

★★ ***Station*** Birmingham Rd DY1 4RA (Crown & Raven) ☎(0384)53418 Telex no 335464
Situated opposite Dudley Zoo, the hotel is just 800 yards from the town centre. Bedrooms have been attractively furnished in pine, whilst the public areas are rather old fashioned and awaiting attention.
31rm(20⇌11♠)(7fb) CTV in all bedrooms ® **T**
Lift ☾ 75P
V ♦ Last dinner 10pm
Credit Cards 1 2 3

★ ***Ward Arms*** Birmingham Rd DY1 4RN (Crown & Raven) ☎(0384)458070 Telex no 335464
Large hotel with popular bar.
48⇌♠ CTV in all bedrooms ® **T**
☾ 150P
☋ English & French V ♦ ☡ ⅟ Last dinner 10pm
Credit Cards 1 2 3

All hotels awarded three or more stars are now also given a percentage grading for the quality of their facilities. Please see p 16 for a detailed explanation.

DULNAIN BRIDGE Highland *Morayshire* Map **14** NH92

★★Muckrach Lodge
PH26 3LY
☎(047985)257

Formerly a shooting lodge, now a family-run hotel. Muckrach Lodge stands in 10 acres of grounds.

10⇌(3fb) CTV in all bedrooms ® **T** (ex guide dogs) sB&B⇌£26.25 dB&B⇌£52.50
50P 3
British & French Lunch £6.50-£8 Dinner £17.75 Last dinner 8.45pm
Credit Cards 1 2 3 5

DULVERTON Somerset Map **03** SS92

★★★72% Carnarvon Arms Brushford TA22 9AE (2m S on B3222)
☎(0398)23302
Closed 8-26 Feb

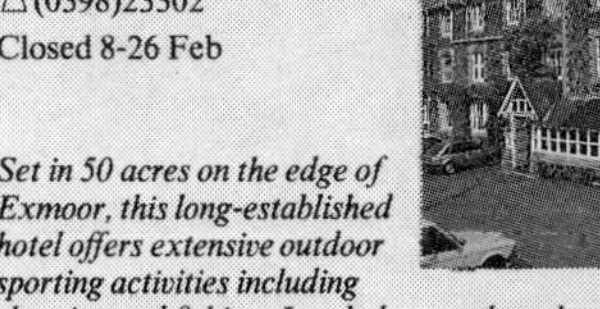

Set in 50 acres on the edge of Exmoor, this long-established hotel offers extensive outdoor sporting activities including shooting and fishing. Lovely lounges have log fires, the bedrooms are traditional in style, and service is warm and friendly.

25rm(22⇌1)(2fb) CTV in all bedrooms **T**
sB&B⇌£45-£47.50 dB&B⇌£90-£125 (incl dinner)
P (heated) (hard) snooker *xmas*
V Lunch fr£7.90&alc Dinner fr£14.90 Last dinner 8.30pm
Credit Cards 1 3

★★ ASHWICK HOUSE
TA22 9QD (3m NW off B3223) ☎(0398)23868

Summer breakfasts on the terrace and log fires in winter are just two of the attractions of Ashwick House. Set on the edge of Exmooor, with splendid views of the River Barle, it is run by the Sherwood family, who combine informality with meticulous attention to detail. Fresh flowers and local mineral water are among the thoughtful touches in the comfortable and spacious bedrooms, while the en suite bathrooms have talking weighing scales The galleried lounge, library and sitting room make pleasant places to while away the evenings, and excellent local produce is provided in the 4-course menu ▶

(choice of starter and sweet). All in all, a most relaxing and tranquil place to stay.
6⇨ CTV in all bedrooms ✕ sB&B⇨£44.75-£64 dB&B⇨£71.50-£112 (incl dinner) ⊟
25P 2⌂ (£2.00 per car) ⌂ ✲ solarium nc8yrs *xmas*
International ♁ ⊻ ⊁ Lunch fr£9.75 Dinner fr£16.95 Last dinner 8.30pm
£

D

DUMBARTON Strathclyde *Dunbartonshire* Map **10** NS37

★★**Dumbuck** Glasgow Rd G82 1EG ☏(0389)34336
Telex no 778303
Popular and friendly privately owned hotel in a converted 18th-century house. Bedrooms have recently been refurbished to a good standard and public areas offer character and style.
22⇨(2fb) CTV in all bedrooms ® T ✳ sB&B⇨£35 dB&B⇨£46
(200P ✲ pool table
V ♁ ⊻ Lunch fr£6 High tea £6 Dinner fr£9 Last dinner 9.30pm
Credit Cards 1 2 3 4 5

○ ***TraveLodge*** Milton G82 2TY (1m E) (Trusthouse Forte)
☏(0389)65202
32⇨
P

DUMFRIES Dumfries & Galloway *Dumfriesshire* Map **11** NX97

See also **Carrutherstown**

★★★ **57%** ***Cairndale*** English St DG1 2DF (Inter) ☏(0387)54111
Telex no 777530
60rm(52⇨8↱)(4fb) CTV in all bedrooms ® T
Lift (CTV 70P
♁ ⊻
Credit Cards 1 2 3 4 5

★★★ **64% Station** 49 Lovers Walk DG1 1LT (Consort)
☏(0387)54316 FAX (0387) 50388
Convenient for the station and the town centre, this hotel, dating from 1896, provides well equipped and attractively appointed bedrooms. There is a spacious lounge bar, and a small team of friendly staff provide good service in the comfortable restaurant.
32rm(19⇨13↱)(1fb) CTV in all bedrooms ® T
sB&B⇨↱£25-£50 dB&B⇨↱£30 £60 ⊟
Lift (40P
V ♁ ⊻ Lunch £6 Dinner £12-£15&alc Last dinner 9.30pm
Credit Cards 1 2 3 5 £

★ ***Skyline*** 123 Irish St DG1 2NS ☏(0387)62416
Closed 25 Dec & 1-2 Jan
A small homely, nicely decorated hotel in convenient central location.
6rm(2↱)(2fb) CTV in all bedrooms ® ✕
CTV 20P
V

DUNBAR Lothian *East Lothian* Map **12** NT67

★★**Bayswell** Bayswell Park EH42 1AE (Exec Hotel)
☏(0368)62225
A friendly atmosphere prevails at this comfortable sea-front hotel. It has cheery, well-equipped bedrooms, a cosy bar and a smart restaurant where good, wholesome food is served.
14rm(13⇨1↱)(2fb) CTV in all bedrooms ® T ✳
sB&B⇨↱£36.30-£44.30 dB&B⇨↱£47-£54 ⊟
20P ✲ ♫ *xmas*
V ♁ ⊻ Lunch £8.95-£14&alc High tea £5-£7&alc Dinner £10-£15&alc Last dinner 9pm
Credit Cards 1 2 3

★★**Redheugh** Bayswell Park EH42 1AE ☏(0368)62793
A small, homely hotel, situated in a residential part of the town, offers compact but well-maintained public areas and bedrooms well suited to modern needs; modest cuisine is presented by a willing young staff.
10rm(8⇨2↱)(3fb) CTV in all bedrooms ® T
sB&B⇨↱£30.80 dB&B⇨↱£39.50 ⊟
P̸ ⌂
V ♁ Lunch £7-£14alc Dinner £10-£20alc Last dinner 9pm
Credit Cards 1 2 3 £

✕**The Courtyard** Woodbush Brae EH42 1HB ☏(0368)64169
Imaginative, homely dishes and a tempting array of rich desserts are on offer at this attractive family-run restaurant.
Closed 3 wks Jan
Dinner not served Sun (mid Oct-Mar)
V 26 seats ✳ Lunch fr£5alc Dinner fr£12.50alc Last lunch 2pm Last dinner 9pm 7P 7 bedrooms available
Credit Cards 1 3

DUNBLANE Central *Perthshire* Map **11** NN70

❀★★★ **CROMLIX HOUSE**
Kinbuck FK15 9JT (3 m NE B8033) (Pride of Britain)
☏(0786)822125
Telex no 779959
FAX (0786) 825450
Closed 1-14 Feb
(Rosette awarded for dinner only)
The stresses of the late 20th century seem very far away from this charming Victorian and Edwardian country house. The Edwardian conservatory has recently been restored, and makes a further attractive public area in addition to the fascinating library, comfortable morning room and spacious halls. There is also a chapel where weddings are held to this day. Fine prints and paintings, porcelain, silver and other antiques abound, and welcoming touches include good toiletries, books and magazines in the bedrooms. Eight of these have sitting rooms. The setting is a beautiful, 5,000-acre family estate, and both estate game and locally caught salmon often feature in the memorable fixed-price menu of 6 courses. Chef Mark Salter shows his imagination and skill in such dishes as a timbale of sea trout and a lobster sauce to start with, then crêpe soufflé with strawberry sauce, followed by fillet of lamb with millefeuille of braised lentils and tomato fondue. A good range of Scottish cheese is also provided, and the fine food is complemented by an outstanding wine list. The young staff are all trained in the Cromlix manner, being courteous, pleasant and helpful at all times.
14⇨↱ CTV in all bedrooms T sB&B⇨↱£75-£110 dB&B⇨↱£110-£175 ⊟
50P 1⌂ ⌂ ✲ ℘ (hard) ⌐ ∪ clay pigeon shooting croquet *xmas*
British, French, German & Swiss V ♁ ⊻ Lunch £12-£19 Dinner £30 Last dinner 10.30pm
Credit Cards 1 2 3 5

D

DUNDEE Tayside *Angus* Map **11** NO33

★★★ 60% **Angus Thistle** 10 Marketgait DD1 1QU (Thistle) ☎(0382)26874 Telex no 76456 FAX (0382) 22564
This busy tourist, business and conference hotel is conveniently located in the city centre. Modern public areas are tastefully appointed, and the bedrooms are comfortable and well equipped.
58⇌↱(4fb)2⊞⊬in 11 bedrooms CTV in all bedrooms ® **T** ✳ sB⇌↱£55-£65 dB⇌↱£65-£80 (room only) ⊟
Lift ☾ 20P CFA games room whirlpool
☋ International ♆ ⌂ ⊬ Lunch fr£7.75&alc Dinner fr£12.95&alc Last dinner 10pm
Credit Cards 1 2 3 4 5

★★★ 63% **Queens** 160 Nethergate DD1 4DU (Inter) ☎(0382)22515 FAX (0382) 202668
A privately-owned city centre hotel with comfortable public rooms. The refurbished bedrooms provide a good range of facilities with some enjoying views of the estuary. The friendly and efficient staff serve wholesome and enjoyable food.
31⇌(4fb) CTV in all bedrooms ® **T** ✗ sB&B⇌£27.50-£55 dB&B⇌£35-£70 ⊟
Lift ☾ 40P
☋ Scottish & French **V** ♆ ⌂ Lunch £4.45-£6.45 High tea £6 Dinner £9.50-£12.95&alc Last dinner 9.30pm
Credit Cards 1 2 3 4 5 £

★★★ 65% **Swallow** Kingsway West, Invergowrie DD2 5JT (3.5 W off A972 Dundee Ring Road) (Swallow) ☎(0382)641122 Telex no 76694 FAX (0382) 568340
This former mansion house has been considerably extended and refurbished to a high standard. Public rooms are warm and inviting, and meals are served in the attractive Garden Restaurant. Bedrooms are comfortably appointed and well equipped.
110⇌↱2⊞⊬in 21 bedrooms CTV in all bedrooms ® **T** ✳ S% sB&B⇌↱£62 dB&B⇌↱£72 ⊟
☾ 80P ✲ ⊡(heated) sauna solarium gymnasium ♫ *xmas*

▶

Scottish & French V S% Lunch fr£8.75&alc Dinner £14.25&alc Last dinner 9.45pm
Credit Cards 1 2 3 5

DUNDONNELL Highland *Ross & Cromarty* Map **14** NH08

★★★69% **Dundonnell** IV23 2QS (Inter) (085483)234
Closed Nov-Mar
This tourist hotel is run by the family proprietors. It is situated by the roadside and backs onto the hills at the north-eastern end of Loch Broom. The decoration and furniture is attractive throughout, with pleasing public rooms and a good range of facilities in the bedrooms.
24rm(23 1)(2fb) CTV in all bedrooms ® T
sB&B £29.50-£34.50 dB&B £49-£59
60P
Bar Lunch £3.50-£8.50 Dinner £12.75-£14.50&alc Last dinner 8.30pm
Credit Cards 1 3

DUNFERMLINE Fife Map **11** NT08

★★★64% **Keavil House** Crossford KY12 8NY (2m W A994) (Best Western) (0383)736258 Telex no 728227
FAX (0383) 621600
The converted fortified mansion has an elegant new bedroom wing and two attractive restaurants, the main dining room and a cocktail bar being complemented by a characterful lounge bar and adjoining supper restaurant. The hotel attracts both tourists and business trade.
32rm(28 4)(1fb)1 CTV in all bedrooms ® T
sB&B £35-£50 dB&B £45-£68
CTV 100P xmas
International V Lunch £7.50-£12.50alc Dinner £12.50-£15&alc Last dinner 9.30pm
Credit Cards 1 2 3 5 £

★★★65% **King Malcolm Thistle** Queensferry Rd, Wester Pitcorthie KY11 5DS (Thistle) (0383)722611 Telex no 727721
FAX (0383) 730865
Located on the southern outskirts of town and convenient for the Forth Road Bridge, this purpose-built hotel offers friendly service and well-equipped bedrooms.
48 in 12 bedrooms CTV in all bedrooms ® T ✱
sB £45-£55 dB £53-£65 (room only)
60P
International Lunch fr£7.25&alc Dinner fr£11.95&alc Last dinner 9.30pm
Credit Cards 1 2 3 4 5

★★★67% **Pitbauchlie House** Aberdour Rd KY11 4PB
(0383)722282 Telex no 727756 FAX (0383) 620738
A modern hotel attracting both business travellers and tourists. Bedrooms are well-equipped, those in the main extension being particularly spacious and comfortable.
32rm(26 6)(2fb) CTV in all bedrooms ® T S%
sB&B £36-£39 dB&B £46-£49
70P solarium
V S% Lunch £7.50&alc Dinner £11.50&alc Last dinner 9pm
Credit Cards 1 2 3 5 £

★★★62% **Pitfirrane Arms** Main St, Crossford KY12 8NJ (half mile W A994) (0383)736132 Telex no 728255
Situated in the village of Crossford, 1.5 miles west of Dunfermline, this modern hotel has evolved from an old coaching inn. The bedrooms are mostly compact, with those in the modern wing more suited to business clientele. The menus offer a good choice of food, including some Italian dishes, and generous portions.
38rm(26 12)(1fb) CTV in all bedrooms ® T (ex guide dogs) ✱ sB&B £34-£42 dB&B £39-£54
72P sauna solarium *xmas*

Italian V Bar Lunch £4.50-£13.50alc Dinner £7.55-£15.95alc Last dinner 10.15pm
Credit Cards 1 2 3

★★**City** 18 Bridge St KY12 8DA (0383)722538
Closed 1 & 2 Jan
Town centre commercial hotel with neat well-equipped bedrooms.
17(2fb)1 CTV in all bedrooms ® T ✱ sB&B £29-£31
dB&B £42.50-£45
15P
French V Bar Lunch £3.25-£6alc High tea £3.85-£6.35alc Dinner £6.60-£14alc Last dinner 9pm
Credit Cards 1 3

DUNHOLME Lincolnshire Map **08** TF07

★★★50% **Four Seasons** Scothern Ln LN2 3QP
Welton(0673)60108 FAX (0673) 62728
Restaurant/entertainment centre with a separate block of modern bedrooms.
24rm(8 16)(1fb) CTV in all bedrooms ® T ✱
sB&B £30 dB&B £45
200P *xmas*
English & French V Lunch fr£7 Dinner £8-£12 Last dinner 10pm
Credit Cards 1 2 3

DUNKELD Tayside *Perthshire* Map **11** NO04

★★**Atholl Arms** Bridgehead PH8 0AQ (03502)219
Closed Feb
Family run traditional hotel standing by the famous bridge over the River Tay.
20rm(4)(1fb) CTV in 4bedrooms ✱ sB&Bfr£16.50
CTV 20P
V Bar Lunch fr£2.15 Dinner fr£10 Last dinner 9.15pm
Credit Cards 1 2 3

★★**Birnam** Birnam PH8 0BQ (Consort) (03502)462
Telex no 57515 ATTN 209
28rm(25 3)(1fb)1 CTV in all bedrooms ® T ✱
sB&B £38 dB&B £60-£85
Lift 50P *xmas*
English & French Lunch £2.50-£10alc Dinner £15-£16 Last dinner 8.30pm
Credit Cards 1 2 3 5 £

DUNMOW, GREAT Essex Map **05** TL62

★★**The Saracen's Head** High St CM6 1AG (Trusthouse Forte)
(0371)3901 FAX (0371) 5743
17th century inn, now well run hotel with cosy lounges and spacious, comfortable well-equipped bedrooms.
24 in 5 bedrooms CTV in all bedrooms ® sB fr£64
dB fr£80 (room only)
60P *xmas*
V S% Lunch fr£7.95 Dinner fr£11.50 Last dinner 9.30pm
Credit Cards 1 2 3 4 5

✕✕**Starr** Market Place CM6 1AX
Great Dunmow(0371)4321 FAX (0371) 6337
A comfortable and attractive 14th century restaurant, which produces fine food from many local ingredients. It also offers an outstanding wine list.
Closed 1 wk Xmas & 3 wks Aug
Lunch not served Sat
Dinner not served Sun
English & French V 60 seats Lunch £16.50 Dinner fr£16.50&alc Last lunch 1.30pm Last dinner 9.30pm 16P
8 bedrooms available
Credit Cards 1 2 3 5

DUNNET Highland *Caithness* Map **15** ND27

★★Northern Sands KW14 8DX ☎Barrock(084785)270
A small tourist hotel close to a delightful sandy beach. All bedrooms now have en-suite facilities and there are three comfortable bars. French and Italian cuisine is served in the neat dining room.
9rm(3⇌6♠)(3fb) CTV in all bedrooms ® ✖ sB&B⇌♠fr£20 dB&B⇌♠fr£36 ⊟
CTV 50P
French & Italian **V** ♉ Lunch £8.50-£12alc Dinner £9.50-£15alc Last dinner 8.30pm
Credit Cards [3]

DUNOON Strathclyde *Argyllshire* Map **10** NS17

★★Abbeyhill Dhailing Rd PA23 8EA ☎(0369)2204
This hillside hotel is named after an old folly resembling an abbey. It has a tidy garden and excellent views.
14rm(8⇌6♠)(3fb) CTV in all bedrooms ® **T** ✱
sB&B⇌♠£26-£28 dB&B⇌♠£40-£44 ⊟
40P ✿
♉ Bar Lunch 90p-£6.80 Dinner £11 Last dinner 8.30pm
Credit Cards [2] [3]

★★Enmore Marine Pde, Kirn PA23 8HH ☎(0369)2230 & 2148
Closed Xmas & New Year RS Nov-Feb
Friendly sea front hotel with tasteful bedrooms, interesting home cooking and some leisure facilities.
12rm(4⇌3♠)(2fb)3 CTV in all bedrooms **T** sB&B£42 sB&B⇌♠£49 dB&B⇌♠£48.50-£62 (incl dinner) ⊟
20P ✿ squash games room
Scottish & French **V** ♉ Bar Lunch fr£1 High tea fr£5&alc Dinner £14&alc Last dinner 8.30pm
Credit Cards [1] [3] [5]

★★*Firpark* Ardnadam PA23 8QG (3m N A815) ☎(0369)6506
A small, well-appointed hotel with wood panelled drawing room and individually decorated bedrooms.
6⇌↱ CTV in all bedrooms ®
CTV 30P ⌘ ✲
✪
Credit Cards [3]

★★**Hunter's Quay** Marine Pde, Hunter's Quay PA23 8JH ☎(0369)4190
This friendly, family-run hotel stands opposite the ferry terminal, overlooking the Firth of Clyde. In its comfortable dining room the menu reflects good, imaginative cooking with an emphasis on Scottish game dishes.
18rm(5⇌2↱)(5fb) CTV in all bedrooms ® sB&B£23-£30 sB&B⇌↱fr£30 dB&B£33-£40 dB&B⇌↱£40-£50 ⊟
☾CTV 20P ✲ solarium sailing ♫ *xmas*
♉ Scottish & French **V** ✪ ⚐ Lunch £5.50-£10.50 High tea £4.50-£6 Dinner £12&alc Last dinner 10pm
Credit Cards [1] [3] [5] (£)

✕✕**Beverley's** Ardfillayne Hotel, West Bay PA23 7QJ ☎(0369)2267
The charming, comfortable surroundings of this friendly, relaxed little restaurant – built in the style of Charles Rennie Mackintosh, and forming part of the Ardfillayne Hotel – provide an ideal background for the enjoyment of a sound, freshly-prepared meal. Cuisine is essentially Scottish in style, though with some French influence, and its excellent use of fresh produce results in an interesting range of seafood dishes. The accompanying wine list offers a wide choice that should accommodate most tastes. Advance booking is advisable.
Lunch not served (by arrangement only)
♉ French **V** 40 seats ✱ Lunch £15-£25alc Dinner £15-£25alc Last lunch 2pm Last dinner 9.30pm 20P 8 bedrooms available
Credit Cards [2] [3] [5]

DUNSTABLE Bedfordshire Map **04** TL02

★★★ 69% **Old Palace Lodge** Church St LU5 4RT ☎(0582)662201 FAX (0582) 696422
This is a charming old ivy-clad building with plenty of character. The spacious bedrooms have been thoughtfully furnished and equipped, and although lounge facilities are limited, the bar lounge is very comfortable. The well-appointed restaurant offers a varied menu of English-style dishes, well prepared from good ingredients. A very friendly and well-managed hotel.
49⇌(6fb)2⊞⚟in 6 bedrooms CTV in all bedrooms ® **T** ✱ S% sB⇌£61.50-£79.50 dB⇌£66-£91 (room only)
Lift ☾ 70P ⌘
♉ Continental **V** ✪ ⚐ Lunch £11.50-£30alc Dinner £15-£30alc Last dinner 10pm
Credit Cards [1] [2] [3] [4] [5]

★★**Highwayman** London Rd LU6 3DX ☎Luton(0582)601122 Telex no 825353 FAX (0582) 471131
This friendly, informal hotel offers comfortable and well-equipped accommodation. The small, intimate restaurant has a short, but interesting menu. There is a large comfortable bar lounge.
38rm(20⇌18↱) CTV in all bedrooms ® **T** ✱ sB&B⇌↱£25-£35 dB&B⇌↱£36-£46 ⊟
☾60P
V ✪ ⚐
Credit Cards [1] [2] [3] [5]

DUNSTER Somerset Map **03** SS94

★★★ 61% **The Luttrell Arms** High St TA24 6SG (Trusthouse Forte) ☎(0643)821555
A successful mix of old and new, this historic building occupies a prime location in the town. The hotel has two bars and two restaurants, and the bedrooms provide good modern facilities. The first-floor oak lounge features a hammerbeam roof.
25⇌4⊞⚟in 2 bedrooms CTV in all bedrooms ® ✱ sB⇌£64 dB⇌£95 (room only) ⊟
3⌂ ⌘ ✲ *xmas*
V ✪ ⚐ ⚟ Lunch £15.70-£21.15alc Dinner £12.50&alc Last dinner 9.30pm
Credit Cards [1] [2] [3] [4] [5]

★★**Exmoor House** West St TA24 6SN ☎(0643)821268
Closed Dec & Jan
This small hotel, located close to the town centre, provides comfortable lounges and friendly service by the proprietors.
6rm(3⇌3↱)⚟in all bedrooms CTV in all bedrooms sB&B⇌↱£28 dB&B⇌↱£41 ⊟
CTV ℙ ⌘ nc12 yrs
✪ ⚐ ⚟ Lunch £5-£7alc Dinner fr£13 Last dinner 7.30pm
Credit Cards [1] [2] [3] [5]

DUNVEGAN

See **Skye, Isle of**

DURHAM Co Durham Map **12** NZ24

See also **Thornley**
★★★★ 68% **Royal County** Old Elvet DH1 3JN (Swallow) ☎091-386 6821 Telex no 538238 FAX 091-386 0704
Overlooking the river, this historic hotel has a Georgian façade and new bedroom wing.
154⇌↱(9fb)1⊞⚟in 30 bedrooms CTV in all bedrooms ® **T** sB&B⇌↱fr£75 dB&B⇌↱fr£85 ⊟
Lift ☾ 120P CFA ⊡(heated) sauna gymnasium Steam room plunge pool impulse showers ♫ *xmas*
♉ International **V** ✪ ⚐
Credit Cards [1] [2] [3] [4] [5]

★★★ 57% ***Bowburn Hall*** Bowburn DH6 5NT (3m SE junc A177/A1(M)) ☎091-377 0311 Telex no 537681
Standing in its own grounds, this hotel has well-appointed bedrooms and a most attractive dining room and lounge.
19⇌ CTV in all bedrooms ® **T** ✈
CTV 100P ✲ ⌂
V ✪ ⚐ Last dinner 10pm
Credit Cards [1] [2] [3] [5]

★★★ 56% **Bridge Toby** Croxdale DH1 3SP (2.25m S off A167) (Toby) ☎091-378 0524 Telex no 538156 FAX 091-378 9981
The restaurant and bar here have been converted from a roadside inn; the bedrooms are in a separate single-storey purpose-built building at the back.
46⇌↱(2fb)⚟in 16 bedrooms CTV in all bedrooms ® **T** ✱ sB&B⇌↱£30-£40 dB&B⇌↱£40-£50 ⊟
☾ 150P ✲
♉ Mainly grills **V** ✪ ⚐ ⚟ Lunch £5.95-£6.50 Dinner fr£5.95 Last dinner 9.45pm
Credit Cards [1] [2] [3] [5]

★★★ 72% **Hallgarth Manor** Pittington DH6 1AB (3m E between A690 & B2183) (Best Western) ☎091-372 1188 Telex no 537023
A country mansion, popular with both business people and tourists. Public rooms are comfortable and the bedrooms are decorated and furnished in keeping with the style of the house. A high standard of food and service is enjoyed in the restaurant.
23rm(14⇌9↱) CTV in all bedrooms ® **T** sB&B⇌↱£54-£60 dB&B⇌↱£65-£71 ⊟
☾ 101P ✲
♉ International **V** ✪ ⚐ Lunch £7.95-£12 Dinner £12.50-£14.50&alc Last dinner 9.15pm
Credit Cards [1] [2] [3] [5]

Book as early as possible for busy holiday periods.

★★★ 65% ***Ramside Hall*** Belmont DH1 1TD (3m NE A690) ☎091-386 5282 Telex no 537681 FAX 091-386 0399
Lying in extensive grounds off the A690 and close to the A1(M), this hotel caters for business people, and offers a choice of restaurants and some luxury bedrooms. A new extension opened in 1989.
34⇌(4fb)⊬in 12 bedrooms CTV in all bedrooms ® T ✗ (ex guide dogs)
☾ 700P ✲ ♫ ⚘
☋ English & French V ♧ ⊻ Last dinner 10pm
Credit Cards 1 2 3 5

★★★ 62% **Three Tuns** New Elvet DH1 3AQ (Swallow) ☎091-386 4326 Telex no 583238 FAX 091-386 1406
A short walk from the city centre, this old coaching inn retains some of its original features, whilst providing modern facilities for the business traveller.
54⇌↱(4fb)1⊞⊬in 16 bedrooms CTV in all bedrooms ® T sB&B⇌↱£52-£56 dB&B⇌↱£70-£75 ⊟
☾ 60P CFA ⚘ *xmas*
☋ English & French V ♧ ⊻ Lunch £4-£9.50 Dinner £11.50&alc Last dinner 9.30pm
Credit Cards 1 2 3 5

★***Redhills*** Redhills Lane, Crossgate Moor DH1 4AN ☎091-386 4331 Telex no 537681
The hotel is comfortable, having been modernised recently, and the restaurant can be specially recommended for its good-value menus.
6rm CTV in all bedrooms ✗
100P
V ♧ ⊻ Last dinner 10pm
Credit Cards 1 2 3 5

DUROR Highland *Argyllshire* Map **14** NM95

★★**Stewart** PA38 4BW (Best Western) ☎(063174)268 Telex no 94014994 BEST
Closed Nov-Etr
A comfortable and nicely appointed Highland hotel successfully blending modern facilities with original features.
20⇌↱(2fb) CTV in all bedrooms ® T sB&B⇌↱fr£37.50 dB&B⇌↱fr£65
CTV 30P ⊞ ✲ sauna solarium clay pigeon shooting sailing *xmas*
V ♧ ⊻ ⊬ Bar Lunch £1-£9 Dinner fr£21.85 Last dinner 9.30pm
Credit Cards 1 2 3 5

DUXFORD Cambridgeshire Map **05** TL44

★★★ 65% **Duxford Lodge** Ickleton Rd CB2 4RU ☎Cambridge(0223)836444 FAX (0223) 832271
RS Sat
Convenient for Cambridge, this hotel offers well-appointed country house-style bedrooms, each individually decorated. Annexe rooms in the converted stable block are more uniform. The bar and lounge are compact, but cosy and relaxing. Chef John Burrows offers an interesting dinner menu with a good choice of well prepared dishes.
11rm(10⇌1↱)Annexe5⇌ CTV in all bedrooms ® T sB&B⇌↱£45-£50 dB&B⇌↱£60-£70 ⊟
34P ⊞ ✲
☋ English & French V Lunch £12-£12.50&alc Dinner fr£15&alc Last dinner 10pm
Credit Cards 1 2 3 5

E

EAGLESHAM Strathclyde Map **11** NS55

★★***Eglinton Arms Hotel*** Gilmour St G76 0 ☎(03553)2631
Pleasant, and popular inn situated in centre of picturesque village.
14⇌ CTV in all bedrooms ® T
(50P shooting ♫ ⌂
☊ French V ♡
Credit Cards 1 2 3 5

EARL SHILTON Leicestershire Map **04** SP49

★★**Fernleigh** 32 Wood St LE9 7ND ☎(0455)47011
Friendly, family run hotel, extended and modernised to provide comfortable accommodation.
28rm(3⇌25↑)(4fb)2⊞ CTV in all bedrooms ® T
sB&B⇌↑£25-£35 dB&B⇌↑£35-£50 ⊟
CTV 100P 10⌂ solarium
☊ English, French & Italian V ♡ ⊥ Lunch £6.25-£7.95&alc
Dinner £7.95&alc Last dinner 9.30pm
Credit Cards 1 3

EARL STONHAM Suffolk Map **05** TM15

✕✕**Mr Underhill's** Norwich Rd IP14 5DW
☎Stowmarket(0449)711206
This is a small restaurant but it is homely and comfortable with attractive furnishings. There is a set menu and the cooking is of a very high standard. The wine list presents the customer with a good selection and service is friendly.
Closed Sun, Mon & BH's
Lunch not served Tue-Sat (by arrangement only)
☊ English & French 24 seats Lunch £19.45 Dinner £19.45 Last dinner 8.30pm 10P 1 bedroom available
Credit Cards 1 2 3

EASINGTON Cleveland Map **04** NZ71

★★★72% **Grinkle Park**
TS13 4UB (2m S off unclass rd linking A174/A171)
☎Guisborough(0287)40515

Recently modernised to a high standard, this hotel stands in 400 acres of grounds.
20rm(14⇌6↑)2⊞ CTV in all bedrooms ® T S5%
sB&B⇌↑fr£51.50 dB&B⇌↑£68-£76 ⊟
130P 2⌂ (£2 per night) ✻ ℘ (hard) ⅃ snooker croquet ♫
xmas
☊ English & French V ♡ ⊥ Lunch £7.95-£8.95 Dinner
£13.95-£16.95&alc Last dinner 9.30pm
Credit Cards 1 2 3 5

EASTBOURNE East Sussex Map **05** TV69

See **Town Plan Section**

★★★★★64% **Grand** King Edwards Pde BN21 4EQ (De Vere)
☎(0323)412345 Telex no 87332 FAX (0323) 412233
The sheer grandeur of this white, palatial hotel at one end of Eastbourne's promenade, is a visual delight. Public areas are spacious, with high ceilings and nearly all the bedrooms have been refurbished. Recent additions include a leisure club and the small, select Mirabelle restaurant. Manager, Peter Hawley, is a dedicated professional and his team of young staff provide a friendly, welcoming atmosphere.
178rm(175⇌3↑)(10fb)1⊞ CTV in all bedrooms T S%
sB&B⇌↑£75-£90 dB&B⇌↑£120-£150 ⊟
Lift (60P ⊞ ✻ CFA ▭(heated) ⌂(heated) snooker sauna solarium gymnasium spa bath hairdressing beauty & massage
♫ ⌂ *xmas*
☊ English & French V ♡ ⊥ S% Lunch £15&alc Dinner
£21&alc Last dinner 10.30pm
Credit Cards 1 2 3 4 5

★★★★70% **Cavendish** Grand Pde BN21 4DH (De Vere)
☎(0323)410222 Telex no 87579 FAX (0323) 410941
Occupying a fine seafront position, this hotel is undergoing extensive refurbishment, with some work still in progress at the time of our inspection. A variety of bedrooms is available, some with balconies. There is a new rear entrance, a games room and a good car park.
114rm(109⇌5↑) CTV in all bedrooms ® T
sB&B⇌↑£65-£100 dB&B⇌↑£105-£140 ⊟
Lift (50P CFA snooker games room ♫ *xmas*
☊ English & French V ♡ ⊥ Lunch fr£10&alc High tea
£2.40-£4.75 Dinner fr£16&alc Last dinner 9.30pm
Credit Cards 1 2 3 4 5 £

★★★★51% **Queens** Marine Pde BN21 3DY (De Vere)
☎(0323)22822 Telex no 877736 FAX (0323)31056
Situated opposite the pier, this busy hotel has long been popular with small conference groups and weekend visitors. It offers well-equipped bedrooms of good size, some facing the sea. There is also a large restaurant, feature bars and service which is both extensive and helpful.
108rm(104⇌4↑)(5fb) CTV in all bedrooms ® T S%
sB&B⇌↑£60-£65 dB&B⇌↑£100-£120 ⊟
Lift (90P CFA snooker ♫ *xmas*
☊ English & French V ♡ ⊥ Lunch fr£10 Dinner fr£14 Last dinner 9pm
Credit Cards 1 2 3 5 £

★★★63% **Chatsworth** Grand Pde BN21 3YR ☎(0323)411016
FAX (0323)643270
Closed Jan-mid Mar
This traditional hotel benefits from a superb seafront location and the accommodation, though old fashioned, is comfortable and well equipped. The personal involvement of the proprietor ensures friendly and helpful service.
45rm(14⇌31↑)(2fb) CTV in all bedrooms T ✳
sB&B⇌↑£29.90-£41.40 dB&B⇌↑£59.80-£82.80 ⊟
Lift (CTV ℙ CFA *xmas*
♡ ⊥ Lunch fr£9.50 Dinner fr£11 Last dinner 8pm
Credit Cards 1 3

★★★53% **Cumberland** Grand Pde BN21 3YT ☎(0323)30342
Occupying a wonderful position facing the sea and opposite the band stand, accommodation here is currently being refurbished and upgraded. Service is generally acceptable with a reasonable standard of cooking. A large function room is available.
70rm(65⇌5↑)(5fb) CTV in all bedrooms ® T ✳
sB&B⇌↑£26.50-£45 dB&B⇌↑£53-£80 (incl dinner) ⊟
Lift (CTV ℙ CFA ♫ ⌂ *xmas*
☊ English & French V ♡ ⊥ Lunch £6.95-£7.50 Dinner
£9.25-£9.75&alc Last dinner 8.30pm
Credit Cards 1 2 3

★★★68% **Lansdowne** King Edward's Pde BN21 4EE (Best Western) ☎(0323)25174 Telex no 878624 FAX (0323)39721
Closed 1-13 Jan
In a prime sea-front position, this fine, well-managed hotel has been owned by the same family since 1912. They provide traditional hospitality and service, along with well-furnished bedrooms, excellent lounges and good standards of cooking.
130rm(108⇌18↑)(7fb) CTV in all bedrooms ® T S10%
sB&B£34-£37 sB&B⇌↑£39-£50 dB&B£56-£58
dB&B⇌↑£66-£84 ⊟
Lift (CTV 22⌂ (£2.50 per night) CFA snooker games room ♫
xmas

V ♔ ☐ ⚡ S10% Lunch £2.50-£7.50alc High tea £5.75 Last high tea 5.30pm
Credit Cards [1] [2] [3] [5] (£)

★★★52% **Princes** Lascelles Ter BN21 4BL ☎(0323)22056 FAX (0323) 27469
This long-established, family-run hotel offers traditional services and management. There is a comfortable lounge, friendly restaurant, a bar and conference rooms.
48rm(37⇌7♪)(3fb) CTV in all bedrooms ® **T** ✈ ✱ sB&B£25-£28 sB&B⇌♪£32-£37 dB&B⇌♪£59-£69 ⊟
Lift ☾ P CFA table tennis pool table ♫ *xmas*
☋ English & French ♔ ☐ Lunch £9 Dinner £12 Last dinner 8.15pm
Credit Cards [1] [2] [3] [5] (£)

★★★65% **The Wish Tower** King Edward's Pde BN21 4EB (Trusthouse Forte) ☎(0323)22676 FAX (0323) 21474
Situated on the promenade, most of the well-furnished bedrooms at this hotel overlook the sea. The lounge and restaurant are very popular and service is efficient.
67rm(59⇌)⚡in 6 bedrooms CTV in all bedrooms ® **T** S% sB£63-£65 sB⇌£63-£65 dB£77-£80 dB⇌£77-£80 (room only) ⊟
Lift ☾ 🚗 (£2 per day) CFA *xmas*
☋ English & French **V** ♔ ☐ ⚡ Lunch £9.30-£10 Dinner £12.50-£15 Last dinner 9pm
Credit Cards [1] [2] [3] [4] [5]

★★**Croft** 18 Prideaux Rd BN21 2NB ☎(0323)642291
Quietly situated, this small, family-run hotel and restaurant offers friendly, attentive service and accommodation in well-equipped rooms of various sizes. 'Le Jardin' offers an à la carte menu in addition to the table d'hôte of the hotel dining room, and the overall standard of cooking is enterprising and reliable.
11rm(10⇌) CTV in all bedrooms ® ✈ sB&B£21.50-£28.50 sB&B⇌£40-£44 dB&B⇌£50-£64

▶

CTV 20P ⛟ ❋ ⛱(heated) ♪ (hard) *xmas*
♀ English & French **V** ♁ S10% Lunch £9.75&alc Dinner £15-£25alc Last dinner 9.30pm
Credit Cards [1] [2] [3] [5]

★★Farrar's 3-5 Wilmington Gardens BN21 4JN ☎(0323)23737
With easy access to the theatres and enjoying a good open aspect to the rear, this hotel has steadily improved its accommodation to provide comfortable, very well-equipped bedrooms. The relaxing atmosphere is complemented by personal service.
42rm(32⇌10⬈)(2fb) CTV in all bedrooms ® **T**
sB&B⇌⬈£22-£30 dB&B⇌⬈£44-£60 ⊟
Lift ☾ CTV 26P *xmas*
♀ English & French **V** ♁ ⊻ Lunch £6-£9alc Dinner £9-£11&alc Last dinner 8pm
Credit Cards [1] [2] [3]

★★Langham Royal Pde BN22 7AH ☎(0323)31451
Closed 6 Nov-24 Mar
This comfortable and well maintained hotel enjoys uninterrupted views of the sea. A high standard of management and the comfort of generous public rooms combine to make the visitor's stay a pleasant one.
94rm(64⇌17⬈) CTV in all bedrooms ® sB&B£21-£27 sB&B⇌⬈£24-£30 dB&B£36-£54 dB&B⇌⬈£42-£60 ⊟
Lift ☾ CTV 3⛟ (£3 per night) ♫
♀ European ♁ ⊻ Lunch £5.95 Dinner £8.25 Last dinner 7.30pm
Credit Cards [1] [3]

★★New Wilmington 25 Compton St BN21 4DU ☎(0323)21219
Closed Jan & Feb
Friendly, family-run hotel with comfortable, well-equipped bedrooms.
41rm(20⇌21⬈)(4fb) CTV in all bedrooms ® **T**
sB&B⇌⬈£23-£27 dB&B⇌⬈£40-£48 ⊟
Lift ☾ CTV 3⛟ (£1.50 per day) ♫ *xmas*
♀ English, French & Italian ♁ ⊻ ⚟ Bar Lunch £4-£6 Dinner £9 Last dinner 8pm
Credit Cards [1] [2] [3] £

★★West Rocks Grand Pde BN21 4DL ☎(0323)25217
Closed mid Nov-mid Mar
Well established sea front hotel with comfortable lounges and friendly staff.
54rm(8⇌32⬈)(4fb) CTV in all bedrooms ® **T** ✖ S10%
sB&B£20-£25 sB&B⇌⬈£25-£32 dB&B⇌⬈£36-£72 ⊟
Lift ☾ CTV ₱ ⛟ nc3yrs
♀ English & French ♁ ⊻ S10% Lunch £6-£7 Dinner £7-£8 Last dinner 7.30pm
Credit Cards [1] [2] [3] [5] £

★Downland 37 Lewes Rd BN21 2BU (Minotels) ☎(0323)32689
Closed 2-31 Jan
Conveniently located just off the A22. The accommodation has been recently upgraded and more improvements are planned. There is an attractive restaurant and bar, a separate lounge and compact modern bedrooms. Cooking is very creditable, reflecting the flair and individualistic style of the chef/proprietor.
15rm(7⇌8⬈)(4fb)1 ⊟ CTV in all bedrooms ® **T** ✖ (ex guide dogs) sB&B⇌⬈£21.50-£34.50 dB&B⇌⬈£43-£69 ⊟
CTV 10P ⛟ ⛳ *xmas*
V ♁ ⊻ Lunch £7.95&alc Dinner £9.50&alc Last dinner 9pm
Credit Cards [1] [2] [3] [5] £

★Lathom 4-6 Howard Square, Grand Pde BN21 4BG ☎(0323)641986
Closed Nov-Feb (ex Xmas & New Year)
The comfortable, privately-owned hotel provides nicely-appointed bedrooms and an attractive lounge. The proprietors and their team of young staff are particularly helpful.
45rm(2⇌41⬈)(5fb) CTV in all bedrooms ® ✖ sB&B£20-£24 sB&B⇌⬈£22-£26 dB&B⇌⬈£36-£44
Lift ☾ 6P (£2 per day) ♫ *xmas*
V ♁ Lunch £3.75 Dinner £5.75 Last dinner 8.30pm
Credit Cards [1] [2] [3] £

★Oban King Edward's Pde BN21 4DS ☎(0323)31581
Closed Dec-Etr RS Mar & Nov
In an excellent position facing the sea, this family-run hotel is also close to the shops and theatres. It has a good lounge and small bar, a verandah and a basement dining room. Service is available 24 hours.
31rm(13⇌18⬈)(3fb) CTV in all bedrooms ®
sB&B⇌⬈£20-£28 dB&B⇌⬈£40-£56 ⊟
Lift ☾ CTV ₱ ♫
V ♁ ⊻ Lunch £4.50 Dinner £7.50 Last dinner 7.30pm
£

✕Byrons 6 Crown St, Old Town BN21 1NX ☎(0323)20171
Closed Sun, 1 wk Xmas & BH
Lunch not served Sat (bookings only Mon-Fri)
♀ French **V** 22 seats Last lunch 1.30pm Last dinner 10.30pm ₱ nc8yrs
Credit Cards [2] [3] [5]

EAST BUCKLAND Devon Map 02 SS63

✕✕Lower Pitt EX32 0TD ☎Filleigh(05986)243
Situated near the church, this charming 16th-century cottage is now a 'restaurant with rooms'. A low doorway (mind your head) leads to a pleasant lounge/bar, where a log fire burns in winter, and the restaurant. The menu features British dishes, ably prepared with fresh ingredients by the proprietress, Suzanne Lyons. There are three letting bedrooms.
Closed Sun & Xmas
Lunch not served
Dinner not served Mon
♀ International 30 seats ✱ Dinner fr£15alc Last dinner 9pm
12P nc10yrs 3 bedrooms available
Credit Cards [1] [2] [3]

See advertisement under BARNSTAPLE

EAST DEREHAM Norfolk Map 09 TF91

★★King's Head Norwich St NR19 1AD
☎Dereham(0362)693842 & 693283
Small modernised 17th-century inn with a walled garden.
10rm(4⇌2⬈)Annexe5rm(2⇌3⬈)(1fb) CTV in all bedrooms ® **T** sB&B£29.50 sB&B⇌⬈£32.50 dB&B⇌⬈£45 ⊟
CTV 30P 3⛟ ♪ (grass) bowling green
♀ English, French & Italian **V** ♁ Lunch £6.50-£11 Dinner £7-£10.50 Last dinner 9pm
Credit Cards [1] [2] [3] [5] £

★★The Phoenix Church St NR19 1DL (Trusthouse Forte)
☎Dereham(0362)692276
Modern hotel in town centre, small and with friendly service.
23⇌⚟in 4 bedrooms CTV in all bedrooms ® **T** S% sB⇌£53 dB⇌£69-£77 (room only) ⊟
40P 2⛟ ♫ *xmas*
V ♁ ⊻ S% Sunday Lunch £8.90&alc High tea £7-£9alc Dinner £11&alc Last dinner 9.30pm
Credit Cards [1] [2] [3] [4] [5]

★George Swaffham Rd NR19 2AZ (Berni/Chef & Brewer)
☎Dereham(0362)696801
This small coaching inn offers comfortable accommodation and a good range of modern facilities.
8rm(5⇌3⬈)(1fb) CTV in all bedrooms ® **T** ✖ (ex guide dogs) sB&B⇌⬈fr£36 dB&B⇌⬈fr£48 ⊟
40P
V ♁ ⊻ Lunch £8 Dinner £9 Last dinner 9.30pm
Credit Cards [1] [2] [3] [5]

EAST GRINSTEAD West Sussex Map **05** TQ33

★★★★ **GRAVETYE MANOR**

RH19 4LJ (3m SW off unclass rd joining B2110 & B2028)
(Relais et Châteaux)
☎Sharpthorne
(0342)810567
Telex no 957239
FAX (0342)810080
RS 25 Dec

Built in 1598, this celebrated hotel stands in magnificent grounds. There are formal gardens, a trout lake and a croquet lawn, and in early summer the rhododendrons and azaleas are stunning. Inside are comfortable, wood-panelled public rooms with big fireplaces. Some of the bedrooms are panelled too, and one has an Art Deco bathroom. All are well furnished, most with antiques, and luxuries include good linen, thick bathrobes and chilled Gravetye spring water. In the evenings the candle-lit dining room sparkles with fine glassware on damask linen, raising expectations which are more than met by chef Mark Raffan's menus of light English dishes. Many of the vegetables are grown at Gravetye, and there is a predominance of fish, such as roast baby brill, freshwater perch and red mullet. The natural flavours of the good ingredients shine through, and the wine list has some 450 bins, including a range of vintages and half bottles. Peace and tranquility prevail, but even at Gravetye time has not stood still. New manager, Andrew Coutts has brought a lighter, ▶

friendlier touch to the unfailingly courteous and professional service, a change that will be appreciated by guests.
14rm(12⇌2↱)1⊟ CTV in all bedrooms ✗ (ex guide dogs) sB⇌↱£75.25-£80.50 dB⇌↱£86.25-£161 (room only)
25P ⛟ ✽ ⛳ croquet nc7yrs
⚟ Lunch £15-£17.20&alc Dinner £19-£21.20&alc Last dinner 9.30pm

★★ ***Woodbury House*** Lewes Rd RH19 8UD ☎(0342)313657
Closed 25-26 Dec
Small, family-run hotel providing comfortable accommodation and friendly, attentive service. The attractive restaurant offers an enterprising menu of skilfully cooked dishes.
6rm(1⇌5↱)Annexe1↱(1fb)1⊟ CTV in all bedrooms ® T
30P ⛟ ✽
♆ ⛉
Credit Cards 1 2 3 4 5

EAST HORNDON Essex Map **05** TQ68

⌂**TraveLodge** CM13 3LL (3m E of M25 junc 29) (Trusthouse Forte) ☎Brentwood(0277)810819
22⇌↱(22fb) CTV in all bedrooms ® sB⇌↱£21.50 dB⇌↱£27 (room only)
☾22P
♉ Mainly grills
Credit Cards 1 2 3

EAST HORSLEY Surrey Map **04** TQ05

★★★58% **Thatchers** Epsom Rd KT24 6TB (Best Western) ☎(04865)4291 FAX (04865) 4222
This pleasant hotel has a large open-plan lounge area which leads through to the bar. Newer bedrooms are generally more spacious than the pool-side rooms, but all are equipped with the same modern facilities, including those in the charming cottage. The oak-beamed restaurant is quite popular with a local clientele.
36⇌↱Annexe23⇌↱(4fb)2⊟ CTV in all bedrooms ® T ✗ (ex guide dogs)
☾60P ✽ ⛱(heated) ♫
♉ English & French **V** ♆ ⛉ Last dinner 9.30pm
Credit Cards 1 2 3 5

EAST KILBRIDE Strathclyde *Lanarkshire* Map **11** NS65

★★★57% **Bruce** Cornwall St G74 1AF (Swallow) ☎(03552)29771 Telex no 778428 FAX (03552) 42216
Situated in the centre of the village, this hotel has attractive well-appointed bedrooms and friendly attentive staff. Lounge facilities are limited to comfortable seating in the newly refurbished lounge bar.
80rm(32⇌48↱) CTV in all bedrooms ® T ✱
sB&B⇌↱£45-£58 dB&B⇌↱£65-£75
Lift ☾ 15P 25⛟ CFA
♉ International ♆ ⛉ Lunch £4.95 High tea £5.15-£6 Dinner £11.95-£12.50&alc Last dinner 9.45pm
Credit Cards 1 2 3 5

★★★62% **Stuart** 2 Cornwall Way G74 1JR ☎(03552)21161 Telex no 778504 FAX (03552)64410
Situated in the busy New Town Centre, this modern low-rise hotel is ideal for the business traveller and offers good bedrooms and spacious public and function rooms.
39⇌↱(1fb)1⊟ CTV in all bedrooms ® T ✱
sB&B⇌↱£40-£46 dB&B⇌↱£51-£56 ⛿
Lift ☾ ⊞ CTV Ᵽ ♫ *xmas*
♉ French **V** ♆ ⛉ Last high tea 8.30pm
Credit Cards 1 2 3 5

EASTLEIGH Hampshire Map **04** SU41

★★★61% ***Crest*** Leigh Rd, Passfield Av SO5 5PG (Crest) ☎(0703)619700 Telex no 47606 FAX (0703) 643945
RS 25 Dec & 1 Jan
An attractive and well-designed, modern hotel with generous bedrooms and extensive, friendly service. There are particularly good standards of cooking in the Beatrix Restaurant.
120⇌(10fb)⚟in 18 bedrooms CTV in all bedrooms ® T
Lift ☾ 200P ⛫
♉ English & French **V** ♆ ⛉ ⚟ Last dinner 9.45pm
Credit Cards 1 2 3 4 5

EAST LINTON Lothian Map **11** NT57

★★**The Harvesters** EH40 3DP ☎(0620)860395
This attractive Georgian house stands in 3 acres of grounds and is popular with tourists and business people alike. It has an elegant restaurant, a grill room and two lounges which offer traditional comforts. Bedrooms vary in size and style.
4rm(2⇌2↱)Annexe7rm(4⇌)(3fb) CTV in all bedrooms ® T
sB&B£25 sB&B⇌↱£38 dB&B£50 dB&B⇌↱£56 ⛿
40P ✽ ⛳ ⛫
♉ Scottish French **V** ♆ ⛉ Lunch £5.85-£9.45alc Dinner £10.50&alc Last dinner 9.30pm
Credit Cards 1 2 3 5

EAST MOLESEY Surrey

See LONDON plan 5*B1*(page 412). Telephone codes are due to change on 6th May 1990. See page 421.

✕✕***Lantern*** 20 Bridge Rd KT8 9HA ☎01-979 1531
Tastefully decorated restaurant with conservatory, run by the chef-patron and his wife.
Closed Sun, Aug & BH's
Lunch not served Mon & Sat
♉ French **V** 50 seats Last lunch 2.15pm Last dinner 10.30pm
Ᵽ nc8yrs
Credit Cards 1 2 3 5

EAST PORTLEMOUTH Devon Map **03** SX73

★★**Gara Rock** TQ8 8PH (Minotels) ☎Salcombe(054884)2342
Closed Nov-Etr
A converted coastguard station on the cliff edge has been converted to provide comfortable hotel accommodation with panoramic views. There are good facilities for children and service is friendly.
22rm(14⇌5↱)(15fb) CTV in 7bedrooms ® sB&B£21-£29 dB&B⇌↱£44-£64 ⛿
CTV 60P ⛟ ✽ ⛱(heated) 🎾 (hard) ⛳ barbeque area games room ⛫
♉ English & French **V** ♆ ⛉ S% Bar Lunch £1.50-£6 Dinner fr£11.50&alc Last dinner 8.45pm
Credit Cards 1 3 5

See advertisement under SALCOMBE

EATHORPE Warwickshire Map **04** SP36

★★**Eathorpe Park** Fosse Way CV33 9DQ (Exec Hotel) ☎Marton(0926)632245 FAX (0926) 632481
Closed 25 Dec evening & 26 Dec
Large early-Victorian building situated amid eleven acres of woodland.
10rm(5⇌3↱)(1fb) CTV in all bedrooms ® T ✱ sB&B£36.50 sB&B⇌↱£36.50-£55 dB&B£42.50-£50 dB&B⇌↱£50-£65 ⛿
CTV 200P ✽ solarium ⛫
♉ English & French **V** ♆ ⛉ Lunch £8.50-£14.50&alc Dinner £8.50-£14.50&alc Last dinner 9.45pm
Credit Cards 1 2 3 5

ECCLESHALL Staffordshire Map **07** SJ82

★★St George Hotel Castle St ST21 6DF ☎(0785)850300
Telex no 367257 FAX (0785) 850940
10rm(8⇌2♠)1⊟ CTV in all bedrooms ® **T** ✗ (ex guide dogs)
S% sB&B⇌♠£40.50-£45
dB&B⇌♠£60-£80 Continental breakfast
17P nc
English & French **V** Lunch £5.75-£7.45&alc High tea £5.50 Dinner £9.45 Last dinner 9.30pm
Credit Cards [1] [2] [3] [5] £

EDDLESTON Borders *Peeblesshire* Map **11** NT24

See also **Peebles**
★★★63% *Black Barony* EH45 8QW (Best Western)
☎(07213)395 FAX (07213) 275
Set in its own grounds on the edge of the village, this 16th-century mansion has been completely renovated and now operates as an hotel for the second time. Aimed at the leisure market, it also specialises in small conferences and weddings. There is a small, elegant restaurant (closed Sunday and Monday evenings) and a coffee shop/carvery.
29rm(26⇌3♠)(4fb)in 8 bedrooms CTV in all bedrooms ® **T**
Lift 98P (heated) sauna solarium gymnasium putting, croquet, clay pigeon shooting
V Last dinner 10pm
Credit Cards [1] [2] [3] [5]

EDENBRIDGE Kent Map **05** TQ44

✕✕✕Honours Mill 87 High St TN8 5AU ☎(0732)866757
The fixed price menus for lunch and dinner offer an appealing choice of French dishes at this tastefully restored mill.
Closed Mon, 2 wks Jan & 2 wks Jun
Lunch not served Sat

▶

Dinner not served Sun
French 38 seats ✱ S15% Lunch £15.75-£25.95 Dinner fr£25.95 Last lunch 2pm Last dinner 10pm nc10yrs
Credit Cards 1 3

EDENHALL Cumbria Map **12** NY53

★★**Edenhall** CA11 8SX ☎Langwathby(076881)454
The hotel dining room, with its large expanse of windows, offers fine views of the garden.
29⇌Annexe8⇌(3fb) CTV in 29bedrooms
CTV 80P 2
English French & Italian **V** Lunch £4.95 Dinner £9.50 Last dinner 9pm
Credit Cards 1 3

EDINBURGH Lothian *Midlothian* Map **11** NT27

See **Town Plan Section**

★★★★★ 61% **Caledonian** Princes St EH1 2AB (Norfolk Capital)(Pride of Britain) ☎031-225 2433 Telex no 72179 FAX 031-225 6632
This splendid city-centre hotel provides good standards of service, accommodation and food, with friendly staff offering a special welcome. A continuing programme of improvement and redecoration ensures high standards – lounges have ben newly decorated and furnished, and all bedrooms and corridors have been upgraded and refurbished.
237⇌(38fb)in 36 bedrooms CTV in all bedrooms **T** (ex guide dogs) S% sB⇌fr£95 dB⇌£135-£145 (room only)
Lift 180P CFA ♫ *xmas*
Scottish & French **V** S% Lunch fr£13&alc Dinner fr£17.50 Last dinner 10.30pm
Credit Cards 1 2 3 4 5

★★★★ 62% **Carlton Highland** North Bridge EH1 1SD (Scottish Highland) ☎031-556 7277 Telex no 727001 FAX 031-556 2691
An attractive hotel in the city centre with spacious, tastefully furnished bedrooms and public areas. Other attractions include a leisure complex, the elegant Quills Restaurant and a new Patisserie.
207⇌(20fb) CTV in all bedrooms ® **T** sB&B⇌£75-£92 dB&B⇌£106-£126
Lift CFA (heated) squash snooker sauna solarium gymnasium jacuzzi table tennis *xmas*
Scottish & French **V** Lunch fr£13.50&alc High tea fr£8.50 Dinner fr£13.50&alc Last dinner 10.30pm
Credit Cards 1 2 3 4 5

★★★★ 63% **George** George St EH2 2PB ☎031-225 1251 Telex no 72570 FAX 031-226 5644
This popular business and tourist hotel is located in the city centre just a short walk from Princes Street. It has elegant and tastefully-appointed public rooms and offers a choice of restaurants. Bedrooms, some of which are compact, have been thoughtfully equipped.
195⇌(10fb)in 4 bedrooms CTV in all bedrooms ® **T** S10% sB⇌£85-£105 dB⇌£120-£132 (room only)
Lift 24P CFA *xmas*
Scottish, English & French **V** S% Lunch £12.95-£19 Dinner £13-£24&alc Last dinner 10pm
Credit Cards 1 2 3 5 £

★★★ 58% **Albany** 39-43 Albany St EH1 3QY ☎031-556 0397 Telex no 727079
Closed 24-26 Dec & 1-2 Jan
An attractive Georgian building with a smartly refurbished basement restaurant and bar. Bedrooms are more practical, with modest appointments, though improvements are planned.
20rm(15⇌5)(2fb) CTV in all bedrooms ® **T** Continental breakfast

Scottish & French **V** Last dinner 9.30pm
Credit Cards 1 2 3 4 5

★★★ 67% **Barnton Thistle** Queensferry Rd, Barnton EH4 6AS (Thistle) ☎031-339 1144 Telex no 727928 FAX 031-339 5521
On the western outskirts of the city, this extended and refurbished hotel offers elegant public areas and modern, well-equipped bedrooms. Two restaurants provide contrasting styles of cuisine, 'Crichtons' being particularly recommended.
50⇌(9fb)1in 10 bedrooms CTV in all bedrooms ® **T** ✱ sB⇌£59-£70 dB⇌£68-£88 (room only)
Lift 100P sauna hairdresser ♫
International S Lunch fr£8.95&alc Dinner fr£12alc Last dinner 10pm
Credit Cards 1 2 3 4 5

★★★ 56% **Braid Hills** 134 Braid Rd, Braid Hills EH10 6JD (2.5m S A702) ☎031-447 8888 Telex no 72311 FAX 031-452 8477
This popular tourist/commercial hotel offers an interesting blend of the old and the new. Comfortable public rooms have a traditional air, while the well-equipped bedrooms are furnished in the modern style.
68rm(42⇌26)2in 8 bedrooms CTV in all bedrooms ® **T** ✱ sB&B⇌£50-£55 dB&B⇌£65-£75
38P *xmas*
Scottish & French **V** Lunch £7-£8&alc Dinner £12-£13&alc Last dinner 9pm
Credit Cards 1 2 3 5 £

★★★ 63% **Bruntsfield** 69/74 Bruntsfield Place EH10 4HH (Best Western) ☎031-229 1393 Telex no 727897 FAX 031-229 5634
Closed 24-26 Dec
Situated to the south of the city centre, this friendly hotel continues its programme of improvements, a new leisure complex being the next project. Bedrooms are comfortable and well-equipped, though some are a little compact. Meals are now served in the 'Potting Shed', an informal, continental-style operation which is proving quite popular.
51rm(42⇌9)(1fb)1 CTV in all bedrooms ® **T** sB&B⇌£47.50-£55 dB&B⇌£65-£75 Continental breakfast
Lift 25P CFA *xmas*
International **V** Lunch fr£5.50&alc Dinner fr£14.50&alc Last dinner 10pm
Credit Cards 1 2 3 5 £

★★★ 65% **Capital Hotel & Leisure Club** Clermiston Rd EH12 6UA ☎031-334 3391 Telex no 728284
98rm(93⇌5)(10fb)1 CTV in all bedrooms ® **T** S% sB&B£35-£65 dB&B£45-£105 dB&B⇌£45-£105
Lift 150P (heated) sauna solarium gymnasium hairdressing *xmas*
Scottish & French **V** Sunday Lunch £6.95-£7.95 Dinner £13.25-£25&alc Last dinner 9.45pm
Credit Cards 1 2 3 4 5

★★★ 64% **Crest** Queensferry Rd EH4 3HL (Crest) ☎031-332 2442 Telex no 72541 FAX 031-332 3408
This comfortable, modern high-rise hotel enjoys a fine outlook over the capital. It offers a range of comfortable modern bedrooms, each well equipped and of ample proportions. The attractive foyer lounge leads to the popular lounge bar and smart restaurant. Conference and business facilities are available.
118rm(79⇌39)(8fb)in 26 bedrooms CTV in all bedrooms ® **T** S% sB⇌£45-£72 dB⇌£68-£91 (room only)
Lift CTV 150P ♫
International **V** S% Lunch £8.50-£9.50 Dinner £11.50-£15 Last dinner 9.45pm
Credit Cards 1 2 3 5

★★★ 61% ***Donmaree*** 21 Mayfield Gardens EH9 2BX ☎031-667 3641
An attractive hotel south of the city centre with richly appointed Victorian-style public areas and consistently good cuisine.
9rm(5⇨4↱)Annexe8rm(3⇨2↱) CTV in all bedrooms ® T
☾ CTV 6P
French Last dinner 10pm
Credit Cards 1 2 3 5

★★★ 56% **Ellersly House** 4 Ellersly Rd EH12 6HZ (Embassy) ☎031-337 6888 Telex no 727860 FAX 031-313 2543
Refurbished public rooms have done much to improve the appeal of this extended Edwardian house. The well-equipped bedrooms are next on the list for upgrading.
55rm(54⇨1↱)(3fb)1 ⚟in 10 bedrooms CTV in all bedrooms ® T ✱ sB⇨↱£62 dB⇨↱£75 (room only)
Lift ☾ 50P croquet pool table *xmas*
V S% Lunch £8.95-£20&alc Dinner £13.75-£25&alc Last dinner 9.30pm
Credit Cards 1 2 3 4 5

★★★ 61% **Howard** Great King St EH3 6QH (Select) ☎031-557 3500 Telex no 727887 FAX 031-557 6515
Splendidly appointed hotel in the city's Georgian New Town area with club-style lounges and cocktail bars and individually-styled bedrooms.
25rm(18⇨7↱)(2fb) CTV in all bedrooms ® T ✱ sB&B⇨↱fr£52 dB&B⇨↱£75-£98
Lift ☾ 14P CFA
Scottish & French Lunch £8.50 Dinner £11.50-£20alc Last dinner 9.30pm
Credit Cards 1 2 3 5

★★★ 68% **King James Thistle** 107 St James Centre EH1 3SW (Thistle) ☎031-556 0111 Telex no 727200 FAX 031-557 5333
This well-appointed city-centre hotel has attractive public areas and comfortable bedrooms which have been furnished and decorated to a high standard. Service is extensive and efficient.
147⇨↱(20fb)⚟in 14 bedrooms CTV in all bedrooms ® T ✱ sB⇨↱£60-£80 dB⇨↱£75-£108 (room only)
Lift ☾ 21P 8 CFA
International Lunch fr£12.50alc Dinner fr£15alc Last dinner 10.20pm
Credit Cards 1 2 3 4 5

See advertisement on page 263

★★★ 55% **Mount Royal** 53 Princes St EH2 2DG (Embassy) ☎031-225 7161 Telex no 727641 FAX 031-220 4671
Occupying a central position looking out over Princes Street Gardens and the Castle, the hotel has recently been effectively refurbished.
159rm(155⇨4↱)(14fb)⚟in 2 bedrooms CTV in all bedrooms ® T ✱ S% sB⇨↱£60-£85 dB⇨↱£75-£95 (room only)
Lift ☾ CFA *xmas*
Scottish & French S% Lunch £7.50-£8.50 High tea £5.25-£6.35 Dinner £11.50-£14.50&alc Last dinner 9.30pm
Credit Cards 1 2 3 4 5

★★★ 57% **Norton House Hotel** Ingliston EH28 8LX ☎031-333 1275 Telex no 727232 FAX 031-333 5303
A comfortable hotel, set in its own gardens and conveniently located beside Edinburgh airport, offers accommodation in bedrooms equipped to meet the needs of the modern traveller. Its cuisine enjoys a good local reputation, and service (in particular, porterage) is commendable, whilst those desiring less formal surroundings should visit the adjacent Norton Tavern for a pub snack.
19⇨↱(3fb) CTV in all bedrooms ® T S% sB&B⇨↱£62-£80 dB&B⇨↱£78-£105
☾ 100P putting green pool table *xmas*
French V Lunch £9.50&alc Dinner £13.95&alc Last dinner 9.30pm
Credit Cards 1 2 3 5

★★★57% **Old Waverley** Princes St EH2 2BY (Scottish Highland) ☎031-556 4648 Telex no 727050 FAX 031-557 6316
A modernised city centre hotel. The carvery dining room is particularly popular at lunchtime when it serves keenly-priced, straightforward dishes.
66rm(58⇌8↱)(6fb)1⊞ CTV in all bedrooms ® T
sB&B⇌↱£55-£60 dB&B⇌↱£80-£89 ⊟
Lift ☾ ₱ CFA *xmas*
V ♧ ⚐ Lunch £3.65-£6 Dinner £8.50-£10.50&alc Last dinner 9.30pm
Credit Cards 1 2 3 5

★★★65% **Post House** Corstorphine Rd EH12 6UA (Trusthouse Forte) ☎031-334 0390 Telex no 727103 FAX 031-334 9237
On western city approach and backed by Edinburgh Zoo this comfortable and spacious hotel offers fine views over the city.
207⇌(98fb)⊁in 12 bedrooms CTV in all bedrooms ® ✱
sB⇌£75-£78 dB⇌fr£85 (room only) ⊟
Lift ☾ 158P CFA
V ♧ ⚐ ⊁ Lunch £8.25-£9.50&alc Dinner £15.50-£16.50&alc Last dinner 10pm
Credit Cards 1 2 3 4 5

★★★69% **Roxburghe** Charlotte Square EH2 4HG (Best Western) ☎031-225 3921 Telex no 727054 FAX 031-220 2518
A handsome Georgian building, featuring some fine examples of Adam architecture, situated in the heart of the city close to Princes Street. Public rooms are elegant and offer a club atmosphere with traditional comforts, whilst bedrooms are thoughtfully equipped, though they do vary in size and style.
75⇌1⊞ CTV in all bedrooms ® T ✱ sB&B⇌£47-£65
dB&B⇌£67-£110 Continental breakfast ⊟
Lift ☾ ₱ ✈ CFA *xmas*
♕ French V ♧ ⚐ S% Lunch £8.50-£10&alc Dinner £13.50-£15&alc Last dinner 10pm
Credit Cards 1 2 3 5 £

★★★57% **Royal Scot** 111 Glasgow Rd EH12 5NF (Swallow) ☎031-334 9191 Telex no 727197 FAX 031-316 4507
This large, purpose-built hotel is convenient for the airport. Facilities include a choice of restaurants and a leisure centre. The best bedrooms are in the north wing, though major refurbishment to the remaining rooms is in progress.
252⇌↱(18fb) CTV in all bedrooms ® T sB&B⇌↱fr£72
dB&B⇌↱fr£92 ⊟
Lift ☾ 200P ✿ CFA ⊡(heated) sauna solarium gymnasium pitch & putt ♫ *xmas*
♕ French ♧ ⚐
Credit Cards 1 2 3 5

★★★58% **Stakis Grosvenor** Grosvenor St EH12 5EF (Stakis) ☎031-226 6001 Telex no 72445 FAX 031-220 2387
The recently refurbished hotel caters for business and coach markets with a choice of two attractive restaurants.
136rm(109⇌27↱)(18fb)1⊞⊁in 18 bedrooms CTV in all bedrooms ® T ✱ sB⇌↱£45-£79
dB⇌↱£80-£102 (room only) ⊟
Lift ☾ CTV ₱ *xmas*
V ♧ ⚐ ⊁ Sunday Lunch £6-£7.50 High tea £4.50-£7 Dinner £8-£12 Last dinner 10pm
Credit Cards 1 2 3 5 £

★★**Cairn** 10-18 Windsor St EH7 5JR ☎031-557 0175 FAX 031-556 8221
This informal hotel, conveniently situated to the east of the city centre, has been completely refurbished to provide well-equipped bedrooms and bright public areas.
52rm(24⇌28↱)(12fb) CTV in all bedrooms ® T ✱
sB&B⇌↱£25-£55 dB&B⇌↱£45-£75 ⊟
☾ CTV ₱
♕ Mainly grills V ♧ ⚐ Lunch £5.50-£10.50 High tea £4.50-£7.50 Dinner £10.50-£12.50&alc Last dinner 9.30pm
Credit Cards 1 2 3 5 £

★★**Clarendon** Grosvenor St EH12 5EG (Scottish Highland) ☎031-337 7033 Telex no 72450 FAX 031-346 7606
Recently refurbished, the quiet, friendly hotel is situated in the attractive West End of the city.
51rm(48⇌3↱)(5fb) CTV in all bedrooms ® T
sB&B⇌↱£45-£50 dB&B⇌↱£70-£75 ⊟
Lift ☾ CTV ₱ *xmas*
V ♧ ⚐ S% Lunch £4.75-£8alc Dinner £10-£12&alc Last dinner 9.30pm
Credit Cards 1 2 3 5

★★**Harp Toby** St John's Rd, Corstorphine EH12 (3.5m W on A8) (Toby) ☎031-334 4750
The recently refurbished public areas of this hotel provide superior bars and a split-level carvery restaurant; bedrooms, though compact, are tastefully appointed and well equipped.
27rm(11⇌16↱)(2fb)⊁in 9 bedrooms CTV in all bedrooms ® T ✱ sB&B⇌↱£44 dB&B⇌↱£54
☾ 50P
♧ ⚐ ⊁
Credit Cards 1 2 3 5

★★**Iona** Strathearn Place EH9 2AL ☎031-447 6264 & 031-447-5050 FAX 031-452 8574
This informal and friendly hotel has well-maintained bedrooms, a busy lounge bar and a quiet, comfortable first floor lounge.
21rm(2⇌2↱)(2fb) CTV in all bedrooms ® T sB&Bfr£26.75
sB&B⇌↱fr£39.40 dB&Bfr£47.75 dB&B⇌↱fr£54.60
CTV 20P ✈
V ♧ Lunch fr£5.45 High tea fr£5.50 Dinner £8.40-£13alc Last dinner 9pm
Credit Cards 1 3 £

★★**Lady Nairne** 228 Willowbrae Rd EH8 7NG (Berni/Chef & Brewer) ☎031-661 3396
33rm(24⇌9↱)(1fb) CTV in all bedrooms ® T ✘ (ex guide dogs) sB&B⇌↱fr£42 dB&B⇌↱fr£63.50 ⊟
Lift ☾ 100P
V ♧ ⚐ ⊁ Lunch £8 Dinner £9 Last dinner 10pm
Credit Cards 1 2 3 5

See advertisement on page 265

★★**Murrayfield** 18 Corstorphine Rd EH12 6HN ☎031-337 1844
A modest commercial hotel south of the city centre with a popular function suite.
23rm(18⇌5↱) CTV in all bedrooms ® T sB&Bfr£29.50
sB&B⇌↱fr£48 dB&Bfr£42 dB&B⇌↱fr£63 ⊟
☾ CTV 30P
♧ ⚐ Lunch fr£5.50&alc Dinner fr£8.75&alc Last dinner 9.30pm
Credit Cards 1 2 3 5 £

★★**Rothesay** 8 Rothesay Place EH3 7SL ☎031-255 4125 Telex no 727025
This well-maintained hotel – part of a Georgian row in the city's New Town – is busy throughout the summer with coach parties from abroad. Bedrooms are compact and functional, equipped with the business user in mind, and this is reflected in its moderate charges.
35rm(26⇌3↱)(1fb) CTV in all bedrooms ® T ✱
sB&B£20-£25 sB&B⇌↱£25-£38 dB&B£30-£42
dB&B⇌↱£40-£60
Lift ☾ CTV ₱
♕ Mainly grills ♧ ⚐ Dinner £6.50-£14.50alc Last dinner 9pm
Credit Cards 1 2 3 4 5

★★***Suffolk Hall*** 10 Craigmillar Park EH16 5NE ☎031-667 9328
Family-run tourist/commercial hotel in residential suburb close to student halls of residence.
12rm(4⇌5↱)(3fb) CTV in all bedrooms ® T ✘
☾ CTV 12P (charged) ✈ ✿
♕ French V ♧ ⚐ Last dinner 9pm
Credit Cards 1 2 3 4 5

★★

Eskbank Motor Hotel

29 Dalhousie Road, Eskbank
EDINBURGH EH22 3AT
Tel: 031 663 3234

Ideally situated for central Edinburgh (7ML) & Airport. All 16 rooms are to a high standard, and all have full facilities. Inc direct dial telephones, bath & shower, colour TV, hair dryer, trouser press, tea/coffee, central heating & double glazed. Well stocked cellar & traditional warm Lounge Bar. Old Worlde Restaurant proudly offering a varied choice of fresh cuisine. Beautiful gardens & large car park. On A7 South Edinburgh. *See gazetteer under Dalkeith.*

Res Proprietors: Charles & Jane Ross

★★★

A traditon of fine food and service that has been its hallmark for over 150 years. The 75 elegantly furnished bedrooms including 2 Suites, all with private bath facilites, enable guests to enjoy the atmosphere of a private house in comfort and style. Situated in Charlotte Square and designed by Robert Adam, the Hotel is just a minute's walk from Princes Street.

A la Carte Restaurant, Cocktail Bar & Buffet, Melrose Room Buttery.

Charlotte Square
Edinburgh EH2 4HG
Telephone: 031-225 3921
Telex: 727054
Fax: 031-220 2518

THE

HOTEL

★★

10/18 Windsor Street,
Edinburgh EH7 5JR
Telephone: 031 557 0175

Situated within the Georgian area of the city and minutes from Princes Street. A warm and friendly welcome awaits. 52 comfortable bedrooms fully equipped. Relax in the cosy Windsor Lounge and enjoy a delicious bar meal in the Shaftesbury Lounge. The restaurant offers a varied à la carte menu and a wide selection of good wines.

Why not visit a sister hotel with similar facilities.

*** AA

King James Thistle Hotel

St. James Centre,
Edinburgh EH1 3SW.
Tel: 031-556 0111. Telex: 727200.

Adjoining Princes Street, in the heart of the city's commercial centre and only a short walk from Edinburgh castle.

The King James boasts a fine French Brasserie, an American cocktail bar, 147 tastefully decorated bedrooms and conference and banqueting facilities for up to 250 people.

Jamie's – the renowned Scottish cabaret – runs from April to October.

For Reservations at Thistle Hotels throughout Britain, tel: 01-937 8033.

THISTLE HOTELS

As individual as you are.

E

○ ***Travelodge*** A720 Ring Rd South(6m S) (Trusthouse Forte)
☎Central reservations 01-567 3444
Due to open winter 1989
40⇌
P

✕✕Alp-Horn 167 Rose St EH2 4LS ☎031-225 4787
Intimate Swiss restaurant with a non-smoking dining area. Our inspector was particularly impressed with the Escalope de Chevreuil a la Mirza served with Spätzli. Short but interesting wine list. Booking is essential.
Closed Sun, 1st wk Jan & 2 wks Jul
Swiss 66 seats S10% Lunch fr£10&alc Dinner £18-£22alc Last lunch 2pm Last dinner 10pm
Credit Cards 1 3

✕✕L'Auberge 56 St Mary's St EH1 1SX ☎031-556 5888
An attractively appointed restaurant on two levels stands close to the city's Royal Mile. A change of chef has resulted in a more polished style of cuisine, strongly influenced by the Perigord region of France. Seafood is excellent, as are such desserts as Le Feuillete aux Deux Chocolats, well worth the extra ten minutes wait. A well-chosen wine list is available, and service is professional. Dinner here can prove rather expensive, though the lunchtime table d'hote menu continues to offer good value for money.
Closed 26 Dec-2 Jan
French **V** 55 seats Lunch £10-£16&alc Dinner £18-£28alc Last lunch 2pm Last dinner 9.30pm
Credit Cards 1 2 3 5

✕✕*Champany Grill* 2 Bridge Rd, Colinton EH13 0LF ☎031-441 2587
A small, attractive, wood-panelled restaurant specialising in outstandingly good char-broiled steaks. Seafood is also featured, and commendable use is made of good raw materials and fresh produce, including an excellent selection of vegetables. Service is friendly and very attentive.
Closed Sun 3 wks Jan
International 36 seats Last lunch 2pm Last dinner 10pm
Credit Cards 1 2 3 5

✕✕Martins 70 Rose St, North Ln EH2 3DX ☎031-225 3106
Tucked away in a small lane off the city's famous Rose Street, this popular and now well-established little restaurant continues to offer reliable and imaginatively prepared food. The menu is constantly changing, but may include dishes such as Mousseline of Salmon with a delicate red pepper sauce, or pigeon breast in a sauce of strawberry and port. Service is friendly and attentive.
Closed Sun & Mon, 26 Dec-3 Jan & 2 wks May/Jun
Lunch not served Sat
28 seats ✱ Lunch £10-£12&alc Dinner £18-£25alc Last lunch 2pm Last dinner 10pm nc8yrs
Credit Cards 1 2 3 5

✕North Sea Village Restaurant 18 Elm Row, Leith EH7 4AA ☎031-556 9476
This is the second of two restaurants of the same name under the ownership of David Ng, and it seems that he is to be personally in control of the cuisine at the bright, unassuming little establishment. His skills are displayed in a range of seafood dishes such as fresh scallop in a black bean sauce and steamed whole sea bass or Dover sole with ginger and spring onion. Service is helpful and charming.
Chinese **V** 50 seats ✱ Lunch £4.20-£6&alc Dinner £8.80-£12.50&alc Last lunch 12.30pm Last dinner 12.30am 15P
Credit Cards 1 2 3 5

Book as early as possible for busy holiday periods.

✕Shamiana 14 Brougham St EH3 9JH ☎031-228 2265
Closed Xmas & New Years Day
Lunch not served Sat & Sun
Kashmiri & North Indian **V** 42 seats ✱ S12.5% Lunch £7.50-£14alc Dinner £7.50-£18alc Last lunch 1.30pm Last dinner 11.30pm
Credit Cards 1 2 3 4 5

EDZELL Tayside *Angus* Map **15** NO56

★★★58% Glenesk High St DD9 7TF ☎(03564)319
Popular golfing hotel with access to the neighbouring course.
25rm(13⇌8)(2fb) CTV in all bedrooms ® **T** ✱
sB&B⇌fr£32 dB&B⇌fr£55
150P 8 (heated) snooker sauna solarium gymnasium *xmas*
V
Credit Cards 2 3 5

★★Central DD9 7TQ ☎(03564)218
A small three-storey hotel standing in a quiet street.
19rm(3⇌8)(2fb) CTV in 11bedrooms **T** sB&B£16-£26 sB&B⇌£26-£28 dB&B£28-£30 dB&B⇌£36-£38
CTV 75P 2 (charged) snooker
V Lunch £4.25-£4.50 High tea £3.50-£5.75alc Dinner fr£8.50&alc Last dinner 8.30pm
Credit Cards 2 3

★★Panmure Arms 52 High St DD9 7TA (Inter)
☎(03564)420 & 427
16rm(5⇌11)(2fb) CTV in all bedrooms ® **T** ✱
sB&B⇌£22-£26 dB&B⇌£34-£40
30P (heated) squash snooker sauna solarium *xmas*
Scottish **V** Bar Lunch £3.55-£6.70alc Dinner £6.25-£12.65alc Last dinner 9pm
Credit Cards 1 2 3 5

EGHAM Surrey Map **04** TQ07

✕✕La Bonne Franquette 5 High St TW20 9EA ☎(0784)439494
Cosy Anglo-French restaurant and bar featuring seasonal dishes with a good wine list and efficient service.
Closed BH's
Lunch not served Sat
French 46 seats ✱ S% Lunch £12.50&alc Dinner £18-£32.50&alc Last lunch 2pm Last dinner 9.30pm 16P
Credit Cards 1 2 3 5

EGLWYSFACH Dyfed Map **06** SN69

★★★ 55% Ynyshir Hall
SY20 8TA
☎Glandyfi(065474)209

Comfortable manor house set amidst gardens next to RSPB bird sanctuary.

9rm(6⇌2)(1fb)1 CTV in all bedrooms **T**
sB&B⇌£30-£35 dB&B⇌£55-£60
20P
English & French **V** Lunch £15-£16 Dinner £15-£16 Last dinner 8pm
Credit Cards 1 2 3 5

EGREMONT Cumbria Map **11** NY01

★★★54% **Blackbeck Bridge Inn** CA22 2NY (Blackbeck 2.75m A595) ☎Beckermet(094684)661

After extensive refurbishment this hotel now offers an elegant carvery restaurant, a spacious and comfortable lounge bar and well appointed bedrooms.

22rm(21⇌1🚿)(1fb)1⊟ CTV in all bedrooms ® T ✱
sB&B⇌🚿£22-£39.50 dB&B⇌🚿£32-£49.50 ⊟
60P ❊
♀ Mainly grills V ♁ ⊈ Lunch £6.50 High tea £2.95-£6.50 Dinner £9.95&alc Last dinner 10pm
Credit Cards 1 2 3 5

ELCOT Berkshire Map **04** SU36

★★★65% **Elcot Park** RG16 8NJ (1m N off A4) (Best Western) ☎Kintbury(0488)58100 Telex no 846448 FAX 0488 58288

Smart hotel, popular with small conferences, set in a peaceful location. There are lots of extra facilities in the recently refurbished bedrooms. Quality cooking displays the flair of the chef.

19⇌Annexe18⇌(2fb)4⊟ CTV in all bedrooms ® T ✱
sB⇌£58-£68 dB⇌£68-£78 (room only) ⊟
(100P ❊ ℛ (hard) hot air ballooning at weekends ⌂ *xmas*
♀ English & Continental V ♁ ⊈ Lunch fr£15 Dinner fr£19.50 Last dinner 9.30pm
Credit Cards 1 2 3 5

ELGIN Grampian *Morayshire* Map **15** NJ26

★★★57% **Eight Acres** Sheriffmill IV30 3UN (Consort) ☎(0343)3077 due to change to 543077 Telex no 73347

This purpose-built hotel stands on the A96, on the western outskirts of the town. The bedrooms vary in size and are mainly functional, but those built in 1985 in conjunction with the sports and leisure complex are very tastefully appointed.

▶

57rm(33⇌24♠)(5fb) CTV in all bedrooms ® T
sB&B⇌♠£42-£47 dB&B⇌♠£60-£65 ⊟
(CTV 200P ✲ CFA ⊡(heated) squash snooker sauna solarium gymnasium *xmas*
♡ Scottish, French & Italian V ✿ ⊻ Lunch fr£6.50 High tea fr£6 Dinner fr£12.50 Last dinner 9pm
Credit Cards 1 2 3 5 £

★★★68% **Mansion House** The Haugh IV30 1AW
☎(0343)548811 FAX (0343) 547916
This mid-19th-century hotel is being extended to provide additional high-quality bedrooms and good leisure facilities. The accommodation is very comfortable, with the attractive restaurant offering cooking of a very good standard. A warm and friendly atmosphere is created by very helpful staff, personally supervised by Fernando Olivera, the proprietor.
18⇌♠(3fb)8⊟ CTV in all bedrooms ® T ✗
sB&B⇌♠£50-£60 dB&B⇌♠£80-£100 ⊟
(30P ✲ ⊡(heated) sauna solarium gymnasium ⌂ *xmas*
V ✿ ⊻ Lunch £10-£12.50&alc High tea £5-£10alc Dinner £15-£20alc Last dinner 9pm
Credit Cards 1 2 3

★★**Laichmoray** Station Rd IV30 1QR ☎(0343)547832
Friendly, commercial hotel with some good modern bedrooms.
32rm(11⇌11♠)(3fb) CTV in all bedrooms T ✱ S%
sB&B£24.50-£34.75 sB&B⇌♠£30-£34.75 dB&B£34-£38
dB&B⇌♠£40-£50 ⊟
CTV 60P ✲ pool table
V ✿ ⊻ Last high tea 6.30pm
Credit Cards 1 2 3 5

★★**Park House** South St IV30 1JB ☎(0343)547695
The basement restaurant of this impressive Georgian house on the western perimeter road enjoys a fine reputation, and the bedrooms are thoughtfully furnished and equipped (though rather compact in some cases).
6rm(2⇌4♠) CTV in all bedrooms ® T sB&B⇌♠£32-£35
dB&B⇌♠£44-£48 ⊟
(30P
♡ Scottish & French V ✿ ⊻ Lunch fr£5.50 High tea fr£5.50 Dinner £16.30-£19.50alc Last dinner 9.30pm
Credit Cards 1 2 3 5

★**St Leonards** Duff Av IV30 1QS ☎(0343)547350
Homely, commercial hotel in a residential area.
16rm(7⇌4♠)(2fb) CTV in all bedrooms ® ✱ sB&B£20
sB&B⇌♠£27.60-£30 dB&B£30 dB&B⇌♠£40-£50 ⊟
CTV 60P ✲
♡ Scottish & French V ✿ ⊻ Lunch £5.75-£6.50 High tea £4-£8 Dinner £11.50-£13 Last dinner 8.30pm
Credit Cards 1 3 £

ELLESMERE Shropshire Map **07** SJ33

★***Red Lion*** Church St SY12 0HD ☎(069171)2632 due to change to (0691) 622632
Comfortable, homely 17th-century inn with modern accommodation.
7rm(1♠)(1fb) CTV in all bedrooms ® ✗ (ex guide dogs)
12P
V ✿ ⊻ Last dinner 11pm
Credit Cards 1 2 3 5

ELLON Grampian *Aberdeenshire* Map **15** NJ93

★***Buchan*** ☎(0358)20208
A commercial/tourist hotel with neat, modern bedrooms.
17♠(2fb) CTV in all bedrooms ®
CTV 60P ♩ ♫
V ✿ ⊻

★***New Inn*** Market St AB4 9JD ☎(0358)20425
An historic inn, rebuilt in a modern style and overlooking the River Ythan. It offers pleasant, comfortable bedrooms and friendly informal service.
12rm(3⇌4♠)(2fb) CTV in all bedrooms ® T
63P
✿ ⊻ ⅟
Credit Cards 1 2 3 5

ELTERWATER Cumbria Map **07** NY30

★★★69% **Langdale Hotel & Country Club** LA22 9JR
☎Langdale(09667)302 FAX (09667) 694
This hotel combines stylish interiors and extensive leisure facilities within the 23 acres of landscaped woodlands and streams in which it stands. A commendable range of slate lodge and cottage bedrooms, which blend perfectly with the environment, have been tastefully decorated and furnished, some with spa baths. The pine-canopied Purdeys Restaurant offers interesting, imaginative cuisine, and service throughout is prompt and friendly.
53⇌♠(12fb) CTV in all bedrooms ® T ✗ (ex guide dogs) S%
sB&B⇌♠£96-£107 dB&B⇌♠£103.50-£115 ⊟
(100P ✲ ⊡(heated) ዖ (hard) ♩ squash snooker sauna solarium gymnasium croquet mountain bicycle hire ♫ ⌂ *xmas*
♡ International V ✿ ⊻ Sunday Lunch £13.50 Dinner £17.90-£19.50&alc Last dinner 10pm
Credit Cards 1 2 3 5

★★♛***Eltermere Country House*** LA22 9HY (On unclass rd between A593 & B5343)
☎Langdale(09667)207
Closed 25-26 Dec

Charming, peaceful old mansion, standing in its own grounds.

15rm(5⇌7♠) CTV in all bedrooms ®
25P ⛟ ✲ nc10 yrs
✿ ⅟ Last dinner 7.30pm
Credit Cards 1 3

★**Britannia Inn** LA22 9HP ☎Langdale(09667)210 & 382
Closed 25 & 26 Dec
With an extensive range of bar meals and real ales, this traditional little inn has great character and is very popular with hill walkers. Travellers will also appreciate the thoughtfully equipped bedrooms and excellent dinners, with an emphasis on fresh ingredients.
10rm(4♠) CTV in all bedrooms ® sB&B£17-£21
dB&B£34-£42 dB&B♠£39.50-£47.50
10P ⛟ bowling green ⌂
✿ ⊻ Bar Lunch £4.65-£6.95alc Dinner £12.25-£15alc Last dinner 7.30pm
Credit Cards 1 3

ELY Cambridgeshire Map **05** TL58

★★★63% **Fenlands Lodge** Soham Rd, Stuntney CB7 5TR (2m SE A142) ☎(0353)667047
Situated on the A142, 2 miles south of Ely, the restaurant is housed in the original farmhouse whilst the motel-style bedrooms are adjacent in low brick and tile buildings, set in a square.
Annexe9⇌♠ CTV in all bedrooms ® T ✱ sB&B⇌♠£45
dB&B⇌♠£57 ⊟
(25P *xmas*

☺ English & French V ♔ ☕ Lunch £11&alc High tea fr£5 Dinner £13&alc Last dinner 9.30pm
Credit Cards [1] [2] [3] [5] Ⓔ

★★**Lamb** 2 Lynn Rd CB7 4EJ (Queens Moat) ☎(0353)663574
The bulk of the cathedral dominates Ely, and close by is The Lamb Hotel, on a busy central road junction. The décor is light and fresh, bedrooms are comfortable and well-equipped and there is a choice of bars as well as restaurant and buttery. The staff are friendly and predominantly young.
32rm(31⇌1♠)(6fb)2⊟ CTV in all bedrooms **T** ✱
sB&B⇌♠£46-£50 dB&B£60-£62 dB&B⇌♠£60-£80 ⊟
☾ 2🚗 *xmas*
☺ English & French V ♔ ☕
Credit Cards [1] [2] [3] [5]

❀✕**Old Fire Engine House** 25 Saint Mary's St CB7 4ER ☎(0353)662582
Close to the cathedral in the centre of Ely, this restaurant once housed the city's fire engine. The emphasis is on fresh ingredients simply prepared and served. The menu features traditional English dishes – steak and kidney pie and beef braised in beer. Puddings are irresistable, and home-made ice creams are superb. Portions are generous and reasonably priced. Service is friendly and attentive.
Closed 2 wks fr 24 Dec & BH's
Dinner not served Sun
36 seats ✱ Lunch £11-£15alc Dinner £11-£15alc Last lunch 2pm Last dinner 9pm 8P ⚡

EMBLETON Northumberland Map **12** NU22

★★***Dunstanburgh Castle*** NE66 3UN ☎(066576)203
The family hotel stands in rural surroundings within easy reach of the sea.
17rm(9⇌)(3fb) ®
CTV 20P 1🚗 ⛟
☺ English & French ♔ ☕
Credit Cards [1] [3]

EMBOROUGH Somerset Map **03** ST65

★★***Court*** BA3 4SA ☎Stratton-on-the-Foss(0761)232237
This busy, little, country hotel, personally run by the owners, provides a good choice of menus with the emphasis on interesting dishes, fresh ingredients and careful cooking.
10rm(7⇌3♠)(2fb)2⊟ CTV in all bedrooms ® **T**
40P ✿
☺ English & French V ♔ ☕ ⚡ Last dinner 9.00pm
Credit Cards [1] [2] [3]

EMSWORTH Hampshire Map **04** SU70

★★★64% **Brookfield** Havant Rd PO10 7LF ☎(0243)373363
FAX (0243)376342
Closed 25 Dec-1 Jan
This friendly family-run hotel with good bedrooms has now been by-passed by the new road. The Hermitage Restaurant, completely refurbished, overlooks a colourful garden and offers table d'hôte and à la carte menus which represent good value for money.
31rm(25⇌6♠)1⊟ CTV in all bedrooms ® **T** ✖ (ex guide dogs) sB&B⇌♠£45-£48 dB&B⇌♠£58-£65 ⊟
☾ 80P ⛟ ✿
☺ English & French V ♔ ☕ Lunch £10.95&alc Dinner £10.95&alc Last dinner 9.30pm
Credit Cards [1] [2] [3] [5]

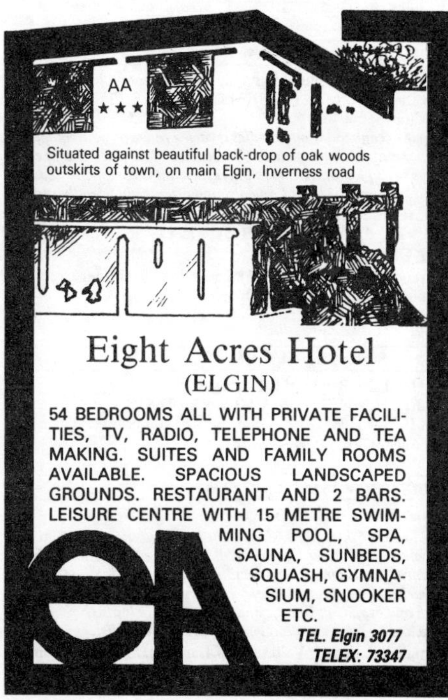

AA
★★★
Situated against beautiful back-drop of oak woods outskirts of town, on main Elgin, Inverness road
Eight Acres Hotel
(ELGIN)
54 BEDROOMS ALL WITH PRIVATE FACILITIES, TV, RADIO, TELEPHONE AND TEA MAKING. SUITES AND FAMILY ROOMS AVAILABLE. SPACIOUS LANDSCAPED GROUNDS. RESTAURANT AND 2 BARS. LEISURE CENTRE WITH 15 METRE SWIMMING POOL, SPA, SAUNA, SUNBEDS, SQUASH, GYMNASIUM, SNOOKER ETC.
8A
TEL. Elgin 3077
TELEX: 73347

✕✕*36 On The Quay* 57 South St PO10 7EG
☎Chichester(0243)375592 & 372257
Don't be confused by the name – this charming little restaurant is actually at 57 South Street, but it is on the quay. In the 3 small, but stylish interconnecting dining rooms, Vivian Abady offers some unusual combinations of flavours, the more simple dishes being the most successful. Daily specials include lobsters from the tank, oysters, turbot with a herb crust and breast of pheasant with cranberry sauce. The cooking, in the modern British style, tends to be rich, and at times cloying, but the combination of originality, location and service (diners press the bell beside each table for attention) make a visit here well worthwhile.
Lunch not served Mon & Sat
V 36 seats Last dinner 9pm 6P ⅍

ENFIELD Greater London Map **04** TQ39

Telephone codes are due to change on 6th May 1990. See page 421.
★★***Holtwhites*** 92 Chase Side EN2 0QN ☎01-363 0124
Telex no 299670
Small, privatly owned hotel with friendly atmosphere.
30⇌⌐(2fb) CTV in all bedrooms **T**
(CTV 30P 4🚗 ⛟ nc4yrs
♉ International **V** ♡ ⚓ Last dinner 8pm
Credit Cards [1] [2] [3] [5]

✕✕**Norfolk** 80 London Rd EN2 6HU ☎01-363 0979 & 01-363 1153
This is an old fashioned, but friendly, restaurant with roasts and flambé dishes featured on the menu. The wines are reasonably priced.
Closed Sun, 1st 3 wks Aug & BH's
Lunch not served Sat
Dinner not served Mon
♉ English & French **V** 90 seats Last lunch 2pm Last dinner 10pm ₽
Credit Cards [1] [2] [3] [4] [5]

EPPING Essex Map **05** TL40

★★★**69% Post House** High Rd, Bell Common CM16 4DG (Trusthouse Forte) ☎(0378)73137 Telex no 81617
FAX (0378) 560402
Annexe accommodation provides a varied range of well-equipped bedrooms at this modern hotel. The choice of set price or à la carte menus in its pleasantly-appointed restaurant is complemented by a simple, reasonably-priced wine list and attentively friendly service.
Annexe82⇌⌐(22fb)⅍in 11 bedrooms CTV in all bedrooms ® **T** ✱ S% sB⇌⌐£65-£75 dB⇌⌐£75-£83 (room only) ⊟
(95P CFA ♫ *xmas*
♉ French **V** ♡ ⚓ ⅍ Lunch £8.25-£9.75&alc Dinner £14.50&alc Last dinner 10.30pm
Credit Cards [1] [2] [3] [4] [5]

EPSOM Surrey Map **04** TQ26

★★**Heathside** Brighton Rd KT20 6BW
☎Burgh Heath(0737)353355 Telex no 929908
FAX (0737) 370857
(For full entry see Burgh Heath)

ERBISTOCK Clwyd Map **07** SJ34

✕**Boat Inn** LL13 0DL ☎Bangor-on-Dee(0978)780143
This lovely 16th-century, stone-built inn stands near the church on the banks of the River Dee. A small flag-stoned bar leads to the basement restaurant, where the table d'hôte and à la carte menus are varied. Chef, Martin Rae, creates interesting sauces, such as peach and brandy or orange and mango. There is also a vegetarian menu and a recent introduction is an organic wine list.
♉ English & French **V** 70 seats ✱ Lunch fr£8.95&alc Dinner fr£10.95&alc Last lunch 2.15pm Last dinner 9pm 50P
Credit Cards [1] [2] [3] [5]

ERISKA Strathclyde *Argyllshire* Map **10** NM94

★★★🏠 **ISLE OF ERISKA**
PA37 1SD
☎Ledaig(063172)371
Telex no 777040
Closed Dec-mid Mar

Peacefully located 4 miles off the A828 Oban/Fort William road on its own private island, this hotel provides above all, quiet and seclusion, and the owners Robin and Sheena Buchanan-Smith are keen to preserve this atmosphere. Accommodation is in traditional country house type bedrooms, all named after islands. Most guests enjoy relaxing in the peaceful lounges, whilst for the energetic there are facilities for tennis, croquet and water-skiing. Improvements have been made to the food; chef Simon Burns now presents a choice of starter and main course, usually fish, to augment the otherwise set six course menu. Breakfasts continue to excel with self-service from chafing dishes on the sideboard. All bread is homemade, as are jams and preserves. The garden continues to yield good vegetables and the cream from the hotel's Jersey cow herd is rich and plentiful. After a stay here guests are almost guaranteed to leave feeling rested and re-charged.
16⇌(1fb) CTV in all bedrooms ® **T** sB&B⇌£67-£130 dB&B⇌£110-£130 ⊟
(36P ⛟ ✲ 𝒫 (hard) ∪ croquet watersports 🏠
Lunch £6.50-£11alc High tea £13 Dinner £32 Last dinner 8.30pm
Credit Cards [1] [2] [3]

ERMINGTON Devon Map **02** SX65

★★**Ermewood House** Totnes Rd PL21 9NS (Exec Hotel)
☎Modbury(0548)830741
Closed 23 Dec-9 Jan
Friendly, country-house-style hotel catering for the tourist and commercial trade.
12rm(10⇌2⌐)(1fb)1⊟ CTV in all bedrooms ® **T** ✱
sB&B⇌⌐£35 dB&B⇌⌐£47.50 ⊟
15P ⛟ ✲
♉ English & Continental ⅍ Dinner £14.50 Last dinner 8.30pm
Credit Cards [1] [3] Ⓔ

See advertisement under PLYMOUTH

ERSKINE Strathclyde *Renfrewshire* Map **11** NS47

★★★**64% Crest Hotel-Erskine Bridge** North Barr, Inchinnan PA8 6AN (Crest) ☎041-812 0123 Telex no 777713 FAX 041-812 7642
Standing on the banks of the Clyde with views over Erskine Bridge, this modern hotel is designed for the residental conference trade and business clientele. There is an extensive leisure complex.
168⇌⌐(4fb)⅍in 35 bedrooms CTV in all bedrooms ® **T** ✱
sB⇌⌐£60-£72 dB⇌⌐£80-£85 (room only) ⊟
Lift (300P ✲ CFA ▭(heated) snooker sauna solarium gymnasium *xmas*
V ♡ ⚓ ⅍ Lunch £10.50-£12&alc Dinner £14.50-£16&alc Last dinner 10pm
Credit Cards [1] [2] [3] [4] [5]

For key to symbols see the inside front cover.

ESHER Surrey

See LONDON plan 5*B1*(page 412). **Telephone codes are due to change on 6th May 1990. See page 421.**

★★**Haven** Portsmouth Rd KT10 9AR (1 m NE on A307) (Inter) ☏01-398 0023

This pleasant family-run commercial hotel is near Sandown Park. It provides a homely atmosphere, with refurbished bedrooms providing modern facilities. Good, home-cooked meals are served in the nicely appointed dining room.

16rm(8⇨8↱)Annexe4rm(2⇨2↱)(4fb) CTV in all bedrooms ® T sB&B⇨↱£50-£60 dB&B⇨↱£60-£70 ⊟

20P 1🚗 ⛟

☋ International V ♧ ☕ Bar Lunch £3.50-£5 High tea £3.50-£5 Dinner £8.50-£10 Last dinner 8.30pm

Credit Cards 1 2 3 4 5

✕✕**Good Earth** 14-18 High St KT10 9RT ☏(0372)62489 & 66681

An attractive restaurant where pleasant, attentive staff serve well-prepared regional Chinese dishes. Our inspector particularly enjoyed the Beef with Pickled Ginger. The extensive menu is complemented by a selection of typical Chinese beverages.

Closed 24-27 Dec

☋ Chinese V 100 seats ✱ Lunch £13.50-£25 Dinner £13.50-£25 Last lunch 2.30pm Last dinner midnight P̸

Credit Cards 1 2 3 5

ESKDALE GREEN Cumbria Map **07** NY10

★★**Bower House Inn** CA19 1TD (Best Western) ☏Eskdale(09403)244

This country inn is popular with tourists and hillwalkers. Most of the bedrooms are contained in 2 annexe buildings.

5rmAnnexe17⇨↱(3fb) CTV in all bedrooms ® ✗ sB&B⇨↱fr£32 dB&B⇨↱fr£48 ⊟

60P ✲ *xmas*

V ♧ Bar Lunch fr£6 Dinner fr£14 Last dinner 8.30pm

Credit Cards 1 3

ESKDALEMUIR Dumfries & Galloway *Dumfriesshire* Map **11** NY29

★★**Hart Manor** DG13 0QQ ☏(03873)73217

Closed 25 Dec

Remotely situated in beautiful countryside, this charming small hotel offers neat, comfortable bedrooms and reliable meals. Friendly and attentive service is provided by the Medcalf family, who offer true hospitality to their guests.

7rm(2⇨3↱)(2fb) CTV in all bedrooms ® ✱ sB&Bfr£22 sB&B⇨↱fr£27 dB&Bfr£43 dB&B⇨↱fr£48 ⊟

CTV 30P ⛟ ✲ ♪ deer stalking shooting

V ♧ ⅟ Lunch fr£6.10alc Dinner £12.50-£16 Last dinner 8pm

ETTINGTON Warwickshire Map **04** SP24

★★🏛**The Chase Hotel at Ettington** Banbury Rd CV37 7NZ (Best Western)

☏Stratford-upon-Avon(0789)740000

Telex no 312241

FAX (0789) 740942

Closed 26-31 Dec & 1 Jan

At the time of going to print, we learned of a change of ownership at The Chase, and we are unable to comment on its new style of operation. However, we do know that the Victorian building has undergone many improvements recently.

12rm(11⇨1↱)(2fb) CTV in all bedrooms ® T ✗ (ex guide dogs) S% sB&B⇨↱£55-£60 dB&B⇨↱£68-£70 ⊟

50P ⛟ ✲

♧ Lunch £11.50 Dinner £15.50-£18.95 Last dinner 9pm

Credit Cards 1 2 3 £

EVERCREECH Somerset Map **03** ST63

★★**Pecking Mill Inn & Hotel** BA4 6PG (On A371 1m W of village) (Best Western) ☏(0749)830336

A tollhouse dating back to the 16th century has been sympathetically extended to create this small, personally run hotel. The bedrooms, though compact, are well-equipped. There is also a cosy bar and a busy restaurant.

6↱ CTV in all bedrooms ® T sB&B↱£27.50 dB&B↱£38

23P ⛟

☋ Mainly grills ♧ Lunch £9.50-£15alc Dinner £9.50-£15alc Last dinner 10pm

Credit Cards 1 2 3 5

EVERSHOT Dorset Map **03** ST50

★★**Summer Lodge** DT2 0JR ☏(0935)83424

Closed 2-18 Jan

11⇨Annexe6⇨(1fb) CTV in 6bedrooms ® T ✱ sB&B⇨£60-£77.50 dB&B⇨£100-£145 ⊟

CTV 40P ⛟ ✲ ⛱(heated) 🎾 (hard & grass) croquet nc8yrs *xmas*

V ♧ ☕ Lunch £12.50 Dinner £18.50 Last dinner 8.30pm

Credit Cards 1 2 3

E

EVESHAM Hereford & Worcester Map 04 SP04

★★★66% **The Evesham** Coopers Ln, off Waterside WR11 6DA ☎(0386)765566 Telex no 339342 FAX (0386) 765443
Closed 25 & 26 Dec
Situated close to the river and convenient for the town centre, this is a pleasant family-run hotel with attractive gardens. Built as a mansion house in 1540, it now offers comfortable, modern accommodation, complemented by an imaginative menu and an extensive selection of wines.
40rm(36⇌4♪)(1fb) CTV in all bedrooms ® T ✱ S% sB&B⇌♪£40-£48 dB&B⇌♪£62-£66 ⊟
50P ✿ croquet putting
♀ International V ♡ ☐ Lunch £6-£21.50alc Dinner £13-£21.50alc Last dinner 9.30pm
Credit Cards 1 2 3 5

★★★63% **Northwick Arms** Waterside WR11 6BT ☎(0386)40322 Telex no 333686 FAX (0386) 41070
This small hotel is set next to the River Avon, south-east of the town centre. The bedrooms are modern, comfortable and well equipped, and the public areas are pleasant and attractive. The hotel caters for tourists and business people, and offers a small conference facility.
25rm(22⇌3♪)1⊞ CTV in all bedrooms ® T sB&B⇌♪fr£50 dB&B⇌♪fr£60 ⊟
☾ 90P
♀ English & French V ♡ ☐ Lunch £11-£15alc Dinner £11-£12&alc Last dinner 10pm
Credit Cards 1 2 3 5

★**Park View** Waterside WR11 6BS ☎(0386)442639
Closed 24 Dec-3 Jan
Standing by the River Avon, the small, family-run hotel offers guests a warm welcome.
29rm(2fb) sB&B£15-£16.50 dB&B£28.60-£32
CTV 40P
♡ ☐ Sunday Lunch £7.25-£9 Dinner £7.25-£9.50 Last dinner 7pm
Credit Cards 1 3 £

EXEBRIDGE Somerset Map 03 SS92

★**Anchor Inn** TA22 9AZ ☎Dulverton(0398)23433
Recently refurbished, this hotel on the banks of the River Exe offers smart, modern bedrooms, most of which have good views. There are 2 bars and a cosy, country style dining room.
6rm(2⇌4♪)(2fb)1⊞ CTV in all bedrooms ® T sB&B⇌♪fr£30 dB&B⇌♪£50-£53
CTV 100P ✿ ⌐
V ♡ Sunday Lunch fr£6.50

EXETER Devon Map 03 SX99

See **Town Plan Section**
See also **Stoke Canon & Topsham**

★★★71% ***Buckerell Lodge Crest*** Topsham Rd EX2 4SQ (Crest) ☎(0392)52451 Telex no 42410 FAX (0392) 412114
Close to the city centre, this attractive hotel sits in its own grounds and offers well-equipped bedrooms. An extensive choice of well-cooked, imaginative dishes is available from à la carte and table d'hôte menus in the friendly restaurant. The wine list carries a wide selection.
54⇌♪(2fb)⚡in 8 bedrooms CTV in all bedrooms ® T
☾ 200P ✿ ✿
♀ English & French V ♡ ☐ ⚡ Last dinner 9.45pm
Credit Cards 1 2 3 4 5

★★★61% **Countess Wear Lodge** Topsham Rd, Exeter bypass EX2 6HE (Queens Moat) ☎Topsham(039287)5441 Telex no 42551 FAX (0392) 876174
The motel-style bedrooms, the majority of which are on the ground floor, are set around an open car park. They have recently been refurbished to provide a high standard of accommodation and necessary facilities for the business traveller. The traditional dining room, in the main building, offers an à la carte menu whilst Reillys Food and Wine Bar provides home-made fare and light snacks.
44⇌♪(1fb)⚡in 4 bedrooms CTV in all bedrooms ® T ✱ sB&B⇌♪fr£43.50 dB&B⇌♪fr£55 ⊟
☾ 120P CFA ⚲ (hard) *xmas*
♀ English & French V ♡ ☐ Lunch £11.50-£18alc Dinner £5.75-£12.95&alc Last dinner 10pm
Credit Cards 1 2 3 5 £

★★★53% **Devon Motel** Exeter By Pass, Matford EX2 8XU (Brend) ☎(0392)59268 Telex no 42551 FAX (0392) 413142
Situated close to the Exeter bypass, with modern extensions.
Annexe41rm(35⇌4♪)(3fb) CTV in all bedrooms ® T sB&B⇌♪£42-£47 dB&B⇌♪£55-£60 ⊟
☾ 250P ♫
♀ English & French ♡ ☐ S% Lunch £7&alc Dinner £7-£16alc Last dinner 9pm
Credit Cards 1 2 3 5

★★★50% **Exeter Arms Toby** Rydon Ln, Middlemoor PH7 4BP (Toby) ☎(0392)435353 FAX (0392) 420826
Modern purpose-built complex alongside primary road on outskirts of city.
37⇌♪(6fb)⚡in 10 bedrooms CTV in all bedrooms ® T ✗ (ex guide dogs) ✱ S10% sB&B⇌♪fr£37 dB&B⇌♪fr£47 ⊟
☾ 380P
V ♡ ☐ ⚡ S% Lunch £5.95-£6.50&alc Dinner fr£5.95&alc Last dinner 10pm
Credit Cards 1 2 3 5

★★★54% **Gipsy Hill** Gipsy Hill Ln, Pinhoe EX1 3RN (3m E on B3181) (Consort) ☎(0392)65252 Telex no 57515 FAX (0392)64302
Closed 25-30 Dec
Located in a peaceful position with views over East Devon, yet convenient for the city and airport. There are well equipped bedrooms and service is friendly in this hotel, which is popular with businessmen.
20rm(19⇌1♪)(3fb)2⊞⚡in 3 bedrooms CTV in all bedrooms ® T ✱ sB&B⇌♪£40-£48 dB&B⇌♪£55-£65 ⊟
☾ 60P ✿ ♫
♀ English & French V ♡ ☐
Credit Cards 1 2 3 5

★★★64% **Granada Lodge** Moor Ln, Sandygate EX2 4AR (Granada) ☎(0392)74044 FAX (0392) 410406
This modern, purpose-built hotel on the edge of the motorway service area, has comfortable bedrooms, a small restaurant and conference facilities.
52⇌(7fb)⚡in 8 bedrooms CTV in all bedrooms ® T ✗ (ex guide dogs) S% sB⇌£28-£32 dB⇌£32-£38 (room only)
☾ CTV 80P ✿
♀ English & French V ♡ ☐ ⚡ S% Lunch £5-£8 Dinner £5-£12alc Last dinner 9.30pm
Credit Cards 1 2 3 5

See advertisement on page 273

★★★56% **Imperial** St David's Hill EX4 4JX ☎(0392)211811 Telex no 42551 FAX (0392) 420906
Built as a mansion during the Queen Anne period, this hotel is situated in five acres of spacious sheltered grounds.
27rm(21⇌2♪)(1fb) CTV in all bedrooms T sB&B£28 sB&B⇌♪£45-£50 dB&B£40 dB&B⇌♪£60 ⊟
☾ CTV 70P 3🚘 ✿ CFA riding, water ski-ing, windsurfing ♫ ⌂
♀ European V ♡ ☐ Lunch £8.75-£10.75 High tea fr£3.50 Dinner £11.50-£17 Last dinner 9pm
Credit Cards 1 2 3 5 £

Book as early as possible for busy holiday periods.

Gipsy Hill Hotel

GIPSY HILL LANE (Nr. Sowton Ind. Estate)
PINHOE, EXETER, DEVON EX1 3RN
Tel. (0392) 65252

* Country House Hotel in lovely gardens with views over Devon countryside.
* Close to Exeter Airport and City Centre.
* Convenient to M5 juction 30 (1 mile).
* All the centrally heated rooms have private bathroom, colour TV, telephone (direct dial), radio, tea and coffee making, trouser press and hair dryer.
* Excellent cuisine from our Table d'Hôte and à la Carte.
* Bar snacks.
* A variety of meeting rooms and function suites for up to 120 guests.
* Personally managed by proprietor Geoffrey Stockman, MHCIMA

HOTEL · RESTAURANT · CONFERENCE CENTRE

★★★

398 Topsham Road, Exeter, Devon, EX2 6HE
Telephone: (0392) 875441 Fax: (0392) 876174

Enjoy the warmth and friendliness of the West Country with the Kitchen Garden Restaurant and Reilly's Food and Wine Bar at the Countess Wear Lodge, Hotel, Restaurant and Conference Centre.
A character hotel ideally situated 1 mile from the M5 (Junction 30) and 2½ miles from the City Centre.
Children sharing parents' room – FREE.

Rates (based on twin occupancy): Bed and Breakfast from £21 per guest. Dinner, Bed and Breakfast from £30 per guest.

For more information please contact: David Adams

The Devon Motel

AA ★★★

ENJOY LUXURY 3 STAR COMFORTS IN DEVON'S HEARTLAND

Conveniently situated close to Exeter by-pass and town centre with easy access to the M5 – yet surrounded by beautiful countryside.

Family owned and managed offering excellent service and value.

Very popular bar, entertainments and function rooms. All rooms with colour T.V., radio, direct dial telephones, coffee facilities, en suite shower/bath etc. First class menu and wine list. **For free colour brochure contact: Mr. A. Brend, Devon Motel, Matford, Exeter, Devon. EX32 8XU Tel: (0392) 59268 Fax No: (0392) 413142**

The Barton Cross Hotel

xvii century

17th Century Charm – 20th Century Luxury

The only six bedroom hotel in Great Britain with a ★★★ AA rating.
British Tourist Authority Commended Hotel.

International Standard Accommodation with Superb Cuisine. Set in glorious Devon Countryside yet only five miles Exeter.

Easy access Dartmoor, Exmoor and Coast.

Relaxing Weekend and Midweek Breaks. Christmas House Party.

BARTON CROSS HOTEL & RESTAURANT
at Huxham, Exeter, EX5 4EJ
Telephone: (0392) 841245
Telex: 42603 Fax: (0392) 50402

★★★66% ***Rougemont*** Queen St EX4 3SP (Mount Charlotte) ☎(0392)54982 Telex no 42455
Recently modernised hotel in a central position, catering for the tourist and commercial trade.
99⇌♠(5fb)⊁in 13 bedrooms CTV in all bedrooms ® T
Lift ☾ 40P CFA
English & French V ♣ ☕ ⊁ Last high tea 5pm
Credit Cards 1 2 3 5

★★★73% ***Royal Clarence*** Cathedral Yard EX1 1HD (Norfolk Capital) ☎(0392)58464 Telex no 23241
After almost a year's closure and a top-to-toe refurbishment, this character city-centre hotel now provides an exceptionally high standard of accommodation. The upgrading has been sympathetically carried out to retain many original features, and the well-equipped bedrooms are individually styled. All departments are well managed, with willing and friendly staff. The modern-style cuisine shows promise, but at the time of going to press was very much in the formative stage.
62rm(56⇌6♠)(4fb) CTV in all bedrooms ® T
Lift ☾ 20P CFA
English & French V ♣ ☕
Credit Cards 1 2 3 4 5

★★★66% **St Olaves Court** Mary Arches St EX4 3AZ ☎(0392)217736 FAX (0392) 413054
Closed 25 Dec-4 Jan
Built in 1827 and standing in its own walled garden, this city-centre hotel is only 300 yards from the cathedral. The bedrooms are well equipped and attractively decorated. The popular restaurant is most attractive, and the food is enjoyable and imaginative.
13rm(10⇌1♠)Annexe4⇌(4fb) CTV in all bedrooms ® T ✈
S% sB&B£32 sB&B⇌♠£46-£50 dB&B⇌♠£39-£64 ⊟
☾ CTV 15P 2🚗 ⊞ ❊
French V ♣ ☕ S% Lunch fr£8.95&alc Dinner fr£13.95&alc Last dinner 9.30pm
Credit Cards 1 2 3 5 £

★★★62% ***White Hart*** 65 South St EX1 1EE ☎(0392)79897 Telex no 42521
Closed Xmas day & Boxing day
The main building of this city-centre hotel is steeped in history, and the public areas and bars are full of character. Most of the well-equipped bedrooms are in a new wing. The first-floor restaurant offers an extensive à la carte menu, with simpler fare available in the wine bar and coffee shop.
61rm(42⇌16♠) CTV in 60bedrooms T ✈ (ex guide dogs)
Lift ☾ CTV 80P ⊞
♣ ☕ Last dinner 9.15pm
Credit Cards 1 2 3 5

★★**Fairwinds Hotel** EX6 7UD ☎(0392)832911
(For full entry see Kennford)

★★**Red House** 2 Whipton Village Rd EX4 8AR ☎(0392)56104
This is a small commercial hotel on the outskirts of the city, and provides comfortable bedrooms and popular bars. There is an extensive à la carte menu, as well as table d'hôte and bar snacks.
12rm(7⇌5♠)(2fb) CTV in all bedrooms ® T ✱
sB&B⇌♠£23-£32 dB&B⇌♠£35-£42 ⊟
28P
English & French V ♣ ☕ Lunch fr£6.50 High tea fr£2.50 Dinner fr£7.50&alc Last dinner 9.30pm
Credit Cards 1 3 £

★★**St Andrews** 28 Alphington Rd EX2 8HN (Exec Hotel) ☎(0392)76784 & 50249
Closed Xmas/New Year
Comfortable, family-run hotel with good home cooking. The bright modern bedrooms have cable television facility.
17rm(7⇌10♠)(2fb) CTV in all bedrooms ® T
sB&B⇌♠£31-£38.50 dB&B⇌♠£48-£57 ⊟
20P ⊞
♣ ☕ Bar Lunch £2-£4 Dinner £7.50-£18alc Last dinner 8.15pm
Credit Cards 1 2 3

○**The Forte Hotel** Southernhay East EX1 1QF (Trusthouse Forte) ☎(0392)412812 FAX (0392)413549
This luxury city-centre hotel is located near to the cathedral and the Georgian terraces of Southernhay and is due to open in Autumn 1989.
110⇌

EXMOUTH Devon Map **03** SY08

★★★58% **The Imperial** The Esplanade EX8 2SW (Trusthouse Forte) ☎(0395)274761
Stands in four acres of gardens, facing south.
58⇌(9fb)⊁in 4 bedrooms CTV in all bedrooms ® T
sB⇌fr£60 dB⇌fr£82 (room only) ⊟
Lift ☾ 55P ⊞ ❊ ⇒(heated) ♪ (hard) *xmas*
V ♣ ☕ ⊁ Sunday Lunch fr£7.50 Dinner fr£12.50&alc Last dinner 9pm
Credit Cards 1 2 3 4 5

★★★57% **Royal Beacon** The Beacon EX8 2AF (Best Western) ☎(0395)264886 Telex no 94016961 FAX (0395) 268890
Sympathetically modernised Georgian posting house, overlooking the sea.
35rm(32⇌3♠)(3fb)2⊟⊁in 1 bedroom CTV in all bedrooms ® T sB&B⇌♠£36-£40 dB&B⇌♠£62-£68 ⊟
Lift CTV 20P 10🚗 CFA snooker ♧ *xmas*
English & French V ♣ ☕ ⊁ Lunch £7.50 High tea £2.75 Dinner £10.75 Last dinner 9.30pm
Credit Cards 1 2 3 4 5 £

★★

Ebford House Hotel

Exmouth Road, Ebford, Devon EX3 0QH
TEL. Exeter (0392) 877658

A beautifully restored Georgian country house set in lovely gardens in rural Devon. Our fine restaurant is renowned for its imaginative cuisine, quality and presentation, and service. Central for Exeter, Dartmoor and beaches.

BTA Highly Commended.
Ashley Courtenay Recommended.

See gazetteer under Topsham

SALSTON MANOR HOTEL

OTTERY ST MARY, NR EXETER, DEVON

AA ★★★

Ashley Courtenay Recommended

Former home of the Coleridge family, set in 6 acres of beautiful East Devon countryside. An ideal base from which you can explore the local countryside, towns, villages and beaches, all of which are only a few minutes drive away. All 27 bedrooms have en suite bathrooms, colour televisions, trouser presses and hair dryers. Indoor heated swimming pool and two squash courts. Special discounts at local golf courses; private salmon fishing, clay pigeon shooting can be arranged. Week-end breaks available.

Please phone 0404 815581 for tariff and brochure

St Olaves Court Hotel

AA★★★

The Country House Hotel
In The Heart Of The City

A small, exclusive, Georgian Hotel set in its own delightful walled garden.
The candlelit Golsworthy's Restaurant has fast earned a reputation as the leading place to eat in the city. Nouvelle and classical French cuisine are served in a warm intimate atmosphere.
The restaurant and cocktail bar overlook the pond and gardens.
Helpful friendly staff and the many facilities available will make your stay a delightful experience.

MARY ARCHES STREET
Exeter EX4 3AZ Tel: 217736

GOLSWORTHY'S
RESTAURANT

GRANADA
Hotel
EXETER

Granada Hotel
Moor Lane,
Sandygate, Exeter,
Devon EX2 4AR
Tel: (0392) 74044
Fax: (0392) 410406

AA★★★ ETB

Close to J30 of M5

A high standard of accommodation at competitive prices

- 75 bedrooms with private bathroom, colour television, radio, wake-up alarm, tea & coffee making facilities and direct dial telephone
- Platters Restaurant, Lounge and Bar
- Conference Facilities for up to 60 people
- Syndicate Rooms
- Ample free parking

For further information or central reservations call (05255) 5555

★★**Barn** Foxholes Hill, off Marine Dr EX8 2DF ☎(0395)274411
Set in its own well-kept gardens, this hotel occupies an elevated site and commands excellent sea views. Bedrooms are clean and bright and there is a comfortable lounge and informal reception bar. Good plain home cooking and a warm welcome are offered to guests.
11rm(8⇨1↱)(4fb) CTV in all bedrooms ® ✗
sB&B⇨↱£29-£33 dB&B⇨↱£48-£56 ⊟
30P 3🚗(£1 per night) ⊞ ✲ ⛆ ⚲ (grass) croquet *xmas*
V ✧ ☕ ⚟ Lunch £7.25-£11.50&alc High tea fr£5.75 Dinner fr£11.50&alc Last dinner 8pm
Credit Cards [1] [3] £

★**Aliston House** 58 Salterton Rd EX8 3EW ☎(0395)274119
The Aperitif Bar of this friendly, welcoming hotel features an old, black-leaded range. Throughout, rooms are attractively decorated and the standard of service is good.
12rm(2⇨5↱)Annexe2↱(2fb) CTV in all bedrooms ®
sB&B£18-£20 sB&B⇨↱£20-£22 dB&B£34-£36
dB&B⇨↱£38-£40 ⊟
CTV 16P ⌂ *xmas*
V ✧ ☕ Lunch fr£5.50&alc High tea £2.25-£3 Dinner fr£7&alc Last dinner 8.30pm

FAIRBOURNE Gwynedd Map **06** SH61

★★**Brackenhurst** LL38 2HX ☎(0341)250226
Country house whose high position affords good views over the Mawddach Estuary.
10rm(3⇨1↱)(2fb) CTV in all bedrooms ® **T** sB&Bfr£18.50 dB&Bfr£37 dB&B⇨↱fr£40 ⊟
CTV 11P ⊞ ✲ *xmas*
V ✧ ☕ ⚟ Lunch £5-£7.50 Dinner £8-£9 Last dinner 8pm
Credit Cards [5]

FAIRFORD Gloucestershire Map **04** SP10

★★★58% **Hyperion House** London St GL7 4AH (Consort)
☎Cirencester(0285)712349 & 712449 FAX (0285) 713126
RS New Year & 1st wk Jan
A Cotswold-stone hotel offers accommodation of a high standard, many of its bedrooms having recently been upgraded to boast quality fabrics and fine furniture. Imaginative food, making good use of fresh produce and catering for all palates, is complemented by friendly, caring service.
27rm(25⇨2↱)Annexe6rm(4fb) CTV in 27bedrooms ® **T** ✱
sB&B⇨↱£44.50-£55.50 dB&B⇨↱£55-£65 ⊟
40P ✲ *xmas*
☋ English & French **V** ✧ ☕ Lunch £7.50-£15 Dinner £13.50-£15.50&alc Last dinner 9.30pm
Credit Cards [1] [2] [3] [5] £

FAIRY CROSS Devon Map **02** SS42

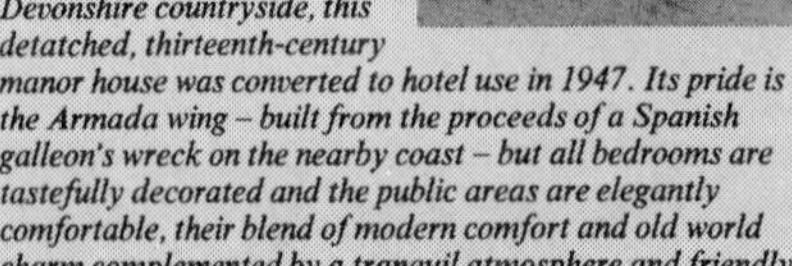

★★★ 71% ***Portledge***
EX39 5BX (off A39) (Best Western)

☎Horns Cross(02375)262
Telex no 265451
FAX (02375) 717

Steeped in history and surrounded by beautiful Devonshire countryside, this detached, thirteenth-century manor house was converted to hotel use in 1947. Its pride is the Armada wing – built from the proceeds of a Spanish galleon's wreck on the nearby coast – but all bedrooms are tastefully decorated and the public areas are elegantly comfortable, their blend of modern comfort and old world charm complemented by a tranquil atmosphere and friendly

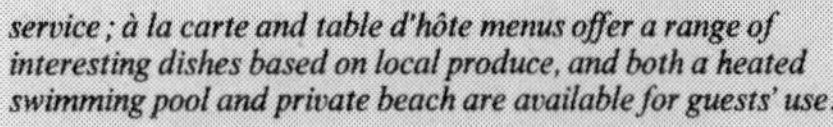

service; à la carte and table d'hôte menus offer a range of interesting dishes based on local produce, and both a heated swimming pool and private beach are available for guests' use.

25⇨↱(5fb)1⊠ CTV in all bedrooms **T**
CTV 40P ✲ CFA ⛆(heated) ⚲ (hard) ⚓ table tennis pool table ⌂
☋ English & French **V** ✧ ☕ Last dinner 8.45pm
Credit Cards [1] [2] [3] [5]

See advertisement under BIDEFORD

FAKENHAM Norfolk Map **09** TF92

★★**Crown** Market Place NR21 9BP (Berni/Chef & Brewer)
☎(0328)51418
A 17th-century coaching inn has been sympathetically restored to provide modern facilities; it has lost none of its original character, and the bar features a 'listed' fireplace.
11rm(5⇨6↱) CTV in all bedrooms ® **T** ✗ (ex guide dogs)
sB&B⇨↱£36 dB&B⇨↱£48 ⊟
25P
V ✧ ☕ ⚟ Lunch £8 Dinner £9 Last dinner 9.30pm
Credit Cards [1] [2] [3] [5]

★★**Old Mill** Bridge St NR21 9AY ☎(0328)2100
Many original features have been preserved in this attractive conversion of a former mill house. The friendly hotel now features Thai food cooked by the propriotor's wife.
9↱1⊠ CTV in all bedrooms ® **T** ✗
30P ⊞ ⚓
☋ International ✧ ☕
Credit Cards [1] [2] [3] [5] £

FALKIRK Central *Stirlingshire* Map **11** NS87

★★★59% **Stakis Park** Arnot Hill, Camelon Rd FK1 5RY (Stakis) ☎(0324)28331 Telex no 776502 FAX (0324) 611593
Modern purpose-built business and tourist hotel on the edge of the town. It offers a choice of bars, good function facilities and well-equipped bedrooms which have been upgraded to a comfortable standard.
55⇨↱(3fb)⚟in 12 bedrooms CTV in all bedrooms ® **T**
sB⇨↱fr£55 dB⇨↱fr£68 (room only) ⊟
Lift ☾ 151P CFA ♫
☋ English, French & Italian **V** ✧ ☕ ⚟ Lunch £3.50-£6.50 Dinner fr£11.50&alc Last dinner 9.45pm
Credit Cards [1] [2] [3] [5] £

✕**Pierre's** 140 Graham's Rd FK2 7BQ ☎(0324)35843
Closed Sun, Mon & 25-26 Dec & 1-2 Jan
Lunch not served Sat
☋ French 38 seats ✱ Lunch £4.60-£6.10&alc Dinner £10.50&alc Last lunch 2.15pm Last dinner 9.30pm 12P
Credit Cards [1] [2] [3] [5]

FALMOUTH Cornwall & Isles of Scilly Map **02** SW83

See **Town Plan Section**
See also **Mawnan Smith**
★★★50% ***Bay*** Cliff Rd TR11 4NU ☎(0326)312094
Telex no 45262 FAX (0326) 319533
Closed Nov-Feb
Large, traditional hotel on the sea front, overlooking Gyllynvase beach, yet close to the town centre.
36⇨(3fb) CTV in all bedrooms ® **T**
Lift ☾ 50P ✲ ⛆(heated) sauna solarium nc12yrs
☋ English & French ✧ ☕ ⚟ Last dinner 9pm
Credit Cards [1] [2] [3] [5]

★★★57% ***Falmouth*** TR11 4NZ ☎(0326)312671 Telex no 45262 FAX (0326) 319533
Closed Xmas
An elegant hotel with an outdoor swimming pool in its grounds overlooks the beaches and harbour of Falmouth. Bedrooms with good facilities and warm, comfortable public areas attract commercial traveller and holidaymaker alike. The spacious dining room offers a table d'hôte menu of well-prepared dishes, and both conference facilities and a ballroom are available.
72⇌(8fb)1 CTV in all bedrooms ® T
Lift ☾ 150P ❋ CFA ⛱(heated) snooker sailing ♫
French & Italian V Last dinner 9.30pm
Credit Cards 1 2 3 5

See advertisement on page 277

★★★67% **Greenbank** Harbourside TR11 2SR ☎(0326)312440 Telex no 45240 FAX (0326) 211362
Closed 1st 2wks Jan
Beautifully situated on the river's edge, with views across to Flushing, the harbour and the docks, this hotel offers spacious accommodation with good facilities, suitable for both business client or holidaymaker, the skilful combining of antiques with modern decor and furnishings in the public rooms creating a comfortablle atmosphere. Both à la carte and table d'hôte menus are available in the river-fronting restaurant.
43rm(36⇌6)(1fb) CTV in all bedrooms ® T ✱
sB&B⇌£29-£57 dB&B⇌£65-£95
Lift ☾ 50P 24 solarium hairdressing & beauty salons ♫
English & French V Lunch £8-£9&alc High tea fr£5 Dinner £13&alc Last dinner 9.45pm
Credit Cards 1 2 3 5

★★★62% **Green Lawns** Western Ter TR11 4QJ ☎(0326)312734 Telex no 45169 FAX (0326) 211427
Closed 24-30 Dec
Built in 1910 in the style of a French château, and set amid terraced lawns, the hotel offers purpose-built, well-equipped bedrooms; the extensive menus of the Garras Restaurant should satisfy most tastes, and there is a modern leisure complex for guests' use.
40rm(38⇌2)(8fb)2 CTV in all bedrooms ® T
sB&B⇌£39.10-£55.60 dB&B⇌£52.90-£80.50
☾ 60P ❋ CFA (heated) (hard & grass) squash sauna solarium gymnasium jacuzzi ♫
English & French V Lunch £7-£35alc High tea £1.50-£10 Dinner £13.50-£14.50&alc Last dinner 10pm
Credit Cards 1 2 3 4 5 £

★★★57% **Gyllyngdune** Melvill Rd TR11 4AR ☎(0326)312978
Closed Jan
An attractive, Georgian manor house with secluded gardens and views towards Falmouth Bay offers simply furnished bedrooms and a lower ground floor games room.
35rm(29⇌)(3fb)3 CTV in all bedrooms ® T ✱
sB&B⇌£25-£32.50 dB&B⇌£50-£65
☾ 35P 4 (charged) ❋ (heated) sauna solarium gymnasium pool table table tennis ♫ *xmas*
Continental
Credit Cards 1 2 3 5

See advertisement on page 277

Entries for rosetted restaurants, red-star and country-house hotels are highlighted by a tinted panel. For a full list of these establishments, consult the Contents page.

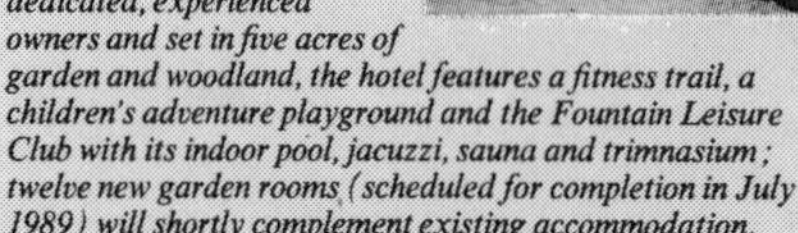

★★★ 72% **Penmere Manor** Mongleath Rd TR11 4PN (Best Western)
☎(0326)211411 Telex no 45608 FAX (0326) 317588
Closed 24-26 Dec

Under the control of dedicated, experienced owners and set in five acres of garden and woodland, the hotel features a fitness trail, a children's adventure playground and the Fountain Leisure Club with its indoor pool, jacuzzi, sauna and trimnasium; twelve new garden rooms (scheduled for completion in July 1989) will shortly complement existing accommodation.

39rm(35⇌4↱)(15fb)⊬in 8 bedrooms CTV in all bedrooms ® T sB&B⇌↱£42-£51 dB&B⇌↱£63-£85 ⊟
50P ✿ ❊ ◫(heated) ⌂(heated) sauna solarium gymnasium jacuzzi croquet table tennis ♫
☋ Cosmopolitan ✪ ⊻ ⊬ Bar Lunch fr£1.50 High tea fr£5 Dinner fr£14.50&alc Last dinner 9.45pm
Credit Cards [1] [2] [3] [5]

See advertisement on page 279

★★★ 70% **Royal Duchy** Cliff Rd TR11 4NX (Brend)
☎(0326)313042 Telex no 42551 FAX (0326) 319420
Facing the sea from its own terraced grounds, the hotel provides bright, pleasant public rooms and comfortable, well-appointed bedrooms. Staff are professional, welcoming and attentive.
50⇌(9fb) CTV in all bedrooms **T** sB&B⇌£37-£43 dB&B⇌£68-£103 ⊟
Lift ☾ CTV 35P ❊ ◫(heated) sauna solarium spa bath table tennis ♫ ⌂ *xmas*
☋ English & French **V** ✪ ⊻ Lunch £6.50&alc Dinner £12&alc Last dinner 9pm
Credit Cards [1] [2] [3] [5]

★★★ 63% **Hotel St Michaels** Stracey Rd TR11 4NB (Consort)
☎(0326)312707 & 318084 Telex no 45540 FAX (0326) 319147
Recently upgraded to a high standard, the hotel offers picturesque views of the bay from its situation close to the beach; bedrooms are well-equipped and public areas spacious, a wide range of indoor and outdoor leisure facilities also being available.
135⇌↱Annexe15⇌↱(38fb) CTV in all bedrooms ® **T** ✳ sB&B⇌↱£42-£49 dB&B⇌↱£78-£95 (incl dinner)
☾ 100P ❊ ◫(heated) ℘ (hard & grass) squash snooker sauna solarium gymnasium jacuzzi hair salon ♫ ⌂ *xmas*
☋ English & French **V** ✪ ⊻ ⊬ Lunch £6.45 High tea £7 Dinner £14&alc Last dinner 10pm
Credit Cards [1] [2] [3] [5]

★★ ***Carthion*** Cliff Rd TR11 4AP ☎(0326)313669
Closed Nov-Feb
Comfortable, family owned hotel with fine views over Falmouth Bay.
18rm(12⇌6↱) CTV in all bedrooms
18P ✿ ❊ nc10yrs
☋ English & French **V** ✪ ⊻ ⊬ Last dinner 8pm
Credit Cards [1] [2] [3] [5]

★★ **Crill House** Golden Bank TR11 5BL (2.5m W on unclass rd)
☎(0326)312994
Closed end Oct-mid Mar
Small, comfortable, friendly hotel in a peaceful rural location.
11⇌(3fb) CTV in all bedrooms ® sB&B⇌£27-£30 dB&B⇌£54-£60 ⊟
22P 1⌂ ❊ ⌂(heated)

▶

The Royal Duchy Hotel

AA ★★★

3 STAR LUXURY OVERLOOKING BAY & BEACHES

Situated in palm-fringed gardens overlooking the bay, The Royal Duchy has all bedrooms with private bath & colour T.V. and offers indoor heated pool, sauna, solarium, spa bath and billiards room. Ideal for summer family holidays or early and late season breaks, here you will enjoy first class cuisine, comfort and personal service. OPEN ALL YEAR.

For free colour brochure and tariff please contact: Mr. A. Allen, The Royal Duchy Hotel, Cliff Road, Falmouth, Cornwall.

Tel: (0326) 313042
Fax No: (0326) 319420

The Gyllyngdune Manor Hotel

AA ★ ★ ★

Melville Road, Falmouth, Cornwall TR11 4AR
Telephone: (0326) 312978

Old Georgian manor house, romantically situated in one acre of beautiful gardens, overlooking the Bay and Estuary. Guaranteed away from traffic, but within ten minutes' walk of the town centre and two minutes from the beach. Very large car park, covered space if required. Luxury indoor heated swimming pool, games room, Sauna and Solarium. Golf at Falmouth Golf club. 95% rooms en-suite all with colour TV, direct dial telephone and tea/coffee making facilities. Every comfort with personal attention the primary consideration.

F

FALMOUTH HOTEL ***

Castle Beach
Seafront, Falmouth
Cornwall TR11 4NZ

Telephone: (0326) 312671
Telex: 45262
Fax: (0326) 319533

A LUXURY HOTEL FOR ALL THE FAMILY

An elegant Victorian hotel situated right on the sea front yet only ten minutes stroll to harbour and town. Open all year except Xmas. 73 bedrooms all with en suite, colour TV and tea/coffee making facilities. Ample car parking. Large garden with outdoor heated swimming pool. Egon Ronay recommended.

Send for illustrated brochure and tariff.

⚲ English & Continental ♔ ⚲ Bar Lunch £1-£6.50alc Dinner £12 Last dinner 8pm
Credit Cards [1] [3]

★★Lerryn De Pass Rd TR11 4BJ ☎(0326)312489
Closed 7 Oct-Apr
Small hotel in a quiet position near seafront.
20rm(10⇦10⇗)(2fb) CTV in all bedrooms ® ✈
sB&B⇦⇗£17-£22 dB&B⇦⇗£30-£38
13P 2🚗(£12) ⛟ nc6yrs
♔ ⚲ Dinner £8-£10&alc Last dinner 8pm

★★*Melville* Sea View Rd TR11 4NL ☎(0326)312134
Set in 2 acres of sub-tropical gardens, this Victorian hotel has distant sea views and a friendly atmosphere.
22rm(7⇦15⇗)(3fb) ®
CTV 20P 10🚗(charged) ✲ croquet lawn putting green
⚲ English & Continental

★★Park Grove Kimberley Park Rd TR11 2DD ☎(0326)313276
Closed Dec-Feb
Bright, family-run hotel, close to the harbour, with modern bedrooms and an intimate cocktail bar.
17rm(15⇗)(4fb) CTV in all bedrooms ® sB&B£16-£18
sB&B⇗£16-£18 dB&B⇗£32-£36
25P
♔ ⚲
Credit Cards [1] [3] £

★★Somerdale Seaview Rd TR11 4EF ☎(0326)312566
Closed 21 Dec-Jan
Enjoying a peaceful location, this hotel provides well equipped bedrooms, many of which have en suite facilities. Special interest holidays are available, notably Golf and Historic House and Garden holidays.
18rm(11⇦4⇗)Annexe4rm(2⇦)(5fb) CTV in all bedrooms ®
T sB&B£21-£23 sB&B⇦⇗£23-£25 dB&B£42-£46
dB&B⇦⇗£46-£50 ⊟
13P ✲ sailing windsurfing
V ♔ ⚲ Bar Lunch £1-£3.50 High tea £2.50 Dinner £11.50&alc
Last dinner 8.15pm
Credit Cards [1] [2] [3] [5] £

FAREHAM Hampshire Map **04** SU50

★★Maylings Manor 11A Highlands Rd PO16 7XJ
☎(0329)286451 FAX (0329) 822584
Quietly situated in a mainly residential area and surrounded by three acres of grounds, this family run hotel provides well-equipped bedrooms, a restaurant whose table d'hôte menu represents excellent value for money and an attractive, new, fully licensed bar.
26rm(24⇦)(2fb)2⊞ CTV in all bedrooms ® **T** ✱ S%
sB&Bfr£45 sB&B⇦fr£45 dB&B⇦fr£55 ⊟
87P ✲
⚲ English & French ♔ ⚲ Lunch fr£8.50&alc Dinner fr£8.50&alc Last dinner 9.30pm
Credit Cards [1] [2] [3] [5]

★★Red Lion East St PO16 0BP (Lansbury) ☎(0329)822640
Telex no 86204 FAX (0329) 823579
Well-appointed coaching inn with excellent bedrooms.
44⇦(3fb)1⊞⚟in 6 bedrooms CTV in 33bedrooms ® **T** ✈ (ex guide dogs) sB&B⇦£30-£55 dB&B⇦£60-£65 ⊟
☾ CTV 80P 3🚗 ⛟
⚲ English & Continental **V** ♔ Lunch fr£8.50 Dinner fr£12.50
Last dinner 10pm
Credit Cards [1] [2] [3] [5]

Book as early as possible for busy holiday periods.

MELVILLE HOTEL★★

Sea View Road, Falmouth,
Cornwall TR11 4NL
Telephone (0326) 312134

★ Delightful private owned and managed hotel ★ Set in two acres of sub-tropical gardens ★ Magnificent views of Falmouth Bay from the front door ★ Twenty-two bedrooms with private facilities ★ Traditional breakfast and five course dinner, well stocked Bar ★ Nine hole putting green and fun croquet ★ Music and dancing in season by arrangement, Barbecue in summer ★ Can cater for parties of up to forty guests ★ Safe coach parking in our large enclosed car park ★ Membership of the Falmouth Club free to our guests ★

Resident Proprietors Toni and Terri Tonnesen

Crill House Hotel AA ★★

Budock Water, Falmouth, Cornwall TR11 5BL
Tel: (0326) 312994

Down a quiet country lane just outside Falmouth, 1½ miles from the sea, 11 bedrooms with private bathroom, colour TV, radio/intercom, tea/coffee making facilities. Licensed bar. Heated outdoor swimming pool. Close to golf course. Free squash & tennis nearby. Special Spring Garden holidays. Enjoy the caring hospitality of the Fenton family. Colour brochure from A. Fenton.

A Fine Georgian Country House

Situated in 5 acres of garden and woodland overlooking Falmouth Bay, the hotel is owned and managed by the Pope family.
The elegant ambience of a country house is retained throughout and the lounges and Fountain Bar are peaceful and relaxing. Excellent food and wine in the restaurant are accompanied by entertainment from our Yamaha Grand Piano each evening. The attractive bedrooms are individually decorated and all have private facilities en suite, colour TV, hair dryer, clock radio, telephone and tea/coffee making facilities.

THE FOUNTAIN LEISURE CLUB Offers indoor and outdoor swimming pools, jacuzzi spa, sauna, trimnasium, solarium, ¾ size snooker table, games cellar, croquet, compendium games tables, outdoor giant chess, playground and woodland fitness trial.

THE GARDEN ROOMS New rooms superior in size, luxury and facilities. Please ask for details and prices.

Mongleath Road, Falmouth, Cornwall, TR11 4PN Tel: (0326) 211411
Fax: (0326) 317588 Telex: 45608

AA★★★

F

FARNBOROUGH Hampshire Map **04** SU85

★★★63% **Queens** Lynchford Rd GU14 6AZ (Trusthouse Forte) ☎(0252)545051 Telex no 859637 FAX (0252) 377210
The imposing character façade of this hotel conceals a redesigned interior with generous public areas; Berties Coffee Shop offers two or three course buffet lunches at fixed prices and a grill menu in the evening, whilst the à la carte and fixed price menus of the Club Room emphasise fresh ingredients presented in modern style. Some particularly spacious and comfortable bedrooms are available, as are the facilities of the Glades Leisure Club should guests wish to keep in trim, the atmosphere throughout being welcoming and friendly.
110⇌(2fb)2⊞ ⅟in 20 bedrooms CTV in all bedrooms ® T S%
sB⇌£78-£88 dB⇌£91-£101 (room only) ⊟
☾170P CFA ⊡(heated) sauna solarium gymnasium health & fitness centre ⌂
V ♧ ⊥ ⅟ Lunch £12-£18&alc Dinner £16-£22&alc Last dinner 10pm
Credit Cards 1 2 3 4 5

★★**Falcon** Farnborough Rd GU14 6TH ☎(0252)545378
RS Xmas
30rm(29⇌1↱)(2fb)1⊞ CTV in all bedrooms ® T ✈
sB&B⇌↱fr£48 dB&B⇌↱fr£58
30P ⛟
☋ International V ♧ ⊥ Lunch fr£10.50&alc Dinner fr£10.50&alc Last dinner 9.30pm
Credit Cards 1 3

✕**Wings Cottage Chinese** 32 Alexandra Rd, North Camp GU14 6DA ☎(0252)544141
☋ Chinese 70 seats ✱ Lunch fr£12.50alc Dinner fr£12.50alc Last lunch 2pm Last dinner 10.30pm 20P nc10yrs ♫
Credit Cards 1 2 3 5

FARNHAM Surrey Map **04** SU84

★★★56% **Bush** The Borough GU9 7NN (Trusthouse Forte) ☎(0252)715237 Telex no 858764 FAX (0252) 733530
A 17th-century Coaching House with well equipped bedrooms, friendly, helpful staff, coffee shop and restaurant.
68rm(66⇌2↱)(2fb)1⊞ ⅟in 6 bedrooms CTV in all bedrooms ® T S% sB⇌↱£74-£85 dB⇌↱£86-£100 (room only) ⊟
☾60P ✿ CFA ⌂ *xmas*
V ♧ ⊥ ⅟ S% Lunch fr£15&alc High tea fr£5.50 Dinner fr£15.50&alc Last dinner 9.30pm
Credit Cards 1 2 3 4 5

★★★56% **Hog's Back Hotel** GU10 1EX (Embassy) ☎Runfold(02518)2345 Telex no 859352 FAX (02518) 3113
(For full entry see Seale)

★★**Trevena House** Alton Rd GU10 5ER ☎(0252)716908
Telex no 94013011
Closed 24 Dec-4 Jan
In a peaceful and secluded setting, this country house hotel has modernised bedrooms which retain some of their original character. There is a cosy lounge/bar and additional seating in the foyer.
20rm(17⇌3↱) CTV in all bedrooms ® T ✈
sB&B⇌↱£43-£48 dB&B⇌↱£52-£58 ⊟
30P ⛟ ✿ ⊃ ℛ (hard)
♧ ⊥ S10% Dinner £10-£17alc Last dinner 9.15pm
Credit Cards 1 2 3 5

FARRINGTON GURNEY Avon Map **03** ST55

★★**Country Ways** Marsh Ln BS18 5TT
☎Temple Cloud(0761)52449
Desmond and Susan Pow offer a warm welcome to their guests at this small country house. The bedrooms have every modern comfort, whilst the public rooms, a neat bar and small lounges, are equally relaxing and well-furnished. Well-prepared, fresh dishes can be selected from the short, but imaginative, menu in the dining room.
6rm(5⇌1↱) CTV in all bedrooms ® T ✈ (ex guide dogs) S5%
sB&B⇌↱£39.35-£45 dB&B⇌↱£49.85 ⊟
10P ⛟ ✿
V ♧ ⊥ S5% Lunch £12-£15 Dinner £12-£15 Last dinner 8.30pm
Credit Cards 1 2 3 5

See advertisement under WELLS

FARTHING CORNER MOTORWAY SERVICE AREA (M2) Kent Map **05** TQ86

⌂**Farthing Corner Lodge** Hartlip ME8 8PW (between juncts 4 & 5 M2) (Rank) ☎Medway(0634)377337
58⇌(12fb)⅟in 6 bedrooms CTV in all bedrooms ® S%
sB&B⇌£24.75 dB&B⇌£31.75 Continental breakfast
☾60P
V ♧ ⊥ ⅟ S%
Credit Cards 1 2 3 5

FAUGH Cumbria Map **12** NY55

★★★54% **String of Horses Inn** CA4 9EG ☎Hayton(0228)70297
A village inn of charm and character features oak beams and roaring log fires; bedrooms are very elaborate, most having canopied or four-poster beds and double sunken baths.
14rm(9⇌5↱)3⊞ CTV in all bedrooms ® T S%
sB&B⇌↱£50-£62 dB&B⇌↱£58-£84 ⊟
☾50P ⊃(heated) sauna solarium whirlpool spa
☋ English & French V ♧ S% Lunch £8.50&alc Dinner £14.50&alc Last dinner 10pm
Credit Cards 1 2 3 5 £

FAVERSHAM Kent Map **05** TR06

★★★72% **Barons** Ashford Rd, Sheldwich ME13 0LT (2m S of M2 jnct 6 on A251) ☎Sittingbourne(0795)539168
Set in 16 acres of gardens and parkland this charming country house, built in 1710, is a listed building. The comfortable bedrooms have been refurbished in keeping with the elegance of the building whilst the public rooms have a gracious yet comfortable atmosphere. There is a good selection of well-presented and prepared dishes on the fixed price menu.
12⇌↱(1fb) CTV in all bedrooms T ✈ (ex guide dogs) ✱
sB&B⇌↱£65-£85 dB&B⇌↱£80-£100
☾65P ⛟ ✿ U putting green nc11yrs *xmas*
☋ French V ♧ ⊥ ⅟ Lunch £10.50-£12.50&alc High tea £3.50-£6.50 Dinner £22.50-£28.50alc Last dinner 10pm
Credit Cards 1 2 3 5

See advertisement under CANTERBURY

❀✕✕**Read's** Painters Forstal ME13 0EE (2m S A251) ☎Sittingbourne (0795)535344
A pretty restaurant in a sleepy village, where the chef/patron continues to provide a consistently high standard of imaginative and well-constructed dishes which combine exciting flavours and textures. The wine list is extensive and the service pleasant and attentive. The table d'hôte lunch menu is particularly good value.
Closed Sun, Mon & 26 Dec
☋ French 44 seats Lunch £12 Dinner £20-£26.50alc Last lunch 2pm Last dinner 10pm 40P
Credit Cards 1 2 3 5

Red-star hotels offer the highest standards of hospitality, comfort and food.

FEARNAN Tayside *Perthshire* Map **11** NN74

★**Tigh-an-Loan** PH15 2PF (Guestaccom) ☎Kenmore(08873)249
Closed Oct-Etr
Cosy, personally-run hotel overlooking Loch Tay.
8rm(3⇌)(1fb) ® sB&Bfr£19 sB&B⇌fr£21.50 dB&Bfr£38 dB&B⇌fr£43
CTV 25P ✲
V Bar Lunch fr£4.50 Dinner fr£10 Last dinner 7.30pm
Credit Cards 1 2 3 5

FELIXSTOWE Suffolk Map **05** TM33

★★★★51% **Orwell Moat House** Hamilton Rd IP11 7DX (Queens Moat) ☎(0394)285511 Telex no 987676
FAX (0394) 670687
This traditional, Victorian-built hotel has been sympathetically updated and equipped to meet the needs of the modern guest. Comfortable, and hospitably run by friendly, competent staff, it features good bedrooms, well-appointed bars and an elegant restaurant run on classic lines, whilst its town-centre position offers easy access to the A45 and ferry links.
60⇌(10fb) CTV in all bedrooms T ✳ sB⇌£49.50-£62.50 dB⇌£62.50-£75 (room only)
Lift ☾ 150P 20 ✲ CFA ♫
English & French V Lunch £12&alc Dinner £15&alc
Last dinner 9.45pm
Credit Cards 1 2 3 5 £

★★★62% ***Brook*** Orwell Rd IP11 7PF ☎(0394)278441
Telex no 987674
A modern, well-furnished hotel situated in a residential area close to the town centre and the sea.
25⇌(1fb) CTV in all bedrooms ® T
☾ 20P
Credit Cards 1 2 3 5

★★**Marlborough** Sea Front IP11 8BJ ☎(0394)285621
Telex no 987047 FAX (0394) 670724
The hotel is located on the sea front, 250 yards south of the new pier leisure complex. Recently refurbished, it provides accommodation in a range of comfortable bedrooms.
47rm(45⇌2)(2fb)1 CTV in all bedrooms ® T ✳
sB⇌£32.95-£45 dB⇌£38.50-£56 (room only)
Lift ☾ CTV 19P flying windsurfing *xmas*
English & French V Lunch £7.50-£8&alc Dinner £9.75&alc Last dinner 9.45pm
Credit Cards 1 2 3 5

★★***Ordnance*** 1 Undercliff Rd West IP11 8AN (Exec Hotel)
☎(0394)273427 Telex no 987129 FAX (0394) 271348
RS Xmas Day
11rm(4)(1fb) CTV in all bedrooms ® T
☾ 55P
European V Last dinner 10.30pm
Credit Cards 1 2 3 5

FELLING Tyne & Wear Map **12** NZ26

○***Travelodge*** A194 Lean Ln, Wardley(Trusthouse Forte)
☎Tyneside(091)43833333
41⇌
P

FENNY BENTLEY Derbyshire Map **07** SK14

★★**Bentley Brook** DE6 1LF ☎Thorpe Cloud(033529)278
Detached, gabled house on the edge of the Peak District National Park.
8rm(3⇌)(1fb) CTV in all bedrooms ® T ✳ sB&B⇌£30-£35
dB&B£40-£45 dB&B⇌£45-£50
CTV 65P ✲ *xmas*
V Lunch £8.50-£10 High tea £3.50-£6 Dinner £10&alc
Last dinner 9.30pm
Credit Cards 1 3 £

FENNY BRIDGES Devon Map **03** SY19

★**Fenny Bridges** EX14 0BQ ☎Honiton(0404)850218
Set in its own grounds beside the A30, a small, inn-style hotel, personally run by the resident proprietor, offers cosy bars and a small restaurant.
8⇌ CTV in all bedrooms ® T sB&B⇌£24.50 dB&B⇌£35
CTV 75P ✲
English & French V Lunch £5.95-£10alc High tea £3-£5alc Dinner £5.95-£10alc Last dinner 10pm
Credit Cards 1 2 3 5 £

★**Greyhound Inn** EX14 0BJ (Berni/Chef & Brewer)
☎Honiton(0404)850380
10rm(3⇌7)1 CTV in all bedrooms ® T (ex guide dogs)
sB&B⇌£32.50 dB&B⇌£44.50
80P
V Lunch £8 Dinner £9 Last dinner 10pm
Credit Cards 1 2 3 5

FENSTANTON Cambridgeshire

○***Travelodge*** A604, Huntingdon Rd(Trusthouse Forte)
☎Central reservations 01-567 3444
Due to open winter 1989
40⇌
P

For key to symbols see the inside front cover.

FENWICK Strathclyde *Ayrshire* Map **11** NS44

★★***Fenwick*** Kilmaurs Rd KA3 6AY ☎(05606)478
A small, comfortable, roadside hotel with a popular restaurant.
9rm(5⇌) CTV in all bedrooms ® **T**
200P
♀ French ♦ ☐
Credit Cards [1] [3]

FERMAIN BAY

See **Guernsey under Channel Islands**

FERNDOWN Dorset Map **04** SU00

★★★★**61% Dormy** New Rd BH22 8ES (De Vere)
☎Bournemouth(0202)872121 Telex no 418301
FAX (0202) 895388
Attractive hotel with well-appointed bedrooms, some in individual bungalows in hotel's extensive grounds.
130rm(122⇌8⇌)(8fb)2⊞ CTV in all bedrooms ® **T** ✱
sB&B⇌⇌fr£75 dB&B⇌⇌fr£105 ⊟
Lift ☾ CTV 220P ✲ CFA ⊠(heated) ℘ (hard) squash snooker sauna solarium gymnasium ♫ ⌂ *xmas*
V ♦ ☐ Lunch fr£10&alc High tea fr£2&alc Dinner £15-£16&alc Last dinner 9.30pm
Credit Cards [1] [2] [3] [4] [5]
See advertisement under BOURNEMOUTH

★★**Coach House Inn** Tricketts Cross BH22 9NW (junc A31/A348) (Consort) ☎(0202)861222 Telex no 265871
FAX (0202) 894130
This modern hotel, with its friendly, informal atmosphere and keen, attentive staff, provides accommodation in good-sized bedrooms furnished with all modern amenities and contained in four blocks outside the main building.
Annexe44rm(32⇌12⇌) CTV in all bedrooms ® **T** ✱
sB&B⇌⇌£38-£44 dB&B⇌⇌£54-£60 ⊟
100P 25♠ CFA
♀ English & Italian **V** ♦ ☐ Lunch £3.50-£7 Dinner £7.75-£8.50&alc Last dinner 9.30pm
Credit Cards [1] [2] [3] [5] £

FERRYBRIDGE SERVICE AREA West Yorkshire Map **08** SE44

○***Granada Lodge*** (junct of A1/M62)
☎Knottingley(0977)782767
Due to open Summer 1988
34⇌
P

FILEY North Yorkshire Map **08** TA18

★★**Wrangham House** Stonegate, Hunmanby YO14 0NS (3m SW off A165) ☎Scarborough(0723)891333
This one-time vicarage has lost nothing of its former charm. The friendly atmosphere, the excellent home-cooking and the log fires lit in the two very comfortable lounges on chillier days provide a warm welcome. Bedrooms are all attractively decorated and individually styled.
9rm(4⇌5⇌)⚟in all bedrooms CTV in all bedrooms ® ✈ (ex guide dogs) S% sB&B⇌⇌£25.50-£28 dB&B⇌⇌£51-£56 ⊟
20P ⊞ ✲ nc12yrs
V ♦ ☐ ⚟ S% Lunch £5.50-£9 Dinner £9.75-£11&alc Last dinner 8pm
Credit Cards [1] [2] [3] [5]

FINDON West Sussex Map **04** TQ10

★★***Findon Manor Hotel*** High St BN14 0TA ☎(090671)2733
The hotel dates from the sixteenth century, when it was a rectory, and it enjoys a charming setting in this village which goes back as far as the Domesday Book. The proprietors personally supervise its running, creating a warm, friendly atmosphere and offering bedrooms that are tastefully and comfortably appointed, with all modern facilities.
11rm(10⇌1⇌)2⊞ CTV in all bedrooms ® **T**
30P
♦ ☐
Credit Cards [1] [2] [3] [5]

FIR TREE Co Durham Map **12** NZ13

★★★**70% Helme Park Hall Country House** DL13 4NW
☎Bishop Auckland(0388)730970
This much extended farmhouse, converted to hotel use in 1987, stands in its own grounds just off the A68/A689 two miles north of Fir Tree; tastefully appointed and offering the services of friendly, attentive staff, it commands superb views west over Wealdale and the North Pennines from its elevated position.
10rm(9⇌1⇌)(3fb)1⊞ CTV in all bedrooms ® **T** ✈ (ex guide dogs) sB&B⇌⇌£39.50 dB&B⇌⇌£55-£75 ⊟
40P ✲ solarium ⌂ *xmas*
♀ English & French **V** ♦ ☐ Lunch £7.50-£15&alc High tea £5-£7.50 Dinner £13.50&alc Last dinner 9.45pm
Credit Cards [1] [2] [3]

FISHGUARD Dyfed Map **02** SM93

★★***Cartref*** High St SA65 9AW ☎(0348)872430
Comfortable hotel situated in the town centre.
14rm(2⇌4⇌) CTV in 8bedrooms ✈
CTV 20P 2♠ ⊞ nc7yrs
♦ ☐ Last dinner 8pm
Credit Cards [1] [3]

★**Abergwaun** The Market Square SA65 9HA ☎(0348)872077
A commercial hotel in the town centre conveniently situated for the Irish ferries.
12rm(1fb) CTV in all bedrooms ® ✱ sB&B£15 dB&B£28-£32
CTV ⚑
♀ English & French **V** ♦ ☐ Lunch £2.95-£6.95alc High tea £2.95-£6.95alc Dinner £6.50-£16.90alc Last dinner 9pm
Credit Cards [1] [2] [3] £

★***Hotel Plâs Glyn-y-Mel*** Lower Town SA65 9LY ☎(0348)872296
Closed Jan
A well-proportioned Georgian house set in twenty-acre grounds retains many of its original features whilst providing good public rooms, friendly service and excellent food.
6rm(5⇌) CTV in all bedrooms ®
20P ✲ ⚓
V ♦ ☐

FITTLEWORTH West Sussex Map **04** TQ01

★★**Swan** Lower St RH20 1EW (Berni/Chef & Brewer)
☎(079882)429
An attractive, 14th-century village inn has been thoughtfully upgraded to preserve its original character. In the dining room hang some 18th-century paintings, once given in lieu of payment. Bedrooms are well appointed, and the dining room serves English and French cuisine of a very high standard, three set-price menus offering a good choice.
10rm(6⇌2⇌)2⊞ CTV in all bedrooms ® **T** ✈ (ex guide dogs)
sB&B⇌⇌£31.50-£34 dB&B⇌⇌£43-£49.50 ⊟
25P ✲ ∪
♦ ☐ ⚟ Lunch £8 Dinner £9 Last dinner 9.30pm
Credit Cards [1] [2] [3] [5]

FIVE OAKS West Sussex Map **04** TQ02

○ ***Travelodge*** A29 RH14 9AE (Trusthouse Forte)
☎Billingshurst(0403)812711
26⇌
P

FLAMBOROUGH Humberside Map **08** TA26

★***Flaneburg*** North Marine Rd YO15 1LF
☎Bridlington(0262)850284
Closed Jan & Feb
A three-storey building on the edge of the village near the famous cliffs, this friendly hotel provides accommodation in nicely appointed bedrooms, which are complemented by comfortable public rooms.
13rm(8↱)(2fb) CTV in all bedrooms ® ✗
CTV 20P ⇼
V ♧

FLEET Hampshire Map **04** SU85

★★★56% **Lismoyne** Church Rd GU13 8NE ☎(0252)628555
Set in a quiet residential area and surrounded by over two acres of pleasant gardens, a Victorian hotel offers a variety of bedrooms, public rooms with old world charm, and the services of pleasant, friendly staff.
40rm(29⇌2↱) CTV in all bedrooms ® **T** ✱ S% sB&B£42 sB&B⇌↱£52 dB&B£67 dB&B⇌↱£67 ⊟
☾ 80P ✲ ♫
♉ English & French **V** ♧ ☕ S% Lunch £9.95&alc Dinner £10.95&alc Last dinner 9.30pm
Credit Cards 1 2 3 4 5

FLEETWOOD Lancashire Map **07** SD34

★★★60% **North Euston** The Esplanade FY7 6BN
☎(03917)6525 Telex no 67231
In a prominent position overlooking the Wyre Estuary this hotel, which dates back to 1841, has attractive bedrooms equipped with modern facilities. The restaurant has recently undergone refurbishment and the Chatterbox Bistro is being extended.
60rm(45⇌13↱)(2fb) CTV in all bedrooms ® **T** ✗ (ex guide dogs) sB&B⇌↱£33 dB&B⇌↱£49-£58 ⊟
Lift ☾ 60P *xmas*
♧ ☕ Lunch £7.50-£8.50&alc Dinner £10.50-£11.50&alc Last dinner 9.30pm
Credit Cards 1 2 3 5

FLIMWELL East Sussex Map **05** TQ73

✗ ***Woods'*** High St TN5 7PB ☎(058087)342
Closed Mon
Lunch not served (ex Sun by reservation only)
Dinner not served Sun
♉ International **V** 26 seats Last dinner 9.30pm 6P
Credit Cards 1 3

Entries for rosetted restaurants, red-star and country-house hotels are highlighted by a tinted panel. For a full list of these establishments, consult the Contents page.

FLITWICK Bedfordshire Map **04** TL03

★★★ 76% **Flitwick Manor** Church Rd MK45 1AE
☎(0525)712242
Telex no 825562
FAX (0525) 712242
Closed 24-28 Dec

Attractively converted to hotel use and tastefully appointed, this 17th-century house offers accommodation in comfortable, well-equipped bedrooms. A Regency-style restaurant provides interesting à la carte dinner menus and a good set lunch, both comprised of skilfully-prepared, imaginative dishes and complemented by a carefully chosen wine list.

15rm(13⇌2♪)(2fb)5 CTV in all bedrooms **T** (ex guide dogs) ✻ sB&B⇌♪£70-£125 dB&B⇌♪£100-£160

50P ✲ (hard) croquet table tennis bicycles putting

English **V** Lunch fr£17.50&alc Dinner fr£17.50 Last dinner 9.30pm

Credit Cards 1 2 3

FLORE Northamptonshire Map **04** SP66

★★★ 67% **The Heyford Manor Hotel** The High St NN7 4LP ☎Weedon(0327)349022 Telex no 311430 FAX (0327) 349017
This modern, purpose-built hotel, located on the A45 just a mile from junction 16 of the M1, has been carefully designed to provide comfortable, well-equipped bedrooms with en suite facilities. The restaurant offers both table d'hôte and à la carte menus, dishes being well-prepared and served by a helpful young staff. Adjoining the restaurant are a small bar, an attractive, open-plan lounge area and a conservatory. Guests also have the use of a small fitness room and sauna.
60⇌(7fb) in 15 bedrooms CTV in all bedrooms ® **T** ✻ S% sB&B⇌£35-£53 dB&B⇌£43-£60
(CTV 117P sauna gymnasium ♫
English & French **V** S% Lunch £7.95-£9.95&alc Dinner £13.75&alc Last dinner 9.30pm
Credit Cards 1 2 3 5

FOCHABERS Grampian *Morayshire* Map **15** NJ35

★★**Gordon Arms Hotel** High St IV32 7DH ☎(0343)820508
The former coaching inn, lying close to the River Spey on the main Aberdeen-Inverness road, offers comfortable and well-equipped bedrooms, a spacious residents' lounge and a choice of two bars, both of which are popular with the fishing fraternity who frequent this conveniently-sited hotel.
14⇌♪(2fb) CTV in all bedrooms ® **T**
CTV 50P 2 (£5 per day) ✲
Scottish, French & Italian **V** Last dinner 9.45pm
Credit Cards 1 2 3

FOLKESTONE Kent Map **05** TR23

★★★ 63% **Clifton** The Leas CT20 2EB (Consort)
☎(0303)851231 Telex no 57515
An imposing hotel in a commanding cliff-top position. Bedrooms offer most modern facilities and public areas include a spacious lounge, a cosy bar and an elegant restaurant. Staff are friendly and helpful, creating a very pleasant atmosphere.
84rm(67⇌11♪)(4fb) CTV in all bedrooms ® **T** ✻ sB&B⇌♪£39-£49.50 dB&B⇌♪£55-£63
Lift (✲ solarium games room ♫ *xmas*
English & French Lunch £8.25-£8.75&alc Dinner £12.50-£13.50&alc Last dinner 9pm
Credit Cards 1 2 3 5

★★**Garden House** 142 Sandgate Rd CT20 2TE (Inter)
☎(0303)52278 FAX (0303) 41376
The modernised and refurbished Victorian hotel has well-equipped bedrooms, an efficiently-managed restaurant and limited lounge accommodation.
42rm(34⇌8♪)(7fb)1 CTV in all bedrooms ® **T** ✻ sB&B⇌♪£35 dB&B⇌♪£55-£65
Lift (16P ✲ *xmas*
Continental **V** Lunch £5.25-£6.50&alc Dinner £11.50&alc Last dinner 9.30pm
Credit Cards 1 2 3 5 £

✕✕**La Tavernetta** Leeside Court, Clifton Gardens CT20 2EP
☎(0303)54955 & 55044
Closed Sun, 25-26 Dec & BH's
Italian **V** 65 seats ✻ Last lunch 2.30pm Last dinner 10.30pm
Credit Cards 1 2 3 5

FONTWELL West Sussex Map **04** SU90

○ ***Travelodge*** A27 BN18 0SB (Trusthouse Forte)
☎Eastergate(0243)543973
32⇌
P

FORD Wiltshire Map **03** ST87

★★**White Hart Inn** SN14 8RP ☎Castle Combe(0249)782213
Quiet 15th-century stone inn with beams and log fires.
3♪Annexe8⇌(1fb)4 CTV in all bedrooms ® ✻ sB&B⇌♪£35 dB&B⇌♪£49
CTV 100P ✲ (heated) *xmas*
English & French **V** Sunday Lunch £6.45 Dinner £6.95-£12.95alc Last dinner 9.30pm
Credit Cards 1 3

FORDINGBRIDGE Hampshire Map **04** SU11

★★**Ashburn Hotel & Restaurant** Station Rd SP6 1JP
☎(0425)52060 52150 FAX (0425) 55915
Situated on a quiet hillside on the edge of town this hotel offers a choice of original and modern new wing bedrooms most with good views over the lawn and swimming pool. Service is friendly and personally supervised and the standard of cooking is very reliable. Fully equipped conference room.
22⇌♪(3fb)1 CTV in all bedrooms ® **T** ✻ sB&B⇌♪£30-£32.50 dB&B⇌♪£52-£58
CTV 60P ✲ (heated)
English & French **V** Sunday Lunch £6.25 Dinner £9-£9.50&alc Last dinner 9pm
Credit Cards 1 2 3 5

✕✕**Hour Glass** Burgate SP6 1LX ☎(0425)52348
Lunch not served Mon
Dinner not served Sun
English & French **V** 45 seats ✻ Lunch £7.95 Dinner £15.95 Last lunch 1.45pm Last dinner 9.45pm 40P nc12yrs
Credit Cards 1 2 3 5

✕**The Three Lions** Stuckton SP6 2HF
☎(0425)52489
June and Karl Wadsack have run this cottage-style free-house pub and restaurant for 11 years. Plenty of plants, pine and copper decorations enhance the friendly atmosphere, and menus are written on two blackboards. Melon with Black Forest ham, fresh breast of farm chicken with mango and

passion fruit sauce, and steamed fillets of Avon salmon with fresh asparagus sauce exemplify Karl's resfreshing cuisine, which has an emphasis on fish. The extensive wine list includes over 200 bins.

Closed Mon, 10 days Xmas, 4 wks Feb, 2 wks Jul/Aug & 2 wks Oct

Dinner not served Sun

☋ International 56 seats ✱ Lunch £8.25-£21.20alc Dinner £12.45-£22.60alc Last lunch 1.30pm Last dinner 9pm 40P nc14yrs

Credit Cards [1] [3]

FOREST ROW East Sussex Map **05** TQ43

★★★ 55% **Roebuck** Wych Cross RH18 5JL (2m S junc A22/A275) (Embassy) ☎(034282)3811 Telex no 957088 FAX (0342) 824790

This busy, commercial Georgian country inn offers a friendly, informal atmosphere, well-equipped bedrooms and comfortable public rooms.

28rm(27⇌1↱) CTV in all bedrooms ® T S% sB⇌↱fr£50 dB⇌↱fr£60 (room only) ⊟

(150P ✲ *xmas*

☋ English & French V ✿ S% Lunch fr£10.50 Dinner fr£11.50 Last dinner 9.15pm

Credit Cards [1] [2] [3] [4] [5]

FORFAR Tayside *Angus* Map **15** MO45

★★ ***Royal*** Castle St DD8 3AE ☎(0307)62691

This modernised town-centre hotel has well-equipped bedrooms, though some are compact and standards do vary. The smart leisure complex is a popular attraction.

19rm(11⇌8↱)(1fb)1⊟ CTV in all bedrooms ® T ✗ (ex guide dogs)

50P ⊡(heated) sauna solarium gymnasium hairdressing salon ♫

☋ International V ✿ ☐ Last dinner 9.30pm

Credit Cards [1] [2] [3] [5] £

FORRES Grampian *Morayshire* Map **14** NJ05

★★ **Ramnee** Victoria Rd IV36 0BN ☎(0309)72410

Fine two-storey stone villa standing back from the main road in well-kept grounds.

21rm(10⇌10↱)(3fb)1⊟ CTV in all bedrooms ® T ✱ sB&Bfr£24 sB&B⇌↱£30-£47.50 dB&B£38 dB&B⇌↱£45-£65 ⊟

CTV 50P ⊟ ✲ shooting ⌂ *xmas*

☋ Scottish & French V ✿ ☐ Lunch £6.50-£7.50 Dinner £12.50&alc Last dinner 9pm

Credit Cards [1] [2] [3] [5]

★★ ***Royal*** Tytler St IV36 0EL ☎(0309)72617

Three-storey building, standing in a quiet area of the town, opposite the market and near the station.

19rm(1⇌5↱)(4fb) CTV in all bedrooms ®

CTV 40P ✲ pool room

☋ European V ✿ ☐ Last dinner 8.30pm

Credit Cards [1] [2] [3]

FORT AUGUSTUS Highland *Inverness-shire* Map **14** NH30

★★ **Caledonian** PH32 4BQ ☎(0320)6256

Closed Oct-Etr

This small family-run hotel is especially noted for its warm and friendly hospitality.

12rm(2⇌2↱)(2fb) ® ✗ (ex guide dogs) ✱ sB&B£14.50-£19.50 dB&B£29-£33 dB&B⇌↱£35-£41 ⊟

CTV 20P ✲

☋ Scottish & French V ✿ ☐ Bar Lunch £5-£9alc Dinner £10-£12alc Last dinner 9.30pm

★★ **Inchnacardoch Lodge** Loch Ness PH32 4BL (Consort) ☎(0320)6258

Closed Dec-Feb

A converted hunting lodge overlooking Loch Ness.

16rm(6⇌5↱)(5fb) CTV in 8bedrooms ® sB&B£15-£35 sB&B⇌↱£25-£35 dB&Bfr£25 dB&B⇌↱£40-£50 ⊟

CTV 40P 2⌂ ✲

☋ International V ✿ ☐ ⁄ Lunch £7.50&alc Dinner £12.95 Last dinner 9pm

Credit Cards [1] [2] [3] [5] £

★★ **Lovat Arms** PH32 4BH ☎(0320)6206

This traditional hotel, with spacious and comfortable lounges, is situated in an elevated position overlooking the Benedictine monastery and Loch Ness. It is ideal for those wishing to tour the Highlands.

20rm(18⇌)(3fb) CTV in all bedrooms ® sB&B⇌£20.50-£27 dB&B⇌£41-£54 ⊟

CTV 50P ✲ Putting Green ♫ *xmas*

V ✿ ☐ Lunch £6.50 Dinner £13.50-£15 Last dinner 8.30pm

Credit Cards [3] [4] [5]

★★ **The Brae Hotel** PH32 4DG ☎(0320)6289

mid Jan-Oct

A friendly, homely little hotel situated on the outskirts of the town provides accommodation in bedrooms which are pleasant, if modestly appointed, and public areas which include a bright dining room serving good home cooking.

8rm(2⇌3↱)(1fb) CTV in all bedrooms ® ✱ sB&B£15-£16.50 dB&B£26-£29 dB&B⇌↱£32-£36 ⊟

▶

CTV 12P ⛟ ❋ nc7yrs
⅟ Bar Lunch fr£3 Dinner £10.50 Last dinner 8.15pm
Credit Cards [1] [3]

FORTINGALL Tayside *Perthshire* Map **14** NN74

★★Fortingall PH15 2NQ ☎Kenmore(08873)367
RS Nov-Feb
Crow-stepped gables are a feature of this 18th-century hotel with a coaching history. Set in an attractive village, it reflects a traditional standard of accommodation coupled with the personal attention of the owners.
11rm(3⇨1♠) ® S% sB&B£18-£20 sB&B⇨♠£21-£23 dB&B£36-£40 dB&B⇨♠£42-£44 ⊟
CTV 15P 5🚘 ❋ ♪ sailing pony trekking
☋ British & French V ♁ ⊻ Lunch £5.50-£8&alc Dinner £12.50-£14&alc Last dinner 8.30pm
Credit Cards [1] [2] [3] £

FORTON MOTORWAY SERVICE AREA (M6) Lancashire Map **07** SD45

○***Rank Motor Lodge*** LA2 9DU (Between juncs 32 & 33)
☎Lancaster(0524)792227
Due to open Feb 1990
40⇨♠

FORTROSE Highland *Ross & Cromarty* Map **14** NH76

★***Royal*** Union St IV10 8SU ☎(0381)20236
Small, family-run hotel overlooking cathedral square.
11rm(3⇨1♠)(2fb) ® ✕
CTV 8P ⛟
☋ Scottish & French V ♁ ⊻ Last dinner 9pm
Credit Cards [1] [3]

FORT WILLIAM Highland *Inverness-shire* Map **14** NN17

See also **Banavie**

❀❀★★★★ INVERLOCHY CASTLE

PH33 6SN (3m NE A82)
(Relais et Châteaux)
☎(0397)2177
Telex no 776229
FAX (0397) 2953
Closed mid Nov-mid Mar

Although Grete Hobbs is the guiding light of this fine baronial hotel, set in 50acres of lovely grounds and overlooked by Ben Nevis, it is the Managing Director Michael Leonard who is the driving force. It is he who ensures that the highest levels of service are maintained, and when one considers that each season he has to recruit and train an almost completely new team of staff, it is greatly to his credit that he succeeds so well in ensuring that guests are treated as individuals and with courtesy and consideration. He and his engaging deputy, Mr Jack, are much in evidence, keeping a watchful, yet unobtrusive, eye on things, whilst the charming staff react accordingly. Bedrooms are all large and comfortable and are kept spotlessly clean and in immaculate condition. Five have recently been refurbished, including the installation of excellent powerful showers. Chef Graham Newbould produces first class British food, with clear honest flavours, and though the choice is somewhat limited, the quality of the raw materials, together with the cooking of them, more than compensate – indeed it is a rare delight these days to be able to taste what is written on the menu. Guests are expected to order dinner in advance, from their room, where the menu and the extensive wine list are available. The combination of location, comfort, quality, peace and quiet, excellent food and caring efficient service set this hotel apart, and it is a joy and a privilege to experience hotel keeping at its very best.
16⇨♠ CTV in all bedrooms **T** ✕ ✱ sB&B⇨♠£110-£120 dB&B⇨♠£150-£210
☾ 16P 1🚘 ⛟ ❋ ⚲ (hard) ♪ snooker
☋ International V ⊻ ⅟ Lunch £19-£29 Dinner £35-£38.50 Last dinner 9.15pm
Credit Cards [1] [2] [3]

★★★58% Alexandra The Parade PH33 6AZ ☎(0397)2241
Telex no 777210 FAX (0397) 3695
Traditional in style and situated close to the main shopping area, the hotel offers compact bedrooms which have recently been upgraded. The popular Great Food Shop provides meals and snacks from 9.30am until 11.00pm, supplementing the main restaurant which serves only dinner.
102⇨(7fb) CTV in all bedrooms ® **T** sB&B⇨£46-£52 dB&B⇨£68-£78 ⊟
Lift ☾ 50P ♫ *xmas*
☋ Scottish & French V ♁ ⊻ Lunch fr£6 High tea fr£4 Dinner £7-£13 Last dinner 11pm
Credit Cards [1] [2] [3] [5] £

★★★50% *Mercury Hotel* Achintore Rd PH33 6RW (Mount Charlotte) ☎(0397)3117 Telex no 778454
Modern, low-rise building, standing by the main road on the southern outskirts of town, with splendid views over Loch Linnhe. The bedrooms have recently been extended and refurbished to a high standard.
86⇨♠(12fb)⅟in 2 bedrooms CTV in all bedrooms ® **T**
Lift ☾ 160P CFA sauna
☋ European V ♁ ⊻ Last dinner 9.30 pm
Credit Cards [1] [2] [3] [5]

★★*Cruachan* Achintore Rd PH33 6RQ (Consort) ☎(0397)2022
Closed Nov-Etr
Large hotel overlooking Loch Linnhe with modern bedroom extension at rear. Caters for tour parties.
54⇨♠(2fb) CTV in all bedrooms ®
☾ 30P snooker ♫
Last dinner 9pm

★★Grand Gordon Square PH33 6DX ☎(0397)2928
FAX (0397) 5060
Three-storey hotel on a corner site at west end of shopping centre and adjacent to Pier.
33⇨(4fb) CTV in all bedrooms ® sB&B⇨fr£20 dB&B⇨fr£40 ⊟
20P
V ♁ ⊻ Lunch fr£6.50 Dinner fr£12.50 Last dinner 8.30 pm
Credit Cards [1] [2] [3] [5] £

★★Imperial Fraser's Square PH33 6DW ☎(0397)2040 & 3921
Closed 3-31 Jan
An extended, large Victorian building, near the main shopping area and with views of Loch Linnhe.
34rm(25⇨9♠)(3fb) CTV in all bedrooms ® **T** sB&B⇨♠£38-£45 dB&B⇨♠£48-£58 ⊟
CTV 20P *xmas*
☋ Scottish & French ⅟ Lunch £4.50-£6.50 Dinner £12.50-£14.50&alc Last dinner 9pm
Credit Cards [1] [3]

A rosette is the AA's highest award for quality of food and service in a restaurant.

★★Milton North Rd PH33 6TG ☎(0397)2331 Telex no 777210 FAX (0397) 3695
Closed mid Oct-late Apr
Recently refurbished hotel, at the foot of Ben Nevis, with comfortable bedrooms. Popular with coach parties.
56⇌♠ Annexe67⇌♠(6fb) CTV in all bedrooms ® ✱ S% sB&B⇌♠£41 dB&B⇌♠£62 ⛿
☾ 150P ♫
♈ ☕ Dinner £7-£12 Last dinner 8.30 pm
Credit Cards [1] [2] [3] [4] [5]

★★Nevis Bank Belford Rd PH33 6BY (Best Western) ☎(0397)5721 Telex no 9401689
Tourist and commercial hotel with well-appointed bedrooms is situated on A82 north of town, at access road to Glen Nevis.
31rm(17⇌14♠)Annexe8rm(4⇌4♠)(2fb) CTV in all bedrooms ® T sB&B⇌♠£31-£40 dB&B⇌♠£50-£60 ⛿
25P sauna solarium gymnasium ♫ *xmas*
V ♈ ☕ Bar Lunch £5-£7.50alc Dinner fr£13.50alc Last dinner 9pm
Credit Cards [1] [2] [3] [5] ⓔ

See advertisement on page 289

★ FACTOR'S HOUSE

Torlundy PH33 6SN
☎(0397)5767
Telex no 776229
FAX (0397) 2953
Closed 16 Dec-15 Jan RS 16 Jan-14 Mar

This charming little hotel was once the Inverlochy estate manager's house, and has been converted so as to combine modern comfort with the warmth and character of a private home. The 7 attractive bedrooms are all very well equipped and most have views of Ben Nevis or the surrounding countryside. Guests can also relax among the magazines in the comfortable lounges, but most of all it is the hospitality provided by Peter Hobbs and his team which makes this such a pleasant place to stay – not least among the staff being Mr Hobbs's dog, Pancho. The cuisine is of a high standard as well, and the fixed-price menu, with its choice of 4 main dishes, is very good value. A blackboard gives details of the evening's fare.

7rm(5⇨2♠) CTV in all bedrooms **T** (ex guide dogs) sB&B⇨♠£40.25-£63.25 dB&B⇨♠£69
CTV 30P ✲ (hard) sailing nc6yrs
Dinner £17.50 Last dinner 9.30pm
Credit Cards 1 2 3 5

FOSSEBRIDGE Gloucestershire Map **04** SP01

★★Fossebridge Inn GL54 3JS ☎(028572)721 due to change to (0285) 720721
The centrepiece of this hotel is the popular and characterful Bridge Bar, which dates back to the original fifteenth-century inn. It remains much as it was then, with fine Yorkshire floors, oak beams and inglenook fireplaces, and offers a comprehensive range of bar snacks.
9rm(6⇨3♠)Annexe4⇨(3fb) CTV in all bedrooms ® **T** ✳ sB&B⇨♠£40-£60 dB&B⇨♠£55-£75
40P ✲ clay pigeon shooting
English & French **V** Lunch £21.50&alc Dinner £21.50&alc Last dinner 9.30pm
Credit Cards 1 2 3 5

FOUR MARKS Hampshire Map **04** SU63

○ ***TraveLodge*** 156 Winchester Rd GU34 5HZ (on A31) (Trusthouse Forte) ☎Alton(0420)62659
31⇨
P

FOWEY Cornwall & Isles of Scilly Map **02** SX15

★★★51% ***Fowey Hotel*** The Esplanade PL23 1HX ☎(072683)2551
This privately owned and personally supervised resort hotel enjoys an excellent setting overlooking the bay. Bedrooms are, for the most part, spacious, many commanding fine views, and a friendly, informal atmosphere prevails.
26rm(11⇨11♠)(4fb) CTV in all bedrooms ® **T**
Lift CTV 22P ✲
Last dinner 9.30
Credit Cards 1 2 3 5

Book as early as possible for busy holiday periods.

★★Marina Esplanade PL23 1HY ☎(0726)833315
Closed Nov-Feb
Comfortable hotel where good food is served in the waterside restaurant.
11rm(10⇨1♠) CTV in all bedrooms **T** sB&B⇨♠£21-£31 dB&B⇨♠£42-£60
windsurfing sailing
English & French **V** Bar Lunch £2-£5 High tea fr£2.50 Dinner fr£13&alc Last dinner 8.30pm
Credit Cards 1 2 3 5

★★*Old Quay* Fore St PL23 1AQ ☎(072683)3302
Closed Dec-Jan
Backing onto the estuary, with a spacious sun terrace, this small hotel offers friendly relaxed service and a good dinner menu.
13rm(7⇨2♠)(3fb) CTV in all bedrooms ®
CTV

Credit Cards 1 3

✕Food for Thought The Quay PL23 1AT ☎(072683)2221
Fresh fish, transformed by the innovative skill of the chef/proprietor, is the speciality of this intimate restaurant set on the quayside of the picturesque Cornish village. Well-flavoured dishes are attractively presented and complemented by a wine list of medium length. Quenelles of Fowey River salmon, and the Rendezvous of freshly caught fish and shellfish with a lobster sauce are two popular choices.
Closed mid Jan-early Mar
Lunch not served
French 40 seats Dinner £16&alc Last dinner 9.30pm
nc10yrs
Credit Cards 1 3

FOWLMERE Cambridgeshire Map **05** TL44

✕✕Chequers Inn SG8 7SR ☎(076382)369
A fine little inn dating back to the 16th century displays among its ancient timbers such relics of the past as mid 17th-century talismans, some business cards from around 1850 and photographs of airmen from fighter squadrons who, in two world wars, made this their second home. Food of a high standard is served in a tiny restaurant where some tables are set up in the gallery, the skilfully prepared dishes on the menu including such delicacies as flowering courgettes stuffed with a light salmon mousse, or chicken breasts stuffed with smoked trout, wrapped in lettuce, steamed and served with a nettle, fromage blanc and yogurt sauce – though a traditional roast is usually also featured. A small but carefully selected list of wines accompanies the meal, some of them being available by the glass.
Closed 25 Dec
English & French **V** 30 seats ✳ Lunch £14.41-£25.90alc Dinner £14.41-£25.90alc Last lunch 2pm Last dinner 10pm
50P
Credit Cards 1 2 3 5

FOWNHOPE Hereford & Worcester Map **03** SO53

★★Green Man Inn HR1 4PE ☎(043277)243
Situated on the B5224 in the centre of the village, this half-timbered inn dates back to 1485 and has a great deal of character. Bedrooms are comfortable and well equipped with modern amenities. The hotel is popular with both tourists and business people.
10rm(6⇨4♠)Annexe5rm(1⇨4♠)(3fb)1 CTV in all bedrooms ® **T** ✳ sB&B⇨♠£27 dB&B⇨♠£36.50
CTV 75P ✲ *xmas*
Lunch £6.75 Dinner £8.50-£11alc Last dinner 9pm
Credit Cards 1 3

Marina Hotel

ESPLANADE, FOWEY, CORNWALL PL23 1HY
Telephone: 072683 3315
AA ★★ Ashley Courtenay

The Marina has a unique waterfront position overlooking the harbour. It is a charming Georgian residence with some bedrooms having balconies and the majority of bedrooms overlooking the water and harbour activities.

The restaurant also has panoramic views across the harbour and the menu provides a delicious range of local fish, meat & game.

The Hotel has its own quayside access to the water and moorings are available to guests.

NEVIS BANK HOTEL

★★

BELFORD ROAD,
FORT WILLIAM PH33 6BY
Telephone: (0397) 5721

Nevis Bank Hotel is a privately owned hotel situated on the eastern side of the town 10 minutes walk from the Main Street & Travel Centre and at the foot of the access road to Ben Nevis, Britain's highest mountain. The Hotel is famous for its Home Cooking and comfortable surroundings. Cabaret in Ceilidh Bar most weekends throughout the year.

Onich Hotel – Onich ★★

INVERNESS-SHIRE PH33 6RY
Telephone:
Onich (STD 08553) 214 Visitors 266

Occupying one of the finest situations in the Scottish Highlands this hotel is the only one in the area with gardens extending to the lochside. The views over Loch Linnhe to Glencoe & Morvern are absolutely breathtaking. This family run hotel has a very real reputation for excellent food and a warm welcoming atmosphere. The new Deerstalker Lounge is open all day for meals and drinks and offers a large selection of malt whisky & real ale on draught. This is an ideal base for climbing, hillwalking, windsurfing, skiing, touring or just relaxing. All 27 rooms have Bath/Shower, TV/Radio, Phone and Tea/Coffee maker. In-house facilities includes Solarium, Jacuzzi, Exercise Equipment, Games Room.

& RESTAURANT
BANAVIE, FORT WILLIAM
Telephone (039 77) 550

AA★★

Access Visa & Diners Accepted

Resident Proprietors:
James and Mary Sinclair

This family run hotel stands in its own grounds beside the Caledonian Canal, at Neptune's Staircase 3 miles from Fort William. Magnificent views of Ben Nevis and the surrounding mountain range can be enjoyed from the hotel. The hotel offers first class facilities in all 24 bedrooms.

The hotel's Jacobean styled restaurant is one of the most popular in the area, renowned for its Scottish cuisine with a French flavour with the emphasis on using fresh local produce. Choose from our Taste of Scotland, à la carte or 4 course table d'hôte menus. To compliment this there is an extensive wine list.

The hotel is located in a perfect situation for day tours to Skye, Mallaig, Inverness, Oban, Pitlochry, Glencoe and Aviemore. Private car park. Brochure & terms on request. Ashley Courtenay Recommeded Exechotels Taste of Scotland.

See gazetteer under Banavie

FRAMLINGHAM Suffolk Map **05** TM26

Telephone numbers are due to change during the currency of this guide.

★★**The Crown** Market Hill IP13 9AN (Trusthouse Forte) ☏(0728)723521
Conveniently set in the market place, and dating from the 16th century, this hotel has much character, retaining its old beams and real log fires. The refurbishment which has been undertaken to provide modern facilities in the bedrooms has been carried out with a sympathetic awareness of period. The cosy bar and popular restaurant offer friendly and welcoming service.
14⇌1 ⊞ ⊁in 1 bedroom CTV in all bedrooms ® **T** ✱
sB⇌£55-£60 dB⇌£60-£80 (room only) ⊟
15P *xmas*
V ✿ ⊻ ⊁ Lunch £8-£8.50&alc Dinner £13-£20alc Last dinner 9.30pm
Credit Cards 1 2 3 4 5

F

FRANKLEY MOTORWAY SERVICE AREA (M5) West Midlands Map **07** SO98

⌂**Granada Lodge** Illey Ln, Frankley B32 4AR (3m SE at M5 Service Area) (Granada) ☏021-550 3261 FAX 021-501 2880
Meals in adjacent service area restaurant.
41⇌↱(13fb)⊁in 9 bedrooms CTV in all bedrooms ® ⋈ (ex guide dogs) sB⇌↱£23-£26 dB⇌↱£26-£28 (room only)
☾CTV 50P
✿ ⊻
Credit Cards 1 2 3 5
See advertisement under BIRMINGHAM

FRASERBURGH Grampian *Aberdeenshire* Map **15** NJ96

★★**Royal** Broad St AB4 5AV ☏(0346)28524
Situated at the centre of the town, close to the harbour, this commercial hotel offers modest, reasonably priced accommodation, most of the rooms having en suite facilities.
15rm(12⇌)(1fb) CTV in all bedrooms ® S% sB&B£15 sB&B⇌£18 dB&B£28 dB&B⇌£32
CTV ⊮ ♫
V ✿ ⊻
Credit Cards 3

★★**Station** Seaforth St AB4 5BB ☏(0346)23343
FAX (0346) 23171
The ground floor of this commercial, town centre hotel has been refurbished to provide attractive facilities which include a smart dining room, a large function suite and a lounge bar which has been furnished and decorated to resemble train carriages. Bedroom accommodation remains modest but is reasonably priced, as are all meals.
20rm(3⇌2↱)(3fb) CTV in all bedrooms ® **T** ✱ ⊟
☾CTV 30P snooker solarium *xmas*
V ✿ ⊻ Last high tea 6.30pm
Credit Cards 1 2 3 5

FRESHFORD Avon Map **03** ST75

❀★★★★ ⅱ
HOMEWOOD PARK

Hinton Charterhouse
BA3 6BB (Between A36 & village) ☏Limpley Stoke (022122)3731
Telex no 444937
FAX (022122) 3820
Closed 24 Dec-6 Jan

A Victorian home with a more charming apppearance than is normally associated with the period, Homewood Park is set in delightful lawns and gardens. Throughout the hotel, the staff reflect the gentle, caring attitude that is the hallmark of owners, Stephen and Penny Ross. Nothing is too much trouble. Though the bedrooms vary in style and size, they are all spacious and it is in this domain that Penny Ross has used colours and fabrics with such skill. Bathrooms are particularly comfortable and the lighting a feature. The kitchen is Stephen Ross's province and he has an impeccable history there, although these days he concentrates more on the planning than the cooking. Chef Darren McGrath cooks with the same dedication and skill, to produce contemporary English dishes. At first glance, the menu appears to contain the type of dishes which are found almost everywhere, but there the similarity ends. Calf's liver, beef fillet, loin of lamb, etc, are cooked so lightly and the sauces are of just the right intensity that flavours are enhanced, while remaining identifiable. Vegetables are cooked to perfection. As one would expect, the wine list is of a comparable standard, with around 200 items on offer.
15⇌↱(2fb) CTV in all bedrooms **T** ⋈ S%
sB&B⇌↱£75-£105
dB&B⇌↱£95-£115 Continental breakfast ⊟
30P ⊯ ✲ ℘ (hard) ⌂
V ✿ ⊻ S% High tea £7.50-£9.50alc Dinner £23-£27.50alc Last dinner 9.30pm
Credit Cards 1 2 3 4 5

FRESHWATER

See **Wight, Isle of**

FRESSINGFIELD Suffolk Map **05** TM27

✕**Fox & Goose** IP21 5PB ☏(037986)247
Built in 1509 (the year that Henry VIII came to the throne) the attractive inn is situated next to the church. A good range of well-cooked dishes is available from the seasonal menus and the wine list is extensive. Sevice is friendly and polite.
Closed Tue, 24-27 Dec, 2 wk late Jan/Feb & 2 wks Sep
Dinner not served Sun (ex BH's)
⊽ English & French 26 seats Lunch £16-£16.50&alc Dinner £16-£16.50&alc Last lunch 1.30 Last dinner 9pm 29P nc10yrs
Credit Cards 1 2 3 5

FREUCHIE Fife Map **11** NO20

★★**Lomond Hills** Parliament Square KY7 7EY (Exec Hotel) ☏Falkland(0337)57329 & 57498
Modernised and extended former coaching inn.
25rm(13⇌12↱)(3fb)2⊞ CTV in all bedrooms ® **T**
sB&B⇌↱£28-£32 dB&B⇌↱£41-£45 ⊟
40P sauna ⌂
⊽ Scottish & French **V** ✿ ⊻ Lunch fr£8alc Dinner fr£12.50&alc Last dinner 9pm
Credit Cards 1 2 3 5

FRINTON-ON-SEA Essex Map **05** TM21

★★**Maplin** Esplanade CO13 9EL ☏(0255)673832
Closed Jan
Welcoming, family-run hotel with comfortable, impeccably kept bedrooms and sound home cooking.
12rm(9⇌1↱)(2fb) CTV in all bedrooms ® **T** ✱ S10%
sB&B£33-£55 sB&B⇌↱£36-£58 dB&B⇌↱£70-£74
⊞ CTV 15P 2⛟ ⊯ ⌓(heated) nc10yrs *xmas*
V ✿ Lunch fr£12.75 Dinner fr£13.75 Last dinner 9.30pm
Credit Cards 1 2 3 5

★**Rock** The Esplanade, 1 Third Av CO13 9EQ ☎(0255)677194
Closed Jan
Friendly and efficiently-run family hotel with a warm welcome.
6rm(5⮫)(3fb)1⊟ CTV in all bedrooms ® S10%
sB&B⮫£31.50-£34 dB&B⮫£50.50-£56
CTV 12P ⛟ solarium
V Lunch £10&alc Dinner £10.50&alc Last dinner 9pm
Credit Cards 1 2 3 5

FROME Somerset Map **03** ST74

★★★62% **Mendip Lodge** Bath Rd BA11 2HP ☎(0373)63223
Telex no 44832 FAX (0373) 51196
A motel block of bedrooms, built in the 1960s and 1970s, has now been updated to today's standards, whilst extensions to the original Edwardian building beside it have made good use of the potential for country views. Staff are friendly and helpful throughout the hotel, and the standard of food served is better than that in many similar establishments.
40⇌(12fb)⊬in 10 bedrooms CTV in all bedrooms ® **T**
sB&B⇌£43-£49 dB&B⇌£62-£72 Continental breakfast ⊟
☾ 60P 12🚗 ✿ CFA ⌂
V ♆ ⛾ Lunch fr£14.50&alc Dinner fr£14.50&alc Last dinner 9.30pm
Credit Cards 1 2 3 5

★★**George** 4 Market Place BA11 1AF ☎(0373)62584
FAX (0373) 51945
A former coaching inn situated in the town centre. The bedrooms have recently been decorated and re-furnished. There is a grill restaurant and an all-day coffee shop-cum-bar.
20rm(14⇌6⮫)(1fb)2⊟ CTV in all bedrooms ® **T** ✱
sB&B⇌⮫£39.50-£44 dB&B⇌⮫£49.50-£60.50 ⊟
17🚗 solarium *xmas*
☋ English & Continental **V** ♆ ⛾ Lunch £5.35-£6.50alc Dinner £9.50-£14.50alc Last dinner 9.30pm
Credit Cards 1 2 3 5 ⓔ

GAINSBOROUGH Lincolnshire Map **08** SK88

★★**Hickman-Hill** Cox's Hill DN21 1HH ☎(0427)3639
Built in the late 16th century as a school, this pleasant and comfortable hotel stands in spacious grounds on the eastern outskirts of the town.
8rm(3⇌3⮫)(1fb) CTV in all bedrooms ® **T** S% sB&B⇌⮫£33 dB&B⇌⮫£45 ⊟
CTV 25P ⛟ ✿ solarium *xmas*
V ♆ ⛾ Lunch £5.25 Dinner £8.50 Last dinner 9.00pm
Credit Cards 1 3

GAIRLOCH Highland *Ross & Cromarty* Map **14** NG87

★★**The Old Inn** IV21 2BD ☎(0445)2006
14rm(11⇌3⮫)(4fb) CTV in all bedrooms ® **T**
sB&B⇌⮫£19.50-£24.50 dB&B⇌⮫£39-£49 ⊟
50P ⛟
♆ ⛾ Lunch fr£5.50 High tea fr£5.50 Dinner fr£11.95 Last dinner 9pm
Credit Cards 1 2 3

GALASHIELS Borders *Selkirkshire* Map **12** NT43

★★★61% **Kingsknowes** Selkirk Rd TD1 3HY ☎(0896)58375
A Victorian mansion built of red sandstone, standing in well-tended grounds overlooking the River Tweed. Its comfortable, well-appointed bedrooms are complemented by elegant public rooms.
11rm(8⇌2⮫)(2fb) CTV in all bedrooms ® **T** ✱
sB&B⇌⮫£40-£45 dB&B⇌⮫£60-£70 ⊟
50P ⛟ ✿ ℘ (hard)
V ♆ Lunch £12.50 Dinner £12.50&alc Last dinner 8.45pm
Credit Cards 1 2 3 4 5

★★★57% ***Woodlands House*** Windyknowe Rd TD1 1RG
☎(0896)4722
Victorian Gothic style mansion in tree studded grounds with good looking spacious rooms.
9rm(8⇌1⮫) CTV in all bedrooms ® **T**
30P ✿ ⌂
V ♆ ⛾ Last dinner 9pm
Credit Cards 1 2 3 5

★★***Abbotsford Arms*** 63 Stirling St TD1 1BY
☎(0896)2517 & 4734
RS 24, 25, 31 Dec & 1Jan
a family-run hotel situated close to the centre of the town providing modern accommodation and helpful service, meals being available throughout the day in the comfortable lounge bars and attractive restaurant.
10rm(5⮫)(2fb) CTV in all bedrooms ® **T** ⛌ (ex guide dogs)
CTV ℙ ⛟
♆ ⛾ Last dinner 9pm
Credit Cards 1 3

GANLLWYD Gwynedd Map **06** SH72

★***Tyn-Y-Groes*** LL40 2NH ☎(0341)40275
This attractive stone-built inn offers newly refurbished bedrooms and serves food of a good standard in its delightful restaurant.
8rm(4⇌3⮫)(1fb) CTV in 3bedrooms ®
CTV 24P ⛟
☋ French **V** ♆ ⊬ Last dinner 9pm

GARFORTH West Yorkshire Map **08** SE43

★★★64% **Hilton National** Wakefield Rd, Garforth Rdbt LS25 1LH (junc A63/A642 6m E of Leeds) (Hilton)
☎Leeds(0532)866556 Telex no 556324 FAX (0532) 868326
Modern and functional, this purpose-built hotel offers comfortable, well appointed bedrooms.
142⇌⮫(21fb)⊬in 4 bedrooms CTV in all bedrooms ® **T** ✱
sB⇌⮫£66-£81 dB⇌⮫£84-£114 (room only)
☾ 250P ✿ CFA ⛆(heated) sauna gymnasium pool *xmas*
V ♆ ⛾ ⊬ Lunch £6.95-£9.95 Dinner £11.75-£12.95&alc Last dinner 10pm
Credit Cards 1 2 3 5

GARSTANG Lancashire Map **07** SD44

★★**Crofters** Cabus PR3 1PH (A6) (Consort) ☎(09952)4128
A comfortable, family-run hotel with attractive public rooms and well-appointed bedrooms.
19rm(4⇌15⮫)(4fb) CTV in all bedrooms ® **T**
sB&B⇌⮫£39.50-£43.50 dB&B⇌⮫£44-£48 ⊟
☾ 200P ♫ *xmas*
☋ French & English **V** ♆ S% Lunch £6.50-£11&alc Dinner £11-£11&alc Last dinner 10pm
Credit Cards 1 2 3 5 ⓔ

★★⌂ **The Pickerings**
Garstang Rd, Catterall
PR3 0HA (2m S B6430)
☎(09952)2133 due to change to (0995) 602133
FAX (0995) 602100

The delightfully furnished country-house hotel and restaurant stands in two acres of well-tended gardens. Bedrooms are very comfortable, and the resident owners take pains to ensure that guests feel at home.
▶

9rm(8⇌1🚿)(2fb)3🛏 CTV in all bedrooms ® T ✗ (ex guide dogs) sB&B⇌🚿£32-£48 dB&B⇌🚿£52-£88 ⊟
50P ✽ *xmas*
♉ English & Continental V ♉ Lunch £8-£9 Dinner fr£16
Last dinner 10pm
Credit Cards [1] [3] [5]

GARVE Highland *Ross & Cromarty* Map **14** NH36

★★***Garve*** IV23 2PR ☎(09974)205
Closed 2 Nov-Mar
Large stone building set on the main road in the shadow of Ben Wyvis.
36rm(16⇌1🚿)(3fb)
CTV 50P ✽ ♩
♉ Scottish & French V ♉ ♉
Credit Cards [1] [2] [3]

★★**Inchbae Lodge** Inchbae IV23 2PH ☎Aultguish(09975)269
Comfortable, family-run hotel offering good food and located 6m W of Garve on A835.
6rm(3⇌)Annexe6🚿(2fb) ® sB&B⇌🚿£20.50-£23.50
dB&B⇌🚿£33-£39 ⊟
CTV 30P ✽ ♩ clay pigeon shooting *xmas*
♉ Scottish & French ♉ ♉ Bar Lunch £1.95-£10.50alc High tea £1.95-£10.50alc Dinner £14.50 Last dinner 8.30pm

GATEHOUSE OF FLEET Dumfries & Galloway
Kirkcudbrightshire Map **11** NX55

★★★★64% **Cally Palace** DG7 2DL ☎Gatehouse(05574)341
Telex no 777088 FAX (05574) 522
Closed 3 Jan-Feb
Enjoying a splendid situation, secluded in spacious grounds and gardens, the hotel features traditional service by friendly staff and provides excellent value for money. Its warm, relaxing atmosphere combines with such outdoor leisure activities as putting, croquet, tennis and swimming to make it a popular choice for the whole family.
59⇌🚿(21fb)1🛏 CTV in all bedrooms ® T ✱
sB&B⇌🚿£35-£45 dB&B⇌🚿£65-£95 (incl dinner) ⊟
Lift ☾ 100P ✽ ⇌(heated) ♔ (hard) ♩ sauna solarium croquet putting green ♫ *xmas*
♉ French V ♉ ♉ ⁄ Lunch £6 Dinner £14-£15 Last dinner 9.30pm
Credit Cards [3]

★★★62% **Murray Arms** DG7 2HY (Best Western)
☎Gatehouse(05574)207 Telex no 9312110663
FAX (05574) 370
A traditional, long-established hotel extends a warm welcome to guests, providing relaxing lounges and comfortable bedrooms with bathrooms, many of them having been modernised to a high standard.
12⇌Annexe1⇌(3fb) CTV in all bedrooms ® T
sB&B⇌£29-£30 dB&B⇌£58-£60 ⊟
☾ CTV 50P ✽ croquet lawn ♔ *xmas*
V ♉ ♉ Bar Lunch £3.25-£10&alc Dinner £12-£13.50 Last dinner 8.45pm
Credit Cards [1] [2] [3] [5] £

GATESHEAD Tyne & Wear Map **12** NZ26

★★★69% **Springfield** Durham Rd NE9 5BT (Embassy) ☎091-477 4121 Telex no 538197 FAX 091-477 7213
Recently modernised to a most comfortable standard. The elegant restaurant offers a carvery as well as the standard menu.
60⇌🚿(4fb)⁄in 7 bedrooms CTV in all bedrooms ® T
Lift ☾ CTV 100P
V ♉ ♉ Lunch fr£7.95 Dinner fr£10.95 Last dinner 9.30pm
Credit Cards [1] [2] [3] [4] [5]

★★★66% **Swallow** NE8 1PE (Swallow) ☎091-477 1105
Telex no 53534 FAX 091-478 7214
Situated just off the southern approach to Newcastle, this modern hotel offers spacious accommodation.
106⇌🚿(6fb)⁄in 19 bedrooms CTV in all bedrooms ® T
sB&B⇌🚿£63-£78 dB&B⇌🚿£73-£88 ⊟
Lift ☾ CTV 90P 50🚗 CFA ▭(heated) sauna solarium gymnasium spa bath steam room ♫
♉ International V ♉ ♉ S% Lunch £6.95-£9.95&alc Dinner £12.50-£15.50&alc Last dinner 10pm
Credit Cards [1] [2] [3] [4] [5]

★★**Eslington Villa Hotel** 8 Station Rd, Low Fell NE9 6DR
☎091-487 6017
14rm(8⇌6🚿)(1fb) CTV in all bedrooms ® T ✱
sB&B⇌🚿£34.50-£39.50 dB&B⇌🚿£44.50-£49.50 ⊟
15P ✽
♉ English & French ⁄ Lunch £8.95-£11.95&alc Dinner £14.95-£15.95&alc Last dinner 10pm
Credit Cards [1] [2] [3] [5]

GATTONSIDE Borders *Roxburghshire* Map **12** NT53

✗✗**Hoebridge Inn** TD6 9NB ☎Melrose(089682)3082
Closed Mon, 3 wks Jun, 1 wks Oct, Xmas & New Year
Lunch not served
♉ British, French & Italian V 46 seats Dinner £8-£15alc Last dinner 10pm 15P
Credit Cards [1] [3]

GATWICK AIRPORT (LONDON) West Sussex
Map **04** TQ24

See **Town Plan Section** under **London Airports**
See also **Burgh Heath, Dorking, East Grinstead, Oxted, Reigate and South Godstone**

★★★★69% **Copthorne** Copthorne Road, Copthorne RH10 3PG (on A264 2m E of A264/B2036 rbt) (Best Western)
☎Copthorne(0342)714971 Telex no 95500 FAX (0342) 717375
Peacefully set in 100 acres of grounds and woodland, yet only minutes from the airport, an hotel centred around a 16th-century farmhouse complements a choice of well appointed, modern bedrooms with restaurants, bars and a range of banquetting, conference, health and leisure facilities; a high level of service is provided in all areas.
223rm(177⇌46🚿)(10fb)4🛏⁄in 14 bedrooms CTV in all bedrooms ® T ✱ sB⇌🚿£75-£80
dB⇌🚿£90-£95 (room only) ⊟
☾ 300P ✽ CFA squash sauna solarium gymnasium croquet putting ♔ *xmas*
♉ English & Continental V ♉ ♉ ⁄ Lunch £11.95-£15&alc Dinner fr£12&alc Last dinner 10.30pm
Credit Cards [1] [2] [3] [4] [5] £

★★★★72% **Effingham Park Hotel** Copthorne RH10 3EU
☎Copthorne(0342)714994 Telex no 95649 FAX (0342) 716039
Set in 40 acres of parkland and gardens, this purpose-built hotel offers a range of well equipped and tastefully appointed bedrooms. There is a choice of restaurants, in addition to the popular leisure club bar lounge, and there are extensive facilities, including a 9-hole golf course, indoor swimming pool and beauty salon. Staff are efficient, helpful and friendly.
122🚿(6fb) CTV in all bedrooms ® T ✗ (ex guide dogs)
Lift ☾ CTV 500P ✽ ▭(heated) ▶9 ♩ sauna solarium gymnasium Dance studio, Jacuzzi & plunge pool
♉ English & French V ♉ ♉ ⁄ Last dinner 11 pm
Credit Cards [1] [2] [3] [5]

★★★★71% **Gatwick Hilton International** RH6 0LL (Hilton)
☎Gatwick(0293)518080 Telex no 877021 FAX (0293) 28980
This hotel provides excellent access to the airport, being directly linked to the terminals. Bedrooms are equipped to a high standard, featuring air-conditioning, mini-bars and television displays of flight information. The reception lobby holds a replica of the Gypsy

Moth aeroplane flown by Amy Johnson, after whom the lounge is named. Garden restaurant and bar, with their efficient, well-managed service, will please the discerning diner, while the amenities include hairdressing salon, bank, shop, business centre, satellite television and indoor swimming pool.
552⇨🚿(4fb)⊬in 34 bedrooms CTV in all bedrooms **T** S%
sB⇨🚿£87.50-£92.50 dB⇨🚿£98-£103.50 (room only) ⊟
Lift ☾ ⊞ 100P (80p per/hr) ❊ CFA ⊡(heated) sauna solarium gymnasium *xmas*
☋ Continental **V** ♉ ⊻ ⊬ S% Lunch fr£13.60 Dinner fr£20.30 Last dinner 11pm
Credit Cards 1 2 3 4 5

★★★62% Chequers Thistle Brighton Road, Horley RH6 8PH (Thistle) ☎Horley(0293)786992 Telex no 877550 FAX (0293) 820625
Once a Tudor coaching inn, this pleasant, friendly hotel offers well appointed bedrooms, equipped with the most modern facilities. The Halfway Halt lounge bar has a low oak-beamed ceiling, while restaurant and cocktail bar favour a more formal style.
78⇨🚿(54fb)⊬in 5 bedrooms CTV in all bedrooms ® **T** ⋈ ✱
sB⇨🚿£65-£75 dB⇨🚿£75-£85 (room only) ⊟
☾ 190P CFA ⊡(heated) ♫
☋ International ♉ ⊻ ⊬ Lunch fr£7.95&alc Dinner fr£14.50&alc Last dinner 10pm
Credit Cards 1 2 3 4 5

★★★57% Gatwick Concorde Church Rd, Lowfield Heath, Crawley RH11 0PQ (Queens Moat) ☎Crawley(0293)33441 Telex no 87287 FAX (0293) 35369
Recently completely refurbished, this hotel now offers well furnished bedrooms equipped to a high standard, some overlooking the runway and others situated in the new wing. Facilities include the Aviators Brasserie, Rounds Pub – a popular meeting place and lunchtime diner – and several function rooms.
▶

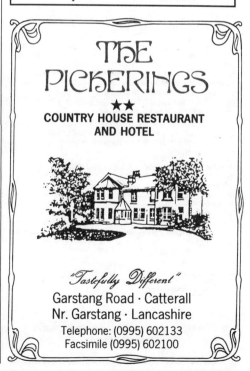

121⇨🚿(7fb) CTV in all bedrooms ® T sB⇨🚿£60-£75 dB⇨🚿£75-£95 (room only) ⊟
Lift ☾ ⊞ 137P (charged) CFA
English, French & Italian V Lunch £9.50-£11.50 Dinner £4-£15alc Last dinner 10.45pm
Credit Cards 1 2 3 5 £

★★★62% The George High Street, Crawley RH10 1BS (Trusthouse Forte) ☎Crawley(0293)24215 Telex no 87385 FAX (0293) 548565
This historic inn stands in the centre of Crawley, easily recognised by its rare gallows sign which spans the High Street. Its interior combines the old world charm of exposed beams and timbers with modern standards of comfort, particularly in the bedrooms of both the main building and its new rear extensions. The Shire Restaurant features cuisine in English style, whilst other amenities include coffee shops, a historic public bar and good car parking.
76⇨(12fb)in 20 bedrooms CTV in all bedrooms ® T ✱ S% sB⇨£73-£85 dB⇨£83-£95 (room only) ⊟
☾ 89P (charged) CFA ♫ *xmas*
V Lunch £6.95-£9.95&alc High tea fr£5&alc Dinner fr£13.95&alc Last dinner 9.30pm
Credit Cards 1 2 3 4 5

G

★★★62% Goffs Park 45 Goffs Park Road, Crawley RH11 8AX ☎Crawley(0293)35447 Telex no 87415 FAX (0293) 542050
Situated in a residential area south of Crawley, this busy commercial hotel offers a choice of well equipped, modern bedrooms and service of a good standard. Other amenities include a popular bar and restaurant, and fine conference facilities.
37rm(18⇨19🚿)Annexe28rm(21⇨7🚿) CTV in all bedrooms ® T sB&B⇨🚿fr£62.50 dB&B⇨🚿fr£74.50 ⊟
☾ 92P CFA
English & French V S% Lunch £9&alc Dinner £11&alc Last dinner 9.30pm
Credit Cards 1 2 3 5

★★★62% Post House Povey Cross Road, Horley RH6 0BA (Trusthouse Forte) ☎Horley(0293)771621 Telex no 877351 FAX (0293) 771054
A modern, purpose-built hotel – much used by airport passengers, for whom it operates a courtesy bus service – offers accommodation in well equipped bedrooms with up-to-date facilities, executive rooms providing additional comforts. Both table d'hote and a la carte menus are available in the restaurant, while a lighter meal can be obtained in the coffee shop.
216⇨in 43 bedrooms CTV in all bedrooms ® T S% sB⇨£78-£87 dB⇨£99-£108 (room only)
Lift ☾ 350P (charged) ✲ CFA (heated)
English & French V Lunch £9.50-£12.50&alc Dinner £15.50-£16.50&alc Last dinner 10.30pm
Credit Cards 1 2 3 4 5

★★Gatwick Manor London Rd, Lowfield Heath, Crawley RH10 2ST (Berni/Chef & Brewer) ☎Crawley(0293)26301 & 35251 Telex no 87529
Original beamed Tudor buildings in the grounds of this spacious hotel have been skilfully extended to offer well equipped modern bedrooms with friendly and efficiently managed service. Guests have a choice of two bars and two Berni restaurants, grill cooking is of a high standard and supplemented by a self-service salad bar.
30⇨🚿(3fb) CTV in all bedrooms ® T (ex guide dogs) sB&B⇨🚿fr£63 dB&B⇨🚿fr£69.50 ⊟
☾ CTV 250P ✲ ♫
Mainly grills V Lunch £8 Dinner £9 Last dinner 10.30pm
Credit Cards 1 2 3 5

GERRARDS CROSS Buckinghamshire Map 04 TQ08

★★Ethorpe Packhorse Rd SL9 8HY (Berni/Chef & Brewer) ☎(0753)882039
The bedrooms at this friendly commercial-style hotel are comfortable and spacious with co-ordinating soft furnishings and fabrics.
29rm(28⇨1🚿)(4fb)1 CTV in all bedrooms ® T sB&B⇨🚿£62 dB&B⇨🚿£72.50 ⊟
☾ 80P ✲
Mainly grills V Lunch £8 Dinner £9 Last dinner 10.30pm
Credit Cards 1 2 3 5

GIFFNOCK Strathclyde *Renfrewshire* Map 11 NS55

★★★67% MacDonald Thistle Eastwood Toll G46 6RA (Thistle) ☎041-638 2225 Telex no 779138 FAX 041-638 6231
Modern hotel at the Eastwood Toll roundabout (A77), on the southern outskirts of Glasgow.
56⇨🚿(1fb) CTV in all bedrooms ® T ✱ sB⇨🚿£55-£70 dB⇨🚿£65-£75 (room only) ⊟
☾ 200P CFA sauna solarium gymnasium games room ♫
International Lunch fr£7.50&alc Dinner fr£12.95&alc Last dinner 10pm
Credit Cards 1 2 3 4 5

See advertisement under GLASGOW

✕Turban Tandoori 2 Station Rd G45 6JF ☎041-638 0069
Standing conveniently close to the railway station, on the southern access road to the city, this well-established restaurant boasts a reputation achieved largely by attentive service and an innovative range of curries, Karami, Jaipuri, Nentara and Masaledar specialities being featured as well as the more popular 'sizzling' Tandoori dishes. Dim lighting adds to the intimate atmosphere created by clever partitioning.
Closed 25 Dec & 1 Jan
Lunch not served
Indian V 70 seats ✱ Dinner £7.50-£9.50alc Last dinner mdnt 150P
Credit Cards 1 2 3

See advertisement under GLASGOW

GIFFORD Lothian *East Lothian* Map 12 NT56

★★*Tweeddale Arms* EH41 4QU (Consort) ☎(062081)240
This character village hotel offers good modern comforts combined with old world charm and traditional hospitality. The smart restaurant serves British and continental cuisine. Bedrooms are comfortable and well equipped and the relaxing lounge has an inviting log fire when the weather demands it.
15rm(13⇨2🚿)(2fb) CTV in all bedrooms ® T
snooker
V Last dinner 9pm
Credit Cards 1 2 3

GIGHA ISLAND Strathclyde *Argyllshire* Map 10 NR64

(Car ferry from Tayinloan (mainland))
★★Gigha PA41 7AD ☎Gigha(05835)254 FAX (05835) 275
Closed mid Jan-Mar
This extended and modernised inn has won an architectural award; equally commendable are the hospitality and home baking.

9rm(3⇨) sB&Bfr£24 sB&B⇨fr£27 dB&Bfr£48 dB&B⇨fr£54
CTV 20P
Lunch fr£7 Dinner fr£15 Last dinner 8pm
Credit Cards 1 3

For key to symbols see the inside front cover.

GILLAN Cornwall & Isles of Scilly Map **02** SW72

★★Tregildry TR12 6HG ☎Manaccan(032623)378
Closed 15 Oct-Etr
Imaginative menus of well-cooked dishes are offered at this family-run hotel with elevated views over Falmouth Bay.
10rm(9⇌1⊓)(2fb) CTV in 6bedrooms ® sB&B⇌⊓£35-£42 dB&B⇌⊓£60-£71.50 (incl dinner) ⊟
CTV 20P ✱
♀ International V ☕ ⚒ S% Bar Lunch £5-£9 Dinner fr£9.50&alc Last dinner 8.30pm
Credit Cards 1 3

See advertisement under HELFORD

GILLINGHAM Dorset Map **03** ST82

★★ STOCK HILL HOUSE
Wyke SP8 5NR
☎(07476)3626 due to change to (0747)823626
Closed 2 wks Jun & Nov

Set in 10 acres of park and woodland, this attractive Victorian manor house is the ideal place for a peaceful, relaxing stay. Public rooms are comfortable and bedrooms are spacious and well equipped. Here, as elsewhere, there are some fine pieces of furniture. A cabinet of china makes an attractive display outside the elegant restaurant, where chef patron, Peter Hauser, provides excellent, honest and unfussy cuisine. Good use is made of fresh produce, much of it local or from the well-kept kitchen garden, and the interesting puddings are hard to resist. A well-chosen wine list complements the food. Luxurious features include an indoor swimming pool, a jacuzzi and a sauna, with an exercise room for the energetic. The gardens and lawns are additional attractions, and Peter Hauser's personal involvement is evident in the efficient but friendly service provided by the willing staff.
7rm(5⇌2⊓)1⊟ CTV in all bedrooms T ✗ ✱
sB&B⇌⊓£65 dB&B⇌⊓£130 (incl dinner)
25P ✱ ⊡(heated) croquet nc7yrs *xmas*
♀ English, French & Austrian V ⚒ Lunch £16 Dinner £22
Last dinner 8.45pm
Credit Cards 1 3

GILLINGHAM Kent Map **05** TQ76

⌂Rank Motor Lodge Hartlip ME8 8PW (Rank)
☎Medway(0634)377337
(For full entry see Farthing Corner Service Area (M2))

GIRVAN Strathclyde *Ayrshire* Map **10** NX19

★★King's Arms Dalrymple St KA26 0DU ☎(0465)3322
This family-run hotel places the emphasis on good food and friendly service, whilst golfing cocktails such as 'The Perfect Slice' are a feature of the Bunker Bar.
25rm(14⇌11⊓)(4fb) CTV in all bedrooms ® T ✗ (ex guide dogs) sB&B⇌⊓£28 dB&B⇌⊓£39 ⊟
(100P 1⊓ (£2) snooker ♫ *xmas*
♀ Scottish & French V ☕ ⚒ Lunch fr£5.50alc Dinner £9.50
Last dinner 9.30pm
Credit Cards 1 3 £

GISBURN Lancashire Map **07** SD84

★★★61% Stirk House BB7 4LJ (Consort) ☎(02005)581 Telex no 635238 FAX (02005) 744
Once an impressive country house, this hotel offers accommodation in a modern wing to complement the comfortable, interesting lounges and bars in the old building.
38⇌♠Annexe12⇌(2fb) CTV in all bedrooms ® **T** ✗ (ex guide dogs) ✱ sB&B⇌♠£55-£60 dB&B⇌♠£65-£70 ⊟
☾ 100P ✲ CFA ▭(heated) squash sauna solarium gymnasium ♫
♡ English & French **V** ♡ ☖ Lunch £6.95-£10 Dinner £13-£15&alc Last dinner 9.45pm
Credit Cards 1 2 3 4 5 £

GITTISHAM Devon Map **03** SY19

★★★67% Combe House EX14 0AD (Pride of Britain)
☎Honiton (0404)42756 & 43560 FAX (0404) 46004
Closed 7 Jan-1 Mar

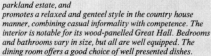

This large, impressive Elizabethan manor house stands in an extensive parkland estate, and promotes a relaxed and genteel style in the country house manner, combining casual informality with competence. The interior is notable for its wood-panelled Great Hall. Bedrooms and bathrooms vary in size, but all are well equipped. The dining room offers a good choice of well presented dishes.
15⇌2⊞ CTV in all bedrooms **T** S12.5% sB&B⇌£52-£76.50 dB&B⇌£80-£103.50 ⊟
50P 1⊜ (£2.50 per night) ⊞ ✲ ♩ croquet *xmas*
♡ English & French **V** ♡ ☖ S12.5% High tea fr£2.50alc Dinner fr£18.50alc Last dinner 9.30pm
Credit Cards 1 2 3 5

GLASBURY Powys Map **03** SO13

★★Llwynaubach Lodge HR3 3PT ☎(04974)473
A modernised hotel, close to Hay-on-Wye, with comfortable bedrooms and a character bar converted from an old mill and forge.
6⇌♠Annexe1⇌♠ CTV in all bedrooms ® **T** sB&B⇌♠£22.50-£25 dB&B⇌♠£45 (incl dinner) ⊟
30P ✲ ⩦ ♩ ♫ *xmas*
♡ English & French **V** ♡ ☖ ⚟ Lunch £6.50-£11&alc Dinner £11&alc Last dinner 9.30pm
Credit Cards 1 3 5 £

GLASGOW Strathclyde *Lanarkshire* Map **11** NS56

See **Town Plan Section**

★★★★60% The Albany Bothwell St G2 7EN (Trusthouse Forte) ☎041-248 2656 Telex no 77440 FAX 041-221 8986
A large city centre business hotel offers a mixture of compact and spacious bedrooms complemented by two restaurants and extensive banqueting and conference facilities. Recently completely renovated, it plans to open a health and fitness club incorporating a swimming pool by Easter 1990.
251⇌⚟in 27 bedrooms CTV in all bedrooms ® **T** ✱ S% sB⇌fr£80 dB⇌fr£100 (room only) ⊟
Lift ☾ ⊞ 25P CFA snooker
♡ Scottish & French **V** ♡ ☖ ⚟ S% Lunch £9.95&alc Dinner £9.95&alc Last dinner 10pm
Credit Cards 1 2 3 4 5

★★★★61% Holiday Inn Glasgow Argyle St, Anderston G3 8RR (Holiday Inns) ☎041-226 5577 Telex no 776355 FAX 041-221 9202
This typical, large, city-centre hotel has some efficient staff, but the general atmosphere can be rather impersonal. Although the restaurant layout is interesting, our inspector found the dishes on its à la carte menu to be expensive and unmemorable. The cocktail bar, where a pianist plays in the evenings, is comfortable, with a pleasant outlook over the pool, and the hotel is well equipped to cater for meetings and functions.
298⇌♠(80fb)⚟in 38 bedrooms CTV in all bedrooms ® **T** sB⇌♠fr£90 dB⇌♠fr£98 (room only) ⊟
Lift ☾ ⊞ 180P ▭(heated) squash sauna solarium gymnasium heated whirlpool *xmas*
♡ European **V** ♡ ☖ ⚟ Lunch fr£16.15&alc High tea fr£7alc Dinner fr£16.15&alc Last dinner 10.30pm
Credit Cards 1 2 3 4 5

★★★★62% *Hospitality Inn* 36 Cambridge St G3 3HN (Mount Charlotte) ☎041-332 3311 Telex no 777334 FAX 041-332 4050
This large city centre hotel, offering spacious, well-appointed bedrooms and having its own car park underneath, is ideal for business traveller and holidaymaker alike.
316⇌(3fb) CTV in all bedrooms ® **T**
Lift ☾ 250⊜ CFA ♫
♡ Scottish, Danish & American **V** ♡ ☖ Last high tea 5.30pm
Credit Cards 1 2 3 4 5

★★★★63% Stakis Grosvenor 1/10 Grosvenor Ter, Great Western Rd G12 0TA (Stakis) ☎041-339 8811 Telex no 776247 FAX 041-334 0710
Situated in the popular west of the city, overlooking the Botanic Gardens, an hotel with a fine façade offers well-equipped bedrooms and spacious public areas. Guests can choose between the Steakhouse and the attractive Lafayette restaurant, attentive and friendly staff providing the same high standard of service in both.
95⇌♠(12fb)1⊞⚟in 50 bedrooms CTV in all bedrooms ® **T** ✱ sB⇌♠£77-£87 dB⇌♠£95-£105 (room only) ⊟
Lift ☾ 12P 70⊜
♡ French **V** ♡ ☖ ⚟ Lunch £6.50-£9&alc High tea £5-£11 Dinner £15.95-£16.95&alc Last dinner 10.30pm
Credit Cards 1 2 3 4 5

★★★71% Copthorne Hotel George Square G2 1DS (Best Western) ☎041-332 6711 Telex no 778147 FAX 041-332-4264
141⇌ CTV in all bedrooms ® **T** ✗ (ex guide dogs) sB⇌£68-£76 dB⇌£80-£88 (room only) ⊟
Lift ☾ ₱ *xmas*
♡ International **V** ♡ ☖ ⚟ Lunch fr£12.95 Dinner fr£13.95&alc Last dinner 9.45pm
Credit Cards 1 2 3 5

★★★62% Crest Hotel Glasgow-City Argyle St G2 8LL (Crest) ☎041-248 2355 Telex no 779652 FAX 041-221 1014
Conveniently situated in the city centre, this refurbished hotel offers a high level of comfort, with relaxing bedrooms and attractive public areas which include a first-floor restaurant where vegetarian and diabetic diets are catered for. Well managed and maintained, providing friendly care from attentive staff, this hotel appeals to business traveller and leisure guest alike.
121⇌♠(6fb)⚟in 30 bedrooms CTV in all bedrooms ® **T** ✗ (ex guide dogs) sB⇌♠£70-£73 dB⇌♠£82-£85 (room only) ⊟
Lift ☾ ₱ CFA *xmas*
♡ Continental **V** ♡ ☖ ⚟
Credit Cards 1 2 3 5

★★★54% Kelvin Park Lorne 923 Sauchiehall St G3 7TE (Queens Moat) ☎041-334 4891 Telex no 778935 FAX 041-337 1659
Conveniently located close to the town centre and M8, the hotel is undergoing vast refurbishment (nearing completion at the time of going to print) which should result in accommodation of a much improved standard.

98⇨↱(7fb)2⊟⅟in 20 bedrooms CTV in all bedrooms ® T S% sB&B⇨↱£54.95-£57.95 dB&B⇨↱£63.95-£66.95 ₽
Lift ☾ 40⛟ ♫ *xmas*
♉ French V ♧ ⅅ Lunch £6.50-£10.95&alc High tea £4.50-£9.50 Dinner £11.25-£15.25&alc Last dinner 10.30pm
Credit Cards 1 2 3 4 5

★★★69% One Devonshire Gardens 1 Devonshire Gardens G12 0UX ☎041-339 2001 & 041-334 9494 FAX 041-337 1663
This elegant hotel is housed in a fine, end-terrace Victorian mansion house and provides spacious and comfortable accommodation. The restaurant attracts an extensive local clientele, and service is unobtrusive but efficient.
18rm(16⇨2↱)(2fb)6⊟ CTV in all bedrooms T S%
sB&B⇨↱£87-£98
dB&B⇨↱£110-£125 Continental breakfast ₽
☾ 8P ⛟
♉ French ♧ ⅅ S% Lunch £12-£14alc High tea £5-£8 Dinner £25 Last dinner 10pm
Credit Cards 1 2 3 4 5

★★★50% Stakis Ingram Ingram St G1 1DQ (Stakis) ☎041-248 4401 Telex no 776470 FAX 041-226 5149
Modern-city centre hotel.
90⇨↱(1fb)⅟in 62 bedrooms CTV in all bedrooms ® T ✱ S%
sB⇨↱£66.73-£73 dB⇨↱£80-£90 (room only) ₽
Lift ☾ 30P CFA *xmas*
♉ Scottish, English & French V ♧ ⅅ ⅟ Lunch £6-£12 Dinner fr£12.95&alc Last dinner 9.45pm
Credit Cards 1 2 3 5 ⓔ

★★★55% Stakis Pond Great Western Rd G12 0XP (Stakis) ☎041-334 8161 Telex no 776573 FAX 041-334 3846
Modern hotel in the north-west suburbs of the city.
132⇨↱(6fb)⅟in 55 bedrooms CTV in all bedrooms ® T ✱
sB⇨↱fr£66 dB⇨↱fr£74 (room only) ₽
Lift ☾ CTV 200P ❊ ⊡(heated) sauna solarium gymnasium *xmas*
V ♧ ⅅ ⅟ Lunch fr£6.35 Dinner fr£9.95 Last dinner 10pm
Credit Cards 1 2 3 5

See advertisement on page 299

★★★58% Swallow Hotel Glasgow 517 Paisley Rd West G51 1RW (Swallow) ☎041-427 3146 Telex no 778795 FAX 041-427 4059
Situated near to the M8, a purpose-built hotel currently undergoing a programme of improvements now boasts attractive, new public areas and a smart, modern leisure complex. All bedrooms are well equipped and comfortable, though some have still to be refurbished.
119rm(105⇨14↱)(1fb)⅟in 8 bedrooms CTV in all bedrooms ® T ✱ sB&B⇨↱fr£62 dB&B⇨↱fr£70 ₽
Lift ☾ 150P CFA ⊡(heated) sauna solarium gymnasium ♫
♉ English & French V ♧ ⅅ Lunch fr£8.75&alc Dinner fr£13&alc Last dinner 9.30pm
Credit Cards 1 2 3 5

See advertisement on page 299

★★★66% Tinto Firs Thistle 470 Kilmarnock Rd G43 2BB (Thistle) ☎041-637 2353 Telex no 778329 FAX 041-633 1340
A modern purpose built hotel set in a residential area on the south side of the city combines style and comfort in its bedrooms and attractive public rooms.
28⇨↱(4fb)⅟in 2 bedrooms CTV in all bedrooms ® T ✱
sB⇨↱£60-£70 dB⇨↱£70-£75 (room only) ₽
☾ 46P ❊ ♫
♉ International ♧ ⅅ ⅟ Lunch fr£7.75&alc Dinner fr£12.50&alc Last dinner 9.45pm
Credit Cards 1 2 3 4 5

Book as early as possible for busy holiday periods.

★★Ewington 132 Queens Dr, Queens Park G42 8QW ☎041-423 1152
Friendly, traditional hotel in a terrace overlooking the park.
45rm(19⇌17♠)(1fb) CTV in all bedrooms ® T ✱ sB&Bfr£25 sB&B⇌♠fr£40 dB&B⇌♠fr£58 ₿
Lift ☾ 18P snooker
♡ ☕ Lunch £5-£6 High tea fr£4.50 Dinner £9-£11 Last dinner 8.45pm
Credit Cards 1 2 3 5

★★Newlands 290 Kilmarnock Rd G43 2XS ☎041-632 9171
Closed 1 Jan
Set on the south side of the city, this small hotel offers comfortable, compact bedrooms with a lively lounge bar providing non-stop music.
17⇌♠ CTV in all bedrooms ® T ✱ sB&B⇌♠£25-£35 dB&B⇌♠£50-£55 ₿
☾ ₱ ♫
♀ French & Italian V ♡ Lunch £5.65-£18.15alc Dinner £5.65-£18.15alc Last dinner 9.30pm
Credit Cards 1 2 3 5

★★Sherbrooke 11 Sherbrooke Av, Pollokshields G41 4PG ☎041-427 4227 FAX 041-427 5685
Traditional red sandstone building located on south side of city with convenient access to motorway.
11rm(7⇌4♠)(3fb)⊁in 2 bedrooms CTV in all bedrooms ® T ✱ sB&B⇌♠£54.90 dB&B⇌♠£65 ₿
☾ CTV 50P ❊
♀ English & French V ♡ ☕ ⊁ Lunch £4.70-£7.50&alc Dinner £12.20&alc Last dinner 9.15pm
Credit Cards 1 2 3 5 £

○***Forum*** Congress Rd G3 8QT ☎041-204 0733 Telex no 776244
Due to have opened Aug 1989
300⇌

✕✕✕Fountain 2 Woodside Crescent G3 7UL ☎041-332 6396
Closed Sun
Lunch not served Sat
♀ French V 70 seats Last lunch 2.30pm Last dinner 11pm ₱ nc3yrs
Credit Cards 1 2 3 5

✕✕L'Ariosto Ristorante 92-94 Mitchell St G1 3NQ ☎041-221 0971 FAX 041-226 4264
Closed Sun, Xmas day & New Years day
♀ Italian V 110 seats ✱ Lunch £6.20-£9.10 Dinner £12-£19.50alc Last lunch 2.30pm Last dinner 11pm ₱ ♫
Credit Cards 1 2 3 5

✕✕Buttery 652 Argyle St G3 8UF ☎041-221 8188
In contrast to the urban development surrounding it, this restaurant is reminiscent of yesteryear, with its plush bar area and well appointed wood-panelled dining room. Carefully prepared dishes are based on sound ingredients and acccompanied by a well-balanced and reasonably priced wine list.
Closed Sun & BH's
Lunch not served Sat
♀ Scottish & French V 50 seats S10% Lunch fr£12.50&alc Dinner £19-£25alc Last lunch 2.30pm Last dinner 10pm 30P
Credit Cards 1 2 3 5

❀✕✕Colonial 25 High St G1 1LX
☎041-552 1923
The key to this unpretentious restaurant's success is the good quality Scottish ingredients, which are lovingly prepared and simply served here; a good value business and executive lunch menu is offered daily, the à la carte selection being changed every four weeks. Among the tempting and original dishes featured, seafood raviolis with a lobster and basil sauce, fine pheasant and flavoursome noisettes of lamb have been particularly popular. Service is friendly, relaxed and efficient, and a splendid wine list ranges from the house wine by Bouchard Ainé to the fine Burgundies of Trapet and Dujac.
Closed Sun & BH's
Lunch not served Sat
Dinner not served Mon
♀ Scottish & French V 45 seats ✱ Lunch £5.85-£9.95&alc Dinner £17-£28&alc Last lunch 2.30pm Last dinner 10.30pm ₱ nc3yrs
Credit Cards 1 2 3

✕✕Kensingtons 164 Darnley St, Pollokshields G41 2LL ☎041-424 3662 FAX 041-221 2762
Closed Sun & 4 days New Year
Lunch not served Sat
♀ International V 30 seats ✱ Lunch £8.75-£10&alc Dinner fr£16.95&alc Last lunch 2pm Last dinner 9.30pm ₱
Credit Cards 1 2 3 5

✕✕Rogano 11 Exchange Place G1 3AN ☎041-248 4055 & 4913
Closed Sun & BH's
V 50 seats ✱ Lunch £17.50-£25alc Dinner £17.50-£25alc Last lunch 2.30pm Last dinner 10.30pm ₱
Credit Cards 1 2 3 5

✕✕The Triangle 37 Queen St G1 3EF ☎041-221 8758
This stylish newcomer to the Glasgow scene offers the choice of a popular brasserie or a more formal dining room. It is the latter which has pleased our inspectors with its spacious and elegant style. The food is innovative, following the modern trend, with the addition of some classical dishes such as Beef Wellington and Tornedos Rossini and a variety of fish dishes. Staff are enthusiastic and friendly.
♀ International V 70 seats Lunch £7.50-£9.50&alc Dinner £17.75-£19.95&alc Last lunch 3pm Last dinner 11pm ₱
Credit Cards 1 2 3 4 5

✕Killermont House Restaurant 2022 Maryhill Rd, Maryhill Park G20 0AB ☎041-946 5412
Located in the northern suberbs, this converted manse provides comfortable and elegant surroundings in which to enjoy reliable and straightforward cuisine based on good quality Scottish ingredients. The fixed-price lunch and dinner menus are varied monthly to take advantage of seasonal produce, and on warm summer days one can eat al fresco in the sheltered walled garden.
Closed Mon
Lunch not served Sat
Dinner not served Sun
♀ British & French 60 seats ✱ Lunch £10 Dinner £18.50 Last lunch 2.15pm Last dinner 10pm 22P
Credit Cards 1 2 3

✕*Loon Fung* 417 Sauchiehall St G2 3LG ☎041-332 1240
Standing at the western end of Glasgow's famous Sauchiehall Street, this Chinese restaurant is constantly filled with bustle, for its extensive range of authentic Cantonese dishes is appreciated by the local population at lunch and dinner times and the Chinese community in the afternoon.
♀ Cantonese V 140 seats Last lunch 2pm Last dinner 11.30pm ₱
Credit Cards 1 2 3 5

✕Peking Inn 191 Hope St G2 2 ☎041-332 8971
Closed Sun & Chinese New Year
♀ Cantonese & Pekinese V 60 seats ✱ Lunch £14.50&alc Dinner £14.50&alc Last lunch 2pm Last dinner 11.30pm ₱
Credit Cards 1 2 3 5

G

GLASGOW AIRPORT Strathclyde *Renfrewshire* Map **11** NS46

★★★★ 55% **The Excelsior** Abbotsinch, Paisley PA3 2TR (Trusthouse Forte) ☎041-887 1212 Telex no 777733 FAX 041-887 3738
Standing alongside the city's airport terminal, this modern tower block hotel offers bedrooms of varying standards and styles.
300⇌(8fb)⅟in 35 bedrooms CTV in all bedrooms ® **T** ✱ S% sB⇌£73-£81 dB⇌£91-£97 (room only) ⊟
Lift ☾ ⊞ 35P CFA solarium ♫
V ♈ ♉ ⅟ Lunch £6.50-£9.95 Dinner £9.95&alc Last dinner 10.30pm
Credit Cards 1 2 3 4 5

★★★ 64% **Crest Hotel-Erskine Bridge** North Barr, Inchinnan PA8 6AN (Crest) ☎041-812 0123 Telex no 777713 FAX 041-812 7642
(For full entry see Erskine)

★★★ 60% **Dean Park** 91 Glasgow Road, Renfrew PA4 8YB (3m NE A8) (Queens Moat) ☎041-886 3771 Telex no 779032 FAX 041-885 0681
118⇌(5fb) CTV in all bedrooms ® **T** ✱ S% sB&B⇌£49.50 dB&B⇌£59.50 ⊟
☾ 200P ✽ CFA ♫ *xmas*
♉ Scottish & French **V** ♈ ♉ Bar Lunch £2.25-£4.25 Dinner £9.95&alc Last dinner 9.45pm
Credit Cards 1 2 3 5 £

★★★ 58% **Glynhill Hotel & Leisure Club** Paisley Road, Renfrew PA4 8XB (2m E A741) (Consort) ☎041-886 5555 Telex no 779536
Well placed for motorway and airport, this much-extended commercial hotel now has a smart new bar, the Carverie Restaurant and a leisure complex.
125⇌(34fb)2⊠ CTV in all bedrooms ® **T** sB&B⇌£47.50-£69 dB&B⇌£57.50-£79 ⊟
☾ 200P 30⌂ CFA ⊡(heated) snooker sauna solarium gymnasium spa bath steam room *xmas*
♉ International **V** ♈ ♉ ⅟ S10% Lunch £8.25-£8.75&alc Dinner £11.45-£15.95&alc Last dinner 10.30pm
Credit Cards 1 2 3 5

★★★ 64% **Stakis Normandy** Inchinnan Rd, Renfrew PA4 5EJ (2m NE A8) (Stakis) ☎041-886 4100 Telex no 778897 FAX 041-885 2366
A well run modern hotel offers compact, well-equipped bedrooms with 24 hour room service from a friendly, helpful staff. A choice of eating options is available, the buffet breakfast in the Juliana's restaurant being particularly impressive. The hotel also provides a courtesy bus service to the airport.
141⇌↱(3fb)⅟in 16 bedrooms CTV in all bedrooms ® **T** S8% sB⇌↱£65-£75 dB⇌↱£76-£86 (room only) ⊟
Lift ☾ 350P ♫
♉ International ♈ ♉ Lunch £7.95-£15.50 High tea £1.35-£2.95 Dinner £14.25-£15 Last dinner 10pm
Credit Cards 1 2 3 5

★★ **Rockfield** 125 Renfrew Rd, Paisley PA3 4EA (2m SE off A741) ☎041-889 6182
20rm(9⇌11↱)(1fb)1⊠ CTV in all bedrooms ® **T** sB&B⇌↱fr£36 dB&B⇌↱fr£57 ⊟
50P
♉ European ♈ ⅟ Bar Lunch fr£4 Dinner fr£10.50&alc Last dinner 9.30pm
Credit Cards 1 3 5 £

All the information in the guide is annually updated, but details of prices and facilities may change during the currency of this guide.

GLASTONBURY Somerset Map **03** ST53

✕✕ **Number Three Dining Rooms** 3 Magdalene St BA6 9EW ☎(0458)32129
Closed Mon & 3 wks Jan
Lunch not served Tue & Sat
Dinner not served Sun
♉ English & French **V** 28 seats Lunch £14.50-£30 Dinner £22-£30 Last lunch 1.30pm Last dinner 9pm 8P 3 bedrooms available ⅟
Credit Cards 2 3

GLEMSFORD Suffolk Map **05** TL84

✕✕ **Barret's** 31 Egremont St CO10 7SA ☎(0787)281573
Closed Mon & 10 days Jan
Lunch not served Tue-Sat
Dinner not served Sun
18 seats Last lunch 2pm Last dinner 9.30pm 10P
Credit Cards 1 3

GLENCAPLE Dumfries & Galloway *Dumfriesshire* Map **11** NX96

★★ **Nith** DG1 4RE ☎(038777)213
A modestly furnished small hotel standing close to the banks of the River Nith. It is particularly popular with the fishing fraternity.
10rm(2⇌5↱)(1fb) CTV in all bedrooms ® **T** ✱ sB&Bfr£17.50 sB&B⇌↱fr£20 dB&B⇌↱fr£36
20P
♉ Mainly grills ♈ ♉ Last high tea 7.00pm
Credit Cards 1 3

GLENCARSE Tayside *Perthshire* Map **11** NO12

★★★ 63% **Newton House** PH2 7LX (Inter) ☎(073886)250 FAX (073886) 717
Personally run by friendly new owners, this former dower house standing on the fringe of the village offers comfortable accommodation and serves good food in its smart restaurant.
10rm(5⇌5↱)(2fb) CTV in all bedrooms ® **T** sB&B⇌↱£36 dB&B⇌↱£52 ⊟
CTV 40P ✽ ⌂ *xmas*
♈ ♉ Lunch £13.75&alc High tea £6.25-£13.75alc Dinner £16.50 Last dinner 9pm
Credit Cards 1 3 5

See advertisement under PERTH

GLENCOE Highland *Argyllshire* Map **14** NN15

★★ **Glencoe** PA39 4HW ☎Ballachulish(08552)245 & 673
Modernised stone building at the western end of Glencoe overlooking Loch Leven.
13rm(4⇌1↱)(3fb) CTV in all bedrooms ® sB&B£18-£20 sB&B⇌↱£19-£21 dB&B£36-£40 dB&B⇌↱£38-£42 ⊟
CTV 30P ✽ games room ♫ *xmas*
V ♈ ♉ ⅟ Bar Lunch £3.75-£4.75alc Dinner £10.50-£15alc Last dinner 10pm
Credit Cards 1 2 3 5

★★ ***Kings House*** PA39 4HY (12m SE A82) ☎Kingshouse(08556)259
Closed 24-25 Dec
A long-established small hotel in an isolated situation of rugged beauty, it was originally a drover's inn. It is a popular stop for today's walkers who appreciate its good Scottish cuisine and warm hospitality.
21rm(10⇌)(1fb) ®
CTV 70P ⊞ ✽ ♩ ♫
V ♈ ♉ Last dinner 8.15pm
Credit Cards 1 2 3

GLENCOE, ARGYLL

This traditional 22 bedroomed hotel stands amid breathtaking scenery at the head of one of Scotland's most famous glens. An ideal centre for either an activity holiday – skiing, walking, climbing, mountain-biking and fishing and all readily available or just a relaxing, 'away from it all break'.

Tel. KINGS HOUSE (08556) 259

GLYNHILL HOTEL AA★★★
and Leisure Club
Paisley Road, Renfrew
(Glasgow Airport 1 mile)
Telephone: 041-886 5555

The Glynhill Hotel and Leisure Club
The Hotel of the Nineteen Nineties

★★

Glencoe Hotel

'The Spot to Stop'
OPEN ALL YEAR

Visit our comfortable Restaurant overlooking Loch Leven and choose from our extensive á la carte Dinner Menu where local fare is evident

Well stocked Wine Cellar

TEAS · COFFEES · BAR & SNACK MEALS

LOUNGE · PUBLIC · COCKTAIL BARS
Regular Entertainment and Good Cheer

We can cater for
Weddings · Dinner Dances · Buffet Dances
Parties · Ceilidhs · Conferences
in our self-contained
GLENCOE CEILIDH PLACE

Telephone
Ballachulish (085 52) 245

THE TURBAN TANDOORI

×

Indian Licensed Restaurant

2 Station Road, Giffnock.
Telephone: 041-638 0069

Full range of Indian cuisine, including Special Tandoori dishes.

5pm – last order midnight

Phone for reservations. Carry out orders available.

G

GLENEAGLES
See **Auchterarder**

GLENFARG Tayside *Perthshire* Map **11** NO11

★★Bein Inn PH2 9PY ☎(05773)216
Former drovers inn nestling in a beautiful glen, provides comfortable and modern accommodation.
9rm(7⇨)Annexe4⇨(4fb) CTV in all bedrooms ® **T** ✈ S7.5% sB&B£23.26 sB&B⇨£29 dB&B£36.55 dB&B⇨£41 ⊟
60P ⛟ ✲ *xmas*
♉ Scottish, English & French **V** ✧ ♀ S7.5% Lunch £3.60-£8&alc High tea £6.50-£8alc Dinner £14-£18alc Last dinner 9.30pm
Credit Cards 1 3

See advertisement under PERTH

★★*Glenfarg* Main St PH2 9NU ☎(05773)241
The small village hotel reflects Victorian charm in its tower and crow-stepped gables. Recent upgrading, sensitively carried out, has produced comfortable bedrooms, open-plan public areas and a traditional dining room where home cooking can be sampled at its best.
10rm(3⇨4↱)(2fb) CTV in all bedrooms ®
39P ⛟ ✲ ♫ nc12yrs
V ✧ ♀ ✂ Last dinner 9pm
Credit Cards 1 2 3 5

See advertisement under PERTH

GLENLIVET Grampian *Banffshire* Map **15** NJ12

★★♛*Blairfindy Lodge*
Ballindalloch AB3 9DJ
☎(08073)376

12rm(7⇨2↱)®
CTV 30P ✲ ⌡
♉ British & French ✧ Last dinner 9pm
Credit Cards 1 2 3

GLENRIDDING Cumbria Map **11** NY31

★★Glenridding CA11 0PB (Best Western) ☎(08532)228 due to change to (07684) 82228
Closed 4-23 Jan
Standing in the centre of the village, commanding fine views of Ullswater and the distant peaks, this spacious and friendly hotel offers bedrooms in a variety of styles and sizes complemented by public rooms where coal fires burn in season; a local pub, a diner serving budget meals and a coffee shop are attached to the hotel.
45rm(34⇨11↱)(6fb) CTV in all bedrooms ® **T** sB&B⇨↱£29-£35 dB&B⇨↱£53-£58 ⊟
Lift CTV 40P *xmas*
V ✧ ♀ ✂ Bar Lunch £2.75-£4.25alc Dinner £13.75-£14.75 Last dinner 9.30pm
Credit Cards 1 2 3 5 £

Red-star hotels offer the highest standards of hospitality, comfort and food.

GLENROTHES Fife Map **11** NO20

★★★68% Balgeddie House Balgeddie Way KY6 3ET
☎(0592)742511
Closed 1 & 2 Jan
Large privately owned mansion dating from 1936 standing on a hillside in six acres of land.
18rm(16⇨2↱) CTV in all bedrooms ® **T** ✈ (ex guide dogs) ✱ S10% sB&B⇨↱£47.85 dB&B⇨↱£72.60 ⊟
CTV P ⛟ ✲ U pool table
♉ English & French **V** ✧ ♀ S10% Lunch £8&alc Dinner £10.90&alc Last dinner 9.30pm
Credit Cards 1 2 3

★★Greenside High St, Leslie KY6 3DA (2m W A911)
☎(0592)743453 FAX (0592) 756341
Closed 1 Jan
This family run commercial hotel offers mainly purpose-built bedrooms and limited lounge facilities.
12rm(3⇨9↱) CTV in all bedrooms ® **T** sB&B⇨↱£32-£35.75 dB&B£38.50-£42.45 dB&B⇨↱£43-£49.45 ⊟
☾ 50P
♉ English & French **V** ✧
Credit Cards 1 2 3 £

★★Rescobie Valley Dr, Leslie KY6 3BQ ☎(0592)742143
Secluded mansion offering country house atmosphere, comfortable lounges and first class cooking.
8rm(3⇨5↱) CTV in all bedrooms ® **T** sB&B⇨↱fr£38 dB&B⇨↱£55-£60 ⊟
20P ⛟ ✲ putting green
♉ International **V** ✧ ♀ Lunch £6.75-£8.50&alc Dinner £13.50-£13.50&alc Last dinner 9pm
Credit Cards 1 2 3 5 £

GLENSHEE (Spittal of) Tayside *Perthshire* Map **15** NO16

★★♛Dalmunzie House
PH10 7QG
☎Glenshee(025085)224
Closed 16 Nov-27 Dec

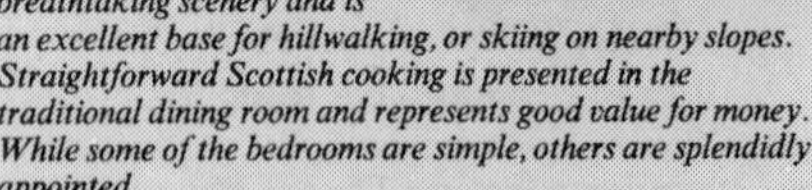

Said to be the highest hotel in Scotland, this imposing baronial lodge is set amongst breathtaking scenery and is an excellent base for hillwalking, or skiing on nearby slopes. Straightforward Scottish cooking is presented in the traditional dining room and represents good value for money. While some of the bedrooms are simple, others are splendidly appointed.
19rm(18⇨) sB&B⇨£25-£31 dB&B⇨£50-£62
Lift CTV 30P 2🚗 ⛟ ✲ ▶9 ዖ (hard) ⌡ stalking, shooting, clay pigeon shooting *xmas*
♉ Scottish & French **V** ✧ ♀ Bar Lunch £4-£6.50alc Dinner £14.50 Last dinner 8.45pm
Credit Cards 1 3 5

★*Dalrulzion Highland* PH10 7LJ ☎Blacklunans(025082)222
The family-run hotel has been created from a historically interesting building that was originally a hunting lodge.
12rm(5⇨)(4fb) CTV in 7bedrooms ® **T** ✈ (ex guide dogs)
CTV 60P ✲ ⌡ hang gliding pony trekking shooting ♫
♉ Scottish & Continental **V** ✧ ♀ Last dinner 9pm
Credit Cards 3

GLENSHIEL (SHIEL BRIDGE) Highland *Ross & Cromarty*
Map **14** NG91

★★Kintail Lodge IV40 8HL ☎Glenshiel(059981)275
Closed 24 Dec-1 Jan RS Nov-Mar
Set at the head of Loch Duich, the small, family-run hotel provides comfortable accommodation.
12rm(7⇔3♠)(2fb) CTV in all bedrooms ® S% sB&B£33-£40 sB&B⇔♠£35-£43 dB&B£66-£80 dB&B⇔♠£70-£86 (incl dinner) ⊟
20P ⛟ ✻ ♫
♡ Scottish & French **V** ♉ ⊻ ✂ S% Bar Lunch £2-£7alc Dinner £14-£20 Last dinner 8.30pm
Credit Cards [1] [3]

GLOSSOP Derbyshire Map **07** SK09

★★Wind in the Willows Derbyshire Level, (off) Sheffield Rd (A57) SK13 9PT ☎(04574)68001 (Due to change to (0457)86001)
Closed Xmas & New Year
Comfort, quality and a relaxed atmosphere are the hallmarks of this Victorian country house, pleasantly set in 5 acres of grounds adjacent to the local golf course.
8rm(2⇔6♠)(1fb) CTV in all bedrooms ® **T** ✗ (ex guide dogs) S% sB&B⇔♠£45-£60 dB&B⇔♠£55-£80
CTV 12P ⛟ ✻ nc10yrs
♉ S% Dinner fr£17 Last dinner 7.30pm
Credit Cards [1] [2] [3]

GLOUCESTER Gloucestershire Map **03** SO81

★★★63% Crest Crest Way, Barnwood GL4 7RX (Crest) ☎(0452)613311 Telex no 437273 FAX (0452) 371036
A new bedroom block now complements the existing comfortable and well-equipped accommodation provided by this modern hotel, conveniently situated for the city centre. Restaurant, bar and lounge amenities are also in the process of extension, and a Sensations Leisure Club offers a variety of facilities to guests.
123⇔(30fb)✂in 24 bedrooms CTV in all bedrooms ® **T** S% sB⇔£70 dB⇔£82 (room only) ⊟
☾ 200P ✻ ▭(heated) sauna solarium gymnasium spa pool steam room games room ♫ ♧ *xmas*
♡ English & French **V** ♉ ⊻ ✂ S% Lunch £7.95-£9.95 Dinner £15.75 Last dinner 10pm
Credit Cards [1] [2] [3] [4] [5]

★★★63% Gloucester Hotel & Country Club Robinswood Hill GL4 9EA (2.5m SE off B4073) (Embassy) ☎(0452)25653 Telex no 43571 FAX (0452) 307212
Squash courts, golf courses, a dry ski slope and a swimming pool are among the facilities provided by this large, well managed complex 3 miles from the city. The main block's comfortable, well-equipped accommodation has recently been upgraded, and guests have a choice of 4 bars. The original barn houses a restaurant, extensive conference and banquetting facilities are available, and service throughout the hotel is considerate and attentive.
97⇔Annexe19⇔(11fb)1⊞✂in 5 bedrooms CTV in all bedrooms ® **T** S% sB⇔£65 dB⇔£78 (room only) ⊟
☾ CTV 300P ✻ ▭(heated) ▶ 18 ℘ (hard) squash snooker sauna solarium gymnasium jacuzzi dry skiing skittle alley pool ♫ *xmas*
♡ French **V** ♉ ⊻ S% Lunch £10.75 Dinner £13 Last dinner 10pm
Credit Cards [1] [2] [3] [5]

★★★75% Hatton Court Upton Hill, Upton St Leonards GL4 8DE (3m SE B4073) ☎(0452)617412 Telex no 437334 FAX (0452) 612945
Standing in its own grounds with fine views over the Severn Valley this hotel has recently been refurbished to a very high standard and has a new wing of good bedrooms.
18rm(16⇔2♠)Annexe28⇔1⊞ CTV in all bedrooms **T** ✗ (ex guide dogs) sB&B⇔♠£66-£76 dB&B⇔♠£88-£98 ⊟
▶

☾75P ❉ ⛱(heated) croquet *xmas*
☋ English & French V ♦ ☐ Lunch fr£14 High tea fr£5 Dinner fr£18&alc Last dinner 10pm
Credit Cards 1 2 3 5

★Rotherfield House 5 Horton Rd GL1 3PX ☎(0452)410500
9rm(1⇨3♠)(2fb) CTV in all bedrooms ® sB&Bfr£16.95 sB&B⇨♠fr£25.95 dB&Bfr£34.10 dB&B⇨♠fr£34.10 ☰
CTV 9P ⛟
☋ English & Continental V ♦ ☐ ⚡ Dinner £7.25&alc Last dinner 6.30pm
Credit Cards 1 2 3 5 £

GLYN CEIRIOG Clwyd Map 07 SJ23

★★★ 58% Golden Pheasant LL20 7BB ☎(069172)281
Telex no 35664
Enjoying beautiful country views this unpretentious, tranquil hotel, with the character of an inn, is ideal for a relaxing break. Popular with the locals.
18rm(16⇨2♠)(7fb)3⊟ CTV in all bedrooms ® T ✱
sB&B£28-£49 dB&B£56-£78 ☰
45P ❉ U game shooting during season ⌂ *xmas*
☋ English & French & Italian V ♦ ☐ Lunch £9.50-£9.50 High tea £3.50-£6.50 Dinner £15.95-£15.95 Last dinner 9pm
Credit Cards 1 2 3 5 £

GOATHLAND North Yorkshire Map 08 NZ80

★★Inn On The Moor YO22 5LZ ☎Whitby(0947)86296
28rm(20⇨2♠)(4fb)2⊟ CTV in all bedrooms ® T ✱
sB&B⇨♠£30.50-£40 dB&B⇨♠£61-£80 (incl dinner) ☰
CTV 20P ❉ croquet lawn ⌂
V ♦ ☐ ⚡ Lunch fr£6.50 High tea fr£1.50alc Dinner fr£12.50 Last dinner 7.45pm
Credit Cards 1 3

★★Mallyan Spout YO22 5AN ☎Whitby(0947)86206 & 86341
The charming, comfortable hotel provides cottage-style accommodation, very good dinners and friendly service.
22⇨♠(4fb)2⊟ CTV in all bedrooms sB&B⇨♠£25-£35 dB&B⇨♠£55-£80 ☰
50P ❉ *xmas*
☋ English & French ♦ ☐ ⚡ Lunch fr£8.25&alc High tea fr£3alc Dinner fr£15&alc Last dinner 8.30pm
Credit Cards 1 2 3 5 £

★Whitfield House Darnholm YO22 5LA (Guestaccom)
☎Whitby(0947)86215
Closed 13 Nov-12 Jan
A converted stone-built 'period' style cottage on the North Yorkshire moors.
10rm(2⇨3♠)(1fb) ® sB&B£14-£16.50 sB&B⇨♠£15-£17.50 dB&B£26-£31 dB&B⇨♠£30-£35 ☰
CTV 10P ⛟ nc3yrs
♦ ☐ ⚡ Dinner £7.50&alc Last dinner 6.30pm

GODALMING Surrey Map 04 SU94

✕✕Inn on the Lake Ockford Rd GU7 1RH ☎(04868)5575
An elegant and attractively decorated restaurant, centred round an indoor ornamental pool, supplements its à la carte range of dishes with two reasonable fixed-price menus. Enterprising cuisine shows a definite French influence and is complemented by a fairly extensive wine list. Good bar facilities are available and pleasant service is provided by cheerful young staff.
☋ International V 80 seats Lunch £14&alc Dinner £14&alc Last lunch 3pm Last dinner 10pm 100P
Credit Cards 1 2 3 5

For key to symbols see the inside front cover.

GOLANT Cornwall & Isles of Scilly Map 02 SX15

★★Cormorant PL23 1LL ☎Fowey(072683)3426
In a picturesque setting overlooking the Fowey Estuary, this peaceful hotel offers tranquility with caring hospitality. The thoughtfully furnished bedrooms and comfortable lounge have superb views of the river and wooded slopes beyond. Good food, using fresh local produce, is served in the intimate restaurant.
11⇨ CTV in all bedrooms ® T ✱ sB&B⇨£36.50-£45 dB&B⇨£57-£66 ☰
24P ⛟ ❉ ⛱(heated) *xmas*
☋ French V ♦ ☐ Lunch £10 High tea fr£4.50 Dinner fr£14.50&alc Last dinner 8.45pm
Credit Cards 1 3 £

GOLSPIE Highland *Sutherland* Map 14 NH89

★★*Golf Links* KW10 6TT ☎(04083)3408
A comfortable little hotel situated beside the beach and close to the golf course.
10rm(8⇨2♠) CTV in 12bedrooms ®
20P ⛟ ❉
☋ Scottish & French V
Credit Cards 1 2 3 5

★★Sutherland Arms Old Bank Rd KW10 6RS
☎(04083)3234 & 3216
A traditional Highland hotel dating from 1808 when established as the first coaching station in Sutherland.
16rm(9⇨1♠)(4fb)1⊟ CTV in all bedrooms ® ✱
sB&B£17-£25 sB&B⇨♠£20-£25 dB&B£40-£45 dB&B⇨♠£45-£50 ☰
CTV 25P ❉ ♫
V ♦ ☐ Last high tea 6pm
Credit Cards 3 £

GOODRICH Hereford & Worcester Map 03 SO51

★★Ye Hostelrie HR9 6HX ☎Symonds Yat(0600)890241
8rm(2⇨2♠)(1fb) ® ✱ sB&B£18 sB&B⇨♠£24 dB&B£30 dB&B⇨♠£36
CTV 25P ⛟ ❉
V ♦

See advertisement under ROSS-ON-WYE

GOODRINGTON

See Paignton

GOODWOOD West Sussex Map 04 SU80

★★★ 72% Goodwood Park PO18 0QB
☎Chichester(0243)775537 Telex no 869173
FAX (0243) 533802
Recent extensions have transformed what was originally a coaching inn into this modern, purpose-built leisure development. A choice of bedrooms with every up-to-date facility is complemented by the classic cuisine and professionally efficient service of Dukes Restaurant.
89⇨♠(3fb)1⊟ CTV in all bedrooms ® T ✱
sB&B⇨♠£40-£85 dB&B⇨♠£60-£100 ☰
☾100P ❉ ⛱(heated) ▶ 18 ℘ (hard) squash snooker sauna solarium gymnasium beauty salon *xmas*
☋ British V ♦ ☐ ⚡ Lunch £11.50-£12.50&alc Dinner fr£14.50&alc Last dinner 9.30pm
Credit Cards 1 2 3 5

All AA-appointed establishments are inspected regularly to ensure that required standards are maintained.

Mallyan Spout Hotel

★★
Goathland, Whitby
N Yorkshire
YO22 5AN
Telephone:
(0947) 86206

A stone-built, ivy clad building situated on the green of a beautiful Yorkshire village overlooking the wide expanses of the famous moors. The hotel takes its name from a small picturesque waterfall flowing into a wooded valley, a short walk below the hotel. Three spacious lounges command a view of the garden, moors and the beautiful Esk Valley, and in the winter you are warmed by roaring fires. Mallyan Spout is an ideal location for outdoor pursuits or the peaceful pleasures of fine food, good wine and friendly hospitality. 24 cottage style bedrooms with private bath including 2 new rooms with balconies and superb views.

GOLDEN PHEASANT HOTEL

★★★
GLYN CEIRIOG, NR. CHIRK (LLANGOLLEN), CLWYD
Telephone: 069172 281/674 Telex: 35664

This traditional inn and elegant country Hotel nestles in the breathtaking Ceiriog Valley. Within easy reach of main motorway networks it is the perfect base for visiting National Trust Properties Chirk Castle, Powys Castle & Erddig Hall. The ambience of the hotel is enhanced by the wealth of antiques, individually styled rooms and choice of two bars. Conference facilities. Elegant restaurant.

INN ON THE MOOR

GOATHLAND, NORTH YORKS MOOR
0947-86296 **AA★★**

Ashley Courtenay recommended

- **Fully licensed**
- **Family suites available**
- **28 rooms with direct dial telephone**
- **Tea/coffee facilities**
- **Private bathrooms**
- **Baby listening service**
- **Colour television with satellite channels**
- **Rachel's Hairdressing Salon**
- **A country location within 45 minutes of York city**
- **Prices include VAT no service charges**

HATTON COURT

Nestling in rolling hills with magnificent views, across the Severn Valley, ideally located for Bath, Cheltenham and touring the Cotswolds. Luxurious accommodation, excellent food and superb hospitality.

2 Night breaks • Romantic breaks • Executive Meetings. 'Loo of the Year' award 1987/88

Telephone now for colour brochure
Hatton Court, Upton Hill, Upton St Leonards, Gloucester GL4 8DE.
Tel: 0452 617412

AA ★★★

Part of the Hatton Hotel Group

GOOLE Humberside Map **08** SE72

★★Clifton 1 Clifton Gardens, Boothferry Rd DN14 6AL
☎(0405)61336
This small, cosy hotel operates under the friendly management of its resident proprietor.
10rm(5⇌3♠)1⊞ CTV in all bedrooms ® **T** ✳ sB&Bfr£23 sB&B⇌♠fr£29 dB&B⇌♠fr£38 ⊟
CTV 8P
☋ English & Continental **V** ♡ Lunch £5.50-£16.75alc Dinner £5.50-£16.75alc Last dinner 9pm
Credit Cards 1 2 3 5 £

GORDANO MOTORWAY SERVICE AREA (M5) Avon Map **03** ST57

○ ***Travelodge*** BS20 9XG (Trusthouse Forte)
☎(027581)3709
40⇌
P

GOREY

See **Jersey under Channel Islands**

GORLESTON-ON-SEA

See **Yarmouth, Great**

GOSPORT Hampshire Map **04** SZ69

★★Anglesey Crescent Rd, Alverstoke PO12 2DH
☎(0705)582157 & 523932
Part of a Regency terrace, this unusual hotel provides modernised and well appointed bedrooms. An elegant restaurant offers a wide range of à la carte dishes, many of them based on fish.
18rm(5⇌13♠)(1fb)1⊞ CTV in all bedrooms ® **T** ✳ sB&B⇌♠fr£37.38 dB&B⇌♠fr£45.43 ⊟
CTV 2🚗(£1.50) ♫
☋ Continental **V** ♡ Lunch £3.95&alc Dinner £7.95-£16.50alc Last dinner 9.45pm
Credit Cards 1 2 3 £

GOUDHURST Kent Map **05** TQ73

★★Star & Eagle High St TN17 1AL ☎(0580)211512
An attractive 14th-century inn combining a homely atmosphere and good cooking.
11⇌♠1⊞ CTV in all bedrooms ® **T** ✗ (ex guide dogs) sB&B⇌♠£45-£50 dB&B⇌♠£60-£68 ⊟
24P *xmas*
☋ European **V** ♡ ☳ Lunch fr£10.25&alc High tea £3.60 Dinner £12-£15alc Last dinner 9.30pm
Credit Cards 1 2 3

GRANGE (In-Borrowdale) Cumbria Map **11** NY21

See also **Borrowdale and Rosthwaite**
★★★51% Borrowdale Gates Country House CA12 5UQ
☎Borrowdale(059684)204 & 606
Comfortable relaxing hotel with panoramic views of surrounding countryside and fells.
23rm(19⇌4♠)(2fb) CTV in all bedrooms ® ✳ sB&B⇌♠fr£26.50 dB&B⇌♠fr£48 ⊟
CTV 35P ⊯ ✲ *xmas*
☋ International **V** ♡ ☳ Lunch fr£5.50 Dinner fr£14 Last dinner 8.45pm
Credit Cards 1 2 5

A rosette is the AA's highest award for quality of food and service in a restaurant.

GRANGE-OVER-SANDS Cumbria Map **07** SD47

★★Grange Lindale Rd, Station Square LA11 8EJ (Consort)
☎(05395)33666
This constantly improving hotel now offers an attractive and comfortable lounge bar, well-appointed à la carte restaurant and good conference facilities.
40rm(32⇌8♠)(6fb) CTV in all bedrooms ® **T** sB&B⇌♠£33.50-£38.50 dB&B⇌♠£59-£69 ⊟
☾ CTV 100P ✲ CFA ♫ *xmas*
☋ English & French **V** ♡ ☳ Lunch fr£7.50 Dinner fr£12.50&alc Last dinner 9.30pm
Credit Cards 1 2 3 5 £

★★🏛*Graythwaite Manor*
Fernhill Rd LA11 7JE
☎(05395)32001 & 33755

Large country house in beautiful grounds, with home grown produce used in restaurant.
22rm(15⇌2♠)(1fb) CTV in all bedrooms ® **T** ✗ (ex guide dogs)
18P 14🚗(£1) ⊯ ✲ 🎾 (hard) helicopter landing area putting
☋ English & French **V** ♡ ☳ ⊬ Last dinner 8.30pm
Credit Cards 1 3

★★Netherwood Lindale Rd LA11 6ET ☎(05395)32552
This imposing mansion, with magnificent carved woodwork and panelling, sits in its own grounds on the edge of town. It provides comfortable accommodation and a good value dinner menu.
23rm(15⇌2♠)(6fb) CTV in all bedrooms ® **T** sB&B£23.50-£25.50 sB&B⇌♠£25.50-£27.50 dB&B£47-£51 dB&B⇌♠£51-£55 ⊟
☾ CTV 60P ✲ 🏠
☋ English & French **V** ♡ ☳ Lunch £6.75-£7.25&alc High tea £6-£6.50 Dinner £10.25-£10.75 Last dinner 8.15pm

★Methven Kents Bank Rd LA11 7DU ☎(05395)32031
Closed Nov-Feb
Small detached family-run hotel overlooking Morecambe Bay.
12rm(3⇌5♠)(2fb) CTV in 5bedrooms ® sB&Bfr£15 sB&B⇌♠£20-£27 dB&Bfr£30 dB&B⇌♠£38-£44 ⊟
CTV 12P ⊯ ✲ nc4yrs
V ♡ Bar Lunch £1-£4 Dinner £7.50 Last dinner 6pm

GRANTHAM Lincolnshire Map **08** SK93

★★★55% Angel & Royal High St NG31 6PN (Trusthouse Forte)
☎(0476)65816 FAX (0476) 67149
One of the oldest inns in England, tracing its history back to the Knights Templar, the Angel & Royal retains such tangible evidence of its past as a medieval banquetting hall – now the Kings Room Restaurant – and the grandiose arch with its angel carving. Accommodation is well up to present standards of comfort, however, modern facilities being provided in all bedrooms.
24⇌⊬in 6 bedrooms CTV in all bedrooms ® **T** S% sB⇌£57-£61 dB⇌£67-£73 (room only) ⊟
☾ 60P *xmas*
☋ English & French **V** ♡ ☳ ⊬ S% Lunch fr£7 Dinner fr£12.50 Last dinner 9pm
Credit Cards 1 2 3 4 5

★★Kings North Pde NG31 8AU ☎(0476)590800
Located just north of the town centre, close to the railway line, the hotel provides sound accommodation with modern facilities. Guests can choose between the menus of the traditional restaurant and the range of lighter meals served in the Orangery.
23rm(16⇌5⌐) CTV in all bedrooms ® T S% sB&Bfr£23 sB&B⇌⌐fr£35 dB&B⇌⌐fr£45 ⊟
☾ 36P ❋ ⚲ (hard) ♫
♉ French V ♧ ♨ Lunch £7-£12.95&alc Dinner £8.50-£12.95 Last dinner 9.30pm
Credit Cards [1] [2] [3] [5] (£)

○ ***TraveLodge*** Grantham Service Area NG32 2AB (4m S of Gratham) (Trusthouse Forte) ☎(0476)77500
41⇌

GRANTOWN-ON-SPEY Highland *Morayshire* Map **14** NJ02

★★★61% Garth Castle Rd PH26 3HN (Inter) ☎(0479)2836 & 2162
Set in its own grounds close to the town centre, this hotel, converted from a 17th-century building, has a country house atmosphere, combined with friendly informal service. Bedrooms are equipped to modern standards.
14rm(10⇌4⌐) CTV in all bedrooms ® T ✗ sB&B⇌⌐£22-£30 dB&B⇌⌐£44-£60
10P ⛟ ❋
♉ French V ♧ ♨ ⚔ Lunch £6.50-£7alc Dinner £16.50&alc Last dinner 8.30pm
Credit Cards [1] [3] [4] [5]

★★Ben Mhor 57 High St PH26 3EG ☎(0479)2056
This spacious hotel with modern bedrooms is situated in the main street in the centre of town.
24rm(20⇌4⌐)(2fb) CTV in all bedrooms ® ✳ sB&B⇌⌐£18.75-£20 dB&B⇌⌐£33-£36 ⊟
24P *xmas*
♉ Scottish & French V ♧ ♨ Bar Lunch 90p-£10 High tea £5-£7.50 Dinner £12.50-£20&alc Last dinner 8.30pm
Credit Cards [1] [3] [5]

★★Coppice Grant Rd PH26 3LD (Exec Hotel) ☎(0479)2688
Closed Nov
This comfortable hotel stands in its own grounds in a pleasant residential area. Bedrooms offer modern facilities. The lounges overlook the gardens and the dining room is traditional in style.
26⌐(3fb) CTV in all bedrooms ® ✳ sB&B⌐£20.50 dB&B⌐£38 ⊟
CTV 50P ❋ shooting *xmas*
V ♧ ♨ Lunch £5-£9 High tea £5-£7 Dinner £10.50 Last dinner 9pm
Credit Cards [1] [3]

★★*Rosehall* The Square PH26 3JU ☎(0479)2721
Distinctive stone building standing in The Square.
14rm(5⇌4⌐)(2fb) ®
CTV 20P ⛟ ⌂
V ⚔

★★Seafield Lodge Woodside Av PH26 3JN (Minotels) ☎(0479)2152
Closed 4 Nov-9 Dec
Comfortable, family run hotel with special facilities for fishing, shooting and curling.
14rm(8⇌6⌐)(2fb) CTV in all bedrooms ® T sB&B⇌⌐£25-£59 dB&B⇌⌐£31-£90 ⊟
15P *xmas*
♨ Bar Lunch £2.60-£10 Dinner fr£12.50&alc Last dinner 9pm
Credit Cards [1] [3] (£)

See advertisement on page 309

G

★Dunvegan Heathfield Rd PH26 3HX ☎(0479)2301
Closed 16-31 Oct & 20-30 Dec
Small family-run hotel in a quiet area opposite playing fields and the golf course.
9rm(2⋔)(5fb) sB&B£11.50-£12.50 dB&B£23-£25 dB&B⋔£29-£31 ⊟
CTV 9P 1⌂(£1) ⇼ *xmas*
♉ ⊻ Bar Lunch fr£1.50 Dinner fr£9.50 Last dinner 7.30pm
Ⓔ

GRASMERE Cumbria Map **11** NY30

★★★★ 64% Wordsworth LA22 9SW ☎(09665)592
Telex no 65329
The hotel has been steadily improving since it reopened under private ownership in 1987 ; the most recent phase of development has added some splendid bedrooms – including two suites – on the second floor and a sun lounge extension to the attractive swimming pool, overlooking the well-tended gardens. Serivce is of a good standard throughout, friendly management and staff creating as relaxed atmosphere.
37rm(36⇌1⋔)2⊞ CTV in all bedrooms **T** ✗ (ex guide dogs) sB&B⇌⋔£43-£46 dB&B⇌⋔£78-£110 ⊟
Lift ☾ 60P ⇼ ❊ CFA ⊡(heated) sauna solarium gymnasium table-tennis pool table jacuzzi darts *xmas*
♉ English & French **V** ♉ ⊻ Lunch £10-£12&alc High tea £3.50 Dinner £19-£25alc Last dinner 9pm
Credit Cards 1 2 3 5

★★★ 63% Gold Rill Country House Red Bank Rd LA22 9PU ☎(09665)486
Closed Jan
This comfortable hotel, peacefully situated just to the west of the village and enthusiastically run by resident proprietors, commands fine views on every side. Bedrooms vary in size, but public areas offer ample space in which to relax, with an attractive restaurant overlooking the well-kept gardens.
17⇌(2fb) CTV in all bedrooms ® **T** ✗ (ex guide dogs) sB&B⇌£28-£34 dB&B⇌£56-£76 ⊟
35P ❊ ⊃(heated) putting green croquet lawn *xmas*
♉ ⊁ High tea £14
Credit Cards 1 2 3 Ⓔ

★★★ 61% Grasmere Red Lion Hotel Red Lion Square LA22 9SS (Consort) ☎(09665)456
A tourist hotel set at the heart of this popular village commands fine views over surrounding countryside.
36rm(35⇌1⋔)(4fb) CTV in all bedrooms ® **T** sB&B⇌⋔£22.50-£30 dB&B⇌⋔£45-£60 ⊟
Lift 26P ❊ CFA *xmas*
V ♉ ⊻ ⊁ Bar Lunch £1-£4.50 Dinner £13&alc Last dinner 8.50pm
Credit Cards 1 2 3 5 Ⓔ

❀★★★♛ MICHAEL'S NOOK
LA22 9RP (Pride of Britain)
☎(09665)496
Telex no 65329
(Rosette awarded for dinner only)
The perfect base for exploration of the Lake District, this charming Victorian hotel is run by Reg Gifford, whose interest in antiques is reflected in the handsome furnishings. There are fresh flowers and roaring fires, the young staff are friendly and attentive, and the bedrooms are stocked with Roger et Gallet toiletries. Best of all, though, is the wonderful cooking, with a 5-course or gourmet 7-course

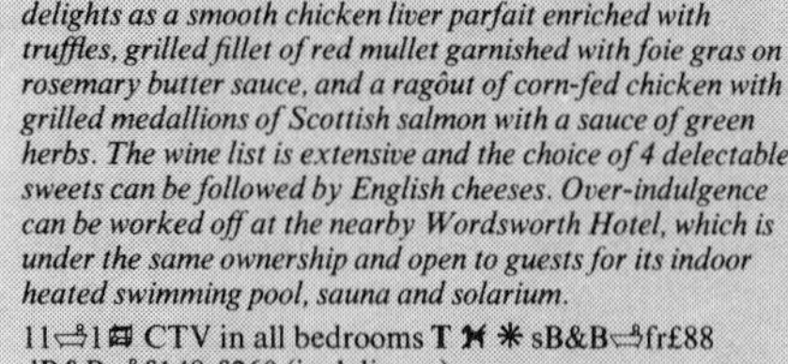

menu to choose from. Stylishly presented dishes include such delights as a smooth chicken liver parfait enriched with truffles, grilled fillet of red mullet garnished with foie gras on rosemary butter sauce, and a ragoût of corn-fed chicken with grilled medallions of Scottish salmon with a sauce of green herbs. The wine list is extensive and the choice of 4 delectable sweets can be followed by English cheeses. Over-indulgence can be worked off at the nearby Wordsworth Hotel, which is under the same ownership and open to guests for its indoor heated swimming pool, sauna and solarium.
11⇌1⊞ CTV in all bedrooms **T** ✗ ✳ sB&B⇌fr£88 dB&B⇌£148-£260 (incl dinner)
20P ⇼ ❊ *xmas*
♉ English & French ⊁ Lunch fr£21 Dinner fr£29.50 Last dinner 8.30pm
Credit Cards 2 5

★★★ 64% *Prince of Wales* LA22 9PR (Mount Charlotte) ☎(09665)666 Telex no 65364
Comfortable accommodation and friendly service are provided by a traditional hotel on the shore of the lake.
77⇌⋔(7fb)1⊞ CTV in all bedrooms ®
☾ 100P ❊ CFA ♩
♉ English & French **V** ♉ ⊻ Last dinner 9pm
Credit Cards 1 2 3 4 5

★★★ 64% The Swan LA22 9RF (Trusthouse Forte) ☎(09665)551 FAX (09665) 741
An attractive 17th-century hotel, the Swan has a great deal of character and exhibits a magnificent collection of horse brasses, copper jugs, old pewter and fine china.
36⇌(2fb)⊁in 3 bedrooms CTV in all bedrooms ® ✳ sB⇌£64-£74 dB⇌£80-£100 (room only) ⊟
40P ⇼ ❊ *xmas*
V ♉ ⊻ ⊁ Lunch £8.50&alc Dinner £15&alc Last dinner 9pm
Credit Cards 1 2 3 4 5

★★Grasmere Broadgate LA22 9TA ☎(09665)277
Closed Jan
Good home cooking and a friendly atmosphere are features of this comfortable hotel in a secluded riverside setting.
12rm(5⇌7⋔)1⊞ CTV in all bedrooms ® **T** sB&B⇌⋔£28-£32 dB&B⇌⋔£49-£68 ⊟
14P ⇼ ❊ croquet nc7yrs ⌂ *xmas*
♉ English & French ♉ ⊻ ⊁ Bar Lunch £2-£3.50 Dinner fr£12.50 Last dinner 8pm
Credit Cards 1 3 Ⓔ

★★Oak Bank Broadgate LA22 9TA (Guestaccom) ☎(09665)217
Closed Xmas-Jan
A pleasant, comfortable hotel with attractive bedrooms and a friendly atmosphere. A very good five-course dinner is served.
14rm(6⇌8⋔)(1fb)2⊞ CTV in all bedrooms ® **T** sB&B⇌⋔£24-£30 dB&B⇌⋔£48-£60 ⊟
CTV 14P ⇼ ❊
♉ English & Continental **V** ♉ ⊻ ⊁ Bar Lunch £2-£8alc Dinner £12.50-£15alc Last dinner 8pm
Credit Cards 1 3

★★Rothay Garden Broadgate LA22 9RH ☎(09665)334
Closed Dec-Jan RS New Year
This charming hotel, set in attractive gardens, offers pretty bedrooms and an elegant restaurant where very good food is served.
20rm(18⇌2⋔)(2fb)5⊞⊁in 2 bedrooms CTV in all bedrooms ® **T** sB&B⇌⋔£40.50-£50 dB&B⇌⋔£65-£100 (incl dinner) ⊟
30P ⇼ ❊ ♩ ⌂
V ♉ ⊻ ⊁ Dinner £16.50-£17.50 Last dinner 8.15pm
Credit Cards 1 2 3

❀★ WHITE MOSS HOUSE

Rydal Water LA22 9SE
☎(09665)295
Closed mid Nov-mid Mar
(Rosette awarded for dinner only)

This delightful little gem of a hotel continues to charm our readers. Regulars will confirm that standards are as good as ever, thanks to the dedication and enthusiasm of Susan and Peter Dixon. Situated between Grasmere and Ambleside, this lakeland stone-built house is run in the style of a country house – indeed, it is the Dixon's home. Synonymous with that style, service is discreet rather than outgoing and is mainly in the capable hands of Susan Dixon. The highlight of any visit to White Moss House will be the food. Peter Dixon's 5-course set dinner – there is no choice until pudding – continues to impress, no more so than when our inspector enjoyed a superb crispy lakeland mallard with plum, portand pinot noir sauce. Traditional puddings also merit mention, but do leave room for the excellent selection of English cheeses. To complement the food there is a first-class wine list offering something to suit everyone's palate and pocket. Bedrooms are compact but pretty and are exceptionally well equipped, down to the thoughtful little touches such as dimmer switches on the lighting. There is no bar, but the very attractive and comfortable lounge is the meeting place for aperitifs before dinner, which is served at 8 o'clock. For those who value peaceful seclusion, the hotel's annexe – a cottage sitting in splendid isolation high above the hotel – is a must. Let as a ▶

G

complete unit, it has 2 bedrooms and a lounge as well as a small kitchen. Its location means a 5-minute car journey or 10 minutes trek on foot; either is well worth the effort.
5⇌Annexe2rm(1⇌1♠) CTV in all bedrooms **T** ✗
dB&Bfr£60 dB&B⇌♠£60-£85
10P ✿ ✲
✗ Dinner £21 Last dinner 8pm

GRASSINGTON North Yorkshire Map **07** SE06

★**Black Horse** Garrs Ln BD23 5AT ☎(0756)752770
A charming, 200-year-old cottage in the centre of the village is pleasantly furnished throughout and offers a warm, friendly welcome to guests.
11rm(5⇌6♠)(1fb)2⊞ CTV in all bedrooms ® ✱
sB&B⇌♠£24.50-£32.50 dB&B⇌♠£38.50-£46.50 ₹
CTV 2P
V ♡ Lunch £5.50-£9alc Dinner £9&alc Last dinner 9.30pm
Credit Cards [1] [3]

★***Grassington House*** 5 The Square BD23 5AQ ☎(0756)752406
Closed Nov-Feb
Charming, privately run village-centre hotel with attractive furnishings.
12rm(1⇌6♠)Annexe6rm(2fb) ®
CTV 20P
V ♡ ☐

GRAVESEND Kent Map **05** TQ67

★★★62% **Inn on the Lake** Watling St (A2) DA12 3HB
☎Shorne(047482)3333 Telex no 966356 FAX (047482) 3175
(For full entry see Shorne)

GRAYSHOTT Hampshire Map **04** SU83

❀ ✗**Woods** Headley Rd GU26 6LB (1m SW B3002 off A3)
☎Hindhead(042873)5555
This former butcher's shop retains its original tiling and meat racks, complementing them with simple pine furniture and fresh flowers. Its short à la carte menu offers a range of dishes carefully prepared from the finest ingredients, enhancing natural flavours with delicate sauces. Fillet of Brill with Saffron Sauce might be followed by Saddle of Hare, with Crumbed Brie as a savoury or Nutty Meringue as a sweet to end the meal. All this can be enjoyed in a pleasant, relaxed atmosphere and a setting suitable for any occasion.
Closed Sun, Mon & 1 wk Xmas
Lunch not served
♡ Continental 35 seats S10% Last dinner 11pm ✗
Credit Cards [1] [2] [3] [5]

GREAT Places incorporating the word 'Great' will be found under the actual placename – eg Great Yarmouth is listed under Yarmouth, Great.

All the information in the guide is annually updated, but details of prices and facilities may change during the currency of this guide.

GREENLAW Borders *Berwickshire* Map **12** NT74

★★***Purves Hall*** TD10 6UJ
(4m SE off A697)
☎Leitholm(089084)558

An attractive and comfortable country hotel, set well back from the main road. Good home cooking is served in the elegant dining room and the young staff are polite and friendly.
7rm(2⇌5♠)(1fb) CTV in all bedrooms ®
20P ✿ ✲ ⇌(heated) ♪ (hard)
♡ International ♡ ☐ Last dinner 8.45pm
Credit Cards [1] [3]

GRETA BRIDGE Co Durham Map **12** NZ01

★★**Morritt Arms** DL12 9SE ☎Teesdale(0833)27232 & 27392
Old coaching inn retaining Dickensian character.
23rm(16⇌)(3fb)1⊞ CTV in 18bedrooms TV in 5bedrooms ®
T S1% sB&B£24 sB&B⇌£33 dB&B£40 dB&B⇌£50 ₹
100P 3⌂ ✿ ✲ ♪ *xmas*
♡ English & French ♡ ☐ Lunch £9.75 Dinner fr£15.50 Last dinner 8.45pm
Credit Cards [1] [2] [3] [5]

GRETNA (with Gretna Green) Dumfries & Galloway *Dumfriesshire* Map **11** NY36

★★**Gretna Chase** CA6 5JB (0.25 S on B721 in England)
☎Gretna(0461)37517
Closed Jan
Once a magnificent house, it has now been modernised while retaining much of its original character and beautiful gardens.
9rm(3⇌3♠)1⊞ CTV in all bedrooms ✗ (ex guide dogs)
sB&B£30-£32 sB&B⇌♠£32-£40 dB&B£38 dB&B⇌♠£48-£70
40P ✲
♡ English & French **V** ♡ Bar Lunch £6-£13 Dinner £8.50-£15alc Last dinner 9.30pm
Credit Cards [1] [2] [3] [5]

★★**Solway Lodge** Annan Rd CA6 5DN (Minotels)
☎Gretna(0461)38266 FAX (0461) 37791
Closed 25 & 26 Dec RS 10 Oct-Mar
The public areas of this small hotel have been refurbished to a high standard to provide an attractive, spacious lounge bar and dining room, together with a homely lounge. Bedrooms in the house are tastefully and comfortably furnished, with excellent bathrooms, whilst those in the chalet annexe offer a more functional style of accommodation.
3⇌♠Annexe7⇌♠1⊞ CTV in all bedrooms ® **T**
sB&B⇌♠fr£25 dB&B⇌♠fr£35
25P ✿
V ♡ ☐ Bar Lunch £2.50-£11.50 Dinner £8-£14alc Last dinner 9pm
Credit Cards [1] [2] [3] [5]

⌂**TraveLodge** Gretna Green CA6 5HQ (on A74) (Trusthouse Forte) ☎Gretna(0461)37566
41⇌♠(41fb) CTV in all bedrooms ® sB⇌♠£21.50
dB⇌♠£27 (room only)
(41P ✿
♡ Mainly grills ✗
Credit Cards [1] [2] [3]

GRIMSBY Humberside Map **08** TA20

★★★63% **Crest** St James' Square DN31 1EP (Crest) ☎(0472)359771 Telex no 527741 FAX (0472) 241427
Closed Xmas
A modern, city-centre hotel offers well-appointed bedrooms.
128⇌♪(6fb)⊬in 20 bedrooms CTV in all bedrooms ® T S%
sB⇌♪£53-£55 dB⇌♪£65-£67 (room only) ⊟
Lift ☾ 100P CFA sauna
☋ English & French V ✧ ☕ ⊬ S% Lunch £6.95-£8.95 High tea £1-£6 Dinner £11.95-£16.50 Last dinner 10pm
Credit Cards 1 2 3 4 5

★★★66% **Humber Royal Crest** Littlecoates Rd DN34 4LX (Crest) ☎(0472)350295 Telex no 527776 FAX (0472) 241354
Comfortable accommodation and a good restaurant are the attractions of this modern hotel.
52⇌♪(2fb)⊬in 8 bedrooms CTV in all bedrooms ® T ✱
sB⇌♪£62-£66 dB⇌♪£78-£88 (room only) ⊟
Lift ☾ 250P ✲ CFA *xmas*
☋ English & French V ✧ ☕ ⊬ Lunch fr£7.45 High tea fr£3.60 Dinner £11.95-£17.70&alc Last dinner 10pm
Credit Cards 1 2 3 4 5

GRIMSTON Norfolk Map **09** TF72

❀★★★ **CONGHAM HALL COUNTRY HOUSE**

Lynn Rd PE32 1AH (Pride of Britain)
☎Hillington(0485)600250
Telex no 81508

Forty acres of parkland with orchards, a paddock and colourful gardens are the setting for this elegant Georgian house. Fresh flowers, magazines and open fires provide a most welcoming atmosphere, and the comfortable sitting room is filled with fine porcelain, pictures and antiques. A resident pianist performs on the grand piano at weekends. The dining room has been enlarged, but remains an attractive setting for menus such as the gourmet, 8-course, fixed-price example. The wine list is comprehensive and reasonably priced. Bedrooms are individually decorated and well equipped. Some are small, but all are provided with thoughtful touches.
11rm(10⇌1♪)2⊞ CTV in all bedrooms T ✗
sB&B⇌♪£65-£70 dB&B⇌♪£85-£98 ⊟
50P 1⌂ ⊕ ✲ ⇒(heated) ♪ (hard) croquet jacuzzi cricket nc12 yrs *xmas*
V ✧ ⊬ Lunch £9.50-£12.50alc
Credit Cards 1 2 3 5

See advertisement under KING'S LYNN

GRINDLEFORD Derbyshire Map **08** SK27

★★★67% **Maynard Arms** Main Rd S30 1HN
☎Hope Valley(0433)30321 FAX (0433) 30445
Though busy, this traditional-style hotel manages to retain a relaxed atmosphere- perhaps most evident in the elegantly comfortable lounge, with its views across the gardens to the Derwent Valley.
13rm(9⇌2♪)(1fb)2⊞ CTV in all bedrooms ® T
sB&B⇌♪£43-£45 dB&B⇌♪£55-£65 ⊟
90P 6⌂ ⊕ ✲ *xmas*
☋ English & French V ✧ Lunch fr£8.50 Dinner fr£14.50 Last dinner 9.30pm
Credit Cards 1 2 3 5

GRIZEDALE Cumbria Map **07** SD39

★★**Grizedale Lodge** LA22 0QL ☎Hawkshead(09666)532
Closed Jan
Elegant former shooting lodge in the heart of Grizedale Forest midway between Coniston Water and Windermere.
6rm(2⇌4♪)(1fb)1⊞⊬in all bedrooms CTV in all bedrooms ® ✗ sB&B⇌♪£36-£41 dB&B⇌♪£60-£70 (incl dinner) ⊟
20P ⊕ *xmas*
☋ English & French ✧ ☕ ⊬ Bar Lunch £1.50-£6alc Dinner £14.50 Last dinner 8.30pm
Credit Cards 1 3

GROBY Leicestershire Map **04** SK50

★**Brant Inn** Leicester Rd LE6 0DU ☎Leicester(0533)872703
Large two-storey building with grounds and gardens, situated in a residential area, just off the A50 4 m NW of Leicester.
10rm(8♪) CTV in all bedrooms ® T ✱ sB&B£24
sB&B♪£26.50 dB&B♪£45
200P ✲
☋ English & French V Lunch £7.45-£7.95&alc Dinner £7.45-£7.45 Last dinner 10.30pm
Credit Cards 1 3 5

G

GUERNSEY

See **Channel Islands**

GUILDFORD Surrey Map **04** SU94

★★★★64% **Post House** Egerton Rd GU2 5XZ (Trusthouse Forte) ☎(0483)574444 Telex no 858572 FAX (0483) 302960
121⇌⊬in 25 bedrooms CTV in all bedrooms ® T S%
sB⇌£81-£91 dB⇌£96-£106 (room only) ⊟
☾ 190P ✲ ⊡(heated) sauna solarium gymnasium *xmas*
▶

French V Lunch £12-£14&alc Dinner fr£16.50&alc Last dinner 10pm
Credit Cards 1 2 3 4 5

★★★70% The Manor at Newlands Newlands Corner GU4 8SE (3m E A25) ☎(0483)222624 FAX (0483) 211389
Set in the peace and tranquility of nine acres of well-kept gardens and grounds, this charming hotel offers tastefully decorated bedrooms of individual character, comfortably furnished and well-equipped. Public areas include a wood-panelled bar, a pleasant restaurant and a relaxing bar off the foyer. Courteous, hospitable staff provide pleasant and efficient service throughout.
20⇌ CTV in all bedrooms T (ex guide dogs) ✱ S% sB&B⇌fr£60 dB&B⇌fr£80
100P 5 nc5yrs
English & French V S% Lunch fr£10.50&alc Dinner £14.50-£16.50&alc Last dinner 9.30pm
Credit Cards 1 2 3 4 5

G

★★The Angel High St GU1 3DR (Trusthouse Forte) ☎(0483)64555 FAX (0483) 570864
Modernised 14th-century coaching inn with modestly furnished bedrooms, coffee shop and 13th-century Crypt Restaurant.
27⇌ in 8 bedrooms CTV in all bedrooms ® T ✱ sB⇌fr£62 dB⇌fr£84 (room only)
xmas
V Lunch £7.95-£15 Dinner £12.50-£17.50&alc Last dinner 10pm
Credit Cards 1 2 3 5

✕Rum-Wong 16-18 London Rd GU1 2AF ☎(0483)36092
A smart modern restaurant offering carefully prepared authentic food is split into two sections. The first, the 'Khan Tok' room, features Tai dancers and low tables from which to eat your meal while reclining on cushions in the traditional way; while the other allows the less brave to dine in a more conventional manner, with standard furnishings and service.
Closed Mon, 25-29 Dec & 2 wks Aug
Thai V 100 seats ✱ Lunch £8-£10alc Dinner £12.50&alc Last lunch 2.30pm Last dinner 10.30pm
Credit Cards 1 3

GULLANE Lothian *East Lothian* Map **12** NT48

★★★75% Greywalls
Duncar Rd EH31 2EG (Pride of Britain)
☎(0620)842144
Telex no 72294
FAX (0620) 842241
Closed Nov-mid Apr

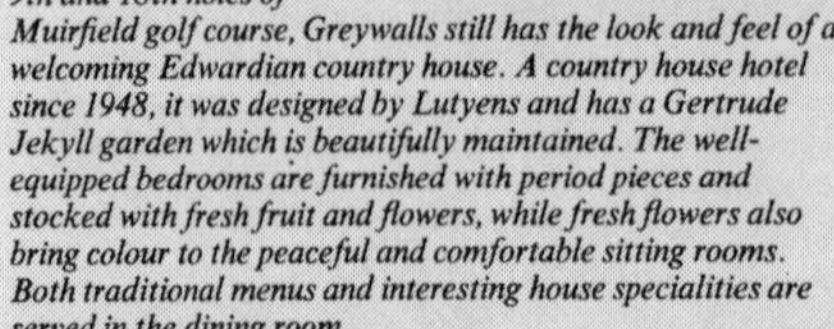

With its gravelled drive and views over the immaculate 9th and 18th holes of Muirfield golf course, Greywalls still has the look and feel of a welcoming Edwardian country house. A country house hotel since 1948, it was designed by Lutyens and has a Gertrude Jekyll garden which is beautifully maintained. The well-equipped bedrooms are furnished with period pieces and stocked with fresh fruit and flowers, while fresh flowers also bring colour to the peaceful and comfortable sitting rooms. Both traditional menus and interesting house specialities are served in the dining room.
18⇌ 1 CTV in all bedrooms T ✱ sB&B⇌£55-£60 dB&B⇌£105-£115
CTV 40P (hard) croquet shooting

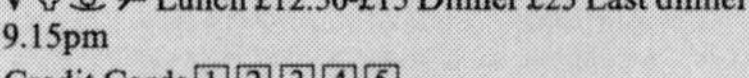

V Lunch £12.50-£15 Dinner £25 Last dinner 9.15pm
Credit Cards 1 2 3 4 5

✕La Potinière Main St EH31 2AA
☎(0620)843214
Owned and run by Hilary and a David Brown, this is a charming little restaurant serving well-cooked food with an excellent wine list. A light courgette soufflé makes a fine introduction to a main course of duck, served with a red-wine sauce flavoured with juniper, accompanied by cabbage and dauphinoise potatoes. Only two things marred our inspectors visit – cold plates and very leisurely service.
Closed Wed, 1 wk Jun & Oct
Lunch not served Sat
Dinner not served Sun-Fri (dinner served Sat only)
French 32 seats Lunch £13.50 Dinner £21 Last lunch 1pm 10P

GULWORTHY Devon Map **02** SX47

✕✕✕Horn of Plenty PL19 8JD ☎Tavistock(0822)832528
This peaceful country restaurant with rooms has marvellous views which extend as far as Bodmin Moor. Under the personal supervision of Sonia Stevenson, the food is wholesome and hearty and a fine mélange of classical and French provincial styles. À la carte and French regional menus feature such dishes as quenelles of fresh Tamar salmon in a cream sauce, followed, perhaps, by Lobster Charontaise or a hefty fillet of beef, roasted in pastry with an intense, almost sticky truffle sauce. The wine list is interesting and the staff are polite.
Closed 25 & 26 Dec
Lunch not served Thu & Fri
Continental V 60 seats ✱ Lunch £16.50&alc Dinner fr£24&alc Last lunch 2pm Last dinner 9.30pm 30P nc10yrs 6 bedrooms available
Credit Cards 1 2 3

GWBERT-ON-SEA Dyfed Map **02** SN15

★★★51% Cliff SA43 1PP ☎Cardigan(0239)613241
Telex no 48440 FAX (0239) 615361
A family, holiday hotel with a friendly atmosphere, the Cliff stands perched on its own 30 acres of headland with fine sea views and offers a good range of facilities.
75rm(65⇌10)(4fb)2 CTV in all bedrooms T
CTV 200P CFA (heated) 9 squash snooker sauna solarium gymnasium sea fishing
Welsh, English & French Last dinner 9pm
Credit Cards 1 2 3 5

GWITHIAN Cornwall & Isles of Scilly Map **02** SW54

★Sandsifter Godrevy Towans TR27 5ED ☎Hayle(0736)753314
This small hotel, adjacent to the sand dunes, has compact, well-equipped bedrooms and a busy bar which is popular with the locals. The restaurant offers a choice of menu and service is happy and relaxed.
8⇌(1fb) CTV in all bedrooms ® sB&B⇌£14-£22 dB&B⇌£28-£44
80P nc8yrs *xmas*
English & French V Lunch £5.50-£7&alc Dinner £7-£8.50&alc Last dinner 9pm
£

HACKNESS North Yorkshire Map **08** SE99

★★★ 66% ***Hackness Grange Country*** North Yorkshire National Park YO13 0JW (Best Western)
☎Scarborough(0723)82345
Telex no 527667

An elegant country house in a superb setting, the family-run hotel offers very comfortable accommodation, a relaxing atmosphere and courteous service.
11⇨Annexe15rm(13⇨2♠)(4fb)2 CTV in all bedrooms ® ✈
(CTV 60P ✿ (heated) ▶9 (hard) Croquet nc5
V ♥
Credit Cards 1 2 3 5

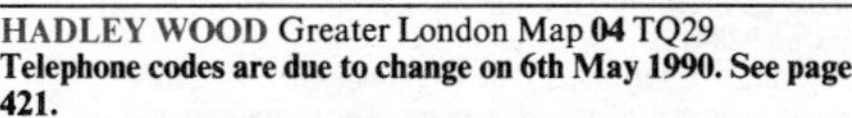

HADLEY WOOD Greater London Map **04** TQ29
Telephone codes are due to change on 6th May 1990. See page 421.

★★★★58% **West Lodge Park** Cockfosters Rd EN4 0PY ☎01-440 8311 Telex no 24734 FAX 01-449 3698
Set in 34 acres of parkland and gardens which include a lake and an arboretum, this pleasant country house dates back to the 16th century, though it was rebuilt in the time of William IV. Facilities include a comfortable lounge, cosy bar and timbered restaurant.
48⇨3 CTV in 50bedrooms ® **T** ✈ (ex guide dogs) sB&B⇨£75-£90 dB&B⇨£90-£120
Lift (200P ✿ CFA putting croquet bar billiards ♫
International **V** ♥ Lunch fr£15alc Dinner fr£15alc Last dinner 9.30pm
Credit Cards 1 2 3 5

HADLOW Kent Map **05** TQ65

★★**Leavers Manor** Goose Green TN11 0JH
☎Tonbridge(0732)851442
The elegant Georgian house offers attractively decorated bedrooms and comfortably furnished public areas; meals are soundly cooked and efficiently served.
10rm(8⇨2♠)(2fb) CTV in all bedrooms ® **T** ✈ (ex guide dogs) ✱ S% sB&B⇨♠£40-£47 dB&B⇨♠£50-£57
60P ✿ (hard)
English & French Dinner fr£8.50 Last dinner 10.30pm
Credit Cards 1 2 3 5 £

HAILSHAM East Sussex Map **05** TQ50

★★**The Olde Forge** Magham Down BN27 1PN ☎(0323)842893
Conveniently located on the A271 a mile and a half east of the town, this small but good quality cottage hotel complements a beautifully furnished interior with personal service from the resident proprietors. The cosy, low-beamed lounge bar and restaurant are made welcoming by fresh flower displays and a log-burning fire.
8rm(1⇨5♠)1 CTV in all bedrooms ®
Lift 12P
English & French **V**
Credit Cards 1 2 3 5

HALESOWEN West Midlands

Granada Lodge Illey Ln, Frankley B32 4AR (3m SE at M5 Service Area) (Granada) ☎021-550 3261 FAX 021-501 2880
(For full entry see Frankley Motorway Service Area (M5))

H

HALIFAX West Yorkshire Map **07** SE02

★★★73% **Holdsworth House** Holmfield HX2 9TG (3m NW off A629 Keighley Road) ☎(0422)240024 Telex no 51574 FAX (0422) 245174
Closed 25 & 26 Dec
Three miles from the town centre, a seventeenth-century house in its own gardens offers forty individually furnished and decorated bedrooms together with public areas that have been carefully restored to preserve the character of the original building. These standards of accommodation combine with excellent cuisine and friendly, caring service to create a hotel that is attractive to business clients and holiday makers alike.
40rm(38⇌2⋒)(1fb)4⊞ CTV in all bedrooms **T**
sB&B⇌⋒£60-£75 dB&B⇌⋒£70-£90 ⊟
☾40P ✲ CFA
♁ French **V** ♉ ♃ Lunch £17-£22alc Dinner £17.50-£25alc Last dinner 9.30pm
Credit Cards [1] [2] [3] [5]

★★★54% **Wool Merchants** Mulcture Hall Rd HX1 1SP
☎(0422)368783
A former woollen warehouse has been converted to provide modern accommodation whilst retaining much of the character of the original building. Bedrooms are well-equipped, and the hotel provides a good base from which to tour Yorkshire.
25⇌⋒(2fb) CTV in all bedrooms ® **T** ✱
sB&B⇌⋒£23-£39.50 dB&B⇌⋒£35.50-£49.50
Lift CTV 200P
♁ International **V** ♉ ♃ Lunch fr£4.95alc Dinner fr£8.75alc Last dinner 11pm
Credit Cards [1] [2] [3]

HALKYN Clwyd Map **06** SJ27

○**TraveLodge** CH8 8RF (on A55) (Trusthouse Forte)
☎(0352)780952
31⇌
P

HALLAND East Sussex Map **05** TQ41

★★**Halland Forge** BN8 6PW (Inter) ☎(082584)456 FAX (082584) 773
Conveniently situated on the A22, with easy access and parking, this family-run motel offers a choice of well-equipped, self-contained bedrooms complemented by a lounge bar, a restaurant and a separate coffee shop that serves light meals throughout the day.
Annexe20rm(17⇌3⋒)(2fb) CTV in all bedrooms ®
sB⇌⋒£35-£37 dB⇌⋒£44-£46 (room only) ⊟
70P ✲ nc5yrs
♁ English & French **V** ♉ ♃ Lunch £8.95-£10.95&alc Dinner £13.50-£14.50&alc Last dinner 9.30pm
Credit Cards [1] [2] [3] [5] £

HALSTEAD

See **Yeldham, Great**

HAMBLETON North Yorkshire Map **08** SE52

★★**Owl** Main Rd YO8 9JH (4m W A63) ☎Selby(0757)82374
A 15th-century gentleman's residence has been converted and extended to provide an hotel of character and interest. Standing about three miles west of Selby, it has well-proportioned and nicely equipped bedrooms, a good lounge bar, dining room and banqueting room.
9rm(8⇌1⋒)(1fb) CTV in all bedrooms ® **T** ⤫ ✱
sB&B⇌⋒£28.50-£32.50 dB&B⇌⋒£38.50-£42.50
50P ⊕
♉ ♃ Lunch £5.50&alc Dinner £6-£11alc Last dinner 10pm
Credit Cards [1] [3] £

HAMILTON MOTORWAY SERVICE AREA (M74) Strathclyde Map **11** NS75

○***Roadchef Lodge*** M74 Northbound GA2 5BA ☎(0698)890904 FAX (0698) 891682
Due to have opened July 1989
36rm

HAMPSON GREEN Lancashire Map **07** SD55

★★***Hampson House*** Hampson Ln LA2 0JB (off A6 at M6 junct 33) ☎Galgate(0524)751158
Pleasantly set in its own grounds, this comfortable, well-furnished hotel is within easy reach of both the M6 Motorway and Lancaster city.
13rm(6⇌5⋒)(3fb) CTV in all bedrooms ®
45P ✲ ⅋ (grass)
♉ ♃
Credit Cards [1] [3]

HAMPTON COURT Greater London

See **London plan 5***B2*(page 412) **Telephone codes are due to change on 6th May 1990. See page 421.**
★★***Liongate*** Hampton Court Rd KT8 9BZ ☎01-977 8121 Telex no 928412
Welcoming, friendly hotel with well equipped, comfortable bedrooms and attractive public areas. The restaurant overlooks picturesque Bushey Park.
9⇌Annexe15⇌2⊞ CTV in all bedrooms ® **T** ⤫ (ex guide dogs)
☾25P
♁ International **V** ♉ ♃ ⊁ Last dinner 10.30pm
Credit Cards [1] [2] [3] [5]

HANCHURCH Staffordshire Map **07** SJ84

★★★79% ***Hanchurch Manor Hotel*** ST4 8SD ☎Stoke-On-Trent(0782)643030 FAX (0782) 643035
Having a pleasant approach along a winding drive flanked by swimming pools on one side and shrubs on the other, a mullion-windowed main house contains luxury styled bedrooms and comfortable, elegant lounges. A thatched mews house annexe offers rooms of a similar standard overlooking the grounds and central fountain, and the restaurant provides a seasonally changing à la carte menu with a set menu including Italian dishes and service by friendly staff.
7⇌Annexe5rm(4⇌1⋒)2⊞ CTV in all bedrooms **T** ⤫
☾25P ⊕ ✲ ♩ nc12yrs
V ⊁ Last dinner 9.30pm
Credit Cards [1] [2] [3] [5]

HANDFORTH Cheshire Map **07** SJ88

★★★★61% **Belfry** Stanley Rd SK9 3LD ☎061-437 0511 Telex no 666358 FAX 061-499 0597
A family-run hotel, conveniently situated for Manchester Airport or the city centre, offers every facility for business traveller and tourist alike. Recent refurbishment has improved its compact bedrooms, but the restaurant takes pride of place, serving such mouthwatering delicacies as wholemeal pancake filled with seafood and served with tomato flavoured Hollandaise sauce, a whole roast crispy duck served with port and orange essence, all meals being accompanied by an outstanding wine list.
82⇌ CTV in all bedrooms **T** ✱ sB⇌£62-£75 dB⇌£72-£84 (room only) ⊟
Lift ☾ 150P ✲ CFA ♫
♁ International **V** ♉ ♃ Lunch fr£9&alc Dinner fr£11&alc Last dinner 10pm
Credit Cards [1] [2] [3] [5]

HARBERTONFORD Devon Map **03** SX75

★★★67% ***Old Mill Country House*** TQ9 7SW ☎(080423)349
This former mill, peacefully located in riverbank setting, has been tastefully converted to provide comfortable bedrooms, and an intimate lounge and bar; the restaurant is popular locally, offering an interesting table d'hôte menu of carefully prepared dishes, whilst the proprietors, who live in the grounds, do everything in their power to ensure guests' enjoyment.
5⇌Annexe1⇌1 ⊞ ⅄in 1 bedroom CTV in all bedrooms **T** ✗
☾60P ✲ ♪
♀ English & French ✿ ☕ Last dinner 9.30pm
Credit Cards [1] [3]

HAREWOOD West Yorkshire Map **08** SE34

★★★66% **Harewood Arms** Harrogate Rd LS17 9LH
☎(0532)886566 FAX (0532) 886064
Once a coaching inn, and dating back to 1815, the hotel has been carefully restored and renovated to provide comfortable accommodation with modern amenities, whilst at the same time retaining its original character.
24rm(17⇌7↱)(1fb) CTV in all bedrooms ® **T** ✳
sB&B⇌↱£45-£56 dB&B⇌↱£60-£70 ⊟
100P ✲ *xmas*
♀ English & French **V** ✿ ☕ Lunch £6.85-£8.50 Dinner £10.95-£12.95&alc Last dinner 10pm
Credit Cards [1] [2] [3] [4] [5]

HARLECH Gwynedd Map **06** SH53

See also **Talsarnau**

★★**The Castle Hotel** Castle Square LL36 2YH ☎(0766)780529
Standing beside the castle, with fine views over the bay, this recently refurbished hotel maintains high standards both in bedrooms and in public areas, resident owners providing good all-round service.
10rm(4⇌6↱)(2fb)1 ⊞ CTV in all bedrooms ® ✳ S%
sB&B⇌↱fr£25 dB&B⇌↱£34-£60 ⊟
CTV 30P ⊞ ▶18 ⚲ (hard) ∪
♀ English & French **V** ✿ ☕ ⅄ S% Lunch £5.50-£6 Dinner £7-£12alc Last dinner 9.30pm
Credit Cards [1] [3]

★**Noddfa** Lower Rd LL46 2UB ☎(0766)780043
Small family-run hotel in an elevated position, with views of Royal St David's Golf Course, the sea and mountains. The hotel offers very good value for money, and archery facilities are available to guests.
6rm(3⇌)(1fb) CTV in 3bedrooms TV in 1bedroom ® ✗ (ex guide dogs) sB&B£15 sB&B⇌£18-£23 dB&B£26 dB&B⇌£32-£36 ⊟
CTV 40P ⊞ ✲ solarium archery nc3 yrs *xmas*
♀ International **V** Lunch £10.50-£11.50&alc Dinner £10.50-£11.50&alc Last dinner 8.30pm
Credit Cards [1] [3] ⓔ

✕**Cemlyn** High St LL46 2YA ☎(0766)780425
Cemlyn is Welsh for frog, and small models of frogs can be found throughout this charming, small restaurant. Owner/chef Ken Goody produces a good array of dishes with fresh fish featuring predominently on the menu – Gravadlax is a speciality – and, of course, Welsh lamb in season. Service is friendly and efficient. It is advisable to book in advance.
Closed mid Oct-Etr
Lunch not served (by arrangement only)
♀ International **V** 42 seats Dinner £14-£17.50 Last dinner 9.30pm ℙ nc8yrs 1 bedrooms available ⅄
Credit Cards [2] [5]

Book as early as possible for busy holiday periods.

HARLESTON Norfolk Map **05** TM28

★★***Swan*** The Thoroughfare IP20 9 ☎(0379)852221
14rm(11⇌3↱)(1fb) CTV in all bedrooms ® **T**
CTV 45P
♀ English & French **V** ✿ ☕ ⅄ Last dinner 9.30pm
Credit Cards [1] [3] ⓔ

HARLOSH

See **Skye, Isle of**

HARLOW Essex Map **05** TL41

★★★68% **Churchgate Manor** Churchgate St, Old Harlow CM17 0JT (Best Western) ☎(0279)20246 due to change to 420246 Telex no 818289 FAX (0279) 37720
This country house style hotel has well-equipped bedrooms, extensive conference facilities and a good indoor leisure complex. Public areas have recently been refurbished and a new wing of suites has been added.
85⇌(8fb) CTV in all bedrooms ® **T** ✳ sB&B⇌£45-£65 dB&B⇌£55-£75 ⊟
☾120P ✲ ▣(heated) sauna solarium gymnasium *xmas*
♀ English & French **V** ✿ ☕ Lunch £8.95-£10&alc Dinner £12.50-£13.50&alc Last dinner 9.45pm
Credit Cards [1] [2] [3] [5]

★★★50% **Green Man** Mulberry Green, Old Harlow CM17 0ET (Trusthouse Forte) ☎(0279)442521 Telex no 817972 FAX (0279) 626113
Interesting coaching inn with comfortable well-equipped bedrooms in modern annexe.
Annexe55⇌⅄in 8 bedrooms CTV in all bedrooms ® **T** ✳
sB⇌fr£61 dB⇌fr£71 (room only) ⊟
▶

☾75P *xmas*
V ♁ ⌻ ⊬ Lunch fr£9.50 Dinner fr£12.50 Last dinner 10pm
Credit Cards [1] [2] [3] [4] [5]

★★★ 65% **Harlow Moat House** Southern Way CM18 7BA (Queens Moat) ☎(0279)22441 Telex no 81658 FAX (0279) 635094
Large hotel with modern and well-equipped bedrooms and recently refurbished public rooms. The hotel offers conference and banqueting facilities.
120⇌↱⊬in 12 bedrooms CTV in all bedrooms ® T ✈ (ex guide dogs) ✱ sB&B⇌↱£40-£70 dB&B⇌↱£50-£85 ⊟
☾180P CFA
♉ English & French V ♁ ⌻ Lunch £8.50-£12.50&alc Dinner fr£12.50&alc Last dinner 10pm
Credit Cards [1] [2] [3] [5] £

HARLYN BAY Cornwall & Isles of Scilly Map **02** SW87

★**Polmark** PL28 8SB (off B3276) ☎Padstow(0841)520206
A small, attractive stone house, quietly situated near the beach, with comfortable public rooms and simple bedrooms.
6rm(1fb) ® ✱ sB&Bfr£23.50 dB&Bfr£47 (incl dinner)
CTV 40P ✿ ⇌(heated) *xmas*
V ♁ ⌻ Lunch £6.95 High tea £3 Dinner fr£8.50&alc Last dinner 8.30pm
Credit Cards [3]

HAROME

See **Helmsley**

HARPENDEN Hertfordshire Map **04** TL11

★★★ 60% ***Glen Eagle*** 1 Luton Rd AL5 2PX ☎(05827)60271 Telex no 825828
An attractive hotel within walking distance of the town centre. Bedrooms vary in style and offer most modern conveniences. The elegant restaurant provides good food and service and the small, well-kept gardens are ideal for pre-dinner drinks in the summer.
51rm(48⇌3↱)2⊟ CTV in all bedrooms T
Lift ☾100P CFA
♉ English & French V ♁ ⌻ Last dinner 10pm
Credit Cards [1] [2] [3] [4] [5]

★★★ 63% ***Harpenden Moat House*** 18 Southdown Rd AL5 1PE (Queens Moat) ☎(05827)64111 Telex no 826938
Closed 26-31 Dec
Many Georgian features survive in the main building of this hotel – formerly St Dominic's Convent. Bedrooms vary, those in the original house displaying more originality but others having been refurbished to supply spacious, comfortable and well-equipped accommodation, whilst public areas, though not extensive, are attractively appointed.
18rm(15⇌3↱)Annexe37⇌(3fb)2⊟⊬in 5 bedrooms CTV in all bedrooms ® T
☾70P ✿ boules croquet lawn ⌂
♉ French V ♁ ⌻ Last dinner 10pm
Credit Cards [1] [2] [3] [5]

All hotels awarded three or more stars are now also given a percentage grading for the quality of their facilities. Please see p 16 for a detailed explanation.

HARRIS, ISLE OF Western Isles *Inverness-shire* Map **13**

SCARISTA Map **13** NG09

★★ **Scarista House**
PA85 3HX
☎(085985)238
Closed Oct-Apr

This charming Georgian house, formerly a manse, is set in an imposing position overlooking miles of beautiful, golden, sandy beaches. Over the years it has built up a sound reputation under the caring ownership of Andrew and Allison Johnson. It is tastefully furnished throughout and peat fires burn, when required, in the sitting rooms. Bedrooms are individually decorated and furnished, with those in the adjoining cottage possibly being the most appealing . The kitchen is Mrs Johnson's domain and although the set menu offers no choice, the cooking is innovative and the quality of food consistently high.
7⇌ ® T sB&B⇌£45-£47 dB&B⇌£64-£70
12P ⊞ ✿ nc8yrs
⊬ Dinner £18 Last dinner 8pm

TARBERT Map **13** NB10

★★**Harris** PA85 3DL ☎Harris(0859)2154 FAX (0859) 2281
Convenient for the ferry terminal, this popular holiday hotel provides practical accommodation, traditional comforts, good home cooking and a warm welcome.
25rm(13⇌4↱)(2fb) ✱ sB&Bfr£20.50 sB&B⇌↱fr£24.50 dB&Bfr£37.30 dB&B⇌↱fr£44.30 ⊟
CTV 30P ✿ ⌂ *xmas*
♁ ⌻ ⊬

HARROGATE North Yorkshire Map **08** SE35

★★★★ 57% **The Crown** Crown Place HG1 2RZ (Trusthouse Forte) ☎(0423)567755 Telex no 57652 FAX (0423) 502284
18th-century building near Valley Gardens and the Royal Baths.
121⇌(3fb)⊬in 5 bedrooms CTV in all bedrooms ® T S% sB⇌fr£70 dB⇌fr£86 (room only) ⊟
Lift ☾50P CFA ♫ *xmas*
♉ French V ♁ ⌻ ⊬ S% Lunch fr£9.50 Dinner fr£14.50 Last dinner 9.30pm
Credit Cards [1] [2] [3] [4] [5]

★★★★ 62% **The Majestic** Ripon Rd HG1 2HU (Trusthouse Forte) ☎(0423)568972 Telex no 57918 FAX (0423) 502283
Situated near Harrogate's new conference centre, this hotel is very imposing, with spacious and lofty public rooms, well-tended gardens and good leisure facilities. A bedroom-refurbishment programme is nearly complete, providing every bedroom with modern facilities.
156⇌(7fb)⊬in 20 bedrooms CTV in all bedrooms ® T ✱ sB⇌fr£75 dB⇌fr£96 (room only) ⊟
Lift ☾180P ✿ CFA ⊡(heated) ℘ (hard) squash snooker sauna solarium gymnasium Health & Fitness Centre ♫ *xmas*
♉ International V ♁ ⌻ ⊬ Lunch fr£9.50 Dinner fr£15.50 Last dinner 9.45pm
Credit Cards [1] [2] [3] [4] [5]

★★★★ 60% **Moat House International** Kings Rd HG1 1XX (Queens Moat) ☎(0423)500000 Telex no 57575 FAX (0423) 524435
The modern, purpose-built, multi-storey hotel stands adjacent to the Conference Centre, providing accommodation in smart, modern

bedrooms, a spacious reception lounge and conference facilities. The restaurant, with its popular lounge bar, offers high quality cuisine, or guests may eat at the Orangery Coffee Shop.
214⇨♪ ⚟in 15 bedrooms CTV in all bedrooms ® T S%
sB&B⇨♪fr£77 dB&B⇨♪fr£95 ⊟
Lift ☾ ⊞ 130P *xmas*
English & French V ♧ ☐ Lunch fr£8 Dinner £13-£15.50&alc Last dinner 10pm
Credit Cards [1] [2] [3] [4] [5]

★★★★ 67% **Old Swan** HG1 2SR (Norfolk Capital)
☎(0423)500055 Telex no 57922 FAX (0423) 501154
Close to the town centre and conference centre, Agatha Christie took refuge in this ivy-clad hotel in 1926. Although a conference centre clientele is catered for, tourists are equally welcome. Recent improvements have resulted in an attractive library, cocktail bar, lounge and dining room.
137⇨♪(5fb) CTV in all bedrooms ® T sB&B⇨♪£34-£82
dB&B⇨♪£68-£96 ⊟
Lift ☾ 200P ❊ CFA ℘ (hard) putting green & croquet lawn *xmas*
V ♧ ☐ Lunch fr£11.50&alc Dinner fr£15&alc Last dinner 9.30pm
Credit Cards [1] [2] [3] [5]

★★★ 63% **Grants** 3-11Swan Rd HG1 2SS ☎(0423)560666
FAX (0423) 502550
A smart hotel with a friendly atmosphere features the popular Chimney Pots restaurant.
17rm(7⇨10♪)(2fb) CTV in all bedrooms ® T sB&B⇨♪£55
dB&B⇨♪£75 ⊟
Lift ☾ 21P *xmas*
V ♧ ⚟ Lunch £8.95 Dinner £12.95&alc Last dinner 9.30pm
Credit Cards [1] [2] [3] [5] Ⓔ

★★★64% ***Hospitality Inn*** Prospect Place, West Park HG1 1LB (Mount Charlotte) ☎(0423)64601 Telex no 57530
Standing in the city centre but overlooking urban greenery, the hotel offers a tranquility rarely found in a town setting; accommodation is comfortable and well-appointed.
71⇌(5fb) CTV in all bedrooms ® **T**
Lift ☾ 40P CFA
☋ English & French **V** ♡ ☐
Credit Cards 1 2 3 5

★★★64% **Hotel St George** 1 Ripon Rd HG1 2SY (Swallow) ☎(0423)561431 Telex no 57995 FAX (0423) 530037
A busy hotel with well-appointed bedrooms, a good leisure suite and a delightfulnew bar lounge and brasserie.
93rm(88⇌5↱)(14fb)1⊠ CTV in all bedrooms ® **T**
sB&B⇌↱fr£70 dB&B⇌↱fr£95 ⊟
Lift ☾ 60P CFA ⊡(heated) sauna solarium gymnasium boutique beautician/massage ♫ *xmas*
☋ English & French **V** ♡ ☐ S% Lunch £10.50-£11.50 Dinner fr£14.50&alc Last dinner 9.30pm
Credit Cards 1 2 3 5

★★★63% ***Studley*** Swan Rd HG1 2SE ☎(0423)60425
Telex no 57506
This busy, popular hotel features a very attractive and comfortable new lounge, together with well-appointed bedrooms. The French restaurant maintains its reputation for a high standard of cuisine, whilst service is efficient and friendly throughout.
36⇌ CTV in all bedrooms ® **T**
Lift ☾ CTV 14P nc8 yrs
☋ French ♡ Last dinner 10pm
Credit Cards 1 2 3 5

★★**Albany** 22-23 Harlow Moor Dr HG2 0JY ☎(0423)565890
A charming small hotel converted from a pair of town houses, the Wessex overlooks the Valley Gardens and complements well-fitted bedrooms with cosy public rooms including lounge and separate bar.
14↱(3fb) CTV in all bedrooms ® ✗ (ex guide dogs)
sB&B↱£20-£25 dB&B↱£40-£45 ⊟
☋ English & Continental **V** ⊬ Dinner £10-£12.50&alc Last dinner 7.30pm
Credit Cards 1 3

★★***Ascot House Hotel*** 53 Kings Rd HG1 5HJ ☎(0423)531005
Centrally situated close to the town centre and conference centre, this hotel provides good old-fashioned service. The lounges are comfortable and the menus offer good value for money.
25rm(7⇌4↱)(1fb) CTV in all bedrooms ® **T**
14P ⇔
☋ English Italian French **V** ♡ ☐ Last dinner 9.00pm
Credit Cards 1 2 3 5 £

★★***Fern*** Swan Rd HG1 2SS (Inter) ☎(0423)523866
Telex no 57583
A pair of stone-built houses have been tastefully converted into this comfortable hotel which offers up-to-date accommodation near the town centre.
27rm(26⇌)(4fb) CTV in all bedrooms ® **T** ✗ (ex guide dogs)
☾ ₱
☋ French **V** Last dinner 9.30pm
Credit Cards 1 2 3 5

★★**Green Park** Valley Dr HG2 0JT (Consort) ☎(0423)504681
Telex no 57515 ATTN 31 FAX (0423) 530811
A three-storey stone building on a corner position overlooking the Valley Gardens.
43rm(28⇌15↱)(2fb) CTV in all bedrooms ® sB&B⇌↱fr£42 dB&B⇌↱fr£60 ⊟
Lift ☾ 10P *xmas*
☋ Cosmopolitan **V** ♡ ☐ ⊬ Bar Lunch 95p-£5.50alc Dinner £10.25&alc Last dinner 8.30pm
Credit Cards 1 2 3 5

★★**Russell** Valley Dr HG2 0JN ☎(0423)509866
Closed 27-30 Dec
Large converted Victorian house overlooking Valley Gardens.
34rm(24⇌10↱)(4fb) CTV in all bedrooms **T** ✱
sB&B⇌↱£42.95-£42.95 dB&B⇌↱£53-£65.50 ⊟
Lift ☾ ₱ ♪ *xmas*
☋ French **V** ♡ ☐ Bar Lunch 75p-£4.95alc Dinner £13.75&alc Last dinner 10pm
Credit Cards 1 2 3 4 5

★★***White House*** 10 Park Pde HG1 5AH (Exec Hotel) ☎(0423)501388
This elegant hotel, overlooking 'The Stray', has many interesting features including a lovely Italian tiled floor in the hall. An interesting à la carte menu is offered in the restaurant and the food is of a very good standard. There is a comfortable lounge and lounge bar.
13rm(7⇌6↱)(1fb)1⊠ CTV in all bedrooms ® **T**
CTV 10P ⇔ ✲
V ♡ ☐ Last dinner 9pm
Credit Cards 1 2 3 5

★**Alvera Court** 76 Kings Rd HG1 5JX ☎(0423)505735
This comfortable and friendly hotel has well-equipped bedrooms and is situated near the conference centre.
12rm(3⇌9↱)(4fb) CTV in all bedrooms ® **T** ✗ (ex guide dogs) S% sB&B⇌↱£20-£28.50 dB&B⇌↱£40-£53.40 ⊟
4P ⇔ *xmas*
S% Dinner £10 Last dinner 7pm

★**Britannia Lodge** 16 Swan Rd HG1 2SA ☎(0423)508482
Pleasant and friendly family-run hotel with a cosy lounge and comfortable bedrooms. Good, home cooked-dinners are served.
12rm(10⇌2↱)(4fb) CTV in all bedrooms ® **T** ✗
sB&B⇌↱£30-£35 dB&B⇌↱£42-£48 ⊟
⊞ CTV 6P 1⌂ ⇔
☋ French **V** ♡ ☐ ⊬ Lunch £6 Dinner £11 Last dinner 7pm
Credit Cards 1 3 £

★**Caesars** 51 Valley Dr HG2 0JH ☎(0423)565818
Closed Xmas & New Year
An hotel overlooking the park from its elevated position close to the town centre offers comfortable, well-appointed accommodation and interesting menus.
12rm(6⇌6↱)(4fb) CTV in all bedrooms ® **T** ✗ (ex guide dogs) sB&B⇌↱fr£34 dB&B⇌↱fr£48 ⊟
CTV ₱ ⇔
☋ English & French ♡ ☐ Bar Lunch £1.20-£5 Dinner fr£10&alc Last dinner 8.30pm
Credit Cards 1 3 £

★**Gables** 2 West Grove Rd HG1 2AD ☎(0423)505625
The converted Victorian house aptly named, stands conveniently close to the shopping area and Conference Centre. The interior is immaculate, offering a spacious and comfortable lounge with separate bar and an attractive and well-appointed restaurant.
9rm(4⇌4↱)(2fb) CTV in all bedrooms ® **T**
sB&B⇌↱£20-£23 dB&B⇌↱£40-£46 ⊟
9P reduced size snooker table
☋ Continental ♡ ☐ Dinner fr£9.25alc Last dinner 8.30pm
Credit Cards 1 3 £

★**Young's** 15 York Rd HG1 2QL ☎(0423)567336 & 521231
Friendly little hotel with a spacious, comfortable lounge and attractive, well-equipped bedrooms.
16rm(10⇌6↱)(2fb) CTV in all bedrooms ® **T** ✱
sB&B⇌↱£28-£36 dB&B⇌↱£42-£54 ⊟
18P ✲
☋ English & French Dinner fr£9.75 Last dinner 7pm
Credit Cards 1 3

✕✕**Emilio's** 3 Ripon Rd HG1 2SX ☎(0423)565267
FAX (0423) 568701
Closed Sun, 25-26 Dec, 1 Jan & BH's
French & Spanish **V** 70 seats ✱ Lunch £7.50&alc Dinner £12.50&alc Last lunch 2pm Last dinner 11pm 22P
Credit Cards [1] [2] [3]

✕**Grundy's** 21 Cheltenham Crescent HG1 1DH ☎(0423)502610
A smart, attractive little restaurant situated near the Conference Centre offers an interesting and varied menu; Crab Terrine, for example, might be followed by Roast Duckling in a Cream, White Wine and Green Peppercorn Sauce, the meal being concluded by a deliciously sticky Toffee Sponge.
Closed Sun
Lunch not served
V 40 seats Dinner £10.75&alc Last dinner 9.30pm P nc5yrs
Credit Cards [1] [2] [3]

HARROW Greater London

See **LONDON plan 5***B5*(page 412) **Telephone codes are due to change on 6th May 1990. See page 421.**

★★**Cumberland** 1 St Johns Rd HA1 2EF ☎01-863 4111
Telex no 917201
Privately owned commercial hotel with informal, friendly atmosphere.
28rm(8⇌20↱)Annexe51rm(25⇌26↱)(3fb) CTV in all bedrooms ® **T** ✗ (ex guide dogs) sB&B⇌↱£55-£62 dB&B⇌↱£70-£77 ⊟
☾ 55P
English & French **V** S10% Lunch £5.99-£8.50&alc Dinner £10.95&alc Last dinner 9.30pm
Credit Cards [1] [2] [3] [5]

★★**Harrow Hotel** Roxborough Bridge, 12-22 Pinner Rd HA1 4HZ ☎01-427 3435 Telex no 917898 FAX 01-861 1370
RS Xmas
The hotel is in a good position for transport to the city, being close to both bus and tube systems, and it also provides ample car-parking space. Much of the well-equipped accommodation is annexed, the Park House having its own bar/lounge and dining room.
76rm(30⇌46♠)(4fb)1⊟ CTV in all bedrooms ® **T** ✱
sB&B⇌♠£48-£55 dB&B⇌♠£65-£85 ⊟
☾67P
International **V** ♉ ⊒ Lunch fr£9.95 Dinner fr£14.95&alc Last dinner 9.45pm
Credit Cards 1 2 3 5 £

HARTINGTON Derbyshire Map **07** SK16

★***Charles Cotton*** SK17 0AL ☎(029884)229
Situated in the centre of this popular Peak District village, the old, stone-built inn provides simple but adequate accommodation. It is named after the famous 17th-century angler and author, who lived locally.
8rm(3fb) CTV in all bedrooms ®
CTV 50P ✲ ♩ ♫
V ♉ ⊒ Last dinner 9pm

HARTLAND Devon Map **02** SS22

★**Hartland Quay** EX39 6DU ☎(02374)218
Closed mid Nov-mid Mar RS mid Mar-Etr
Standing beside the old harbour, the hotel was converted from the harbour master's cottage and stores.
16rm(7⇌1♠)(2fb) ® S% sB&B£14-£15 sB&B⇌♠£15-£17 dB&B£28-£30 dB&B⇌♠£30-£32
CTV 100P ⛆
♉ ⊒ Bar Lunch £1-£7alc Dinner £7-£9&alc Last dinner 8pm
Credit Cards 1 3

HARTLEPOOL Cleveland Map **08** NZ53

✕**Krimo's** 8 The Front, Seaton Carew TS25 1BS (2m S A178) ☎(0429)266120
Charming Italian restaurant overlooking the sea, offering a large choice of appetising dishes.
Closed Sun, Mon, & 1st 2 wks Aug
Lunch not served Sat
Italian **V** 26 seats Lunch £4.50-£6.90&alc Dinner £8.40-£17.45alc Last lunch 1.30pm Last dinner 9.30pm ⅌
Credit Cards 1 3

HARWICH Essex Map **05** TM23

★★**Cliff** Marine Parade, Dovercourt CO12 3RD ☎(0255)503345 Telex no 98372
This informal sea-front hotel improves each year and bedrooms are now equipped with modern facilities. The restaurant offers a choice of menu and the main bar is popular with the locals. Staff are friendly and helpful.
28rm(26⇌2♠) CTV in all bedrooms ® **T** sB&B⇌♠fr£35 dB&B⇌♠fr£45 ⊟
☾60P 4🚗 (£1.50)
V ♉ ⊒ Lunch fr£8.50&alc Dinner fr£9.50&alc Last dinner 9pm
Credit Cards 1 2 3 4 5 £

★★**The Pier at Harwich** The Quay CO12 3HH ☎(0255)241212 Telex no 987083 FAX (0206) 322752
Standing on the quay, with splendid views over the estuary, an establishment which has long been renowned for its fish restaurant now offers six quality bedrooms.
6⇌(2fb) CTV in all bedrooms ® **T** ✗ (ex guide dogs) ✱ S% sB⇌£35-£50
dB⇌£45-£55 Continental breakfast (room only) ⊟
☾10P ♫
English & French **V** Lunch fr£9.50&alc Dinner £11.75-£20alc Last dinner 9.30pm
Credit Cards 1 2 3 5

★★**Tower** Main Rd, Dovercourt CO12 3PJ ☎(0255)504952
RS 25 & 26 Dec
In this recently converted Victorian building modern bedrooms are complemented by friendly service.
15rm(8⇌7♠)(2fb) CTV in all bedrooms ® **T** sB&B⇌♠fr£32 dB&B⇌♠fr£48 ⊟
☾50P 1🚗 ⛟
V ♉ ⊒ Lunch £7-£7.75&alc Dinner £10-£20alc Last dinner 10pm
Credit Cards 1 2 3 5

HASLEMERE Surrey Map **04** SU93

★★★67% **Lythe Hill** Petworth Rd GU27 3BQ (1.25m E B2131) ☎(0428)51251 Telex no 858402 FAX (0428) 4131
Nestled among the Surrey hills and once an ancient hamlet, this charming hotel preserves some marvellous Tudor architecture; modern wings have been added, but they are sympathetically blended in with the original farmhouse. Most of the main building's spacious, modern and comfortable rooms offer attractive views over surrounding countryside, whilst the separate Auberge de France provides six delightful period rooms as well as an additional restaurant. Good service is rendered by pleasant, helpful staff throughout the hotel.
38⇌(8fb)1⊟ CTV in all bedrooms **T** ✱ sB⇌£72-£128 dB⇌£85-£150 (room only) ⊟
☾200P ✲ CFA ℘ (hard) ♩ sauna solarium gymnasium boules clay pigeon shooting croquet *xmas*
English & French **V** ♉ ⊒ Lunch £14.50-£25&alc Dinner £14.50-£25&alc Last dinner 9.15pm
Credit Cards 1 2 3 5

❀ ✕✕**Morels** 23/27 Lower St GU27 2NY ☎(0428)51462
Chef patron, Jean Morel, is a favourite among our inspectors for his fine French cooking. Dishes range from tender pigeon breast with moist langoustines in the delicate modern style, to more hearty dishes of honest provincial derivation, such as a terrine of duck breast with lentils and a confit of the leg. The surroundings are bright and fresh, and service is attentive without being too solemn.
Closed Sun, Mon, 2 wks Feb, 2 wks Sep & BH's (ex Good Fri)
Lunch not served Sat
French **V** 48 seats ✱ Lunch fr£14&alc Dinner fr£17&alc Last lunch 1.45pm Last dinner 10pm ⅌
Credit Cards 1 2 3 5

✕**Shrimpton's of Kingsley Green** 2 Grove Cottages, Midhurst Rd GU27 3LF ☎Haselmere(0428)3539
In this cosy, converted 16th century cottage, the English and Continental menu is supplemented by daily special dishes.
Closed Sun, 26 Dec, 1 Jan, BH
Lunch not served Sat
English & French **V** 42 seats S10% Lunch £13.75&alc Dinner £18-£26alc Last lunch 1.45pm Last dinner 9.45pm 4P nc3yrs
Credit Cards 1 2 3 5

The AA's star-rating scheme is the market leader in hotel classification.

H

HASTINGS & ST LEONARDS East Sussex Map **05** TQ80

★★★75% **Beauport Park** Battle Rd TN38 8EA (3m N off A2100) (Best Western) ☎Hastings(0424)651222
Telex no 957126 FAX (0424) 652465
Set in 33 acres of formal gardens and parkland, with extensive outdoor leisure facilities, this lovely Georgian manor house has been tastefully furnished throughout. Formal levels of service are provided and the standard of cuisine is good.
23⇌♠(2fb)1⊠ CTV in all bedrooms ® T S%
sB&B⇌♠£45-£48 dB&B⇌♠£62-£65 ⊟
60P 4⌂(£1.50) ❊ ⌒(heated) ▶ 18 ⚲ (hard) squash ∪ snooker putting croquet *xmas*
♀ French V ♡ ⊡ Lunch fr£10.50&alc Dinner fr£12.50&alc Last dinner 9.30pm
Credit Cards 1 2 3 5

❀✕ **Roser's** 64 Eversfield Place TN37 6DB
☎Hastings(0424)712218
The chef/proprietor of this small, seafront restaurant continues to produce an interesting and well balanced range of dishes, his creative style being reflected in such specialities as Rye Bay scallops with saffron sauce flavoured with Pernod and garnished with young vegetables, or calves' sweetbreads with Madeira sauce and slivers of truffle. Reliable and honest standards of cuisine are complemented by attentive, friendly service.
Closed Sun, 1st 2 wks Jan & BH Mons
Lunch not served Sat
♀ French 40 seats S10% Lunch fr£15&alc Dinner £18.80-£29.60alc Last lunch 2pm Last dinner 10.30pm ⊁
Credit Cards 1 2 3 5

HATFIELD Hertfordshire Map **04** TL20

★★★50% **Comet** 301 St Albans Rd West AL10 9RH (junc A1/A414) (Embassy) ☎(07072)65411
RS Xmas
This hotel is named after the De Havilland Comet, a model of which stands in the forecourt.
57rm(52⇌2♠)(3fb)⊁in 12 bedrooms CTV in all bedrooms ® T ✱ sB£20-£38 sB⇌♠£58-£68 dB⇌♠£68-£78 (room only) ⊟
☾150P ❊
V ♡ ⊡ ⊁ Lunch £7.95-£9.95&alc Dinner £9.95&alc Last dinner 9.55pm
Credit Cards 1 2 3 5

✕✕✕**Salisbury** 15 The Broadway, Old Hatfield AL9 5JB ☎(07072)62220 & 67957
An elegant and spacious restaurant with a large lounge bar where aperitifs may be enjoyed whilst selecting from the imaginative à la carte and good-value table d'hôte menus. Staff are courteous and efficient.
Closed Mon, 26 Dec for 2 weeks
Lunch not served Sat
Dinner not served Sun
V 60 seats Lunch £13-£13.75 Dinner £22-£23.50 Last lunch 2pm Last dinner 9.30pm 16P
Credit Cards 1 2 3 5

HATHERSAGE Derbyshire Map **08** SK28

★★**George** Main Rd S30 1BB (Lansbury)
☎Hope Valley(0433)50436 Telex no 547196
FAX (0433) 50099
A 16th-century coaching inn has been restored and modernised to provide a well equipped hotel with spacious bedrooms, attractive restaurant, lounge bar and separate private bar.
18⇌(3fb)1⊠⊁in 6 bedrooms CTV in all bedrooms ® T ✗ (ex guide dogs) sB&B⇌fr£52 dB&B⇌fr£64 ⊟
50P ❊ ⌂ *xmas*
♀ International V ♡ Lunch fr£7.85&alc Dinner fr£13.50&alc Last dinner 10pm
Credit Cards 1 2 3 5

★★***Hathersage Inn*** Main St S30 1BB (Best Western)
☎Hope Valley(0433)50259
This comfortable, creeper-clad hotel offers guests a warm welcome and traditional English cooking. The relaxing lounge has a log fire and lots of books.
11rm(9⇌2♠)Annexe3rm1⊠ CTV in all bedrooms ® T ✗ (ex guide dogs)
20P
V ♡ ⊡ ⊁ Last dinner 9.30pm
Credit Cards 1 2 3 5

HAVANT Hampshire Map **04** SU70

★★★60% **The Bear** East St PO9 1AA (Lansbury)
☎(0705)486501 Telex no 869136
This sixteenth-century coaching inn, used for Divisional Petty Sessions before the Court House was built, offers upgraded bedroom accommodation which is provided with trouser presses and hairdriers, a character beamed bar, a Henekey's Restaurant which serves grills plus a range of more imaginative dishes at both lunch and dinner time, and good parking at the rear of the hotel.
42⇌(3fb)1⊠⊁in 5 bedrooms CTV in all bedrooms ® T ✗ (ex guide dogs) ✱ sB&B⇌£30-£60 dB&B⇌£60-£70 ⊟
Lift ☾ 100P *xmas*
♀ European V ♡ ⊡ Lunch fr£8.50 Dinner fr£12.50 Last dinner 10.30pm
Credit Cards 1 2 3 5

HAVERFORDWEST Dyfed Map **02** SM91

★★**Hotel Mariners** Mariners Square SA61 2DU ☎(0437)763353
FAX (0437) 764258
Closed 26-27 Dec & 1 Jan
An historic inn, extended several times since its beginnings, now provides modern, well-appointed accommodation with two friendly bars where you can soak up the local atmosphere.
26rm(22⇌3♠) CTV in all bedrooms ® T sB&Bfr£25 sB&B⇌♠fr£35 dB&B⇌♠fr£52 ⊟
☾40P
♀ British & French V ♡ ⊡ Bar Lunch £5-£12 Dinner £9-£10.50&alc Last dinner 9.30pm
Credit Cards 1 2 3 5

★★**Pembroke House** Spring Gardens SA61 2EJ
☎(0437)3652 & 5511
A Georgian, town-centre hotel, its façade attractively clad in Virginia creeper, features bright, well furnished public rooms. Bedrooms, though compact, are well equipped, and the restaurant offers a good choice of food.
21rm(13⇌6♠)(4fb)1⊠ CTV in all bedrooms ® T ✱ S10%
sB&B£24 sB&B⇌♠£28 dB&B£35 dB&B⇌♠£40 ⊟
CTV 18P
♡ ⊡ Dinner £8.90&alc Last dinner 10pm
Credit Cards 1 2 3 5

HAWES North Yorkshire Map **07** SD88

★★***Fountain*** Market Place DL8 3RD ☎(09697)206
Modernised town centre hotel, family owned and run.
13rm(5⇌8♠)(2fb) CTV in all bedrooms ®
10P
♡ Last dinner 9pm
Credit Cards 1 3

★★***Rookhurst Country House*** Gayle DL8 3RT ☎(09697)454
Closed 16 Dec-Jan
This charming, tranquil hotel, set on the fringe of the hamlet, offers comfortable accommodation in rooms boasting a wealth of antiques; dinner is specially recommended.
▶

This Georgian style country house hotel lies at the heart of one of the most beautiful and unspoilt areas of England.

Each of the 14 bedrooms has a private bathroom, colour TV, radio and direct dialling telephone.

Standing in 30 acres Netherfield Place is a haven for those who enjoy peace and tranquility in a grand setting; with two hard tennis courts, putting green and croquet lawn within the grounds.

Conference and Banqueting information on request.

Helen and Michael Collier
Netherfield Place, Battle, East Sussex.
Tel: Battle (04246) 4455 Telex: 95284

Architecturally unique, the Comet Hotel was built to honour the local aircraft industry. Today with a friendly atmosphere and comfortable surroundings, the Comet is well patronised by holiday makers and business people who appreciate the good value and high standards of service in which the Comet staff take pride.

The 54 bedrooms each have private bathrooms and there is parking for 150 cars.

Comet Hotel,
301 St, Albans Road West, Hatfield,
Herts AL10 9RH. Tel: 070 7265411

Embassy Hotels ★★★

The Beauport Park Hotel

Hastings, Sussex TN38 8EA
Telephone: 0424 51222

A Georgian country house hotel set in 33 acres of parkland with its own swimming pool, tennis courts, putting green, croquet lawn and country walks. Candle-lit restaurant and open log fires. Adjacent to an 18 hole golf course, riding stables and squash courts.

Resident proprietors:
Kenneth and Helena Melsom

Special country house bargain breaks available all year. Please send for our colour brochure and tariff.

Telex: 957126. ★★★

H

6rm(3⇋1⮣)2⊞⊁in all bedrooms CTV in all bedrooms ® ⌘ (ex guide dogs)
10P ⊯ nc
♡ ⊻ ⊁ Last dinner 7.30pm

★★Simonstone Hall Simonstone DL8 3LY ☎(09697)255 due to change to (0969) 667255
Delightfully restored Hall with spacious rooms and fine home cooking.
10rm(9⇋1⮣)1⊞ CTV in all bedrooms ®
dB&B⇋⮣£64.50-£80 ⊟
24P ⊯ ✲ potholing hang gliding ⌂ *xmas*
V ♡ ⊻ Lunch £10.20 Dinner £16.50&alc Last dinner 8.30pm
Credit Cards [1] [2] [3] [5] £

★★⊕Stone House Sedbusk DL8 3PT N
☎(09697)571
RS mid Nov-mid Mar

Dating back to the turn of the century, this country house has been carefully modernised to preserve the good features and atmosphere. Managed by the resident proprietors, the service is very courteous. Dinner is especially recommended.
15rm(9⇋5⮣) CTV in all bedrooms ® sB&B⇋⮣£22.50 dB&B£37 dB&B⇋⮣£45-£55
15P *xmas*
V ♡ Lunch £3-£5 Dinner £11.50 Last dinner 8pm
Credit Cards [1] [3]

★Herriots Hotel Main St DL8 3QU ☎(09697)536 due to change to (0969) 667536
Closed Nov-mid Feb RS Feb-Etr
Courteous resident proprietors manage this small, friendly hotel, ensuring that its restaurant offers excellent value for money.
6⮣(1fb) CTV in all bedrooms ® sB&B⮣fr£25
dB&B⮣fr£38 ⊟
Ᵽ
V ♡ Bar Lunch £1.25-£3.30alc Dinner £8-£10.70alc Last dinner 9.30pm
Credit Cards [1] [3]

HAWICK Borders *Roxburghshire* Map **12** NT51

★★Buccleuch 1 Trinity St TD9 9NR ☎(0450)72368
A friendly tourist/commercial hotel in the town centre.
18rm(4⇋)(1fb) CTV in all bedrooms ® T sB&B£16-£18.50 sB&B⇋£21.50 dB&B£32 dB&B⇋£36 ⊟
6⊜
♡ ⊻ Sunday Lunch £4.95-£5.50 High tea £3.75-£4.50 Dinner £5.50-£10.95 Last dinner 8.45pm
Credit Cards [1] [2] [3] [5] £

★★Kirklands West Stewart Place TD9 8BH (Exec Hotel)
☎(0450)72263
Small well-appointed hotel with attractive dining room and thoughtfully equipped bedrooms.
6rm(2⇋1⮣)Annexe7rm(6⇋1⮣) CTV in all bedrooms ® T ✳ sB&B£30 sB&B⇋⮣£35.80 dB&B£48 dB&B⇋⮣£50 ⊟
20P ⊯ ✲ snooker games room ⌂
♀ International V ♡ Lunch £2.50-£7.95&alc Dinner £11.95-£12.95&alc Last dinner 9.30pm
Credit Cards [1] [2] [3] [5]

★★Mansfield House Weensland Rd TD9 9EL ☎(0450)73988
An attractive house overlooking the Cheviot Valley, offering most enjoyable cuisine served in the spacious dining room by friendly, informal staff. Bedrooms, though modest in style are well equipped, and those in the basement are accessible only from the outside.
5rm(2⇋)Annexe5rm(1⇋4⮣)(2fb) CTV in all bedrooms ® T sB&B£27 sB&B⇋⮣£34-£38 dB&B£42 dB&B⇋⮣£50 ⊟
CTV 20P ✲ ⌂
V ♡ ⊻ Lunch fr£9 Dinner £9-£11&alc Last dinner 9pm
Credit Cards [1] [2] [3] [5]

✕The Old Forge Newmill-on-Teviot TD9 0JU (3m SW A7)
☎Teviotdale(04585)298
This delightful restaurant, run by Mr and Mrs Irving, is housed in what used to be the village smithy, hence the name. Cooking is of Cordon Bleu standard and the dinners – they no longer serve lunches – are good value for money.
Closed Sun, Mon, 2 wks May & 2 wks Nov
Lunch not served
Dinner not served Sun & Mon
♀ International V 28 seats S% Dinner £10-£12.50 Last dinner 9.30pm 10P
Credit Cards [1] [2] [3]

HAWKCHURCH Devon Map **03** ST30

★★★⊕ 71% Fairwater Head EX13 5TX
☎(02977)349
Closed Jan & Feb RS Dec

Commanding panoramic views of the countryside from its setting in beautiful gardens above the Axe Valley, an elegant hotel dating from the turn of the century offers warm, comfortable bedrooms complemented by public areas with a peaceful, relaxed atmosphere. The restaurant provides both table d'hôte and à la carte dinner menus, and special diets can be catered for. Resident proprietors offer a warm welcome to guests and take a personal interest in their well-being.
14⇋Annexe4⇋ CTV in all bedrooms ® T sB&B⇋£55 dB&B⇋£95 (incl dinner) ⊟
30P ⊯ ✲ croquet ♫ ⌂
♡ ⊻ Lunch fr£8.50 Dinner fr£16 Last dinner 8.30pm
Credit Cards [1] [2] [3] [5]

See advertisement under LYME REGIS

HAWKHURST Kent Map **05** TQ73

★★Tudor Court Rye Rd TN18 5DA (Best Western)
☎(0580)752312 Telex no 957565 FAX (0580) 753966
A pleasant, rural hotel with attractive gardens, located in the lovely Weald of Kent. Bedrooms are cosy and in keeping with the character of the hotel and are equipped with modern facilites. The restaurant offers a choice of menus and there is a wood-panelled bar.
18rm(12⇋6⮣)(1fb)2⊞ CTV in all bedrooms ® T S%
sB&B⇋⮣fr£35 dB&B⇋⮣£65-£68 ⊟
CTV 50P 2⊜(£1.50) ✲ ⚲ (hard) croquet clock golf *xmas*
♀ International ♡ ⊻ ⊁ Lunch £9.50&alc Dinner £11-£12&alc Last dinner 9.15pm
Credit Cards [1] [2] [3] [5] £

HAWKRIDGE Somerset Map 03 SS83

★★ *Tarr Steps* TA22 9PY
☎Winsford(064385)293
Closed mid Nov-mid Mar

This former Georgian rectory, 200 yards from the Bronze-Age Tarr Steps, is peacefully situated in beautiful countryside. There is a large lounge, a cosy bar, and a romantic candle-lit restaurant. The bedrooms are individual in style and some are furnished with antiques. The proprietors personally supervise the pleasant young staff and provide enjoyable, uncomplicated cuisine.

12rm(6⇌)Annexe3rm(2⇌)2
20P ✽ rough & clay pigeon shooting
Last dinner 8.45pm
Credit Cards 2 3

This is one of many useful guidebooks published by the AA. The complete range is available in AA Centres and most bookshops.

HAWKSHEAD (near Ambleside) Cumbria Map 07 SD39

★★★ 53% Tarn Hows
Hawkshead Hill LA22 0PR
☎Hawkeshead(09666)330
FAX (09662) 3438

Situated at Tarn Hows on an unclassified road between Ambleside and Hawkshead, this comfortable hotel offers the ultimate in peace and tranquility. Guests will find service friendly and attentive. Dinner is especially recommended.

15rm(14⇌1)(2fb)2 CTV in all bedrooms ® T S10% sB&B⇌£25-£40 dB&B⇌£50-£80
CTV 40P ✽ (heated) sauna solarium putting *xmas*
V S10% Lunch £7.50 High tea £5.50 Dinner £17
Last dinner 9.00pm
Credit Cards 1 2 3 5 £

★★Field Head House LA22 0PY ☎Hawkshead(09666)240
Closed 16 Jan-2 Feb RS Tue
7rm(4⇌3)(2fb) in all bedrooms CTV in all bedrooms ® T S% sB&B⇌£33-£36 dB&B⇌£50-£56
15P ✽ Croquet *xmas*
S% Dinner fr£18 Last dinner 8pm

★★*Queen's Head* Main St LA22 0NS ☎Hawkshead(09666)271
A charming inn with low ceilings, oak beams and brasses offers a good choice of meals in bar or restaurant.
8rm(1⇌3♠)Annexe2⇌(3fb) CTV in all bedrooms ® ✗
CTV 10P nc8 yrs
English & Continental V Last dinner 9.30pm
Credit Cards 1 2 3

★Highfield House
Hawkshead Hill LA22 0PN
☎Hawkshead(09666)344
Closed 24-26 Dec

Sitting in its own grounds, three quarters of a mile from the village, this country house enjoys magnificent panoramic Lakeland views. Some of the comfortable bedrooms are extremely spacious, there is a relaxing lounge and the inventive country cooking offers excellent value for money.
11rm(6⇌2♠)(2fb) CTV in all bedrooms ® sB&Bfr£19.50 sB&B⇌♠fr£24.50 dB&Bfr£37 dB&B⇌♠fr£43
12P
English & Continental V Bar Lunch fr£3.50alc High tea fr£3.50alc Dinner fr£10.50alc Last dinner 8pm
Credit Cards 3

HAWORTH West Yorkshire Map **07** SE03

★★Old White Lion 6 West Ln BD22 8DU ☎(0535)42313
Stone-built coaching inn standing at the top of the main road.
14rm(6⇌8♠)(2fb) CTV in all bedrooms ® T ✗ (ex guide dogs) ✱ sB&B⇌♠£26 dB&B⇌♠£36.50
CTV 10P 2 *xmas*
English & French V Lunch £4.55-£7.50 Dinner £7.50&alc Last dinner 9.30pm
Credit Cards 1 2 3 5

See advertisement under KEIGHLEY

✕Weavers 15 West Ln BD22 8DU ☎(0535)43822
Comfortable and informal, a restaurant converted from roadside cottages retains the atmosphere of its origins, offering such dishes as Shepherd's Pie and Beef Pie alongside Salmon, Pork Normandie and Breast of Duck, Spotted Dick and Custard as an alternative to Creme Brulée – all dishes, including the excellent bread rolls, being home-made.
Closed Mon, 1 wk Xmas & 3 wks Jun/July
Lunch not served Tue-Sat & Sun (Etr-Oct)
Dinner not served Sun
V 60 seats Sunday Lunch £9.50 Dinner £10.50&alc Last dinner 9pm
Credit Cards 1 2 3

HAYDOCK Merseyside Map **07** SJ59

★★★66% Post House Hotel Lodge Ln, Newton-Le-Willows WA12 0JG (adj to M6 junc 23) (Trusthouse Forte)
☎Wigan(0942)717878 Telex no 677672 FAX (0942) 718419
A modern hotel situated in wooded parkland overlooking Haydock Park racecourse. In addition to an international à la carte menu and a 'Huntsman's Table', hot and cold snacks are available throughout the day and there is a room service menu. A leisure centre has recently been opened.
99⇌in 21 bedrooms CTV in all bedrooms ® T ✱
sB⇌£70-£80 dB⇌£80-£90 (room only)
(197P CFA (heated) sauna solarium gymnasium *xmas*
International V Lunch £8-£12.50&alc Dinner £11.30-£15.75&alc Last dinner 10.30pm
Credit Cards 1 2 3 4 5

HAYDON BRIDGE Northumberland Map **12** NY86

★★Anchor John Martin St NE47 6AB (Exec Hotel)
☎(043484)227
Friendly hotel supervised by resident proprietors.
12rm(10♠)(1fb) CTV in all bedrooms ® T sB&Bfr£25 sB&B♠fr£30 dB&Bfr£36 dB&B♠fr£42
25P
English & French V Bar Lunch £2-£4alc Dinner £10-£12alc Last dinner 8.30pm
Credit Cards 1 2 3 5 £

✕General Havelock Inn Ratcliffe Rd NE47 6ER ☎(043484)376
Closed Mon, Tue, 2 wks Jan & last wk Aug-1st wk Sep
Lunch not served Mon-Tue
Dinner not served Sun-Tue
English & French V 28 seats Lunch £6.75-£9.75 Dinner £14-£17 Last lunch 1.30pm Last dinner 9pm 12P

HAYLE Cornwall & Isles of Scilly Map **02** SW53

★★Hillside Angarrack TR27 5HZ (1m E of Hayle on unclass rd off A30) ☎(0736)752180
Closed 23-31Dec
Peacefully situated within a walled garden, this personally-run hotel offers spotlessly clean bedrooms, good home cooking and a friendly atmosphere.
10rm(1⇌4♠)(3fb) ✗ (ex guide dogs) sB&B£19-£20.50 sB&B⇌♠£23.50-£25 dB&B£33-£37 dB&B⇌♠£38.50-£40
CTV 8P
V Lunch £6.50 High tea £4.25-£5.15 Dinner £8.15-£8.75 Last dinner 7.30pm
Credit Cards 1 3 £

HAYLING ISLAND Hampshire Map **04** SU70

★★★61% Post House Northney Rd PO11 0NQ (Trusthouse Forte) ☎(0705)465011 Telex no 86620 FAX (0705) 466468
The hotel is situated off the A3023, overlooking the estuary from the north shore of the island. Facilities include a well-run coffee shop and bar, the dignified Club House Restaurant with cocktail lounge, and a modern health and fitness club. Accommodation is in a choice of comfortable and well-equipped bedrooms.
96⇌(6fb)in 16 bedrooms CTV in all bedrooms ® T S%
sB⇌£70-£76 dB⇌£81-£87 (room only)
(CTV 150P CFA (heated) sauna solarium gymnasium *xmas*
V S% Lunch £9.25-£9.75&alc High tea £6-£7 Dinner £14.50-£18.75&alc Last dinner 10pm
Credit Cards 1 2 3 4 5

HAY-ON-WYE Powys Map **03** SO24

★★★64% The Swan Church St HR3 5DQ
☎(0497)821177 & 821188
This Georgian hotel has been completely modernised and refurbished with all modern facilities. The lounge is particularly elegant, and the two bars offer a choice of atmosphere. Service is professional.
15rm(13⇌2♠)(1fb)1 CTV in all bedrooms ® T ✱
sB&B⇌♠£25-£30 dB&B⇌♠£45-£50
24P *xmas*
British & French V Lunch £10-£20alc Dinner £10-£20alc Last dinner 9.30pm
Credit Cards 1 3

★★***Kilvert Country*** Bull Ring HR3 5AG ☎(0497)821042 Telex no 35315 FAX (0497) 821004
The Jacobean origins of this town-centre hotel have been carefully preserved in its restoration to provide quality bedroom accommodation backed by good service.
11rm(1⇌10↖)(1fb)⊬in 3 bedrooms CTV in all bedrooms ® **T**
☾ CTV 10P ✲ ♩
♉ International **V** ♧ ⊒ ⊬ Last dinner 10pm
Credit Cards [1] [2] [3]

★★**Olde Black Lion** 26 Lion St HR3 5AD ☎(0497)820841
A village inn of charm and character, personally owned and with friendly service, the hotel has cosy, comfortable bedrooms and a nice cottage restaurant offering imaginative menus and good home cooking.
6↖Annexe4rm(2⇌)(2fb) CTV in all bedrooms ® **T** sB&B£16.50-£25 sB&B⇌↖£25 dB&B£33 dB&B⇌↖£35.50-£39.50 ⊟
CTV 20P ⊞ ♩ *xmas*
♉ European **V** ♧ ⊒ Lunch £5.95-£10.50alc Dinner £5.95-£12.50alc Last dinner 9pm
Credit Cards [1] [2] [3]

HAYTON Cumbria Map **12** NY55

★★★71% ***Edmond Castle*** CA4 8QD ☎(022870)651
24⇌↖ CTV in all bedrooms **T** ⋈
☾ 150P ✲ ⊡(heated) ♇ (grass) ♩ snooker sauna solarium nc14yrs
♧ ⊒ ⊬
Credit Cards [1] [2] [3] [4]

HAYTOR Devon Map **03** SX77

★★★⚑70% Bel Alp House
TQ13 9XX
☎(03646)217
RS Dec-Feb

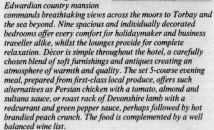

Set in an elevated position on the south-eastern edge of Dartmoor, this elegant Edwardian country mansion commands breathtaking views across the moors to Torbay and the sea beyond. Nine spacious and individually decorated bedrooms offer every comfort for holidaymaker and business traveller alike, whilst the lounges provide for complete relaxation. Décor is simple throughout the hotel, a carefully chosen blend of soft furnishings and antiques creating an atmosphere of warmth and quality. The set 5-course evening meal, prepared from first-class local produce, offers such alternatives as Persian chicken with a tomato, almond and sultana sauce, or roast rack of Devonshire lamb with a redcurrant and green pepper sauce, perhaps followed by hot brandied peach crunch. The food is complemented by a well balanced wine list.
9rm(8⇌1↖) CTV in all bedrooms ® **T** sB&B⇌↖£54-£66 dB&B⇌↖£84-£108
Lift 20P ⊞ ✲ snooker
♉ English & French ⊬ Lunch £17.50 Dinner £27.50 Last dinner 8.30pm
Credit Cards [1] [3]

★★**Rock Inn** Haytor Vale TQ13 9XP ☎(03646)305 & 465
Busy, family-run, convivial inn, with well appointed bedrooms and good food.
9rm(7⇌2↖)(2fb)1⊠⊬in 2 bedrooms CTV in all bedrooms ® **T** ⋈ (ex guide dogs) ✱ sB&B⇌↖£18.50-£30.50 dB&B⇌↖£37-£59.50 ⊟
CTV 20P ⊞ ✲ *xmas*
♉ English & French **V** ♧ ⊬ Bar Lunch £1.50-£10.50 Dinner £15.90 Last dinner 9pm
Credit Cards [1] [2] [3] £

HEATHROW AIRPORT (LONDON) Greater London Map **04** TQ07

See **Town Plan Section** under **London Airports. Telephone codes are due to change on 6th May 1990. See page 421.**
See also **Ashford (Surrey), Hounslow, Staines**

★★★★59% **The Excelsior** Bath Rd, West Drayton UB7 0DU (adj M4 spur at junc with A4) (Trusthouse Forte) ☎01-759 6611 Telex no 24525 FAX 01-759 3421
A massive refurbishment programme is well under way at this large hotel, which now has a new leisure centre. A choice of restaurants includes the popular 'Draitone'.
580⇌⊬in 12 bedrooms CTV in all bedrooms ® **T** S12% sB⇌£110-£120 dB⇌£120-£130 (room only) ⊟
Lift ☾ ⊞ 350P CFA ⊡(heated) sauna solarium gymnasium health & fitness centre jacuzzi ♫
♉ French Italian English **V** ♧ ⊒ ⊬ S12% Lunch £12.95-£22.95&alc Dinner £12.95-£22.95&alc Last dinner 10.45pm
Credit Cards [1] [2] [3] [4] [5]

★★★★64% ***Heathrow Penta*** Bath Rd, Hounslow TW6 2AQ ☎01-897 6363 Telex no 934660 FAX 01-897 1113
Bedrooms are functional rather than luxurious at this airport hotel, but they are all air-conditioned and double-glazed. Public areas include an impressive marbled entrance hall, two theme bars – one providing evening entertainment – and the London Chop House Restaurant featuring good set meal and à la carte menus; the popular leisure complex and swimming pool have recently reopened ▶

after refurbishment. Room service and the coffee shop offer 24-hour service and the hotel runs a courtesy coach to and from the airport.
670⇨🚿⊬in 4 bedrooms CTV in all bedrooms ® T
Lift ☾ ▦ 600P (£1.80) ⛟ CFA ⛆(heated)
♈ French V ♔ ♖ ⊬ Last dinner 11.00pm
Credit Cards 1 2 3 5

★★★★61% **Holiday Inn** Stockley Rd, West Drayton UB7 9NA (2m N junc M4/A408) ☏West Drayton(0895)445555
Telex no 934518 FAX (0895) 445122
A modern transit/conference hotel with spacious, well-equipped bedrooms is in process of improvement which will provide more ladies and non-smoking rooms. The Farmhouse Kitchen serves refreshments throughout the day, or you can choose a more formal meal from the comprehensive menu of the Tudor Restaurant. Good leisure facilities are available.
396⇨🚿(220fb)⊬in 21 bedrooms CTV in all bedrooms ® T
sB⇨🚿£78-£85 dB⇨🚿£89-£97 (room only) ⊟
Lift ☾ ▦ 400P ⛟ ✲ CFA ⛆(heated) ⚑ 9 ℘ (hard) sauna solarium gymnasium ⌂
♈ International V ♔ ♖ ⊬
Credit Cards 1 2 3 4 5

H

★★★56% **The Ariel** Bath Rd, Hayes UB3 5AJ (1.5m E junc A4/A437) (Trusthouse Forte) ☏01-759 2552 Telex no 21777
FAX 01-564 9265
Many aspects of this popular, compact hotel have been improved by ongoing modernisation, and it now has a delightful, unpretentious fish restaurant in addition to the Willow Carvery; bedrooms are adequately equipped, and service is provided by helpful, friendly staff.
177⇨🚿(6fb)⊬in 12 bedrooms CTV in all bedrooms ® T ✱
S% sB⇨🚿£85-£97 dB⇨🚿£95-£107 (room only) ⊟
Lift ☾ ▦ 100P CFA *xmas*
V ♔ ♖ ⊬ Lunch £13.50&alc Dinner £14.50&alc Last dinner 11pm
Credit Cards 1 2 3 4 5

★★★64% **Berkeley Arms** Bath Road, Hounslow TW5 9QE (2.5m E on A4) (Embassy) ☏01-897 2121 Telex no 935728
FAX 01-897 7014
An additional sixteen well-equipped bedrooms have recently been added to the comfortable accommodation of this modern, purpose-built hotel. Meals are taken in a carvery-style restaurant which also features a short à la carte menu, and staff are pleasant and friendly throughout.
56⇨🚿 CTV in all bedrooms ® T ✱ sB⇨🚿£60-£70
dB⇨🚿£66.50-£80 (room only) ⊟
Lift ☾ 85P ✲ ♫
♈ International V ♔ ♖ Lunch £8.95-£11.95&alc Dinner fr£11.95&alc Last dinner 9.45pm
Credit Cards 1 2 3 5

★★★63% **Master Robert Motel** 366 Great West Rd TW5 0BD
☏01-570 6261 Telex no 9413782 FAX 01-569 4016
(For full entry see Hounslow)

★★★62% **Post House** Sipson Road, West Drayton UB7 0JU (2m N A408) (Trusthouse Forte) ☏01-759 2323
Telex no 934280 FAX 01-897 8659
Conveniently situated for terminals 1, 2, and 3, this large, purpose-built hotel offers good, well-equipped accommodation; carvery and popular restaurants are open at times to suit both transit and business clients.
569⇨(176fb)⊬in 60 bedrooms CTV in all bedrooms ® T
sB⇨£80-£100 dB⇨£90-£110 (room only) ⊟
Lift ☾ ▦ 400P CFA ♫
V ♔ ♖ ⊬ Bar Lunch fr£30
Credit Cards 1 2 3 4 5

★★★50% ***The Skyway*** Bath Road, Hayesa UB3 5AW (Trusthouse Forte) ☏01-759 6311 Telex no 23935 FAX 01-759 4559
Spacious hotel with well-appointed restaurant.
411⇨(7fb)⊬in 20 bedrooms CTV in all bedrooms ® T
Lift ☾ ▦ 230P CFA ⛆(heated) snooker
V ♔ ♖ ⊬
Credit Cards 1 2 3 4 5

★★**Hotel Ibis Heathrow** 112/114 Bath Road, Hayes UB3 5AL
☏01-759 4888 Telex no 929014 FAX 01-564 7894
Modern and inexpensive, the hotel offers basic but reasonably comfortable accommodation with a limited range of service.
244⇨🚿(4fb) CTV in all bedrooms T ✱ sB⇨🚿fr£44
dB⇨🚿fr£49 (room only) ⊟
Lift ▦ 120P *xmas*
♈ International V ♔ ♖ Lunch fr£8.50 Dinner fr£8.50 Last dinner 10.30pm
Credit Cards 1 2 3 5

⌂**Granada Lodge** M4 Service Area, North Hyde Ln TW5 9NA (Granada) ☏01-574 7271 FAX 01-574 1891
(For full entry see Heston)

HEBDEN BRIDGE West Yorkshire Map 07 SD92

★★***Hebden Lodge*** New Rd HX7 8AD (Exec Hotel)
☏(0422)845272
Attractively situated opposite the newly developed Marina, this is a friendly hotel with comfortable bedrooms.
13rm(9🚿)(3fb) CTV in all bedrooms ® ✖ (ex guide dogs)
₱
♈ English, French & Italian V ♔ ♖ Last dinner 9.30pm
Credit Cards 1 2 3 5

HEDGE END Hampshire Map 04 SU41

★★★64% **Botleigh Grange** SO3 2GA (Best Western)
☏Botley(0489) 787700 FAX 0489 788535
This period hotel forms the centre of a new small business park – all the bedrooms have been tastefully refurbished. The Squire's Restaurant provides imaginative cooking with fresh local ingredients in season; the Carvery offers a good value-for-money meal. The gardens overlook the hotel's own lakes. Riding and hunting can be arranged at the hotel's own stables and fishing is also available.
44rm(22⇨22🚿)(4fb)2⊠ CTV in all bedrooms ® T S%
sB&B⇨🚿£57.50-£71.50 dB&B⇨🚿£71.50-£89.50 ⊟
☾ 200P ✲ ♩ *xmas*
♈ English & French V ♔ ♖ S% Lunch £5.85-£11&alc High tea £4.50-£6 Dinner £8.50-£11&alc Last dinner 10pm
Credit Cards 1 2 3

HELENSBURGH Strathclyde *Dunbartonshire* Map 10 NS28

★★★61% **Commodore Toby** 112 West Clyde St G84 8ER (Toby)
☏(0436)76924 Telex no 778740
Set on the seafront of this popular coastal town, the hotel provides well-equipped bedrooms and modern public rooms which include a carvery restaurant.
45⇨ CTV in all bedrooms ® T ✱ sB&B⇨fr£43
dB&B⇨fr£61 ⊟
Lift ☾ 120P *xmas*
V ♔ ♖ ⊬ Lunch £3-£10&alc Dinner £5-£9alc Last dinner 9.30pm
Credit Cards 1 2 3 5

HELFORD Cornwall & Isles of Scilly Map 02 SW72

✕✕**Riverside** TR12 6JU ☏Manaccan(032623)443
FAX (032623) 443
Situated in the village centre, this intimate restaurant is run by Edward and Susan Darrell, who provide good food in a friendly and relaxed atmosphere. The extensive menu changes daily, with an emphasis on fresh fish: an unusual fish terrine and light,

mouthwatering soufflés feature among the starters. Duck, lamb and game can also be found on the main course selection, and there is an extensive wine list.
Closed Nov-Mar
Lunch not served Mon-Thu, May-Jul
☋ English & French 30 seats S% Lunch £10-£15alc Dinner fr£24 Last dinner 9.30pm 10P 7 bedrooms available

HELMSDALE Highland *Sutherland* Map **14** ND01

★★***Navidale House*** KW8 6JS (1m NE A9) ☎(04312)258
Closed Dec & Jan
This delightful, country-house hotel has breathtaking sea views and extends a warm welcome, providing a relaxed atmosphere and good food. It is an ideal base for those fishing the famed Sutherland rivers.
11rm(7⇌1↱)Annexe5rm(2⇌) CTV in 12bedrooms ® CTV 30P ✲ clay pigeon shooting
☋ Scottish & French V ♡ ⊻ Last dinner 8.30pm
Credit Cards [1] [3]

HELMSLEY North Yorkshire Map **08** SE68

★★★73% **Black Swan** Market Place YO6 5BJ (Trusthouse Forte) ☎(0439)70466 Telex no 57538 FAX (0439) 70174
Overlooking the market square, this delightful hotel combines the best of old world charm with modern facilities, both in the original building and in the tasteful extension to the rear. In the public rooms, however, low beamed ceilings, frock-coated management and waitresses in the uniform of Victorian maidservants vividly recall a bygone era. The restaurant also successfully blends the best of old and new, bringing traditional and more innovative dishes together in its table d'hôte and à la carte menus.
40⇌(1fb)⊬in 3 bedrooms CTV in all bedrooms ® **T** S% sB⇌fr£70 dB⇌fr£103 (room only) ⊟

▶

☾ CTV 60P ✲ croquet *xmas*
English & French V S% Lunch fr£9.65 High tea fr£3.50alc Dinner fr£19.50&alc Last dinner 9.30pm
Credit Cards 1 2 3 4 5

★★★64% **Feversham Arms** 1 High St YO6 5AG (Best Western) ☎(0439)70766 Telex no 57966
Carefully modernised old inn providing comfort and a peaceful atmosphere.
18⇌(4fb)5 CTV in all bedrooms ® T sB&B⇌£44-£54 dB&B⇌£66-£76
30P ✲ ⇌(heated) (hard)
English, French & Spanish V Lunch £10-£17 Dinner £15-£20 Last dinner 9.30pm
Credit Cards 1 2 3 5

★★**Crown** Market Square YO6 5BJ ☎(0439)70297
Originally a 16th-century inn, this hotel has been sympathetically renovated to preserve its identity. It offers a warm welcome in the English tradition of hospitality, providing accommodation in small characterful rooms that are comfortably furnished and well equipped; the cosy bars and dining room serve wholesome English fare, afternoon tea proving particularly popular.
14rm(3⇌9)(1fb) CTV in all bedrooms ® sB&B£20-£23 sB&B⇌£22-£25 dB&B⇌£44-£50
CTV 17P 3 ✲
V Lunch £6.50-£7.25alc High tea £3-£5.50alc Dinner £12-£13alc Last dinner 8pm
Credit Cards 1 3

★★**Feathers** Market Place YO6 5BH ☎(0439)70275
Closed 23 Dec-1 Jan
Local stone house, partly 14th century and partly 17th century, with Georgian modifications.
18rm(6⇌7)(4fb) CTV in all bedrooms ® ✱ S% sB&Bfr£18.50 sB&B⇌£23-£46 dB&Bfr£37 dB&B⇌fr£46
CTV 12P 1 ✲
English & Continental V Lunch fr£6.75 Dinner £11-£17 Last dinner 9.00pm
Credit Cards 1 2 3 5

★★**Pheasant** Harome YO6 5JG (2.5m SE on unclass rd) ☎(0439)71241
Closed Jan-Feb
A very comfortable hotel has been established in premises that once housed the village blacksmith and shop. Bedrooms are furnished to a very high standard, several of them looking out onto the duck pond, and the resident proprietors create an atmosphere in which it is easy to relax and unwind.
12⇌Annexe2⇌ CTV in all bedrooms ® T sB&B⇌£42-£46 dB&B⇌£84-£92 (incl dinner)
20P ✲ nc12 yrs
Bar Lunch £2-£7alc Dinner £16 Last dinner 8pm

HELSTON Cornwall & Isles of Scilly Map 02 SW62

★★**The Gwealdues** Falmouth Rd TR13 8JX ☎(0326)572808
The compact bedrooms of this small, commercial hotel are well-equipped, though uninspired in their decor as yet. Both lunch and dinner can be chosen from an extensive range of bar meals, though à la carte and table d'hôte menus are also available in the evening.
12rm(4⇌5)(2fb) CTV in all bedrooms ® T ✱ sB&B£25 sB&B⇌£30 dB&B£30 dB&B⇌£40
60P ⇌
V Sunday Lunch £4.50 Dinner £8.50&alc Last dinner 9.30pm
Credit Cards 1 3 £

★★**Nansloe Manor**
Meneage Rd TR13 0SB
☎(0326)574691
Closed 25-30 Dec

Run in friendly style by Angela and Harry Dary Thomas, the hotel has chintzy bedrooms and a delightful lounge and bar. The restaurant is popular for dinner and excellent light lunches are served in the lounge.
7rm(4⇌3)1 CTV in all bedrooms ® T sB&B⇌£28.50-£42 dB&B⇌£44-£72
40P ✲ croquet nc10 yrs
English & Continental V Lunch £5.95-£6.70 Dinner £13.50-£20alc Last dinner 9.30pm
Credit Cards 1 3

HEMEL HEMPSTEAD Hertfordshire Map 04 TL00

★★★60% **Aubrey Park Hotel** Hemel Hempstead Rd AL3 7AF ☎Redbourn(058285)2105 Telex no 82195 FAX (058285) 2001
(For full entry see Redbourn)

★★★55% **Post House** Breakspear Way HP2 4UA (Trusthouse Forte) ☎(0442)51122 Telex no 826902 FAX (0442) 211812
Attractively decorated and furnished hotel about 2 miles from the town centre.
Annexe107⇌(8fb)in 21 bedrooms CTV in all bedrooms ® T sB⇌fr£75 dB⇌fr£90 (room only)
Lift ☾ 140P ✲ CFA *xmas*
V Lunch fr£10.95 Dinner fr£14.50 Last dinner 10pm
Credit Cards 1 2 3 4 5

HENLEY-IN-ARDEN Warwickshire Map 07 SP16

✕✕**Le Filbert Cottage** 64 High St B95 5BX ☎(05642)2700
Set in the main street of this attractive small town, a cosy, cottage-style restaurant offers a good range of French cuisine in its quaint, simple surroundings; meat and fish are complemented by excellent sauces and accompanied by a comprehensive wine list – the intimate little bar providing an opportunity to enjoy an aperitif before you sit down to eat.
Closed Sun, Mon, & 26 Dec, BH
French 30 seats Lunch fr£17alc Dinner fr£23alc Last lunch 1.45pm Last dinner 9.45pm nc6yrs
Credit Cards 1 2 3 4 5

HENLEY-ON-THAMES Oxfordshire Map 04 SU78

★★★62% ***Red Lion*** RG9 5LB ☎(0491)572161 Telex no 83343 FAX (0491) 410039
A recent change of ownership has prompted significant improvement and upgrading throughout this character hotel, which stands next to the river at the heart of the town. Public rooms are particularly comfortable, comprising cosy lounges, public and cocktail bars and an elegant restaurant, all attractively decorated, richly furnished, and softened by the skilful use of colourful quality fabrics. Bedrooms have been refurbished to some extent and are scheduled for improvement work to bring them up to the standard of the public areas. Imaginative food is commendably well prepared, whilst traditional standards of service result in prompt, friendly attention.
26rm(21⇌)(1fb)1 CTV in all bedrooms ® T
☾ 25P
V Last dinner 10.00pm
Credit Cards 1 2 3

All AA-appointed establishments are inspected regularly to ensure that required standards are maintained.

THE PHEASANT HOTEL ★★

Harome, Helmsley,
North Yorkshire YO6 5JG
Telephone:
Helmsley (0439) 71241 & 70416

Former blacksmith's premises, this charming friendly hotel overlooks millstream and village pond. The hotel has 12 bedrooms all with private bathroom, colour TV and tea/coffee making facilities. Log fires. Large Garden. Bar. Car park. *Please write or telephone for brochure and tariff.*

1637 — Over 350 — 1989
YEARS OF GOOD SERVICE

Formerly a posting house in coaching days, and full of character, a convenient centre for the North Yorkshire Moors, and east coast, with Castle Howard, and Rievaulx and Byland Abbeys within easy distance. 14 rooms (12 en suite) and all with colour TV. Tea and coffee facilities, and radio. Two private lounges. Full central heating throughout. Jacobean dining room offering traditional country-style cooking, with many choices. Winter bargain breaks October to May. Dogs welcome (no charge). Under the same ownership for 30 years. Brochure sent on request. Access and Visa cards accepted.

CROWN HOTEL

Helmsley, York, ★★
North Yorkshire YO6 5BJ
Telephone: Helmsley (0439) 70297

H

THE FEATHERS HOTEL ★★

MARKET PLACE, HELMSLEY,
YORK YO6 5BH
Telephone (0439) 70275

Fronting onto Helmsley marketplace with the picturesque outlines of the ruined Castle in the background, the Feathers Hotel could not be more centrally or pleasantly situated.

The Hotel contains 18 bedrooms, 15 of which have private facilities, colour TV and tea making equipment. Special out of season breaks are available.

A wide choice of excellent food is served in the Dining Room, together with a variety of bar-snacks, sandwiches and morning coffee.

Family run, it combines efficiency with charm. which is highlighted by the cheerful and helpful staff.

The Feversham Arms Hotel

Helmsley (North Yorkshire) YO6 5AG
Tel: (0439) 70766
Situated in the unique North York Moors National Park

AA
★★★

Rebuilt by the Earl of Feversham in 1855, now luxuriously modernised retaining its old charm, this friendly Inn has 18 bedrooms all with bathroom, hair-dryer, trouser press, telephone, safe, radio, colour TV, and tea-coffee facilities. Some bedrooms with four-poster beds and de luxe bathrooms. Central heating throughout. Tennis court, swimming pool and gardens. The Goya restaurant is well known for the shell fish and game specialities.

The hotel is central to over 20 Golf courses and for touring the Moors, Dales, East Coast and York. Attractive bargain breaks for all year round and an incredible super-bargain break in winter. Six ground floor bedrooms available for senior citizens. Brochure on request.

HEREFORD Hereford & Worcester Map **03** SO54

See also **Much Birch**

★★★**62% The Green Dragon** Broad St HR4 9BG (Trusthouse Forte) ☎(0432)272506 Telex no 35491 FAX (0432) 352139

A large hotel in traditional style, located in the city centre, features a very attractive oak panelled restaurant complemented by a spacious, pleasant and comfortable lounge. Bedrooms also offer a good standard of comfort, being well equipped and providing accommodation that is equally suitable for business clients or tourists.

88⇌2⊠⅟in 9 bedrooms CTV in all bedrooms ® T ✻ sB⇌£61-£66 dB⇌£77-£87 (room only) ⊟

Lift ☾ 90⌂ CFA *xmas*

♀ English V ♡ ⚻ ⅟ S% Lunch £8-£9.75&alc Dinner fr£15.50&alc Last dinner 10.15pm

Credit Cards 1 2 3 4 5

★★★**68% Hereford Moat House** Belmont Rd HR2 7BP (Queens Moat) ☎(0432)354301 FAX (0432) 275114

Closed Xmas

Recently completed extensions and improvements have provided this hotel with an elegant new restaurant and spacious, comfortable foyer lounge, as well as an additional 28 bedrooms to supplement the existing motel-type accommodation; it is a popular venue for functions, and conference facilities are also available, its position on the A465 south-west of the city centre making for easy access.

28⇌♪ Annexe32⇌♪ CTV in all bedrooms ® T ✻ S% sB&B⇌♪£50-£55 dB&B⇌♪£63-£66 ⊟

☾ 150P ✲

♀ English & French V ♡ ⚻ ⅟ Lunch £9-£9.50&alc High tea £4.50-£8 Dinner £12&alc Last dinner 9.45pm

Credit Cards 1 2 3 5

★★**Castle Pool** Castle St HR1 2NR (Exec Hotel) ☎(0432)356321

Set in a quiet, secluded area of the city, this hotel offers guests a comfortable stay with a friendly family atmosphere.

26rm(20⇌6♪)(3fb)2⊠ CTV in all bedrooms ® T sB&B⇌♪fr£39.50 dB&B⇌♪fr£55 ⊟

CTV 14P ✲

♀ International V ♡ ⚻ Lunch fr£6.50 Dinner fr£13.75 Last dinner 9.30pm

Credit Cards 1 2 3 5

★★***Graftonbury*** Grafton Ln HR2 8BN ☎(0432)356411

A large house has been considerably altered and extended to form this hotel, which now includes a small health club.

21rm(11⇌4♪)Annexe11⇌(2fb) CTV in all bedrooms ® T ✗

Lift CTV 100P ✲ ⌒(heated) sauna solarium gymnasium

♀ English & French ♡ ⚻ Last dinner 9pm

Credit Cards 1 2 3 5

★★**Merton Hotel & Governors Restaurant** Commercial Rd HR1 2BD ☎(0432)265925 FAX (0432) 354983

RS Sun

Situated just a few minutes walk from the city centre, this small, comfortable hotel provides modern accommodation, ideal for both business people and tourists.

15rm(11⇌4♪)Annexe4rm(2⇌)(1fb) CTV in all bedrooms T sB&B£30 sB&B⇌♪£39-£44 dB&B⇌♪£61-£67.50 ⊟

CTV 6P sauna solarium gymnasium *xmas*

♀ International V ♡ ⚻ ⅟ Lunch fr£10.50&alc High tea £5-£10 Dinner fr£13.50&alc Last dinner 9.30pm

Credit Cards 1 2 3 5 £

See the preliminary section 'Hotel and Restaurant Classification' for an explanation of the AA's appointment and award scheme.

★★**Netherwood Restaurant & Country House Hotel** Tupsley HR1 1UT

☎(0432)272388

A fine Georgian house in two-acre grounds offers guests a peaceful, relaxing stay, providing comfortable rooms and a short, innovative menu of home-cooked food.

7⇌(1fb) CTV in all bedrooms ® ✻ sB&B⇌£34-£36 dB&B⇌£44-£48 ⊟

CTV 30P ✲ *xmas*

V Lunch £7.50 Dinner £12.50 Last dinner 9pm

Credit Cards 1 2 3

★★**Somerville** 12 Bodenham Rd HR1 2TS ☎(0432)273991

Quietly situated in a residential area, yet close to the city centre, this large, Victorian mansion provides comfortable, well-equipped bedrooms and friendly, informal service.

10rm(2⇌4♪)(2fb) CTV in all bedrooms ® T ✗ (ex guide dogs) ✻ sB&Bfr£19 sB&B⇌♪fr£23 dB&Bfr£35 dB&B⇌♪fr£39

CTV 10P ⇎

V ♡ ⚻ ⅟ Dinner £6-£9alc Last dinner 8pm

★**Dormington Court Country House** Dormington HR1 4DA (3.5m E off A438) ☎(0432)850370

7rm(6⇌)(1fb)1⊠ CTV in all bedrooms ® sB&B⇌£30-£38 dB&B⇌£52-£62 ⊟

16P ⇎ ✲

♀ English & French V ♡ ⚻ Lunch £5-£12alc Dinner £12-£16alc Last dinner 8.45pm

Credit Cards 1 3 £

✕**Fat Tulip Wine Bar & Bistro** The Old Wye Bridge, 2 St Martin's St HR2 7RE ☎(0432)275808

A simple but pleasant little restaurant stands beside the River Wye, close to the city centre and cathedral. Run in a pleasantly informal manner by a husband and wife team, it offers a short but imaginative menu – a starter of crab meat pancakes, for example, might be followed by a main course of roast, boned quail stuffed with calves' liver.

Closed Sun & 24-30 Dec, B/H's

♀ English, French & Italian 35 seats ✻ Lunch £15.90-£20.80alc Dinner £15.90-£20.50alc Last lunch 2pm Last dinner 10pm ₱

Credit Cards 1 2 3

HERM

See **Channel Islands**

HERSTMONCEUX East Sussex Map **05** TQ61

✕✕**Sundial** BN27 4LA ☎(0323)832217

Set in rural, village surroundings, the elegant, country restaurant has a warm, friendly atmosphere and is personally supervised by the chef/patron and his charming French wife. The French cuisine, which specialises in fish cookery, is prepared to a very high standard.

Closed Mon, 10 Aug-10 Sep & 23 Dec-20 Jan

Dinner not served Sun

♀ French V 60 seats ✻ Lunch fr£14.50&alc Dinner fr£19.50&alc Last lunch 2pm Last dinner 9.30pm 25P ⅟

Credit Cards 1 2 3 5

HERTFORD Hertfordshire Map **04** TL31

★★★51% **White Horse** Hertingfordbury SG14 2LB (1m W on A414) (Trusthouse Forte) ☎(0992)586791 Telex no 83326 FAX (0992) 550809

Most of the bedrooms of this characterful roadside hotel have been refurbished to provide a good standard of well-equipped, modern accommodation. The restaurant features a conservatory-style section overlooking the gardens, and a new reception area, lounge and bar will offer further space in which to relax; cheerful service from friendly young staff creates a warm, pleasant atmosphere throughout.

42⇨(7fb)⚟in 7 bedrooms CTV in all bedrooms ® **T** ✳
sB⇨£62-£67 dB⇨£76-£82 (room only) 🖪
☾ 60P ❊ *xmas*
V ♤ ⚐ ⚟ Lunch £8.95-£9.95 High tea £3.25-£5.85 Dinner £13.95-£14.95&alc Last dinner 9.30pm
Credit Cards 1 2 3 4 5

HESLEDEN Durham Map **08** NZ43

★★**Hardwicke Hall Manor** TS27 4PA (2.5m N of town on A1086) ☎Hartlepool(0429)836326

An old manor house, boasting a wealth of historical features and interesting stories, offers comfortable accommodation and meals that can be recommended both for quality and value.

11rm(8⇨3⚑)(2fb)2⊠ CTV in all bedrooms ® **T** ✳
sB&B⇨⚑£35-£45 dB&B⇨⚑£45-£55 🖪
50P ❊
☋ French **V** ♤ ⚐ Lunch £2.50-£15alc Dinner £10-£18alc Last dinner 9.30pm
Credit Cards 1 2 3 5 ⓔ

Book as early as possible for busy holiday periods.

HESTON MOTORWAY SERVICE AREA (M4) Greater London

See **LONDON plan 5***A3*(page 412) **Telephone codes are due to change on 6th May 1990. See page 421.**

Granada Lodge M4 Service Area, North Hyde Ln TW5 9NA (Granada) ☎01-574 7271 FAX 01-574 1891

Conveniently situated between London and Heathrow, on the westbound carriageway, the Lodge provides accommodation in well equipped, modern bedrooms with fully tiled bathroom facilities. Meals can be taken at the Country Kitchen Restaurant in the adjoining service area.

46⇌(15fb)⅟in 6 bedrooms CTV in all bedrooms ®
sB⇌£30-£36 dB⇌£36-£38 (room only)
(300P
V ♈ ⊻ ⅟
Credit Cards 1 2 3 5

See advertisement under HEATHROW AIRPORT (LONDON)

HESWALL Merseyside Map **07** SJ28

★★**Hill House** Mount Av L60 4RH (Berni/Chef & Brewer) ☎051-342 5535

A friendly hotel with a popular bar and well-appointed bedrooms stands amid sweeping lawns in its own grounds, close to the centre of the village.

8⇌ CTV in all bedrooms ® **T** ✗ (ex guide dogs) ✱
sB&B⇌fr£35 dB&B⇌fr£50 ⊟
(34P ✿
☋ Mainly grills **V** ♈ Lunch £4.99-£12alc Dinner £4.95-£12alc Last dinner 10pm
Credit Cards 1 2 3 5

HETHERSETT Norfolk Map **05** TG10

★★★65% **Park Farm** NR9 3DL ☎Norwich(0603)810264 FAX (0603) 812104

Closed 25-29 Dec

Its buildings grouped around attractive gardens featuring a fountain, this family-run hotel stands in a quiet, secluded position off the A11, 5 miles south of Norwich. Bedrooms are individually designed and very well equipped, many of them are located in garden buildings or new, purpose-built blocks; amenities include an indoor swimming pool and sauna.

6rm(5⇌1♠)Annexe30rm(25⇌4♠)(1fb)14⊞ CTV in all bedrooms ® **T** ✗ (ex guide dogs) S% sB&B⇌♠£45-£78 dB&B⇌♠£58-£88 ⊟
100P 1⌂ ⊞ ✿ ⊡(heated) ℘ (hard) sauna solarium table tennis pool table putting croquet
☋ English & French **V** ♈ ⊻ ⅟ Lunch £8.50-£9.50 High tea £2-£4 Dinner £9.50-£10.50&alc Last dinner 9.30pm
Credit Cards 1 2 3 4 5

See advertisement under NORWICH

HEVERSHAM Cumbria Map **07** SD48

★★★62% **The Blue Bell at Heversham** Prince's Way LA7 7EE (Consort) ☎Milnthorpe(04482)2018

Closed Xmas day & Boxing day

This characterful former coaching inn standing beside the A6 now provides individually styled bedrooms with modern facilities; enjoyable meals are served in a comfortable restaurant where service is both friendly and efficient.

26rm(16⇌5♠) CTV in all bedrooms ® **T**
CTV 100P ✿
☋ English & Swiss ♈ ⊻
Credit Cards 1 2 3

Red-star hotels offer the highest standards of hospitality, comfort and food.

HEXHAM Northumberland Map **12** NY96

★★**Beaumont** Beaumont St NE46 3LT ☎(0434)602331

Closed 25-26 Dec & 1 Jan

This very pleasant hotel offers an elegant restaurant, a comfortable cocktail bar and several well appointed bedrooms overlooking the Abbey grounds.

23rm(5⇌18♠)(3fb)1⊞ CTV in all bedrooms ® **T** ✗
sB&B⇌♠£35 dB&B⇌♠£50-£55
(6P
☋ International **V** ♈ ⊻ Lunch £7.50 Dinner fr£8&alc Last dinner 9.45pm
Credit Cards 1 2 3 5

★★**County** Priestpopple NE46 1PS ☎(0434)602030

Warm, comfortable, small hotel with good wholesome food.

9rm(2⇌6♠)(3fb) CTV in all bedrooms ® **T**
(2P
☋ International **V** ♈ ⊻ Last dinner 9.30pm
Credit Cards 1 2 3

★★**Royal** Priestpopple NE46 1PQ (Consort) ☎(0434)602270 Telex no 57515 ATTN 115

An old-established inn with the original coaching arch, located in the town centre.

25rm(21⇌2♠)(3fb) CTV in all bedrooms ®
sB&B⇌♠£31.50-£35.50 dB&B⇌♠£49.50-£53.50 ⊟
(25P
☋ English Scottish & French **V** ♈ ⊻ ⅟ Lunch £7.50 High tea £5-£6 Dinner £12&alc Last dinner 9.30pm
Credit Cards 1 2 3 5 £

HIGHBRIDGE Somerset Map **03** ST34

★★**Sundowner** 74 Main Road, West Huntspill TA9 3QU (1m S on A38) ☎Burnham on Sea(0278)784766

This small, family-run hotel, standing on the main road, was originally a thatched cottage and has been completely refurbished to provide pleasant bedrooms, a comfortable bar lounge. English home cooking is served in a friendly atmosphere, and a first class breakfast is provided.

8rm(4⇌4♠)(1fb) CTV in all bedrooms ® **T** ✱
sB&B⇌♠£28-£32 dB&B⇌♠£43-£48 ⊟
CTV 24P ✿ solarium
☋ Mainly grills **V** ♈ ⊻ Lunch £4.65-£19.45alc Dinner £4.65-£19.45alc Last dinner 10pm
Credit Cards 1 2 3 5

HIGH WYCOMBE Buckinghamshire Map **04** SU89

★★★65% ***Crest*** Crest Rd, Handy Cross HP11 1TL (Crest) ☎(0494)442100 Telex no 83626 FAX (0494) 39071

A modern commercial hotel with good conference facilities provides accommodation specially geared to the needs of the business person. Bedrooms are comfortable and spacious, whilst the well-appointed restaurant serves a range of interesting dishes, well prepared from fresh produce of a high quality, on both à la carte and table d'hôte menus; service is efficient and friendly throughout the hotel.

110⇌♠(12fb)⅟in 21 bedrooms CTV in all bedrooms ® **T**
(173P CFA
☋ English & French **V** ♈ ⊻ ⅟ Last dinner 10.30pm
Credit Cards 1 2 3 4 5

HILLINGDON Greater London

See **LONDON plan 5***A4*(page 412) **Telephone codes are due to change on 6th May 1990. See page 421.**

★★★61% **Master Brewer Motel** UB10 9NX ☎Uxbridge(0895)51199 Telex no 946589 FAX (0895) 810330

Conveniently situated for Heathrow and the M25, the motel offers a range of popular eating options, well-equipped bedrooms being provided in separate modern blocks.

106⇨(22fb) CTV in all bedrooms ® T sB⇨£37-£54.50 dB⇨£37-£72 (room only) 🛏
(200P ❊ CFA ⌂
☺ Continental V ✧ ☕ Lunch £5-£20alc Dinner £5-£20alc Last dinner 11pm
Credit Cards 1 2 3 5

HILTON PARK MOTORWAY SERVICE AREA (M6) West Midlands Map **07** SJ90

⌂ ***Rank Motor Lodge*** Hilton Park Services (M6), Essington WV11 2DR (on M6 between juncts 10a & 11) (Rank)
☎Cheslyn Hay(0922)414100 FAX (0922) 418762
This modern lodge, located at the Hilton Park Service Area on the southbound side of the M6, provides accommodation in well-furnished bedrooms which represent very good value for money; meals can be taken at the service area restaurant.
60⇨(22fb)⚟in 6 bedrooms CTV in all bedrooms ®
(60P
V ✧ ☕ ⚟
Credit Cards 1 2 3 5

HIMLEY Staffordshire Map **07** SO89

★★★68% **Himley Country Club & Hotel** School Rd DY3 4LG
☎Wombourne(0902)896716 Telex no 333688
FAX (0902) 896668
A comfortable, modern hotel with two restaurants – one a carvery – has been created from the old school house. Elegantly furnished bedrooms have all amenities and the staff spare no effort to make guests feel welcome.
36rm(24⇨12↱) CTV in all bedrooms ® T ✗ (ex guide dogs) ✱ sB⇨↱£45-£48 dB⇨↱£53-£65 (room only)
(⊞ 126P ⛟ ⌂
☺ Continental V ☕ Lunch fr£12 Dinner £9.95-£12 Last dinner 10pm
Credit Cards 1 2 3 5
See advertisement under DUDLEY

★★**Himley House** DY3 4LD (On A449 N of Stourbridge) (Berni/Chef & Brewer) ☎Wombourne(0902)892468
17rm(9⇨8↱)Annexe7rm(4⇨3↱)(2fb) CTV in all bedrooms ® T ✗ (ex guide dogs) sB&B⇨↱£42.50 dB&B⇨↱£55 🛏
(120P ❊
☺ Mainly grills V ✧ ☕ Lunch £8 Dinner £9 Last dinner 10.30pm
Credit Cards 1 2 3 5

HINCKLEY Leicestershire Map **04** SP49

★★***Sketchley Grange*** Sketchley Ln, Burbage LE10 3HU (Best Western) ☎(0455)251133 Telex no 34694 FAX (0455) 631384
This friendly, privately-owned hotel is pleasantly situated in four acres of grounds with views of unspoilt countryside, yet is conveniently placed for the M69 and A5.
34rm(22⇨12↱)2⊟⚟in 10 bedrooms CTV in all bedrooms ® T ✗ (ex guide dogs)
(200P
☺ English & French V ✧ ☕ ⚟ Last dinner 10.45pm
Credit Cards 1 2 3 5
See advertisement under LEICESTER

★**Kings Hotel & Restaurant** 13/19 Mount Rd LE10 1AD
☎(0455)637193 FAX (0455) 636201
This large Victorian house is set in a quiet road close to the town centre. It provides comfortable, well-equipped accommodation. There is an interesting choice of food and the wine list is extensive.
7rm(2⇨5↱)⚟in 3 bedrooms CTV in all bedrooms ® T ✗ ✱ sB&B⇨↱£45-£55 dB&B⇨↱£55-£65 🛏
12P 1🚘 (£5) ♫

☺ English, French & Hungarian V ✧ Lunch £12.50-£17.50&alc Dinner £14.50-£19.50&alc Last dinner 9.30pm
Credit Cards 1 2 3 5 £

HINDHEAD Surrey Map **04** SU83

★★★54% **Devils Punch Bowl** London Rd GU26 6AG (Consort)
☎(042873)6565 Telex no 858918 FAX (042873) 5713
The hotel offers a sound standard of modern accommodation in recently decorated and refurbished bedrooms. There are two bars and an open-plan restaurant and lounge area.
36⇨↱(1fb) CTV in all bedrooms ® T ✱ S% sB&B⇨↱£55.50-£65.50 dB&B⇨↱£65.50-£72.50 🛏
(85P CFA
☺ English ✧ ☕ Lunch £9-£18alc Dinner £9-£18alc Last dinner 10pm
Credit Cards 1 2 3 5

HINDON Wiltshire Map **03** ST93

★★**Lamb at Hindon** SP3 6DP ☎(074789)573 FAX (074789) 605
This attractive inn provides modern accommodation, healthy home cooking and a refreshing style of friendly service.
15rm(10⇨1↱)(2fb)1⊟ CTV in all bedrooms ® T ✗ (ex guide dogs) ✱ sB&B£25-£50 sB&B⇨↱£25-£50 dB&B£40-£50 dB&B⇨↱£40-£50 🛏
CTV 26P 2🚘 ⛟ ❊ ⚲ shooting fishing *xmas*
✧ ☕ Lunch £9.50&alc Dinner £12.50 Last dinner 9.30pm
Credit Cards 1 2 3

HINTLESHAM Suffolk Map **05** TM04

❀★★★⚜ **HINTLESHAM HALL**
IP8 3NS (Relais et Châteaux)
☎(047387)268 & 334
Telex no 98340
FAX (047387) 463
RS Sat
This beautiful country house, with its charming façade and reputation for excellent cuisine receives the Red Star accolade for the first time this year. No hotel has been more discussed for the award over the last few years, and Hintlesham Hall's near-misses in the past have been due to the hotel's layout, rather than to the quality of service, which has been of a consistently good standard, staff showing a high degree of skill and professionalism. A very considerable redevelopment, due for completion before this guide is published, will improve this hotel still further. Chief among the improvements will be more central and spacious kitchens. Also in the scheme is the addition of more suites to the bedrooms, with ground floor rooms giving better access for less nimble guests. Hintlesham Hall has been famous for its cuisine for many years, and under the ownership of Ruth and David Watson, this reputation has been maintained by chef Robert Mabey. He draws on modern French sources of inspiration, but has a style all of his own in the use he makes of fresh local produce, including many ingredients from the hotel's 18 acres of gardens and grounds.
33⇨↱2⊟⚟in 12 bedrooms CTV in all bedrooms ® T ✱ S% sB&B⇨↱£85-£100 dB&B⇨↱£90-£300 Continental breakfast 🛏
(100P ⛟ ❊ ⚲ (hard) ⚲ ∪ snooker croquet clay & game shooting *xmas*
▶

English & French V S% Lunch £18.50-£30.50&alc Dinner fr£35&alc Last dinner 10pm
Credit Cards 1 2 3 5

HITCHIN Hertfordshire Map **04** TL12

★★★55% **Blakemore** Little Wymondley SG4 7JJ (3m SE A602) (Thistle) ☎Stevenage(0438)355821 Telex no 825479
FAX (0438) 742114
Originally a Georgian house, and still enjoying a peaceful location in its own grounds, this popular commercial hotel has been extended to provide modern bedroom accommodation, whilst the style of the public areas is more in keeping with that of the original building.
82rm(69⇌13)(6fb) CTV in all bedrooms ® T ✱
sB⇌£49-£64 dB⇌£55-£75 (room only)
Lift ☾ 200P ✲ (heated) sauna games room
International Lunch fr£11.25&alc Dinner fr£13.50&alc Last dinner 9.30pm
Credit Cards 1 2 3 4 5

HOCKLEY HEATH West Midlands Map **07** SP17

★★★77% **Nuthurst Grange Country House**
Nuthurst Grange Ln B94 5NL (off A34, 2m S junction 4 M42)
☎Lapworth(05643)3972
Telex no 333485
FAX (05643) 3919

A visit to this hotel is a memorable experience, not least because of the outstanding and imaginative cuisine of its chef/proprietor, whose tempting menu features dishes that are predominantly English in style, though cooked in the light French manner. The house – delightfully situated in 7 1/2 acres of gardens and grounds, its location offering easy access to both Birmingham and Stratford-upon-Avon – is comfortably and elegantly furnished, bedrooms withn en suite facilities being provided with many thoughtful extras, while service is attentive throughout.
8⇌1 CTV in all bedrooms T (ex guide dogs)
sB&B⇌fr£75
dB&B⇌£95-£125 Continental breakfast
50P 6 ✲ croquet
English & French V Lunch £15.50 Dinner £24.50-£29.50 Last dinner 9.30pm
Credit Cards 1 2 3 5 £

HODNET Shropshire Map **01** SJ62

★★**Bear** TF9 3NH ☎(063084)214 & 787 FAX (063084) 351
A friendly village hotel offers guests comfortable bedrooms and a good selection of meals from bar snack, table d'hôte or à la carte menus. Neat, lawned gardens provide the perfect setting for relaxation on a summer's afternoon, and for that special occasion you can hire a baronial hall on the first floor.
6rm(5⇌1)(1fb)2 CTV in all bedrooms ® T ✱
sB&B⇌fr£30 dB&B⇌£40-£45 Continental breakfast
80P ✲ shooting
English, French & Italian V Lunch £7.50-£10.50 Dinner £3.50-£15 Last dinner 10pm
Credit Cards 1 3

HOLBETON Devon Map **02** SX65

★★★65% **Alston Hall**
Battisborough Cross
PL8 1HN
☎(075530)259 & 262
FAX (0752) 881522

Pleasantly set in its own gardens and ideally situated for touring the South Hams, this stone-built manor house complements comfortable bedrooms with elegant public areas where log fires burn in winter, the reception lounge with its original panelling being of particular interest. A recently completed leisure centre comprises gym, sauna, solarium and indoor pool, and there is also an outdoor pool in the gardens.
9rm(7⇌2) CTV in all bedrooms T sB&B⇌£45-£50 dB&B⇌£70-£84
60P ✲ (heated) (heated) (hard) sauna solarium gymnasium
English & French V Lunch £12.50 High tea £2.75-£4.50 Dinner £18.95-£21 Last dinner 9.15pm
Credit Cards 1 2 3 5

HOLDENBY Northamptonshire Map **04** SP66

✕✕**Lynton House Country Restaurant & Hotel** The Croft NN6 8DJ ☎Northampton(0604)770777
In this Victorian, red-brick house, in rolling countryside just 6 miles north-west of Northampton, Carlo and Carol Bertozzi provide Italian cooking which is rich and flavoursome. Seafood dishes include octopus, squid and scallops, and the home-made pastas and sauces have been particularly praised by our inspectors. The food is complemented by a well-chosen wine list. There are also five letting bedrooms.
Closed Xmas 3 days, 1 wk in spring, 2 wks Aug
Lunch not served Sat & Mon
Dinner not served Sun
Italian V 55 seats ✱ Lunch £12.75 Dinner £17.95 Last dinner 9.45pm 25P nc10yrs 5 bedrooms available
Credit Cards 1 3

HOLFORD Somerset Map **03** ST14

★★***Alfoxton Park***
TA5 1SG
☎(027874)211
Closed Nov-Mar

White 18th-century house, home of poet William Wordsworth in 1797, set in 50 acres of parkland.
18⇌(3fb) CTV in all bedrooms ®
25P ✲ (heated) (hard) croquet
English & French
Credit Cards 1 2 3 5

For key to symbols see the inside front cover.

★★ ♛ Combe House
TA5 1RZ
☎(027874)382
Closed Jan RS mid Nov-Dec & Feb-mid Mar

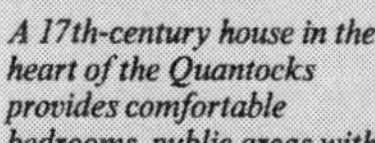

A 17th-century house in the heart of the Quantocks provides comfortable bedrooms, public areas with exposed beams and open fires, and a popular restaurant in which a table d'hôte menu, changed daily, is complemented by good, old-fashioned service and a genuine country house atmosphere. Leisure facilities include a hard tennis court, a croquet lawn, an indoor swimming pool and a sauna.

20rm(13⇨2♠)(2fb)1▣ CTV in all bedrooms T sB&B£24-£29 sB&B⇨♠£31-£35 dB&B£46-£52 dB&B⇨♠£54-£75 ⊟

15P ⊞ ✲ ⊠(heated) ℘ (hard) sauna solarium

♡ ⊥ ⊁ Bar Lunch £1.50-£6 Dinner £9.75-£11 Last dinner 8.30pm

Credit Cards 1 2 3

HOLKHAM Norfolk Map 09 TF84

See also **Wells-next-the-Sea**

★Victoria NR23 1RG ☎Fakenham(0328)710469
A compact building, constructed of local flints, and situated at the entrance to Holkham Hall.
8rm ® sB&B£17-£20 dB&B£34-£40 ⊟
CTV 50P ⊞ ✲
♀ English & French ♡ Bar Lunch £2-£10 Dinner £9.50&alc Last dinner 8.30pm
£

HOLLINGBOURNE Kent Map 05 TQ85

★★★66% Great Danes Ashford Rd ME17 1RE (Embassy)
☎Maidstone(0622)30022 Telex no 96198 FAX (0622) 35290
A house dating back to the 1840's has been greatly enlarged and modernised to provide well-equipped, modern accommodation. As well as pleasant service and a choice of bars and eating places, this popular hotel offers extensive leisure facilities.
126⇨♠(4fb)⊁in 13 bedrooms CTV in all bedrooms ® T S% sB⇨♠£69 dB⇨♠£82 (room only) ⊟
Lift ☾ 400P ✲ CFA ⊠(heated) ℘ (hard) ♩ snooker sauna solarium gymnasium pool table pitch & putt croquet ♫ *xmas*
♀ English & French V ♡ ⊥ S% Dinner fr£11&alc Last dinner 11pm
Credit Cards 1 2 3 5

See advertisement under MAIDSTONE

HOLMES CHAPEL Cheshire Map 07 SJ76

★★Old Vicarage Knutsford Road, Cranage CW4 8EF
☎(0477)32041
Built in 1623, this former vicarage, situated on the banks of the River Dane, though recently extended and modernised, retains much of its original character. The restaurant offers a high standard of cuisine and the atmosphere throughout is warm and friendly.
5rm(3⇨2♠)Annexe4⇨ CTV in all bedrooms ® T ✗ (ex guide dogs) sB&B⇨♠£42.50-£44.50 dB&B⇨♠£54-£56 ⊟
70P ♩
♀ English & French V ♡ ⊥ Lunch £8.50-£9.50&alc Dinner £12-£13.50&alc Last dinner 10pm
Credit Cards 1 2 3

HOLT Norfolk Map 09 TG03

★★Feathers 6 Market Place NR25 6BW (Berni/Chef & Brewer)
☎(0263)712318
The ancient coaching inn is now well equipped to meet the needs of modern business travellers or tourists, but its original character has been carefully preserved. It is ideally situated, being in the centre of the town and within easy reach of the coastal resorts of Cromer and Sheringham.
13rm(10⇨) CTV in all bedrooms ® T ✗ (ex guide dogs) sB&B⇨fr£35.50 dB&B⇨fr£47.50 ⊟
50P
V ♡ ⊥ ⊁ Lunch £8 Dinner £9 Last dinner 9.30pm
Credit Cards 1 2 3 5

HOLYHEAD

See **Trearddur Bay**

HOLYWELL Clwyd Map 07 SJ17

★★Stamford Gate Halkyn Rd CH8 7SJ (Best Western)
☎(0352)712942 & 712968
This modern hotel offers all creature comforts, and its excellent restaurant is supplied with fresh fish by the hotel's own trawler.
12⇨♠ CTV in all bedrooms ® ✗ ✳ S% sB&B⇨♠£28 dB&B⇨♠£40
100P
♀ English & Italian V ♡ S10% Lunch £5.50-£6.50&alc Dinner £8.75-£10.75&alc Last dinner 10pm
Credit Cards 1 3 4

H

HOLYWELL GREEN West Yorkshire Map 07 SE01

★★*Rock Inn* HX4 9BS ☎Halifax(0422)79721 Telex no 517284
Peacefully situated, though only a mile and a half from junction 24 of the M62, the comfortable village hotel offers friendly service, pleasant bedrooms and inviting lounges.
18♠ CTV in all bedrooms ® T
100P 2⌂ ✲ solarium
♀ English & French V ♡ ⊥ Last dinner 9.45pm
Credit Cards 1 2 3 5

HONITON Devon Map 03 ST10

★★★ ♛ 67% Deer Park
Weston EX14 0PG (2.5m W off A30)
☎(0404)41266

Old stone manor house built in 1777, set in its own grounds of 26 acres.

15⇨Annexe14⇨(2fb) CTV in all bedrooms T ✗ S10% sB&B⇨£40-£90 dB&B⇨£70-£120 ⊟
CTV 100P 4⌂ ⊞ ✲ CFA ⊠(heated) ℘ (hard) ♩ squash snooker sauna solarium croquet putting shooting ♔ *xmas*
♀ English & French V ♡ ⊥ S10% Lunch £12.50-£20&alc High tea fr£6.50 Dinner £20-£25&alc Last dinner 10pm
Credit Cards 1 2 3 5 £

See advertisement on page 339

★★**Home Farm** Wilmington EX14 9JR (2m E)
☎Wilmington(040483)278
Closed Dec-Jan
A cottage-style family-run hotel standing about 3 miles from the town features individually decorated bedrooms, some of them located in an annexe; characterful public rooms include a small, informal restaurant offering an à la carte menu.
7rm(3⇌)Annexe5⇌↱(3fb) CTV in 13bedrooms ® ✱ sB&B£22 sB&B⇌↱£26 dB&B£44 dB&B⇌↱£48 ⊟
CTV 25P ❋ golf practice nets
☋ English V ♈ ☞ Lunch £1.50-£7.50alc Dinner £9.50-£9.50&alc Last dinner 9pm
Credit Cards 1 2 3 £

★★***New Dolphin*** High St EX14 8HE ☎(0404)2377
A town-centre hotel with an inn-style atmosphere, recently upgraded, it now has attractive public areas and pleasant modern bedrooms. Service is personal and attentive.
10rm(5⇌3↱)Annexe5rm(3⇌2↱) CTV in all bedrooms ® T
12P ⇻ ⌂
V ♈
Credit Cards 1 3

HOOK Hampshire Map 04 SU75

★★**Raven** Station Rd RG27 9HS (0.75m N of M3 junc 5 on B3349) (Lansbury) ☎(0256)762541 Telex no 858901
FAX (0256) 768677
Ideal for either business or leisure, and conveniently located near the station, this popular commercial hotel has been completely refurbished. Bedrooms are particularly well-equipped. The spacious, lively bar lounge and the busy restaurant present a welcoming atmosphere.
38⇌(3fb)1⊟ ⚟in 5 bedrooms CTV in all bedrooms ® **T** ✗ (ex guide dogs) sB&B⇌£30-£65 dB&B⇌£60-£75 ⊟
☾100P CFA sauna *xmas*
☋ European V ♈ ☞ ⚟ Lunch fr£8.50 Dinner fr£12.50 Last dinner 10.30pm
Credit Cards 1 2 3 4 5

HOPE COVE Devon Map 03 SX64

★★**Cottage** Inner Hope Cove TQ7 3HJ
☎Kingsbridge(0548)561555
Closed 2-30 Jan
This converted and extended cottage hotel is set in two acres of grounds with panoramic views of Hope Cove. Family owned, it promotes high standards of hospitable service throughout, providing comfortable, traditional lounges and a well-appointed restaurant. All the bedrooms are cosy, but eight of them have recently been totally refurbished to an excellent standard.
35rm(17⇌2↱)(5fb) CTV in 19bedrooms **T** S10%
sB&B£26.35-£36 dB&B£52.70-£72
dB&B⇌↱£72-£93.50 (incl dinner) ⊟
CTV 50P ⇻ ❋ ⌂ *xmas*
☋ English & French ♈ ☞ S10% Lunch £7 Dinner £13.35&alc
Last dinner 8.45pm

★★**Lantern Lodge** TQ7 3HE ☎Kingsbridge(0548)561280
Closed Dec-Feb
Situated in its own gardens overlooking the sea and fishing village of Hope Cove, this hotel provides comfortable bedrooms and lounges. Imaginative food, making use of local produce, is served in the dining room and there is an indoor swimming pool.
14rm(11⇌3↱)(1fb)3⊟ CTV in all bedrooms ® ✗ (ex guide dogs) ✱ sB&B⇌↱£33.50-£37.50
dB&B⇌↱£67-£75 (incl dinner)
CTV 15P 1🚗 ⇻ ▭(heated) sauna solarium putting green nc8yrs
☋ English & French V ♈ ⚟ Dinner £12.50 Last dinner 8.30pm
Credit Cards 1 3

★★***Sun Bay*** Inner Hope Cove TQ7 3HH
☎Kingsbridge(0548)561371
Closed 19 Oct-27 Mar
Commanding attractive sea views from its elevated position on the edge of a peaceful village, the hotel offers comfortable bedrooms and pleasant public areas.
14rm(10⇌2↱)(7fb) CTV in all bedrooms ®
CTV 12P ⇻ ❋
V ♈ ☞ Last dinner 8.30pm

★***Greystone Hotel*** TQ7 3HH ☎Kingsbridge(0548)561233
The comfortable public rooms of the hotel have large windows giving magnificent views of Hope Cove. The substantial home-prepared meals and friendly informal service make for an enjoyable stay.
9rm(2⇌1↱)(1fb) ®
CTV 15P 3🚗 (£1 per night) ⇻ ❋
♈ ☞ Last dinner 9.30pm
Credit Cards 1 2 3

HORDLE Hampshire Map 04 SZ29

❀✕✕**Provence** Gordleton Mill, Silver St SO41 6DJ
☎Lymington(0590)682219
The tastefully modernised interior of this pretty, ivy-clad mill house on the Avon Water provides an ideal setting in which to enjoy such specialities from the Provence region as Bavelle à l'échalote (beef skirt with shallots), or Pintadeau à l'anis (roasted guinea fowl cooked in aniseed). The lunch menu provides particularly good value for money, but all meals are of high quality and complemented by a good wine list. Five bedrooms are available for guests desiring overnight accommodation.
Closed Jan
☋ French V 35 seats ✱ Lunch £11.90-£18.90 Dinner fr£19.50&alc Last lunch 2pm Last dinner 10pm 20P nc8yrs
5 bedrooms available
Credit Cards 1 2 3 5

HORLEY Hotels are listed under Gatwick Airport

HORNBY Lancashire Map 07 SD56

★★***Castle*** Main St LA2 8JT ☎(0468)21204
Stone-built inn situated in the centre of the village.
13rm(4⇌4↱)(2fb) CTV in all bedrooms
50P ⇻
☋ English & Continental V ♈ ☞
Credit Cards 1 2 3

HORNCASTLE Lincolnshire Map 08 TF26

★**Bull** Bull Ring LN9 5HU ☎(06582)3331
Closed 25 & 26 Dec
A 16th-century inn, with a historically decorated banqueting hall, and a cobbled yard.
7rm(2⇌5↱)(1fb)1⊟ CTV in all bedrooms ®
25P
☋ English & French V ♈ Last dinner 9.30pm
Credit Cards 1 2 3 5 £

HORNCHURCH Greater London Map 05 TQ58

★★★59% **Hilton National** Southend Arterial Rd RM11 3UJ (Hilton) ☎Ingrebourne(04023)46789 Telex no 897315
FAX (04023) 41917
This modern hotel with comfortable bedrooms is under new ownership. The popular 'Palms' cocktail bar and eating house is due to be enlarged and the new leisure centre should be open by, or soon after our publication date.

137⇌↱(10fb)⊁in 25 bedrooms CTV in all bedrooms ® **T** ✳
sB⇌↱£45-£80 dB⇌↱£45-£90 (room only) ⊟
☾180P ❊ CFA ♫
☋ English & American **V** ♉ ⊥ Lunch £9-£20alc Dinner £13-£25alc Last dinner 10.30pm
Credit Cards [1] [2] [3] [5]

HORNING Norfolk Map **09** TG31

★★★66% **Petersfield House** Lower St NR12 8PF
☏(0692)630741 FAX (0692) 630745
Overlooking the River Bure from its pleasant position in Horning village, this hospitable, family-run hotel offers an ideal retreat for businessmen and holidaymakers alike. Bedrooms are well furnished and comfortable, while an elegantly appointed restaurant with views across landscaped gardens provides an attractive setting in which to enjoy a meal from the extensive range available.
18rm(13⇌5↱)(1fb) CTV in all bedrooms **T** ✳ sB&B⇌↱fr£42 dB&B⇌↱fr£55 ⊟
70P ⊞ ❊ ♪ *xmas*
☋ English & Continental **V** ♉ ⊥ Lunch £10-£15.50 High tea fr£3 Dinner fr£12&alc Last dinner 9.30pm
Credit Cards [1] [2] [3] [5]

★**Swan** Lower St NR12 8AA (Berni/Chef & Brewer)
☏(0692)630316
The hotel is attractively set on the banks of the River Bure, at the centre of a charming Broads village. It offers comfortable, well-equipped bedrooms – many with superb views over the river – and a traditional beamed restaurant.
11rm(9⇌2↱)(2fb) CTV in all bedrooms ® **T** ✗ (ex guide dogs) sB&B⇌↱£35.50 dB&B⇌↱£47.50 ⊟
150P ❊ ♪ billiards
V ♉ ⊥ Lunch £8 Dinner £9 Last dinner 9.30pm
Credit Cards [1] [2] [3] [5]

H

HORN'S CROSS Devon Map **02** SS32

★★★ **67% Foxdown Manor** EX39 5PJ (Signed from A39 W of village)

☎Horns Cross (02375)325 & 642

Closed Jan & Feb

Secluded, personally-run country hotel with many facilities, in large grounds.

7rm(5⇌2♠)(1fb)2 CTV in all bedrooms ® T S10% sB&B⇌♠£25.50-£35.50 dB&B⇌♠£43-£60

30P ❋ ⇌(heated) (hard) sauna solarium croquet putting *xmas*

English & French V S10% Lunch £7.50 High tea £5 Dinner £13.50 Last dinner 8.45pm

Credit Cards 1 2 3 ⓔ

H

HORRABRIDGE Devon Map **02** SX56

★★**Overcombe** PL20 7RN ☎Yelverton(0822)853501

In village centre position close to the main road, the hotel complements comfortable, well-moderised bedrooms with ample public areas where open fires burn in the colder months. Relaxed, friendly service and the provision of thoughtful extras combine to give a real 'home from home' feeling.

11rm(2⇌7♠)(2fb) CTV in all bedrooms ® ✱ sB&Bfr£17 sB&B⇌♠fr£22 dB&Bfr£34 dB&B⇌♠fr£39 (incl dinner)

CTV 10P croquet

English V Lunch fr£6 Dinner fr£9.75 Last dinner 7.15pm

Credit Cards 1 3 ⓔ

HORSFORTH West Yorkshire Map **08** SE23

✕✕✕**Low Hall** Calverley Ln LS18 4EF ☎Leeds(0532)588221

An elegant Tudor house has been converted into a comfortable hotel where the relaxing atmosphere is largely due to the attentive but unobtrusive service provided by its courteous staff. The restaurant features an interesting range of menus – particularly for the evening meal – starters such as smoked salmon, terrines, home-made soups and Yorkshire puddings with onion and red wine gravy being followed by a choice of main courses including lobster, lamb and beef; puddings, also home made, are a delight, while the wine list has been carefully chosen to complement the menu as a whole.

Closed Sun, Mon & Xmas, 26 & 27 May, & BH's

Lunch not served Sat

English & French V 80 seats ✱ Lunch fr£10.50&alc Dinner fr£18.50&alc Last lunch 2pm Last dinner 9.30pm 70P

Credit Cards 1 3

See advertisement under LEEDS

HORSHAM West Sussex Map **04** TQ13

★★★ **74% South Lodge** Brighton Rd RH13 6PS (Prestige)

☎Lower Beeding (0403891)711 Telex no 877765

FAX (0403891) 253

(For full entry see Lower Beeding)

★★**Ye Olde King's Head** RH12 1EG ☎(0403)53126

Closed 25 & 26 Dec

A part-timbered inn dating from the 15th century, with 13th-century cellars. This is a comfortable, well-managed hotel, where spacious modern bedrooms are complemented by extensive menus and friendly service. Access and parking can be difficult, so guests are recommended to ask for directions.

43rm(6⇌35♠)(2fb)1 CTV in all bedrooms ® T sB&Bfr£47 sB&B⇌♠£58 dB&B⇌♠£70-£75

40P CFA

V Lunch fr£5.95&alc Dinner £10.95&alc Last dinner 9.45pm

Credit Cards 1 2 3 5

HORTON Northamptonshire Map **04** SP85

❀✕✕**French Partridge** NN7 2AP

☎Northampton(0604)870033

(Rosette awarded for dinner only)

A calm, dignified atmosphere distinguishes this family-run house where Mrs Partridge attends to the bar and takes orders whilst her husband creates carefully balanced dishes of French flair and flavour. Pastries and mousses are his specialities, but savoury dishes such as his feuilleté of lambs' tongue and kidneys are becoming very popular. The predominantly French wine list includes many well-chosen regional wines and is reasonably priced.

Closed Sun & Mon, 2 wks Xmas, 2 wks Etr & 3 wks Jul-Aug

Lunch not served

French 40 seats S10% Dinner £18.50 Last dinner 9pm

50P

HORTON-CUM-STUDLEY Oxfordshire Map **04** SP51

❀★★★ **54% Studley Priory** OX9 1AZ (Consort)

☎Stanton St John (086735)203 & 254

Telex no 23152

FAX (086735) 613

Founded in the 12th-century as a Benedictine nunnery, the priory today is a comfortable hotel standing in 13 acres of grounds. Bedrooms are well equipped, public areas are elegant and full of character, and chef Glen Purcell provides modern English cuisine of note in the restaurant. A brioche filled with warm quail's eggs and spinach served with a beautifully seasoned tomato and chive sabayon makes a delectable starter, to be followed by main dishes such as a tender fillet of lamb, stuffed with apricots on a fragrant port sauce. An extensive wine list complements the fine food, and staff are most attentive.

19rm(15⇌4♠)2 CTV in all bedrooms ® T S% sB&B⇌♠£65-£95 dB&B⇌♠£80-£120

100P 1 ❋ (grass) croquet clay pigeon shooting *xmas*

English & French V S% Lunch £22.50-£25&alc Dinner £22.50-£25&alc Last dinner 9.30pm

Credit Cards 1 2 3 4 5

HORWICH Greater Manchester Map **07** SD61

★★***Swallowfield*** Chorley New Rd BL6 6HN ☎(0204)697914

A warm and friendly hotel on the A673, not far from junction 6 of the M61, popular with tourists and business people alike. The public rooms are comfortable and bedrooms are well appointed.

19rm(10⇌5♠)(3fb) CTV in all bedrooms ® T

25P 2 ❋

Last dinner 9pm

Credit Cards 1 2 3 5

HOUNSLOW Greater London

See **LONDON plan 5***B3*(page 412) **Telephone codes are due to change on 6th May 1990. See page 421.**

★★★ 63% **Master Robert Motel** 366 Great West Rd TW5 0BD (A4) ☎01-570 6261 Telex no 9413782 FAX 01-569 4016

The hotel stands on land once grazed by the horse whose name it bears – the Master Robert who, having gone lame, later went on to win the Grand National in 1934. Comfortable bedroom accommodation includes the recently opened Hogarth wing, well equipped with modern amenities, and the restaurant has also been extended. Recent refurbishment has brought the bar to a good standard and visitors are welcomed in a new reception area.

100⇔(8fb) CTV in all bedrooms ® T ✗ (ex guide dogs) ✱ sB⇔£42-£61 dB⇔£47.50-£72 (room only) ⊟

☾ 100P 35🚗 ❊

☋ Mainly grills V ♡ ☕

Credit Cards 1 2 3 5

HOVE

See **Brighton & Hove**

HOVINGHAM North Yorkshire Map **08** SE67

★★★ 59% ***Worsley Hotel Arms*** YO6 4LA ☎(065382)234 & 320

Closed 25-26 Dec

The hotel, a charming Georgian building at the centre of a historic village in the Howardian Hills, offers accommodation in well-fitted and restful bedrooms, comfortable, spacious lounge areas and an elegant restaurant of a reliable standard.

14⇔1⊟ T

Lift CTV 50P 2🚗 (£1) ❊ ⌂

☋ International V ♡ ☕ Last dinner 8.45pm

Credit Cards 1 3

HOWARTH West Yorkshire Map **08** SE03

★★★ 58% ***Five Flags*** Manywells Heights BD13 5DY (nr junc A629/B6429) ☎Bradford(0274)834188 FAX (0274) 833340

A stone building in the middle of moorland, but it is close enough to Bradford and Keighley for convenience. There are two restaurants serving different styles of food and the bedrooms have good facilities.

26⇔♠(4fb) CTV in all bedrooms ® T ✗

☾ CTV 100P ❊

☋ French, Greek & Italian V ♡ ⚟ Last dinner 11pm

Credit Cards 1 2 3 5

HOW CAPLE Hereford & Worcester Map **03** SO63

★★**How Caple Grange** HR1 4TF ☎(098986)208

In a quiet village setting, surrounded by attractive gardens, the family-run hotel offers a large function room which is ideal for conferences or receptions

26rm(18⇔) CTV in 18bedrooms ® T ✱ sB&B⇔£33.50 dB&B⇔£57 ⊟

CTV 100P ❊ ⩫ sauna solarium gymnasium putting *xmas*

♡ Lunch £7.50 Dinner £9 Last dinner 9pm

HOWDEN Humberside Map **08** SE72

★★**Bowmans** Bridgegate DN14 7JG ☎(0430)430805

A quaint inn situated on the main street of this tiny town offers good-value restaurant and bar meals both at lunchtime and in the evening.

13rm(10⇔)(1fb) CTV in all bedrooms ® T ✗ (ex guide dogs) ✱ S% sB&B⇔£27.95-£29.95 dB&B⇔£47.95-£49.95 ⊟

80P

☋ Continental V ♡ ☕ ⚟ Lunch £9.50&alc Dinner £9.50&alc Last dinner 9.30pm

Credit Cards 1 2 3 5

HOWTOWN (near Pooley Bridge) Cumbria Map **12** NY41

❀❀★★★⚘ **SHARROW BAY COUNTRY HOUSE**

Sharrow Bay CA10 2LZ (at Pooley Bridge take unclass. road S for 4m (Relais et Châteaux) ☎Pooley Bridge (08536)301 due to change to (07684) 86301

Fax (08536) 349 due to change FAX to (07684) 86349

Closed early Dec-early Mar

To maintain such excellence over 41 years is a tribute to both Brian Sack and Francis Coulson, but to continually improve it places Sharrow Bay as one of the great British hotel experiences. Equal credit must also go to the Manager, Nigel Lawrence and his smart young staff, while not forgetting the team of chefs who work so well under Francis Coulson to produce truly wonderful food. The style ofcooking really doesn't change much, thank goodness, and remains wholesome, honest and satisfying. Starters such as a moist terrine of duckling, venison and foie gras, or fresh prawns in cream and wine with tarragon and vegetables, daintily served in a little copper sauteuse, might be followed by a robust saddle of venison or, more delicately, some fresh scallops with spinach and a light orange sauce. The marvellous traditional puddings should not be missed on any account. It is unfortunate that, at times, the popularity of the hotel robs it of the calm and tranquility which have made it famous – particularly when afternoon tea is being served in the comfortable lounges, but this really is a feast not to be missed Peace and quiet are absolutely assured in the annexe rooms of the Lodge and Bank House – the latter having its own lounge and breakfast room. This elegant hotel is set amid beautiful scenery, with a number of its rooms looking out over Ullswater.

12rm(8⇔)Annexe18rm(16⇔2♠) CTV in all bedrooms ® T ✗ ✱ sB&B£73 sB&B⇔♠£93-£97 dB&B£146 dB&B⇔♠£180-£220 (incl dinner)

25P 2🚗 ⛟ ❊ nc13yrs

☋ English & French V ♡ ☕ ⚟ Lunch £16.50-£21.50 Dinner £32.50 Last dinner 8.45pm

HUDDERSFIELD West Yorkshire Map **07** SE11

★★★ 61% **Briar Court** Halifax Road, Birchencliffe HD3 3NT ☎(0484)519902 Telex no 518260

This is a busy, modern hotel, near junction 24 of the M62 leading into the town. A feature of the hotel is the Da Sandro Italian restaurant, renowned for its pizza, baked in the traditional Neopolitan way.

48⇔♠(3fb) CTV in all bedrooms ® T ✗ (ex guide dogs) sB&B⇔♠£50 dB&B⇔♠£57 ⊟

☾ 140P ❊

☋ English French & Italian V ♡ ☕ Lunch £5.45&alc Dinner £14.50&alc Last dinner 11.0pm

Credit Cards 1 2 3 5

★★★ 65% **The George** St George's Square HD1 1JA (Trusthouse Forte) ☎(0484)515444 FAX (0484) 435056

At this traditional hotel, convenient for the station and the town centre, there are good facilities for both business travellers and holiday-makers. The Shines Restaurant offers à la carte and table d' hôte menus, and many items are Yorkshire specialities – some with interesting sauces. The staff are friendly and the atmosphere relaxed and comfortable.

▶

62rm(38⇌)⊁in 15 bedrooms CTV in all bedrooms ® T ✻
sB£47 sB⇌£56-£66 dB£61 dB⇌£70-£80 (room only) ⊟
Lift ☾ 12P CFA *xmas*
V ♈ ⅅ ⊁ Lunch £7.50&alc Dinner £13.95&alc Last dinner 10pm
Credit Cards [1] [2] [3] [4] [5]

★★★63% **Pennine Hilton** HD3 3RH (Hilton)
☏Elland(0422)375431 Telex no 517346 FAX (0422) 310067
This comfortable modern hotel, situated just off the M62 at junction 24, provides accommodation in well appointed bedrooms.
119⇌⊁in 25 bedrooms CTV in all bedrooms ® T
sB⇌£71-£90 dB⇌£86-£101 (room only) ⊟
Lift ☾ 250P CFA ⊡(heated) sauna gymnasium children's pool *xmas*
♉ English, French & Italian V ♈ ⅅ Lunch £7.50-£10.70 Dinner £13-£14&alc Last dinner 10pm
Credit Cards [1] [2] [3] [5]

★★**Huddersfield** 33-47 Kirkgate HD1 1QT ☏(0484)512111
Telex no 51575 FAX (0484) 435262
The hotel, standing close to the central ring road, has compact, well-fitted bedrooms with stylish decor, a reception lounge and nightclub access through the bistro-style restaurant. Staff are friendly and helpful.
40rm(20⇌20)(4fb)2⊟ CTV in all bedrooms ® T ✻
sB&B⇌£26-£45 dB&B⇌£39-£60
Lift ☾ CTV 30P sauna solarium jacuzzi pool-table darts ♫ *xmas*
Dinner £7.95-£9.95&alc Last dinner 12.30am
Credit Cards [1] [2] [3] [4] [5] £

✕**Weavers Shed** Knowl Rd, Golcar HD7 4AN (3m W off A62)
☏(0484)654284
The restaurant is housed in a quaint old weavers shed, which has been delightfully converted to retain the original character and atmosphere. The menu of traditional British dishes features unusual home-made soups. Main course dishes change regularly to make the best use of seasonal produce: fish, meat and game are all used. Sweets range from light trifles to crumbles and sticky toffee pudding.
Closed Sun & Mon, 1st 2 wks Jan & last 2 wks Jul
Lunch not served Sat
40 seats Lunch £10-£15alc Dinner £14-£19alc Last lunch 1.45pm Last dinner 9pm 30P nc10yrs
Credit Cards [1] [2] [3]

HULL Humberside Map **08** TA02

★★★★67% **Post House** Castle St HU1 2BX (Trusthouse Forte)
☏(0482)225221 Telex no 592777 FAX (0482) 213299
Attractively set by the marina, within the redeveloped docks area and near the city centre, this hotel has spacious public areas, pleasant bedrooms and a health and fitness club.
99⇌(12fb)⊁in 11 bedrooms CTV in all bedrooms ® T
sB⇌£75-£85 dB⇌fr£91 (room only) ⊟
Lift ☾ 130P ✲ ⊡(heated) ℘ (grass) sauna solarium gymnasium marina heritage trail *xmas*
♉ English & French V ♈ ⅅ ⊁ S% Lunch £9-£20&alc Dinner £15-£20&alc Last dinner 10.30pm
Credit Cards [1] [2] [3] [4] [5]

★★★67% **Crest Hotel-Humber Bridge** Ferriby High Rd HU14 3LG (Crest) ☏(0482)645212 Telex no 592558
FAX (0482) 643332
(For full entry see North Ferriby)

★★★75% **Grange Park Hotel** Main St HU10 6EA (Best Western) ☏(0482)656488 Telex no 592773 FAX (0482) 655848
(For full entry see Willerby)

★★★57% ***Royal Hotel*** Ferensway HU1 3UF (Consort)
☏(0482)25087 Telex no 592450 FAX (0482) 23172
Spacious public areas complement well appointed bedrooms at this traditional city centre hotel.
123rm(80⇌43)(4fb)2⊟⊁in 19 bedrooms CTV in all bedrooms ® T
Lift ☾ CTV 60P gymnasium
V ♈ ⅅ ⊁ Last dinner 9.30pm
Credit Cards [1] [2] [3] [4] [5] £

★★★63% ***Stakis Paragon*** Paragon St HU1 3JP (Stakis)
☏(0482)26462 Telex no 592431 FAX (0482) 213460
A modern, town-centre hotel offers well appointed bedrooms accommodation..
125⇌(4fb)⊁in 50 bedrooms CTV in all bedrooms ® T
Lift ☾ CTV Ᵽ CFA
♉ French V ♈ ⅅ Last dinner 10pm
Credit Cards [1] [2] [3] [5]

★★★56% **Valient House Hotel** 11 Anlaby Rd HU1 2PJ
☏(0482)23299 FAX (0482) 214730
Good-value menus are offered by this modern, city-centre hotel.
58rm(43⇌15) CTV in all bedrooms ® T sB⇌£42
dB⇌£54 (room only) ⊟
Lift ☾ 10P
♉ English & French V ♈ ⅅ Lunch £7.50&alc Dinner £10.75&alc Last dinner 10pm
Credit Cards [1] [2] [3] [5] £

★★★69% **Willerby Manor Hotel** Well Ln HU10 6ER
☏(0482)652616 Telex no 592629 FAX (0482) 653901
(For full entry see Willerby)

★★**Pearson Park** Pearson Park HU5 2TQ ☏(0482)43043
FAX (0482) 447679
Closed 24 Dec-1 Jan
This comfortable hotel, managed by the proprietors, enjoys a delightful location overlooking parkland yet conveniently close to the main Beverley road.
35rm(26⇌3)(4fb)1⊟ CTV in all bedrooms ® T
sB&B⇌fr£38.50 dB&B⇌fr£48 ⊟
☾ 30P
♉ English & French V ♈ ⅅ Lunch fr£5.50&alc Dinner fr£8.25&alc Last dinner 9pm
Credit Cards [1] [2] [3]

★***Maxim's Hotel*** 394 Anlaby Rd HU3 6PB ☏(0482)509660
14rm(7⇌6)(1fb)1⊟ CTV in all bedrooms ® T
CTV 25P
♈ ⅅ Last dinner 9.30pm
Credit Cards [1] [3]

⌂**Campanile** Beverley Rd HU2 9AN (Campanile)
☏(0482)25530 Telex no 592840
A modern, purpose-built unit provides simple bedrooms as an annexe to the restaurant.
Annexe48⇌ CTV in all bedrooms ® T sB⇌fr£29
dB⇌fr£29 (room only) ⊟
60P *xmas*
♉ English & French Lunch £3.75-£8.90 Dinner £6.80-£8.90 Last dinner 10pm
Credit Cards [1] [3]

✕✕**Cerutti's** 10 Nelson St HU1 1XE ☏(0482)28501
Closed Sun & 24 Dec-3 Jan
Lunch not served Sat
♉ International fish cuisine 36 seats ✻ Lunch £15-£30alc Dinner £15-£30alc Last lunch 2.00pm Last dinner 9.30pm 10P
Credit Cards [1] [3]

H

HUMBIE Lothian *East Lothian* Map **12** NT46

★★★66%
Johnstounburn House
EH36 5PL (1m S on A6137)
(Mount Charlotte)
☎(087533)696
Telex no 557934

Set in forty acres of secluded grounds and gardens, this charming seventeenth-century house offers well-equipped, individually styled bedrooms and comfortable public rooms which make it easy to relax.
11⇌↱Annexe9⇌↱(14fb) CTV in all bedrooms ® T
20P ✿ clay pigeon shooting
V ✿
Credit Cards 1 2 3 5

HUNGERFORD Berkshire Map **04** SU36

★★★64% **Bear** Charnham St RG17 0EL ☎(0488)82512
FAX (0488) 84357
The red plush dining room of this ancient inn serves food in the modern style, and there is a large bar; an interesting range of bedrooms includes some with old beams and some having river views.
14⇌Annexe27rm(24⇌3↱)(2fb)1 CTV in all bedrooms ® T
sB⇌↱£55-£65 dB⇌↱£65-£80 (room only)
☾ 60P *xmas*
✿ Lunch £12.95&alc Dinner £16.95&alc Last dinner 9.30pm
Credit Cards 1 2 3 5

HUNSTANTON Norfolk Map **09** TF64

★★★58% **Le Strange Arms Hotel,** Golf Course Rd, Old Hunstanton PE36 6JJ (Consort) ☎(04853)34411
Telex no 817403
Set in a commanding position, overlooking the sea and with views across the Wash, this Victorian hotel forms part of the characterful older part of the town. Its comfortable public areas and friendly staff combine to make it ideal for holidaymakers and business clients alike.
28⇌↱2 CTV in all bedrooms ® T sB&B⇌↱£43-£48.50
dB&B⇌↱£62-£67
200P ✿ (grass) snooker *xmas*
V ✿ Lunch £13&alc Dinner fr£13&alc Last dinner 9pm
Credit Cards 1 2 3 5

★★***Lodge*** Hunstanton Rd, Old Hunstanton PE36 6HX
☎(04853)2896
The small, family-run hotel, located near to the well-known golf course and beach, provides comfortable accommodation and friendly service.
15rm(6⇌9↱)(2fb) CTV in all bedrooms ®
70P ✿ snooker
English & Italian ✿ Last dinner 8.45pm
Credit Cards 1 3

★**Sunningdale Hotel** 3-5 Av Rd PE36 5BW ☎(04853)2562
You are assured of a warm welcome at this small, comfortable hotel where the proprietors work hard to provide a friendly, informal atmosphere and good food.
11rm(4⇌7↱)(1fb) CTV in all bedrooms ®
sB&B⇌↱£18-£19.50 dB&B⇌↱£36-£39
nc7yrs *xmas*
English & Continental ✿ Lunch £7.50 Dinner £7.50&alc Last dinner 8pm

★**Wash & Tope** Le Strange Ter PE36 5AJ ☎(04853)2250
This small family-run hotel is just across the road from the seafront and convenient for the town centre. The unusual name is taken from the sea inlet, and the tope – a small species of shark. The rooms have been improved – some with en-suite facilities – and offer simple, comfortable accommodation.
10rm(4⇌2↱)(1fb)1 CTV in all bedrooms ® ✱
sB&B£13.50-£17.50 sB&B⇌↱£17.50 dB&B£25
dB&B⇌↱£30-£35
12P 2 pool table
V ✿ Lunch £6-£8&alc Dinner £8&alc Last dinner 10.30pm
Credit Cards 1 2 3

HUNSTRETE Avon Map **03** ST66

★★★78% ***Hunstrete House*** Chelwood BS18 4NS
(Relais et Châteaux)
☎Compton Dando
(07618)578 (due to change to (0761) 490490)
Telex no 449540

Long a West Country favourite, Hunstrete House, has all the appurtenances of a stately home – from the 90-acre deer park to the Italian fountain in the courtyard, the impressive library and delightful drawing room. The décor is tasteful and elegant and there are two dining rooms. Hunstrete House has changed hands since the previous edition of this guide, and it is our policy to withdraw Red Stars in such instances until we have been able to properly gauge any changes in the style of operation.
13⇌Annexe11⇌2 CTV in all bedrooms T (ex guide dogs)
☾ 40P ✿ (heated) (hard) croquet nc9yrs
English & French ✿ Last dinner 9.15pm
Credit Cards 1 2 3 5

HUNTINGDON Cambridgeshire Map **04** TL27

★★★57% **The George** George St PE18 6AB (Trusthouse Forte)
☎(0480)432444 FAX (0480) 53130
A hotel set just off the High Street was once the home of Oliver Cromwell's grandfather, and parts of it date back to early Stuart times. Most bedrooms are spacious, and all of them offer modern facilities, while Chaucer's Restaurant features some tradtional English dishes.
24rm(23⇌1↱)(2fb) in 4 bedrooms CTV in all bedrooms ® T
✱ sB⇌↱£61-£65 dB⇌↱£72-£76 (room only)
71P *xmas*
V ✿ Lunch £8.75-£11&alc Dinner £10-£18alc Last dinner 9.30pm
Credit Cards 1 2 3 4 5

★★★69% **The Old Bridge** PE18 6TQ ☎(0480)52681
Telex no 32706 FAX (0480) 411017
An ivy-clad Georgian property, set only a short walk from the town centre in gardens which run down to the River Ouse, offers individually decorated bedrooms with modern facilities. Guests can choose between the restaurant's good range of well prepared dishes and the lighter, more informal meals served in the Terrace Lounge.

26rm(24⇌2↱)(3fb)1 CTV in all bedrooms T
sB&B⇌↱£63.25-£77 dB&B⇌↱£93.50-£110
☾ 50P private mooring for boats *xmas*
V ✿ Lunch fr£25alc High tea fr£10.50alc Dinner fr£25alc Last dinner 10.15pm
Credit Cards 1 2 3 5

HUNTLY Grampian *Aberdeenshire* Map **15** NJ53

★★Castle AB5 4SH
☎(0466)2696
Closed Jan-Feb

Once the family home of the Gordons, this personally managed, traditional hotel in an elevated position on the ourskirts of the town is popular with anglers. Although facilities are somewhat limited, bedrooms are generally spacious and comfortable, as are the lounges.

24rm(7⇌2♠)(2fb)1 Ⓡ sB&Bfr£25 sB&B⇌♠fr£28 dB&Bfr£45 dB&B⇌♠fr£48
CTV 20P 3 ✿
V Lunch fr£6.50 High tea fr£5 Dinner fr£12.50 Last dinner 10pm
Credit Cards [1] [2] [3] [5] £

HURLEY Berkshire Map **04** SU88

★★Ye Olde Bell SL6 5LX (Trusthouse Forte)
☎Littlewick Green(062882)5881 FAX (062882) 5939
This ancient inn traces its history back to 1136 and retains much original character plus comfortable bedrooms and friendly, willing service.
10⇌♠Annexe15⇌♠(1fb)3 CTV in all bedrooms Ⓡ **T**
sB⇌♠£65-£87 dB⇌♠£87-£100 (room only)
90P ✿ *xmas*
French **V** S% Lunch £16.50&alc Dinner £16.50&alc Last dinner 9.30pm
Credit Cards [1] [2] [3] [4] [5]

HURSTBOURNE TARRANT Hampshire Map **04** SU35

★★Esseborne Manor
SP11 0ER (Pride of Britain)
☎(0264)76444
FAX (0264) 76473

Well-kept gardens and parkland are the setting for this Georgian and Victorian manor house, which was bought by Michael Yeo and family in 1988. Antiques and magazines enhance the welcoming country house atmosphere and the comfortable public rooms are decorated with taste and flair. The bedrooms are attractive and well supplied with thoughtful touches. Six are in the main building and 6, more spacious, are in the annexe. In the dining room, chef Mark Greenfield provides a well-balanced table d'hôte using the finest local ingredients, and breakfast is an equally enjoyable experience. Relaxed efficiency and a refreshing, unpretentiousness prevail throughout, and we very much hope that, as the new owners settle in, a red star award can be considered for this splendid little hotel.

6⇌♠Annexe6⇌♠1 CTV in all bedrooms **T** (ex guide dogs) ✱ sB&B⇌♠£65-£70 dB&B⇌♠£78-£95
30P ✿ (hard) croquet golf practice net nc12yrs *xmas*

English & French Lunch £7.50-£10.50 Dinner £23-£25.50 Last dinner 9.30pm
Credit Cards [1] [2] [3] [5]

HURST GREEN Lancashire Map **07** SD63

★★Shireburn Arms BB6 9QJ ☎Stonyhurst(025486)518
A 17th-century coaching inn, furnished with several fine antiques.
16rm(14⇌2♠)(1fb)1 CTV in all bedrooms Ⓡ **T** ✱
sB&B⇌♠£29.50-£34.50 dB&B⇌♠£46-£60
CTV 71P ✿ putting green *xmas*
English & French **V** Bar Lunch £4.75-£7.50alc Dinner £8.50-£12.50&alc Last dinner 9.30pm
Credit Cards [1] [3]

HYTHE Kent Map **05** TR13

★★★★65% Hotel Imperial Princes Pde CT21 6AE (Best Western) ☎(0303)67441 Telex no 965082 FAX (0303) 264610
The impressive hotel stands in a magnificent seafront location and enjoys extensive views. Attractive public areas include a split-level restaurant, two bars and a lounge, whilst the bedrooms are comfortable and well equipped. Indoor and outdoor leisure facilities include a golf course, swimming pool, squash courts and a new spa bath.
83rm(79⇌4♠)(5fb)2 CTV in all bedrooms Ⓡ **T**
Lift 150P 10 (charged) ✿ (heated) 9 (hard & grass) squash snooker sauna solarium gymnasium croquet bowls putting beauty salon karts
English & French **V** Lunch £11&alc High tea £4-£7.50 Dinner £15&alc Last dinner 9pm
Credit Cards [1] [2] [3] [5]

★★★ 60% **Fredericks** 95 Seabrook Rd CT21 5QY (on A259 between Hythe & Folkestone) ☎(0303)67279
Spacious, well appointed bedrooms with every modern facility are an attractive feature of this friendly hotel, personally run by the owners to meet guests' every need. The intimate restaurant offers an interesting menu of well prepared dishes, with dancing on occasions.
8⇌↱ CTV in all bedrooms ® **T** sB&B⇌↱fr£50 dB&B⇌↱£68-£98 ⊟
☾CTV 25P
V Lunch fr£9.95&alc Dinner fr£9.95&alc
Credit Cards 1 2 3 5 £

★★★ 62% **Stade Court** West Pde CT21 6DT (Best Western) ☎(0303)68263 Telex no 965082 FAX (0303) 264610
A friendly, informal hotel in an impressive seafront position, featuring a cosy bar lounge and a first floor sun lounge. Bedrooms are well equipped and maintained, with some split-level rooms which are ideal for families. Guests can make use of the leisure facilities in a neighbouring hotel.
39rm(29⇌10↱)(5fb)⅟in 4 bedrooms CTV in all bedrooms ® **T** sB&B⇌↱£35-£41 dB&B⇌↱£55-£64 ⊟
Lift 12P 2⛟(£3.00 per night) CFA ▭(heated) ▶9 ℘ (hard & grass) squash snooker sauna solarium gymnasium *xmas*
English & Continental **V** ⅟ Lunch £7.25-£9.50 High tea £5 Dinner £13.50-£14.50 Last dinner 9pm
Credit Cards 1 2 3 5

H

ILFRACOMBE Devon Map 02 SS54

★★★ 56% **Cliffe Hydro** Hillsborough Rd EX34 9NP ☎(0271)63606
An owner-managed hotel, attractively sited to overlook the harbour, features comfortable, well-equipped bedrooms, good public areas and an indoor swimming pool/health complex with excellent heat and humidity controls.
37rm(26⇌7↱)(4fb) CTV in all bedrooms ® **T** ✱ sB&B£20-£35 sB&B⇌↱£28-£40 dB&B£40-£55 dB&B⇌↱£50-£70 ⊟
Lift 5P ❊ ▭(heated) sauna solarium gymnasium spa bath steam room ♫ *xmas*
V Bar Lunch £1.20-£4.95 Dinner £8.95 Last dinner 8.30pm
Credit Cards 1 3

★★ ***Arlington*** Sommers Crescent EX34 9DT ☎(0271)62252
Closed Jan
This privately owned and run hotel stands in an elevated position, overlooking the sea, within easy reach of shops and the front; it offers bright, well-equipped bedrooms and pleasant public areas.
29rm(25⇌3↱)(7fb) CTV in all bedrooms ® **T**
Lift ☾ 30P 1⛟ ❊ ⛀(heated) sauna solarium
French Last dinner 8.45pm
Credit Cards 1 2 3 4 5

★★ **Elmfield** Torrs Park EX34 8AZ ☎(0271)63377
Closed Nov-Mar (ex Xmas)
From an elevated position overlooking Ilfracombe and the surrounding countryside, this friendly hotel offers well-equipped bedrooms, comfortable public rooms and the use of a heated swimming pool.
12rm(11↱) CTV in all bedrooms ® ✗ sB&B↱£21 dB&B↱£42 ⊟
12P ❊ ▭(heated) sauna solarium gymnasium pool table darts jacuzzi spa bath nc8yrs *xmas*
English & Continental **V** ⅟ Dinner £9.50&alc Last dinner 7.30pm
Credit Cards 1 2 3

For key to symbols see the inside front cover.

★★ **Ilfracombe Carlton** Runnacleave Rd EX34 8AR (Consort) ☎(0271)62446
Closed Dec-Feb RS Mar & Nov
Detached holiday and touring hotel with popular bar, located in the centre of town.
50rm(20⇌16↱)(6fb) CTV in all bedrooms ® ✗ (ex guide dogs) sB&B£17.50-£20.50 sB&B⇌↱£19-£22 dB&B£35-£41 dB&B⇌↱£38-£44 ⊟
Lift ☾ CTV 25P ♫ *xmas*
⅟ Sunday Lunch £4.50-£6.50 Dinner £9.50-£10.50 Last dinner 8.30pm
Credit Cards 1 2 3 £

★★ **St Helier** Hillsborough Rd EX34 9QQ ☎Barnstaple(0271)64906
Closed Oct-Apr
The family-run hotel occupies a commanding position with sea views, yet is within comfortable walking distance of shops, amusements, sports facilities and beaches.
23rm(15⇌)(8fb) CTV in all bedrooms ® sB&B£16-£16.50 dB&B£32-£33 dB&B⇌£35-£36 ⊟
CTV 20P 9⛟ ❊ pool-table, table-tennis
Austrian, French & Italian Dinner £6.50-£7.50 Last dinner 7.30pm
Credit Cards 1 3

★★ ***Tracy House*** Belmont Rd EX34 8DR ☎(0271)63933
Closed Nov
Small, secluded, privately-owned hotel.
11rm(4⇌5↱)(2fb) CTV in all bedrooms ® **T**
11P 1⛟(£2) ❊ solarium putting green
English & Continental Last dinner 8pm

★ ***Torrs*** Torrs Park EX34 8AY ☎(0271)62334
Closed Nov-Feb
Set high in its own grounds, this family-run resort hotel offers views over sea, town and surrounding countryside. All bedrooms are equipped with en suite facilities, and the dining room offers a range of simple fare.
14rm(7⇌7↱)(5fb) CTV in all bedrooms ®
16P solarium nc5 yrs
V Last dinner 7.30pm
Credit Cards 1 2 3 4 5

ILKLEY West Yorkshire Map 07 SE14

★★★ 56% **Cow & Calf** Moor Top LS29 8BT ☎(0943)607335
Closed Xmas
Situated on a hillside above the town and overlooked by the Cow and Calf Rocks, this popular tourist hotel offers a choice of bars and eateries. Many of the bedrooms have lovely views and all are well equipped.
17rm(11⇌6↱)(1fb)1⊠ CTV in all bedrooms ® **T** sB&B⇌↱£45-£57.50 dB&B⇌↱£52.50-£67.50 ⊟
100P ❊
English & French **V** Lunch £4-£8.50 Dinner £11-£12.50&alc Last dinner 9.30pm
Credit Cards 1 2 3 4 5 £

★★ **Greystones** 1 Ben Rhydding Rd LS29 8RJ ☎(0943)607408
Closed Xmas Day & New Years Day
An interesting house with lovely views over the moors. Personal service from the resident proprietor.
10⇌↱(1fb) ® **T** ✱ sB&B⇌↱fr£36 dB&B⇌↱fr£48.50
CTV 17P ❊

Credit Cards 1 2 3 5

A rosette is the AA's highest award for quality of food and service in a restaurant.

★★**Rombalds** 11 West View, Wells Rd LS29 9JG
☎(0943)603201 Telex no 51593 FAX (0943) 816586
Personally supervised by the proprietors, this elegant, carefully-restored Georgian house stands on the edge of the moor. Dinner, where dishes range from the local to the more exotic, is particularly recommended.
15rm(6⇌9♠)(5fb) CTV in all bedrooms ® T
sB&B⇌♠£46-£63 dB&B⇌♠£68-£80 ⊟
(22P ⊯ ♫ *xmas*
☋ Cosmopolitan V ♈ ⊻ Lunch £4.50-£7.50&alc Dinner £16-£24alc Last dinner 10pm
Credit Cards [1] [2] [3] [5]

★**Grove** 66 The Grove LS29 9PA ☎(0943)600298
Closed 24-31 Dec
A comfortable hotel managed by the resident proprietor, offering well-appointed bedrooms and friendly services.
6rm(2⇌4♠)(2fb) CTV in all bedrooms ® sB&B⇌♠£30-£33
dB&B⇌♠£44-£47 ⊟
CTV 5P ⊯ nc3yrs
Bar Lunch £3.50-£5alc Dinner £5-£9.50alc Last dinner 7.30pm
Credit Cards [1] [3]

❀✕✕✕**Box Tree** Church St LS29 9DR
☎(0943)608484
(Rosette awarded for dinner only)
This pretty little restaurant has managed to uphold its reputation as one of the finest eating houses in the North. To some the compact rooms, richly decorated and filled to capacity with prints, paintings, and objets d'art may seem a little over the top while to others it is the ideal venue for a cosy and intimate evening. Whatever diners views on the décor might be, it is the expertise of Chef Edward Penny that really achieves for this restaurant its rosette accolade. Definitely a ▶

place for that special occaision. Diners will be well looked after by the friendly and efficient waiters.
Closed Mon, 25-26 Dec & 1 Jan
Lunch not served Tue-Sat
Dinner not served Sun
French 50 seats Sunday Lunch fr£13.95 Dinner fr£17.50&alc Last dinner 10pm
Credit Cards 1 2 3 5

ILMINSTER Somerset Map **03** ST31

★★Shrubbery TA19 9AR (Consort) (0460)52108
Telex no 46379 FAX (0460) 53660
The busy, owner-run, function, commercial and touring hotel offers well equipped accommodation, whilst the original 15th-century section has been carefully renovated to house the restaurant and banqueting suites. Service throughout is by pleasant and helpful staff.
12(3fb) CTV in all bedrooms ® **T** sB&B£45-£50 dB&B£60-£70
CTV 100P (heated) (grass) deep-sea fishing
English & French **V** Lunch £9.50&alc High tea fr£6 Dinner fr£14.50&alc Last dinner 9.30pm
Credit Cards 1 2 3 4 5 £

INCHNADAMPH Highland *Sutherland* Map **14** NC22

★★Inchnadamph IV27 4HL Assynt(05712)202
Closed Nov-14 Mar
A haven for anglers and an ideal base from which to explore the beautiful north west Highlands, this friendly family hotel is run on traditional lines, many a fishing yarn being swapped over a glass of malt in its comfortable lounges.
27rm(10)(5fb) sB&B£22.50-£24.75 dB&B£45-£49.50 dB&B£49-£53.50
CTV 30P 4 (£1.50)
V Lunch fr£7.15 Dinner fr£10.15 Last dinner 7.30pm
Credit Cards 1 3 5 £

INGATESTONE Essex Map **05** TQ69

★★★ 67% Heybridge Moat House Roman Rd CM4 9AB (Queens Moat) (0277)355355 Telex no 995186
FAX (0277) 353288
The original 15th-century building has been carefully renovated and now houses the restaurant and banqueting suites. The modern bedroom wing offers well equipped accommodation.
22(3fb) CTV in all bedrooms **T** ✱ S% sBfr£62 dBfr£70 (room only)
CTV 200P
International **V** Lunch £11-£21.50 Dinner fr£21.50 Last dinner 10.30pm
Credit Cards 1 2 3 4 5 £

INGLESHAM Wiltshire Map **04** SU29

✕✕Inglesham Forge SN6 7QY Faringdon(0367)52298
This old forge and cottage has been converted into a smart restaurant whilst still retaining its character with exposed beams, stone walls and a log fire. The comprehensive menus contain interesting dishes prepared from fresh ingredients.
Closed last 2 wks Aug & 24-31 Dec
Lunch not served Sat & Mon
Dinner not served Sun
V 30 seats ✱ Lunch £17.50-£24.50 Dinner £17.50-£24.50&alc Last lunch 2pm Last dinner 9.30pm 15P
Credit Cards 1 2 3 5

INSTOW Devon Map **02** SS43

★★★61% Commodore Marine Pde EX39 4JN (0271)860347
FAX (0271) 861233
This modern hotel has a commanding position with views across the river to Appledore. The bedrooms are comfortable and well equipped, the public areas relaxing and the views from the recently refurbished restaurant (which offers both table d'hôte and à la carte menus) are simply glorious.
20(3fb) CTV in all bedrooms ® **T** sB&B£39-£45 dB&B£59-£72
150P *xmas*
English & Continental **V** Lunch £8.50&alc Dinner £14.50&alc Last dinner 9.15pm
Credit Cards 1 2 3

See advertisement under BARNSTAPLE

INVERARAY Strathclyde *Argyllshire* Map **10** NN00

★*Fernpoint* PA32 8UX (0499)2170
Closed Nov-wk before Etr
The oldest house in town, featuring a spiral stair tower, the personally-run hotel offers a range of traditional Scottish fare which includes a special Scottish Dinner.
6rm(4)(4fb) CTV in 4bedrooms ®
CTV 12P boating
V Last dinner 9pm

INVERGARRY Highland *Inverness-shire* Map **14** NH30

★★Glengarry Castle
PH35 4HW
(08093)254
5 Apr-26 Oct

Ruins of Invergarry Castle are to be found in the grounds of this Victorian mansion.

28rm(24 1)(4fb)2 CTV in 4bedrooms ® sB&B£23-£25 sB&B£30-£32 dB&B£19-£21 dB&B£24.50-£33.50
CTV 30P 2 (hard)
V Lunch £6.75 Dinner £12 Last dinner 8.15pm
Credit Cards 1 3

INVERKEILOR Tayside *Angus* Map **15** NO64

✕Gordon's Homewood House, Main Rd DD11 5RN (02413)364
Enjoyable and affordable French dishes are reliably well prepared at this cosy little village restaurant. Chef/patron Gordon Watson's modern influence on traditional French cooking together with his excellent use of fresh produce is a successful combination.
Closed Mon, 1st 2 wks Jan
Lunch not served Sat
Dinner not served Sun
French 25 seats Dinner £14.20-£20.35alc Last dinner 9.30pm 6P nc8yrs 2 bedrooms available
Credit Cards 1 3

Places with AA hotels and restaurants are identified on the location atlas at the back of the book.

INVERMORISTON Highland *Inverness-shire* Map **14** NH41

★★ ***Glenmoriston Arms*** Glenmoriston IV3 6YA
☎Glenmoriston(0320)51206
This traditional Highland hotel offers friendly service with the proprietors fully involved. The bar also boasts a fine collection of malt whiskies.
8⇌1 CTV in all bedrooms ® **T**
CTV 28P ✲ stalking & shooting
British **V** Last dinner 8.30pm
Credit Cards 1 3 £

INVERNESS Highland *Inverness-shire* Map **14** NH64

See **Town Plan Section**
★★★★ 58% **Culloden House** Culloden IV1 2NZ (2m E off A96) (Prestige) ☎(0463)790461 Telex no 75402 FAX (0463) 792181
This fine country house was Bonnie Prince Charlie's base during the Battle of Culloden, and is furnished in keeping with the period. Proprietors Mr and Mrs MacKenzie offer real hospitality, and cuisine of a good standard is accompanied by an excellent wine list.
20⇌(1fb)5 CTV in all bedrooms **T** sB&B⇌fr£85 dB&B⇌£115-£155
50P 2 ✲ (hard) snooker sauna solarium nc10yrs *xmas*
Scottish & French **V** Lunch fr£12alc Dinner £27 Last dinner 9pm
Credit Cards 1 2 3 5 £

★★★ 71% **Bunchrew House Hotel** Bunchrew IV3 6TA (3m W off A862)
☎(0463)234917
Closed 16 Nov-17 Dec

This charming 17th-century Scottish mansion stands in 15 acres of landscaped gardens and woodlands. Inside the wood panelled sitting room with its log fire provides comfort and relaxation while the restaurant offers an interesting menu with dishes expertly prepared from fresh local produce. A well-balanced wine list with some good vintage wines complements the cooking. Bedrooms are spacious, tasteful and well equipped. The hospitality of proprietors Alan and Patsy Wilson and their staff in the true, sincere Scottish style ensures guests of a welcome visit.
6⇌(2fb)1 in 1 bedroom CTV in all bedrooms **T** sB&B⇌£47-£65 dB&B⇌£60-£95
40P 2 ✲ clay pigeon shooting *xmas*
International **V** Lunch £6.50-£9.50 Dinner £18.50 Last dinner 9pm
Credit Cards 1 2 3 5 £

★★★ 65% **Caledonian** Church St IV1 1DX (Embassy) ☎(0463)235181 Telex no 75232 FAX (0463) 711206
This smart town-centre hotel has been tastefully refurbished to provide attractive accommodation with an extended range of services and facilities. Comfortable, well-equipped bedrooms are furnished and decorated in modern style, and guests are offered a choice of bars, meals in a pleasant restaurant with views over the river, and the use of a new leisure club.
100⇌(12fb) CTV in all bedrooms ® **T** sB⇌£57-£72 dB⇌£76-£90 (room only)
Lift 80P (charged) CFA (heated) snooker sauna solarium gymnasium whirlpool spa-bath *xmas*
International **V** Lunch fr£7.50&alc High tea fr£8.50 Dinner fr£14.50&alc Last dinner 9pm
Credit Cards 1 2 3 5

★★★ 69% **Craigmonie** 9 Annfield Rd IV2 3HX (Best Western) ☎(0463)231649 Telex no 94013304 FAX (0463) 233720
Gabled, turreted red sandstone mansion (1832) with modern extension.
35⇌(3fb)3 in 10 bedrooms CTV in all bedrooms ® **T** (ex guide dogs) ✱ sB&B⇌£48.50-£52 dB&B⇌£70-£88
Lift 60P ✲ (heated) sauna solarium gymnasium beauty therapy treatments *xmas*
Scottish & French **V** Lunch £5.95-£7.95 Dinner £14-£16&alc Last dinner 9pm
Credit Cards 1 2 3 5

★★★ 64% **Kingsmills** Culcabock Rd IV2 3LP (Swallow) ☎(0463)237166 Telex no 75566 FAX (0463) 225208
The first phase of a major upgrading and refurbishment programme is nearing completion at this popular business and tourist hotel. It offers a range of bedroom styles and standards – though all are comfortable and well equipped. The smart new leisure complex is a welcome development.
64⇌(12fb) CTV in all bedrooms ® **T** sB&B⇌£58-£80 dB&B⇌£78-£175
100P ✲ (heated) squash sauna solarium gymnasium putting green *xmas*
V Lunch £7.50-£12.50 Dinner fr£15.75&alc Last dinner 9.45pm
Credit Cards 1 2 3 5

★★★ 58% ***Mercury*** Nairn Rd IV2 3TR (junc A9/A96) (Mount Charlotte) ☎(0463)239666 Telex no 75377
This purpose-built modern hotel is situated on the outskirts of town with convenient access to the A9. The major refurbishment programme started in 1989 is a welcome development and will provide a high standard of comfort when complete.
118⇌(11fb) in 6 bedrooms CTV in all bedrooms ® **T**
Lift 150P ✲
V
Credit Cards 1 2 3 5

★★★ 50% **Palace** Ness Walk IV3 5NE ☎(0463)223243 Telex no 777210
Situated near the river, this hotel caters for business and tourist trade. Bedrooms are well equipped and the atmosphere friendly and informal.
43⇌Annexe41⇌(12fb) CTV in all bedrooms ® ✱ sB&B⇌£48-£58 dB&B⇌£74-£84
Lift 40P *xmas*
Scottish & French Lunch fr£6 High tea fr£5 Dinner £7-£13 Last dinner 9pm
Credit Cards 1 2 3 5 £

See advertisement on page 351

★★★ 57% ***Station*** 18 Academy St IV1 1LG ☎(0463)231926 Telex no 75275
Closed 10 days at Xmas/New Year
Situated next to the railway station, this well-established hotel offers traditional comforts combined with modern day facilities. The public rooms are large, the bedrooms well equipped and the foyer/lounge is a popular rendezvous.
66rm(43⇌10)(6fb) CTV in all bedrooms ® **T**
Lift 10P
British & French **V** Last dinner 9.15pm
Credit Cards 1 2 3 4 5

★★ ***Beaufort*** 11 Culduthel Rd IV2 4AG ☎(0463)222897
The hotel stands in its own grounds in the best area of the town, a few minutes walk from the centre. There is generous car-parking space.
31⇌(6fb) CTV in all bedrooms **T**

Lift ⊞ 50P
V ♈ ⚲
Credit Cards [1] [2] [3] [5]

★★Cummings Church St IV1 1EN ☎(0463)232531
Modernised, commercial and tourist hotel.
34rm(14⇔5↱)(2fb) CTV in all bedrooms **T** ⌘ (ex guide dogs) sB&B£25-£28 sB&B⇔↱£28-£33 dB&B£20-£23 dB&B⇔↱£22-£25
Lift ☾ CTV 25P
♈ Lunch £3.90-£4.50alc Dinner £6-£8.50&alc Last dinner 8pm
£

★★Dunain Park IV3 6JN
☎(0463)230512
RS 2wks Nov & Feb

Delightful country house in 6 acres of grounds near Loch Ness, it is run in a friendly and congenial manner by Ann and Edward Nicoll. Good country cooking is provided in the well appointed dining room, and the charming bedrooms are thoughtfully equipped with many extras.
6rm(4⇔)(2fb)1⊟ CTV in all bedrooms **T** ✱
dB&B⇔£78-£90 ⊟
20P ⊞ ✲ ⊡(heated) sauna croquet badminton *xmas*
⊖ Scottish & French **V** ♈ ⚲ ⊬ Lunch £12.50 Dinner £19.50 Last dinner 9pm
Credit Cards [1] [2] [3] [5]

★★Glen Mhor 10 Ness Bank IV2 4SG ☎(0463)234308
Telex no 75114
Closed 31 Dec-3 Jan
Conversion of Tarradale stone mansion dating from 1870, in a quiet residential area of the town.
21rm(8⇔10↱)Annexe10rm(3⇔7↱)(1fb)1⊟ CTV in all bedrooms ® **T** sB&Bfr£20 sB&B⇔↱fr£40 dB&B⇔↱£40-£70 ⊟
30P pool table ♫ *xmas*
⊖ International **V** ♈ ⚲ Lunch £7.50 High tea £4-£8.50alc Dinner fr£14.50 Last dinner 9.30pm
Credit Cards [1] [2] [3] [5] £

★★Lochardil House Stratherrick Rd IV2 4LF ☎(0463)235995
This handsome, castellated, Victorian house set in 3 acres of grounds still retains much of its original charm. Bedrooms are modern with modern-day facilities.
11rm(7⇔4↱)(2fb) CTV in all bedrooms ® **T** ⌘ (ex guide dogs) ✱ sB&B⇔↱£39-£42.50 dB&B⇔↱£44-£55 ⊟
120P 3⌂ ✲
⊖ Scottish & French **V** ♈ ⚲ Lunch fr£7.50 Dinner £9.50-£18alc Last dinner 9.00pm
Credit Cards [1] [2] [3] [5] £

★★Loch Ness House Glenurquhart Rd IV3 6JL (Consort)
☎(0463)231248
The commercial hotel is situated on the outskirts of the town.
23rm(4⇔13↱)(1fb)2⊟ CTV in all bedrooms ® **T** ✱
sB&Bfr£25 sB&B⇔↱fr£38 dB&Bfr£46 dB&B⇔↱fr£56 ⊟
60P ⊞ ✲ ♫ *xmas*
⊖ Scottish & French **V** ♈ ⚲ Lunch fr£6.50 High tea fr£6.50 Dinner fr£13.50&alc Last dinner 9pm
Credit Cards [1] [2] [3]

★*Redcliffe* 1 Gorden Ter IV2 3HD ☎(0463)232767
Friendly and comfortable little family-run hotel standing close to the town centre and featuring good food.
6rm(3↱)(2fb) CTV in all bedrooms ®
12P ⊞ ✲
V ♈ ⚲
Credit Cards [1] [2] [3]

INVERSHIN Highland *Sutherland* Map **14** NH59

★*Invershin* IV27 4ET ☎(054982)202
Closed 25 Dec & 1st 2 wks Jan
Formerly a drovers inn, this simple friendly hotel serves good honest food at reasonable prices.
17rm(7⇔3↱)Annexe4rm(2fb) CTV in 17bedrooms ®
50P ⊞ ✲ ⌐
V ♈ ⚲ Last dinner 8.30pm
Credit Cards [1] [3] [5]

INVERURIE Grampian *Aberdeenshire* Map **15** NJ72

★★★63% *Strathburn* Burghmuir Dr AB5 9GY ☎(0467)24422
This small, purpose-built hotel on the northern outskirts of town is personally run by the proprietors and their friendly staff. Public areas are attractive and the bedrooms, though not large, are well equipped.
15rm(11⇔4↱)(1fb) CTV in all bedrooms ® **T**
40P ⊞ ⌂
V ♈ ⚲ Last dinner 9.30pm
Credit Cards [1] [2] [3]

★★Gordon Arms Market Place AB5 9SA ☎(0467)20314
A commercial hotel in the centre of town, the Gordon Arms has a homely first floor lounge and dining room and a popular lounge bar only recently refurbished. Several of the bedrooms have en suite facilities.
11rm(6↱) CTV in all bedrooms ® ✱ sB&B£17.95 sB&B↱£19.95 dB&B£28.50 dB&B↱£30.50 ⊟
CTV ⊅
⊖ European **V** ♈ Lunch £4.50-£5alc High tea £2.50-£5.50alc Dinner £5-£7alc Last dinner 8pm
Credit Cards [1] [2] [3] [5] £

IPSWICH Suffolk Map **05** TM14

❀★★★ **HINTLESHAM HALL HOTEL, HINTLESHAM**
IP8 3NS (Relais et Châteaux) ☎Hintlesham (047387)268 & 334
Telex no 98340 FAX (047387) 463
(For full entry see Hintlesham)

★★★56% *Ipswich Moat House* London Rd IP8 3JD (just off A12 near Copdock village) (Queens Moat) ☎Copdock(047386)444
Telex no 987207 FAX (047386) 801
Modern hotel, geared to short-stay guests, with extensive function facilities.
45⇔(17fb)1⊟ CTV in all bedrooms ® **T**
☾ P ✲ ♫
⊖ English & Continental **V** ♈ ⚲ Last dinner 9.20pm
Credit Cards [1] [2] [3] [5]

★★★71% The Marlborough at Ipswich Henley Rd IP1 3SP
☎(0473)257677 FAX (0473) 226927
RS 25 Dec
Situated opposite Christchurch Park and close to the town centre, the original hotel has now been much extended. Bedrooms are well equipped, the lounge area comfortable and there is also a small study with writing desk and chess set for guests' use. The restaurant which overlooks the garden offers a choice of well prepared dishes.
22⇔(3fb) CTV in all bedrooms **T** ✱ S% sB⇔£58-£65 dB⇔£70-£90 (room only) ⊟
☾ CTV 60P ⊞ ✲ mini croquet lawn *xmas*

♀ British & French V ✿ ⊥ ⅟ S% Lunch £9.50-£12.25&alc Dinner £20-£26alc Last dinner 9.30pm
Credit Cards [1] [2] [3] [5] (£)

See advertisement on page 353

★★★64% Novotel Ipswich Greyfriars Rd IP1 1UP (Novotel)
☎(0473)232400 Telex no 987684 FAX (0473) 232414
Convenient modern hotel for business and family use, with all-day restaurant.
101⇌↱(6fb)⅟in 38 bedrooms CTV in all bedrooms ® T ✳
S% sB⇌↱fr£53 dB⇌↱fr£53 (room only) ⊟
Lift 50P
♀ International V ✿ ⊥ ⅟ Lunch £9.50-£10.50 Dinner £10.95-£11.95 Last dinner 11.30pm
Credit Cards [1] [2] [3] [5]

See advertisement on page 353

★★★52% Post House London Rd IP2 0UA (Trusthouse Forte)
☎(0473)690313 Telex no 987150 FAX (0473) 680412
Popular hotel for business clients, with two restaurants and an outdoor swimming pool.
118⇌⅟in 11 bedrooms CTV in all bedrooms ® T ✳
sB⇌£67-£81 dB⇌£78-£92 (room only) ⊟
☾ 175P ❄ CFA ⛆(heated) *xmas*
♀ English & French V ✿ ⊥ ⅟ Lunch fr£5.95&alc High tea fr£2.50 Dinner fr£12.95&alc Last dinner 10pm
Credit Cards [1] [2] [3] [4] [5]

★★Great White Horse Tavern St IP1 3AH ☎(0473)256558
FAX (0473) 253396
Historic hotel having links with Dickens and George II.
60rm(47⇌11↱)(2fb)2⊞ CTV in all bedrooms ® T ✕ ✳
sB£32 sB⇌↱£47.50-£65 dB⇌↱£55-£65 (room only)
☾ CTV 6P 18🚗

▶

⌂ English & French V ✿ ⌒ Bar Lunch fr£1 Dinner fr£9.75&alc Last dinner 9.30pm
Credit Cards 1 2 3 5

✕✕The A La Carte Orwell House, 4A Orwell Place IP4 1BB ☎(0473)230254 FAX (0449) 677970
Closed Sun, 26 Dec, 1 Jan & BH Mons
Dinner not served Mon & Tue
⌂ British & French **V** 28 seats ✱ Lunch £15-£26.50alc Dinner £15-£26.50alc Last lunch 2pm Last dinner 9.30pm 10P ⚟
Credit Cards 1 2 3

IRVINE Strathclyde *Ayrshire* Map **10** NS33

★★★★63% *Hospitality Inn* Roseholm, Annickwater KA11 4LD (Mount Charlotte) ☎(0294)74272 Telex no 777097
This popular business, tourist and conference hotel is conveniently situated close to the A78. There is a choice of restaurants including one which is beside the spectacular tropical lagoon. Bedrooms are comfortable and well equipped.
128⇌(44fb) CTV in all bedrooms ® **T**
☾ ⊞ 300P ✲ ⊡(heated) ♪ jacuzzi football pitch ⌂
V ✿ ⌒
Credit Cards 1 2 3 4 5

ISLAY, ISLE OF Strathclyde *Argyllshire* Map **10**

BOWMORE Map **10** NR35

★★*Lochside* 19 Shore St PA43 7LB ☎(049681)244 & 266
7rm(2⇌) CTV in all bedrooms ®
P̸
V ✿ ⌒ Last dinner 8.30pm
Credit Cards 1 3

PORT ASKAIG Map **10** NR46

★★Port Askaig PA46 7RD ☎(049684)245 & 295
9rm(2⇌2↱)(1fb) CTV in all bedrooms ® S10%
sB&B£25-£27.50 sB&B⇌↱£28-£30.50 dB&B£46-£50
dB&B⇌↱£50-£54 ⊟
CTV 15P 6⌂ ⛟ ✲
V ✿ ⌒ S10% Lunch £6-£10 Dinner fr£10 Last dinner 9pm
£

ISLE OF Places incorporating the words 'Isle of' or 'Isle' will be found under the actual name, eg Isle of Wight is listed under Wight, Isle of.

ISLE OF WHITHORN Dumfries & Galloway *Wigtownshire* Map **11** NX43

★Queens Arms DG8 8LF ☎Whithorn(09885)369
10rm(4⇌)(2fb) CTV in all bedrooms ® **T**
☾ P sea fishing
V ✿ ⌒ Last high tea 6.30pm
Credit Cards 3

ISLE ORNSAY

See **Skye, Isle of**

IXWORTH Suffolk Map **05** TL97

✕✕Theobalds 68 High St IP31 2HJ ☎Pakenham(0359)31707
Closed 25-26 Dec & BH's
Lunch not served Mon & Sat
Dinner not served Sun
⌂ English & French **V** 36 seats S% Lunch £11.95&alc Dinner £17.50-£22.50alc Last lunch 2pm Last dinner 10pm nc8 ⚟
Credit Cards 1 3

JEDBURGH Borders *Roxburghshire* Map **12** NT62

★★*Jedforest Country House* Camptown TD8 6PJ (3m S of Jedburgh off A68) ☎Camptown(08354)274
Mansion dating from 1870, standing in 50 acres of tree-studded parkland bordering the River Jed.
7rmAnnexe4↱(3fb) CTV in all bedrooms ®
CTV 50P ✲ ♪ pool table
⌂ English & French ✿ ⌒ Last high tea 4.30pm
Credit Cards 1 3

JERSEY

See **Channel Islands**

JEVINGTON East Sussex Map **05** TQ50

✕✕Hungry Monk BN26 5QF ☎Polegate(03212)2178
Situated in the heart of the charming village of Jevington, this is a restaurant of character with a cosy and comfortable lounge area and an intimate and well appointed dining room. The blackboard menu changes according to the season and good use is made of local produce – especially game. The wine list is extensive and good value. Good service is provided by the long-skirted waitresses. A relaxed and enjoyable experience at this restaurant is ensured.
Closed 24-26 Dec & BH Mons
Lunch not served Mon-Sat (ex by reservation)
Lunch by arrangement
⌂ English & French **V** 38 seats S% Sunday Lunch £15.95-£17.45 Dinner £15.95-£17.45 Last dinner 10.15pm 14P nc3yrs ⚟

JOHN O'GROATS Highland *Caithness* Map **15** ND37

★★*John O'Groats House* KW1 4YR ☎(095581)203 FAX (095581) 408
Said to be the most northerly house on the British mainland. it overlooks the harbour with views across Stroma to the Orkneys.
16rm(2⇌1↱)(2fb)1⊠ CTV in 4bedrooms ®
CTV 20P ⛟ ⌂
✿ ⌒ Last dinner 9.45pm
Credit Cards 1 2 3

JURA, ISLE OF Strathclyde *Argyllshire* Map **10**

CRAIGHOUSE Map **10** NR56

★★Jura PA60 7XU ☎Jura(049682)243
Closed 20 Dec-6 Jan
17rm(4⇌1↱)(1fb) CTV in 1bedroom ® ✱ S10%
sB&Bfr£19.50 sB&B⇌↱fr£21.50 dB&Bfr£39 dB&B⇌↱fr£43
CTV 10P 6⌂ ✲ ♪
✿ ⌒ S10% Bar Lunch £1-£6alc Dinner fr£11.25&alc Last dinner 9pm
Credit Cards 1 2 3 5

KEGWORTH Leicestershire Map **08** SK42

★★★61% Yew Lodge 33 Packington Hill DE7 2DF ☎(0509)672518 Telex no 341995 FAX (0509) 674730
Situated close to the East Midlands Airport and the M1, this busy hotel is popular with commercial visitors and conference delegates. The accommodation is modern and well equipped.
54rm(44⇌10↱)(3fb) CTV in all bedrooms ® **T**
sB&B⇌↱fr£50 dB&B⇌↱fr£80 ⊟
Lift ☾ 120P
⌂ English & French **V** ✿ ⌒ Lunch £7-£7.50 Dinner £11.50-£12.50 Last dinner 10pm
Credit Cards 1 2 3 5

K

KEIGHLEY West Yorkshire Map **07** SE04

★★*Beeches* Bradford Rd BD21 4BB ☎(0535)607227
Victorian manor house with bedrooms of charm and interest and a spacious public bar. The restaurant has acquired a growing reputation.
11rm(2⇌)Annexe9(6fb) CTV in all bedrooms ® T
☾ CTV 120P 2 ✻ ♫
V Last dinner 9pm
Credit Cards 1 2 3

★★**Dalesgate** 406 Skipton Rd, Utley BD20 6HP (2m NW A629) ☎(0535)664930
Standing about a mile from the town centre, a family-operated hotel of modest dimensions offers smartly decorated, comfortable bedrooms – some with the original Victorian features and some newly built in modern style, but all well-equipped; the lounge bar provides an ideal spot for relaxation, and guests are assured of friendly service throughout the hotel.
11rm(2⇌9)(1fb) CTV in all bedrooms ® T ✻
sB&B⇌£19.50-£26.50 dB&B⇌£32-£35
☾ 22P
Dinner £4.95-£12.95alc Last dinner 8pm
Credit Cards 1 2 3 5 £

KELSO Borders *Roxburghshire* Map **12** NT73

★★★60% **Cross Keys** 36-37 The Square TD5 7UL (Exec Hotel) ☎(0573)23303 FAX (0573) 257921
One of Scotland's oldest coaching inns, now bedecked with window boxes and offering spotless accommodation. Overlooks Kelso's cobbled square.
24rm(10⇌14)(4fb) CTV in all bedrooms ® T
Lift ☾ CTV snooker sauna solarium gymnasium
Scottish & Continental V Lunch £5.90-£7.90 Dinner £11.50-£13.50&alc Last dinner 9.15pm
Credit Cards 1 2 3 5 £

★★★64% **Ednam House** Bridge St TD5 7HT ☎(0573)24168
Closed 25 Dec-10 Jan
A fine Georgian mansion situated in 3 acres of gardens overlooking the River Tweed. The hotel is renowned for its warm and friendly atmosphere and tastefully combines modern facilities with traditional values. Popular with fishing and shooting enthusiasts.
32rm(28⇌4)(2fb) CTV in all bedrooms T S%
sB&B⇌£27.50-£30.80 dB&B⇌£47.30-£66
CTV 100P ✻
V S% Sunday Lunch fr£8.25 Dinner fr£14 Last dinner 9pm
Credit Cards 3

★★★ 75% **Sunlaws House** Heiton TD5 8JZ (2m SW A698)
☎Roxburgh(05735)331
Telex no 728147
FAX (05735) 611

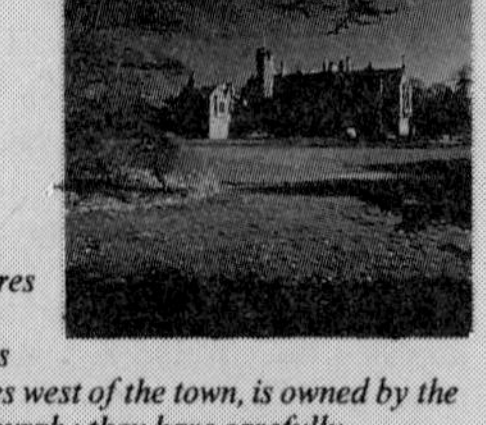

The fine country mansion, standing in two hundred acres of well tended gardens and woodland close to the banks of the Teviot and three miles west of the town, is owned by the Duke and Duchess of Roxburgh; they have carefully converted the hotel to reflect their own tastes whilst retaining an aura of homeliness and comfort. The carefully-chosen décor of the public rooms, comfortably furnished and warmed by log fires, is enhanced by soft lighting and potted plants. Extra facilities make the hotel popular with the sporting fraternity – its attractive new stable courtyard bedrooms being ideally suited to those who come and go at odd hours – and the cuisine of chef Robert Grindle should satisfy the healthy appetites of those who have spent an energetic day in the country. Good use is made of local produce, dishes generally being presented in the modern style, and the dessert trolley's contents are all freshly prepared. Management and staff exhibit a friendly, relaxed manner in keeping with the style of the establishment.
16rm(15⇌1)Annexe6rm(4fb)2 CTV in all bedrooms ® T (ex guide dogs)
☾ 30P ✻ (hard) shooting croquet
Scottish & French V Last high tea 7.30pm
Credit Cards 1 2 3 5 £

★*Bellevue House Hotel* Bowmont St TD5 7DZ ☎(0573)24588
A friendly and homely atmosphere prevails at this comfortable hotel which overlooks the bowling green and tennis courts, just north of the town centre. Just a short distance away is Floors Castle.
9rm(1⇌4) ®
CTV 8P
Credit Cards 1 3

KENDAL Cumbria Map **07** SD59

★★★60% **Woolpack** Stricklandgate LA9 4ND (Swallow) ☎(0539)723852 Telex no 53168 FAX (0539) 728608
Modernised coaching inn with character bars including the Crown Carvery and popular Laurels coffee House. The Crown Bar, with its beams and open fires, was Kendal's wool auction room.
38⇌Annexe15⇌(5fb) in 6 bedrooms CTV in all bedrooms ® T sB&B⇌£52-£55 dB&B⇌£65-£70
☾ 60P CFA *xmas*
English & French V Lunch fr£7.25 High tea fr£6 Dinner fr£12&alc Last dinner 9.30pm
Credit Cards 1 2 3 4 5

★★**Garden House** Fowl-ing Ln LA9 6PH ☎(0539)731131
FAX (0539) 740064
Closed 4 days Xmas
A delightfully furnished house standing in two acres of grounds. It is personally owned and run and provides good standards of food and service.
10rm(8⇌2)(2fb)1 in 8 bedrooms CTV in all bedrooms ® T (ex guide dogs) S% sB&B⇌£39.50-£44 dB&B⇌£49.50-£56
40P ✻
English & French V Dinner £14.50-£16.50 Last dinner 9pm
Credit Cards 1 2 3 5 £

KENILWORTH Warwickshire Map **04** SP27

★★★53% *Chesford Grange* CV8 2LD (0.5m SE Jct A46/A452) (Consort) ☎(0926)59331 & 52371 Telex no 311918
FAX (0926) 59075
This busy hotel with modern facilities is particularly popular for its large conference rooms and the compact restaurant with its choice of carvery and à la carte menus.
133⇌(40fb) CTV in all bedrooms ® T
Lift ☾ 500P ✻
English & French V Last dinner 10.15pm
Credit Cards 1 2 3 4 5

★★★56% **Kenilworth Moat House** Chesford Bridge CV8 2LN (Queens Moat) ☎(0926)58331 FAX (0926) 58153
Situated to the south of the town on the A452, convenient for the A46. Public areas have recently been upgraded along with the bedrooms, which are now equipped with modern facilities, but as a result are more compact.

48⇨ CTV in all bedrooms ® T sB&B⇨£40-£65 dB&B⇨£50-£75 ⊟
☾ 160P ✲ ♩ *xmas*
☋ English, French & Italian V ♈ ⊡ Lunch fr£9&alc Dinner fr£15&alc Last dinner 10pm
Credit Cards [1] [2] [3] [4] [5]

★★Clarendon House Old High St CV8 1LZ ☎(0926)57668
Telex no 311240 FAX (0926)50669
An old oak tree still supports part of the main roof of this charming Tudor building in the old town, and a deep well has been renovated in the cocktail bar.
30rm(22⇨8♠)(1fb)4⊟ CTV in all bedrooms ® T sB&B⇨♠£41-£44 dB&B£60-£65 dB&B⇨♠£60-£65 ⊟
30P ⊞
☋ European V ♈ Lunch £7.50 Dinner £10.50-£13.50 Last dinner 9.30pm
Credit Cards [1] [3] £

✕Restaurant Bosquet 97A Warwick Rd CV8 1HP
☎(0926)52463
Closed Sun, Mon, BH's, 10 days Xmas & 3 wks Jul
Lunch not served (ex reservation only)
☋ French 26 seats ✱ Lunch fr£15.50&alc Last dinner 9.30pm
P̸
Credit Cards [1] [2] [3]

KENNFORD Devon Map **03** SX98

★★Fairwinds EX6 7UD ☎Exeter(0392)832911
Closed 4Dec-3Jan
Conveniently positioned close to the A38/M5, the useful, small, personally owned and run hotel offers value for money and friendly service, appealing to tourists and commercial clients alike. Cosy, warm, well-equipped bedrooms are spotlessly clean, and the ▶

compact public rooms are brightly decorated and furnished in modern style.
8rm(4⇨2♠)⊁in 1 bedroom CTV in all bedrooms ® T ✱ ✳ sB&B£16-£20 sB&B⇨♠£25-£30 dB&B⇨♠£32-£39 ⊟
8P ⊞ nc12 yrs
V ⊁ Lunch £7.25-£10.25 Dinner £7.65-£10.25 Last dinner 8pm
Credit Cards 1 3 £

KENTALLEN Highland *Argyllshire* Map **14** NN05

❀★★ *Ardsheal House*
PA38 4BX
☎Duror(063174)227
Closed Nov-Mar
(Rosette awarded for dinner only)

A house party atmosphere prevails at this former home of the Stuarts of Appin, now run by hospitable Americans Robert and Jane Taylor. Set in 900 acres on a peaceful peninsular with superb views over Loch Linnhe, it has antique furnishings and relaxing open fires, and the bedrooms are individually decorated. We are delighted to report that talented new chef Graeme Cockburn has settled in well, and makes excellent use of fresh Scottish produce in his French-influenced cuisine. Dining at Ardsheal remains a most pleasurable experience.
13rm(9⇨2♠)(2fb)
CTV 20P ⊞ ✲ ℘ (hard) snooker
♡ International ♆ ⊈ ⊁
Credit Cards 1 2 3

★★Holly Tree Kentallen Pier PA38 4BY ☎Duror(063174)292
Closed Nov-mid Feb
Set on the hillside, this charming hotel was converted from a railway station built in the Glasgow style – two bedrooms actually being created from the old waiting rooms. The new bedrooms, which have been elegantly furnished and decorated, share the view across Loch Linnhe with a restaurant where chef/patron Alasdair Robertson produces interesting and imaginative meals.
12rm(11⇨1♠)(3fb) CTV in all bedrooms ® T sB&B⇨♠£58 dB&B⇨♠£110 (incl dinner) ⊟
30P ✲ ♩
♡ International ♆ ⊈ ⊁ Lunch £10.50&alc Dinner £21 Last dinner 9.30pm
Credit Cards 1 3

KESWICK Cumbria Map **11** NY22

See **Town Plan Section**
See map 11 for details of other hotels in the vicinity

★★★ 73% *Brundholme Country House Hotel* Brundholme Rd CA12 4NL ☎(07687)74495
Closed 20 Dec-Jan
Converted to a contry house hotel of style in 1988, this fine Georgian mansion commands superb views across the town to the surrounding hills. The emphasis is on quality throughout from the cosy cocktail lounge and large comfortable drawing room, to the well-equipped, and often spacious bedrooms. Chef/proprietor Ian Charlton's cooking is excellent, and his wife Lynn and their staff offer friendly and personal attention to guests at all times.
11rm(9⇨2♠)2⊟ CTV in all bedrooms ® T
20P ⊞ ✲ croquet bowls nc11yrs
♡ English & French V ♆ ⊁ Last dinner 8.45pm
Credit Cards 1 3

★★★57% Derwentwater Portinscale CA12 5RE (Consort)
☎(07687)72538 Telex no 57515 FAX (07687) 71002
This large, old, lake-side house stands amid vast gardens in a tiny village near Keswick.
52rm(35⇨17♠)(2fb)2⊟ CTV in all bedrooms ® T sB&B⇨♠£43.50-£46.50 dB&B⇨♠£67-£70 ⊟
Lift ☾ CTV 120P ✲ ♩ Putting ♫ *xmas*
♡ English & French ♆ ⊈ Bar Lunch £2.75-£4.95 High tea £2.75-£4.85 Dinner £12.75-£13.50&alc Last dinner 9.30pm
Credit Cards 1 2 3 5 £

★★Chaucer House Ambleside Rd CA12 4DR ☎(07687)72318
Closed 29 Oct-2 Apr
In the public areas of this friendly, comfortable hotel, several spacious lounges (including one warmed by a real fire) are complemented by a very attractively appointed dining room and lounge bar.
36rm(5⇨17♠)(7fb)⊁in 6 bedrooms CTV in all bedrooms ® S% sB&B£13.50-£17.80 sB&B⇨♠fr£23 dB&B£27-£35.20 dB&B⇨♠fr£42 ⊟
CTV 25P
♡ English & French ♆ ⊈ ⊁ Bar Lunch £4.60 Dinner £8.50 Last dinner 7.30pm
Credit Cards 1 2 3 4

★★Crow Park The Heads CA12 5ER ☎(07687)72208
Closed Xmas & New Year
Well-furnished family-run hotel, offering very good value, standing at the head of Borrowdale.
26rm(14⇨12♠)(1fb) CTV in all bedrooms ® T sB&B⇨♠£18.50-£22.50 dB&B⇨♠£37-£47 ⊟
CTV 26P ⊞
♡ English & Continental ♆ ⊁ Dinner £9.50-£10 Last dinner 8.00pm
Credit Cards 1 3

★★Grange Country House Manor Brow, Ambleside Rd CA12 4BA ☎(07687)72500
RS Feb & Mar
A delightful hotel on the outskirts of the town, the Grange is elegantly furnished and extremely comfortable. Owners Mr and Mrs Miller are most hospitable and devote themselves to ensuring that guests enjoy their stay.
11rm(5⇨6♪)(1fb)2⊞ CTV in all bedrooms ® sB&B⇨♪£22-£30 dB&B⇨♪£43-£51 ⊟
12P 1⌂ ⊯ ✲ nc5 yrs *xmas*
V ♔ ⊒ ⊁ Lunch £4.50-£7 Dinner £11.75-£13.50 Last dinner 8pm
Credit Cards 3 £

★★*Lairbeck* Vicarage Hill CA12 5QB ☎(07687)73373
Family hotel with clean accommodation and good home cooking.
14rm(5⇨1♪)(6fb) CTV in all bedrooms ® ✗ (ex guide dogs) 25P ⊯ ✲
♕ English & French Last dinner 8.00pm
Credit Cards 1 3

★★♛Lyzzick Hall Country House Under Skiddaw CA12 4PY
☎(07687)72277
Closed Feb

Warm and friendly hotel with fine views from the spacious lounges and some bedrooms.

19rm(13⇨6♪)Annexe1⇨(4fb) CTV in all bedrooms ® T ✗ ✳ sB&B⇨♪£21.50-£23 dB&B⇨♪£43-£46 ⊟
40P ⊯ ✲ ⇰(heated) ⌂ *xmas*
♕ International V ♔ Lunch £4.50-£9alc Dinner £8.50-£10&alc Last dinner 9.30pm
Credit Cards 1 2 3 5

★★Queen's Main St CA12 5JF (Exec Hotel) ☎(07687)73333 FAX (07687) 71144
Closed 24th Dec – 26th Dec
Built of local stone and standing in the centre of town, this hotel is one of the oldest in Keswick.
35rm(29⇨6♪)(16fb) CTV in all bedrooms ® T ✗ sB&B⇨♪£26-£32.40 dB&B⇨♪£42-£54 ⊟
Lift 12⌂ (£) *xmas*
♕ English & French V ♔ ⊒ Lunch £7 Dinner £12.95&alc Last dinner 9pm
Credit Cards 1 2 3 5 £

★★♛Red House Under Skiddaw CA12 4QA on A591
☎(07687)72211
Closed Dec-Feb

Set amidst 8 acres of woodland just north of Keswick, this Victorian country house commands superb views of northern Lakeland. Always a popular hotel with families – its games and recreation cellar proves a boon in wet weather.

22rm(20⇨)(7fb)1⊞ CTV in all bedrooms ® sB&B⇨£38-£45 dB&B⇨£72-£80 (incl dinner) ⊟
CTV 25P ⊯ ✲ ⇰ putting green games room ⌂
♕ European ♔ ⊁ Dinner £14 Last dinner 8.30pm
Credit Cards 1 £

★★Skiddaw Main St CA12 5BN ☎(07687)72071
Closed Xmas & New Year
Situated in the town centre, this well-run hotel offers good value for money.
40rm(38⇨2♪)(7fb) CTV in all bedrooms ® T sB⇨♪fr£22 dB⇨♪fr£38 (room only) ⊟
Lift 12P ⊯ sauna solarium gymnasium
♕ English & French V ♔ ⊒ Lunch fr£5alc Dinner fr£11alc Last dinner 9pm
Credit Cards 1 2 3

★★Walpole Station Rd CA12 4NA ☎(07687)72072
About 100 years old and one of the finest examples of local slate work.
17rm(6⇨4♪)(6fb) CTV in all bedrooms ® sB&Bfr£21 sB&B⇨♪fr£22.50 dB&Bfr£42 dB&B⇨♪fr£45 ⊟
9P ⊯ Qtr Size Billiards Table *xmas*
♕ English & French V Dinner fr£11.50&alc Last dinner 8pm
Credit Cards 1 3

★Highfield The Heads CA12 5ER ☎(07687)72508
Closed Nov-Mar
A friendly, family-run hotel serving good home cooking.
19rm(2⇨13♪)(3fb) ® sB&B£14 sB&B⇨♪£20.50 dB&B⇨♪£34.50-£41
CTV 19P ⊯ nc5yrs
V ♔ ⊒ ⊁ Dinner £10 Last dinner 6.30pm

★Latrigg Lodge Lake Rd CA12 5DQ ☎(07687)73545
This family-run hotel, set in a cul-de-sac near the town centre, provides accommodation of very good quality and a warm welcome; its restaurant is particularly popular.
7rm(2⇨5♪)1⊞ CTV in all bedrooms ® T sB&B⇨♪£25-£27.50 dB&B⇨♪£40-£45 ⊟
CTV 7P ⊯ *xmas*
♕ English & French V ♔ Lunch fr£7.50&alc Dinner £7.50-£15&alc Last dinner 11pm
Credit Cards 1 3 £

See advertisement on page 361

★Linnett Hill 4 Penrith Rd CA12 4HF ☎(07687)73109
The cosy little family-run hotel has pretty bedrooms and offers a friendly welcome.
7rm(2⇨5♪)(2fb)⊁in all bedrooms CTV in all bedrooms ® ✳ sB&B⇨♪£18.25 dB&B⇨♪£32.50 ⊟
12P nc4yrs *xmas*
♕ International V ♔ ⊒ ⊁ Bar Lunch £3.50-£5.50 Dinner £8&alc Last dinner 7pm
Credit Cards 1 3

★Priorholm Borrowdale Rd CA12 5DD ☎(07687)72745
Closed Dec
A compact, friendly and well-maintained tourist hotel featuring good home cooking, served in an attractive dining room. Use of the lounge bar is restricted to residents and diners.
9rm(3⇨1♪)(1fb) CTV in 4bedrooms ® ✗ (ex guide dogs) S% sB&Bfr£17 sB&B⇨♪fr£22 dB&Bfr£34 dB&B⇨♪fr£44
CTV 7P ⊯
⊁ Dinner £13 Last dinner 7.30pm
Credit Cards 1 3 £

Book as early as possible for busy holiday periods.

The Walpole Hotel ★★ AA

A FRIENDLY FAMILY RUN TOWN CENTRE HOTEL & RESTAURANT

- ★ COLOUR TV's – TEA/COFFEE (ALL ROOMS)
- ★ RESTAURANT – OPEN TO NON-RESIDENTS
- ★ CLOSE TO ALL AMENITIES

Keswick (07687) 72072

33 STATION ROAD, KESWICK

Lyzzick Hall Country House Hotel

UNDERSKIDDAW, KESWICK-ON-DERWENTWATER ★★
CUMBRIA, CA12 4PY.
Tel. (07687) 72277.

An enchanting country home set in rambling gardens (with outdoor swimming pool) in glorious unspoilt northern lakeland, Lyzzick Hall has a very special character with the emphasis very much on personal care and attention to detail.

The hotel enjoys an excellent local reputation for food and service and offers much in terms of traditional hospitality and courtesy with every modern amentiy to ensure a pampered stay.

Brochure with pleasure on request.

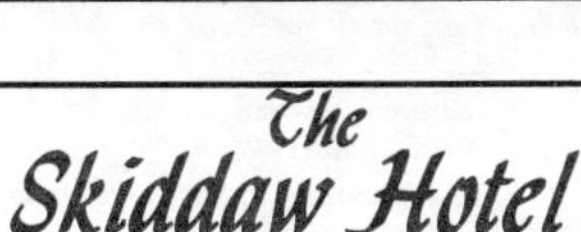

Market Square
Keswick-on-Derwentwater
Cumbria CA12 5BN
Tel: (07687) 72071

English Tourist Board

AA ★★

Overlooking the Market Square and famous Moot Hall, the Skiddaw Hotel is centrally situated in the Old Market Town of Keswick. The Hotel offers a high standard of comfort and cuisine to help make your stay in the Lake District a memorable one. All 40 bedrooms have private facilities, television, tea and coffee making, telephone and hairdryer. The Hotel has its own Saunas & Solarium with Golf and Squash available through the Hotel.

A full brochure is available.

Manor Brow, Keswick, Cumbria. CA12 4BA
Telephone (07687) 72500

The Grange, 19th Century built, is a graceful Hotel with individually decorated bedrooms and lovely lounges with log fires which create an atmosphere of a cosy Country House Hotel. Quietly situated on the hillside overlooking Keswick and commanding magnificent views of the mountains from bedrooms, restaurant and garden terrace. The highest standards are maintained at the Grange with our excellent cuisine, attentive service and first-class wines complementing the splendour of a Lakeland holiday. Duncan and Jane Miller look forward to welcoming you to the Grange.

Ashley Courtenay recommended

K

★**Skiddaw Grove** Vicarage Hill CA12 5QB ☎(07687)73324
Closed 1st 2 Weeks November RS Jan & Feb
Family-run hotel with bright cheerful bedrooms and comfortable public rooms.
12rm(5⇌)(1fb) ® ✱ sB&B£13-£14 dB&B£26-£28 dB&B⇌£30-£34 ⊟
CTV 12P ✿ *xmas*
✿ ⊬ S% Dinner £8 Last dinner 7.00pm
£

KETTERING Northamptonshire Map **04** SP87

★★★**60% Ketterings Royal** Market Place NN16 8ST (Associated Leisure) ☎(0536)520732 FAX (0536) 411036
The warm, comfortable, traditional-style hotel stands in the town centre, attracting commercial and local trade.
39rm(34⇌4⌐)(3fb)2⊟ CTV in all bedrooms ® **T** ✱ sB&B⇌⌐£35-£58 dB&B⇌⌐£45-£68 ⊟
(CTV 45⊟
English & French **V** ✿ Lunch £3.50-£7.50 Dinner £11.50&alc Last dinner 9.45pm
Credit Cards 1 2 3 5

KETTLEWELL North Yorkshire Map **07** SD97

★★***Racehorses*** BD23 5QZ ☎(075676)233
An 18th-century former coaching inn, situated on the riverside in village centre.
16rm(3⇌13⌐)(2fb) CTV in all bedrooms ®
CTV 20P private trout fishing
V ✿
Credit Cards 1 3

KEYSTON Cambridgeshire Map **04** TL07

✕✕**Pheasant Inn** PE18 0RE ☎Bythorn(08014)241
English & French **V** 55 seats Lunch £10.95-£17.40&alc Dinner £10.95-£17.40&alc Last lunch 2pm Last dinner 10pm
50P
Credit Cards 1 2 3 5

KIDDERMINSTER Hereford & Worcester Map **07** SO87

★★★★**57% Stone Manor** Stone DY10 4PJ (2m SE on A448)
☎Chaddesley Corbett(056283)555 Telex no 335661
FAX (056283) 834
RS Xmas Day
The hotel stands in 24 acres of grounds, just two miles from the centre of the town. Its bedrooms are comfortable, willing service is offered, and there is a popular restaurant.
53⇌(1fb)4⊟ CTV in all bedrooms ® **T** ✱ sB⇌£57.50-£60 dB⇌£70-£75 (room only) ⊟
(CTV 400P ✿ CFA (hard) ♫
International **V** ✿ Lunch fr£10.25&alc Dinner £15-£29alc Last dinner 10pm
Credit Cards 1 2 3 5

★★**Gainsborough House** Bewdley Hill DY11 6BS (Best Western)
☎(0562)820041 Telex no 333058 FAX (0562) 66179
Modern hotel with large banqueting facilities.
42⇌⌐(4fb)1⊟⊬in 8 bedrooms CTV in all bedrooms ® **T** ✱ sB&B⇌⌐£46.50-£55 dB&B⇌⌐£62-£72 ⊟
(130P CFA ♫ *xmas*
English & Continental **V** ✿ S% Lunch £7.25-£8.95 High tea fr£2.25 Dinner £11.95-£11.50 Last dinner 10.00pm
Credit Cards 1 2 3 5 £

KILCHRENAN Strathclyde *Argyllshire* Map **10** NN02

★★★ **ARDANAISEIG**
PA35 1HE (Pride of Britain)
☎(08663)333
FAX (08663) 222
Closed mid Oct-mid Apr
(Rosette awarded for dinner only)
A 10-mile drive from the A85 will bring you to this peaceful haven on the north shore of Loch Awe. Built in the Scottish baronial style in 1834, Ardanaiseig has been the Brown family's home for 25 years and Jonathan and Jane Brown are natural hosts, offering a warm and friendly welcome to their guests. The standards of accommodation and hospitality provided here are what good hotel-keeping is all about, and we are pleased to award our coveted Red Stars to this fine hotel. The comfortable drawing room, with chunky chintz-covered chairs, high ceilings and polished wood floor, is the main focal point, though the adjacent library bar is equally welcoming. Bedrooms are of assorted shapes and sizes, and some have recently been refurbished by Jane Brown, who is also an interior decorator. The cooking of chef Lindsay Little again achieves our rosette award. His 5-course dinner features such dishes as Charlotte of wood pigeon, Gratinée of pickled salmon and breast of guinea fowl in a sunberry and truffle sauce. Puddings are also interesting, featuring exotic babaco in various guises. a choice is available for starters and puddings and, for a supplement to the table d'hôte price, additional main course items are available. The hotel is run on country house lines and the enthusiasm of the owners is also evident in their pleasant young staff.
14⇌ CTV in all bedrooms **T** sB&B⇌£82-£114 dB&B⇌£124-£168 (incl dinner)
20P ✿ (hard) snooker croquet clay pigeon shooting boating nc8 yrs
✿ Lunch £1.75-£15alc Dinner fr£25&alc Last dinner 9pm
Credit Cards 1 2 3 5

★★★**66% Taychreggan**
PA35 1HQ
☎(08663)211
Closed 23 Oct-2 Apr
A lochside hotel, only 20 minutes drive from the Oban to Tyndrum road, Taychreggan was formerly a ferry inn and, though the ferry has since ceased to operate, the hotel retains much of its character. Owners John and Tove Taylor continue to make improvements year by year, and Taychreggan is not only beautifully decorated but also very comfortable, with a choice of several lounges and a central courtyard which is a real suntrap in summer. The table d'hôte dinners are to be recommended, and at lunchtime the bar meals are proving extremely popular.
17rm(15⇌)1⊟ **T** sB&B⇌£55-£59 dB&B⇌£110-£118 (incl dinner)
CTV 30P ✿ *xmas*

♔ ☕ Lunch £10-£12 High tea fr£5 Dinner £20 Last dinner 9pm
Credit Cards [1] [2] [3]

KILCREGGAN Strathclyde *Dunbartonshire* Map **10** NS28

★★ ***Kilcreggan*** G84 0JP ☎(043684)2243
Closed 1 Jan
Set high up overlooking gardens and River Clyde.
10rm(5⇌5♠)(2fb) **T**
CTV 40P ✈ ✲
V ♔ Last dinner 8pm
Credit Cards [1] [3] [5]

KILDRUMMY Grampian *Aberdeenshire* Map **15** NJ41

★★★ 75% **Kildrummy Castle** AB3 8RA (Best Western)
☎(09755)71288
Telex no 9401252
FAX (09755) 71345
Closed 3 Jan-3 Mar

Situated in peaceful Donside and overlooking the ruins and beautiful gardens of the 13th-century Kildrummy Castle, this most comfortable hotel manages to blend old and new to great effect. The public areas have all the features expected in a grand house, such as ▶

K

elaborate impressive fireplaces and tapestry-covered walls, and the bedrooms are spacious and well equipped.
16rm(15⇔1♠)(4fb)1⊞ CTV in all bedrooms ® T
sB&B⇔♠fr£42 dB&B⇔♠fr£75 ⊟
30P ⊞ ✲ ⅃ snooker shooting ⌂ *xmas*
☋ Scottish & French V ✿ ⅅ Lunch £10.50-£11.50 Dinner fr£18.50&alc Last dinner 9pm
Credit Cards 1 2 3 4

KILDWICK West Yorkshire Map **07** SE04

★★★66% ***Kildwick Hall*** BD20 9AE ☎Cross Hills(0535)32244
An impressive Jacobean house sympathetically converted to retain atmosphere and character. The comfortable restaurant offers interesting menus.
16rm(12⇔1♠)Annexe2rm2⊞ CTV in 16bedrooms ® T
☾CTV 60P ✲
☋ French ✿ ⅅ
Credit Cards 1 2 3 5

See advertisement under SKIPTON

KILFINAN Strathclyde *Argyll* Map **10** NR97

★★**Kilfinan** PA21 2EP ☎(070082)201 FAX (070082)205
Total renovation has added a touch of elegance to this old coaching inn. A friendly and informal atmosphere prevails in this hotel which is also gaining a deserved reputation for its delightful food. Attractive bedrooms have luxury bathrooms and thoughtful little extras. The cocktail bar doubles as the lounge.
11⇔♠(1fb) CTV in all bedrooms T sB⇔♠fr£32
dB⇔♠fr£44 (room only)
30P ⊞ ✲ ⅃ clay pigeon shooting deer stalking *xmas*
☋ Scottish & French V ✿ ⅅ Lunch fr£8&alc Dinner £18&alc Last dinner 9pm
Credit Cards 1 2 3 £

KILLIECRANKIE Tayside *Perthshire* Map **14** NN96

★★**Killiecrankie** PH16 5LG ☎Pitlochry(0796)3220
FAX (0796) 2451
Closed Dec-mid Feb
This delightful hotel stands in 6 acres of wooded grounds beside the Pass of Killiecrankie. High standards of comfort and personal service feature prominently on Duncan and Jennifer Hattersley-Smith's list of priorities. Of equal importance is the flair and skill demonstrated by chef Paul Booth and his young team. The daily changing table d'hôte menu offers imaginative Scottish cuisine featuring speciality soups, a range of fish, beef, venison and game dishes as well as delicious homemade sweets.
12rm(3⇔5♠)(2fb) sB&B£27-£30 sB&B⇔♠£29.50-£32.50
dB&B£52-£58 dB&B⇔♠£57-£63 ⊟
CTV 30P ⊞ ✲ croquet putting ⌂
V ✿ ⅅ ⁄ Bar Lunch £2-£10alc High tea £2.50-£7.50alc
Dinner £16.50-£18 Last dinner 8.30pm
Credit Cards 1 3 £

KILLIN Central *Perthshire* Map **11** NN53

★★**Morenish Lodge** Loch Tayside FK21 8TX ☎(05672)258
Closed mid Oct-Etr
Conversion of traditional shooting lodge, overlooking Loch Tay.
13rm(4⇔8♠)(1fb)2⊞ ® ✗ sB&B⇔♠£28-£32
dB&B⇔♠£56-£64 (incl dinner) ⊟
CTV 20P ⊞ ✲ nc4yrs
Dinner £12&alc Last dinner 8.15pm
Credit Cards 1 3

For key to symbols see the inside front cover.

★***Falls of Dochart*** Main St FK21 8UW ☎(05672)237
Informal hotel situated in the main street.
9rm(1⇔4♠)(2fb) ® ✗ (ex guide dogs)
CTV 20P
V ✿ ⅅ Last dinner 9pm
Credit Cards 1 3

KILMARNOCK Strathclyde *Ayrshire* Map **10** NS43

★★★55% **Howard Park** Glasgow Rd KA3 1UT (Swallow)
☎(0563)31211 Telex no 53168 FAX (0563) 27795
A modern purpose-built hotel situated just to the north of town. The ground floor of this hotel has recently been refurbished to provide an attractive restaurant, cocktail bar and foyer lounge area. Bedrooms are compact and funtional.
46⇔(6fb)⁄in 14 bedrooms CTV in all bedrooms ® T S%
sB&B⇔£30-£50 dB&B⇔£55-£85 ⊟
Lift ☾ 200P *xmas*
☋ Scottish & French V ✿ ⅅ S% Lunch £11&alc Dinner £11&alc Last dinner 9.30pm
Credit Cards 1 2 3 5

KILMARTIN Strathclyde *Argyllshire* Map **10** NR89

✕***Cairn*** PA31 8RQ ☎(05465)254
Closed Nov-Mar
Lunch not served (ex by arrangement)
☋ Continental 40 seats Last lunch 3pm Last dinner 10pm 25P nc10yrs
Credit Cards 2 3 5

KILMELFORD Strathclyde *Argyllshire* Map **10** NM81

★★**Cuilfail Hotel** PA34 3XA ☎(08522)274
Closed Jan-mid Feb
Friendly, informal and family-run, the hotel has retained much of its original coaching inn character.
12rm(4⇔3♠)(1fb) ® sB&B£20-£23 sB&B⇔♠£23-£26
dB&B£34-£40 dB&B⇔♠£40-£46
CTV 20P ⊞ ✲
✿ ⅅ Bar Lunch £6-£9alc Dinner £14.50-£16.50alc Last dinner 8.30pm
Credit Cards 1 3

KILNSEY North Yorkshire Map **07** SO96

★★***Tennant Arms*** BD23 5PS (Consort)
☎Grassington(0756)752301
Situated right by the impressive Kilnsey Crags, this busy, popular inn offers good bedrooms and an oak-panelled restaurant.
10rm(9⇔1♠)(2fb) CTV in all bedrooms ®
40P ⅃
✿ Last dinner 8.30pm
Credit Cards 1 2 3

KILWINNING Strathclyde *Ayrshire* Map **10** NS34

★★★♛67% **Montgreenan Mansion House**
Montgreenan Estate
KA13 7QZ (4m N of Irvine off A736, 3m E B785)
☎(0294)57733
Telex no 778525
FAX (0294) 85397

A fine country mansion set in 45 acres of wooded grounds features elegant and comfortably-appointed public rooms.

Bedrooms are thoughtfully equipped, the larger among them being provided with en suite spa baths.
16⇌1 CTV in all bedrooms ® T ✗ (ex guide dogs) ✱ sB&B⇌£44-£49.50 dB&B⇌£72.50-£100
Lift ☾ 50P ✤ ▶ 5 (hard) snooker clay-pigeon shooting croquet *xmas*
Scottish & French V Lunch £9.50-£13.50 Dinner fr£17.75 Last dinner 9.30pm
Credit Cards [1] [2] [3] [5]

KIMBOLTON Cambridgeshire Map **04** TL06

✕ **La Côte d'Or** 19 High St PE18 0HB
☎Huntingdon(0480)861587
Closed Tue & 25-26 Dec
Dinner not served Sun
French 30 seats ✱ S10% Lunch £4.25-£9.95&alc Dinner £19.95&alc Last lunch 1.45pm Last dinner 9pm nc6yrs
Credit Cards [1] [3]

All hotels awarded three or more stars are now also given a percentage grading for the quality of their facilities. Please see p 16 for a detailed explanation.

KINCLAVEN Tayside *Perthshire* Map **11** NO13

★★★ 75% **Ballathie House** PH1 4QN (Best Western)
☎Meikleour(025083)268
Telex no 76216
Closed Feb RS Dec-Jan

An ambitious refurbishment programme is nearing completion at this delightful coutry house hotel which is peacefully set in its own grounds beside the River Tay. The elegant public rooms and comfortable bedrooms of varying size and style are well equipped. Visitors to this hotel are assured of a warm welcome.

22rm(19⇌3↑)(2fb)1 CTV in 34bedrooms ® T sB&B⇌↑£42-£55 dB&B⇌↑£75-£100

50P ✲ CFA (hard) putting croquet *xmas*

Scottish & Continental Lunch £10-£11&alc Dinner £16.75-£18&alc Last dinner 8.30pm

Credit Cards 1 2 3 5

KINGHAM Oxfordshire Map **04** SP22

★★★ 69% **Mill House Hotel & Restaurant** OX7 6UH ☎(060871)8188 Telex no 849041 TVH 003 FAX (060871) 492
The recent appointment of Stephen Taylor (one-time 2nd chef to Chris Oakes at the Royal Crescent in Bath and at the Castle in Taunton) as head chef has introduced commendable standards of cuisine to the restaurant of this delightful Cotswold-stone hotel. Dishes worthy of mention are his mousseline of Lemon Sole with flevrons of puff pastry and wild mushrooms in a delicate fish stock with dill sauce; his breast of grouse with cranberries and Calvados, and the delicious sweets such as a chocolate and hazelnut soufflé. The hotel has recently upgraded its bedrooms, and the standards of decoration and furnishings are exceptionally pleasing, as is the hospitality offered by the owners Mr and Mrs Barnett and their staff. The Mill House enjoys delightful rural surroundings and a mill stream running through its attractive grounds has given the hotel its name. and takes its name from th mill stream that winds its way through the grounds.
21rm(20⇌)(1fb)1 CTV in all bedrooms ® T ✱ sB&B⇌£40-£42.50 dB&B⇌£60-£80
60P ✲ croquet nc5yrs *xmas*
English & French V Lunch fr£11.50&alc High tea £6-£7 Dinner fr£16.50&alc Last dinner 10pm
Credit Cards 1 2 3 4 5 £

KINGSBRIDGE Devon Map **03** SX74

★★★ 78% **Buckland-Tout-Saints** Goveton TQ7 2DS (2.5 m NE on unclass rd) (Prestige)
☎(0548)3055
Telex no 42513
FAX (0548) 6261
Closed 2 Jan-2 Feb

From its garden setting, this charming Queen Anne house commands views of the South Devon countryside. The hotel forms part of an estate whose written history goes back for nine centuries and, with its panelled lounges and dining room, offers true country-house hospitality. Standards of comfort are high and the restaurant menu, in the French and modern English style, offers such dishes as salad of wood pigeon (smoked on the premises), noisettes of lamb served with celeriac and a madeira sauce, with pear frangipan for dessert.

12⇌1 CTV in all bedrooms T S10% sB&B⇌£85 dB&B⇌£95-£140

14P ✲ croquet putting nc8yrs *xmas*

S10% Lunch £15.50-£17.50 Dinner £25-£30 Last dinner 9pm

Credit Cards 1 2 3 4 5

★★ **Kings Arms** Fore St TQ7 1AB (Exec Hotel) ☎(0548)2071
Historic coaching inn with character bedrooms (many with four poster beds), a popular bar and restaurant, and a small indoor swimming pool.
11rm(8⇌1↑)10 ® ✱ sB&B£25 sB&B⇌↑£25 dB&B£47 dB&B⇌↑£47
CTV 40P (heated) nc8yrs
English & French V Lunch £4.60-£5.50&alc Dinner £10-£16alc Last dinner 9.00pm
Credit Cards 1 3 £

★★ **Rockwood** Embankment Rd TQ7 1JZ ☎(0548)2480
Closed 24-27 Dec
Small villa with new extension overlooking estuary.
6rm(4⇌2↑) CTV in all bedrooms ®
CTV 9P 3
English & Continental V Last dinner 9pm
Credit Cards 1 3 £

KING'S LYNN Norfolk Map **09** TF62

★★★ 65% **Butterf**' Beveridge Way, Hardwick Narrows PE30 4NB (junct A10/A17) (Consort) ☎(0553)771707
Telex no 818360 FAX (0553) 768027
50rm(25⇌25↑)(2fb) CTV in all bedrooms ® T
sB⇌↑£53-£55 dB⇌↑£57.50-£60 (room only)
CTV 125P ✲
British & European V Lunch £6.75-£8.75&alc Dinner £6.75-£8.75&alc Last dinner 10pm
Credit Cards 1 2 3 5

See advertisement on page 367

★★★ 64% **The Duke's Head** Tuesday Market Pl PE30 1JS (Trusthouse Forte) ☎(0553)774996 Telex no 817349
FAX (0553) 763556
A classical building with modern extensions in the centre of town overlooking the market square. This hotel has a choice of bars, a restaurant and a coffee shop where light snacks are served throughout the day.
72⇌(1fb) in 10 bedrooms CTV in all bedrooms ® T ✱
sB⇌£56 dB⇌£72 (room only)
Lift 41P CFA *xmas*
English & French V Lunch £8.50 Dinner £14&alc Last dinner 9.30pm
Credit Cards 1 2 3 4 5

★★★ 65% **Knights Hill Hotel** Knights Hill Village, South Wootton PE30 3HQ (junct A148/A149) (Best Western)
☎(0553)675566 Telex no 818118 FAX (0553) 675568
7⇌Annexe18⇌1 CTV in all bedrooms ® T sB⇌fr£50 dB⇌fr£60 (room only)
250P ✲ (heated) snooker sauna solarium gymnasium jogging circuit croquet ♫ *xmas*
International V Lunch fr£8.50&alc Dinner fr£9.50alc Last dinner 9.30pm
Credit Cards 1 2 3 5 £

K

★★**Globe** Tuesday Market Pl PE30 1EZ (Berni/Chef & Brewer) ☎(0553)772617
The restaurant of this busy, town-centre hotel is extremely popular with local families attracted by its reasonable prices and friendly service, whilst the Tuesday Market in particular attracts visitors to the area. Bedroom accommodation has been upgraded to provide comfortable, well-equipped rooms.
40⇌↱(2fb) CTV in all bedrooms ® **T** ✗ (ex guide dogs) sB&B⇌↱fr£36 dB&B⇌↱fr£51 ⊟
(15P 8🚗
V ♧ ☕ ⊬ Lunch £8 Dinner £9 Last dinner 10.30pm
Credit Cards 1 2 3 5

★★**Grange** Willow Park, South Wootton Ln PE30 3BP ☎(0553)673777 & 671222
An impressive, Edwardian hotel with an attractive garden situated on the outskirts of King's Lynn. This is a family-run hotel where the atmosphere is homely and the service personal and friendly.
6rm(3⇌2↱)Annexe4⇌ CTV in all bedrooms ® ✳ sB&B⇌↱£30 dB&B⇌↱£43 ⊟
15P 1🚗
♧ ☕ Lunch £5.95 Dinner £8.90&alc Last dinner 8.30pm
Credit Cards 1 2 3

★★**Hotel Mildenhall** Blackfriars St PE30 1NN ☎(0553)775146 Telex no 818318 FAX (0553) 766957
Commercial hotel overlooking small park.
40⇌Annexe8⇌(3fb) CTV in all bedrooms ® **T**
Lift (40P ♫
V ♧ ☕ Last dinner 9.15pm
Credit Cards 1 2 3 5 £

★★**Stuart House** 35 Goodwins Rd PE30 5QX ☎(0553)772169 Telex no 817209
Closed Xmas & New Year
The large, detached house with its pleasant garden is set in a quiet, residential part of the town. Bedrooms in the older part of the house, though compact, are fully equipped with modern furnishings, whilst those in a newer extension are considerably larger and very comfortable indeed. Friendly staff offer attentive service under the personal direction of the owners.
19rm(12⇌3↱)(6fb) CTV in all bedrooms ® **T** ✗ sB&B£25 sB&B⇌↱£29-£36 dB&B£38 dB&B⇌↱£45-£50 ⊟
CTV 25P
🍷 European **V** Dinner £9&alc Last dinner 8.30pm
Credit Cards 1 2 3 £

★★**The Tudor Rose** St Nicholas St, off Tuesday Market Pl PE30 1LR ☎(0553)762824 Telex no 818752 FAX (0553) 764894
Town-centre hotel, parts of which date to Tudor times.
14rm(4⇌7↱)(1fb) CTV in all bedrooms ® **T** sB&B£19.95 sB&B⇌↱£30 dB&B⇌↱£45 ⊟
P̸
🍷 English & French **V** ♧ ☕ Bar Lunch £3.15-£6alc Dinner fr£8.50&alc Last dinner 9.00pm
Credit Cards 1 2 3 5

KINGSTEIGNTON Devon Map **03** SX87

★★★71% **Passage House** Hackney Ln TQ12 3QH ☎Newton Abbot(0626)55515 FAX (0626) 63336
Modern hotel with conference facilities and leisure complex including indoor pool, jet stream, jacuzzi, sauna and solarium. Overlooks the Teign Estuary and its wild-life.
39⇌↱ CTV in all bedrooms ® **T** ✳ sB&B⇌↱£48-£64 dB&B⇌↱£75-£88 ⊟
Lift (300P ⊞ ✲ ⊡(heated) ♪ sauna solarium gymnasium *xmas*
V ♧ ☕ Lunch £7.50-£8.50&alc Dinner fr£12.50&alc Last dinner 9.30pm
Credit Cards 1 2 3 5

KINGSTON UPON THAMES Greater London

See LONDON plan 5*B2*(page 412) **Telephone codes are due to change on 6th May 1990.** **See page 421.**
★★★63% **Kingston Lodge** Kingston Hill KT2 7NP (Trusthouse Forte) ☎01-541 4481 Telex no 936034 FAX 01-547-1013
Modern hotel with cocktail bar and popular courtyard restaurant. Some bedrooms have courtyard balconies.
61⇌↱1⊠⊬in 10 bedrooms CTV in all bedrooms ® **T** ✳ sB⇌↱fr£87 dBfr£92 dB⇌↱fr£106 (room only) ⊟
(74P ♫ *xmas*
V ♧ ☕ ⊬ S% Lunch £10.50-£14.50&alc Dinner £14.50-£17.50&alc Last dinner 9.45pm
Credit Cards 1 2 3 5

KINGTON Hereford & Worcester Map **03** SO25

★★**Burton** Mill St HR5 3BQ (Exec Hotel) ☎(0544)230323
A former coaching inn, situated at the centre of a quiet market town, has been modernised to appeal to tourists and business people alike, providing comfortable, well-equipped accommodation with attractive bars and a pleasant restaurant.
15rm(13⇌2↱)(3fb)1⊠ CTV in all bedrooms ® **T** sB&B⇌↱fr£33 dB&B⇌↱fr£42 ⊟
50P ✲
🍷 International **V** ♧ ☕ Lunch fr£10.50 Dinner fr£10.50 Last dinner 9.30pm
Credit Cards 1 2 3 5

KINGUSSIE Highland *Inverness-shire* Map **14** NH70

★**Columba House** Manse Rd PH21 1JF ☎(0540)661402
Closed Nov
Former manse set in its own secluded garden. Personal service by the proprietors is friendly and sincere. Residential/table licence only.
7rm(2⇌5↱)(2fb) CTV in all bedrooms ® **T** dB&B⇌↱£69 (incl dinner) ⊟
12P ⊞ ✲ 🎾 (grass) croquet, 9-hole putting *xmas*
V ♧ ☕ Lunch £6.50-£8.50 Dinner £13.50 Last dinner 8.30pm
£

See advertisement on page 369

★**Osprey** Ruthven Rd PH21 1EN ☎(0540)661510
Closed 28 Dec-31 Oct
A compact, homely hotel on the main street where the owners, Mr & Mrs Reeves have built up a sound reputation for their standard of hospitality and cuisine. There is a welcoming, informal atmosphere, which appeals to summer holidaymakers and winter skiers alike, though the inevitable table-sharing for meals will not suit everyone. Dinner, with its set main course and range of starters and puddings, is prepared by Mrs Reeves in a straightforward, wholesome manner using good, fresh ingredients.
8rm(1⇌3↱) sB&B£30-£40 sB&B⇌↱£35-£46 dB&B£60-£68 dB&B⇌↱£66-£92 (incl dinner)
CTV 10P ⊞ nc3yrs
🍷 Scottish, English & French ♧ ☕ ⊬ Dinner £17.50 Last dinner 8pm
Credit Cards 1 2 3 4 5

❀ ✕**The Cross** High St PH21 1HX ☎(0540)661762
(Rosette awarded for dinner only)
This small, shop-fronted restaurant in the main street continues to gain the acclaim of our inspectors. Whilst perhaps lacking in the formality expected, one is almost cosseted by Tony Hadley, who takes great care to explain all the items on the short 4-course menu and then guides guests through the massive wine list. While Tony excels as front of the house host, his wife Ruth constantly achieves very high standards of creatively cooked dishes of fish and game in the kitchen. ▶

Hotel Mildenhall

& Motel ★★

KINGS LYNN PE30 1NN

Tel: 0553 775146

This old established Hotel with its friendly relaxed atmosphere has 50 beautifully refurbished en-suite bedrooms, with every modern facility, including courtesy tea/coffee facilities and direct dial BT telephones. Our Edwardian Restaurant is open for dinner every evening, serving an interesting and varied menu of both traditional and Continental meals. Enjoy a glass of real ale in the Bar. Our SANDRINGHAM SUITE seats up to 120 guests for meetings, conferences, trade shows and family celebrations of all kinds.

RESIDENT MANAGERS BARRY AND HELENA ANDERSON

A member of the Baron Hotel Group

★★★

Congham Hall

COUNTRY HOUSE HOTEL
& RESTAURANT

KING'S LYNN NORFOLK PE32 1AH

TELEPHONE HILLINGTON 0485 600250

1984 BEST NEWCOMER – MIDLANDS

1988 3 RED STARS AND ROSETTE

"One of the best Country House Hotels in Great Britain".

Under personal supervision of the owners, offering quiet and peaceful atmosphere.

Boardroom conference facilities.
Weekend breaks all year.

See gazetteer entry under Grimston

K

The Grange Hotel AA★★

Willow Park, Off South Wootton Lane
King's Lynn, Norfolk PE30 3BP
Telephone: (0553) 673777/671222

Our impressive Edwardian Hotel offers you a warm welcome. Set in its own grounds. Spacious centrally heated, en-suite, bedrooms, with C.T.Vs, direct dial telephones, coffee & tea making facilities. Ideal base to explore North West Norfolk. Resident & Restaurant licence.

★★★

HOTEL – RESTAURANT – BAR

King's Lynn new hotel – informal, comfortable and relaxing – full of style
At the BUTTERFLY you will find all the modern facilities today's travellers require, in a rustic traditional setting, that's welcoming and friendly. Bedrooms fully equipped, all with private bathroom or shower rooms

Walt's Place – Restaurant and Bar – Where you can enjoy good food, wines and service at affordable prices

BEVERIDGE WAY – HARDWICK NARROWS
Next to A10-A47 ROUNDABOUT,
KING'S LYNN, NORFOLK

For reservations please 'phone (0553) 771707

Inspectors applauded the scallop mousse served as a starter, and wild mountain hare which was cooked rare and almost melted in the mouth. Puddings range from lovely light chiffon pie to chocolate fudge cake.
Closed Mon, Sun, 1-25 Dec & 3 wks May/Jun
Lunch not served
20 seats ✱ Dinner £18.50-£24 Last dinner 9.30pm ⅊ nc12 yrs 3 bedrooms available ⅍

KINLOCHBERVIE Highland *Sutherland* Map **14** NC25

★★★ 60% Kinlochbervie IV27 4RP ☎(097182)275
FAX (097182) 438
RS mid Nov-Feb
This comfortable, modern hotel stands in a delightful position overlooking the harbour. Personally supervised by the owners, it has well equipped bedrooms and specialises in Cordon Bleu cookery.
14⇌(3fb) CTV in all bedrooms ® **T** sB&B⇌£40-£80 dB&B⇌£50-£90 ⊟
30P ⛟ *xmas*
☋ French ♆ ⅅ Bar Lunch £3-£10.80 High tea £4.50-£6.50 Dinner £21.50-£23.50 Last dinner 8.30pm
Credit Cards 1 2 3 5

KINLOCHEWE Highland *Ross & Cromarty* Map **14** NH06

★★ *Kinlochewe* IV22 2PA (Minotels) ☎(044584)253
Small, relaxing, family-run hotel offering well-appointed accommodation and honest cooking based on good ingredients.
10rm(3⇌2↱)
20P ⛟
V ♆ ⅅ Last dinner 8pm
Credit Cards 1 3

KINROSS Tayside *Kinross-shire* Map **11** NO10

★★★ 61% Green 2 The Muirs KY13 7AS (Best Western)
☎(0577)63467 Telex no 76684 FAX (0577) 64525
RS 23-28 Dec
A wide range of leisure and sporting activities is available at this popular erstwhile coaching inn. Standards are continually rising, and it offers bedrooms which, though for the most part compact and simply appointed, are neatly decorated and furnished, whilst public rooms are homely and welcoming.
40rm(34⇌6↱)(6fb) CTV in all bedrooms ® **T**
sB&B⇌↱£45-£48 dB&B⇌↱£60-£66 ⊟
☾ 60P ✲ CFA ⊡(heated) ▶ 18 ♩ squash sauna solarium gymnasium curling croquet putting ♫ ⛬ *xmas*
☋ French **V** ♆ ⅅ Sunday Lunch £6.75-£7.50 High tea £5-£6.50 Dinner £13.50-£14.50&alc Last dinner 9.30pm
Credit Cards 1 2 3 5

★★★ 66% Windlestrae The Muirs KY13 7AS (Consort)
☎(0577)63217 FAX (0577) 64733
Extensively refurbished, the former restaurant is now a comfortable hotel with 18 attractive bedrooms and a striking split-level lounge bar.
18⇌(2fb)1⊟ CTV in all bedrooms ® **T** sB&B⇌£39.50-£44 dB&B⇌£56-£75 ⊟
☾ ⊞ 60P 1⌂ (charged) ✲ sauna ⛬ *xmas*
☋ International **V** ♆ ⅅ Lunch £7.50-£9.50&alc Dinner fr£12.50&alc Last dinner 9.30pm
Credit Cards 1 2 3 5 £

★★Kirklands 20 High St KY13 7AN ☎(0577)63313
Conveniently situated in the High Street, this former coaching inn has been substantially refurbished to provide comfortable modern accommodation.
8rm(3⇌5↱) CTV in all bedrooms ® **T** ⅍ (ex guide dogs) ✱
sB&B⇌↱£25 dB&B⇌↱£35
30P ✲
V ♆ ⅅ Bar Lunch £3.60-£5.50alc Dinner £5.40-£14.75alc Last dinner 9pm
Credit Cards 1 2 3

⌂Granada Lodge Kincardine Rd KY13 7HQ (on A977, off junct 6 of M90) (Granada) ☎(0577)64646 & 63123 FAX (0577) 64108
Meals available from adjacent Country Kitchen restaurant.
34⇌(15fb)⅍in 6 bedrooms CTV in all bedrooms ®
sB⇌£23-£26 dB⇌£26-£28 (room only) ⊟
34P
♆ ⅅ
Credit Cards 1 2 3 4 5

KINTBURY Berkshire Map **04** SU36

✕✕Dundas Arms RG15 0UT ☎(0488)58263 & 58559
A sensibly-chosen, mainly French menu with consistently high standards of cuisine is offered by this smart, cosy, international restaurant, which forms part of a popular pub. Its desirable location, quiet, comfortable lounge, cheerful service and good wine list make it a popular choice with local people.
Closed Sun & Mon & Xmas-New Year
☋ English & French 36 seats ✱ Lunch £12.50-£16.50 Dinner £18.50-£24.50 Last lunch 1.30pm Last dinner 9.15pm 50P ⅍
Credit Cards 1 2 3 5

KIRBY MISPERTON North Yorkshire Map **08** SE77

★★Beansheaf Restaurant Motel Malton Rd YO18 0UE
☎(065386)614 & 488
RS Monday
The established and noteworthy restaurant, set in rural surroundings, has added an accommodation wing and now offers well-equipped bedrooms, charmingly fitted out with pine furniture and modern fabrics.
20rm(1⇌19↱)(2fb)1⊟ CTV in all bedrooms ® **T** S%
sB&B⇌↱£20.50-£21.50 dB&B⇌↱£32-£33 ⊟
60P ✲ sauna solarium *xmas*
☋ English & Continental **V** ♆ ⅅ ⅍ Lunch £5.50-£7 Dinner £7.50-£8.50&alc Last dinner 10pm
Credit Cards 1 3 £

See advertisement under PICKERING

KIRKBY FLEETHAM North Yorkshire Map **08** SE29

★★★ ⛫ 72% *Kirkby Fleetham Hall* DL7 0SU
☎Northallerton (0609)748226
An impressive Georgian house in 30 acres of parkland, the hotel boasts its own lake and offers the advantages of a really peaceful atmosphere, spacious, comfortable lounges and bedrooms, charming staff and good, interesting cooking.
15⇌(2fb)3⊟ CTV in all bedrooms **T**
40P ⛟ ✲ ⌓(heated) croquet
☋ British & French **V** ♆ ⅅ Last dinner 9pm
Credit Cards 1 2 3 4 5

KIRKBY LONSDALE Cumbria Map **07** SD67

★★★50% Royal Main St LA6 2AE (Minotels) ☎(05242)71217 FAX (05242) 72228
A pleasant, friendly hotel, full of character, features a very good and popular restaurant; bar meals are also available.
20rm(15⇌1♠)1⊟ CTV in all bedrooms ® **T** S10% sB&B£30-£35 sB&B⇌♠£30-£35 dB&B£35-£55 dB&B⇌♠£35-£55 ⊟
CTV 25P 8🚗 snooker ♫ *xmas*
V ♡ ⊻ Lunch fr£7.50 High tea £1.50-£6.50 Dinner fr£11.50&alc Last dinner 10pm
Credit Cards 1 2 3 5 £

KIRKBYMOORSIDE North Yorkshire Map **08** SE68

★★George & Dragon Market Place YO6 6AA ☎(0751)31637
Welcoming 13th-century inn with modern bedrooms in converted stables.
14rm(10⇌4♠)Annexe8rm(7⇌1♠)(3fb) CTV in 20bedrooms TV in 1bedroom ® **T** ✗ sB&B⇌♠fr£32 dB&B⇌♠fr£56 ⊟
25P ⊞ ✲ *xmas*
☺ International **V** ♡ ⊻ Lunch fr£7 Dinner fr£14.50&alc Last dinner 9.30pm
Credit Cards 1 3 £

KIRKBY STEPHEN Cumbria Map **12** NY70

★★King's Arms Market St CA17 4QN ☎(07683)71378
Closed Xmas day
Situated in the centre of town, this 17th-century former posting inn offers plenty of old world charm. Bedrooms vary in size, but are freshly decorated, if simply furnished. In addition to the two intimate bars there is a comfortable residents' lounge. Good quality local produce features on the dinner and bar lunch menus which are served in the dining room.
9rm(1⇌2♠)(1fb) ® **T** sB&B£22.50-£27.50 dB&B£37.50 dB&B⇌♠£45 ⊟
CTV 4P 5🚗
V ♡ Sunday Lunch £7 Dinner £14.25 Last dinner 9.00pm
Credit Cards 1 3

KIRKCALDY Fife Map **11** NT29

★★★62% Dean Park Chapel Level KY2 6QW ☎(0592)261635 Telex no 727071
Two miles to the north of the town, off the A910, this business hotel offers modern bedrooms, a formal restaurant and limited lounge facilities.
20⇌♠Annexe12♠(3fb)1⊟ CTV in all bedrooms ® **T** ✗ (ex guide dogs) ✱ sB&B⇌♠£37.50-£42.50 dB&B⇌♠£50.50-£56.50
☾100P ⊞ ✲ snooker
☺ Scottish & French **V** ♡ Lunch fr£5.95 Last high tea 6pm
Credit Cards 1 2 3 5

KIRKCOLM Dumfries & Galloway *Wigtownshire* Map **10** NX06

★Corsewall Arms Main St DG9 0NN ☎(0776)853228
A small, modestly-appointed hotel, run by its cheerful proprietors, provides compact but neatly maintained bedrooms and serves good pub food in the character bar.
11rm(9⇌1♠)(2fb) CTV in all bedrooms ® ✱ sB&B⇌♠fr£17.50 dB&Bfr£30 dB&B⇌♠fr£30
40P ✲ ♩ U *xmas*
V ♡ ⊻ Lunch fr£6.50 High tea fr£4.50 Dinner fr£12 Last dinner 8.30pm
Credit Cards 1 2 3 5 £

KIRKCUDBRIGHT Dumfries & Galloway *Kirkcudbrightshire* Map **11** NX65

★★Selkirk Arms Old High St DG6 4JG ☎(0557)30402
Robert Burns is reputed to have written the 'Selkirk Grace' here. Today, the popular, traditionally-appointed hotel reflects a recent change of ownership in its new emphasis on high standards of cuisine, making good use of local seafood and game, and in the ongoing refurbishment of both the bedrooms and the public areas.
15rm(6⇌4♠)Annexe1⇌(2fb) CTV in all bedrooms ® **T** sB&Bfr£25 sB&B⇌♠fr£33 dB&Bfr£45 dB&B⇌♠fr£53 ⊟
4P 16🚗 ✲ *xmas*
☺ Scottish & Continental **V** ♡ ⊻ Sunday Lunch £6&alc Dinner £12&alc Last dinner 9pm
Credit Cards 1 2 3 5

KIRKHILL Highland *Inverness-shire* Map **14** NH54

★Inchmore IV5 7PX (at jnct A862/B9164) ☎Inverness(0463)83240
The small, friendly, family-run hotel set at the roadside offers a relaxed and informal atmosphere.
6rm(4⇌) CTV in all bedrooms ® **T** sB&B£18-£20 sB&B⇌£22-£25 dB&B£32-£36 dB&B⇌£36-£40 ⊟
80P
♡ ⊻ Lunch £5.50-£6.50&alc Dinner £7.50-£10&alc Last dinner 8.30pm
Credit Cards 1 3 £

KIRK LANGLEY Derbyshire Map **08** SK23

★★Meynell Arms Ashbourne Rd DE6 4NF (Minotels) ☎(033124)515
Standing on the A52 just north of Derby and offering comfortable accommodation, this popular hotel was built in 1776 as a Georgian manor farmhouse.
10rm(5⇌2♠)(2fb)2⊟ CTV in all bedrooms ® ✱ sB&B£18-£22 sB&B⇌♠£21-£28 dB&B£29-£35 dB&B⇌♠£35-£42 ⊟
100P ✲
V ♡ Lunch £6.50-£10alc Dinner £7-£12alc Last dinner 9.30pm
Credit Cards 1 2 3 5 £

See advertisement under DERBY

KIRKMICHAEL Tayside *Perthshire* Map **15** NO06

★★Aldchlappie PH10 7NS ☎Strathardle(025081)224
A comfortable, attractively modernised, personally managed hotel.
7rm(5⇌)(1fb) ® sB&B£14-£16 sB&B⇌£19-£24 dB&B⇌£32-£38 ⊟
CTV 20P 2🚗 ✲ ♩ nc5 yrs
♡ ⊻ S% Lunch fr£4.50 Dinner fr£10.50 Last dinner 9.30pm
Credit Cards 1 3 £

★★Log Cabin PH10 7NB (Exec Hotel) ☎Strathardle(025081)288
Built from Norwegian pine logs and roofed with turf, this attractive, modern hotel stands nine hundred feet up amid rugged moorland, offering glorious views over the surrounding countryside.
13rm(7⇌6♠)(5fb) TV available ® ✱ sB&B⇌♠£24.95-£31.95 dB&B⇌♠£39.90-£43.90 ⊟
CTV 50P ✲ ♩ shooting ski-ing *xmas*
V ♡ ⊻ ⊬ Sunday Lunch £7&alc High tea £7.20-£9.65alc Dinner £15.95 Last dinner 9pm
Credit Cards 1 2 3 5 £

★Strathlene Main Rd PH10 7NT ☎Strathardle(025081)347
Small family-run hotel whose emphasis is on hospitality and good food.
7rm(1⇌4♠)(1fb) ® ✱ sB&B£14 sB&B⇌♠£16 dB&B£28 dB&B⇌♠£32 ⊟

CTV 3P
Scottish V Dinner £8.95-£8.95 Last dinner 8.30pm
Credit Cards 1 3 £

KIRKWALL

See **Orkney**

KIRKWHELPINGTON Northumberland Map **12** NY98

★★ ***The Knowesgate*** Knowesgate NE19 2SH (Inter)
Otterburn(0830)40261
Modern hotel complex.
16rm(8⇌8) CTV in all bedrooms ® T
100P games room
V
Credit Cards 1 2 3 5

KNARESBOROUGH North Yorkshire Map **08** SE35

★★★64% **Dower House** Bond End HG5 9AL (Best Western)
Harrogate(0423)863302 Telex no 57202 FAX (0423) 867665
Closed Xmas Day
Evidence can still be seen of the Tudor origins of this impressive building, although the hotel is now substantially modernised, with up-to-date facilities. Privately-operated, it is nicely placed between the town centre and the river and its stylish restaurant overlooks well-kept gardens.
26rm(22⇌2)Annexe4rm(3⇌1)(2fb) CTV in all bedrooms ® T S% sB&B⇌fr£42.50 dB&B⇌fr£60
80P (heated) sauna solarium gymnasium
English & French V Lunch fr£8.25&alc Dinner fr£12.50 Last dinner 9pm
Credit Cards 1 2 3 5

★★**Mitre** Station Rd HG5 9AA ☎Harrogate(0423)863589
A Georgian-type building set in a picturesque part of town.
9rm(4⇌5↱) CTV in all bedrooms ® **T** ✗ (ex guide dogs)
CTV sauna solarium
V ♧ ⊈ Last dinner 10pm
Credit Cards 1 2 3 5 £

✕✕**Four Park Place** 4 Park Place HG5 0ER
☎Harrogate(0423)868002
A delightful and intimate restaurant to be found just off the High Street. The menu features interesting dishes skillfully prepared. Salmon, scallops, scampi, pigeon and veal are all to be found cooked and served in many different ways. There is also a good selection of starters and desserts. Service is attentive and unobtrusive.
Closed Sun, 1 wk Jan, 1 wk Aug & 25-26 Dec
Lunch not served Sat
28 seats Lunch fr£10.95&alc Dinner fr£17.95&alc Last lunch 2.30pm Last dinner 9.30pm 5P nc5yrs ⚟
Credit Cards 1 3

KNIGHTON Powys Map **07** SO27

★★★ 66% **The Knighton Hotel** Broad St LD7 1BL
☎(0547 520)530 FAX (0547520) 529
15rm
10P
♔ International **V**
Credit Cards 1 2 3 5

★★**Milebrook House** Milebrook LD7 1LT ☎(0547)528632
This eighteenth-century dower house to Stannage Castle has been tastefully converted into a country hotel offering high standards of food, comfort and hospitality.
6⇌↱ CTV in all bedrooms ® ✗ sB&B⇌↱£35
dB&B⇌↱£42 ⊟
20P ✲ Croquet nc8yrs
♔ English & French **V** ♧ Lunch £9.50-£13.50&alc Dinner £10.50-£13.50&alc Last dinner 8.30pm
Credit Cards 1 3 £

KNIGHTWICK Hereford & Worcester Map **03** SO75

★***Talbot*** WR6 5PH ☎(0886)21235
Quietly situated on the banks of the River Teme, this inn offers modern accommodation to tourists and business people alike. Meals are available in the dining room or the bar. Facilities include squash courts and a sauna.
10rm(5⇌2↱)(2fb) ®
CTV 50P ⛟ ✲ ♩ squash sauna
V ♧ Last dinner 9.30pm
Credit Cards 1 3

KNIPOCH Strathclyde *Argyllshire* Map **10** NM82

★★★ 74% **Knipoch** PA34 4QT (6m S of Oban)
☎Kilninver(08526)251 FAX (08526) 249
Closed Jan-mid Feb RS Mar Apr & Nov
The original building of this tastefully extended hotel dates from the 16th century. Standing in its own grounds and offering panoramic views over Loch Feochan, it couples tranquil natural surroundings with the country house atmosphere of its spacious, well-appointed bedrooms and fine, wood-panelled lounges. In the three period dining rooms a set 5-course dinner – based on quality ingredients, imaginatively cooked and presented – is complemented by an extensive wine list.
18⇌↱(2fb) CTV in all bedrooms **T** ✗ (ex guide dogs) ✱
sB&B⇌↱£46 dB&B⇌↱£92
40P ⛟ ✲
♧ ⊈ Lunch £12.50 Dinner £26 Last dinner 9pm
Credit Cards 1 2 3 5

KNUTSFORD Cheshire Map **07** SJ77

★★★ 65% **Cottons** Manchester Rd WA16 0SU (Shire)
☎(0565)50333 Telex no 669931 FAX (0565) 55351
Situated in rural surroundings just north-west of Knutsford, this hotel is only minutes away from Junction 19 of the M6 and Manchester Airport. The hotel has comprehensive conference facilities and a leisure club with swimming pool, gym and a floodlit tennis court.
86⇌↱(6fb)3⊞ ⚟in 12 bedrooms CTV in all bedrooms ® **T** ✱
sB&B⇌↱fr£75 dB&B⇌↱fr£86 ⊟
Lift ☾ CTV 180P ✲ ⊡(heated) ℘ (hard) sauna solarium gymnasium spa bath ♫ *xmas*
♔ English & French **V** ♧ ⊈ Lunch £9.95-£10&alc High tea 85p-£4.95 Dinner £14.50-£22.25alc Last dinner 9.45pm
Credit Cards 1 2 3 5

★★**Royal George** King St WA16 6EE (Berni/Chef & Brewer)
☎(0565)4151
Standing at the centre of the well-known Cheshire town – which owes its fame to authoress Mrs Gaskell – this elegant Georgian hotel offers bedrooms which have been modernised to a high standard and provided with en suite facilities, three also having four-poster beds.
25rm(18⇌7↱)Annexe6⇌(1fb)3⊞ CTV in all bedrooms ® **T**
✗ (ex guide dogs) sB&B⇌↱fr£53.50 dB&B⇌↱fr£64 ⊟
Lift ☾ 40P 7⌂
♔ Mainly grills **V** ♧ ⊈ ⚟ Lunch £8 Dinner £9 Last dinner 10.30pm
Credit Cards 1 2 3 5

○ ***TraveLodge*** Chester Rd, Tabley WA16 0PP (A556) (Trusthouse Forte) ☎(0565)52187
Close to junction 19 of the M6, with meals available at the adjacent Little Chef.
32⇌

✕✕**La Belle Epoque** 60 King St WA16 6DT
☎(0565)3060 & 2661
A charming restaurant steeped in history fittingly decked out with objets d'art and curios. Chef David Williams conjures up delicious fare in the modern French style. Diners are strongly advised not to miss out on the excellent cheese board. Service in this restaurant is friendly and attentive assuring diners of a relaxed and enjoyable (as well as delicious) meal.
Closed Sun, & 1st wk Jan
Lunch not served
♔ French 85 seats ✱ Dinner £25-£35alc Last dinner 10.30pm
P̸ nc14yrs 5 bedrooms available
Credit Cards 1 2 3 4 5

✕✕***David's Place*** 10 Princess St WA16 6DD ☎(0565)3356
Smoked salmon pancakes, oysters in champagne, collops of veal in marsala sauce with onion marmalade, steak en croute and delicious home-made sweets indicate the variety of dishes which can be sampled at this High Street restaurant – a symbol of good eating in Knutsford for several years.
Closed Sun & BH's
♔ International 60 seats Last lunch 2pm Last dinner 10pm P̸
Credit Cards 1 2 3 5

KYLE OF LOCHALSH Highland *Ross & Cromarty*
Map **13** NG72

★★★ 52% **Lochalsh** Ferry Rd IV40 8AF ☎Kyle(0599)4202
Telex no 75318
A busy tourist hotel beautifully situated on a rocky promontory overlooking the Isle of Skye beside the ferry terminal. Bedrooms and restaurant have been vastly improved by a recent programme of refurbishment.
40rm(38⇌)(8fb) CTV in all bedrooms ® **T** ✱ sB&B⇌£30-£58
dB&B⇌£55-£85

Lift ☾ 20P 6🚗 *xmas*
V ♔ ☕ Lunch fr£6 Dinner fr£15&alc Last dinner 9pm
Credit Cards [1] [2] [3] [4] [5]

★★Kyle Main St IV40 8AB ☎Kyle(0599)4204
A reasonably-priced hotel, with a modern extension, offering compact, comfortable accommodation.
34⇌⫯(1fb) CTV in all bedrooms ® ✱ sB&B⇌⫯£25-£27 dB&B⇌⫯£50-£54 ⊟
CTV 80P ⚑9 ♫ ♔
V ♔ ☕ Lunch fr£5.25&alc Dinner £10.50 Last dinner 9.30pm
Credit Cards [3]

KYLESKU Highland *Sutherland* Map **14** NC23

★Kylesku IV27 4HW ☎Scourie(0971)2231
Closed Nov-Mar
The simple, homely hotel stands beside the now-obsolete ferry ramp; its restaurant features freshly caught seafood at very reasonable prices.
7rm ® ✱ sB&B£14-£15 dB&B£28-£30
CTV 10P
♕ English & French V ♔ ☕ Bar Lunch £1.50-£6 Dinner £11.50 Last dinner 9pm
Credit Cards [1] [3]

LACEBY Humberside Map **08** TA20

★★★66% Oaklands Barton St DN37 7LE
☎Grimsby(0472)72248
A Victorian country house set in attractive grounds with bedroom wings built on to provide spacious and modern accommodation. A recent addition to this hotel is the leisure facilities for residents' sole use.
46⇌⫯(3fb)1⊞ CTV in all bedrooms ® T
sB&B⇌⫯£48.50-£55 dB&B⇌⫯£65-£70 ⊟

▶

☾100P ⇄ ✲ ▭(heated) sauna solarium gymnasium golf driving range ♫ ⌂
♀ International V ♁ ⊻ Lunch £3.50-£3.75&alc Dinner £10.50&alc Last dinner 10pm
Credit Cards [1] [2] [3] [5] (£)

LAGG

See **Arran, Isle of**

LAGGAN BRIDGE Highland *Inverness-shire* Map **14** NN69

★★★62% Gaskmore House PH20 1BS ☎Laggan(05284)250
Just east of Laggan Bridge, this tastefully modernised family-run hotel has well-equipped bedrooms and comfortable public rooms where log fires burn in season.
9rm(7⇌2↱)Annexe1↱(3fb) CTV in all bedrooms ® T sB&B⇌↱fr£27.50 dB&B⇌↱fr£55
40P ✲ *xmas*
V ♁ ⊻ ⚟ Lunch £7.50-£6.50alc Dinner £10-£15alc Last dinner 9.00pm
Credit Cards [1] [3]

LAIRG Highland *Sutherland* Map **14** NC50

★★★60% Sutherland Arms IV27 4AT (Scottish Highland) ☎(0549)2291 Telex no 778215
Closed Nov-Mar
Situated in the village with views of Loch Shin, this traditional Highland holiday hotel serves good home cooking.
25rm(18⇌2↱)(3fb) CTV in all bedrooms ® sB&B£38 sB&B⇌↱£41 dB&B£65 dB&B⇌↱£71 ⊟
30P ✲ ♪
♁ ⊻ Bar Lunch £2.50-£5 Dinner fr£13.50 Last dinner 8.30pm
Credit Cards [1] [2] [3] [5]

LAMORNA COVE Cornwall & Isles of Scilly Map **02** SW42

★★★♣59% *Lamorna Cove*
TR19 6XH (Inter)
☎Penzance(0736)731411

This former church for Cornish miners has been tastefully converted to provide comfortable accommodation. Cosy lounges, good home cooking using local produce and beautiful views of Lamorna Cove all make for an enjoyable stay.
18rm(14⇌4↱)(3fb)1⊠ CTV in all bedrooms T
Lift 30P ⇄ ✲ ⌓(heated) sauna Diving ⌂
♁ ⊻ ⚟
Credit Cards [1] [2] [3]

LAMPETER Dyfed Map **02** SN54

★★★55% Falcondale Country House SA48 7RX ☎(0570)422910
Set in 14 acres of attractive parkland, this Italianate mansion, built in the 19th century, is undergoing gradual improvement. Many bedrooms are now comfortably appointed, but a few are more modest. The food is good, with a kitchen garden supplying most of the produce.
22rm(13⇌8↱)(6fb)2⊠ CTV in all bedrooms ® T ✈
sB&B⇌↱£32-£38 dB&B⇌↱£45-£57 ⊟
Lift 80P ✲ ♪(hard) ♪ *xmas*

♀ English & French V ♁ ⊻ Lunch £9 Dinner £12.50 Last dinner 9.30pm
Credit Cards [1] [3]

LAMPHEY Dyfed Map **02** SN00

★★★♣64% Court
SA71 5NT (Best Western)
☎(0646)672273
Telex no 48587
FAX (0646) 672480

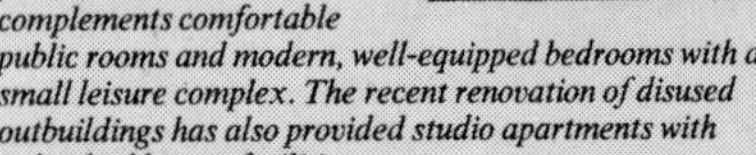

An elegant Georgian mansion, set amid lawns and pleasant woodland, complements comfortable public rooms and modern, well-equipped bedrooms with a small leisure complex. The recent renovation of disused outbuildings has also provided studio apartments with individual lounge facilities.
22rm(21⇌1↱)(6fb)6⊠ CTV in all bedrooms T
sB&B⇌↱£44-£48 dB&B⇌↱£78-£90 ⊟
▦ CTV 50P ✲ ▭(heated) sauna solarium gymnasium ⌂ *xmas*
♀ English & French V ♁ ⊻ Bar Lunch £3-£8&alc High tea £3-£6 Dinner £14&alc Last dinner 9pm
Credit Cards [1] [2] [3] [5]

See advertisement under PEMBROKE

★★Lamphey Hall Hotel SA71 5NR ☎(0646)672394
This newly refurbished hotel, standing close to the Bishop's Palace, offers comforable, well-equipped bedrooms and friendly service.
10rm(5⇌5↱)(2fb)1⊠ CTV in all bedrooms ® T ✳
sB&B⇌↱£35 dB&B⇌↱£67-£84 (incl dinner) ⊟
30P
♀ English & French V ♁ ⊻ Sunday Lunch £4.95 Dinner fr£12.50 Last dinner 8.30pm
Credit Cards [1] [3]

LANCASTER Lancashire Map **07** SD46

★★★★59% Post House Waterside Park, Caton Rd LA1 3RA (close to junc 34 M6) (Trusthouse Forte) ☎(0524)65999
Telex no 65363 FAX (0524) 841265
Modern, well-furnished riverside hotel with very comfortable bedrooms.
117⇌(23fb)1⊠⚟in 25 bedrooms CTV in all bedrooms ® T ✳
S% sB⇌£70-£81 dB⇌£86-£95 (room only) ⊟
Lift ☾ 180P ✲ ▭(heated) sauna solarium gymnasium health & fitness centre *xmas*
V ♁ ⊻ ⚟ S% Lunch £7.75-£10&alc Dinner £12.95&alc Last dinner 10.30pm
Credit Cards [1] [2] [3] [4] [5]

★★Slyne Lodge Slyne LA2 6AZ (2m N on A6)
☎Hest Bank(0524)823389
10⇌(3fb) CTV in all bedrooms ® T sB&B⇌£27.50-£30 dB&B⇌£38-£40
100P ✲ ⌂
♀ Mainly grills V ♁ ⊻ ⚟ Lunch £7.30-£13alc Dinner £7.30-£13alc Last dinner 10.30pm
Credit Cards [1] [2] [3] [4] [5] (£)

Book as early as possible for busy holiday periods.

LANDCROSS Devon Map **02** SS42

★★***Beaconside*** EX39 5JL (1m SW on A388)
☎Bideford(02372)77205
Comfortable small, secluded hotel with good food and atmosphere.

9rm(4⇌2♨)(2fb) CTV in all bedrooms ✗
CTV 16P ✽ ⛱(heated) ♈ (hard)
♈ ♈ ✗
Credit Cards [1] [5]

LANGBANK Strathclyde *Renfrewshire* Map **10** NS37

✽★★★♛71% ***Gleddoch House*** PA14 6YE

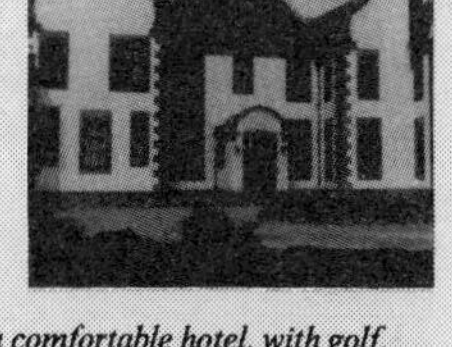

☎(047554)711
Telex no 779801
Closed 26-27 Dec & 1-2 Jan

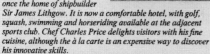

With its wonderful views over the Firth of Clyde, this gracious country house was once the home of shipbuilder Sir James Lithgow. It is now a comfortable hotel, with golf, squash, swimming and horseriding available at the adjacent sports club. Chef Charles Price delights visitors with his fine cuisine, although the à la carte is an expensive way to discover his innovative skills.

33rm(31⇌2♨)(6fb)1⊞ CTV in all bedrooms ® **T**
☾ 100P ✽ ⊡(heated) ▶ 18 squash ∪ snooker sauna ♨
V ♈ ♈ Last dinner 9pm
Credit Cards [1] [2] [3] [5]

LANGDALE, GREAT

See **Elterwater**

LANGHO Lancashire Map **07** SD73

★★★67% **Mytton Fold Farm** Whalley Rd BB6 8AB
☎Blackburn(0254)40662
RS Xmas week
Comfortable bedrooms, friendly service and a very good restaurant are provided at this family-run hotel.
27rm(18⇌9♨)2⊞ CTV in all bedrooms ® **T** ✗ (ex guide dogs) sB&B⇌♨£28-£43 dB&B⇌♨£44-£62 ⊟
60P ✽ nc6yrs
V ♈ Lunch £6.50-£20alc High tea £6.75 Dinner £6.50-£20alc
Last dinner 9.30pm
Credit Cards [1] [3] £

✕✕✕**Northcote Manor** Northcote Rd BB6 8BE
☎Blackburn(0254)40555
A comfortable country house off the A59 which offers an interesting menu and wine list that caters for all tastes and pockets – complemented by genteel service. An exceptionally good value table d'hôte menu is offered at lunchtime, while the evening meal is à la carte. The puddings are irresistible.
Closed Xmas-1 Jan
Lunch not served Sat
V 70 seats ✱ Lunch £8.95-£10.95 Dinner £20-£26alc Last lunch 1.30pm Last dinner 9.30pm 60P ♫
Credit Cards [1] [2] [3] [5]

LANGHOLM Dumfries & Galloway *Dumfriesshire* Map **11** NY38

★★Eskdale Market Place DG13 0JH (Minotels) ☎(03873)80357
An historic coaching hostelry providing modernised accommodation. Popular with businessmen.
16rm(3⇌7⥮)(2fb)⊁in 3 bedrooms CTV in all bedrooms ® **T**
sB&Bfr£20 sB&B⇌⥮fr£22 dB&Bfr£33 dB&B⇌⥮fr£37
10P ♪
V ♡ ⊡ Bar Lunch £1.95-£3.50alc Dinner £10&alc Last dinner 8.30pm
Credit Cards [1] [3] [4] £

LANGLAND BAY West Glamorgan Map **02** SS68

See also **Mumbles and Swansea**
★★★55% *Osborne* Rotherslade Rd SA3 4QL (Embassy)
☎Swansea(0792)366274
Popular hotel on cliff top, offering warm and friendly service.
36rm(29⇌3⥮)(3fb) CTV in all bedrooms ® **T**
Lift ☾ 40P ♫
⊕ Welsh, English & French **V** ♡ ⊡
Credit Cards [1] [2] [3] [4] [5]

★★*Langland Court* Langland Court Rd SA3 4TD (Best Western)
☎Swansea(0792)361545 Telex no 498037
The small, personally-run hotel has received major upgrading recently and now offers very comfortable, modern bedrooms, well equipped and individually decorated . In the wood panelled dining room you can rely on quality cooking standards and prompt, friendly service, whilst outside there are attractive small gardens with good views over Swansea Bay.
16rm(10⇌6⥮)Annexe5rm(3⇌2⥮)(5fb)1⊠⊁in 2 bedrooms.
CTV in all bedrooms ® **T**
45P 4⌂ (£2) ✲
⊕ English & Continental **V** ♡ Last dinner 9.30pm
Credit Cards [1] [2] [3] [5]

See advertisement under SWANSEA

LANGSTONE Gwent Map **03** ST38

★★New Inn Motel NP6 2JN (Porterhouse)
☎Newport(0633)412426 FAX (0633) 413679
Conveniently sited just off the M4 north-east of Newport, this comfortable small motel has quality bedrooms and popular restaurant and bar facilities.
34rm(1⇌32⥮)(1fb) CTV in all bedrooms ® **T** ✈
CTV 250P
V ♡
Credit Cards [1] [2] [3] [5] £

LANREATH Cornwall & Isles of Scilly Map **02** SX15

★★Punch Bowl Inn PL13 2NX ☎(0503)20218
Originally a coaching inn dating from the early 17th century, and once the haunt of smugglers, the hotel today features well-equipped rooms named after Punch characters. Its busy bars serve an extensive range of bar meals, whilst both à la carte and table d'hôte menus are available in the popular restaurant.
18rm(11⇌2⥮)(2fb)3⊠ CTV in all bedrooms ®
sB&B£14-£17.50 sB&B⇌⥮£19-£21.50 dB&B£28-£35
dB&B⇌⥮£38-£43 ⊟
CTV 50P
V ♡ Lunch £5.95 High tea fr£5alc Dinner £8.50 Last dinner 9.30pm
Credit Cards [1] [3]

See advertisement under LOOE

The AA's star-rating scheme is the market leader in hotel classification.

LARGS Strathclyde *Ayrshire* Map **10** NS25

★★Elderslie John St, Broomfields KA30 8DR ☎(0475)686460
Closed Xmas Day & Boxing Day
A 19th-century building on Largs seafront commanding magnificent views.
25rm(9⇌4⥮) CTV in all bedrooms ® sB&B£23
sB&B⇌⥮£28 dB&B£46 dB&B⇌⥮£56
CTV 30P ✲ ⌂ *xmas*
♡ Lunch £7.50-£10.50 Dinner £9.50-£11.50 Last dinner 8.30pm
Credit Cards [1] [2] [3] [5] £

★★Springfield Greenock Rd KA30 8QL ☎(0475)673119
Set on the seafront of this popular resort, the hotel caters for both tourist and coach trade, offering pleasant comfortable bedrooms – with en suite facilities in many cases – and spacious, neatly appointed public rooms.
47rm(3⇌38⥮)(5fb) CTV in all bedrooms ® sB&B£21
sB&B⇌⥮£28 dB&B£37 dB&B⇌⥮£43 ⊟
Lift CTV 80P ✲ putting green ♫ *xmas*
⊕ Scottish, French & Italian **V** ♡ ⊡ ⊁ Lunch £3.95-£5.75&alc High tea £4.50-£10 Dinner £9.50-£10.50&alc Last dinner 8.30pm
Credit Cards [1] [2] [3] [5]

LARKFIELD Kent Map **05** TQ65

★★★57% Larkfield ME20 6HJ (Trusthouse Forte)
☎West Malling(0732)846858 Telex no 957420
FAX (0732) 846786
Professional, well-managed hotel with modern, well-appointed bedrooms, an à la carte restaurant and welcoming staff.
52rm(48⇌4⥮)1⊠⊁in 5 bedrooms CTV in all bedrooms ® **T**
S% sB⇌⥮£64-£74 dB⇌⥮£74-£84 (room only) ⊟
☾ 95P ✲ CFA ♫ *xmas*
⊕ French & International **V** ♡ ⊡ ⊁ S% Lunch £8.95-£10.95 Dinner £14.50-£18.75&alc Last dinner 10pm
Credit Cards [1] [2] [3] [4] [5]

See advertisement under MAIDSTONE

LASTINGHAM North Yorkshire Map **08** SE79

★★*Lastingham Grange*
YO6 6TH
☎(07515)345
Closed mid Dec-Feb
A 17th-century house of local stone set in attractive gardens and providing a comfortable lounge, with a real fire, well appointed bedrooms and excellent service.
12⇌ CTV in all bedrooms ® **T**
30P 2⌂ ⊞ ✲ ⌂
V ♡ ⊡ ⊁
Credit Cards [2] [5]

LAUNCESTON Cornwall & Isles of Scilly Map **02** SX38

★★White Hart Broad St PL15 8AA ☎(0566)2013
FAX (0566) 3668
A High Street coaching inn providing modest accommodation.
25rm(13⇌7⥮)(4fb) CTV in 20bedrooms ® **T** ✱ sB&B£16-£23
sB&B⇌⥮£21-£23 dB&B£30-£45 dB&B⇌⥮£37-£45 ⊟

▶

THE ARUNDELL ARMS HOTEL

Lifton, Devon. PL16 0AA

★ ★ ★

A 250-year-old former coaching inn near Dartmoor, now a famous sporting hotel with 20 miles of our own salmon and trout rivers, pheasant and snipe shoots, riding and golf. Log-fire comfort with superb food and wines; winter gourmet evenings by our French-trained chef. Splendid centre for exploring Devon and Cornwall. Excellent conference facilities.

Details: Anne Voss-Bark.
Tel. Lifton (0566) 84666
BTA Commended Country Hotel.
On A30, 38 miles from M5 motorway at Exeter.

★★

Langholm, Dumfriesshire DG13 0JH
Telephone: Langholm (03873) 80357

The Eskdale Hotel is a former coaching inn in the centre of Langholm on the Scottish border. The hotel offers a high degree of comfort, facilities and good quality home cooking. There are tea/coffee making facilities, colour TV, radio and full central heating in all rooms, ⅔ of rooms have en suite facilities. Lively atmosphere with two bars, games room and à la carte restaurant. Ample parking is available in the hotel which is a good base for touring the Border region. Fishing, shooting and golf are all available in the area. Fishing permits available from Hotel.

L

ELDERSLIE HOTEL LARGS

★★ AA

Situated on the sea front at Largs 'Elderslie' commands breathtaking views over the Firth of Clyde.

Fully licensed with central heating throughout.
Extensive Lounges ★ Private car park
Wide choice of menus ★ A warm welcome guaranteed

All bedrooms are equipped with television, wash basin, radio & tea making facilities
Many have private bathroom or shower.

Send now for our colour brochure and tariff

ELDERSLIE HOTEL,
BROOMFIELDS, LARGS, AYRSHIRE KA30 8DR.
Tel: Largs 686460

CTV 24P CFA snooker *xmas*
V ☕ Lunch fr£5.75 Dinner fr£9.25 Last dinner 9.30pm
Credit Cards 1 2 3 5

LAVENHAM Suffolk Map **05** TL94

★★★70% **The Swan** High St CO10 9QA (Trusthouse Forte)
☎(0787)247477 Telex no 987198 FAX (0787) 248286
Four attractive timbered houses dating back to the 14th century make up this lovely hotel. Spacious lounges clustered around upen fires make an ideal setting for afternoon tea – especially to the accompaniment of a harpsichord. Meals are served in the heavily timbered restaurant with its minstrels' gallery. Bedrooms come in all shapes and sizes.
47⇨(1fb)2 ⊬in 4 bedrooms CTV in all bedrooms ® T ✳ S% sB⇨£74.50-£77.50 dB⇨£96.12-£131 (room only)
(60P ✣ ♫ *xmas*
V ☕ ⊬ S% Lunch £10.75-£21.55&alc Dinner £17.20-£18.95&alc Last dinner 9.30pm
Credit Cards 1 2 3 4 5

✕✕**The Great House** Market Place CO10 9QZ ☎(0787)247431
This beautifully renovated building, providing a wealth of charm and character, is an ideal setting for the restaurant. The food is competently cooked and ranges from the classic to the imaginatively new and light dishes. Fresh fish features strongly on the menu and is particularly good. Light snacks or full meals are served at lunchtime.
Closed last 3 wks Jan
Lunch not served Mon (in winter)
Dinner not served Sun (in winter)
Continental V 40 seats Lunch £7.50-£15 Dinner fr£13.50&alc Last lunch 2.30pm Last dinner 10.30pm 6P 4 bedrooms available
Credit Cards 1 3

LAWSHALL Suffolk Map **05** TL85

★★**Corders** Bury Rd IP29 4PJ ☎(0284)830314
Small and charming family-run hotel set in its own grounds.
8⇨(2fb)1 CTV in all bedrooms ® T (ex guide dogs) S10% sB&B⇨£34-£39 dB&B⇨£50-£64
CTV 30P ✣ sauna jacuzzi nc5yrs *xmas*
English & French V ⊬ Lunch £7.50-£9.50&alc Dinner £7.50-£9.50&alc Last dinner 9pm
Credit Cards 1 2 3 5 £

LEAMINGTON SPA (ROYAL) Warwickshire Map **04** SP36

★★★50% **Falstaff** 20 Warwick New Rd CV32 5JQ
☎Royal Leamington Spa(0926)312044 Telex no 333388
FAX (0926) 450574
Neat Victorian house with attractive wood-faced modern extension and a small garden.
68rm(44⇨18)(3fb)2 CTV in all bedrooms ® T ✳ sB&B⇨£36-£49 dB&B⇨£48-£58
Lift (80P ✣ CFA *xmas*
English & French V ☕ Lunch £6.50&alc Dinner £10&alc Last dinner 9.15pm
Credit Cards 1 2 3 4 5 £

Entries for rosetted restaurants, red-star and country-house hotels are highlighted by a tinted panel. For a full list of these establishments, consult the Contents page.

❀★★★ **MALLORY COURT**

Harbury Ln, Bishop's Tachbrook CV33 9QB (2m S off A452) (Relais et Châteaux) ☎Royal Leamington Spa (0926)330214
Telex no 317294
FAX (0926) 451714

Set in 10 acres of terraces and rose gardens, this turn-of-the-century house offers an outdoor swimming pool, squash and tennis courts and a croquet lawn. Inside, open fires warm the luxurious and welcoming sitting rooms, and the immaculate bedrooooms are equally agreeable. All are provided with every conceivable extra that the guest might want, to the point, it must be said, of creating clutter. This minor grumble aside, the rooms are warm, comfortable and very well equipped. Owners Jeremy Mort and Allan Holland, who have built up Mallory Court's reputation, are to be congratulated on the impeccable, discreet and efficient service which makes this such a tranquil and relaxing place to stay. Allan has recently handed over the reins in the kitchen, but Anthony Wright shows no less flair and originality in such creations as a game terrine of rabbit, hare, woodcock, wild duck and venison with Cumberland sauce, or a breast of chicken filled with a mousse of lobster, truffle and sweetbreads, poached and served with a lemon butter sauce.
10⇨(1fb)1 CTV in all bedrooms T sB&B⇨fr£95 dB&B⇨£87-£165 Continental breakfast
50P 2 (£5) ✣ (hard) squash croquet nc12yrs
French ☕ Lunch fr£19.50 Dinner fr£36 Last dinner 9.45pm
Credit Cards 1 3

★★★54% **Manor House** Avenue Rd CV31 3NJ (Trusthouse Forte) ☎Royal Leamington Spa(0926)423251
FAX (0926) 425933
Large hotel near station with choice of restaurants and ample conference facilities.
53rm(46⇨7)(2fb)⊬in 12 bedrooms CTV in all bedrooms ® T S% sB⇨fr£64 dB⇨fr£80 (room only)
Lift (100P CFA *xmas*
English V ☕ ⊬ Lunch fr£8 Dinner fr£13 Last dinner 10pm
Credit Cards 1 2 3 4 5

★★★50% **Regent** 77 The Parade CV32 4AX (Best Western)
☎Royal Leamington Spa(0926)427231 Telex no 311715
FAX (0926) 450728
Conveniently sitauated within the town centre, a Regency hotel which still retains some examples of classical décor and provides an appropriately traditional style of service.
80⇨(7fb)1 CTV in all bedrooms ® T sB&B⇨£50-£65 dB&B⇨£67.50-£78
Lift (CTV 70P 30 CFA table tennis pool table ♫ *xmas*
English, French & Italian ☕ Lunch fr£9.25 Dinner fr£12.85 Last dinner 10.45pm
Credit Cards 1 2 3 5

★★**Abbacourt** 40 Kenilworth Rd CV32 6JF
☎Royal Leamington Spa(0926)451755
Large converted house, popular with business people.
27rm(8⇨13)(4fb) CTV in 20bedrooms TV in 7bedrooms ® T

30P
Continental **V** Last dinner 10pm
Credit Cards [1] [2] [3] [4] [5]

★★Adams 22 Av Rd CV31 3PQ
☎Royal Leamington Spa(0926)450742 & 422758
FAX (0926) 313110
An impressive Georgian residence on the outskirts of the town has been lovingly restored by the proprietors to create a very comfortable hotel with well-appointed bedrooms and public rooms which still include many original features and antique pieces. Home-cooked food and personal service ensure a most comfortable and relaxing stay.
14rm(1⇨12↱)(1fb) CTV in 11bedrooms **T**
sB&B⇨↱£29-£36 dB&B⇨↱£45-£48
14P
V Lunch £14-£18 Dinner £17&alc Last dinner 8pm
Credit Cards [1] [2] [3] [5]

★★Angel 143 Regent St CV32 4NZ (Consort)
☎Royal Leamington Spa(0926)881296
Standing near to the town centre, the Regency-style hotel has timbered interior decor and a select, friendly restaurant.
37rm(29⇨7↱)(7fb)4 CTV in all bedrooms ® **T**
sB&B£17.50-£30 sB&B⇨↱£25.50-£42.50 dB&B⇨↱£35-£55
Lift 40P
English & French **V** Lunch fr£7.95 Dinner £9.95-£10.95&alc Last dinner 9.30pm
Credit Cards [1] [2] [3] £

★★Beech Lodge Warwick New Rd CV32 5JJ
☎Royal Leamington Spa(0926)422227
RS 24 Dec-3 Jan
Public rooms are airy, pleasantly furnished and comfortable in this large Regency house midway between Warwick and Leamington Spa, though bedrooms tend to be more compact. Friendly, personal service is provided by the proprietors, John and Janet Hayward, and their family.
12rm(1⇨8↱) CTV in all bedrooms ® **T** sB&B£26.50
sB&B⇨↱£33 dB&B⇨↱£52
CTV 16P
English & French **V** Lunch fr£5 Dinner fr£8.25 Last dinner 9pm
Credit Cards [1] [2] [3] £

★ LANSDOWNE

87 Clarendon St CV32 4PF
☎Royal Leamington Spa (0926)450505
Telex no 337556
RS 24 Dec-7 Jan

This small, elegant Regency hotel is conveniently situated close to the town centre, and what it lacks in size is more than adequately compensated by a warm and happy atmosphere. Guests can really relax and feel at home here – a feat that few hotels ever achieve – and David and Gillian Allen are enthusiastic and caring, working hard to meet the needs of their guests with a genuine hospitality. Little wonder that we receive so many letters of praise about the Lansdowne. Bedrooms vary considerably in size, but all are comfortable, and during the coming year alterations should help to alleviate some of the more compact rooms. Gillian Allen takes an active part in choosing the soft furnishings for the hotel, but is most often found busy in the kitchen, preparing carefully selected dishes from the best quality ingredients. David's personal choice of wines complement the food; the list includes some unusual items, but all are good quality and value for money. We were particularly impressed by the willingness to split a bottle of wine for single guests if a half bottle was not available.
10rm(2⇨2↱)(1fb) sB&B£24.95-£27.95
sB&B⇨↱£36.95-£39.95 dB&B£39.30-£42
dB&B⇨↱£49.90-£53
CTV 8P nc5yrs
English, French & Italian Dinner £11.95-£14.95 Last dinner 8.30pm
Credit Cards [1] [3] £

LECKMELM Highland *Ross & Cromarty* Map **14** NH19

★Tir-Aluinn IV23 2RJ
☎Ullapool(0854)2074
Closed Oct-19 May

Country house hotel quietly situated on the shores of Loch Broom.

16rm(3⇨) ® sB&B£14 dB&B£28 dB&B⇨£33
CTV 30P
V Dinner £6.75 Last dinner 8pm

LEDBURY Hereford & Worcester Map **03** SO73

★★★ 63% **Feathers** High St HR8 1DS ☎(0531)5266
FAX (0531) 2001
This attractive former coaching inn has recently undergone major improvements. Accommodation is modern and well equipped and yet still retains charm and character. This hotel is equally suitable for tourists and business people.
11⇌♠(2fb)1 ⊠ CTV in all bedrooms ® **T** sB&B⇌♠£40-£55 dB&B⇌♠£65-£79 ⊟
☾10P 6⊠ squash *xmas*
English & French **V** Lunch fr£9.50alc Dinner fr£13.50alc Last dinner 9.30pm
Credit Cards 1 2 3 5

❀★★ **Hope End Country House** Hope End HR8 1JQ (2.5m NE unclass rd)
☎(0531)3613
Closed Dec-Feb RS Mar-Nov
(Rosette awarded for dinner only)
This delightfuly countrty house surrounded by 40 acres of tranquil parkland and woods was once the home of Elizabeth Barratt Browning. Tastefully converted into a small and comfortable hotel by John and Patricia Hegarty, the crowning glory of a stay here is undoubtedly the traditional English-style food – many of the fresh ingredients are grown in an enormous 18th-century walled garden. many of the recipes used are included in Patricia Hegarty's own book, An English Flavour.
7⇌Annexe2⇌ CTV in 1bedroom ® ✱
sB&B⇌£63-£97 dB&B⇌£70-£104 ⊟
10P ✿ nc14yrs
Dinner £25 Last dinner 8.30pm
Credit Cards 1 3

★★ ***Verzons*** Trumpet HR8 2PZ (3m W A438)
☎Trumpet(053183)381
Situated 3 miles west of Ledbury on the A438, this large Georgian farmhouse provides simple but comfortable accommodation. Informally run, it is equally suitable for both tourists and business guests.
10rm(6⇌1♠)(2fb) CTV in all bedrooms ®
45P ✿
English & French **V** Last dinner 9.30pm
Credit Cards 1 2 3 5

★★ **Ye Olde Talbot Hotel** New St HR8 2DX ☎(0531)2963
At this popular, timber-framed inn guests can enjoy good home cooking served in a dining room which features a magnificent carved overmantle.
6rm(2♠)(1fb) CTV in 3bedrooms ® sB&B£23-£25 sB&B♠£28 dB&B£35 dB&B♠£42 ⊟
CTV 5P *xmas*
V Lunch £6.50-£9&alc High tea £1.50 Dinner £6.50-£9&alc Last dinner 9pm
Credit Cards 3

All the information in the guide is annually updated, but details of prices and facilities may change during the currency of this guide.

LEE Devon Map **02** SS44

★★ ***Lee Manor Country House Hotel & Restaurant*** Lee Bay EX34 8LR (3m W on unclass road)
☎Ilfracombe(0271)63920
Closed Nov-Mar (ex Xmas & New Year)

An original 19th-century coach house, a fine replica of a Tudor mansion, has been sympathetically restored by owners, Alan and Pamela Jordan, to create a charming small hotel providing bright, comfortable bedrooms and character public rooms which include a galleried dining room. Food standards are commendable, imagination and flair being brought to bear on quality local produce. Peacefully secluded and commanding sea views, Lee Manor offers an ideal retreat in which to relax.
11⇌♠1 ⊠ CTV in all bedrooms ®
20P nc12yrs
English & Continental **V** Last dinner 8.30pm

LEEDS West Yorkshire Map **08** SE33

★★★★ 64% **Hilton International** Neville St LS1 4BX (Hilton) ☎(0532)442000 Telex no 557143 FAX (0532) 433577
A comfortable city-centre hotel close to the railway station and with good access to the M1. Choice of menus in the restaurant – interesting à la carte and very good value buffet.
234rm(205⇌29♠)(3fb) in 30 bedrooms CTV in all bedrooms ® **T** sB⇌♠£83-£150 dB⇌♠£95-£150 (room only) ⊟
Lift ☾ ⊞ 5P 70⊠ CFA ♫
International **V** Lunch £10-£16&alc Dinner £15-£18&alc Last dinner 10pm
Credit Cards 1 2 3 5

★★★★ 60% **The Queen's** City Square LS1 1PL (Trusthouse Forte) ☎(0532)431323 Telex no 55161 FAX (0532) 425154
Friendly staff offer spontaneous and courteous service in this traditional city centre hotel. Bedrooms are well-appointed.
188rm(186⇌2♠) in 37 bedrooms CTV in all bedrooms ® **T** S% sB⇌♠£75-£91 dB⇌♠£91-£107 (room only) ⊟
Lift ☾ CFA *xmas*
British & French **V** S% Lunch £9-£12&alc Dinner £11-£13&alc Last dinner 10pm
Credit Cards 1 2 3 4 5

★★★ 62% **Grove Crest** The Grove LS26 8EJ (Crest) ☎(0532)826201 Telex no 557646 FAX (0532) 829243
(For full entry see Oulton)

★★★ 64% **Hilton National** Wakefield Rd, Garforth Rdbt LS25 1LH (6m E at junc A63/A642) (Hilton) ☎(0532)866556 Telex no 556324 FAX (0532) 868326
(For full entry see Garforth)

★★★ 50% ***Merrion*** Merrion Centre LS2 8NH (Mount Charlotte) ☎(0532)439191 Telex no 55459 FAX (0532) 423527
A functional city centre hotel.
120⇌ in 42 bedrooms CTV in all bedrooms ® **T**
Lift ☾ P CFA ♫
English & French **V** Last dinner 10.30pm
Credit Cards 1 2 3 5

Red-star hotels offer the highest standards of hospitality, comfort and food.

★★★ 65% **Parkway** Otley Rd LS16 8AG (Embassy) ☎(0532)672551 Telex no 556614 FAX (0532) 674410
Situated on the A660 just one mile north of the ring road, this hotel offers a choice of restaurants, well-appointed bedrooms and new leisure facilities.
103rm(97⇔6♠)(8fb)⅄in 11 bedrooms CTV in all bedrooms ® **T** ✗ (ex guide dogs) sB⇔♠fr£65 dB⇔♠fr£79 (room only) 🅱
Lift ☾ 250P ✿ ⊠(heated) ℘ (hard) snooker sauna solarium gymnasium ♫
English & French **V** ♡ ☕ Lunch £7.95-£9.75 Dinner fr£12.50&alc Last dinner 10pm
Credit Cards [1] [2] [3] [4] [5]

★★★ 66% **The Post House Hotel, Leeds/Selby** LS25 5LF (Trusthouse Forte) ☎South Milford(0977)682711 Telex no 557074 FAX (0977) 685462
(For full entry see Lumby)

★★★ 64% **Stakis Windmill** Mill Green View, Seacroft LS14 5QP (Stakis) ☎(0532)732323 Telex no 55452 FAX (0532) 323018
A modern, comfortable hotel on the ring road and convenient for the city centre and major roads. Service is spontaneous, friendly and courteous.
100⇔♠(12fb)⅄in 22 bedrooms CTV in all bedrooms ® **T** ✱ sB⇔♠fr£76 dB⇔♠fr£86 (room only) 🅱
Lift ☾ 200P *xmas*
English, French & Italian ♡ ☕ Lunch £7.50&alc Dinner £12.95&alc Last dinner 10pm
Credit Cards [1] [2] [3] [4] [5]

★ ***Hartrigg*** Shire Oak Road, Headingley LS6 2DL (2.5m NW A660) ☎(0532)751568
A very modest, old fashioned hotel.
28♠(2fb) ®
CTV 12P 3🚗
Credit Cards [1] [2] [3]

○ ***Leeds Crest*** Wellington St(Crest) ☎(0532)825877
Due to open Jan 1990
125⇔

LEEK Staffordshire Map **07** SJ95

★★ **Jester At Leek** 81 Mill St ST13 8EU ☎(0538)383997
A century ago this modern and popular hotel, standing on the A523 to the north of the town centre, was a small inn and adjoining cottages.
14rm(9⇔2♠)(4fb) CTV in all bedrooms ® **T** sB&B⇔♠£24.50-£26.50 dB&B⇔♠£35.50-£37.50 🅱
70P snooker
English & Continental **V** ♡ ☕ ⅄ Lunch £5.95-£6.50&alc High tea £4.50-£5.50 Dinner £8.50-£12.95alc Last dinner 10pm
Credit Cards [3] £

LEEMING BAR North Yorkshire Map **08** SE28

★★ ***Motel Leeming*** DL8 1DT ☎Bedale(0677)23611
(For full entry see Bedale)

★★ **White Rose** DL7 9AY ☎Bedale(0677)22707 & 24941
Modest, clean roadside hotel,
18rm(8⇔10♠) CTV in all bedrooms ® **T** ✱ sB&B⇔♠fr£23 dB&B⇔♠fr£39 🅱
CTV 50P
♡ ☕ Lunch £6.25-£6.75 High tea £5.75 Dinner £8.75&alc Last dinner 9.30pm
Credit Cards [1] [2] [3] [5] £

Entries for rosetted restaurants, red-star and country-house hotels are highlighted by a tinted panel. For a full list of these establishments, consult the Contents page.

LEICESTER Leicestershire Map **04** SK50

★★★★58% **Grand** Granby St LE1 6ES (Embassy)
☎(0533)555599 Telex no 342244 FAX (0533) 544736
Impressive Victorian city-centre building standing on the main A6.
92rm(86⇌6♠)(2fb)2 CTV in all bedrooms ® **T** S%
sB⇌♠£60-£70 dB⇌♠£68-£100 (room only)
Lift ☾ 120P ♫
English & French V ✿ S10% Lunch £9.50&alc High tea £1.75-£3.75 Dinner £9.50&alc Last dinner 10pm
Credit Cards 1 2 3 4 5

★★★★60% **Holiday Inn** St Nicholas Circle LE1 5LX
☎(0533)531161 Telex no 341281 FAX (0533) 513169
Large, modern purpose-built hotel close to the city centre, adjacent to multi-storey car park.
188♠(106fb)⊬in 58 bedrooms CTV in all bedrooms ® **T** S%
sB♠£63-£68 dB♠£69-£75 (room only)
Lift ☾ CFA (heated) sauna gymnasium ♫
International **V** ✿ ⊬ Lunch £10-£15&alc Dinner £15-£20&alc Last dinner 10.15pm
Credit Cards 1 2 3 4 5

★★★67% **Belmont** De Montfort St LE1 7GR (Best Western)
☎(0533)544773 Telex no 34619 FAX (0533) 470804
Closed 25 Dec-2 Jan
Personally run by the family who have owned it for more than 50 years, and set conveniently close to the railway station, just south of the city centre, this large hotel caters mainly for the business person. Its Victorian exterior conceals modern, well-equipped accommodation, good conference/function facilities, a pleasant restaurant and a choice of bars.
36rm(33⇌3♠)Annexe21rm(19⇌2♠)(7fb)⊬in 9 bedrooms CTV in all bedrooms ® **T** ✱ sB&B⇌♠£58-£70
dB&B⇌♠£68-£80
Lift ☾ 40P CFA ♫
English & French **V** ✿ Lunch £8-£9.50&alc Dinner £11.50-£12.50&alc Last dinner 10pm
Credit Cards 1 2 3 5

★★★60% **Leicester Forest Moat House** Hinckley Rd, Leicester Forest East LE3 3GH (Queens Moat) ☎(0533)394661
FAX (0533) 394952
A well furnished, modern-style, mainly commercial hotel situated on the A47 Hinckley Road.
34⇌♠ CTV in all bedrooms ® **T** ✱ sB⇌♠£27-£52
dB⇌♠£42-£62 (room only)
☾ 200P ✿ putting
English & French **V** ✿ Lunch £6.50-£8.50 Dinner £10.50&alc Last dinner 9.45pm
Credit Cards 1 2 3 5

★★★62% **Leicestershire Moat House** Wigston Rd, Oadby LE2 5QE (3m SE A6) (Queens Moat) ☎(0533)719441
Telex no 34474 FAX (0533) 720559
A major refurbishment programme is transforming this hotel. Its new public areas and bedrooms are comfortable and well-equipped.
57⇌♠(4fb)⊬in 14 bedrooms CTV in all bedrooms ® **T**
sB⇌♠£27-£51 dB⇌♠£40-£61 (room only)
Lift ☾ CTV 190P ✿
English & French **V** ✿ Lunch £9.20&alc High tea £2-£4.50alc Dinner £9.20&alc Last dinner 9.45pm
Credit Cards 1 2 3 5

★★★61% ***Penguin*** Humberstone Rd LE5 3AT ☎(0533)20471
Telex no 341460 FAX (0533) 514211
Closed 25-31 Dec
A large, busy, city-centre hotel providing well equipped accommodation, catering mainly for business people and conference delegates.
209⇌(7fb)⊬in 22 bedrooms CTV in all bedrooms ® **T**
Lift ☾ P 25
V ✿ Last dinner 10.30pm
Credit Cards 1 2 3 4 5

★★★61% **Post House** Braunstone Ln East LE3 2FW
(Trusthouse Forte) ☎(0533)630500 Telex no 341009
FAX (0533) 823623
A large and busy hotel on the A46, conveniently placed for access to the M1, M69 and city centre. Popular with business people and a conference centre this hotel has three grades of well-equipped bedrooms and a choice of restaurants.
172⇌(6fb)⊬in 4 bedrooms CTV in all bedrooms ® **T** S%
sB⇌fr£67 dB⇌fr£80 (room only)
Lift ☾ 240P CFA *xmas*
International **V** ✿ ⊬ S% Lunch £8-£9&alc Dinner fr£14&alc Last dinner 10pm
Credit Cards 1 2 3 4 5

★★★63% **Hotel Saint James** Abbey St LE1 3TE
☎(0533)510666 Telex no 342434 FAX (0533) 515183
Completely modernised and with good conference facilities, this hotel has panoramic views of the city. Public areas are comfortable and bedrooms well equipped.
73⇌(3fb) CTV in all bedrooms ® **T** ✱ sB⇌£30.50-£51.50
dB⇌£39.50-£59.50 (room only)
Lift ☾ sauna solarium gymnasium steam room jacuzzi
English & French **V** ✿ Lunch £7.50&alc High tea £1.80-£3.45 Last high tea 6pm
Credit Cards 1 2 3 5 £

★★**Regency** 360 London Rd LE2 2PL ☎(0533)709634
Conveniently situated on the A6 just 1 1/2 miles south of the city centre, this hotel is well equipped and provides good value for money. It is popular with business people, but equally suitable for tourists and others visiting the area.
37rm(24⇌13♠)(2fb) CTV in all bedrooms ® **T** (ex guide dogs) ✱ sB&B⇌♠£35-£40 dB&B⇌♠£50-£55
☾ 40P *xmas*
English & Continental **V** ✿ Lunch £5&alc Dinner £10-£15&alc Last dinner 11.30pm
Credit Cards 1 2 3 5 £

★***Rowans*** 290 London Rd LE2 2AG ☎(0533)705364
Closed 23 Dec-4 Jan
Situated on the A6, just one mile south of the city centre, this hotel offers simple accommodation and informal service and caters mainly for commercial guests.
14rm(1⇌1♠)(1fb) CTV in 7bedrooms TV in 7bedrooms ®
CTV 15P croquet
English, French & Italian ✿
Credit Cards 1

✕✕✕**The Manor** Glen Parva Manor, The Ford, Little Glen Rd, Glen Parva LE2 9TL 3m SW on A426 ☎(0533)774604
A 16th-century house just south of the city in Glen Parva village. June and John Robson have worked wonders since coming here in 1987, most notably with the appointment of chef Martin Zalesny to lead the kitchen brigade. An extensive à la carte menu is offered, but most popular are the speciality lunch and dinner menus, featuring the best of the day's market. Thin slices of calf's liver on a potato pancake, strips of salmon and plaice in a watercress sauce, steamed chocolate and rum pudding, coffee and petit fours came to under £10 in 1989, and a dinner with two more courses was not much dearer. The extensive wine list features some classic chateaux and outstanding years.
Closed 25-26 Dec
Lunch not served Sat
Dinner not served Sun
French **V** 70 seats Lunch £10.50&alc Dinner £17.50&alc Last lunch 2pm Last dinner 10pm 90P
Credit Cards 1 2 5

A rosette is the AA's highest award for quality of food and service in a restaurant.

L

LEIGH Greater Manchester Map **07** SJ69

★★★60% ***Greyhound*** Warrington Rd WN7 3XQ (Embassy) ☎(0942)671256

An attractive restaurant, a flower-decked conservatory and popular public bars are the main features of this friendly hotel situated on a roundabout at the junction of the A580 and A574, just south of Leigh. Bedrooms, though dated, are functional with modern facilities.

54⇨♠⅟in 2 bedrooms CTV in all bedrooms ® **T**
Lift ☾ ▦ 80P 16🚗
♉ English & French **V** ♈ ♉ Last dinner 9.45pm
Credit Cards 1 2 3 5

LEIGH DELAMERE MOTORWAY SERVICE AREA (M4) Wiltshire Map **03** ST87

⌂**Granada Lodge** M4 Service Area SN14 6LB (Granada) ☎Chippenham(0666)837097 FAX (0666) 837691

Bedroom accommodation of a high standard, tastefully furnished and equipped with en suite facilities, is provided at a budget price in this modern, two-storey block (which can also cater for the needs of disabled clients). The Country Kitchen Restaurant serves a range of refreshments, snacks and full meals 24 hours a day, whilst a shop in an adjacent building sells confectionery, gifts, newspapers and magazines.

35⇨(6fb)⅟in 8 bedrooms CTV in all bedrooms ®
sB⇨£23-£26 dB⇨£26-£28 (room only)
100P 🚗
V ♈ ♉ ⅟
Credit Cards 1 2 3 5

See advertisement under CHIPPENHAM

LEIGHTON BUZZARD Bedfordshire Map **04** SP92

★★★72% **Swan** High St LU7 7EA ☎(0525)372148 FAX (0525) 370444
RS 25 & 31 Dec

A tastefully restored 18th-century inn with well-equipped and well-appointed bedrooms. The charming restaurant offers some well-prepared and interesting dishes and the atmosphere throughout is relaxing and friendly.

38⇨(1fb)1⊞ CTV in all bedrooms ® **T** ✈ ✳
sB&B⇨£61.50-£65 dB&B⇨£75-£85 ⊟
☾ 10P 🚗
V ♈ ♉ ⅟ Lunch £10.95-£12.50 Dinner fr£16.50&alc Last dinner 9.30pm
Credit Cards 1 2 3 5

LEISTON Suffolk Map **05** TM46

★**White Horse** Station Rd IP16 4HD ☎(0728)830694

A warm welcome on arrival and continuing hospitality are offered to guests by proprietors Mr and Mrs Doyle. Accommodation is modest with some modern facilities.

10rm(1⇨5♠)(1fb) CTV in all bedrooms ® **T** ✳
sB&B£27.50-£31 sB&B⇨♠fr£31 dB&Bfr£36 dB&B⇨♠fr£42 ⊟
CTV 14P 3🚗 🚗 ✿ ♫ ♘ *xmas*
♉ English & French **V** ♈ ♉ Lunch £3.25&alc Dinner £4.25-£8.50&alc Last dinner 9.30pm
Credit Cards 1 3 £

LEOMINSTER Hereford & Worcester Map **03** SO45

★★★54% **Talbot** West St HR6 8EP (Best Western) ☎(0568)6347 Telex no 35332

The cruck-framed hotel, parts of which date from 1470, will please both individual and conference guests with its period furniture, log fires and relaxed atmosphere.

25rm(20⇨5♠)(4fb) CTV in all bedrooms ® **T** ✈ ✳
sB&B⇨♠£42-£45 dB&B⇨♠£70-£76 ⊟
30P *xmas*
♉ English & French **V** ♈ ♉ Lunch £8-£8.50&alc Dinner £13-£13.50&alc Last dinner 9.30pm
Credit Cards 1 2 3 5

★★**Royal Oak** South St HR6 8JA (Minotels) ☎(0568)2610

Close to the town centre, this former Georgian coaching inn provides simple but comfortable accommodation and informal service. Equally suitable for tourists and business people, its ground floor annexe bedroom with access from the car park makes it accessible for disabled guests.

17rm(16⇨1♠)Annexe1⇨(2fb)1⊞ CTV in all bedrooms ® ✳
sB&B⇨♠£25.50-£28.50 dB&B⇨♠£38-£42 ⊟
CTV 24P 1🚗
V ♈ ♉ Lunch fr£11alc Dinner fr£11alc Last dinner 9pm
Credit Cards 1 2 3 5

LERWICK

See **Shetland**

L'ETACQ

See **Jersey under Channel Islands**

LETHAM Fife Map **11** NO31

★★★♛63% ***Fernie Castle***
KY7 7RU
☎(033781)381
Telex no 295141
FAX (033781) 422

An imposing castle modernised to meet the needs of both the business person and tourist. Bedrooms are of varying sizes and all well-equipped. There is a comfortable drawing room and interesting vaulted cocktail bar.

16rm(6⇨10♠)(2fb)1⊞ CTV in all bedrooms ® **T**
CTV 50P ✿ putting clay pigeon shooting
♉ French **V** ♈ ♉
Credit Cards 1 2 3 5

LETHAM Tayside *Angus* Map **15** NO54

★★★♛63% **Idvies House**
DD8 2QJ
☎(030781)787
Telex no 76252
Closed 26 & 27 Dec RS 24 & 25 Dec

Set in 12 acres of wooded grounds, this fine Victorian mansion house offers peaceful relaxation, friendly service and sound country house cooking. Public rooms are homely and bedrooms well-equipped.

6⇨♠(1fb)1⊞ CTV in all bedrooms ® **T** ✳
sB&B⇨♠£25-£35 dB&B⇨♠£35-£45 ⊟
60P ✿ squash croquet clay pigeon shooting
V ♈ ♉ Lunch fr£9&alc High tea £4.75-£7.25 Dinner £11.50-£15&alc Last dinner 9.30pm
Credit Cards 1 2 3 5

LETTERFINLAY Highland *Inverness-shire* Map **14** NN29

★★**Letterfinlay Lodge** PH34 4DZ (off A82)
☎Spean Bridge(039781)622
Closed Nov-Feb
A friendly and comfortable family-run hotel delightfully situated overlooking Loch Lochy.
15rm(8⇌3⌐)(4fb) ✻ S10% sB&B⇌⌐£16-£27
dB&B⇌⌐£30-£60
⊞ CTV 100P ✿
V ♈ ☕ S10% Bar Lunch £9-£10 Dinner fr£14 Last dinner 8.30pm
Credit Cards 1 2 3 4 5

LEVEN Fife *Fife*

★★★59% **New Caledonian** 81 High St KY8 4NG ☎(0333)24101
FAX (0333) 21241
Modern business hotel replacing one which was damaged by fire some years ago.
16⇌⌐ CTV in all bedrooms ® ✻ sB&B⇌⌐£35-£45
dB&B⇌⌐£47-£57
CTV 50P
Lunch £6.95 High tea £3.25-£7.50 Dinner £10.95&alc Last dinner 9.30pm
Credit Cards 1 2 3 5

LEWDOWN Devon Map **02** SX48

✿★★ **Lewtrenchard Manor** EX20 4PN
☎(056683)256 222

This splendid early 17th-century manor house is set in a 1,000 acre estate on the edge of Dartmoor, and is approached by a sweeping drive through well-tended gardens, complete with fountain. The lounge areas are comfortable and crammed with antiques and objets d'art and there is an abundance of fresh flower arrangements. Many fine architectural features are preserved, including wood panelling, frescoes, ornate ceilings and a delightful gallery. Chef David Shepherd produces an interesting Menu Gourmande, together with a sensible à la carte, based on local produce, the more straightforward dishes being the most successful. The wine list is short, but bottles are generally from highly reputable vineyards. Proprietors James and Sue Murray, together with their charming staff, place the emphasis very much on personal service.
8rm (7⇌) 2⊟ CTV in all bedrooms ®
P ✿
☕ English & French ☕ Last dinner 9.30pm.

LEWES East Sussex Map **05** TQ41

★★★54% ***Shelleys*** High St BN7 1XS (Mount Charlotte)
☎(0273)472361 Telex no 86719
Its comfortable, skilfully restored public rooms elegantly furnished with antiques, this gracious Georgian-style hotel makes an ideal base for visits to Glyndebourne.
21⇌⌐2⊟ CTV in all bedrooms **T**
☾25P 3⌂ ✿ CFA
V ♈ ☕ Last dinner 9.15pm
Credit Cards 1 2 3 5

★★**White Hart** High St BN7 1XE (Best Western)
☎(0273)474676 & 473794 Telex no 878468
Much of the original character and olde worlde charm of this 15th-century town centre hotel has been retained. Facilities include a carvery, conservatory restaurant and coffee shop.
19rm(13⇌1⌐)Annexe14⇌(3fb)2⊟ CTV in all bedrooms ® **T**
S10% sB&B£32-£35 sB&B⇌⌐£51-£53 dB&B£45-£50
dB&B⇌⌐£68-£75 ⊟
☾ 40P *xmas*
☕ English & French V ♈ ☕ ✂
Credit Cards 1 2 3 5 £

LEWIS, ISLE OF Western Isles *Ross & Cromarty* Map **13**

STORNOWAY Map **13** NB43

★★★56% **Caberfeidh** PA87 2EU (Best Western) ☎(0851)2604
FAX (0851) 5572
RS 1 Jan
Purpose-built hotel on the edge of town, for holidaymakers, business and functions.
40⇌⌐ CTV in all bedrooms ® **T** ✻ sB&B⇌⌐£45-£51
dB&B⇌⌐£60-£66 ⊟
Lift ☾ CTV 100P ✿
☕ French V ♈ ☕ Lunch £6-£8 Dinner £11-£12&alc Last dinner 9.30pm
Credit Cards 1 2 3 5

LEYBURN North Yorkshire Map **07** SE19

★**Golden Lion** Market Place DL8 5AS
☎Wensleydale(0969)22161
Closed 25 & 26 Dec
A good range of both bar meals and à la carte dinners is served at this busy, popular village inn.

14rm(10⇌1↱)(5fb) CTV in all bedrooms ® T sB&B£13-£16 sB&B⇌↱£14-£19 dB&B£26-£32 dB&B⇌↱£32-£38 ⊟
Lift ⊁ ⛟
V ✿ S% Lunch £5-£10alc Dinner £8-£15alc Last dinner 9pm
Credit Cards 1 3 £

LEYLAND Lancashire Map **07** SD52

★★★55% Penguin Hotel Leyland Way PR5 2JX
☎Preston(0772)422922 Telex no 677651 FAX (0772) 622282
Functional modern hotel just off junction 28 of the M6.
93⇌↱(9fb)⊁in 6 bedrooms CTV in all bedrooms ® T ✱ sBfr£47 sB⇌↱fr£47 dBfr£59 dB⇌↱fr£59 (room only) ⊟
(CTV 150P CFA *xmas*
☋ English & French V ✿ ⊥ Lunch £5.50-£7.75&alc Dinner £10.25-£10.25&alc Last dinner 9.45pm
Credit Cards 1 2 3 5 £

★★★69% Pines Clayton-le-Woods PR6 7ED (1m S of M6 junc 29 on A6) ☎Preston(0772)38551 Telex no 67308
Closed 25 & 26 Dec
A well-furnished, late-Victorian house with modern extensions.
24⇌ CTV in all bedrooms ® T ✗ ✱ S10% sB&B⇌£30-£50 dB&B⇌£55-£60 ⊟
(130P ⛟ ✲ squash solarium
V ✿ ⊥ S10% Lunch £8.25-£9.52&alc Dinner £11.35-£20.92alc Last dinner 9.30pm
Credit Cards 1 2 3 5

LICHFIELD Staffordshire Map **07** SK10

★★★57% George Bird St WS13 6PR (Embassy) ☎(0543)414822 FAX (0543) 415817
RS Xmas
Large Georgian inn near Cathedral. (The nearby Swan Hotel, under the same ownership, is used as an annexe).
38rm(34⇌4↱)(3fb)⊁in 5 bedrooms CTV in all bedrooms ® T S% sB⇌↱fr£52 dB⇌↱fr£63 (room only) ⊟
(40P 3⌂ CFA ♫ *xmas*
☋ International V ✿ ⊥ S% Lunch £8.25&alc Dinner £10.95 Last dinner 9.30pm
Credit Cards 1 2 3 4 5

★★★60% Little Barrow Beacon St WS13 7AR ☎(0543)414500
Popular central hotel with modern, well-equipped bedrooms.
24⇌ CTV in all bedrooms ® T ✗ (ex guide dogs) sB&B⇌£50 dB&B⇌£60 ⊟
(⊞ CTV 70P
☋ French V ✿ ⊥ Lunch £6.50&alc Dinner £9.50&alc Last dinner 9.30pm
Credit Cards 1 2 3 5

★★Angel Croft Beacon St WS13 7AA ☎(0543)258737 FAX (0543) 415605
Closed 25 & 26 Dec RS Sun evenings
A well-run, family hotel with large comfortable rooms and friendly service. Situated almost opposite the Cathedral and with rear gardens backing onto Beacon Park, it is ideal for tourists and business people alike.
11rm(3⇌6↱)Annexe8⇌(2fb)1⊟ CTV in all bedrooms ® T ✗ (ex guide dogs) ✱ sB&B£25-£31 sB&B⇌↱£34.50-£50 dB&B£36-£45 dB&B⇌↱£44-£60 ⊟
60P ✲
✿ ⊥ Lunch £7.50-£13.75 Dinner £10.15-£14.65 Last dinner 9pm
Credit Cards 1 3 5

★★Fradley Arms Rykneld St, Fradley WS13 8RD (on A38, 3m NE) ☎Burton-on-Trent(0283)790186 & 790977
Small Georgian inn beside A38, offering friendly service.
6rm(1⇌5↱)(1fb) CTV in all bedrooms ® T sB&B⇌↱£30-£35 dB&B⇌↱£40-£48 ⊟
CTV 200P ✲ ♫
☋ English & French V ✿ ⊥ S% Lunch fr£5.50 Dinner fr£9.45&alc Last dinner 9.30pm
Credit Cards 1 2 3 5

LIFTON Devon Map **02** SX38

★★★71% Arundell Arms PL16 0AA (Best Western)
☎(0566)84666
Closed 4 days Xmas
An old coaching inn owned and managed since 1961 by Mrs. Voss-Bark who has taken great care in her refurbishment of the place to provide attractive, comfortable and well-equipped bedrooms, lounges and bars. The dining room makes an elegant setting for the interesting menu skilfully conjured up by young English chef Philip Burgess.
24rm(19⇌5↱) CTV in all bedrooms ® T sB&B⇌↱£41-£46 dB&B⇌↱£67-£74 ⊟
80P ⛟ ✲ CFA ⌡ skittle alley games room *xmas*
☋ English & French ✿ ⊥ ⊁ Lunch £12-£14 Dinner £18-£20 Last dinner 9pm
Credit Cards 1 2 3 5

See advertisement under LAUNCESTON

★★Lifton Cottage PL16 0DR ☎(0566)84439
Small, friendly, family-run cottage hotel of character with a pleasant atmosphere, popular bar and restaurant and good bedrooms. Conveniently situated for touring the West Country.
13rm(2⇌8↱)(2fb) CTV in all bedrooms ® T sB&B£18.25-£20.50 sB&B⇌↱£22.50-£24.50 dB&B£36.50 dB&B⇌↱£44
CTV 25P ✲
V ✿ ⊥ ⊁ Lunch £5.95 Dinner £8.50 Last dinner 9pm
Credit Cards 1 2 3 5

LIMPLEY STOKE (near Bath) Wiltshire Map **03** ST76

★★★⚑59% Cliffe Tracey Mallinson, Crowe Hill BA3 6HY (Best Western)
☎(022122)3226
Telex no 445731
Closed 22 Dec- 15 Jan
This small hotel with a terraced garden overlooks the Avon Valley and offers a cosy, well-decorated lounge and a candle-lit dining room. Bedrooms are newly decorated and furnished. The hotel is popular with tourists.
11rm(8⇌3↱)(3fb)1⊟ CTV in all bedrooms ® T ✗ (ex guide dogs) sB&B⇌↱£65-£85 dB&B⇌↱£70-£85 ⊟
40P ⛟ ✲ ⌂(heated)
☋ English & French V ✿ ⊥ Lunch £11.50-£16 High tea £3.50-£6 Dinner £15-£17alc Last dinner 9pm
Credit Cards 1 2 3 5

★★Limpley Stoke Hotel BA3 6HZ (Consort) ☎(022122)3333
Telex no 57515 ATTN 13
Approached up a private road, this country house is situated in the heart of the River Avon Valley.
54rm(42⇌12↱)(4fb)3⊟ CTV in all bedrooms ® T
Lift CTV 60P ✲ CFA
V ✿ Last dinner 8.30pm
Credit Cards 1 2 3 5

See advertisement under BATH

LINCOLN Lincolnshire Map **07** SK97

★★★★63% **The White Hart** Bailgate LN1 3AR (Trusthouse Forte) ☎(0522)26222 Telex no 56304 FAX (0522) 531798
Early Georgian house with a slate Victorian façade, standing in the shadow of Lincoln cathedral.
50⇌(4fb)⊬in 12 bedrooms CTV in all bedrooms ® **T** ✱ sB⇌£65-£70 dB⇌£85-£90 (room only) ⛿
Lift ☾ CTV 25P 35🚘 CFA ♫ *xmas*
V ♈ ☕ ⊬ Lunch £6.50-£11.50&alc High tea £2.50-£6.50 Dinner £13.75-£15&alc Last dinner 9.45pm
Credit Cards [1] [2] [3] [5]

★★★54% **Eastgate Post House** Eastgate LN2 1PN (Trusthouse Forte) ☎(0522)20341 due to change to 520341 Telex no 56316 FAX (0522) 510780
Modern hotel with ample parking facilities, situated opposite the Cathedral.
71⇌(1fb)⊬in 10 bedrooms CTV in all bedrooms ® **T** sB⇌£67 dB⇌£84 (room only) ⛿
Lift ☾ 110P ❊ CFA *xmas*
♉ English & French **V** ♈ ☕ ⊬ S% Lunch £8.50-£11.50&alc Dinner £10.50-£11.50&alc Last dinner 10pm
Credit Cards [1] [2] [3] [4] [5]

★★★50% **Four Seasons** Scothern Ln LN2 3QP
☎Welton(0673)60108 FAX (0673) 62728
(For full entry see Dunholme)

★★★52% **Moor Lodge Hotel** LN4 1HU (Consort)
☎(0522)791366 Telex no 56396 FAX (0522) 510720
(For full entry see Branston)

★★★🏠62%
Washingborough Hall Country House Church Hill, Washingborough LN4 1BE (3m E B1190) (Minotels)
☎(0522)790340

Mr and Mrs Shillaker and their small team provide a friendly informal and relaxed service in this beautifully restored Georgian manor house set in 3 acres of gardens and woodland. Bedrooms are individually designed and well equipped, whilst the comfortable lounge, which dominates the ground floor, has an open log fire which burns for most of the year.
12rm(9⇌3↱)1⊟⊬in 2 bedrooms CTV in all bedrooms ® **T** sB&B⇌↱£38-£45 dB&B⇌↱£55-£65 ⛿
50P ⊞ ❊ ⇒ ⌂
♉ International **V** ♈ ☕ ⊬ Lunch £6.50-£8.50 Dinner fr£10&alc Last dinner 9.30pm
Credit Cards [1] [2] [3] [5] £

★★**Barbican** Saint Marys St LN5 7EQ ☎(0522)528374 & 543811
An unusual feature of this hotel is the Barnum's Lager Bar. Decorated and furnished on the Barnum's Circus theme, it certainly provides a lively atmosphere. Good standards of décor prevail throughout the public areas and the modern bedrooms which are individually furnished and well equipped, though some are rather compact.
20rm(13↱)(2fb) CTV in all bedrooms ® **T** sB&B£29 sB&B↱£34 dB&B£41.50 dB&B↱£46 ⛿
CTV P̸
♉ Mainly grills **V** ♈ ☕ ⊬ Lunch £6-£14alc High tea £3.80-£7.60alc Dinner £6-£14alc Last dinner 9.30pm
Credit Cards [1] [2] [3] [5] £

★★*Castle* Westgate LN1 3AS ☎(0522)38801
Lovely old building, built as a school in 1852, tastefully modernised and converted.
15⇌Annexe6↱(2fb) CTV in all bedrooms ® T
21P nc8yrs
Continental V
Credit Cards 1 2 3 5

★★*Duke William* 44 Bailgate LN1 3AP ☎(0522)33351
Closed 25 Dec
Located a few minutes' walk from the Cathedral, the comfortable and friendly hotel has been an inn since 1791.
10↱(2fb) CTV in all bedrooms ® T
(12P
V Last dinner 9.30pm
Credit Cards 1 2 3 5

★★**Grand** Saint Mary's St LN5 7EP ☎(0522)524211
Telex no 56401
This busy commercial hotel, ideally situated for the city's transport terminals, offers sound, modern accommodation with a good range of facilities and services.
48rm(42⇌6↱)(2fb) CTV in all bedrooms ® T
sB&B⇌↱£34-£37 dB&B⇌↱£45-£48
(40P
V Lunch £6.50-£8.80&alc High tea £2.70-£5.15alc Dinner £9-£11.50&alc Last dinner 10pm
Credit Cards 1 2 3 5

★★**Hillcrest** 15 Lindum Ter LN2 5RT (Guestaccom)
☎(0522)510182
Closed 20 Dec-3 Jan
A former Victorian rectory with rose gardens standing in a quiet road north-east of the city centre, the hotel provides comfortable, well-equipped rooms and has good views over part of the city.
17rm(2⇌15↱)(4fb) CTV in all bedrooms ® T
sB&B⇌↱£28-£32.50 dB&B⇌↱£41-£45
8P
International V Bar Lunch £2-£5 Dinner £6.50-£12.50alc Last dinner 9pm
Credit Cards 1 3

★★**Loudor** 37 Newark Rd, North Hykeham LN6 8RB (3m SW A1434) ☎(0522)680333
A small, attractive house has been completely remodelled and enlarged to create a compact, modern hotel where personal attention ranks high.
9⇌↱Annexe1↱(1fb) CTV in all bedrooms ® T
sB&B⇌↱£28.50-£33 dB&B⇌↱£38-£42
12P
English & French
Credit Cards 1 2 3 5 £

LINLITHGOW Lothian *West Lothian* Map 11 NS97

✕✕✕**Champany** EH49 7LU (2m NE off A904)
☎Philipstoun(050683)4532 & 4388
Closed Sun, 24 Dec-9 Jan
Lunch not served Sat
International 48 seats Lunch £18.50-£30.50alc Dinner £18.50-£30.50alc Last lunch 2pm Last dinner 10pm 100P nc8yrs
Credit Cards 1 2 3 5

LIPHOOK Hampshire Map 04 SU83

✕✕*Lai Quilla* 15 The Square GU30 7AB ☎(0428)722095
Indian Last dinner 11.30pm
Credit Cards 1 2 3 5

For key to symbols see the inside front cover.

LISKEARD Cornwall & Isles of Scilly Map 02 SX26

★★**Country Castle**
Station Rd PL14 4EB
☎(0579)42694
Closed Nov RS Jan & Feb

Quietly set in 2.5 acres of grounds, with magnificent views over the Looe Valley, this hotel provides individually decorated and attractively furnished bedrooms and an elegant lounge. The personal involvement of the proprietors maintains old-fashioned standards of hospitality, serving wholesome food and offering individual service.
11rm(5⇌5↱)(1fb) CTV in all bedrooms ® *
sB&B⇌↱£32 dB&B⇌↱£48-£56
50P croquet boule *xmas*
English & French V Lunch £7.50 High tea fr£6 Dinner £10.75&alc Last dinner 8.30pm
Credit Cards 1 3 £

★★**Lord Eliot** Castle St PL14 3AQ ☎(0579)42717
Small hotel built around the character house of a one-time country landlord.
15rm(4⇌10↱)(3fb) CTV in all bedrooms ® T
sB&B⇌↱£33.35-£36.80 dB&B⇌↱£46-£57.50
(CTV 60P ♫ *xmas*
English & French V Lunch £5.50-£7 High tea £4.50-£5 Dinner £7.50-£8&alc Last dinner 9.30pm
Credit Cards 1 3 £

★★ **WELL HOUSE**
St Keyne PL14 4RN
☎(0579)42001

The running of this well-proportioned Victorian house is a labour of love for owner Nick Wainsford, who is determined to ensure that his guests' every need is met with a combination of attentive and friendly service. The bedrooms are very individual, well equipped and furnished with taste; fresh flowers, nice pictures and perfumed toiletries complete the scene. The cosy sitting room, with its pleasant outlook over the garden, is very comfortable, with deep settees and an open fire in the cooler months. Dining at Well House is an enjoyable and memorable experience. Chef David Pope is both skilled and imaginative, and his background has well prepared him for this opportunity to create innovative dishes which not only look good, but have realistic flavour combinations. Every attention is paid to detail, his light breads and brioche being as important as his terrine of foie gras and his noisettes of young English lamb, the latter being accompanied by a natural enriched robust sauce of port wine. The wine list is carefully researched, with some 180 bins catering for all tastes, and is realistically priced, ensuring excellent value for money. We strongly recommend you to be advised by the knowledgeable Nick Wainsford in your choice of wine.

7⇌(1fb) CTV in all bedrooms T ✳ sB&B⇌£42.50-£47.50 dB&B⇌£54-£85 Continental breakfast
30P 🚗 ✿ ⇌(heated) 🎾 (hard) croquet nc10yrs
♔ 🍸 Lunch fr£18&alc Dinner fr£27.50&alc Last dinner 9pm
Credit Cards 1 2 3

LITTLE HALLINGBURY

See **Bishop's Stortford**

LITTLE LANGDALE Cumbria Map 11 NY30

★★Three Shires Inn LA22 9NZ ☎Langdale(09667)215
Closed Jan RS mid Nov-mid Feb
A few miles west of Ambleside and north of Coniston, this former AA Norhtern Region "Inn of the Year" offers spotless accommodation for walkers, climbers and other holidaymakers. The slate-floored Cavalier bar and landscaped gardens are popular for substantial bar meals.
11rm(5⇌2♪)(1fb) ® ✖ sB&B£22-£26 dB&B£44-£52 dB&B⇌♪£50-£58
CTV 20P 2🚗 🚗 ✿
☋ British & Continental ♔ 🍸 ⚡ Bar Lunch £1-£8alc Dinner £12.95-£14.95 Last dinner 8pm

See advertisement under AMBLESIDE

LITTLE WEIGHTON Humberside Map 08 SE93

★★★🏠 66% Rowley Manor HU2 3XR
☎Hull(0482)848248
FAX (0482) 849900

This interesting country house, set in a most attractive and tranquil location, offers courteously attentive service and an evening meal that can be highly recommended.
16rm(13⇌3♪)3🛏 CTV in all bedrooms T ✳
sB&B⇌♪£40-£55 dB&B⇌♪£55-£75 🛏
☾ 80P ✿ solarium croquet *xmas*
☋ International V ♔ 🍸 Lunch £10&alc Dinner £10&alc Last dinner 9.30pm
Credit Cards 1 2 3 5

LIVERPOOL Merseyside Map 07 SJ39

See **Town Plan Section**
See also **Blundellsands and Bootle**
★★★★ 56% *Atlantic Tower* Chapel St L3 9RE (Mount Charlotte) ☎051-227 4444 Telex no 627070 FAX 051-236 3973
A distinctive building on Liverpool's famous waterfront, with fine views over the Mersey from many of the compact, but well-appointed bedrooms. The Stateroom restaurant offers a high standard of cuisine and the Clubcar Carver, designed like a Pulman carriage, is noted for its tasty roasts.
226⇌♪(6fb)⚡in 48 bedrooms CTV in all bedrooms ® T
Lift ☾ ▦ 60P 45🚗 CFA ♫
☋ European V ♔ 🍸
Credit Cards 1 2 3 4 5

Book as early as possible for busy holiday periods.

★★★★57% **Liverpool Moat House** Paradise St L1 8JD (Queens Moat) ☎051-709 0181 Telex no 627270 FAX 051-709 2706
Closed 24-28 Dec
Modern purpose-built hotel close to city centre.
251⇌♪(202fb) CTV in all bedrooms ® T sB&B⇌♪fr£70 dB&B⇌♪fr£90 ⊟
Lift ☾ ⊞ ⊁ CFA ⊡(heated) sauna solarium gymnasium whirlpool
☋ English & French V ✲ ⊒ S12.5% Lunch £10-£12&alc High tea £6-£10 Dinner £16-£18&alc Last dinner 10.30pm
Credit Cards [1] [2] [3] [4] [5] [£]

★★★63% **Crest Hotel Liverpool-City** Lord Nelson St L3 5QB (Crest) ☎051-709 7050 Telex no 627954 FAX 051-709 2193
Large, city-centre hotel with comfortable public areas and its own adjacent car park. Bedrooms are spacious but rather dated, although progressive upgrading is underway. Staff are friendly and helpful.
150⇌(2fb)⊁in 53 bedrooms CTV in all bedrooms ® T S% sB&B⇌£35-£64 dB&B⇌£60-£85 ⊟
Lift ☾ 300P (charged) CFA snooker
☋ French V ✲ ⊒ ⊁ S% Lunch £5.95-£7.80&alc High tea £2.50-£3.50 Dinner £10.50-£12.95&alc Last dinner 9.45pm
Credit Cards [1] [2] [3] [4] [5]

★★★62% **St George's** St John's Precinct, Lime St L1 1NQ (Trusthouse Forte) ☎051-709 7090 Telex no 627630 FAX 051-709 0137
Built in 1972 as part of an extensive city centre development, this large hotel provides well-equipped accommodation and is popular with a wide range of customers from tourists to business people using the extensive conference facilities.
155⇌⊁in 15 bedrooms CTV in all bedrooms ® T sB⇌fr£50 dB⇌fr£77 (room only) ⊟
Lift ☾ 1⌂ CFA
V ✲ ⊒ ⊁ Lunch £6.25-£6.50&alc Dinner fr£9.95&alc Last dinner 10pm
Credit Cards [1] [2] [3] [4] [5]

★★★ ***Trials*** 56-62 Castle St L2 7LQ ☎051-227 1021
Telex no 626125
A building that once housed a bank has been converted into a luxury hotel where the delightfully furnished bedrooms all have corner spa baths. Attentive service successfully combines friendliness with professionalism.
20⇌(2fb)4⊠⊁in 3 bedrooms CTV in all bedrooms ® T ✗
Lift ☾ 24⌂ ⊞ ⊡ ⚲ (grass) ⌂
✲ ⊒ Last dinner 10.30pm
Credit Cards [1] [2] [3] [4] [5]

★★**Grange** Holmfield Rd, Aigburth L19 3PQ ☎051-427 2950
Telex no 298928 FAX 051-427 9055
Standing in its own grounds, four miles from the city centre in a surburban area.
25rm(19⇌6♪)(1fb)4⊠ CTV in all bedrooms ® T ✗ (ex guide dogs) sB&B⇌♪fr£27.75 dB&B⇌♪£45.50-£57.50 ⊟
CTV 50P ✲
☋ French V ✲ ⊒ ⊁ Lunch £7.65 Dinner £11.95&alc Last dinner 9pm
Credit Cards [1] [2] [3] [5]

★★**Green Park** 4/6 Greenbank Dr L17 1AN ☎051-733 3382
A Victorian building, situated close to Sefton Park and within easy reach of the city centre, offering comfortable accommodation with up-to-date facilities.
23rm(8⇌8♪)(6fb) CTV in all bedrooms T sB&B£23 sB&B⇌♪£27 dB&B£32 dB&B⇌♪£37 ⊟
☾ ⊞ CTV 25P ✲ ⌂
V ✲ ⊒ Lunch £5.50-£7.50&alc Dinner £5.50-£7.50&alc Last dinner 9pm
Credit Cards [1] [2] [3] [5] [£]

○***Campanile*** Wapping and Chaloner St, Albert Docks(Campanile) ☎Central reservation 01-569 5757
Due to open Feb 1990
83⇌

✕✕**Far East** 27-35 Berry St L1 9DF ☎051-709 3141 & 6072
Situated on the outskirts of the city, this is a restaurant where Cantonese cooking at its best can be tasted. The spacious restaurant is on the first floor while for those only wanting Dim Sum there are many delicious varieties to be sampled on the ground floor.
Closed 25 & 26 Dec
☋ Cantonese V 250 seats ✱ S5% Lunch £4.50-£12.90&alc Dinner £9.20-£12.90alc Last lunch 2pm Last dinner 11.25pm 35P
Credit Cards [1] [2] [3] [5]

LIVINGSTON Lothian *West Lothian* Map 11 NT06

★★★60% ***Hilton National*** Almondvale East(Hilton) ☎(0506)31222 Telex no 727680 FAX (0506) 34666
Popular business hotel with conference and leisure facilities.
120♪(18fb)⊁in 15 bedrooms CTV in all bedrooms ® T
☾ ⊞ ⊁ ✲ ⊡(heated) snooker sauna gymnasium
V ✲ ⊒ ⊁ Last dinner 10pm
Credit Cards [1] [2] [3] [5]

LIZARD, THE Cornwall & Isles of Scilly Map 02 SW71

★★**Housel Bay** Housel Cove TR12 7PG
☎The Lizard(0326)290417 FAX (0326) 290359
Closed Jan-Feb 10
House of Victorian origin superbly situated in cliffside grounds. Breathtaking views from all the public rooms & gardens.
23rm(20⇌3♪)1⊠⊁in 2 bedrooms CTV in all bedrooms ® sB&B⇌♪£18-£36 dB&B⇌♪£36-£66 ⊟
Lift CTV 25P 4⌂ (£2 per night) ✲ *xmas*
☋ International V ✲ ⊒ ⊁ Lunch £6.90 Dinner £11&alc Last dinner 9pm
Credit Cards [1] [2] [3] [£]

★**Kynance Bay House Hotel** Penmenner Rd TR12 7NR
☎The Lizard(0326)290498
Closed Jan
Commanding fine coastal views from its position at the edge of the village, a well-run hotel with a happy family atmosphere offers comfortable bedrooms, a good choice of meals from its short à la carte menu and the charm of a sheltered hidden garden.
9rm(7♪)⊁in all bedrooms ® sB&Bfr£24.50 sB&B♪fr£32 dB&Bfr£49 dB&B♪fr£64 (incl dinner) ⊟
CTV 9P ⊞ ✲ *xmas*
☋ British & Continental V ✲ ⊒ ⊁ Lunch £8.50-£10 Dinner £10.50-£11.50&alc Last dinner 8.30pm
Credit Cards [1] [2] [3] [5]

LLANARMON DYFFRYN CEIRIOG Clwyd Map 07 SJ13

★★★65% **Hand** LL20 7LD ☎(069176)666 FAX (069176) 262
Closed Feb-mid Mar
A peaceful and relaxing country hotel set in the heart of a village that seems ruled by the Berwyn Mountains. Here guests can be assured of peace and quiet as there are no TVs or telephones in bedrooms, and personal service from the proprietors and their staff.

14⇌ CTV in 1bedroom sB&B⇌fr£41 dB&B⇌fr£64 ⊟
CTV 30P ⊞ ✲ ⚲ (hard) ♩ *xmas*
☋ English & Continental V ✲ ⊒ Lunch £9.25 Dinner £15.95 Last dinner 9pm
Credit Cards [1] [2] [3] [5]

★★West Arms LL20 7LD ☎(069176)665 FAX (069176) 262
Country hotel, over 400 years old, situated in a small picturesque village 950ft above sea level.
14⇌(1fb)⊁in 5 bedrooms CTV in 2bedrooms sB&B⇌£41-£46 dB&B⇌£64-£70 ⊟
CTV 30P 2⊞ ❄ ♩ *xmas*
♡ English & Continental **V** Bar Lunch £1.50-£9.50 High tea £1.75 Dinner £15.95 Last dinner 9pm
Credit Cards [1] [2] [3] [5]

LLANBEDR Gwynedd Map **06** SH52

★★Cae Nest Hall
LL45 2NL
☎(034123)349
Closed Dec-Feb (ex Xmas & New Year)

Dating back to the 1480s this stone built manor house stands in three acres of grounds. The hotel is pleasantly furnished and offers warm, friendly service.
10rm(3⇌7)(2fb) CTV in all bedrooms ® ✗ (ex guide dogs)
12P ❄
♡ British & Continental **V** ⊁ Last dinner 7.30pm

See advertisement on page 393

★★Ty Mawr LL45 2NH ☎(034123)440
Comfortable, personally-run hotel, with good home cooking.
10rm(4⇌6♠)(2fb) CTV in all bedrooms ® sB&B⇌♠£22 dB&B⇌♠£44 ⊟
☾ CTV 30P ⊞ ✲ *xmas*
♉ British & Continental **V** ♡ ☐ Lunch £7.50-£10&alc High tea fr£4.50 Dinner £8.50-£10&alc Last dinner 8.45pm

LLANBERIS Gwynedd Map **06** SH56

★Gallt-y-Glyn Caernarfon Rd LL55 4EL ☎(0286)870370
RS Boxing Day
Although extended over the years, part of this hotel dates back to the 17th-century. Now a comfortable small hotel personally owned and run.
8rm(1♠)(1fb) ✗ ✱ sB&B£13.50 dB&B£27
CTV 12P ⊞ ✲
V
Credit Cards [1]

✗✗Y Bistro Glandwr, 43-45 Stryd Fawr LL55 4EU ☎(0286)871278
The pleasures of French and Welsh cooking are combined to good effect in a delightful restaurant at the centre of this very Welsh village. Locally produced lamb is notable for its quality, menus always feature a fresh fish of the day, a more-than-adequate wine list is available and service is both friendly and expert. In addition to the attractively furnished restaurant and comfortable cocktail bar, there are also lounges in which to relax.
Closed 3 wks Jan
Lunch not served
♉ Welsh & French **V** 50 seats ✱ Dinner £15.75-£18 Last dinner 9.30pm ⊁ ⊁
Credit Cards [1] [3]

LLANDDEWI SKYRRID Gwent Map **03** SO31

✿ ✗ *Walnut Tree Inn* NP7 8AW (3m NE of Abergavenny) ☎Abergavenny(0873)2797
In its attractive setting beneath the wooded hill of Ysgyryd Fawr, on the Ross-on-Wye to Abergavenny road, the Walnut Tree has been serving its excellent food for more than 25 years – owners Franco and Ann Taruschio celebrated their Silver Jubilee in November 1988. The cooking, naturally, owes much to the Italian tradition, making use of only the best fresh ingredients, beautifully flavoured, and fish dishes are particularly good. The restaurant is open only for dinner, and at lunchtime, meals and snacks are served at highly polished Britannia tables in the comfortable bars.
Closed Sun , 4 days Xmas & 2 wks Feb
Lunch not served Mon
♉ French & Italian **V** 45 seats 30P

LLANDEGAI Gwynedd Map **06** SH57

○***Rank Motor Lodge*** Bangor Services LL57 4BG (Rank) ☎Central reservations 01-569 7120
Due to open May 1990
35⇌♠

LLANDEILO Dyfed Map **02** SN62

★★★60% *Cawdor Arms* SA19 6EN ☎(0558)823500
Elegant, very comfortable Georgian house offering good quality food.
17rm(13⇌4♠)2⊟ CTV in all bedrooms **T**
7P
♉ English & French ♡ ☐
Credit Cards [1] [2] [3] [5]

LLANDOVERY Dyfed Map **03** SN73

See also **Crugybar**
★★Castle Hotel Kings Rd SA20 0AW (Minotels) ☎(0550)20343
Formerly a coaching inn, this attractive hotel dates back to the 16th century and, historically, has associations with Lord Nelson. Standards of comfort are high, and three popular bars contribute much local character and warmth.
26rm(4fb)2⊟ CTV in all bedrooms ® **T** sB&Bfr£18 sB&Bfr£26 dB&Bfr£35 dB&Bfr£44
CTV 40P ℛ (hard) ♩
V ♡ ☐ Lunch fr£5.80alc High tea £3.50-£5.50alc Dinner £5.80-£8.90alc Last dinner 9.30pm
Credit Cards [1] [3] £

LLANDRILLO Clwyd Map **06** SJ03

★★♛Tyddyn Llan Country House Hotel & Restaurant
LL21 0ST
☎(049084)264
Closed Feb

Set in three acres of attractive gardens and lawns, this elegant eighteenth-century country house has been very carefully furnished to provide comfortable accommodation. Elizabethan-style kitchen gardens produce vegetables and herbs which, together with other local produce, contribute much to the excellence of the meals served.
9rm(7⇌2♠)(2fb) ® **T** sB&B⇌♠£33.75-£37 dB&B⇌♠£53.50-£60 ⊟
CTV 20P ⊞ ✲ ♩ croquet lawn *xmas*
V ♡ ☐ Lunch £3-£10alc Dinner £15 Last dinner 9.30pm
Credit Cards [1] [3]

LLANDRINDOD WELLS Powys Map **03** SO06

See also **Newbridge-on-Wye and Penybont**
★★★61% Hotel Metropole Temple St LDI 5DY ☎(0597)2881
Telex no 35237 FAX (0597) 4828
This large, well run town-centre hotel, under the same family ownership for the past 100 years, is currently being refurbished. Most of the bedrooms are now completed and all are well equipped. There are good conference facilities, an excellent leisure complex and staff are friendly and helpful.
121rm(114⇌7♠)(2fb) CTV in all bedrooms ® **T** sB&B⇌♠£42-£45 dB&B⇌♠£58-£62 ⊟
Lift ☾ 150P ✲ ⊡(heated) sauna solarium steamroom whirlpool beauty salon *xmas*
V ♡ ☐ Lunch £9-£15 Dinner £12-£15 Last dinner 9pm
Credit Cards [1] [2] [3] [4] [5] £

All hotels awarded three or more stars are now also given a percentage grading for the quality of their facilities. Please see p 16 for a detailed explanation.

L

LLANDUDNO Gwynedd Map **06** SH78

See **Town Plan Section**

★★★

★★★ **BODYSGALLEN HALL**

LL30 1RS (on A470 Llandudno link road) (Prestige)
☎Deganwy(0492)84466
Telex no 617163
FAX (0492) 82519

The restoration of this delightful 17th-century house has created a warm, welcoming atmosphere in magnificent surroundings. The public rooms still reflect the origins of the Hall, with fine oak panelling, large fireplaces and several comfortable seating areas of various styles. The bedrooms, however, have 20th-century facilities – modern, comfortable beds, colour television, telephones and such luxuries as toiletries, magazines and swift room service. For those who crave solitude, there are a number of cottages in the grounds which provide accommodation of the same high standard. Chef Martin James has made the restaurant one of the finest in North Wales, using local produce to provide a good choice of dishes on a fixed price menu. Cooking is in the modern style, with intense flavours and lightly cooked vegetables, and is complemented by a wine list of over 200 items, including a good selection of half bottles. Surrounding the hotel are beautifully kept gardens, including a 17th-century knot garden, which produces many culinary herbs, and a walled garden which produces the cut flowers so lovingly displayed throughout the hotel. Beyond the gardens are lovely views towards Snowdonia and the Conwy Valley, and there is no finer panorama that that from the Watch Tower – well worth the climb on a fine day.

19⇌Annexe9rm(8⇌1⋔)(3fb)1⊞ CTV in all bedrooms ® T S5% sB⇌⋔£68-£98 dB⇌⋔£86-£123 (room only) ⊟

☾70P 1⊜ ⊞ ✲ ⚲ (hard) croquet ♫ nc8yrs *xmas*

V ⊕ ⊡ S10% Lunch £10-£12 Dinner £21.50 Last dinner 9.45pm

Credit Cards 1 2 3 5

★★★65% Chatsworth House Central Promenade LL30 2XS ☎(0492)860788
Closed 28 Dec-12 Jan
This well-furnished sea-front hotel offers a good range of facilities and entertainment.
58rm(48⇌10⋔)(13fb)1⊞ CTV in all bedrooms ® T sB&B⇌⋔£35-£44 dB&B⇌⋔£66-£82 (incl dinner) ⊟
Lift ☾ 9P ⊡(heated) sauna solarium jacuzzi *xmas*
⊕ ⊡ ⚟ Lunch fr£4.95 Dinner fr£11 Last dinner 8.30pm
Credit Cards 1 3

★★★64% Empire Church Walks LL30 2HE ☎(0492)860555
Telex no 617161 FAX (0492) 860791
Closed 17 Dec-2 Jan
Family owned and run, this large well-furnished hotel offers an extensive range of facilities including 3 restaurants, an indoor pool and roof garden with a children's paddling pool. A small annexe of bedrooms is furnished in Victorian style to a very high standard.
56⇌Annexe8⇌(7fb)1⊞ CTV in all bedrooms ® T S% sB&B⇌£41.50-£52.50 dB&B⇌£55-£82.50 ⊟
Lift 35P 5⊜ (£5) ⊞ CFA ⊡(heated) ⊇(heated) sauna solarium ♫
⊖ French V ⊕ ⊡ S10% Lunch £9.50 Dinner £14.50 Last dinner 9.30pm
Credit Cards 1 2 3 4 5

★★★65% Gogarth Abbey West Shore LL30 1QY ☎(0492)76211
Closed 18 Dec-20 Jan
A well-furnished and comfortable hotel that has fine views of the Snowdonia Mountains and Conwy Estuary towards Anglesey. The bedrooms are well-equipped, the four lounges delightful and the welcome from the resident owners warm and friendly.
40rm(34⇌6⋔)(4fb) CTV in all bedrooms ® T ✗ (ex guide dogs) ✱ sB&B⇌⋔£25-£40 dB&B⇌⋔£50-£80 ⊟
☾ 40P ✲ ⊡(heated) sauna solarium table tennis pool table ♫
V ⊕ ⊡ ⚟
Credit Cards 1 2 3 £

★★★63% Imperial The Promenade LL30 1AP (Best Western) ☎(0492)77466 Telex no 61606 FAX (0492) 78043
Imposingly placed on the promenade and close to the central shopping areas. Extensive improvements of the last few years include a new leisure centre and refurbished bedrooms.
100rm(98⇌2⋔)(10fb) CTV in all bedrooms ® T
Lift ☾ 40P CFA ⊡(heated) snooker sauna solarium gymnasium ♫
⊕ ⊡ Last dinner 9pm
Credit Cards 1 2 3 5

★★★66% Risboro Clement Av LL30 2ED (Inter) ☎(0492)76343
Telex no 617117 FAX (0492) 79881
Family-owned and run hotel, in a residential area, with a pleasant atmosphere and friendly staff.
65rm(47⇌18⋔)(7fb)1⊞ CTV in all bedrooms ® T S% sB&B⇌⋔£25-£30 dB&B⇌⋔£50-£60 ⊟
Lift ☾ 40P CFA ⊡(heated) ∪ snooker sauna solarium gymnasium ♫ *xmas*
⊖ English & French V ⊕ ⊡ S% Lunch £7.50&alc High tea £9 Dinner £9-£11.50&alc Last dinner 8.30pm
Credit Cards 1 2 3 5 £

★★Bedford Promenade LL30 1BN ☎(0492)76647
Detached Victorian building, three quarters of a mile from the main shopping area. Hotel undergoing major alterations during the currency of this guide.
27⇌(2fb) CTV in all bedrooms ® T
Lift ☾ CTV 20P
⊖ English, French & Italian V ⊕ ⊡
Credit Cards 1 3

★★Belle Vue 26 North Pde LL30 2LP ☎(0492)79547
Closed Nov-Mar
Comfortable hotel overlooking sea provides well-appointed accommodation and good food.
17rm(7⇌10⋔)(2fb) CTV in all bedrooms ® T
sB&B⇌⋔£20-£24 dB&B⇌⋔£40-£48 ⊟
Lift 12P ⊞ table tennis
⊖ French & Italian ⊕ Bar Lunch £3.50-£5 Dinner £8 Last dinner 8pm
Credit Cards 1 2 3 5 £

★★Bromwell Court Promenade LL30 1BG ☎(0492)78416 & 74142
A well-furnished seafront hotel offering a good standard of accommodation. Bedrooms are thoughtfully designed and equipped and public areas are comfortable.
11rm(3⇌6⋔)(2fb) CTV in all bedrooms ® T ✗ (ex guide dogs) ✱ sB&B⇌⋔fr£21 dB&B⇌⋔fr£38 ⊟
P ⊞ nc4yrs *xmas*
V ⊕ ⊡ Lunch £2.50-£4.75 Dinner fr£8 Last dinner 7.30pm
Credit Cards 1 3

For key to symbols see the inside front cover.

★★

26 North Parade, Llandudno, Gwynedd LL30 2LP

This comfortable, family run hotel is ideally situated on the sea front, facing south, with delightful views of the bay.
All rooms are en suite with colour TV, video, telephone, hair dryer and tea/coffee making facilities. Bar. Lift. Car park. Snooker and table tennis. Good food. Self contained luxury flat also available.

Brochure? With pleasure.

Telephone: (0492) 79547

one of Llandudno's largest hotels, set proudly on the promenade with 111 bedrooms, 3 bars and a new leisure complex.

and a friendly Welcome!

The Promenade, Llandudno, Gwynedd, North Wales, LL30 1AP
Telephone: (0492) 77466/9
Telex: 61606 IMPOTL G
Facsimile: (0492) 78043

A privately owned and professionally run hotel in a central position, facing South it boasts sunshine all day long. All 65 bedrooms are en suite and have been luxuriously refurnished to modern yet extremely elegant taste, each equipped with direct dial telephone, colour satellite TV, video service and some rooms with jacuzzi baths. 2 Lifts service all floors from our magnificent ballroom, probably the most sought after in town; to our roof top sun garden. Open all year with Special Mini, Maxi, Ski-Swim, Golf, Xmas and New Year packages. Superb indoor heated swimming pool, maintained at 80°F complimented by 'Gym & Toni'' health Club, containing Spa, Sauna, Steam room, full multi-gym lastest high speed tanning. Conferences are a speciality with 4 suites on site telex, fax and secretarial service, inclusive delegate rates available. Car Parks holds 40 cars – **for information contact Mr COLIN A IRVING. Clement Avenue, Llandudno, LL30 2ED. Tel (0492) 76343.**

Chatsworth House Hotel

Central Promenade, Llandudno, North Wales

AA ★★★

A superbly positioned, central Seafront Hotel. All 57 bedrooms have private bathroom, colour TV, radio-intercom/baby-listening; tea/coffee making facilities, as well as hair driers and direct dial telephone. Facilities include, indoor heated swimming pool, toddlers pool, leisure complex and gamesroom. Coffee Shop open daily. Sun Terrace. Lift. Fully licensed bar. Lounge/ballroom with dancing several nights during Season, & Fridays & Saturdays during Winter months. Championship Golf – 2 miles. Artificial Ski slope and Tobogganing 1 mile. Zoo 5 miles.

Open Christmas. Winter/Spring Breaks. Children Welcome.

Write or telephone (0492) 860788 for Brochure.

Llandudno

★★Bryn-y-Bia Lodge Craigside LL30 3AS
☎(0492)49644 & 40459
A delightful detached house set in its own grounds on the Coastal Road, near the Little Orme, features well-equipped modern bedrooms and elegantly furnished public areas. Good food, ably prepared by the resident owner and served in an attractive dining room, high standards of hospitality and quality accommodation combine to make this hotel something a little special.
13rm(1⇌12↱)(2fb)1▭ CTV in all bedrooms ® T
sB&B⇌↱£20-£24.50 dB&B⇌↱£38-£45 ⛪
20P 🏠 ❋
♕ English & Continental V ✈ ⚡ Bar Lunch £2.50-£5 Dinner £15 Last dinner 8pm
Credit Cards [1] [2] [3]

★★Dunoon Gloddaeth St LL30 2DW ☎(0492)860787
Closed Nov-mid Mar
Centrally situated hotel with attractive, comfortable bedrooms, and a pleasant dining room. Staff are friendly and attentive.
56rm(48⇌8↱)Annexe14⇌(22fb) CTV in all bedrooms ® T
✈ (ex guide dogs) S% sB&B⇌↱£20-£25 dB&B⇌↱£37-£50
Lift CTV 24P solarium
V ✈ ♕ Lunch £6.50-£7.50 Dinner £8.50-£9.50&alc Last dinner 8pm
Credit Cards [1]

★★Esplanade Glan-y-Mor Pde, Promenade LL30 2LL
☎(0492)860300 Telex no 61155
55rm(44⇌11↱)(16fb) CTV in all bedrooms ® T
sB&B⇌↱£28.50-£35 dB&B⇌↱£50-£63 ⛪
Lift ☾ CTV 30P ⚑ 18 games room ♫ *xmas*
♕ English & French V ✈ ♕ Sunday Lunch £6-£7 Dinner £9-£10 Last dinner 8pm
Credit Cards [1] [2] [3] [5] £

★★*Four Oaks* Promenade LL30 1AY ☎(0492)76506
RS Nov-Feb
Large holiday hotel, family run and with modern facilities.
57rm(19⇌8↱)(25fb) CTV in all bedrooms ®
Lift ☾ CTV ⚐ ♫ ⌂
V ✈ ♕ Last dinner 7.30pm

★★Headlands Hill Ter LL30 2LS (Exec Hotel) ☎(0492)77485
Closed Jan-Feb
A relaxed atmosphere prevails in this personally-run hotel, a detached house situated on the Great Orme with superb sea and mountain views.
17rm(12⇌3↱)(4fb)3▭ CTV in all bedrooms ® T ✻
sB&Bfr£21 sB&B⇌↱fr£21 dB&Bfr£42 dB&B⇌↱fr£42 ⛪
CTV 7P 🏠 *xmas*
✈ ⚡ Bar Lunch fr£1.50 Dinner fr£13 Last dinner 8.30pm
Credit Cards [1] [3] [5] £

★★Merrion South Pde LL30 2LN ☎(0492)860022
A well furnished and comfortable hotel occupying a prime position on the Promenade. Family owned and run, it offers good bedrooms, relaxing lounges and well prepared food from an imaginative menu.
67rm(46⇌21↱)(7fb) CTV in all bedrooms ® T
sB&B⇌↱fr£35 dB&B⇌↱fr£55 ⛪
Lift ☾ CTV 16P 25🚗 snooker ♫ ⌂ *xmas*
♕ English & French ✈ ♕ Lunch £8 High tea £2 Dinner £13 Last dinner 8.30pm
Credit Cards [1] [2] [3]

★★Ormescliffe Promenade LL30 1BE ☎(0492)77191
Closed Jan
This large sea-front hotel is family owned and run. It offers good value and has a comfortable lounge.
65rm(28⇌16↱)(10fb) CTV in 44bedrooms ® ✻ sB&B£16-£21
sB&B⇌↱£18-£21 dB&B£32-£34 dB&B⇌↱£36-£40 ⛪
Lift CTV 15P pool table table tennis ♫ ⌂ *xmas*

♕ International ✈ Lunch fr£6.50 Dinner fr£9.50 Last dinner 8pm
Credit Cards [1] [3]

★★Plas Fron Deg 48 Church Walks LL30 2HL
☎(0492)77267 & 860226
Closed Nov-Jan
An elegantly furnished Victorian house in a sheltered position in its own gardens at the foot of the Great Orme. The resident owners provide good standards of food and service and bedrooms are comfortable.
9rm(3⇌6↱)(1fb) CTV in all bedrooms ® T ✈ (ex guide dogs)
S% sB&B⇌↱£20.50-£23 dB&B⇌↱£58-£63 (incl dinner) ⛪
7P 🏠 nc7yrs
V ⚡
Credit Cards [1] [3] [5] £

★★Royal Church Walk LL30 2HW ☎(0492)76476
Closed 24 Dec-29 Jan
Pebble-dashed building located under Great Orme in a residential area.
36rm(14⇌12↱)(11fb) CTV in all bedrooms ® T ✈ (ex guide dogs)
Lift 30P ❋ dry ski slope ♫
V ✈ ♕ Last dinner 8pm
Credit Cards [1] [3] £

❀★★ ST TUDNO

Promenade LL30 2LP
☎(0492)74411
Telex no 61400
Closed 24 Dec-12 Jan

From the moment you enter the St Tudno you know that this is a very special hotel. Martin aned Janette Bland have created something that is quite unique and they and their caring, smiling staff offer warm personal service. Every attention has been paid to the décor and furnishings throughout the hotel, providing individually designed bedrooms and charming public rooms. As well as the cosy lounge, there is a bar lounge, both having good views over the bay. The dining room is pretty and refreshing and here guests can enjoy fine food complemented by a well-balanced wine list. We are confident that guests will be delighted with this hotel of great charm and character.
21rm(19⇌2↱)(4fb)1▭ CTV in all bedrooms ® T ✈ (ex guide dogs) ✻ sB&B⇌↱£45-£59.50 dB&B⇌↱£58-£95 ⛪
Lift 4P 2🚗 (£3) 🏠 ◫(heated)
V ✈ ♕ ⚡ Lunch £8.50-£24alc High tea £5-£12.50alc Dinner £18.25-£18.25&alc Last dinner 9.30pm
Credit Cards [1] [2] [3]

★★Sandringham West Pde LL30 2BD ☎(0492)76513 & 76447
Closed Nov-Feb
A pleasant, family-run hotel, overlooking the sea at West Shore. It offers good standards of comfort, service and food.
17rm(12⇌5↱)(4fb) CTV in all bedrooms ® T ✈
sB&B⇌↱£18-£21 dB&B⇌↱£36-£42 ⛪
CTV 6P games room
V ✈ ⚡ Lunch £5.50-£7.50alc Dinner £8-£9alc Last dinner 7.30pm
Credit Cards [1] [3] £

MERRION HOTEL ★★

South Parade
Llandudno, Gwynedd
Tel: (0492) 860022
Fax: (0492) 860378

A sea front hotel with
all rooms en suite.
Excellent cuisine.
High standards throughout.

Telephone for brochure & tariff.

ESPLANADE Hotel ★★

PROMENADE, LLANDUDNO LL30 2LL
Tel: 0492-860300 (5 lines) Telex: 61155

Premier sea front position. Ideally located for town and leisure facilities. Brochure and tariff on request from the resident manager.

57 comfortable rooms all with bathroom/shower and toilet en suite, colour TV, tea and coffee making facilities and trouser press – all with radio/intercom, baby listening and shaver points, most with direct dial telephone. Central heating in all bedrooms and public rooms. Car park at rear. Fully licensed. 2 resident lounges, lift, games room, small ballroom. Buttery open all year. Free membership of North Wales Golf Club for two. Open all year round – Xmas and New Year inclusive terms available – conferences – parties – Spring and Autumn breaks.

L

★★

HEADLANDS HOTEL

Hill Terrace, Llandudno, Gwynedd LL30 2LS
Telephone: 0492 77485

Where comfort and cuisine are the most important ingredients for your holiday. Simply superb views over the Bay, Conwy Estuary and Snowdonia. Direct access to the country park and only 5 minutes to the shops. Bedrooms have en suite or private bath/shower, TV, radio, direct dial telephone, teas maid and central heating, some four poster beds. Why not spoil yourself – you deserve a holiday with a touch of luxury.

Recommended by Les Routier and Ashley Courtenay.

Deganwy Castle

★★

Station Road
Deganwy
Gwynedd
Telephone:
(0492) 83555

Excellent views from the hotel across the Conwy estuary to Conwy Castle and the Snowdonia mountains.

★★Sefton Court Church Walks LL30 2HL ☎(0492)75262
Set in a quiet road, this pleasantly furnished hotel stands within its own grounds. Good service and hospitality is provided by the resident owners.
14rm(10⇌1↖)(6fb)⅟in 1 bedroom CTV in all bedrooms ® sB&B£16.50-£20 sB&B⇌↖£16.50-£20 dB&B£33-£40 dB&B⇌↖£33-£40 ⊟
CTV 13P *xmas*
☊ Welsh, English & French V ♧ ☕ ⅟ Lunch £7.50 Dinner £7.50 Last dinner 8pm
Credit Cards 1 3

★★Somerset St Georges Crescent, Promenade LL30 2LF ☎(0492)76540
Closed 16 Nov-Feb
Family-run, Victorian seafront hotel with good views of the bay.
37rm(29⇌8↖)(4fb) CTV in all bedrooms ® ✱ sB&B⇌↖£30 dB&B⇌↖£56 (incl dinner)
Lift 20P ♫
V ♧ Bar Lunch 90p-£2.50 Dinner £6 Last dinner 7.30pm
Credit Cards 1 3

★★Tan-Lan Great Orme's Rd, West Shore LL30 2AR ☎(0492)860221
Closed Nov-18 Mar
This elegant family-run hotel provides comfortable bedrooms and warm hospitality.
18rm(10⇌8↖)(4fb) CTV in all bedrooms ® sB&B⇌↖£17-£19 dB&B⇌↖£34-£38 ⊟
15P ⛟
☊ English, French & Italian ♧ ☕ Lunch £6-£7 Dinner £9 Last dinner 8pm
Credit Cards 1 3 £

★Branksome Lloyd St LL30 2YP ☎(0492)75989
Closed Jan-Mar
Good food and service are provided in the pleasantly furnished family-run hotel which stands in a residential area only a short distance from the sea.
48rm(7⇌10↖)Annexe5rm(10fb)
CTV 12P sauna solarium gymnasium ♫
☊ English, French & Italian V ♧ ☕

★Bron Orme 54 Church Walks LL30 2HL ☎(0492)76735
Closed Nov-Feb
Located at the foot of Great Orme, only a short distance from beach and town centre.
9rm(3↖)(4fb) ® ✗ (ex guide dogs) sB&B£11-£12 sB&B↖£13.50-£14.50 dB&B£20-£22 dB&B↖£25-£27
CTV ₱ ⛟ nc5yrs
☊ English & French ♧ ☕ ⅟ Lunch £3-£7.50 Dinner £12.50-£15 Last dinner 7pm

★Clontarf 1 Great Ormes Rd, West Shore LL30 2AR ☎(0492)77621
Closed 30 Dec-Feb
Detached hotel situated in residential area close to the West Shore.
10rm(1⇌3↖)(2fb) ® ✗
CTV 10P ⛟ ✲ nc3yrs
V ♧ ☕ ⅟ Last dinner 7.30pm

★Cornerways 2 St David's Place LL30 2UG ☎(0492)77334
Closed Nov-Etr
This small, family-run, private hotel stands in a quiet residential area only a few minutes' walk from the town centre.
8rm(6⇌1↖)(1fb) CTV in all bedrooms ® ✗ sB&Bfr£13 sB&B⇌↖fr£18 dB&B⇌↖£26-£30
5P ⛟ nc10yrs
☊ British & Continental ☕ ⅟ Lunch fr£6 Dinner fr£9 Last dinner 7pm
Credit Cards 1 2 3

★Gwesty Leamore 40 Lloyd St LL30 2YG ☎(0492)75552
Closed Dec
"Croeso" means "welcome" and this you will find at Leamore, a bright, clean hotel with well-equipped bedrooms and comfortable public areas, personally-run by the Welsh-speaking proprietors.
12rm(1⇌6↖)(4fb) CTV in all bedrooms ® ✗ S% sB&B£15-£16.50 sB&B⇌↖£17-£18.50 dB&B£26-£29 dB&B⇌↖£30-£33 ⊟
CTV 4P ⛟
V ⅟ S% Bar Lunch £2-£4 Dinner £7-£8 Last dinner 7.30pm
£

★Hilbre Court Great Ormes Rd, West Shore LL30 2AR ☎(0492)76632
Closed Nov-Mar
Edwardian house in residential area, near West Shore.
10rm(3⇌3↖)(1fb)⅟in 2 bedrooms CTV in all bedrooms ® sB&B£18.50-£19.50 sB&B⇌↖£21.50-£22.50 dB&B£39 dB&B⇌↖£43-£45 (incl dinner) ⊟
CTV 6P ⛟ *xmas*
V ♧ ☕ ⅟ Lunch £4.50&alc Dinner £6.50&alc Last dinner 8pm
Credit Cards 1 2 3 £

★Min-y-Don North Pde LL30 2LP ☎(0492)76511
Closed Nov-Jan
Family-run holiday hotel on the sea-front, near the shops.
20rm(2⇌9↖)(9fb) CTV in all bedrooms ® ✗ sB&B£15 sB&B⇌↖£16.70 dB&B£30 dB&B⇌↖£33.40 ⊟
⊞ CTV 5P *xmas*
V ♧ ☕ ⅟ Lunch £3.95-£5.95 High tea £2.50 Dinner £6.95 Last dinner 7.30pm
£

★Oak Alyn Deganwy Av LL30 2YB ☎(0492)76497 due to change to 860320
Closed Jan-mid Feb RS Feb
Centrally located for the beach and shops, the friendly family-run hotel, with its pleasantly-appointed bedrooms and lounges, represents good value for money.
14rm(4⇌10↖)(2fb) CTV in all bedrooms ® sB&B⇌↖£12.25 dB&B⇌↖£24.50 Continental breakfast ⊟
CTV 16P
☊ British & Continental ♧ ⅟ Lunch £6.50 Dinner £6.50 Last dinner 7.30pm
Credit Cards 1 3

★Quinton 36 Church Walks LL30 2HN ☎(0492)76879 & 75086
Closed Nov-Jan (ex Xmas)
This family-run hotel stands in a quiet part of the town, both beaches being within walking distance.
15rm(4⇌5↖)(8fb) CTV in all bedrooms ® T ✱ sB&B£16.50 sB&B⇌↖£18-£18.50 dB&B£33-£35 dB&B⇌↖£36-£38 (incl dinner) ⊟
20P *xmas*
♧ ☕
Credit Cards 1

★Ravenhurst West Pde LL30 2BB ☎(0492)75525
Closed mid Nov-Feb
The family-run hotel, set on the town's west shore, offers well-equipped bedrooms and comfortable lounges.
23rm(17⇌6↖)Annexe1⇌(4fb) CTV in all bedrooms ® sB&B⇌↖£26-£29 dB&B⇌↖£52-£58 (incl dinner) ⊟
15P table tennis pool table ♫
V ♧ ☕ Lunch fr£4&alc Dinner £7.50&alc Last dinner 7.30pm
Credit Cards 1 3 5

The AA's star-rating scheme is the market leader in hotel classification.

★Sunnymede West Pde LL30 2BD ☎(0492)77130
Closed mid Nov-Feb
The caring, family-run hotel enjoys a good location, and very high standards of comfort prevail in bedrooms and public rooms.
18rm(14⇌3↑)(3fb)2⊟ CTV in all bedrooms ® ✱
sB&B⇌↑£13-£17 dB&B£26-£34 dB&B⇌↑£26-£34 ⊟
18P
♈ ⊒ Bar Lunch £1.50-£6 Dinner £7-£9 Last dinner 7pm
Credit Cards [1] [3] ⓔ

✕✕The Floral Victoria St, Craig-y-Don LL30 1LJ
☎(0492)75735
A friendly, well-furnished restaurant standing in a side street just off the Promenade offers a wide choice of dishes, all well prepared from fresh ingredients, including such specialities as Chicken Buckingham (breast of chicken in a cream and prune sauce). An extensive wine list carries a full description of each item, staff are particularly helpful and attractive décor enhances the pleasant atmosphere.
Lunch not served Sat
Dinner not served Sun
V 60 seats ✱ Lunch £6.95-£8.10 Dinner £12-£18alc Last lunch 1.30pm Last dinner 9.30pm P nc10yrs
Credit Cards [1] [3]

✕✕Lanterns 7 Church Walks LL30 2HD ☎(0492)77924
Closed Sun, Mon, 25-30 Dec & mid Feb-mid Mar
Lunch not served
☋ French **V** 24 seats Dinner £15-£30alc Last dinner 9.30pm
P nc10yrs
Credit Cards [1] [2] [3] [5]

LLANELLI Dyfed Map **02** SN50

★★★55% Diplomat Felinfoel SA15 3PJ ☎(0554)756156
FAX (0554) 751649
A warm, relaxing atmosphere pervades the open-plan public areas of this family-run hotel, which also features recently upgraded bedrooms and excellent leisure facilities, furnished to a high standard.
31⇌(2fb) CTV in 23bedrooms ® **T** sB&B⇌£45-£55
dB&B⇌£55-£60 ⊟
Lift 300P ✼ ▭(heated) sauna solarium gymnasium turkish bath ♫
☋ English & French **V** ♈ ⊒ Lunch £9.95&alc Dinner £9.95&alc Last dinner 9.45pm
Credit Cards [1] [2] [3] [5] ⓔ

★★★52% Stradey Park Furnace SA15 4HA (Trusthouse Forte)
☎(0554)758171 Telex no 48521
Conveniently positioned company-owned hotel with purpose-built accommodation designed for business clients.
80⇌(3fb)⚟in 8 bedrooms CTV in all bedrooms ® S%
sB⇌£54-£60 dB⇌£65-£70 (room only) ⊟
Lift ☾ 120P CFA ♫ *xmas*
☋ International **V** ♈ ⊒ ⚟ S% Lunch £7.50-£7.95 Dinner £10.25-£10.95&alc Last dinner 9.30pm
Credit Cards [1] [2] [3] [4] [5]

LLANFAIR PWLLGWYNGYLL Gwynedd Map **06** SH57

★★★62% *Carreg Bran Country* Church Ln LL61 5YH
☎Llanfairpwll(0248)714224 Telex no 61464
FAX (0248) 715983
Well furnished modern hotel offering a good standard of accommodation. Situated on the Menai Straits close to the Britannia Bridge.
29⇌Annexe4⇌(5fb) CTV in all bedrooms ® **T**
☾ 150P ✼ ⌂
☋ French **V** ♈ ⊒ Last dinner 10pm
Credit Cards [1] [2] [3] [5]

See advertisement on page 401

LLANFYLLIN Powys Map **06** SJ11

★★ Bodfach Hall
SY22 5HS
☎(069184)272
Closed 19 Nov-24 Dec & Jan-2 Mar

A warm relaxed atmosphere awaits the guests at this 17th century country house. Ornate ceilings, wood-panelled walls and some original William Morris wallpaper in the lounge are noteworthy features.
9rm(7⇌2)(2fb) CTV in all bedrooms ® sB&B⇌fr£25 dB&B⇌fr£50
20P ✲ xmas
V Lunch fr£7.50 Dinner fr£11.75 Last dinner 8.45pm
Credit Cards 1 2 5

LLANGAMMARCH WELLS Powys Map **03** SN94

★★★ 76% Lake
LD4 4BS
☎(05912)202

Popular with fishermen and birdwatchers, this elegant and hospitable Victorian house stands in 50 acres of beautiful grounds. Tennis, pitch-and-putt, horseriding, billiards and clay pigeon shooting are available as well as fishing. Individually styled bedrooms combine character with comfort, and the innovative cooking uses local produce. Smoked duck and chicken in filo pastry with a wild bramble sauce, and a selection of seafoods in a lemon butter sauce, have been recommended by our inspectors.
19⇌(1fb)3 in 6 bedrooms CTV in all bedrooms ® T
sB&B⇌£58.50 dB&B⇌£78.50
70P 2 ✲ 9 (hard) snooker clay pigeon shooting xmas
English & French Lunch £10.50-£11.50 Dinner £18.50 Last dinner 8.45pm
Credit Cards 1 2 3

LLANGEFNI Gwynedd Map **06** SH47

★★ *Nant-yr-Odyn* Llanfawr LL77 7YE (S of junction A5/A5114)
☎(0248)723354
14rm(7⇌7) CTV in all bedrooms ® T
30P
Credit Cards 1 3

Entries for rosetted restaurants, red-star and country-house hotels are highlighted by a tinted panel. For a full list of these establishments, consult the Contents page.

LLANGOLLEN Clwyd Map **07** SJ24

★★★ 65% *Bryn Howel*
LL20 7UW (2.75m E A539)
☎(0978)860331
Closed Xmas Day

This Tudor-style hotel with modern extensions is situated down a quiet country lane on the outskirts of Llangollen. The large restaurant which has panoramic views of the Dee Valley is renowned for its quality meals created from the freshest of ingredients, often locally produced. Visitors to Bryn Howel can also explore the 6-acre grounds and take advantage of the game fishing facilities This hotel is also popular for all types of conferences and functions.
38⇌ CTV in all bedrooms ® T
CTV 200P ✲ CFA sauna solarium
International V
Credit Cards 1 2 3

★★★ 56% The Royal Bridge St LL20 8PG (Trusthouse Forte)
☎(0978)860202 FAX (0978) 861824
Three-storey stone hotel, situated in the centre of town on the bank of the River Dee.
33⇌(3fb) in 6 bedrooms CTV in all bedrooms ®
sB⇌£52-£57 dB⇌£67-£72 (room only)
20P xmas
V Lunch fr£7.50 Dinner fr£10.25 Last dinner 9.30pm
Credit Cards 1 2 3 4 5

★★ Ty'n-y-Wern Shrewsbury Rd LL20 7PH (1m E on A5) (Exec Hotel) ☎(0978)860252
Originally a farm cottage, this small family-run hotel has been thoughtfully extended to offer comfortable accommodation. The interesting menu uses fresh ingredients and bar snacks are readily available. Trout and salmon rods are available on the River Dee.
12rm(10⇌2) in 2 bedrooms CTV in all bedrooms ® T ✳
sB&B⇌£25-£32.50 dB&B⇌£32-£42
CTV 80P ✲ ♫ xmas
English & French V Lunch £2.50-£9.50 Dinner £2.50-£10&alc Last dinner 9.30pm
Credit Cards 1 3

See advertisement under CHESTER

LLANGURIG Powys Map **06** SN98

★★ *Glansevern Arms* Pant Mawr SY18 6SY (4m W on Aberystwyth Rd) ☎(05515)240
Closed 10 Days at Xmas
Comfortable modern facilities, good food, and a welcome as warm as its log fires are the hallmarks of this cosy inn, set just above the River Wye on the main A44 road.
8rm(7⇌1) CTV in all bedrooms ®
40P

LLANGYBI Gwent Map **03** ST39

★★★★ 67% Cwrt Bleddyn Llangybi NP5 1PG
☎Tredunnock(0633)49521
Originally a small country manor house set in fine gardens, Cwrt Bleddyn has been extensively but sympathetically extended over the years. A leisure complex is a recent addition.
▶

Bryn Howel Hotel

Llangollen, Clwyd. ★★★

Telephone: 0978 860331

Set in 6 acres of its own grounds, this 19th Century Manor House has been extended in a style that provides comfortable, pleasant and restful surroundings, ideal for conferences, dinners/dances and weddings, large or small. Noted for good food, wine and hospitality. Parking for 200 cars. Game fishing on hotel's private waters. Telephone, TV etc in all rooms. Full central heating throughout. Golf and stables nearby. Barclaycard and Access credit cards.

Awarded the European Gold Crown. 2 miles east of Llangollen along the A539. The personal supervision of A Lloyd MHCIMA and family ensure your comfort.

BODFACH HALL ★★

LLANFYLLIN
POWYS SY22 5HS

An exceptionally attractive Country House, secluded in 4 acres of mature garden, well off the Oswestry/Lake Vyrnwy road. All of the nine bedrooms have private bathrooms, all have colour TV. Good homely fare is complemented by an interesting wine list. Llanfyllin is an ideal centre from which to visit the many places of interest in Mid and North Wales.

Brochure: Mr and Mrs Ian Gray,
Llanfyllin (069184) 272.

Nant yr Odyn

COUNTRY HOTEL ★★

Llanfawr, Llangefni, Isle of Anglesey LL77 7YE

Telephone: Llangefni (0248) 723354

The present house and buildings were built circa 1700 with the original dwelling standing in 1282. The hotel is located near the centre of this picturesque island. Within easy reach are the fine sandy beaches, various National Trust properties and castles of Beaumaris and Caernarvon. Tennis, golf, fishing and wind surfing are available in the area. All 14 bedrooms are en suite and have colour TV, telephone, radio alarm and tea/coffee making facilities. The licensed restaurant offers excellent food and drink. The Studio has facilities for practising artists or as a conference or lecture room. Open to non residents.

Church Lane, Llanfair PG, Gwynedd

Tel: (0248) 714224 Fax: (0248) 715983

Ideally situated for businessmen and tourists, easily located off the first exit from Brittannia Bridge.

The Proprietors, Managers and staff pride themselves on the quality of service offered to guests.

All 33 en-suite bedrooms have full central heating, remote control satellite television, direct dial telephone, beverage facilities, hair dryer and trouser press.

Our elegant restaurant offers à la carte and table d'hôte meals.

Our conference/function room accommodating approximately 150 people is ideal for seminars/trade shows and buffets are available.

For your Business Lunch/Conference/ Function or Seminar visit the Carreg Bran.

L

27⇌↱Annexe3⇌↱(5fb)3⊟ CTV in all bedrooms ® **T** ✈ (ex guide dogs) ✱ sB&B⇌↱£58.50-£105 dB&B⇌↱£74.50-£105 ⊟
☾CTV 200P ✲ ⊡(heated) ⚲ (hard) squash snooker sauna solarium gymnasium ♫ ⌂ *xmas*
☋ Welsh & French **V** ♧ ⊻ Lunch £12.25-£16.95&alc Dinner £16.95&alc Last dinner 10pm
Credit Cards [1] [2] [3] [5]

See advertisement under USK

LLANGYNOG Powys Map **06** SJ02

★**New Inn** SY10 0EX ☏Pennant(069174)229
Comfortable family-run inn set in mountain hamlet.
7rm(2⇌)(1fb) sB&B£14 dB&B£28 dB&B⇌£32
CTV 18P pool
V ♧ ⊻ Lunch £3.95 Dinner £4.75-£10.50alc Last dinner 9.45pm
£

LLANIDLOES Powys Map **06** SN98

★***Red Lion*** Longbridge St SY18 6EE ☏(05512)2270
Closed 25 Dec
Good-value meals, clean but modest accommodation and a friendly atmosphere are provided by this family-run inn at the centre of a small market town.
6rm(1fb) CTV in all bedrooms ®
CTV 10P
V ♧
Credit Cards [1] [2] [3]

LLANRUG Gwynedd Map **06** SH56

★★★♛79% **Seiont Manor**
LL55 2AQ
☏Caernarfon (0286)76887 & 77349
FAX (0286) 2840

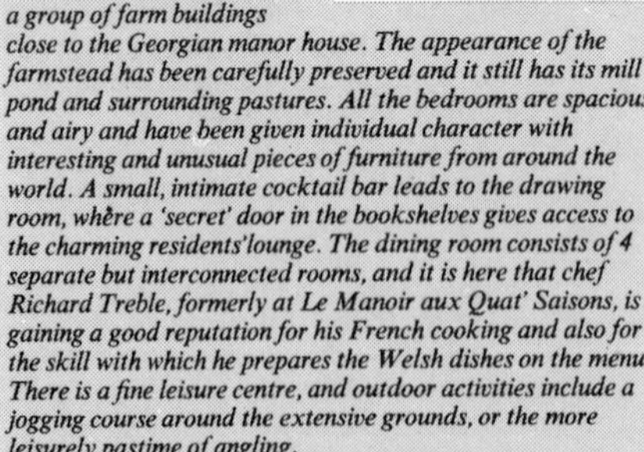

Midway between Caernarfon and Llanberis, Seiont Manor Hotel has been created from a group of farm buildings close to the Georgian manor house. The appearance of the farmstead has been carefully preserved and it still has its mill pond and surrounding pastures. All the bedrooms are spacious and airy and have been given individual character with interesting and unusual pieces of furniture from around the world. A small, intimate cocktail bar leads to the drawing room, where a 'secret' door in the bookshelves gives access to the charming residents' lounge. The dining room consists of 4 separate but interconnected rooms, and it is here that chef Richard Treble, formerly at Le Manoir aux Quat' Saisons, is gaining a good reputation for his French cooking and also for the skill with which he prepares the Welsh dishes on the menu. There is a fine leisure centre, and outdoor activities include a jogging course around the extensive grounds, or the more leisurely pastime of angling.
28⇌↱(7fb)1⊟ CTV in all bedrooms **T** ✱ sB&B⇌↱£60 dB&B⇌↱£80-£125
⊞ 30P ✲ ⊡(heated) ▶ 18 ♪ sauna solarium gymnasium *xmas*
☋ French **V** ♧ ⊻ ⚟ Lunch £16.50 Dinner fr£16.50 Last dinner 10pm
Credit Cards [1] [2] [3] [5]

LLANRWST Gwynedd Map **06** SH76

★★★62% ***Maenan Abbey*** Maenan LL26 0UL (Exec Hotel) ☏Dolgarrog(049269)247 & 230
This 19th-century stone building, with an impressive carved oak staircase, is situated on the site of an old monastery. Bedrooms are well furnished and have good facilities, and roaring open log fires burn in the bars during the winter months.
12rm(9⇌3↱)(2fb) CTV in all bedrooms ®
60P ✲ ♪ clay pigeon shooting ♫
☋ Welsh, English & French **V** ♧ ⊻
Credit Cards [1] [2] [3] [5]

★★★♛63% ***Plas Maenan Country House*** Maenan
LL26 0YR (3m N)
☏Dolgarrog(049269)232

Standing in an elevated position overlooking the Conwy Valley, this large, elegant country house has excellent river and mountain views. Set in 15 acres of grounds and terraced gardens, it is well furnished throughout and offers a relaxed and friendly atmosphere together with well-cooked food, including Welsh and vegetarian specialities.
15⇌(2fb)1⊟⚟in 3 bedrooms CTV in all bedrooms ®
80P ✲ ⌂
☋ Welsh, English & French **V** ♧ ⊻ Last dinner 9pm
Credit Cards [1] [3] [5]

★★**Eagles** LL26 0LG ☏(0492)640454 FAX (069 02) 777
An impressive stone-built hotel set on the banks of the Conwy at the centre of the market place offers good facilities in all areas.
12rm(10⇌2↱)(5fb) CTV in all bedrooms ® **T** ✱ sB&B⇌↱£25-£30 dB&B⇌↱£35-£40 ⊟
CTV 50P ♪ sauna solarium gymnasium pool ⌂
☋ Welsh, English & French **V** ♧ ⚟ Lunch fr£6.50 Dinner fr£11&alc Last dinner 9pm
Credit Cards [1] [3] [5]

★★**Meadowsweet** Station Rd LL26 0DS ☏(0492)640732
A well furnished, comfortable hotel on the edge of the village and close to the River Conwy. The very good standard of cooking is matched by an extensive wine list.
10↱(3fb) CTV in all bedrooms **T** ✱ sB↱£28.50-£36 dB↱£38-£48 (room only) ⊟
10P ⊞
☋ French ♧ ⚟ Dinner £17.75 Last dinner 9.30pm
Credit Cards [1] [3] £

LLANTWIT MAJOR South Glamorgan Map **03** SS96

★★**West House** West St CF6 9SP ☏(04465)2406 & 3726
Pleasantly positioned in a quiet village setting, yet also convenient for businessmen, the attractive little country house hotel has a cosy bar and lounge plus an intimate dining room which maintains commendable standards of cooking.
20rm(16⇌)(1fb)1⊟ CTV in all bedrooms ® **T** ✱ sB&B£28 sB&B⇌£35 dB&B£38 dB&B⇌£45 ⊟
☾CTV 60P ♫ *xmas*
☋ English & French **V** ♧ ⊻ ⚟ Lunch £3.75-£7.50 High tea £1.50-£3.50 Dinner £7.50-£9.50&alc Last dinner 9pm
Credit Cards [1] [2] [3]

See advertisement under CARDIFF

✕✕✕ **Colhugh Villa Restaurant** Flanders Rd CF6 9RL
☎(04465)2022
Lunch not served Tue-Sat
Dinner not served Monday
V 75 seats Sunday Lunch fr£7.95 Dinner fr£14.95&alc Last dinner 9.30pm 40P
Credit Cards 1 2 3 5

LLANWDDYN Powys Map **06** SJ01

★★★ 68% Lake Vyrnwy
SY10 0LY
☎(069173)692
FAX (069173) 259

The hotel, which enjoys a superb location overlooking the lake, has been totally refurbished to provide facilities befitting the 1980's. Private fishing is available, together with shooting over 18, 000 acres.

30rm(29⇌1↱)(12fb)2 CTV in all bedrooms **T**
sB&B⇌↱£45 dB&B⇌↱£50-£100
70P 4 (hard) clay & game shooting sailing *xmas*
British & French **V** Lunch fr£8.45 High tea fr£2.50 Dinner fr£18.75 Last dinner 9.30pm
Credit Cards 1 2 3 4 5 £

L

LLANWNDA Gwynedd Map **06** SH45

★★★63% **Stables** LL54 5SD (Inter) ☎(0286)830711 & 830935 FAX (0286) 830413
A motel-style operation with well-equipped bedrooms. The restaurant, which serves good food, is situated in converted stables.

Annexe14rm(13⇨1↱)(2fb)1⊞ CTV in all bedrooms ® T sB&B⇨↱£35 dB&B⇨↱£52 ⊟
40P ✲ ⩯
♡ International V ♦ ⊻ Lunch £5.25-£5.95 Dinner fr£10.50&alc Last dinner 9.30pm
Credit Cards 1 2 3

LLECHRYD Dyfed Map **02** SN24

★★★⚜52% ***Castell Malgwyn*** SA43 2QA (0.5m S unclass rd towards Boncath)
☎(023987)382

An elegant 18th-century mansion set in 40 acres of gardens and woodland. Inside, the hotel's public areas are spacious and comfortable while outside guests can use the heated swimming pool. Salmon and trout fishing in the Teifi is also available.
22rm(20⇨2↱)(3fb) CTV in 23bedrooms ® T
50P ✲ ⩯(heated) ⌡ putting croquet
V ♦ ⊻ Last dinner 9.30pm
Credit Cards 1 2 3 5

LLYSWEN Powys Map **03** SO13

★★**Griffin Inn** LD3 0UR ☎(087485)241
An ideal base for touring, beside the A470 south of Builth Wells, the small, personally-run inn has character bars and comfortable bedrooms.
6rm(4⇨2↱) ® T ✻ sB&B⇨↱£21.50-£23.50 dB&B⇨↱£38.50-£42.50 ⊟
CTV 14P ⛟ ⌡
V ♦ Lunch £8-£12.50 Dinner £8-£13.50&alc Last dinner 9pm
Credit Cards 1 2 3 5

LOCHAILORT Highland *Inverness-shire* Map **13** NM78

★**Lochailort Inn** PH38 4LZ ☎(06877)208
The small roadside inn offers genuine Highland hospitality and a practical standard of accommodation.
7rm(1fb) ® ✻ sB&B£15-£17 dB&B£30-£34 ⊟
CTV 20P ⛟ pool table deer stalking
V ♦ ⊻ S10% Lunch £5-£10alc
£

LOCHBOISDALE

See **South Uist, Isle of**

LOCHEARNHEAD Central *Perthshire* Map **11** NN52

★**Lochearnhead** Lochside FK19 8PU ☎(05673)229
Closed mid Nov-mid Mar
Homely little hotel with lovely views.
14rm(1⇨3↱) CTV in all bedrooms ®
sB&B⇨↱£18.15-£23.75 dB&B⇨↱£28.90-£36.90
CTV 80P ⛟ ✲ ⌡ squash water sking windsurfing sailing
♡ Scottish & French V ♦ ⊻ Bar Lunch £1-£8alc Dinner £6-£15alc Last dinner 9pm
Credit Cards 1 2 3 5

★**Mansewood Country House** FK19 8NS ☎(05673)213
Set amidst beautiful scenery, this charming little family-run hotel offers a cosy atmosphere, peaceful relaxation and good home cooking. Bedrooms are compact, but cheery and comfortable.
7rm(4⇨1↱) ® ✻ sB&B£18 sB&B⇨↱£20 dB&B£36 dB&B⇨↱£40
16P ⛟ ✲ surfing sailing canoeing water-skiing
♦ ⚟ Dinner £12 Last dinner 8.30pm
Credit Cards 1 3

LOCHINVER Highland *Sutherland* Map **14** NC12

★★★77% **Inver Lodge** IV27 4LU (Best Western) ☎(05714)496 Telex no 75206 FAX (05714) 395
Closed 15 Oct-1 May
Literally hewn out of the hillside, this modern tourists' and sporting hotel has attractive rooms with magnificent views of harbour, loch and mountains.
20⇨(2fb) CTV in all bedrooms ® T ✻ S10% sB&B⇨fr£58.30 dB&B⇨fr£88 ⊟
30P ⛟ ✲ ⌡ snooker sauna solarium
♦ ⊻ S10% Lunch fr£13.75 Dinner £20.35&alc Last dinner 9pm
Credit Cards 1 2 3 5

LOCKERBIE Dumfries & Galloway *Dumfriesshire* Map **11** NY18

★★★53% **Lockerbie House** Boreland Rd DG11 2RG (1m N off B273) (Consort) ☎(05762)2610 Telex no 57515 ext 17 FAX (05762) 3046
New resident owners continue to improve this Georgian country mansion. The lounges are spacious and comfortable, the bedrooms attractively refurbished and the service, provided by the young, local staff, friendly and informal.
26⇨↱(2fb)3⊞ CTV in all bedrooms ® T sB&B⇨↱£38.50 dB&B⇨↱£55-£75 ⊟
CTV 100P 1⌂ ✲ *xmas*
♡ English & French V ♦ ⊻ ⚟ Lunch £7.50 High tea £5.90-£10.45 Dinner £13-£18.50alc Last dinner 9.30pm
Credit Cards 1 2 3 5 £

★★**Dryfesdale** DG11 2SF ☎(05762)2427
Peacefully situated in its own grounds and yet conveniently close to the A74, this former manse offers comfortable accommodation and is personnally managed by the resident proprietors. In the attractive restaurant guests can enjoy not only well-prepared meals but also fine views of the surrounding countryside.
16rm(13⇨1↱)(1fb) CTV in all bedrooms ® T sB&B£28 sB&B⇨↱£36 dB&B£44 dB&B⇨↱£56 ⊟
CTV 50P ⛟ ✲ ⌂
V ♦ ⊻ Lunch £8.50&alc Dinner £11.75 Last dinner 9.00pm
Credit Cards 1 2 3

★★**Queens Hotel** Annan Rd DG11 2RB ☎(05762)2415
Conveniently situated adjacent to the A74, this sturdy Victorian house has been extended and improved to provide well-equipped, modern bedrooms, a leisure complex and conference facilities.
21rm(12⇨9↱)(2fb) CTV in all bedrooms ® T ✻
sB&B⇨↱fr£30 dB&B⇨↱fr£48 ⊟
200P ⩯(heated) snooker sauna solarium gymnasium
V ♦ ⊻ ⚟ Lunch fr£8.25 Dinner fr£10.50&alc Last dinner 9.15pm
Credit Cards 1 3

See advertisement on page 407

The Dryfesdale Hotel

★★

Lockerbie
Telephone 05762 2427

Quietly situated very close to the A74 overlooking Lockerbie with panoramic views of the surrounding countryside.

A beautifully appointed family run hotel where comfort and relaxation are the keywords. 16 bedrooms all but 2 en suite and 6 on the ground floor with full facilities for disabled persons.

The restaurant has a renowned reputation and a wide selection of bar meals is also available.

Open all the year round.

Mansewood

COUNTRY HOUSE

Lochearnhead, Perthshire, Scotland FK19 8NS
Telephone: 05673 213

Farm Holiday Guide Award Winner 1986
Recommended Scottish Good Hotels Book

GUESTACCOM **AA★** **RELAIS ROUTIERS**

Mansewood Country House is a small informal, friendly hotel, ideally situated for touring some of the loveliest areas of Scotland. As there is no television, guests can enjoy an evening of friendly conversation with each other in the lounge, sun lounge or small residents' bar. We offer a good standard of food. Dinner is served between 19.30 and 20.30 hrs and breakfast from 8.30 until 9.30am. All bedrooms are double glazed and beds have electric blankets. There is a log fire in the diningroom and a wood burning stove in the lounge. The hotel has full central heating. Rooms with en-suite available. For brochure please telephone or send a stamp.

Sue and Jeff Jeffrey look forward to welcoming old and new friends to their lovely home.

Lockerbie House Country Hotel

★ ★ ★

Lockerbie, Dumfries & Galloway
DG11 2RG
Telephone: (05762) 2610

A delightful Country Mansion situated in 78 acres of Woodland yet only ½ mile from the main A74 London-Glasgow road, 1 mile North of Lockerbie on the B723, 25 miles North of CARLISLE. An ideal staging post for the traveller. Free Golf on Lockerbie and Moffat courses.

Castell Malgwyn Hotel

Llechryd, Cardigan, Dyfed, SA43 2QA.
Telephone 023 987 382

★ ★ ★

This lovely old country mansion hotel, set in over 4[illegible] acres of its own gardens and woodland with salmon and trout fishing, offers comfortable rooms, all ensuite. Excellent traditional cooking. Heated outdoor pool. Colour TV in rooms, radio and baby listening, tea and coffee facilities and BT telephone . Bargain breaks, Winter weekends, Christmas Holidays. Children sharing parents rooms accommodated free. For full details and colour brochure please telephone or write to the above address.

★★**Somerton House** Carlisle Rd DG11 2DR
☎(05762)2583 & 2384
A charming small hotel, enthusiastically run by the resident proprietors. The comfortable well-equipped bedrooms are generally spacious and some have been redecorated with pretty wallpapers and fabrics. Fresh local produce features on the reasonably priced menus on offer in the popular restaurant.
7rm(6⇨1♠)(2fb) CTV in all bedrooms ® T ✱
sB&B⇨♠£25-£30 dB&B⇨♠£40-£45
CTV 150P ❊
International V Lunch £7.75-£8.95alc Dinner £10.50-£12.75alc Last dinner 9.30pm
Credit Cards 1 2 3

LOLWORTH Cambridgeshire Map **05** TL36

○**TraveLodge** Huntingdon Rd CB3 8DR (A604) (Trusthouse Forte) ☎Crafts Hill(0954)81335
20⇨♠(20fb) CTV in all bedrooms ® sB⇨♠fr£21.50 dB⇨♠fr£27 (room only)
50P
V
Credit Cards 1 2 3

Alphabetical Index of
LONDON HOTELS & RESTAURANTS

	Page No.	*Key No.*	*Plan Reference*
Ajimura Japanese (WC2) ✕	443	2	Plan 1 D4
Alastair Little (W1) ❀✕	437		(not on plan)
Annas Place (N1) ✕	422		Plan 5 D4
Arirang (W1) ✕	437	3	Plan 1 A4
Ark (W8) ✕	440	2	Plan 2 A3
L'Arlequin (SW8) ❀✕✕	429		Plan 5 D3
Athenaeum (W1) ★★★★	432	4	Plan 2 E4
Auberge de Provençe (SW1) ✕✕✕	425	3	Plan 3 B2
Au Jardin des Gourmets (W1) ❀✕✕	436	4	Plan 1 B4
Aunties (W1) ✕	437	4	Plan 3 A6
Avoirdupois (SW3) ✕✕	427	5	Plan 2 C1
Basil Street (SW3) ★★★	427	71	Plan 2 D3
La Bastide (W1) ✕✕	436	5	Plan 1 B4
La Bastille (EC1) ✕	422	1	Plan 4 A4
Bayleaf Tandoori (N6) ✕✕	422		Plan 5 D5
Belvedere (W8) ✕✕✕	440		Plan 5 C3
Berkeley (SW1) ★★★★★	424	8	Plan 2 D4
Bibendum (SW3) ❀✕✕	427	9	Plan 2 C2
Bloomsbury Crest (WC1) ★★★	441		(not on plans)
Bombay Brasserie (SW7) ✕✕✕	429	10	Plan 2 B2
Boulestin (WC2) ❀✕✕✕	443	7	Plan 1 D3
Boyd's Glass Garden (W8) ✕✕	440	11	Plan 2 A4
Brinkley's (SW10) ✕✕	429		Plan 5 C3
Britannia (W1) ★★★★	432	12	Plan 2 E5
Brown's (W1) ★★★★	432	5	Plan 3 A4
Le Café des Amis du Vin (WC2) ✕	443	9	Plan 1 D4
Café Flo (NW3) ✕	423		Plan 5 D4
Le Café du Jardin (WC2) ✕	443	12	Plan 1 E4
Cannizaro House (SW19) ★★★★	430		Plan 5 C2
Capital (SW3) ❀★★★★	426	13	Plan 2 D3
Carnarvon (W5) ★★★	439		Plan 5 B4
Cavalier's (SW8) ❀✕✕	429		Plan 5 D3
Cavendish (SW1) ★★★★	424	14	Plan 1 A2
Central Park (W2) ★★★	438	14	Plan 2 A5
Chambeli (W1) ✕✕	436	6	Plan 3 A5
Chesa (Swiss Centre) (W1) ✕✕	436	15	Plan 1 C3
Chez Nico (W1) ❀❀❀✕✕	436	16	(not on plan)
Chesterfield (W1) ★★★	434	16	Plan 2 E5
Chinon (W14) ✕	441		Plan 5
Churchill (W1) ★★★★★	430	18	Plan 2 D6
Ciboure (SW1) ❀✕	426	19	Plan 2 E3
Claridges (W1) ★★★★★	430	20	Plan 2 E6
Clarke's (W8) ★★	440		
Clifton-Ford (W1) ★★★	434	21	Plan 2 E6
Connaught (W1) ❀❀★★★★★	431	22	Plan 2 E5
La Croisette (SW10) ✕	429	23	Plan 2 A1
Crowthers (SW14) ✕	430		Plan 5 C3
Cumberland (W1) ★★★★	432	24	Plan 2 D6
Dan's (SW3) ✕	428	25	Plan 2 C1
Daphne's (SW3) ✕✕	427	26	Plan 2 C2
Drury Lane Moat House (WC2) ★★★	442	19	Plan 1 D5
Duke's (SW1) ★★★★	424	20	Plan 1 A1
Eatons (SW1) ✕	426	30	Plan 2 E2
Ebury Court (SW1) ★	425	31	Plan 2 E3
English Garden (SW3) ✕✕	427	32	Plan 2 D2
English House (SW3) ✕✕	427	33	Plan 2 D2
Frederick's (N1) ✕✕	422		Plan 5 D4
Frith's (W1) ✕	438	21	Plan 1 B4
Fuji Japanese (W1) ✕	438	22	Plan 1 B3

London

Gallery Rendezvous (W1) ✕✕	436	23	Plan 1 A3
Le Gavroche (W1) ❀❀❀✕✕✕✕	434	36	Plan 2 E5
Gavvers (SW1) ✕✕	425	37	Plan 2 E2
Gay Hussar (W1) ✕✕	436	24	Plan 1 B4
Ginnan (EC4) ✕	422	2	Plan 4 A4
Gloucester (SW7) ★★★★	428	38	Plan 2 A2
Good Earth (NW7) ✕✕	423		Plan 5 C5
Good Earth, Brompton Rd (SW3) ✕✕	427	40	Plan 2 C3
Goring (SW1) ★★★★	424	8	Plan 3 A2
The Greenhouse (W1) ✕✕✕	436	41	Plan 2 E5
Grosvenor House (W1) ★★★★★	431	43	Plan 2 E5
Happy Wok (WC2) ✕	443	25	Plan 1 D4
Harvey's (SW17) ❀❀✕✕	430		Plan 5 C2
Hilaire (SW7) ❀✕✕	429	44	Plan 2 B2
Hilton International Kensington (W11) ★★★	440		Plan 5 C3
L'Hippocampe (SW6) ✕	428		Plan 5 C3
Holiday Inn-Marble Arch (W1) ★★★★	433	46	Plan 2 C6
Holiday Inn-Swiss Cottage (NW3) ★★★★	423		Plan 5 D4
Hospitality Inn on the Park (W2) ★★★	438	47	Plan 2 A5
Hyatt Carlton Tower (SW1) ★★★★★	424	48	Plan 2 D3
Hyde Park (SW1) ★★★★★	424	49	Plan 2 D4
Ibis Greenwich	423		Plan 5 E3
Inigo Jones (WC2) ✕✕✕✕	442	28	Plan 1 D3
Inn on the Park (W1) ★★★★★	431	50	Plan 2 E4
Inter-Continental (Le Soufflé) (W1) ❀★★★★★	431	51	Plan 2 E4
Interlude de Tabaillau (WC2) ✕✕	443	29	Plan 1 D4
Kalamara's (W2) ✕	438	53	Plan 2 A5
Ken Lo's Memories of China (SW1) ❀✕✕	426	10	Plan 3 A1
Kensington Close (W8) ★★★	439		Plan 5 C3
Kensington Palace Thistle (W8) ★★★★	439	54	Plan 2 A3
Kensington Place (W8) ✕	440		(not on plan)
Kerzenstuberl (W1) ✕	438	55	Plan 2 E6
Koto Japanese (NW1) ✕	422		Plan 5 D4
Lai Qila (W1) ✕✕	437	11	Plan 3 A1
Langan's Brasserie (W1) ✕✕	437	12	Plan 3 A3
Lee Ho Fook (W1) ✕	438	31	Plan 1 B3
Leith's (W11) ✕✕✕	440		Plan 5 C3
Hotel Lexham (W8) ★★	439	56	Plan 2 A2
Lindsay House (W1) ✕✕	437	32	Plan 1 C4
Little Akropolis (W1) ✕	438		(not on plan)
London Embassy (W2) ★★★	438	58	Plan 2 A5
London Hilton (W1) ★★★★★	436	45	Plan 2 E4
London Hilton Hotel (Trader Vic's) (W1) ✕✕✕✕	436	45	Plan 2 E4
London Marriot (W1) ★★★★	433	60	Plan 2 E6
London Ryan (WC1) ★★★	442		(not on plans)
London Tara (W8) ★★★★	439		Plan 5 C3
Ma Cuisine (SW3) ✕	428	62	Plan 2 C2
Mandeville (W1) ★★★	434	63	Plan 2 E6
Mario (SW3) ✕✕	427	64	Plan 2 C2
Marlborough Crest (WC1) ★★★★	441	33	Plan 1 C5
Martin's (NW1) ✕✕	422	65	Plan 2 D6
May Fair Inter-Continental (W1) ★★★★★	431	13	Plan 3 A4
Maxim Chinese (W13) ✕	441		Plan 5
Maxim's Wine Bar (SW1) ✕✕	426	67	Plan 2 D3
Le Mazarin (SW1) ❀✕✕	426		Plan 5 D3
Ménage à Trois (SW3) ✕✕	428	68	Plan 2 D3
Meridiana (SW3) ✕✕	427	69	Plan 2 C2
Le Meridien (Oak Room) (W1) ❀★★★★★	431	35	Plan 1 A2
Michel (W8) ✕	440		Plan 5 C3
Mijanou (SW1) ✕✕	426	70	Plan 2 E2
Mr Kai of Mayfair (W1) ✕✕	437	71	Plan 2 D6
Mr Ke (NW3) ✕	423		Plan 5 D4
Montcalm (W1) ★★★★	433	72	Plan 2 D6
Mount Royal (W1) ★★★	434	73	Plan 2 D6
M'sieur Frog (N1) ✕	422		Plan 5 D4
Nayab Indian (SW6) ✕✕	428		Plan 5 C3
Neal Street (WC2) ✕✕✕	443	36	Plan 1 D4
New World (W1) ✕	438	37	Plan 1 C3
Ninety Park Lane (W1) ❀✕✕✕✕✕	434	43	Plan 2 E5
Novotel London (W6) ★★★	439		Plan 5 C3

Number 10 (W1) ✕✕	437	14	Plan 3 A4
Odin's (W1) ❀✕✕	437		(not on plan)
Park Court (W2) ★★★	438	74	Plan 2 A5
Park Lane (W1) ★★★★	433	75	Plan 2 E4
Peter's Bistro (NW6) ✕	423		Plan 5 C4
Le Plat du Jour (NW1) ✕	423		Plan 5 D4
Pollyanna's (SW11) ✕	430		Plan 5 D3
La Pomme d'Amour (W11) ✕✕	440		Plan 5 C3
Poons (WC2) ✕	444		
Poon's of Russell Square (WC1) ✕✕	442	15	Plan 3 C6
Portman Inter-Continental (W1) ★★★★	433	77	Plan 2 D6
Post House (NW3) ★★★	423		Plan 5 D4
Le Poulbot (EC2) ❀✕✕✕	422	3	Plan 4 B4
Princess Garden of Mayfair (W1) ✕✕✕	436	79	Plan 2 E6
Quincy's 84 (NW2) ✕	423		Plan 5 C4
Ramada (W1) ★★★★	433	42	Plan 1 A5
Red Fort (W1) ✕✕	437	43	Plan 1 B3
Regent Palace (W1) ★★	424	44	Plan 1 B3
The Regency (SW7) ★★★	429		(not on plan)
Rembrandt (SW7) ★★★	429	81	Plan 2 C3
Restaurant 192 (W11) ✕	440		Plan 5 C3
Ritz (W1) ★★★★★	432	16	Plan 3 A3
Royal Garden (W8) ★★★★★	439	82	Plan 2 A4
Royal Horseguards Thistle (SW1) ★★★	425	46	Plan 1 D1
Royal Lancaster (W2) ★★★★	438	83	Plan 2 B5
Royal Trafalgar Thistle (WC2) ★★★	442	47	Plan 1 C2
Royal Westminster Thistle (SW1) ★★★★	425	17	Plan 3 A1
RSJ The Restaurant on the South Bank (SE1) ✕	423	18	Plan 3 E3
Rubens (SW1) ★★★	425	19	Plan 3 A2
La Ruelle (W8) ❀✕✕	440		Plan 5 C3
Rue St Jacques (W1) ❀✕✕✕	436	48	Plan 1 B5
Hotel Russell (WC1) ★★★★	441	20	Plan 3 C6
St George's (W1) ★★★★	433	21	Plan 3 A5
St Quentin (SW3) ✕✕	428	84	Plan 2 C3
Salloos (SW1) ❀✕✕	426	85	Plan 2 D3
Santini (SW1) ✕✕	426	22	Plan 3 A1
Savoy (WC2) ❀★★★★★	442	50	Plan 1 E3
Savoy Grill (WC2) ✕✕✕✕✕	442	50	Plan 1 E3
Selfridge (W1) ★★★★	433	87	Plan 2 E6
Seven Dials (WC2) ✕✕	443	51	Plan 1 C4
Sheraton Park Tower (SW1) ★★★★★	424	88	Plan 2 D4
Stafford (SW1) ★★★★	425	52	Plan 1 A1
Strand Palace (WC2) ★★★	442	53	Plan 1 E3
Le Suquet (SW3) ✕	428	90	Plan 2 C2
Sutherlands (W1) ❀✕✕	437	54	Plan 1 A4
Swallow International (SW5) ★★★	428	91	Plan 2 A2
Tante Claire (SW3) ❀❀✕✕	428	92	Plan 2 D1
Tast of India (WC2) ✕	444	55	Plan 1 E4
Thomas de Quincey's (WC2) ✕✕	443	56	Plan 1 E3
Tiger Lee (SW5) ✕✕	428	93	Plan 2 A1
Tower Thistle (E1) ★★★★	422	4	Plan 4 C3
Turners (SW3) ❀✕✕	428	95	Plan 2 C2
Wakaba (NW3) ✕	423		Plan 5 D4
Waldorf (WC2) ★★★★	442	57	Plan 1 E4
Waltons (SW3) ✕✕✕✕	427	96	Plan 2 C2
Westbury (W1) ★★★★	433	26	Plan 3 A4
White's (W2) ★★★★	438	97	Plan 2 B5
Yumi (W1) ✕✕	437	98	Plan 2 D6
Zen Chinese (SW3) ✕✕✕	427	99	Plan 2 D1
Zenw 3 Chinese (NW3) ✕	423		Plan 5 D4

London Postal Districts and ways in and out of London

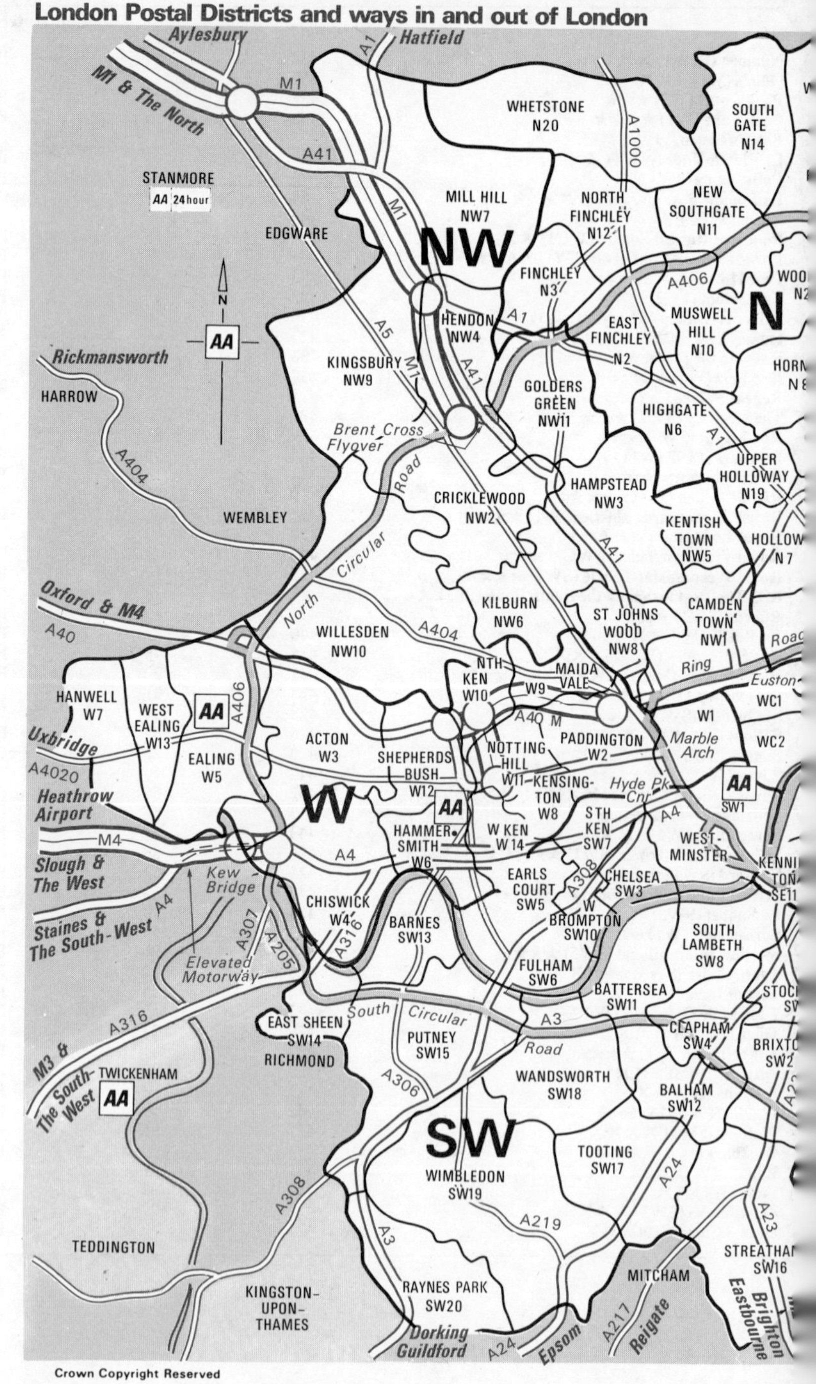

London

London Postal Area Boundary
London Postal District Boundaries
Main Roads into and out of London
Signposted North and South Circular
Roads & Ring Road
Other Main Roads
Service Centre
AA
Scale of Miles
0
1
2
3
4
ambridge
A10
LOWER EDMONTON N9
CHINGFORD E4
UPPER EDMONTON N18
Epping
A104
A11
M11
TOTTENHAM N17
SOUTH WOODFORD E18
A1400
A406
A12
Chelmsford
Southend
SOUTH TOTTENHAM N15
A503
WALTHAMSTOW E17
GANTS HILL
A12
A114
Romford
North Circular Road
TOKE WINGTON N16
LEYTON E10
LEYTONSTONE E11
A118
A106
ILFORD
ILFORD
CLAPTON E5
MANOR PARK E12
FOREST GATE E7
HACKNEY WICK E9
E
A11
A406
HACKNEY E8
A102 (M)
BARKING
A117
BOW E3
STRATFORD E15
Tilbury
BETHNAL GREEN E2
PLAISTOW E13
EAST HAM E6
A13
R THAMES
A13
STEPNEY E1
Road
LIMEHOUSE E14
NORTH WOOLWICH E16
THAMESMEAD SE28
Ring
Free Ferry
ROTHERHITHE SE16
ABBEY WOOD SE2
DEPTFORD SE8
CHARLTON SE7
Erith
A102 M
A205
WOOLWICH SE18
A206
NEW CROSS SE14
GREEN WICH SE10
A202
A2
SE
PECKHAM SE15
BLACKHEATH SE3
WELLING
BROCKLEY SE4
A21
A207
EAST DULWICH SE22
LEWISHAM SE13
A20
A2
A2
South
ELTHAM SE9
FOREST HILL SE23
A205
LEE SE12
A20
Rochester
Motorway
Dover
CATFORD SE6
SYDENHAM SE26
SIDCUP
PENGE SE20
A20
A21
BROMLEY
AA
Sevenoaks
Sevenoaks
Hastings
A224

London Plan 1

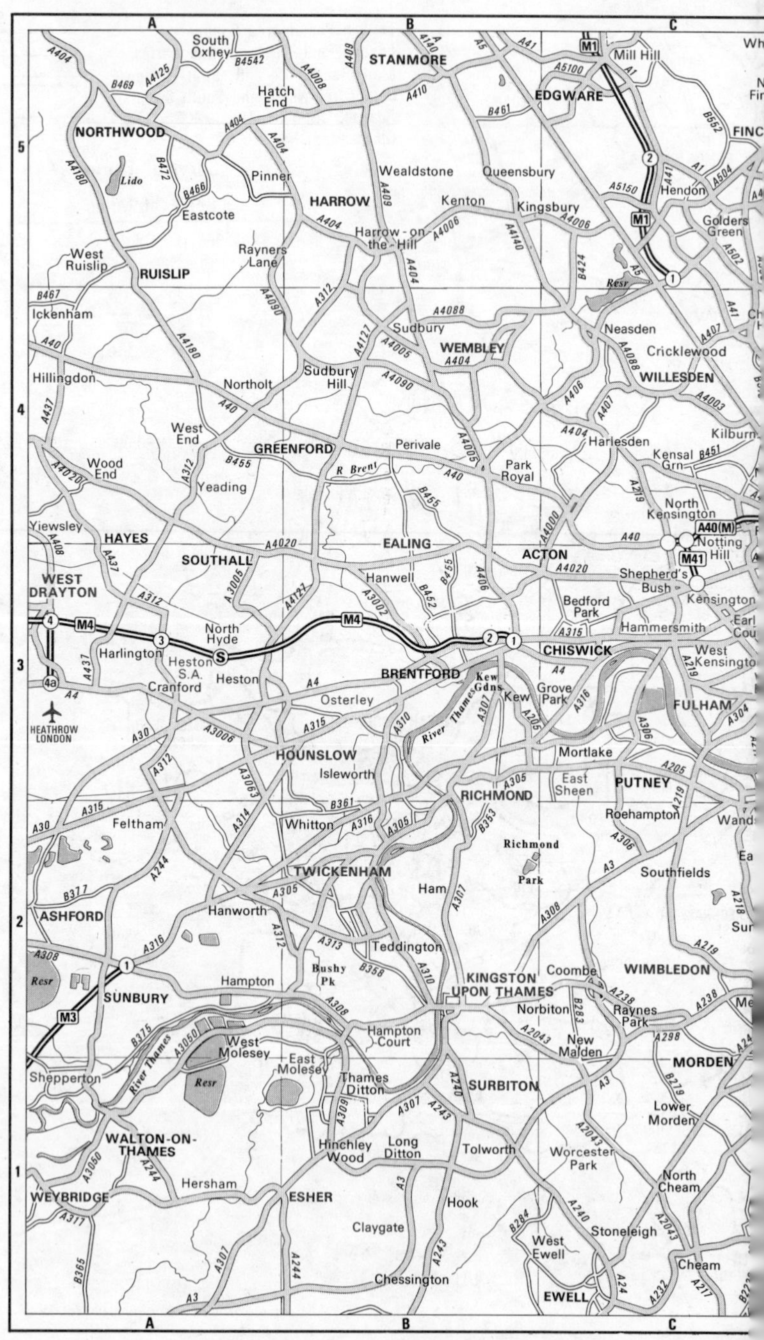

London

London Plan 1

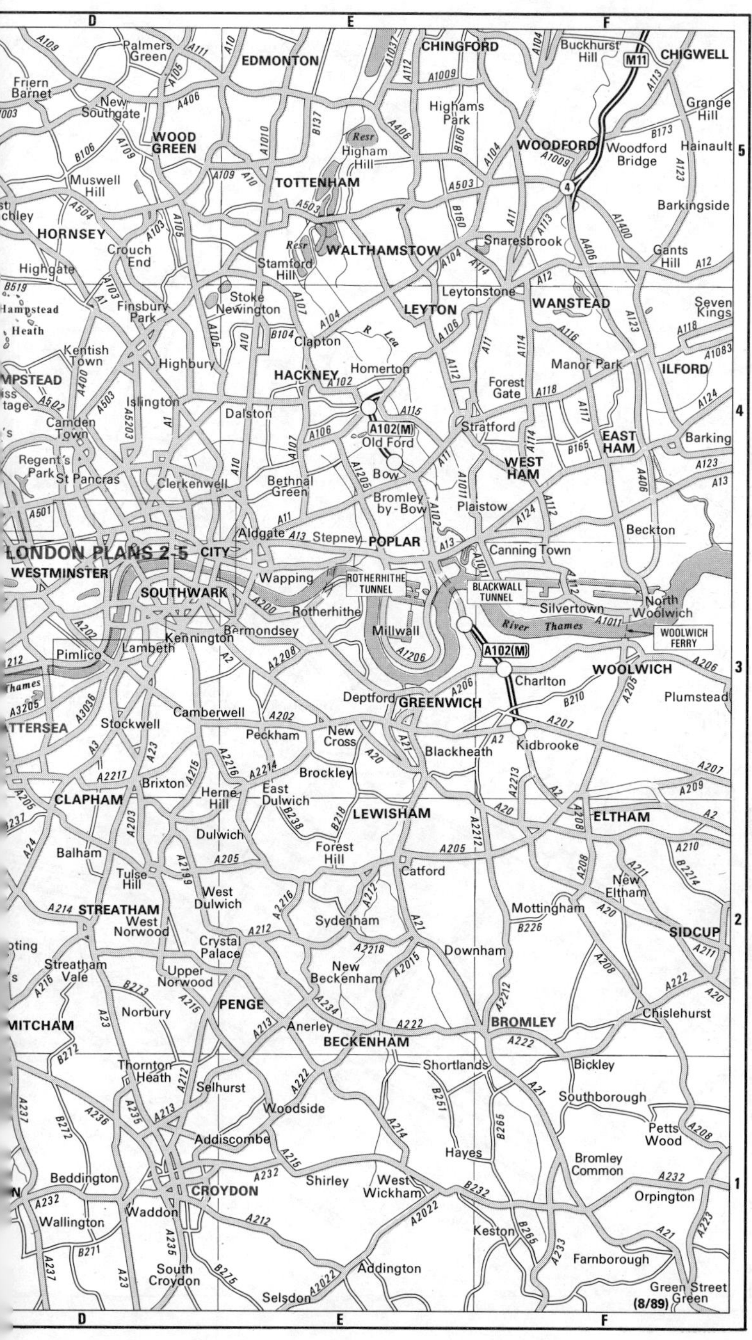

London

London Plan 2

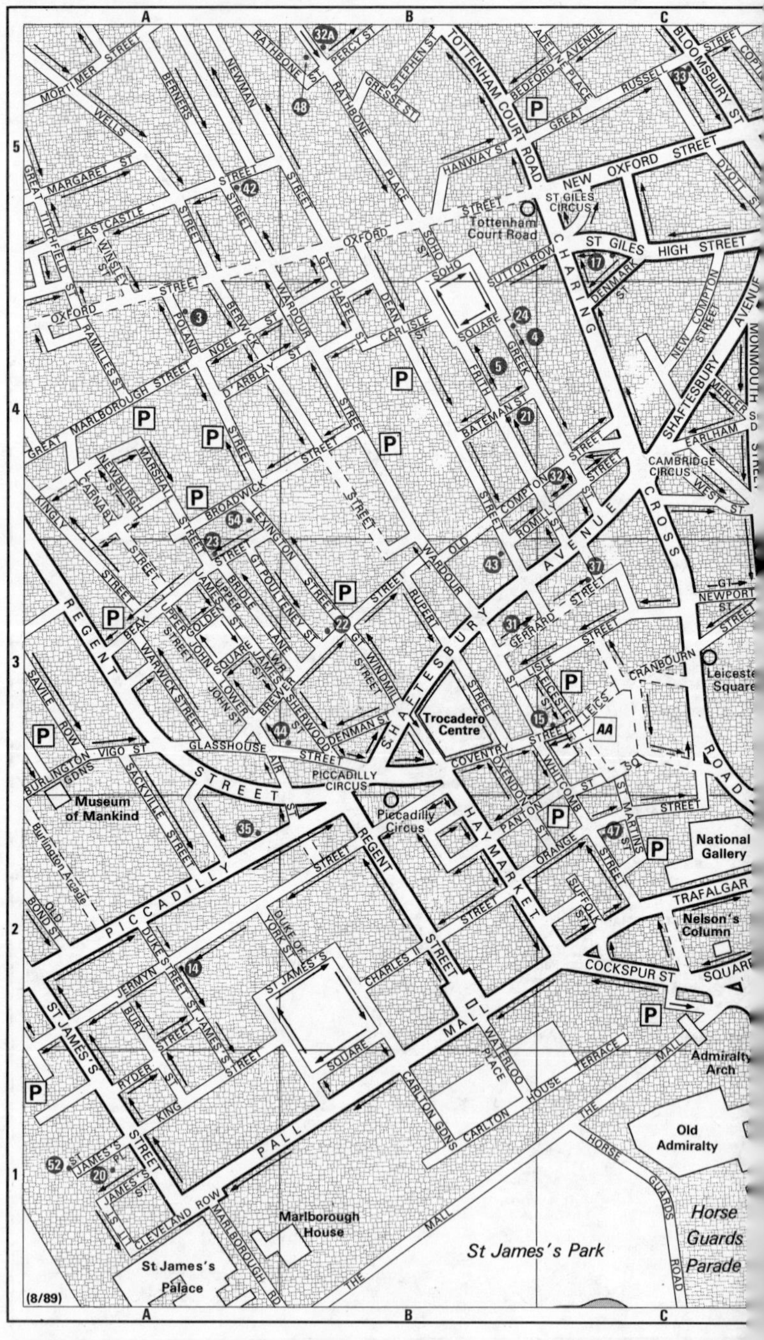

London

London Plan 2

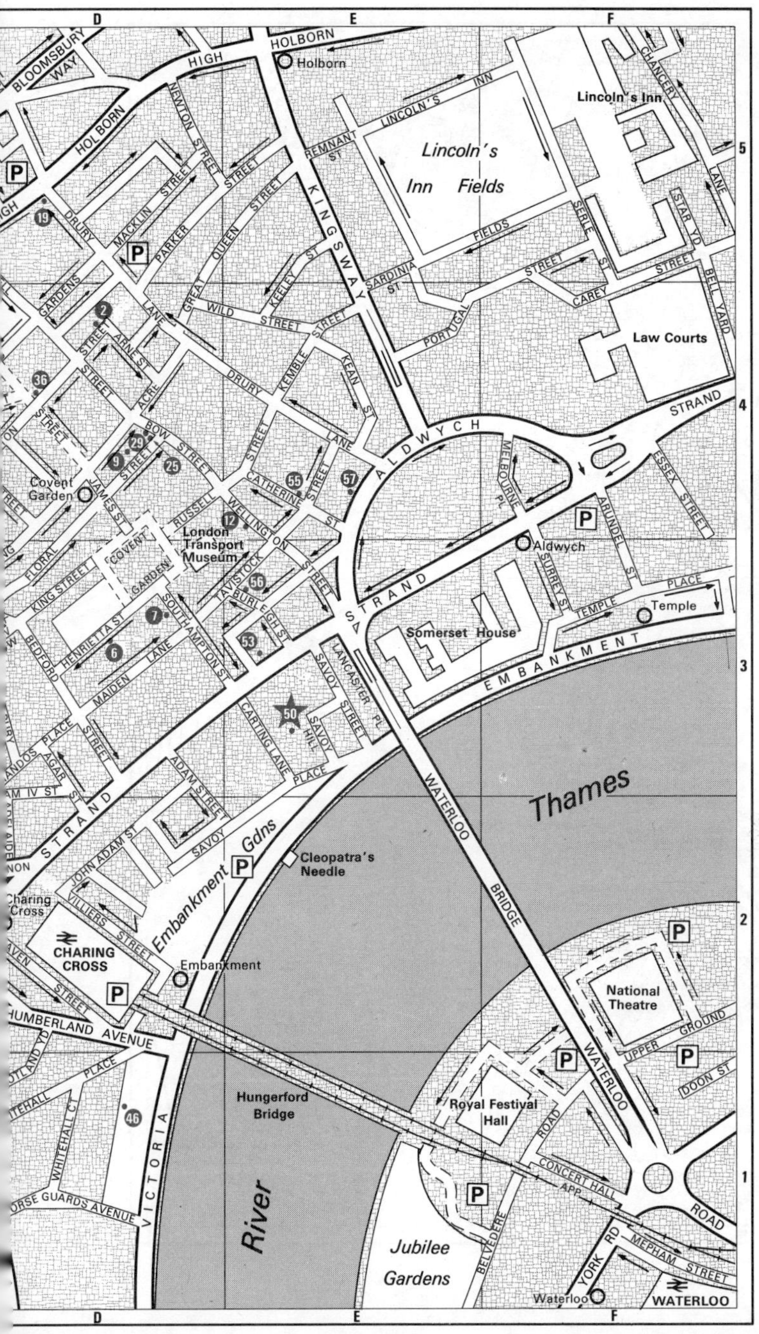

London

London Plan 3

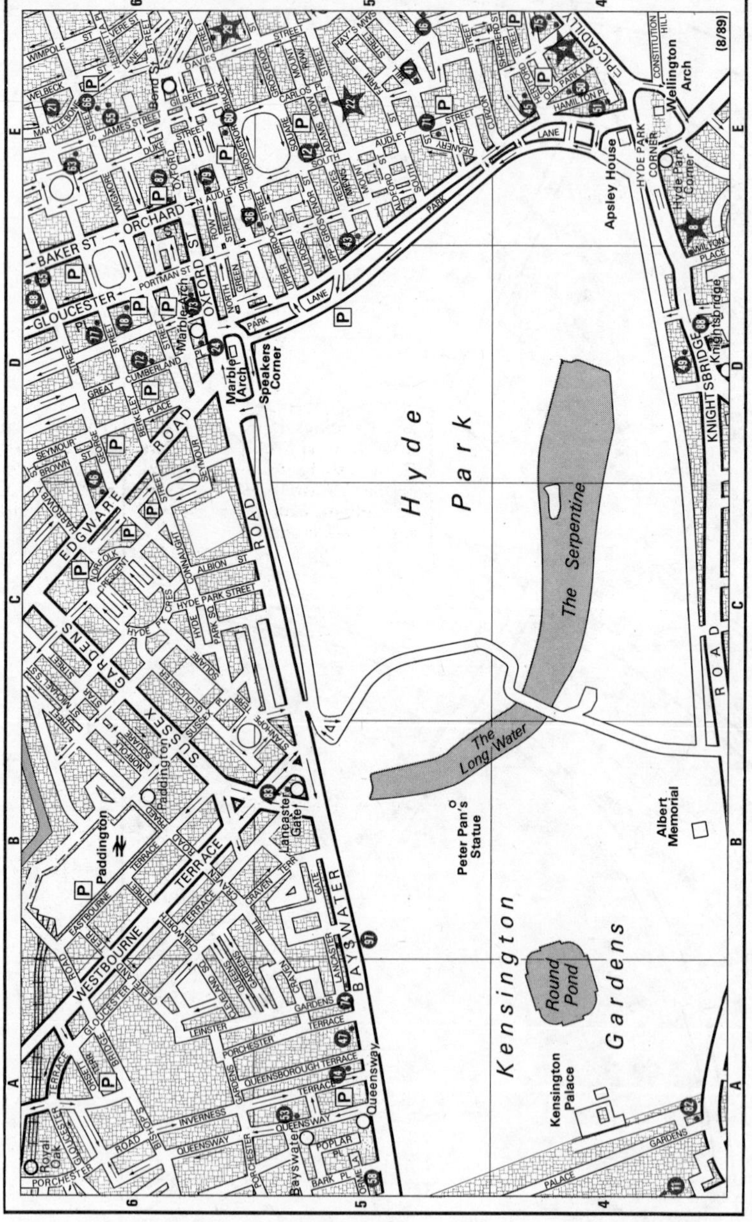

London Plan 3

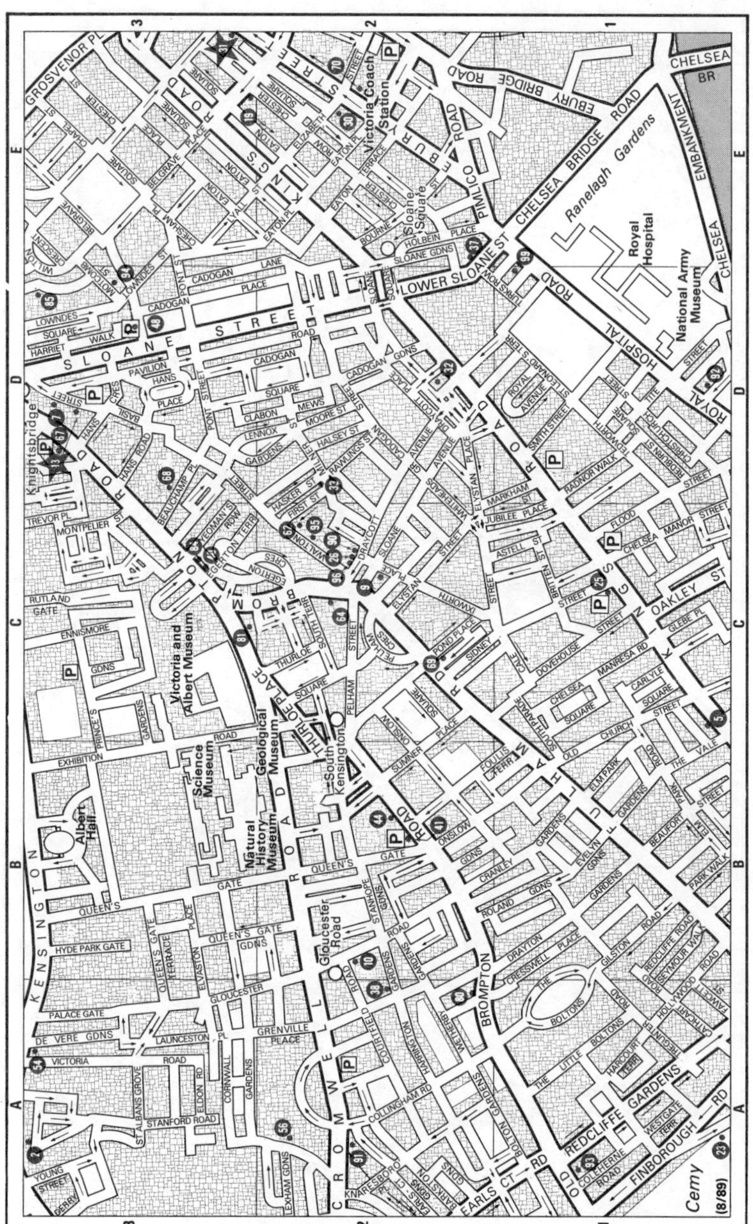

London

London Plan 4

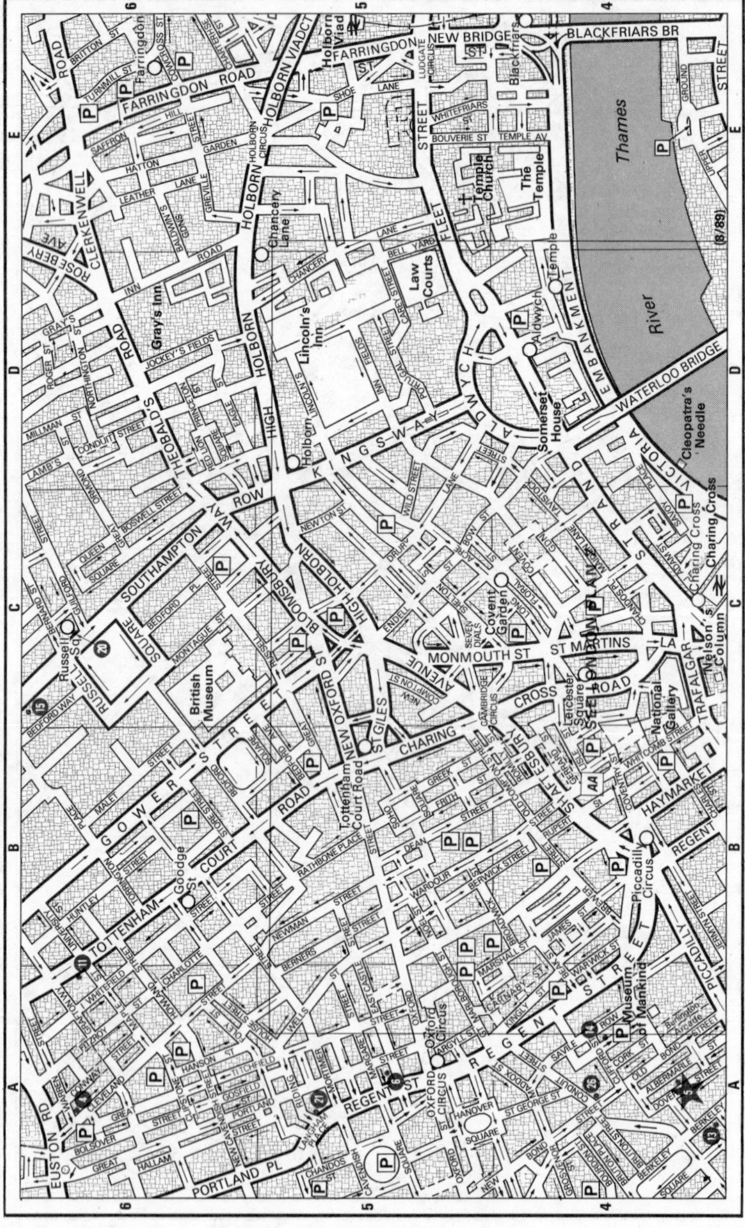

London Plan 4

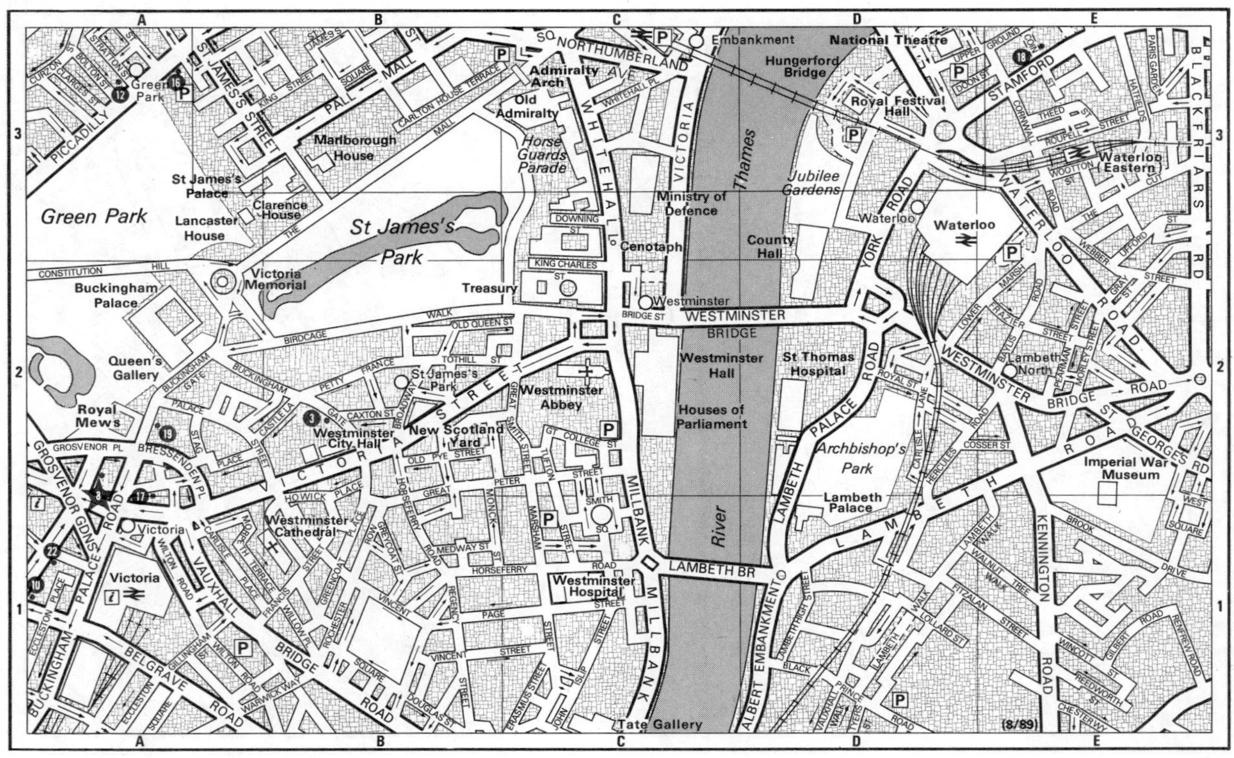

London Plan 5

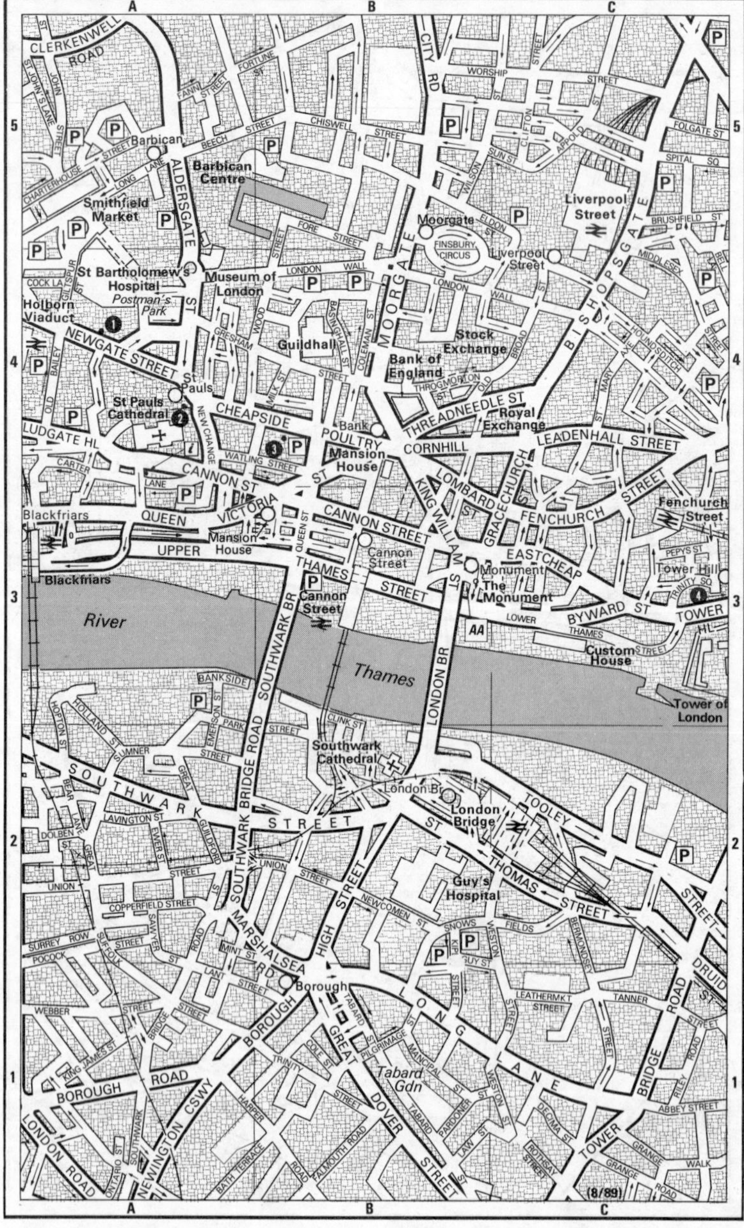

NEW LONDON CODES From 6th May 1990

From 6th May, 1990 some London telephone numbers will have a new code, to replace the currently used 01-. If you have difficulty in obtaining a London number after that date, check, the chart below.

Simply look through the numbers listed below and find the first three digits of the present telephone number. The new code is printed beside these first three digits.
For example, 01-434 000 will become 071-434 000. And 01-666 0000 will become 081-666 0000.

1st 3 digits of no.	New code
200	081
202	081
203	081
204	081
205	081
206	081
207	081
208	081
209	081
210	071
214	071
215	071
217	071
218	071
219	071
220	071
221	071
222	071
223	071
224	071
225	071
226	071
227	071
228	071
229	071
230	071
231	071
232	071
233	071
234	071
235	071
236	071
237	071
238	071
239	071
240	071
241	071
242	071
243	071
244	071
245	071
246	071
247	071
248	071
249	071
250	071
251	071
252	071
253	071
254	071
255	071
256	071
257	071
258	071
259	071
260	071
261	071
262	071
263	071
265	071
266	071
267	071
268	071
269	071
270	071
271	071
272	071
273	071
274	071
276	071
277	071

1st 3 digits of no.	New code
278	071
279	071
280	071
281	071
283	071
284	071
286	071
287	071
288	071
289	071
290	081
291	081
293	081
294	081
295	081
297	081
298	081
299	081
300	081
301	081
302	081
303	081
304	081
305	081
308	081
309	081
310	081
311	081
312	081
313	081
314	081
316	081
317	081
318	081
319	081
320	071
321	071
322	071
323	071
324	071
325	071
326	071
327	071
328	071
329	071
330	081
332	081
335	081
336	081
337	081
339	081
340	081
341	081
342	081
343	081
345	081
346	081
347	081
348	081
349	081
350	071
351	071
352	071
353	071
354	071
355	071
356	071
357	071
358	071
359	071
360	081

1st 3 digits of no.	New code
361	081
363	081
364	081
365	081
366	081
367	081
368	081
370	071
371	071
372	071
373	071
374	071
375	071
376	071
377	071
378	071
379	071
380	071
381	071
382	071
383	071
384	071
385	071
386	071
387	071
388	071
389	071
390	081
391	081
392	081
393	081
394	081
397	081
398	081
399	081
400	071
401	071
402	071
403	071
404	071
405	071
406	071
407	071
408	071
409	071
420	081
421	081
422	081
423	081
424	081
426	081
427	081
428	081
429	081
430	071
431	071
432	071
433	071
434	071
435	071
436	071
437	071
438	071
439	071
440	081
441	081
442	081
443	081
444	081
445	081
446	081

1st 3 digits of no.	New code
447	081
448	081
449	081
450	081
451	081
452	081
453	081
455	081
456	081
458	081
459	081
460	081
461	081
462	081
463	081
464	081
466	081
467	081
468	081
469	081
470	081
471	081
472	081
473	071
474	071
475	081
476	071
478	081
480	071
481	071
482	071
483	071
484	071
485	071
486	071
487	071
488	071
489	071
490	071
491	071
492	071
493	071
494	071
495	071
496	071
497	071
498	071
499	071
500	081
501	081
502	081
504	081
505	081
506	081
507	081
508	081
509	081
511	071
512	071
514	081
515	071
517	081
518	081
519	081
520	081
521	081
523	081
524	081
526	081
527	081
529	081

1st 3 digits of no.	New code
530	081
531	081
532	081
533	081
534	081
536	081
537	071
538	071
539	081
540	081
541	081
542	081
543	081
544	081
545	081
546	081
547	081
549	081
550	081
551	081
552	081
553	081
554	081
555	081
556	081
558	081
559	081
560	081
561	081
562	081
563	081
564	081
566	081
567	081
568	081
569	081
570	081
571	081
572	081
573	081
574	081
575	081
576	081
577	081
578	081
579	081
580	071
581	071
582	071
583	071
584	071
585	071
586	071
587	071
588	071
589	071
590	081
591	081
592	081
593	081
594	081
595	081
597	081
598	081
599	081
600	071
601	071
602	071
603	071
604	071
605	071

1st 3 digits of no.	New code
606	071
607	071
608	071
609	071
618	071
620	071
621	071
622	071
623	071
624	071
625	071
626	071
627	071
628	071
629	071
630	071
631	071
632	071
633	071
634	071
635	071
636	071
637	071
638	071
639	071
640	081
641	081
642	081
643	081
644	081
645	081
646	081
647	081
648	081
650	081
651	081
653	081
654	081
655	081
656	081
657	081
658	081
659	081
660	081
661	081
663	081
664	081
665	081
666	081
667	081
668	081
669	081
670	081
671	081
672	081
673	081
674	081
675	081
676	081
677	081
678	081
679	081
680	081
681	081
682	081
683	081
684	081
685	081
686	081
687	081
688	081

1st 3 digits of no.	New code
689	081
690	081
691	081
692	081
693	081
694	081
695	081
697	081
698	081
699	081
700	071
701	071
702	071
703	071
704	071
706	071
707	071
708	071
709	071
720	071
721	071
722	071
723	071
724	071
725	071
726	071
727	071
728	071
729	071
730	071
731	071
732	071
733	071
734	071
735	071
736	071
737	071
738	071
739	071
740	081
741	081
742	081
743	081
744	081
745	081
746	081

1st 3 digits of no.	New code
747	081
748	081
749	081
750	081
751	081
752	081
754	081
755	081
756	081
758	081
759	081
760	081
761	081
763	081
764	081
766	081
767	081
768	081
769	081
770	081
771	081
773	081
776	081
777	081
778	081
780	081
783	081
785	081
786	081
788	081
789	081
790	071
791	071
792	071
793	071
794	071
796	071
798	071
799	071
800	081
801	081
802	081
803	081
804	081
805	081
806	081

1st 3 digits of no.	New code
807	081
808	081
809	081
820	071
821	071
822	071
823	071
824	071
826	071
828	071
829	071
831	071
832	071
833	071
834	071
835	071
836	071
837	071
839	071
840	081
841	081
842	081
843	081
844	081
845	081
846	081
847	081
848	081
850	081
851	081
852	081
853	081
854	081
855	081
856	081
857	081
858	081
859	081
861	081
863	081
864	081
866	081
868	081
869	081
870	081
871	081

1st 3 digits of no.	New code
874	081
875	081
876	081
877	081
878	081
879	081
881	081
882	081
883	081
884	081
885	081
886	081
888	081
889	081
890	081
891	081
892	081
893	081
894	081
897	081
898	081
900	081
902	081
903	081
904	081
905	081
906	081
907	081
908	081
909	081
920	071
921	071
922	071
923	071
924	071
925	071
927	071
928	071
929	071
930	071
931	071
932	071
933	071
934	071
935	071
936	071

1st 3 digits of no.	New code
937	071
938	071
940	081
941	081
942	081
943	081
944	081
946	081
947	081
948	081
949	081
950	081
951	081
952	081
953	081
954	081
958	081
959	081
960	081
961	081
963	081
964	081
965	081
968	081
969	081
974	081
976	071
977	081
978	071
979	081
980	081
981	081
983	081
984	081
985	081
986	081
987	071
988	081
989	081
991	081
992	081
993	081
994	081
995	081
997	081
998	081

LONDON Greater London Plans 1-5, pages 412-420 (Small scale maps 4 & 5 at back of book) A map of the London postal area appears on pages 410-411, listed below in postal district order, commencing East, then North, South and West, with a brief indication of the area covered. Detailed plans 1-4 show the locations of AA-appointed hotels and restaurants within the Central London postal districts which are indicated by a number, followed by a grid reference e.g. A5 to help you find the location. Plan 5 shows the districts covered within the outer area keyed by a grid reference e.g. A1. Other places within the county of London are listed under their respective place names and are also keyed to this plan or the main map section. If more detailed information is required the AA Motorists map of London, on sale at AA offices, is in two parts : the 'West End and the City' shows one-way systems, banned turns, car parks stations, hotels, places of interest etc. 'Outer London' gives primary routes, car parks at suburban stations etc. A theatre map of the West End is included. For London Airports see town plan section at the back of the book.

E1 Stepney and east of the Tower of London

★★★★60% **Tower Thistle** St Katherine's Way E1 9LD (Thistle) ☎01-488 4134 Telex no 885934 FAX 01-488 4106
Situated next to the Tower of London and overlooking Tower Bridge and St Katherine's Dock, this hotel has a lovely location. There are two standards of bedroom – both air-conditioned – and a choice of three very different restaurants.
808 (24fb) CTV in all bedrooms ® T ✱
sB £89-£112 dB £102-£125 (room only)
Lift ☾ 136P (charged) 116 (charged) CFA ♫
International Lunch fr£18.75&alc Dinner fr£24.50&alc Last dinner 10.30pm
Credit Cards 1 2 3 4 5

EC1 City of London

✕ ***La Bastille*** 116 Newgate St EC1 ☎01-600 1134
The small, intimate, city restaurant has some good wood carvings, and the portraits of Victorian judges on the walls set an atmosphere. A sound standard of French provincial cuisine is provided, the menu changing daily.
Closed Sat, Sun, 1 wk Aug, 2 wks Dec & BH's
Dinner not served
French 55 seats Last lunch 2.30pm
Credit Cards 1 2 3 4 5

EC2 City of London

✕✕✕ **Le Poulbot** 45 Cheapside EC2
☎01-236 4379 FAX 01-622 5657
(Rosette awarded for lunch only)
Chef Philippe Vandewalle has yet to make as firm a mark at this Roux Brothers city restaurant as his predecessor, Rowley Leigh. The light French cuisine is ideal for lunchtime though, and the fixed-price menu, which includes an aperitif, is still good value for money. Starters might include a carefully prepared boudin blanc de volaille aux truffes, or a ballotine de foie gras, and might be followed by dishes such as a good magret de canard with an apricot sauce of sufficient finesse to suggest that the second rosette could be regained in due course. As always, the sometimes inexperienced waiters are supervised by the wonderful Maitre d', Jean Cottard.
Closed Xmas & BH's
Dinner not served
French V 50 seats ✱ Lunch £27.50 Last lunch 3pm
Credit Cards 1 2 3 4 5

EC4 City of London

✕ ***Ginnan*** 5 Cathedral Place EC4 ☎01-236 4120
Simple, modern Japanese restaurant with small party room.
Closed Sun & BH's
Dinner not served Sat
Japanese 60 seats Last dinner 10pm
Credit Cards 1 2 3 5

N1 Islington

See LONDON plan 5*D4*
✕✕ ***Frederick's*** Camden Passage N1 8EG ☎01-359 2888
Dating back from the 18th-century, and originally called 'The Gun', this very popular and well-appointed restaurant was renamed in honour of Prince Augustus Frederick who died in 1813. The enterprising menu is changed fortnightly but always includes some delectable puddings, and the formal service is very efficient.
Closed Sun, 26 Dec, 1 Jan, Good Fri & BH Mons
International 150 seats Last lunch 2.30pm Last dinner 11.30pm
Credit Cards 1 2 3 4 5

✕ **Annas Place** 90 Mildmay Park N1 4PR ☎01-249 9379
A small very friendly Swedish café where simplicity and honesty combine to produce outstanding and authentic Swedish cooking. Anna's warm and sincere involvement is complemented by her loyal team of friendly staff. There is a good selection of wines on offer. This restaurant is marvellous value for money.
Closed Sun, Mon, 2 wks Xmas, 2 wks Etr & 4 wks Aug
Swedish V 50 seats ✱ S10% Lunch £11.85-£16.75alc Last lunch 2.15pm Last dinner 10.45pm
Credit Cards

✕ ***M'Sieur Frog*** 31A Essex Rd N1 ☎01-226 3495
A good choice of dishes is available at this lively and very popular bistro.
Closed Sun, 1 wk Xmas & 1 wk Aug
Lunch not served Sat
French 63 seats Last lunch 2.30pm Last dinner 11.15pm
Credit Cards 1 3

N6 Highgate

See LONDON plan 5*D5*
✕✕ ***Bayleaf Tandoori*** 2 North Hill N6 4PU ☎01-340 1719 & 01-340 0245
Well-appointed contemporary restaurant and take-away featuring specialities and seafoods. All dishes are grilled on charcoal. Service is dignified and attentive.
Indian V 100 seats Last lunch 2.45pm Last dinner 11.15pm 20P
Credit Cards 1 2 3 5

NW1 Regent's Park

See LONDON plan 5*D4*
✕✕ **Martin's** 239 Baker St NW1 6XE ☎01-935 3130 & 01-935 0997 Plan 65 *D6*
A contemporary and very smart restaurant bar where the menu offers particularly good value, skilfully-prepared dishes.
Closed Sun BH's
Lunch not served Sat
English & French 60 seats Lunch £18.50-£23.50 Dinner £25-£30alc Last lunch 3pm Last dinner 11pm nc10yrs
Credit Cards 1 2 3 5

✕ ***Koto Japanese*** 75 Parkway NW1 ☎01-482 2036
A small and very friendly traditional restaurant is personally run by the proprietor, Yoko Arai. Specialities include Sashimi and Tempora, and there are others which can be cooked at your table. Service is very attentive, and there is a traditional dining room upstairs.

Closed Sun
☋ Japanese 22 seats Last dinner 10.30pm ₱
Credit Cards 1 2 3 4 5

✕Le Plat du Jour 19 Hampstead Rd NW1 3JA ☎01-387 9644 & 01-387 7291
Popular lunchtime restaurant/wine bar offering excellent value for money with French regional dishes and daily specialities.
Closed Sat, Sun, 24 Dec-1 Jan & BH's
☋ French **V** 70 seats ✱ S12.5% Lunch fr£13.50&alc Dinner fr£13.50&alc Last lunch 4pm Last dinner 10pm ₱
Credit Cards 1 2 3 5

NW2 Cricklewood, Willesden

See LONDON plan 5*C4*
✕Quincy's 84 675 Finchley Rd NW2 2JP ☎01-794 8499
Flair and imagination are evident in the cooking at this restaurant, where dishes from a short but interesting menu are served in a friendly, informal atmosphere under the personal supervision of the owner.
Closed Sun, Mon & 24 Dec-14 Jan
Lunch not served
☋ English & French **V** 30 seats ✱ Dinner £18.50 Last dinner 11.30pm ₱
Credit Cards 1 3

NW3 Hampstead and Swiss Cottage

See LONDON plan 5*D4*
★★★★65% Holiday Inn Swiss Cottage 128 King Henry's Rd, Swiss Cottage NW3 3ST (Holiday Inns) ☎01-722 7711
Telex no 267396 FAX 01-586 5822
A modern, multi-storey hotel ideally placed for access to Central London. Bedrooms, recently refurbished, are spacious and well equipped, the split-level lounge and cocktail bar extremely comfortable and the restaurant pleasant and airy. This hotel also has a leisure club with an indoor heated pool.
303⇨🚿(166fb)⅟in 52 bedrooms CTV in all bedrooms **T** ✱
sB⇨🚿fr£110 dB⇨🚿fr£135 (room only) ⊟
Lift ☾ ⊞ 50P 100🚗 ⊡(heated) sauna solarium gymnasium *xmas*
☋ International **V** ♧ ℒ ⅟ Lunch fr£15.50 Dinner fr£16 Last dinner 10.30pm
Credit Cards 1 2 3 4 5

★★★66% Post House Haverstock Hill NW3 4RB (Trusthouse Forte) ☎01-794 8121 Telex no 262494 FAX 01-435 5586
Situated on high ground, this hotel has fine south-westerly views across the city. Bedrooms are tastefully appointed and well equipped. The Heathroom restaurant offers an interesting à la carte menu, whilst the daily roast on our last visit was well worth a recommendation. Service by young staff is attentive.
140⇨⅟in 28 bedrooms CTV in all bedrooms ® ✱
sB⇨£79-£85 dB⇨£90-£95 (room only) ⊟
Lift ☾ 70P *xmas*
☋ English & French **V** ♧ ℒ ⅟ Lunch fr£10.95&alc Dinner fr£10.95&alc Last dinner 10.30pm
Credit Cards 1 2 3 4 5

✕Cafè Flo 205 Haverstock Hill NW3 ☎01-435 6744
Closed 1 week at Xmas
☋ French **V** 38 seats ✱ S% Lunch £6.50-£10&alc Dinner £6.50-£10&alc Last lunch 3.00pm Last dinner 11.30pm ₱
Credit Cards 1 3

✕Mr Ke 7 College Pde NW3 5EP ☎01-722 8474
Small, family-run contemporary restaurant specialising in Peking and Szechuan cuisine. All dishes are cooked to order and offer excellent value for money.
☋ Jiangnan, Pekinese & Szechuan **V** 55 seats ✱ S10% Lunch £13.50-£22&alc Dinner £13.50-£22&alc Last lunch 2.30pm Last dinner 11.30pm ₱
Credit Cards 1 2 3 5

✕*Wakaba* 122a Finchley Rd NW3 ☎01-586 7960
The functional bland interior design of this restaurant, by architect John Paulson, is both modern and unusual. A range of set dinners based on traditional Japanese recipes is available, together with old favourites like Tempura and Sashimi; many specialities are cooked at the table, and there is a separate Sushi Bar.
Closed Mon, 4 days Xmas, 4 days Etr & 1 wk Aug
Lunch not served
☋ Japanese **V** 38 seats Last dinner 11pm ₱
Credit Cards 1 2 3 5

✕Zenw 3 Chinese 83 Hampstead High St NW3 ☎01-794 7863 FAX 01-437 7863
Interior and furnishings are in the 'Art Deco' style at this restaurant which provides the 'New Wave' style of cooking with salads, charcoal grills and iron plate food.
Closed Xmas
☋ Chinese **V** 140 seats Last dinner 11.30pm ₱
Credit Cards 1 2 3 4 5

NW6 Kilburn

See LONDON plan 5*C4*
✕*Peter's Bistro* 63 Fairfax Rd NW6 ☎01-624 5804
Green awning and fresh plants make the frontage of this restaurant very impressive. Inside the relaxed intimate atmosphere provides the ideal setting for a well-cooked meal chosen from a bistro-type menu.
Lunch not served Sat
Dinner not served Sun
☋ French 60 seats ₱ ⅟
Credit Cards 1 2 3 5

NW7 Mill Hill

See LONDON plan 5*C5*
✕✕Good Earth 143-145 Broadway, Mill Hill NW7 ☎01-959 7011 FAX 01-823 8769
Smart, cheerful and popular restaurant with appealing menu of authentic Cantonese cooking.
☋ Chinese **V** 100 seats ✱ Lunch £13-£35&alc Dinner £13-£35&alc Last lunch 2.30pm Last dinner 11.15pm 12P ⅟
Credit Cards 1 2 3 5

SE1 Waterloo

✕RSJ The Restaurant on the South Bank 13A Coin St SE1 ☎01-928 4554 & 01-928 9768
Stylish and elegant restaurant where chef Ian McKenzie demonstrates his flair for 'New Wave' cooking. There are some excellent wines from the Loire region.
Closed Sun & 25-28 Dec
Lunch not served Sat
☋ French 60 seats ✱ S10% Lunch £13.47-£15.12&alc Dinner £13.47-£15.12&alc Last lunch 2pm Last dinner 11pm ₱
Credit Cards 1 2 3

SE10 Greenwich

See LONDON plan 5*E3*
○*Ibis Greenwich* 30 Stockwell St, Greenwich SE10 9JN ☎01-305 1177 Telex no 929647 FAX 01-858 7139
Due to open May 1990
82⇨

All hotels awarded three or more stars are now also given a percentage grading for the quality of their facilities. Please see p 16 for a detailed explanation.

London

SW1 Westminster

★★★★★**THE BERKELEY**

Wilton Place,
Knightsbridge SW1X 7RL
☎01-235 6000
Telex no 919252 FAX 01-235 4330

Over the past 2 or 3 years considerable refurbishment has been carried out here, which includes the provision of a more attractive restaurant, the 'softening' of the corridors, re-decoration of the drawing room and bedrooms and further improvement of some of the already fine suites. There is a heated swimming pool on the top floor, together with a sauna and mini-gym. The standard of French cuisine in the restaurant is sound, and the popular 'Le Perroquet' bar and adjoining Buttery offer a wide range of good-value dishes. Service thoughout is formal, extensive and traditional – staff tend to smile more when greeting customers they know. At other times it has to be said that an air of aloofness prevails, until one comes to appreciate the distinctive style of The Berkeley. Discretion is considered to be as important as meeting the high standards of a discerning clientele, which in turn helps to explain why it attracts such a loyal following.

160⇨⌐ CTV in all bedrooms **T** ✘ S15%
sB⇨⌐£140-£200 dB⇨⌐£200-£250 (room only) ⊟
Lift ☾ ⊞ 50🚗 (£17 per night) 🚗 ⊡(heated) sauna solarium gymnasium *xmas*
♀ French & Italian ♥ ☐ S15% Lunch £11.50-£16
Credit Cards [1] [2] [3] [5]

London

★★★★★72% **Hyatt Carlton Tower** Cadogan Place, Westminster SW1X 9PY ☎01-235 5411 Telex no 21944 FAX 01-235-9129
A somewhat regimented, modern hotel with some good facilities. These include the refurbished Rib Room Restaurant, attractive Chelsea Room Restaurant and a new health centre that also has a relaxing lounge. Bedrooms are modestly furnished and prices comparatively expensive.
224⇨⌐⊬in 23 bedrooms CTV in all bedrooms **T** ✘ (ex guide dogs) ✳ sB⇨⌐£170-£190 dB⇨⌐£170-£190 (room only) ⊟
Lift ☾ ⊞ 40🚗 (£2 per hour) 🚗 CFA ♪ (hard) sauna solarium gymnasium beauty treatment hair salon ♫
♀ International **V** ♥ ☐ S% Lunch fr£22.50&alc Dinner fr£28 Last dinner 11.15pm
Credit Cards [1] [2] [3] [4] [5]

★★★★★76% **The Hyde Park** Knightsbridge SW1Y 7LA (Trusthouse Forte) ☎01-235 2000 Telex no 262057 FAX 01-235 4552
This elegant and dignified hotel is situated in the centre of fashionable Knightsbridge overlooking Hyde Park. A stately entrance leads to the reception area – ornate with marble, high, gilded ceilings and huge, fresh flower displays. The lounge and bar is a popular rendezvous which leads into the Park Room Restaurant where the piano is played. Downstairs, the oak-panelled Grill Room offers English roasts and French specialities. Bedrooms and suites, individually decorated by leading designers, are superbly equipped.
186⇨⊬in 6 bedrooms CTV in all bedrooms **T** sB⇨£175-£250 dB⇨£200-£250 (room only)
Lift ☾ ⊞ **P** 🚗 CFA ♫ *xmas*
♀ English & French **V** ♥ ☐ ⊬ Lunch £20-£22&alc Dinner £25-£50alc Last dinner 11pm
Credit Cards [1] [2] [3] [4] [5]

★★★★★63% ***Sheraton Park Tower*** 101 Knightsbridge SW1X 7RN ☎01-235 8050 Telex no 917222 FAX 01-235 8231
Modern facilities, elegant furnishings and exceptional views are the distinguishing features of the Sheraton Park's bedrooms, and the upper-floor executive rooms, with their TV/videos, individual air-conditioning, mini-bars, etc, are ideally suited for business travellers. The Edwardian-style restaurant and conservatory make an inviting setting for the tempting menus, while light meals and snacks are served throughout the day in the Champagne Bar.
295⇨⌐⊬in 20 bedrooms CTV in all bedrooms **T** ✘
Lift ☾ ⊞ 70🚗 (£7 per day) 🚗
V ♥ ☐ Last dinner 11.30pm
Credit Cards [1] [2] [3] [4] [5]

★★★★63% **The Cavendish** Jermyn St SW1Y 6JF (Trusthouse Forte) ☎01-930 2111 Telex no 263187 FAX 01-839 2125
The Cavendish is carrying out a programme of refurbishment, designed to improve the comfort of the bedrooms, some of the best of which have balconies affording superb views over London. The restaurant is well supervised and meals are served by friendly and attentive staff. There is also a gallery lounge where drinks and snacks, including traditional afternoon tea, can be ordered throughout the day.
253⇨⊬in 63 bedrooms CTV in all bedrooms **T** ✳ S%
sB⇨£105-£130 dB⇨£140-£162 (room only) ⊟
Lift ☾ 80🚗 (fr £16) 🚗 CFA ♫ *xmas*
♀ French **V** ♥ ☐ ⊬ Lunch £16.50&alc Dinner £18.50&alc Last dinner 11pm
Credit Cards [1] [2] [3] [4] [5]

★★★★74% ***Duke's*** St James' Place SW1A 1NY (Prestige) ☎01-491 4840 Telex no 28283 FAX 01-493 1264
A charming, Edwardian hotel in a peaceful, secluded setting where the highly professional staff manage to create a relaxed and friendly atmosphere. In addition to the superbly furnished and equipped bedrooms, this hotel now has well-appointed suites as well. Public areas are comfortable and the small intimate restaurant offers a short but interesting menu of English and French cuisine skilfully prepared by chef Tony Marshall.
58⇨(22fb)1⊞ CTV in all bedrooms **T** ✘ (ex guide dogs)
Lift ☾ **P** 🚗 nc5yrs
♥ ☐ Last dinner 10pm
Credit Cards [1] [2] [3] [4] [5]

★★★★**GORING**

Beeston Place, Grosvenor Gardens SW1W 0JW ☎01-834 8211 Telex no 919166 FAX 01-834 4393

For over 75 years, successive generations of the Goring family have owned and run this unique hotel with total dedication and enthusiasm, and discerning guests have long ranked it among the most pleasant places to stay in London. A loyal following numbers among the Goring's virtues its understated style and an emphasis on the highest standards, for which William Cowpe, General Manager for 20 years, must take considerable credit. Recent and continuing refurbishment reflects the changes required to keep abreast with other London hotels, and a bright pink scheme throughout the marbled foyer area has attracted a mixed reaction. There is uniform approval however for the upgrading of 30 of the bedrooms to a very high standard, including splendid marbled bathrooms. Unfortunately, the contrast with some of the other compact rooms is quite marked. We are happy to record that the improvements here have not been made at the expense of the Goring's strengths. The hotel is spotlessly clean, the staff are uniformly smart, professional and, at the same time, friendly and caring and the elegant restaurant continues to offer a good blend of English and French cuisine. Perhaps, though, the greatest compliment we can pay the Goring is that there is never a shortage of inspectors volunteering to stay here – not only is it a pleasure, but it serves as a reminder of what can be achieved by concentrating on those old fashioned virtues of hospitality, comfort, cleanliness and good manners. In short, a rare and shining beacon in this age of uniformity and gimmickry.

90⇨↱ CTV in all bedrooms **T** ✗ ✱ S10%
sB⇨↱£95-£105 dB⇨↱£138-£150 (room only)
Lift ☾ 10P (£7) 4🚗 (£7) ⌗ ♫
☋ English & French **V** ✩ ☐ Lunch £18&alc Dinner fr£21&alc Last dinner 10pm
Credit Cards [1] [2] [3] [5]

★★★★67% **Royal Westminster Thistle** 40 Buckingham Palace Rd SW1W 0QT (Thistle) ☎01-834 1821 Telex no 916821 FAX 01-931 7542
Bedrooms here are spacious and well appointed, there is a comfortable lounge and impressive entrance lobby. The two options when it comes to eating are the formal restaurant – the St Germain Brasserie – or the more casual Café St Germain and the service in both is helpful and friendly.
134⇨↱(69fb)⚟in 67 bedrooms CTV in all bedrooms **T** ✗ ✱
sB⇨↱fr£105 dB⇨↱fr£130 (room only) ⛿
Lift ☾ ⊞ P̸ ♫
☋ French ✩ ☐ ⚟ Lunch fr£15.95&alc Dinner fr£15.95&alc Last dinner 11.30pm
Credit Cards [1] [2] [3] [4] [5]

★★★★75% **Stafford** 16-18 St James's Place SW1A 1NJ (Prestige) ☎01-493 0111 Telex no 28602 FAX 01-493 7121
Nestling in a quiet cul-de-sac off St James's, this lovely town-house hotel attracts a discriminating clientele who appreciate the personal service no less than the elegantly furnished bedrooms and luxurious ambience of all the public rooms. The American cocktail bar has become something of an institution and is well worth a visit.
62⇨1⊟ CTV in all bedrooms **T** ✗ ✱ sB⇨£150-£155
dB⇨£186-£385 (room only) ⛿
Lift ☾ 5🚗 (£12 per night) ⌗ *xmas*
☋ French ✩ ☐ S10% Lunch £20 Dinner £25.50 Last dinner 10pm
Credit Cards [1] [2] [3] [4] [5]

★★★68% **Royal Horseguards Thistle** Whitehall Court SW1A 2EJ (Thistle) ☎01-839 3400 Telex no 917096 FAX 01-925 2263
A luxurious new wing, offering more spacious bedrooms than those in the original building, which tend to be somewhat compact, has been added to this imposing hotel with its splendid public areas and opulently furnished foyer.
376⇨↱(98fb)⚟in 95 bedrooms CTV in all bedrooms ® **T** ✗
✱ sB⇨↱£87-£120 dB⇨↱£97-£130 (room only) ⛿
Lift ☾ P̸ CFA ♫
☋ International ✩ ☐ ⚟ Lunch fr£15.75&alc Dinner fr£15.75&alc Last dinner 10.30pm
Credit Cards [1] [2] [3] [4] [5]

★★★68% **Rubens** Buckingham Palace Rd SW1W 0PS
☎01-834 6600 Telex no 916577 FAX 01-828 5401
An efficient, well-managed hotel offering extensive services and very well-equipped modern bedrooms; public areas include the Master Restaurant, a cocktail bar and the library lounge. Guests should note that parking is particularly difficult.
191rm(173⇨18↱)(3fb)⚟in 44 bedrooms CTV in all bedrooms **T** sB⇨↱£72-£82 dB⇨↱£99-£100 (room only) ⛿
Lift ☾ P̸ ♫ *xmas*
☋ International **V** ✩ ☐ S10% Lunch fr£14.50
Credit Cards [1] [2] [3] [5]

★ **EBURY COURT**

26 Ebury St SW1 0LU
☎01-730 8147 &
01-730 7002

Small is beautiful at Ebury Court. For over 50 years it has been run by Mrs Topham, whose care and thoroughness set the standard for the rest of the loyal staff, and service is always good natured and helpful. Pretty fabrics, cushions and china bring charm to the small and spotless rooms, which have notably comfortable beds. Direct dial telephones and radios are provided, but televisions must be arranged in advance. Downstairs one of the little lounges has a writing desk, another has a television, and, downstairs again, the dining room is decked out in pink and navy stripes. If Ebury Court lacks space and modern facilities, it more than compensates with its unique and delightful atmosphere. The food is British, simple and good, and fresh soda bread is baked daily on the premises.
38rm(11⇨)4⊟ TV available **T** ✱ sB&Bfr£39
sB&B⇨fr£42 dB&Bfr£62 dB&B⇨fr£72
Lift ☾ CTV P̸ ⌗
☋ English & Continental **V** Lunch £7.50-£11alc Dinner fr£11alc Last dinner 9pm
Credit Cards [1] [3]

✕✕✕ **Auberge de Provence** (St James Court Hotel), Buckingham Gate SW1E 6AF ☎01-821 1899 Telex no 938075 FAX 01-630 7587
Chef Yves Gravelier shows his flair for the cooking of Provence with well-constructed dishes, authentic sauces and home-made pâtisserie. Service, under the direction of Monsieur Perrodin, remains traditionally French and thoroughly professional, with knowledgeable advice about the wine list.
Closed Sun, BH's & 26 Dec
Lunch not served Sat
☋ French **V** 88 seats ✱ Lunch £17.50-£30&alc Dinner £30-£50alc Last lunch 2.30pm Last dinner 11pm P̸ nc10yrs ⚟
Credit Cards [1] [2] [3] [4] [5]

✕✕ **Gavvers** 61 Lower Sloane St SW1 8HD ☎01-730 5983 & 01-823 4772 FAX 01-622 5657
A Roux Brothers enterprise, the restaurant offers a very popular, value for money, fixed price menu, the charge covering not only half a bottle of wine but also service and VAT.
Closed Sun, Xmas-1 Jan & BH's
Lunch not served Sat
☋ French 60 seats ✱ Lunch £15.50 Dinner £27.50 Last lunch 2.30pm Last dinner 11pm P̸
Credit Cards [1] [2] [3] [5]

❀ ✕✕ ***Ken Lo's Memories of China*** 67 Ebury St SW1
☎01-730 7734
Still the top Chinese restaurant in London, the elegant repertoire of classical and regional dishes assures diners an enjoyable experience. Our inspector particularly recommends the Cantonese Quick Fried Beef with oyster sauce and Peking Ma Shu Rou. Preparation of sauces is excellent, flavours are superb; the staff are helpful and efficient.
Closed Sun & BH's
🍷 Chinese **V** 80 seats Last dinner 10.45pm ₽
Credit Cards 1 2 3 5

✕✕ **Maxim's Wine Bar** 143 Knightsbridge SW1 7PA
☎01-225 2553 & 01-584 9399
Closed 25-28 Dec
🍷 Pekinese **V** 80 seats ✻ Lunch £7.50-£15&alc Dinner £6.50-£12.50alc Last lunch 3pm Last dinner 11pm ₽ ♫
Credit Cards 1 2 3 5

❀ ✕✕ **Le Mazarin** 30 Winchester St, Pimlico SW1V 4NE
☎01-828 3366 & 01-630 7604
(Rosette awarded for dinner only)
René Bajard has firmly established himself as one of the most talented and consistent of the Roux Brothers' protegés, and the cooking in this attractive basement restaurant has an individuality that makes Le Mazarin one of our best single-rosetted establishments. Robust and flavoursome cuisine is typified by an excellent gâteau provençal aux fines pointes d'asperges, while commendable restraint is shown in a supreme de sandre roti au beurre rouge à la moelle, with sauces in general being outstanding. The fixed-price menu offers a good choice, and, for London, good value, although the adequate French wine list is pricey. Le Mazarin is now also open for lunch from Tuesday to Saturday and service is attentive and friendly.
Closed Sun & Mon, 1 wk Xmas & BH's, 2 last wks in Aug
🍷 French 55 seats Lunch £16-£35 Dinner £28-£35&alc Last lunch 2pm Last dinner 11pm ₽
Credit Cards 1 2 3 5

✕✕ **Mijanou** 143 Ebury St SW1 ☎01-730 4099
FAX 01-823 6402
Sonia Blech, continues to maintain a high standard in her imaginative cooking. The menu is not large, but will suit most tastes, and good fresh produce is well used. A good, comprehensive wine list accompanies the food and some interesting wines are available. There is a friendly, informal atmosphere, with Nevelle Blech keeping a watchful eye on the service. The décor is tasteful and the atmosphere pleasant, enhanced for some by the provision of a no-smoking area.
Closed Sat, Sun, 2 wks Xmas, 1 wk Etr, 3 wks Aug & BH's
🍷 French **V** 30 seats ✻ Lunch £14-£26.50 Dinner £23-£32 Last lunch 2pm Last dinner 11pm ₽ ⚟
Credit Cards 1 2 5

❀ ✕✕ **Salloos** 62-64 Kinnerton St SW1 ☎01-235 4444
An unassuming first floor Pakistani restaurant tucked away in a quiet area of Knightsbridge. The menu boasts that no artificial colours are used in cooking and certainly the cuisine is of a style and standard not usually found in this type of restaurant. Spicy marinated meats from the Tandoori oven, the chicken in cheese (a souffle dish) and the nan bread which almost melts in the mouth are all recommended. Salloo himself is a genial host. Beware the hefty cover and service charges.
Closed Sun & BH's
🍷 Pakistani **V** 70 seats Lunch £18.40&alc Dinner £23&alc Last lunch 2.30pm Last dinner 11.15pm ₽
Credit Cards 1 2 3 5

✕✕ **Santini** 29 Ebury St SW1W 0NZ ☎01-730 4094 & 01-730 8275 FAX 01-730 0544
A bright and stylish very Italian restaurant where tables are close together and the atmosphere is noisy and convivial. The menu is à la carte supplemented by daily specials, and the fresh pasta, fresh fish and the Italian dishes that are served are of a quality not often found in this country. Good, value-for-money Italian and fine French wines complement the menu and the puddings should not be missed.
Closed Xmas, Etr & BH's
Lunch not served Sat & Sun
🍷 Italian **V** 60 seats ✻ S12% Lunch fr£12.50&alc Dinner fr£35alc Last lunch 2.30pm Last dinner 11.30pm ₽
Credit Cards 1 2 3 5

❀ ✕ **Ciboure** 21 Eccleston St SW1W 9LX ☎01-730 2505
Bright, modern restaurant offering wholesome dishes tastefully prepared by the newly appointed chef Melanie Dixon. Service is professional but informal.
Closed Sun & Sat 14/08/89-04/09/89
🍷 French 36 seats ✻ S15% Lunch £14.50 Dinner £17.50-£19.50alc Last lunch 2.30pm Last dinner 11.15pm ₽ nc5yrs
Credit Cards 1 2 3 5

✕ **Eatons** 49 Elizabeth St SW1W 9PP ☎01-730 0074
Artichoke and cucumber soup and boneless, stuffed quail with a cream and brandy sauce are just two examples from the menu of this cosy and friendly restaurant. The normal menu has seasonal additions. Service is pleasant and courteous.
Closed Sat, Sun & BH's
🍷 Continental 40 seats ✻ S12.5% Lunch £18.40-£24alc Dinner £18.40-£24alc Last lunch 2pm Last dinner 11.15pm ₽
Credit Cards 1 2 3 5

SW3 Chelsea, Brompton

❀★★★★ **CAPITAL**

Basil St, Knightsbridge
SW3 1AT ☎01-589 5171
Telex no 919042
FAX 01-225 0011

This modern hotel has a reputation as a place of character, and the news this year is of a refurbishment in 'fin de siècle' style. The particularly pleasant atmosphere remains unchanged, however, as do the high standards which amply compensate for the hotel's lack of space. Bedrooms vary in size, but all are furnished to a high standard of comfort, with extras such as bathrobes and seasonal fresh fruit, as well as air-conditioning and other good modern facilities. Valet room service is pleasant and polite, and efficiency prevails in all departments. The prettily decorated restaurant, in pastel pink,

green and beige, is now under the supervision of a recently promoted and charming manager, who, with Maître Chef Elliot, deserves a special mention for the combination of skilful cooking and welcoming atmosphere. Together they create a sense that this is somewhere very special, and the wine list is naturally very good too. The proprietor, David Levin, is continually improving the hotel, and is once again to be congratulated on making it such a delightful place. It enjoys a quiet setting for London, and nearby is another of its assets, the very good Le Metro wine bar.

48⇌ CTV in all bedrooms T ✱ S15% sB⇌£135-£160 dB⇌£160-£185 (room only)

Lift ☾ ⊞ 12 (£8)

French V S15% Lunch £16.50-£18.50&alc Dinner £32-£36.50alc Last dinner 11pm

Credit Cards 1 2 3 4 5

★★★ 62% **Basil Street** Basil St, Knightsbridge SW3 1AH ☎01-581 3311 Telex no 28379 FAX 01-581 3693

A well-established hotel stylishly and comfortably furnished. The lounge area, wine bar, Punch Restaurant and the Ladies Club are especially attractive and popular.

92rm(81⇌) CTV in all bedrooms T S% sBfr£45 sB⇌fr£85 dBfr£69 dB⇌fr£110 (room only)

Lift ☾ *xmas*

International V S% Lunch £13.50 Dinner £13-£18alc Last dinner 9.45pm

Credit Cards 1 2 3 4 5

✕✕✕✕ **Waltons** 121 Walton St SW3 ☎01-584 0204

Chef Tony Cameron has brought his own adventurous style of cooking to this long-established and famous restaurant. Surroundings are opulent, the wine list excellent, and diners may choose between the prix fixe and the more expensive à la carte menus. Service is very professional, but impersonal.

Closed Xmas, New Year & Etr

International V 65 seats Last lunch 2.30pm Last dinner 11.30pm nc2yrs

Credit Cards 1 2 3 4 5

✕✕✕ **Zen Chinese** Chelsea Cloisters, Sloane Av SW3 ☎01-589 1781 FAX 01-437 0641

A popular restaurant serving an appealing selection of well-prepared dishes. The staff are attentive and courteous and offer good Chinese hospitality.

Closed Xmas

Chinese V 120 seats Last lunch 2.30pm Last dinner 11.30pm

Credit Cards 1 2 3 4 5

✕✕ ***Avoirdupois Restaurant*** 334 Kings Rd SW3 ☎01-352 4071

Well prepared, varied and imaginative menu served in friendly atmosphere with soft live music.

Closed 25 & 26 Dec

English & French V 140 seats Last dinner 11.45pm ♫

Credit Cards 1 2 3 4 5

✕✕ **Bibendum** 1st Floor Michelin House, 81 Fulham Rd SW3 6RD

☎01-581 5817 FAX 01-823 7925

Simon Hopkinson has firmly established himself with a style of his own at this cool, elegant, Conran-designed restaurant, whose setting is the splendid old Michelin building. Now open on Sundays, this bustling restaurant continues to gain popularity, and deservedly so. Service is not always as welcoming as it might be, but the hearty cuisine is robust and satisfying. Roast guinea fowl with lemon and basil is packed with flavour, while a dish of grilled scallops with a fennel salad is more delicate, and neither is unnecessarily fussy.

Closed 24-28 Dec & BH's

Continental V 74 seats ✱ S15% Lunch £22.45-£24.75 Dinner £45-£55alc Last lunch 2.30pm Last dinner 11.30pm nc5yrs

Credit Cards 1 3

✕✕ **Daphne's** 110-112 Draycott Av, Chelsea SW3 3AE ☎01-584 6883 & 01-589 4257

Warm cosy restaurant with fine French and English cuisine.

Closed Sun & Bank Hols

Lunch not served Sat

English & French 95 seats ✱ Lunch £10-£14alc Dinner £18-£25alc Last lunch 2.30pm Last dinner mdnt

Credit Cards 1 2 3 5

✕✕ **English Garden** 10 Lincoln St SW3 2TS ☎01-584 7272

Well-researched old English recipies, cooked with considerable skill, are featured in a fashionable conservatory, English-garden setting.

Closed 25-26 Dec & Good Fri

V 65 seats Lunch £15&alc Dinner £21-£27alc Last lunch 2.30pm Last dinner 11.30pm

Credit Cards 1 2 3 5

✕✕ **The English House** 3 Milner St SW3 ☎01-584 3002

This elegant, well-appointed restaurant serves thoroughly researched traditional English dishes; supervision and service are excellent.

Closed 25-26 Dec & Good Fri

V 40 seats Lunch £14.50-£15.50&alc Dinner £19.50&alc Last lunch 2.30pm Last dinner 11.30pm

Credit Cards 1 2 3 5

✕✕ **Good Earth** 233 Brompton Rd SW3 ☎01-584 3658 FAX 01-823 8769

A loyal and appreciative clientèle ensure that this good, serious Chinese restaurant is always busy. Cantonese, Pekinese and Szechuan specialities offer a choice of styles ranging from fiery chilli dishes to the milder, delicate flavour of crispy lamb wrapped in lettuce and served with yellow plum sauce. Whole fish and fresh lobster are generally available at a market price.

Closed 4 days Xmas

Cantonese, Pekinese & Szechuan V 155 seats ✱ Lunch £12-£35&alc Dinner £12-£35&alc Last dinner 11.15pm 5P

Credit Cards 1 2 3 5

✕✕ **Mario** 260-262A Brompton Rd SW3 2AS ☎01-584 1724

An interesting selection of Italian wines complements the reliable and authentic regional dishes produced by Chef Cannas. Pasta is fresh and made on the premises, sauces well flavoured, the vegetables fresh and cooked with care.

Closed Mon & BH's

Italian V 80 seats Lunch £16.50&alc Dinner £15-£35alc Last lunch 3pm Last dinner 11.30pm

Credit Cards 1 2 3 5

✕✕ ***Meridiana*** 169 Fulham Rd SW3 ☎01-589 8815

Well managed and efficient Italian restaurant featuring open air balcony terrace, interesting authentic and home-made pasta.

Italian 165 seats Last dinner mdnt

Credit Cards 1 2 3 5

The AA's star-rating scheme is the market leader in hotel classification.

London

✕✕Ménage à Trois 15 Beauchamp Place SW3 1NQ ☎01-589 4252 & 01-589 0984 FAX 01-589 8860
This lively, basement restaurant has an intimate atmosphere, open fires in season and live piano music. The menu consists of starters and sweets only and the cheerful young staff are happy to help diners make their selections. Especially recommended by our inspector was the "menage a trois" cheese-filled parcels and the splendid array of chocolate puds.
Closed 25-25 Dec & Good Fri
Lunch not served Sat & Sun
French V 70 seats S12.5% Lunch £15-£20alc Dinner £22.50-£30alc Last lunch 3.15pm Last dinner 12.15am ♫
Credit Cards 1 2 3 4 5

✕✕St Quentin 243 Brompton Rd SW3 2EP ☎01-589 8005 & 01-581 5131 FAX 01-584 6064
This small, intimate brasserie offers a well chosen menu where the fish dishes are highly to be recommended. The wine list is comprehensive and offers a choice of reasonably priced bottles, the staff are friendly and efficient.
French 80 seats ✱ Lunch fr£10.90&alc Dinner fr£12.90&alc Last lunch 3pm Last dinner mdnt nc
Credit Cards 1 2 3 5

❀❀✕✕ TANTE CLAIRE 68 Royal Hospital Rd SW3 4HP (Relais et Châteaux)
☎01-352 6045 & 01-351 0227
A very French restaurant, which does not give an immediate impression of luxury, but shows its style in gleaming tablecloths and well-groomed polite staff, who serve with care and attention to detail. Outstanding dishes have included a casolette d'escargots, full of fresh flavours, and a rouelle de bar a la crême de laitue, which lived up to its reputation with a delicious sauce – in the matter of sauces, says at least one inspector, Maître Koffman remains unique. Vegetables lack potatoes on occasion, but are always well presented and properly cooked. Desserts are delicious, and a gratin de poire aux amandes et sorbet has been praised, although it was, perhaps, too rich in eau de vie. Excellent petits fours accompany richly fragrant coffee, and the wine list is well and truly comprehensive. One leaves this establishment in the assurance that not only is it one of London's best restaurants, but feeling grateful for its many years of consistent excellence.
Closed Sat, Sun, BH's 10 days Xmas, 10 days Etr & 3 wks Aug/Sep
French 38 seats ✱ S15% Lunch £19&alc Dinner £40-£55alc Last lunch 2pm Last dinner 11.15pm
Credit Cards 1 2 3 5

❀✕✕ *Turners* 87-89 Walton St SW3 2HP
☎01-584 6711
Brian Turner spends much time with his customers, and with his infectious enthusiasm has created a warm and friendly restaurant. The cuisine is modern French in style with good use made of fresh ingredients. Diners make their selection from the set menu du jour or a longer menu.
Lunch not served Sat
French 52 seats Last dinner 11pm
Credit Cards 1 2 3 5

✕Dans 119 Sydney St SW3 6NR ☎01-352 2718
The warm, cheerful atmosphere and attractive décor have helped to make this a popular restaurant. The cooking is of good quality and dishes are unpretentious and well prepared. Terrine of game, followed by a succulent loin of lamb en croûte with a dessert of poached pear attractively presented on a raspberry sauce are typical of the lunch dishes.
Closed Sun, BH's & Xmas-New Year
Lunch not served Sat
English & French 50 seats ✱ Lunch £13.50-£15.50alc Dinner fr£19 Last lunch 2.30pm Last dinner 10.45pm
Credit Cards 1 2 3 5

✕Ma Cuisine 113 Walton St SW3 ☎01-584 7585
A cosy little Chelsea restaurant specialising in robust French provincial cuisine. The cooking seems to have lost some edge since a change of ownership in 1988, but hearty dishes such as daube de canard continue to be enjoyable, and are served by good-humoured staff.
French 32 seats Lunch £10.45-£19.30alc Dinner £10.45-£19.30alc Last lunch 2pm Last dinner 11pm
Credit Cards 1 2 3 4 5

✕*Le Suquet* 104 Draycott Av SW3 ☎01-581 1785
With French Riviera connections it comes as no surprise to find seafood a speciality at this corner-sited restaurant. Commendable dishes include Loup de Mer au beurre blanc and lobster fresh from the tank. Booking is essential, particularly if a single diner.
French 50 seats Last dinner 11.30pm
Credit Cards 1 2 3 5

SW5 Earl's Court

★★★ 64% Swallow International Cromwell Rd SW5 0TH (Swallow) ☎01-370 4200 Telex no 27260 FAX 01-244-8194
Large, friendly hotel with well-equipped bedrooms.
417⇌(36fb) CTV in all bedrooms ® T sB&B⇌£80-£90 dB&B⇌£90-£105 Continental breakfast
Lift ☾ 50P (£10 per day) (heated) sauna solarium gymnasium spa jacuzzi hydro massage jets steamroom ♫
English & French V Lunch £13-£15alc High tea £4-£6alc Dinner fr£14&alc Last dinner mdnt
Credit Cards 1 2 3 5

✕✕ *Tiger Lee* 251 Old Brompton Rd SW5 9HP ☎01-370 2323 Telex no 919660 FAX 01-370 0440
The elegantly modern Chinese restaurant specialises in seafood and offers dishes with such evocative names as "Shadow of a Butterfly". The attentive and professional service is excellent and there are some fine French wines on the wine list.
Lunch not served
Cantonese V 56 seats Last dinner 11.15pm
Credit Cards 1 2 3

SW6 Fulham

See LONDON plan 5*C3*

✕✕Nayab Indian 309 New King's Rd SW6 4RF ☎01-731 6993 & 01-736 9596
Closed 25-26 Dec & 1 Jan
Indian V 50 seats Lunch £9-£22alc Dinner £9-£22alc Last lunch 2.45pm Last dinner 11.45pm nc5yrs
Credit Cards 1 2 3 5

✕L'Hippocampe 131A Munster Rd SW6 6DD ☎01-736 5588 FAX 01-736 3287
Lunch not served Sat
French 40 seats ✱ Lunch £9-£14.50&alc Dinner £14-£18alc Last lunch 2.30pm Last dinner 11pm
Credit Cards 1 2 3

SW7 South Kensington

★★★★ 65% Gloucester 4-18 Harrington Gardens SW7 4LH (Rank) ☎01-373 6030 Telex no 917505 FAX 01-373 0409
A pleasant modern hotel with an open-plan foyer/lounge and two restaurants, one of which offers a traditional à la carte menu, whilst the other provides an all day light meal and snack service. Bedrooms are spacious and well equipped, and pleasant, cheerful

London

staff provide 24-hour room service. In addition to the cocktail lounge there is also a wine cellar and real ale pub.
550⇔(2fb)⅍in 51 bedrooms CTV in all bedrooms ® T ✱ sB⇔£105-£120 dB⇔£120-£140 (room only)
Lift ☾ ⊞ 100🚘 (fr £6.50) CFA ♫ *xmas*
☋ English & Continental V ♉ ☊ ⅍ Lunch £13.25-£15.50 Dinner £14.25-£18.25&alc Last dinner 10.30pm
Credit Cards 1 2 3 4 5

★★★66% **The Regency** One Hundred Queens Gate, Kensington SW7 5AG ☎01-370 4595 Telex no 267594 FAX 01-370 5555
Peaceful, courteous and welcoming hotel with modern bedrooms, attractive restaurant and health spa.
200⇔⅍in 25 bedrooms CTV in all bedrooms T ⛓ (ex guide dogs) ✱ S% sB⇔£85 dB⇔£99 (room only)
Lift ☾ sauna solarium gymnasium health spa
☋ French V ♉ ☊ S% Lunch £15-£40alc High tea £5-£10alc Dinner £15-£40alc Last dinner 10.30pm
Credit Cards 1 2 3 4 5

★★★59% **Rembrandt** Thurloe Place SW7 2RS ☎01-589 8100 Telex no 295828 FAX 01-225 3363
This hotel boasts a comfortable lounge, good carvery restaurant and the Aquilla Health Club. Recently-refurbished bedrooms are well furnished and equipped.
200⇔(25fb)⅍in 17 bedrooms CTV in all bedrooms T ⛓ (ex guide dogs) S% sB⇔fr£79 dB⇔fr£99 (room only)
Lift ☾ P̸ ⊡(heated) sauna solarium gymnasium beauty parlour massage spa bath ♫
♉ ☊ Lunch £10.55-£14.25&alc High tea fr£6.95 Dinner £10.55-£14.25&alc Last dinner 9.30pm
Credit Cards 1 2 3 4 5

✕✕✕ **Bombay Brasserie** Courtfield Close, 140 Gloucester Rd SW7 ☎01-370 4040 & 01-373 0971 Telex no 264221
This restaurant serves authentic regional dishes in an elegant colonial atmosphere.
☋ Indian V 175 seats ✱ Lunch £11.50 Last lunch 2.45pm Last dinner mdnt P̸ ♫
Credit Cards 1 2 3 5

❀✕✕ **Hilaire** 68 Old Brompton Rd SW7 ☎01-584 8993
(Rosette awarded for dinner only)
This two-storey Kensington restaurant maintains a high standard of cooking. Here Bryan Webb uses his skill and flair to produce flavoursome dishes accompanied by well-prepared fresh vegetables. The puddings will not disappoint and the wine list is well balanced and reasonably priced. A plainer menu is available at lunchtime.
Closed Sun, 1 wk Xmas & BH's
Lunch not served Sat
☋ French V 48 seats Lunch £15.50-£18.50 Dinner £23.50-£27.50 Last lunch 2.30pm Last dinner 11pm P̸
Credit Cards 1 2 3 4 5

SW8 Battersea

See LONDON plan 5*D3*
See also SW11

❀✕✕ ***L'Arlequin*** 123 Queenstown Rd SW8 ☎01-622 0555
Christian Delteil continues to delight with his refreshingly understated menu concealing dishes of great finesse. The virtues of modern French cuisine are exemplified by stunning presentation, gentle cooking and shiny sauces, resulting in highly satisfying food. An honest fish mousseline with butter sauce, chosen from the excellent prix fixe luncheon menu, was outstanding, and a tender breast of Mallard, served with an intense, red-wine glaze was accompanied by the crispy legs. The wine list complements the cuisine and service in this smart little restaurant under the supervision of Madame Delteil, is relaxed and 'sympathique'.
Closed Sat, Sun, 1 wk winter & 3 wks Aug
☋ French 45 seats Last dinner 10.30pm P̸ nc5yrs
Credit Cards 1 2 3 5

❀✕✕ **Cavaliers'** 129 Queenstown Rd SW8 3RH ☎01-720 6960
Chef, David Cavalier, continues to cook in his distinctively creative and original style. Sauces have a new refinement that complements dishes with exciting combinations of texture, colour and flavour. Newly discovered delights include lobster ravioli infused with its own oil and spiked with herbs, sweetbreads and roasted crab, terrine of foie gras with muscat jelly, canon of new season's lamb scented with sweet basil, and seabass steamed with ginger. Service, under the eye of Susan Cavalier, is unobtrusive, but very attentive.
Closed 2 wks Aug
Lunch not served Sun & Mon
50 seats ✱ Lunch fr£16.50&alc Dinner fr£25alc Last lunch 2pm Last dinner 10.30pm P̸ nc8yrs
Credit Cards 1 2 3 5

SW10 West Brompton

See LONDON plan 5*C3*

✕✕ **Brinkley's** 47 Hollywood Rd SW10 9HX ☎01-351 1683 FAX 01-376 5083
Located off the Fulham Road, Brinkley's is allied to a wine bar and wine shop. Whether you choose from the 'Dishes of the Day' or the à la carte menu, you are sure to enjoy the skilful cooking of Chef Graham Day. This is a deservedly popular restaurant, offering good value for money, and friendly, attentive service. The candlelight and soft lighting create an intimate atmosphere in the evenings. Located off the Fulham Road, Brinkley's is allied to a wine bar and wine shop. Whether you choose from the 'Dishes of the Day' or the à la carte menu, you are sure to enjoy the skilful cooking of chef Graham Day. This is a deservedly popular restaurant, offering good value for money and friendly, attentive service. The candlelight and soft lighting create an intimate atmosphere in the evenings.
Closed Sun, Xmas & Etr
Lunch not served
☋ English & French V 60 seats Dinner £17-£19alc Last dinner 11.30pm P̸
Credit Cards 1 3

✕ ***La Croisette*** 168 Ifield Rd SW10 ☎01-373 3694
Popular small French restaurant specialising in shellfish. Good main basement ambience.
Closed Mon & 2 wks Xmas
Lunch not served Tue
☋ French 55 seats Last dinner 11.30pm P̸
Credit Cards 1 2 3 5

All AA-appointed establishments are inspected regularly to ensure that required standards are maintained.

SW11 Battersea

See LONDON plan 5*D3*
See also SW8
✕Pollyanna's 2 Battersea Rise SW11 ☎01-228 0316
Fashionable bistro-style décor is complemented by skilful and reliable cooking supervised by the proprietor.
Closed 4 days Xmas & 1 Jan
Lunch not served Mon-Sat
Dinner not served Sun
🍸 French **V** 80 seats Bar Lunch £10.95 Dinner £10-£20alc Last dinner mdnt ⁄P
Credit Cards 1 3

SW14 East Sheen

See LONDON plan 5*C3*
✕Crowthers 481 Upper Richmond Rd West, East Sheen SW14 ☎01-876 6372
Small family-run, tastefully decorated restaurant offering a fixed price menu.
Closed Sun, 1 wk Xmas & 2 wks summer
Lunch not served Sat
🍸 French **V** 28 seats Lunch £14 Dinner £23 Last lunch 1.45pm Last dinner 10.45pm ⁄P
Credit Cards 1 2 3

SW17 Wandsworth Common

See LONDON plan 5*C2*

❀❀ ✕✕ **HARVEY'S** 2 Bellevue Rd, Wandsworth Rd SW17 7EQ ☎01-672 0114
Marco Pierre White has taken culinary London by storm. A major refurbishment and a television series in the past year have not taken the slightest edge off the cooking here, which seems to get better and better. There are times when you will find nothing else in the country to match. Memorable dishes are so numerous that it is impossible to list them all, but particularly impressive have been a tagliatelle of oysters with caviar, and a superb ravioli of lobster to start with, a Bresse pigeon with cèpes and a fragrant fumet of red wine, and an innovative roast fillet of lamb stuffed with kidneys rolled in fresh mint and served with a delicious herby 'jus'. Desserts are equally good, and service, perhaps the weakest point of the operation, will hopefully continue to improve. The comprehensive wine list includes vintages from 1947. Murals, fresh flowers and air-conditioning all add to the pleasure. It is our own pleasure and delight that the forecast of awarding two 'roses' last year has been extended to two rosettes.
Closed Sun, last 2 wks Aug & last wk Dec-1st wk Jan
Lunch not served Sat
45 seats Last dinner 11pm ⁄P nc5yrs
Credit Cards 1 2 3

SW19 Wimbledon

See LONDON plan 5*C2*
★★★★72% **Cannizaro House** West Side, Wimbledon Common SW19 4UF (Thistle) ☎01-879 1464 Telex no 9413837 FAX 01-879 7338
Set in its own beautiful parkland, this historic Georgian mansion provides guests with all the peace and tranquillity of the countryside. Bedrooms are beautifully furnished and have marble-tiled bathrooms. Cuisine is reliable and service highly professional.
51⇌↱4⊟ CTV in all bedrooms **T** ✱ sB⇌↱£79-£90 dB⇌↱£95-£130 (room only) ⊟
☾ 60P ✲ ♫
🍸 International ♰ ⊒ Lunch fr£16.50&alc Dinner fr£16.50&alc Last dinner 10.30pm
Credit Cards 1 2 3 4 5

W1 West End

★★★★★66% **Churchill** W1A 4ZX ☎01-486 5800
Telex no 264831 FAX 01-486 1255
This hotel has a lovely location overlooking Portman Square Gardens. The flower-filled lobby, attractive arcade of shops, the sunken lounge where afternoon tea is served to the accompaniment of a harp, and the choice of bar, coffee shop and sophisticated restaurant are just some of the facilities made available to guests staying here.
452⇌↱⁄in 66 bedrooms CTV in all bedrooms **T** ✱
sB⇌↱£132-£150 dB⇌↱£145-£165 (room only) ⊟
Lift ☾ ⊞ 60🚗 (£2.50 per 2hrs) ✲ CFA ℘ (hard) ♫
🍸 International **V** ♰ ⊒ ⁄ Lunch fr£25&alc Dinner £30-£60alc Last dinner 11pm
Credit Cards 1 2 3 4 5

★★★★★ **CLARIDGE'S**
Brook St W1A 2JQ ☎01-629 8860 Telex no 21872 FAX 01-499 2210

This Grande Dame of hotels, favourite of royalty and celebrities, is not resting on its laurels. The majority of the bedrooms and nearly all the superb suites have been refurbished, and work continues on upgrading the rest, with air-conditioning among other welcome new features. The kitchens have also undergone a major transformation costing several million pounds. None of these improvements have been carried out at the expense of the supremely high standards which make Claridge's the epitome of fine English hotel-keeping. Standing in the heart of Mayfair, it adheres rigidly to its traditional values of exclusiveness, discretion and professional service of the highest order. Much of the credit for preserving the ambience and individual style must go to Michael Bentley, manager now for 20 years. To witness his greeting of loyal guests and to hear him talk with pride and affection for this distinguished hotel is to understand why Claridge's attracts such a devoted following. The Managing Director, Ron Jones, has brought such life, enthusiasm and personality that it has lifted the spirits of all the staff, and these two gentlemen will undoubtedly ensure that Claridge's remains a very special and uniquely British hotel.
190⇌↱ CTV in all bedrooms **T** ✗ (ex guide dogs) S15%
sB⇌↱£175-£200 dB⇌↱£220-£250 (room only)
Lift ☾ ⁄P ✲ ♫
🍸 International **V** ♰ ⊒ Lunch £11-£14.75 High tea £8-£8alc Dinner fr£38 Last dinner 11pm
Credit Cards 1 2 3 5

All hotels awarded three or more stars are now also given a percentage grading for the quality of their facilities. Please see p 16 for a detailed explanation.

⊛⊛★★★★★ CONNAUGHT

Carlos Place W1Y 6AL
☎01-499 7070

One of the last bastions of immaculate, traditional hotel-keeping, the Connaught was judged Europe's best hotel in a survey conducted by the AA in 1988. Managing Director, Mr P Zago, shields the hotel from the glare of publicity, and since much of the business consists of long and well-established repeat bookings, there is no need for constant media attention. The public rooms gleam with old polished panelling, antiques and flower arrangements. From afternoon tea in the Regency drawing room to cocktails in the 'clubby' bar, service is charming and highly attentive. The bedrooms and suites vary considerably, but even the smallest rooms (and there are a few small ones) are elegantly appointed. Newly decorated rooms tend to have lighter, fresher designs, while others are more restrained and masculine. Modern facilities are provided without gimmickry. The handsome restaurant and grill room are the setting for the fine cuisine of Michel Bourdin and his brigade, and although the cooking has been strangely inconsistent recently, the many fine dishes, such as superb teal with truffle sauce, an excellent fillet of brill with a delicious lobster sauce, and lunchtime favourites such as boiled silverside brisket with pickled tongue and dumplings, have outshone some overseasoned sauces and overcooked vegetables. Roasts from the trolley are always outstanding and the cuisine is complemented by a sensible cellar.

90⇨ CTV in all bedrooms **T** ✗

Lift ☾ P ⇎

☋ English & French ☕

Credit Cards [1]

★★★★★72% ***Grosvenor House*** Park Ln W1A 3AA (Trusthouse Forte) ☎01-499 6363 Telex no 24871 FAX 01-493 3341

After several years of refurbishment, this hotel has been restored to its rightful position as one of the leading 5-star hotels in the country. Besides the renowned banqueting suites, there are a number of shops, and a large lounge where afternoon tea is especially popular. There is a choice of three restaurants – 90 Park Lane, the Pavilion Restaurant (particularly good value at lunchtime) and the attractive Pasta Vino e Fantasia where Italian cuisine is served.

472⇨⊁in 47 bedrooms CTV in all bedrooms ® **T**

Lift ☾ 20P 100🚗 (charged) CFA ⊡(heated) sauna solarium gymnasium health & fitness centre

V ♈ ☕ ⊁

Credit Cards [1] [2] [3] [4] [5]

★★★★★75% **Inn on the Park** Hamilton Place, Park Ln W1A 1AZ (Prestige) ☎01-499 0888 Telex no 22771 FAX 01-493 1895/6629

This year the Inn on the Park has been awarded Red Stars and we believe it to be possibly the best modern hotel in London. It is certainly elegant and attractive, with every attention paid to the comfort and convenience of its guests. The entrance lobby, with marbled floors and dark wood panelling, is enhanced by lots of fresh flowers and greenery. There are places to sit and a variety of quality shops. The foyer lounge provides snacks and drinks throughout the day and traditional afternoon teas to the sound of the harp or piano. A double staircase leads to the first floor where there is a further sitting area, the Four Seasons Restaurant with cocktail lounge and the Lanes Restaurant where a pianist plays each evening. Executive Chef, Eric Deblonde, and Phillipe Boulot, are in charge of the catering and have created menus with some imaginative dishes. The bedrooms are spacious, well appointed and individually decorated with tasteful soft furnishings and the added benefit of air conditioning. The valet room service is pleasantly polite and an efficient service prevails throughout the hotel. Overseeing the whole operation, with the same commitment, attention to detail, professionalism and care, is the most charming and courteous Ramon Pajares.

228⇨♪⊁in 48 bedrooms CTV in all bedrooms **T** ✗ S%
sB⇨♪£195.50-£212.75 dB⇨♪£235.75 (room only) ⊟

Lift ☾ ⊞ 65🚗 (£8) ⇎ ♫ *xmas*

☋ International **V** ♈ ☕ ⊁ Lunch £19-£25&alc Dinner £35&alc Last dinner mdnt

Credit Cards [1] [2] [3] [4] [5]

⊛★★★★★73% ***Inter-Continental*** 1 Hamilton Pl, Hyde Park Corner W1V 0QY
☎01-409 3131 Telex no 25853 FAX 01-493 3476

This huge cosmopolitan hotel continues to hold a rosette award for Le Soufflé restaurant, although our inspectors' reports have been less favourable than in other years. Under the direction of Peter Kromberg, soufflés remain the highlight of the meal, while more hearty dishes such as mignonettes de boeuf au foie gras, and cotelettes de pigeonneau aux cèpes et petit pois are well sauced and enjoyable. Service under the supervision of Josef Lanser, remains exceptionally good.

490⇨♪⊁in 5 bedrooms CTV in all bedrooms **T** ✗ (ex guide dogs)

Lift ☾ ⊞ 100🚗 (charged) ⇎ CFA sauna gymnasium leisure spa

☋ French **V** ♈ ☕ Last dinner 11.30pm

Credit Cards [1] [2] [3] [4] [5]

★★★★★73% **London Hilton** 22 Park Ln W1A 2HH (Hilton)
☎01-493 8000 Telex no 24873 FAX 01-493 4957

From its prime position at the heart of Mayfair the Hilton's rooms command superb views over Hyde Park, Green Park and St James's Park. Bedrooms are well equipped and offer free cable and satellite TV as well as the usual facilities. The lively Polynesian restaurant beneath the hotel is very popular and there is also a roof restaurant and a discotheque. Staff are cosmopolitan, well trained and very helpful, contributing much to the character of the hotel.

446⇨♪⊁in 23 bedrooms CTV in all bedrooms **T**
sB⇨♪£166.75-£235.75
dB⇨♪£189.75-£264.50 (room only) ⊟

Lift ☾ ⊞ P sauna solarium ♫

☋ International **V** ♈ ☕ ⊁

Credit Cards [1] [2] [3] [4] [5]

See advertisement on page 433

★★★★★50% ***May Fair Inter-Continental*** Stratton St W1A 2AN
☎01-629 7777 Telex no 262526 FAX 01-629 1459

Long-established hotel, with friendly service. Facilities include a popular coffee house, elegant restaurant, small cinema and the Mayfair theatre.

322⇨♪(14fb) CTV in all bedrooms **T** ✗ (ex guide dogs)

Lift ☾ ⊞ P ⇎

☋ English & French **V** ♈ ☕ Last dinner 10.30pm

Credit Cards [1] [2] [3] [4] [5]

⊛★★★★★73% **Le Meridien** 21 Piccadilly W1V 0BH
☎01-734 8000 Telex no 25795 FAX 01-437 3574

▶

Visually stunning, luxury hotel with many virtues, including a superb leisure and health club with a swimming pool, jacuzzi, sauna, billiard tables, library and a restaurant and bar. There are a variety of restaurants and bars as well as an elegant lounge to satisfy most thirsts and appetites. Bedrooms and bathrooms are the only disappointment in an otherwise excellent 5-star hotel.
284⇔↱1⊞ CTV in all bedrooms **T** ✕ (ex guide dogs) ✻ sB⇔↱£166.75-£195.50
dB⇔↱£189.75-£218.50 (room only)
Lift ☾ ⊞ 𝑃 ⇎ ⊡(heated) squash snooker sauna solarium gymnasium health & leisure club ♫ *xmas*
☋ International **V** ♁ ⊻ ⊁ Lunch fr£15&alc Last high tea 6pm
Credit Cards 1 2 3 4 5

★★★★★74% **Ritz** Piccadilly W1V 9DG (Prestige) ☎01-493 8181 Telex no 267200 FAX 01-493 2687
With its glitteriong gold leaf and chandeliers, the Ritz remains the prettiest and most elegant London hotel. The bedrooms have been recently refurbished and the suites are now quite outstanding. In the magnificent restaurant with its trompe l'oeil ceiling, Chef Keith Stanley offers inventive British cooking, while the Palm Court lounge remains popular for those taking afternoon tea.
130⇔↱ CTV in all bedrooms **T** ✕ ✻ sB⇔↱fr£155
dB⇔↱£185-£240 (room only) ⊟
Lift ☾ 𝑃 ⇎ ♫ *xmas*
☋ International **V** ♁ ⊻ Lunch £18.50-£25&alc High tea fr£9.50 Dinner fr£39.50&alc Last dinner 10.45pm
Credit Cards 1 2 3 4 5

London

★★★★**ATHENAEUM**

Piccadilly W1V 0BJ
(Rank)(Pride of Britain)
☎01-499 3464
Telex no 261589 FAX 01-493 1860

It says much for Rank hotels that the 15-year-old Athenaeum is one of the few group-owned hotels to be awarded Red Stars. General Manager, Nicholas Rettie, is to be congratulated for ensuring that the standards of service remain as high as ever. The staff are professionally discreet but welcoming, polite and pleasant too, all of which helps to create a distinctive and understated style. The recent refurbishment of all the very well-appointed bedrooms is now complete, and the lounge has been revamped to become warmer and more colourful. The small, almost club-like bar is notable for serving over 50 types of single malt whiskies, while in the elegant restaurant chef Derek Fuller continues to offer unusual combinations of ingredients and flavours. A usefully central West End setting with views over Green Park is also a bonus.
112⇔↱⊁in 27 bedrooms CTV in all bedrooms **T** ✕ (ex guide dogs) ✻ sB⇔↱£145-£155
dB⇔↱£155-£170 (room only) ⊟
Lift ☾ ⊞ 300⌂ (£14.50) ⇎ CFA ♫ *xmas*
☋ International **V** ♁ ⊻ Lunch £17.50-£19.50&alc Dinner £27.50-£35&alc Last dinner 10.30pm
Credit Cards 1 2 3 4 5

★★★★75% **Britannia Inter-Continental** Grosvenor Square W1X 3AN ☎01-629 9400 Telex no 23941 FAX 01-629 7736
High standards continue to be maintained in this friendly and popular hotel. Service is professional and the staff helpful. Bedrooms range from small singles to spacious de luxe, but all are tastefully decorated and well equipped. The Adams Restaurant offers a number of imaginative dishes, well and freshly prepared by an enthusiastic staff. Puddings are also a delight.
353⇔⊁in 5 bedrooms CTV in all bedrooms **T** ✕ (ex guide dogs) sB⇔£120.75-£184 dB⇔£149.50-£184 (room only) ⊟
Lift ☾ ⊞ 15P CFA Satellite TV ♫ *xmas*
☋ English, American & Japanese **V** ♁ ⊻ ⊁ Lunch £18.65-£18.95&alc Dinner £18.95-£24.75&alc Last dinner 10.30pm
Credit Cards 1 2 3 4 5

★★★★ **BROWN'S**

Dover St, Albermarle St
W1A 4SW (Trusthouse Forte)
☎01-493 6020
Telex no 28686 FAX 01-493 9381

Spanning 12 houses among the fine antique shops and art galleries of Mayfair, Brown's is one of London's oldest hotels. This is a place of oak panelling, stained glass and deep calm – not unlike the gentlemen's clubs nearby. A discreet air prevails in the lounge, where log fires burn in winter and afternoon tea is served among chintz-covered armchairs under the eye of the grandfather clock. An open fire also warms the intimate St George's bar, with its deep leather sofas and oil paintings. The elegant panelled dining room, 'l'Aperitif', offers both French and English specialities such as gratin of deep scallops and boneless saddle of rabbit with fresh figs and juniper syrup, followed by home-made puddings from the trolley. Bedrooms are individually decorated in traditional style, with Victorian luggage racks as well as the modern amenities of direct-dial telephones and mini-bars. Good-humoured, attentive staff, despite some hiccups, enhance the character of this very individual hotel. Although it cannot be described as the smartest of our Red Star selection, it remains one of the best loved.
133⇔↱(14fb)⊁in 12 bedrooms CTV in all bedrooms **T** ✕ (ex guide dogs) ✻ sB⇔↱£125-£140
dB⇔↱£160-£180 (room only) ⊟
Lift ☾ 𝑃 ⇎ CFA *xmas*
☋ English & French **V** ♁ ⊻ ⊁ S% Lunch £19-£24.75&alc High tea £11.50-£14.25&alc Dinner £26.50-£29&alc Last dinner 10pm
Credit Cards 1 2 3 4 5

★★★★58% **The Cumberland** Marble Arch W1A 4RF (Trusthouse Forte) ☎01-262 1234 Telex no 22215 FAX 01-724 4621
This popular commercial and tourist hotel is continuing to upgrade its accommodation and most rooms are now both well equipped and comfortable, as are the lounges and reception area. The choice of restaurants includes a carvery and a coffee-shop as well as the main restaurant and, for those who like the exotic, one in Japanese style.
905⇔⊁in 50 bedrooms CTV in all bedrooms **T** ✻
sB⇔£85-£95 dB⇔£108-£116 (room only) ⊟
Lift ☾ 𝑃 ⇎ CFA *xmas*
☋ International **V** ♁ ⊻ ⊁ Lunch £13
Credit Cards 1 2 3 4 5

★★★★58% **Holiday Inn – Marble Arch** 134 George St W1H 6DN (Holiday Inns) ☎01-723 1277 Telex no 27983 FAX 01-402 0666
Well-managed, modern high-rise hotel with varied international clientele. As we went to print a new European restaurant was being introduced to complement the existing coffee shop. Staff are willing and helpful, and the well-equipped bedrooms are particularly spacious. Free parking for residents is a bonus.
241(135fb) in 32 bedrooms CTV in all bedrooms **T** S15% sB£119-£132 dB£132-£152 (room only)
Lift 5P 60 CFA (heated) sauna solarium gymnasium *xmas*
European **V** Lunch fr£14.50 Dinner fr£14.50&alc Last dinner 11pm
Credit Cards 1 2 3 4 5 £

★★★★75% **London Marriott** Grosvenor Square W1A 4AW ☎01-493 1232 Telex no 268101 FAX 01-491 3201
Overlooking Grosvenor Square, this tastefully-furnished hotel offers a choice of eateries, particularly well-equipped bedrooms and good business and function facilities.
223 CTV in all bedrooms **T** (ex guide dogs)
sB£178.25-£189.75 dB£201.25-£212.75 (room only)
Lift CFA *xmas*
International **V** Lunch fr£15.50&alc Dinner £18-£30alc Last dinner 1am
Credit Cards 1 2 3 4 5 £

★★★★73% **Montcalm** Great Cumberland Place W1A 2LF ☎01-402 4288 Telex no 28710 FAX 01-724 9180
This terraced Georgian building has been tastefully modernised to provide comfortable accommodation and well-equipped bedrooms. The Celebrités restaurant offers an interesting menu of skilfully prepared dishes and service is professional and friendly.
114(9fb) CTV in all bedrooms **T** S12% sBfr£146 dBfr£168 (room only)
Lift
French **V** S% Lunch £12-£14.75&alc Dinner £18-£20&alc Last dinner 10pm
Credit Cards 1 2 3 4 5 £

★★★★73% **Park Lane** Piccadilly W1Y 8BX ☎01-499 6321 Telex no 21533 FAX 01-499 1965
The old-fashioned atmosphere based on traditional levels of service and hospitality coupled with good management are the secrets of this hotel's success. In addition, residents can enjoy the Palm Court lounge, Bracewells Restaurant and the Brasserie. Leisure facilities are also available.
321(32fb) in 44 bedrooms CTV in all bedrooms **T**
sB£133-£154 dB£154-£176 (room only)
Lift 180 (charged) CFA gymnasium
International **V** S% Lunch £17-£18.50&alc Dinner £24.50-£27&alc Last dinner 10.30pm
Credit Cards 1 2 3 5

★★★★74% **Portman Inter-Continental** 22 Portman Square W1H 9FL ☎01-486 5844 Telex no 261526 FAX 01-935 0537
An inviting lobby with clusters of comfortable armchairs, the popular bakery and pub, Truffles Restaurant, a choice of modern bedrooms or penthouse suites and superb function facilities – just some of the services to be enjoyed in this hotel.
273 in 14 bedrooms CTV in all bedrooms **T** (ex guide dogs)
Lift CFA (hard)
French **V**
Credit Cards 1 2 3 4 5

★★★★64% **Ramada** 10 Berners St W1A 3BA ☎01-636 1629 Telex no 25759 FAX 01-580 3972
235(10fb) in 105 bedrooms CTV in all bedrooms **T**
S% sB£76-£118 dB£118-£140 (room only)
Lift *xmas*
English & French **V** Lunch £13.75-£14.95&alc High tea £3-£5 Dinner £13.75-£14.95&alc Last dinner 10.30pm
Credit Cards 1 2 3 5

★★★★53% **St George's** Langham Place W1N 8QS (Trusthouse Forte) ☎01-580 0111 Telex no 27274 FAX 01-436 7997
The hotel shares its building just north of Oxford Circus with the BBC and bedrooms, recently refurbished and upgraded, are all above the ninth floor. The Summit Restaurant, bar and lounge afford panoramic views over London.
86(5fb) in 16 bedrooms CTV in all bedrooms ® **T** S%
sB£98-£150 dB£125-£250 (room only)
Lift P (£10) *xmas*
English & French **V** S% Lunch £16.50-£18.50&alc Dinner £16.50-£18.50&alc Last dinner 10pm
Credit Cards 1 2 3 4 5

★★★★68% **Selfridge** Orchard St W1H 0JS (Thistle) ☎01-408 2080 Telex no 22361 FAX 01-629 8849
A modern hotel with fine public rooms including a panelled lounge and country pub-style cocktail bar. There are two restaurants – one formal and very comfortable and the other very informal. Bedrooms tend to be small but very well equipped.
298(25fb) in 110 bedrooms CTV in all bedrooms **T**
sB£115-£140 dB£135-£155 (room only)
Lift
International Lunch fr£16.95&alc Dinner fr£16.95&alc Last dinner 10.30pm
Credit Cards 1 2 3 4 5

★★★★63% **The Westbury** Bond St, Conduit St W1A 4UH (Trusthouse Forte) ☎01-629 7755 Telex no 24378
An hotel, with attractive appearance and décor, constantly improving and providing a good range of traditional services. Public areas, whilst compact, are particularly pleasant and feature ▶

London

a fine wood-panelled lounge. Reasonable French cuisine is served in the Polo Restaurant.
243⇌⚡in 40 bedrooms CTV in all bedrooms T ✻
sB⇌£130-£150 dB⇌£165-£185 (room only) ⊟
Lift ☾ ⊞ P ⇌ CFA ♫ *xmas*
French V ⚘ ⚡ Lunch £23.30-£41.40alc Dinner fr£21.50&alc Last dinner 10.30pm
Credit Cards 1 2 3 4 5

★★★ 70% ***Chesterfield*** 35 Charles St W1X 8LX ☎01-491 2622 Telex no 269394 FAX 01-491 4793
This traditional hotel in the centre of Mayfair now has the new Butlers restaurant, which offers an outstanding buffet lunch in addition to its à la carte menu . The colourful bedrooms are furnished to a high standard, and a warm atmosphere is created by flowers and antiques in the ground floor public rooms, which include a wood-panelled library.
113⇌1 CTV in all bedrooms T ✗ (ex guide dogs)
Lift ☾ P ⇌
⚘ Last dinner 10.30pm
Credit Cards 1 2 3 5

★★★ 69% **Clifton-Ford** 47 Welbeck St W1M 8DN ☎01-486 6600 Telex no 22569 FAX 01-486 7492
It is rare to find an hotel of such quality, elegance and tranquillity in the heart of the West End. Traditional style and modern facilities blend harmoniously, and the top-floor rooms and suites, with their panoramic views of London, have been equipped with every comfort, while rooms on other floors have recently been upgraded.
230⇌(6fb) CTV in all bedrooms T ✻
sB⇌£109.25-£132.25
dB⇌£132.25-£172.50 (room only) ⊟
Lift ☾ 10 (£12) ♫
International V ⚘ Bar Lunch £3-£15alc Dinner £19-£30alc Last dinner 11pm
Credit Cards 1 2 3 5

★★★ 66% **Mandeville** Mandeville Place W1M 6BE ☎01-935 5599 Telex no 269487 FAX 01-935 9588
An inviting hotel, well placed for Oxford Street shopping and the West End, the Mandeville's rooms are well equipped and attractive. The coffee shop, residents' lounge bar and Boswell's Pub Bar are all popular and management and staff give guests a friendly reception.
165⇌ CTV in all bedrooms T
Lift ☾ P ⇌
V ⚘
Credit Cards 1 2 3 5

★★★ 65% ***Mount Royal*** Bryanston St, Marble Arch W1A 4UR (Mount Charlotte) ☎01-629 8040 Telex no 23355 FAX 01-499 7792
A large commercial and tourist hotel just near Marble Arch – ideally placed for those visiting the capital. This hotel has a number of boutiques and kiosks, conference and banqueting facilities as well as a variety of places for guests to eat. Bedrooms are being tastefully refurbished.
701⇌(31fb)⚡in 40 bedrooms CTV in all bedrooms ® T ✗
Lift ☾ P CFA
Mainly grills ⚘ ⚡ Last dinner 11pm
Credit Cards 1 2 3 4 5

★★**Regent Palace** Glasshouse St, Piccadilly W1A 4BZ (Trusthouse Forte) ☎01-734 7000 Telex no 23740 FAX 01-734 6435
Good accommodation in this outstanding value-for-money hotel, adjacent to Piccadilly Circus.
999rm(34fb)⚡in 210 bedrooms CTV in all bedrooms ® ✻
sB&B£44 dB&B£59 ⊟
Lift ☾ P CFA ♫ *xmas*
V ⚘ ⚡ Lunch £11.95&alc Dinner £11.95&alc Last dinner 9pm
Credit Cards 1 2 3 4 5

✻ ✕✕✕✕✕ ***Ninety Park Lane*** 90 Park Ln W1
☎01-409 1290 Telex no 24871 FAX 01-493 3341
One of the few really opulent restaurants remaining in London, where the tail-coated professional staff seem to glide from one table to another amidst an elegant international clientele. The lunch menu was particularly praised by our inspector as were the excellent selection of sweets and the café filtre served with delicious petits fours.
Closed Sun
Lunch not served Sat
French V 78 seats Last lunch 2.45pm Last dinner 10.45pm 10P nc3yrs ⚡
Credit Cards 1 2 3 4 5

✻✻✻ ✕✕✕✕ **LE GAVROCHE** 43 Upper Brook St W1Y 1PF
☎01-408 0881 & 01-499 1826
Our visits early in 1989 indicated that Albert Roux's superb restaurant was failing to live up to its reputation for serving some of the best food in the country. The introduction of son, Michel, as head chef may have played as significant a part as outside pressures, but, happily, more recent visits have seen a return to the highest standards, and we are pleased to be able to award our most coveted accolade once again. Immaculate service, a fine cellar and air-conditioning all play a part, but most important is the cuisine itself. Dishes are decidedly non-experimental, drawing influence from both classical and ▶

London

London

modern French roots. A ragôut de langoustines aux artichauts et persil, and a mousseline de homard, sauce Champagne, have been memorable starters. Among the main courses you might find an earthy pöelée de rognon, ris et pied de veau au basilic, or delicious cotelettes d'agneau au vinaigre à l'estragon. A delicate soufflé or a satisfying tarte tatin would complete a memorable meal.

Closed Sat, Sun & 22 Dec-2 Jan

French **V** 65 seats S% Lunch £22-£50&alc Dinner fr£50&alc Last lunch 2pm Last dinner 11pm nc6yrs

Credit Cards 1 2 3 4 5

✕✕✕✕ ***London Hilton Hotel (Trader Vic's)*** 22 Park Ln W1A 2HH ☎01-493 7586 Telex no 24873 FAX 01-493 4957

Lively Polynesian restaurant below Hilton Hotel.

Closed Xmas Day

Lunch not served Sat

French & Chinese **V** 150 seats Last dinner 11.45pm

Credit Cards 1 2 3 4 5

✕✕✕ **The Greenhouse** 27A Hay's Mews W1X 7RJ ☎01-499 3331 Telex no 919042

Modern elegant dining room with formal but friendly service accompanying English and French cuisine.

Closed Sun, 1wk after Xmas & BH's

Lunch not served Sat

English & French 85 seats ✱ Lunch £15-£25alc Last lunch 2.30pm Last dinner 11pm nc5yrs

Credit Cards 1 2 3 4 5

✕✕✕ ***Princess Garden of Mayfair*** 8-10 North Audley St W1V 1FA ☎01-493 3223

Closed Xmas & Etr

Pekinese **V** 150 seats Last dinner 11.20pm nc7yrs

Credit Cards 1 2 3 5

❀✕✕✕ **Rue St Jacques** 5 Charlotte St W1P 1HD ☎01-637 0222 FAX 01-637 0224

Chef Gunther Schlender continues to produce appealing, imaginative menus, but recent changes behind the scenes may have resulted in a standard of cuisine that is not quite as refined and careful as in the past. Nevertheless, excellent sauces have been praised by our inspectors, including one of chervil butter with a warm crab terrine, and a fragrant truffle 'jus' with pigeon. Service is courteous, and there is an extensive French wine list.

Closed Sun, Xmas, Etr & BH's

Lunch not served Sat

French **V** 70 seats Lunch fr£19.50 Dinner fr£32alc Last lunch 2.30pm Last dinner 11.15pm

Credit Cards 1 2 3 5

❀✕✕ **Au Jardin Des Gourmets** 5 Greek St W1 ☎01-437 1816 FAX 01-437 0043

A popular restaurant, long established and located in the heart of Soho, continues to offer well-prepared and appealing French dishes. The fixed price menu is good value, while the gourmet menu offers an impressive meal. Extensive wine list with some good vintages reasonably priced.

Closed Sun, Xmas & Etr

Lunch not served Sat & BH's

French 85 seats Lunch £15.50-£28.50&alc Dinner £15.50-£28.50&alc Last dinner 11.30pm

Credit Cards 1 2 3 5

✕✕ **La Bastide** 50 Greek St W1V 5LQ ☎01-734 3300

This elegant Georgian style restaurant creates a pleasant and caring ambience. Regional French dishes are the speciality, executed with a high degree of competance and there are fixed price menus as well as the à la carte. The wine list is comprehensive, with a good general appeal.

Closed Sun & Bank Hols

Lunch not served Sat

French 45 seats ✱ Lunch £16.50-£18.50&alc Dinner £17.20-£22alc Last lunch 2.30pm Last dinner 11.30pm nc12yrs

Credit Cards 1 2 3 5

✕✕ ***Chambeli*** 12 Great Castle St W1N 7AD ☎01-636 0662

Predominantly North Indian dishes are well prepared in this modern restaurant whose two floors are air-conditioned. The staff are helpful, efficient and attentive and the atmosphere is friendly.

Closed Sun & 25-26 Dec

Indian **V** 86 seats Last dinner 11.30pm

Credit Cards 1 2 3 5

✕✕ **Chesa Restaurant** (Swiss Centre), 10 Wardour St W1V 3HG ☎01-734 1291 Telex no 8811646 FAX 01-439 6129

Closed 25 Dec

Swiss **V** 54 seats ✱ Lunch £13-£27alc Dinner £19.50 Last lunch 2.30pm Last dinner 11pm

Credit Cards 1 2 3 5

❀❀❀✕✕ **CHEZ NICO** 35 Great Portland St W1N 5DD ☎01-436 8846

We welcome the controversial Nico Ladenis back to the pages of our guide this year, after his request not to be included in the previous edition. In this new, more central restaurant we have found the cooking to be just as impressive and popular as ever. One would travel far – and across the Channel – to taste sauces comparable to those served here. The balance, clarity and intensity of flavour are masterful, as demonstrated in dishes such as Poitrine de Pintade au Vieux Xeres et sa Ballotine Pistachée. To begin, a cassolette de St Jacques is accompanied by excellent noodles, or, at a small supplement, it is difficult to pass by the Mosaique de Foie Gras. Puddings and pastries have yet to achieve the same perfection, but overall the quality of cooking by Nico's brigade is truly outstanding – many would say the best in the country – and we are very pleased (despite the occasional service hiccup) to give due and proper recognition to Nico's talents, professionalism and dedication by the award of 3 rosettes.

Closed Sun & Xmas/New Year, 3 wks Aug-Sep

French **V** 45 seats ✱ Lunch £25&alc Dinner fr£42alc Last lunch 2pm Last dinner 11pm nc10yrs

---

✕✕ **Gallery Rendezvous** 53 Beak St W1R 3LF ☎01-734 0445

Chinese paintings are permanently exhibited in the restaurant.

Closed Xmas & New Year

Chinese & Pekinese **V** 140 seats S10% Lunch £10-£17alc Dinner £10-£21alc Last lunch 2.30pm Last dinner 10.45pm

Credit Cards 1 2 3 5

✕✕ ***Gay Hussar*** 2 Greek St W1V 6NB ☎01-437 0973

A popular, intimate restaurant with a distinctive character offers good, honest Hungarian cuisine which is both wholesome and well flavoured. Guests can sample a range of interesting Hungarian wines, and service though informal, is attentive and efficient.

Closed Sun

Hungarian 35 seats Last dinner 10.30pm

London

✕✕Lai Qila 117 Tottenham Court Rd W1P 9HL ☎01-387 4570
Smart, air-conditioned Tandoori restaurant with a short but interesting menu composed mainly of specialities. The pungent and highly spiced sauces compliment the good quality ingredients used. A take-away service is also available.
Closed 25 & 26 Dec
Indian V 75 seats Lunch fr£10&alc Dinner £10-£30alc Last dinner 11.30pm P
Credit Cards [1] [2] [3] [5]

✕✕Langan's Brasserie Stratton St W1 ☎01-491 8822
Very fashionable, popular and sometimes noisy brasserie and first-floor Venition Room. The stylish menu changes daily and the standard of cooking is always reliable.
Closed Sun & Public hols
Lunch not served Sat
English & French V 200 seats ✱ S12.5% Lunch £16.48-£31.89alc Dinner £16.48-£31.89alc Last lunch 3.00pm Last dinner 11.45pm P ♫
Credit Cards [1] [2] [3] [5]

✕✕Lindsay House 21 Romilly St W1V 5TG ☎01-439 0450
The elegant, tastefully-appointed restaurant specialises in traditional English cuisine, offering meals of a high standard and a very high level of service, excellently supervised.
English & French V 30 seats ✱ Lunch fr£14.75&alc Dinner £30-£40alc Last lunch 2.30pm Last dinner mdnt P ♫
Credit Cards [1] [2] [3] [5]

✕✕*Mr Kai of Mayfair* 65 South Audley St W1Y 5FD ☎01-493 8988
Sophisticated, elegant restaurant serving both classical and regional Chinese dishes.
Closed Xmas & Bank Hols
Pekinese 120 seats Last lunch 2.30pm Last dinner 11.15pm P nc6yrs
Credit Cards [1] [2] [3] [5]

✕✕*Number 10* 10 Old Burlington St W1X 1LA ☎01-439 1099 & 01-734 5010
A modern restaurant which has, as its name suggests, a political flavour in its décor, with many pictures and caricatures of past Prime Ministers and politicians. Not surprisingly, the menu offers typically English dishes such as sausage and mash, black pudding and fish cakes.
Closed Sat, Sun, 1 wk Xmas & 1 wk Aug BH
Dinner not served Mon
V 68 seats Last lunch 3.30pm Last dinner 10.30pm
Credit Cards [1] [2] [3] [5]

❀✕✕Odin's 27 Devonshire St W1N 1RJ ☎01-935 7296
Always busiest at lunchtime, this attractive restaurant just off Marylebone High Street is one of those under the joint ownership of Richard Shephard and Michael Caine. It is richly appointed and the walls are adorned with fine paintings, but the cuisine is refreshingly unfussy. The list of starters is indeed quite straightforward, but is lifted above the average by ingredients of the best quality. Commendable main dishes include loin of lamb baked in pastry and served with an intense Madeira sauce, and medallion of venison with beetroot and port. Mrs Langan's chocolate pudding is a classic which should not be missed. The short wine list is well balanced and service is good humoured, but sensible prices are unfortunately boosted by hefty service and cover charges.
Closed Sun & Public hols
Lunch not served Sat
French 60 seats ✱ S15% Lunch £21.39-£32.89alc Dinner £21.39-£32.89alc Last lunch 2.30pm Last dinner 11.30pm P
Credit Cards [1] [2] [3] [5]

✕✕*Red Fort* 77 Dean St W1V 5HA ☎01-437 2525
The exterior of this new Indian restaurant has the air of a pink palace. Inside, exquisite girls in red saris serve cocktails and such regional dishes as spiced and marinated quail baked in a charcoal fire.
Closed 25-27 Dec
Indian V 160 seats Last dinner 11.15pm P nc5yrs
Credit Cards [1] [2] [3] [5]

❀✕✕Sutherlands 45 Lexington St W1R 3LG ☎01-434 3401
A stylish and well-frequented restaurant housed in a listed Georgian terrace in Soho. The service provided by the young staff is warm and friendly and the innovative but delicious dishes prepared by chef Garry Hollihead are prepared from top-quality ingredients.
Closed Sun & B H's
Lunch not served Sat
V 55 seats Lunch £25&alc Dinner fr£27alc Last lunch 2.15pm Last dinner 11.15pm P
Credit Cards [1] [2] [3]

✕✕*Yumi* 110 George St W1H 6DJ ☎01-935-8320
The typical Japanese menu offers well prepared and interesting dishes. Guests are welcomed by traditionally dressed waitresses and at lunchtime there is a choice of reasonably priced set menus.
Closed Sun, 2 wks Xmas, 1 wk Aug & Public Hols
Lunch not served Sat
Japanese 70 seats Last dinner 10.30pm P
Credit Cards [1] [2] [3] [5]

❀✕*Alastair Little* 49 Frith St W1 ☎01-734 5183
The high standards of cooking ensure that this small, fashionable restaurant maintains its popularity, so much so that advance booking is always advisable. The menu, changed at every meal, is short but imaginative; the wine list, on the other hand, is comprehensive and reasonably priced.
Closed Sat, Sun 3 wks Aug & 2 wks Xmas
International 36 seats Last lunch 2.30pm Last dinner 11.30pm P

✕Arirang 31-32 Poland St W1 ☎01-437 6633 & 01-437 9662
There is an authentic atmosphere in this intimate little Korean restaurant, where the interesting menu of delicately prepared meals is served by friendly, young, national waitresses.
Closed Sun, Xmas & New Year
Korean V 120 seats ✱ S10% Lunch £8.50-£19.50&alc Dinner £13.50-£19.50&alc Last lunch 3pm Last dinner 11pm P
Credit Cards [1] [2] [3] [4] [5]

✕Aunties 126 Cleveland St W1 ☎01-387 1548 & 01-387 3226
English restaurant specialising in home-made pies.
Closed Sun, 25-26 Dec, 1 Jan, PH's & 2 wks Aug
Lunch not served Sat

▶

London

30 seats ✳ Lunch £16.50 Dinner £16.50 Last lunch 2pm Last dinner 11pm ₱
Credit Cards 1 2 3 5

✕Frith's 14 Frith St W1V 5TS ☎01-439 3370 & 01-734 7535
Tasteful design in modern style has created a bright and fresh atmosphere in this black and white Soho restaurant which features a table d'hôte lunchtime menu augmented by an à la carte selection in the evening. Wine by the glass is good, though the wine list itself is short, and service is friendly and polite.
Closed Sun, 2 wks Xmas, Etr & BH's
Lunch not served Sat
British & Italian **V** 60 seats ✳ Lunch £18-£25alc Dinner £18-£25alc Wine £8.50 Last lunch 2.30pm Last dinner 11.15pm ₱
Credit Cards 3

✕*Fuji Japanese* 36-40 Brewer St W1 ☎01-734 0957
Closed 2 wks Xmas
Lunch not served Sat & Sun
Japanese 54 seats Last dinner 10.45pm ₱
Credit Cards 1 2 3 5

✕Kerzenstuberl 9 St Christopher's Place W1M 5HB ☎01-486 3196 & 01-486 8103
Here you can relax in a typically Austrian atmosphere to enjoy authentic Austrian food and wine. Personal service is provided by the proprietors, and in the late evenings staff and guests sing along together to the strains of an accordion.
Closed Sun, Xmas, Etr & 31 Jul-27 Aug
Lunch not served Sat
Austrian **V** 50 seats Lunch £13.50-£16.50&alc Dinner £20-£25alc Last lunch 2.15pm Last dinner 11pm ₱ ♫
Credit Cards 1 2 3 5

✕Lee Ho Fook 15 Gerrard St W1 ☎01-734 9578
Authentic Chinatown atmosphere in this intimate restaurant.
Closed 25 & 26 Dec
Chinese **V** 150 seats ✳ Lunch £6-£9&alc Dinner £6-£9&alc Last dinner 11.30pm ₱
Credit Cards 1 2 3 5

✕*Little Akropolis* 10 Charlotte St W1P 1HE ☎01-636 8198
Small, intimate, candlelit, Greek restaurant.
Closed Sun & BH's
Lunch not served Sat
Greek **V** 32 seats Last dinner 10.30pm ₱
Credit Cards 1 2 3 5

✕New World 1 Gerrard Place W1 ☎01-734 0677 & 01-434 2508
This large and popular Chinese restaurant offers a wide selection of dishes based on good-quality ingredients. Throughout the day, heated trolleys circulate among the tables, enabling guests to choose from a tempting array of Dim Sum; service is generally courteous and friendly.
Closed 25 Dec
Chinese **V** 600 seats Last lunch 5.45pm Last dinner 11.30pm ₱
Credit Cards 1 2 3 5

W2 Bayswater, Paddington

★★★★70% Royal Lancaster Lancaster Ter W2 2TY (Rank) ☎01-262 6737 Telex no 24822 FAX 01-724 3191
A large modern hotel just minutes away from Marble Arch and overlooking Hyde Park. There are two bars and two restaurants in addition to the spacious lounge. The Reserve Club rooms offer particularly comfortable sleeping accommodation.
418⇌♠(40fb)⊬in 22 bedrooms CTV in all bedrooms **T** ✖ (ex guide dogs) sB⇌♠£125-£140
dB⇌♠£145-£160 (room only) ⊟
Lift ☾ ⊞ 50P (£7.50) 50🚗 (£7.50) CFA *xmas*
International **V** ♥ ⊥ ⊬ Lunch £15-£17&alc High tea fr£4.30alc Dinner £20-£23&alc Last dinner 10.45pm
Credit Cards 1 2 3 4 5

★★★★74% *White's* Lancaster Gate W2 3NR (Mount Charlotte) ☎01-262 2711 Telex no 24771 FAX 01-262 2147
The well equipped bedrooms of this elegant hotel are particularly attractive, furnished in light oak and decorated in pastel shades. Public rooms, though not large, have a peaceful and relaxing atmosphere. In the restaurant, chef Peter Brown offers an interesting and varied menu with skilfully prepared dishes.
54⇌1⊟⊬in 4 bedrooms CTV in all bedrooms **T** ✖ (ex guide dogs)
Lift ☾ ⊞ 25P ✽
English & French **V** ♥ ⊥ Last dinner 10.30pm
Credit Cards 1 2 3 4 5

★★★50% Central Park Queensborough Ter W2 3SS ☎01-229 2424 Telex no 27342 FAX 01-229 2904
A contemporary, well-managed hotel offering adequate comfort complemented by the attractive Terrace Restaurant and friendly, helpful service.
251rm(210⇌31♠)(10fb) CTV in all bedrooms **T** S15% sB&B⇌♠fr£57 dB&B⇌♠fr£78 Continental breakfast
Lift ☾ 10P (£1.50) 20🚗 (£1.50) sauna solarium gymnasium *xmas*
International **V** ♥ ⊥ Lunch fr£10.75 Dinner fr£11.75 Last dinner 10pm
Credit Cards 1 2 3 5

★★★50% *Hospitality Inn on the Park* 104/105 Bayswater Rd W2 3HL (Mount Charlotte) ☎01-262 4461 Telex no 22667
This popular and efficiently-managed hotel offers a choice of particularly well-equipped modern bedrooms, most having excellent views of Kensington Gardens. The buffet-style restaurant and lounge facilities are very restricted, but 24-hour room service is available, and the range of services offered is extensive.
175⇌♠ CTV in all bedrooms ® **T**
Lift ☾ ⊞ 20P 40🚗 CFA
International **V** ♥ ⊥
Credit Cards 1 2 3 4 5

★★★65% London Embassy 150 Bayswater Rd W2 4RT (Embassy) ☎01-229 1212 Telex no 27727 FAX 01-229 2633
Modern commercial and tourist hotel overlooking Hyde Park. A pre-theatre meal, fixed price carvery and small à la carte menu are available in the restaurant. Helpful staff provide some lounge and room service.
193⇌♠⊬in 12 bedrooms CTV in all bedrooms ® **T** ✖ (ex guide dogs) ✳ S% sB⇌♠£80-£90
dB⇌♠£95-£105 (room only) ⊟
Lift ☾ 20P 20🚗 (£2) CFA
International **V** ♥ ⊥ S% Lunch fr£11.50&alc Dinner fr£11.50&alc Last dinner 10.15pm
Credit Cards 1 2 3 5

★★★62% *Park Court* 75 Lancaster Gate, Hyde Park W2 3NN (Mount Charlotte) ☎01-402 4272 Telex no 23922
The well-equipped bedrooms of this large busy hotel include some executive rooms, and there is an informal, bistro-style restaurant.
404⇌♠(41fb)⊬in 64 bedrooms CTV in all bedrooms ® **T**
Lift ☾ ₱ ✽ CFA
V ♥ ⊥ ⊬
Credit Cards 1 2 3 4 5

✕Kalamara's 76-78 Inverness Mews W2 3JQ ☎01-727 9122 & 01-727 2564
There are two Kalamara's restaurants in Inverness Mews – a smaller, unlicenced one and this, which provides an all-Greek wine list to complement the authentic Greek cuisine.

London

Lunch not served
Greek V 86 seats ✱ Dinner £15&alc Last dinner mdnt
Credit Cards 1 2 3 5

W5 Ealing

See LONDON plan 5*B4*
See also **W13 Ealing (Northfields)**

★★★ 70% **Carnarvon** Ealing Common W5 3HN (Consort) ☎01-992 5399 Telex no 935114 FAX 01-992 7082
A modern hotel, on the edge of Ealing Common and handy for the North Circular Road, looks from the outside severely functional, but inside is spacious, bright and comfortable with well equipped bedrooms. A first-class management team and well organised, personable staff prove that good hotelkeeping standards can still flourish. A bonus for visitors to London are the extensive car-parking facilities.
145 in 10 bedrooms CTV in all bedrooms ® **T** (ex guide dogs) sB£75 dB£95 (room only)
Lift 150P CFA
English & European Lunch fr£15alc Dinner fr£15alc Last dinner 9.30pm
Credit Cards 1 2 3 5

W6 Hammersmith

See LONDON plan 5*C3*

★★★ 51% ***Novotel London*** 1 Shortlands W6 8DR (Novotel) ☎01-741 1555 Telex no 934539 FAX 01-741 2120
Large purpose-built hotel offering spacious accommodation. In addition to the à la carte restaurant, there is 'Le Grill', with a small terrace area. A business centre and shop in the main lobby area add to the facilities.
640 in 20 bedrooms CTV in all bedrooms **T**
Lift CTV 230 (£6.50)
English & French **V** Last dinner mdnt
Credit Cards 1 2 3 5

W8 Kensington

See LONDON plan 5*C3*

★★★★★ 68% **Royal Garden** Kensington High St W8 4PT (Rank) ☎01-937 8000 Telex no 263151 FAX 01-938 4532
Suites, studios and bedrooms are all tastefully furnished, equipped with all five-star facilities and afford views over Kensington Gardens and Hyde Park or the lively scene of Kensington High Street. The Garden Cafe serves meals throughout the day, and shares beautiful views over the park with the adjacent Garden Bar, where a resident pianist entertains. If you prefer a club-like atmosphere, there is the comfortable Gallery Bar, and the Roof Restaurant is an ideal rendezvous for dining and dancing.
380 7 in 10 bedrooms CTV in all bedrooms **T** (ex guide dogs) ✱ sB£117.50-£175 dB£147.50-£175 (room only)
Lift 142 (£6 per night) CFA ♫ *xmas*
International **V** Lunch £9.75 Dinner £8-£20alc Last dinner 11pm
Credit Cards 1 2 3 4 5

★★★★ 68% **Kensington Palace Thistle** De Vere Gardens W8 5AF (Thistle) ☎01-937 8121 Telex no 262422 FAX 01-937 2816
The rooms in this busy hotel have been upgraded to provide modern amenities. The restaurant offers interesting and enjoyable dishes and there is also a coffee shop for lighter meals. Service from the friendly and willing staff is attentive and efficient.
298 (27fb) in 32 bedrooms CTV in all bedrooms ® **T** ✱ sB£83-£115 dB£99-£130 (room only)
Lift CFA ♫
International Lunch fr£17.50&alc Dinner fr£17.50&alc Last dinner 10.45pm
Credit Cards 1 2 3 4 5

★★★★ 55% **London Tara** Scarsdale Place, off Wrights Ln W8 5SR (Best Western) ☎01-937 7211 Telex no 918834 FAX 01-937 7100
Well into a major bedroom and public area improvement programme, this hotel also offers a good range of eating options and very good check-in facilities.
831 in 96 bedrooms CTV in all bedrooms **T** (ex guide dogs) ✱ sB£80-£95 dB£95-£110 (room only)
Lift 30P 80 (£8 per 24hours) CFA *xmas*
French **V** Lunch £12.20-£13.20&alc Dinner £12.20-£13.20&alc Last dinner 11pm
Credit Cards 1 2 3 4 5

★★★ 58% **Kensington Close** Wright's Ln W8 5SP (Trusthouse Forte) ☎01-937 8170 Telex no 23914 FAX 01-937 8289
A busy hotel, popular with a wide clientele who appreciate the amenity of the leisure complex and the West End location. Bedrooms are on the small side and there is a choice of restaurants – the informal Rendezvous or the more sophisticated Kensington Grill.
522 in 11 bedrooms CTV in all bedrooms sB£74-£110 dB£86-£125 (room only)
Lift 40P (£3.50 2 hours) 60 (£3.50 2 hours) CFA (heated) squash sauna solarium gymnasium health & fitness centre *xmas*
Mainly grills **V** Lunch £12.50&alc Dinner £12.50&alc Last dinner 11pm
Credit Cards 1 2 3 4 5

★★ **Hotel Lexham** 32-38 Lexham Gardens W8 5JU ☎01-373 6471
Closed 23 Dec-2 Jan
Accommodation in this traditional hotel is very good value, especially for central London. What it lacks in modern facilities it makes up for in service. There is no bar, but a choice of two lounges, and the staff are pleasant and cheerful. ▶

London

63rm(26⇨8⛆)(12fb) ✗ S10% sB&B£25.50-£28.50 sB&B⇨⛆£31.50-£36.50 dB&B£34.50-£38.50 dB&B⇨⛆£46.50-£56.50
Lift ☾ CTV ₱ ✲
English & Continental S10% Lunch fr£6alc Dinner £6.95-£7.75 Last dinner 8pm
Credit Cards 1 3

✕✕✕Belevedere Holland House, Holland Park W8 ☎01-602 1238
The elegantly-situated, aristocratic house retains its formal English flower garden and its peaceful atmosphere. The chef has a particular flair with white fish, and many daily specialities appear among the reliable and enterprising dishes on the menu. Service is efficient and very attentive.
Lunch not served Sat
French V 60 seats ✱ S12.5% Lunch fr£18&alc Last lunch 2.30pm Last dinner 10.30pm ₱
Credit Cards 1 2 3 5

✕✕Boyd's Glass Garden 135 Kensington Church St W8 7LP ☎01-727 5452
Closed Sat, Sun & 1 wk Xmas
French V 36 seats ✱ S15% Lunch £12.50-£14.75 Dinner £27.50-£32.50 Last lunch 2.30pm Last dinner 10.30pm ₱
Credit Cards 1 2 3

✕✕Clarke's 124 Kensington Church St W8 ☎01-221 9225
This fresh, bright restaurant offers a short lunch menu and no choice at all in the evenings – but its quality is beyond question. Chef/patronne Sally Clarke's light, American and Eastern-influenced style is exemplified in dishes such as a deliciously spicy corn chowder, and char-grilled meat and fish with imaginative sauces and crisp vegetables. Breads and pastries are excellent, and the wine list includes a good North American range. The bakery and coffee shop next door also sells Californian wines and splendid home-made pickles.
Closed Sat & Sun, Xmas, Etr & 3 weeks Aug-Sep
V 90 seats ✱ Lunch £14-£16 Dinner £28 Last lunch 2pm Last dinner 11pm ₱
Credit Cards 1 3

❀✕✕La Ruelle 14 Wright's Ln W8 6TF ☎01-937 8525 Telex no 918834 FAX 01-937 7100
Close to Kensington High Street, this attractively decorated restaurant offers various French menus. Dishes, reliably cooked and deliciously flavoured, are served by attentive French staff.
Closed Sat, Mon & Bank Hols
French V 70 seats ✱ Lunch £13.50-£19&alc Dinner £19&alc Last lunch 2.30pm Last dinner 11.30pm 10P nc12yrs
Credit Cards 1 2 3 4 5

✕The Ark 35 Kensington High St W8 5BA ☎01-937 4294
Long established and extremely popular, this restaurant maintains very reliable standards. Freshly prepared dishes include daily specialities, and a limited selection of good value French wines is available.
Closed 4 days Xmas & 4 days Etr
Lunch not served Sun
French V 95 seats ✱ Lunch £15-£20alc Dinner £15-£20alc Last lunch 3pm Last dinner 11.30pm ₱
Credit Cards 1 2 3 5

Red-star hotels offer the highest standards of hospitality, comfort and food.

✕*Kensington Place* 201/205 Kensington Church St W8 ☎01-727 3184
Rowley Leigh presides over this lively, popular restaurant, situated at the Notting Hill end of Kensington Church Street, and open 12 hours a day. Cooking is excellent and dishes range from the homely (cod with parsley sauce or rabbit stew, for example), to the more imaginative, such as griddled foie gras with sweetcorn pancake, or the red and grey mullet with wild rice and ginger particularly enjoyed by our inspector. Service is relaxed and friendly but tables are very close together, so not ideal for private conversation. The set lunch is good value and there is a range of reasonably priced wines.

✕Michel 343 Kensington High St W8 6NW ☎01-603 3613
This small, lively restaurant, pretty in pink, has a French/Mediterranean style menu of sound innovative cooking.
Closed Sun & BH's
French V 55 seats ✱ Lunch fr£18.50&alc Last lunch 2.30pm Last dinner 11pm
Credit Cards 1 2 3 4 5

W11 Holland Park, Notting Hill

See LONDON plan 5*C3*

★★★ 72% Hilton International Kensington Holland Park Av W11 4UL (Hilton) ☎01-603 3355 Telex no 919763 FAX 01-602 9397
Large and exceptionally comfortable hotel with a distinctly international flavour, well placed for access to and from the West End and A40. A choice of three places to eat – the à la carte/carvery Market Restaurant, a 24-hour drink and snack bar and the Hiroko where authentic Japanese cuisine is served. There are several shops in the foyer and car parking for 100 (£5 for residents) available underneath the hotel.
606⇨ CTV in all bedrooms ® T S10% sB⇨£89-£120 dB⇨£110-£140 (room only)
Lift ☾ 100 (£5) CFA *xmas*
International V S10% Lunch fr£12.50&alc Dinner fr£14.50&alc Last dinner 10.30pm
Credit Cards 1 2 3 4 5

✕✕✕Leith's 92 Kensington Park Rd W11 2PN ☎01-229 4481
Popular, well-established restaurant that continues to offer reliable and unusual food, particularly the varied starters. Good fixed price menu.
Closed 27-28 Aug & 24-27 Dec
Lunch not served
International V 85 seats S15% Dinner £26-£35 Last dinner 11.30pm ₱ nc7yrs
Credit Cards 1 2 3 5

✕✕La Pomme d'Amour 128 Holland Park Av W11 ☎01-229 8532
French regional cooking of a reliable standard forms the basis of the menu here, complemented by a choice of imaginative specialities devised by the chef and combining good-quality ingredients with well constructed sauces. Service is attentive and agreeably supervised.
Closed Sun & BH's
Lunch not served Sat
French V 64 seats ✱ Lunch £11.50&alc Dinner fr£13.50&alc Last lunch 2.15pm Last dinner 10.45pm ₱ nc10yrs
Credit Cards 1 2 3 5

✕*Restaurant 192* 192 Kensington Park Rd W11 2ES ☎01-229 0482
A simple restaurant-cum-wine-bar on two floors which offers a short, high-quality menu of mostly English dishes well prepared from good, basic ingredients. The atmosphere is friendly and informal and the service attentive.
Closed BH's
Dinner not served Sun

French V 80 seats Last lunch 2.30pm Last dinner 11.30pm
P
Credit Cards 1 2 3

W13 Ealing (Northfields)

See LONDON plan 5*B4*
See also **W5**

✕ **Maxim Chinese** 153-155 Northfield Av W13 9QT ☎01-567 1719 & 01-840 1086
Fashionable restaurant where the menu features a large selection of dishes using best quality ingredients. A good choice of wine is also available.
Closed 25-28 Dec
Lunch not served Sun
Pekinese V 120 seats Lunch £7-£25&alc Dinner £7-£25&alc Last lunch 2.30pm Last dinner mdnt P
Credit Cards 1 2 3 5

W14 West Kensington

✕ **Chinon** 25 Richmond Way W14 ☎01-602 5968 & 01-602 4082
This small, candlelit restaurant specialises in its own original variations on British cuisine, dishes being beautifully presented and garnished. A choice of two fixed price menus offers excellent value for money.
Closed Sun, Mon, Etr & Aug BH
Dinner not served Tue-Fri
V 28 seats ✻ Last lunch 10.30pm Last dinner 11pm P nc10yrs
Credit Cards 1 2 3

WC1 Bloomsbury, Holborn

★★★★ 69% **Marlborough Crest** Bloomsbury St WC1B 3QD (Crest) ☎01-636 5601 Telex no 298274 FAX 01-636 0532
The hotel provides comfortable accommodation and has an attractive restaurant offering a wide choice of dishes. Service is efficient and friendly.
169rm(151⇨18♠) in 57 bedrooms CTV in all bedrooms ® T ✻ sB⇨♠£126 dB⇨♠£146-£152 (room only)
Lift ☾ P *xmas*
French V Lunch fr£14.50&alc Dinner fr£14.50&alc Last dinner 11.30pm
Credit Cards 1 2 3 4 5 £

★★★★ 61% **Hotel Russell** Russel Square WC1B 5BE (Trusthouse Forte) ☎01-837 6470 Telex no 24615 FAX 01-837 3612
The imposing entrance hall, with large chandelier, marble pillars and staircase, ushers guests into this large, commercial hotel. Bedrooms are on the whole comfortable, though some can only be described as 'compact'. Service is good, however, and there are two restaurants – an informal, colourful brasserie and a well appointed carvery which also offers an à la carte menu.
326⇨(1fb) in 20 bedrooms CTV in all bedrooms **T** S15% sB⇨£90-£95 dB⇨£110-£115 (room only)
Lift ☾ P CFA *xmas*
V
Credit Cards 1 2 3 4 5

★★★ 67% **Bloomsbury Crest** Coram St WC1N 1HT (Crest) ☎01-837 1200 Telex no 22113 FAX 01-837 5374
Major new features include a spacious lobby, a business centre, air-conditioned meeting facilities, and an extra floor of well-equipped executive bedrooms. The Café Shaws serves "tapas" with drinks amid stained glass, stone urns and wicker chairs. The first floor also has a brasserie and more formal restaurant with cocktail lounge.
284⇨(29fb) in 67 bedrooms CTV in all bedrooms ® **T** (ex guide dogs) ✻ sB⇨£92-£105 dB⇨£106-£114 (room only)
Lift ☾ 100 (£8.40 per night) ♫

▶

London

International V ♁ ⊈ ⚡ Lunch £12.50-£17&alc High tea £1.50-£8 Dinner £14.50-£18&alc Last dinner 10.45pm
Credit Cards 1 2 3 4 5

★★★53% ***London Ryan*** Gwynne Place, Kings Cross Rd WC1X 9QN (Mount Charlotte) ☎01-278 2480 Telex no 27728
Though bedrooms are simply furnished and a little clinical at this Mount Charlotte hotel, they are nevertheless well equipped and some have double glazing. The compact restaurant becomes very busy in the evening, so it is advisable to make a table reservation.
210⇌⌂(73fb) CTV in all bedrooms ® T ✖ (ex guide dogs)
Lift ☾ 28P 8🚗
English & Continental V ♁ ⊈
Credit Cards 1 2 3 5

✕✕**Poons of Russell Square** 50 Woburn Place, Russell Square WC1 ☎01-580 188
Elegant Chinese restaurant offering an extensive choice of authentic dishes.
Closed 25-26 Dec & Sun prior to BH
Cantonese V 120 seats ✱ Last lunch 3pm Last dinner 11.30pm ₽
Credit Cards 1 2 3 5

WC2 Covent Garden

★★★★★

❀★★★★★ **THE SAVOY**

Strand WC2R 0EU ☎01-836 4343 Telex no 24234 FAX 01-240 6040

(Rosette awarded for Savoy Restaurant)

For over 100 years the Savoy has set a standard that many hotels aspire to and few achieve. It did for some time lose its vitality, but the buzz and sheer magic returned once more under the regime of indefatigable managing director Willy Bauer, now sadly departed. There are splendid suites and wonderful spacious rooms overlooking the Thames, and if some of the rooms (especially some compact singles) seem drab when compared to those in other international 5-star hotels, there are more than adequate compensations in the quality of the beds and linen, the huge towels and the splendid old baths with their 'thunderstorm' showers. Not that the Savoy hasn't moved with the times – apart from satellite television in the bedrooms (some of which are air-conditioned), the 'Upstairs' eating place offers fish, wine and champagne, and equally popular is the American bar, while the facilities for meetings and functions are excellent. The renowned Grill Room attracts a loyal following, as does the restaurant where Alan Hill continues to display his considerable talents. Here, dancing to a trio of musicians takes place on most nights, with the River Thames providing a romantic backdrop. The essence of the unique Savoy spirit remains its emphasis on courtesy, comfort and cuisine. In all departments – linkman, room service, maids, valet and the rest – staff are not only efficient and formal, but warm and hospitable as well. In short, the Savoy remains one of the Great Hotels of the world and it is still the place to visit for a special occasion and a memorable experience.

200⇌⚡in 30 bedrooms CTV in all bedrooms T ✖ (ex guide dogs) S15% sB⇌fr£140 dB⇌£170-£230 (room only) ⊟
Lift ☾ 58🚗 (£6.50-£17) ⛟ CFA ♫ *xmas*
English & French V ♁ ⊈ S15% Lunch fr£20.50 Dinner £25.50-£36 Last dinner 11.30pm
Credit Cards 1 2 3 5

★★★★69% **The Waldorf** Aldwych WC2B 4DD (Trusthouse Forte) ☎01-836 2400 Telex no 24574 FAX 01-836 7244
Edwardian elegance is the keynote of this hotel, which originally opened in 1908, and this is now combined with modern amenities. Bedrooms vary considerably in size, but in compensation the hotel has many outstanding attractions – notably the Palm Court, the two bars and the Waldorf Restaurant.
310⇌(11fb)⚡in 40 bedrooms CTV in all bedrooms T ✖ (ex guide dogs) S10% sB⇌fr£115 dB⇌fr£145 (room only) ⊟
Lift ☾ ₽ CFA Hairdresses ♫ *xmas*
V ♁ ⊈ ⚡ S10% Lunch £14-£19.50&alc High tea £15 Dinner £17.50-£21.50&alc Last dinner 10pm
Credit Cards 1 2 3 4 5

★★★66% **Drury Lane Moat House** 10 Drury Ln WC2B 5RE (Queens Moat) ☎01-836 6666 Telex no 8811395 FAX 01-831 1548
A stylish purpose-built Covent Garden hotel providing accommodation in comfortably appointed bedrooms and a choice of à la carte or buffet-style meals. Efficient service is rendered by friendly staff.
153⇌(15fb) CTV in all bedrooms T sB⇌£99-£120 dB⇌£126-£139 (room only) ⊟
Lift ☾ ⊞ 10🚗 (£6)
French V ♁ ⊈
Credit Cards 1 2 3 4 5

★★★62% **Royal Trafalgar Thistle** Whitcomb St WC2H 7HG (Thistle) ☎01-930 4477 Telex no 298564 FAX 01-925 2149
Modern but cosy, this comfortable hotel stands just off Trafalgar Square, offering compact but well-equipped bedrooms and friendly, helpful service. The new brasserie offers a French-style menu and mulled wine.
108⇌⌂⚡in 36 bedrooms CTV in all bedrooms ® T ✱ sB⇌⌂£79-£95 dB⇌⌂£93-£108 (room only) ⊟
Lift ☾ ₽
French ♁ ⊈ ⚡ Lunch fr£12.50&alc Dinner fr£12.50&alc Last dinner 11.30pm
Credit Cards 1 2 3 4 5

★★★53% **Strand Palace** Strand WC2R 0JJ (Trusthouse Forte) ☎01-836 8080 Telex no 24208 FAX 01-836 2077
Modernised compact Regency-style hotel.
775⇌⚡in 80 bedrooms CTV in all bedrooms ® T ✱ S% sB⇌£71-£77 dB⇌£85-£91 (room only) ⊟
Lift ☾ ₽ *xmas*
International V ♁ ⊈ ⚡ Lunch £11.95 Dinner £11.95 Last dinner mdnt
Credit Cards 1 2 3 4 5

✕✕✕✕✕**Savoy Grill** Strand WC2R 0EU ☎01-836 4343 Telex no 24234 FAX 01-240 6040
Maître chef Alan Hill combines his talented creativity with the traditional dishes that are now synonymous with the Grill Room. Service is highly professional and very discreet in the fine Savoy tradition.
Closed Sun & Aug
Lunch not served Sat
English & French V 80 seats ✱ Lunch £22-£46.50alc Dinner £17.50-£20.50&alc Last lunch 2.30pm Last dinner 11.15pm ₽ nc12yrs
Credit Cards 1 2 3 5

✕✕✕✕**Inigo Jones** 14 Garrick St WC2E 9BJ ☎01-836 6456 & 01-836 3223 FAX 01-226 9580
This one-time workhouse with its stained glass windows and gothic arches, was converted into a restaurant in 1968. It will be closed for a 12-month refurbishment programme when this guide is published, and will re-open in October 1990.

London

Closed Sun & BH's
Lunch not served Sat
♀ French V 75 seats ✱ Lunch fr£21.75 Last lunch 2.30pm Last dinner 11.30pm P̸
Credit Cards 1 2 3 5

❀ ✕✕✕ **Boulestin** 1A Covent Garden, Covent Garden WC2E 8PS
☎01-836 3819 & 01-836 7061

The Edwardian luxury of the décor makes a fine setting for this traditional French restaurant, where the house speciality, their soufflé, is an experience worth savouring time and again. The menu gives the skilful kitchen staff ample opportunity to demonstrate their talents, and the wine list, although not cheap, will excite the interest of most wine lovers. French waiters provide professional service, efficient without being intrusive.

Closed Sun, 1 wk Xmas, BH's & last 3 wks Aug
Lunch not served Sat
♀ French V 70 seats ✱ S15% Lunch £17.50-£22.50&alc Dinner £29.25-£39.75alc Last lunch 2.30pm Last dinner 11.15pm P̸ nc5yrs
Credit Cards 1 2 3 4 5

✕✕✕ ***Neal Street*** 26 Neal St WC2H 9PH ☎01-836 8368

Modern restaurant with tasteful basement cocktail bar; serving very original cuisine.

Closed Sat, Sun & 1 wk Xmas
♀ International V 70 seats Last dinner 11pm P̸
Credit Cards 1 2 3 5

✕✕ **Oh! Poivrier** 7-8 Bow St WC2 ☎01-836 9864 FAX 01-379 6859

Informal atmosphere, honest French cooking and good value for money.

V 70 seats ✱ Lunch £6-£9&alc Dinner £6-£9&alc Last dinner 11.30pm P̸
Credit Cards 1 3

✕✕ ***Seven Dials*** 5 Neal's Yard, Covent Garden WC2 9DP ☎01-836 0984

This pleasant, airy restaurant is attractively designed in conservatory style. Its atmosphere is friendly, service being cheerful and helpful, and an international menu is supported by a fairly priced wine list. Set-priced menus are available for two or three course meals.

♀ French V 80 seats Last dinner 11.30pm P̸
Credit Cards 1 2 3 4 5

✕✕ **Thomas de Quincey's** 36 Tavistock St WC2E 7PB ☎01-240 3972 & 01-240 3773

The menu makes interesting reading, offering a range of unusual and original dishes. Standards of cooking are fairly consistent, the restaurant is attractive and friendly, but front-of-house management could occasionally be thought lacking. The sweet trolley may present an overwhelming temptation, but do give the waiter a chance to explain how very good the selection of cheeses can be.

Closed Sun, 2 wks Aug & BH's
Lunch not served Sat
♀ French 50 seats Lunch £17.40&alc Dinner £30-£45alc Last lunch 3pm Last dinner 11.15pm P̸
Credit Cards 1 2 3 4 5

✕ **Ajimura Japanese** 51-53 Shelton St WC2H 9HE ☎01-240 0178 & 01-240 9424

This Japanese restaurant, run bistro-style, has an interesting menu of authentic dishes.

Lunch not served Sat & Sun
♀ Japanese V 55 seats ✱ Lunch £6.20-£25&alc Dinner £8.50-£25&alc Last lunch 3pm Last dinner 11pm P̸
Credit Cards 1 2 3 5

✕ **Le Café Des Amis Du Vin** 11-14 Hanover Place WC2 9JP ☎01-379 3444

French provincial cooking of a very high standard has made this traditional French restaurant and brasserie an extremely popular eating place. The atmosphere is relaxed, informal and friendly, and the well balanced wine list offers some interesting bottles.

Closed Sun
♀ French V 116 seats ✱ Last lunch 4.45pm Last dinner 11.30pm P̸
Credit Cards 1 2 3 5

✕ ***Le Cafe du Jardin*** 28 Wellington St WC2 ☎01-836 8769

In the heart of theatreland, this popular brasserie with its delicious and wholesome food, attentive and friendly French staff and pianist who plays each evening, has a lively and very French atmosphere.

Closed Sun, 25-26 Dec & Public hols
Lunch not served Sat
♀ French V 116 seats Last dinner 11.30pm P̸ ⅟ ♫
Credit Cards 1 2 3 4 5

✕ **Happy Wok Restaurant** 52 Floral Stret WC2 ☎01-836 3696
Closed Sun
Lunch not served Sat

▶

Chinese V 50 seats ✱ Dinner £16.90-£27.50&alc Last dinner 11.30pm
Credit Cards 1 2 3 5

✕Poon's 4 Leicester St WC2 ☎01-437 1528
Closed Sun & Xmas period
Cantonese V 100 seats ✱ S10% Last lunch 11.30am Last dinner 11.30pm

✕Taste of India 25 Catherine St WC2B 5JS ☎01-836 6591 & 01-836 2538
A modern Indian restaurant on two floors offering an interesting menu with some specialities. Dishes are freshly prepared with skilful use of herbs and spices. Service is friendly, helpful and efficient.
Closed 25 & 26 Dec
Indian V 125 seats ✱ Lunch £7.95-£8.50&alc Dinner £7.95-£8.50&alc Last lunch 2.30pm Last dinner mdnt
Credit Cards 1 2 3 5

LONDON AIRPORTS

See under Gatwick & Heathrow

LONG EATON Derbyshire Map 08 SK43

See also **Sandiacre**
★★★58% Novotel Nottingham Derby Bostock Ln NG10 4EP (S of M1 junc 25) (Novotel) ☎(0602)720106 Telex no 377585
A purpose-built hotel almost adjacent to junction 25 of the M1. Bedrooms are spacious and functional and the Grill Restaurant is open from 6am for light snacks and more substantial meals.
110(110fb) CTV in all bedrooms ® T sBfr£50 dBfr£50 (room only)
Lift 180P CFA (heated) mini golf course putting green *xmas*
English & French V Lunch £11-£12.50alc High tea £1.60-£2alc Dinner £11-£13alc Last dinner mdnt
Credit Cards 1 2 3 5

★★Europa 20 Derby Rd NG10 1LW ☎(0602)728481 Telex no 377494
Three-storey Victorian building standing by the A6005 close to the town centre.
20rm(8 3)(2fb) CTV in all bedrooms ® T (ex guide dogs) ✱ S% sB&B£26-£32 sB&B£32 dB&B£40
CTV 27P
V Lunch £4.75-£6.50 Dinner £8.45-£12.75 Last dinner 8.30pm
Credit Cards 1 2 3 5 £

LONGHAM Dorset Map 04 SZ09

★★★72% *Bridge House* 2 Ringwood Rd BH22 9AN ☎Bournemouth(0202)578828 Telex no 418484
Closed 25 & 26 Dec
Situated on the banks of the River Stour, this is a modern 'Mediterranean-style' hotel, providing comfortable, well-equipped accommodation. Public rooms are bright and colourful. The attractive restaurant offers good table d'hôte and à la carte menus of well-prepared food, using good basic ingredients. Service is helpful and attentive.
36 3 CTV in all bedrooms ® T
200P
English, French & Greek Last dinner 10.30pm
Credit Cards 1 2 3

LONGHORSLEY Northumberland Map 12 NZ19

★★★★76% Linden Hall NE65 8XG (Prestige) ☎Morpeth(0670)516611 Telex no 538224 FAX (0670) 88544
Dating back to the early 19th century, this fine, classical, ivy-clad converted mansion house stands in 300 acres of well-tended grounds. It is the friendliness and efficiency of manager John Moore and his staff that makes staying in such fine and elegant surroundings such a special treat. Bedrooms vary from palatial to compact but all are comfortable and prettily decorated. Food continues to be of a high standard and the table d'hôte menu is excellent value.
45(16fb)4 CTV in all bedrooms ® T ✱ sB&Bfr£70 dB&B£82.50-£92.50
Lift 260P CFA (hard) snooker sauna solarium croquet putting clay-pigeon shooting *xmas*
V Lunch £11.95-£12.50&alc High tea £2.75-£5 Dinner fr£15.95 Last dinner 10pm
Credit Cards 1 2 3 5 £

See advertisement under MORPETH

LONG MELFORD Suffolk Map 05 TL84

★★★59% The Bull Hall St CO10 9JG (Trusthouse Forte) ☎Sudbury(0787)78494 FAX (0787) 880307
Parts of this hotel date back to the 15th century and much fine timberwork has been uncovered. Rooms vary in size but all have up-to-date facilities. There is an attractive restaurant and two comfortable lounge areas.
25(4fb) in 4 bedrooms CTV in all bedrooms ® T ✱ sBfr£56 dBfr£71 (room only)
40P *xmas*
V Lunch £8.95&alc Dinner £12.95&alc Last dinner 9.30pm
Credit Cards 1 2 3 4 5

★★Crown Inn Hall St CO10 9JL ☎Sudbury(0787)77666 FAX (0787) 881883
A family-run, high street inn that dates back to the early 17th century. Some bedrooms are in the main inn, while others are in the converted courtyard rooms – but all are newly decorated and offer modern facilities. There is a homely lounge for guests' use and an attractive restaurant which overlooks the garden.
7rm(3 3)Annexe5rm(4 1)(1fb)4 CTV in all bedrooms ® T ✱ sB&B£29.50-£31.50 sB&B£29.50-£31.50 dB&B£39.50-£47.50 dB&B£39.50-£47.50
6P gymnasium
English & French V Lunch £2.95-£7.95&alc
Credit Cards 1 3

✕✕Chimneys Hall St CO10 9JR ☎Sudbury(0787)79806
This attractive timber-framed 16th-century building houses a very pleasant restaurant and bar. Well prepared ingredients are presented in an attractive manner, still very much in the modern style. Sauces are light and restrained, vegetables straightforward and desserts imaginative. There is a good wine list and service is friendly and informal.
Dinner not served Sun
English & French V 55 seats ✱ Lunch £11.50&alc Dinner £20-£23alc Last lunch 2pm Last dinner 9.30pm
Credit Cards 1 3

LONGRIDGE Lancashire Map 07 SD63

★★Blackmoss Country House Thornley PR3 2TB (2m NE off Chipping rd) ☎(077478)3148 due to change to (0772) 783148
Closed Xmas Day
The personally-owned sandstone house, set in three and a half acres of grounds, offers bright, well-furnished bedrooms and good home cooking.
10(1fb) in 2 bedrooms CTV in all bedrooms ®
sB&B£22-£27 sB&B£27 dB&B£38
65P (heated) sauna solarium pool table
Lunch £7.50-£14&alc Dinner £8-£10&alc Last dinner 9pm
Credit Cards 1 2 3 5

LOOE Cornwall & Isles of Scilly Map **02** SX25

★★★60% Hannafore Point Marine Dr, Hannafore PL13 1BH (Best Western) ☎(05036)3273 Telex no 45604 FAX (05036) 3272

In a spectacular position, with views over the bay, this hotel has upgraded over half of its bedrooms, which now offer good facilities. Table d'hôte and à la carte menus are available at dinner, whilst a wide range of hot and cold bar meals are on offer in St Georges bar at lunchtime. A leisure complex is due to be completed by the end of 1989.

38⇌(10fb) CTV in all bedrooms ® **T** sB&B⇌£38.50-£53.50 dB&B⇌£62-£86 ⊟

Lift ☾ 24P ⊡(heated) squash sauna solarium gymnasium *xmas*

☋ English, French & Italian **V** ♦ ☋ Sunday Lunch fr£5.95 High tea fr£4.55 Dinner fr£12.25&alc Last dinner 9pm

Credit Cards [1] [2] [3] [5]

★★*Commonwood Manor* St Martin's Rd PL13 1LP ☎(05036)2929

Closed Nov-Feb

The well-appointed, personally-run hotel enjoys rural surroundings, nestled into the hillside overlooking the harbour. Comfortable lounges, well-appointed bedrooms and a warm, friendly atmosphere combine to make your stay a pleasant one.

10rm(1⇌7↱)(2fb) CTV in all bedrooms **T**

CTV 20P ⛟ ✲ ⩯(heated) nc8yrs

☋ English & Continental ♦ ☋ Last dinner 8pm

Credit Cards [1] [2] [3]

★★Fieldhead Portuan Rd PL13 2DR ☎(05036)2689

Closed Dec-Jan

Family-run hotel with relaxed, friendly atmosphere, overlooking Looe Harbour and the coastline.

14rm(9⇌3↱)(2fb)1⊟ CTV in all bedrooms ® ✈ sB&B£20-£25.50 sB&B⇌↱£25-£30.50 dB&B£40-£50 dB&B⇌↱£40-£55 ⊟

9P 5⛟ ✲ ⩯(heated) nc5yrs

V ♦ ☋ Lunch £5.25-£6.80alc Dinner fr£9.90&alc Last dinner 8.30pm

Credit Cards [1] [2] [3]

★Portbyhan West Looe Quay PL13 2BU ☎(05036)2071 & 2830

Basic accommodation with a friendly, informal atmosphere is provided at this family holiday hotel.

43rm(17↱)(7fb) CTV in all bedrooms ® **T** ✱ sB&B£17 sB&B↱£17.50 dB&B£34 dB&B↱£35 ⊟

Lift ℙ sauna ♫ *xmas*

V ♦ ☋ Dinner fr£6 Last dinner 7.45pm

LORTON Map **11** NY12

LOSTWITHIEL Cornwall & Isles of Scilly Map **02** SX15

★★Restormal Lodge Hillside Gardens PL22 0DD (Consort) ☎Bodmin(0208)872223

Small comfortable motel conveniently situated on the A390 in the ancient town of Lostwithiel.

20rm(13⇌7↱)Annexe12⇌(3fb) CTV in all bedrooms ® **T** sB⇌↱£27-£30 dB⇌↱£37-£40 (room only) ⊟

40P ✲ ⩯(heated) solarium ♫ ⛮ *xmas*

V ♦ ☋ Bar Lunch £1.25-£5 Dinner £10-£11.50&alc Last dinner 9.30pm

Credit Cards [1] [2] [3] [5] Ⓔ

LOUGHBOROUGH Leicestershire Map **08** SK51

★★★63% King's Head High St LE11 2QL (Embassy) ☎(0509)233222 FAX (0509) 262911

RS Xmas

Situated in the town centre and only 3 miles from the M1, this hotel, with its well-equipped accommodation, conference and function facilities, is understandably popular with business people. It is also popular for weekend breaks.

▶

86rm(69⇌9↑)(4fb)⚟in 14 bedrooms CTV in all bedrooms ® **T** S% sB⇌↑£50-£60 dB⇌↑£60-£78 (room only) ⛿
Lift ☾ 80P CFA games room ♫
☋ English & French **V** ✿ ⚲ S% Lunch £5.95-£8.95&alc High tea fr50p Dinner £8.95&alc Last dinner 9.15pm
Credit Cards [1] [2] [3] [4] [5] (£)

★★Great Central Great Central Rd LE11 1RW (Minotels)
☎(0509)263405 FAX (0509) 264130
RS 24-31 Dec
Large Victorian hotel close to the Old Great Central railway line.
18rm(10⇌8↑)(1fb) CTV in all bedrooms ® **T**
sB&B⇌↑£22.50-£37.50 dB&B⇌↑£37.50-£45 ⛿
40P ⌂
☋ English & French **V** ✿ Lunch £2.25-£9.50 Dinner £10-£12.50&alc Last dinner 9pm
Credit Cards [1] [2] [3] [5] (£)

✕✕Restaurant Roger Burdell The Manor House, Sparrow Hill LE11 1BT ☎(0509)231813
Restaurateur Roger Burdell has created a delightfully furnished restaurant in this restored manor house, close to the church in the centre of town. Cooking is light and in the modern style, with influences from both England and France. Dishes are well cooked with flair and imagination and are attractively presented to the table by friendly, professional staff. Naturally there is a very good wine list to complement the fine food.
Closed Sun
Lunch not served Mon
☋ English, French & Italian **V** 65 seats Lunch fr£8.50&alc Dinner £22-£24&alc Last lunch 2pm Last dinner 9.15pm 6P
Credit Cards [1] [2] [3]

LOUTH Lincolnshire Map **08** TF38

★★Priory Eastgate LN11 9AJ ☎(0507)602930
Closed 24 Dec-2 Jan
Magnificent Gothic-style building set in its own impressive gardens, approximately a quarter of a mile from the town centre.
12rm(6⇌3↑)(2fb) CTV in all bedrooms ® ✖ (ex guide dogs)
sB&B£22-£25 sB&B⇌↑£27-£35 dB&B£38-£42
dB&B⇌↑£42-£47
CTV 24P ⛫ ✲
V ✿ Dinner fr£8.95 Last dinner 8.30pm
Credit Cards [1] [3] (£)

LOWER BEEDING West Sussex Map **04** TQ22

★★★⛪74% South Lodge
Brighton Rd RH13 6PS
(Prestige)
☎(0403891)711
Telex no 877765
FAX (0403891) 253

Built towards the end of the 19th century, South Lodge is set in 90 acres of woodland, with a glorious display of rhododendrons and azaleas in the season. There is also a trout lake where guests can fish, and other activities include tennis, croquet, riding and clay pigeon shooting. The interior of the house is splendid, with a grand staircase, wood panelling, attractive plasterwork and fine period furniture. Bedrooms range in style from the cottagey to the grandiose, but all are well equipped and comfortable. Fixed price and à la carte menus are provided in the dining room, with service by cheerful and friendly young staff.
39⇌2⛫ CTV in all bedrooms **T** ✱ sB⇌£75-£80
dB⇌£115-£125 (room only) ⛿
☾ 50P ⛫ ✲ ⚲ (hard & grass) ⚸ golf-driving net croquet shooting ♫ *xmas*
☋ English & French **V** ✿ ⚲ Lunch fr£15 High tea fr£5.50 Dinner fr£25alc Last dinner 10.30pm
Credit Cards [1] [2] [3] [4] [5]

LOWER SLAUGHTER Gloucestershire Map **04** SP12

★★★⛪ LOWER SLAUGHTER MANOR

GL54 2HP (Prestige)
☎Cotswold(0451)20456
Telex no 437287
FAX (0451) 22150

Originally the home of the High Sheriff of Gloucestershire and later a convent, this fine old Cotswolds manor house is steeped in history and enjoys a tranquil setting amid extensive gardens in one of the Cotswolds' most beautiful villages. We are delighted to welcome the Manor to that select number of hotels which have been awarded our highest accolade of red stars, and we feel sure that guests will appreciate the genuinely friendly welcome, high standards of comfort, and attentive service as much as our inspector did. The dinner menus are carefully chosen and offer dishes such as Pannequets of smoked salmon filled with a salad of cucumber and chervil, served on a tomato coulis, or terrine of chicken liver with foie gras and pistachio, served with a truffle vinaigrette, followed by fricassee of veal kidneys, seasoned with juniper berries and served on a bed of spinach with a jus lie, or aiguillettes of beef garnished with roasted shallots and served with a rich red-wine sauce. The desserts, too, are delicious, particularly the Dariole of dark chocolate served with a salad of of oranges marinated in Grand Marnier. There is also a notable wine list.
11⇌Annexe8⇌2⛫ CTV in all bedrooms **T**
sB&B⇌£80-£100
dB&B⇌£95-£185 Continental breakfast ⛿
☾ 60P ⛫ ✲ ▣(heated) ⚲ (hard) ⚸ sauna solarium croquet nc8yrs *xmas*
☋ French **V** ✿ ⚲ Lunch £14.95-£17.95&alc Dinner £24.95-£33.95 Last dinner 9.30pm
Credit Cards [1] [2] [3] [5] (£)

LOWESTOFT Suffolk Map **05** TM59

★★★62% Broadlands Bridge Rd, Oulton Broad NR32 3LN (Consort) ☎(0502)516031 Telex no 975621
Guests can choose between a carvery-style restaurant and a Spaghetti House at this modern, purpose-built hotel in a small shopping precinct near Oulton Broad. Well-equipped bedrooms all receive satellite TV and a video channel, leisure facilities include an indoor swimming pool and Turkish bath, and friendly service is provided throughout by helpful young staff.
52⇌(2fb)1⛫⚟in 6 bedrooms CTV in all bedrooms ® **T**
sB&B⇌£45 dB&B⇌£56 ⛿
☾ CTV 120P ▣(heated) snooker sauna solarium gymnasium *xmas*
☋ English & Italian ✿ ⚲
Credit Cards [1] [2] [3] [5] (£)

For key to symbols see the inside front cover.

★★★56% **Victoria** Kirkley Cliff Rd NR33 0BZ ☎(0502)574433
Modernised Victorian hotel situated on the cliff top at the southern end of town.
36rm(30⇨6♠)(6fb)1⊞ ⊁in 25 bedrooms CTV in all bedrooms ® T ✳ sB&B⇨♠fr£38.50 dB&B⇨♠fr£55 ⊟
Lift ☾ CTV 50P ❖ ⛆(heated) *xmas*
☋ French V ♈ ⩍ ⊁ Lunch £8-£10 High tea £5-£7 Dinner £9.95 Last dinner 10pm
Credit Cards 1 2 3 5

★**Denes** Corton Rd NR32 4PL (Toby) ☎(0502)564616 & 500679
Set in a residential area, this hotel, with a popular carvery and bar, offers reasonable accomodation.
12♠ CTV in all bedrooms ® T ✳ sB&B♠£30.50 dB&B♠£31-£40.50 ⊟
15P
☋ Mainly grills V ♈ ⩍ ⊁ Lunch £6.15-£9.15 Dinner £6.15-£9.15 Last dinner 10pm
Credit Cards 1 2 3 5

LOWESWATER Cumbria Map **11** NY12

★★Scale Hill CA13 9UX
☎Lorton(090085)232
Closed Dec-Feb (ex Xmas & New Year)

A friendly, family-run hotel, nestling into the fells, offers a tranquil atmosphere and delightful views across the valley; its substantial home-cooked dinners are particularly recommended.
15rm(14⇨1♠)Annexe2⇨(2fb)1⊞ ✳ S% sB&B⇨♠£40-£50 dB&B£60-£76 dB&B⇨♠£66-£92 (incl dinner)
25P ⊞ ❖ *xmas*
♈ ⩍ S% Bar Lunch fr£1 Dinner £12-£15 Last dinner 7.45pm

★**Grange Country House** CA13 0SU
☎Lamplugh(0946)861211 & 861570
Closed 20 Dec-4 Jan RS 1-19 Dec & 5 Jan-Feb
Comfortable, 17th-century country hotel situated in its own grounds at the head of Loweswater.
7rm(6⇨)Annexe5rm(4⇨)(1fb)2⊞ CTV in 6bedrooms TV in 6bedrooms ® ✳ sB&B£21-£22.50 dB&B£42-£45
CTV 20P 2🚗(charged) ⊞ ❖
V ♈ ⩍ Lunch £6.50-£9 High tea £6-£7.50 Dinner £10-£12.50 Last dinner 8pm

LUDLOW Shropshire Map **07** SO57

★★★61% **The Feathers at Ludlow** Bull Ring SY8 1AA
☎(0584)5261 due to change to (0584) 875261 Telex no 35637
This fully restored and extended Jacobean building in the centre of town has retained many of its original features. All rooms have modern facilities and the restaurant offers a choice from a seasonal à la carte menu or a daily set menu, for both lunch and dinner.
40⇨♠(3fb)10⊞ CTV in all bedrooms ® T ✗ ✳ sB&B⇨♠£49-£54 dB&B⇨♠£78-£92 ⊟
Lift ☾ 37P CFA snooker *xmas*
V ♈ ⩍ ⊁ Lunch £9.50-£10.50&alc Dinner £2.50-£17.50alc Last dinner 9pm
Credit Cards 1 2 3 4 5 £

★★Cliffe Dinham SY8 2JE
☎(0584)2063 due to change to (0584) 872063
Set in attractive grounds, this family-run hotel has fine views of Ludlow Castle. With well-furnished rooms and a popular bar, guests are assured of an informal, friendly stay.
10rm(3⇨4↿)(1fb) CTV in all bedrooms Ⓡ ✻ sB&Bfr£16.50 sB&B⇨↿fr£23 dB&Bfr£32 dB&B⇨↿fr£36 ⊟
CTV 50P ⊯ ✽
V ♁ Lunch £5.20-£7&alc Dinner £7-£8&alc Last dinner 8.45pm
Credit Cards 1 3 £

★★Dinham Weir Hotel Dinham Bridge SY8 1EH (Minotels)
☎(0584)4431 due to change to (0584)874431
6rm(1⇨5↿)1⊞ CTV in all bedrooms Ⓡ **T** ✘ ✻
sB&B⇨↿£27.50-£30.50 dB&B⇨↿£45-£49.50 ⊟
10P ⊯ nc5yrs
V ♁ S10% Lunch £9.50-£10.50&alc Dinner £9.50-£10.50&alc Last dinner 9pm
Credit Cards 1 2 3 5 £

LUDWELL Wiltshire Map **03** SY92

★★Grove House SP7 9ND (2m E A30) ☎Donhead(074788)365
Closed Dec-Jan
A warm welcome is extended at this small, comfortable and personally-run hotel which provides good food and pleasant gardens for the enjoyment of its guests.
11rm(4⇨6↿)(1fb) CTV in all bedrooms Ⓡ sB&B£23-£26 sB&B⇨↿£23-£26 dB&B⇨↿£46-£52 ⊟
12P ⊯ ✽ nc5yrs
♉ English & Continental ⍻ Bar Lunch £6-£10alc Dinner £12.50-£15 Last dinner 8pm
Credit Cards 1 3

LUGWARDINE Hereford & Worcester Map **03** SO53

★★⌂Longworth Hall
HR1 4DF
☎Hereford(0432)850223

This 18th-century mansion was built of rich, red brick, its unusual turret-like corners creating interesting features inside. Public rooms are finely proportioned and carefully furnished in compatible style to offer a high degree of comfort, whilst spacious bedrooms promote a rural atmosphere with bright, co-ordinating colours and fabrics. Welcoming, friendly staff and the hotel's location in lush valley countryside make this the ideal spot if you are looking for peace and relaxation, but the energetic can also enjoy a value-for-money outdoor persuits break.
10⇨↿(1fb)1⊞ CTV in all bedrooms Ⓡ **T**
sB&B⇨↿£31.05-£49.45 dB&B⇨↿£62.10-£98.90 ⊟
30P ✽ ♩ ⌂ *xmas*
V ♁ ♅ Lunch £8.95 High tea £1.75-£5 Dinner £10.95&alc Last dinner 9.45pm
Credit Cards 2 3 5 £

See advertisement under HEREFORD

A rosette is the AA's highest award for quality of food and service in a restaurant.

LUMBY North Yorkshire Map **08** SE43

★★★66% The Post House Hotel, Leeds/Selby LS25 5LF (southern junc A1/A63) (Trusthouse Forte)
☎South Milford(0977)682711 Telex no 557074
FAX (0977) 685462
A modern, purpose-built hotel situated at the junction of the A1/A63 and close to the M62. Recently refurbished, this hotel offers greatly improved bedrooms, a leisure centre, two bars and the Traders' Restaurant.
109rm(59⇨50↿)(3fb)⍻in 12 bedrooms CTV in all bedrooms Ⓡ **T** ✻ sB⇨↿£60-£67 dB⇨↿£70-£78 (room only) ⊟
☾ 300P ✽ CFA ▭(heated) ℘ (hard) sauna 9 hole pitch & putt *xmas*
♉ European V ♁ ♅ ⍻ Lunch £7.50-£11.10&alc Dinner £10.50-£14.10&alc Last dinner 10pm
Credit Cards 1 2 3 4 5

LUNDIN LINKS Fife Map **12** NO40

★★★67% *Old Manor* Leven Rd KY8 6AJ ☎(0333)320368
Telex no 727606
Tasteful extension and conversion of the original mansion have produced this elegant hotel looking across the golf course to the Firth of Forth.
19rm(15⇨)(2fb) CTV in all bedrooms Ⓡ **T** ✘
☾ 80P ✽
♉ Continental **V** ♁ ♅
Credit Cards 1 2 3

★★Lundin Links Leven Rd KY8 6AP (Inter) ☎(0333)320207
FAX (0333) 320930
20rm(8⇨10↿)(4fb)1⊞ CTV in all bedrooms Ⓡ **T**
sB&B⇨↿£33-£49 dB&B£44-£60 dB&B⇨↿£52-£98 ⊟
CTV 50P *xmas*
♉ Scottish & French **V** ♁ ♅ Lunch £5.50-£15&alc High tea £5.50-£15 Dinner £10-£25&alc Last dinner 9.30pm
Credit Cards 1 2 3 5 £

LUSS Strathclyde *Dunbartonshire* Map **10** NS39

★★*Inverbeg Inn* Inverbeg G83 8PU (3m N on A82)
☎(043686)678
An attractive inn with modern, comfortable facilities, the Inverbeg stands close to the banks of Loch Lomond.
14rm(7⇨)(1fb) CTV in all bedrooms Ⓡ
☾ 80P ✽ squash ⌂
♉ British & French **V** ♁ ♅ ⍻
Credit Cards 1 2 3 5

LUSTLEIGH Devon Map **03** SX78

★★*Eastwrey Barton* Moretonhampstead Rd TQ13 9SN (On A382 NE Bovey Tracey) ☎(06477)338
Standing amid acres of woodland in the beautiful Wrey Valley on the southern edge of Dartmoor National Park, this small hotel has been transformed to provide hospitable, country house-style accommodation of a commendably high standard. Cosy, attractive bedrooms retain their distinct character, despite modernisation, and in the attractive dining room guests can enjoy freshly prepared English and Provençale dishes.
6⇨ CTV in 2bedrooms Ⓡ ✘ (ex guide dogs)
CTV 32P ⊯ ✽
♉ English & French **V** ♁ Last dinner 9pm
Credit Cards 1 3

LUTON Bedfordshire Map **04** TL02

★★★62% Chiltern Waller Av, Dunstable Rd LU4 9RU (Crest)
☎(0582)575911 Telex no 825048 FAX (0582) 581589
This modern commercial hotel, with good conference facilities, has comfortable bedrooms, well-equipped with the business guest in mind. The restaurant offers some interesting dishes, accompanied

by a well-balanced wine list. The friendly, helpful staff create a relaxed, informal atmosphere.
93⇨↱⊁in 17 bedrooms CTV in all bedrooms ® T ✱
sB⇨↱£67-£79 dB⇨↱£67-£91 (room only) 𝔅
Lift ☾ 150P CFA
♔ English & French V ♔ ☕ ⊁ Lunch £12.95&alc High tea £3.45 Dinner £13.95&alc Last dinner 10pm
Credit Cards 1 2 3 4 5

★★★60% Crest Hotel – Luton Dunstable Rd LU4 8RQ (Crest) ☎(0582)575955 Telex no 826283 FAX (0582) 490065
This good, well-equipped conference/commercial hotel offers an attractive restaurant and helpful service from friendly staff.
117⇨⊁in 21 bedrooms CTV in all bedrooms ® T
sB⇨£70-£74 dB⇨£82-£86 (room only) 𝔅
Lift ☾ 130P CFA pool table small snooker table
♔ International V ♔ ☕ ⊁ Lunch £8-£15&alc Dinner £15-£17&alc Last dinner 10pm
Credit Cards 1 2 3 4 5

★★★68% Strathmore Thistle Arndale Centre LU1 2TR (Thistle) ☎(0582)34199 Telex no 825763 FAX (0582) 402528
The hotel has been tastefully modernised to provide comfortable accommodation with well-equipped bedrooms, and helpful staff offer friendly service.
150⇨↱(7fb)⊁in 33 bedrooms CTV in all bedrooms ® T ✗ ✱
sB⇨↱£63-£80 dB⇨↱£75-£93 (room only) 𝔅
Lift ☾ 44P CFA
♔ International ♔ ☕ ⊁ Lunch fr£12.50&alc Dinner fr£16&alc Last dinner 10pm
Credit Cards 1 2 3 4 5

★★Red Lion Castle St LU1 3AA (Lansbury) ☎(0582)413881 Telex no 826856 FAX (0582) 23864
Recently refurbished, the bedrooms and public areas of this town centre hotel have been decorated in keeping with its character. Friendly service is offered in the busy coffee shop and restaurant.
38rm(36⇨2↱)(2fb)1▣⊁in 6 bedrooms CTV in all bedrooms ® T ✗ (ex guide dogs) sB&B⇨↱fr£58 dB&B⇨↱fr£68
☾ 48P
V ♔ Lunch fr£8alc Dinner fr£12alc Last dinner 10.30pm
Credit Cards 1 2 3 5

LUTTERWORTH Leicestershire Map 04 SP58

★★★72% Denbigh Arms High St LE17 4AD (Consort) ☎(0455)553537 Telex no 342545 FAX (0455) 556627
Closed 24-26 Dec & 1-2 Jan
An 18th-century coaching inn in the centre of this small town, thoroughly and yet sympathetically modernised to provide warm, comfortable bedrooms and bright, modern public rooms. Very popular as a venue for lunch and dinner, this hotel provides value for money and attentive service.
34⇨(1fb) CTV in all bedrooms ® T ✗ (ex guide dogs) ✱
sB&B⇨£61.50-£70 dB&B⇨£75-£85 𝔅
☾ 30P ⛟
V ♔ ☕ S10% Lunch £9.50-£10.50&alc Dinner £14.50-£16&alc Last dinner 10pm
Credit Cards 1 2 3 5

LYDDINGTON Leicestershire Map 04 SP89

★★★61% Marquess of Exeter Main Rd LE15 9LT (Best Western) ☎Uppingham(0572)822477 FAX (0572) 821343
Charming 17th-century rural village inn, with modern bedrooms in annexe.
Annexe17rm(12⇨5↱) CTV in all bedrooms ® T ✗
sB&B⇨↱£52-£58 dB&B⇨↱£64-£74 𝔅
70P ⛟ ✽ ♫
♔ English & French V ♔ ☕ Lunch £8-£12&alc Dinner £10.50-£12.50&alc Last dinner 9.45pm
Credit Cards 1 2 3 5

LYDFORD Devon Map 02 SX58

★★♣Lydford House
EX20 4AU (Minotels)
☎(082282)347

This delightful, granite-built country house was formerly the home of the Victorian artist William Widgery, whose scenes of Dartmoor still hang in the cosy residents' lounge. The Boulter family have gradually been upgrading the accommodation over a number of years. Service is personal and attentive, and the home cooking very enjoyable. Eight acres of gardens and pasture surround the property, and there is a riding school run by the owners' daughter.
13rm(10⇨1↱)(2fb)1▣⊁in 1 bedroom CTV in all bedrooms ® T sB&B⇨↱£23.50 dB&B⇨↱£47 𝔅
30P ⛟ ✽ U nc5yrs
♔ ⊁ Lunch fr£5.50 Dinner fr£10 Last dinner 8pm
Credit Cards 1 2 3 5

LYDNEY Gloucestershire Map 03 SO60

★★Feathers High St GL15 5DN ☎Dean(0594)842815 & 842826
There is a friendly atmosphere in this popular town-centre hotel, which offers a choice of à la carte dining room or carvery, and there are also good bar menus available.
14rm(13⇨1↱)(3fb)1▣ CTV in all bedrooms ® T ✱
sB&B⇨↱fr£35.50 dB&B⇨↱fr£47.50 𝔅
▶

50P
V ♆ ☑ ⚟ Lunch £4.95-£15alc Dinner £6.50-£15alc Last dinner 10pm
Credit Cards [1] [3]

LYME REGIS Dorset Map **03** SY39

See also **Rousdon**

★★★60% Alexandra Pound St DT7 3HZ ☎(02974)2010 & 3229
Closed 18 Dec-3 Feb
Built in 1735, this hotel occupies a prime position with beautiful views over Lyme Bay. Public rooms, though tastefully modernised, still retain their charm and character, and bedrooms are comfortable. The table d'hôte menu changes daily.
24rm(22⇌2♠)(6fb) CTV in all bedrooms ® **T**
sB&B⇌♠£36-£48 dB&B⇌♠£72-£96 (incl dinner) ⛿
24P ⇎ ✲
☋ English & French **V** ♆ ☑ Lunch £6.95-£7.50&alc Dinner £13.50-£13.95&alc Last dinner 8.30pm
Credit Cards [1] [3]

★★★50% Devon Hotel Lyme Rd DT7 3TQ (Best Western)
☎(02974)3231 Telex no 42513
(For full entry see Uplyme)

★★★62% *Mariners* Silver St DT7 3HS ☎(02974)2753
Closed 8 Jan-13 Feb
A 17th-century coaching inn with a friendly and relaxing atmosphere, personally supervised by the owners. Considerable improvements are making this hotel very comfortable. It also has an attractive restaurant which specialises in dishes using fresh local fish.
16rm(9⇌5♠)(1fb) CTV in all bedrooms **T**
26P croquet
☋ International **V** ♆ ☑ Last dinner 9pm
Credit Cards [1] [2] [3] [5]

★★*Bay* Marine Pde DT7 3JQ ☎(02974)2059
Closed Dec-Feb
A family-run, seafront hotel with a friendly and welcoming atmosphere. Bedrooms are adequately equipped and the lounge is comfortable, while the attractive restaurant offers a varied menu at a reasonable price.
21rm(9⇌3♠)(3fb) ®
CTV 5P 20🚘 ⇎
☋ English & French ♆ ☑ Last dinner 8.30pm
Credit Cards [1]

★★Buena Vista Pound St DT7 3HZ ☎(02974)2494
A detached Regency house with good sea views, comfortable lounges and well-equipped bedrooms maintains its warm friendly atmosphere under the personal supervision of the proprietor.
20rm(13⇌4♠)(2fb) CTV in all bedrooms ® **T** sB&B£19-£23 sB&B⇌♠£21-£26 dB&B£42-£68 dB&B⇌♠£42-£68 ⛿
CTV 18P ⇎ ✲
♆ Dinner fr£9 Last dinner 8pm
Credit Cards [1] [2] [3] [5] Ⓔ

★★Dorset Silver St DT7 3HX ☎(02974)2482
Closed Nov-Feb
A clean, well-maintained, family-run hotel with a warm and friendly atmosphere. Bedrooms are of a good size and the lounge comfortable. A reasonably-priced table d'hote menu is served in the bright and airy dining-room.
12rm(3⇌7♠)(2fb) CTV in all bedrooms ® ✱
sB&B£17.50-£20.50 dB&B£51-£58 dB&B⇌♠£56-£63 ⛿
13P
V ♆ ☑
Credit Cards [1] [3]

Book as early as possible for busy holiday periods.

★★*Royal Lion* Broad St DT7 3QF ☎(02974)5622
Fine panelling and oak beams still exist in this 16th-century coaching inn.
30rm(20⇌10♠)(4fb)1⊟ CTV in all bedrooms ® **T**
36P ⇎ snooker games room
♆ ☑ ⚟ Last dinner 10pm
Credit Cards [1] [2] [3] [5]

★★St Michael's Pound St DT7 3HZ ☎(02974)2503
A small, friendly, family-run hotel offering comfortable accommodation. Bedrooms are nicely equipped. A table d'hôte menu is available in the dining room at a reasonable price.
14rm(5⇌7♠)(1fb)1⊟ CTV in all bedrooms ® ✱
sB&B£22.50-£27.50 sB&B⇌♠£22.50-£27.50 dB&B£45-£55 dB&B⇌♠£45-£55
12P 1🚘 ⇎
♆ ☑ ⚟
Credit Cards [1] [3]

★Tudor House Church St DT7 3BU ☎(02974)2472
Closed Nov-mid Mar
Historic Elizabethan hotel with comfortable accommodation. Bar contains old water well.
17rm(4⇌)(10fb) S10% sB&B£14-£16 sB&B⇌£16-£18 dB&B£28-£32 dB&B⇌£32-£36
CTV 12P
♆ ☑ S10% Bar Lunch fr£1.50 Dinner fr£5.50 Last dinner 7.30pm
Credit Cards [1] [3] Ⓔ

LYMINGTON Hampshire Map **04** SZ39

★★★♛73% Passford House Mount Pleasant Ln SO41 8LS (2m NW on Sway rd)
☎(0590)682398
Telex no 47502
Quietly standing in 9 acres of gardens and paddocks on the edge of the New Forest, this hotel has three comfortable lounges, an elegant restaurant and well-equipped and co-ordinated bedrooms. There are separate modern leisure facilities.
54⇌♠(4fb)1⊟ CTV in all bedrooms ® T ✱
sB&B⇌♠fr£60 dB&B⇌♠£86-£95 ⛿
☾ CTV 100P 4🚘 (£3) ⇎ ✲ CFA ▭(heated) ⌒(heated) ✎ (hard) sauna solarium gymnasium croquet putting table tennis pool table ⌂ *xmas*
☋ English & French ♆ ☑ Lunch fr£9.50&alc Dinner fr£16.50&alc Last dinner 9pm
Credit Cards [1] [2] [3]

See advertisement on page 453

★★★72% Stanwell House High St SO41 9AA ☎(0590)677123
Telex no 477463 FAX (0590) 677756
Set in the heart of the town, yet within an acre of walled gardens, this is a modernised Georgian house with a recently built business suite. Food, fresh from the market, is well cooked in the traditional English style and the wine list is quite outstanding. Conveniently situated for sailing or exploring the New Forest.
35⇌1⊟ CTV in all bedrooms ® **T** ✗ (ex guide dogs)
sB&B⇌fr£52.50 dB&B⇌fr£75 ⛿
✗ ⇎ ✲ *xmas*

▶

South Lawn Hotel & Restaurant ★★★

Milford-on-Sea, Lymington, Hampshire SO41 0RF
Tel: Lymington (0590) 43911 – 4 lines

Delightful Country House Hotel in peaceful surroundings where comfort and good food predominate. Owner/Chef Ernst Barten supervises excellent cuisine. Specially imported wines from Germany.

All rooms en-suite, colour TV, phone and trouser press. Facilities nearby include windsurfing and sailing from Keyhaven, Golf at Brockenhurst and Barton-on-Sea, the Beach at Milford and walking or riding in the beautiful New Forest.

FAIRWATER HEAD HOTEL ★★★

near Lyme Regis, HAWKCHURCH, AXMINSTER, DEVON EX13 5TX

BTA Commended, Egon Ronay, Ashley Courtenay – Best 10 Hotel Gardens in Britain Award

See gazetteer under Hawkchurch

Set in glorious open countryside, in peaceful tranquillity. Where guests return year after year for the excellent food and wine, cheerful log fires, 18 en suite bedrooms, comfortable lounge and garden lounge . . . and family hospitality. Ideal location for walking, birdwatching, photography, visiting gardens and National Trust properties, the coast at Lyme Regis . . . or just total relaxation.

Golf concession at Lyme Regis. **Bargain Breaks.**
NEW colour brochure: Hawkchurch (029 77) 349

Comfort, good food and friendly service

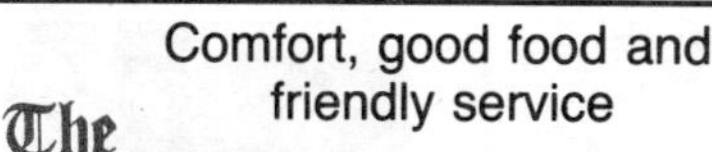

Silver Street
Lyme Regis
Dorset DT7 3HS
(02974) 2753

AA ★★★

Former 17th century coaching inn, scheduled as of historical interest and illustrated by Beatrix Potter in 'Tales of a Little Pig Robinson'. Superbly preserved to include all the modern comforts with en suite bathrooms. Retaining the charm and ambience of the period with its crooked rooms. A 325 year old tulip tree in the garden from where there are spectacular views of the Dorset coast. Finest cuisine with local fish specialities. Bargain Breaks Available.

For colour brochure please telephone or write.

ALEXANDRA HOTEL

Pound Street, Lyme Regis, Dorset DT7 3HZ

AA ★ ★ ★

Ashley Courtenay, Egon Ronay and Signpost Recommended

Built in 1735, the Alexandra occupies a prime position in this attractive and historic town. Tastefully modernised, but retaining its charm, this peaceful hotel, in its beautiful garden, with panoramic views over Lyme Bay, is ideal for relaxing Summer holidays or short Spring and Autumn breaks. Golf concessions available to guests.

For full details and colour brochure, please ring Lyme Regis (02974) 2010

English & French V Lunch fr£10.50 Dinner fr£17.50
Last dinner 9.30pm
Credit Cards 1 3

LYMM Cheshire Map **07** SJ68

★★★ **56% Lymm** Whitbarrow Rd WA13 9AQ (De Vere)
☎(092575)2233 Telex no 629455 FAX (092575) 6035
RS New Year
Conveniently situated for easy access to the M6 and Manchester Airport, this hotel offers bedrooms of a good standard and a large lounge with plenty of comfortable seating.
22rm(7⇌15↱)Annexe47rm(43⇌4↱)(1fb) CTV in all bedrooms ® **T** sB&B⇌↱£70 dB&B⇌↱£85
120P CFA nc
English & French V Lunch £13&alc Dinner £13&alc
Last dinner 10pm
Credit Cards 1 2 3 5 £

LYMPSHAM Avon Map **03** ST35

★★ **Batch Farm Country**
BS24 0EX
☎Weston-Super-Mare(0934)750371
Closed Xmas
A peaceful place to stay, this small, personally-run hotel is also a 100-acre working farm. Bedrooms are well maintained and comfortable and the lounge and bar areas are very homely.
8⇌(4fb) in 2 bedrooms CTV in all bedrooms ®
sB&B⇌£25-£26 dB&B⇌£42-£44
CTV 50P ✻ snooker croquet
V Bar Lunch £4.95-£5.95 Dinner £9.50-£10.50&alc Last dinner 8pm
Credit Cards 1 2 3 £

See advertisement under WESTON-SUPER-MARE

LYMPSTONE Devon Map **03** SX98

✕✕ **River House** The Strand EX8 5EY
☎Exmouth(0395)265147
The entrance to this detached red brick building is in the main street of the village, but there are fine views of the estuary from the lounge and dining room. The menu offers a good selection of freshly prepared dishes. The atmosphere is relaxing and the service attentive.
Dinner not served Sun
English & French V 34 seats Lunch £27.50 Dinner £27.50
Last lunch 1.30pm Last dinner 9.30pm nc6yrs 2 bedrooms available
Credit Cards 1 2 3

LYNDHURST Hampshire Map **04** SU30

★★★ **68% Crown** High St SO43 7NF (Best Western)
☎(042128)2922 Telex no 9312110733 FAX (042128) 2751
An attractive hotel of considerable charm situated in the centre of this New Forest town. Comfortable public areas have a traditional appeal, and major bedroom refurbishment is well under way at the time of going to print. Straightforward cuisine is served by pleasant young staff, and bar meals in particular are very reasonably priced.
41⇌(6fb)1 CTV in all bedrooms ® **T** sB&B⇌£44-£50
dB&B⇌£66-£78
Lift CTV 60P CFA board & computer games *xmas*
European V Lunch £11.25-£12.50&alc Dinner fr£12.50&alc Last dinner 9.30pm
Credit Cards 1 2 3 5

See advertisement under SOUTHAMPTON

★★★ **63% Forest Lodge Hotel** Pikes Hill, Romsey Rd SO43 7AS
☎(042128)3677 FAX (042128) 3828
An attractive small Georgian hotel on the edge of Lyndhurst and the New Forest. Totally refurbished during 1989, it now provides bedrooms which are comfortable and well equipped. The spacious restaurant offers table d'hôte and à la carte menus which are good value for money.
19rm(15⇌4↱)(1fb)1 in 5 bedrooms CTV in all bedrooms ® **T** ✻ sB&B⇌↱£45-£59 dB&B⇌↱£65-£85
50P ✻ (heated) pitch & putt *xmas*
English & French V Lunch £8.50 High tea £2.50-£5
Dinner £10&alc Last dinner 9.45pm
Credit Cards 1 2 3 5

★★★ **60% Lyndhurst Park** High St SO43 7NL (Forestdale)
☎(042128)3923 Telex no 477802 FAX (042128) 3019
This Georgian hotel has been extended by a new bedroom wing, and south-facing rooms overlook attractive gardens. The Highwayman's Bar is well known in this part of the New Forest, and by the end of 1989 a large conservatory will have been added to the restaurant.
59rm(58⇌1↱)(3fb)4 in 3 bedrooms CTV in all bedrooms ® **T**
Lift 100P ✻ CFA (heated) (hard) snooker sauna solarium ♫
English & Continental V Last dinner 10pm
Credit Cards 1 2 3 4 5

★★★ **66% Parkhill**
Beaulieu Rd SO43 7FZ
(Select)
☎(042128)2944
FAX (042128) 3268

An elegant Georgian hotel in park-like surroundings achieves a genuine country house atmosphere, with comfortable public rooms decked with fresh flowers and liberally provided with magazines, cheerfully warmed by log fires throughout the cooler months. The dining room offers guests a choice of table d'hôte and à la carte menus based on modern British cuisine, and bedrooms are, at the time of going to press, about to undergo refurbishment.
15rm(13⇌2↱)Annexe5⇌↱(4fb)1 CTV in all bedrooms ® **T**
75P ✻ (heated) croquet
French V Last dinner 10pm
Credit Cards 1 2 3 4 5 £

★★ **Evergreens** Romsey Rd SO43 7AR (Minotels)
☎(042128)2175 & 2343
Standing in its own gardens on the town's fringe, the hotel provides accommodation in bedrooms which are for the most part tastefully refurbished and well equipped. The Austrian chef/proprietor, Gernot Schwetz, and his friendly staff pride themselves particularly on a 4-course dinner which represents excellent value for money.
20rm(10⇌8↱)Annexe2⇌(1fb)3 CTV in all bedrooms ® **T**
S% sB&B£35-£42 dB&B⇌↱£48-£80
34P 3 ✻ *xmas*

L

English & Continental V S% Bar Lunch £1.50-£4alc Dinner £11-£12&alc Last dinner 9pm
Credit Cards 1 3 5 £

LYNMOUTH Devon Map 03 SS74

See also **Lynton**

★★★ 63% **Tors** EX35 6NA Lynton(0598)53236
Closed 4 Jan-9 Mar
Comfortable hotel in five acres of grounds, set on a hill above Lynmouth. There are fine views over the bay.
35rm(33⇌2)(5fb) CTV in all bedrooms ® T ✱ sB&B⇌£32-£52 dB&B⇌£53-£67
Lift CTV 40P ❊ CFA (heated) *xmas*
English & French S% Lunch £6 Dinner £12-£12&alc Last dinner 8.45pm
Credit Cards 1 2 3 5

★★ **Bath** Sea Front EX35 6EL (Exec Hotel) Lynton(0598)52238
Closed Nov-Feb RS Mar
Traditional, family-run hotel situated in the centre of the village.
24rm(16⇌1)(9fb) CTV in all bedrooms ® T S10% sB&Bfr£18 sB&B⇌£25-£27.50 dB&Bfr£36 dB&B⇌£50-£55
11P 4 (£1.50 per night)
English & French S10% Lunch fr£6 Dinner fr£11 Last dinner 8.30pm
Credit Cards 1 2 3 5 £

★★ **Rising Sun** The Harbour EX35 6EQ Lynton(0598)53223
Closed 2 Jan-11 Feb
Stone built inn, set into the hill beside the harbour.
11rm(3⇌8)Annexe5rm(3⇌2)(2fb)2 in 6 bedrooms CTV in all bedrooms ® T ✱ S10% sB&B⇌£37.50-£37.50 dB&B⇌£59-£75
CTV ❊ nc5yrs *xmas*
English & French V Lunch £7.50-£9.50 Dinner £15.50&alc Last dinner 8.45pm
Credit Cards 1 2 3 £

★ **Bonnicott** Watersmeet Rd EX35 6EP Lynton(0598)53346
Closed Jan
Family-run hotel with entrance through steep, terraced garden. Public areas are all sea-facing and the bedrooms are simple and clean.
10rm(1⇌3)(2fb)1 CTV in all bedrooms ® ✱ sB&B£15.50-£17.50 dB&B£31-£35 dB&B⇌£37-£41
❊ *xmas*
English, French & Italian V Lunch £2-£7.50 High tea £1-£3.50 Dinner fr£9.50&alc Last dinner 8.30pm
Credit Cards 1 2 3 £

★ **Rock House** EX35 6EN Lynton(0598)53508
A busy tea garden is one of the attractions of this delightful little Georgian hotel. Overlooking the harbour, it occupies a unique position beside the River Lyn, the foreshore and the Manor Gardens.
6rm(1⇌3)(2fb)1 CTV in all bedrooms ® sB&B£20 sB&B⇌£25 dB&B£40 dB&B⇌£50
CTV 7P
English & French V Bar Lunch £1.15-£6.95alc High tea £2.50-£4.50alc Dinner £10&alc Last dinner 8.45pm
Credit Cards 1 2 3 5

Entries for rosetted restaurants, red-star and country-house hotels are highlighted by a tinted panel. For a full list of these establishments, consult the Contents page.

LYNTON Devon Map 03 SS74

See also **Lynmouth**

★★★ 69% **Lynton Cottage** North Walk EX35 6ED (0598)52342 FAX (0598) 52597
RS Mon-Thu (Dec-Feb)
Perched literally 500 feet above Lynmouth Bay, this cottage hotel is surrounded by countryside of outstanding beauty and has lovely views. Bedrooms, most of which have recently been refurbished, are attractively decorated and offer a high standard of comfort and facilities – including sumptuous bathrooms. Food standards are commendable as are the warmth and hospitality offered to guests by hotel proprietors John and Maisie Jones and their dedicated staff. An ideal retreat and good touring base for North Devon.
18rm(14⇌4) CTV in all bedrooms ® T dB&B⇌£70-£95
26P ❊ nc10yrs *xmas*
French Lunch fr£12.50&alc Dinner fr£17.50&alc Last dinner 8.45pm
Credit Cards 1 2 3 5 £

★★ ***Castle Hill House*** Castle Hill EX35 6JA (0598)52291
Closed Nov-Etr
Situated in the town centre, this tall, Victorian house is personally run by owners Mr and Mrs Smart, who provide friendly and attentive service. Bedrooms are pretty and well equipped and imaginative food is served in the tented restaurant.
9rm(7⇌2)(2fb) in 2 bedrooms CTV in all bedrooms ® (ex guide dogs)
nc5yrs
English & Continental V Last dinner 9.30pm
Credit Cards 1 3

★★ ***Crown*** Sinai Hill EX35 6AG (Inter) (0598)52253
Closed Jan
Dating back to 1760 and once a coaching inn, this character hotel maintains its position as the local hostelry, with a reputation for fine beer. Family run, it combines soundly equipped, cosy bedrooms with a popular restaurant and bars, whilst its central yet secluded position makes it an ideal base from which to tour the area.
16rm(15⇌1)(6fb)5 CTV in all bedrooms ® T
20P
English & French V Last dinner 8.30pm
Credit Cards 1 2 3 5

★★ **Hewitts** North Walk EX35 6HJ
(0598)52293
RS mid Nov-mid Mar

Retaining the same manager, Simon Evans, despite a recent change of ownership, this small Victorian mansion in its 27 acres of woodland continues to provide the relaxed atmosphere of a country house by the sea. Stylish public rooms include a splendid galleried lounge, and the intimate restaurant features imaginative menus, based on English cuisine with some French influence. Chef David Lamprell was a finalist in the 1986 'Young Chef of the Year' competition.
12rm(9⇌)(1fb)1 in 2 bedrooms CTV in all bedrooms T S10% sB&B£28-£60 sB&B⇌£36-£56 dB&B£52-£78 dB&B⇌£51-£84
10P ❊ clay pigeon shooting jaccuzi *xmas*
V S10% Lunch £7.95-£12.50&alc Dinner £15.50-£16.95&alc Last dinner 9.30pm
Credit Cards 1 2 3 5 £

★★**Neubia House** Lydiate Ln EX35 6AH (Guestaccom)
☎(0598)52309
Closed 20 Nov-11 Feb
12rm(9⇌3♪)(3fb) CTV in all bedrooms ®
sB&B⇌♪£20.75-£21.75 dB&B⇌♪£41.50-£43.50 ₽
14P ⇼ nc4yrs
V ⚘ Dinner £9-£10 Last dinner 7.30pm
Credit Cards 1 3

★★**Sandrock** Longmead EX35 6DH ☎(0598)53307
Closed Dec-Jan
This small touring/holiday hotel, owned by the same family for many years, offers modestly-appointed bedrooms and compact, cosy public rooms. It stands conveniently close to the town centre.
9rm(5⇌2♪)(3fb) CTV in all bedrooms ® ✱ sB&B£15-£18
dB&B⇌♪£32-£36 ₽
9P ⇼
♔ ☐ Bar Lunch £3-£6alc Dinner £9.50-£11.50 Last dinner 7.45pm
Credit Cards 1 2 3 £

See advertisement on page 457

★**Chough's Nest** North Walk EX35 6HJ ☎(0598)53315
Closed mid Oct-Etr
Comfortable holiday hotel, situated high above the bay.
12rm(7⇌5♪)(2fb)2⊞ CTV in all bedrooms ® ✗
sB&B⇌♪£18.30-£20 dB&B⇌♪£36.60-£40
₱ ⇼ ✲ nc2yrs
V ♔ ☐ ⚘ Dinner £7.50 Last dinner 7.30pm

The AA's star-rating scheme is the market leader in hotel classification.

★🏠**Combe Park** Hillsford Bridge EX35 6LE
☎(0598)52356
Closed mid Nov-mid Mar (ex Xmas)

Former hunting lodge set in six acres of woodland.

9rm(6⇌2♠)(3fb)®
CTV 11P ⛟ ❖ bird watching nc12yrs
♈ ☕ Last dinner 7.30pm

★**Fairholme** North Walk EX35 6ED ☎(0598)52263
Closed Oct-Mar
The small hotel stands in a breathtaking position overlooking the Bristol Channel.
12rm(7⇌1♠)(2fb) TV available ✗ ✳ sB&Bfr£15 sB&B⇌♠£15 dB&Bfr£30 dB&B⇌♠£30
CTV 12P ⛟ ❖ ▣(heated)
♈ ☕

★**North Cliff** North Walk EX35 6HJ ☎(0598)52357
Closed Nov-Feb
This small, family-run hotel, commanding unrestricted sea views from its elevated position, provides cosy bedrooms, a relaxed atmosphere and friendly service.
16rm(12⇌2♠)(2fb) CTV in 4bedrooms ® sB&B£22-£23 sB&B⇌♠£24.50-£25.50 dB&B£44-£46 dB&B⇌♠£49-£51 (incl dinner)
CTV 15P ⛟ table tennis pool table
♈
£

★**Rockvale** Lee Rd EX35 6HW ☎(0598)52279 & 53343
Closed Nov
Former Bristol merchant's holiday home, the hotel has been modernised and offers comfortable accommodation.
8rm(4⇌1♠)(2fb)1⊞ CTV in 7bedrooms TV in 1bedroom ® T S% sB&B£15.75-£17 sB&B⇌♠£16.50-£18 dB&Bfr£33 ⊟
10P ⛟ ❖ nc4yrs
♈ ☕ Lunch £2-£5 Dinner £9.50 Last dinner 7.30pm
Credit Cards 3

★**Seawood** North Walk EX35 6HT ☎(0598)52272
Closed Dec-Feb
Overlooking the sea from its rising, wooded grounds, this pink-painted house offers quiet, comfortable accommodation, the bedrooms having good facilities.
12rm(4⇌8♠)(1fb)4⊞ CTV in all bedrooms ® ✳ sB&B⇌♠£20-£24 dB&B⇌♠£38-£42 ⊟
10P ⛟ ❖
🍷 English & Continental V
£

LYTHAM ST ANNES Lancashire Map **07** SD32

★★★★61% **Clifton Arms** West Beach, Lytham FY8 5QJ (Lansbury) ☎(0253)739898 Telex no 677463 FAX (0253) 730657
Guests will experience delightfully courteous service in every area of this very comfortable hotel.
41rm(37⇌4♠)1⊞ CTV in all bedrooms ® T sB&B⇌♠fr£65 dB&B⇌♠fr£75 ⊟
Lift ☾ 50P CFA sauna solarium jacuzzi ♫ *xmas*
🍷 English & French V ♈ ☕ Lunch fr£8.75&alc Dinner £12.50-£18.50&alc Last dinner 10pm
Credit Cards 1 2 3 5

★★★68% **Bedford** 307-311 Clifton Dr South FY8 1HN (Exec Hotel) ☎(0253)724636 FAX (0253) 729244
A very friendly hotel, managed by the resident proprietors, providing comfortable accommodation throughout. There is a choice of eating options – the main restaurant, a coffee shop and a quaint lower-ground-floor bistro.
36rm(20⇌16♠)(6fb)1⊞ CTV in all bedrooms ® T sB&B⇌♠£24-£30 dB&B⇌♠£45-£60 ⊟
Lift ☾ CTV 20P sauna solarium gymnasium jacuzzi steam room *xmas*
🍷 English & Continental V ♈ ☕ Lunch fr£5.95 High tea fr£3.25 Dinner fr£10.50&alc Last dinner 8.30pm
Credit Cards 1 3 £

★★★67% **Grand Osprey** South Promenade, St Annes FY8 1NB (Toby) ☎(0253)721288 Telex no 67481
Grand Edwardian building now modernised throughout, situated on the sea front.
40rm(38⇌2♠)(5fb)⊬in 12 bedrooms CTV in all bedrooms ® T ✳ sB&B⇌♠£53.50-£58.50 dB&B⇌♠£63.50-£68.50 ⊟
Lift ☾ 250P ❖ CFA ♫ *xmas*
🍷 International V ♈ ☕ Lunch fr£7.25&alc Dinner fr£10.75&alc Last dinner 9.30pm
Credit Cards 1 2 3 5

★★**Chadwick** South Promenade FY8 1NP ☎(0253)720061
This spacious, sea-front hotel offers good service and excellent value for money.
70rm(61⇌9♠)(24fb)1⊞ CTV in all bedrooms T ✗ (ex guide dogs) sB&B⇌♠£27.50-£29.50 dB&B⇌♠£36-£42.50 ⊟
Lift ☾ 40P ⛟ CFA ▣(heated) sauna solarium turkish bath jacuzzi games room ⌂ *xmas*
🍷 English & French ♈ ☕ ⊬ Lunch £5.50-£6.50 Dinner £9.50-£10.50 Last dinner 8.30pm
Credit Cards 1 2 3 5

★★**Fernlea** 15 South Promenade FY8 1LU (Consort) ☎(0253)726726 Telex no 677150 FAX (0253) 721561
Modern, sea-front hotel with extensive leisure facilities.
95⇌(50fb)2⊞⊬in 10 bedrooms CTV in all bedrooms ® T ✳ sB&B⇌£36.50-£40 dB&B⇌£60-£100 ⊟
Lift ☾ CTV 60P CFA ▣(heated) squash snooker sauna solarium gymnasium *xmas*
V ♈ ☕ Lunch £7.50-£9.50 High tea £3.50-£8 Dinner £12.50-£12.50 Last dinner 8pm
Credit Cards 1 2 3 5

★★**New Glendower** North Promenade FY8 2 N (Consort) ☎(0253)723241
Large stone building overlooking the sea front.
60⇌(17fb) CTV in all bedrooms ® T ✳ sB&B⇌£24.50-£30 dB&B⇌£49-£60 ⊟
☾ CTV 45P ▣(heated) solarium mini-gym, pool table, badminton ♫ *xmas*
V ♈ Bar Lunch £2-£4 High tea £3.25-£4.50 Dinner £10-£12 Last dinner 8pm
Credit Cards 2 3 5

★★**St Ives** 7-9 South Promenade FY8 1LS ☎(0253)720011
Spacious lounge areas, well-appointed bedrooms and leisure facilities are features of this comfortable, well-managed hotel.
73rm(64⇌2♠)(44fb) CTV in all bedrooms ® T ✗ sB&B£28-£33 sB&B⇌♠£30-£35 dB&B⇌♠£43-£61 (incl dinner) ⊟
☾ ⊞ CTV 100P ⛟ CFA ▣(heated) snooker sauna solarium ♫ *xmas*
🍷 English & French V ♈ ☕ Lunch 95p-£3alc Dinner £7.95-£7.95&alc Last dinner 8.30pm
Credit Cards 1 2 3 5

★**Carlton** 61 South Promenade FY8 1LZ ☎(0253)721036
Closed Jan & Feb
Pleasant, family-run hotel overlooking the promenade gardens.
21rm(5⇌5⋒)(6fb) CTV in all bedrooms ® ✱ sB&B£20 dB&B£20 dB&B⇌⋒£21 (incl dinner)
CTV 10P *xmas*
V ♈ ☕ ⅟ Bar Lunch £1-£2 Dinner £6-£7.50 Last dinner 7pm
Credit Cards [1]

★***Ennes Court*** 107 South Prom FY8 1ND ☎(0253)723731
Closed Nov-Feb
10rm(6⇌4⋒)(1fb) CTV in all bedrooms ® ✈
CTV 9P ⛟ nc3yrs
⅟ Last dinner 7pm

★**Lindum** 63-67 South Promenade FY8 1LZ
☎(0253)721534 722516 FAX (0253) 721364
Conveniently situated sea front hotel.
80rm(72⇌8⋒)(25fb) CTV in all bedrooms ® T
sB&B⇌⋒£22-£24 dB&B⇌⋒£34-£38 ⊟
Lift ☾ CTV 20P CFA sauna solarium jacuzzi *xmas*
V ♈ ☕ Lunch £5.75 High tea £3 Dinner £8 Last dinner 7pm
Credit Cards [1] [2] [3]

MACCLESFIELD Cheshire Map **07** SJ97

See also **Bollington**

★**Crofton** 22 Crompton Rd SK11 8DS ☎(0625)34113
A warm welcome is assured at this small, tastefully furnished hotel close to the centre of this old silk-weaving town. All the bedrooms have en suite facilities colour TV and tea/coffee making facilities. Excellent dinners are provided until late in the evening and the 'Crofton Breakfast Grill' is recommended.
7rm(2⇌5⋒)(2fb) CTV in all bedrooms ® ✈ ✱
sB&B⇌⋒£35-£45 dB&B⇌⋒£55-£65
P̸
♉ English & Continental V ♈ ☕ Dinner £10.40-£15&alc Last dinner 11pm
Credit Cards [1] [3]

MACDUFF Grampian *Banffshire* Map **15** NJ76

★★★**59% Highland Haven** Shore St AB4 1UB (Inter)
☎(0261)32408
Overlooking the harbour of this small fishing port, and appealing to tourists and business people alike, the hotel offers attractively appointed, well-equipped bedrooms and a modern leisure centre.
20⇌⋒(2fb) CTV in all bedrooms ® T
sB&B⇌⋒£19.95-£28.95 dB&B⇌⋒£38-£49 ⊟
☾ CTV 6P snooker sauna solarium gymnasium turkish bath whirlpool spa *xmas*
V ♈ ☕ Lunch £4-£7&alc High tea £3-£7&alc Dinner £11&alc Last dinner 9pm
Credit Cards [1] [2] [3] [4] [5] ⓔ

MACHYNLLETH Powys Map **06** SH70

★★**Dolguog Hall** SY20 8UJ ☎(0654)2244
Set alongside the River Dulas, this 17th-century gentleman's residence has been carefully modernised to provide elegant and comfortable accommodation.
9rm(4⇌5⋒)(1fb) CTV in all bedrooms ® T ✈ ✱
sB&B⇌⋒£24-£32 dB&B⇌⋒£40-£52 ⊟
20P ✿ ♩ *xmas*
♉ Continental V ♈ ☕ ⅟ Sunday Lunch £6.25-£6.75alc Dinner £12.50&alc Last dinner 9pm
Credit Cards [1] [3] [5]

See advertisement on page 459

For key to symbols see the inside front cover.

M

MADINGLEY Cambridgeshire Map **05** TL36

✕✕ ***Three Horseshoes*** High St CB3 8AB ☎(0954)210221
Though situated only a few miles from Cambridge, this is a picture-postcard, thatched, village inn, its setting park-like and its interior beamed and panelled. Food is mainly British, with a French country influence, and game figures prominently.
English & French **V** 32 seats Last dinner 10pm 70P
Credit Cards 1 2 3 5

MAIDENCOMBE

See **Torquay**

MAIDENHEAD Berkshire Map **04** SU88

★★★★ **Fredrick's** Shoppenhangers Rd SL6 2PZ
☎(0628)35934 Telex no 849966 FAX (0628) 771054
Closed 24-30 Dec
Herr Losel continues to upgrade the hotel, offering beautifully-appointed bedrooms and willing service. His strong views on food are reflected in the consistently high standards of cuisine.
38rm(28⇌10↱) CTV in all bedrooms **T**
sB&B⇌↱£79.50-£98 dB&B⇌↱£125-£195
90P
English & French **V** Lunch £19.50-£21.50&alc Dinner £32.50-£35alc Last dinner 9.45pm
Credit Cards 1 2 3 5

★★★57% ***Thames Riviera*** At the Bridge SL6 8DW
☎(0628)74057 Telex no 846687
This efficiently-run hotel is situated next to the 13th-century bridge which brought wealth to medieval Maidenhead. Jerome's Restaurant and the modern coffee shop offer a good choice of food.
35rm(29⇌6↱)(3fb)1 CTV in all bedrooms ® **T**
50P 10
English & French **V** Last dinner 10pm
Credit Cards 1 2 3 4 5

✕✕✕ ***Shoppenhangers Manor*** Manor Ln SL6 2RA
☎(0628)23444 Telex no 847502 FAX (0628) 770035
The present Manor House, with its beautiful antique appearance, is actually a replica of the original 16th-century merchant's house, re-built after a disastrous fire in 1937. An ideal venue for private parties and business meetings, the à la carte menu is imaginative and well complimented by the list of wines. Service by the smart young staff is efficient and courteous.
Closed Sun BH's
Lunch not served Sat
International 40 seats Last lunch 2pm Last dinner 10.30pm 80P nc12yrs
Credit Cards 1 2 3 5

MAIDSTONE Kent Map **05** TQ75

★★★57% **Larkfield Hotel** ME20 6HJ (Trusthouse Forte)
☎West Malling(0732)846858 Telex no 957420
FAX (0732) 846786
(For full entry see Larkfield)

★★ **Boxley House** Boxley Rd, Boxley ME14 3DZ (3m N between A249 & A229) (Exec Hotel) ☎(0622)692269
FAX (0622) 683536
A 17th-century house set in open parkland retains traces of its original character, though bedrooms have been updated by the addition of modern appliances. In the restaurant – unusually located beneath a gallery – guests can enjoy a range of mainly English dishes.
11rm(5⇌6↱)Annexe7rm(5⇌2↱)(4fb)2 CTV in all bedrooms ® **T** ✱ sB&B⇌↱fr£39 dB&B⇌↱fr£55
150P (heated)
English & French **V** Lunch fr£8.50 Dinner £12.50-£15.50 Last dinner 9pm
Credit Cards 1 2 3 5

★★ **Grange Moor** St Michael's Rd ME16 8BS (off A26)
☎(0622)677623 & 57222
Friendly family-run hotel with tasteful, compact bedrooms and Tudor-style restaurant.
36rm(1⇌31↱)(3fb)1 CTV in all bedrooms ® **T**
sB&B£26-£34 sB&B⇌↱£35-£40.50 dB&B£37.50-£43.50
dB&B⇌↱£43.50-£53.50
60P
English & French **V** Lunch £10&alc Dinner £10&alc Last dinner 10pm
Credit Cards 1 3

✕✕ ***Suefflé*** The Green, Bearsted ME14 4 (2m E A20)
☎(0622)37065
French 40 seats Last dinner 9.45pm 14P
Credit Cards 1 2 3 5

MALDON Essex Map **05** TL80

★★ **The Blue Boar** Silver St CM9 7QE (Trusthouse Forte)
☎(0621)852681
The proximity of a 13th-century church enhances the charm and character of this period hotel with its beamed restaurant, cosy lounge accommodation and well-equipped bedrooms. Service, though simple, is efficient and the friendly staff create a pleasant atmosphere.
23rm(22⇌1↱)Annexe5⇌ in 3 bedrooms CTV in all bedrooms ® **T** ✱
43P
English **V** S% Lunch £7.95-£9.50alc High tea fr£5alc Dinner £11-£15alc Last dinner 9.45pm
Credit Cards 1 2 3 4 5

✕ **Francine's** 1A High St CM9 7PB ☎(0621)856605
The simplicity of this restaurant and the very easy manner of the chef patron create a most relaxing atmosphere. Here, freshly prepared dishes are cooked with great care, while a selection of good value French wines is also available. An unpretentious restaurant, well worth a visit.
Closed Sun & Mon 1st 2 wks Feb & Aug
Lunch not served (by arrangement only)
French 24 seats ✱ Lunch £13-£17alc Dinner £15-£19alc Last lunch 2pm Last dinner 9.15pm 8P
Credit Cards 1 3

MALLAIG Highland *Inverness-shire* Map **13** NM69

★★ **Marine** PH41 4PY ☎(0687)2217
RS mid Dec-mid Jan
Close to the harbour and the railway station.
22rm(8⇌2↱)(1fb) CTV in 15bedrooms ® sB&B£18-£20
sB&B⇌↱£20-£24 dB&B£32-£36 dB&B⇌↱£40-£44
CTV 6P
Bar Lunch fr£4alc Dinner fr£11.50 Last dinner 8.30pm
Credit Cards 1 2 3 £

★★ **West Highland** PH41 4QZ ☎(0687)2210 FAX (0397) 5060
Closed 10 Oct-21 Apr
Large stone building overlooking the fishing port and the islands of Rhum, Eigg & Skye.
26⇌(6fb) ® ✱ sB&B⇌£22-£23 dB&B⇌£44-£46
CTV 30P
V Lunch £6 Dinner £12 Last dinner 8.30pm
Credit Cards 1 2 3 5 £

Book as early as possible for busy holiday periods.

THE LARKFIELD HOTEL

The Hotel, offers the Clubhouse Bar and Restaurant with its excellent French and International cuisine. We welcome vegetarians. Children under 16 are half price. Weekend leisure breaks throughout the year from £38.00 per person per night, sharing a twin or double with en suite facilities and must include a Saturday night. Includes table d'hote dinner, full English breakfast. Children sharing parents room are free. Conference and private function rooms available. The Larkfield is situated on the A20, 5 miles from Maidstone, 2 miles from the M20 (Junction 4) and 5 miles from the M26/M25 (Junction 2).

SPECIAL LEISURE BREAK OFFER UNTIL 31ST MAY 1990 – 3 NIGHTS FOR THE PRICE OF 2! (FRI-SUN)
PLEASE QUOTE "AA OFFER"

For reservations call (0732) 846858
London Road, Larkfield,
Nr. Maidstone, Kent ME20 6HJ
Fax (0732) 846786 Telex 957420

★★★

Trusthouse Forte Hotels

★ ★ ★ ★

MAIDSTONE/SEVENOAKS

thf

Post House Hotel

THE PERFECT LOCATION
AT WROTHAM HEATH

This luxury Hotel is ideally situated close to the M20 and M26. Built in a new, fresh style, the Post House offers sumptuous accommodation and also offers a choice of luxury suites and Executive rooms. The superb Restaurant, featuring the 'Traders Table', offers exquisite cuisine with authentic dishes from all around the World. The Hotel is also equipped with a magnificent Health and Fitness Club with heated indoor swimming pool, jacuzzi, sauna, solarium and multi-gym. Ideal for your business meeting or training course.

For more information/reservations, Telephone: (0732) 883311

London Road,
Wrotham Heath,
Sevenoaks,
KENT.
TN15 7RS

Fax No: (0732) 885850

Telex No: 957309

Spoil Yourself!

Set in 20 acres of parkland in the heart of Kent, the Great Danes offers the friendly atmosphere of a country house with all the facilities of a modern hotel, including:–

- Luxurious leisure club
- Extensive banqueting and conference facilities
- A la carte restaurant, coffee shop and traditional Kentish pub

All of the luxurious bedrooms have a private bathroom and colour t.v.

The Great Danes Hotel, ★★★
Hollingbourne, Maidstone, Kent ME17 1RE.
Tel: (0622) 30022

Embassy Hotels

DOLGUOG HALL
HOTEL and RESTAURANT

Machynlleth, Powys SY20 8UJ
Telephone: 0654 2244

★★

Guarded by the mountains of Powys and Meirionydd, bounded by the river Dulas and fine timbered slopes are the rich meadowlands originally owned by Guog, son of the warrior Princes of Powys. Here a fine house was built, and since that day in the 6th century when the original building was built and when in the 17th century the existing house was started, Dolguog Hall has been somewhere special.

Today hundreds of years later it is now a special hotel. All nine bedrooms have private facilities, colour television, central heating and tea making facilities. The newly constructed "Victorian Conservatory Restaurant" serves both traditional and vegetarian meals, and affords magnificent views of the Dyfi Valley and the foothills of Snowdonia.

Ideally situated, the hotel makes a superb base for all that Mid Wales has to offer - walking, fishing, watersports, birdwatching and fine sandy beaches amongst many others.

MALLWYD Gwynedd Map **06** SH81

★**Brigand's Inn** SY20 9HJ ☎Dinas Mawddwy(06504)208
Closed Jan-Feb
15th-century coaching inn with good atmosphere, popular with fishing enthusiasts.
14rm(4⇌1♠)(2fb) ® ✳ sB&Bfr£16.95 sB&B⇌♠fr£19.95 dB&Bfr£33.90 dB&B⇌♠fr£39.90 ⊟
CTV 40P ⛟ ♩
♔ ⊒ Lunch £5.25 Dinner £8.50-£9.50 Last dinner 9.15pm
Credit Cards 1 3

MALMESBURY Wiltshire Map **03** ST98

★★★**68% Old Bell** Abbey Row SN16 0BW ☎(0666)822344 FAX (0666) 825145
Possibly the oldest hotel in the county, standing next to the Abbey, the Old Bell retains many interesting features including a 700-year-old fireplace. The spacious dining room serves quality English food, including sumptuous sweets. There is also an elegant lounge, a large bar and a separate cocktail bar, cheerful with fresh flowers and log fires. Some bedrooms are newly built, others are furnished with antiques, but all have the usual modern facilities. The staff are good natured and their attitude makes this hotel a special place to stay.
37rm(35⇌2♠)Annexe1⇌1⊞ CTV in all bedrooms ® ✗ (ex guide dogs) sB&B⇌♠fr£55 dB&B⇌♠fr£75 ⊟
☾ 30P ✲
♕ English & French **V** ♔ ⊒ Lunch fr£10.50 Dinner fr£17.50 Last dinner 9.30pm
Credit Cards 1 3

★★★♛ **72% Whatley Manor** Easton Grey SN16 0RB
☎(0666)822888
Telex no 449380
FAX (0666) 826120
An elegant tree-lined drive leads to this delightful Cotswold Manor House. Bedrooms, both those in the main building and those in the Court House, are charming, spacious and tastefully furnished, whilst the panelled public rooms have roaring log fires. Leisure facilities include all-weather tennis, croquet, swimming pool, sauna, solarium and spa bath.
15⇌Annexe11⇌(3fb)1⊞ CTV in all bedrooms ® **T** sB&B⇌£63-£72 dB&B⇌£88-£104 ⊟
☾ 60P ⛟ ✲ ⏏(heated) ⚲ (hard) ♩ sauna solarium croquet putting table tennis jaccuzzi *xmas*
♕ English & Continental **V** ♔ ⊒ Lunch fr£11 High tea fr£6.50 Dinner fr£22 Last dinner 9pm
Credit Cards 1 2 3 5

MALTON North Yorkshire Map **08** SE77

★★**Leat House** Welham Rd YO17 9DS
☎(0653)692027 & 695333
14⇌(3fb)1⊞⊁in 1 bedroom CTV in all bedrooms ® **T** S% sB&B⇌£25-£35 dB&B⇌£45-£55 ⊟
45P 3⌂ *xmas*
♕ English & French **V** ♔ ⊒ S% Lunch £7.95-£9.95 High tea £6.50-£8.50 Dinner £9.95-£18.50 Last dinner 9.30pm
Credit Cards 1

★**Wentworth Arms** Town St, Old Malton YO17 0HD
☎(0653)692618
Closed Xmas Day
Just on the edge of this market town, this hospitable and well-run hotel has clean, comfortable bedrooms and good home-made food served in the bar and the small cosy dining room.
7rm CTV in all bedrooms ® ✗ sB&B£16-£17 dB&B£32-£34
30P ⛟ nc6yrs
♔ ⊒ Lunch 90p-£6.50alc
Credit Cards 3

MALVERN Hereford & Worcester Map **03** SO74

★★★**65% Abbey** Abbey Rd WR14 3ET (De Vere)
☎(0684)892332 Telex no 335008 FAX (0684) 892662
Standing close to the town centre, beside its 11th-century Benedictine priory church, this large, busy and popular hotel complements well-equipped conference facilities with comfortable bedrooms, attracting both business people and holidaymakers.
105rm(84⇌21♠)(4fb)1⊞ CTV in all bedrooms ® **T** sB&B⇌♠£60 dB&B⇌♠£80 ⊟
Lift ☾ 120P ✲ CFA
V ♔ ⊒ Lunch fr£9.50&alc Dinner fr£12.50&alc Last dinner 8.30pm
Credit Cards 1 2 3 5

★★★**65% Colwall Park** Colwall WR13 6QG (3m SW B4218) (Inter) ☎(0684)40206 Telex no 335626 FAX (0684) 40847
A comfortable, privately-owned hotel, situated just south of Malvern in the village of Colwall, it creates an informal and relaxed atmosphere which appeals to both business travellers and tourists. It is particularly popular for weekend breaks.
20rm(16⇌4♠)(2fb) CTV in all bedrooms ® **T** ✳ sB&B⇌♠£41.50-£46.50 dB&B⇌♠£59.50-£65 ⊟
50P ✲ croquet *xmas*
V ♔ ⊒ Lunch £8.50-£10.50 Dinner £16 Last dinner 9pm
Credit Cards 1 2 3 £

★★★♛ **63% Cottage in the Wood** Holywell Rd, Malvern Wells WR14 4LG (3m S A449) (Consort)
☎(0684)573487
Telex no 57515 ATTN 134
This lovely Georgian dower house is situated in 7 acres of wooded grounds on the eastern slopes of the Malvern Hills. Over half of the bedrooms are situated in two separate annexes, one a converted cottage and the other a former coach house. Under the personal supervision of the owners, who have worked hard to improve standards, the service is informal and the atmosphere relaxed and peaceful. The style is traditional English and this is reflected in the imaginative menu.
8⇌Annexe12⇌3⊞ CTV in all bedrooms ® **T** sB⇌fr£49.50 dB⇌£68-£105 (room only) ⊟
50P ✲ *xmas*
V ♔ ⊒ Lunch £5-£12.50&alc Dinner £16-£25alc Last dinner 9pm
Credit Cards 1 3 £

★★★**60% *Foley Arms*** Worcester Rd WR14 4QS (Best Western)
☎(0684)573397 Telex no 437269 FAX (0684) 892275
Popular, family-run, town-centre hotel with comfortable lounge overlooking River Severn.
26rm(20⇌6♠)(1fb)1⊞⊁in 1 bedroom CTV in all bedrooms ® **T**

▶

M

☾ 45P 4🚗 ✲ CFA
V ✧ ⊒ ⅟ Last dinner 9.30pm
Credit Cards 1 2 3 5

★★*Broomhill* West Malvern Rd, West Malvern WR14 4AY (2m W B4232) ☎(06845)64367
Three-storey Victorian house with magnificent views.
10rm(4⇨2↰) CTV in all bedrooms ®
CTV 10P 🅿 nc5yrs
V ✧ ⅟ Last dinner 7pm

★★Cotford 51 Graham Rd WR14 2JW ☎(0684)572427
Closed 25 Dec-11 Jan
Comfortable, family-run hotel situated in a quiet road leading to the town centre.
15rm(7⇨3↰)(3fb) CTV in all bedrooms ® T ✻ sB&Bfr£22 sB&B⇨↰fr£28 dB&Bfr£38 dB&B⇨↰fr£46 ⊟
10P 🅿 ✲
V ⅟ Dinner fr£13 Last dinner 9pm
Credit Cards 1 3

★★Essington Holywell Rd, Malvern Wells WR14 4LQ (3m S A449) ☎(0684)561177
Small, family-run hotel with 2 acres of terraced gardens. Personal service and home cooking are offered.
9rm(7⇨2↰)(1fb)1⊟ CTV in all bedrooms ® sB&B⇨↰fr£25 dB&B⇨↰fr£46 ⊟
30P 🅿 ✲ *xmas*
✧ ⅟ Dinner £12-£15 Last dinner 8.15pm
Credit Cards 1 3

★★♜Holdfast Cottage
Welland, Malvern Wells
WR13 6NA (4m SE)
☎Hanley Swan (0684)310288
Closed Jan
This 17th-century country house, providing accommodation in rooms decorated with floral wallpapers and matching fabrics and standing in a lovely, lawned garden, really does have the cottage atmosphere that its name suggests. Food is predominantly English, making good use of local produce and serving home-grown vegetables. Situated on A4104 midway between Welland and Little Malvern.
8rm(7⇨1↰) CTV in all bedrooms ® T ✗ (ex guide dogs) sB&B⇨↰£32-£48 dB&B⇨↰£56-£72 ⊟
16P 🅿 ✲ croquet nc10yrs *xmas*
♡ English & French V ✧ ⊒ ⅟ Dinner £18-£24alc Last dinner 9.30pm
Credit Cards 1 £

★★Malvern Hills Wynds Point WR13 6DW (4m S A449) ☎Colwall(0684)40237 FAX (0684) 40327
Situated on the A449 between Malvern and Ledbury, the hotel provides an ideal base from which to explore the attractions of the surrounding area, though its well-equipped bedrooms also offer suitable accommodation for a business clientele.
16rm(11⇨4↰)(1fb)1⊟ CTV in all bedrooms ® T sB&B⇨↰£35-£38 dB&B⇨↰£55-£58 ⊟
CTV 35P 🅿 ✲ solarium *xmas*
♡ English & French V ✧ ⊒ Lunch £8.95-£9.50 Dinner £10.95-£11.50&alc Last dinner 9.45pm
Credit Cards 1 3 £

★★Montrose 23 Graham Rd WR14 2HU ☎(06845)2335
Closed 1 wk Xmas
Reputedly the first purpose-built hotel in this famous spa resort, this large old house is conveniently close to the town centre and provides simple but comfortable accommmodation with friendly service.
14rm(5⇨6↰)(1fb) CTV in 11bedrooms ® ✗
CTV 16P 🅿 ✲ sauna solarium gymnasium
V ⊒
Credit Cards 1 3 £

★★Mount Pleasant Belle Vue Ter WR14 4PZ ☎(0684)561837
Closed Xmas
Set in attractive gardens, this large Georgian house, close to the town centre, stands opposite the priory church. It is run in a friendly and informal manner by the proprietors, who provide comfortable and well-equipped accommodation for both tourists and travelling business people alike. There are also facilities for functions and conferences. The small intimate restaurant offers a mainly Spanish theme menu and there is an adjoining coffee shop.
15rm(11⇨3↰) CTV in all bedrooms ® T ✗ (ex guide dogs) sB&B⇨↰£38.75-£43 dB&B⇨↰£52.50-£58 ⊟
20P ✲ nc7yrs
♡ English & Spanish V ✧ ⊒ Lunch £8.95-£9.95 Dinner £9.95-£10.95&alc Last dinner 9.30pm
Credit Cards 1 2 3 5 £

★★Royal Malvern Graham Rd WR14 2HN (Minotels) ☎(0684)563411 Telex no 9401187
Closed 25 Dec
Equally suitable for business people and tourists, this 18th-century town centre hotel has been tastefully converted to provide comfortable and well-equipped accommodation.
14rm(12⇨) CTV in all bedrooms ® T sB&Bfr£24 sB&B⇨£36-£40 dB&Bfr£36 dB&B⇨£48-£60 ⊟
Lift 10P
V ✧ ⊒ ⅟ Bar Lunch fr£4.50&alc Dinner fr£12.75&alc Last dinner 9pm
Credit Cards 1 2 3 5 £

❀ ✕✕Croque-en-Bouche 221 Wells Rd, Malvern Wells WR14 4HF (3m S A449)
☎(0684)565612
(Rosette awarded for dinner only)
A husband and wife team have turned this attractive old Malverns house into a very popular French-style restaurant, offering an imaginative table d'hôte menu based on the best possible fresh seasonal ingredients. Sauces are particularly good, and an extensive wine list includes some fine vintages at very reasonable prices. Booking is essential.
Closed Sun, Mon, Tue, Xmas & New Year
Lunch not served
♡ French 22 seats ✻ Dinner £27 Last dinner 9.30pm ⅌ ⅟
Credit Cards 1 3

MAN, ISLE OF Map **06**

BALLASALLA Map **06** SC27

✕La Rosette ☎Castletown(0624)822940
It is advisable to book well in advance at this charming little French restaurant, for it is equally popular with local people and tourists. Cosy and well-furnished, it offers an array of attractive, good-value dishes coupled with friendly service.
Closed Sun & Mon
♡ French 45 seats ✻ Lunch £8-£14alc Dinner £18-£25alc Last lunch 4pm Last dinner 10.30pm nc4yrs ⅟
Credit Cards 1 3

CASTLETOWN Map **06** SC26

★★★**62% Castletown Golf Links** Fort Island ☎(0624)822201
Telex no 627636 FAX (0624) 824633
At the southerly extreme of island, surrounded by golf course.
58rm(44⇌12⌐)(1fb)1⊞ CTV in all bedrooms ® **T** ✳
sB&B⇌⌐£50-£75 dB&B⇌⌐£70-£150 ⊟
☾ CTV 80P ✿ CFA ⊡(heated) ▶ 18 snooker sauna solarium shooting *xmas*
♉ French **V** ✿ ⊒ ⁄ Lunch £12.50-£14.50&alc Dinner £14.50-£17.50&alc Last dinner 10pm
Credit Cards 1 2 3 5

DOUGLAS Map **06** SC37

★★★**62% Empress** Central Promenade ☎(0624)27211
Telex no 627772 FAX (0624) 73554
There are two restaurants at this large, well-furnished, seafront hotel overlooking Douglas Bay.
90⇌⌐(8fb) CTV in all bedrooms ® **T** ✖ (ex guide dogs) ✳
S% sB&B⇌⌐£33-£40 dB&B⇌⌐£58-£65
Lift ☾ CTV ⁄P ⌗ ⊡(heated) snooker sauna solarium gymnasium
♉ French ✿ ⊒ S% Lunch £4-£6 Dinner £5-£6&alc Last dinner 10pm
Credit Cards 1 2 3 5 £

★★★**63% Sefton** Harris Promenade ☎(0624)26011
Telex no 627519 FAX (0624) 76004
This friendly hotel, centrally situated on the seafront, features well-designed leisure facilities, including an excellent snooker room and conference and banqueting facilities. Bedrooms are well-equipped, with penthouse and private suites available.
80rm(78⇌2⌐)(5fb) CTV in all bedrooms ® **T** ✖ ✳
sB&B⇌⌐£35 dB&B⇌⌐£43 ⊟
Lift ☾ 40P ⌗ ⊡(heated) sauna solarium gymnasium

▶

V ♔ ⊒ ⊁ Lunch £4-£5.50alc Dinner £11-£13alc Last dinner 10pm
Credit Cards 1 2 3 5

★**Woodbourne** Alexander Dr ☎(0624)21766
Closed 29 Sep-23 May
Friendly, comfortable public house in residential area.
10rm ✖ ✳ sB&B£12.50-£14.50 dB&B£21-£23
CTV P ⇎ nc12yrs
♔

✗✗✗ ***Boncompte's*** King Edward Rd, Onchan ☎(0624)75626
Impressively situated, with panoramic views over Douglas Bay, this smart, friendly restaurant offers a very high standard of international cuisine and is popular with both locals and visitors alike. Dishes are cooked to order using the best fresh produce and although fish is prominently featured, the menu is wide ranging, with prime meat and game in season and flambé specialities. The seafood soufflé can be especially recommended. A wide choice of wines complements the excellent cooking.
Lunch not served Sat
☋ French V 85 seats Last lunch 2pm Last dinner 10pm 20P nc3yrs
Credit Cards 1 3 5

RAMSEY Map **06** SC49

★★★★61% **Grand Island** Bride Rd ☎(0624)812455 Telex no 629849 FAX (0624) 815291
After extensive refurbishment this friendly hotel now offers a very good standard of accommodation and an elegant restaurant with superb views.
54rm(51⇌3↱)(4fb)1⊞ CTV in all bedrooms ® T ✖ (ex guide dogs) sB&B£45-£138 sB&B⇌↱£45-£138 dB&B£74-£138 dB&B⇌↱£74-£138 ☰
Lift ☾ 150P ⇎ ✲ ⊡(heated) U snooker sauna solarium gymnasium clay-pigeon shooting steam room croquet *xmas*
☋ International V ♔ ⊒ Lunch £9.95-£9.95&alc Dinner £13-£13&alc Last dinner 10pm
Credit Cards 1 2 3 5 £

MANCHESTER Greater Manchester Map **07** SJ89

See **Town Plan Section**
See also **Salford**

★★★★66% **Holiday Inn Crowne Plaza** Peter St M60 2DS ☎061-236 3333 Telex no 667550 FAX 061-228 2241
Neither Mr Rolls nor Mr Royce, who first met at this splendid Edwardian building, would recognise the interior now, although modernisation has not detracted from the luxury and elegance for which the hotel is renowned. In addition to the 3 restaurants, there are excellent conference and banqueting facilities and, in the lower areas, comprehensive leisure facilities. Efficient service is provided by friendly and helpful staff.
303⇌↱(23fb)⊁in 54 bedrooms CTV in all bedrooms T ✳ S% sB⇌↱£85-£101 dB⇌↱£113-£119 (room only) ☰
Lift ☾ ⊞ P ⊡(heated) squash sauna solarium gymnasium jacuzzi *xmas*
☋ English & French V ♔ ⊒ Lunch £14.50-£15.95 Dinner £14.50-£15.95&alc Last dinner 11.30pm
Credit Cards 1 2 3 5

★★★★66% **Hotel Piccadilly** Piccadilly M60 1QR (Embassy) ☎061-236 8414 Telex no 668765 FAX 061-228 1568
Situated in the city centre, this hotel has been totally refurbished over recent years to provide comprehensive facilities. Bedrooms, though not large, are well equipped, public rooms are spacious and comfortable and a high standard of cuisine has been achieved in the elegant Pavilion and Verandah Restaurants.
271⇌↱3⊞⊁in 35 bedrooms CTV in all bedrooms ® T ✳ sB⇌↱£79-£97 dB⇌↱£97-£114 (room only) ☰
Lift ☾ 80P CFA ⊡(heated) sauna solarium gymnasium *xmas*
☋ English & French V ♔ ⊒ ⊁ Lunch £8-£12&alc Dinner £14.50&alc Last dinner 10.30pm
Credit Cards 1 2 3 4 5

★★★★64% **Portland Thistle** 3/5 Portland St, Piccadilly M1 6DP (Thistle) ☎061-228 3400 Telex no 669157 FAX 061-228 6347
A small, but attractively decorated hotel that prides itself on its extensive champagne list and 170 different whiskies. The Winstons Restaurant, where chef Peter Marshall prepares delectable dishes with care and devotion, can also be recommended.
208⇌↱(6fb)2⊞⊁in 51 bedrooms CTV in all bedrooms ® T ✳ sB⇌↱£75-£88 dB⇌↱£90-£95 (room only) ☰
Lift ☾ ⊞ P ⊡(heated) sauna solarium gymnasium whirlpool hairdresser
☋ International ♔ ⊒ ⊁ Lunch fr£11.95&alc Dinner fr£13.95&alc Last dinner 10pm
Credit Cards 1 2 3 4 5

★★★★65% **Ramada Renaissance** Blackfriars St M3 2EQ ☎061-835 2555 Telex no 669699 FAX 061-835 3077
A large, modern, city-centre hotel with spacious and well-appointed bedrooms. The young staff provide service in a cheerful and helpful manner.
205⇌↱⊁in 48 bedrooms CTV in all bedrooms T ✖ (ex guide dogs) ✳ sB⇌↱£72.50-£79.50 dB⇌↱£80-£89 (room only) ☰
Lift ☾ 80⌂ ⇎
V ♔ ⊒ Lunch £13.50&alc Dinner £16&alc Last dinner 11pm
Credit Cards 1 2 3 4 5

★★★60% **Novotel Manchester West** Worsley Brow M28 4YA (Novotel) ☎061-799 3535 Telex no 669586 FAX 061-703 8207
(For full entry see Worsley)

★★★56% **Post House** Palatine Rd, Northenden M22 4FH (Trusthouse Forte) ☎061-998 7090 Telex no 669248 FAX 061-946 0139
One of the earlier Post House Hotels, built very much with the motorist in mind, conveniently situated on the B5167 midway between the city centre and the airport and close to the M56 and M63. There is ample car parking, mostly under cover, and light meals are served in the coffee shop throughout the day, in addition to the normal restaurant service.
200⇌↱(50fb)⊁in 12 bedrooms CTV in all bedrooms ® S% sB⇌↱£70-£90 dB⇌↱£80-£100 (room only) ☰
Lift ☾ 123P 120⌂ CFA
V ♔ ⊒ ⊁ S% Lunch £7.50-£15&alc High tea £3-£7.50 Dinner £14-£17.50&alc Last dinner 10.30pm
Credit Cards 1 2 3 4 5

★★★60% **Willow Bank** 340-342 Wilmslow Rd, Fallowfield M14 6AF ☎061-224 0461 Telex no 668222 FAX 061-257 2561
Situated 3 miles from the city centre, this popular business hotel has been enhanced by recent refurbishment of the restaurant and other public rooms. Facilities will be further improved when planned bedroom upgrading is completed.
124rm(110⇌12↱)(2fb) CTV in all bedrooms T ✖ (ex guide dogs) S% sB⇌↱£37-£42 dB⇌↱£50-£54 (room only) ☰
☾ CTV 70P 30⌂ ♫
☋ English & Continental V ♔ ⊒ ⊁ S% Lunch fr£5.50&alc High tea fr£3 Dinner fr£9&alc Last dinner 10.15pm
Credit Cards 1 2 3 5

★★**Crescent Gate** Park Crescent, Victoria Park M14 5RE ☎061-224 0672 FAX 061-257 2822
Closed Xmas
Small, friendly hotel in quiet crescent off the A6061 Wilmslow Road, south of the city centre.
15rm(2⇌3↱)Annexe11rm(2⇌9↱)(1fb) CTV in all bedrooms ® T sB&B£22 sB&B⇌↱£27 dB&B⇌↱£40
CTV 18P ⇎
♔ ⊒ ⊁ Bar Lunch £1-£3.35alc Dinner fr£7.50 Last dinner 8pm
Credit Cards 1 2 3 5

M

★★***Mitre*** Cathedral Gates M3 1SW ☎061-834 4128
Telex no 669581
A pleasantly-furnished, family-run hotel close to Victoria Station and the Cathedral.
28rm(3⇨6♠)(1fb) CTV in all bedrooms ® T ✱ (ex guide dogs)
☾ CTV ₱
♀ English & French V ♈ ⊈ Last dinner 9.45pm
Credit Cards [1] [2] [3] [5]

✕✕***Brasserie St Pierre*** 57/63 Princess St M2 4EQ ☎061-228 0231
This bright, lively French brasserie offers an interesting regularly-changed à la carte menu, featuring such dishes as Filet de Boeuf au Roquefort, Sauce Bordelaise and Saumon au Gingembre.
Lunch not served Sat
♀ English & French V 70 seats Last lunch 2pm Last dinner 11pm ₱
Credit Cards [1] [2] [3] [4] [5]

✕✕**Gaylord** Amethyst House, Marriot's Court, Spring Garden M2 1EA ☎061-832 6037 & 061-832 4866
Part of a group renowned internationally, this relaxing restaurant serves authentic Tandoori and Mughlai cuisine. Diners can also watch the chef at work through a large window. Tandoori food is subtly flavoured, and the friendly, helpful staff make eating at this restaurant a very pleasant experience.
Closed 25 Dec & 1 Jan
♀ Indian V 102 seats Last lunch 3pm Last dinner 11.30pm ₱ ⁄
Credit Cards [1] [2] [3] [5]

✕✕**Rajdoot** St James House, South Kings St M2 6DW ☎061-834 2176
One of a small chain of restaurants specialising in Tandoori cooking, where the standard is very reliable and the atmosphere elegant and exotic. Fish Tandoori is just one dish particularly praised by our inspector, but the popular shish kebabs and the lamb curry roghan josh are also highly recommended. This is a colourful restaurant, with statuettes, framed Indian paintings and Indian background music to set the scene.
Lunch not served Sun
♀ Indian 87 seats Last lunch 2.30pm Last dinner 11.30pm ₱
Credit Cards [1] [2] [3] [5]

✕✕**Woodlands** 33 Shepley Rd, Audenshaw M34 5DJ ☎061-336 4241
A double-fronted, detached house in a suburb of the city has been decorated and furnished in a relaxed, comfortable style to create an intimate restaurant. Family run, it offers warm, friendly service, and a good French menu of particularly well cooked dishes – fish being a speciality – which is accompanied by a worthwhile wine list.
Lunch not served Sat (ex party bookings)
♀ French V 40 seats Lunch fr£10.50&alc Dinner fr£12.50&alc Last lunch 2pm Last dinner 9.30pm 10P
Credit Cards [1] [3]

✕✕**Woo Sang** 19-21 George St M1 4AG ☎061-236 3697
Attractive Chinese paintings, green pot plants and an interesting fish tank feature in this friendly Cantonese restaurant, situated in the heart of Manchester's Chinatown. The extensive and varied menu includes a number of specialities as well as a wide range of Dim Sum. A low price menu is offered at lunchtime and service is helpful and attentive.
Closed 25-26 Dec
♀ Cantonese V 220 seats ✱ S10% Lunch £3-£5.50 Dinner £10-£20&alc Last lunch 2pm Last dinner 11.45pm ₱
Credit Cards [1] [2] [3] [5]

For key to symbols see the inside front cover.

✕✕**Yang Sing** 34 Princess St M1 4JY ☎061-236 2200
Very popular, bustling Chinese restaurant serving familiar and more exotic dishes of mainly Cantonese food. Service is on the brisk side because of the great demand for tables, but a meal is an experience to remember. Booking is recommended.
Closed Xmas Day
♀ Cantonese V 140 seats ✱ S10% Last dinner 11pm ₱
Credit Cards [1] [2]

✕***Hopewell City*** Ground Floor, 45-47 Faulkner St M1 4EE ☎061-236 0091
Barbecue roasts, Dim Sum and Cantonese cooking are featured in this deliciously friendly and efficient restaurant situated in the heart of Manchester's Chinatown. The food served here has been much praised and eating here is a thoroughly enjoyable experience.
♀ Chinese & Cantonese V 100 seats Last lunch 2pm Last dinner 11.45pm ₱
Credit Cards [1] [2] [3] [5]

✕**The Koreana** Kings House, 40 King St West M3 2WY ☎061-832 4330
A family-run restaurant, situated below street level, providing delicious Korean cuisine and friendly service.
Closed Sun, 25 Dec, 1 Jan & BH's (ex party bookings)
Lunch not served Sat
♀ Korean V 60 seats ✱ Lunch £4.20-£15.50&alc Dinner £8.65-£15.50&alc Last lunch 2.30pm Last dinner 11pm ₱
Credit Cards [1] [2] [3] [5]

✕***Kosmos Taverna*** 248 Wilmslow Rd, Fallowfield M14 6LD ☎061-225 9106
The traditional, authentic Greek dishes served at this friendly and cheerful little taverna include Houmous, Taramasalata, Dolmades, Kieftedes and Lamb Kebabs. A good variety of wines is available on the reasonably priced wine list.
Lunch not served
♀ Greek V 70 seats ₱
Credit Cards [1] [3]

✕**Lime Tree** 8 Lapwing Ln, West Didsbury M20 8WS ☎061-445 1217
A superb little restaurant with a cheerful atmosphere offers an imaginative menu of well-prepared dishes which includes such specialities as roast quail in a port and orange sauce and sole fillets filled with salmon mousse.
Closed Mon
Lunch not served Tue-Sat
Dinner not served Sun
♀ French V 80 seats ✱ Sunday Lunch £8.50 Dinner £12 Last lunch 2.30pm Last dinner 10pm 3P
Credit Cards [1] [3]

✕**Market** Edge St, 104 High St M4 1HQ ☎061-834 3743
This intriguing little restaurant close to the former Smithfield Market in the heart of old Manchester has a simple décor and a 'junk shop' collection of bric-a-brac. A collection of recipes begged and borrowed from around the world form the basis for an unusual range of dishes which include stewed lamb with rhubarb.
Closed Sun & Mon, Aug, 1 wk Xmas & 1 wk Spring
Lunch not served
V 40 seats Dinner £9.50-£17.50alc Last dinner 9.30pm ₱
Credit Cards [1] [2] [3]

✕**Mina-Japan** 63 George St M1 4NS ☎061-228 2598 FAX 061-872 1197
This Japanese restaurant features an extensive choice of well-prepared and presented dishes, many of them being cooked at the table by the friendly and experienced staff, whose national dress adds colour to the oriental setting which has been created from a city-centre basement.
Closed Sun & 2 Jan
Lunch not served
♀ Japanese V 50 seats Dinner £2-£5&alc Last dinner 11.30pm
Credit Cards [1] [2] [3] [5]

MANCHESTER AIRPORT Greater Manchester
Map **07** SJ78

★★★★57% **The Excelsior** Ringway Rd M22 5NS (Trusthouse Forte) ☎061-437 5811 Telex no 668721 FAX 061-436 2340
A good-sized hotel, incorporating a leisure centre with swimming pool, sauna and gym, forms part of the airport complex and is within easy reach of the national motorway network.
300⇨(3fb)⅟in 46 bedrooms CTV in all bedrooms ® T
sB⇨£80-£90 dB⇨£97-£107 (room only) ⊟
Lift ☾ ⊞ 350P ✲ CFA ⊡(heated) sauna solarium gymnasium health & fitness centre
V ♦ ⊡ ⅟ Lunch £10.50&alc Dinner £14.50&alc Last dinner 10.15pm
Credit Cards [1] [2] [3] [4] [5]

★★★★66% **Hilton International** Outwood Ln M22 5WP (Hilton) ☎061-436 4404 Telex no 668361 FAX 061-436 1521
A large, modern hotel which features lots of greenery and an attractive little stream running through its public areas. Enhanced recently by the opening of a stylish new restaurant and additional well-appointed bedrooms, it is busy, with a lively atmosphere. There are extensive conference and banqueting facilities and an appealing leisure complex.
223⇨⌐(10fb)⅟in 20 bedrooms CTV in all bedrooms ® T ✱
S% sB&B⇨⌐£78.50-£120 dB&B⇨⌐£98.50-£125 ⊟
Lift ☾ ⊞ 260P ⊡(heated) sauna gymnasium ♫
V ♦ ⊡
Credit Cards [1] [2] [3] [5]

See advertisement on page 469

★★★59% **Valley Lodge** SK9 4LR ☎Wilmslow(0625)529201 Telex no 666401 FAX (0625) 531876
Behind its distinctive Swiss Chalet exterior, this hotel offers every modern amenity, including excellent leisure facilities. Some of the bedrooms are compact, but the newer ones are sizeable. The public ▶

rooms in the older part of the hotel are due to be refurbished. Food is enjoyable and the staff are helpful.
125⇌2⊟ CTV in all bedrooms ® **T** ✳ sB⇌£31-£65.50 dB⇌£42-£75 (room only) ⊟
Lift ☾ 400P ✲ CFA ⊡(heated) squash snooker sauna solarium gymnasium jacuzzi steam room beauty therapy
☋ International **V** ♡ ⊒ Lunch fr£7.95&alc Dinner fr£9.75&alc Last dinner 10.30pm
Credit Cards 1 2 3 5

❀✕✕**Moss Nook** Ringway Rd M22 5NA
☎061-437 4778
Plush, Edwardian-style restaurant, only minutes from the airport but surprisingly undisturbed by noise. Chef Robert Thornton is an inventive exponent of the modern French style, and those who find it hard to choose from the enjoyable à la carte menu should opt for the Menu Surprise, featuring the best of the day's market. A wine and passion fruit sauce with fish and shellfish has attracted praise, as have light starters such as lobster mousse with saffron sauce, while the filet gourmet is a must for garlic lovers. Soufflés and crêpes are a speciality, but a recent visit suggested that more care was needed in the pastry department. Owners Derek and Pauline Harrison can take credit for a deservedly popular restaurant, however, and booking is usually essential.
Closed Sun, Mon & 25 Dec-8 Jan
Lunch not served Sat
☋ French 50 seats S% Lunch fr£24&alc Dinner fr£24&alc Last lunch 1.30pm Last dinner 9.30pm 50P nc12yrs
Credit Cards 1 2 3 5

M

MANORBIER Dyfed Map 02 SS09

★★**Castle Mead** SA70 7TA ☎(0834)871358
Closed Nov-Etr
Situated at the head of a small wooded valley that runs down to the beach a few hundred yards away, this small, family-run hotel has beautiful views of the sea and church and of the castle ruins nearby. Bedrooms are modest but cosy, and food is well-cooked and enjoyable.
5⇌Annexe3⇌(2fb) CTV in all bedrooms ® S% sB&B⇌fr£22 dB&B⇌fr£44 ⊟
20P ⛟ ✲
V ♡ ⊒ Bar Lunch £2.50 Dinner £9 Last dinner 8pm
Credit Cards 1 2 3

MANSFIELD Nottinghamshire Map 08 SK56

★★***Midland*** Midland Place NG5 6BW ☎(0623)24668
This former private house, standing close to the town centre, was built in 1704 and converted into a hotel by the Midland Railway Company in 1874. Today it offers comfortable and well-equipped accommodation.
27rm(16⇌4⩘)(2fb) CTV in all bedrooms ® **T** ⋈
CTV 20P
♡ Last dinner 9.30pm
Credit Cards 1 2 3

★★**Pine Lodge** 281-283 Nottingham Rd NG18 4SE
☎(0623)22308
Comfortable, homely hotel providing modern, well-equipped accommodation to suit both tourist and commercial customers. Situated on the A60, a quarter of a mile south of the town centre.
21rm(13⇌3⩘)(2fb) CTV in all bedrooms ® **T** ⋈ ✳ sB&B£29.95 sB&B⇌⩘£34.50-£40 dB&B⇌⩘£41.50-£50 ⊟
40P ⛟ sauna solarium
♡ ⊒
Credit Cards 1 2 3 £

MARAZION Cornwall & Isles of Scilly Map 02 SW53

★★**Mount Haven** Turnpike Rd TR17 0DQ (Minotels)
☎Penzance(0736)710249
Closed 17 Dec-4 Jan
Personally-run in a friendly atmosphere this one time coaching inn has a fascinating galleried restaurant, comfortable bedrooms and excellent parking.
17⇌(4fb)1⊟ CTV in all bedrooms ® **T** sB&B⇌£18-£31 dB&B⇌£36-£52 ⊟
40P ⛟
☋ English & French **V** ♡ ⊒ ⁄ Lunch fr£4.60alc Dinner fr£10.50&alc Last dinner 9pm
Credit Cards 1 2 3

See advertisement under PENZANCE

MARCH Cambridgeshire Map 05 TL49

★**Olde Griffin** High St PE15 9EJ ☎(0354)52517
The husband and wife team at the Olde Griffin have made many recent improvements to this 17th-century market-place coaching inn. They offer a warm, welcoming atmosphere and friendly service.
21rm(15⇌3⩘)(2fb) CTV in all bedrooms ® **T** ⋈ S5% sB&Bfr£30 sB&B⇌⩘fr£35 dB&Bfr£40 dB&B⇌⩘fr£42.50
CTV 50P ⛟ ♫
☋ English & Continental **V** ♡ S5% Lunch £5.50&alc Dinner fr£7.50&alc Last dinner 9.30pm
Credit Cards 1 3 £

All AA-appointed establishments are inspected regularly to ensure that required standards are maintained.

MARCHWIEL Clwyd Map **07** SJ34

★★**Cross Lanes Hotel & Restaurant** Cross Lanes LL13 0TF
☎Bangor-on-Dee(0978)780555
Popular and relaxing hotel with function facilities, set in seven acres of grounds south-east of Wrexham.
18rm(9⇌9⋔)(1fb)1⊟ CTV in all bedrooms ® **T** ✱
sB&B⇌⋔£29-£39 dB&B⇌⋔£56 Continental breakfast ⊫
80P ✲ ⊡(heated) sauna
♉ International **V** ✿ ♨ Lunch £8.50&alc Dinner £12.95&alc Last dinner 9pm
Credit Cards 1 2 3 5

MARFORD Clwyd Map **07** SJ35

★**Trevor Arms** Springfield Ln LL12 8TA ☎Chester(0244)570436
The inn, and other buildings in the village, were constructed by Flemish builders in the early 1800's and have a unique architectural style. Inside there are old beams and open fires, and bedrooms are well equipped and comfortable. Varied meals are served, with 'specials' displayed on boards.
7⋔1⊟ CTV in all bedrooms ® **T** ⊠ (ex guide dogs) ✱
sB&B⋔£20-£24 dB&B⋔£25-£29.50 Continental breakfast ⊫
70P ✲
V ✿ ♨ Lunch £3.50-£6.50&alc High tea £2.50 Dinner £3.50-£6.50&alc Last dinner 10pm
Credit Cards 1 3 £

MARGATE Kent Map **05** TR37

★★**Walpole Bay** Fifth Av, Cliftonville CT9 2JJ (1m E)
☎Thanet(0843)221703
Closed Oct-Apr
A charmingly traditional seaside hotel that offers fine sea views, a peaceful atmosphere, good services and pleasant accommodation, rather than the very latest in 'mod cons'.
44rm(22⇌)(10fb) CTV in 2bedrooms TV in 4bedrooms ® ✱
sB&B£20-£35 sB&B⇌£25-£40 dB&B£35-£45
dB&B⇌£40-£55 ⊫
Lift ☾ CTV ₱
✿ ♨ Dinner £7.50 Last dinner 8pm
Credit Cards 1 2 3 5

MARKET DRAYTON Shropshire Map **07** SJ63

★★**Corbet Arms** High St TF9 1PY ☎(0630)2037 & 2961
This historic inn where Thomas Telford once stayed, is believed to have a ghost that appears only to bachelors. Bars are cosy and the bedrooms are well equipped.
12rm(8⇌2⋔)(2fb) CTV in all bedrooms ® **T** sB&B£25-£28
sB&B⇌⋔£28-£32 dB&B£32-£36 dB&B⇌⋔£40-£44 ⊫
CTV 60P 2⊜ (£1.50) crown green bowling
♉ Mainly grills **V** ✿ ♨ ⊬ Lunch £5.50-£6.25 Dinner £7.50-£8.75&alc Last dinner 9pm
Credit Cards 1 2 3 5 £

★★**Tern Hill Hall** TF9 3PU (on A53) ☎Tern Hill(063083)310
RS 24-27 Dec
Large, detached hotel in spacious grounds.
12rm(7⇌)(3fb) CTV in all bedrooms ® ⊠ (ex guide dogs) S%
sB&B£26 sB&B⇌£30 dB&B£40 dB&B⇌£36-£40
CTV 90P ✲
♉ English & French **V** ✿ ♨ S10% Lunch £7.50 Dinner £5-£12alc Last dinner 9pm
Credit Cards 1 2 3

See the preliminary section 'Hotel and Restaurant Classification' for an explanation of the AA's appointment and award scheme.

MARKET HARBOROUGH Leicestershire Map **04** SP78

★★★61% **Three Swans** 21 High St LE16 7NJ (Best Western)
☎(0858)66644 Telex no 342375 FAX (0858) 33101
This historic inn, dating from the 15th century, stands on the A6 in the town centre.
21rm(10⇌10⋔)2⊟⊬in 8 bedrooms CTV in all bedrooms ® **T**
⊠ (ex guide dogs) sB&B⇌⋔£58-£64 dB&B⇌⋔£68-£74 ⊫
☾ 40P 8⊜
♉ International **V** ✿ ♨ Lunch fr£8.95 High tea fr£2.50 Dinner fr£13.95 Last dinner 10.00pm
Credit Cards 1 2 3 4 5

MARKFIELD Leicestershire Map **08** SK41

○***Granada Lodge*** Little Shaw Ln LE6 0PP (Granada)
☎(0530)244237
39⇌

MARKHAM MOOR Nottinghamshire Map **08** SK77

○***TraveLodge*** A1 Northbound DN22 0QU (Trusthouse Forte)
☎Retford(0777)838091
40⇌

MARKINGTON North Yorkshire Map **08** SE26

★★★♔74% **Hob Green**
HG3 3PJ
☎Harrogate(0423)770031
Telex no 57780
Beautifully placed hotel in 870 acres of farm and woodland, with splendid views. The drawing room and hall are relaxing with their antique furnishings and open fires, and the traditionally styled bedrooms have very up-to-date facilities. Service by mainly young staff is hospitable and discreet.
12⇌⋔1⊟ CTV in all bedrooms ® **T** sB&B⇌⋔£53-£59
dB&B⇌⋔£68.50-£77.50 ⊫
40P ⊕ ✲ croquet
♉ English & French **V** ✿ ♨ Lunch fr£9.95 Dinner fr£14.50alc Last dinner 9.30pm
Credit Cards 1 2 3 5

See advertisement under HARROGATE

MARKS TEY Essex Map **05** TL92

★★★50% **Marks Tey** London Rd CO6 1DU
☎Colchester(0206)210001 Telex no 987176
This purpose-built hotel stands close to the A12 and offers modern bedroom facilities. The friendly staff provide a good range of services.
108⇌(11fb) CTV in all bedrooms ® **T** sB&B⇌£49-£55
dB&B⇌fr£62 ⊫
☾ CTV 160P CFA ℘ (hard) gymnasium *xmas*
♉ English & French **V** ✿ ♨ S% Lunch fr£9.75&alc Dinner fr£9.75&alc Last dinner 10pm
Credit Cards 1 2 3 5

Places with AA hotels and restaurants are identified on the location atlas at the back of the book.

MARLBOROUGH Wiltshire Map **04** SU16

★★★ 64% **The Castle & Ball** High St SN8 1LZ (Trusthouse Forte) ☎(0672)55201 FAX (0672) 55895

Located in the centre of this lovely market town, this 17th-century inn, with an attractive tile-hung Georgian façade, offers prompt and friendly standards of service. The interior has been completely modernised, yet retains its charm and character. Public rooms are cosy and traditional.

36⇨ ⅟in 4 bedrooms CTV in all bedrooms ® T ✻
sB⇨£70-£80 dB⇨£80-£90 (room only) ⊟
50P *xmas*
V ✿ ⊻ ⅟ Lunch fr£8&alc High tea fr£3.95 Dinner fr£13&alc
Last dinner 9.30pm
Credit Cards [1] [2] [3] [4] [5]

★★★ 68% **Ivy House Hotel & Garden Restaurant** High St SN8 1HJ (Best Western) ☎(0672)55333 due to change to 515333 Telex no 449703 FAX (0672) 515338

An attractive, ivy-clad house in the town centre, with its own rear car park and sun terrace. It provides comfortable, modern bedroom accommodation (some in a recently completed annexe), attractive public rooms and friendly service. The restaurant offers interesting menus which can be complemented by some excellent wines from the comprehensive wine list.

12⇨↑Annexe16⇨↑(4fb) CTV in all bedrooms ® T ✻
sB⇨↑£55-£65 dB⇨↑£58-£75 (room only) ⊟
30P ⊞ nc12yrs *xmas*
⊽ English & French V Lunch fr£12&alc Dinner £12-£20alc
Last dinner 9.30pm
Credit Cards [1] [2] [3] [5] £

Book as early as possible for busy holiday periods.

MARLOW Buckinghamshire Map **04** SU88

★★★★ 73% **The Compleat Angler** Marlow Bridge SL7 1RG (Trusthouse Forte) ☎(06284)4444 Telex no 848644 FAX (06284) 6388
Ideally situated on the Thames and set in its own lovely gardens, the hotel complements tastefully appointed accommodation with willing, helpful service and a relaxing atmosphere.
46⇌4 in 5 bedrooms CTV in all bedrooms **T** ✳ S%
sB⇌£88 dB⇌£108-£118 (room only)
100P 6 CFA (hard) *xmas*
English & French **V** S% Lunch fr£17.50&alc Dinner £25-£35&alc Last dinner 10pm
Credit Cards 1 2 3 4 5

MARPLE Greater Manchester Map **07** SJ98

★**Springfield** Station Rd SK6 6PA ☎061-449 0721
A small but very well-appointed hotel situated in a pleasant residential area within easy reach of important business centres, Manchester airport, the motorway network and the Peak District. Attractive, well-equipped bedrooms, good home cooking and a warm and friendly atmosphere can be found here.
6rm(4⇌2) CTV in all bedrooms ® **T** sB&Bfr£33 sB&B⇌fr£33 dB&Bfr£46 dB&B⇌fr£46
CTV 10P
British Lunch £7.50 High tea £6 Dinner £12.50 Last dinner 8.30pm
Credit Cards 1 2 3 5

MARSTON MORETAINE Bedfordshire Map **04** SP94

○ ***Travelodge*** A421 Beancroft Rd Junction MK43 0PQ (Trusthouse Forte) ☎Bedford(0234)766755
32⇌
P

MARSTON TRUSSELL Northamptonshire Map **04** SP68

★★ ***Sun Inn Hotel & Restaurant*** LE16 9TY
☎Market Harborough(0858)65531
Modern accommodation is provided in the extension of this traditional, rural, village inn.
10⇌ CTV in all bedrooms ® **T**
CTV 35P 2
English & Continental **V** Last dinner 9.30pm
Credit Cards 1 2 3

See advertisement under MARKET HARBOROUGH

MARTINHOE Devon Map **03** SS64

★ **Old Rectory** EX31 4QT
☎Parracombe(05983)368
Closed Dec-Feb

In a quiet location close to Lynton, the Old Rectory is a charming house set in three acres of landscaped gardens. Both bedrooms and public rooms are tastefully furnished. Proprietors Tony and Anna Pring are always on hand to ensure your visit is a happy one.
9rm(7⇌2) CTV in 5bedrooms sB&B⇌fr£39 dB&B⇌£70 (incl dinner)
14P putting nc12yrs
Bar Lunch £2-£4 Dinner £11.50-£12.50 Last dinner 7.45pm
£

See advertisement under LYNTON

MARYPORT Cumbria Map **11** NY03

★★**Ellenbank** Birkby CA15 6RE (2m NE A596) ☎(0900)815233
Attractive sandstone building, with a friendly atmosphere, standing in its own grounds.
14rm(12⇌2)(3fb) CTV in all bedrooms ® **T** S10%
sB&B⇌£25-£30 dB&B⇌£40-£50
CTV 40P *xmas*
English & Continental **V** S% Lunch £5.30-£10.50 Dinner £10.50&alc Last dinner 9.30pm
Credit Cards 1 3

★**Waverley** Curzon St CA15 6LW ☎(0900)812115
Homely commercial hotel with an extensive bar/dining room menu offering honest home cooking.
20rm(2⇌2)(2fb) CTV in 16bedrooms ® ✳ sB&Bfr£15 sB&B⇌fr£22 dB&Bfr£27 dB&B⇌fr£33
CTV pool table
V Last high tea 4.30pm
Credit Cards 1 3 5 £

✕✕**Retreat** Birkby CA15 6RG (1.25m NE A596)
☎(0900)814056
This elegant Georgian house has been sympathetically converted to provide pleasant surroundings in which to enjoy the careful cooking of chef/proprietor Rudi Geissler.
Continental **V** 40 seats ✳ Lunch £3.10-£14alc Dinner £13&alc Last lunch 1.45pm Last dinner 9.45pm 21P
Credit Cards 1 3

MARY TAVY Devon Map **02** SX57

★★ **Moorland Hall**
Brentor Rd PL19 9PY
☎(082281)466

Converted from a farmhouse in 1877 the hotel stands gracefully in four acres of private gardens, offering attractive and comfortable accommodation in peaceful suroundings.
10rm(4⇌4)(1fb) CTV in 8bedrooms TV in 2bedrooms ® ✳ sB&B⇌fr£25 dB&B⇌fr£38.50
20P croquet lawn *xmas*
English & French **V**
Credit Cards 1 3 £

Entries for rosetted restaurants, red-star and country-house hotels are highlighted by a tinted panel. For a full list of these establishments, consult the Contents page.

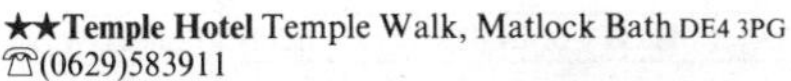

MASHAM North Yorkshire Map **08** SE28

★★⚘Jervaulx Hall HG4 4PH
☎Bedale(0677)60235
Closed mid Nov-mid Mar

Early 19th century country house adjoining Jervaulx Abbey, with its own attractive gardens. It is a comfortable and friendly hotel serving good food.

8⇨(1fb) ® ✱ sB&B⇨£45-£54 dB&B⇨£80-£98 (incl dinner) ⊟
CTV 15P ⊞ ❉ croquet
♆ ☑ Dinner £14 Last dinner 8pm

MATLOCK Derbyshire Map **08** SK36

★★★52% The New Bath New Bath Rd DE4 3PX (2m S A6) (Trusthouse Forte) ☎(0629)583275 FAX (0629) 580268
Large, much extended, Georgian-style building high above the A6.
55⇨⊬in 11 bedrooms CTV in all bedrooms ® **T** S% sB⇨fr£70 dB⇨£75-£83 (room only) ⊟
(250P ❉ CFA ⊐ ⚲ (hard) sauna solarium thermal pool *xmas*
V ♆ ☑ ⊬ S% Lunch £8-£9&alc High tea £3.50-£5 Dinner £12.25&alc Last dinner 9.30pm
Credit Cards 1 2 3 4 5

★★★⚘70% Riber Hall DE4 5JU (Pride of Britain)
☎(0629)582795
FAX (0629) 580475

A quiet country house hotel full of charm and character dating back to Elizabethan times, that has been tastefully and thoughtfully restored to maintain its period feel. The bedrooms, all in the annexe, are extremely well appointed and in keeping with the rest of the house, with much exposed woodwork and antique furniture. Chef Jeremy Brezelle has created an interesting menu which is augmented by the quality, comprehensive wine list.

Annexe11⇨9⊞ CTV in all bedrooms ® **T** ✗ (ex guide dogs) sB&B⇨£58 dB&B⇨£78 Continental breakfast ⊟
50P ⊞ ❉ ⚲ (hard) nc10yrs
♕ English & French **V** ♆ ☑ Lunch £12.50 High tea fr£7alc Dinner fr£23alc Last dinner 9.30pm
Credit Cards 1 2 3 4 5

★★Red House Old Rd, Darley Dale DE4 2ER (2.5m N A6)
☎(0629)734854
6rm(3⇨3↱) CTV in all bedrooms ® **T** ✱ sB&B⇨↱£35-£40 dB&B⇨↱£50-£60 ⊟
16P ❉
♕ English & French ♆ ☑ Lunch fr£9 Dinner £14.50-£16.50 Last dinner 9pm
Credit Cards 1 2 3 5 £

★★Temple Hotel Temple Walk, Matlock Bath DE4 3PG
☎(0629)583911
Perched on a steep, wooded hillside overlooking the River Derwent, this completely modernised hotel has smart, comfortable bedrooms. There are two styles of restaurant, one a small carvery, the other offers an à la carte menu specialising in game.
14⇨(1fb) CTV in all bedrooms ® **T** ✗ ✱ sB&B⇨£40-£44 dB&B⇨£50 ⊟
(CTV 40P ❉ *xmas*
♕ English, French & Austrian **V** ♆ ☑ ⊬ Lunch £8-£18alc Dinner £12-£18alc Last dinner 9.45pm
Credit Cards 1 2 3 5

★★*Woodland Lodge* Temple Walk, Matlock Bath DE4 3PG
☎(0629)3654
Annexe10⇨(4fb) CTV in all bedrooms ® **T** ✗
30P ⊞
♆ ☑
Credit Cards 1 3

MAWGAN PORTH Cornwall & Isles of Scilly Map **02** SW86

★★Tredragon TR8 4DQ (Inter) ☎St Mawgan(0637)860213 FAX (0637) 860269
Comfortable, family holiday hotel, with fine views of the beach and direct access to it.
29rm(14⇨12↱)(12fb) CTV in all bedrooms ® **T** sB&B⇨↱£27-£38 dB&B⇨↱£38-£63
CTV 30P ❉ ⊡(heated) sauna solarium ♫ ⌂ *xmas*
♕ English & French ♆ ☑ Sunday Lunch £9.50 Dinner £9.50 Last dinner 8pm
Credit Cards 1 3 £

MAWNAN SMITH Cornwall & Isles of Scilly Map **02** SW72

★★★69% Budock Vean TR11 5LG ☎Falmouth(0326)250288
Telex no 45795 FAX (0326) 250892
Closed early Jan-mid Feb
This very professionally run hotel stands in its own golf course, which runs down to the Helford River.
59⇌(6fb)1⊟ CTV in all bedrooms **T** sB&B⇌£33-£63
dB&B⇌£66-£126 (incl dinner)
Lift ☾ 100P ⊞ ❋ ⊡(heated) ▶9 ℘ (hard) ♩ snooker ♫ *xmas*
☋ English & French **V** ♔ ⊒ Lunch £10.50 Dinner
£15.50-£29.50 Last dinner 9pm
Credit Cards 1 2 3 5

See advertisement under FALMOUTH

★★★♛73% Meudon
TR11 5HT
☎Falmouth(0326)250541
Telex no 45478
FAX (0326) 250543
Closed Jan-14 Feb

Friendly, relaxing manor house where comfortable lounges overlook superb subtropical gardens.
30⇌♠(1fb)1⊟ CTV in all bedrooms ® **T**
sB&B⇌♠£50-£55 dB&B⇌♠£80-£90 ⊟
☾ 50P 2⊜ (£5 per night) ⊞ ❋ CFA ♩ U nc5yrs *xmas*
☋ English & French **V** ♔ ⊒ ⊬ Lunch £12.50 High tea
£3-£7 Dinner £15-£19.50&alc Last dinner 8.45pm
Credit Cards 1 3 5

★★★62% Trelawne TR11 5HS ☎Falmouth(0326)250226
FAX (0326) 250909
Closed 30 Dec-28 Feb
Set in rural surroundings, with its own 2.5-acre grounds, and within easy reach of the sea, this spotlessly clean, family-run holiday hotel maintains good standards of cooking, menus exhibiting some flair and imagination. Bedroom accommodation is cosy, public rooms pleasant and the atmosphere is comfortably homely.
15rm(11⇌2♠)(2fb) CTV in all bedrooms ® **T**
sB&B⇌♠£29-£32 dB&B⇌♠£52-£58 ⊟
20P ⊞ ❋ ⊡(heated) *xmas*
♔ ⊒ ⊬ Bar Lunch £1.10-£4.70 Dinner £14.90&alc Last dinner 8.30pm
Credit Cards 1 2 3 5

See advertisement under FALMOUTH

MAYPOOL (near Churston) Devon Map **03** SX85

★★★64% Lost & Found Inn TQ5 0ET ☎Churston(0803)842442
Owned and run by the hospitable Giblett family, this hotel lies in a peaceful setting, from which you can look down across the valley of the River Dart. The 16 bedrooms combine modern standards with charm and character. The public rooms include a large lounge bar and well-appointed dining room and there is a particularly pleasant sun terrace with lovely views. Imaginative food, all cooked to order, is served in an informal and friendly manner.
16rm(8⇌8♠)1⊟ CTV in all bedrooms ® **T**
sB&B⇌♠£50-£57 dB&B⇌♠£90-£104 (incl dinner)
25P ⊞ ❋
☋ English & French **V** ♔ ⊒ Lunch £7.95-£10.95&alc Dinner
£16.95-£19.95&alc Last dinner 10pm
Credit Cards 1 2 3

MEALSGATE Cumbria Map **11** NY24

★★Pink House CA5 1JP ☎Low Ireby(09657)229
31 Dec-24 Dec
The small hotel is friendly and cosy, with a comfortable lounge and an attractive bar where enjoyable meals are served.
6rm(4⇌2♠)(2fb) CTV in all bedrooms ® **T** ✗ (ex guide dogs)
sB&B⇌♠£28-£28 dB&B⇌♠£39-£39
CTV 30P ❋ ⌂
☋ English **V** ♔ Lunch £5.75-£11alc Dinner £5.75-£11alc Last dinner 8.45pm
Credit Cards 1 3

MELKSHAM Wiltshire Map **03** ST96

★★★♛74% Beechfield House Beanacre SN12 7PU
(1m N A350)
☎(0225)703700
FAX (0225) 790118

A great treat for business or pleasure, this ornate Victorian country house sits in 8 acres of lovely grounds, which include a pool that is inside a walled garden. Bedrooms are delightfully decorated and equipped. Chef John Williams provides a short à la carte menu of unusual dishes which can be complemented with wines from the comprehensive wine list.
16⇌Annexe8⇌1⊟ CTV in all bedrooms **T** ✗ (ex guide dogs) ✱ sB&B⇌fr£74.25
dB&B⇌£93.50-£110 Continental breakfast ⊟
40P ⊞ ❋ ⊃(heated) ℘ (grass) croquet ⌂ *xmas*
☋ English & French **V** ♔ ⊒ ⊬ Lunch £13.95-£15.35
Dinner £18.50-£27.95alc Last dinner 9.30pm
Credit Cards 1 2 3 5 £

★★Conigre Farm Semington Rd SN12 6BX ☎(0225)702229
The 17th century farmhouse offers a warm friendly atmosphere and comfortable bedrooms in a variety of sizes, some of them in a converted stable block. Rooms are all named after Dickens characters, Mr Bumble's Restaurant offers a good selection of well-prepared dishes.
4rm(1⇌)Annexe5rm(2⇌3♠)1⊟ CTV in all bedrooms ® **T** ✗
✱ sB&B£23.50-£29.50 sB&B⇌♠£23.50-£29.50
dB&B£38-£42.50 dB&B⇌♠£38-£42.50 ⊟
☾ 12P 2⊜ ⊞ ❋
V ♔ ⊒ S% Lunch £11.50&alc Dinner £11.50&alc Last dinner 10pm
Credit Cards 1 2 3

★★Kings Arms Market Place SN12 6EX ☎(0225)707272
This attractive, fully-licensed hotel in the town centre provides attentive, very friendly service. Well maintained and comfortable bedrooms are equipped with a good range of facilities.
14rm(9⇌1♠) CTV in all bedrooms ® **T** ✱ sB&B£27
sB&B⇌♠£37 dB&B⇌♠£48 ⊟
40P
V ♔ ⊒ Lunch £3.85-£8.50&alc Dinner £8.50&alc Last dinner 9pm
Credit Cards 1 2 3 5 £

★★Shaw Country Bath Rd, Shaw SN12 8EF (2m NW A365)
☎(0225)702836 FAX (0225) 790275
A 400 year-old building, set in its own grounds on the edge of the town centre, has been tastefully restored to provide comfortable accommodation. Staff are friendly and attentive, and meals are chosen from extensive menus of freshly prepared dishes.

10rm(5⇨5♪)(1fb)1 ⊠ CTV in all bedrooms ® T ✗ S%
sB&B⇨♪£36-£46 dB&B⇨♪£48-£60 ⊟
25P ✲ ⇨(heated) ⊕
☋ English & French V ✧ ⊒ S% Lunch fr£7 High tea fr£2.50 Dinner fr£9.50&alc Last dinner 9pm
Credit Cards [1] [2] [3] (£)

MELLING Lancashire Map **07** SD57

★★Melling Hall LA6 2RA (Exec Hotel) ☎Hornby(05242)21298
A converted 17th-century manor house, set in open country on the edge of the village.
14rm(7⇨3♪)(1fb) CTV in all bedrooms ® sB&B£22 sB&B⇨♪£30-£32 dB&B£34 dB&B⇨♪£44 ⊟
40P ✲ *xmas*
☋ English & French ✧ Lunch fr£5.95 Dinner £10.50&alc Last dinner 9.30pm
Credit Cards [1] [2] [3] [5] (£)

MELROSE Borders *Roxburghshire* Map **12** NT53

★★Burt's The Square TD6 9PN ☎(089682)2285
FAX (089682) 2870
Dating from 1722, this converted town house is of architectural interest.
21rm(16⇨5♪) CTV in all bedrooms ® T sB&B⇨♪£30 dB&B⇨♪£52 ⊟
40P ⊠ ✲ snooker shooting game fishing
☋ English & French V ✧ Lunch £9-£11 Dinner £12.50-£16alc Last dinner 9.30pm
Credit Cards [1] [2] [3] [5]

For key to symbols see the inside front cover.

★★George & Abbotsford TD6 9PD (Consort) ☎(089682)2308 FAX (089682) 3363
A former coaching inn, situated in the centre of town with comfortable and recently upgraded public areas and friendly helpful staff.
31rm(15⇨16↱)(3fb) CTV in all bedrooms ® **T** sB&B⇨↱£32-£38 dB&B⇨↱£50-£58 ⊟
⊞ CTV 150P 1🚗 ❁
☋ British & French **V** ♧ Bar Lunch £3-£6alc High tea £5.50-£6.50 Dinner £12-£14&alc Last dinner 9.30pm
Credit Cards [1] [2] [3] [5]

MELTON MOWBRAY Leicestershire Map **08** SK71

★★★★♛73% Stapleford Park Stapleford LE14 2EF (Prestige)
☎Wymondham (057284)522
Telex no 342319
FAX (057284)651

Bob and Wendy Payton have created a unique and exciting luxury hotel within this fine mansion. Bedrooms have been individually designed by 'famous names' such as Liberty and Wedgwood and throughout the hotel no expense has been spared to provide opulent surroundings and the best in comfort and convenience. The service is particularly friendly and informal. Extensive grounds and parkland surround the house and include many recreational facilities.
35⇨↱1⊟ CTV in all bedrooms **T** sB&B⇨↱£95-£175 dB&B⇨↱£190-£350 Continental breakfast ⊟
Lift ☾ 120P ⊟ ❁ ♬ (hard) ↲ ∪ minature golf croquet basketball nc10yrs *xmas*
V ⊻ ⅟ Lunch £15-£20alc Dinner £20-£35alc Last dinner 11pm
Credit Cards [1] [2] [3] [4] [5]

★★★58% The George High St LE13 0TR ☎(0664)62112 FAX (0664) 410457
A town centre coaching inn dating from the 17th century, the George provides comfortable accommodation, and a good range of bar snacks is available in the cosy atmosphere of its three bars.
20rm(19⇨1↱)4⊟ CTV in all bedrooms ® ✳ sB&B⇨↱£35-£45 dB&B⇨↱£45-£61 ⊟
☾ CTV 20P
☋ Continental **V** ♧ ⊻ Lunch £4.25-£8.95 Dinner £10.25-£10.85 Last dinner 9.45pm
Credit Cards [1] [2] [3] [4] [5]

★★★57% Harboro' Burton St LE13 1AF (Trusthouse Forte) ☎(0664)60121 Telex no 341713
Commercial hotel, which was formerly a coaching inn, situated on the A606.
27rm(23⇨4↱)(1fb)⅟in 5 bedrooms CTV in all bedrooms ® **T** S% sB⇨↱fr£50 dB⇨↱fr£60 (room only) ⊟
☾ 40P *xmas*
V ♧ ⊻ ⅟ S% Lunch £6.85-£9.50&alc Dinner £11.35&alc Last dinner 10pm
Credit Cards [1] [2] [3] [4] [5]

★★*Kings Head* Nottingham St LE13 1NW ☎(0664)62110
The town-centre hotel, popular with commercial guests, provides modern, well-equipped accommodation and simple but wholesome meals that represent good value for money.
15rm(4⇨8↱)(1fb) CTV in all bedrooms ®
CTV 100P 20🚗
♧ Last dinner 9pm
Credit Cards [1] [2] [3]

★★Sysonby Knoll Asfordby Rd LE13 0HP ☎(0664)63563 FAX (0664) 410364
Closed Xmas
This comfortable little hotel stands in its own grounds on the outskirts of the market town, having plesant views over the River Eye and surrounding countryside .
25rm(16⇨3↱)(2fb)1⊟ CTV in all bedrooms ® **T** sB&B£24 sB&B⇨↱£33 dB&B£33 dB&B⇨↱£42-£44 ⊟
CTV 30P ❁ ⛶
☋ English & French **V** ♧ Sunday Lunch fr£6.50 Dinner fr£8alc Last dinner 8.30pm
Credit Cards [1] [3]

MELVICH Highland *Caithness* Map **14** NC86

★★*Melvich* KW14 7YJ ☎(06413)206
This friendly roadside hotel, with a modern bedrooms wing, has stunning coastal views from its elevated position.
14↱ CTV in all bedrooms ®
10P ⊟ ❁ ↲
V ♧ ⊻ ⅟ Last dinner 8pm

MENAI BRIDGE Gwynedd Map **06** SH57

★★Anglesey Arms LL59 5EA ☎(0248)712305
Standing at the end of the Menai Suspension Bridge, at the gateway to Anglesey, this hotel provides comfortable, modern accommodation.
17rm(10⇨6↱) CTV in all bedrooms ® sB&B⇨↱fr£29 dB&B⇨↱fr£46 ⊟
CTV 25P ❁ *xmas*
V ♧ ⊻ Lunch fr£10 Dinner fr£10 Last dinner 9.30pm
Credit Cards [1] [3]

★★Gazelle Glyn Garth LL59 5PD (2m NE A545) (Frederic Robinson) ☎(0248)713364 & 713167
Pleasant and well furnished, commanding views of the Snowdonia mountains across the estuary, the hotel serves well-cooked meals of a good standard in its restaurant and bars.
9rm(4⇨1↱) CTV in all bedrooms ® **T** sB&B⇨↱fr£27.50 dB&Bfr£38.50 dB&B⇨↱fr£48.50
40P ❁ sailing sea fishing watersports
V Lunch £8&alc Dinner £8&alc Last dinner 9.30pm
Credit Cards [1] [3]

MERE Wiltshire Map **03** ST83

★★Old Ship Castle St BA12 6JE ☎(0747)860258 FAX (0747) 860501
16th-century building of architectural interest with comfortable bedrooms and modern annexe, with good range of meals served in restaurant.
14rm(6⇨)Annexe10rm(8⇨2↱)(3fb)2⊟ CTV in all bedrooms ® **T** ✳ sB&Bfr£27 sB&B⇨↱fr£31 dB&Bfr£38 dB&B⇨↱fr£44 ⊟
50P
☋ English & French **V** Lunch £10-£17alc Dinner £10-£17alc Last dinner 9.30pm
Credit Cards [1] [3] [4] [£]

MERIDEN West Midlands Map **04** SP28

★★★66% Manor CV7 7NH (De Vere) ☎(0676)22735 Telex no 311011 FAX (0676) 22186
Recently refurbished and extended, this large hotel provides a very good standard of bedrooms and public areas. A varied choice of dishes is served in the restaurant, whilst the buttery offers a more simple style of food. Situated in a delightful village in the centre of England and convenient for the National Exhibition Centre.

M

74⇨ CTV in all bedrooms ® T sB&B⇨fr£62 dB&B⇨fr£74 ⊟
☾ 250P ✻ CFA ⌂(heated) ♫
♀ English & French V ♧ ☕ S% Lunch fr£13.50&alc Dinner fr£13.50&alc Last dinner 10pm
Credit Cards 1 2 3 5

MERTHYR TYDFIL Mid Glamorgan Map **03** SO00

See also **Nant Ddu**

★★★62% Baverstock The Heads Of Valley Rd CF44 0LX ☎(0685)6221 FAX (0685) 723670
Comfortable modern hotel with extensive conference facilities, just north of town on the A465 Heads of the Valleys road.
53⇨↱(2fb) CTV in all bedrooms ® T ✗ (ex guide dogs) ✱ S% sB&B⇨↱£38 dB&B⇨↱£40-£45 ⊟
☾ CTV 300P ✻ snooker pool table *xmas*
♀ Welsh, English & Continental V ♧ ☕ ⊁ S% Lunch fr£7.50 High tea £1.75-£2.50 Dinner fr£9.50 Last dinner 10.30pm
Credit Cards 1 2 3 5

★★Tregenna Park Ter CF47 8RF ☎(0685)723627 & 82055 FAX (0685) 721951
This modern hotel, a short walk from the town centre, is very well run and has cheerful, friendly staff. The wide-ranging menu offers good value food and bedrooms are all well equipped with modern comforts.
14⇨↱Annexe7⇨(6fb)1⊞ CTV in all bedrooms ® T sB&B⇨↱£30-£35 dB&B⇨↱£40-£45 ⊟
☾ CTV 21P *xmas*
V ♧ ☕ Lunch fr£7&alc High tea fr£1.25&alc Dinner fr£7&alc Last dinner 10pm
Credit Cards 1 2 3 £

See advertisement on page 479

M

MEVAGISSEY Cornwall & Isles of Scilly Map **02** SX04

★★Spa Polkirt Hill PL26 6UY ☏(0726)842244
Family-run hotel in commanding position on Polkirt Hill, with well-equipped bedrooms and a pleasant garden.
12rm(10⇔1↱)(4fb) CTV in all bedrooms ® ✱
sB&B⇔↱£18-£22 dB&B⇔↱£36-£44 ⊟
CTV 14P ⊞ ✲ putting green pool table *xmas*
☋ English & French **V** ♡ ⊻ Bar Lunch £1-£2.95 Dinner £8.50-£9 Last dinner 8.00pm
Credit Cards 1 2 3

★★Tremarne Polkirt Hill PL26 6UY ☏(0726)842213
Closed Dec-Feb
Comfortable, friendly family holiday hotel with good food, pleasant garden and fine views.
14rm(4⇔10↱)(2fb) CTV in all bedrooms ® ✗ (ex guide dogs)
sB&B⇔↱£19-£24 dB&B⇔↱£32-£42 ⊟
14P ⊞ ✲ ⌒(heated) nc3yrs
♡ ⊻ ⊁ Dinner £12.25 Last dinner 6pm
Credit Cards 1 3

★★Trevalsa Court Polstreath PL26 6TH
☏(0726)842468 & 843794
Closed Dec-Jan
Country house of character in a peaceful situation overlooking the sea.
10rm(8⇔2↱)(2fb) CTV in 8bedrooms TV in 2bedrooms ®
sB&B£20-£21 sB&B⇔↱£20-£21 dB&B⇔↱£40-£50 ⊟
40P ⊞ ✲ sea fishing trips shooting horse riding nc10yrs
☋ English, French & Italian **V** ♡ ⊻ Bar Lunch £2.50-£7 High tea fr£2 Dinner fr£9.50&alc Last high tea 5pm
Credit Cards 1 2 3 5

★Sharksfin The Quay PL26 6QU ☏(0726)843241
Closed Dec & Jan
This former sardine cannery, in a unique quayside position, has been converted to provide a restaurant where cheerful local staff serve a good range of meals. Accommodation is available in second-floor bedrooms.
11rm(2↱)(2fb) CTV in all bedrooms ® ✗ ✱
sB&B£16.20-£19.50 sB&B↱£16.20-£19.50 dB&B£26.40-£33 dB&B↱£37.40-£44
CTV ₱ ⊞
V ♡ ⊻
Credit Cards 1 2 3 5 £

MICKLETON Gloucestershire Map **04** SP14

★★★64% Three Ways GL55 6SB (Inter) ☏(0386)438429
Telex no 337242 FAX (0386) 438118
A modern bedroom wing, attractive restaurant and conference room are features of this convenient touring hotel.
40rm(33⇔7↱)(5fb) CTV in all bedrooms ® **T** S%
sB&B⇔↱£32-£40 dB&B⇔↱£52-£61 ⊟
☾ 37P ✲ CFA ♫ *xmas*
☋ English & Continental **V** ♡ ⊻ Lunch £8.50-£10 Dinner £12.50-£15.50 Last dinner 9pm
Credit Cards 1 2 3 5 £

MIDDLEHAM North Yorkshire Map **07** SE18

★★Millers House Market Place DL8 4NR
☏Wensleydale(0969)22630
Closed Jan
Friendly attentive service and good cooking using fresh produce can be found at this small Georgian 'country house hotel in town'.
7rm(6⇔)1⊞ CTV in all bedrooms ® **T** ✗ (ex guide dogs)
sB&B⇔fr£26 dB&B⇔£52-£58 ⊟
8P ⊞ nc11yrs *xmas*
☋ English & French ♡ ⊁ Bar Lunch £5-£6.50 Dinner £13.50 Last dinner 8.30pm
Credit Cards 1 3

MIDDLESBROUGH Cleveland Map **08** NZ42

★★★50% Blue Bell Vaux Inn Acklam Rd, Acklam TS5 7HL
☏(0642)593939 Telex no 53168
A two-storey hotel with a modern wing, standing by a busy roundabout.
60⇔↱ CTV in all bedrooms ® **T** sB&B⇔↱£34-£38
dB&B⇔↱£42-£46.50
Lift ☾ 200P CFA ♫ *xmas*
☋ Mainly grills **V** ♡ S% Lunch fr£5.45 Dinner £7.65-£6.45&alc Last dinner 9.45pm
Credit Cards 1 2 3 5

★★★50% Marton Hotel & Country Club Stokesley Rd, Marton TS7 8DS (3m S of A172) ☏(0642)317141
A modern functional three-storey hotel at the junction of the A172 and A174. There are spacious public areas, conference and banqueting facilities, and bright and cheerful bedrooms which are warm and comfortable.
52⇔(2fb) CTV in all bedrooms **T** ✱ sB&B⇔£19.50-£27
dB&B⇔£30-£37
☾ CTV 300P CFA snooker ♫
☋ English, French & Italian ♡ ⊻ Lunch £5.95&alc Dinner £6.95-£7.25&alc Last dinner 10pm
Credit Cards 1 2 3 5

★★★55% Marton Way Toby Marton Rd TS4 3BS (Toby)
☏(0642)817651 Telex no 587783
Closed 25 Dec
This comfortable, modern hotel surrounds a courtyard car park. Both lunch and dinner are available from the popular, good-value carvery.
53⇔(4fb)⊁in 18 bedrooms CTV in all bedrooms ® **T** ✱
sB&B⇔£33.50 dB&B⇔£43.50 ⊟
☾ 500P CFA
☋ British & Continental **V** ♡ ⊻
Credit Cards 1 2 3 5

★★Highfield 358 Marton Rd TS4 2PA (Berni/Chef & Brewer)
☏(0642)817638
Exceptionally comfortable accommodation and warm, friendly service attract visitors to this large, old house, which stands in its own grounds.
23rm(19⇔4↱)2⊞ CTV in all bedrooms ® **T** ✗ (ex guide dogs) sB&B⇔↱fr£36 dB&B⇔↱fr£51 ⊟
☾ 100P 4⌂
☋ Mainly grills **V** ♡ ⊻ ⊁ Lunch £8 Dinner £9 Last dinner 10.30pm
Credit Cards 1 2 3 5

★The Grey House 79 Cambridge Rd, Linthorpe TS5 5NL
☏Middlesborough(0642)817485
Charming Edwardian house in well-tended gardens, owner-run with friendly informality. All bedrooms have en suite facilities.
7↱(1fb) CTV in all bedrooms ® sB&B↱£24-£29
dB&B↱£33-£38
10P ⊞
Dinner fr£7 Last dinner 7pm

MIDDLETON-IN-TEESDALE Co Durham Map **12** NY92

★★Teesdale Market Place DL12 0QG ☏Teesdale(0833)40264
The friendly, family-run hotel offers very comfortable accommodation and good home cooking.
14rm(7⇔)(1fb) CTV in 13bedrooms **T** sB&Bfr£27
sB&B⇔fr£28 dB&Bfr£48 dB&B⇔fr£50 ⊟
CTV 14P ⊞ *xmas*
☋ English, French, German & Italian ♡ ⊻ Dinner fr£13.50&alc Last dinner 8.30pm
Credit Cards 1 3 £

MIDDLETON STONEY Oxfordshire Map **04** SP52

★★Jersey Arms OX6 8SE ☎(086989)234 & 505
FAX (086989) 565
Granite lintels, exposed beams and large open fires set the scene at this charming Cotswold inn beside the A43. Main-building bedrooms are cosy and well equipped, but courtyard suites offer more comfort and spaciousness, the Langtry in particular, with its delightful four-poster bed, being reminiscent of bygone days. Public rooms include an attractive new wood-panelled restaurant and a stylish quiet lounge for residents, whilst meals – whether enjoyed al fresco in the courtyard or formally in the restaurant – are of a commendable standard. Service is friendly and a relaxed atmosphere pervades the hotel.
6⇌Annexe10⇌1⊞ CTV in all bedrooms **T** ✱
sB&B⇌£47.50-£75 dB&B⇌£60-£89.50 ⊟
55P ⊞ ✲
☋ English & French **V** ♁ ☕ Lunch £12-£21alc Dinner £15-£21alc Last dinner 9.30pm
Credit Cards [1] [2] [3] [5]

MIDDLE WALLOP Hampshire Map **04** SU23

★★*Fifehead Manor* SO20 8EG ☎Andover(0264)781565
Closed 2wks Xmas
A small manor house on the fringe of the village has been tastefully restored to provide comfortable accommodation in both the main building and annexe. In the restaurant a sophisticated à la carte menu of French cuisine is served by a willing young staff.
10⇌ CTV in all bedrooms **T**
50P ⊞ ✲ croquet
☋ English & French ♁ ☕ Last dinner 9.30pm
Credit Cards [1] [2] [3] [5]

M

✕**Old Drapery Stores** SO20 8HN ☎Andover(0264)781301
English & French **V** 48 seats ✱ Lunch £8.50-£28 Last lunch 2.30pm Last dinner 10pm 17P
Credit Cards 1 2 3 5

MIDHURST West Sussex Map **04** SU82

See also **Trotton**

★★★67% **Spread Eagle** South St GU29 9NH (Best Western) ☎(073081)6911 Telex no 86853 FAX (073081) 5668
The Spread Eagle has been welcoming guests since it originated as a tavern in 1430 and throughout its long and well documented history as a famous coaching inn. Today, the hotel has been sympathetically extended and renovated to provide individually and tastefully decorated bedrooms and comfortable public areas. The food served here is varied and innovative and can be enjoyed in the candle-lit restaurant.
37 Annexe4 5 in 4 bedrooms CTV in all bedrooms **T** ✱ S10% sB&B £58-£80 dB&B £65-£140
80P CFA *xmas*
English & French S10% Lunch fr£15.50&alc Dinner £21.50-£25.50 Last dinner 9.30pm
Credit Cards 1 2 3 5 £

★★***Angel*** North St GU29 9DJ (Embassy) ☎(073081)2421
This country-town, commercial hotel, recently refurbished to provide comfortable accommodation, has character and a friendly, informal atmosphere.
17rm(12 4)2 CTV in all bedrooms ® **T**
CTV 60P
English & French
Credit Cards 1 2 3 4 5

✕**Hindle Wakes** 1 Church Hill GU29 9NX ☎(073081)3371
A delightful small restaurant, meticulously run by a sister and brother team and still little-known at the time of printing. Chef Lisa Francis-Lang offers a short, fixed-price menu of imaginative and stylishly cooked starters and main courses. Terrines are particularly good, and light sauces complement main courses such as lamb cutlets with tarragon mousse, and pigeon with honey and fresh fig. Service is very attentive, and a good selection of wines is available too.
Closed Sun & Mon, 2 wks Oct & 2 wks Feb
Lunch not served Tue
20 seats ✱ Lunch £12.50 Dinner £16.50 Last lunch 1.45pm Last dinner 9.30pm nc12yrs
Credit Cards 1

MIDSOMER NORTON Somerset Map **03** ST65

★★★59% **Centurion** Charlton Ln BA3 4BD ☎(0761)417711 FAX (0761) 418351
A well-established sports club and golf course, with the recent addition of some particularly well-furnished, pleasant bedrooms. Public areas tend in style to be more in keeping with the sports club.
17 CTV in all bedrooms ® **T** (ex guide dogs) sB&B £42-£48 dB&B £53-£66
100P (heated) 9 squash snooker sauna
English & Continental **V** Lunch £12.50-£15.50&alc Dinner £13-£16&alc Last dinner 10pm
Credit Cards 1 2 3 5

MILDENHALL Suffolk Map **05** TL77

★★★61% **Smoke House Inn** Beck Row IP28 8DH ☎(0638)713223 Telex no 817430 FAX (0638) 712202
Situated in the centre of the village of Beck Row, this busy inn is housed in a range of modern buildings which include a restaurant and cocktail bar. Service and facilities are available over long hours.
105 Annexe10 (20fb) CTV in all bedrooms ® **T** (ex guide dogs) S10% sB&B £48-£52 dB&B £60-£65
CTV 200P *xmas*
V S10% Lunch £7-£10&alc High tea £6-£8 Dinner £10-£12&alc Last dinner 10pm
Credit Cards 1 2 3 £

See advertisement on page 483

★★**Bell** High St IP28 7EA (Best Western) ☎(0638)717272 Telex no 94011647 FAX (0638) 717057
Situated in the heart of Mildenhall, parts of this inn date back to the 1600s. Accommodation is modest with reasonable facilities, and a large bar continues to be very popular.
17rm(11 2)(3fb) CTV in all bedrooms ® **T** sB&B£31-£34 sB&B £36-£39 dB&B£45-£49 dB&B £50-£55
25P *xmas*
V Lunch fr£8.95&alc High tea fr£3.50 Dinner £9-£14alc Last dinner 9pm
Credit Cards 1 2 3 5 £

★★**Riverside** Mill St IP28 7DP (Best Western) ☎(0638)717274 Telex no 94011647
Popular with families from the nearby Air Force Base, the listed red brick house stands at the end of the town's main road, its rear lawns stretching down to the River Lark.
19rm(9 6)(4fb) CTV in all bedrooms ® **T** ✱ sB&B£30 sB&B £33 dB&B £44
Lift 45P *xmas*
International **V** Lunch £8-£20alc High tea £2.50-£4.50 Dinner £8-£20alc Last dinner 9pm
Credit Cards 1 2 3 5 £

MILFORD HAVEN Dyfed Map **02** SM90

★★**Lord Nelson** Hamilton Ter SA73 3AL ☎(06462)5341 Telex no 48622 FAX (06462) 2274
Comfortable, modern hotel.
32rm(16 16)(1fb)1 in 2 bedrooms CTV in all bedrooms ® **T** ✱ sB&B £36 dB&B £55
CTV 26P
English & French **V** Lunch £10.55-£15.35alc Dinner £10.55-£15.35alc Last dinner 9.30pm
Credit Cards 1 2 3 5 £

★★**Sir Benfro** Herbrandston SA73 3TD (3m W on unclass rd) ☎(06462)4242 due to change to (0646) 694242
RS 25 Dec
A small, friendly hotel.
12 (1fb) CTV in all bedrooms ® **T** sB&B £25.88 dB&B £35
50P
English & French **V** Lunch £6.95-£12.55alc Dinner £6.95-£12.55alc Last dinner 9.45pm
Credit Cards 1 3 £

MILFORD-ON-SEA Hampshire Map **04** SZ29

★★★72% **South Lawn** Lymington Rd SO41 0RF ☎Lymington(0590)43911
Closed 22 Dec-13 Jan
This former Dower House, set in well-kept grounds, provides a warm welcome and personal service. There is a comfortable lounge and spacious dining room, and bedrooms and bathrooms are also of a good size and spotlessly clean. Fresh food, full of flavour, is complemented by a well-chosen wine list, neither being over priced. Many of the guests return regularly.
24 (2fb) CTV in all bedrooms **T** sB&B fr£41 dB&B fr£71
50P nc7yrs
International **V** Lunch fr£9.25 Dinner fr£12.25 Last dinner 8.30pm
Credit Cards 1 3

See advertisement under LYMINGTON

★★★ 64% **Westover Hall** Park Ln SO41 0PT
☏Lymington(0590)43044 FAX (0590) 44490
Swiss owned and managed, you are assured of the personal attention of the proprietors at this hotel, where service is warm and informal. It is a late Victorian house with fine, wood-panelled walls, well appointed bedrooms and fine sea views across to the Isle of Wight. The carefully produced table d'hôte menus are imaginative.
13⇨ CTV in all bedrooms ® **T** sB&B⇨£32-£50 dB&B⇨£64-£100 ⊟
50P ✽ *xmas*
English **V** Lunch £8.50-£16.95 High tea £2.50-£7 Dinner £12.95-£16.95
Credit Cards [1] [2] [3] [5] £

MILNGAVIE Strathclyde *Dunbartonshire* Map **11** NS57

★★★ 59% **Black Bull Thistle** Main St G62 6BH (Thistle) ☏041-956 2291 Telex no 778323 FAX 041-956 1896
A former coaching inn has been tastefully restored to retain the character of its historic past. Quality and tradition are reflected in the beamed ceilings, polished oak and tapestries of the public rooms, whilst bedrooms offer all modern facilities.
27⇨♠(2fb) CTV in all bedrooms ® **T** ✱ sB⇨♠£50-£60 dB⇨♠£58-£70 (room only) ⊟
(120P ♫
International Lunch fr£6.75&alc Dinner fr£12.75&alc Last dinner 9.30pm
Credit Cards [1] [2] [3] [4] [5]

MILTON Dyfed Map **02** SN00

★★**Milton Manor** SA70 8PG (Exec Hotel)
☎Carew(0646)651398 FAX (0646) 651897
Set in 7 acres of secluded woodlands, this Georgian manor house is family run by experienced hoteliers with the chef/proprietor ensuring good quality food.
19rm(14⇨5↱)(1fb) CTV in all bedrooms ® **T** sB&B⇨↱£30 dB&B⇨↱£44 ⊟
CTV 40P ✲ putting *xmas*
☋ International **V** ♢ ☕ Lunch £11.50-£14alc Dinner fr£8.50&alc Last dinner 9.30pm
Credit Cards [1] [3] Ⓔ

MILTON ABBAS Dorset Map **03** ST80

★★♛**Milton Manor**
DT11 0AZ
☎(0258)880254

Tudor style hotel in its own grounds.

12rm(6⇨3↱)(2fb)1⊞ CTV in all bedrooms ® **T** ✗ (ex guide dogs) sB&B£36 sB&B⇨↱£38 dB&B£59 dB&B⇨↱£63 ⊟
CTV 50P ⊞ ✲ putting green croquet *xmas*
V ♢ ☕ Lunch £10.50 High tea £3.50-£7.50 Dinner £14 Last dinner 9pm
Credit Cards [1] [3] Ⓔ

MILTON COMMON Oxfordshire Map **02** SP60

See also **Oxford**
★★★64% **Belfry** Brimpton Grange OX9 2JW (Inter)
☎Great Milton(0844)279381 Telex no 837968
FAX (0844) 279624
Closed 25-30 Dec
Large, half-timbered country house in extensive grounds.
60rm(52⇨8↱) CTV in all bedrooms ® **T**
sB&B⇨↱£57.50-£70
dB&B⇨↱£70-£85 Continental breakfast ⊟
☾ 200P ✲ CFA ⇨ volley ball ♫
☋ English & Continental **V** ♢ ☕ Lunch fr£11&alc Dinner £14.50-£16&alc Last dinner 9.30pm
Credit Cards [1] [2] [3] [5]

MILTON, GREAT Oxfordshire Map **04** SP60

❀❀❀★★★♛
LE MANOIR AUX QUAT' SAISONS

OX9 7PD (Relais et Châteaux) ☎(0844)278881
Telex no 837552
FAX (0844) 278847
Closed 22 Dec-20 Jan

(9m SE of Oxford, follow signs to Wallingford from junc A40/A329 (M40 junc 7) then second turning right).

There are few more refreshing experiences than a night or two at Raymond Blanc's marvellous 15th-century manor house. It feels like a little corner of France, and a friendly, welcoming atmosphere prevails. Floral displays abound in the public areas, which include a bright reception foyer and comfortable salon. Although most come here for Blanc's legendary cuisine, guests will want for nothing in the sumptuous bedrooms. Individually styled, with antique furnishings and pretty fabrics, each is well equipped and provided with an array of extras. Breakfast is taken in the bedroom, and those who might prefer a cooked breakfast will surely be impressed by the standard of coffee, croissants and preserves, with other delights such as French yoghurt. A boiled egg may be had on request. A view over part of Le Manoir's 27 acres of gardens and parkland makes a backcloth to the elegant, pretty restaurant. This is Raymond Blanc's stage, the setting for his splendid French cuisine. The extensive à la carte, together with a menu gourmand, can occasionally stretch the kitchen to the limit, resulting in some minor disappointments, but the norm is the near perfection found by our inspectors in dishes such as a superb courgette en fleur farcie, and a rich, intense millefeuille de pommes de terres et navets au foie gras, sauce au vieux Xeres. The wine list is generally pricey but comprehensive and service is immaculate.
10⇨(2fb)2⊞ CTV in all bedrooms **T** ✗ S10% dB&B⇨£150-£300 Continental breakfast ⊟
☾ 60P ✲ ⇨(heated) ♀ (hard) U clay pigeon shooting croquet nc8yrs
☋ French **V** ♢ ☕ ✗ S10% Lunch £21.50-£48&alc Dinner fr£48&alc Last dinner 10.30pm
Credit Cards [1] [2] [3] [4] [5]

MILTON KEYNES Buckinghamshire Map **04** SP83

See also **Newport Pagnell, Wicken and Woburn**

★★★★**57% Post House** 500 Saxon Gate West MK9 2HQ (Trusthouse Forte) ☎(0908)667722 Telex no 826893 FAX (0908) 674714

Spacious public areas, comfortable, well-equipped bedrooms and good leisure facilities are provided at this modern commercial hotel.

163⇌(4fb)⊁in 8 bedrooms CTV in all bedrooms ® **T** ✱ S% sB⇌£67-£79 dB⇌£82-£95 (room only) ⋿

Lift ☾ ⊞ 80P ▣(heated) sauna solarium gymnasium health & fitness centre *xmas*

V ✿ ☕ ⊁ Lunch fr£8.95&alc Dinner fr£14.50&alc Last dinner 11pm

Credit Cards 1 2 3 5

★★★**63% Friendly Lodge** Monks Way, Two Mile Ash MK8 8LY (junct A5/A422) (Consort) ☎(0908)561666 Telex no 826152 FAX (0908) 568303

A modern hotel with conference facilities, which has the spacious well-equipped and comfortable bedrooms expected of a busy commercial hotel. The restaurant has a carvery and à la carte menu. Service is friendly and informal.

50⇌(8fb)2⊟⊁in 8 bedrooms CTV in all bedrooms ® **T** ✱ sB&B⇌£49.50-£59.50 dB&B⇌£65-£69.50 Continental breakfast

☾ CTV 76P (charged) ❁

V ✿ ☕ Lunch £9.25-£10.50&alc Dinner £10.50-£11.75&alc Last dinner 10pm

Credit Cards 1 2 3 5 £

MINCHINHAMPTON

See **Amberley**

MINEHEAD Somerset Map **03** SS94

During the currency of this publication Minehead telephone numbers are liable to change.

★★★**Beacon Country House** Beacon Rd TA24 5SD ☎(0643)3476

Family-run Edwardian house set in 20 acres high above the town. Recently restored to a high standard, the hotel offers fresh, comfortable rooms, imaginative cuisine and caring service.

7rm(5⇌2↱) CTV in all bedrooms ® **T** ✗ (ex guide dogs) ✱ S5% dB&B⇌↱£48-£54 (incl dinner) ⋿

14P ⇍ ❁ ≏ ∪

♀ French **V** ✿ ☕ S5% Lunch 90p-£12alc Dinner £16.50 Last dinner 9.30pm

Credit Cards 1 3

★★★ **70% Benares** Northfield Rd TA24 5PT (Consort) ☎(0643)4911

Closed 23 Nov-mid Mar (ex Xmas)

Friendly holiday and business hotel, with good restaurant and fine gardens.

20rm(18⇌1↱)(2fb) CTV in all bedrooms ® **T** sB&B⇌↱£26.50-£33 dB&B⇌↱£53-£64 ⋿

20P 2🚗 (£1.25) ⇍ ❁ ⌂ *xmas*

♀ English, French & Italian **V** ✿ ☕ ⊁ Bar Lunch £5-£12alc Dinner £13.50 Last dinner 8.30pm

Credit Cards 1 2 3 5

★★★ **67% Northfield** Northfield Rd TA24 5PU (Best Western) ☎(0643)5155 Telex no 42513

Set in 2 acres of interesting gardens, just 100 yards from the sea, this beautifully kept hotel offers good lounges as well as indoor sports facilities. It is very popular with retired British holidaymakers.

24rm(23⇌1↱)(7fb) CTV in all bedrooms ® **T** sB&B⇌↱£36-£43 dB&B⇌↱£74-£96 ⋿

Lift 44P ⇍ ❁ ▣(heated) gymnasium putting green steam room spa bath *xmas*

V ✿ ☕ ⊁ Lunch £5.25-£7.95 Dinner £11.95 Last dinner 8.30pm

Credit Cards 1 2 3 5

★★**Beaconwood** Church Road, North Hill TA24 5SB ☎(0643)2032

Closed Xmas

Peaceful, family-run hotel outside the town centre.

16rm(8⇌3↱)(3fb) CTV in all bedrooms ® sB&B£21 sB&B⇌↱£26 dB&B£38 dB&B⇌↱£48 ⋿

CTV 25P ❁ ≏(heated) ℘ (grass) ⌂

V ✿ ☕ ⊁ Bar Lunch £1.25-£2.50 High tea £3.50-£7 Dinner £10 Last dinner 8pm

Credit Cards 1 3

★★***Merton*** Western Ln, The Parks TA24 8BZ ☎(0643)2375

Small, holiday and business hotel, that is comfortable and personally run.

12rm(3⇌3↱)(3fb) CTV in all bedrooms ®

CTV 15P ❁

✿ ☕

Credit Cards 1 3

★★**Winsor** The Avenue TA24 5AW ☎(0643)2171

Closed 4 Oct-5 May

Large, seasonal, holiday hotel run by the owners.

33rm(10⇌1↱)(4fb) CTV in all bedrooms ® ✱ sB&B£15 dB&B£30 dB&B⇌↱£36 (incl dinner)

CTV 26P ⇍

V ✿ ⊁ Bar Lunch fr£2.50 Dinner fr£7 Last dinner 8pm

Credit Cards 1 2 3 5

★★**York** The Avenue TA24 5AN ☎(0643)5151 due to change t o 705151

The detached, stone-built, gabled hotel stands on the main road from the town centre to the beach. The large bar offers a good range of bar foods, and facilities are sound throughout.

21rm(8⇌4↱)(5fb) CTV in 12bedrooms ® **T** ✗ ✱ sB&B£13-£14 sB&B⇌↱£17-£19 dB&B£26-£28 dB&B⇌↱£36-£38

CTV 12P nc5yrs

✿ Dinner £5.50-£10.50alc Last dinner 9pm

Credit Cards 1 2 3 5

★**Kingsway** Ponsford Rd TA24 5DY ☎(0643)2313

Closed 7 Nov-21 Mar

Comfortable, privately-owned and run hotel.

8rm(6⇌2↱)(2fb) CTV in all bedrooms ® S% sB&B⇌↱£20-£25 dB&B⇌↱£32-£42 ⋿

CTV 8P ⇍ nc3yrs *xmas*

✿ ☕ ⊁ S% Dinner £8.50-£10.50 Last dinner 7pm

Credit Cards 1 3

★**Mentone** The Parks TA24 8BS ☎(0643)5229 due to change t o 705229

Closed Nov-Mar

The small, privately owned and personally run hotel offers thoughtfully prepared, imaginative menus and provides an ideal centre for touring.

9rm(5⇌2↱) CTV in all bedrooms ® ✗ sB&B£15-£19 dB&B⇌↱£30-£38 ⋿

5P 2🚗 ⇍ nc8yrs

♀ English, Asian & Continental ✿ ☕ ⊁ Bar Lunch fr£2alc Dinner £5-£6.50 Last dinner 6.45pm

MINSTEAD Hampshire Map **04** SU21

✕***Honeysuckle Cottage*** SO43 7FX ☎Southampton(0703)813122

Lunch not served

♀ English & French 45 seats Last dinner 9.30pm 20P

Credit Cards 1

MISKIN Mid Glamorgan Map **03** ST08

★★★ **69%** ***Miskin Manor*** CF7 8ND ☎Llantrisant(0443)224204
Telex no 444969 FAX (0443) 237606
Recently refurbished to a high standard, this stone-built hotel has comfortable public rooms and bedrooms.
32⇌🚿(3fb)2🛏⚡in 6 bedrooms CTV in all bedrooms **T** ✈
☾ 100P 🚗 ✲ (heated) squash snooker sauna solarium gymnasium steam room, badminton ⌂.
V ♥ ☕ Last dinner 9.45pm
Credit Cards [1] [2] [3] [5]

See advertisement under CARDIFF

MOCHRUM Dumfries & Galloway *Wigtownshire*
Map **10** NX34

★***Greenmantle*** DG8 9LY ☎Port William(09887)357
Converted from a 17th century manse, this hotel stands in its own grounds in the centre of this small country village.
7rm(6🚿)(1fb)
CTV 20P 🚗 ✲
V ♥ ☕

MOFFAT Dumfries & Galloway *Dumfriesshire* Map **11** NT00

See also **Beattock**

★★★ **60% Moffat House** High St DG10 9HL (Exec Hotel)
☎(0683)20039
Closed Jan-mid Mar
Fine 18th-century Adam mansion with wide country views at rear. Nicely decorated rooms and attentive service.
16rm(8⇌8🚿)(3fb) CTV in all bedrooms ® **T**
sB&B⇌🚿£30-£32.50 dB&B⇌🚿£49-£54 ⊟
40P 2🚘 ✲ ⌂
☺ Scottish & French **V** ♥ ⚡ Bar Lunch £5-£8 Dinner £11.50-£19alc Last dinner 8.45pm
Credit Cards [1] [2] [3] [5]

★★**Beechwood Country House** Harthorpe Place DG10 9RS
☎(0683)20210
Charmingly set on a hillside above the town, backed by woods and farmland, the small hotel provides accommodation in bedrooms which are, for the most part, spacious and individually decorated. Light lunches are served in an elegant new conservatory, the more adventurous evening meal is accompanied by a well laid out wine list, and guests are unobtrusively pampered by the enthusiastic proprietors and their friendly staff.
7rm(6⇌1🚿) CTV in all bedrooms ® **T** sB&B⇌🚿fr£51.15
dB&B⇌🚿fr£85 (incl dinner)
15P 🚗 ✲ *xmas*
V ♥ ☕ ⚡ Lunch £2.50-£4.50alc Dinner £14.95 Last dinner 9pm
Credit Cards [1] [2] [3]

See advertisement on page 487

★**The Star Hotel** 44 High St DG10 9EF ☎(0683)20156
This central, family-run hotel is reputed to be Britain's narrowest. An attractive dinning room, comfortable lounge bar and well-equipped first floor bedrooms are the result of steady improvements.
8rm(5🚿) CTV in 5bedrooms TV in 3bedrooms ® **T** ✱
sB&B£15-£25 sB&B🚿£22-£25 dB&B£30-£36 dB&B🚿£36 ⊟
CTV 🅿̸
V ♥ ☕ ⚡ Lunch £3-£7.95 High tea fr£4.40 Dinner £3.50-£8
Last dinner 9pm
Credit Cards [1] [3]

★**Well View** Ballplay Rd DG10 9JU ☎(0683)20184
7rm(1⇌4🚿)(1fb)1🛏⚡in 2 bedrooms CTV in all bedrooms ®
✱ sB&B£18-£21 sB&B⇌🚿£34-£37 dB&B£36-£42
dB&B⇌🚿£48-£66 ⊟
8P 🚗 ✲ *xmas*

▶

M

☋ Scottish & French ✿ ☐ ⊁ Lunch £6.50-£8.50 Dinner £10.50-£13 Last dinner 8pm
Credit Cards [1] [3]

MOLD

See **Northop Hall**

MONIAIVE Dumfries & Galloway *Dumfriesshire* Map **11** NX79

★★Woodlea DG3 4EN ☏(08482)209
Closed 6 Jan-mid Mar RS Xmas
This off-beat country hotel caters particularly for family holidays, the exuberantly youthful enthusiasm of its proprietors creating a very lively atmosphere and providing a comprehensive range of pursuits during the high season. Prospective guests can send for the hotel's video.
14rm(7⇌)(7fb) CTV in all bedrooms Ⓡ ✳ sB&B£20-£30 sB&B⇌£25-£35 dB&B£40-£60 dB&B⇌£50-£70 (incl dinner) ⊟
CTV 20P ✿ ▭(heated) ℘ (hard) sauna solarium gymnasium pony riding croquet putting games room *xmas*
V ✿ ☐ ⊁ Bar Lunch 55p-£10.55 Dinner £10-£11 Last dinner 8.30pm

MONK FRYSTON North Yorkshire Map **08** SE52

★★★ 68% Monk Fryston Hall LS25 5DU
☏South Milford (0977)682369
Telex no 556634
FAX (0977) 683544

This historic, characterful, stone-built house, set in beautiful gardens and retaining open fires in its oak-panelled bar and bar-lounge, offers a good standard of cuisine in its pleasant restaurant.
29⇌▶(2fb)1⊞ CTV in all bedrooms Ⓡ T S10% sB&B⇌▶£50-£58 dB&B⇌▶£70-£85 ⊟
☾ 60P ✿ ✿ *xmas*
✿ S10% Lunch £8.85-£9.50&alc Dinner £13.25-£14&alc Last dinner 9.30pm
Credit Cards [1] [2] [3]

MONMOUTH Gwent Map **03** SO51

★★★ 61% Kings Head Agincourt Square NP5 3DY (Inter) ☏(0600)2177 Telex no 497294
Professionally-run by the Geogh family for over two decades, this comfortable 17th-century inn provides good food and conference facilities.
29rm(20⇌9▶)(2fb)1⊞ CTV in all bedrooms T sB⇌▶£42-£50 dB⇌▶£62 (room only) ⊟
☾ 20P CFA *xmas*
☋ English, French & Italian V ✿ Lunch £12.50 Dinner £20-£22 Last dinner 9pm
Credit Cards [1] [2] [3] [5]

★★Riverside Cinderhill St NP5 3EY (Minotels) ☏(0600)5577 & 3236
6▶Annexe6▶(1fb) CTV in all bedrooms Ⓡ T ✗ (ex guide dogs)
30P
☋ European V ✿ ☐ Last dinner 9.30pm
Credit Cards [1] [3] [5]

★*Talocher Farmhouse* Wonastow Rd NP5 4DN ☏Dingestow(060083)236 & 450
Small, character, rural hotel.
9rm(1⇌1▶)⊁in 5 bedrooms CTV in all bedrooms Ⓡ
CTV 20P ✿ ✿ ⇌ sauna solarium
☋ English& Continental V ✿ ☐ Last dinner 10pm
Credit Cards [1] [2] [3]

MONTACUTE Somerset Map **03** ST41

★★Kings Arms Inn TA15 6UU ☏Martock(0935)822513
Dating back to the 16th century, this attractive, Ham stone inn stands at the centre of the village. Run by a young, enthusiastic management team, it has a good dining room serving popular modern dishes. Whilst some bedrooms are compact, they are all smart and have many facilities.
11⇌1⊞ CTV in all bedrooms Ⓡ T sB⇌£43-£56 dB⇌£59-£75 (room only) ⊟
15P ✿ ✿
☋ English & French V ✿ ☐ ⊁ Sunday Lunch £6.50 Dinner fr£12.50alc Last dinner 9pm
Credit Cards [1] [2] [3] ⓔ

See advertisement under YEOVIL

MONTGOMERY Powys Map **07** SO29

★★Dragon SY15 6AA ☏(068681)359
This fine, former coaching inn, dating back to the sixteenth century, offers friendly hospitality, a warm atmosphere and good food.
14rm(13⇌1▶)(2fb) CTV in all bedrooms Ⓡ T ✗ (ex guide dogs) sB&B⇌▶£32-£39 dB&B⇌▶£49-£60 ⊟
21P *xmas*
☋ Welsh & French V ✿ Lunch £9.75-£20&alc Dinner fr£13.50&alc Last dinner 9.30pm
Credit Cards [1] [3]

MONTROSE Tayside *Angus* Map **15** NO75

★★★ 60% Park 61 John St DD10 8RJ ☏(0674)73415
Telex no 76367 FAX (0674) 77091
A popular and efficiently run business hotel with a friendly atmosphere. Bedrooms are comfortable with practical modern furniture and décor.
59rm(45⇌5▶)(4fb) CTV in all bedrooms Ⓡ T sB&Bfr£28 sB&B⇌▶£30-£48 dB&B⇌▶£42-£65 ⊟
☾ CTV 50P ✿ CFA ⌂ *xmas*
V ✿ ☐ Last high tea 6pm
Credit Cards [1] [2] [3] [5]

MORAR Highland *Inverness-shire* Map **13** NM69

★★Morar PH40 4PA ☏Mallaig(0687)2346
Closed 21 Oct-Mar
Family-run hotel above the white sands of Morar.
27⇌(3fb) Ⓡ
CTV 50P ⌐
V ✿ ☐ Last dinner 8.30pm

MORECAMBE Lancashire Map **07** SD46

★★★Elms Bare LA4 6DD (Consort) ☏(0524)411501
Telex no 57515
Pleasant, comfortable hotel serving home grown English food.
37⇌(1fb)1⊞ CTV in all bedrooms Ⓡ T ✗ sB&B⇌£30-£40 dB&B⇌£50-£60 ⊟
Lift ☾ 60P ✿ CFA *xmas*
V ✿ ☐ ⊁ Lunch £5.75-£7.50 High tea £5-£7.50 Dinner £10.25-£11.50&alc Last dinner 9pm
Credit Cards [1] [2] [3] [4] [5] ⓔ

★★★69% **Headway** Marine Rd East LA4 5AN ☎(0524)412525
Closed 18 Dec-4 Jan RS Nov-Apr
Modern, comfortable and providing courteously attentive service, the hotel offers views across the bay to the Cumbrian fells.
53⇨⌐(4fb) CTV in all bedrooms ® **T** ✖ ✱
sB&B⇨⌐£32-£37 dB&B⇨⌐£51-£67
Lift ☾ 20P
V ♦ ☕ Bar Lunch £1.50-£5 Dinner £9&alc Last dinner 8pm
Credit Cards [1] [2] [3] [5]

★★★65% **Strathmore** East Promenade LA4 5AP (Best Western)
☎(0524)421234 Telex no 65452 FAX (0524) 414242
Friendly traditional hotel with resident proprietors.
51rm(35⇨10⌐)(6fb) CTV in all bedrooms ® **T** ✖ (ex guide dogs) sB&B⇨⌐£42-£50 dB&B⇨⌐£54-£62 ⊟
Lift ☾ 30P 12🚗 ♫ *xmas*
♀ French **V** ♦ ☕ Lunch £7.25-£8.50&alc Dinner £10.50-£12&alc Last dinner 9.30pm
Credit Cards [1] [2] [3] [5] £

★★**Clarendon** Promenade, West End LA4 4EP ☎(0524)410180
Closed Xmas wk
A sea-front hotel providing accommodation in well-appointed bedrooms.
33rm(20⇨7⌐)(4fb) CTV in all bedrooms ® **T** S10%
sB&B⇨⌐£26 dB&B£39 dB&B⇨⌐£39 ⊟
Lift ☾ CTV ⊁ games room
S% Lunch £5 High tea £4-£6 Dinner fr£7&alc Last dinner 9pm
Credit Cards [1] [2] [3] [4] [5] £

MORETONHAMPSTEAD Devon Map **03** SX78

★★♣***Glebe House*** North Bovey TQ13 (1.5m SW)
☎(0647)40544
Closed 20 Dec-Feb

Welcoming former Victorian vicarage offering well-prepared food.
9rm(5⇨4⌐)(1fb) **T**
CTV 40P ✈ ✿
♀ International ♦ ☕
Credit Cards [1] [3]

★★**The White Hart** The Square TQ13 8NF (Minotels)
☎(0647)40406
A traditional inn, built in 1637 and enthusiastically run by the owner, Mr P Morgan and his friendly team of staff, offering a relaxing retreat for the tourist. Though the original character of the hotel has been preserved, modernisation has provided cosy bedrooms, popular bars and a choice of restaurants, meals ranging from a wide variety of bar food to the more imaginative dishes of the à la carte menu. A stay here will give you an excellent base from which to explore South Devon and the Dartmoor National Park.
20⇨(3fb) CTV in all bedrooms ® sB&B⇨£30-£33
dB&B⇨£48-£52.50 ⊟
12P snooker nc10yrs *xmas*
♀ English & French **V** ♦ ☕ ⊁ Bar Lunch £1.60-£3.75 Dinner £9.75-£10.25 Last dinner 8.30pm
Credit Cards [1] [2] [3] [5] £

M

MORETON-IN-MARSH Gloucestershire Map **04** SP23

★★★70% **Manor House** High St GL56 0LJ ☎(0608)50501 Telex no 837151 FAX (0608) 51481
Fine Cotswold hotel, with very comfortable well furnished rooms and candlelit restaurant.
38rm(34⇌)4 CTV in all bedrooms **T** S8% sB&Bfr£27 sB&B⇌fr£49 dB&B⇌fr£68.50
Lift ☾ 25P 4 (charged) (heated) (hard) sauna spa bath nc12yrs *xmas*
Lunch £9-£12 Dinner £18-£22 Last dinner 9pm
Credit Cards 1 2 3 5 £

★★**Redesdale Arms** High St GL56 0AW ☎(0608)50308 Telex no 837928 FAX (0608) 51843
Comfortable well run hotel with good restaurant.
9rm(8⇌1)Annexe8rm(5⇌3)(2fb) CTV in all bedrooms ® **T** (ex guide dogs) sB&B⇌£44.75-£49.50 dB&B⇌£63.25-£82.50
20P *xmas*
V Lunch £9.95-£10.95 High tea £1.75-£5.25 Dinner £11.95-£13.50&alc Last dinner 9.30pm
Credit Cards 1 2 3

★★**The White Hart Royal** High St GL56 0BA (Trusthouse Forte) ☎(0608)50731
A company-owned hotel with a cobbled hallway and a character lounge bar.
18rm(7⇌)in 1 bedroom CTV in all bedrooms ® sB£38-£41 sB⇌£46-£50 dB£51-£55 dB⇌£61-£66 (room only)
10P *xmas*
V Lunch fr£9.50 Dinner fr£11.50alc Last dinner 9.30pm
Credit Cards 1 2 3 4 5

M

MORFA NEFYN Gwynedd Map **06** SH24

★★**Linksway** LL53 6BG ☎Nefyn(0758)720258
Ideally located for golfing and beaches, this comfortable, modernised hotel maintains good standards in accommodation and food, backing these with friendly service.
26rm(11⇌10)(1fb) CTV in all bedrooms ® sB&B£14-£21.50 sB&B⇌£15-£22.50 dB&B£28-£43 dB&B⇌£30-£45
60P 2 ♫ *xmas*
English & Italian Sunday Lunch £5 Dinner £8.50 Last dinner 9pm
£

MORPETH Northumberland Map **12** NZ28

★★★★76% **Linden Hall Hotel** NE65 8XG (Prestige) ☎(0670)516611 Telex no 538224 FAX (0670) 88544
(For full entry see Longhorsley)

MORTEHOE

See **Woolacombe**

MOTTRAM ST ANDREW Cheshire Map **07** SJ87

★★★67% **Mottram Hall** Prestbury SK10 4QT (De Vere) ☎Prestbury(0625)828135 Telex no 668181 FAX (0625) 829284
Georgian mansion built in 1721, standing in formal gardens surrounded by 120 acres of parkland.
95⇌(10fb)7in 12 bedrooms CTV in all bedrooms ® **T** S% sB&B⇌fr£80 dB&B⇌fr£100
☾ 250P CFA (heated) (hard & grass) squash snooker sauna solarium gymnasium croquet putting ♫
English & French **V** Lunch fr£11.50 Dinner fr£17.50 Last dinner 9.45pm
Credit Cards 1 2 3 5

MOULSFORD-ON-THAMES Oxfordshire Map **04** SU58

★★***Beetle & Wedge*** Ferry Ln OX10 9JF ☎Cholsey(0491)651381
This pretty, rose-brick hotel, its garden bordering the Thames, provides neat, attractive bedrooms. Restaurant and bars are popular.
10⇌Annexe2(2fb)1 CTV in 15bedrooms ® **T**
54P
V Last dinner 9.45pm
Credit Cards 1 2 3 5

MOULTON North Yorkshire Map **08** NZ20

✕✕**Black Bull Inn** DL10 6QJ ☎Barton(032577)289 FAX (032577) 422
Closed Sun & 23-31 Dec
Lunch not served Sat
100 seats ✱ Lunch £8.75&alc Dinner £16.25-£31alc Last lunch 2pm Last dinner 10.15pm 80P nc7yrs
Credit Cards 1 2 3

MOUNT HAWKE Cornwall & Isles of Scilly Map **02** NZ20

★**Tregarthen Country Cottage** Banns Rd TR4 8BW ☎Porthtowan(0209)890399
A charming, cottage-style hotel, set on the edge of the village and enthusiastically managed by Clive and Mavis Hutton. Wholesome, home-cooked meals, with a limited choice, are served at dinner. Co-ordinating fabrics have been used to good effect in the bedrooms, several of which have queen-sized beds – one also boasting a corner spa bath – whilst the well-appointed dining room and two comfortable lounges maintain the overall air of quality.
6rm(5⇌1) (ex guide dogs) sB&B⇌£25-£27 dB&B⇌£50-£54 (incl dinner)
CTV 12P
Dinner fr£9 Last dinner 8pm

MOUSEHOLE Cornwall & Isles of Scilly Map **02** SW42

★★**Carn Du** Raginnis Hill TR19 6SS ☎Penzance(0736)731233
Closed 5 Feb-9 Mar
The small, personally-run hotel serves home-cooked food with an emphasis on fresh local fish and vegetables. Its windows offer panoramic views across Mount's Bay.
7rm(1⇌5) CTV in 3bedrooms TV in 1bedroom ® sB&B⇌£23-£27 dB&B⇌£38-£46
CTV 12P *xmas*
English & German **V** Bar Lunch fr£3 Dinner fr£11.45 Last dinner 8pm
Credit Cards 1 2 3

★★**Lobster Pot** South Cliff TR19 6QX ☎Penzance(0736)731251 FAX (0736) 731140
Closed early Jan-mid Mar
Well-appointed character hotel and restaurant overhanging the small village harbour.
14rm(12⇌2)Annexe12rm(7⇌2)(5fb) CTV in all bedrooms ® **T** S10% sB&B£20.50-£30.50 sB&B⇌£25.20-£36.20 dB&B£41-£61 dB&B⇌£50.40-£72.40
xmas
English & French S10% Sunday Lunch £7.70 Dinner £13.75&alc Last dinner 9.45pm
Credit Cards 1 2 3

MUCH BIRCH Hereford & Worcester Map **03** SO53

★★★60% **Pilgrim** HR2 8HJ (Inter) ☎Golden Valley(0981)540742 Telex no 35332
With splendid views of the countryside from most of its rooms, this hotel offers comfort and relaxation for the traveller.
19rm(16⇌2)1 CTV in all bedrooms ® **T** (ex guide dogs) sB&B⇌£39.50-£45 dB&B⇌£52-£58

40P ✻ croquet putting pitch & putt *xmas*
English & French **V** Lunch £7.75 Dinner £15.75&alc Last dinner 9.45pm
Credit Cards [1] [2] [3] [5] (£)

See advertisement under HEREFORD

MUCH WENLOCK Shropshire Map **07** SO69

★★Gaskell Arms Bourton Rd TF13 6AQ ☎(0952)727212
This pleasant and comfortable hotel, originally a 17th-century coaching inn, has been tastefully modernised and stands conveniently close to the town centre.
11rm(3⇌)(2fb) CTV in 3bedrooms TV in 8bedrooms ® sB&Bfr£22 sB&B⇌£30 dB&Bfr£35 dB&B⇌£45
30P 1 ✻
V S% Lunch £7.95 Dinner £10-£15alc Last dinner 9.30pm
Credit Cards [1] [3]

MUDEFORD

See **Christchurch**

MUIRHEAD Strathclyde *Lanarkshire* Map **11** NS66

✕✕*La Campágnola* 112 Cumbernauld Rd G69 9AA ☎041-779 3405 & 041-779 3020
Smart little Italian restaurant with good atmosphere.
French & Italian **V** 80 seats Last lunch 2.45pm Last dinner 10.30pm 30P ♫
Credit Cards [1] [2] [3] [5]

MUIR OF ORD Highland *Ross & Cromarty* Map **14** NH55

★★Ord Arms Great North Rd IV6 7XR
☎Inverness(0463)870286
Attractive, sandstone building set back from the main road on the northern outskirts of town.
11rm(4⇌3)(2fb) CTV in all bedrooms ® **T** sB&B£20-£22 sB&B⇌£25-£28 dB&B£30-£34 dB&B⇌£38-£44
CTV 120P 6 ✻ solarium ♫ *xmas*
V Last high tea 7pm
Credit Cards [1] [3] (£)

MULL, ISLE OF Strathclyde *Argyllshire* Map **10**

CRAIGNURE Map **10** NM73

★★★ 58% Isle Of Mull PA65 6BB (Scottish Highland)
☎(06802)351 Telex no 778215
Closed Nov-Mar
Comfortable, friendly tourist hotel with panoramic views from all rooms.
60⇌(8fb) CTV in all bedrooms ® sB&B⇌fr£41 dB&B⇌fr£71
(50P ✻ ♫
Scottish & French **V** Bar Lunch £4 Dinner fr£12 Last dinner 8.30pm
Credit Cards [1] [2] [3] [5]

TOBERMORY Map **13** NM55

★*Mishnish* Main St PA75 6NU ☎(0688)2009
Small, traditional, Highland hotel overlooking the picturesque Tobermory Bay.
12rm(7⇌3)(2fb) CTV in all bedrooms ®
CTV squash snooker ♫
V Last dinner 9pm

★*Tobermory* 53 Main St PA75 6NT ☎(0688)2091
RS Oct-Apr
Delightful, little waterfront hotel with charming lounges, bright, cheerful bedrooms and a cosy dining room.

▶

15rm(3⇨2🚿)(2fb) ®
CTV ₱ ⛟ sailing on hotel yacht
European V ♈ Last dinner 7.45pm

★Ulva House PA75 6PR ☎(0688)2044
Closed Nov-Feb
On the hillside with views of the bay, this small friendly, family-run hotel has pretty, compact bedrooms, and an excellent local reputation for their home cooking.
6rm(1🚿)(3fb) TV available ® ✳ sB&B£17.50-£27.50 dB&B£35 dB&B🚿£42
8P ⛟ ✲ wildlife expeditions
International V ♈ Lunch £10.95&alc Dinner £10.95&alc Last dinner 8pm

MULLION Cornwall & Isles of Scilly Map **02** SW61

★★★69% Polurrian TR12 7EN ☎(0326)240421
Telex no 94015906 FAX (0326) 240083
Closed 8 Dec-14 Mar
Family holiday hotel superbly situated in 12 acres of terraced grounds overlooking Polurrian Cove with its fine surfing beach.
39⇨🚿(20fb)5⊞ CTV in all bedrooms **T** ✳ S%
sB&B⇨🚿£35-£61 dB&B⇨🚿£64-£140 (incl dinner) ⊟
☾ CTV 60P 3🚗(£5) ⛟ ✲ CFA ⊡(heated) ⛱(heated) ⚲ (hard) squash snooker sauna solarium gymnasium cricket net whirlpool putting ♫
English & French V ♈ ⊻ S% Lunch £5-£8 High tea £5-£6 Dinner £12-£15&alc Last dinner 8.30pm
Credit Cards 1 2 3 5

★★Mullion Cove TR12 7EP ☎(0326)240328
Closed 6 Nov-2 Mar
The hotel offers a relaxed, friendly atmosphere and panoramic views over Mount's Bay.
36rm(17⇨4🚿)(8fb) CTV in all bedrooms ® sB&B£19-£22 dB&B£38-£44 dB&B⇨🚿£42-£54 ⊟
CTV 50P 5🚗(charged) ✲ ⛱(heated) ⚲ (hard) sauna solarium *xmas*
English & Continental V ♈ ⊻ Sunday Lunch £4-£6 Dinner £11-£13.50 Last dinner 8.30pm
Credit Cards 1 3 5 £

MUMBLES (near Swansea) West Glamorgan Map **02** SS68

See also **Langland Bay and Swansea**
★St Anne's Western Ln SA3 4EY ☎Swansea(0792)369147
Telex no 498450 FAX (0222) 374671
Small, quiet, modern hotel overlooking Swansea Bay.
24rm(15⇨1🚿)Annexe4rm(2🚿)(1fb) CTV in all bedrooms ® **T** ✖ sB&B£20 sB&B⇨🚿£25 dB&B£32 dB&B⇨🚿£38 ⊟
CTV 50P ✲ snooker
V ♈ ⊻ Lunch £6-£7 High tea £3 Dinner £6-£7 Last dinner 8.30pm
Credit Cards 1 £

MUNDESLEY-ON-SEA Norfolk Map **09** TG33

★★Manor NR11 8BG ☎Mundesley(0263)720309
Closed 3-15 Jan
26rm(9⇨12🚿)(2fb) sB&B£20 sB&B⇨🚿fr£22.50 dB&B£30-£34 dB&B⇨🚿£32.50-£36.50 ⊟
CTV 50P ⛱(heated) ♫ *xmas*
V ♈ ⊻ Lunch fr£5.95 High tea £6.90-£20alc Dinner £6.95-£8.95 Last dinner 8.50pm

All the information in the guide is annually updated, but details of prices and facilities may change during the currency of this guide.

MUNGRISDALE Cumbria Map **11** NY33

★The Mill CA11 0XR (Guestaccom) ☎Threlkeld(059683)659
Closed Dec & Jan
Charming, country hotel providing hospitality, comfort and good home cooking.
8rm(5⇨)(1fb) CTV in 5bedrooms ® ✳ sB&B£23.50-£26.50 sB&B⇨£28.50-£31.50 dB&B£39-£43 dB&B⇨£49-£53
CTV 15P ⛟ ✲ ⚓ games room
English & French V ♈ ⊻ ⚡ S% Dinner £12.75 Last dinner 8pm

MUSSELBURGH Lothian *Midlothian* Map **11** NT37

○***Granada Lodge*** A1 Old Craighall EH21 8RE (Granada) ☎031-653 6070
Due to have opened Sep 1989
44⇨

NAIRN Highland *Nairnshire* Map **14** NH85

★★★★55% Golf View Seabank Rd IV12 4HG ☎(0667)52301
Telex no 75134
Well situated hotel overlooking Moray Firth, and offering fine, mainly nouvelle cuisine.
55rm(46⇨9🚿)(5fb)1⊞ CTV in all bedrooms **T**
sB&B⇨🚿£47-£54 dB&B⇨🚿£78-£93 ⊟
Lift ☾ 40P ✲ CFA ⛱(heated) ⚲ (hard) sauna gymnasium putting green ♫ *xmas*
♈ ⊻ Dinner fr£17.50 Last dinner 9.15pm
Credit Cards 1 2 3 5 £

★★★★51% Newton Inverness Rd IV12 4RX (Consort)
☎(0667)53144 Telex no 739248 FAX (0667)54026
A mixture of Georgian and Scottish baronial architecture, set in 27 secluded acres with excellent views of the Moray Firth. The interesting table d'hôte and à la carte dishes are well-prepared from good ingredients, and the friendly service is efficient and helpful.
30⇨🚿Annexe14⇨🚿(6fb)1⊞ CTV in all bedrooms ® **T** ✳
sB&B⇨🚿£30.50-£43 dB&B⇨🚿£41-£68 ⊟
Lift ☾ CTV 100P ✲ ⚲ (hard) sauna solarium putting *xmas*
Scottish & French V ♈ ⊻ Lunch £6 Dinner £12.50 Last dinner 9.15pm
Credit Cards 1 2 3 5

★★★57% *Windsor* Albert St IV12 4HP ☎(0667)53108
This well-decorated and maintained family-run hotel has modern bedrooms of varying sizes.
60rm(30⇨24🚿)(7fb) CTV in all bedrooms ® **T**
Lift ☾ CTV 40P ✲ CFA ∪ bowling ♫
Scottish & French V ♈ ⊻ Last dinner 9.30pm
Credit Cards 1 2 3 5

★★*Alton Burn* Alton Burn Rd IV12 5ND ☎(0667)52051
RS Oct-Mar
Only the golf course stands between the Moray Firth and this family-run hotel which offers good food, friendly service and some nice family bedrooms.
19rm(14⇨3🚿) CTV in 18bedrooms
CTV 30P ✲ ⛱(heated) ⚲ ∪ putting green
International ♈
Credit Cards 1 3

★★Carnach House Delnies IV12 5NT (2m W A96)
☎(0667)52094
Three miles west of the town, set in 8 acres of wooded grounds beside the A96, this hospitable, family-run hotel offers modestly furnished bedrooms. Good food is served in the small restaurant, and a welcoming atmosphere is created by the log fires that blaze in both the attractive lounge and the cosy bar on cooler days.
9rm(5⇨2🚿)1⊞ CTV in all bedrooms ® **T**
sB&B⇨🚿£28.50-£31.50 dB&B⇨🚿£57 ⊟

15P 🅶 ✲ ∪ *xmas*
V ✆ ☕ ⅟ Lunch fr£6.50 Dinner £12.50-£30 Last dinner 9pm
Credit Cards 1 3

★★Clifton IV12 4HW ☎(0667)53119
Closed Nov-Feb
An ivy-clad, Victorian house, Clifton retains much of its original character. The owners, Mr and Mrs Macintyre, have, over the years, built up a large collection of works of art, paintings, books and antique furniture, which fill every corner of the hotel with interest and originality. Their second love, the theatre, is reflected in the sense of occasion at dinner, as well as in the programme of plays and recitals staged during the winter months. The food is imaginative, and local produce is prepared with a lovely, light touch.
16rm(15⇨1♠)(2fb)3🛏
CTV 20P 🅶 ✲
🍷 Scottish & French V ✆ ☕ ⅟
Credit Cards 1 2 3 5

NANT-DDU (near Merthyr Tydfil) Powys Map **03** SO01

★★*Nant Ddu Lodge Country House* Cwm Taf CF48 2HY (5m N of Merthyr Tydfil on A470 near Brecon) (Minotels)
☎Merthyr Tydfil(0685)79111 FAX (0685) 89136
A former hunting lodge of Lord Tredegar, situated in spectacular scenery of the Brecon Beacons.
15rm(12⇨3♠)(4fb)1🛏⅟in 2 bedrooms CTV in all bedrooms ® T
☾ 60P ✲ 🏠
🍷 English & French V ✆ ☕ Last dinner 10pm
Credit Cards 1 2 3 5

See advertisement on page 493

NANTWICH Cheshire Map **07** SJ65

★★★🏅75% Rookery Hall
Worleston CW5 6DQ (2m N B5074) (Select)

☎(0270)626866
Telex no 367169
FAX (0270)626027

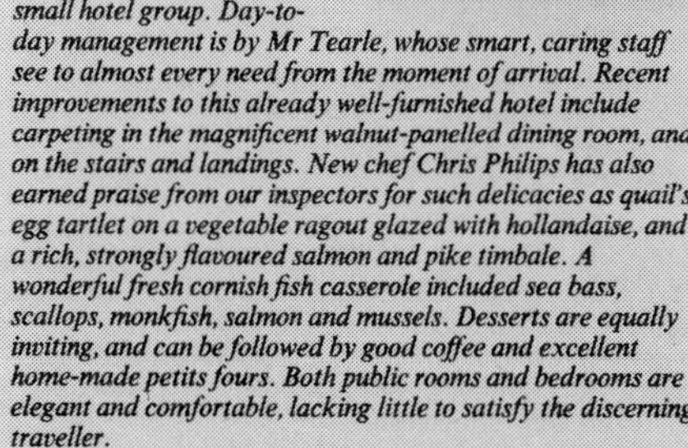

Fine Georgian hall in 28 acres of parkland by the River Weaver, now owned by small hotel group. Day-to-day management is by Mr Tearle, whose smart, caring staff see to almost every need from the moment of arrival. Recent improvements to this already well-furnished hotel include carpeting in the magnificent walnut-panelled dining room, and on the stairs and landings. New chef Chris Philips has also earned praise from our inspectors for such delicacies as quail's egg tartlet on a vegetable ragout glazed with hollandaise, and a rich, strongly flavoured salmon and pike timbale. A wonderful fresh cornish fish casserole included sea bass, scallops, monkfish, salmon and mussels. Desserts are equally inviting, and can be followed by good coffee and excellent home-made petits fours. Both public rooms and bedrooms are elegant and comfortable, lacking little to satisfy the discerning traveller.
9⇨Annexe2⇨1🛏 CTV in all bedrooms T ✘ (ex guide dogs) sB&B⇨fr£75 dB&B⇨fr£120 🅱
CTV 50P 2🚗 ✲ 🎾 (hard) ⛳ clay pigeon shooting putting green nc10yrs *xmas*
🍷 English & French V ✆ ☕ ⅟ Lunch fr£13.50 Dinner fr£27 Last dinner 9.15pm
Credit Cards 1 2 3 5

N

★★Alvaston Hall Middlewich Rd CW5 6PD (Associated Leisure) ☎(0270)624341 Telex no 36311 FAX (0270) 623395
This Victorian house, situated in open countryside off the A530 just north of the town, has been extended to provide a standard of accommodation that will appeal to both tourists and businessmen, facilities include a wide variety of leisure activities and good conference/banquet facilities.
38rm(23⇌15♠)Annexe53rm(33⇌20♠)(4fb) CTV in all bedrooms ® **T** ✻ S% sB&B⇌♠£35-£65 dB&B⇌♠£50-£70 ₿
☾ 250P ✿ CFA ⊡(heated) ♬ (hard) squash sauna solarium gymnasium whirlpool bath beauty therapist ♫ *xmas*
V ♡ ☐ ⅟ Lunch £9.50 Dinner fr£12 Last dinner 9.30pm
Credit Cards 1 2 3 4 5

★★*Cedars* Crewe Rd CW5 6NB ☎(0270)626455
A pleasantly furnished family-owned house with a good restaurant.
25rm(2⇌13♠)(2fb) CTV in all bedrooms ® **T**
☾ CTV 50P pool table
☋ English & French **V** ♡ ☐ Last dinner 9.30pm
Credit Cards 1 3

★★The Lamb Hospital St CW5 5RH ☎(0270)625286
Two hundred years old, and formerly a coaching inn, this hotel at the centre of historic Nantwich offers a varied menu in both the à la carte restaurant and the popular lounge bar.
16rm(10⇌3♠)(1fb) CTV in 13bedrooms ® ✗ (ex guide dogs) sB&B£22 sB&B⇌♠£30 dB&B£38.50 dB&B⇌♠£44 ₿
CTV 15P 10🚗
☋ English & French **V** ♡ Lunch £7.50 Dinner £11.50 Last dinner 9.30pm
Credit Cards 1 3

NARBERTH Dyfed Map **02** SN11

★★*Plas-Hyfryd* Moorfield Rd SA67 7AB (Guestaccom) ☎(0834)860653
A family-run hotel in an 18th-century mansion, which was formerly the rectory.
12rm(9⇌3♠)(1fb)⅟in 2 bedrooms CTV in all bedrooms ® **T**
CTV 30P ✿ ⇑(heated) putting green
☋ British, French & Spanish **V** ♡ ☐ Last dinner 9.30pm
Credit Cards 1 2 3 5

NARBOROUGH Leicestershire Map **04** SP59

★★Charnwood 48 Leicester Rd LE9 5DF (off A46 2m S of M1, junc21) ☎Leicester(0533)862218 FAX (0533) 750119
Closed 1 wk from 25 Dec RS Sun
Well placed for the M1, M69 and Leicester city centre, this friendly hotel with its large garden is popular with business clients.
20rm(5⇌15♠) CTV in all bedrooms ® **T**
50P ⛟ ✿
☋ English & French **V** ♡ ☐ Last dinner 9.30pm
Credit Cards 1 2 3 £

NEASHAM Co Durham Map **08** NZ31

★★★ 66% **Newbus Arms Hotel & Restaurant** Hurworth Rd DL2 1PE (Best Western) ☎Darlington(0325)721071 Telex no 58664 FAX (0325)721770
Elegant period house in its own gardens, with impressive public and conference areas.
15⇌♠3⛟ CTV in all bedrooms ® **T** sB&B⇌♠£45-£55 dB&B⇌♠£45-£75 ₿
80P 2🚗 ⛟ ✿ squash
☋ European **V** ♡ ☐ Lunch £14.25-£25alc Dinner £14.25-£25alc Last dinner 10pm
Credit Cards 1 2 3 5 £

NEATH West Glamorgan Map **03** SS79

★★Castle Hotel The Parade SA11 1RB (Lansbury) ☎(0639)641119 & 643581 Telex no 48119 FAX (0639) 641624
28⇌♠(8fb)1⛟ CTV in all bedrooms ® **T** sB&B⇌♠fr£48 dB&B⇌♠fr£58 ₿
☾ ⊞ CTV 20P sauna solarium exercise bike
☋ English & Continental **V** ♡ ☐ ⅟ Lunch £6-£8alc Dinner £7-£12alc Last dinner 10.30pm
Credit Cards 1 2 3 5

NEEDHAM MARKET Suffolk Map **05** TM05

★★*Limes* IP6 8DQ ☎(0449)720305
Closed Xmas
The original building dates back to 1485, but has substantial Georgian additions.
11⇌(4fb) CTV in all bedrooms ® **T**
60P
☋ English & French **V** ♡ ☐
Credit Cards 1 2 3 5

NEFYN Gwynedd Map **06** SH34

★Caeau Capel Rhodfar Mor LL53 6EB ☎(0758)720240
Closed Nov-Etr
Detached holiday hotel set in its own grounds in a quiet cul-de-sac.
15rm(1⇌7♠)(4fb) ® sB&B£17.50-£18.75 sB&B⇌♠£20.63-£22.50 dB&B£35-£37.50 dB&B⇌♠£41.26-£45 ₿
CTV 20P ⛟ ✿ ♬ (grass) putting
V ♡ ☐ Bar Lunch £4-£6alc Dinner £10.50 Last dinner 7pm
Credit Cards 1 3 £

NELSON Lancashire Map **07** SD83

★★*Great Marsden* Barkerhouse Rd BB9 9NL ☎(0282)64749
Standing within its own walled grounds, this hotel offers good value.
12rm(4⇌6♠)(2fb) CTV in all bedrooms ®
Lift ⊞ CTV 120P ✿ pool table
V ♡ ☐ Last dinner 8.30pm
Credit Cards 1 3

NEVERN Dyfed

★★Trewern Arms SA42 0NB ☎Newport(0239)820395
Modernised and extended 18th-century inn of some character, in a picturesque and secluded valley.
8rm(1⇌7♠)(1fb) CTV in all bedrooms ® ✻ S% dB&B⇌♠fr£36
CTV 100P ✿ ♩ ∪ solarium gymnasium pool table *xmas*
V ♡ S% Sunday Lunch £5-£6.50 Dinner £11.75-£13.50 Last dinner 9.30pm
Credit Cards 1

NEW ABBEY Dumfries & Galloway *Kirkcudbrightshire* Map **11** NX96

★*Abbey Arms* 1 The Square DG2 8BU ☎(038785)215
Situated in the centre of an interesting abbey village, this simply-furnished hotel is personally run by the resident proprietors.
6rm(3fb) CTV in 4bedrooms ®
CTV 6P
♡ ☐

Red-star hotels offer the highest standards of hospitality, comfort and food.

NEWARK-ON-TRENT Nottinghamshire Map **08** SK75

★★**Grange** 73 London Rd NG24 1RZ ☎(0636)703399
Closed 24 Dec-2 Jan
A warm, friendly and comfortable hotel, personally run by the resident owners, who offer well-cooked food and good bedrooms. Located just south of the town centre in a residential area.
8rm(7⇌1♠)(2fb) CTV in all bedrooms ® ✗ (ex guide dogs) ✱
sB&B⇌♠fr£35 dB&B⇌♠£44-£48
9P
V Dinner £8.50-£12.80alc Last dinner 9pm
Credit Cards [1] [3]

★★***Midland*** Muskham Rd NG24 1BL ☎(0636)73788
Small inn with modest accommodation.
10rm(2⇌)(2fb) CTV in all bedrooms ® ✗
CTV 20P
V ♈ Last dinner 8.30pm
Credit Cards [1] [2] [5]

★★***Ram*** ☎(0636)702255
This coaching inn stands near the castle in town centre.
15rm(11⇌1♠)(1fb) CTV in all bedrooms ® T ✗
CTV 10
♈ Last dinner 8.45pm
Credit Cards [1] [2] [3]

TraveLodge North Muskham NG23 6HT (3m N A1) (Trusthouse Forte) ☎(0636)703635
30⇌♠ CTV in all bedrooms ®
☾ 60P
Mainly grills
Credit Cards [1] [2] [3]

NEWBRIDGE Cornwall & Isles of Scilly Map **02** SW43

✗✗**Enzo of Newbridge** TR20 8QH ☎Penzance(0736)63777
Situated in a small hamlet between Penzance and St Just, the restaurant is in two sections – a small, stone-walled area, and the modern plant-adorned conservatory where cooking is carried out under a copper canopy in the corner. An extensive menu features Italian food, with pastas as starters or main courses and a good selection of other dishes, whilst a separate menu concentrates on the use of local fish and fresh well-cooked vegetables. A list of mainly Italian wines is available, and smiling attentive service is offered by uniformed waitresses.
Closed Thu (Dec-Apr) & 1-21 Nov
Lunch not served
Italian V 70 seats ✱ Dinner £11.50&alc Last dinner 9.30pm
25P
Credit Cards [1] [2] [3] [5]

See advertisement under PENZANCE

NEWBRIDGE-ON-WYE Powys Map **03** SO05

★***New Inn*** LD1 6HY ☎Newbridge on Wye(059789)211
Closed Xmas
A 16th-century village inn with a modern restaurant.
9rm(2⇌1♠)(3fb) CTV in 8bedrooms ®
CTV 100P (heated)
V ♈
Credit Cards [1]

NEW BRIGHTON

See **Wallasey**

Book as early as possible for busy holiday periods.

NEWBURGH Grampian *Aberdeenshire* Map **15** NJ92

★★**Udny Arms** Main St AB4 0BL ☎(03586)44489
A popular business and sport hotel, retaining much of its original Victorian character, and offering good fresh food in both bar and bistro and friendly service.
26rm(17⇌9↖) CTV in all bedrooms ® **T**
☾ 50P CFA ▶9 ♩ petanque
♔ ☋ Last dinner 9.30pm
Credit Cards 1 2 3

NEWBURY Berkshire Map **04** SU46

See also **Elcot**

★★★63% **The Chequers** Oxford St RG13 1JB (Trusthouse Forte) ☎(0635)38000 Telex no 849205 FAX (0635) 37170
Bedrooms vary in style and standard, but improvements are continuing steadily at this former coaching inn. Public areas are pleasant and comfortable, whilst service throughout is helpful and friendly.
56⇌↖(3fb)⊬in 12 bedrooms CTV in all bedrooms ® **T**
sB⇌↖£57-£75 dB⇌↖£80-£100 (room only) ⊟
☾ 60P CFA *xmas*
V ♔ ☋ ⊬ Lunch £9.95-£11.50 Dinner £12.95 Last dinner 9.45pm
Credit Cards 1 2 3 4 5

NEWBY BRIDGE Cumbria Map **07** SD38

★★★63% **The Swan** LA12 8NB (Exec Hotel) ☎(05395)31681 Telex no 65108 FAX (05395)31917
Closed 2-8 Jan
Guests may arrive by car, boat or helicopter at this modernised coaching inn, attractively set on the River Leven at the southern end of Lake Windermere. Spacious bedrooms are well furnished and equipped, and the de luxe rooms are provided with many thoughtful extras. Dinner is in the first-floor restaurant, full of character and next to an elegant and comfortable cocktail bar. Lighter meals and lunches are served in the Mailcoach Wine bar, open all day.
36⇌(8fb) CTV in all bedrooms ® **T** ✗ (ex guide dogs) S%
sB&B⇌£42-£60 dB&B⇌£70-£98 ⊟
CTV 100P 4⌂ ⌗ ❋ ♩ croquet table tennis ♫ ⌂ *xmas*
☋ English & French **V** ♔ ☋ S% Lunch £7.95 Dinner fr£13.50&alc Last dinner 9.30pm
Credit Cards 1 2 3 5

★★★69% **Whitewater** The Lakeland Village LA12 8PX ☎(05395)31133 Telex no 54173 FAX (05395) 31881
Imaginatively converted from what was originally a mill standing beside the turbulent River Leven, this is a smart complex, built of local stone and slate. The hotel has spacious, well-appointed and comfortable bedrooms and, together with an excellent health and leisure club, forms part of the Lakeland Village time-share resort.
35⇌↖(10fb)1⌗ CTV in all bedrooms ® **T** ✗ (ex guide dogs) ✱ sB&B⇌↖£53.50 dB&B⇌↖£75 ⊟
Lift ☾ 50P ⌗ ⊡(heated) ℘ (hard & grass) squash sauna solarium gymnasium putting ♫ *xmas*
V ♔ ☋ Lunch fr£6.95alc Dinner fr£12.95&alc Last dinner 9pm
Credit Cards 1 2 3 5 £

NEWCASTLETON Borders *Roxburghshire* Map **12** NY48

✗ ***Copshaw Kitchen*** TD9 0RB ☎Liddesdale(054121)250
This attractive restaurant was once a grocer's shop; today, a thriving antique business has developed in parallel with the restaurant trade, and many of the delightful articles that surround you as you eat are actually for sale. It is for its interesting and varied menu and the standard of its cuisine, however, that the Copshaw Kitchen is particularly noteworthy.
Closed Tue
Dinner not served Sun & Mon
V 36 seats Last dinner 9pm 12P ⊬

NEWCASTLE-UNDER-LYME Staffordshire Map **07** SJ84

★★★62% ***Clayton Lodge*** Clayton Rd ST5 4AF (A519) (Embassy) ☎(0782)613093
A modernised hotel extended to include its own pub, the Copeland Arms, and a large banqueting suite.
50rm(48⇌2↖)(8fb)⊬in 8 bedrooms CTV in all bedrooms ® **T**
☾ 400P ❋ CFA ⌂
☋ English & French **V** ♔ ☋
Credit Cards 1 2 3 4 5

★★★55% **Post House** Clayton Rd ST5 4DL (Trusthouse Forte) ☎(0782)717171 Telex no 36531 FAX (0782) 717138
This long, purpose-built hotel provides extensive parking space within easy reach of busy public rooms and bedrooms. It is conveniently situated adjacent to junction 15 of the M6, and many of its rooms have views across the motorway to wooded hills.
126⇌(46fb)⊬in 8 bedrooms CTV in all bedrooms ® **T** S%
sB⇌fr£70 dB⇌fr£81 (room only) ⊟
☾ 128P ❋ *xmas*
V ♔ ☋ ⊬ S% Lunch fr£9.95 Dinner fr£14 Last dinner 10.30pm
Credit Cards 1 2 3 4 5

★**The Deansfield** 98 Lancaster Rd ST5 1DS ☎(0782)619040
This small, privately-owned hotel provides a high standard of hospitality, whether guests are housed in the main building or the more compact rooms of the annexe.
6↖Annexe5↖(2fb) CTV in all bedrooms ® **T** sB&B↖£26.50 dB&B↖£38 ⊟
CTV 30P 1⌂ ⌗ ❋ *xmas*
☋ English & Continental **V** ♔ ☋ ⊬ Lunch fr£4alc High tea fr£4alc Dinner fr£10alc Last dinner 9pm
Credit Cards 1 2 3 5 £

NEWCASTLE UPON TYNE Tyne & Wear Map **12** NZ26

See **Town Plan Section**
See also **Seaton Burn**

★★★★70% **Gosforth Park Thistle** High Gosforth Park, Gosforth NE3 5HN (Thistle) ☎091-236 4111 Telex no 53655 FAX 091-236 8192
Modern hotel with extensive leisure facilities and choice of restaurants serving interesting, well-prepared food.
178⇌↖(67fb)⊬in 30 bedrooms CTV in all bedrooms ® **T** ✱
sB⇌↖£78-£86 dB⇌↖£90-£98 (room only) ⊟
Lift ☾ 300P ❋ CFA ⊡(heated) ▶18 ℘ (hard) squash sauna solarium gymnasium games room trim trail whirlpool ♫
☋ International ♔ ☋ ⊬ Lunch fr£12.50&alc Dinner fr£18.95&alc Last dinner 10.30pm
Credit Cards 1 2 3 4 5

★★★★54% **Holiday Inn** Great North Rd NE13 6BP (Holiday Inns) ☎091-236 5432 Telex no 53271 FAX 091-236 8091
(For full entry see Seaton Burn)

★★★63% **County Thistle** Neville St NE99 1AH (Thistle) ☎091-232 2471 Telex no 537873 FAX 091-232 1285
Comfortable city-centre hotel opposite the main railway station. The delightful Café Mozart serves good food.
115⇌↖(4fb)⊬in 10 bedrooms CTV in all bedrooms ® **T** ✱
sB⇌↖£60-£70 dB⇌↖£70-£85 (room only) ⊟
Lift ☾ 25P CFA ♫
☋ International ♔ ☋ ⊬ Lunch fr£8.45&alc Dinner fr£12&alc Last dinner 9.45pm
Credit Cards 1 2 3 4 5

★★★70% **George Washington Hotel** Stone Cellar Rd NE37 1PH ☎091-417 2626 Telex no 537143 FAX 091-415 1166
(For full entry see Washington)

★★★ 55% ***Hospitality Inn*** 64 Osborne Rd, Jesmond NE2 2AT (Mount Charlotte) ☎091-281 7881 Telex no 53636
Comfortable executive hotel converted from terraced houses in the residential area of Jesmond, close to the city centre. Dinner is currently restricted to the coffee house, open all day.
89⇌(6fb)1 ⊟ ⊁in 10 bedrooms CTV in all bedrooms ® T ✗ (ex guide dogs)
Lift ☾ 90P 10🚗 (£3)
♡ English & French V ♡ ☐ ⊁
Credit Cards 1 2 3 5

★★★ 61% **Imperial** Jesmond Rd NE2 1PR (Swallow) ☎091-281 5511 Telex no 537972 FAX 091-281 8472
Mainly commercial, modernised city centre hotel with neat bedrooms, open plan public areas and an attractive leisure complex. Restaurant and coffee shop facilities.
129⇌(6fb)⊁in 28 bedrooms CTV in all bedrooms ® T S10% sB&B⇌fr£64 dB&B⇌fr£75 ⊟
Lift ☾ ⊞ 150🚗 CFA ⊡(heated) sauna solarium gymnasium steam room spa bath ♫ *xmas*
V ♡ ☐ S% Lunch £8&alc Dinner £12&alc Last dinner 9.45pm
Credit Cards 1 2 3 5

★★★ 62% **Newcastle Crest** New Bridge St NE1 8BS (Crest) ☎091-232 6191 Telex no 53467 FAX 091-261 8529
Functional accommodation and a choice of restaurants are offered by this modern city centre hotel.
166⇌⊁in 58 bedrooms CTV in all bedrooms ® T ✱ S% sB⇌fr£66.50 dB⇌fr£78.50 (room only) ⊟
Lift ☾ P CFA
V ♡ ☐ ⊁ Lunch fr£13.95&alc Last high tea 6pm
Credit Cards 1 2 3 4 5

★★★ 59% **Newcastle Moat House** Coast Rd NE28 9HP (Queens Moat) ☎091-262 8989 & 091-262 7044 Telex no 53583 FAX 091-263 4172
(For full entry see Wallsend)

★★★ 58% ***Northumbria*** Osborne Rd, Jesmond NE2 2BR (Mount Charlotte) ☎091-281 4961 Telex no 53636
Situated near the city centre, this unpretentious hotel offers pleasant bedrooms, designed with the business guest in mind.
67⇌(2fb) CTV in all bedrooms ® T ✗ (ex guide dogs)
Lift ☾ 20P ❊ sauna
♡ English & French V ♡ ☐
Credit Cards 1 2 3 5

★★★ 61% **Post House** Emerson Distrist 5 NE37 1LB (Trusthouse Forte) ☎091-416 2264 Telex no 537574
(For full entry see Washington)

★★★ 69% **Springfield Hotel** Durham Rd NE9 5BT (Embassy) ☎091-477 4121 Telex no 538197 FAX 091-477 7213
(For full entry see Gateshead)

★★★ 63% **Swallow** Newgate Arcade NE1 5SX (Swallow) ☎091-232 5025 Telex no 538230 FAX 091- 232 8428
Purpose-built hotel with sixth-floor cocktail lounge and restaurant giving good views across the city. A leisure complex is planned.
93rm(92⇌1)⊁in 41 bedrooms CTV in all bedrooms ® T ✱ S% sB&B£65-£70 sB&B⇌£65-£70 dB&B£72-£78 dB&B⇌£72-£78 ⊟
Lift ☾ 120P CFA ♫ *xmas*
♡ English & French V ♡ ☐ Lunch £7.50-£8.50&alc Dinner £13-£15&alc Last dinner 10pm
Credit Cards 1 2 3 5

★★★ 66% **Swallow Hotel-Gateshead** NE8 1PE (Swallow) ☎091-477 1105 Telex no 53534 FAX 091-478 7214
(For full entry see Gateshead)

For key to symbols see the inside front cover.

N

★★Cairn 97/103 Osborne Road, Jesmond NE2 2TJ ☎091-281 1358 FAX 091-281 9031
This family-run, commercial hotel stands close to the town centre.
55rm(39⇌5↖)(7fb)2▣ CTV in all bedrooms ® T ✱ sB&B£29-£30 sB&B⇌↖£40-£42.50 dB&B£40-£42.50 dB&B⇌↖£55-£57.50
☾ 20P *xmas*
V ♡ ☕ Lunch £5.95-£6.50
Credit Cards 1 2 3 5 £

★★*Morrach* 82-86 Osborne Road, Jesmond NE2 2AP ☎091-281 3361
Modest accommodation is available at this family-run hotel. Dinners represent good value, and there is also a small coffee shop which remains open throughout the day and evening.
34rm(7⇌5↖)(1fb)1▣ CTV in all bedrooms ®
20P 3🚗 pool table
V ♡ ☕ Last dinner 9pm
Credit Cards 1 2 3

★★Whites 38-40 Osborne Road, Jesmond NE2 2AL ☎091-281 5126
Modern, comfortable hotel behind impressive Victorian façade, where friendly proprietors create a welcoming atmosphere.
25rm(15⇌7↖)(1fb) CTV in all bedrooms ® ✗ ✱ sB&B£25-£33 sB&B⇌↖£33 dB&B£34 dB&B⇌↖£43 ⊟
☾ CTV 30P
V ♡ ☕ Lunch £5.50 Dinner £6.95-£7.95 Last dinner 9.30pm
Credit Cards 1 2 3 5

★Osborne Osborne Road, Jesmond NE2 2AE ☎091-281 3385
Comfortable hotel in residential area with modern facilities.
26rm(1⇌9↖)(2fb) CTV in all bedrooms ® T ✱ sB&B£18-£28 sB&B⇌↖£23-£36 dB&B£36-£40 dB&B⇌↖£38-£50 ⊟
CTV 6P 1🚗 (£2)
V ♡ ☕ Bar Lunch fr£2 Dinner £5.50-£7 Last dinner 8.30pm
Credit Cards 1 3

N

✕✕✕Fishermans Lodge Jesmond Dene, Jesmond NE7 7BQ ☎091-281 3281 & 091-281 3724
Hugely popular and busy restaurant specialising in fresh seafood in Jesmond Dean Park. The à la carte dinner menu (half of it hand written) reflects the best of the day's market with dishes such as baked monkfish with a vermouth sauce, grilled halibut with herbs, and lobster. Fillet steaks are also popular, and most of the puddings include homemade ice cream or sorbet. Booking is essential.
Closed Sun, 25-28 Dec & BH's
Lunch not served Sat
♡ French V 65 seats Lunch £12.50-£13.50&alc Dinner £18-£35alc Last lunch 2pm Last dinner 11pm 45P nc9yrs
Credit Cards 1 2 3 5

✕✕✕21 Queen Street Quayside ☎091-222 0755
Stylish restaurant with comfortable little aperitif lounge, owned and run with flair by Terence Laybourne. The menu is dictated by the season, with game figuring strongly and fresh fish and seafood bought daily from the market. Textures, flavours and sauces have all impressed our inspectors, who have praised a beautifully light terrine of fresh fishes and garden herbs, served warm with a vegetable butter sauce, medallions of Kielder venison with a spicy game sauce, and the smoothest of crêmes brulées.
Lunch not served Sat
♡ French 50 seats ✱ Lunch £11.40&alc Dinner fr£18alc Last lunch 2pm Last dinner 10.45pm P̸
Credit Cards 1 2 3 5

✕✕*King Neptune* 34-36 Stowell St NE1 4XB ☎091-261 6657 & 091-261 6660
Friendly Cantonese restaurant in the heart of the city's small Chinatown, specialising in seafood and szechuan dishes.
♡ Cantonese V 50 seats Last dinner 11pm P̸
Credit Cards 1 2 3 5

✕✕Le Roussillon 52/54 Saint Andrews St NE1 5SF ☎091-261 1341
Attractive, French-style, city-centre restaurant with an interesting menu and good wine list.
Closed Sun
Lunch not served Sat
Dinner not served Mon
♡ French V 45 seats Lunch £4.50-£10&alc Dinner £15-£26alc Last lunch 2pm Last dinner 10pm
Credit Cards 1 2 3 5

NEWCASTLE UPON TYNE AIRPORT Tyne & Wear Map 12 NZ17

★★★ 64% Stakis Airport Woolsington NE13 8PJ (Stakis) ☎Ponteland(0661)24911 Telex no 537121 FAX (0661) 860157
Situated within the airport complex, this modern hotel has comfortable and well-appointed bedrooms, open-plan lounge areas and an attractive restaurant and cocktail bar.
100⇌↖(2fb)⊁in 30 bedrooms CTV in all bedrooms ® T ✱ sB⇌↖£59 dB⇌↖£70 (room only) ⊟
Lift ☾ 200P ✲ CFA *xmas*
V ♡ ☕ ⊁
Credit Cards 1 2 3 5

NEWMARKET Suffolk Map 05 TL66

★★★ 62% Newmarket Moat House Moulton Rd CB8 8DY (Queens Moat) ☎(0638)667171 FAX (0638) 666533
Comfortable and close to both 'the Gallops' and the town centre. Popular for conferences.
49⇌(2fb) CTV in all bedrooms ® T sB&B⇌£52-£55 dB&B⇌£68-£73 ⊟
Lift ☾ CTV 60P 10🚗 CFA
♡ English & French V ♡ ☕ Lunch £10.50-£14.95&alc Dinner £10.50-£14.95&alc Last dinner 9.45pm
Credit Cards 1 2 3 5 £

★★Bedford Lodge Bury Rd CB8 7BX (Best Western) ☎(0638)663175 Telex no 97267 FAX (0638) 667391
Built in 1861, and owned by Lord Derby and other horseracing enthusiasts when it was a private residence, the hotel preserves its racing connections in a décor that is at its most effective in the bar. Continual upgrading has provided individually-designed, well-equipped bedrooms (including some in newly converted courtyard buildings) and an elegant restaurant where very competently prepared meals are served.
11rm(6⇌5↖)Annexe7rm(1fb)1▣ CTV in 11bedrooms ® T ✱ sB&B⇌↖£42 dB&B⇌↖£54-£72 ⊟
☾ 60P ✲
♡ English & French V ♡ ☕ Lunch £11.95-£11.95&alc Dinner £13.95-£13.95&alc Last dinner 9.30pm
Credit Cards 1 2 3 5 £

★★Rosery Country House 15 Church St, Exning CB8 7EH (2m NW B1103) ☎Exning(063877)312
11rm(7⇌1↖)1▣ CTV in all bedrooms ® T ✗ (ex guide dogs) sB&B£36-£38 sB&B⇌↖£46-£48 dB&B⇌↖£57-£60
20P ✲ croquet
♡ English & French V ♡ ☕ Lunch £4.90-£10alc Dinner £8-£20alc Last dinner 9.30pm
Credit Cards 1 2 3 5

See advertisement on page 499

★★Rutland Arms High St CB8 8NB ☎(0638)664251 Telex no 329265
The main building is a Georgian coaching house built round a cobbled courtyard.
45⇌(2fb) CTV in all bedrooms ® T sB&B⇌£46-£52.50 dB&B⇌fr£57.50 ⊟
☾ 26P 8🚗 CFA *xmas*

▶

N

V ✿ ☐ Lunch fr£9.75&alc Dinner fr£9.75&alc Last dinner 9pm
Credit Cards 1 2 3 5

★★White Hart High St CB8 8JP (Consort) ☎(0638)663051 FAX (0638) 667284
Three-storey gabled building standing on the site of a 17th-century inn.
23rm(19⇌4♨)1⊟ CTV in all bedrooms ® T
☾ 30P
♀ English & French V ✿ ☐ Last dinner 9pm
Credit Cards 1 2 3 5

NEW MILTON Hampshire Map 04 SZ29

❀★★★★ ♜ **CHEWTON GLEN**
Christchurch Rd BH25 6QS
(Relais et Châteaux)
☎Highcliffe(0425)275341
Telex no 41456
FAX (0425)272310

Nothing stands still at this classic country house hotel bordering the New Forest. Arriving guests can feast their eyes on the beautifully developed grounds, with their tennis courts, golf course and croquet lawn. New suites are furnished to the highest standards and comprehensively equipped, with an array of quality toiletries and other extras. A few of the other rooms are more compact, but overall the quality and comfort shine through. Public rooms are airy and pleasant, with a large lounge and pretty restaurant filled with fresh flowers and objects d'art. Some minor lapses apart, service is well managed, polite and professional, and the restaurant is particularly hospitable. Chef Pierre Chevillard's cuisine continues to earn a rosette, and while reports from our inspectors early in 1989 were not wholly favourable, later visits confirmed that the cooking had significantly improved. A jambrette of smoked duck with a warm lentil salad, and a succulent fillet of turbot with a spicy butter sauce have been especially praised. A superbly appointed hotel of great quality throughout, Chewton Glen remains a firm favourite with users of our guide.
46⇌1⊟ CTV in all bedrooms T ✗ (ex guide dogs) S15%
sB⇌£138-£187 dB⇌£138-£363 (room only) ⊟
☾ 100P ✲ CFA ⇌(heated) ▶9 ♟(hard) snooker ♫ nc7yrs *xmas*
♀ French V ✿ ☐ S15% Lunch fr£20 Dinner fr£38alc Last dinner 9.30pm
Credit Cards 1 2 3 4 5

NEWPORT

See Wight, Isle of

NEWPORT Gwent Map 03 ST38

★★★★63% Celtic Manor Coldra Woods NP6 2YA
☎Llanwern(0633)413000 Telex no 497557 FAX (0633) 412910
The 19th-century manor, once used as a maternity home, is situated close to the motorway. It offers well-appointed bedrooms, elegant public rooms, two good restaurants and a cellar bar.
75⇌(1fb)2⊟ CTV in all bedrooms T ✗ (ex guide dogs) ✱
sB⇌fr£72 dB⇌fr£93 (room only) ⊟
Lift ☾ 150P 1♠ ✲ ⊡(heated) sauna solarium gymnasium trim trail ♫ *xmas*
♀ French V ✿ ☐ ⚟ Lunch fr£14.50&alc Dinner fr£17.75&alc Last dinner 10.30pm
Credit Cards 1 2 3 5 £

★★★55% Hilton National The Coldra NP6 2YG (Hilton)
☎(0633)412777 Telex no 497205 FAX (0633) 413087
Busy commercial hotel just off the M4. A 1989 refurbishment programme included the upgrading of bedrooms, and a new leisure complex.
119⇌♨(20fb)⚟in 22 bedrooms CTV in all bedrooms ® T ✱
S% sB⇌♨£60-£75 dB⇌♨£75-£90 (room only) ⊟
☾ 400P ✲ ⊡(heated) sauna gymnasium steam room ♫ *xmas*
V ✿ ☐ ⚟ Lunch £5.95-£8.95&alc Dinner £1.75-£14.95alc Last dinner 10.30pm
Credit Cards 1 2 3 5

★★★59% Kings High St NP9 1QU ☎(0633)842020
Telex no 497330
Closed 25-30 Dec
Convenient for the railway station and M4, with well-equipped bedrooms and extensive conference and function facilities.
47⇌♨(10fb)⚟in 2 bedrooms CTV in all bedrooms ® T ✗ (ex guide dogs) sB&B⇌♨£54 dB&B⇌♨£64 ⊟
Lift ☾ 20P 10♠ ♫
♀ International V ✿ ☐ ⚟ Lunch £5.95-£8.95&alc Dinner £7.50-£11.45&alc Last dinner 9.30pm
Credit Cards 1 2 3 5

★★New Inn Motel NP6 2JN (Porterhouse) ☎(0633)412426
FAX (0633) 413679
(For full entry see Langstone)

★★*Priory* High St, Caerleon NP6 1XD (3m NE B4236) (Porterhouse) ☎Caerleon(0633)421241
Character hotel in village. Comfortable bedrooms and popular restaurant.
16⇌♨Annexe5⇌♨(1fb) CTV in all bedrooms ® T ✗
70P ✲ ▶9
♀ English & French ✿ ☐ Last dinner 9.45pm
Credit Cards 1 2 3

NEWPORT Shropshire Map 07 SJ71

★★*Royal Victoria* St Mary's St TF10 7AB (Crown & Raven)
☎(0952)820331 Telex no 335464
Simple comfortable accommodation is available at this 18th-century town-centre hotel.
24rm(16⇌7♨)(1fb) CTV in all bedrooms ® T
100P
♀ English & French V ✿ ☐ Last dinner 10pm
Credit Cards 1 2 3

NEWPORT PAGNELL Buckinghamshire Map 04 SP84

★★Swan Revived High St MK16 8AR ☎(0908)610565
Telex no 826801 FAX (0908) 210995
15th-century coaching inn with a friendly, welcoming atmosphere.
40rm(12⇌27♨)1⊟ CTV in all bedrooms ® T
sB&B⇌♨£22-£48 dB&B⇌♨£34-£54 ⊟
Lift ☾ 15P 3♠
♀ English & Continental V ✿ ☐ Lunch £9-£14.50alc Dinner £9-£14.50alc Last dinner 10pm
Credit Cards 1 2 3 5

NEWQUAY Cornwall & Isles of Scilly Map 02 SW86

See **Town Plan Section**

★★★61% Barrowfield Hillgrove Rd TR7 1EG ☎(0637)878878
FAX (0637)879490
A spacious, modern hotel with well-equipped bedrooms, in a quiet residential area, though only a short walk to the beach. Ideal for both holidaymakers and business people.
81rm(77⇌4♨)(18fb)11⊟ CTV in all bedrooms ® T ▶

N

Lift ☾ CTV 34P 16🚗 CFA ⊡(heated) ⌂(heated) snooker sauna solarium gymnasium ♫
☋ French V ♆ ☗ Last dinner 8.30pm
Credit Cards [1] [3]

★★★ 62% **Hotel Bristol** Narrowcliff TR7 2PQ ☎(0637)875181 FAX (0637) 879347
In an ideal position directly overlooking Tolcarne beach, this hotel has been under the same ownership since 1927.
86rm(66⇨)(18fb) CTV in all bedrooms T ✳ sB&B£30-£35 sB&B⇨£36-£42 dB&B£50-£60 dB&B⇨£60-£70 ⊟
Lift ☾ CTV 100P 5🚗 (£3 daily) CFA ⊡(heated) snooker sauna solarium *xmas*
V ♆ ☗ Lunch £8.50-£8.50&alc Dinner £13.50-£13.50&alc Last dinner 8.30pm
Credit Cards [1] [2] [3] [5]

★★★ 60% **Edgcumbe** Narrowcliff TR7 2RR ☎(0637)872061 FAX (0637) 877320
Excellent indoor and outdoor leisure facilities 'for the young at heart'.
85rm(65⇨19↱)(43fb) CTV in all bedrooms ® T
Lift ☾ CTV 70P ⊡(heated) ⌂(heated) snooker sauna solarium games room whirlpool ⌂
V ♆ ☗ Last dinner 8.30pm
Credit Cards [1] [3]

★★★ 56% ***Glendorgal*** Lusty Glaze Rd TR7 3AE ☎(0637)874937
RS Oct-Apr
Friendly, personally-run, secluded hotel in 15 acres of grounds and headland.
40rm(38⇨)(8fb)1⊞ CTV in all bedrooms T
70P ✲ ⌂(heated) ℘ (hard) ♩ sauna solarium ⌂
☋ English & Continental V ♆ ☗
Credit Cards [1] [3]

★★★ 57% ***Kilbirnie*** Narrowcliff TR7 2RS ☎(0637)875155
Occupying a commanding position overlooking the bay, this owner-managed hotel offers spacious, comfortable public areas and simply-appointed, but well-equipped bedrooms. Additional facilities include indoor and outdoor swimming pools.
74⇨(17fb) CTV in all bedrooms ® T
☾ ⊞ CTV 60P ⊡(heated) snooker sauna solarium
♆ ☗
Credit Cards [1] [3]

★★★ 56% ***Hotel Mordros*** 4 Pentire Av TR7 1PA ☎(0637)876700
This modern, family, holiday-hotel offers good bedrooms, a non-smokers' lounge and a well-equipped gymnasium. It is personally run by the owners, and the atmosphere is friendly and informal.
30⇨↱(10fb) CTV in all bedrooms ® T ✈
Lift CTV 1P ⌂(heated) sauna solarium gymnasium ♫
☋ English & Continental ♆ ☗

★★★ 60% **Trebarwith** Island Estate TR7 1BZ ☎(0637)872288
Closed Jan-10 Apr & 7 Oct-Dec
Family owned and run hotel, with a garden having its own steps to the beach.
44rm(33⇨6↱)(7fb)4⊞ CTV in all bedrooms T ✈ (ex guide dogs) ✳ sB&B£22-£34 dB&B£30-£54 dB&B⇨↱£36-£68 (incl dinner)
☾ CTV 40P ⊞ ✲ ⊡(heated) ♩ snooker sauna solarium spa bath video theatre games room ♫
V ♆ ☗ Bar Lunch £1-£3 Dinner £12&alc Last dinner 8.30pm
Credit Cards [1] [3]

★★★ 60% ***Windsor*** Mount Wise TR7 2AY ☎(0637)875188
Closed Dec-Feb
Spacious family hotel close to seafront, with excellent leisure facilities.
42rm(35⇨1↱)(14fb)1⊞ CTV in all bedrooms T ✈ (ex guide dogs)
50P ⊞ ✲ ⊡(heated) ⌂(heated) squash sauna solarium gymnasium jacuzzi putting green ♫ ⌂
☋ English & French ♆ ☗ ⚟ Last dinner 8.30pm
Credit Cards [1] [3]

★★ ***Beachcroft*** Cliff Rd TR7 1SW ☎(0637)873022
Closed early Oct-mid Apr
Large family hotel in its own gardens, close to the town centre and beach.
69rm(29⇨25↱)(12fb) CTV in 59bedrooms ®
Lift ☾ CTV 80P ✲ ⊡(heated) ⌂(heated) ℘ (hard) sauna solarium games room ⌂
V ♆ ☗ Last dinner 8pm
Credit Cards [1]

★★ ***Bewdley*** 10 Pentire Rd TR7 1NX ☎(0637)872883
RS Nov-Mar
On the outskirts of town overlooking Fistral Beach and the Gannel Estuary.
29rm(8⇨19↱)(6fb) CTV in all bedrooms ®
CTV 40P ⌂(heated) ♫ ⌂
♆
Credit Cards [1] [3]

★★ **Cedars** Mount Wise TR7 2BA ☎(0637)874225
Closed Dec-Mar (ex Xmas)
Small friendly country-house style hotel.
36rm(15⇨16↱)(8fb) CTV in all bedrooms ® T
CTV 40P 2🚗 ✲ ⌂(heated) sauna solarium gymnasium
♆ ☗ ⚟

★★ **Corisande Manor** Riverside Avenue, Pentire TR7 1PL (Exec Hotel) ☎(0637)872042
Closed 14 Oct-4 May
This uniquely designed and quietly situated holiday hotel overlooking the Gannel estuary has been run for twenty years by the Painter family, who pride themselves particularly on the quality of the meals they provide.
19rm(4⇨11↱)(3fb) sB&B£15-£20 sB&B⇨↱£16.50-£22 dB&B£30-£40 dB&B⇨↱£33-£44 ⊟
CTV 19P ⊞ ✲ solarium croquet putting green outdoor chess nc3yrs
☋ English, French & Italian ♆ ☗ Bar Lunch £3.75-£5.60 Dinner £8-£10 Last dinner 8pm
Credit Cards [1] [3]

★★ **Cross Mount** 58-60 Church St, St Columb Minor TR7 3EX ☎(0637)872669
Closed 1 wk New Year
Dating from the 17th century, the small hotel retains old stone walls and beams.
12rm(4⇨2↱) CTV in all bedrooms ® ✈
CTV 10P ⊞
☋ English & French V ♆ Last dinner 9.45pm
Credit Cards [1] [3]

★★ ***Cumberland*** 8-10 Henver Rd TR7 3BJ ☎(0637)873025
This comfortable, modern hotel has a convivial atmosphere and is a short walk from the beach and town centre.
33rm(1⇨6↱) CTV in all bedrooms ®
CTV 38P ⌂(heated) solarium ♫ nc
♆ ☗
Credit Cards [1]

See advertisement on page 503

★★ **Minto House** 38 Pentire Crescent, Pentire TR7 1PU ☎(0637)873227
Family hotel situated on the banks of the Gannel Estuary.
40⇨↱ Annexe5rm(3⇨2↱)(15fb) CTV in all bedrooms ® T
40P ✲ ⌂(heated) ♩ sauna solarium dinghy, windsurfing ♫
☋ English & Continental V ♆ ☗ Last dinner 8pm
Credit Cards [1] [3]

GLENDORGAL HOTEL

AA ★★★

Lusty Glaze Road · Newquay · Cornwall

Tel. Newquay (0637) 874937

A 40 Bedroom Hotel set in 15 Acres of Private Headland with 1 Mile of Coastline owned by the Hotel.

- ★ Heated swimming pool 90°
- ★ Sauna
- ★ Solarium (Tan both sides)
- ★ Jacuzzi
- ★ Tennis Court
- ★ Shuffle Board Court
- ★ Putting Green
- ★ Private Cove
- ★ Children's Play Garden (swings, slides, table tennis)
- ★ Pool Side Restaurant and Bar

★★★★★★

- ★ Cocktail Bar
- ★ Pool Room
- ★ Entertainment nightly
- ★ Colour TV and radio in all rooms
- ★ Most rooms have private bathroom ensuite, sea-views
- ★ Hairdryers
- ★ Baby listening
- ★ Large Car Park

★★★★★★

English and Continental food, table d'hôte and flambé menu, extensive wine list

Kilbirnie Hotel ★★★

Narrowcliff,
Newquay,
Cornwall TR7 2RS

Telephone:
Newquay (0637) 875155

A luxury hotel for all the family

The hotel occupies one of the finest positions in Newquay, where you can enjoy a really relaxing holiday with the accent on comfort and attention to detail. Particular care has been taken in choosing the furnishings, decor and colour schemes, from the bedrooms to public rooms. All the bedrooms have colour television with video and en suite facilities, central heating, radio, shaver point and telephone. Family rooms have baby listening service. Heated indoor & outdoor swimming pool, sauna and solarium plus Games Room with full size snooker table and pool table are all available for your relaxation. Entertainment during the high season provides enjoyment for all the family.

★★Philema 1 Esplanade Rd, Pentire TR7 1PY ☎(0637)872571
Closed Nov-Feb
Comfortable, friendly hotel with convivial atmosphere, overlooking golf course.
31rm(15⇨11⌐)(20fb)1⊞ CTV in all bedrooms ® ✳
sB&B£18-£24 sB&B⇨⌐£20-£26 dB&B£36-£48
dB&B⇨⌐£40-£52 (incl dinner) ⊟
CTV 34P ⊞ ⊡(heated) sauna solarium table tennis pool table *xmas*
⊕ English & Continental V ♦ ⊡ Bar Lunch £1-£2.50 Dinner £5.50-£7.50 Last dinner 7.30pm
Credit Cards 1 3

★★Porth Veor Manor House Porthway TR7 3LW
☎(0637)873274
Closed Nov
The family-run hotel provides peace and comfort, with a good choice of well-cooked meals.
16rm(12⇨4⌐)(3fb) CTV in all bedrooms ®
sB&B⇨⌐£24.50-£29 dB&B⇨⌐£49-£58 (incl dinner) ⊟
48P ⊞ ✲ ℘ (grass) putting
⊕ International ♦ ⊡ Sunday Lunch £5.50-£8 Dinner £6.95-£9.50&alc Last dinner 9pm
Credit Cards 1 3

★★*Tremont* Pentire Av TR7 1PB ☎(0637)872984 & 873148
Closed end Nov-Feb ex Xmas & New Years eve
A modern family hotel, standing in an elevated position overlooking Fistral Bay, offers a value-for-money holiday with a full timetable of entertainments.
53rm(23⇨24⌐)(26fb) CTV in all bedrooms ® T
Lift ☾ CTV 60P ✲ ⊡(heated) ℘ (hard) squash snooker sauna solarium gymnasium putting ♫ ⌂
⊕ English & French ♦ ⊡ Last dinner 5pm
Credit Cards 1 3

★★Water's Edge Esplanade Rd, Pentire TR7 1QA
☎(0637)872048
Closed Nov-Apr
Small family-owned hotel near Fistral Bay.
20rm(12⇨4⌐)(3fb)1⊞ CTV in all bedrooms ® T ✗ (ex guide dogs) sB&B£27.50-£36.50 dB&B⇨⌐£55-£73 (incl dinner) ⊟
18P
⊕ English & French V ♦ ⊡ Dinner fr£11.95 Last dinner 8pm
Credit Cards 1 3 £

★★Whipsiderry Trevelgue Road, Porth TR7 3LY
☎(0637)874777
Closed Oct-Etr
Friendly hotel offering good restaurant, comfort and excellent value.
20rm(2⇨16⌐)(5fb) CTV in all bedrooms ®
sB&B£18.50-£24.50 sB&B⇨⌐£20.50-£27.50
dB&B£41.50-£54.50 dB&B⇨⌐£44.50-£57.50
CTV 30P ⊞ ✲ ⊃(heated) putting green pool table ⌂
⊕ English & Continental V ♦ ⊡ Bar Lunch £2-£5 Dinner £7.50-£11.50 Last dinner 8pm
£

★Lowenva 103 Mount Wise TR7 2BT ☎(0637)873569
Closed Nov-Feb
A small, friendly, modern hotel which is centrally situated.
18rm(12⌐)(8fb) CTV in all bedrooms ® S% sB&B£16-£24
sB&B⌐£18-£26 dB&B£32-£48 dB&B⌐£36-£52 (incl dinner)
CTV 15P ⊃(heated) pool table *xmas*
V ♦ ⊡ ⊁ Bar Lunch £1-£3 Dinner £2.50-£5.50 Last dinner 7pm
Credit Cards 1 3 £

Book as early as possible for busy holiday periods.

★Trevone Mount Wise TR7 2BP ☎(0637)873039
mid Apr-21 Oct
Small family hotel situated close to town centre and beaches.
32rm(5⇨22⌐)(3fb) ® ✗ (ex guide dogs)
CTV 20P ✲ games room ♫
⊕ English, French, Indian & Italian ♦ ⊁

NEW QUAY Dyfed Map 02 SN35

★★Black Lion SA45 9PT ☎(0545)560209
Built at the same time (1830) and of the same stone as the harbour at New Quay. This small character hotel offers comfortable accommodation, commendable food standards and friendly local service. Overlooking the bay from its elevated position, it is a firm favourite with locals and tourists alike.
7rm(4⇨2⌐)(3fb) CTV in all bedrooms ® ✳ sB&B£24-£28
sB&B⇨⌐£28-£34 dB&B£38-£40 dB&B⇨⌐£40-£45 ⊟
CTV 40P ⊞ ♫
⊕ British & Continental V ♦ Lunch £6-£13.50alc Dinner £6-£15alc Last dinner 9.30pm
Credit Cards 1 2 3 5 £

NEWTON ABBOT Devon Map 03 SX87

★★Queens Queen St TQ12 2EZ ☎(0626)63133 & 54106
Tony and Fay Jolley's family-run hotel has been extensively upgraded and offers spotless comfort for the business and tourist trade alike. A relaxing atmosphere and friendly, prompt service complement the traditional Devon cooking. This is a hotel of character, well placed for the station, town centre and racecourse, and also a good touring base for the South Devon and Dartmoor National Park.
26rm(15⇨1⌐)(2fb) CTV in all bedrooms ® T sB&B£32
sB&B⇨⌐£38 dB&B£46 dB&B⇨⌐£58 ⊟
▶

Porth Veor Manor

AA★ ★ ETB♛♛♛

A Family run Country House Hotel

One of the finest positions on the North Cornish Coast. With Panoramic Views from all rooms. Two acres of garden and private path to beach. All rooms Ensuite, Colour TV and full central heating.

High Class Restaurant offering a choice of superb food with table d'hôte and à la Carte menu.

9 Hole Putting Green. Grass Tennis Court.

Special Autumn, Spring & Winter Breaks

PORTH VEOR MANOR HOTEL
PORTH WAY, PORTH BEACH
NR. NEWQUAY, CORNWALL TR7 3LW
TELEPHONE (0637) 873274

AA ★★ E.T.B.

Dalswinton

Country House Hotel

ST. MAWGAN (Nr. NEWQUAY)
CORNWALL TR8 4EZ.
TEL. (0637) 860385

Standing in 1½ acres of secluded grounds with superb views over wooded valley to sea.

Ideally situated between Newquay and Padstow, reputed to be the finest coastline in Europe. Excellent beaches and coves within 2 miles.

All rooms en-suite, with colour television, tea/coffee making facilities, log fires in bar and lounge.

Superb cooking in a friendly atmosphere.

Philema Hotel ★★

PENTIRE · NEWQUAY · CORNWALL
Telephone: Newquay (0637) 872571
Resident Proprietor: Jim Nettleton

A family run Hotel gloriously situated overlooking the beach & golf course. All bedrooms have tea-making facilities, colour TV, radio/intercom, most have private bathrooms. Full central heating, heated indoor swimming pool, sauna, solarium, games room. Excellent food & wines. Enjoy the view of the surf from the comfortable bar Lounge. Ideal for early & late breaks. Open Christmas.

Cumberland Hotel AA ★★

8 Henver Road, Newquay,
Cornwall TR7 3BJ
Telephone (0637) 873025

A bright, modern family run hotel, 34 bedrooms all with colour TV, radio, intercom and en suite. Heated outside pool and sun patio. Large ballroom and cocktail bar. Entertainment nightly. Two large car parks. Open all year, including Christmas. Modern sequence dance tours and bowls tours catered for.

Please send for full colour brochure to Mrs Marion Faulkner.

N

8P *xmas*
V ✿ ⅅ Lunch £8.95&alc Dinner £10.95&alc Last dinner 9pm
Credit Cards [1] [3] (£)

★Hazlewood House 33A Torquay Rd TQ12 2LW ☎(0626)66130
This cosy little hotel and restaurant stands only five minutes walk from the town centre and is also within easy reach of the station. Its well-appointed dining room features ecclesiastical panelling and offers imaginative menus, whilst bedrooms have been upgraded with the addition of more en suite facilities.
7rm(1⇨4↱)(1fb) CTV in all bedrooms ® **T** ✳ sB&B£24.50-£30 sB&B⇨↱£24.50-£30 dB&Bfr£34.50 dB&B⇨↱fr£40
6P
♀ English & French **V** ✿ ⅅ Lunch fr£7.95&alc High tea fr£2 Dinner fr£7.95&alc Last dinner 9pm
Credit Cards [1] [3] (£)

NEWTON FERRERS Devon Map **02** SX54

★★Court House Court Rd PL8 1AQ (Exec Hotel)
☎Plymouth(0752)872324
Closed 24 Dec-15 Jan

Fine, creeper-clad Georgian hotel combining modern facilities with comfort and character. Owned and run by Alan and Mary Ann Gilchrist, with friendly service complemented by the latter's imaginative cooking.
10⇨1 ⊟ CTV in all bedrooms ® **T** sB&B⇨£35-£50 dB&B⇨£50-£80 ⊨
20P ⊞ ✲ ⩤(heated) croquet nc8yrs
♀ British & French **V** ✿ ⅅ Dinner fr£15.50&alc Last dinner 9pm
Credit Cards [1] [3]

See advertisement under PLYMOUTH

NEWTON LE WILLOWS Merseyside Map **07** SJ59

★★Kirkfield 2/4 Church St WA12 9SU ☎(09252)28196 & 20489
This family-run hotel offering good value for money stands in the centre of the town, opposite the church.
16rm(7⇨9↱)(1fb)1⊟ CTV in all bedrooms ® **T** ✖ (ex guide dogs) ✳ sB&B⇨↱£30-£35 dB&B⇨↱£42-£50 ⊨
CTV 50P
✿ ⅅ
Credit Cards [1]

NEWTON MEARNS Strathclyde *Renfrewshire* Map **11** NS55

✕*Royal Garden Restaurant* Harvie Av, Crookfur Shopping Precinct G77 ☎041-639 8097 & 6261
Stephen Ho is an enthusiastic proprietor, carefully explaining the many regional specialities that are available at this Chinese restaurant discreetly tucked away in a small shopping precinct. Daily specialities are chalked on a blackboard at the entrance.
Lunch not served Sat & Sun
♀ Pekinese & Cantonese **V** 85 seats Last dinner mdnt 49P
Credit Cards [1] [2] [3] [5]

A rosette is the AA's highest award for quality of food and service in a restaurant.

NEWTON POPPLEFORD Devon Map **03** SY08

★★Coach House Hotel Southerton EX11 1SE
☎Colaton Raleigh(0395)68577
Closed 2-31 Jan
In a rural situation and within 2.5 acres of landscaped gardens lies this personally-run small country house hotel and restaurant, tastefully converted from the coach house of a former country estate. Stylish bedrooms are well-equipped and comfortable with some nice personal touches whilst good cooking standards prevail in the restaurant.
6rm(5⇨1↱)2⊟ CTV in all bedrooms ® **T** ✖ (ex guide dogs) sB&B⇨↱£27.50-£40 dB&B⇨↱£50-£55
CTV 16P ⊞ ✲ nc14yrs *xmas*
♀ International **V** ⊬ Lunch £3-£5.90 Dinner £9.50&alc Last dinner 9pm
Credit Cards [1] [3]

NEWTON SOLNEY Derbyshire Map **08** SK22

★★★56% The Newton Park DE15 0SS (Embassy) ☎Burton-on-Trent(0283)703568 FAX (0283)703214
A restored manor house set on the edge of a quiet village offers comfortable accommodation in peaceful surroundings and is popular for conferences and business meetings.
46⇨(1fb)⊬in 2 bedrooms CTV in all bedrooms ® **T** sB⇨£48-£58 dB⇨£57-£67 (room only) ⊨
Lift ☾ 150P ✲ *xmas*
♀ English & French **V** ✿ ⅅ Lunch £8.95-£9.95&alc Dinner £10.95-£11.95&alc Last dinner 9.30pm
Credit Cards [1] [2] [3] [4] [5]

NEWTON STEWART Dumfries & Galloway *Wigtownshire* Map **10** NX46

★★★★61% Kirroughtree Minnigaff DG8 8AN
☎(0671)2141
Closed 4 Jan-3 Feb
Now a charming and relaxing hotel, this 18th-century mansion is set in eight acres of landscaped grounds and gardens, and offers comfort and excellent cuisine. The splendidly elegant lounge is matched by two equally elegant dining rooms, and the well-equipped bedrooms are indivdually furnished to a high standard. Service is friendly and helpful.
20⇨↱Annexe2⇨↱(2fb) CTV in all bedrooms **T** ✳ sB&B⇨↱£39 dB&B⇨↱£70-£92 ⊨
☾ 40P ⊞ ✲ bowls croquet pitch and putt nc10yrs
♀ French ✿ ⅅ ⊬ Sunday Lunch £10-£15alc Dinner £23 Last dinner 9.30pm
Credit Cards [1] [2] [3] [5]

See advertisement on page 507

★★★57% Bruce 88 Queen St DG8 6JL ☎(0671)2294
Telex no 934999
Closed Dec & Jan
An informal, family-run hotel with friendly personal service from the proprietors and their young staff, offering guests enjoyable, freshly prepared meals. There is an attractive and comfortable lounge bar and some bedrooms have recently been redecorated.
18⇨↱(2fb) CTV in all bedrooms ® **T** sB&B⇨↱£29-£31 dB&B⇨↱£48-£52 ⊨
20P ⊞ solarium gymnasium ⌂

🍷 English & French V ⚘ Lunch £5-£10&alc Dinner £12.50-£14.95 Last dinner 8.30pm
Credit Cards [1] [2] [3] [5]

See advertisement on page 507

★★Creebridge House DG8 6NP (Consort) ☎(0671)2121
An attractive hotel in the country house style, with tastefully appointed bedrooms. Dinners are particularly enjoyable, the food being well prepared and presented.
17rm(16⇨1↱)(2fb) CTV in all bedrooms ® T ✳ sB&B⇨↱£32-£37 dB&B⇨↱£54-£60 ₪
CTV 50P ❊ *xmas*
🍷 Scottish & French V ⚘ ⛾ Bar Lunch £5.50-£12 Dinner £12.95-£14.50 Last dinner 8.30pm
Credit Cards [1] [3]

★★Crown 101 Queen St DG8 6JW ☎(0671)2727
This modestly appointed but pleasant former coaching inn stands adjacent to the town's market.
10rm(4⇨1↱)(1fb) CTV in all bedrooms ® ✗ (ex guide dogs) sB&Bfr£15.50 sB&B⇨↱fr£21 dB&Bfr£31 dB&B⇨↱fr£35
CTV 20P ♩ ♫
V ⚘ ⚟ Bar Lunch £2-£8 Dinner fr£10&alc Last dinner 8.30pm
Credit Cards [1] [3]

NEWTOWN Powys Map **06** SO19

★★Elephant & Castle Broad St SY16 2BQ ☎(0686)626271
RS 24 – 26 Dec
Now completely modernised, the hotel dates from the early 19th-century and was the birth place of Robert Owen, the famous Welsh pioneer. It enjoys a pleasant setting beside the River Severn and complements its comfortable, well-equipped bedrooms with enjoyable meals, skilfully prepared.
25rm(22⇨2↱)(11fb) CTV in all bedrooms ® T sB&B⇨↱£32 dB&B⇨↱£45
▶

(⊞ CTV 60P ♩
☋ English V ♁ ⌧ S% Lunch £7.50 High tea fr£5 Dinner fr£10 Last dinner 9.30pm
Credit Cards 1 2 3 5

○ ***The Riverdale Hotel*** Llanidloes Rd
☎Central reservation 0800-838155
Due to open May 1990
51⇌

NEWTOWN LINFORD Leicestershire Map **04** SK50

★★Johnscliffe Hotel & Restaurant 73 Main St LE6 0AF
☎Markfield(0530)242228 & 243281
Closed 24 Dec-4 Jan
Fine rural views are available from this converted Edwardian house with its extensive grounds.
8rm(2⇌5↑)(1fb)3⊞ CTV in all bedrooms ® T
CTV 30P ✽
☋ English & French V ♁ ⌧ Last dinner 9.45pm
Credit Cards 1 2 3 5

NOLTON HAVEN Dyfed Map **02** SM81

★★*Mariners Inn* SA62 3NH ☎Camrose(0437)710469
The small, family-run inn stands near to the sea and within the Pembrokeshire National Park. It provides modern bedrooms which are cosy and compact, character bars and a new restaurant complex which serves a good standard of food.
11rm(4⇌7↑)(3fb) CTV in all bedrooms ®
10P
☋ Welsh, English & French V ♁ ⌧ Last dinner 10pm
Credit Cards 1 2 3

NORMAN CROSS Cambridgeshire Map **04** TL19

★★★57% Crest Great North Rd PE7 3TB (Crest)
☎Peterborough(0733)240209 Telex no 32576
FAX (0733) 244455
Situated on the southbound side of the busy A1, with access off the roundabout at Norman Cross. This sound hotel has modern facilities. One wing has recently been refurbished to a good standard, with executive, studio and Lady Crest bedrooms. Other bedrooms, though equipped with the same facilities, are looking more dated.
97rm(77⇌20↑)⊬in 24 bedrooms CTV in 98bedrooms ® T ✱
sB⇌↑£57.50 dB⇌↑£69.50-£81.50 (room only) ⊟
(120P ✽ CFA games room *xmas*
V ♁ ⌧ ⊬ Lunch £7.80-£11 High tea £2.25 Dinner £12.60-£14.90&alc Last dinner 10pm
Credit Cards 1 2 3 4 5 £

NORMANTON Leicestershire Map **04** SK90

★★★♔75% Normanton Park LE15 8RP (1m E unclass)
☎Stamford(0780)720315

The huge 18th-century mansion which once stood here was demolished in the 1920's, but the derelict coach house – a magnificent building in its own right, complete with clock tower – was acquired by the present owners and converted into luxurious modern hotel accommodation. From its beautifully appointed restaurant, diners can enjoy splendid views across Rutland Water whilst sampling the delights of the sensibly priced à la carte menu with its imaginative selection of seventeen main courses, all carefully prepared and attractively presented.
8rm(6⇌1↑)Annexe8⇌(5fb) CTV in all bedrooms ® T ✗ (ex guide dogs) ✱ sB&Bfr£40 sB&B⇌↑£45-£55 dB&Bfr£45 dB&B⇌↑£55-£65 ⊟
⊞ CTV 60P ✽ sailing canoeing windsurfing
☋ English & French V ♁ ⌧ Lunch fr£8&alc Dinner fr£11.75&alc Last dinner 10pm
Credit Cards 1 2 3 5 £

See advertisement under OAKHAM

NORTHALLERTON North Yorkshire Map **08** SE39

★★★♔67% Solberge Hall Newby Wiske DL7 9ER (3.25m S off A167) (Best Western)
☎(0609)779191
FAX (0609) 780472

This gracious, porticoed country house dates from the Victorian era and stands in fifteen acres of grounds. Carefully chosen furnishings enhance its character, the comfortable bedrooms offer many extra facilities, and service is friendly.

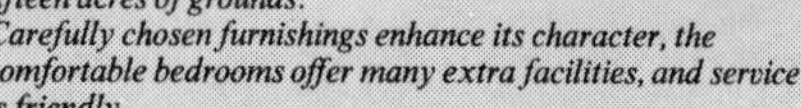

30⇌(2fb)2⊞ CTV in all bedrooms ® T ✱
sB&B⇌£58-£65 dB&B⇌£70-£85 ⊟
100P ✽ snooker croquet clay pigeon shooting *xmas*
☋ English & French V ♁ ⌧ Lunch fr£9.50&alc High tea fr£5 Dinner £15-£20&alc Last dinner 9.30pm
Credit Cards 1 2 3 5

See advertisement on page 509

★★★67% Sundial Darlington Rd DL6 2PN ☎(0609)780525
FAX (0609) 780491
Modern hotel a mile north of town on the A167. Bedrooms are well-equipped for the business client, and the elegant restaurant offers an interesting menu.
28⇌(8fb)⊬in 22 bedrooms CTV in all bedrooms ® T ✱
sB&B⇌£25-£49 dB&B⇌£50-£58 Continental breakfast ⊟
(⊞ 60P ✽ ♫
☋ English & French V ♁ ⌧ ⊬ Lunch £7.50-£7.95 High tea £2.25-£4.75 Dinner fr£13.75&alc Last dinner 9.30pm
Credit Cards 1 2 3 5

★★The Golden Lion Market Place DL7 8PP (Trusthouse Forte)
☎(0609)777411
Sympathetically modernised inn with Georgian façade offering comfortable old world atmosphere and stylish dining room.
28rm(15⇌)⊬in 12 bedrooms CTV in all bedrooms ® T
sBfr£48 sB⇌fr£56 dBfr£62 dB⇌fr£72 (room only) ⊟
CTV 60P *xmas*
V ♁ ⌧ ⊬ S% Lunch £9 High tea £6 Last high tea 6pm
Credit Cards 1 2 3 4 5

NORTHAMPTON Northamptonshire Map **04** SP76

★★★★55% Swallow Eagle Dr NN4 0HW (off A5, between A428 & A508) (Swallow) ☎(0604)768700 Telex no 31562
FAX (0604) 769011
An imaginativly designed modern hotel with well-equipped bedrooms, two restaurants and an excellent leisure centre.
122⇌↑⊬in 38 bedrooms CTV in all bedrooms ® T ✱
sB&B⇌↑£73-£110 dB&B⇌↑£95-£110 ⊟
▶

(166P ⛾(heated) sauna solarium gymnasium jacuzzi steam room
V ✿ ☕ Lunch fr£10.50 High tea fr£7 Dinner fr£11.25 Last dinner 10.30pm
Credit Cards 1 2 3 5

★★★ 50% Grand Gold St NN1 1RE ☎(0604)250511
Telex no 311198 FAX (0604)234534
62⇌♨(2fb) CTV in all bedrooms ® T ✱ sB&B⇌♨fr£50 dB&B⇌♨fr£60 ⊟
Lift (16P 10⛟ (£1.50) CFA
Lunch fr£8.50&alc Dinner fr£10&alc Last dinner 9.30pm
Credit Cards 1 2 3 5 £

★★★ 70% Northampton Moat House Silver Street, Town Centre NN1 2TA (Queens Moat) ☎(0604)22441 Telex no 311142 FAX (0604) 230614
Centrally located, the hotel is just 5 miles from the M1 junctions 15 and 16. The attractive 'Le Jardin' restaurant offers an à la carte, a table d'hôte and an 'all-day' menu of lighter meals. There are also two bars, a comfortable open-plan lounge area and extensive conference and function facilities.
142⇌♨(4fb) CTV in all bedrooms ® T sB&B⇌♨£64.50 dB&B⇌♨£79.50 ⊟
Lift (200P (£2.50) CFA sauna solarium gymnasium jacuzzi hairdresser
☋ English & French V ✿ ☕ Lunch £7.50-£15alc Dinner fr£11&alc Last dinner 10.30pm
Credit Cards 1 2 3 4 5

★★★ 69% Westone Moat House Ashley Way, Weston Favell NN3 3EA (3m E off A45) (Queens Moat) ☎(0604)406262
Telex no 312587 FAX (0604)415023
Closed Xmas-New Years Day
30⇌Annexe36⇌(3fb) CTV in all bedrooms ® T
sB&B⇌£21-£59 dB&B⇌£42-£69 ⊟
Lift (CTV 100P 2⛟ (£5) ❊ sauna solarium gymnasium croquet putting *xmas*
☋ International V ✿ ☕ Lunch £9.90&alc Dinner £10.50&alc Last dinner 9.45pm
Credit Cards 1 2 3 5

★★*Lime Trees* 8 Langham Place, Barrack Rd NN2 6AA (from city centre follow sign A508 Leicester) (Inter)
☎Gullane(0620 84)2123
Closed 25-26 Dec RS 27 Dec-New Year
Friendly, family-run hotel offering comfortable accommodation to mainly commercial clientele.
20rm(2⇌13♨)(2fb) CTV in all bedrooms ® T ✗
CTV 20P ⛟
V ✿ ☕ Last dinner 9pm
Credit Cards 1 2 3 5

★★Thorplands Toby Talavera Way, Round Spinney NN3 4RN (Toby) ☎(0604)494241
Closed 25, 26 Dec & 1 Jan
30⇌(2fb)⚟in 8 bedrooms CTV in all bedrooms ® T ✗ ✱
sB&B⇌£44.50 dB&B⇌£51.50 ⊟
(100P ❊ pool table
V ✿ ☕ ⚟ Lunch £5.95&alc Dinner £5.95&alc Last dinner 10.30pm
Credit Cards 1 2 3 5

○***TraveLodge*** (A45, towards M1 junct 16) (Trusthouse Forte)
☎(0604)758395
40⇌
P

✗***Vineyard*** 7 Derngate NN1 1TU ☎(0604)33978
☋ French V 30 seats Last lunch 1.50pm Last dinner 10.10pm
P ⚟
Credit Cards 1 2 3 5

NORTH BALLACHULISH Highland *Inverness-shire*
Map **14** NN06

★★Loch Leven PH33 6DA ☎Onich(08553)236
Family run hotel on the shores of Loch Leven with magnificent views.
12rm(4⇌1♨)(2fb) CTV in 5bedrooms ✱ sB&B£17-£20
dB&B£34-£40 dB&B⇌♨£40-£44
CTV 60P ⛟ ❊
☋ Scottish & Continental V ✿ ☕ Bar Lunch £2.75-£8alc High tea £2.75-£8alc Last high tea 9pm
Credit Cards 1 3

NORTH BERWICK Lothian *East Lothian* Map **12** NT58

★★★ 64% The Marine Cromwell Rd EH39 4LZ (Trusthouse Forte) ☎(0620)2406 Telex no 72550 FAX (0620) 4480
This popular golfing and conference hotel stands beside the championship golf links overlooking the Firth of Forth. Public rooms have been upgraded to a good standard, as have also most of the comfortable and well-equipped bedrooms.
83⇌⚟in 10 bedrooms CTV in all bedrooms ® T ✱
sB⇌£59-£65 dB⇌£68-£100 (room only) ⊟
Lift (200P 20⛟ ❊ CFA ⛾(heated) ℘ (hard) squash snooker sauna solarium ♫ ⌂ *xmas*
☋ International V ✿ ☕ ⚟ S% Lunch £7.50-£8.50&alc Dinner £12.50&alc Last dinner 9.30pm
Credit Cards 1 2 3 4 5

★★*Blenheim House* Westgate EH39 4AF ☎(0620)2385
The hotel stands close to the town centre, commanding fine views across West Bay to the coast of Fife. It offers bedrooms which are comfortable though modestly equipped and appointed, pleasant public rooms and informal service.
11rm(5⇌1♨)(2fb) CTV in all bedrooms ®
30P ⛟ ❊
✿

★★Nether Abbey 20 Dirleton Av EH39 4BQ ☎(0620)2802
Modest and traditional in style, the hotel stands on the northern approach to the town centre. Its comfortable lounge bar is popular with local people, and the bedrooms are rather simple, though improvements are planned.
16rm(4⇌6♨)(5fb) CTV in all bedrooms ® sB&Bfr£20
sB&B⇌♨fr£23.50 dB&Bfr£40 dB&B⇌♨fr£43.50
CTV 40P ❊
✿ Bar Lunch fr£3.80alc Dinner £12.50 Last dinner 8.30pm
Credit Cards 1 3

★★Point Garry West Bay Rd EH39 4AW ☎(0620)2380
Closed Nov-Mar
Popular with golfers, this family-run hotel overlooks the West Course and sea front. Some of the public areas have recently been refurbished and the modest bedrooms are gradually being improved.
16rm(5⇌6♨)(6fb) CTV in all bedrooms ® sB&Bfr£20
sB&B⇌♨fr£30 dB&Bfr£40 dB&B⇌♨fr£58 ⊟
14P ⛟ snooker
☋ International V ✿ ☕ Dinner fr£9.95&alc Last dinner 9pm

NORTH FERRIBY Humberside Map **08** SE92

★★★ 67% Crest Hotel-Hull Ferriby High Rd HU14 3LG (Crest)
☎Hull(0482)645212 Telex no 592558 FAX (0482) 643332
RS Xmas & New Year
Situated just off the M62/A63, the hotel is in a rural setting with views over the River Humber to the impressive Humber Bridge. Comfortable accommodation and interesting menus are complemented by warm, courteous service.
102⇌(6fb)⚟in 20 bedrooms CTV in all bedrooms ® T ✱
sBfr£65 sB⇌fr£65 dBfr£77 dB⇌fr£77 (room only) ⊟

☾120P ❊ CFA
International V Lunch fr£8.50 Dinner fr£14.75 Last dinner 10pm
Credit Cards 1 2 3 4 5 £

NORTH HUISH Devon Map **03** SX75

★★ BROOKDALE HOUSE

TQ10 9NR ☎Gara Bridge (054882)402 & 415
Closed 3-24 Jan

Tucked away in a wooded valley in Devon's lush South Hams, this family-run hotel is charming and welcoming. Charles Trevor ensures the guest's well-being with touches such as fresh flowers, home-made biscuits, books and magazines in the prettily furnished bedrooms, two of which are in a cottage annexe. All are very well equipped, and the bathrooms, well-stocked with good toiletries, are notably spacious. Everywhere antiques and attractive decorations create a pleasant atmosphere, and the public rooms are warm and comfortable. The recent appointment of Terry Rich as head chef has brought a new flair and expertise to the kitchen, and in particular our inspectors have praised the chicken and wild mushroom ravioli with tomato and basil sauce, hot mushroom strudel, steamed fillet of brill with saffron potatoes, and succulent breast of local duck in a honey and ginger sauce. The home-made sweets and puddings are equally tempting.

▶

N

6⇨Annexe2⇨ CTV in all bedrooms ® T ✗
sB&B⇨£55-£65 dB&B⇨£70-£90 ₿
20P ✽ nc10yrs *xmas*
✗ Dinner £23 Last dinner 9pm
Credit Cards [1] [3]

NORTHIAM East Sussex Map **05** TQ82

★★**Hayes Arms** Village Green TN31 6NN (Exec Hotel)
☎(07974)3142
This 15th-century farmhouse, skilfully extended in Georgian times, lies close to the 12th-century village church. Well-equipped bedrooms are individually furnished, mostly with antiques, and log burning inglenook fires complement the traditional, relaxing atmosphere. The standard of cooking is good and will satisfy most tastes.
7⇨1⊟ CTV in all bedrooms ® T ✗ ✱ sB&B⇨£29.50-£38 dB&B⇨£48-£58
40P ✽ nc10yrs
Bar Lunch £2.10-£10.50alc Dinner £9-£16alc Last dinner 9.30pm
Credit Cards [1] [2] [3]

NORTHLEACH Gloucestershire Map **04** SP11

★**Wheatsheaf** GL54 3EZ ☎Cotswold(0451)60244
Small, family-run, Cotswold stone inn of character, with good food and simple but spotless bedrooms.
9rm(2⇨5♠)(1fb) CTV in 8bedrooms TV in 1bedroom ® ✱
sB&Bfr£20 sB&B⇨♠fr£24 dB&Bfr£30 dB&B⇨♠fr£38 ₿
20P 3🚗
V ♥ ☕ Lunch fr£7.50 Dinner £9.75-£11.60alc Last dinner 9.30pm
Credit Cards [1] [2] [3] [5]

NORTH MUSKHAM Nottinghamshire Map **08** SK75

○ ***TraveLodge*** A1 NG23 6HT (Trusthouse Forte)
☎Newark(0636)703635
30⇨

NORTHOP Clwyd Map **07** SJ26

★★★75% **Soughton Hall**
CH7 6AB (Pride of Britain)
☎(035286)207
Telex no 61267
FAX (035286)382

You pass through rolling parkland with grazing sheep and up an avenue of lime trees towards this lovely Georgian mansion. There are plans to develop some further neat, formal gardens to include a tennis court. The interior has been carefully restored: fine public rooms include a first floor drawing room, with tapestries, comfortable seating and carved doors, the hall-lounge with a carved chimney-piece, a library with log fire, and the small 'Justice Bar' (once a courtroom). Good food prepared by Chef Malcolm Warham, is served in the elegant dining room in the evenings; breakfast is served in country-house style in the old Servants' Hall. The bedrooms are all individually furnished in keeping with the house, and bathrooms are superb. The Rodenhurst family are most friendly hosts, and all the staff offer pleasant and attentive service.

12⇨♠1⊟ CTV in all bedrooms T ✱
dB&B⇨♠£90-£130 ₿
☾ CTV 40P ✽ croquet nc10yrs *xmas*
♥ ☕ ✗ Lunch £14 Dinner £20.50&alc Last dinner 9.30pm
Credit Cards [1] [2] [3] £

NORTHOP HALL Clwyd Map **07** SJ26

★★★58% **The Chequers Country House Hotel** Chester Rd CH7 6HJ (Inter) ☎Deeside(0244)816181 Telex no 617112 FAX (0244) 814661
Old manor house in wooded parkland has well-equipped bedrooms, and some Welsh dishes on an extensive menu.
29⇨♠(2fb)1⊟✗in 2 bedrooms CTV in all bedrooms ® T
sB&B⇨♠£40-£45 dB&B⇨♠£55-£65 ₿
100P 2🚗 ✽
☋ International V ♥ ☕ ✗ Lunch £6.95&alc Dinner £11.95&alc Last dinner 9.45pm
Credit Cards [1] [2] [3] [5] £

NORTH QUEENSFERRY Fife Map **11** NT18

○ ***Queensferry Lodge*** St Margaret's Head KY11 1HP
☎(0383)410000 Telex no 727553 FAX (0383) 419708
Due to have opened summer 1989
30⇨

NORTH STOKE Oxfordshire Map **04** SU68

★★★74% **Springs** Wallingford Rd OX9 6BE
☎Wallingford(0491)36687 Telex no 849794 FAX (0491)36877
A pleasing country house hotel which has been extended and refurbished over the last few years to provide comfortable, character public rooms and individually-styled and furnished bedrooms. Many rooms enjoy beautiful views, either over the lake (which is flood-lit at night) or the quiet woodland which surrounds the hotel. Food standards here are worthy of commendation; expertise and flair combine with the good use of quality seasonal ingredients.
34rm(33⇨1♠)(4fb)2⊟ CTV in all bedrooms T S10%
sB&B⇨♠£65-£77 dB&B⇨♠£85-£105 ₿
☾ 130P ✽ ⇨(heated) 🎾 (hard) sauna croquet putting *xmas*
☋ English & French V ♥ ☕ S10% Lunch £14.50-£25alc Dinner fr£22alc Last dinner 10.15pm
Credit Cards [1] [2] [3] [4] [5] £

NORTH WALTHAM Hampshire Map **04** SU54

★★**Wheatsheaf** RG25 2BB (on A30) (Lansbury)
☎Dummer(0256)758282 due to change to (0256) 398282
Telex no 859775 FAX (0256) 398253
A popular meeting place for over three hundred years and now skilfully modernised, the hotel retains its historic atmosphere whilst offering easy access to junctions 7 and 8 of the M3. Meals from the Farmers Kitchen and popular cuisine from Henekey's Restaurant can be enjoyed in the atmosphere of a rural pub.
28⇨♠(1fb)1⊟ CTV in all bedrooms ® T sB&B⇨♠£30-£63
dB&B⇨♠£60-£75 ₿
☾ 100P ✽
♥ ☕ Lunch fr£8.50 Dinner fr£12.50 Last dinner 10.20pm
Credit Cards [1] [2] [3] [4] [5]

NORTHWICH Cheshire Map **07** SJ67

★★★63% ***Hartford Hall*** School Ln, Hartford CW8 1PW (2m SW off bypass A556) (Consort) ☎Hartford(0606)75711
A 16th-century country mansion standing in its own extensive grounds with a small lake, just off the A556 Northwich by-pass. Bedrooms are well appointed and the public rooms are in character with the historical style of the house.

21⇌(1fb) CTV in all bedrooms ® T
☾ CTV 50P ✲ ⌂
V ♈
Credit Cards [1] [2] [3] [5]

★★Woodpecker London Rd CW9 8EG ☎(0606)45524
Telex no 668025
Closed Xmas Day (pm)
This well-furnished hotel, situated just off the bypass road, has bedrooms in a modern extension block.
33rm(31⇌2♠)(3fb) CTV in all bedrooms ® T ✳
sB&B⇌♠£46-£58 dB&B⇌♠£65-£80 ⊟
☾ 100P ✲
♀ English & French V ♈ ⊻ Lunch £7-£8&alc Dinner £9-£11&alc Last dinner 9.45pm
Credit Cards [1] [2] [3] [5]

★Blue Cap 520 Chester Rd, Sandiway CW8 2DN (Berni/Chef & Brewer) ☎(0606)883006
12rm(6⇌6♠)1⊞ CTV in all bedrooms ® T ✕ (ex guide dogs)
sB&B⇌♠fr£37 dB&B⇌♠fr£48.50 ⊟
200P ⊞
♀ Mainly grills V ♈ ⊻ ⚡ Lunch £8 Dinner £9 Last dinner 9.30pm
Credit Cards [1] [2] [3] [5]

○***Friendly Floatel*** London Rd ☎(0606)44443
FAX (0606) 42592
Due to open Nov 1989
60⇌

NORTON Shropshire Map **07** SJ70

★★*Hundred House* Bridgnorth Rd TF11 9EE (on A442 6m N of Bridgnorth) (Exec Hotel) ☎(095271)353 Telex no 35815
FAX (0952) 462557
The bedrooms at this roadside hotel are attractively decorated with patchwork quilts and curtains; Mrs Phillips has an eye for detail and this is reflected in each room. The busy bar and restaurant serves well-prepared food in a friendly, informal manner.
9⇌(5fb) CTV in all bedrooms ® T ✕
40P
♈ ⊻ Last dinner 10pm
Credit Cards [1] [2] [3]

See advertisement under TELFORD

NORWICH Norfolk Map **05** TG20

★★★64% Arlington 10 Arlington Ln Newmarket Rd NR2 2DA (Best Western) ☎(0603)617841 Telex no 975392
FAX (0603) 663708
Five minutes from the city centre, with compact well-equipped rooms and two restaurants – the elegant Le Papillon and the Grill Room Carvery.
44⇌(3fb)1⊞ CTV in all bedrooms ® T ✳ sB&B⇌fr£54
dB&B⇌fr£75 ⊟
☾ 60P ♫ *xmas*
♀ English & French V ♈ ⊻ Lunch £7.95 High tea fr£7.95 Dinner fr£7.95 Last dinner 10pm
Credit Cards [1] [2] [3] [5]

★★★57% Lansdowne 116 Thorpe Rd NR1 1RU (Embassy)
☎(0603)620302 FAX (0603) 761706
Situated just half a mile from the historic city centre, the Lansdowne provides comfortable accommodation for both leisure and commercial guests. Bedrooms are well equipped and there is a cocktail bar and a restaurant decorated in pastel colours.
39rm(28⇌10♠)(1fb)⚡in 4 bedrooms CTV in all bedrooms ®
T ✳ sB⇌♠£46-£56 dB⇌♠£56-£70 (room only) ⊟
Lift ☾ CTV 60P CFA *xmas*

►

N

French Lunch £7.50-£9.85&alc Dinner £9.85&alc Last dinner 9.15pm
Credit Cards 1 2 3 4 5

★★★62% Maids Head Tombland NR3 1LB (Queens Moat) (0603)761111 Telex no 975080 FAX (0603) 613688
Historic hotel with 13th-century features, in the shadow of the cathedral. There are three bars and many lounge areas. Some rooms have recently been refurbished.
81(1fb)1 CTV in all bedrooms ® T sB&B£57-£77 dB&B£71.50-£89
Lift 80P 20 CFA *xmas*
English & French V Lunch £4.75-£8.25 Dinner fr£10.25&alc Last dinner 9.45pm
Credit Cards 1 2 3 5 £

★★★63% Hotel Nelson Prince of Wales Rd NR1 1DX (0603)760260 Telex no 975203 FAX (0603) 620008
Modern hotel set attractively on the River Wensum, with two riverside restaurants.
121(24fb) CTV in all bedrooms ® T (ex guide dogs) sB&B£58.50-£66.50 dB&B£69.50-£77.50
Lift 119P 30 sauna *xmas*
V Lunch £7.95&alc Dinner £10.50&alc Last dinner 9.45pm
Credit Cards 1 2 3 4 5

★★★63% Hotel Norwich 121-131 Boundary Rd NR3 2BA (Best Western) (0603)787260 Telex no 975337 FAX (0603) 400466
A pleasing modern hotel, easily accessible from the ring road to the north-west of the city, offers a good range and quality of facilities.
102(16fb) in 5 bedrooms CTV in all bedrooms ® T (ex guide dogs) * sB&B£53-£60 dB&B£63-£70
225P CFA *xmas*
International V Lunch £11-£13&alc High tea £6-£7.50 Dinner £10.50-£12.25&alc Last dinner 10pm
Credit Cards 1 2 3 5 £

N

★★★68% Post House Ipswich Rd NR4 6EP (Trusthouse Forte) (0603)56431 Telex no 975106 FAX (0603) 506400
Commercial hotel on outskirts with consistently satisfactory standards.
120 in 2 bedrooms CTV in all bedrooms ® T *
sB£67-£77 dB£77-£87 (room only)
200P CFA (heated) sauna solarium gymnasium health & fitness centre *xmas*
English & French V Lunch £7.25-£9.75&alc High tea fr£6.75 Dinner fr£13.95&alc Last dinner 10pm
Credit Cards 1 2 3 4 5

★★★63% Sprowston Manor Wroxham Road, Sprowston NR7 8RP (2m NE A1151) (Best Western) (0603)410871 Telex no 975356 FAX (0603) 423911
A hotel of 16th-century origin, just north of Norwich and also convenient for the Broads. Extensive improvements to rooms and conference facilities were underway in 1989.
25rm(19 6)Annexe14rm(13 1)(1fb)2 CTV in all bedrooms ® T
120P CFA croquet
English & French V Last dinner 10pm
Credit Cards 1 2 3 5 £

★★Annesley 6 Newmarket Rd NR2 2LA (0603)624553
Closed Xmas
This small, friendly and family-run hotel is made up of two Georgian buildings which are linked by a sun lounge containing a fifty year old grape vine.
19rm(1 10)(1fb) CTV in all bedrooms ® T (ex guide dogs) * sB&Bfr£25 sB&B fr£31.50 dB&Bfr£36.50 dB&B fr£41
30P
English & French V Lunch fr£9.95 Dinner fr£10.95&alc Last dinner 9pm
Credit Cards 1 2 3 5

★★Oaklands 89 Yarmouth Rd, Thorpe St Andrew NR7 0HH (0603)34471 FAX (0603) 700318
Tucked away in the leafy suburb of Thorpe St Andrew, the hotel is set in a secluded position, with views of the valley of the River Yare. Most bedrooms are en suite and are simply furnished, yet comfortable and well equipped. The restaurant provides both a carvery and à la carte meals, and the food is competently cooked.
43rm(24 3)(5fb) CTV in all bedrooms ® T sB&B£38-£45 sB&B £48-£60 dB&B£50-£60 dB&B £60-£80
90P *xmas*
V S% Lunch £7.95-£15 Dinner £9.95-£18 Last dinner 9.30pm
Credit Cards 1 2 3 5 £

○***Friendly Lodge*** Derehand Rd, Bowthorpe (0603)741161
Due to have opened Oct 1989
84

✕✕Adlard's 79 Upper St Giles St NR2 1AB (0603)633522
This attractive restaurant was a well-established favourite in the nearby market town of Wymondham until David and Mary Adlard moved it to larger premises in Norwich. The candlelit tables, lovely collection of paintings, and green and white decor make a relaxing atmosphere in which to enjoy David Adlard's excellent cooking. His dishes, such as poached supreme of salmon with a chive butter sauce, or Spring lamb cutlets with a crust of fresh herbs served on a garnish of oyster mushrooms are immaculately prepared, and his sauces have a wonderful lightness of flavour. The wine list is notable and extensive.
Lunch not served All week
30 seats Dinner £22-£24 Last dinner 9pm
Credit Cards 1 3

✕✕Marco's 17 Potter-Gate NR2 1DS (0603)624044
Centrally situated, this busy and popular little restaurant produces both classic and some more imaginative Italian dishes. Competent service and a relaxing atmosphere complement the highly enjoyable food. Not a run-of-the-mill pizzeria by any means.
Closed Sun, Mon & 20 Aug-20 Sep
Italian V 40 seats * Lunch fr£12&alc Dinner £25-£30alc Last lunch 2pm Last dinner 10pm
Credit Cards 1 2 3 4 5

✕*Greens Seafood* 82 Upper St Giles St NR1 1AQ (0603)623733
Interesting and friendly city-centre restaurant with striking décor, offering a wide range of fresh fish dishes and a good wine list. Some meat dishes also available.
Closed Sun, Mon, 2 wks Xmas & BH's
Lunch not served Sat
V 52 seats Last lunch 2pm Last dinner 10.30pm nc8yrs
Credit Cards 1 3

NOTTINGHAM Nottinghamshire Map **08** SK54

See **Town Plan Section**
★★★★53% The Albany Saint James's St NG1 6BN (Trusthouse Forte) (0602)470131 Telex no 37211 FAX (0602) 484366
Just off the central ring road, with good views of city and castle from many rooms. Extensive refurbishment was planned in 1989.
139 in 20 bedrooms CTV in all bedrooms ® T sBfr£67 dBfr£82 (room only)
Lift CFA *xmas*
English & French V Lunch fr£9.95&alc High tea fr£4.95alc Dinner fr£9.95&alc Last dinner 10.15pm
Credit Cards 1 2 3 4 5

★★★★ 61% **Royal Moat House International** Wollaton St NG1 5RH (Queens Moat) ☏(0602)414444 Telex no 37101 FAX (0602) 475667
Large, well-equipped city-centre hotel with a wide range of facilities and four restaurants. Ample parking available in multi-storey car park next door.
201⇌⌐(20fb)⁄in 44 bedrooms CTV in all bedrooms ® T
Lift ☾ ⊞ 600P squash solarium gymnasium ♫
☋ English & French V ♧ ⚐
Credit Cards 1 2 3 5

★★★★ 56% ***Savoy*** Mansfield Rd NG5 2BT ☏(0602)602621 Telex no 377429 FAX (0602) 691506
This large, busy, modern hotel stands less than a mile from the city centre and provides good parking facilities.
173⇌⌐⁄in 66 bedrooms CTV in all bedrooms ® T ✈
Lift ☾ 250P 90🚗
☋ International V ♧ ⚐ ⁄ Last dinner 11pm
Credit Cards 1 2 3 5

★★★ 62% **Stakis Victoria** Milton St NG1 3PZ (Stakis) ☏(0602)419561 Telex no 37401 FAX (0602) 484736
This attractive, red-brick building in the city centre, formerly a railway hotel, has undergone extensive modernisation. There are spacious public areas and a good range of function facilities, as well as a choice of different styles of well-equipped bedrooms.
166⇌⌐(15fb)1⊠⁄in 23 bedrooms CTV in all bedrooms ® T
✳ S3% sB⇌⌐£56-£66 dB⇌⌐£70-£81 (room only) ⊟
Lift ☾ 25P *xmas*
V ♧ ⚐ ⁄ Bar Lunch £1.75-£3.75 Dinner £13.50-£15&alc Last dinner 9.45pm
Credit Cards 1 2 3 5

See advertisement on page 515

★★★ 61% **Strathdon Thistle** Derby Rd NG1 5FT (Thistle) ☎(0602)418501 Telex no 377185 FAX (0602) 483725
Modern city-centre hotel with high standard of cuisine.
69rm(25⇨44↱)(8fb)⊁in 8 bedrooms CTV in all bedrooms ® **T** ✱ sB⇨↱£52-£60 dB⇨↱£67-£74 (room only) 🖹
Lift ☾ 10P 5🚗 CFA ♫
☋ International ♲ ☑ ⊁ Lunch fr£9.40&alc Dinner fr£10.75&alc Last dinner 10.30pm
Credit Cards [1] [2] [3] [4] [5]

★★★ 66% **Waltons** 2 North Road, The Park NG7 1AG ☎(0602)475215 FAX (0602)475053
Closed Boxing Day
Just west of the city centre, this large Georgian house stands adjacent to the A6200 and offers accommodation in comfortable, well-equipped bedrooms, complemented by elegant public areas.
10rm(4⇨5↱)1🛏 CTV in all bedrooms ® **T** ✱ sB&B⇨↱£37-£50 dB&B⇨↱£60-£70
☾ CTV 14P 4🚗 ⛫ ✲ ⛼ sauna solarium ♫ *xmas*
☋ French **V** ♲ ☑ Lunch fr£10.50 Dinner fr£12.50 Last dinner 9.45pm
Credit Cards [1] [2] [3]

★★ **Priory** Derby Rd, Wollaton Vale NG8 2NR (Toby) ☎(0602)221691
This large public house has a modern extension housing a grill restaurant and bar, and a wing of comfortable well-equipped bedrooms.
31⇨(4fb)⊁in 7 bedrooms CTV in all bedrooms ® **T** ✗ (ex guide dogs) ✱ sB&B⇨£36.50-£48.50 dB&B⇨£46.50-£59 🖹
☾ 200P
☋ Mainly grills **V** ♲ ☑ ⊁ Lunch fr£5.95&alc Dinner fr£5.95&alc Last dinner 10.15pm
Credit Cards [1] [2] [3] [5]

★★ **Rufford** 53 Melton Road, West Bridgford NG2 7NE ☎(0602)814202 Telex no 455801
Closed Xmas
This popular commercial hotel, situated in a suburb of Nottingham, has well-equipped bedrooms and a basement games room.
35↱ CTV in all bedrooms ® **T** ✗ (ex guide dogs) S% sB&B↱£35.40 dB&B↱£55.66 🖹
☾ CTV 35P
♲ ☑ S% Dinner £9.20-£10.93 Last dinner 8pm
Credit Cards [1] [2] [3] [5]

★★ **Westminster Hotel** 310-318 Mansfield Rd, Carrington NG5 2EF (on A60 1.5m N of town centre) ☎(0602)623023 FAX (0602) 691156
Situated 1.5 miles north of the city centre on the A60, this comfortable hotel provides well-equipped accommodation, a pleasant restaurant and an attractive lounge bar.
57⇨ CTV in all bedrooms ® **T** ✗ ✱ sB&B⇨£38-£40 dB&B⇨£48-£50 🖹
Lift ☾ 38P
☋ Cosmopolitan ♲ ☑ Dinner £10-£11 Last dinner 9.15pm
Credit Cards [1] [3]

✕✕ **Les Artistes Gourmands** 61 Wollaton Rd, Beeston NG9 2NG ☎(0602)228288
Closed Sun & 1 wk Jan
Lunch not served Sat & Mon
☋ French **V** 70 seats ✱ Lunch £10-£14&alc Dinner £19.90&alc Last lunch 1.45pm Last dinner 9.30pm 1P ⊁
Credit Cards [1] [2] [3] [5]

✕ ***Shogun*** 95 Talbot St, Canning Circus NG1 5GN ☎(0602)475611 FAX (0602) 400318
Truly Japanese, and an experience not to be missed, the simply furnished city-centre restaurant is embellished with prints, paintings and a life-size figure of a Samurai warrior. Its well-designed menu offers a wide choice, enabling visitors to sample such delights as Tempurs (deep-fried prawns and vegetables in the lightest of batters), Sukiyaki (thin slices of beef cooked with vegetables at the table) and of course Sashimi (raw fresh fish). A limited range of wines is available, but you may choose to complement your meal with Japanese beer or green tea.
Closed Sun
Lunch not served Mon
☋ Japanese **V** 50 seats Last lunch 1.45pm Last dinner 11pm ₱
Credit Cards [1] [2] [3] [5]

NUNEATON Warwickshire Map **04** SP39

★★ **Chase** Higham Ln CV11 6AG (Porterhouse) ☎(0203)341013 FAX (0203) 383406
Modernised hotel, popular with business clientele.
28⇨↱ CTV in all bedrooms ® **T**
CTV 300P ⛫ ✲
☋ English & French **V** ♲ ☑
Credit Cards [1] [2] [3] [5] £

★★ **Longshoot Toby** Watling St CV11 6JH (Toby) ☎(0203)329711 Telex no 311100
Closed 24 Dec-4 Jan
Busy motel at the A5/A47 junction.
Annexe47⇨↱(5fb)⊁in 11 bedrooms CTV in all bedrooms ® **T** ✗ ✱ sB&B⇨↱£24.50-£34.50 dB&B⇨↱£34.50-£44.50 🖹
☾ 120P
V ♲ ⊁ Lunch fr£6.35 Dinner fr£6.35 Last dinner 10pm
Credit Cards [1] [2] [3] [5]

⌂ ***Griff House Travel Inn*** Coventry Rd CV10 7PJ ☎(0203)343584
Closed Christmas Day & Boxing Day
The childhood home of writer George Eliot has been tastefully converted to provided a popular, value-for-money restaurant and comfortable, modern, en-suite accommodation in a position on the A444 north of junction 3 of the M6.
38⇨ CTV in all bedrooms ✗
120P
☋ Mainly grills Wine £5.20 Last dinner 10.30
Credit Cards [1] [2] [3] [5]

NUNNINGTON North Yorkshire Map **08** SE67

✕✕ **Ryedale Lodge** YO6 5XB ☎(04395)246
Elegant small restaurant, delightfully converted from a Victorian railway station on the edge of the Vale of Pickering. The four-course table d'hôte offers mainly English dishes such as pigeon pie, roast duck, breast of smoked goose and duck, and local Ryedale red deer, with a stimulating wine list and delicious desserts. Seven bedrooms provide commendable accommodation and more are planned.
Lunch not served
☋ European **V** 30 seats ✱ Dinner £19.50-£21.50 Last dinner 9.30pm 30P 70 bedrooms available ⊁
Credit Cards [1] [3]

NUTFIELD Surrey Map **04** TQ35

★★★ 70% **Nutfield Priory** RH1 4EN ☎Redhill(0737)822066 FAX (0737) 823321
Impressive country house built in romantic style in 1872, offering good cuisine and magnificent views over Surrey and Sussex. One of the best vantage points is the comfortable library. The hall and cocktail lounge provide further sitting areas, and the spacious bedrooms are individually styled.
32⇨ CTV in all bedrooms **T**
Lift ☾ 30P ⛫ ✲
☋ European **V** ♲ ☑ Last dinner 10.15pm
Credit Cards [1] [2] [3] [5]

Book as early as possible for busy holiday periods.

N

OAKHAM Leicestershire Map **04** SK80

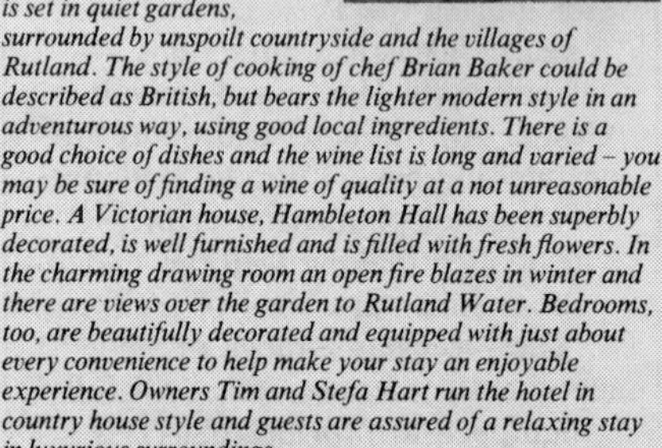

✿★★★♛
HAMBLETON HALL

Hambleton LE15 8TH (3m E off A606) (Relais et Châteaux) ☎(0572)756991
Telex no 342888

This attractive manor house is set in quiet gardens, surrounded by unspoilt countryside and the villages of Rutland. The style of cooking of chef Brian Baker could be described as British, but bears the lighter modern style in an adventurous way, using good local ingredients. There is a good choice of dishes and the wine list is long and varied – you may be sure of finding a wine of quality at a not unreasonable price. A Victorian house, Hambleton Hall has been superbly decorated, is well furnished and is filled with fresh flowers. In the charming drawing room an open fire blazes in winter and there are views over the garden to Rutland Water. Bedrooms, too, are beautifully decorated and equipped with just about every convenience to help make your stay an enjoyable experience. Owners Tim and Stefa Hart run the hotel in country house style and guests are assured of a relaxing stay in luxurious surroundings.

15⇌↱1⊞ CTV in all bedrooms **T** sB&B⇌↱£90 dB&B⇌↱£90-£190 Continental breakfast ⊟
Lift 40P ⊞ ✲ ⅄ (hard) *xmas*
V ♔ Lunch £19.50-£23&alc Dinner £19.50-£35&alc Last dinner 9.30pm
Credit Cards 1 2 3 4 5

★★★♛ 75% Normanton Park LE15 8RP
☎Stamford(0780)720315
(For full entry see Normanton)

★★★ 68% Whipper-in Hotel Market Place LE15 6DT
☎(0572)756971 FAX (0572) 757759
Furnished with antiques, this 17th-century inn has been transformed into a comfortable hotel. Chef Paul Cherrington promotes modern British cuisine with refreshing skill, and the restaurant is popular. Parking may be restricted on market days – check when booking.
21rm(19⇌2↱)Annexe3⇌2⊞ CTV in all bedrooms **T** ✱ sB&B⇌↱£42.50-£59 dB&B⇌↱£64-£84 ⊟
☾ ⅊ *xmas*
V ♔ ⚘ Lunch fr£9.95&alc Dinner fr£16.95&alc Last dinner 9.30pm
Credit Cards 1 2 3 5

★★Boultons 4 Catmose St LE15 6HW ☎(0572)722844
In the centre of this old market town this hotel, with comfortable accommodation, is an ideal base for touring.
14rm(12⇌2↱)(2fb)⊬in 7 bedrooms CTV in all bedrooms ® **T** sB&B⇌↱fr£40 dB&B⇌↱fr£48 ⊟
15P 1⌂ *xmas*
♕ French ♔ ⚘ Lunch fr£8.50 Dinner fr£10&alc Last dinner 9.30pm
Credit Cards 1 2 3 5 £

★*Rutland Angler* Mill St LE15 6EA ☎(0572)55839
Simple but comfortable bedrooms and modest public areas with a choice of bars are provided by a small stonebuilt inn which stands close to the city centre and is popular with both tourists and commercial guests.
9rm(1⇌)(1fb) CTV in all bedrooms **T**
20P ♫
♕ Spanish **V**
Credit Cards 1 2 5

OAKHILL Somerset Map **03** ST64

✕✕Oakhill House Hotel Restaurant Bath Rd BA3 5AQ
☎(0749)840180
In the relaxed, informal atmosphere of this delightful 17th-century country house with its elegant bar and spacious dining room, the proprietors present a short, mainly English, menu of imaginative dishes based on local produce and making effective use of fruit sauces; poultry is raised on the premises and herbs are gathered from the garden.
Closed Mon
Lunch not served Sat
Dinner not served Sun
V 45 seats ✱ Lunch £8.95-£14.75 Dinner £16.45-£28.95alc Last lunch 2pm Last dinner 9.30pm 40P 6 bedrooms available
Credit Cards 1 2 3

OBAN Strathclyde *Argyllshire* Map **10** NM83

See town plan section page
★★★ 52% Alexandra Corran Esplanade PA34 5AA (Scottish Highland) ☎(0631)62381 Telex no 778215
Closed Nov-Mar
The hotel occupies a quiet position towards the northern end of the Promenade, most of its public rooms enjoying fine views of the bustling harbour and bay.
55⇌(1fb) CTV in all bedrooms ® **T** ✱ sB&B⇌£43 dB&B⇌£73 ⊟
Lift ☾ 35P pool table
V ♔ ⚘
Credit Cards 1 2 3 5 £

★★★ 55% Caledonian Station Square PA34 5RT ☎(0631)63133
Telex no 777210
Set in the town centre close to the railway and bus station, this five-storey Victorian building overlooks the bay and harbour.
70⇌(10fb) CTV in all bedrooms ® ✱ sB&B⇌£46-£53 dB&B⇌£68-£78 ⊟
Lift ☾ 6P ⊞ *xmas*
♕ Scottish & French ♔ ⚘ Lunch fr£6 High tea fr£5 Dinner £7-£13 Last dinner 11pm
Credit Cards 1 2 3 5 £

★★Argyll Corran Esplanade PA34 5PZ ☎(0631)62353
Situated on the front, near the north pier, the hotel has good views of the bay. The comfortable accommodation has recently been modernised, and a friendly atmsphere prevails.
28rm(3⇌6↱)(3fb) ® ✱ sB&B£16-£22 sB&B⇌↱£22-£28 dB&B£34-£44 dB&B⇌↱£34-£44 ⊟
☾ CTV 6P ♫
♕ European **V** ♔ ⚘ Last high tea 8.30pm
Credit Cards 1 3 £

★★Lancaster Corran Esplanade PA34 5AD ☎(0631)62587
RS 26 Dec-3 Jan
Seafront hotel popular with tourist and business trade alike.
27rm(3⇌21↱)(3fb) CTV in all bedrooms ® ✱ sB&B£20-£22 sB&B⇌↱£25-£30 dB&B⇌↱£44-£50
20P ⊞ ⊡(heated) sauna solarium jacuzzi
V ♔ ⚘ Lunch £5&alc Dinner £8.50&alc Last dinner 8pm

★★Manor House Gallanach Rd PA34 4LS ☎(0631)62087
Closed Xmas Day & 1-2 Jan & (Sun-Mon Nov-Mar)
This small, comfortable hotel on the waterfront provides a relaxed atmosphere and good food.
11⇌↱⊬in 2 bedrooms CTV in all bedrooms ® **T** ✱ sB&B⇌↱£25-£84 dB&B⇌↱£50-£100 (incl dinner) ⊟
20P ⊞ ✲ nc5yrs

Scottish & French & German V Lunch £16-£25alc Dinner £16-£18&alc Last dinner 8.30pm
Credit Cards 1 3

★**King's Knoll** Dunollie Rd PA34 5JH ☎(0631)62536
Good value accommodation is provided by this small, family-owned hotel which stands on a hillside overlooking the bay.
15rm(2)(8fb) CTV in all bedrooms ® ✱ sB&B£16-£20 dB&B£32-£36 dB&B£37-£41
CTV 7P
V Bar Lunch £3.50-£5alc Dinner fr£7.50alc Last dinner 7.30pm
Credit Cards 1 £

ODIHAM Hampshire Map **04** SU75

★★**George** High St RG25 1LP ☎(0256)702081 Telex no 858797 FAX (0256) 704213
Set at the centre of the small town, a coaching inn dating back to the 16th century retains much of its original character whilst offering modern standards of comfort with the provision of a new bedroom annexe. Bar meals are modest, but you can enjoy a good meal in the restaurant featuring 16th-century panelling and used for ministerial courts in the 1700's.
9(bath)Annexe6(bath)(1fb)2 CTV in all bedrooms ® T ✱ sB&B(bath)fr£48 dB&B(bath)fr£56
20P
English & French V Lunch fr£10.50 Dinner fr£15.50alc Last dinner 10pm
Credit Cards 1 3 5

OKEHAMPTON Devon Map **02** SX59

○ ***TraveLodge*** EX20 4LY (A30) (Trusthouse Forte) ☎(0837)2124
32(bath)
P

CALEDONIAN HOTEL · OBAN

AA ★★★

Station Square. PH34 5RT
Telephone: 0631 63133
Telex: 777210

Panoramic bedrooms overlook the bustling fishing harbour towards the Isle of Mull. Experience a taste for the Highlands by staying at this attractive hotel. The modern bedrooms are well equipped to ensure your comfort and the restaurant is well renowned for its standards of cuisine.

Whether on holiday or on business, the Caledonian is the place to stay. Send for our colour brochure or phone to secure.

The Boultons ★★

Hotel & Accommodation

The Boultons is a beautiful 16th century hotel which has retained its many charming traditional features and offers hotel accommodation of a very high standard.

Restaurant & Bars

Enjoy a superb meal in the quiet relaxed atmosphere of our restaurant with its original oak beams, or pay a visit to our comfortable lounge bar.

Oakham, Rutland, Leics. LE15 6HW
Tel. Oakham 722844

NORMANTON PARK HOTEL

Normanton Park, Nr Oakham, Rutland, Leics LE15 8RP
Telephone: Stamford (0780) 720315

Family owned and run hotel situated in 4 acres of grounds, with direct access to Europe's largest man made lake. Luxury bedrooms with all facilities, superb restaurant overlooking the water. Sailing, windsurfing, fishing, cycling, riding and bird watching are available on and around the shores of Rutland Water. Located 5 minutes from A1 in the heart of Rutland. ★★★

Award winning conversion of listed Coach House.

OLD BURGHCLERE Hampshire Map **04** SU45

✕✕ ***The Dew Pond*** RG15 9LH ☎Burghclere(063527)408
This charming 16th-century house has been converted into a comfortable restaurant. Offering the best of English foods in a French style, Mr and Mrs Smallthwaite personally supervise the service of the meal.
6.25 miles south of Newbury, off A34; follow signs for Beacon Hill, then unclassified road to Old Burghclere.
Closed Sun & Mon
Lunch not served
English & French **V** 40 seats Last dinner 10pm 20P
Credit Cards 1 3

OLDBURY West Midlands Map **07** SO98

○ ***Travelodge*** A4123 Wolverhampton Rd B69 2BH (Trusthouse Forte) ☎021-552 2967
33

OLDHAM Greater Manchester Map **07** SD90

★★★57% ***The Bower*** Hollinwood Av, Chadderton OL9 8DE (2.25 SW A6104) (De Vere) ☎061-682 7254 Telex no 666883
RS 25-31 Dec
Once the home of a well-known local family, this house has been developed and extended to provide modern accommodation; its restaurant is popular with personal and business visitors alike, and function suites are available.
66rm(42 24)(1fb)1 CTV in all bedrooms ® **T**
140P CFA
Continental **V**
Credit Cards 1 2 3 5

★★★62% **Hotel Smokies Park** Ashton Rd, Bardsley OL8 3HX (Consort) ☎061-624 3405 Telex no 667490 FAX 061-627 5262
A new and very well-appointed hotel, midway between Ashton-under-Lyne and Oldham.
47 CTV in 40bedrooms ® **T** (ex guide dogs) *
sB&B £22-£45 dB&B £44-£55
120P
English & French **V** Lunch £10.50&alc High tea £3.50 Dinner £10.50&alc Last dinner 10.30pm
Credit Cards 1 2 3 5

★★ **High Point** Napier St OL8 1TR ☎061-624-4130 FAX 061-627 2767
A friendly, family-run hotel with exceptionally well-appointed bedrooms. Situated in an elevated position looking towards the town centre.
19rm(8 7)(4fb)1 CTV in all bedrooms ® **T** *
sB&B £32.50-£50 dB&B£38 dB&B £40-£65
42P
English & French **V** Lunch fr£5.95&alc Dinner fr£7.50&alc Last dinner 9.45pm
Credit Cards 1 2 3 5 £

OLD MELDRUM Grampian *Aberdeenshire* Map **15** NJ82

★ **Meldrum Arms** The Square AB5 0DS ☎(06512)2238 2505
Family-run village hotel with an attractive lounge bar, neat, compact bedrooms and a wide range of keenly-priced meals.
7 CTV in all bedrooms ® **T** * sB&B £22 dB&B £38
25P
V Bar Lunch £3.55-£5.45alc High tea £3.90-£7.95alc Dinner £6.90-£12.55alc Last dinner 9.30pm
Credit Cards 1 2 3

Red-star hotels offer the highest standards of hospitality, comfort and food.

OLD RAYNE Grampian *Aberdeenshire* Map **15** NJ62

★ ***Lodge*** AB5 6RY ☎(04645)205
Friendly, homely small hotel, just off A96. The attractive annexe comprises modern, timber-clad chalet style bedrooms.
2rmAnnexe4 CTV in 5bedrooms ®
CTV 50P
Last dinner 8pm

OLD SODBURY Avon Map **03** ST78

★★ **Cross Hands** BS17 6RJ ☎Chipping Sodbury(0454)313000
RS Xmas Night
Mellow Cotswold stone building in a rural setting alongside the main A46 Bath/Stroud road.
24rm(3 17)1 CTV in all bedrooms ® **T** sB&B£31.50 sB&B £39.50-£42.50 dB&B£50.50 dB&B £64.50-£71.50 Continental breakfast
200P
International **V** Lunch £9-£18alc Dinner £9-£18alc Last dinner 10.30pm
Credit Cards 1 2 3 5

See advertisement under BRISTOL

OLLERTON Nottinghamshire Map **08** SK66

★ **Hop Pole** NG22 9AB ☎Mansfield(0623)822573
Ivy-covered coaching inn.
12rm(1 5)(2fb) CTV in 2bedrooms ® sB&Bfr£21 sB&B fr£24.50 dB&Bfr£31 dB&B fr£37.50
CTV 45P snooker
V Sunday Lunch £6.25 Dinner £6.50 Last dinner 10pm
Credit Cards 1 2 3

OLNEY Buckinghamshire Map **04** SP85

✕✕ ***Dhaka Dynasty*** 2-3 Stanley Court, Weston Rd MK46 5NH ☎Bedford(0234)713179 & 713188
A modern, tastefully-appointed Indian restaurant featuring traditional Moghul and Tandoori dishes. Among those recommended are Murgh Makhani, Lamb Pasanda, Mawabi, Gosht Makhani, King Prawn Bhuna and Murgh Jalfrezi. Good basic ingredients and fresh produce are used, including, where possible, fresh spices and herbs. The atmosphere is warm and informal, with friendly, efficient service.
Indian & Moghul 50 seats Last dinner 11pm 20P
Credit Cards 1 2 3 4 5

ONICH Highland *Inverness-shire* Map **14** NN06

★★★65% **Lodge on the Loch** Creag Dhu PH33 6RY ☎(08553)237 Telex no 94013696 FAX (08552) 629
Closed Nov-Mar
Relaxing, family-run hotel with magnificent views of Loch Linnhe and surrounding mountains from most bedrooms. A ground floor has been specially designed for disabled guests.
18rm(12 6)(1fb) CTV in all bedrooms ® **T**
sB&B £26.50-£37.50 dB&B £53-£75
25P
Scottish & International **V** Lunch £3.50-£7alc Dinner £15-£16&alc Last dinner 10pm
Credit Cards 1 3 £

See advertisement under FORT WILLIAM

★★ **Allt-Nan-Ros** PH33 6RY ☎(08553)210
Closed Nov-Etr
The friendly, roadside hotel offers good food and views of the loch.
20rm(17 3)(2fb)1 CTV in all bedrooms ® **T** *
sB&B £30-£35 dB&B £60-£70
CTV 50P

O

☋ Scottish & French ♔ ☊ ⊁ Lunch £2-£10alc Dinner £16-£19alc Last dinner 8.30pm
Credit Cards [1] [2] [3] [5]

★★Onich PH33 6RY (Consort) ☎(08553)214 266
RS Nov-Mar
Recently refurbished, the hotel provides comfortable accommodation, and its nicely laid out garden runs down to the lochside.
27rm(25⇌2↱)(6fb) CTV in all bedrooms ® T
sB&B⇌↱£25-£32 dB&B⇌↱£44-£58 ⛿
50P ❁ solarium gymnasium jacuzzi ⌂
☋ International ♔ ☊ Bar Lunch £1.50-£5.75alc Dinner £13.50-£15 Last dinner 8.30pm
Credit Cards [1] [2] [3] [5]
See advertisement under FORT WILLIAM

ORFORD (near Woodbridge) Suffolk Map 05 TM44

★★The Crown & Castle IP12 2LJ (Trusthouse Forte)
☎Orford(0394)450205
An 18th-century posting house once associated with smugglers.
9rm(1⇌)Annexe10⇌⊁in 1 bedroom CTV in all bedrooms ®
✱ sBfr£41 sB⇌fr£53 dBfr£50.50 dB⇌fr£61.50 (room only) ⛿
20P ⛟ ❁ *xmas*
V ♔ ☊ ⊁ Sunday Lunch fr£7.50 Dinner £11-£15 Last dinner 8.30pm
Credit Cards [1] [2] [3] [4] [5]

ORKNEY Map 16

KIRKWALL Map 16 HY41

★★Ayre Ayre Rd KW15 1QX ☎(0856)3001
Closed 1-2 Jan
32rm(4⇌6↱)(2fb) CTV in all bedrooms ® T ✱ sB&B£21
sB&B⇌↱£34 dB&B£38 dB&B⇌↱£52
25P sauna , trout & sea fishing
☋ International V ♔ ☊ Lunch £2-£4.40alc Dinner £5.20-£14alc Last dinner 9pm
Credit Cards [1] [3]

ST MARGARET'S HOPE Map 16 ND48

✕Creel Front Rd KW17 2SL ☎(0856)83311
An unpretentious little restaurant stands on the waterfront, looking across Scapa Flow. Under the personal supervision of the owners, it provides a most enjoyable range of dishes, making good use of local fish and seafood. Service is simple, as befits the surroundings.
Closed Mon, Tue & Jan
Lunch not served
40 seats ✱ Dinner £9-£14alc Last dinner 9.45pm 15P

OSTERLEY Greater London

See **LONDON plan 5**B3(page 412) **Telephone codes are due to change on 6th May 1990. See page 421.**
★★Osterley 764 Great West Rd TW7 5NA (Consort) ☎01-568 9981 Telex no 915059 FAX 01-569 7819
Friendly hotel where improvements are producing an increasing number of good, comfortable bedrooms.
56rm(50⇌6↱)Annexe4rm(9fb) CTV in all bedrooms ® T
sB&Bfr£42 sB&B⇌↱fr£57 dB&Bfr£47
dB&B⇌↱fr£62 Continental breakfast ⛿
☾ 140P
☋ English & French V ♔ ☊ Lunch £7-£8.50&alc Dinner £8.50&alc Last dinner 10pm
Credit Cards [1] [2] [3] [5]

OSWESTRY Shropshire Map **07** SJ22

★★★ 64% **Wynnstay** Church St SY11 2SZ ☎(0691)655261 FAX (0691) 661845
Traditional Georgian town centre hotel, with well-modernised bedrooms and a new conference and function suite. An attractive older feature is the crown bowling green.
26⇌2 in 12 bedrooms CTV in all bedrooms ® T
70P ✽ crown green bowling
V
Credit Cards 1 2 3 4 5 £

★★ **Sweeney Hall** Morda SY10 9EU (1m S on A483)
☎(0691)652450

This hotel is made from two large country houses standing in very spacious grounds.

9rm(6⇌) ® ✱ sB&Bfr£26 sB&B⇌fr£30 dB&Bfr£43 dB&B⇌£49-£54
CTV 50P ✽ putting green
English, French & Italian V Lunch £10&alc Dinner £10&alc Last dinner 9.30pm
Credit Cards 1 3

TraveLodge Mile End Services SY11 4JA (junct A5/A483) (Trusthouse Forte) ☎(0691)658178
Situated at the junction of the A5/A483, this modern lodge unit – busy at all times of the year with tourists and business people – has one room specially equipped for the disabled.
40⇌(40fb) CTV in all bedrooms ® sB⇌£21.50 dB⇌£27 (room only)
40P
Mainly grills
Credit Cards 1 2 3

O

OTHERY Somerset Map **03** ST33

★ ***Sedgemoor House*** Glastonbury Rd TA7 0QL (Guestaccom) ☎Burrowbridge(082369)382
A small, friendly hotel with neat, compact bedrooms and a restaurant converted from a stable block.
7rm(1⇌4)(1fb) CTV in all bedrooms ®
20P ✽
V

OTLEY West Yorkshire Map **08** SE24

★★★ 66% **Chevin Lodge Country Park** Yorkgate LS21 3NU ☎(0943)467818 Telex no 51538 FAX (0943) 850335
Constructed of pine in Scandinavian style, the hotel stands in 50 acres of birchwood. Attractively appointed bedrooms and public areas, maintaining the pinewood theme throughout, offer modern comforts and facilities, whilst the restaurant's three menus provide a choice between local and international dishes, supported by a good wine list.
18⇌Annexe22⇌(5fb) CTV in all bedrooms ® T ✱ sB&B⇌£45-£75 dB&B⇌£59-£85
100P ✽ sauna solarium cycling xmas
English & French V Bar Lunch £1.95-£6.50 Dinner £13.75&alc Last dinner 9.30pm
Credit Cards 1 2 3

OTTERBURN Northumberland Map **12** NY89

★★ **Otterburn Tower** NE19 1NB ☎(0830)20620
RS 25 Dec
This historic building, standing in its own grounds, dates back to 1706 and offers bedrooms which are, for the most part, spacious and attractively decorated, though lounge accommodation is, at present, limited. Friendliness is the keynote of the establishment, and the proprietors have created a genuine country house atmosphere.
12rm(4⇌3)(4fb)2 CTV in 1bedroom TV in 5bedrooms ® sB&Bfr£27.50 sB&B⇌fr£32.50 dB&Bfr£45 dB&B⇌£50-£55
CTV 50P ✽ CFA *xmas*
V Lunch fr£8&alc Dinner £9.50-£10&alc Last dinner 9.30pm
Credit Cards 1 2 3 5 £

OTTERY ST MARY Devon Map **03** SY19

★★★ 56% ***Salston*** EX11 1RQ (1m SW off B3174 towards West Hill) (Best Western) ☎(040481)2310 5581 Telex no 42551
Set on the edge of town is this red-brick 18th-century country house, with modern extensions, enjoying attractive views over the East Devon countryside. A recent change of ownership has seen some improvements with well-equipped bedrooms and a range of recreational amenities on site. The hotel also offers conference facilities.
26rm(24⇌2)(13fb)2 in 10 bedrooms CTV in all bedrooms ® T
100P ✽ CFA (heated) squash sauna solarium gymnasium
English & French
Credit Cards 1 2 3 5

See advertisement under EXETER

OULTON West Yorkshire Map **08** SE32

★★★ 62% **Grove Crest** The Grove LS26 8EJ (Crest) ☎Leeds(0532)826201 Telex no 557646 FAX (0532) 829243
Conveniently located at the junction of the A639 and A642, the up-to-date hotel offers motel-style accommodation in a wing separated from the public areas by spacious car parks. Guests can relax in good lounge bars and an attractive, well-appointed restaurant.
40⇌ in 5 bedrooms CTV in all bedrooms ® S% sB⇌£58 dB⇌£72 (room only)
200P pool table
V
Credit Cards 1 2 3 4 5

OUNDLE Northamptonshire Map **04** TL08

★★★ 58% **The Talbot** New St PE8 4EA (Trusthouse Forte) ☎(0832)73621 due to change to 273621 Telex no 32364 FAX (0832) 274545
Period stone and slate building with the original coaching entrance.
38rm(18⇌17)(3fb) CTV in all bedrooms ® T ✱ sB⇌£65 dB⇌£80 (room only)
60P CFA *xmas*
V Lunch £9 Dinner £15 Last dinner 10pm
Credit Cards 1 2 3 4 5

OVINGTON Northumberland Map **12** NZ06

★★ ***Highlander Inn*** NE42 6DT ☎Prudhoe(0661)32016
The stone-built village inn features a restaurant which offers good-value French cuisine under the personal supervision of the French proprietor.
5rm(2⇌) CTV in all bedrooms ® T
20P ✽
English & French
Credit Cards 2 5

OXFORD Oxfordshire Map **04** SP50

See **Town Plan Section**

★★★★ 56% **The Randolph** Beaumont St OX1 2LN (Trusthouse Forte) ☎(0865)247481 Telex no 83446 FAX (0865) 791678
Not before time, major refurbishment has begun at this splendid old city-centre hotel. As we went to print, the improvement of the public areas had almost been completed, and all had been tastefully decorated to provide a high degree of comfort. We now hope for speedy improvement of the bedrooms, and continuing development of services and cuisine.
109⇌(5fb)⊁in 15 bedrooms CTV in all bedrooms ® **T** ✱ sB⇌£77-£80 dB⇌£98-£190 (room only) ⊟
Lift ☾ 60🚗 (charged) CFA ♫ *xmas*
☉ International **V** ✧ ☕ ⊁ S% Lunch £15&alc Dinner £19&alc Last dinner 10pm
Credit Cards 1 2 3 4 5

★★★ 61% **Cotswold Lodge** 66A Banbury Rd OX2 6JP ☎(0865)512121 Telex no 837127
Closed 25-30 Dec
Continued improvements at this family-owned hotel just on the outskirts of the city include well-equipped and nicely furnished bedrooms in both the main house and the new wing. There is a comfortable lounge and restaurant and service is prompt and conducted in a friendly manner.
52⇌(2fb) CTV in all bedrooms **T** sB&B⇌£62.50-£69.50 dB&B⇌£79.50-£89.50 ⊟
☾ 60P
☉ English & French **V** ✧ ☕ Lunch £9.50-£12.50 Dinner £15-£17.50&alc Last dinner 10.30pm
Credit Cards 1 2 3 5

★★★ 57% **Eastgate** The High OX1 4BE (Trusthouse Forte) ☎(0865)248244 Telex no 83302 FAX (0865) 791681
Standing at the heart of the city, the hotel has recently been remodelled to include elegantly furnished public rooms with a smart carvery restaurant and busy student bar. Bedrooms range from the sumptuous to the more modest, but cheerful service is provided throughout.
43⇌1⊞⊁in 4 bedrooms CTV in all bedrooms ® **T** ✱ sB⇌£67-£80 dB⇌£77-£107 (room only) ⊟
Lift ☾ 43P CFA *xmas*
V ✧ ☕ ⊁ Lunch £13-£14.50&alc Dinner £14-£15.50&alc Last dinner 9.30pm
Credit Cards 1 2 3 4 5

★★★ 58% **Linton Lodge** Linton Rd, Park Town OX2 6UJ (Hilton) ☎(0865)53461 Telex no 837093 FAX (0865) 310365
Situated just north of the city, this commercial style of hotel has recently been refurbished and offers a blend of modern and traditional well-equipped accommodation.
71rm(70⇌1♠)(1fb)1⊞⊁in 6 bedrooms CTV in all bedrooms ® **T** sB⇌♠fr£70 dB⇌♠fr£90 (room only) ⊟
Lift ☾ 40P CFA pool table *xmas*
V ✧ ☕ ⊁ Lunch fr£9.50&alc Dinner fr£12.95&alc Last dinner 9.30pm
Credit Cards 1 2 3 5

❀❀❀★★★★ **LE MANOIR AUX QUAT' SAISON** OX9 7PD (Relais et Châteaux) ☎(0844)278881 Telex no 837552 FAX (0844) 278847
(For full entry see Milton, Great)

A rosette is the AA's highest award for quality of food and service in a restaurant.

★★★ 63% **Oxford Moat House** Godstow Rd, Wolvercote Rbt OX2 8AL (Queens Moat) ☎(0865)59933 Telex no 837926 FAX (0865) 310259
Comfortable, modern hotel on the outskirts of the city, providing well-equipped bedrooms, extensive sport and leisure amenities and prompt service. The comprehensive range of business and conference facilities make the hotel popular with commercial guests.
155⇌(17fb) CTV in all bedrooms ® **T** sB&B⇌fr£80 dB&B⇌fr£90 ⊟
☾ 250P ⊡(heated) squash snooker sauna solarium gymnasium whirlpool pitch & putt
V ✧ ☕ Lunch fr£10 Dinner fr£12 Last dinner 9.45pm
Credit Cards 1 2 3 5

❀★★★ 54% **Studley Priory** OX9 1AZ (Consort) ☎Stanton St John (086735)203 & 254 Telex no 23152 FAX (086735) 613
(For full entry see Horton-cum-Studley)

★★ **Royal Oxford** Park End St OX1 1HR (Embassy) ☎(0865)248432 FAX (0865) 250049
Traditional hotel with modern bedroom facilities.
25rm(12⇌)(2fb) CTV in all bedrooms ® **T** S% sB£33-£35 sB⇌£48-£52 dB£43-£45 dB⇌£58-£62 (room only) ⊟
☾ 12P
V ✧ ☕
Credit Cards 1 2 3 5 £

★★ **The Tree Hotel** Church Way, Iffley OX4 4EY 3m SE off A4158 ☎(0865)775974 & 778190 FAX (0865) 747554
Lying three miles south-east of the city centre in Iffley village, this Victorian public house has been transformed into a friendly and comfortable small hotel by Dave and Ann Bowman. Bedrooms in particular are attractively furnished and well-equipped, as are the spotless en suite facilities. The ground floor has a comfortable bar with character, and a homely little dining room. Honest home ▶

cooking and hospitable service from staff and owners alike make this and excellent base for the business traveller or tourist.
7rm(3⇔4♠)(1fb)1♯ CTV in all bedrooms ® T ✗ (ex guide dogs) ✱ sB&B⇔♠£40 dB&B⇔♠£60-£75
20P ♠ (£1 per night)
♀ English V ♦ ♀ ⚡ Lunch £7.70-£12.70alc High tea £3.10-£3.50alc Dinner £7.70-£12.70alc Last dinner 8.30pm
Credit Cards 1 2 3

★★Victoria 180 Abingdon Rd OX1 4RA ☎(0865)724536
Telex no 837031
Closed 20 Dec-20 Jan
Though the small, family-run hotel stands in a residential area, it is conveniently positioned for access to the city centre and the A4144. Its combination of homely, soundly-equipped accommodation and restricted public areas make it most suitable for commercial and short-stay guests.
23rm(14⇔)(2fb) CTV in all bedrooms ® T ✱ sB&B£35.50 sB&B⇔£45.50 dB&B£47.50 dB&B⇔£55.50 ♯
CTV 15P
♀ Hungarian & Italian V ♦ ♀ ⚡ Lunch £7.50-£12.50 High tea fr£2.50 Dinner £12.50&alc Last dinner 9pm
Credit Cards 1 3

★★Welcome Lodge Peartree Roundabout OX2 8JZ (junc A34/A43) (Trusthouse Forte) ☎(0865)54301 Telex no 83202
FAX (0865) 513474
Modern hotel with a grill and carvery restaurant.
100⇔(41fb)⚡in 10 bedrooms CTV in all bedrooms ®
sB&B⇔fr£49 dB&B⇔fr£59 ♯
120P ✽ CFA ⇔(heated)
♀ Mainly grills V ♦ ♀ ⚡ Dinner £8.50-£11.50alc Last dinner 10pm
Credit Cards 1 2 3 4 5

★River 17 Botley Rd OX2 0AA ☎(0865)243475
Closed Xmas & New Year
A small, friendly, family-run hotel in a riverside setting. Moderately priced accommodation includes a good annexe.
16rm(6⇔5♠)Annexe8rm(3⇔3♠)(3fb) CTV in all bedrooms ® T ✗ (ex guide dogs) sB&Bfr£30 sB&B⇔♠£37.50-£42.50 dB&Bfr£40 dB&B⇔♠fr£47.50 ♯
CTV 25P ♯ ✽ ♩
♦ ♀ Bar Lunch fr£3 Dinner £6-£10 Last dinner 7.30pm
Credit Cards 1 3

✗✗✗Restaurant Elizabeth 82/84 St Aldates OX1 1RA
☎(0865)242230
Stylish, traditional restaurant on the first floor of an early 17th-century building, nicely tucked away, but close to the colleges. Signor Lopez provides commendable French, Spanish and Greek dishes, complemented by an extensive wine list, and service is professional.
Closed Mon, 25-31 Dec & Good Fri
♀ French, Greek & Spanish V 45 seats ✱ Lunch £12.50 Dinner £19-£22.50alc Last lunch 2.30pm Last dinner 11pm
₱ ⚡
Credit Cards 1 2 3 5

✗✗*Gees* 61A Banbury Rd OX2 7DY ☎(0865)53540 & 59736
Pleasant and attractive bistro restaurant within a bright, stylish conservatory providing friendly, informal service and imaginative dishes from a short, well-balanced menu.
Closed 1st 2 wks Jan
♀ French V 80 seats Last dinner 10.30pm 30P
Credit Cards 1 3 4

✗✗Paddyfield 39-40 Hythe Bridge St OX1 2EP ☎(0865)248835
A recent face-lift has provided a bright, stylish, modern interior to this popular Chinese restaurant, but service remains as cheerful and friendly as ever. Well-prepared, authentic Cantonese and Pekinese dishes include such specialities as crispy aromatic duck with plum sauce, sizzling monkfish with black bean sauce and steamed scallops in garlic butter, with plentiful jasmine tea served in pretty china cups to complete the meal.
Closed 25-27 Dec
♀ Cantonese, Pekinese & Szechuan V 150 seats ✱ S10% Lunch fr£5&alc Last lunch 2.15pm Last dinner 11.45pm 20P
Credit Cards 1 2 3 5

✗15 North Parade 15 North Pde Av OX2 6LX ☎(0865)513773
A stylish, modern, small restaurant offering warm hospitality and a good standard of imaginative cuisine is cosily tucked away in the northern outskirts of the city. Its efficiently short menu features a range of mainly English dishes in which quality ingredients are complemented by a range of tasty and unusual sauces. Surroundings are bright and cheerful, service friendly and unhurried, whilst prices – especially for the set lunch – are sensible.
Dinner not served Sun
Lunch by arrangement
V 50 seats ✱ Lunch £10.75&alc Dinner £16.75&alc Last lunch 2pm Last dinner 10pm ₱
Credit Cards 1 3

PADSTOW Cornwall & Isles of Scilly Map 02 SW97

See also **Constantine Bay**

★★★58% The Metropole Station Rd PL28 8DB (Trusthouse Forte) ☎(0841)532486
Large detached traditional hotel in an elevated position overlooking the river estuary.
44⇔(11fb)⚡in 5 bedrooms CTV in all bedrooms ® T
sB⇔£60.50-£61.50 dB⇔£82-£86.50 (room only) ♯
Lift 35P ✽ ⇔(heated) pitch & putt trampoline paddling pool
♠ *xmas*
V ♦ ♀ ⚡ Lunch £9-£10 Dinner £12.75-£13.50&alc Last dinner 9.15pm
Credit Cards 1 2 3 4 5

★★*Old Custom House Inn* South Quay PL28 8ED
☎(0841)532359
Closed Jan & Feb RS Nov, Dec & Etr
Pleasant personally-run inn by harbour's edge and once the old custom house.
25⇔(2fb) CTV in all bedrooms ® T
CTV ₱
♀ English & French V ♦ Last dinner 9.30pm
Credit Cards 1 2 3 5

❀✗✗Seafood PL28 8BY
☎(0841)532485
(Rosette awarded for dinner only)
A bright quayside restaurant, where menus change daily to include the freshest fish, shellfish and herbs, which are skilfully used to enhance flavours rather than mask them. The fish is cooked for maximum succulency, and a superb fish and shellfish soup, followed by steamed turbot with small beach clams, has been commended by our inspectors, who also praise the crisp, flavoursome vegetables. The wine list of some 180 bins has a strong French bias and offers good value, especially in the house wine selection. Friendly and attentive service reflects the care of Jill and Richard Stein, the latter being winner of the 1989 Glenfiddich Cookery Book of the Year award for his 'English Seafood Cookery'.
Closed Sun, 11 Dec-2 Mar
Lunch not served
♀ English & French 75 seats ✱ Dinner fr£19.50&alc Last dinner 9.30pm ₱ 10 bedrooms available
Credit Cards 1 2 3

For key to symbols see the inside front cover.

O

PAIGNTON Devon Map **03** SX86

★★★**62% The Palace** Esplanade Rd TQ4 6BJ (Trusthouse Forte) ☏(0803)555121 FAX (0803) 527974

Commanding fine views of sea and beach from its position on the seafront, this traditional hotel provides comfortable, spacious public rooms, well-equipped bedrooms which have recently been refurbished and a small sports/leisure complex. Service is attentive and pleasant throughout.

52⇌(5fb)⊁in 9 bedrooms CTV in all bedrooms ® **T** ✳ sB⇌£52-£56 dB⇌£72-£87 (room only)

Lift ☾ 60P ✲ CFA ⇌(heated) ⚲ (hard) squash sauna solarium gymnasium jacuzzi health & beauty salon ♫ ⌂ *xmas*

☋ English & French **V** ♱ ⚐ ⊁ Sunday Lunch £6.50 Dinner £10.50 Last dinner 9pm

Credit Cards 1 2 3 5

★★★**61% Redcliffe** Marine Dr TQ3 2NL ☏(0803)526397 FAX (0803) 528030

Set in 5 acres of grounds directly adjoining Paignton's sandy beach, the hotel—a charming, mid-Victorian building with central tower, pinnacles and battlements – offers a range of spacious, traditionally-styled public rooms, many with sea views. Bedrooms, though more modest, are all soundly equipped and provided with en suite facilities. Both grounds and building have been the subject of recent upgrading.

63rm(56⇌7↱)(8fb) CTV in all bedrooms ® **T** ✗ (ex guide dogs) sB&B⇌↱£28-£36 dB&B⇌↱£56-£72 ⊟

Lift ☾ CTV 80P ✲ CFA ⇌(heated) ⚳ putting green, table tennis ♫ *xmas*

☋ English & French **V** ♱ ⚐ Lunch £6.25-£6.75 Dinner £9.75-£10.75&alc Last dinner 8.30pm

Credit Cards 1 2 3

P

★★*Dainton* 95 Dartmouth Rd, Three Beaches, Goodrington TQ4 6NA ☎(0803)550067
Of modern construction, but Tudor in style, the hotel stands on a corner site, with the side road leading to the beach. This small, personally-run hotel has been upgraded under the new ownership to provide spotlessly clean, compact but well-equipped bedrooms, bright public rooms and a cosy intimate restaurant. Service is prompt and conducted in a friendly manner.
10⇌♠(3fb) CTV in all bedrooms ® T
(CTV 20P ⇌ solarium
V ♡ ⊥
Credit Cards 1 3

★★**Seaford** 2-4 Stafford Rd TQ4 6EU (off Sands Road) ☎(0803)557341
Family owned and run hotel, positioned adjacent to playing fields and close to the seafront, which is popular with both holidaymakers and commercial guests alike. Bedrooms, though compact, are brightly decorated and well equipped for the size of the hotel. Public areas are cosy.
23rm(12⇌9♠) CTV in all bedrooms ® T ✗ (ex guide dogs) sB&B£20 dB&B⇌♠£40
Lift 10P *xmas*
☺ English & French V ♡ ⊥ Dinner £9 Last dinner 9pm
Credit Cards 1 3

★★**Torbay Holiday Motel** Totnes Rd TQ4 7PP ☎(0803)558226
Closed 24-31 Dec
Conveniently positioned on the Totnes road just outside Paignton, the friendly family-owned and run motel complex complements spacious, well-equipped bedrooms with pleasant, recently upgraded bars and restaurant. Holiday studio apartments and suites are also available, either self-catering or on a full-board basis, for guests who like to combine greater freedom and space with the convenience of hotel facilities.
16rm(10⇌6♠) CTV in all bedrooms ® T sB&B⇌♠£20-£23 dB&B⇌♠£32-£38
150P ✽ ⊡(heated) ⇌(heated) sauna solarium gymnasium crazy golf, adventure playground
☺ English & French V ♡ Bar Lunch £4-£6alc Dinner £7.50&alc Last dinner 9pm
Credit Cards 1 3

★**Oldway Links Hotel** Barrett, 21 Southfield Rd TQ3 2LZ ☎(0803)559332
13rm(4⇌6♠)(2fb) CTV in all bedrooms ® ✗ (ex guide dogs) ✱ sB&B⇌♠£18-£21 dB&B⇌♠£36-£42 ⊟
40P ⇌ ✽
☺ English & French ♡ Bar Lunch £1.25-£3.75 Dinner £10.50 Last dinner 8.00pm
Credit Cards 1 3 £

★**Preston Sands** 10/12 Marine Pde TQ3 2NU ☎(0803)558718
Attractive, family-run hotel with magnificent sea views, 15 yards from a safe sandy beach and also close to the town centre. The well-equipped bedrooms all have en suite facilities.
26rm(1⇌23♠) CTV in all bedrooms ® ✱ sB&B⇌♠£15-£22 dB&B⇌♠£30-£44
24P nc10yrs
V ♡ Bar Lunch £1.85-£5 Dinner £8.50 Last dinner 7.30pm

PAINSWICK Gloucestershire Map **03** SO80

★★★65% **Painswick** Kemps Ln GL6 6YB ☎(0452)812160
Telex no 43605 FAX (0452) 812160
Although it is located in the centre of the village, this hotel is in a secluded position behind the parish church, and the reception area was once a private chapel. The oak-panelled bar lounge has an open fire and a homely atmosphere prevails throughout. Attentive service and an interesting menu are offered in the restaurant.
15rm(14⇌1♠)(2fb) CTV in all bedrooms ® T ✱
sB&B⇌♠£39-£45 dB&B⇌♠£60 ⊟
25P ⇌ ✽ snooker croquet *xmas*
☺ French V ♡ ⊥ Sunday Lunch fr£7.50 Dinner fr£15.50&alc Last dinner 9.30pm
Credit Cards 1 2 3 5

PAISLEY Hotels are listed under Glasgow Airport.

PANGBOURNE Berkshire Map **04** SU67

★★★72% ***The Copper Inn*** Church Rd RG8 7AR ☎(07357)2244
Telex no 849041 Ref 522 BWH FAX (07357) 5542
A small, welcoming hotel with elegantly furnished bedrooms and lounges. The restaurant, where the emphasis is on fresh, local produce has a good reputation and the attractive bar serves real ale and popular lunchtime snacks.
21⇌♠(1fb)1⊞ CTV in all bedrooms ® T
30P ⇌ ✽
☺ English & French V ♡ ⊥ Last dinner 9.30pm
Credit Cards 1 2 3 5 £

★★**George Hotel** The Square RG8 7AJ ☎(07357)2237
Telex no 849910 FAX (07357) 5396
Situated in the centre of this attractive Thames village, the George has occupied the same site since 1295. Today, under new ownership, it provides comfortable bedroom accommodation, an attractive beamed cocktail bar and a restaurant offering both à la carte and set menus. Hot and cold snacks are served in the Village Bar lounge.
8rm(5⇌3♠) CTV in all bedrooms ® T ✱ sB⇌♠£30-£45 dB⇌♠£50-£55 (room only) ⊟
25P
☺ English & French V ♡ ⊥ Lunch £8.50-£13&alc Dinner fr£10.50&alc Last dinner 10pm
Credit Cards 1 2 3 5

PARBOLD Lancashire Map **07** SD41

★★*Lindley* Lancaster Ln WN8 7AB ☎(02576)2804
Closed 24, 25 & 31 Dec-1 Jan
This well-equipped hotel is located in a quiet suburb.
9rm(2⇌7♠)(1fb) CTV in all bedrooms ®
60P ⇌ ✽
☺ English & French
Credit Cards 1 2 3

PARKGATE Cheshire Map **07** SJ27

★★★57% **The Ship** The Parade L64 6SA (Trusthouse Forte) ☎051-336 3931
Relaxed, traditional small hotel with excellent views of the Dee Estuary and its wild bird life.
26⇌2⊞⊬in 2 bedrooms CTV in all bedrooms ® T ✱
sB⇌fr£50 dB⇌fr£65 (room only) ⊟
(100P *xmas*
V ♡ ⊥ ⊬ Lunch fr£7.50&alc Dinner fr£12&alc Last dinner 9.30pm
Credit Cards 1 2 3 4 5

★★**Parkgate** Boathouse Ln L64 6RD (Lansbury) ☎051-336 5001 Telex no 629469 FAX 051-336 8504
This recently extended and refurbished hotel is well-appointed for the business traveller.
27rm(20⇌7♠)(3fb)1⊞⊬in 5 bedrooms CTV in all bedrooms ® T sB&B⇌♠fr£50 dB&B⇌♠fr£60 ⊟
(150P
☺ English & French V ♡ ⊥ Lunch £5.75-£6.75&alc Dinner fr£12.50&alc Last dinner 10pm
Credit Cards 1 2 3 5

The AA's star-rating scheme is the market leader in hotel classification.

PARKHAM Devon Map **02** SS32

★★★64% **Penhaven Country House** EX39 5PL
☎Horns Cross(02375)388 & 711

Standing on the edge of the village in 11 acres of wooded grounds, a Victorian rectory has been sensitively restored to create a small hotel with a friendly, relaxed atmosphere. Well-equipped country-style bedrooms are individually decorated, while public rooms are cosy and comfortable. A small restaurant offers imaginative menus, making good use of such local specialities as Devon beef or Bideford Bay seafood, complemented by the hotel's own vegetables, and Parkham Cheddar cheese is featured on the cheese board. Accommodation with full use of the hotel's services and facilities is also available in 5 adjoining cottages.

12rm(11⇌1♠)(5fb)1 CTV in all bedrooms ® T ✳
sB&B⇌♠£36.50-£48.50 dB&B⇌♠£73-£97 (incl dinner)
50P ✲ nc10yrs *xmas*
V Lunch £7.50 Dinner £11.50&alc Last dinner 9.30pm
Credit Cards 1 2 3 5 £

PATELEY BRIDGE North Yorkshire Map **07** SE16

✕✕ ***Sportsman's Arms*** Wath-in-Nidderdale HG3 5PP (2m NW unclass rd) ☎Harrogate(0423)711306

Nestling in the beautiful Nidderdale countryside this restaurant is housed in an attractive building dating from the 17th century. Cuisine is basically British with game (in season), salmon, beef, duck, pork and fish expertly cooked and served. The food is complemented by an extensive wine list.

Closed 25-26 Dec
Lunch not served Mon-Sat
Dinner not served Sun
English & Continental V 45 seats Last dinner 9.30pm 30P
Credit Cards 1 2 3 5

P

PATTERDALE Cumbria Map **11** NY31

★★**Patterdale** CA11 0NN (Consort) ☎Glenridding(08532)231
Closed Nov-Etr
This hotel lies at the foot of the Kirkstone Pass facing Ullswater.
57rm(32⇌25♠)(4fb) ® sB&B⇌♠£22.20-£26.40
dB&B⇌♠£44.80-£52.80
CTV 30P 1🚗 ✲ ♩
V ♈ Lunch £5.95 Dinner £10.50 Last dinner 8pm
Credit Cards 1 2 3 £

PATTINGHAM Shropshire Map **07** SO89

★★★56% ***Patshull Park*** Patshull WV6 7HR (1.5m W of Pattingham) (Best Western) ☎(0902)700100 Telex no 334849 FAX (0902) 700874
Popular for functions and residential golfing breaks, with an 18-hole golf course, 65-acre fishing lake and a large leisure/fitness complex within the spacious grounds.
48⇌♠(4fb) CTV in all bedrooms ® **T**
☾ ▦ CTV 200P ▭(heated) ▶ 18 ♩ snooker sauna solarium gymnasium beautician
♈ ⊻ Last dinner 9.30pm
Credit Cards 1 2 3 5

PEASMARSH East Sussex Map **05** TQ82

★★**Flackley Ash** TN31 6YH (Best Western) ☎(079721)651
Telex no 957210 FAX (079721) 510
Spacious, well-appointed bedrooms and quality indoor leisure facilities are now available in the new wing of this Georgian hotel, but it also retains compact and modestly furnished accommodation in the original house. Menus feature locally-caught fish, and service is friendly and helpful.
30rm(21⇌3♠)(3fb)3⊞ CTV in all bedrooms ® **T** S10%
sB&B⇌♠£49.50-£59.50 dB&B⇌♠£74.80-£84.80 ⊟
70P ✲ ▭(heated) sauna solarium gymnasium spa bath croquet *xmas*
♉ English & French **V** ♈ ⊻ Lunch £7.50-£9.50 High tea £3.50-£4.75 Dinner £12.95-£18.50 Last dinner 9.30pm
Credit Cards 1 2 3 5

See advertisement under RYE

PEAT INN Fife Map **12** NO40

❀ ✕✕**The Peat Inn** KY15 5LH
☎(033484)206
Continued success has not spoilt the relaxed atmosphere of this country restaurant with its eight suites. The à la carte menu features the best Scottish produce, and a 'tasting menu' of six or seven small courses is good for groups. David Wilson's style of cooking is unfussy and lets the natural flavours shine through in dishes such as young grouse roasted Peat Inn style, flan of Arbroath smokies with lemon sauce, breast of pigeon with wild mushrooms. Among the excellent puddings the chocolate marquise with orange cream sauce has been particularly recommended. A set-menu lunch served at 1pm represents good value. One of Scotland's best wine lists includes a wealth of classic wines and some of the best from North America, with many very reasonably priced bottles.
Closed Sun, Mon, 2 wks Jan & 2 wks Nov
♉ French 48 seats S10% Lunch £13.50 Dinner £29&alc Last lunch 1pm Last dinner 9.30pm 24P 8 bedrooms available ⅟
Credit Cards 1 2 3 5

Book as early as possible for busy holiday periods.

PEEBLES Borders *Peeblesshire* Map **11** NT24

See also **Eddleston**

★★★60% ***Park*** Innerleithen Rd EH45 8BA (Swallow)
☎(0721)20451 Telex no 53168
Individually styled bedrooms and a panelled dining room are features of this hotel, which stands in well-maintained gardens with views over the Cademuir Hills.
26⇌(3fb)1⊞ CTV in all bedrooms ®
☾ 60P ✲ ♫
♉ Scottish & French **V** ♈ ⊻
Credit Cards 1 2 3 4 5

★★★64% **Peebles Hydro** EH45 8LX (Consort) ☎(0721)20602
Telex no 72568 FAX (0721) 22999
Majestically placed above the town, this elegant Edwardian hotel has a swimming pool, tennis courts and a putting green. The supervised play rooms and other facilities will also appeal to families with young children, and there are excellent conference and function rooms.
137rm(129⇌8♠)(26fb) CTV in all bedrooms ® **T** ✗ (ex guide dogs) S% sB&B⇌♠£54-£62
dB&B⇌♠£75-£107.50 (incl dinner) ⊟
Lift ☾ 200P ✲ CFA ▭(heated) ℘ (hard) squash ∪ snooker sauna solarium gymnasium pitch and putt ♫ ⌂ *xmas*
♉ Scottish **V** ♈ ⊻ ⅟ S% Lunch fr£9.50 Dinner fr£13.75 Last dinner 9pm
Credit Cards 1 2 3 5 £

★★★57% **The Tontine** High St EH45 8AJ (Trusthouse Forte)
☎(0721)20892
Traditional, friendly and well-equipped hotel in the centre of the picturesque town.
37rm(36⇌1♠)(3fb)⅟in 5 bedrooms CTV in all bedrooms ® **T**
S% sB⇌♠£35-£38 dB⇌♠£50-£55 (room only) ⊟
☾ 30P 4🚗 CFA *xmas*
♉ English & French **V** ♈ ⊻ ⅟ Bar Lunch £3.95-£8.75 Dinner £10.50-£11.50&alc Last dinner 9pm
Credit Cards 1 2 3 4 5

★★♣**Cringletie House**
EH45 8PL
☎Eddleston(07213)233
Closed 28Dec-Feb

With its crow-stepped gables and fairytale turrets, Cringletie is a romantically splendid Scottish house which has been transformed into a charming hotel. It is owned and run by the Maguire family, who create an instantly welcoming atmosphere with plenty of flower arrangements in the public rooms. Sound home cooking can always be relied upon, and the bedrooms have an equally straightforward, simple charm. A team of smart, polite staff complete the picture. This is a deservedly popular hotel, with an understated and unpretentious style.
13rm(12⇌1♠)(2fb) CTV in 16bedrooms **T**
sB&B⇌♠£35-£45 dB&B⇌♠£65 ⊟
Lift 40P ⊞ ✲ ℘ (hard) putting croquet
♉ International ♈ ⊻ ⅟ Lunch £4.50-£10.50 Dinner £18.50 Last dinner 8.30pm
Credit Cards 1 3

For key to symbols see the inside front cover.

★★Kingsmuir Springhill Rd EH45 9EP ☎(0721)20151
Tasteful bedrooms are offered at this family-run hotel.
10⇨(2fb) CTV in all bedrooms ® sB&B⇨£26-£32 dB&B⇨£44-£52 [symbol]
27P [symbol] ❋
V [symbol] Lunch fr£6.50 Dinner fr£9.50&alc Last dinner 8.30pm
Credit Cards 1 2 3 £

★★Tweedbridge House Chambers Ter EH45 9DZ ☎(0721)20590
Quiet hotel with panelled dining room and cocktail bar.
5rm(3⇨2↑)1[symbol] CTV in all bedrooms **T** sB&B⇨↑£30-£45 dB&B⇨↑£50-£80
20P [symbol] ❋
V [symbol] [symbol] [symbol] Lunch £9.50-£10.50&alc Dinner £15.95-£17.95&alc Last dinner 9.30pm
Credit Cards 1 2 3 £

★★[symbol]Venlaw Castle
Edinburgh Rd EH45 8QG
☎(0721)20384
Closed Nov-Mar

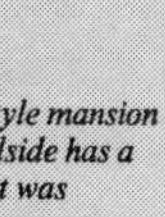

This baronial-style mansion on a wooded hillside has a cocktail bar that was originally a library.
12rm(5⇨4↑)(4fb) CTV in all bedrooms ® S% sB&B£20-£21 sB&B⇨↑£22-£24 dB&Bfr£38 dB&B⇨↑£44-£48 [symbol]
20P [symbol] ❋
V [symbol] Bar Lunch £5-£8 Dinner £11.50-£12.50 Last dinner 8pm
Credit Cards 1 2 4 5 £

See advertisement on page 529

PELYNT Cornwall & Isles of Scilly Map **02** SX25

★★Jubilee Inn PL13 2JZ ☎Lanreath(0503)20312
An inn of charm and character has been tastefully modernised to provide comfortable accommodation; the atmosphere is relaxing and friendly, helpful service being rendered by charming staff.
9rm(8⇨1↑)(2fb)1[symbol] CTV in all bedrooms **T** ✱ sB&B⇨↑£31-£35.30 dB&B⇨↑£53-£61.60 (incl dinner)
CTV 80P 6[symbol] ❋ [symbol] *xmas*
[symbol] English & Continental **V** [symbol] [symbol] Lunch £6.95&alc Dinner £5-£8.70alc Last dinner 10pm
Credit Cards 1 3

PEMBROKE Dyfed Map **02** SM90

See also **Lamphey**

★★Coach House Inn 116 Main St SA71 4HN (Exec Hotel)
☎(0646)684602 Telex no 48407
Closed 24-26 Dec
The original coach house has been extended and modernised to provide comfortable, well-equipped, pine-fitted bedrooms. A pleasant little gallery lounge stands above the old courtyard, and the good food served in the dining room includes a vegetarian selection.
14rm(13⇨1↑)(3fb) CTV in all bedrooms ® **T** [symbol] (ex guide dogs) sB&B⇨↑£29-£32 dB&B⇨↑£40-£44 [symbol]
10P ❋ solarium
[symbol] English & French **V** [symbol] [symbol] Sunday Lunch fr£5.50 Dinner £10.25-£18alc Last dinner 9.30pm
Credit Cards 1 2 3 5 £

★★**Holyland** Holyland Rd SA71 4PP (Minotels) ☎(0646)681444
Georgian mansion converted into a family-run hotel, serving good food.
12rm(6⇨6♠)(1fb)1 CTV in all bedrooms ® T
50P ✲ ♫
V ♡ Last dinner 9.30pm
Credit Cards 1 3 5 £

★★*Old Kings Arms* Main St SA71 4JS ☎(0646)683611
Closed 25-26 Dec & 1 Jan
This small hotel of great character offers friendly, personal service and promotes commendable cooking standards; bedrooms are modern and compact, while the restaurant with its flagged floor, is charmingly reminiscent of bygone days.
21⇨ CTV in all bedrooms ® T
21P
V ♡ Last dinner 10pm
Credit Cards 1 2 3

★★*Underdown Country House* Grove Hill SA71 5
☎(0646)683350 FAX (0646) 621229
Closed 28 Feb-24 Dec
This delightful little country house hotel promotes a personal, homely style. It is splendidly furbished with the owners' own antiques and offers fine home cooking in the warmth and charm of an attractive restaurant. Bedrooms combine character with modern facilities.
6rm(4⇨2♠)(2fb)2 CTV in all bedrooms ® T ✗ (ex guide dogs)
(CTV 20P 4 ✲ nc12yrs
English & French V Last dinner 10pm
Credit Cards 1 3 5

PENARTH South Glamorgan Map 03 ST17

★**Walton House** 37 Victoria Rd CF6 2HY ☎(0222)707782
This small, family-run hotel, standing in a residential area, offers good-value accommodation and a wide range of meals.
11rm(5⇨3♠) CTV in all bedrooms ® T ✗ (ex guide dogs)
sB&B£20-£24 sB&B⇨♠£24-£27 dB&B£32-£37 dB&B⇨♠£37
16P ✲
English French, Italian & Spanish V Bar Lunch £9&alc Dinner £9&alc Last dinner 9pm
Credit Cards 1 3

✕*Il Piccolino* The Esplanade CF6 2 ☎(0222)703428
Standing beside the yacht club, with lovely views over the Bristol Channel, this little restaurant complements its variety of Italian dishes with a few in English style among both main courses and sweets. Pasta items such as Tagliatelli Napoletana or Alfredo, with fish, chicken or even tender veal cooked in sweet Marsala, tempt the palate, and there is a good range of Italian wines available. There is also a more modestly priced Pizzeria, open both at lunchtime and in the evening.
English, French & Italian V 40 seats Last dinner 11.30pm
Credit Cards 1 2 3

PENCOED Mid Glamorgan Map 03 SS98

○*Travelodge* Old Mill, Felindre CF3 5HU (Trusthouse Forte)
☎Central reservations 01-567 3444
Due to have opened July 1989
1m from junction 35 M4, just off A473 towards Felindre and Ruthin.
40⇨

All hotels awarded three or more stars are now also given a percentage grading for the quality of their facilities. Please see p 16 for a detailed explanation.

PENCRAIG Hereford & Worcester Map 03 SO52

★★**Pencraig Court**
HR9 6HR
☎Ross-on-Wye(0989)84306
Closed Xmas, New Year & Jan-Feb

Peaceful small country hotel set in gardens and woodland.
11⇨(2fb)1 CTV in all bedrooms ® ✗ (ex guide dogs)
S% sB&B⇨£27-£32 dB&B⇨£38-£44
25P ✲ U
English & French ♡ Bar Lunch fr£3 Dinner fr£11.50&alc Last dinner 9pm
Credit Cards 1 2 3 5

See advertisement under ROSS-ON-WYE

PENDOGGETT Cornwall & Isles of Scilly Map 02 SX07

★★*Cornish Arms* PL30 3HH ☎Bodmin(0208)880263
Closed Xmas Day & Boxing Day
Delightful, small hotel in a 17th-century former ale house. Comfortable, modern bedrooms, charming character bars and freshly cooked wholesome food.
7rm(5⇨)
CTV 40P ✲ nc14yrs
V ♡ Last dinner 8.45pm
Credit Cards 1 2 3 5

PENMAEN West Glamorgan Map 02 SS58

★★**Nicholaston House** Nicholaston SA3 2HL
☎Swansea(0792)371317
Set in the heart of the Gower, this 19th-century hotel is run by the friendly Lewis family, and has panoramic views of Oxwich Bay from many rooms. A full-size snooker table is available, and bedrooms are bright and well-equipped.
11⇨(4fb)1 CTV in all bedrooms ® ✱ sB&B⇨£17-£25.30 dB&B⇨£30-£46
CTV 35P ✲ snooker 9 hole putting green
V ♡ Sunday Lunch £6.25-£6.75 Dinner £8-£11 Last dinner 8.30pm
Credit Cards 1 3

PENNAL Gwynedd Map 06 SH60

★**Riverside** SY20 9DW ☎(065475)285
Located in the centre of the village by the river bridge, this inn caters for locals and tourists alike.
7rm(1fb) ✱ sB&B£18.50-£19.50 dB&B£37-£39
CTV 60P 4 ✲
♡ Lunch £7.25-£8.25 Dinner £10.50-£12.50 Last dinner 8.45pm

PENRITH Cumbria Map 12 NY53

See also **Edenhall and Shap**
★★★ 73% **North Lakes** Ullswater Rd CA11 8QT
(Shire)(Consort) ☎(0768)68111 Telex no 64257
FAX (0768) 68291
A modern, well-appointed hotel, situated close to the M6, with extensive leisure and conference facilities. It offers every comfort to its guests, whether on holiday or on business. Bedrooms are attractively furnished and very well equipped and public areas are full of character. The Martindale restaurant is particularly efficient and friendly.

85⇌(12fb)4⊞✗in 6 bedrooms CTV in all bedrooms ® T ✱
sB&B⇌fr£68 dB&B⇌fr£88 ⊟
Lift ☾ CTV 150P ⊡(heated) squash snooker sauna solarium gymnasium spa pool *xmas*
V ♈ ⊡ ✗ Lunch £7.50-£9.50&alc Dinner £15-£18&alc Last dinner 9.45pm
Credit Cards 1 2 3 5

★★***Clifton Hill*** Clifton CA10 2EJ (2.75m S A6) ☎(0768)62717
Personally managed by the resident proprietors, this much enlarged traditional hotel organises excursions and entertainment for guests and is a popular venue for private functions.
57rm(55⇌2↱)(2fb) CTV in all bedrooms
CTV 200P 25⌂ ✲
V ♈ ⊡ ✗

See advertisement on page 531

★★**George** Devonshire St CA1 7SU ☎(0768)62696
FAX (0768)68223
Closed Xmas Day, Boxing Day & New Years Day
Former coaching inn, offering courteous and personal service.
31rm(11⇌20↱)(1fb) CTV in all bedrooms ® T
sB&B⇌↱fr£33 dB&B⇌↱fr£45 ⊟
☾ 30P
♉ English & French ♈ ⊡ Lunch £5.50-£7 Dinner fr£9.75 Last dinner 8.30pm
Credit Cards 1 3 £

★**Glen Cottage** Corney Square CA11 7PX ☎(0768)62221
Closed Xmas Day, Boxing Day & New Years Day
White stucco-faced cottage of charm and character, built in 1756.
7rm(4⇌)(3fb) CTV in all bedrooms sB&B£18.50-£20.50
sB&B⇌£22.50-£23.50 dB&B£27-£29 dB&B⇌£31-£33
3⌂ (50p per night)
♈ Lunch £3.50-£5 Dinner £4.95-£6 Last dinner 9pm
Credit Cards 1 2 3 5 £

○ *TraveLodge* Redhills(A66) (Trusthouse Forte)
☎(0768)66958
32⇨
P

PENYBONT Powys Map **03** SO16

★★Severn Arms LD1 5UA ☎(059787)224
Closed Xmas wk
The bedrooms of this white-painted inn beside the A44, though modestly furnished, are bright and clean with private bathroom facilities. Lunches are available at the bar, and both fixed price and à la carte dinners served in the restaurant are popular locally for their unfailing quality.
10⇨(6fb) CTV in all bedrooms ® **T** ✱ sB&B⇨£22
dB&B⇨£40
CTV 20P 2🚗 ✲ ⌡
V ♉ Lunch £5.50 Dinner £8 Last dinner 9pm
Credit Cards 1 3

PENZANCE Cornwall & Isles of Scilly Map **02** SW43

★★★62% Higher Faugan Newlyn TR18 5NS (off B3315)
☎(0736)62076

Built for Stanhope Forbes in 1904, this Cornish stone house stands in 10 acres of gardens and paddocks and is now a relaxing venue for both business and holiday travellers. Bedrooms are individually furnished and a short table d'hôte menu is offered at dinner.
12rm(11⇨1🚿)(2fb)1 ⊟ ⁄in 3 bedrooms CTV in all bedrooms ® **T** ✗ (ex guide dogs) ✱ sB&B⇨🚿£29-£36
dB&B⇨🚿£58-£72 ⊟
20P 3🚗 ⊞ ✲ ⌒(heated) ℛ (hard) snooker , putting green *xmas*
♉ English, French & Italian ♉ ⊥ ⁄ Lunch £5.95-£6.95&alc High tea fr£3.50 Dinner £11.50-£13&alc Last dinner 8.30pm
Credit Cards 1 2 3 5 £

★★★60% Mount Prospect Britons Hill TR18 3AE (Exec Hotel)
☎(0736)63117 FAX (0736) 50970
Well-appointed hotel in gardens overlooking Mounts Bay and Penzance harbour.
26rm(23⇨3🚿)(2fb)⁄in 6 bedrooms CTV in all bedrooms ® **T**
sB&B⇨🚿fr£32.20 dB&B⇨🚿fr£52.90 ⊟
☾ CTV 14P ✲ ⌒(heated)
♉ English & Continental ♉ ⊥ Bar Lunch fr£5.20 Dinner fr£10.35 Last dinner 9pm
Credit Cards 1 2 3 5

★★★52% Queen's The Promenade TR18 4HG ☎(0736)62371
Large, traditional hotel on the sea front with exceptional views over Mount's Bay.
71rm(49⇨22🚿)(9fb)1 ⊟ CTV in all bedrooms ® **T** ✱
sB&B⇨🚿£23.50-£40 dB&B⇨🚿£42-£70 ⊟
Lift ☾ 100P sauna solarium gymnasium *xmas*
♉ English & French **V** ♉ ⊥ ⁄ Lunch £8.50 Dinner £15&alc Last dinner 8.45pm
Credit Cards 1 2 3 5 £

★★Sea & Horses 6 Alexandra Ter TR18 4NX ☎(0736)61961
Closed Xmas
Small, spotless amd friendly hotel on the seafront, with a cellar-style dining room and good views over Mounts Bay.
11rm(2⇨6🚿)(4fb) CTV in all bedrooms ® ✗ S%
sB&B£16-£18 sB&B⇨🚿£17-£19 dB&B£30-£34
dB&B⇨🚿£32-£36 ⊟
8P 1🚗(£1) ⊞
V ♉ ⊥ Bar Lunch 80p-£3 Dinner fr£8 Last dinner 7.30pm
Credit Cards 1 3

★Alexandra Alexandra Ter, Seafront TR18 4NX ☎(0736)62644
Telex no 934999
A double-fronted Victorian holiday hotel in end-of-terrace position provides well-equipped bedrooms, simple wholesome food and a homely atmosphere.
33rm(6⇨24🚿)(12fb) CTV in all bedrooms ® **T**
sB&B£15.50-£19 sB&B⇨🚿£17.50-£21 dB&B£31-£38
dB&B⇨🚿£35-£42 ⊟
21P ♫ *xmas*
♉ International **V** ♉ ⊥ Bar Lunch 95p-£5.95 Dinner £8-£8.50&alc Last dinner 7.45pm
Credit Cards 1 2 3 £

★Estoril 46 Morrab Rd TR18 4EX
☎(0736)62468 & 67471 & 69811
Closed Dec-Feb
At this small hotel, conveniently situated in the town centre, you are assured of a friendly welcome, a homely atmosphere and accommodation in comfortable, well-equipped bedrooms.
10rm(5⇨5🚿)(2fb) CTV in all bedrooms ® **T** ✗
sB&B⇨🚿£20-£21 dB&B⇨🚿£40-£42 ⊟
4P ⊞
V Lunch £4-£5 Dinner £8.50 Last dinner 7.30pm
Credit Cards 1 3

See advertisement on page 533

P

★**Tarbert** 11-12 Clarence St TR18 2NU (Minotels)
☎(0736)63758
Closed Dec
Small comfortable hotel in central situation. Good food and friendly atmosphere.
12rm(1⇌11⇖) CTV in all bedrooms ® **T** ✗
sB&B⇌⇖£19.50-£21.50 dB&B⇌⇖£39-£49 ⊟
CTV 5P ⛟ nc12yrs
♉ English & French **V** ♧ ☕ Bar Lunch 90p-£3.50alc Dinner fr£10.50&alc Last dinner 8pm
Credit Cards [1] [2] [3] [5]

PERELLE

See **Guernsey under Channel Islands**

PERRANPORTH Cornwall & Isles of Scilly Map **02** SW75

★**Beach Dunes** Ramoth Way, Reen Sands TR6 0BY
☎Truro(0872)572263 FAX (0872) 573824
Closed Nov & Dec RS Jan & Feb
Peaceful, friendly hotel, with good facilities, overlooking the sea.
7rm(2⇌1⇖)Annexe3⇌(2fb) CTV in all bedrooms ® **T** ✗ (ex guide dogs) sB&B£17.57-£21.37 sB&B⇌⇖£18.50-£22.50 dB&B£35.14-£42.74 dB&B⇌⇖£37-£45 ⊟
15P ⛟ ✲ ⊡(heated) squash exercise equipment nc3yrs
V ♧ ☕ ⚡ S% Bar Lunch £1.50-£5 Dinner fr£9.50 Last dinner 7.30pm
Credit Cards [1] [2] [3]

PERRANUTHNOE Cornwall & Isles of Scilly Map **02** SW52

★***Ednovean House*** Ednovean Ln TR20 9LZ (on A394 5m E of Penzance) ☎Penzance(0736)711071
A peacefully situated hotel of character, with views of St Michael's Mount. Vegetarian and other diets are catered for in the good cooking.
9rm(6⇖)(2fb) ®
CTV 16P ⛟ ✲ putting green, croquet ⌂
V ♧ ☕ ⚡
Credit Cards [1] [3]

PERSHORE Hereford & Worcester Map **03** SO94

★★★61% **The Angel Inn** High St WR10 1AF ☎(0386)552046
FAX (0386) 552581
Interesting old coaching inn with riverbank grounds and interesting menus, in the centre of the town.
16⇌2⊞ CTV in all bedrooms ® **T** ✳ sB&B⇌£44
dB&B⇌£58 ⊟
50P ✲ ♪
♉ International **V** ♧ ☕ Lunch £4.50-£8 High tea 50p-£1.50 Dinner £10-£18alc Last dinner 9.30pm
Credit Cards [1] [2] [3] [5]

★★**Avonside** Main Rd, Wyre Piddle WR10 2JB (2m NE on B4084) ☎(0386)552654
Guests enjoy the relaxing atmosphere at this hotel set beside the river in the village of Wyre Piddle.
7rm(6⇌1⇖)(3fb) CTV in all bedrooms ® **T** ✗
sB&B⇌⇖fr£38 dB&B⇌⇖fr£50 ⊟
10P ⛟ ✲ ⌓(heated) ♪ nc7 yrs *xmas*
♉ English & French Dinner fr£13 Last dinner 7.30pm
Credit Cards [1] [3]

★***Star*** Bridge St ☎(0386)552704
Town centre inn with a small garden, bordering the banks of the River Avon.
9rmAnnexe4rm CTV in all bedrooms ®
50P ⛟
♧
Credit Cards [1] [3]

PERTH Tayside *Perthshire* Map **11** NO12

See town plan section page

★★★71% **Balcraig House Hotel** Scone PH2 7PG ☎(0738)51123
FAX (0738)33449
Nestling below the Sidlaw Hills, 3 miles north of the town, a lovely Victorian house provides charming, individually decorated bedrooms, all but one being furnished with antiques. Beautifully appointed public rooms invite relaxation, whilst the sound meals served in the smart new conservatory restaurant feature game and seafood to tempt the palate.
10⇌⇖(2fb)1⊞ CTV in all bedrooms **T** ✳ S8%
sB&B⇌⇖£59-£69 dB&B⇌⇖£82-£105 ⊟
35P ✲ ℘ (hard) pony trekking *xmas*
♉ Scottish & Italian **V** ♧ ☕ Lunch £9-£12.50&alc Dinner fr£16&alc Last dinner 9.30pm
Credit Cards [1] [2] [3] [5]

★★★65% **Huntingtower** Crieff Rd, Almondbank PH1 3JT (3m W off A85) ☎(0738)83771 FAX (0738) 83777
Standing in 3.5 acres of landscaped grounds a short drive west of the city, this hotel continues to serve imaginative cuisine in the attractive pine-panelled restaurant.
17⇌⇖Annexe7rm(4⇌)(2fb) CTV in 17bedrooms ® **T** ✳
sB&B£44-£59 sB&B⇌⇖£44-£59 dB&B£61-£84
dB&B⇌⇖£61-£84 ⊟
☾ CTV 100P ✲ putting *xmas*
♉ Scottish & Continental **V** ♧ ☕ ⚡ Lunch £7.75-£9.50 Dinner £16.25-£17.25&alc Last dinner 9.30pm
Credit Cards [1] [2] [3] [5] Ⓔ

★★★59% **Isle of Skye Toby** Queen's Bridge, Dundee Rd PH2 7AB (Toby) ☎(0738)24471 Telex no 76185
Comfortable, spacious bedrooms and bright, modern public areas are provided by this virtually rebuilt hotel. The original building houses the popular Carving Room and additional bedrooms, some of which are rather compact.
56⇌⇖(2fb)⚡in 14 bedrooms CTV in all bedrooms ® **T** ✗ (ex guide dogs) ✳ sB&B⇌⇖fr£42.50 dB&B⇌⇖fr£54 ⊟
Lift ☾ 70P CFA *xmas*
♧ ☕ ⚡ Lunch £6.50-£9 Dinner £6.50-£9 Last dinner 9pm
Credit Cards [1] [2] [3] [5]

★★★60% **Lovat Hotel** 90 Glasgow Rd PH2 0LT ☎(0738)36555
Telex no 76531
Popular business, tourist and conference hotel just south of city centre, with one bar reserved for non-smokers.
26rm(15⇌11⇖) CTV in all bedrooms ® **T** ✗ (ex guide dogs)
✳ sB&B⇌⇖£40 dB&B⇌⇖£58 ⊟
☾ 60P ♫ *xmas*
V ♧ ☕ ⚡ Lunch fr£6.50 High tea fr£4 Dinner fr£9.50&alc Last dinner 9.30pm
Credit Cards [1] [2] [3]

★★★63% ***Queens Hotel*** Leonard St PH2 8HB ☎(0738)25471
Telex no 76531
Close to the station and city centre, this extensively refurbished business and tourist hotel offers a range of conference and leisure facilities.
50rm(40⇌9⇖)(7fb)1⊞ CTV in all bedrooms ® **T** ✗
Lift ☾ 30P ⊡(heated) sauna solarium gymnasium
V ♧ ☕ Last dinner 9.30pm
Credit Cards [1] [2] [3]

★★★58% **The Royal George** Tay St PH1 5LD (Trusthouse Forte) ☎(0738)24455 FAX (0738) 30345
A popular hotel standing beside the river and close to the town centre amenitiies. Refurbishment has considerably enhanced the public areas, but though bedroom improvements are underway, some rooms remain rather dated.
43⇌⚡in 4 bedrooms CTV in all bedrooms ® S% sB⇌£50
dB⇌£66-£77 (room only) ⊟
☾ 20P 12⛫ *xmas*

►

P

🍷 International V ✿ 🍸 ⚡ Lunch £8-£10&alc Dinner £12&alc Last dinner 9.30pm
Credit Cards 1 2 3 4 5

★★★59% **Stakis City Mills** West Mill St PH1 5QP (Stakis) ☎(0738)28281 Telex no 778704
A former water mill, imaginatively converted into an interesting hotel with a choice of bars and restaurants.
78rm(76⇌)(2fb)2⇌⚡in 50 bedrooms CTV in all bedrooms ® T ✱ sB⇌£54-£64 dB⇌£64-£74 (room only) ⊟
☾ 75P CFA ♫ *xmas*
🍷 Scottish & International V ✿ 🍸 ⚡ Lunch £5.95-£7&alc Dinner £8-£10.50&alc Last dinner 10pm
Credit Cards 1 2 3 5

★★**Salutation** South St PH2 8PH (Embassy) ☎(0738)30066 Telex no 76357 FAX (0738) 33598
Established in 1699, was temporary headquarters of Bonnie Prince Charlie.
70rm(23⇌37♿)(6fb) CTV in all bedrooms ® sB&Bfr£30 sB&B⇌♿fr£39 dB&Bfr£43 dB&B⇌♿fr£55 ⊟
☾ CTV 𝒫 CFA *xmas*
🍷 Scottish & French V ✿ 🍸 Lunch fr£6.25 Dinner £9.25&alc Last dinner 9.30pm
Credit Cards 1 2 3 4 5

✕✕**Coach House** 8-10 North Port PH1 5LU ☎(0738)27950
Set close to the river in a quiet, older part of the city, this little restaurant continues to please. The cosy and informal atmosphere suits the unfussy but interesting style of cooking.
Closed Sun & Mon 1st 2 wks Jan
36 seats S% Lunch fr£9.50alc Dinner fr£18.50alc Last lunch 2pm Last dinner 10pm 𝒫
Credit Cards 1 2 3

✕✕***Number Thirty Three*** 33 St George St PH1 5LA ☎(0738)33771
A 1930s theme restaurant serving seafood specialities including mussels, crab, oysters, salmon and a variety of fresh white fish. Sticky toffee pudding is one of a range of delicious homemade sweets. Service is friendly and attentive.
Closed Sun, Mon & 10 days Xmas-New Year
🍷 Scottish & French V 48 seats Last lunch 2.30pm Last dinner 9.30pm 𝒫 nc5yrs
Credit Cards 1 2 3

P

PETERBOROUGH Cambridgeshire Map **04** TL19

★★★56% **Bull** Westgate PE1 1RB ☎(0733)61364 Telex no 329265
Former coaching inn with a 17th-century façade. Extensive modernisation has been carried out on the ground floor and in all rooms.
112⇌(3fb) CTV in all bedrooms ® T sB&B⇌£52-£57.50 dB&B⇌fr£62 ⊟
☾ 100P CFA
🍷 English & French V ✿ 🍸 Lunch fr£10.50&alc Dinner fr£10.50&alc Last dinner 10.30pm
Credit Cards 1 2 3 5

★★★57% **Crest Hotel** Great North Rd PE7 3TB (Crest) ☎(0733)240209 Telex no 32576 FAX (0733) 244455
(For full entry see Norman Cross)

★★★66% **Peterborough Moat House** Thorpe Wood PE3 6SG (Queens Moat) ☎(0733)260000 Telex no 32708 FAX (0733) 262737
A modern, purpose-built hotel on the west side of the city, adjacent to Thorpe Wood Golf Course. Well-equipped for both business guests and holidaymakers, it has a leisure centre and a recently refurbished restaurant and cocktail bar.
125⇌♿⚡in 28 bedrooms CTV in all bedrooms ® T ✱ S% sB⇌♿£62-£69.50 dB⇌♿£73-£79.50 (room only) ⊟
Lift ☾ 230P ❄ CFA ⊡(heated) sauna solarium gymnasium jacuzzi spa pool ♫

🍷 International V ✿ 🍸 S% Lunch £9.45-£11.95&alc Dinner £11.95&alc Last dinner 9.45pm
Credit Cards 1 2 3 5

⌂**TraveLodge** Great North Rd, Alwalton Village PE7 3UR (A1 southbound) (Trusthouse Forte) ☎(0733)231109
32⇌♿(32fb) CTV in all bedrooms ® sB⇌♿£21.50 dB⇌♿£27 (room only)
32P ⇌
🍷 Mainly grills
Credit Cards 1 2 3

○***Butterfly*** Thorpe Meadows, Off Longthorpe Parkway PE3 6GA ☎(0733)64240
Due to have opened August 1989
50⇌

PETERHEAD Grampian *Aberdeenshire* Map **15** NK14

★★★67% **Waterside Inn** Fraserburgh Rd AB4 7BN (Consort) ☎(0779)71121 Telex no 739413 FAX (0779) 70670
This modern hotel is well-equipped for the business traveller and has helpful and friendly staff.
70⇌♿Annexe40⇌♿(40fb) CTV in all bedrooms ® T ✱ sB&B⇌♿£39.60-£51.15 dB&B⇌♿£46.20-£59.40 ⊟
☾ 250P ❄ CFA ⊡(heated) snooker sauna solarium gymnasium steam room spa bath ♫
🍷 Scottish & French V ✿ 🍸 Lunch £5.95-£12.50 Dinner fr£10.95 Last dinner 10pm
Credit Cards 1 2 3 5 £

The AA's star-rating scheme is the market leader in hotel classification.

THE GLENFARG HOTEL

If you enjoy the friendly, informal atmosphere of a smaller hotel but you also appreciate high standards of service, you'll find the perfect combination at the Glenfarg Hotel.

Situated in the picturesque village of Glenfarg, just 2½ miles from the M90, this elegant Victorian hotel is ideal for golf, shooting, fishing, touring or just relaxing.

All bedrooms ensuite with colour TV, tea and coffee making. Excellent restaurant offering delicious home-cooked cuisine. Bar meals also available.

The Glenfarg Hotel,
Glenfarg, Perthshire, Scotland
Tel: (05773) 241 ★★

This converted mill has 78 bedrooms all with en suite bathrooms, colour television, tea and coffee facilities. Our two restaurants offer excellent cuisine. Conference facilities from 2 to 150, Weddings, Dinner Dances and Seminars. Easy access by road and rail.

Tel: 0738-28281

STAKIS ★★★

City Mills Hotel

PERTH

The Bein Inn ★★

Glenfarg

Perthshire PH2 9PY Telephone (05773) 216

Nestling in beautiful Glenfarg, eight miles south of Perth just off the M90, is where you will find the Bein Inn.

The public rooms are in the traditional style, comfortable and full of atmosphere. The bedrooms all with private bath and TV, are spacious, bright and modern.

Edinburgh, Perth, Dundee and St. Andrews, are all within easy motoring distance.

A golfers' paradise with St. Andrews, Gleneagles, Carnoustie and many more within easy reach.

Special Bargain-Break prices available for Spring/ Autumn.

Send for brochure and terms.

Personally supervised by
Mike and Elsa Thompson

NEWTON HOUSE HOTEL

★★★

Glencarse, By Perth, Perthshire PH2 7LX.
Telephone: (073886) 250.
Fax: (073886) 717

An ideal retreat within two hours driving time from Glasgow, Aberdeen, Edinburgh and Inverness. Dundee 15 miles and Perth 6 miles. A former Dower House it retains the character and style of gracious living. Chef takes pride in using local and fresh produce for his menus. Relax in either of the two lounges or the 1½ acres of garden. All the bedrooms have full private facilities, colour TV, radio, tea making facilities and dial out telephone. They are all individually decorated and all overlook the garden. Open all year including New Year and special weekend breaks. **Your hosts: Geoffrey & Carol Tallis.**

P

PETTY FRANCE Avon Map **03** ST78

★★★71% **Petty France** GL9 1AF (on A46 S of junct with A433) ☎Didmarton(045423)361 FAX (045423) 768
Charming, privately-run coaching inn with ambitious menu of well prepared food.
8rm(7⇌1↱)Annexe12rm(11⇌1↱)(1fb)1⊡ CTV in all bedrooms ® **T** sB&B⇌↱£45-£80
dB&B⇌↱£65-£110 Continental breakfast ⊟
☾ 50P ⊞ ✲ *xmas*
♡ International **V** ♡ ⚑ Lunch £13-£17 Dinner £15-£18&alc
Last dinner 10pm
Credit Cards 1 2 3 £

✗✗**The Restaurant at Bodkin House** Badminton GL9 1AF (on A46 S of junct with A433) ☎Didmarton(045423)310 & 422 FAX (0453) 843572
This period roadhouse, dating in parts form the 16th-century has an attractive bar and interesting dining room. The food is enjoyable and is backed by a well-chosen wine list.
♡ English & French **V** 45 seats ✱ Lunch £20-£30alc Dinner £20-£30alc Last lunch 2pm Last dinner 10pm 25P
Credit Cards 1 2 3 5

See advertisement under BADMINTON

PEVENSEY East Sussex Map **05** TQ60

★★**Priory Court Inn** Castle Rd BN24 5LG
☎Eastbourne(0323)763150
Dating from the 15th-century, this agreeable, family-run hotel has some attractive, well-furnished bedrooms, cosy public rooms, reliable cooking standards and offers good value for money.
9rm(5⇌1↱)(1fb)1⊡ CTV in 6bedrooms ® ✱ sB&B£23
sB&B⇌↱£28 dB&B£38 dB&B⇌↱£48-£56
CTV 60P ✲
♡ Mainly grills **V** ♡ ⚑ Lunch fr£7.95&alc
Credit Cards 1 2 3

PICKERING North Yorkshire Map **08** SE78

★★**Burgate House** 17 Burgate YO18 7AU ☎(0751)73463
7rm(2⇌)(2fb) CTV in all bedrooms ® **T** ✗ (ex guide dogs) S%
sB&B£23-£28 sB&B⇌£28-£33 dB&B£36-£48
dB&B⇌£52-£60 ⊟
⊞ CTV 8P ⊞ *xmas*
♡ English & French **V** ♡ ⚑ Lunch fr£6.50 High tea £5-£6.75
Dinner £5-£9.50 Last dinner 9pm
Credit Cards 1 3

★★***Crossways Hotel*** Eastgate YO18 7DW ☎(0751)72804
Friendly little hotel with secluded garden.
10rm(3↱)(3fb) CTV in all bedrooms ®
CTV 15P ⊞
♡ ⚑ Last dinner 9.30pm
Credit Cards 1 3

★★**Forest & Vale** Malton Rd YO18 7DL (Consort)
☎(0751)72722 Telex no 57515
Comfortable country hotel with well-kept garden. Large restaurant serving mainly English food.
16rm(11⇌5↱)Annexe5rm(4⇌1↱)(3fb) CTV in all bedrooms ® **T** sB&B⇌↱£40-£52 dB&B⇌↱£63-£73 ⊟
70P ✲
♡ English & French **V** ♡ ⚑ Lunch £8.50&alc Dinner £13&alc
Last dinner 9.30pm
Credit Cards 1 2 3 5

★★**White Swan** Market Place YO18 7AA ☎(0751)72288
Parts of this tastefully modernised coaching inn date back to the 16th-century, and it retains much of its original character and charm. Under the personal supervision of the proprietors it offers a hospitable and friendly atmosphere, fine cuisine with the emphasis on fresh produce, and competitive prices.
13⇌↱(1fb)⊬in 2 bedrooms CTV in all bedrooms ® **T**
sB&B⇌↱£30 dB&B⇌↱£50-£60 ⊟
35P ⊞ ✲ *xmas*
♡ English & French **V** ♡ Lunch fr£8 Dinner fr£12.50 Last dinner 9pm
Credit Cards 1 3 £

PIDDLETRENTHIDE Dorset Map **03** SY79

★★**Old Bakehouse** DT2 7QR ☎(03004)305
Closed 25 & 26 Dec & Jan
This former bakehouse, under the personal supervision of the owners, has a warm and friendly atmosphere. The unusual galleried restaurant has an inviting menu of well-prepared dishes.
3⇌Annexe7rm(6⇌1↱)3⊡ CTV in all bedrooms ® ✱
sB&B⇌↱£21.50 dB&B⇌↱£37-£43 ⊟
16P ⊞ ✲ ⛆(heated) nc12yrs
♡ English & Continental **V** Dinner £13-£16alc Last dinner 9pm
Credit Cards 1 3

PIMPERNE Dorset Map **03** ST90

★★**The Anvil Hotel & Restaurant** Salisbury Rd DT11 8QU
☎Blandford(0258)53431 480281
Charming, thatched 16th-century inn of great character. Bedrooms vary in size but all are comfortable, and cosy, beamed restaurant offers a varied menu. Owners Mr and Mrs Palmer ensure a warm, friendly atmosphere.
9rm(6⇌3↱) CTV in all bedrooms ® **T** ✱ sB&B⇌↱£35
dB&B⇌↱£50 ⊟
CTV 25P
V ♡ ⚑ Lunch £15&alc Dinner £15&alc Last dinner 9.45pm
Credit Cards 1 2 3 5

PITLOCHRY Tayside *Perthshire* Map **14** NN95

★★★58% **The Atholl Palace** Atholl Rd PH16 5LY (Trusthouse Forte) ☎(0796)2400 Telex no 76406 FAX (0796) 3036
A popular holiday and conference hotel standing in 48 acres of grounds, with a wide range of leisure facilities. Spacious public rooms offer traditional comforts, while bedrooms are modest and somewhat practical.
84rm(78⇌6↱)(6fb)1⊡⊬in 6 bedrooms CTV in all bedrooms ® **T** S% sB⇌↱£47-£54 dB⇌↱£67-£75 (room only) ⊟
Lift ☾ 150P ✲ CFA ⛆(heated) ♪ (hard) snooker sauna solarium gymnasium pitch & putt *xmas*
V ♡ ⚑ ⊬ S% Bar Lunch £1.75-£5.95alc Dinner £13.50-£14.50&alc Last dinner 9pm
Credit Cards 1 2 3 4 5

★★★63% **Green Park** Clunie Bridge Rd PH16 5JY
☎(0796)3248
Closed 2 Nov-26 Mar
Extended country house hotel standing on the banks of Loch Faskally and backed by woodland.
37rm(36⇌1↱)(10fb) CTV in all bedrooms ® **T** ✗
sB&B⇌↱£28-£32 dB&B⇌↱£56-£65 ⊟
50P 4⊞ (£1.50) ⊞ ✲ CFA ⌐ putting table tennis bar billiards
♡ Scottish & French **V** ♡ ⚑ ⊬ Bar Lunch fr£4.40alc Dinner £13-£15&alc Last dinner 8.30pm
Credit Cards 1

See the preliminary section 'Hotel and Restaurant Classification' for an explanation of the AA's appointment and award scheme.

★★★68% Pine Trees
Strathview Ter PH16 5QR
☎(0796)2121
FAX (0796)2460
Closed mid Nov-Etr

Run by the MacLellan family, this delightful Victorian country house is set in 14 acres of secluded grounds. The public rooms are elegant, and the well-equipped bedrooms are constantly being improved.

18rm(15⇌2↱)(3fb) CTV in all bedrooms ® T ✗ (ex guide dogs) sB&B£32 sB&B⇌↱£37 dB&B⇌↱£64 ⊟
CTV 40P ✻ putting
Scottish & French V ☕ Lunch £10 Dinner £15 Last dinner 8.30pm
Credit Cards 1 3

★★★61% Pitlochry Hydro Knockard Rd PH16 5JH (Scottish Highland) ☎(0796)2666 FAX (0796)2238
Closed Dec-Feb
The volume of coach business has been reduced at this upgraded popular tourist hotel, where refurbished bedroom accommodation and an exciting new leisure centre now complement spacious and comfortably-appointed public rooms.
64⇌(4fb) CTV in all bedrooms ® T ✗ (ex guide dogs) sB&B⇌£40-£48 dB&B⇌£68-£78 ⊟
Lift ☾ CTV 100P ✻ (heated) (hard) snooker sauna solarium gymnasium putting green croquet games room
Scottish, English & French V ☕ Bar Lunch £3.50-£6 Dinner £12-£15 Last dinner 8.30pm
Credit Cards 1 2 3 5

★★★55% Scotland's 40 Bonnethill Rd PH16 5BT (Best Western) ☎(0796)2292 Telex no 76392 FAX (0796) 3284
Offering practical accommodation and traditional comforts, this hotel is popular with both tourists and business people alike. Standards in some areas remain rather modest, though improvements are in progress.
56rm(21⇌35↱)(14fb) CTV in all bedrooms ® T S2.5% sB&B⇌↱£30-£44 dB&B⇌↱£50-£72 ⊟
Lift ☾ CTV 60P ✻ CFA pool table *xmas*
V ☕ S2.5% Lunch fr£9 Dinner fr£12 Last dinner 8.30pm
Credit Cards 1 2 3 5 £

★★Acarsaid 8 Atholl Rd PH16 5BX ☎(0796)2389
Closed 7th Jan-2nd Mar
Friendly, family-run hotel in its own grounds, popular as a base for touring holidaymakers.
18rm(15⇌3↱)(1fb) CTV in all bedrooms ® ✗
sB&B⇌↱£19-£22.75 dB&B⇌↱£38-£45.50
CTV 20P ✻ putting green *xmas*
V ☕ Lunch £5.50-£11.50 Dinner £9-£13 Last dinner 8pm
Credit Cards 1 3

★★Airdaniar 160 Atholl Rd PH16 5AR (Guestaccom) ☎(0796)2266
Closed Jan
Set just north of the town centre in 3 acres of beautiful gardens, this friendly, family-run hotel combines bright, modern and comfortable public areas with practically-styled and well-equipped bedrooms, in a range of sizes.
9rm(4⇌5↱)(1fb) CTV in all bedrooms ® T
sB&B⇌↱£34.65-£35.65 dB&B⇌↱£49.30-£50.30
18P ✻ *xmas*

▶

P

V ♈ ⅟ Bar Lunch £4.50-£7alc Dinner £11.50 Last dinner 8.30pm
Credit Cards 1 3

★★Birchwood 2 East Moulin Rd PH16 5DW (Inter) ☎(0796)2477
Closed Xmas-Feb
Secluded, well-appointed hotel with high quality annexe bedrooms.
11rm(7⇌4↱)Annexe5↱(4fb) CTV in all bedrooms ® T ✱ S% sB&B⇌↱£36-£40.50 dB&B⇌↱£64-£73 (incl dinner) ⊟
25P ✣
♈ ⊻ ⅟ Lunch £3-£5 Dinner £11&alc Last dinner 8pm
Credit Cards 1 3

★★Burnside 19 West Moulin Rd PH16 5EA ☎(0796)2203
Closed Nov-late Mar
Comfortable hotel personally-run by the proprietors, with attractive floral arrangements throughout.
17rm(12⇌5↱)Annexe6rm(3⇌1↱)(6fb) CTV in all bedrooms ® sB&Bfr£24.45 sB&B⇌↱fr£27.95 dB&Bfr£42.40 dB&B⇌↱fr£49.90 ⊟
30P ✣
☋ Scottish & Continental V ♈ ⊻ ⅟ Lunch fr£6.50 Dinner fr£12.50&alc Last dinner 8.30pm
Credit Cards 1 2 3 5 £

★★*Castlebeigh* 10 Knockard Rd PH16 5HJ ☎(0796)2925
Closed mid Oct-Mar
A peaceful and welcoming family-run hotel providing comfortably-appointed accommodation and home-cooked meals, the 4-course dinner menu being changed daily.
18⇌ CTV in all bedrooms ®
CTV 36P ⛟ ✣ nc14yrs
V Last dinner 7.50pm
Credit Cards 1 3

★★*Claymore* 162 Atholl Rd PH16 5AR ☎(0796)2888
Closed Jan-Feb
Welcoming hotel run by the owners, Joyce and Harold Beaton.
7rm(4⇌1↱)Annexe4rm(1↱)(1fb) CTV in all bedrooms ®
25P ⛟ ✣
V ♈ ⊻ ⅟ Last dinner 9pm
Credit Cards 1 3

P

★★Craigower 134/136 Atholl Rd PH16 5AB ☎(0796)2590
Set in the town centre, this popular tourist hotel offers neatly appointed bedrooms, comfortable lounges and a choice of two restaurants.
23rm(1⇌15↱)(6fb) CTV in 18bedrooms ® ✱ sB&B£16-£24 sB&B⇌↱£20-£28 dB&B£28-£36 dB&B⇌↱£30-£40
CTV 15P *xmas*
V ♈ ⊻ Lunch £6-£10 High tea £5-£8 Dinner £10.50-£14.50 Last dinner 8.30pm
Credit Cards 1 3

★★Craigvrack West Moulin Rd PH16 5EQ (Minotels) ☎(0796)2399
Closed Jan – March
Friendly, modern privately-owned hotel on Braemar Road.
19rm(7⇌7↱)(2fb) CTV in all bedrooms ® sB&B£17-£20 sB&B⇌↱£26-£29 dB&B£34-£40 dB&B⇌↱£39-£46 ⊟
22P ⛟ ✣ putting green, games room *xmas*
☋ English & French V ♈ ⊻ ⅟ Bar Lunch £2.50-£7 Dinner fr£12 Last dinner 9.15pm
Credit Cards 1 2 3 £

★Balrobin Higher Oakfield PH16 5HT ☎(0796)2901
Closed Nov-Mar
Standing in its own grounds, and enjoying extensive views from its elevated position, the traditional Scottish stone house has recently been extended to provide comfortable bedrooms with modern facilities, and public areas where guests can relax in a friendly atmosphere.
12rm(1⇌9↱)(1fb) CTV in all bedrooms ® sB&B£12-£16 dB&B£24-£32 dB&B⇌↱£28-£40
12P ⛟ ✣ nc10yrs
⅟ Dinner £8 Last dinner 7.30pm

★Craig Urrard 10 Atholl Rd PH16 5BX ☎(0796)2346
Small friendly hotel with smart new lounge bar.
10rm(4↱)Annexe2↱(4fb) CTV in all bedrooms ® ✱ sB&B£12.50-£15 dB&B£25-£30 dB&B↱£28-£33
CTV 12P ⛟ ✣
⅟ Bar Lunch £1.25-£4alc Dinner £8-£9&alc Last dinner 8pm
Credit Cards 1 2 3

★Knockendarroch House Higher Oakfield PH16 5HT ☎(0796)3473
Closed 15th Nov – 31st Mar
An attractive family-run hotel enjoying a pleasant outlook from its own grounds offers bright, airy bedrooms, nicely appointed lounges that invite relaxation and a neat dining room where the short menu is based on local produce.
12rm(7⇌5↱)(1fb)2⊞ CTV in all bedrooms ® ✱ sB&B⇌↱£19.50-£26.50 dB&B⇌↱£39-£56 ⊟
☾ 12P ⛟ ✣
☋ Scottish & French Dinner £11 Last dinner 7.15pm
Credit Cards 1 2 3 5

PLOCKTON Highland *Ross & Cromarty* Map **14** NG83

★★Haven IV52 8TW ☎(059984)223 & 334
Closed 21 Dec-9 Feb
This splendid little hotel on Scotland's western coast is an ideal base for exploring the islands of Skye and Raasay. Bedrooms and public areas have recently been refurbished to provide exceptional comfort and are immaculately maintained. The owners are friendly and knowledgeable about the area, and meals prepared by their kitchen staff are homely and enjoyable.
13rm(10⇌) CTV in all bedrooms ® T sB&B⇌£22-£25 dB&B⇌£44-£50 ⊟
7P ⛟ nc7yrs
♈ ⊻ ⅟ Lunch £5-£10 Dinner £13.50-£15 Last dinner 8.30pm
Credit Cards 1 3

PLYMOUTH Devon Map **02** SX45

See **Town Plan Section**
See also **Down Thomas**

★★★★63% Copthorne Armada Centre, Armada Way PL1 1AR (Best Western) ☎(0752)224161 Telex no 45756
FAX (0752) 670688
Popular modern city-centre hotel, with comfortable and well-equipped bedrooms, attractive public areas and a small leisure centre. The Burlington Restaurant offers an interesting choice of dishes cooked in the modern classical style, while Bentley's Brasserie provides an alternative menu in more informal surroundings. Service is prompt and conducted in a pleasant manner.
135rm(131⇌4↱)(29fb)⅟in 18 bedrooms CTV in all bedrooms ® T ✱ sB⇌↱£43.50-£65 dB⇌↱£57-£75 (room only) ⊟
Lift ☾ 40🚘 ⊡(heated) snooker sauna solarium gymnasium pool
☋ International V ♈ ⊻ ⅟ Lunch £9.75-£15.95alc High tea fr£3.95alc Dinner £13.95-£16.95alc Last dinner 10.30pm
Credit Cards 1 2 3 5 £

★★★★58% Plymouth Moat House Armada Way PL1 2HJ (Queens Moat) ☎(0752)662866 Telex no 45637
FAX (0752) 673816
The 12-storey purpose-built modern hotel commands views over the city and across Plymouth Hoe. It offers a good choice of restaurants – the Penthouse boasting a superb outlook and Mongers, on the ground floor, specialising in seafood – and a variety of bars. Bedrooms, currently undergoing some upgrading, are well equipped, attractively decorated and spacious, although ▶

★★

CLAYMORE HOTEL

Atholl Road, Pitlochry, Perthshire PH16 5AR
Telephone: (0796) 2888

Standing in its own beautiful gardens this lovely traditional hotel enjoys panoramic views across Loch Faskally to the Cluniemore Hills and yet is only two minutes walk from Pitlochry town centre. The Claymore Hotel rightly enjoys an excellent reputation for its good food and high standard of service. All bedrooms have colour TV and tea/coffee trays. Dogs by arrangement.

Proprietors: Mr & Mrs H Beaton

★★

Burnside Hotel

19 WEST MOULIN ROAD, PITLOCHRY PH16 5EA

For those who really value comfort, quietness, quality cuisine and friendly service, the proprietor run Burnside Hotel, situated centrally on the A924 Pitlochry to Braemar Road extends a warm welcome.

All but two of our 23 well appointed bedrooms have en suite facilities, including the ground floor bedroom designed for the use of disabled guests. Central heating throughout, comfortable lounges, adequate car parking.

Our LICENSED RESTAURANT offers the best in Scottish home cooking, traditional breakfasts, appetising lunch snacks and imaginative table d'hôte or à la carte dinners, featuring 'Taste of Scotland' dishes. Vegetarian and other diets catered for.

Colour brochure, tariff, and sample menus, with details of our SPECIAL INTEREST HOLIDAYS, including THEATRE, and HAVE A BREAK TERMS available from resident proprietors: Mr & Mrs W G Falconer.

Telephone (0796) 2203 Reception (0796) 2493 Guests

The Jewel in the Town

Plymouth's newest four star hotel providing the very highest standards of service, accommodation and cuisine for business or pleasure.

FOR THE PLEASURE SEEKER

Close to the modern shopping centre and the historic Barbican, The Copthorne is ideally situated for those visiting the City, beautiful coast and nearby Dartmoor. All rooms have a private bathroom, TV and mini bar and there is free membership to the Plymsoles leisure club.

FOR THE BUSINESSMAN

If style and comfort are what you are looking for our well appointed meeting rooms offer you both. All AV equipment and presentation aids are available plus secretarial and business support. Executive accommodation and dining available.

For details and reservations:-

The Copthorne Plymouth, The Armada Centre,
Armada Way, Plymouth, Devon, PL1 1AR
Telephone: (0752) 224161.

P

some bathrooms are rather small, and the 5th floor is a non-smoking area. A small leisure complex complements the indoor swimming pool.
217 in 14 bedrooms CTV in all bedrooms T ✱ sB £40-£79 dB £50-£84 (room only)
Lift ☾ 30P 100 CFA (heated) sauna solarium gymnasium ♫ *xmas*
Continental V Lunch £8.50-£13.50 Dinner £12.50&alc Last dinner 10pm
Credit Cards 1 2 3 5

★★★ 57% ***Astor*** Elliot Street, The Hoe PL1 2PS (Mount Charlotte) ☎(0752)225511 Telex no 45652
Popular, and therefore busy, commercial hotel, conveniently situated for the city and within walking distance of The Hoe. Bedrooms are being upgraded and are soundly equipped. Service is friendly and prompt.
56rm(49 4)(3fb) CTV in all bedrooms Ⓡ T
Lift ☾ CFA
V Last dinner 9.30pm
Credit Cards 1 2 3 5

★★★ 66% **Mayflower Post House** Cliff Rd, The Hoe PL1 3DL (Trusthouse Forte) ☎(0752)662828 Telex no 45442 FAX (0752) 660974
Situated at the end of Plymouth Hoe, the attractive restaurant and coffee shop of this purpose-built hotel command fine views over Plymouth Sound. Executive bedrooms and private suites are comfortable and well-appointed.
106(69fb) in 8 bedrooms CTV in all bedrooms Ⓡ T sB £70 dB £81 (room only)
Lift ☾ 149P CFA (heated) *xmas*
English & Continental V Lunch £8.95-£9.50&alc Dinner £13&alc Last dinner 10.30pm
Credit Cards 1 2 3 4 5

★★★ 61% ***New Continental*** Millbay Rd PL1 3LD ☎(0752)220782 Telex no 45193 FAX (0752) 227013
Closed 24Dec-3Jan
This large, impressive hotel has undergone major refurbishment over recent times and now has a leisure complex equipped with an excellent range of facilities. The well-equipped bedrooms have attractive soft furnishings and service is friendly and prompt.
76(6fb)2 CTV in all bedrooms Ⓡ T
Lift ☾ 76P (heated) sauna solarium gymnasium games room
English, French & Greek V Last dinner 10pm
Credit Cards 1 2 3 5

★★★ 55% **Novotel Plymouth** Marsh Mills Roundabout, 270 Plymouth Rd PL6 8NH (Novotel) ☎(0752)221422 Telex no 45711
Modern hotel with pleasant atmosphere and a French theme in the restaurant.
101 CTV in all bedrooms Ⓡ T sB £49-£56 dB £56 (room only)
Lift ☾ 140P CFA
French V S% Lunch £10.50&alc Dinner £10.50&alc Last dinner mdnt
Credit Cards 1 2 3 4 5 £

★★ ***Grosvenor*** 9 Elliot Street, The Hoe PL1 2PP ☎(0752)260411
This busy commercial hotel, converted from a Georgian-style house, features a lower-ground restaurant whose wall murals depict various ghouls.
13rm(8 5) CTV in all bedrooms Ⓡ T
CTV
Credit Cards 1 2 3

Book as early as possible for busy holiday periods.

★★**Invicta** 11-12 Osborne Place, Lockyer Street, The Hoe PL1 2PU ☎(0752)664997
Closed 25 Dec-5 Jan
Well-appointed bedrooms are available at this recently-refurbished, city-centre hotel, those at the front facing 'Drake's Bowling Green'.
23rm(6 14)(4fb) CTV in all bedrooms Ⓡ T (ex guide dogs) ✱ sB&B£20-£24 sB&B £30-£34 dB&B£34-£36 dB&B £42-£46
CTV 10P
Mainly grills Dinner fr£7.50&alc Last dinner 9.30pm
Credit Cards 1 3

See advertisement on page 543

★★**Strathmore** Elliot St, The Hoe PL1 2PP (Consort) ☎(0752)662101 Telex no 45193 FAX (0752) 227013
Part of a terrace on the celebrated Plymouth Hoe, this popular commercial hotel has recently completed a major refit of bedrooms and provides well-appointed accommodation.
54(6fb) CTV in all bedrooms Ⓡ T sB&B fr£43 dB&B fr£54
Lift ☾ *xmas*
English & Continental V Lunch fr£6.50 Dinner fr£10.50 Last dinner 10pm
Credit Cards 1 2 3 5 £

★**Drake** 1 & 2 Windsor Villas, Lockyer Street, The Hoe PL1 2QD ☎(0752)229730
Closed Xmas
This hotel offers good facilities, sound food and friendly service.
36rm(11 12)(3fb) CTV in all bedrooms Ⓡ T sB&Bfr£21 sB&B £28-£31 dB&Bfr£34 dB&B £37-£42
25P 2

▶

P

Mainly grills **V** Lunch fr£7.80&alc Dinner fr£7.80&alc Last dinner 9pm
Credit Cards 1 2 3 5

★**Imperial** Lockyer Street, The Hoe PL1 2QD ☎(0752)227311
Closed 25-31 Dec
This detached Victorian hotel near the Hoe has pleasant public rooms where a log fire burns in winter. Friendly, attentive service is given by proprietors and staff.
22rm(4⇌12↱)(5fb) CTV in all bedrooms ® **T** sB&B£23 sB&B⇌↱£30-£35 dB&B£36 dB&B⇌↱£39.50-£43.50
CTV 18P games room
V Bar Lunch £2-£5 Dinner £9.75-£11.25 Last dinner 8.15pm
Credit Cards 1 2 3 5 (£)

⌂**Campanile** Marsh Mills, Longbridge Rd, Forder Valley PL6 8LD (Campanile) ☎(0752)601087 Telex no 45544
48⇌↱ CTV in all bedrooms ® **T** sB⇌↱fr£29 dB⇌↱fr£29 (room only)
56P ✽ *xmas*
English & French Lunch £3.75-£5 Dinner £6.80-£8.90 Last dinner 10pm
Credit Cards 1 3

❀ ✕ **The Chez Nous** 13 Frankfort Gate PL1 1QA
☎(0752)266793
Jacques and Suzanne Marchal's delightful and very French restaurant continues to please. Chef patron Jacques makes imaginative use of the best ingredients in dishes like filets de St Pierre à la Orange, pheasant with apricots and sweetbreads, and confit of duck. Among the puddings which should not be missed are marble gateaux, and hot rum and raisin cake with quennelles of home-made ice cream. Nice touches like home-made brioche and delectable petits fours add to the sense of occasion. The fixed-price menu, displayed daily on a blackboard, offers very good value for lunch and dinner, and late suppers are also provided for theatre-goers. The wine list is commendable.
Closed Sun, Mon , 3 wks Feb, 3 wks Sep & BH's
French 28 seats ✱ Lunch £19.50&alc Dinner £19.50&alc Last lunch 2pm Last dinner 10.30pm ⚐
Credit Cards 1 2 3 5

P

POCKLINGTON Humberside Map 08 SE84

★★**Feathers** Market Square YO4 2AH ☎(0759)303155
A market-place inn offering well-appointed accommodation and good value menus.
6rm(5⇌1↱)Annexe6⇌(1fb)1⛟ CTV in all bedrooms ® **T** (ex guide dogs) sB&B£28.50-£30 sB&B⇌↱£28.50-£30 dB&B£43-£45 dB&B⇌↱£43-£45
CTV 60P 6
V Lunch £5.95-£8.50 Dinner £5.95-£8.50&alc Last dinner 9.30pm
Credit Cards 1 2 3 5

PODIMORE Somerset Map 03 ST51

○ ***TraveLodge*** (A303, S of junct with A37) (Trusthouse Forte) ☎Yeovil(0935)840074
31⇌
P

All AA-appointed establishments are inspected regularly to ensure that required standards are maintained.

POLMONT Central *Stirlingshire* Map 11 NS97

★★★62% **Inchyra Grange** Grange Rd FK2 0YB (Best Western) ☎(0324)711911 Telex no 777693 FAX (0324) 716134
This former country house has been considerably altered and extended to offer sound, well-equipped bedrooms and a good range of conference and function facilities, though lounge accommodation is limited. The hotel's position gives easy access to junction 4 of the M9.
33⇌ CTV in all bedrooms ® **T** sB&B⇌£57-£72 dB&B⇌£84-£100
(150P ✽ (heated) snooker sauna solarium gymnasium Jacuzzi Steam Room & Beauty Therapy Room
Scottish & French **V** Lunch £8-£9 High tea £5-£8alc Dinner £11.50-£12.50&alc Last dinner 9.30pm
Credit Cards 1 2 3 5 (£)

POLPERRO Cornwall & Isles of Scilly Map 02 SX25

★**Claremont** Fore St PL13 2RG ☎(0503)72241
Closed 8 Jan-23 Mar & 16 Oct-15 Dec
A small holiday hotel with a warm French influence providing comfortable accommodation and well-cooked food.
10rm(2⇌7↱)(2fb) CTV in 8bedrooms ® sB&B⇌↱£15.50-£17.50 dB&B£24-£26 dB&B⇌↱£29-£38.50
CTV 16P nc2yrs *xmas*
French Bar Lunch £3.95-£6alc Dinner £9.50-£10.50&alc Last dinner 8.30pm
Credit Cards 1 3 (£)

Red-star hotels offer the highest standards of hospitality, comfort and food.

Lockyer Street
The Hoe, Plymouth
Tel: Plymouth (0752) 229730

36 bedroomed comfortable hotel run by resident proprietors. Ideally situated on Plymouth Hoe within easy walking distance of theatre, cinemas, main shopping centre and sea front. Restaurant and bar open every evening.

Private car park.

Weekend bargain breaks available most weekends.

INVICTA HOTEL

11/12 OSBORNE PLACE
LOCKYER STREET, THE HOE
PLYMOUTH PL1 2PU
Tel: (0752) 664997 AA★★

This modernised Family Run Hotel, is situated directly opposite the famous Plymouth Hoe, very close to the City Centre & Brittany Ferries.

★ 23 appointed bedrooms mostly en-suite, with C/H, Colour TV, telephone & tea/ coffee making facilities.
★ Excellent restaurant food. Bar.
★ Wedding Receptions & Conferences catered for.
★ Private lock-up Car Park.

Enjoy some old fashioned hospitality and personal service at the Imperial.

A warm welcome awaits you . . .

Alan and Prue Jones look forward to meeting you at the Imperial. With their rich naval background and many years experience in running hotels, you can be certain of a most enjoyable stay. The Hotel is ideally situated between the famous Hoe seafront, City Centre and Barbican (the Elizabethan Quarter). It is also the nearest hotel to the Theatre Royal. All transport facilities are nearby including Brittany Ferries, so altogether you couldn't ask for more.

Relax in comfortable surroundings . . .

In our elegant Victorian hotel you will find 22 well appointed, centrally heated bedrooms, mostly ensuite including 5 on the ground floor; colour television, radio/intercom, direct dial telephone and tea making facilities. Enjoy traditional English Fayre and a drink in our intimate 'nautical flavour' cocktail bar. There is also ample free parking on the premises. We regret no pets allowed. **For free brochure and reservations: TEL: PLYMOUTH (0752) 227311**

Lockyer Street, The Hoe, Plymouth PL1 2QD. Tel: (0752) 227311

P

POLZEATH Cornwall & Isles of Scilly Map **02** SW97

★★***Pentire Rocks*** PL27 6US ☎Trebetherick(020886)2213
Comfortable, basic accommodation, a warm, relaxing atmosphere and good meals are the attractions of this family-run hotel.
16rm(1⇨12♠)(3fb) CTV in 7bedrooms TV in 1bedroom ®
CTV 30P ✇ ✲
V ♉ ☕ Last dinner 9.30pm
Credit Cards [1] [2] [3]

POOLE Dorset Map **04** SZ09

For hotel locations see Town Plan Section under Bournemouth
See also **Bournemouth**

★★★★53% ***Hospitality Inn*** The Quay BH15 1HD (Mount Charlotte) ☎(0202)666800 Telex no 418374
Modern, well-equipped commercial hotel with good harbour views and a spacious restaurant.
68⇨♠(65fb) CTV in all bedrooms ® **T**
Lift ☾ 150P CFA ♫
♉ French **V** ♉ ☕
Credit Cards [1] [2] [3] [4] [5]

★★★56% **Dolphin** High St BH15 1DU ☎(0202)673612
Telex no 417205 FAX (0202) 674197
This friendly and informal hotel in the main shopping precinct has recently been upgraded, and serves good food at the Carvery, Brasserie and coffee shop.
66rm(53⇨12♠)1☐ CTV in all bedrooms ® **T** ✻
sB&B⇨♠£50-£70 dB&B⇨♠£60-£80 ☰
Lift ☾ 50P
♉ French **V** ♉ ☕ Lunch £7-£15&alc Dinner £11.95-£14.95&alc Last dinner 11pm
Credit Cards [1] [2] [3] [5] [£]

★★★73% **Harbour Heights** 73 Haven Rd, Sandbanks BH13 7LW ☎(0202)707272 FAX (0202) 708594
Commanding striking views from its setting in lovely gardens high above Poole Harbour, the hotel features particularly pleasant bedrooms – comfortable, modern, attractively decorated in pastel shades and, in many cases, balconied. The Carvery provides an alternative to the formal restaurant, and there is a cocktail bar.
49rm(36⇨13♠) CTV in all bedrooms ® **T** sB&B⇨♠£40
dB&B⇨♠£66-£70 ☰
Lift ☾ 84P ✇ ✲
♉ English & French **V** ♉ ☕ Lunch £10 High tea £4.50 Dinner £12.50-£15&alc Last dinner 9.30pm
Credit Cards [1] [2] [3] [5]

★★★69% **Haven** Sandbanks BH13 7QL ☎(0202)707333
Telex no 41338 FAX (0202) 708796
This historic town centre hotel has been substantially extended and upgraded. The spacious public areas are tasteful and elegant and offer a choice of two restaurants. A leisure complex and further bedrooms are due to be completed around the time of going to print.
96rm(93⇨3♠)(6fb) CTV in all bedrooms ® **T** ✗ (ex guide dogs) ✻ sB&B⇨♠£30-£40 dB&B⇨♠£60-£80 ☰
Lift ☾ 150P ✲ ▭(heated) ⌒(heated) ✓ squash sauna solarium gymnasium Steam Room *xmas*
♉ English & French **V** ♉ ☕ Lunch fr£8.50 High tea fr£1.50 Dinner fr£15.95 Last dinner 8.30pm
Credit Cards [1] [2] [3] [5] [£]

★★★75% **Mansion House** Thames St BH15 1JN
☎(0202)685666 Telex no 41495
Closed 24 Dec-2 Jan
Situated a short distance from the quay, this elegant Georgian town-house has the twin virtues of friendly service and good, honest cooking in the Dining Club Restaurant. A separate breakfast room, an intimate lounge with antique furnishings, and every conceivable facility in the bedrooms, ensure that guests will have a comfortable stay.

►

P

28⇌↱(2fb) CTV in all bedrooms **T** ✱ S10% sB&B⇌↱£65 dB&B⇌↱£83-£95 ⊟
40P ⛟ CFA ♫
☕ English & French ✿ ⊻ Lunch £9.50-£14.50 Dinner £15.75&alc Last dinner 10pm
Credit Cards 1 2 3 5 £

★★★72% **Salterns** 38 Salterns Way, Lilliput BH14 8JR (Best Western) ☏(0202)707321 Telex no 41259 FAX (0202) 707488
Owned and run by Mr and Mrs Smith, this welcoming and attractive hotel enjoys a unique setting overlooking the marina. A very comfortable first-floor lounge gives good harbour views, and the intimate restaurant serves and an interesting menu of well-prepared dishes.
16⇌ CTV in all bedrooms ® **T** ✱ sB⇌£54 dB⇌£72.75 (room only) ⊟
☾150P ⛟ ✽ ↲ squash snooker *xmas*
☕ French & English ✿ ⊻ Lunch fr£11&alc Dinner £14-£20alc Last dinner 10pm
Credit Cards 1 2 3 5

★★★59% **Sandbanks** Banks Rd, Sandbanks BH13 7PS ☏(0202)707377 Telex no 41338 FAX (0202) 708796
Family holiday hotel on the Sandbanks peninsula, with sea views to one side, and Poole Harbour on the other.
115rm(105⇌10↱) CTV in all bedrooms ® **T** ⋈ (ex guide dogs) ✱ sB&B⇌↱£30-£40 dB&B⇌↱£60-£80 ⊟
Lift ☾200P ✽ CFA ⊡(heated) sauna solarium gymnasium Steam Room ♫ ⌂ *xmas*
☕ International **V** ✿ ⊻ Lunch fr£9 High tea fr£1.50 Dinner fr£14 Last dinner 8.30pm
Credit Cards 1 2 3 5 £

★★***Antelope*** High St BH15 1BP ☏(0202)672029 Telex no 418387
Set in the High Street, not far from the quay, and recently completely renovated, the Antelope offers bedrooms with modern facilities and many extras. A cheerful young staff provides helpful service in the rustic-style Henekey's restaurant.
21rm(19⇌2↱)(1fb)⊬in 3 bedrooms CTV in all bedrooms ® **T** ⋈ (ex guide dogs)
☾20P
☕ European **V** ✿ ⊻ Last dinner 10.30pm
Credit Cards 1 2 3 4 5

P

★★***Sea Witch*** 47 Haven Rd, Canford Cliffs BH13 7LH ☏(0202)707697
Closed 25 Dec-3 Jan
The pleasant hotel stands close to Sandbanks, between Bournemouth and Poole. Its attractive restaurant offers a good range of well-prepared dishes, and service is pleasant.
9rm(7⇌2↱)(2fb) CTV in all bedrooms ® **T** ⋈
40P ⛟
☕ International **V** ✿ ⊻
Credit Cards 1 3

★**Fairlight** 1 Golf Links Road, Broadstone BH18 8BE (3m NW B3074) ☏(0202)694316
Closed 23 Dec – 3 Jan
Friendly small hotel offering a good, honest table d'hôte menu.
10rm(6⇌1↱)(1fb) sB&Bfr£20 sB&B⇌↱£22-£25 dB&B£31-£37.50 dB&B⇌↱£35-£42 ⊟
CTV 10P ⛟ ✽
⊬ Dinner £12.50-£13.75 Last dinner 7.30pm
Credit Cards 1 3 £

✕✕**Le Château** 13 Haven Rd, Canford Cliffs BH13 7LE ☏(0202)707400
A pleasant and hospitable little restaurant in Canford Cliffs, offering well-prepared, flavoursome dishes and a wine list of about 38 bins.
Closed Sun & Mon
☕ English & French **V** 35 seats ✱ Lunch £12.45-£19.95alc Dinner £12.45-£19.95alc Last lunch 2pm Last dinner 10pm 4P
Credit Cards 1 2 3

POOLEWE Highland *Ross & Cromarty* Map **14** NG88

★★**Pool House** IV22 2LE ☏(044586)272
Closed 15 Oct – Etr
Small friendly, family-run tourist hotel.
13rm(10⇌1↱)(1fb) CTV in all bedrooms ® ⋈ ✱ sB&B£20-£23 sB&B⇌↱£21-£25 dB&B⇌↱£44-£50 ⊟
20P ⛟
✿ ⊻ ⊬ Bar Lunch fr£1.55alc Dinner £11.50 Last dinner 8.30pm
Credit Cards 1 3

★**Poolewe** IV22 2JX ☏(044-586)241
This modest, but friendly, family-run, Highland hostelry provides reasonably priced food.
5rm(1⇌1↱)(1fb)⊬in 3 bedrooms CTV in all bedrooms ® sB&B£14.50-£18.50 sB&B⇌↱£16.50-£18.50 dB&B£29-£37 dB&B⇌↱£42 ⊟
CTV 50P Ʊ snooker ♫ *xmas*
V ✿ ⊻ ⊬ Lunch fr£6.50&alc High tea fr£5.50 Dinner fr£12 Last dinner 9pm
Credit Cards 1 2 3 £

POOLEY BRIDGE Cumbria Map **12** NY42

★**Swiss Chalet Inn** CA10 2NN ☏(08536)215
Closed 3-18Jan
This pleasant and friendly small hotel offers comfortable, well-appointed bedrooms. There is also an attractive restaurant and lounge bar which is popular with visitors to this picturesque area.
6rm(2⇌4↱)(1fb)1⊞ CTV in all bedrooms ® sB&B⇌↱£22-£28 dB&B⇌↱£36-£44 Continental breakfast
40P ✽
☕ Continental **V** ✿ ⊻ Bar Lunch £5.15-£15.10alc Dinner £5.15-£15.10alc Last dinner 10pm
Credit Cards 1 3

POOL-IN-WHARFDALE West Yorkshire Map **08** SE24

❀❀✕✕✕ **POOL COURT** Pool Bank LS21 1EH ☏Leeds(0532)842288 FAX (0532) 843115
(Rosette awarded for dinner only)
Chef David Watson now leads the brigade at this fine restaurant with rooms. He has been at Pool Court for a year, after gaining experience in London, and our inspectors have noticed some slight changes in style. A chicken and asparagus timbale failed to produce the expected intensity of flavour ; but praise was unreserved for superbly light and flavoursome scallop and trout mousses, and for a perfectly cooked loin of Scottish venison. Steamed barracuda has also been available. Michael Gill, who opened Pool Court in 1966, is still very much the caring host and his enthusiasm infects the young staff who make dining here very much a special occasion. There are six attractive bedrooms, and a continental breakfast is served to house guests.
Closed Sun & Mon Xmas Day & 2 wks mid-summer
Lunch not served (ex parties by arrangement)
☕ British & French **V** 65 seats ✱ Lunch £17.50-£27.50 Dinner £10&alc Last dinner 9.30pm 65P
Credit Cards 1 2 3 5

For key to symbols see the inside front cover.

PORLOCK Somerset Map **03** SS84

★★The Oaks Doverhay TA24 8ES ☎(0643)862265
There are fine views of the Bristol Channel from this hotel, standing in its own grounds and offering accommodation in peaceful comfort. An imaginative range of freshly prepared food is available.
12rm(4⇌8↑)(2fb) CTV in all bedrooms ® **T** S%
12P ✽
English & French ⚘ ⅟ S% Dinner £12-£13.50 Last dinner 8.30pm
£

PORLOCK WEIR Somerset Map **03** SS84

★★Anchor Hotel & Ship Inn TA24 8PB ☎Porlock(0643)862636 FAX (0643) 862843
RS Jan-Feb
Ten yards from the picturesque harbour stands a comfortable, informal establishment offering large, well-furnished bedrooms in the main hotel building and simpler, less expensive accommodation in the Ship Inn.
24rm(19⇌1↑)(2fb)1 CTV in all bedrooms ® **T** S10%
sB&B⇌↑£32.50-£51 dB&B£42-£62 dB&B⇌↑£55-£87
30P 3 ✽ *xmas*
British & French **V** ⚘ Lunch £6.95-£6.95 High tea £3.45-£5.95 Dinner £12.45-£12.45&alc Last dinner 9.15pm
Credit Cards 1 2 3 4 £

See advertisement on page 549

See the preliminary section 'Hotel and Restaurant Classification' for an explanation of the AA's appointment and award scheme.

PORT APPIN Strathclyde *Argyllshire* Map **14** NM94

★★

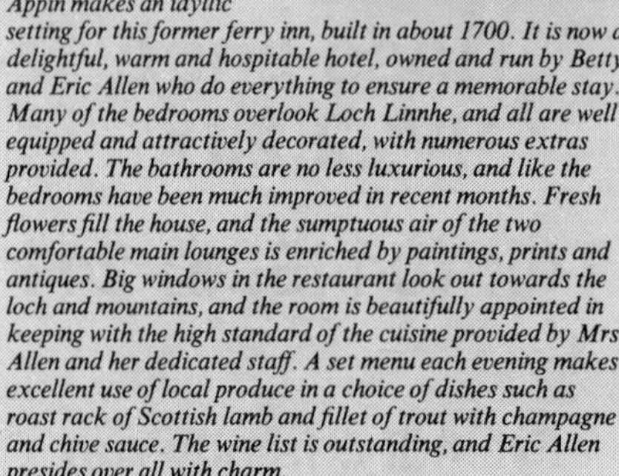

❀★★ **AIRDS**

PA38 4DF (Relais et Châteaux)
☎Appin(063173)236 & 211
Closed mid Nov-mid Mar
(Rosette awarded for dinner only)

The little village of Port Appin makes an idyllic setting for this former ferry inn, built in about 1700. It is now a delightful, warm and hospitable hotel, owned and run by Betty and Eric Allen who do everything to ensure a memorable stay. Many of the bedrooms overlook Loch Linnhe, and all are well equipped and attractively decorated, with numerous extras provided. The bathrooms are no less luxurious, and like the bedrooms have been much improved in recent months. Fresh flowers fill the house, and the sumptuous air of the two comfortable main lounges is enriched by paintings, prints and antiques. Big windows in the restaurant look out towards the loch and mountains, and the room is beautifully appointed in keeping with the high standard of the cuisine provided by Mrs Allen and her dedicated staff. A set menu each evening makes excellent use of local produce in a choice of dishes such as roast rack of Scottish lamb and fillet of trout with champagne and chive sauce. The wine list is outstanding, and Eric Allen presides over all with charm.

12rm(11⇌1♠)Annexe2♠ CTV in all bedrooms **T** ✗ (ex guide dogs) sB&B⇌♠£90 dB&B⇌♠£80-£124
30P ✿ nc5yrs
♥ ☐ ⅟ Bar Lunch £3-£12 Dinner £28 Last dinner 8.30pm

PORT ASKAIG

See **Islay, Isle of**

PORT GAVERNE Cornwall & Isles of Scilly Map **02** SX08

★★**Headlands** PL29 3SH ☎Bodmin(0208)880260
Spectacularly positioned over a rocky inlet, the hotel offers friendly personal service, comfortable well-furnished bedrooms and public areas comprising breakfast room, lounge, bar and restaurant. The menu offers a good range of imaginative dishes, well cooked and attractively presented.
11rm(7⇌4♠)(1fb) CTV in all bedrooms ® S10% sB&B⇌♠£21-£28 dB&B⇌♠£42-£56 ♬
35P ✿ sauna *xmas*
♀ English & European **V** ♥ ☐ S10% Lunch fr£6.25 Dinner fr£9.50&alc Last dinner 9.30pm
Credit Cards 1 2 3 5

★★***Port Gaverne*** PL29 3SQ ☎Bodmin(0208)880244
Closed 8 Jan-24 Feb
Well-appointed, friendly hotel in a valley next to the beach.
16⇌Annexe3⇌(5fb) CTV in 18bedrooms ® **T**
CTV 30P
♀ International **V** ♥ ☐ Last dinner 9.30pm
Credit Cards 1 2 3 5

PORTHCAWL Mid Glamorgan Map **03** SS87

★★★**57% Seabank** The Promenade CF36 3LU (Lansbury) ☎(065671)2261 Telex no 497797 FAX (065671) 5363
This company-owned, character hotel occupies a commanding position overlooking the Bristol Channel. A recent major refurbishment has created comfortable modern bedrooms, spacious public rooms and a small leisure complex.
62rm(56⇌6♠)(4fb) CTV in all bedrooms ® **T** sB&B⇌♠fr£52 dB&B⇌♠fr£62 ♬
Lift ☾ 150P ✿ sauna solarium gymnasium jacuzzi *xmas*
♀ English & French **V** ♥ ☐ Lunch fr£7.50&alc Dinner fr£11.50&alc Last dinner 10pm
Credit Cards 1 2 3 5

★★**Glenaub** 50 Mary St CF36 3YA ☎(065671)8242
Small personally managed hotel with comfortable bedrooms and commendable food standards.
18⇌ CTV in all bedrooms ® **T** ✗ sB&B⇌£32.50 dB&B⇌£39.50 ♬
CTV 12P
♀ International **V** ♥ ☐ Lunch £5.25-£5.50 Dinner £7.75&alc Last dinner 10pm
Credit Cards 1 2 3 4 5 £

★**Brentwood** 37-41 Mary St CF36 3YN ☎(065671)2725
A family-run hotel, convenient for both the seafront and the town centre, offering well-equipped bedrooms and a good choice of food. The bar attracts a busy local trade.
22rm(19⇌2♠)(5fb) CTV in all bedrooms ® **T** ✱ sB&B⇌♠£20-£25 dB&B⇌♠£30-£40 ♬
CTV 12P games room *xmas*
V Lunch fr£4.95 Dinner £6.95-£8.95&alc Last dinner 10.30pm
Credit Cards 1 2 3 5

★**Rose & Crown** Heol-y-Capel, Nottage CF36 3ST (2m N B4283) (Berni/Chef & Brewer) ☎(065671)4850
This small, friendly inn, a short drive from sea and town centre, provides compact but comfortable and well-equipped bedrooms. Though there is no residents' lounge, it offers a choice of 3 popular bars, whilst the Country Carvery restaurant serves a range of good-value meals which always includes a traditional roast.
8⇌(1fb) CTV in all bedrooms ® **T** ✗ (ex guide dogs) sB&B⇌fr£36 dB&B⇌fr£48.50 ♬
30P
♀ Mainly grills **V** ♥ ☐ ⅟ Lunch £8 Dinner £9 Last dinner 9.30pm
Credit Cards 1 2 3 5

✕✕***Lorelei*** Esplanade Av CF36 3YS ☎(065671)2683
Dinner not served Sun
V 24 seats Last lunch 2pm Last dinner 10pm ₱ 15 bedrooms available
Credit Cards 1 2 3 5

PORT ISAAC Cornwall & Isles of Scilly Map **02** SW98

See also **Port Gaverne and Trelights**

★★**Archer Farm** Trewetha PL29 3RU ☎Bodmin(0208)880522
Closed Nov-Feb
Standing on the outskirts of the village and extended from a farmhouse, the hotel provides comfortable bedrooms, good home cooking and the friendly services of the owners.
8rm(1⇌3♠)(1fb) CTV in 1bedroom sB&B£16-£17.50 dB&B£32-£35 dB&B⇌♠£36-£39 ♬
CTV 8P ✿ *xmas*
♀ French Dinner £12 Last dinner 8.30pm

★★**Castle Rock** PL29 3SB ☎Bodmin(0208)880300
Closed Mid Oct-Estr
A friendly hotel with fine sea views has been refurbished to provide very comfortable and well-equipped bedrooms and bright, pleasant public rooms.
19rm(11⇌3♠)(3fb) CTV in 7bedrooms ® sB&B£19-£22 sB&B⇌♠£22-£27 dB&B£38-£44 dB&B⇌♠£44-£54 ♬
CTV 20P ✿
V ♥ ☐ ⅟ Bar Lunch £1.20-£4.50 Dinner fr£11.50 Last dinner 8.30pm
Credit Cards 1 5

CASTLE ROCK HOTEL

★★

Port Isaac,
North Cornwall PL29 3SB
Telephone 0208-880300

"The hotel with the view"

Superb clifftop position overlooking Port Isaac Bay with magnificent panoramic views. High standard of comfort and cuisine with personal service. Spring and Autumn Breaks. Brochure with pleasure.

★★

HEADLANDS

PORT GAVERNE
PORT ISAAC
CORNWALL

Beautiful cliff-top location with magnificent sea views from all rooms. Comfortable bedrooms and friendly atmosphere. Special breaks available all year.

Write for colour brochure and tariff or telephone (0208) 880 260

PORT GAVERNE HOTEL

Near Port Isaac, Cornwall PL29 3SQ
Telephone: Bodmin (0208) 880244
FULLY LICENSED – FREE HOUSE

★★

Gently comfortably restored 17thC Coastal Inn –

- Internationally recognized dining
- All bedrooms en suite with colour TV and direct dial telephones
- Central heating and log fires
- A staff who know how to care

ALSO 7 self-catering character cottages.

Write or telephone for a free brochure
Mr. & Mrs. Frederick P. Ross
Resident Proprietors (21 years)

The ANCHOR HOTEL & SHIP INN ★★

EXMOOR NATIONAL PARK

Just 10 yards from the water's edge of a small picturesque harbour amidst Exmoor's magnificent scenery and dramatic coastline. This is old rural England with wildlife and memorable walks and is ideal for relaxing and unwinding. Very comfortable part 15th century thatched hotel.

Bargain Break terms.
Please phone 0643 862636

THE ANCHOR HOTEL and THE SHIP INN
PORLOCK HARBOUR · SOMERSET TA24 8PB

PORTLAND Dorset Map **03** SY67

★★★**52% Portland Heights** Yeates Corner DT5 2EN (Best Western) ☎(0305)821361 Telex no 418493 FAX (0305) 860081
Modern style hotel with good amenities overlooking Chesil Beach.
67rm(66⇌1♠)(4fb)⅟in 5 bedrooms CTV in all bedrooms ® T ✱ sB&B⇌♠£35-£47 dB&B⇌♠£60-£62 ⊟
☾ 160P CFA ⌂(heated) squash sauna solarium gymnasium steam room ♫ *xmas*
⊖ International V ✿ ⊈ ⅟ Lunch £6.50-£7.50 Dinner £10.80&alc Last dinner 9.30pm
Credit Cards [1] [2] [3] [5] (£)

★★**Pennsylvania Castle** Pennsylvania Rd DT5 1HZ ☎(0305)820561
An 18th-century mock castle standing in grounds overlooking the sea.
13rm(5⇌5♠)(1fb)3⊞ CTV in all bedrooms ® T ✱ S% sB&B£25 sB&B⇌♠£32-£38 dB&B£40 dB&B⇌♠£44-£54 ⊟
☾ CTV 150P ⊞ ❊ *xmas*
⊖ International V ✿ S% Lunch £11.95&alc Dinner £11.95-£12.95&alc Last dinner 11.30pm
Credit Cards [1] [3]

PORTLOE Cornwall & Isles of Scilly Map **02** SW93

★★**Lugger** TR2 5RD (Inter) ☎Truro(0872)501322 FAX (0872) 501691
Closed mid Nov-mid March
Very hospitable, family-run hotel in delightful harbourside position in the picturesque village. Comfortable and pretty public areas include a good-sized terrace for sunny days, and bedrooms are individually styled. The best are in the annexe. Cooking is straightforward and enjoyable.
7rm(1⇌6♠)Annexe13⇌ CTV in all bedrooms ® T ✗ (ex guide dogs) sB&B⇌♠£34-£37 dB&B⇌♠£68-£80 ⊟
27P ⊞ sauna solarium nc12yrs
⊖ English & Continental V ✿ ⊈ ⅟ Lunch fr£7.50 Dinner fr£13.50&alc Last dinner 9pm
Credit Cards [1] [2] [3] [5]

PORTPATRICK Dumfries & Galloway *Wigtownshire* Map **10** NX05

P

★★★**63% Fernhill** DG9 8TD ☎(077681)220
Situated in an elevated position commanding fine panoramic views over the village and out to sea, this enlarged Victorian house provides comfortable accommodation. Bedrooms, although compact and plainly decorated, are clean, fresh and well equipped. Guests can relax in the elegant lounge and enjoyable meals are served by friendly young staff in the bright, modern restaurant.
11rm(8⇌)Annexe4rm(1⇌3♠)(1fb) CTV in all bedrooms ® T sB&B£23-£25.50 sB&B⇌♠£25.50-£40 dB&Bfr£46 dB&B⇌♠fr£51 ⊟
45P ❊ ⌂ *xmas*
⊖ Scottish & French V ✿ ⊈ Bar Lunch fr£5&alc Dinner fr£13.50&alc Last dinner 10pm
Credit Cards [1] [2] [3] [5] (£)

All hotels awarded three or more stars are now also given a percentage grading for the quality of their facilities. Please see p 16 for a detailed explanation.

❀❀★★ **KNOCKINAAM LODGE**

DG9 9AD (2m S on unclass rd) (Pride of Britain) ☎(077681)471
Closed 11Jan-14Mar
(Rosettes awarded for dinner only)
Marcel and Corrina Frichot run this charming little off-the-beaten-track hotel in south-west Scotland, and with their helpful, friendly staff ensure that guests have a peaceful and relaxing stay. The setting is superb, with spacious wooded grounds and cliffs on three sides. A private beach gives wonderful westward views over the sea to the Irish coast. Inside, a considerable refurbishment has taken place, the rooms are individually furnished, and the panelled bar is particularly pleasant. The other great strength of the hotel lies in the cooking of Daniel Galmiche, who makes enticing use of the best ingredients. The menu is kept small, although alternatives are available, and the sauces are quite outstanding. The lobster cream with the assiette de homard et langoustines, the sauce Beaujolaise with Galloway beef, and the 'jus' in the feuillette de pigeon are all experiences to be savoured. Be warned, though, that the 4- or 5-course meal is likely to take two and a half hours, and guests must exercise the same restraint while waiting for the superb dishes as they should when driving along the narrow winding lanes that lead to this gem of a hotel.
10⇌1⊞ CTV in all bedrooms T ✱ sB&B⇌fr£77 dB&B⇌fr£114 (incl dinner) ⊟
25P ⊞ ❊ croquet *xmas*
⊖ French ✿ ⊈ ⅟ Lunch £2.50-£14alc Dinner £24 Last dinner 9pm
Credit Cards [1] [2] [3] [5]

★★***Portpatrick*** DG8 8TQ (Mount Charlotte) ☎(077681)333
Closed Nov-Mar
Large cliff-top resort hotel with good amenities for families with children.
60rm(40⇌1♠)(5fb) CTV in all bedrooms
Lift ☾ CTV 60P ❊ CFA ⌂(heated) ⚑9 ℘ (grass) snooker games room ♫ ⌂
V ✿ ⊈
Credit Cards [1] [2] [3] [5]

★**Mount Stewart** South Crescent DG9 8LE ☎(077681)291
A family-run hotel beside the harbour, commanding imposing sea views. Service is friendly, and local seafoods are a speciality.
7rm(3♠)(2fb) CTV in all bedrooms ® ✱ sB&B£14-£17 dB&B£26-£32 dB&B♠£30-£37
15P ⊞
⊖ Scottish & International V ✿ Lunch £5.95-£8.95&alc High tea £4.50-£11alc Dinner £8.50-£9&alc Last dinner 10pm
Credit Cards [1] [3]

PORTREE

See Skye, Isle of

PORTSCATHO Cornwall & Isles of Scilly Map **02** SW83

★★★**63% Rosevine** Porthcurnick Beach TR2 5EW ☎(087258)206 & 230
Closed Nov-Etr
A bright, spacious hotel set in well-tended, landscaped grounds. It lies 100 yards from the beach, on the beautiful Roevine peninsular.

14rm(11⇌1↑)(2fb) CTV in all bedrooms **T** sB&B£35.75-£43 sB&B⇌↑£37.50-£44.75 dB&B£71.50-£86 dB&B⇌↑£83.50-£92 (incl dinner)
(CTV 40P
International **V** Bar Lunch £5-£7.50alc Dinner £17 Last dinner 8.30pm
Credit Cards 1 3

★★Gerrans Bay Gerrans TR2 5ED ☎(087258)338
Closed Nov-Mar
A small friendly hotel in the heart of the Roseland Peninsula where good food can be enjoyed in a pleasant atmosphere.
14rm(12⇌2↑)(2fb) ® sB&B£26.75-£34 dB&B⇌↑£53.50-£68 (incl dinner)
CTV 16P *xmas*
Lunch £6.75 Dinner fr£12.25 Last dinner 8pm
Credit Cards 1 2 3

★★Roseland House
Rosevine TR2 5EW
☎(087258)644
Closed Dec-Feb 
The well-proportioned Edwardian house stands amid well-tended gardens in a superb cliff-top position with its own private access to the beach. Bedrooms are comfortable and public rooms intimate.
19rm(17⇌2↑)(5fb)2 (ex guide dogs)
CTV 25P 3 private beach nc5yrs
V Last dinner 8pm

PORTSMOUTH & SOUTHSEA Hampshire Map **04** SZ69

★★★67% **Crest** PO1 2TA (Crest) ☎Portsmouth(0705)827651
Telex no 86397 FAX (0705) 756715
A large, modern holiday and commercial hotel, conveniently situated for both the beach and the town centre. Modernised bedrooms are well equipped, though compact; public rooms are more spacious. Guests can enjoy competently-prepared meals, cheerfully served by bright young staff, in a choice of two restaurants.
163⇌↑(12fb) in 36 bedrooms CTV in all bedrooms ® **T** S10% sB⇌↑£69-£75 dB⇌↑£85-£95 (room only)
Lift (80P CFA
English & French **V** S10% Lunch fr£9.75 Dinner £12.95-£14.50&alc Last dinner 9.45pm
Credit Cards 1 2 3 4 5 ©

See advertisement on page 553

★★★67% **Holiday Inn** Southampton Rd, North Harbour PO6 4SH (Holiday Inns) ☎Portsmouth(0705)383151
Telex no 86611 FAX (0705) 388701
Very comfortable hotel with excellent leisure facilities.
170⇌↑(76fb) in 23 bedrooms CTV in all bedrooms **T** ✱
sB⇌↑£70-£83 dB⇌↑£78-£83 (room only)
Lift (200P CFA (heated) squash sauna solarium gymnasium childrens adventure playground *xmas*
English & French **V** Lunch £12.95-£14.95&alc High tea £2.50 Dinner £15&alc Last dinner 11pm
Credit Cards 1 2 3 4 5 ©

A rosette is the AA's highest award for quality of food and service in a restaurant.

★★★55% ***Hospitality Inn*** South Pde PO4 0RN (Mount Charlotte) ☎Portsmouth(0705)731281 Telex no 86719
This impressive and spacious sea front hotel provides some well appointed and attractively decorated bedrooms. Lounge facilities are limited, but there is a gracious restaurant featuring fine chandeliers, and four function rooms.
115⇌♞(6fb) CTV in all bedrooms ® T
Lift ☾ 50P
English & French V ♥ Last dinner 9.45pm
Credit Cards 1 2 3 5

★★★51% **The Pendragon** Clarence Pde PO5 2HY (Trusthouse Forte) ☎Portsmouth(0705)823201 Telex no 86376
Overlooking Southsea Common, this hotel has many modern facilities.
49⇌(1fb)⚡in 5 bedrooms CTV in all bedrooms ® T
sB⇌£53-£59 dB⇌£69-£75 (room only) ⊟
Lift ☾ 4P 6🚗 ✲ CFA *xmas*
V ♥ ⊡ ⚡ Lunch £5-£8.50 Dinner fr£11.50&alc Last dinner 9pm
Credit Cards 1 2 3 4 5

★★**Keppels Head** PO1 3DT (Trusthouse Forte) ☎Portsmouth(0705)833231
Well established modernised hotel with very limited lounge facilities. Some bedrooms enjoy views across the Solent. Close to Royal dockyard, Isle of Wight ferry and Nelson's Victory.
25rm(11⇌14♞)⚡in 3 bedrooms CTV in all bedrooms ® S%
sB⇌♞£53-£59 dB⇌♞£69-£75 (room only) ⊟
Lift ☾ 18P
V ♥ ⊡ ⚡
Credit Cards 1 2 3 4 5

★★**Ocean** St Helens Pde PO4 0RW ☎Portsmouth(0705)734233 FAX (0705) 812199
Comfortable seafront hotel with fine views of the Solent and good leisure facilities. Major refurbishments were planned at time of printing.
48rm(16⇌)(10fb) CTV in all bedrooms ® T sB&B£33 sB&B⇌£38.50 dB&B£55 dB&B⇌£60 ⊟
Lift ☾ 50P squash snooker sauna solarium gymnasium *xmas*
International V ♥ ⊡ Lunch £7.50 Dinner £9.50 Last dinner 10pm
Credit Cards 1 2 3 5 £

P

○***Arcade*** Winston Churchill Av PO1 2DG ☎Portsmouth(0705)821992 Telex no 869429 FAX (0705) 863460
Due to have opened Jul 1989
144⇌

✕**Bistro Montparnasse** 103 Palmerston Rd PO5 3PS ☎Portsmouth(0705)816754
A small bistro, brightly decorated with a friendly informal atmosphere. Cooking is of a very good standard with a few specialities.
Closed Sun, 1st 2 wks Jan & BH's
Lunch not served
French 42 seats Dinner £12-£16alc Last dinner 10pm nc5yrs
Credit Cards 1 2 3 5

PORT TALBOT West Glamorgan Map **03** SS79

★★★51% **Aberafan** Aberavon Beach SA12 6QP (Consort) ☎(0639)884949 FAX (01-706) 0860
A modern sea-front hotel with good bedrooms and open plan public areas. The dining room offers a good choice of meals.
65⇌(6fb) CTV in all bedrooms ® T ✱ sB&B⇌£38.50-£42 dB&B⇌£42-£46 ⊟
Lift ☾ CTV 150P CFA ♫ *xmas*
Welsh, English & French ♥ ⊡ Lunch fr£5.75 Dinner fr£10&alc Last dinner 10.15pm
Credit Cards 1 2 3 5 £

PORT WILLIAM Dumfries & Galloway *Wigtownshire* Map **10** NX34

★★★ 63% **Corsemalzie House** DG8 9RL (Inter)
☎Mochrum(098886)254
Closed 21Jan-5Mar

Very peaceful 19th-century country mansion, surrounded by extensive wooded grounds. Sporting pursuits can be arranged, and the young staff are friendly and efficient.
15rm(10⇌5♞)(1fb) CTV in all bedrooms ® T
sB&B⇌♞£31-£39 dB&B⇌♞£49-£62 ⊟
30P ✲ ✓ croquet, game shooting, putting
Scottish & French V ♥ ⊡ Lunch £8-£10&alc Dinner £13.75 Last dinner 9.15pm
Credit Cards 1 2 3 £

★★***Monreith Arms*** The Square DG8 9SE ☎(09887)232
A modestly appointed coastal hotel close to the town's harbour.
12rm(5⇌6♞)(3fb) CTV in all bedrooms ® T
CTV 10P ✓ snooker
Scottish, English & Italian V ♥ ⊡ Last dinner 9.30pm
Credit Cards 1 3

PORTWRINKLE Cornwall & Isles of Scilly Map **02** SX35

★***Whitsand Bay*** PL11 3BU ☎St Germans(0503)30276
Both golfers and family groups are welcomed by this friendly hotel, which offers extensive leisure facilities as well as a position near the sea. There is ample bar and lounge space, the dining room features an enjoyable variety of homely dishes, and bedrooms are comfortable though simple.
35rm(28⇌)(10fb) CTV in 1bedroom ®
CTV 60P ✲ (heated) ▶18 sauna solarium gymnasium beauty salon games room
English & French V ♥ ⊡ Last dinner 8.30pm

POTT SHRIGLEY Cheshire Map **07** SJ97

★★★★ 65% **Shrigley Hall Golf & Country Club** Shrigley Park SK10 5SB ☎Bollington(0625)75757 FAX (0625) 73323
A magnificent building set in 260 rolling acres which include an 18-hole championship golf course. Many other sports are offered, as are conference and banqueting facilities. Ten miles from Manchester Airport.
58⇌5 CTV in all bedrooms ® T ✗ (ex guide dogs) S%
sB&B⇌£70-£85 dB&B⇌£80-£160 ⊟
Lift ☾ 600P ✲ (heated) ▶18 (hard) ✓ squash snooker sauna solarium gymnasium ♫ *xmas*
V ♥ ⊡ ⚡ S% Lunch £15&alc Dinner £17.50-£21&alc Last dinner 9.45pm
Credit Cards 1 2 3 4 5

All hotels awarded three or more stars are now also given a percentage grading for the quality of their facilities. Please see p 16 for a detailed explanation.

POWBURN Northumberland Map **12** NU01

★★ Breamish House
NE66 4LL
☎(066578)266
Closed Jan

Set back from the A697 in its own well-kept and peaceful grounds, this elegant Georgian house offers a very good standard of accommodation throughout. The withdrawal of its former red-star grading is no reflection on the new proprietors, Alan and Doreen Johnson, but a result of AA policy to reserve the accolade until they have established themselves. We are confident that Breamish House will improve, as the Johnsons are dedicated to the pursuit of excellence, and care very much for the comfort of their guests.
10 CTV in all bedrooms ® T ✱ sB&B £35-£46 dB&B £54-£68 (incl dinner)
30P nc12yrs
Sunday Lunch fr£10.50 Dinner fr£16.50 Last dinner 8pm

POWFOOT Dumfries & Galloway *Dumfriesshire* Map **11** NY16

★★Golf Links Av DG12 5PN ☎Cummertrees(04617)254
On the Solway coast and next to an 18-hole golf course, this hotel offers spacious public areas and a modern wing of superior bedrooms. Friendly young staff offer polite, helpful service.
21rm(7 7)(1fb) CTV in 7bedrooms ® T sB&Bfr£21 sB&B fr£31 dB&Bfr£41.40 dB&B fr£50.60
CTV 100P 10 (heated) 18 *xmas*
V Lunch fr£5&alc Dinner fr£11&alc Last dinner 8.15pm
Credit Cards 1 £

PRAA SANDS Cornwall & Isles of Scilly Map **02** SW52

★★*Prah Sands* Chy An Dour Rd TR20 9SY
☎Penzance(0736)762438
Family hotel positioned at the water's edge.
22rm(12)(7fb) CTV in all bedrooms ®
CTV 20P (heated) (hard) croquet
English & French V Last dinner 8.45pm
Credit Cards 1 3

PRESTBURY Cheshire Map **07** SJ97

✕✕✕Legh Arms SK10 4DG ☎(0625)829130 & 827833
This very popular, chic restaurant, parts of which date back to the 15th century, is set in the centre of the village. Cooking is essentially French, with some variations; a keenly priced luncheon menu and bar meals are also available.
Closed Mon, Xmas Day evening & New Years Day evening
English & French **V** 90 seats ✱ Lunch £9&alc Dinner £13&alc Last lunch 2pm Last dinner 10pm 60P
Credit Cards 1 2 3 5

PRESTEIGNE Powys Map **03** SO36

★★Radnorshire Arms High St LD8 2BE (Trusthouse Forte)
☎(0544)267406
Attractively set amid lawns and gardens, the half-timbered inn offers public rooms of character, and bedrooms which have recently been upgraded to a high standard, those in the annexe being approached by a covered walkway.

▶

P

8⇨Annexe8⇨⅍in 1 bedroom CTV in all bedrooms ® T ✱ S% sB⇨£52 dB⇨£67-£72 (room only)
20P 6 ✲ *xmas*
V ♈ ⅅ ⅍ S% Lunch £6-£15alc Dinner £11.95-£16 Last dinner 9pm
Credit Cards 1 2 3 4 5

PRESTON Lancashire Map 07 SD52

See also **Bartle and Barton**

★★★71% **Broughton Park Hotel & Country Club** Garstang Rd, Broughton PR3 5JB (3m N on A6)
☎Broughton(0772)864087 Telex no 67180 FAX (0772) 861728
A tranquil setting, comfortable accommodation and courteous, helpful service combine to make your stay here a pleasant experience. Two restaurants offer a delightful range of skilfully prepared and attractively presented dishes, including home-made pasta.
98⇨(7fb)3⅍in 11 bedrooms CTV in all bedrooms ® T (ex guide dogs) sB&B⇨£50-£90 dB&B⇨£70-£100
Lift (220P ✲ (heated) squash snooker sauna solarium gymnasium ♫ *xmas*
English & French V ♈ ⅅ ⅍ Lunch £8.95 Dinner £15&alc Last dinner 10.30pm
Credit Cards 1 2 3 5 £

★★★63% **Crest** The Ringway PR1 3AU (Crest) ☎(0772)59411 Telex no 677147 FAX (0772) 201923
Modern, town centre hotel, offering comfortable bedrooms and courteous service.
126⇨(11fb)⅍in 46 bedrooms CTV in all bedrooms ® T (ex guide dogs) ✱ S% sB£62 sB⇨£62 dB£74 dB⇨£74 (room only)
Lift (30P CFA
International V ♈ ⅅ ⅍ Lunch £7.95&alc Dinner £15&alc Last dinner 10pm
Credit Cards 1 2 3 5

★★★55% ***Novotel Preston*** Reedfield Place, Walton Summit PR5 6AB (Novotel) ☎(0772)313331 Telex no 677164
Modern and convenient hotel just off the M6 at junction 29.
100⇨(100fb) CTV in all bedrooms ® T
Lift (120P ✲ (heated) pool table
Continental V ♈ ⅅ Last dinner 11.50pm
Credit Cards 1 2 3 5

★★★55% **Penguin** Leyland Way PR5 2JX ☎(0772)422922 Telex no 677651 FAX (0772) 622282
(For full entry see Leyland)

★★★61% **Swallow Trafalgar** Preston New Rd, Samlesbury PR5 0UL (Swallow) ☎(0772)877351 Telex no 677362 FAX (0772) 877424
A functional, modern hotel offering well-appointed bedrooms and very pleasant service.
78rm(54⇨24)⅍in 18 bedrooms CTV in all bedrooms ® T sB&B⇨fr£57 dB&B⇨fr£68
Lift (P CFA (heated) squash sauna solarium gymnasium steam room & spa pool *xmas*
International V ♈ ⅅ Lunch £7.50-£7.75 Dinner fr£11.75 Last dinner 9.45pm
Credit Cards 1 2 3 5

★★★68% **Tickled Trout** Preston New Rd, Samlesbury PR5 0UJ (Associated Leisure) ☎Samlesbury(077477)671 Telex no 677625 FAX (077477) 463
This comfortable hotel combines modern bedroom accommodation with a quaint old world restaurant and lounge. Situated just off junction 31 of the M6.
66⇨(53fb)2⅍in 10 bedrooms CTV in all bedrooms ® T ✱ S% sB&B⇨£40-£56 dB&B⇨£54-£66
(150P 10 CFA sauna solarium gymnasium wave pool steam room ♫ *xmas*
International V ♈ ⅅ S% Lunch £7-£11.95
Credit Cards 1 2 3 5

★★***Dean Court*** Brownedge Ln, Bamber Bridge PR5 6TB
☎(0772)35114
This well-furnished hotel offers comfortable accommodation, friendly professional service and a good range of well-cooked meals.
9rm(5⇨4)(4fb)5 CTV in all bedrooms ® T
35P
♈ ⅅ Last dinner 9.30pm
Credit Cards 1 3

★★***Vineyard*** Cinnamon Hill, Chorley Rd, Walton-Le-Dale PR5 4JN (2m S A49) (Consort) ☎(0772)54646
Closed Xmas Day night & New Years Day night
Attractive hotel in an elevated position just south of Preston, with a large cosmopolitan restaurant, a Manhattan-style cocktail bar and a piano lounge. Bedrooms are spacious.
14⇨(1fb) CTV in all bedrooms ® T (ex guide dogs)
(200P ♫
French V ♈ ⅅ Last dinner 10.15pm
Credit Cards 1 2 3 5

PRESTWICK Strathclyde *Ayrshire* Map 10 NS32

★★★60% **Carlton Toby** KA9 1TP (Toby) ☎(0292)76811 Telex no 778740
A bright, modern and conveniently placed hotel. It has a lively lounge bar and a carvery restaurant, where service is provided by friendly young staff.
39⇨(2fb)⅍in 9 bedrooms CTV in all bedrooms ® T ✱ sB&B⇨£38.50-£41 dB&B⇨£53-£58
(100P ✲ ♫ *xmas*
European V ♈ ⅅ ⅍ Lunch £4.95-£6.35 High tea fr£4.50 Dinner fr£6.35 Last dinner 10pm
Credit Cards 1 2 3 5

★★**Parkstone** Esplanade KA9 1QN ☎(0292)77286
Looking across the Esplanade to the Isle of Arran, the hotel caters for business and function trade as well as tourists. Bedrooms, though compact for the most part, are equipped with modern facilities, and several offer good views; public areas are pleasantly appointed and include an open-plan central lounge.
15rm(3⇨12)(1fb) CTV in all bedrooms ® sB&B⇨£29-£32 dB&B⇨£46-£48
(30P 4
V ♈ ⅅ Lunch £5.75-£5.95 High tea £4.45-£8.25 Dinner £9.50-£9.95 Last dinner 9pm
Credit Cards 1 2 3

★★***St Nicholas*** 41 Ayr Rd KA9 1SY ☎(0292)79568
Cosy, owner-run hotel which is continually being improved. Bedrooms are attractively decorated, and there are two bars as well as a quieter residents' lounge.
16rm(8)(4fb) CTV in 10bedrooms TV in 6bedrooms ® T (ex guide dogs)
CTV 50P
V ♈ Last dinner 9.30pm
Credit Cards 1 2 3 5

PUDDINGTON Cheshire Map 07 SJ37

✕✕✕**Craxton Wood** Parkgate Rd L66 9PB (on A540 junct A550) ☎051-339 4717 FAX 051-339 1740
Charming country house with elegant attractive restaurant.
Closed Sun, 2 wks end Aug & BH's
French V 85 seats ✱ Lunch £19.85-£27.15alc Dinner £19.85-£27.15alc Last lunch 2pm Last dinner 10pm 60P 14 bedrooms available
Credit Cards 1 2 3 5

P

PUDSEY West Yorkshire Map **08** SE23

✕Tiberio 68 Galloway Ln LS28 8LE ☎Bradford(0274)665895

Charming service is provided in a comfortably intimate restaurant where the international cuisine includes some interesting pasta dishes and is complemented by a wine list on which all countries are represented.

Closed Mon (ex BH's)

Lunch not served Sat

English & Italian **V** 66 seats Lunch £7.95-£8.50&alc Last lunch 2pm Last dinner 11pm 30P

Credit Cards 1 2 3

PULBOROUGH West Sussex Map **04** TQ01

★★Chequers Church Place RH20 1AD (Minotels) ☎(07982)2486 due to change to (0798)872486 Telex no 67596 FAX (0798) 872715

Welcoming, tile-hung house with beautiful views over the Sussex Downs. Good British food is served, and the well-equipped bedrooms have many useful extras.

11rm(7⇌4♠)(2fb)1⊞ CTV in all bedrooms ® sB&B⇌♠£39.50-£44.50 dB&B⇌♠£52-£57 ⊟

11P ✽

Lunch fr£6.50 High tea £3.50-£4.50 Dinner fr£12.50 Last dinner 8.15pm

Credit Cards 1 2 3 5

❀✕Stane Street Hollow Codmore Hill RH20 1BG ☎(07982)2819

Set back from the A29, a cosily charming stone-built cottage restaurant offers a monthly-changing menu which features both Swiss and French style cuisine, dishes being prepared largely from homegrown or local produce. Always in evidence are the daily fresh fish speciality, the beautifully constructed desserts and a fine wine list. Service is unfailingly attentive.

Closed Sun, Mon, Tue 2 wks May, 3 wks Oct & 24 Dec-6 Jan

Lunch not served Sat

French & Swiss **V** 35 seats Lunch £6.50&alc Dinner £14.50-£17.50alc Last lunch 1.15pm Last dinner 9pm 15P

PWLLHELI Gwynedd Map **06** SH33

★★Plas Bodegroes Restaurant LL53 5TH (1.5m W on Nefyd rd)

☎(0758)612363

Closed Jan – Feb

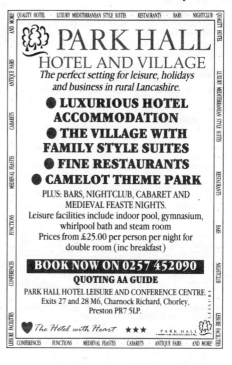

Standing in 6 acres of grounds, this elegant Georgian country house provides comfortable accommodation and high quality food.

8⇌♠2⊞ CTV in 7bedrooms **T** S% sB&B⇌♠£35-£70 dB&B⇌♠£60-£90 ⊟

25P ✽ croquet *xmas*

S% Dinner £14-£20&alc Last dinner 9.30pm

Credit Cards 1 3

The AA's star-rating scheme is the market leader in hotel classification.

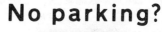

★**The Seahaven** West End Pde LL53 5PN ☎(0758)612572
10rm(5↱)(2fb) CTV in all bedrooms ® ✱ dB&B£12-£14 dB&B↱£16-£18 ⊟
CTV ⇄
Dinner fr£8.50 Last dinner 7.15pm

QUORN Leicestershire Map **08** SK50

★★★★70% **Quorn Country** Charwood House, Leicester Rd LE12 8BB (on A6 in village centre) ☎(0509)415050
Telex no 347166 FAX (0509) 415557
RS Boxing Day & New Year
Standing in spacious grounds alongside the River Soar. Constructed of natural stone and brick the hotel provides well equipped and quite luxurious accommodation, catering mainly for businessmen.
19⇨↱(1fb)1⊠ CTV in all bedrooms ® **T** ✱ sB⇨↱fr£64 dB⇨↱£78-£110 (room only) ⊟
☾⊞ CTV 100P ✲ ♪
♡ English & Continental **V** ♧ ⊈
Credit Cards 1 2 3 5
See advertisement under LOUGHBOROUGH

RAASAY, ISLE OF Highland *Inverness-shire* Map **13** NG53

★★**Isle Of Raasay** IV40 8PB
☎Isle of Raasay(047862)222 & 226
Closed Oct-Mar
12⇨ CTV in all bedrooms ® ✱ sB&B⇨fr£25 dB&B⇨fr£50
CTV 12P ⇄ ✲
♡ English & Scottish **V** ♧ ⊈ ⚟ Bar Lunch fr£2.50 Dinner fr£14 Last dinner 7.30pm

RAGLAN Gwent Map **03** SO40

★★**Beaufort Arms** High St NP5 2DY ☎(0291)690412
Set at the centre of Raglan, overlooking the church, this comfortable and tastefully-appointed hotel has recently been fully renovated. Bedrooms are well-fitted, whilst public rooms present an old world character.
10⇨↱(2fb) CTV in all bedrooms ® **T** ✗ (ex guide dogs) sB&B⇨↱£28.50 dB&B⇨↱£38.50 ⊟
CTV 80P *xmas*
♡ English & French **V** ♧ ⊈ Lunch £6.95-£6.95
Credit Cards 1 2 3 5 £

RAINHILL Merseyside Map **07** SJ49

★**Rockland** View Rd L35 0LG ☎051-426 4603
Set in its own grounds, this detached Georgian house with good annexe bedrooms, is just off the A57, not far from junction 7 of the M62.
10rm(7⇨)Annexe10rm(4⇨6↱)(5fb) CTV in all bedrooms ® sB&B£20-£27 sB&B⇨↱£24-£31 dB&B£33-£43 dB&B⇨↱£37-£47 ⊟
30P ✲
V ♧ ⊈ Lunch £5.50 Dinner £8.50&alc Last dinner 8.15pm
Credit Cards 1 3 £

RAMSBOTTOM Greater Manchester Map **07** SD71

★★**Old Mill** Springwood BL10 9DS ☎(070682)2991
FAX (070682) 2291
A comfortable lounge bar and adjoining beamed restaurant are features of the clean and well-appointed hotel, now extended to incorporate additional bedrooms and a leisure centre.
36⇨(3fb)1⊠ CTV in all bedrooms ® **T** ✗ ✱
sB&B⇨£26.50-£39.50 dB&B⇨£39-£55 ⊟
☾ 85P ⇄ ⊡(heated) sauna solarium gymnasium *xmas*
♡ French & Italian **V** ♧ ⊈ Lunch fr£6.50&alc Dinner fr£10.50&alc Last dinner 10.30pm
Credit Cards 1 2 3 4 5 £

RAMSEY

See **Man, Isle of**

RAMSGATE Kent Map **05** TR36

★★***San Clu*** Victoria Pde CT11 8DT ☎Thanet(0843)592345
Old fashioned family-run hotel.
54rm(22⇨)(7fb) CTV in all bedrooms **T**
Lift ☾ 12P CFA
♡ English & French **V** ♧ ⊈ Last dinner 9pm
Credit Cards 1 2 3

★★**Savoy** Grange Rd, 43 West Cliff CT11 9NA
☎Thanet(0843)592637
Family-run and informal, the hotel offers accommodation in well-equipped bedrooms, those in the annexe being particularly spacious. Traditionally-styled public areas are comfortably appointed, and the cuisine, though modest, is popular.
15rm(1⇨7↱)Annexe11rm(2⇨9↱)(4fb) CTV in all bedrooms ® **T** ✗ (ex guide dogs) ✱ sB&B£22-£33 sB&B⇨↱£29-£33 dB&B£31-£44 dB&B⇨↱£39-£44
☾ 15P 2🚗 (£3 per night) ⇄
♡ French **V** ♧ ⊈ Lunch fr£6.50&alc Dinner fr£10alc Last dinner 10pm
Credit Cards 1 2 3 5

RANGEMORE Staffordshire Map **07** SK12

★★***Needwood Manor***
DE13 9RS
☎Barton-under-Needwood (028371)2932 & 3340
Closed 24-30 Dec
A 19th-century red brick house stands in a park just three miles west of the southern end of the Burton upon Trent bypass. Notable features of the hotel are its fine pitch pine staircase and gallery.
11rm(1⇨1↱)(2fb)1⊠⚟in 1 bedroom CTV in 4bedrooms ® ✗
CTV 30P ⇄ ✲
♧
Credit Cards 1 3

RANGEWORTHY Avon Map **03** ST68

★★***Rangeworthy Court***
Church Ln, Wotton Rd
BS17 5ND (Exec Hotel)
☎(045422)347 & 473
FAX (045422) 8945
Closed 24 Dec-1 Jan RS Sun
Dating from the 14th century, this former manor house is in a peaceful setting by the church. Some of the bedrooms are rather compact, but all are individually decorated and have good facilities. Personal

attention is provided by the proprietors and their friendly staff.
14rm(4⇌10🚿)1⊞ CTV in all bedrooms ® T
CTV 50P ⛟ ✲
V ♔ Last dinner 9pm
Credit Cards [1] [2] [3] [5]

See advertisement under BRISTOL

RAVENGLASS Cumbria Map **06** SD09

★**Pennington Arms** CA18 1SD ☎(06577)222 & 626
Situated in a quiet village on the estuary of the Rivers Esk, Mite and Irt, this friendly hostelry offers fairly simple accommodation in the main building and three annexes.
17rm(5⇌3🚿)Annexe12rm(2⇌1🚿)(7fb) ® ✻ sB&B£14-£19 sB&B⇌🚿£19-£25 dB&B£24-£32 dB&B⇌🚿£30-£38 ⊟
CTV 50P 3🚘 pool table
V ♔ ⊡ Lunch £7.50 High tea £5.50-£9 Dinner £8.50-£11 Last dinner 10pm

RAVENSTONEDALE Cumbria Map **12** NY70

★★**Black Swan** CA17 4NG (Inter) ☎Newbiggin-on-Lune(05873)204
Closed Jan & Feb RS Jan accomodation & bar meals only
A well maintained and characterful hotel, the focal point of the sleepy little village, provides friendly service throughout. Bedrooms have some nice touches, there is a small but comfortable residents' lounge, and the cosy bar complements an attractive dining room where guests enjoy country cooking of a commendably high standard.
14rm(8⇌3🚿)(1fb) ® T sB&B£30-£35 sB&B⇌🚿£33-£38 dB&B£38-£46 dB&B⇌🚿£44-£46 ⊟
CTV 20P 3🚘 ⛟ ✲ 🎾 (hard) ✔ *xmas*
♔ ⊡ ⚡ Lunch fr£8.50&alc High tea fr£3 Dinner fr£14.50&alc Last dinner 9pm
Credit Cards [1] [2] [3] Ⓔ

★★**The Fat Lamb** Cross Bank CA17 4LL (Guestaccom) ☎Newbiggin-on-Lune(05873)242
Surrounded by rolling hills and dales, this tranquil and utterly relaxing 17th-century inn was once a farmhouse. Most of the pleasant, traditionally furnished bedrooms are fairly small, but all have smart modern bathrooms.
10⇌(2fb) ® ✻ sB&B⇌£24 dB&B⇌£38 ⊟
CTV 60P ✲ *xmas*
V Lunch £11.50&alc Dinner £11.50&alc Last dinner 9pm

RAWTENSTALL Lancashire Map **07** SD82

★★***High Croft*** 271-273 Haslingden Old Rd BB4 8RR ☎(0706)215808
Comfortable and peacefully placed house run by the owners.
10rm(2⇌6🚿)(2fb) CTV in all bedrooms ® T ✗
CTV 10P ⛟ ✲ ⛱ ♞
Credit Cards [1] [2] [3]

READING Berkshire Map **04** SU77

★★★★ 59% **Ramada** Oxford Rd RG1 7RH ☎(0734)586222 Telex no 847785 FAX (0734) 597842
A modern purpose-built hotel with good sized bedrooms and attractive public areas. Of the two restaurants the Arabesque offers sound French cooking.
200⇌🚿(100fb)⚡in 49 bedrooms CTV in all bedrooms ® T ✗ (ex guide dogs) sB&B⇌🚿£45-£90 dB&B⇌🚿£60-£110 ⊟
Lift ☾ ⊞ 75🚘 ⊡(heated) sauna solarium gymnasium turkish bath jacuzzi beauty salon ♫
♕ International V ♔ ⊡ ⚡ Lunch £7.75-£11.95&alc Dinner £11.50-£28.50alc Last dinner 11.30pm
Credit Cards [1] [2] [3] [4] [5]

★★★ 66% **Kirtons Farm Country Club** Pingewood RG3 3UN ☎(0734)500885 FAX (0734) 391996
30⇌ CTV in all bedrooms ® T ✻ S% sB⇌fr£64 dB⇌fr£75 (room only) ⊟
Lift ☾ ⊞ CTV 200P ⊡(heated) 🎾 (hard) ✔ squash snooker sauna solarium gymnasium ♫ *xmas*
♕ English & French V ♔ ⊡ Lunch fr£12.50&alc Dinner fr£18.50&alc Last dinner 10pm
Credit Cards [1] [2] [3] [5]

★★★ 68% **Post House** Basingstoke Rd RG2 0SL (Trusthouse Forte) ☎(0734)875485 Telex no 849160 FAX (0734) 311958
After a good meal in the octagonal Icarns restaurant guests at this modern hotel can relax in the Railway bar or the attractive, cosy cocktail bar. Other facilities include a coffee shop and a leisure complex.
143⇌(43fb)⚡in 14 bedrooms CTV in all bedrooms ® T ✻ sB⇌£81-£91 dB⇌£92-£102 (room only) ⊟
☾ 240P ✲ CFA ⊡(heated) sauna solarium gymnasium Health & Fitness Centre *xmas*
♕ English & French V ♔ ⊡ ⚡ Lunch £8.95-£19.75 Dinner £14.50-£19.75 Last dinner 10.30pm
Credit Cards [1] [2] [3] [4] [5]

★★**George** King St RG1 2HE (Berni/Chef & Brewer) ☎(0734)573445
68⇌(2fb) CTV in all bedrooms ® T ✗ (ex guide dogs) sB&B⇌fr£49 dB&B⇌fr£61 ⊟
☾ P̸
V ♔ ⊡ ⚡ Lunch fr£8 Dinner fr£9 Last dinner 10.30pm
Credit Cards [1] [2] [3] [5]

○ ***Travelodge*** 387 Basingstoke Rd RG2 0JE (Trusthouse Forte) ☎(0734)750618
36⇌
P

✕✕***Peking Palace*** 3 Prospect St. Caversham RG4 8JB ☎(0734)483488 & 483888
A welcoming Peking restaurant also offering interesting dishes from Szechuan and Canton.
Closed Xmas Day & Boxing Day
Cantonese, Pekinese & Szechuan **V** 120 seats Last lunch 1.45pm Last dinner 11.20pm
Credit Cards 1 2 3 5

REDBOURN Hertfordshire Map **04** TL11

★★★60% **Aubrey Park** Hemel Hempstead Rd AL3 7AF ☎(058285)2105 Telex no 82195 FAX (058285) 2001
A pleasant hotel, set in 6 acres of gardens and lawns. The oak-beamed Ostler's Restaurant offers traditional English fayre, whilst the Beaumont Restaurant serves dishes of a more international style. The bar has recently been extended and new deluxe bedrooms have all modern facilities.
118(2fb) CTV in all bedrooms ® **T** ✱ sB£66-£75 dB£76-£85 (room only)
160P (heated)
English & French **V** Lunch fr£8.50&alc Dinner £12.50-£15.50&alc Last dinner 9.45pm
Credit Cards 1 2 3 4 5

REDBROOK Clwyd Map **07** SJ54

★★**Redbrook Hunting Lodge** Wrexham Rd SY13 3ET (Inter) ☎Redbrook Maelor(094873)204 & 533
Although located at a busy road junction, this family-run hotel has well-cared-for gardens which give it a country house atmosphere. Guests have a choice between a carvery menu in the lounge bar and an à la carte menu in the restaurant.
12rm(9 3)(3fb)2 CTV in all bedrooms ® **T** sB&B fr£36.50 dB&B fr£50.50
100P *xmas*
English & French **V** Lunch fr£6.75&alc Dinner fr£8.50&alc Last dinner 9pm
Credit Cards 1 2 3 5 £

REDCAR Cleveland Map **08** NZ62

★★★67% **Park** Granville Ter TS10 3AR ☎(0642)490888
An elegant, comfortable, sea-front hotel providing a very good value carvery for both lunch and dinner, as well as a substantial range of bar snacks.
25 CTV in all bedrooms ® **T** (ex guide dogs) ✱ sB&B£20-£38 dB&B£30-£45
20P
V Lunch £6.55-£7.70&alc Dinner £6.55-£7.70&alc Last dinner 9.30pm
Credit Cards 1 2 3 5

See advertisement under MIDDLESBROUGH

REDDITCH Hereford & Worcester Map **07** SP06

★★★63% **Southcrest** Pool Bank, Southcrest B97 4JG (Best Western) ☎(0527)41511 Telex no 338455 FAX (0527) 402600
Closed 24 Dec-2 Jan & BH's RS Sun evenings
Peacefully located in six acres of landscaped grounds and surrounded by woodland, yet giving easy access to the M5 and M42 motorways from its position just half a mile south of the town centre, this much extended former country house specialises in catering for business people, conferences and functions, for which it is well equipped.
58(2fb)2 CTV in all bedrooms ® **T** ✱ sB&B£50-£62 dB&B£62-£72
100P
French **V** Lunch £10-£10.50&alc Dinner £11-£11.50&alc Last dinner 9.15pm
Credit Cards 1 2 3 5

Campanile Farmoore Ln, Winyates Green B98 0FD (Campanile) ☎(0527)510710 Telex no 339608
Modern hotel for business travellers and others seeking pleasant, straightforward accommodation. Well placed for the M42.
Annexe48 CTV in all bedrooms ® **T**
CTV 60P
English & French **V** Last dinner 10pm
Credit Cards 1 3

REDLYNCH Wiltshire Map **04** SU22

✕✕**Langley Wood** SP5 2PB ☎Romsey(0794)390348
An attractive, creeper-clad house, set in its own pleasant grounds among dense woodland at the edge of the village, offers an imaginative menu and a wine list that are both reasonably priced. It is run by a husband and wife team – she cooking with flair and he bringing humour and professionalism to the task of serving.
Closed Mon, Tue & 2-3 wks Jan/Feb
Lunch not served all week (ex by reservation)
Dinner not served Sun
English & French **V** 30 seats Lunch £12.50-£20alc Dinner £12.50-£20alc Last dinner 11pm 30P 3 bedrooms available
Credit Cards 1 2 3 5

REDRUTH Cornwall & Isles of Scilly Map **02** SW64

★★★58% ***Penventon*** TR15 1TE ☎(0209)214141
This family-owned and run Georgian manor house has elegant dining galleries featuring an extensive à la carte menu and a short table d'hôte menu. Bedrooms are rather compact. The Twilight Zone nightclub in the grounds is well insulated for sound.
55rm(45 5)(3fb) CTV in all bedrooms ® **T**
100P (heated) snooker sauna solarium gymnasium
English, French & Italian **V**
Credit Cards 1 2 3

See advertisement under TRURO

★★**Aviary Court** Mary's Well, Illogan TR16 4QZ ☎Portreath(0209)842256
On the edge of Illogan Woods, between Redruth and Portreath, a charming 300-year-old Cornish country house stands in two-and-a-quarter acres of well-tended gardens. Here the Studley family have created a hospitable, welcoming atmosphere, details like flowers and fruit in the warm, attractive bedrooms complementing the high standard of modern facilities. The cosy, comfortably-furnished lounge is heated by log fires in winter, and its windows open onto the garden terrace in summer. Cornish produce is put to good use in the creation of enjoyable meals served in the well-appointed new restaurant.
6rm(4 2)(1fb) CTV in all bedrooms ® **T** sB&B£28.50-£33 dB&B£41.50-£46
25P nc3 yrs
English & French Lunch fr£7 Dinner fr£8.50&alc Last dinner 8.45pm
Credit Cards 2 5

★★**Crossroads Motel** Scorrier TR16 5BP (2m E off A30) ☎(0209)820551 Telex no 45133
A purpose built hotel, conveniently situated for touring and local industry, with a choice of restaurants and modern, well-equipped bedrooms.
35rm(33)(2fb) CTV in all bedrooms ® **T** sB&B£25-£35 dB&B£38-£48
Lift 140P
English & French **V** Lunch £5-£9alc Dinner £9.95&alc Last dinner 9.30pm
Credit Cards 1 2 3 5

Red-star hotels offer the highest standards of hospitality, comfort and food.

RED WHARF BAY Gwynedd Map **06** SH58

★★Bryn Tirion LL75 8RZ ☎Tynygongl(0248)852366
Closed Jan & Feb
A family-owned hotel standing in its own grounds above the bay offers personal service at reasonable prices, all bedrooms having private bathrooms and colour TV.
20⇌(3fb) CTV in all bedrooms ® ✗ (ex guide dogs) sB&B⇌fr£23.50 dB&B⇌fr£42 ⊟
65P ✲
V ♉ ☕ Bar Lunch fr£5alc Dinner fr£7.50alc Last dinner 9pm
Credit Cards 1 3 £

★Min-y-Don LL75 8RJ ☎Tynygongl(0248)852596
RS Nov-Feb
Comfortably appointed family run hotel, only a few miles from the sea.
15rm(3⇌3↱)(4fb) CTV in 6bedrooms ® sB&B£17-£38 sB&B⇌↱£38 dB&Bfr£32 dB&B⇌↱fr£44
CTV 100P ✲ ♫
♉ ☕
Credit Cards 1 3

REETH North Yorkshire Map **07** SE09

★★*The Buck* DL11 6SW ☎Richmond(0748)84210
A charming village inn providing comfortable accommodation and good value dinners and bar meals.
8⇌(1fb) CTV in all bedrooms ® ✗
P̸ ✲ ⌂
♉ Last dinner 9.30pm
Credit Cards 1 2 3 4

See advertisement on page 561

R

★**Burgoyne Hotel** DL11 6SN (Guestaccom)
☎Richmond(0748)84292
Closed end Nov-Etr
A comfortable, peaceful house in an elevated position overlooks village and fells. Resident proprietors offer courteous, friendly service, and the home-cooked dinners are specially to be recommended.
11rm(2⇌2↾)(2fb) CTV in all bedrooms ® sB&B£17.50-£22.50 dB&B£35-£38 dB&B⇌↾£40-£44 ☷
CTV 4P 2🚗 ⛟
Dinner fr£11.50 Last dinner 8pm
Credit Cards [3]

REIGATE Surrey Map **04** TQ25

★★★65% **Bridge House** Reigate Hill RH2 9RP
☎(0737)246801 & 244821 Telex no 268810
Hillside hotel with wonderful views. Most of the spacious bedrooms have balconies, and the large, popular restaurant has a live band playing for dancing on five evenings a week.
40rm(31⇌9↾)(3fb) CTV in all bedrooms ® **T** ✖ S% sB&B⇌↾£46-£58
dB&B⇌↾£64-£79 Continental breakfast ☷
☾110P ⛟ ♫ *xmas*
♕ English & French **V** ✿ S12.25% Lunch fr£11.75&alc Dinner fr£16.50 Last dinner 10.30pm
Credit Cards [1] [2] [3] [5]

★★★68% **Reigate Manor Hotel** Reigate Hill RH2 9PF (Best Western) ☎(0737)240125 Telex no 927845 FAX (0737) 223883
Popular and welcoming hillside hotel with spacious restaurant. A new wing has a gym, sauna and solarium.
51rm(39⇌12↾)(1fb)1⊟ CTV in all bedrooms ® **T** ✖ (ex guide dogs) ✱ S% sB⇌↾£49.50-£69
dB⇌↾£72-£80 (room only) ☷
☾130P ⛟ sauna solarium gymnasium
♕ English & French **V** ✿ ⊈ S% Lunch £8.95-£9.95&alc Dinner £12.95-£13.95&alc Last dinner 10pm
Credit Cards [1] [2] [3] [5]

RENFREW For hotels see **Glasgow Airport**

RENISHAW Derbyshire Map **08** SK47

★★★64% **Sitwell Arms Toby** S31 9WE (Toby)
☎Eckington(0246)435226 Telex no 547303
Closed Xmas day evening
Converted 18th-century coaching inn with good quality, spacious, modern accommodation and imaginative food.
30rm(24⇌6↾)⊁in 10 bedrooms CTV in all bedrooms ® **T** ✱ sB&B⇌↾£35.50-£45.50 dB&B⇌↾£45.50-£55.50 ☷
☾150P ✲ ⌂
♕ English & French **V** ✿ ⊈ ⊁ Lunch £11.95&alc Dinner £11.95&alc Last dinner 9.30pm
Credit Cards [1] [2] [3] [5]

RETFORD (EAST) Nottinghamshire Map **08** SK78

★★★64% ***West Retford*** North Rd DN22 7XG (Situated on A638) (Associated Leisure) ☎East Retford(0777)706333 Telex no 56143 FAX (0777) 709951
This large Georgian country house offers very attractive public areas and two annexes of well-equipped comfortable, modern bedrooms.
Annexe31⇌↾(15fb) CTV in all bedrooms ® **T**
☾CTV 100P ✲ CFA
♕ French **V** ✿ ⊈ Last dinner 10.30pm
Credit Cards [1] [2] [3] [5]

Book as early as possible for busy holiday periods.

REYNOLDSTON West Glamorgan Map **02** SS48

★★🏰**Fairyhill Country House** SA3 1BS
☎Gower(0792)390139
Closed 25-26 Dec & 1st 2 wks Jan
This delightful 18th-century country mansion in 24 acres of park and woodland has been restored and now provides elegant and comfortable accommodation. The food is excellent and the friendly Frayne family and their staff are always on hand.
12⇌↾ CTV in all bedrooms ® **T** sB&B⇌↾£55-£65 dB&B⇌↾£65-£75
50P ⛟ ✲ ♪ sauna
♕ English & French **V** ✿ Lunch fr£10.50 Dinner £15.95-£21.40alc Last dinner 9.15pm
Credit Cards [1] [3]

RHAYADER Powys Map **06** SN96

★★***Elan Valley Hotel*** LD6 5HN (2.50m W of Rhayader)
☎(0597)810448
12rm(2⇌5↾)(1fb) TV available ®
CTV 50P 2🚗 (£2.00) ✲ ♪ snooker
V ✿ Last dinner 8pm
Credit Cards [1] [3]

★***Elan Hotel*** West St LD6 5AF ☎(0597)810373
Situated in the centre of this small market town this small family-run hotel is now being modernised. Bedrooms so far completed are comfortable and well-equipped but others are more modest.
15rm(1⇌)(2fb)
CTV 12P
✿ ⊈

RHOSSILI West Glamorgan Map **02** SS48

★★**Worms Head** SA3 1PP ☎Gower(0792)390512
Closed 24-26 Dec
Bright cliff-top hotel with magnificent views of the sea and the bay.
21rm(2⇌3↾)(2fb) ® ✖ (ex guide dogs) ✱ sB&B£19 dB&B£38 dB&B⇌↾£40 ☷
CTV 20P pool table
V ✿

RICHMOND North Yorkshire Map **07** NZ10

★★**Frenchgate** 59-61 Frenchgate DL10 7AE
☎(0748)2087 &3596
Closed Dec-Feb
Stone-built, Georgian, gentleman's town house, enclosing a 16th-century cottage.
13rm(3⇌4↾) CTV in all bedrooms ® **T** sB&Bfr£22.50 sB&B⇌↾fr£30.50 dB&Bfr£42 dB&B⇌↾fr£48 ☷
6P ⛟ nc7 yrs
Dinner fr£9&alc Last dinner 8.30pm
Credit Cards [1] [2] [3] [5]

★★**King's Head** Market Square DL10 4HS (Consort)
☎(0748)2311
A busy inn in the market square with a coffee shop and a pizzeria.
29⇌↾Annexe4rm(3⇌1↾)(5fb)1⊟⊁in 4 bedrooms CTV in all bedrooms ® **T** ✖ (ex guide dogs) S% sB&B⇌↾fr£39.50 dB&B⇌↾fr£62 ☷

23P *xmas*
🍽 Traditional & Continental **V** ♧ ☕ ⚡ Lunch £5.95-£6.50 High tea fr£4.50 Dinner fr£10.25 Last dinner 9.30pm
Credit Cards [1] [2] [3] [4] [5]

RICHMOND UPON THAMES Greater London

See LONDON plan 5 page 412. **London telephone codes are due to change on 6th May 1990. See page 421.**

★★★63% Richmond Hill 146-150 Richmond Hill TW10 6RW (Best Western) ☎01-940 2247 & 01-940 5466 Telex no 21844 FAX 01-940 5424
Overlooking the Thames Valley from its location near Richmond Park, an hotel with a wealth of interesting architectural features provides accommodation in bedrooms which have been modernised to a comfortable standard, a cosy bar, and the warmth and elegance of a wood-panelled dining room. Visitors to this popular, busy establishment are assured of a warm welcome and pleasant, helpful service.
123⇨🚿(9fb)1⊠ CTV in all bedrooms ® **T** ✱
sB&B⇨🚿£60-£70 dB&B⇨🚿£72-£85 ⊟
Lift ☾ 150P CFA squash ♫ *xmas*
🍽 English & French **V** ♧ ☕ S% Lunch fr£10 Dinner fr£14 Last dinner 9pm
Credit Cards [1] [2] [3] [5]

RINGWOOD Hampshire Map **04** SU10

★★Struan Horton Rd BH24 2EG ☎(0425)473553 & 473029 FAX (0425) 480529
(For full entry see Ashley Heath)

★Moortown Lodge Hotel 244, Christchurch Rd BH24 3AS ☎(0425)471404
Closed 24 Dec-14 Jan
Comfortable and very hospitable small hotel, with cooking of exceptional quality by proprietress Mrs Burrows-Jones. Bedrooms are compact but all are pleasant and well-equipped.
6rm(1⇨4🚿)(1fb) CTV in all bedrooms ® **T** ✗ ✱ sB&B£22 sB&B⇨🚿£29 dB&B£42 dB&B⇨🚿£42 ⊟
7P ⊞
🍽 British & French **V** ⚡ Lunch £4.25-£14alc Dinner £9.95&alc Last dinner 9pm
Credit Cards [1] [2] [3]

RIPON North Yorkshire Map **08** SE37

★★★64% Ripon Spa Park St HG4 2BU (Best Western) ☎(0765)2172 Telex no 57780
The hotel, standing in large and extremely pleasant gardens only a few minutes' walk from the town centre, has been extensively refurbished to offer individually styled and most attractive bedrooms.
40rm(37⇨3🚿)(5fb)2⊠ CTV in all bedrooms ® **T**
sB&B⇨🚿£44-£60 dB&B⇨🚿£56-£80 ⊟
Lift ☾ CTV 80P ❃ CFA *xmas*
V ♧ ☕ Lunch £8.50-£12 Dinner £11.25-£16.50 Last dinner 9pm
Credit Cards [1] [2] [3] [5] (£)

★★Bridge 16-18 Magdalen Rd HG4 1HX ☎(0765)3687
This bay-windowed Victorian house, overlooking the River Ure, offers charming bedrooms and well-restored public rooms.
15⇨🚿(7fb)1⊠ ⚡in 4 bedrooms CTV in all bedrooms ® **T** ✗ (ex guide dogs) sB&B⇨🚿£37-£43 dB&B⇨🚿£52-£70 ⊟
15P ⊞ *xmas*
🍽 English, French & Italian **V** ♧ ☕ ⚡ Lunch £1.75-£7.50&alc Dinner £13.25 Last dinner 9.30pm
Credit Cards [1] [2] [3] [5]

★★**Unicorn** Market Place HG4 1BP (Consort) ☎(0765)2202 Telex no 57515 FAX (0765) 700321
This hotel has stood in the medieval market place since its days as a post house. It provides well-fitted bedrooms, a comfortable first-floor lounge, and bars and a restaurant retaining some original features on the ground floor.
33rm(18⇌15♠)(4fb) CTV in all bedrooms ® T
sB&B⇌♠£36-£38 dB&B⇌♠£42-£49.50
15P 4
English & French V Lunch £4.95&alc High tea £1.50-£6.50alc Dinner £1.50-£6.50alc Last dinner 9pm
Credit Cards 1 2 3 5

RIPPONDEN West Yorkshire Map **07** SE01

✕✕**Over The Bridge** Millfold HX6 4DJ ☎Halifax(0422)823722
This delightful little stone-built restaurant stands beside a packhorse bridge and was once a row of millworkers' cottages. Attractive interior decorations create a relaxing atmosphere, and cuisine of a high standard is provided from the short, interesting, fixed-price menu. An ample wine list is also available.
Lunch not served
English & French 48 seats S% Dinner £18.50 Last dinner 9.30pm 50P nc10yrs
Credit Cards 2 3

ROADE Northamptonshire Map **04** SP75

✕**Roadhouse** 16-18 High St NN7 2NW ☎(0604)863372
Closed Sun, Mon & 3 wks Summer
Lunch not served Sat
French 32 seats S10% Lunch £12.50&alc Dinner £15-£20alc Last lunch 1.45pm Last dinner 10pm 15P nc5yr
Credit Cards 1 3

ROBIN HOOD'S BAY North Yorkshire Map **08** NZ90

★**Grosvenor** Station Rd YO22 4RA ☎Whitby(0947)880320
This friendly, family-run hotel represents good value for money, offering a varied selection of dishes at both lunch and dinner.
13rm(3⇌2♠)(2fb) CTV in 6bedrooms ® T (ex guide dogs) sB&Bfr£15 sB&B⇌♠fr£17 dB&Bfr£30 dB&B⇌♠fr£34
CTV
Lunch fr£4.95 Dinner fr£6.95&alc Last dinner 9pm
Credit Cards 1 3

ROCHDALE Greater Manchester Map **07** SD91

★★★65% **Norton Grange** Manchester Rd, Castleton OL11 2XZ (Associated Leisure) ☎(0706)30788 FAX (0706) 49313
Five minutes drive from Junction 20 of the M62, this Victorian mansion has been modernised and extended for business use and functions.
50rm(48⇌2♠)(28fb)1 CTV in all bedrooms ® T ✱ S%
sB&B⇌♠£33-£57 dB&B⇌♠£47-£65
Lift 150P *xmas*
International V S% Lunch fr£7.95&alc Dinner fr£10.95&alc Last dinner 10pm
Credit Cards 1 2 3 4 5

★★**Midway** Manchester Rd, Castleton OL11 2XX ☎(0706)32881 Telex no 635220 FAX (0706) 53522
Extensively modernised hotel with wine bar and two restaurants.
29rm(2⇌19♠)(2fb)1 CTV in all bedrooms ® T ✱
sB&Bfr£29.50 sB&B⇌♠fr£34.50 dB&B⇌♠fr£48.50
100P *xmas*
English, French & Italian V Bar Lunch 95p-£2.95alc
Credit Cards 1 2 3

For key to symbols see the inside front cover.

ROCHESTER Kent Map **05** TQ76

★★★67% **Crest** Maidstone Rd ME5 9SF (on A229 1m N of M2 jnct 3) (Crest) ☎Medway(0634)687111 Telex no 965933 FAX (0634) 684512
This is a busy, commercial hotel with well-maintained modern bedrooms, an open plan lounge/bar area, a leisure complex and business centre. Staff are friendly and pleasant.
105⇌♠(7fb) in 21 bedrooms CTV in all bedrooms ® T ✱
sB⇌♠£74.50-£79 dB⇌♠£90-£95.50 (room only)
Lift 150P (heated) sauna solarium gymnasium ♫
English & French V Lunch £7.50-£9.50&alc Dinner £15-£17&alc Last dinner 10.30pm
Credit Cards 1 2 3 4 5

ROCHFORD Essex Map **05** TQ89

★★★68% **Hotel Renouf** Bradley Way SS4 1BU ☎Southend-on-Sea(0702)541334 Telex no 995158 FAX (0702) 549563
A new hotel with some style, privately run, offers well-equipped bedrooms which are simply but tastefully decorated. In the split-level restaurant, with its air of grandeur, service is professionally supervised and the imaginative dishes featured on both the table d'hôte and à la carte menus are feshly prepared, well-presented and complemented by a reasonably priced wine list.
24⇌♠(1fb) CTV in all bedrooms ® T ✱ sB&B⇌♠£48-£65
dB&B⇌♠£55-£75
25P *xmas*
French V S10% Lunch £12&alc Dinner £12&alc Last dinner 9.15pm
Credit Cards 1 2 3 5

✕✕**Renoufs** 1 South St SS4 1BL ☎Southend-on-Sea(0702)544393 Telex no 995158 FAX (0702) 549563
Closed Sun, Mon, 1-21 Jan & 2-11 Jul
Lunch not served Sat
English & French V 70 seats S10% Lunch £12&alc Dinner £12&alc Last lunch 2pm Last dinner 10pm
Credit Cards 1 2 3 4 5

ROCK (near St Minver) Cornwall & Isles of Scilly Map **02** SW97

★★**Mariners Motel** Slipway PL27 6LD ☎Trebetherick(020886)2312
RS Nov & Feb
Overlooking the estuary, the motel-type operation is personally run, offering a friendly atmosphere and a choice of good food from the well-priced table d'hôte or slightly more expensive à la carte menus. The main building contains reception, cocktail bar and dining room on the first floor, with the popular bar at ground level, whilst comfortable bedrooms are situated across the side road in Custom House Cottage and a more modern conversion. Some of whose these rooms have lounge areas.
Annexe15⇌(3fb) CTV in all bedrooms ® ✱ sB&B⇌£22-£25
dB&B⇌£36-£44
32P 2 pool table
V Lunch £4.75-£9alc Dinner £6-£15alc Last dinner 9.30pm
Credit Cards 1 3

★★**St Enodoc** PL27 6LA ☎Trebetherick(020886)3394
This elevated hotel has unrestricted views of the Camel Estuary and offers comfortable accommodation in a friendly, relaxed atmosphere; menus are carefully prepared and a new leisure complex is available.
13rm(10⇌3♠)(2fb) CTV in all bedrooms T S10%
sB⇌♠£26.50-£30 dB⇌♠£36-£45 (room only)
33P squash snooker sauna solarium gymnasium water-skiing, windsurfing, pony-trekking *xmas*

☊ English & Continental V ✿ ☕ Lunch £7.50&alc High tea £2.50 Dinner £12.50&alc Last dinner 9.30pm
Credit Cards [1] [2] [3] (£)

ROCKCLIFFE Dumfries & Galloway *Kirkcudbrightshire*
Map **11** NX85

★★★ 68% Baron's Craig
DG5 4QF
☎(055663)225
Closed mid Oct-Etr

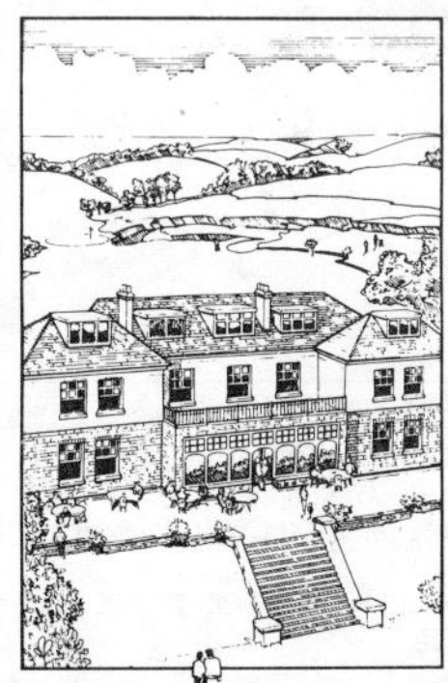

Handsome mansion, set peacefully in woodland with colourful gardens and views of the Solway and Rough Firths. Both traditional modern bedrooms are offered, and there is a smart cocktail bar.
27rm(20⇌)(2fb) CTV in all bedrooms **T**
sB&B£30.25-£34.50 sB&B⇌£42.20-£46.50 dB&B£56-£65 dB&B⇌£71-£86.40 ⊟
50P ❀ ✽ putting
☊ International ✿ ☕ Lunch fr£8 Dinner fr£16 Last dinner 9pm
Credit Cards [1] [3]

ROMALDKIRK Durham Map **12** NY92

★★Rose & Crown DL12 9EB ☎Teesdale(0833)50213
Charming old village inn with wide-ranging inexpensive bar meals.
6rm(4⇌2♪)Annexe5rm(4⇌1♪)(1fb)10⊞ CTV in all bedrooms ® **T** sB&B⇌♪£45-£50 dB&B⇌♪£55-£65 ⊟
60P *xmas*
☊ English & French ✿ ☕ Lunch £8.50-£10.50 Dinner £15-£18 Last dinner 9.30pm
(£)

ROMILEY Greater Manchester Map **07** SJ99

✕Le Bistro 166 Stockport Rd SK6 3AN ☎061-430 4302
Unpretentious French cooking is now the order of the day at this attractive little stone built restaurant situated alongside the Peak Forest Canal. Previously the 'Waterside', Le Bistro offers a good value à la carte menu with dishes such as French onion soup or delightfully sauced Rognons Dijonnaise, Entrecôte au Poivre, Sole Meunière or Dieppoise. Vegetables in particular have been praised.
Closed Mon
Dinner not served Sun
☊ English & French 36 seats Last dinner 10pm 12P
Credit Cards [1] [3]

ROMSEY Hampshire Map **04** SU32

★★★62% Potters Heron Hotel SO51 9ZF (Lansbury)
☎Southampton(0703)266611 Telex no 47459
(For full entry see Ampfield)

★★★61% The White Horse Market Place SO5 8NA (Trusthouse Forte) ☎(0794)512431 FAX (0794) 517485
Part-Tudor coaching inn with a Georgian façade, offering elegance at the LucellaDixon restaurant and a flower-filled courtyard for summer bar meals or drinks.
33⇌(7fb)⊁in 4 bedrooms CTV in all bedrooms ®
sB⇌£64-£66 dB⇌£74.50-£77 (room only) ⊟
60P CFA *xmas*
☊ English & French V ✿ ☕ ⊁ Lunch £8.50-£10.50&alc High tea £3.50-£4.50 Dinner £13-£14&alc Last dinner 9.45pm
Credit Cards [1] [2] [3] [4] [5]

R

❀ ✕✕**Old Manor House** 21 Palmerston St SO5 8GF
☎(0794)517353
Charming and intimate cottage restaurant with low, wooden-beamed ceiling. Fresh fish, supplied daily, is a speciality of the short, fixed-price menu, including succulent dishes such as supreme of Turbot and noisettes. Also worth trying is the 'Bresalo', a dish consisting of home-cured and smoked beef, and the astonishing wine list has nearly 600 bins. The chef patron and his wife ensure that guests are well looked after, and the service by enthusiastic young staff is efficient and attentive.
Closed Mon, 24-30 Dec & last 3 wks Aug
Dinner not served Sun
French 46 seats Lunch £10.50-£18.50 Dinner fr£25 Last lunch 2pm Last dinner 9.30pm 12P
Credit Cards 1 3

ROSEBANK Strathclyde *Lanarkshire* Map **11** NS84

★★★54% **Popinjay** Lanark Rd ML8 5OB (Consort)
☎Crossford(055586)441 Telex no 776496 FAX (055586) 204
Mock-Tudor hotel with gardens by the River Clyde. Popular for functions.
36rm(29⇌7↱)(1fb)2⊟ CTV in all bedrooms ® **T** ✳
sB&B⇌↱£42 dB&B⇌↱£50 ⊟
☾100P ✲ ⤴ ⌂
International **V** ♡ ⊻ Lunch fr£5.95&alc Dinner fr£9.25 Last dinner 10pm
Credit Cards 1 2 3 5

ROSEDALE ABBEY North Yorkshire Map **08** SE79

★★★66% **Blacksmiths Arms** Hartoft End YO18 8EN
☎Lastingham(07515)331
A lovingly converted 16th-century farmhouse in the heart of beautiful moorland. All bedrooms have good views and are attractively decorated, many with Laura Ashley furnishings. The bars are full of old-world charm, and Mr and Mrs Foot work hard to ensure guests' comfort. The atmosphere is very good indeed.
14rm(9⇌3↱) CTV in all bedrooms ® **T** ✗ sB&B⇌↱£39-£53
dB&B⇌↱£76-£96 (incl dinner) ⊟
80P ⊞ ✲
English & French **V** ♡ ⊻ Lunch £7.75-£11 Dinner £14.50-£16.50 Last dinner 8.45pm
Credit Cards 1 3 £

★★**Milburn Arms** YO18 8RA (Guestaccom)
☎Lastingham(07515)312
A very friendly hotel offering an extensive range of well-prepared bar and restaurant meals, and comfortable accommodation.
6⇌↱Annexe8rm(4fb)1⊟ CTV in all bedrooms ® **T** ✳
sB&B⇌↱£28-£32.50 dB&B⇌↱£50-£56 ⊟
35P ⊞ ✲ pool table *xmas*
English **V** ♡ ⊁ Bar Lunch £7.20-£11.65alc Dinner £7.20-£14.90alc Last dinner 9pm
Credit Cards 1 3

★★**White Horse Farm** YO18 8SE (Minotels)
☎Lastingham(07515)239
Closed Xmas day
Converted 17th-century farmhouse overlooking unspoilt Rosedale.
11rm(5⇌5↱)Annexe4rm(2⇌2↱)(2fb) CTV in all bedrooms ® sB&B⇌↱£22-£27 dB&B⇌↱£44 ⊟
50P ⊞ ✲ *xmas*
English & Continental **V** Sunday Lunch £6.50-£7.50 High tea 90p-£5alc Dinner £13.50-£15.50 Last dinner 9pm
Credit Cards 1 2 3 5

ROSEHALL Highland *Sutherland* Map **14** NC40

★★***Achness*** IV27 4BD ☎(054984)239
Closed Oct-Feb
This small Highland fishing hotel's more spacious bedrooms result from the conversion of courtyard outbuildings. Dinner is provided in the form of a self-service buffet.
5rmAnnexe7⇌ TV in 6bedrooms ®
CTV 40P ⊞ ✲ ⤴ clay pigeon shooting
V ♡ ⊻
Credit Cards 1 3

ROSSETT Clwyd Map **07** SJ35

★★★⚑73% **Llyndir Hall**
LL12 0AY
☎Chester(0244)571648

8⇌ CTV in all bedrooms **T** ✗ (ex guide dogs) ✳
sB&B⇌£55-£70
dB&B⇌£75-£95 Continental breakfast ⊟
☾50P ⊞ ✲ croquet *xmas*
English & French **V** ♡ ⊻ Lunch £9-£12.50&alc High tea £7-£7 Dinner £16.50-£16.50&alc Last dinner 9.45pm
Credit Cards 1 2 3 5

See advertisement under CHESTER

ROSSINGTON South Yorkshire Map **08** SK69

★★**Mount Pleasant** Great North Rd DN11 0HP (On A638 Great North Rd 1.5m E of village)
☎Doncaster(0302)868696 & 868219 FAX (0302) 865130
Closed Xmas Day
This charming country house style hotel has small comfortable lounges and well-appointed bedrooms.
38rm(23⇌10↱)(2fb)4⊟ CTV in all bedrooms ® **T** ✗ (ex guide dogs) sB&B£20 sB&B⇌↱£35 dB&B⇌↱£45
☾CTV 100P 2⌂(charged) ✲
V ♡ ⊻ Lunch £5-£7.80&alc High tea £3.75-£8 Dinner £10-£12.50&alc Last dinner 9.30pm
Credit Cards 1 3

See advertisement under DONCASTER

ROSS-ON-WYE Hereford & Worcester Map **03** SO62

See also **Goodrich, Pencraig and Symonds Yat**
★★★61% **Chase** Gloucester Rd HR9 5LH (Consort)
☎(0989)763161 Telex no 35658 FAX (0989) 768330
Set in extensive grounds on the outskirts of town this former country house provides comfortable, well-equipped accommodation, good service and hospitality. It is popular with both conference delegates and tourists.
40rm(36⇌4↱)(2fb)2⊟ CTV in all bedrooms **T** ✗ (ex guide dogs) sB&B⇌↱fr£61 dB&B⇌↱fr£85 ⊟
☾200P ✲ CFA *xmas*
English & French **V** ♡ ⊻ Lunch £10.50 Dinner £15&alc Last dinner 9.45pm
Credit Cards 1 2 3 5

R

★★★🏠61% **Pengethley Manor** HR9 6LL (4m N on A49 Hereford rd) (Best Western)

☎Harewood End (098987)211 Telex no 35332 FAX (098987) 238

Set in extensive grounds with superb views, this Georgian house offers a heated swimming pool, a 9-hole pitch and putt course, and a trout fishing lake. Some bedrooms are in the former stable block and coach house. Both holiday and business use is catered for with conference facilities also available.

11⇌Annexe11⇌(3fb)2⊞ CTV in all bedrooms ® **T** sB&B⇌£60-£115 dB&B⇌£100-£160 ⊟

70P 1🚗 ✿ ⛱(heated) ♪ snooker 9 hole mini golf croquet *xmas*

V ♁ ⊡ S% Lunch fr£12.50 Dinner fr£20&alc Last dinner 9.30pm

Credit Cards 1 2 3 5 £

★★★65% **Royal** Palace Pound HR9 5HZ (Trusthouse Forte) ☎(0989)65105 FAX (0989) 768058

Built in 1837 and overlooking the River Wye from its elevated position west of the castle, the hotel offers comfortable, well-equipped accommodation which will attract both business people and tourists. Good conference and banqueting facilities make it a popular venue for such functions.

40rm(38⇌2↱)(4fb) CTV in all bedrooms ® **T** sB⇌↱fr£59 dB⇌↱£84-£94 (room only) ⊟

☾40P ✿ ♪ *xmas*

V ♁ ⊡ ⚟ S% Lunch £8.50-£9.75&alc High tea £1.95-£5.75 Dinner £13.95-£14.50&alc Last dinner 9.30pm

Credit Cards 1 2 3 4 5

★★**Chasedale** Walford Rd HR9 5PQ ☎(0989)62423

A large detached house with pleasant gardens situated on the B4228 on the southern outskirts of town. Family run, in a friendly informal manner, it provides simple but fairly well-equipped accommodation.

11rm(9⇌)(4fb) CTV in all bedrooms ® sB&B⇌£27-£28.50 dB&B£33.50-£35 dB&B⇌£43-£45 ⊟

14P ⛟ ✿ *xmas*

☊ English & French **V** ♁ ⊡ Lunch £6.50-£7.75 Dinner £9.25-£10&alc Last dinner 9pm

Credit Cards 1 3 4 5 £

★★🏠**Glewstone Court** Glewstone HR9 6AW

☎Llangarron(098984)367

Closed 25-27 Dec

Christine and William Reeve-Tucker fell in love with this 250-year-old manor in 1987. Set prettily in grounds and gardens surrounded by orchards, it is now their family home and charming country house hotel, where informal service and warm hospitality ensure that guests really do feel like guests. The bedrooms are spacious, and tasteful furnishings throughout provide comfort while complementing the character of the house. An imaginative menu using seasonal local produce is offered in the popular restaurant. Christine is a keen balloonist, and, among other activities, adventurous guests can arrange a balloon flight from the grounds

6rm(4⇌2↱) CTV in 2bedrooms ® ✱ sB&B⇌↱fr£33 dB&B⇌↱fr£48 ⊟

CTV 20P ⛟ ✿ croquet lawn ♫ ⌂

☊ English & French **V** ♁ Lunch £8-£14 High tea fr£3 Dinner fr£14 Last dinner 9.30pm

Credit Cards 1 2 3

★★**Hunsdon Manor** Gloucester Rd, Weston-Under-Penyard HR9 7PE (2m E A40) ☎(0989)62748 & 63376

A 16th-century manor house with later additions, standing in two and a half acres of lawns and gardens.

14rm(5⇌7↱)Annexe3⇌(2fb) CTV in all bedrooms ® **T** ✱ sB&B£22 sB&B⇌↱£27-£29 dB&B£30 dB&B⇌↱£37-£40 ⊟

55P ⛟ ✿ sauna solarium

V ♁ ⊡ Lunch £7.50&alc Dinner £9.50 Last dinner 9.30pm

Credit Cards 1 2 3 5 £

★★**King's Head** 8 High St HR9 5HL ☎(0989)763174

Closed 24-26Dec

Situated in the town centre this 14th-century coaching inn, with a Georgian façade, has a cosy atmosphere. The well-equipped bedrooms and honest, enjoyable cuisine make it popular both with tourists and commercial visitors.

14rm(13⇌1↱)Annexe9⇌(4fb) CTV in all bedrooms ® **T** sB&B⇌↱£32-£35 dB&B⇌↱£48-£52 ⊟

20P ⛟

V ♁ ⊡ Lunch £2.75-£8alc Dinner £11-£15alc Last dinner 9pm

Credit Cards 1 3 £

★★**Orles Barn** Wilton HR9 6AE ☎(0989)62155

Closed Nov

Small family-run hotel in well kept gardens, close to the junction of the A40 and the A49.

10rm(4⇌2↱)(2fb) CTV in all bedrooms ® ✱ sB&B£25-£28 sB&B⇌↱£30-£33 dB&B£40-£44 dB&B⇌↱£50-£55 ⊟

☾20P ✿ ⛱(heated) ⌂

☊ English, French & Spanish **V** ♁ ⊡ Lunch £7-£8 Dinner £8.25-£9.25&alc Last dinner 9pm

Credit Cards 1 2 3 5

★**Bridge House** Wilton HR9 6AA (adjacent A40/A49 junc) ☎(0989)62655

A small, family-run hotel offers good, wholesome meals.

7rm(1⇌6↱)1⊞ CTV in all bedrooms ® ✗ sB&B⇌↱£26-£29 dB&B⇌↱£42-£45 ⊟

CTV 14P ⛟ ✿ *xmas*

☊ English & French Lunch fr£7&alc Dinner fr£8.95&alc Last dinner 9pm

Credit Cards 1 3 £

ROSTHWAITE Cumbria Map **11** NY21

See also **Borrowdale and Grange (In-Borrowdale)**

★★★57% **Scafell** CA12 5XB ☎Keswick(059684)208

Closed 2 Jan-9 Feb

Popular former coaching inn, offering traditional hospitality in the peaceful setting of the Borrowdale valley. Bedrooms are gradually being modernised.

20rm(19⇌1↱)(3fb) CTV in all bedrooms ® **T** ✱ sB&B⇌↱£26.50 dB&B⇌↱£53 ⊟

50P ⛟ ✿ *xmas*

☊ International **V** ♁ ⊡ Bar Lunch £6-£12alc Dinner £14.50&alc Last dinner 8.15pm

See advertisement on page 569

R

ROTHBURY Northumberland Map **12** NU00

★★Coquet Vale Station Rd NE65 9QN ☎(0669)20305
Large detached, grey-stone building in an elevated position overlooking the valley.
13rm(4⇌6⇐)(6fb) CTV in all bedrooms ® ✗ (ex guide dogs) ✱ sB&B£20 sB&B⇌⇐£22 dB&B£36 dB&B⇌⇐£36 ⊟
40P ❋ *xmas*
V ♦ Lunch £5.95-£12 High tea £3.50-£4.50 Dinner £8.95-£10.50&alc Last dinner 9pm
Credit Cards [1] [3]

ROTHERHAM South Yorkshire Map **08** SK49

★★★66% Rotherham Moat House Moorgate Rd S60 2BG (Queens Moat) ☎(0709)364902 Telex no 547810 FAX (0709) 368960
A modern, well-appointed hotel offering comfortable accommodation. Situated close to the town centre and motorways.
64⇌⇐(5fb)1⊠ ⊁in 4 bedrooms CTV in all bedrooms ® **T** sB⇌⇐fr£60 dB⇌⇐fr£65 (room only) ⊟
Lift ☾ CTV 75P CFA sauna solarium gymnasium jacuzzi ♫
♀ English & French **V** ♦ ⊻ ⊁ Lunch £6.75 Dinner £10.50-£11.75&alc Last dinner 9.45pm
Credit Cards [1] [2] [3] [4] [5]

★★Brentwood Moorgate Rd S60 2TY ☎(0709)382772 Telex no 547291 FAX (0709) 820289
Closed 26 & 27 Dec RS Bank Hols
A stone-built Victorian residence in its own grounds with a modern extension.
25rm(13⇌7⇐)Annexe10rm(6⇌4⇐)(1fb)1⊠ CTV in all bedrooms ® **T** sB&B⇌⇐£19-£42 dB&B⇌⇐£30-£55 ⊟
60P ❋
♀ English & Continental **V** ♦ Lunch fr£7.95&alc Dinner fr£12.95&alc Last dinner 9.30pm
Credit Cards [1] [2] [3] [5] [£]

★Elton Main St, Bramley S66 0SF (3m E A631) ☎(0709)545681
A two-storey stone building, which was originally a farmhouse.
15rm(2⇌3⇐) CTV in all bedrooms ® **T** sB&B£27.50-£34.50 sB&B⇌⇐£35-£40 dB&B£44 dB&B⇌⇐£48 ⊟
☾ 20P
♀ English & French **V** ♦ ⊻ Lunch £8.25-£12.75&alc Dinner £12.75-£12.75&alc Last dinner 9.30pm
Credit Cards [1] [2] [3] [£]

ROTHERWICK Hampshire Map **04** SU75

★★★★⚑ 79% Tylney Hall
RG27 9AJ (Prestige)
☎Hook(0256)764881
Telex no 859864
FAX (0256) 768141

A grand, country-house-style hotel, Tylney Hall offers its guests a high standard of comfort in an imposing setting of marble, carved woodwork and decorative plasterwork. All the bedrooms and suites are well equipped, and some offer jacuzzis in the spacious en suite bathrooms. Recreational facilities are good, and there is a golf-course adjacent to the hotel.

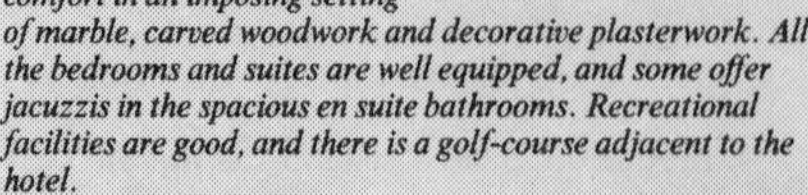

35⇌Annexe56⇌(1fb)3⊠ CTV in all bedrooms **T** ✗ (ex guide dogs) ✱ S10% sB&B⇌£78-£210 dB&B⇌£92-£210 ⊟
Lift ☾ 120P ⊕ ❋ ▭(heated) ⊇(heated) ℘ (hard) snooker sauna gymnasium croquet archery clay pigeon ♫ *xmas*
♀ English & French **V** ♦ ⊻ ⊁ Lunch fr£15&alc Dinner fr£22&alc Last dinner 9.30pm
Credit Cards [1] [2] [3] [5] [£]

See advertisement under BASINGSTOKE

ROTHES Grampian *Morayshire* Map **15** NJ24

★★★⚑ 64% Rothes Glen
IV33 7AH
☎(03403)254
Closed Jan

A baronial-style mansion, designed in grounds where Highland cattle roam. The entrance hall is particularly impressive, and the public rooms are elegant and comfortable. The very well-equipped bedrooms include spacious examples furnished with antiques.
16rm(13⇌)(4fb) CTV in all bedrooms **T** ✱ sB&B£36.30 sB&B⇌£49.65 dB&B£53.46 dB&B⇌£72.60 ⊟
CTV 40P ⊕ ❋
♦ S10% Lunch £9.50 Dinner £18-£25&alc Last dinner 9pm
Credit Cards [1] [2] [3] [5]

ROTHESAY

See **Bute, Isle of**

R

ROTHLEY Leicestershire Map **08** SK51

★★★70% **Rothley Court** Westfield Ln LE7 7LG (Trusthouse Forte) ☎Leicester(0533)374141 Telex no 342811 FAX (0533) 374483
A splendid manor house dating from the 13th-century when a chapel was built by the Knights Templar. Lovingly restored rich wood panelling enhances the comfortable public areas whilst the bedrooms – both in the main house and the converted stable block – are comfortable and very well equipped.
15rm(13⇌2♠)Annexe21⇌(1fb)2 CTV in all bedrooms ® T ✱ S% sB⇌♠£70-£75 dB⇌♠£86-£130 (room only)
(100P ✿ CFA croquet *xmas*
V S% Lunch £11.95&alc High tea £2.75 Dinner £17.50&alc Last dinner 10pm
Credit Cards 1 2 3 4 5

ROTTINGDEAN East Sussex Map **05** TQ30

★★**White Horse** Marine Dr BN2 7HB (Berni/Chef & Brewer) ☎Brighton(0273)300301
Set in a prime position and enjoying fine sea views, this well-equipped modern hotel features quality bedrooms, lively bars and a contemporary restaurant.
17⇌(2fb)2 CTV in all bedrooms ® T (ex guide dogs) sB&B⇌fr£43 dB&B⇌fr£58.50
Lift (45P
V Lunch £8 Dinner £9 Last dinner 10pm
Credit Cards 1 2 3 5

ROUSDON Devon Map **03** SY29

★★**Orchard Country** DT7 3XW ☎Lyme Regis(02974)2972
Closed Nov-Mar
Located in a quiet country setting between Lyme Regis and Seaton, this comfortable family hotel has a good reputation for its freshly prepared foods and varied choice.
11rm(7⇌4♠) CTV in all bedrooms ® sB&B⇌♠£30-£32 dB&B⇌♠£48-£53
CTV 25P ✿ nc8 yrs
Bar Lunch £5 Dinner £11 Last dinner 8.15pm
Credit Cards 1 3 £

ROWARDENNAN Central *Stirlingshire* Map **10** NS39

★**Rowardennan** G63 0AR ☎Balmaha(036087)273
Closed Nov RS Oct-Mar
Personally run historic inn on Loch Lomond.
11rm(1⇌)(2fb) ® S% sB&B£18-£22 dB&B£32-£36 dB&B⇌fr£36
CTV 50P water-skiing boating
Scottish V S% Bar Lunch £4.50-£10.50 Dinner £10.50-£12.50 Last dinner 8.45pm £

ROWEN Gwynedd Map **06** SH77

★**Tir-y-Coed Country House** LL32 8TP
☎Tynygroes(0492)650219
Closed Xmas RS Nov-Feb

Detached, Edwardian house situated in a small peaceful village.

7rm(5⇌2♠)Annexe1♠(1fb) CTV in all bedrooms ® sB&B⇌♠£17.50-£20.50 dB&B⇌♠£32.50-£37.50
8P ✿
Bar Lunch £1.85-£4.50alc Dinner £8.50 Last dinner 7.30pm
£

ROWNHAMS MOTORWAY SERVICE AREA (M27)

○**Roadchef Lodge** M27 Southbound SO1 8AW ☎(0703)734480
39⇌♠ Open late summer 1990.

ROWSLEY Derbyshire Map **08** SK26

★★★53% **Peacock** DE4 2EB (Embassy) ☎Matlock(0629)733518 FAX (06[illegible]) 732671
Relaxed hotel with country house atmosphere on the River Derwent. Guests should book for the popular restaurant. The cottage annexe offers simpler accommodation at a lower price.
14rm(10⇌4♠)Annexe6rm(1⇌)(4fb)1 in 3 bedrooms CTV in all bedrooms ® T sB£37-£45 sB⇌♠£45-£65 dB£45-£50 dB⇌♠£65-£70 (room only)
(45P 2 ✿ *xmas*
Lunch £7-£11.95 Dinner £21-£28 Last dinner 9.00pm
Credit Cards 1 2 3 5

★★**East Lodge Country House** DE4 2EF
☎Matlock(0629)734474

Tranquilly set in ten acres of grounds and once the East Lodge of Haddon Hall, this delightful, stonebuilt hotel is nevertheless close enough to the A6 to offer easy access to the Peak Park and Chatsworth House. It is personally run in the true country house style by proprietors who offer well-equipped accommodation, furnished to a high standard.
6rm CTV in all bedrooms ® T sB&B£48-£58 dB&B£66-£80
P ✿ *xmas*
International Lunch £9.50-£12.50 Dinner £12.50 Last dinner 8.45pm Credit Cards 1 3

ROY BRIDGE Highland *Inverness-shire* Map **14** NN28

★★**Glenspean Lodge** PH31 4AW ☎Spean Bridge(039781)223
This hotel set in its own grounds overlooks Monessie Gorge.
13rm(9⇌2♠)(2fb) CTV in 9bedrooms ® T ✱ sB&B£18-£20 sB&B⇌♠£22-£26 dB&B£36-£40 dB&B⇌♠£44-£52
CTV 30P ✿ rough shooting stalking *xmas*
Scottish & French V Bar Lunch £2-£6.25alc High tea £2.50-£7alc Dinner fr£11.50 Last dinner 9.30pm
Credit Cards 1 2 3

ROZEL BAY

See Jersey, under Channel Islands

RUABON Clwyd Map **07** SJ34

★★**Wynnstay Arms** High St LL14 6BL ☎(0978)822187
A creeper-clad hotel, on a busy road junction, with a large function room, two bars serving bar meals, and a small simply furnished restaurant.
9rm(3⇌)(1fb) CTV in all bedrooms ® ✱ sB&B£25-£29 sB&B⇌fr£29 dB&Bfr£35 dB&B⇌fr£42
80P 2

English & French V Lunch £5-£7.50 Dinner £7.50-£10.50 Last dinner 9.45pm
Credit Cards 1 2 3 4 5 £

RUAN HIGH LANES Cornwall & Isles of Scilly
Map **02** SW93

★★**Hundred House** TR2 5JR ☎Truro(0872)501336
Closed Dec-Feb
Georgian house with cosy, comfortable bedrooms, run very hospitably by Mike and Kitty Eccles.
10rm(6⇌4♪) CTV in all bedrooms ® ✱ sB&B⇌♪£22-£24 dB&B⇌♪£44-£48
15P nc10yrs
Bar Lunch fr£1.95alc Dinner £14 Last dinner 7pm
Credit Cards 1 3 £

★★**Pendower** Gerrans Bay TR2 5LW ☎Truro(0872)501257 FAX (0452)410440
Closed Nov-Easter
Occupying a superb position on Roseland Peninsula with direct access through well-tended gardens to an award-winning beach. The hotel has been totally refurbished and offers a good combination of comfort and facilities together with friendly, attentive service.
14⇌(2fb) ✱ sB&B⇌£30-£37.50 dB&B⇌£60-£75 (incl dinner)
CTV 16P 3 (£2 per day)
V Sunday Lunch £7.50 Dinner £11.50-£15 Last dinner 9pm
Credit Cards 1 2 3

★★*Polsue Manor*
TR2 5LU
☎Truro(0872)501270
RS Jan

Charming 18th century manor in secluded setting and with a relaxed atmosphere.

13rm(10⇌)(3fb) CTV in all bedrooms ® T
17P putting croquet table tennis skittles
Credit Cards 1 3

RUGBY Warwickshire Map **04** SP57

★★★50% **Clifton Court** Lilbourne Rd, Clifton-upon-Dunsmore CV23 0BB ☎(0788)565033 FAX (0788) 541153
Popular business hotel in peaceful surroundings.
16rm(12⇌4♪)(1fb)1 CTV in all bedrooms ® T
75P
English, French & Italian V
Credit Cards 1 3 5

★★★60% **Grosvenor** Clifton Rd CV21 3QQ ☎(0788)535686 FAX (0788) 541297
The proprietors of this small, friendly hotel have worked hard to provide the modern facilities in its tastefully furnished public areas. Most of the charming, individually designed little bedrooms are decorated to a Victorian theme, some being furnished with brass beds – and some also having jacuzzis.
16rm(10⇌6♪)(1fb)1 CTV in all bedrooms ® T ✱ sB&B⇌♪£38-£49.50 dB&B⇌♪£55-£65
16P jacuzzi *xmas*
V Lunch £8.95&alc High tea £2.30-£3.50 Dinner £12.95-£22.95alc Last dinner 10pm
Credit Cards 1 2 3 5

See advertisement on page 573

★★★63% **Post House Hotel** NN6 7XR (Trusthouse Forte)
☎Crick(0788)822101 Telex no 311107 FAX (0788) 823955
(For full entry see Crick)

★★**Dun Cow** The Green, Dunchurch CV22 6NJ (3m S A426)
☎(0788)810233
16th-century coaching inn, well-furnished with antiques.
23rm(16⇌7♪)Annexe4⇌(2fb)4 CTV in all bedrooms ® T S10% sB&B⇌♪£30-£45 dB&B⇌♪£43-£65
150P 6 shooting *xmas*
English & French V S10% Lunch £10.95-£14.95&alc High tea £4.95-£6.95 Dinner £12.95-£14.95&alc Last dinner 10.30pm
Credit Cards 1 2 3 5 £

★★***Hillmorton Manor*** 78 High St, Hillmorton CV21 4EE (2m SE off A428) ☎(0788)565533 & 572403
Located in the centre of a village on the south-east of Rugby, this extended house is ideal for small parties and gatherings of business people.
11⇌♪(1fb) CTV in all bedrooms ® T
40P
English, French & Italian V Last dinner 10pm
Credit Cards 1 2 3 4

Places with AA hotels and restaurants are identified on the location atlas at the back of the book.

R

RUGELEY Staffordshire Map **07** SK01

★★Cedar Tree Main Road, Brereton WS15 1DY
☎(0889)584241
RS Sun evenings
A three-storey, white-painted 18th-century building located between Lichfield and Rugeley.
16rm(11⇌) CTV in all bedrooms ® **T** ✕ ✳ sB&B£16-£21 sB&B⇌£21-£23 dB&B£35-£38 dB&B⇌£38
CTV 200P squash solarium
English & French **V** Lunch fr£5.50&alc Dinner fr£7.50&alc Last dinner 9.30pm
Credit Cards 1 2 3 5 £

○ ***TraveLodge*** Western Springs Rd WS15 2AS (A51) (Trusthouse Forte) ☎(08894)70096
32⇌

RUNCORN Cheshire Map **07** SJ58

★★★ 64% **Crest** Wood Ln, Beechwood WA7 3HA (Crest)
☎(0928)714000 Telex no 627426 FAX (0928) 714611
Just off junction 12 of the M56 this is a modern hotel with a wide range of business facilities including a business centre, executive study bedrooms and a recently opened leisure centre.
134⇌(12fb) in 30 bedrooms CTV in all bedrooms ® **T** ✳ sB⇌£22-£73 dB⇌£35-£85 (room only)
Lift 250P CFA (heated) sauna solarium gymnasium steam room spa bath pool tables ♫ *xmas*
V Lunch £6.95-£9.50&alc Dinner £14.50&alc Last dinner 9.45pm
Credit Cards 1 2 3 4 5

RUSHDEN Northamptonshire Map **04** SP96

★★The Rilton Hotel High St NN10 1BT
☎Wellingborough(0933)312189
Impressive Victorian building with up-to-date facilities, including the popular Steak House restaurant and extensive bars.
10⇌1 CTV in all bedrooms ® **T** ✳ sB&B⇌fr£27.50 dB&B⇌fr£37.50
CTV 50P
V Lunch £5.95
Credit Cards 1 3

★*Westward* Shirley Rd NN10 9BY
☎Wellingborough(0933)312376
Closed 24 Dec-8 Jan
16rm(9)Annexe10(3fb) CTV in 19bedrooms TV in 7bedrooms ®
CTV 16P (heated) pool table darts
Last dinner 8.30pm
Credit Cards 1 3 £

RUSHYFORD Co Durham Map **08** NZ22

★★★ 59% **Eden Arms** DL17 0LL (Swallow)
☎Bishop Auckland(0388)720541 FAX (0388) 721871
A business and conference hotel conveniently situated two miles from the A1(M).
46⇌(4fb)1 in 5 bedrooms CTV in all bedrooms ® **T** ✳ sB&B⇌£52 dB&B⇌£73
200P (heated) sauna solarium gymnasium ♫ *xmas*
English & French **V** S%
Credit Cards 1 2 3 5

RUSPER West Sussex Map **04** TQ23

★★★ 71% **Ghyll Manor** RH12 4PX (Trusthouse Forte)
☎(0293)871571 Telex no 877557 FAX (0293) 871419
The 14th-century Tudor manor house stands in magnificent grounds and offers some spacious, airy bedrooms that have been tastefully appointed with the accent on comfort. The atmosphere is warm and friendly, the menu imaginative and the cooking good.
28rm(27⇌1)6 in 3 bedrooms CTV in all bedrooms ® **T** ✳ sB⇌£40-£80 dB⇌£80-£90 (room only)
150P (heated) (hard) sauna solarium *xmas*
V Lunch £14&alc Dinner £18&alc Last dinner 10pm
Credit Cards 1 2 3 4 5

See advertisement under GATWICK AIRPORT (LONDON)

RUTHIN Clwyd Map **06** SJ15

★★★ 57% **Ruthin Castle** LL15 2NU (Best Western)
☎(08242)2664 Telex no 61169 FAX (08242) 5978
Impressive 15th-century stone castle situated in its own well-kept grounds.
58rm(56⇌2)(6fb)1 CTV in all bedrooms ® **T** ✕ (ex guide dogs) sB&B⇌fr£42 dB&B⇌fr£64
Lift CTV 200P CFA snooker *xmas*
International **V** Sunday Lunch fr£6.95 Dinner fr£11.95 Last dinner 9.30pm
Credit Cards 1 2 3 5 £

RYDE

See **Wight, Isle of**

RYE East Sussex Map **05** TQ92

★★★ 63% **Mermaid Inn** Mermaid St TN31 7EU ☎(0797)223065 Telex no 957141
With beams and panelling dating from its 1420 rebuilding, the Mermaid offers good food and warm hospitality. The inn's charm compensates for the lack of space, and some rooms have four-posters.
29rm(21⇌5)3 CTV in 1bedroom **T** ✕ (ex guide dogs) ✳ S10% sB&B⇌£48-£52 dB&B⇌£75-£90
CTV 25P nc8 yrs *xmas*
Lunch £12-£14&alc Dinner £14-£16&alc Last dinner 9.15pm
Credit Cards 1 2 3 4 5

★★The George High St TN31 7JP (Trusthouse Forte)
☎(0797)222114
An historic coaching inn, whose many original architectural features include an elegant first-floor lounge and banqueting suite, offers bedrooms which are well equipped, though compact in some cases, and a range of enjoyable meals featuring some 'Olde Englishe' recipes in Chaucers restaurant.
22⇌ CTV in all bedrooms ® **T** ✳ sB⇌£60 dB⇌£77-£87 (room only)
9P 8 *xmas*
V Lunch £7.95-£9.50 Dinner £10-£16 Last dinner 9pm
Credit Cards 1 2 3 4 5

✕Flushing Inn Market St TN31 7LA ☎(0797)223292
A 15th-century inn with a 900-year-old vaulted cellar and rare fresco. The timber-framed and panelled restaurant is run by the Mann family, whose fixed-price menus specialise in seafood. Other delectable dishes include fillet steak Tudor style, loin of English lamb, and English sherry trifle in a tea cup.
Closed Tue, 1st 2 wks Jan & 1st 2 wks Jun
Dinner not served Mon
V 34 seats Lunch £8.50-£12&alc Dinner £15-£19&alc Last lunch 1.45pm Last dinner 9.15pm
Credit Cards 1 2 3 5

✕Landgate Bistro 5-6 Landgate TN31 7LH ☎(0797)222829
The success of this beamed cottage bistro bears evidence to the long-established partnership of chefs Toni Ferguson-Lees and Nick Parkin. Local seafood and game are featured regularly, and popular specialities include Duck Paté, Poached Fillet of Trout with Chervil Sauce and Fillet of Lamb en Croute with Rosemary Sauce; vegetables are particularly well selected and there is a limited range of desserts. Service is friendly and casually attentive.
Closed Sun, Mon, Xmas, 1 wk Jun & 2 wks Oct
Lunch not served

☋ British & French V 34 seats S10% Dinner £13-£18.50alc Last dinner 9.30pm ₱
Credit Cards 1 2 3 5

SAFFRON WALDEN Essex Map **05** TL53

★★**Saffron** 10-18 High St CB10 1AY ☏(0799)22676
Telex no 81653 FAX (0799) 26088
A 16th-century hotel combining old-world charm with modern comforts and providing high standards of cuisine.
21rm(8⇌8⌐)(2fb)1⊟ CTV in all bedrooms ® T S% sB&B£25 sB&B⇌⌐£41 dB&B⇌⌐£55 Continental breakfast ⊟
10P
☋ English & French V ♁ Lunch £13.95&alc Dinner £13.95&alc Last dinner 9.30pm
Credit Cards 1 3

See advertisement on page 575

Entries for rosetted restaurants, red-star and country-house hotels are highlighted by a tinted panel. For a full list of these establishments, consult the Contents page.

ST AGNES Cornwall & Isles of Scilly Map **02** SW75

★★Rose in Vale Country House Rose in Vale, Mithian TR5 0QD
☎(087255)2202
Closed Nov-Feb

Attractive Georgian house with modern extension, set in peaceful valley.

15rm(9⇌6♠)(3fb)1⊞ CTV in all bedrooms ® T
sB&B⇌♠£27.50-£32.50
dB&B⇌♠£50-£55 (incl dinner) ⊟
CTV 20P ⇔ ✲ ⇌(heated) solarium croquet badminton table tennis billiards nc5 yrs
♀ English & Continental ♆ ☑ ⚟ Lunch fr£6.10 Dinner fr£11.50&alc Last dinner 8pm
Credit Cards 1 3

★★Rosemundy House Rosemundy TR5 0UF ☎(087255)2101
Closed 8 Oct-10 Apr & 22 Apr-3 May
Delightful country-house style hotel, parts of which date back to 1780, set in 4 acres of wooded gardens close to the village centre. This is a busy holiday hotel offering exceptional value for money.
44rm(33⇌11♠)(16fb) CTV in all bedrooms ®
sB&B⇌♠£14-£27 dB&B£25-£51 dB&B⇌♠£28-£54
CTV 50P ⇔ ✲ ⇌(heated) badminton games room croquet putting
♆ ☑ ⚟ Dinner £8-£8 Last dinner 8pm

★Lamorna House Chapel Porth Rd, Goonvrea TR5 0NG
☎(087255)2670
Closed mid Oct-Etr
This small holiday hotel, quietly situated on the outskirts of St. Agnes, enjoys splendid panoramic views.
10rm(1fb) ® sB&B£12-£16 dB&B£24-£32
CTV 12P ⇔ ✲
♆ ☑ Bar Lunch £1-£3.50alc Dinner £8.50 Last dinner 7.30pm

★Sunholme Goonvrea Rd TR5 0NW ☎(087255)2318
Closed Nov – Mar
Small family holiday hotel in a rural location offering comfortable bedrooms and well-cooked meals.
11rm(9♠)(5fb) CTV in all bedrooms T ✱ sB&B£14.50-£16
sB&B♠£17-£18.50 dB&B£29-£32 dB&B♠£34-£37.50 ⊟
CTV 20P ✲ ⌂
♆ ☑ ⚟ Bar Lunch £1.20-£2.50 Dinner £8-£10 Last dinner 7.30pm
Credit Cards 1 3 £

S

ST ALBANS Hertfordshire Map **04** TL10

★★★66% Noke Thistle Watford Rd AL2 3DS (2.75m S at junct A405/B4630) (Thistle) ☎(0727)54252 Telex no 893834
FAX (0727) 41906
A comfortable, elegant hotel offering modern, well-equipped bedrooms and pleasant, attentive service. Enterprising French and English cuisine is served in the restaurant.
57⇌♠(4fb)⚟in 5 bedrooms CTV in all bedrooms ® T ✱
sB⇌♠£70-£75 dB⇌♠£80-£85 (room only) ⊟
☾150P ✲ CFA
♀ International ♆ ☑ ⚟ Lunch fr£14.50&alc Dinner fr£17.50&alc Last dinner 10pm
Credit Cards 1 2 3 4 5

★★★63% St Michael's Manor Fishpool St AL3 4RY
☎(0727)64444 Telex no 917647
Closed 27-30 Dec
Located within walking distance of the town centre this hotel has comfortable lounge accommodation and a restaurant with a conservatory-style extension overlooking the gardens. Bedrooms vary in size, but all are well-equipped.
26rm(13⇌9♠)4⊞ CTV in all bedrooms T S%
sB&B⇌♠£45-£70 dB&B⇌♠£60-£90
☾ CTV 80P ⇔ ✲ nc12yrs
♀ English & French V Lunch £14-£16&alc Dinner £16-£17.50&alc Last dinner 9pm
Credit Cards 1 2 3 5

★★★60% Sopwell House Cottonmill Ln, Sopwell AL1 2HQ (Best Western) ☎(0727)64477 Telex no 927823
FAX (0727) 44741
An appealing 18th-century mansion surrounded by several acres of well-kept gardens. Bedrooms have been refurbished to offer most modern conveniencies and the restaurant offers an extensive, though perhaps pricey, à la carte menu complimented by efficient service.
70⇌♠(10fb)22⊞⚟in 12 bedrooms CTV in all bedrooms ® T
✱ sB⇌♠£60-£78 dB⇌♠£80-£90 (room only) ⊟
Lift ☾ 150P ✲ CFA *xmas*
V ♆ ☑ ⚟ Lunch £9-£13.50&alc Dinner £15.50-£17.50&alc Last dinner 10.30pm
Credit Cards 1 2 3 5

ST ANDREWS Fife Map **12** NO51

★★★★72% St Andrews Old Course Hotel Old Station Rd KY16 9SP ☎(0334)74371 Telex no 76280 FAX (0334) 77668
Closed 26-30 Dec
A fine, modern hotel overlooking the famous Old Course providing excellent facilities for the international golfing clientele. Traditional standards of hotel keeping are maintained and there are two comfortable restaurants.
125⇌♠ CTV in all bedrooms T
Lift ☾ ⊞ 150P ✲ ⇌(heated) snooker sauna solarium gymnasium health spa jacuzzi
♀ Scottish & French V ♆ ☑
Credit Cards 1 2 3 4 5

★★★★60% Rusack's Pilmour Links KY16 9JQ (Trusthouse Forte) ☎(0334)74321 FAX (0334) 77896
Occupying a prime position overlooking the 1st and 10th Fairways of the Old Course and the fine beach, the hotel has been totally refurbished to high standard.
50⇌⚟in 5 bedrooms CTV in all bedrooms ® T S%
sB⇌£75-£80 dB⇌£113-£138 (room only) ⊟
Lift ☾ 30P ⇔ sauna solarium *xmas*
V ♆ ☑ ⚟ Lunch £6-£9.25 Dinner £24.50-£32 Last dinner 9.30pm
Credit Cards 1 2 3 4 5

★★★68% Rufflets Country House Strathkinness Low Rd KY16 9TX ☎(0334)72594
Closed 7 Jan-19 Feb
An attractive hotel, situated outside the centre of the town, stands amid splendid, formal gardens. Its ongoing programme of refurbishment has provided comfortable, spacious public areas and well-equipped bedrooms, those in Rose Cottage being particularly charming. Polite staff provide service of a professional standard, especially in the restaurant where meals with a strong Scottish emphasis are served.
18⇌♠Annexe3⇌♠(2fb)1⊞ CTV in all bedrooms ® T ✗ (ex guide dogs) sB&B⇌♠£46-£50 dB&B⇌♠£36-£50 ⊟
☾ 50P 2🚗 (£1) ✲ Putting ⌂ *xmas*
♀ Scottish & French V ♆ ☑ ⚟ Lunch £8-£9.50 Dinner £16.75-£20 Last dinner 10pm
Credit Cards 1 2 3 5

★★★67% **St Andrews Golf** 40 The Scores KY16 9AS (Inter)
☎(0334)72611 FAX (0334) 72188
This comfortable hotel continues to improve under the personal supervision of the proprietor.
23rm(20⇌3↱)(10fb) CTV in all bedrooms ® T
sB&B⇌↱£39.50-£50.50 dB&B⇌↱£69-£81 ⊟
Lift ☾ 6P CFA sauna solarium *xmas*
☋ Scottish & French ♡ ☏ Lunch £9 High tea £7.50 Dinner £16.50&alc Last dinner 9.30pm
Credit Cards 1 2 3 4 5 £

See advertisement on page 577

★★★62% **Scores** 76 The Scores KY16 9BB (Best Western)
☎(0334)72451 Telex 94012061 FAX (0334) 73947
Situated close to the famous golf course, this is a spacious hotel with two bars, a restaurant and coffee shop. Bedrooms vary in size and style.
30rm(29⇌)(1fb) CTV in all bedrooms ® T
sB&B⇌£38.50-£52.50 dB&B⇌£50-£90 ⊟
Lift ☾ 10P ✲ *xmas*
☋ English & French V ♡ ☏ Lunch fr£4.95alc High tea fr£5alc Dinner fr£14.50&alc Last dinner 9.30pm
Credit Cards 1 2 3 4 5

★★**Ardgowan** 2 Playfair Ter KY16 9HX (Consort)
☎(0334)72970
Closed 25 Dec-15 Jan RS Nov-24 Dec & 16 Jan-Apr
Family run hotel offering personal attention and friendly service.
13rm(7⇌4↱)(2fb) CTV in all bedrooms ® sB&B£20-£22.50 sB&B⇌↱£27.50-£35 dB&B£40-£45 dB&B⇌↱£50-£55
CTV ℙ
☋ Scottish & French V Bar Lunch £6.50-£7.50alc Dinner £8.50-£12alc Last dinner 9.30pm
Credit Cards 1 3

S

★★Parklands Hotel & Restaurant Kinburn Castle, Double Dykes Rd KY16 9DS ☎(0334)73620
Set back from the road, this friendly hotel is in a quiet setting. Two dinner menus are available, one at 6.30pm and a gourmet menu for the discerning diner from 7.30pm where the chef/proprietor offers first class cooking using the very best ingredients. Lounge facilities are limited but there is a comfortable cocktail lounge.
15rm(8⇌1♠)(2fb)⊁in 3 bedrooms CTV in all bedrooms ® T ✕ (ex guide dogs) ✱ sB&B£21-£22.50 sB&B⇌♠£31-£33 dB&B£38-£40 dB&B⇌♠£54-£57.50 ⊟
30P ⇎
V ♧ ⊁ Lunch £6.30-£10alc Dinner £12.50&alc Last dinner 8.30pm
Credit Cards 1 3

★★Russell Hotel 26 The Scores KY16 9AS ☎(0334)73447
Closed 25 Dec- 14 Jan
Small family-run hotel with views of the sea.
7rm(1⇌6♠)(1fb) CTV in all bedrooms ® T ✕ (ex guide dogs) dB⇌♠£40-£45 (room only)
CTV ⊭ ⇎
☋ Scottish & French V ♧ ⊻ Lunch £10-£15alc High tea £5-£7.50 Dinner £12.50-£15alc Last dinner 9.30pm
Credit Cards 1 2 3

ST ANNES

See **Lytham St Annes**

ST ASAPH Clwyd Map 06 SJ07

★★★61% Oriel House Upper Denbigh Rd LL17 0LW ☎(0745)582716 FAX (0745) 582716
A popular hotel set in large gardens leading down to the banks of the River Elwy. There are busy function rooms, a restaurant and a lounge bar with an extensive snack bar menu.
19rm(12⇌7♠)(1fb)1⊟ CTV in all bedrooms ® T sB&B⇌♠£30-£36 dB&B⇌♠£48-£56 ⊟
200P ✲ ♩ snooker
☋ English, Chinese & French V ♧ ⊻ Lunch fr£7.50&alc High tea fr£3.05 Dinner £8-£17alc Last dinner 9.45pm
Credit Cards 1 2 3 5 £

★★Plas Elwy Hotel & Restaurant The Roe LL17 0LT (Minotels) ☎(0745)582263 & 582089
Closed 26 Dec-1 Jan
Small, family-run hotel on the edge of town with compact, well-equipped bedrooms, a character bar and restaurant and an informal atmosphere.
7♠ CTV in all bedrooms ® T ✕ (ex guide dogs) sB&B♠£32 dB&B♠£44 ⊟
20P ⇎
V ♧ Lunch £7.25 Dinner £10&alc Last dinner 10pm
Credit Cards 1 2 3 5

ST AUSTELL Cornwall & Isles of Scilly Map 02 SX05

★★★★69% Carlyon Bay Sea Rd, Carlyon Bay PL25 3RD (Brend) ☎Par(072681)2304 Telex no 42551 FAX (072681) 4938
Beautifully situated in extensive grounds overlooking the bay, this constantly improving hotel offers extensive all-weather facilities for families and individuals from attractive walks to a choice of golf courses.
70⇌(10fb) CTV in all bedrooms ® T ✕ (ex guide dogs) sB&B⇌£50-£62 dB&B⇌£96-£142 ⊟
Lift ☾ CTV 100P 2⌂ (£1.75) ⇎ ✲ ⊡(heated) ⌓(heated) ▶18 ℛ (hard) snooker sauna solarium spa bath table tennis putting ♫ ⌂ *xmas*
☋ English & French V ♧ ⊻ Lunch £9.50&alc Dinner £15&alc Last dinner 9pm
Credit Cards 1 2 3 4 5

★★★63% Cliff Head Sea Rd, Carlyon Bay PL25 3RB (2m E off A390) ☎Par(072681)2345
Situated close to the beach this modernised hotel provides comfortable public areas and well-equipped bedrooms.
48rm(30⇌4♠)(10fb) CTV in 40bedrooms ® T ✱ S% sB&B£26.54-£29.32 sB&B⇌♠£29.32-£32.20 dB&B⇌♠£51.16-£56.34 ⊟
☾ CTV 60P 8⌂ ✲ ⌓(heated) ♫ *xmas*
V ♧ ⊻ ⊁ Lunch £5.50-£7.75 High tea £2.50-£3.75 Dinner £9.95-£13.45 Last dinner 9pm
Credit Cards 1 2 3 5 £

★★★63% Porth Avallen Sea Rd PL25 3SG ☎Par(072681)2802 & 2183 FAX (072681) 7097
Closed Xmas & New year
Privately-owned resort hotel in an ideal setting, overlooking Carlyon Bay, offering comfortable accommodation. Sound English cooking is nicely prepared and service is friendly and helpful. Good value for money.
23rm(18⇌1♠)(2fb)2⊟ CTV in all bedrooms ® T ✕ (ex guide dogs) ✱ sB&B⇌♠£33.50-£43.50 dB&B⇌♠£53-£59 ⊟
☾ CTV 50P 2⌂ ✲
☋ English & French V ♧ ⊻ Lunch £6.25-£9.55 High tea fr£1.75 Dinner £10.30-£13.60 Last dinner 8.30pm
Credit Cards 1 2 3 5

★★ Boscundle Manor Tregrehan PL25 3RL (2m E off A390)
☎Par(072 681)3557
Closed mid Oct-mid Jan RS mid Jan-mid Apr
A lovely, eighteenth-century manor house, set in secluded grounds and furnished with many fine antiques, features a well-appointed restaurant with a high standard of cuisine.
9rm(4⇌5♠)Annexe2⇌ CTV in all bedrooms ® T S% sB&B⇌♠£50 dB&B⇌♠£75-£90
15P ⇎ ✲ ⌓(heated) gymnasium croquet practise golf course
☋ International S% Dinner £18 Last dinner 9pm
Credit Cards 1 2 3

★★Clifden 36-39 Aylmer Square PL25 5LJ ☎(0726)73691
Closed 24 Dec-1 Jan
Situated above a shopping precinct close to the town centre, this commercial hotel features an 'all day' restaurant.
15rm(3⇌1♠) CTV in all bedrooms ® T S10% sB&B£20-£22 sB&B⇌♠£25.50-£28 dB&B£33.50-£37 dB&B⇌♠£40-£45
CTV ⊭
V ♧ ⊻ Lunch £4.15-£5.25&alc Dinner £1-£10alc Last dinner 9pm
Credit Cards 1 2 3 5

ST BOSWELLS Borders *Roxburghshire* Map 12 NT63

★★Buccleuch Arms The Green TD6 0EW ☎(0835)22243 Telex no 336587 FAX (0835) 23965
Standing on the edge of an appealing village, the attractive hotel has some very comfortable bedrooms and a tastefully appointed lounge.
19⇌♠(1fb) CTV in all bedrooms ® T ✱ sB&B£30-£40 sB&B⇌♠£32.50-£50 dB&B£50 dB&B⇌♠£60 ⊟
☾ 50P 2⌂ ✲ *xmas*
▶

CLIFF HEAD HOTEL ★★★

Carlyon Bay, Nr. St. Austell, Cornwall PL25 3RB
Telephone: Reception (072) 681 2125/2345

The Hotel faces south and stands in its own extensive grounds of over two acres, of delightful multi-coloured hydrangeas in the centre of the Cornish Riviera, ideally situated for touring Cornwall. Privately owned, it is the aim of both proprietors and staff to ensure that your stay is a pleasant one. Thirty-five en suite bedrooms with colour TV, intercom and direct dial telephone system. Business travellers catered for.

English Tourist Board — West Country Tourist Board MEMBER

ST. ANDREWS GOLF HOTEL

★★★

○ *Elegant Old Hotel with every modern facility*

○ *Our comfortable bedrooms all have bath/shower en suite*

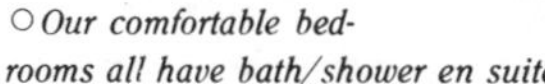

○ *Only 200 yards from the famous "Old Course"*

THE RESTAURANT

Dine in our elegant candlelit restaurant with its superb view over St. Andrews Bay. The very best of fresh local produce complimented by our extensive wine list.

FOR RESERVATIONS TEL: (0334) 72611

St. Andrews Golf Hotel St. Andrews KY16 9AS
Fax (0334) 72188

The Carlyon Bay Hotel AA★★★★

In a world of its own on the Cornish Riviera

The exceptionally mild climate and wealth of firstclass facilities combine to provide the perfect location for your family or golfing holiday. Situated within its own 250 acres of grounds, overlooking this unspoilt bay with its golden beaches, you are assured the highest standards of comfort, cuisine and personal service. Excellent facilities include large indoor and outdoor heated pools, sauna, solarium, spa bath, 2 full size snooker tables, tennis courts, children's play area and amusement room. *FREE GOLF IS AVAILABLE to residents on our 18 hole, 6,400 yard course adjacent to the hotel, with resident professional and clubhouse facilities available.* All bedrooms have private bath, colour TV with video facility, radio and telephone, most having panoramic seaviews. Whether active or relaxing your early and late season break or summer holiday will be complemented by the unrivalled natural splendour of the Cornish Riviera.

For free brochure, tariff, details of Winter, Spring, Early Summer and Autumn Breaks, and child reductions please contact The Manager, The Carlyon Bay Hotel, Nr. St. Austell, Cornwall.

Phone Par (072 681) 2304
Fax: (072 681) 4938

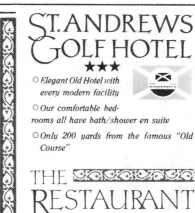

S

☊ International V ♔ ☋ ⁄ Lunch £8-£9 Dinner £11.25-£12.25&alc Last dinner 10pm
Credit Cards [1] [2] [3] [5] £

ST BRELADE

See Jersey **under** Channel Islands

ST CLEARS Dyfed Map **02** SN21

★★Forge Restaurant & Motel SA33 4NA ☎(0994)230300
Closed 25 & 26 Dec
This small, personnally-run motel provides comfortable bedrooms within a small complex well distanced from the A40, together with bars and a separate grill. New bedrooms and a small leisure complex have been finished to a high standard.
Annexe18rm(10⇨8♠)(4fb) CTV in all bedrooms ® T sB&B⇨♠£30 dB&B⇨♠£45
80P ⇼ ✲ ⊡(heated) sauna gymnasium
☊ Mainly grills V ♔ ☋ ⁄ Lunch £3.75-£10alc Dinner £3.75-£10alc Last dinner 9.30pm
Credit Cards [1] [2] [3] £

ST COMBS Grampian *Aberdeenshire* Map **15** NK06

★★Tufted Duck AB4 5YS ☎Inverallochy(03465)2481
Converted and extended, the hotel is in a secluded location close to the beach. The pleasant bedrooms have modern facilities for the businessman and public rooms have been tastefully updated. The à la carte menu offers an interesting range of dishes.
18rm(11⇨7♠)(4fb) CTV in all bedrooms ® T ✳ sB&B⇨♠£25.50-£32.50 dB&B⇨♠£40-£50 ⊟
☾ 50P ✲ ♩
☊ Scottish, French & Italian V ♔ ☋ ⁄ Lunch fr£6.95 High tea £4-£8 Dinner £6.95-£15&alc Last dinner 9.30pm
Credit Cards [1] [2] [3] [5] £

ST DAVID'S Dyfed Map **02** SM72

★★★⚑62% Warpool Court SA62 6BN
☎(0437)720300
Telex no 48390
FAX (0437) 720300

Originally built as St David's Cathedral Choir School in the 1860's, and enjoying spectacular scenery, this country-house hotel looks out over St Bride's Bay from seven acres of Italian gardens. Under new ownership, it offers stylish bedrooms, some containing unique ornamental Victorian tiles, comfortable public rooms and promising food standards.
25rm(16⇨9♠)(3fb) CTV in all bedrooms ® T ✳ sB&B⇨♠£36-£50 dB&B⇨♠£59-£90 ⊟
100P ✲ ⊡(heated) ♐ (hard) sauna gymnasium croquet, pool table, childrens play area *xmas*
☊ English & French V ♔ ☋ Lunch £10.50-£17.50 High tea £3.50-£5.50 Dinner £17.50-£26&alc Last dinner 9.15pm
Credit Cards [1] [2] [3] [4] [5]

★★Old Cross Cross Square SA62 6SP ☎(0437)720387
Closed Nov-Feb
This modernised 18th-century house facing the Market Cross in the Square, and a short walk from the Cathedral, is run by the friendly Lynas family. Bedrooms, though generally small, are well-equipped, the food is good and public areas relaxing.
17rm(14⇨3♠)(5fb) CTV in all bedrooms ® T ✗ (ex guide dogs) sB&B⇨♠£20-£25 dB&B⇨♠£40-£50 ⊟
18P ⇼
☊ English, European & Oriental V ♔ Bar Lunch £3-£5 Dinner fr£10.50&alc Last dinner 8.30pm
Credit Cards [3] £

★★St Non's SA62 6 ☎(0437)720239 FAX (0437) 721839
Named after the mother of the Patron Saint of Wales and a short walk from the Cathedral, this very popular hotel has well-equipped bedrooms and busy bars. Free golf is available just two miles away for residents.
24⇨(5fb) CTV in all bedrooms ® T sB&B⇨£23-£35 dB&B⇨£46-£52 ⊟
60P ♫ *xmas*
☊ International V ♔ ☋ Sunday Lunch £8.50 Dinner £12-£14&alc Last dinner 9pm
Credit Cards [1] [2] [3] £

ST FILLANS Tayside *Perthshire* Map **11** NN62

★★★64% *The Four Seasons Hotel* PH6 2NF ☎(076485)333
Closed Jan & Feb
Delightfully situated at the east end of Loch Earn this hospitable family-run hotel offers modern, well-equipped bedrooms and a choice of small lounges. Sound food is served in the pleasant restaurant overlookimg the loch.
12rm(11⇨1♠)(1fb) CTV in all bedrooms T
25P ⇼
☊ International V ♔ ☋ ⁄ Last dinner 9.30pm
Credit Cards [1] [2] [3]

★★*Drummond Arms* PH6 2NF (Inter) ☎(076485)212
Closed mid Oct-Etr
Four-storey, roadside hotel in an attractive position overlooking the wooded shore of Loch Earn.
26rm(22⇨4♠)(2fb) ®
CTV 40P ✲
♔ ☋
Credit Cards [1] [2] [3] [5]

ST HELENS Merseyside Map **07** SJ59

★★★66% Post House Lodge Ln, Newton-Le-Willows WA12 0JG (Trusthouse Forte) ☎Wigan(0942)717878
Telex no 677672 FAX (0942) 718419
(For full entry see Haydock)

ST HELIER

See Jersey **under** Channel Islands

ST IVES **Cambridgeshire** Map **04** TL37

★★★58% Dolphin Bridge Foot, London Rd PE17 4EP ☎(0480)66966 FAX (0480) 495597
The modern town-centre, purpose-built hotel gives views of the adjacent river and countryside.
10⇨Annexe12⇨(2fb) CTV in all bedrooms ® T sB&B⇨£50-£55 dB&B⇨£60-£65 ⊟
☾ 80P ✲ ♩
☊ English & French V ♔ ☋ Lunch £10.50-£12&alc Dinner £10.50-£12&alc Last dinner 9.30pm
Credit Cards [1] [2] [3] [5]

★★★62% Slepe Hall Ramsey Rd PE17 4RB ☎(0480)63122
FAX (0480) 61175
Closed Xmas Day & Boxing Day
Small, comfortable hotel set back from main road.
13rm(9⇨)(1fb)2⊠ CTV in all bedrooms ® sB&Bfr£40 sB&B⇨fr£52.50 dB&Bfr£54 dB&B⇨fr£65 ⊟
70P 1⌂ ⇼

S

English V Lunch fr£11.95&alc Dinner fr£11.75&alc Last dinner 9.45pm
Credit Cards 1 2 3 5

★★St Ives Motel London Rd PE17 4EX ☎(0480)63857
RS 25 & 26 Dec
Easily located between the A604 and St. Ives this former roadside bungalow has been extended to create a restaurant and bar with two blocks of motel bedrooms at the rear. Popular with businessmen, and locals for the value-for-money meals.
16(2fb) CTV in all bedrooms ® T sB&B£28.50-£39.50 dB&B£46-£55
80P
English & French V Lunch fr£9.50&alc Dinner fr£9.50&alc Last dinner 9.45pm
Credit Cards 1 2 3 5 £

★*Pike & Eel* Overcote Ln, Needingworth PE17 3TW (3m E off A1123) ☎(0480)63336
Closed Xmas Night
Dating from the 16th century, this popular inn enjoys a very pleasant location beside the Great Ouse.
9rm(3)(4fb) CTV in all bedrooms
CTV 100P
English & French V
Credit Cards 1 2 3 4

ST IVES Cornwall & Isles of Scilly Map **02** SW54

★★★58% Carbis Bay Carbis Bay TR26 2NP
☎Penzance(0736)795311
Closed Nov – Mar
A large detatched hotel in a prominent position overlooking its own private beach and the Bay. Recently upgraded bedrooms offer modern standards of comfort, with friendly service from local staff.
32rm(16 12)(9fb)1 CTV in all bedrooms ® T
sB&B£28-£38 sB&B£31-£34 dB&B£50-£60 dB&B£53-£63
CTV 200P 6 (heated) snooker Hotel has own beach
English & Continental Lunch £5-£7
Credit Cards 1 2 3 5 £

See advertisement on page 581

★★★61% Chy-an-Drea The Terrace TR26 2BP (Consort)
☎Penzance(0736)795076
Closed Nov – Feb
A popular, well-established hotel offering a homely atmosphere and prompt, friendly service. Recent upgrading includes a very pleasant foyer lounge and a small leisure complex.
33rm(22 11)(4fb) CTV in all bedrooms ® T
sB&B£24-£31 dB&B£48-£62
5P 20 jacuzzi fitness equipment nc5yrs
English & French Bar Lunch £1.80-£3alc Dinner £11.50 Last dinner 8.30pm
Credit Cards 1 2 3 5

★★★64% Garrack Higher Ayr TR26 3AA
☎Penzance(0736)796199 FAX (0736) 798955
This secluded family owned and run hotel, which enjoys panoramic views over St. Ives Bay, has a country house atmosphere with cosy public rooms and friendly service. The well-equipped bedrooms range from the modern Terrace rooms to the more intimate accommodation within the main house. The small restaurant promotes well-balanced menus and commendable cooking standards.
19rm(14 2)Annexe2rm(3fb) CTV in all bedrooms T
sB&B£23-£26 sB&B£25-£33.50 dB&B£46-£52 dB&B£50-£67
CTV 30P (heated) sauna solarium *xmas*

♀ English & French ✪ ♨ Lunch £5.50-£11alc Dinner £12&alc Last dinner 8.30pm
Credit Cards 1 2 3 4 5

★★★ 67% Porthminster The Terrace TR26 2BN (Best Western) ☎Penzance(0736)795221 FAX (0736) 797043
Traditional hotel in a commanding position overlooking St Ives Bay.
53rm(30⇌23↱)(7fb) CTV in all bedrooms ® T sB&B⇌↱£33-£38 dB&B⇌↱£66-£76 ⊟
Lift ☾ CTV 32P 9⌂ ✽ ⊡(heated) ⌓(heated) sauna solarium gymnasium ♘ *xmas*
♀ English & French ✪ Lunch £11.25-£17.50alc Dinner £11.25&alc Last dinner 8.30pm
Credit Cards 1 2 3 4 5 £

★★ *Boskerris* Boskerris Rd, Carbis Bay TR26 2NQ ☎Penzance(0736)795295
Closed mid Oct-Etr
This well-appointed country-house-style hotel enjoys glorious coastal views. Meals are carefully cooked and well balanced.
19rm(15⇌)(4fb)
CTV 20P ⊞ ✽ ⌓(heated) putting, games room
♀ English & French V ✪ ♨ Last dinner 8pm
Credit Cards 3 5

★★ *Chy-an-Albany* Albany Ter TR26 2BS ☎Penzance(0736)796759
Closed 1-22 Dec & 28 Dec-Feb
Family-holiday hotel in elevated position near the beach and the town centre.
36rm(5⇌9↱)(13fb) CTV in all bedrooms ®
☾ 36P ✽ ♫
✪ ♨ Last dinner 7.45pm
Credit Cards 1 2 3 5

★★Chy-an-Dour Trelyon Av TR26 2AD ☎Penzance(0736)796436
Friendly, personally-run holiday hotel in a peaceful setting with superb views of St Ives and the bay. Public rooms are comfortable and the bedrooms, though compact, are soundly equipped.
23rm(1⇌22↱)(2fb) CTV in all bedrooms ® ✗ (ex guide dogs) dB&B⇌↱£60-£75 (incl dinner) ⊟
Lift CTV 23P ✽ ♫ *xmas*
♀ English & Continental V ✪ ⚟
Credit Cards 1 3

★★ *Cornwallis* Headland Rd, Carbis Bay TR26 2NR ☎Penzance(0736)795294 Telex no 946240
Closed Jan & Feb
In a spectacular position overlooking St Ives Bay, this is a personally-run hotel with traditional bedrooms. Golfing, bowling and birdwatching activity holidays out of main season.
12rm(5⇌3↱)Annexe10⇌(13fb) CTV in 12bedrooms ® T ✗
29P ✽ sauna solarium gymnasium
✪ ♨
Credit Cards 1 2 3 5

★★ *Pedn-Olva* The Warren TR26 2EA ☎Penzance(0736)796222
Pearched right at the water's edge on a rocky promontory with unrestricted views over the bay and harbour. This is a small, personally-managed hotel with a friendly atmosphere, comfortable public rooms, cosy bedrooms, a sun terrace and outdoor pool. The small grill room is a dining alternative to the main restaurant.
20⇌↱Annexe4rm(5fb) CTV in all bedrooms ® T
☾ ℙ ⌓(heated) ♫
♀ English & French V ✪ ♨
Credit Cards 1 3

Book as early as possible for busy holiday periods.

★★St Uny Carbis Bay TR26 2NQ ☎Penzance(0736)795011
Closed early Oct-Etr
Castle-style, comfortable family hotel, set in its own grounds and gardens close to the beach.
30rm(14⇌5↱)(4fb)1⊟ ✗ ✱ sB&B£22-£28 sB&B⇌↱£27-£33 dB&B£44-£56 dB&B⇌↱£54-£66 (incl dinner) ⊟
CTV 28P 4⌂ ✽ snooker table tennis, putting nc5 yrs
♀ English V ✪ ♨ ⚟ Dinner £14.50 Last dinner 8pm
Credit Cards 1 3

★Dunmar Pednolver Ter TR26 2EL ☎Penzance(0736)796117
Small, family hotel overlooking the town and the bay.
17rm(3⇌7↱)(7fb) CTV in all bedrooms ® ✱
sB&B£11.30-£17.75 sB&B⇌↱£13.30-£17.75
dB&B£22.60-£31.50 dB&B⇌↱£26.60-£35.50 ⊟
CTV 20P
✪ ♨ ⚟
Credit Cards 1 3

★ *Trecarrell* Carthew Ter TR26 1EB ☎Penzance(0736)795707
Closed Jan & Feb RS Mar
Personally managed small hotel in a quiet position above the town.
16rm(2⇌7↱)(2fb) TV in 1bedroom ® ✗ (ex guide dogs)
CTV 15P 1⌂ ♘
V ✪ ♨ ⚟ Last high tea 4pm
Credit Cards 1 3

ST LAWRENCE

See **Wight, Isle of**

ST LAWRENCE

See **Jersey, under Channel Islands**

ST LEONARDS Dorset Map 04 SZ19

★★★ 72% St Leonards Hotel BH24 2NP (Lansbury) ☎(0425)471220 Telex no 418215 FAX (0425) 480274
A warm and friendly atmosphere prevails at this hotel. Public areas are limited but the bright, relaxing restaurant serves well-prepared dishes, and there are some exceptionally good bedrooms.
34⇌↱(3fb)1⊟⚟in 5 bedrooms CTV in 29bedrooms ® T ✗
sB&B⇌↱£30-£55 dB&B⇌↱£60-£65 ⊟
☾ 150P ✽ sauna gymnasium
♀ European V ✪ ♨ Lunch fr£8.50 Dinner fr£12.25 Last dinner 10.30pm
Credit Cards 1 2 3 5

ST LEONARDS-ON-SEA

See **Hastings & St Leonards**

ST MARGARET'S HOPE

See **Orkney**

ST MARTIN

See **Guernsey, under Channel Islands**

ST MARY CHURCH

See **Torquay**

ST MARY'S

See **Scilly, Isles of**

ST MARY'S LOCH Borders *Selkirkshire* Map 11 NT22

★ *Rodono* TD7 5LH ☎Cappercleuch(0750)42232
Sandstone shooting lodge set on hillside overlooking loch and Borders hill country.
11rm(2fb) ®
CTV 15P ✽ ⌡
✪ ♨ Last dinner 7.30pm

S

Stay awhile and enjoy our style !

In or out of season you can enjoy our full comfort, superb cuisine and exceptional location. We offer sub-tropical gardens, direct access to the beach and horizon clear sea views, 50 en-suite bedrooms, passenger lift, indoor leisure pool complex, outdoor heated pool (June – Sept), direct dial telephones, 4 channel TV with video and a level of service that is second to none. Short breaks are available out of season.

St. Ives, Cornwall
Tel: (0736) 795221

ST IVES, CORNWALL ★★★
Tel: 0736 796199
Proprietors The Kilby Family

Family owned and managed country house hotel of 21 rooms, with indoor swim-/spa-pool, sauna and solarium, standing in secluded grounds, 10 minutes from town centre, overlooking beach and 30 miles of coastal views. Reputation for good food. Recommended by major guides. Open all year. Ample parking.

CARBIS BAY, ST IVES, CORNWALL TR26 2NP
Telephone 0736-795311

Ideally situated by our own beach. Beautiful views across St Ives Bay. 28 rooms, most with private bathroom, all with Colour Television, radio, intercom and baby listening service.
Holiday flats also available.
Excellent English and French cuisine.
Renowned for our superb selection of wines — definitely the hotel for lovers of fine wines. Heated swimming pool, sheltered sunbathing area.
Good centre for walking, riding, surfing and sight seeing.
One mile from West Cornwall Golf Club.

Open Easter to November.
Special terms for early and late season bookings.
Please write or phone for our colour brochure.
Resident Proprietor Mr M W Baker.

ST MAWES Cornwall & Isles of Scilly Map **02** SW83

★★★50% **Idle Rocks** Tredenhan Rd TR2 5AN (Inter) ☎(0326)270771
Closed Mid Nov-Mar
Family-owned hotel situated on the harbour-side with pleasant views from the public rooms.
15rm(13⇨2↑)Annexe9⇨(5fb) CTV in all bedrooms ® sB&B⇨↑£40 dB&B⇨↑£70-£80 ⊟
P̸ ⊕
⊗ English & Continental V ✿ ⊒ Lunch fr£8 High tea fr£2.75 Dinner £7.50-£13.95&alc Last dinner 9pm
Credit Cards [1] [2] [3] [5] £

★★*Green Lantern* Marine Pde TR2 5DW ☎(0326)270502
Closed mid Dec-mid Feb
This hotel is in a central position on the sea front with views of the harbour.
8rm(4⇨4↑) CTV in 4bedrooms ® ✖
CTV P̸ ⊕ nc12yrs
⊗ English & Continental
Credit Cards [1] [2] [3] [5]

★★**Rising Sun** TR2 5DJ ☎(0326)270233
A delightful little harbourside hotel has recently undergone upgrading to provide comfortable accommodation in pretty bedrooms, some of which are very compact, but all are individually appointed and well equipped. Facilities also include a smart new bar overlooking the water, a sun terrace and a restaurant which offers excellent meals based on fresh produce, presented in a variety of interesting styles and attentively served by willing staff.
12rm(9⇨)⊁in all bedrooms CTV in all bedrooms ® T sB&B£30 sB&B⇨£35 dB&B£60 dB&B⇨£70 ⊟
6P ⊕ nc10 yrs
⊗ English, French & Italian ✿ ⊒ Lunch £8.50 High tea £2 Dinner £16 Last dinner 9pm
Credit Cards [1] [2] [3]

★★**St Mawes** The Seafront TR2 5DW ☎(0326)270266
Closed Dec & Jan
7rm(5⇨) CTV in all bedrooms ® ✳ S10% dB&B£66 dB&B⇨£72-£78 (incl dinner) ⊟
P̸ ⊕ nc5yrs
⊗ English & French V ✿ Lunch £8.50&alc Dinner £11.50&alc Last dinner 8.15pm
Credit Cards [1] [3]

ST MAWGAN Cornwall & Isles of Scilly Map **02** SW86

★★**Dalswinton** TR8 4EZ ☎(0637)860385
A fine Victorian house, overlooking this charming village from a commanding position, has been carefully converted into an hotel of character, with a variety of small public rooms and comfortable, well equipped bedrooms. The hotel also boasts a spacious, well-tended garden and a heated outdoor swimming pool which is available for guests' use during the warmer months.
9rm(4⇨5↑)(4fb) CTV in all bedrooms ® ✳ sB&B⇨↑£21.70-£27.45 dB&B⇨↑£47.40-£58.90 (incl dinner) ⊟
CTV 15P ⊕ ✿ ⇒(heated) ⌂ *xmas*
⊗ English & Continental ✿ ⊒ ⊁ Lunch £5.25 High tea £1.85-£2.85 Dinner £7&alc Last dinner 9pm
Credit Cards [1] [3]

See advertisement under NEWQUAY

ST MELLION Cornwall & Isles of Scilly Map **02** SX36

★★★62% **St Mellion** PL12 6SD ☎Liskeard(0579)50101 FAX (0579) 50116
Closed Xmas RS 23-27 Dec
Modern hotel with excellent leisure facilities including a golf course and sports centre. Bedrooms are in a seperate block and there is a smart lounge bar and formal restaurant.
Annexe24⇨↑ CTV in all bedrooms ® T ✖ sB&B⇨↑fr£53 dB&B⇨↑fr£106 ⊟
☾ CTV 500P ⊕ ✿ ⊡(heated) ▶ 18 ℘ (hard) squash snooker sauna solarium gymnasium badminton table tennis keep fit
⊗ English & Continental V ✿ ⊒ Lunch £8-£8.75 Dinner £16.25 Last dinner 9.15pm
Credit Cards [1] [2] [3] [5]

ST PETER

See **Jersey, under Channel Islands**

ST PETER PORT

See **Guernsey, under Channel Islands**

ST SAVIOUR

See **Jersey, under Channel Islands**

ST WENN Cornwall & Isles of Scilly Map **02** SW69

★ *Wenn Manor*
☎St Austell(0726)890240

Standing on the outskirts of this tiny village, a former Georgian vicarage offers comfortable accommodation with well-equipped bedrooms and a good range of public areas which includes a choice of lounges.
8rm(6⇨1↑)(4fb) ®
CTV 20P 1⌂ ⊕ ✿ ⇒(heated), putting, croquet ⌂
✿ ⊒
Credit Cards [1] [3]

SALCOMBE Devon Map **03** SX73

★★★69% **Bolt Head** TQ8 8LL (Best Western) ☎(054884)3751
Closed 12 Nov-16 Mar
Standing adjacent to National Trust property on the headland 140ft above sea-level, and enjoying outstanding sea views over Salcombe estuary, this personally-owned Swiss-chalet-style hotel has been considerably upgraded over recent years to offer good-quality accommodation. Bright, spotlessly clean, modern bedrooms are furnished in attractive pine and well equipped, whilst comfortable public areas and lounges are richly appointed. Other features available here include private moorings, commendable cuisine based on quality produce, and high standards of service.
28⇨↑(6fb) CTV in all bedrooms ® T sB&B⇨↑£48-£62 dB&B⇨↑£96-£124 (incl dinner) ⊟
30P ⊕ ✿ ⇒(heated) ⌂
⊗ English & French V ✿ ⊒ Lunch £5.50-£10alc High tea £4-£8alc Dinner £18.50-£31 Last dinner 9pm
Credit Cards [1] [2] [3] [5] £

★★★71% **Soar Mill Cove** Soar Mill Cove, Malborough TQ7 3DS (3m W of town off A381 at Malborough) ☎Kingsbridge(0548)561566 FAX (0548) 561223
Closed 29 Dec-11 Feb
Situated 300 yards from the pretty cove of Soar Mill, this hotel has been modernised and extended by the owners Norma and Keith Makepeace to provide high standards of comfort coupled with attentive, friendly service. Bedrooms are spacious and well-equipped with sun patios, and public areas are tastfully decorated. The restaurant offers good quality dishes using local produce including wild mushrooms and lobster.

14➪(2fb) CTV in all bedrooms ® T sB&B➪£48-£60 dB&B➪£96-£120 ⛿
30P 🚗 ✲ ⊡(heated) ⛼ ℘ (grass) *xmas*
☋ International ♆ ☕ Last high tea 5pm
Credit Cards [1] [3]

★★★56% ***South Sands*** TQ8 8LL ☎(054884)3741
Popular holiday hotel with good direct access to the beach. Facilities include an indoor swimming pool and a seasonal beach restaurant.
29➪ CTV in all bedrooms ® T
45P 🚗 ⊡(heated) sauna solarium sailboarding sailing ♫
☋ International V ♆ ☕ Last dinner 9.30pm
Credit Cards [1] [2] [3] [5]

★★★77% **Tides Reach** South Sands TQ8 8LJ ☎(054884)3466
Closed Dec-Feb
Perched right on the water's edge, with glorious views of the estuary and coastline, this well-established hotel maintains its high standards. Recent improvements have invested bedrooms with a degree of luxury, as new furnishings and pastel décor bring them up to the standard of the balconied bed-sitting rooms installed a year ago. Richly furnished lounges with fresh-flower arrangements complement a brightly appointed restaurant serving generous portions of fine food with an emphasis on fresh fish. An indoor leisure complex with health and beauty spa completes a good range of facilities, all well served by a dedicated management and staff.
42rm(39➪3↱)(3fb) CTV in all bedrooms T ✳
sB&B➪↱£39-£65.50 dB&B➪↱£78-£152 (incl dinner) ⛿
Lift ☾ 100P 🚗 ✲ ⊡(heated) squash snooker sauna solarium gymnasium windsurfing nc8yrs
☋ English & Continental V ♆ ☕ Bar Lunch fr£1.50&alc Dinner fr£19.25&alc Last dinner 10pm
Credit Cards [1] [2] [3] [5]

S

★★**Grafton Towers** Moult Rd, South Sands TQ8 8LG (Exec Hotel) ☎(054884)2882
Closed Nov-Mar
Creeper-clad Victorian house, in a fine elevated position overlooking the bay, providing friendly services, comfortable public areas and improving bedrooms.
14rm(9⇌3♠) CTV in 12bedrooms ® sB&B£24-£32 sB&B⇌♠£24-£32 dB&B£48-£52 dB&B⇌♠£52-£62 ⊟
12P ⚘ ❋
V Dinner £12.50-£13.50 Last dinner 8pm
Credit Cards 1 3

★**Charborough House** Devon Rd TQ8 8HB ☎(054884)2260
Closed Oct-Mar
Perched only 100 yards from Salcombe's picturesque harbour this personally-run hotel provides friendly service, good home cooking and well-equipped bedrooms.
9rm(1⇌6♠)(2fb) CTV in all bedrooms ® ✗ sB&B£36-£48 sB&B⇌♠£38-£50 dB&B£56-£76 dB&B⇌♠£60-£80 (incl dinner)
10P
English & Continental Bar Lunch £7.50-£9alc Dinner £11-£14.50 Last dinner 8pm
Credit Cards 1 3

★**Knowle** Onslow Rd TQ8 8HY ☎(054884)2846
Closed Nov-Feb
Small, personally-run hotel in an elevated position with modest accommodation and public rooms of character.
9rm(1⇌5♠)Annexe6rm(1⇌1♠)(3fb) CTV in all bedrooms ® sB&B£19.50-£27.50 sB&B⇌♠£21.80-£28.75 dB&B£39-£55 dB&B⇌♠£43.60-£57.50 ⊟
CTV 30P ⚘ ❋
English & Continental V S% High tea £2.50 Dinner £11.50 Last dinner 7.45pm
Credit Cards 1 3

★**Sunny Cliff** Cliff Rd TQ8 8JU ☎(054884)2207
RS Nov-Mar
Small, friendly holiday hotel on a clifftop location, with grounds sloping down to the water's edge. There are fine estuary views.
14rm(2⇌)Annexe4⇌(5fb) ✱ sB&B£20-£23 sB&B⇌£23-£26 dB&B£40-£46 dB&B⇌£46-£52 ⊟
CTV 14P 1🚗 ❋ ⛆(heated) ✓
English & French Bar Lunch £1.10-£3.75 High tea £2-£5 Dinner £9.50 Last dinner 8pm
Credit Cards 1 3

★**Woodgrange Hotel** Devon Rd TQ8 8HJ (Minotels) ☎(054884)2439 & 2006
Closed Nov-Etr
10rm(7⇌3♠)(1fb) CTV in all bedrooms ® T
sB&B⇌♠£18-£21 dB&B⇌♠£36-£42 ⊟
12P ⚘
Bar Lunch 50p-£5 Dinner £9.50-£12 Last dinner 7.30pm
Credit Cards 1 2 3 5 £

S

SALFORD Greater Manchester Map **07** SJ89

See also **Manchester**

★**Beaucliffe** 254 Eccles Old Rd, Pendleton M6 8ES ☎061-789 5092 FAX 061-787 7739
Closed 25 Dec
Pleasantly furnished hotel with resident proprietor.
21rm(2⇌15♠)(2fb) CTV in 17bedrooms ® ✗ sB&B£18-£25 sB&B⇌♠£20-£35 dB&B£25-£37 dB&B⇌♠£35-£47 ⊟
CTV 25P ⚘
European V Bar Lunch fr£3.25 Dinner fr£8 Last dinner 8.45pm
Credit Cards 1 2 3 5

★**Inn of Good Hope** 226 Eccles Old Rd M6 8AG (Berni/Chef & Brewer) ☎061-707 6178
Situated on the A576, close to its junction with the M602, and almost opposite Hope hospital, this lively public house offers well appointed bedrooms and a small dining room.
8rm(6⇌2♠) CTV in all bedrooms ® T ✗ (ex guide dogs) sB&B⇌♠fr£38 dB&B⇌♠fr£48 ⊟
50P ⚘
V Lunch £8 Dinner £9 Last dinner 9.30pm
Credit Cards 1 2 3 5

SALISBURY Wiltshire Map **04** SU12

★★★69% **Red Lion** Milford St SP1 2AN (Best Western) ☎(0722)23334 Telex no 477674 FAX (0722) 25756
Former coaching inn dating from 1320 containing many items of historic interest.
57rm(56⇌1♠)(4fb)3⊠ CTV in all bedrooms ® T ✗ (ex guide dogs) ✱ sB&B⇌♠£50-£55 dB&B⇌♠£70-£75 ⊟
Lift ☾ 8P 10🚗 CFA *xmas*
English & French V Lunch £10-£15alc Dinner £11.95-£13 Last dinner 9.00pm
Credit Cards 1 2 3 5

★★★58% **Rose & Crown** Harnham Road, Harnham SP2 8JQ (Queens Moat) ☎(0722)27908 Telex no 47224 FAX (0722) 339816
An historic, characterful inn attractively situated on the banks of the River Avon. Accommodation features exposed oak beams, and is well-equipped, although compact and modest in style. Staff are friendly and menus extensive.
28⇌♠(6fb)3⊠ CTV in all bedrooms ® T S% sB&B⇌♠£60.50-£65.50 dB&B⇌♠£92.50-£98.50 ⊟
☾ 40P ❋ CFA *xmas*
English & French V Lunch £8.50-£10.50&alc Dinner £10.25-£11.50&alc Last dinner 9.30pm
Credit Cards 1 2 3 5 £

See advertisement on page 587

★★★63% **The White Hart** St John St SP1 2SD (Trusthouse Forte) ☎(0722)27476 FAX (0722) 412761
The comfortably refurbished foyer lounge of this hotel leads to the Wavells bar, where open fires enhance traditional décor. the Chequers Restaurant, offering pleasant views across the courtyard and garden, serves a varied cuisine from table d'hôte and à la carte menus.
68⇌(3fb)⅟in 8 bedrooms CTV in all bedrooms ® T ✱ sB⇌fr£70 dB⇌fr£88 (room only) ⊟
☾ 85P *xmas*
V Lunch fr£9.25&alc Dinner fr£13.95&alc Last dinner 9.45pm
Credit Cards 1 2 3 4 5

★★***Cathedral*** Milford St SP1 2AJ ☎(0722)20144
Terraced hotel in the middle of town amidst shops and many other attractions.
30rm(15⇌4♠)(3fb)1⊠ CTV in all bedrooms ® T ✗ (ex guide dogs)
Lift ☾
English & French V Last dinner 9pm
Credit Cards 1 3

★★**County** Bridge St SP1 2ND (Berni/Chef & Brewer) ☎(0722)20229
Conveniently central, with private parking, the hotel stands on the banks of the River Severn. It offers a pleasant bar and restaurant, together with very well furnished, comfortable bedrooms and all modern facilities.
31rm(23⇌8♠)(3fb) CTV in all bedrooms ® T ✗ (ex guide dogs) sB&B⇌♠fr£39.50 dB&B⇌♠fr£58.50 ⊟
☾ 31P
Mainly grills Lunch £8 Dinner £9 Last dinner 10pm
Credit Cards 1 2 3 5

S

★★ ***Trafalgar Hotel*** 33 Milford St SP1 2AP ☎(0722)338686
Originally a pick-up point for the Southampton stagecoach, this renovated hotel dates back to the 15th century, though it was extended in the 17th. Bedrooms are tastefully decorated, the restaurant offers interesting meals and good-quality snacks are served in the comfortable bar-lounge.
16⇌ CTV in all bedrooms **T** ✖ (ex guide dogs)
☾ P̸
French **V**
Credit Cards 1 2 3 5

★**King's Arms** 9-11 St John's St SP1 2SP (Berni/Chef & Brewer) ☎(0722)27629
This recently refurbished hotel provides accommodation in well furnished and equipped bedrooms. The character dining room offers a good choice of traditional fare on table d'hôte and à la carte menus, and there are two bars. A friendly atmosphere and good service will do much to make your stay a pleasant one.
12rm(8⇌4↱)Annexe3⇌(1fb)2 CTV in all bedrooms ® **T** ✖ (ex guide dogs) sB&B⇌↱fr£37.50 dB&B⇌↱fr£54.50
V Lunch £8 Dinner £9 Last dinner 10pm
Credit Cards 1 2 3 5

SALTASH Cornwall & Isles of Scilly Map **02** SX45

★**Holland Inn** Hatt PL12 6PJ (Toby) ☎Plymouth(0752)844044
Situated three miles west of Saltash, on the A388, this busy inn provides accommodation in separate chalet bedrooms.
Annexe30⇌↱ in 10 bedrooms CTV in all bedrooms ® **T** ✻ sB&B⇌↱£23.50-£28.50 dB&B⇌↱£28.50-£38.50
250P pool table & skittles ♫
Mainly grills **V** Lunch fr£6.45 Dinner fr£6.45 Last dinner 10pm
Credit Cards 1 2 3 5

Granada Lodge Callington Rd, Carkeel PL12 6LF (Granada) ☎Plymouth(0752)848408 FAX (0752) 848346
31↱(14fb) in 5 bedrooms CTV in all bedrooms ® ✖ (ex guide dogs) S% sB↱£24.50 dB↱£27.50 (room only)
70P
V
Credit Cards 1 2 3 5

SAMPFORD PEVERELL Devon Map **03** ST01

★ ***Green Headland*** EX16 7BJ ☎Tiverton(0884)820255
Conveniently situated just off the M5 at junction 27, its friendly atmosphere popular with tourists and businessmen alike. The well-maintained, family-run hotel is pleasantly set in attractive gardens.
7rm(3fb) CTV in all bedrooms ®
100P ✿ ♫
V Credit Cards 1 3

See advertisement under TIVERTON

TraveLodge Sampford Peverell Service Area EX16 7HD (SE junc 27, M25) (Trusthouse Forte) ☎Tiverton(0884)821087
40⇌↱(40fb) CTV in all bedrooms ® sB⇌↱£21.50 dB⇌↱£27 (room only)
40P
Mainly grills
Credit Cards 1 2 3

SANDBACH Cheshire Map **07** SJ76

★★★65% **Chimney House** Congleton Rd CW11 0ST (Lansbury) ☎Crewe(0270)764141 Telex no 367323 FAX (0270) 768916
Distinguished by its Tudor façade, the hotel is set in spacious grounds on the A534 not far from junction 17 of the M6. Comfortable bedrooms are exceptionally well appointed, being equipped with every modern amenity; and versatile conference facilities are available.
50⇌(2fb) CTV in all bedrooms ® **T** sB&B⇌fr£60 dB&B⇌fr£70
☾ 110P ✿ sauna solarium
English & French **V** Lunch fr£7.50&alc Dinner fr£11&alc Last dinner 10pm
Credit Cards 1 2 3 5

★★★62% **Saxon Cross Motor Hotel** Holmes Chapel Rd CW11 9SE (M6 Junc 17) ☎Crewe(0270)763281 Telex no 367169 P HOTEL G FAX (0270) 768723
The low rise buildings of this motor hotel give little indication of the tasteful standards which can be found here following recent refurbishment. Cars can be parked outside bedrooms. Situated just off junction 17 of the M6.
52⇌↱(13fb) in 5 bedrooms CTV in all bedrooms ® **T** ✻ sB&B⇌↱£30-£52 dB&B⇌↱£39-£62
☾ 200P ✿ CFA
English & French **V** Lunch fr£7.95&alc High tea fr£3.50 Dinner fr£11.95&alc Last dinner 9.30pm
Credit Cards 1 2 3 5 £

★★ ***Old Hall*** Newcastle Rd CW11 0AL (Minotels) ☎Crewe(0270)761221
This delightful building dating from the 17th century contains much of architectural interest including Jacobean fireplaces and panelling.
12rm(7⇌5↱)(1fb) CTV in all bedrooms **T**
50P
English & Continental **V** Last dinner 10pm
Credit Cards 1 2 3 5

SANDBANKS

See Poole

SANDIACRE Derbyshire Map **08** SK43

See also Long Eaton

★★★52% **Post House** Bostocks Ln NG10 5NJ (N of M1 junc 25) (Trusthouse Forte) ☎(0602)397800 Telex no 377378 FAX (0602) 490469
Modern, purpose built hotel, at junction 25 of the M1, with a restaurant and a coffee shop which serves snacks and grills throughout the day.
107⇌(20fb) in 10 bedrooms CTV in all bedrooms ® ✻ sB⇌£67 dB⇌£78 (room only)
☾ 180P ✿ CFA *xmas*
English & French **V** Lunch fr£8.95&alc Dinner £13.50-£17.75&alc Last dinner 9.45pm
Credit Cards 1 2 3 4 5

SANDIWAY Cheshire Map **07** SJ56

★★★ 75% ***Nunsmere Hall Country House***
Tarporley Rd CW8 2ES
☎Northwich(0606)889100
A beautifully-converted late-Victorian mansion peacefully situated on a peninsula in 10 acres of wooded grounds. Bedrooms and bathrooms are individually and sumptuously furnished and decorated – most have fine views over the lawns and garden. The cuisine is especially recommended, with three menus to choose from.
15⇌1 CTV in all bedrooms ® **T**
Lift ☾ CTV 30P ✿
V Last dinner 9.30pm
Credit Cards 1 2 3 5

SANDOWN

See **Wight, Isle of**

SANQUHAR Dumfries & Galloway *Dumfriesshire*
Map **11** NS70

★★**Mennockfoot Lodge** Mennock DG4 6HS
☎(0659)50382 & 50477
This small cottage hotel enjoys a tranquil position beside the Mennock Water where it joins the River Nith, just south of the town. The majority of the bedrooms are contained in a simple cedarwood annexe behind the main building. There is also a dining room and bar which have recently been redecorated.
1rmAnnexe8rm(4⇌4♪)(1fb) CTV in all bedrooms ® T sB&B⇌♪fr£22 dB&B⇌♪fr£36
CTV 25P ✲
♀ British & Continental V ♈ ☕ Lunch £5-£11alc High tea £5.50-£11alc Dinner £9-£14alc Last dinner 8.30pm
Credit Cards 1 3

★**Nithsdale** 1-7 High St DG4 6DJ ☎(0659)50506
Improvements continue at a small hotel which now boasts attractively refurbished public areas; bedrooms, though fairly compact, are clean and freshly decorated.
6rm(1♪)(2fb) CTV in all bedrooms ® ✱ sB&B£15-£18 dB&B£30 dB&B♪£30
2P ✲ bowling ♫ *xmas*
♀ Mainly grills ♈ ☕ Lunch £9.50 High tea fr£5 Dinner fr£9.50&alc Last dinner 9.30pm

See advertisement on page 589

SARN PARK MOTORWAY SERVICE AREA (M4) Mid Glamorgan Map **03** SS98

TraveLodge CF32 9RW (junction 36, M4) (Trusthouse Forte)
Bridgend(0656)59218
Annexe40(40fb) CTV in all bedrooms ® sB£21.50 dB£27 (room only)
40P
Mainly grills
Credit Cards 1 2 3

SAUNDERSFOOT Dyfed Map **02** SN10

★★★ **61% St Brides** St Brides Hill SA69 9NH (Inter)
(0834)812304 Telex no 48350 FAX (0834) 813303
Closed 1-14 Jan
Standing above the harbour with superb views from the restaurant and many of the bedrooms, this is a comfortable, family-run hotel.
45rm(34 11)(4fb)1 CTV in all bedrooms ® T sB&B£48-£65 dB&B£74-£100
70P CFA (heated) sauna sailing *xmas*
English & French V Lunch £6.50-£10.50alc Dinner £13.95-£17.95&alc Last dinner 9.15pm
Credit Cards 1 2 3 5 £

★★ **Glen Beach** Swallow Tree Woods SA69 9DE (0834)813430
Small, personally run family hotel, set in woodlands with access to beach.
13rm(4 9)(3fb)1 CTV in all bedrooms ® T sB&B£19-£30 dB&B£38-£60
35P *xmas*
English & French V Lunch £8.75&alc
Credit Cards 1 2 3 £

★★ **Rhodewood House** St Brides Hill SA69 9NU (0834)812200
This hotel is situated in a quiet road close to the harbour and managed by the owner; it features well-equipped bedrooms, award-winning gardens and a good range of public rooms including an attractive two-tier Victorian restaurant.
34rm(25 9)(6fb) in 6 bedrooms CTV in all bedrooms ® T sB&B£21-£32 dB&B£38-£60
70P snooker solarium *xmas*
V Lunch £5-£7 Dinner £7-£8.25 Last dinner 9.30pm
Credit Cards 1 2 3 5 £

SAUNDERTON Buckinghamshire Map **04** SP70

★★ **Rose & Crown** Wycombe Rd HP17 9NP (Exec Hotel)
Princes Risborough(08444)5299 & 2241
Closed 25-31 Dec
This small, friendly, proprietor-run hotel offers wholesome food in a cosy restaurant, a good bar atmosphere and bedrooms which, though small are clean and comfortable.
17rm(6 8) CTV in all bedrooms ® T (ex guide dogs) sB&B£25-£36.50 sB&B£35-£55 dB&B£45-£65
50P
English & French S10% Lunch £9.95-£12.25 Dinner fr£14.25 Last dinner 9.30pm
Credit Cards 1 2 3 5

SAUNTON Devon Map **02** SS43

★★★★ **65% Saunton Sands** EX33 1LQ (Brend)
Croyde(0271)890212 Telex no 42551 FAX (0271) 890145
A haven for families, this hotel not only overlooks wonderful beaches but also has an excellent range of indoor leisure facilities. Bedrooms are well equipped, attentive service is provided by friendly, skilled staff, and guests may even benefit from the hotel's own private weather station
90(39fb) CTV in all bedrooms ® T (ex guide dogs) sB&B£47-£61 dB&B£81-£106
Lift CTV 140P 2 CFA (heated) (hard) squash snooker sauna solarium putting table tennis spa bath *xmas*
English & French V Lunch £8&alc Dinner £13&alc Last dinner 9pm
Credit Cards 1 2 3 5

See advertisement on page 591

★★ **Preston House** EX33 1LG Croyde(0271)890472
Telex no 890702
RS Dec-Feb
This large, detached house, set in its own grounds with superb views of beach and sea, offers bedrooms which are generally comfortable, and delightful public areas. Personal service is provided by the resident owners and their smart young staff, creating a country-house atmosphere.
12rm(7 5)2 CTV in all bedrooms ® T sB&B£22 dB&B£44-£54
CTV 12P sauna solarium nc12yrs *xmas*
English & Continental V Lunch £7-£8 Dinner £11 Last dinner 8.30pm
Credit Cards 1 3

SAVERNAKE

See **Burbage**

SAWBRIDGEWORTH Hertfordshire Map **05** TL41

Manor of Groves High Wych CM21 0LA
Bishops Stortford(0279)722333
Due to have opened September 1989
40

SCALASAIG

See **Colonsay, Isle of**

SCARBOROUGH North Yorkshire Map **08** TA08

See **Town Plan Section**

★★★★ **61% Holbeck Hall** Seacliff Rd YO11 2XX (Best Western)
(0723)374374 FAX (0723) 351114
In a superb position on a headland overlooking South Bay is this comfortable hotel full of charm and character.
30(3fb) CTV in all bedrooms T sB&B£36-£41 dB&B£72-£100
CTV 50P *xmas*
English & French Lunch £8.50-£15.50 Dinner fr£15.95&alc Last dinner 9.30pm
Credit Cards 1 2 3 5

See advertisement on page 590

★★★★ **50% Royal** St Nicholas St YO11 2HE (0723)364333
Telex no 527609 FAX (0723) 500618
Elegant Regency building by town centre with very comfortable, modern bedrooms.
135rm(104 31)(20fb) CTV in all bedrooms ® T (ex guide dogs) S% sB&Bfr£55 dB&Bfr£90
Lift 25P (£3.5) 25 (£3.50) CFA (heated) snooker sauna solarium gymnasium jacuzzi steam room *xmas*
V Lunch fr£7.50 Dinner fr£16&alc Last dinner 9.30pm
Credit Cards 1 2 3 5 £

★★★ **56% *Clifton*** Queens Pde YO12 7HX (0723)375691
Telex no 527667
Victorian in origin, but modern and well-furnished, the hotel overlooks the magnificent North Bay.
70rm(30 34)1 CTV in all bedrooms T
Lift CTV 30P
Credit Cards 1 2 3

See advertisement on page 591

S

ST BRIDES HILL, SAUNDERSFOOT
DYFED SA69 9NU

AA ★★ WALES TOURIST BOARD

This Hotel full of character under the personal supervision of the resident owners is situated in 1½ acres of award winning gardens only 2 minutes from Glen Beach and offering a warm welcome to all ages. Fully licensed with snooker, solarium, launderette, ballroom, lounge bars, no smoking facilities, children's play park and large car park. There is entertainment 6 nights from April through to October and each weekend during winter months. Acclaimed à la carte restaurant. Fully centrally heated. All bedrooms en suite with teamaker, colour TV with satellite channels, radio, hairdryer and direct dial telephone. Credit cards welcome. Ramped access for disabled. Weekend and short breaks available.

Tel. (0834) 812200 for brochure and tariff

ST. BRIDES HOTEL

Saundersfoot, Dyfed

In the Pembrokeshire Coast National Park

One of Wales' most beautiful resort hotels. Clifftop restaurant with dramatic views over Saundersfoot's golden sands. Angle Bay lobster, freshly caught fish, flambé dishes. Heated Pool. Car Parking for 70 cars.

45 bedrooms with private bath/shower, colour television, direct dial phones, hair-dryers and complimentary tea tray. Elegant Suites.

Reduced green fees for golf at Tenby G.C. and Haverfordwest G.C. Sailing : Fishing : Riding : Walking; AA ★★★

TELEPHONE 0834 812304
Telex: 48350 Fax: 0834 813303

★★ Glen Beach Hotel

SWALLOW TREE WOOD,
SAUNDERSFOOT,
DYFED SA69 9DE
Tel: Saundersfoot (0834) 813430

Unique in character and situation, this hotel stands in acres of woodland just ½ mile off the centre of Saundersfoot. A three minute walk through the tree tunnel and woods takes you onto the beach. Ample car parking. All rooms are en-suite with full facilities. Children and pets are welcome.

Sanquhars

NITHSDALE HOTEL★

HIGH STREET, SANQUHAR
DUMFRIESSHIRE, DG4 6DJ
TEL: 0659-50506

ACCOMMODATION
NEW A LA CARTE RESTAURANT
BAR MEALS : FUNCTION SUITE

S

★★★63% **Esplanade** Belmont Rd YO11 2AA ☎(0723)360382
Large seaside hotel overlooking South Cliffs and the sea.
81rm(60⇌12♠)(9fb) CTV in 73bedrooms ® **T** ✱
sB&B£22-£24 sB&B⇌♠£25-£27 dB&B⇌♠£46-£50 ⊟
Lift ☾ CTV 24P ✲ CFA darts table tennis ♫ *xmas*
♆ ⚐ Lunch £6.50 Dinner £9&alc Last dinner 9pm
Credit Cards 1 2 3 5

★★★61% **Palm Court** Nicholas Cliff YO11 2ES ☎(0723)368161
Telex no 527579 FAX (0723) 371547
Beach and local amenities are both within easy reach of a recently modernised hotel near the town centre which offers comfortable public rooms, an indoor swimming pool with sauna, and attentive service from a friendly young staff.
51rm(33⇌18♠)(11fb) CTV in all bedrooms **T** ✈ (ex guide dogs) sB&B⇌♠fr£32 dB&B⇌♠£53-£70 ⊟
Lift ☾ CTV 6P ⊞ ▭(heated) sauna ♫ *xmas*
♉ English & French **V** ♆ ⚐ Lunch fr£7.50 High tea fr£3 Dinner fr£10&alc Last dinner 9pm
Credit Cards 1 2 3 5

★★★62% ***Hotel St Nicholas*** St Nicholas Cliff YO11 2EU
☎(0723)364101 Telex no 52351 FAX (0723) 500538
This large, seafront hotel, undergoing a continuous programme of upgrading, now offers good conference and leisure facilities.
141⇌♠(18fb)4⊞ CTV in all bedrooms ® **T**
Lift ☾ 15⌂ (£2) ▭(heated) sauna solarium children's games room
V ♆ ⚐ Last dinner 9pm
Credit Cards 1 2 3 5

★★★ 64% **Wrea Head Country** Scalby YO13 0PB (3m NW off A171) (Inter)
☎(0723)378211

Converted Victorian residence standing in 14 acres of landscaped gardens.

21rm(17⇌4♠)(3fb) CTV in all bedrooms ® **T**
sB&B⇌♠£30-£50 dB&B⇌♠£60-£100 ⊟
☾ 50P 40⌂ ✲ putting green croquet *xmas*
♉ English & French **V** ♆ ⚐ S% Lunch £8.50-£10 Dinner fr£15.95 Last dinner 9pm
Credit Cards 1 2 3 5 ⓔ

See advertisement on page 593

★★**Brooklands** Esplanade Gardens, South Cliff YO11 2AW
☎(0723)376576 & 361608
Closed Dec-Feb
A friendly atmosphere prevails in this comfortable, unpretentious hotel, which enjoys the personal supervision of the resident proprietor.
61rm(47⇌)(5fb) CTV in all bedrooms ® **T** ✈ (ex guide dogs)
Lift ☾ (£2) ⊅ CFA Full sized pool table ♫
V ♆ ⚐ Last dinner 8pm
Credit Cards 1 3

See advertisement on page 593

★★**Central** 1-3 The Crescent YO11 2PW ☎(0723)365766
The family-run hotel, overlooking the Crescent gardens, offers a wide choice of menus, the à la carte and table d'hôte dinner selections being supplemented by an extensive bar menu at lunchtime.
39rm(13⇌8♠)(3fb) CTV in all bedrooms ® **T** sB&B£22.50
sB&B⇌♠£26.50 dB&B£45 dB&B⇌♠£53 ⊟
▶

S

S

Lift 18P *xmas*
♕ English & Continental **V** ♆ Bar Lunch £1.25-£5.50 Dinner £7.50&alc Last dinner 10.30pm
Credit Cards 1 2 3 5 £

★★Gridley's Crescent The Crescent YO11 2PP ☎(0723)360929
20⇔1⊟⚟in 5 bedrooms CTV in all bedrooms ® **T** ✗ (ex guide dogs) sB&B⇔£30-£42 dB&B⇔£52-£62 ⊟
Lift ☾ P̸ ⊞ nc6yrs
V ♆ ⊒ Lunch fr£7.50&alc Dinner fr£10.50&alc Last dinner 10pm
Credit Cards 1 3

★★Red Lea Prince of Wales Ter YO11 2AJ ☎(0723)362431 FAX (0723) 371230
Pleasant, family-run hotel, with a smart new leisure centre, offering good value for money.
67rm(48⇔19↱)(7fb) CTV in all bedrooms ® **T** ✗ ✳
sB&B⇔↱£20.50-£22.50 dB&B⇔↱£41-£45
Lift ☾ CTV P̸ ▭(heated) sauna solarium gymnasium *xmas*
♕ International ♆ ⊒ Lunch fr£6 Dinner fr£8.50 Last dinner 8pm
Credit Cards 1 3

★★Southlands 15 West St, Southcliff YO11 2QW (Consort) ☎(0723)361461 Telex no 57515
Closed Dec-Feb
Friendly, family-run hotel with spacious modern bedrooms.
58⇔↱(8fb) CTV in all bedrooms ® **T** sB&B⇔↱£33-£35 dB&B⇔↱£55-£60 ⊟
Lift ☾ CTV 45P CFA
V ♆ ⊒ ⚟ S% Lunch £7 High tea £4.95 Dinner £10 Last dinner 8.30pm
Credit Cards 1 2 3 5 £

✕✕Lanterna Ristorante 33 Queen St YO11 1HQ
☎(0723)363616
Lunch not served
♕ Continental **V** 36 seats Dinner £11-£14alc Last dinner 9.30pm P̸ nc2yrs
Credit Cards 1 3

SCARISTA

See Harris, Isle of

SCILLY, ISLES OF No map

ST MARY'S

★★Godolphin Church St, Hugh Town TR21 0JR
☎Scillonia(0720)22316 FAX (0720) 22252
Closed mid Oct-late Mar
A Georgian house in the town centre offers modern, well-equipped bedrooms and good public areas which include an intimate cocktail bar.
31rm(25⇔2↱)(3fb) CTV in all bedrooms ® **T** ✗
sB&B⇔↱£20-£25 dB&B⇔↱£40-£50
P̸ ⊞ sauna
♕ British & French ♆ ⊒ ⚟ Bar Lunch fr£2 Dinner £12-£14 Last dinner 8pm
Credit Cards 1 3

★★Tregarthens Hugh Town TR21 0PP (Best Western)
☎Scillonia(0720)22540 FAX (0720) 22089
Closed Nov-mid Mar
Overlooking the harbour from its elevated position, a hotel which has undergone major refurbishment over recent years offers modern, well-equipped bedrooms and spacious, comfortable public areas; imaginative food is complemented by friendly and attentive service.
32rm(24⇔)Annexe1rm(5fb) CTV in all bedrooms ® **T** ✗ ✳
sB&B£35-£40.50 sB&B⇔£38.50-£44 dB&B£64-£75
dB&B⇔£68-£99 (incl dinner) ⊟
♕ English & French **V** ♆ ⊒ Sunday Lunch £7.95 High tea £4-£6 Dinner fr£13.50 Last dinner 8pm
Credit Cards 1 2 3 5

TRESCO

★★★73% The Island Old Grimsby TR24 0PU
☎Scillonia(0720)22883
Closed mid Oct-mid Mar
Set in a commanding position, with extensive grounds and a private beach, this character hotel is designed to meet the needs of the modern traveller. Bedrooms are comfortable and particularly well-equipped, many of them having sea views, whilst public areas are bright and comfortable – the restaurant, with its panoramic views, menu of well-cooked dishes and balanced wine list being particularly worthy of note. Attentive service is offered throughout by the resident managers and their team of friendly staff.
29⇔↱ CTV in all bedrooms ® **T** ✗ (ex guide dogs)
sB&B⇔↱£71-£75 dB&B⇔↱£130-£170 (incl dinner)
CTV P̸ ⊞ ✼ ⌓(heated) ♩ croquet boating
♕ English & Continental **V** ♆ ⊒ Lunch £5-£25alc Dinner £20-£22 Last dinner 8.30pm

★★New Inn New Grimsby TR24 0QQ ☎Scillonia(0720)22844
RS end Oct-mid Mar
This historic inn stands by a small harbour. The atmosphere is friendly and informal. The bedrooms, the lounge and the residents' bar have all been tastefully modernised.
12rm(10⇔) ® ✗ (ex guide dogs) sB&B£26-£44.50
dB&B⇔£52-£89 (incl dinner) ⊟
CTV P̸ ⊞ ⌓(heated) sea fishing *xmas*
V ♆ Bar Lunch £5-£15alc Dinner £9.50-£14.50 Last dinner 8.30pm

S

Tregarthen's Hotel ★★

ST MARY'S
ISLES OF SCILLY
Tel: 0720 22 540

A quiet, peaceful and well established hotel, ideally situated within 2 minutes walk of the quay where you can catch boats to the off-islands or saunter through the small "capital" of the island – Hugh Town.

The hotel's comfortable lounge and restaurant look out over panoramic views. You can enjoy our excellent cuisine and service before retiring to one of our 33 well furnished bedrooms, all of which have colour TV, radio, telephone and Tea and Coffee making facilities.

BROOKLANDS

Esplanade Gardens,
Scarborough YO11 2AW ★★
Telephone:
(0723) 376576

- New Conference Suite
- Seating up to 200 Delegates
- Specialised Conference Equipment Available according to requirements
- A few minutes from the Spa

Old established Hotel with every modern convenience. Situated in the most desirable part of the South Cliff, with level approach to Gardens, lift to Spa and beach, central heating, lifts to all floors. The majority of rooms have bathroom en suite all have colour television, radio, tea and coffee-making facilities, BT telephones in all bedrooms. Residential and restaurant licence.

Open all year round

The CENTRAL HOTEL & RESTAURANT

★ Centrally located near to amenities

★ Wine bar with full bar meals menu lunch and evening

★ A La Carte restaurant

★ 40 bedrooms all with colour TV, radio, teamaker and telephone

★ Private Car park

Traditional Yorkshire hospitality at its very best

1-3 The Crescent, Scarborough YO11 2PW Tel: 0723 365766

AA★★ Les Routiers Ashley Courtney ETB

Wrea Head ★★★ Country Hotel

Victorian Country House Hotel set in fourteen acres of glorious parkland adjacent to the North Yorkshire Moors. All bedrooms with private bathroom, colour TV, radio, hairdryer, direct dial telephone. Honeymoon rooms and suites available. Ample free car parking. Good English food with fresh produce from our own gardens. Putting, Croquet, Stabling all within the grounds. Fully licensed. Open all year. *An English Rose Hotel.*

Scalby, Scarborough YO13 0PB Tel: 0723 378211

S

SCOLE Norfolk Map **05** TM17

★★**Scole Inn** IP21 4DR (Best Western) ☎Diss(0379)740481 FAX (0379) 740762
A fine example of 17th-century architecture and a Grade I listed building, Scole Inn offers a choice of bedrooms. Those in the main building have interesting features such as inglenook fireplaces and four-poster beds whilst those in the converted stables are more modern. Character bar and elegant restaurant.
12⇌♠Annexe11⇌♠(2fb)3 CTV in all bedrooms ® T ✱ sB&B⇌♠£40-£45 dB&B⇌♠£55-£62
CTV 60P *xmas*
English & French V Lunch £9.95&alc Dinner £9.95&alc Last dinner 10pm
Credit Cards 1 2 3 5 £

SCONE (NEW) Tayside *Perthshire* Map **11** NO02

★★★**Murrayshall Country House Hotel**
PH2 7PH
☎Perth(0738)51171
Telex no 76197
FAX (0738) 52595

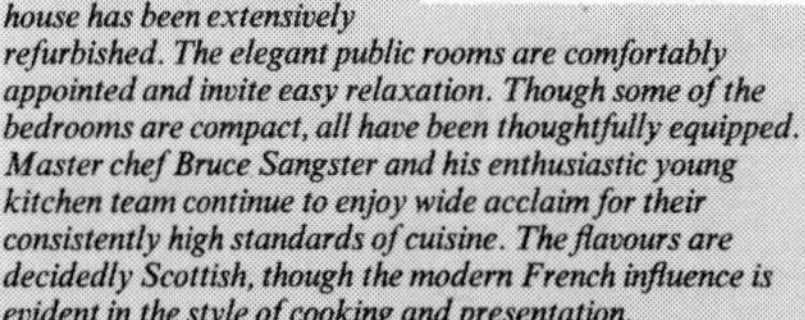

Set in 300 acres of parkland, which includes a golf course, this fine Victorian mansion house has been extensively refurbished. The elegant public rooms are comfortably appointed and invite easy relaxation. Though some of the bedrooms are compact, all have been thoughtfully equipped. Master chef Bruce Sangster and his enthusiastic young kitchen team continue to enjoy wide acclaim for their consistently high standards of cuisine. The flavours are decidedly Scottish, though the modern French influence is evident in the style of cooking and presentation.
19⇌(1fb) CTV in all bedrooms T (ex guide dogs) ✱ sB&B⇌£50-£70 dB&B⇌£85-£185
50P 18 nc10yrs *xmas*
British & French V Lunch £12.75-£15 Dinner £22.50-£25 Last dinner 9.30pm
Credit Cards 1 2 3 5

SCOTCH CORNER (near Richmond) North Yorkshire Map **08** NZ20

○***Rank Motor Lodge*** A1/A66, Middleton Tyas Ln DL10 6PQ (Rank) ☎Darlington(0325)377177
Due to open Feb 1990
50⇌♠

○***TraveLodge*** DL10 5EQ (A1) (Trusthouse Forte) ☎Richmond(0748)3768
40⇌

SCOURIE Highland *Sutherland* Map **14** NC14

★★**Eddrachilles** Badcall Bay IV27 4TH ☎(0971)2080 & 2211
Closed Nov-Feb
Magnificently situated at the head of Badcall Bay this hotel offers modern, comfortable accommodation.
11rm(3⇌8♠)(1fb) CTV in all bedrooms ® T (ex guide dogs) sB&B⇌♠£29.80-£38.75 dB&B⇌♠£49.60-£57.50
25P boats for hire nc3yrs
Bar Lunch fr£2.20 Dinner fr£8.40&alc Last dinner 8pm

★★**Scourie** IV27 4SX (Exec Hotel) ☎(0971)2396 FAX (0971) 2423
Closed Nov-mid Mar RS mid Mar-mid May
A shingle-clad building and part of a 17th-century tower house, make up this hotel.
18rm(16⇌)Annexe2⇌(2fb) ® T sB&Bfr£19.50 sB&B⇌fr£25 dB&Bfr£37 dB&B⇌fr£46
30P
British & French Lunch fr£6 Dinner fr£10 Last dinner 8.30pm
Credit Cards 1 2 3 5

SCUNTHORPE Humberside Map **08** SE81

★★★60% **Wortley House** Rowland Rd DN16 1SU ☎(0724)842223 Telex no 527837 FAX (0724) 280646
The large house, suitably converted and extended, stands near the town centre; spacious public areas of comfort and style are complemented by up-to-date bedrooms.
38rm(37⇌1♠)(2fb)3 CTV in all bedrooms ® T sB&B⇌♠£49-£52 dB&B⇌♠£56-£60
100P *xmas*
English & French V Lunch £7.50-£8&alc High tea £1-£3.75 Dinner £7.50-£8&alc Last dinner 9.30pm
Credit Cards 1 2 3 4 5 £

★★**Royal** Doncaster Rd DN15 7DE (Trusthouse Forte) ☎(0724)282233 Telex no 527479
RS Public Hols
Popular, comfortable villa-style hotel with relaxing atmosphere.
33rm(32⇌1♠)(1fb) in 6 bedrooms CTV in all bedrooms ® S% sB⇌♠£50 dB⇌♠£60 (room only)
33P CFA *xmas*
V S% Lunch £8.95&alc High tea £4.75 Dinner £11.20-£17.20alc Last dinner 10pm
Credit Cards 1 2 3 4 5

SEAHOUSES Northumberland Map **12** NU23

★★**Beach House** Sea Front NE68 7SR ☎(0665)720337
Closed Nov-Mar
A warm welcome is extended by the owners of this very pleasant and well-furnished hotel, and bedrooms have good views towards the Farne Islands.
14rm(7⇌7♠)(3fb)1 CTV in all bedrooms ® T sB&B⇌♠£22-£30 dB&B⇌♠£44-£60
CTV 16P spa bath games table
English & Italian Dinner £12.50-£13.50 Last dinner 8pm
Credit Cards 1 3 £

★★**Olde Ship** NE68 7RD ☎(0665)720200
Closed Nov-Etr
In an elevated situation, overlooking the harbour, the hotel features public areas with a maritime theme. The friendly proprietors, aided by local staff, offer very pleasant service.
10rm(2⇌5♠)(1fb) CTV in all bedrooms ® sB&Bfr£21 sB&B⇌♠fr£23.50 dB&Bfr£42 dB&B⇌♠fr£47
CTV 10P 2 putting green
V Lunch fr£5.50 Dinner fr£10 Last dinner 8pm

★★***St Aidans*** NE68 7SR ☎(0665)720355
Closed 16 Nov-14 Feb
Seafront hotel with a cosy bar and a comfortable restaurant.
8rm(1⇌3♠)(3fb) CTV in all bedrooms ®
10P
English & Continental V Last dinner 8pm
Credit Cards 1 3

For key to symbols see the inside front cover.

S

SEALE Surrey Map **04** SU84

★★★ **56% Hog's Back** GU10 1EX (on A31) (Embassy)
☎Runfold(02518)2345 Telex no 859352 FAX (02518) 3113
A friendly hotel with spectacular views from the rear gardens.
75rm(73⇌2♠)(6fb)2⊞ ⊁in 10 bedrooms CTV in all bedrooms ® T S% sB⇌♠£65-£75 dB⇌♠£70-£85 (room only) ⊟
☾ 130P ✱ snooker *xmas*
♉ English & French V ✿ S% Lunch £8-£12.50&alc Dinner £8-£12.50&alc Last dinner 9.30pm
Credit Cards 1 2 3 4 5

SEATON BURN Tyne & Wear Map **12** NZ27

★★★★ **54% Holiday Inn** Great North Rd NE13 6BP (Holiday Inns) ☎091-236 5432 Telex no 53271 FAX 091-236 8091
Set in open countryside this low rise modern hotel has spacious, attractive bedrooms and a leisure complex.
150⇌♠(77fb)⊁in 10 bedrooms CTV in all bedrooms **T** sB⇌♠£70-£84 dB⇌♠£79-£91 (room only) ⊟
☾ ⊞ 200P ✱ CFA ⊡(heated) sauna solarium gymnasium games room ♫ *xmas*
♉ International V ✿ ⊥ ⊁ Lunch £9.25-£14.50 High tea £4.75-£10alc Dinner £14.50&alc Last dinner 10.30pm
Credit Cards 1 2 3 4 5

SEAVIEW

See **Wight, Isle of**

SEAVINGTON ST MARY Somerset Map **03** ST41

✕✕ **Pheasant** Water St TA19 0QH
☎South Petherton(0460)40502 FAX (0460) 42388
Closed Sun & 26 Dec-10 Jan
Lunch not served
♉ English, French & Italian V 48 seats Dinner fr£12.95&alc Last dinner 9.30pm 40P 10 bedrooms available
Credit Cards 1 2 3 5

SEDGEFIELD Co Durham Map **08** NZ32

★★★ **67%** ***Hardwick Hall*** TS21 2EH ☎(0740)20253
Telex no 537681
Standing in an attractive country park, yet close to the A1(M), this hotel offers charming accommodation in a peaceful environment. Bedroom refurbishment will be complete in 1990, when all bathrooms will offer spa baths. Meals are of good quality, dinner being especially worthy of recommendation.
17⇌(1fb) CTV in all bedrooms **T** ✗
200P ✱ ⌂
♉ English & French V ✿ ⊥ Last dinner 9.30pm
Credit Cards 1 2 3 5

★★ **Crosshill** 1 The Square TS21 2AB ☎(0740)20153 & 21206
Small, friendly hotel, supervised by proprietors.
8rm(5⇌3♠)(2fb) CTV in all bedrooms ® T
sB&B⇌♠£40-£45 dB&B⇌♠£50-£55 ⊟
☾ CTV 9P ⊞ *xmas*
V ✿ ⊥ Lunch £1.50-£7.60 High tea £4-£7.50 Dinner £7.50-£15 Last dinner 9.30pm
Credit Cards 1 2 3 £

SEDGEMOOR MOTORWAY SERVICE AREA (M5)
Somerset Map **03** ST35

○ ***Roadchef Lodge*** M5 Motorway southbound BN26 2US

○ ***Travelodge*** M5 Motorway Northbound BS24 0JL (only accessible from northbound carriageway) (Trusthouse Forte)
☎Weston-Super-Mare(0934)750831
40⇌
P

SEDLESCOMBE East Sussex Map **05** TQ71

★★ **Brickwall** The Green TN33 0QA ☎(042487)253 due to change to (0424870) 253
Overlooking the village green this Tudor manor house c1597 offers comfortable accommodation and modern facilities. The restaurant promotes good standards of cooking and there is a well-stocked wine cellar.
24rm(10⇌8♠)(2fb)4⊞ CTV in all bedrooms ® T sB⇌♠£40 dB⇌♠£51 (room only) ⊟
25P ⊞ ✱ ⩳(heated) *xmas*
♉ English, French & Italian V ✿ ⊥ Lunch £8.50-£10.50 High tea fr£2.50 Dinner £11.50-£13 Last dinner 8.45pm
Credit Cards 1 2 3 5

SELBY North Yorkshire Map **08** SE63

★★ **Londesborough Arms** Market Place YO8 0NS (Berni/Chef & Brewer) ☎(0757)707355
A former coaching inn, located in the town centre close to the Abbey, combines old world charm with the comfort of refurbished and well-fitted bedrooms. Bars are spacious, and an attractive restaurant overlooking the patio provides an interesting à la carte menu.
27rm(14⇌9♠)1⊞ CTV in all bedrooms ® T ✗ (ex guide dogs) sB&B⇌♠£35-£40 dB&B⇌♠£47-£51 ⊟
☾ 18P 6⌂
V ✿ ⊥ ⊁ Lunch fr£8 Dinner fr£8 Last dinner 9.30pm
Credit Cards 1 2 3 5

★★ **Owl** Main Rd YO8 9JH (4m W A63) ☎(0757)82374
(For full entry see Hambleton (4m W A63))

Book as early as possible for busy holiday periods.

SELKIRK Borders *Selkirkshire* Map **12** NT42

★**Heatherlie House** Heatherlie Park TD7 5AL ☎(0750)21200
A friendly hotel, under the personal supervision of the resident owner, set in 2 acres of grounds and gardens.
7rm(6⌐)(2fb) CTV in all bedrooms ® sB&B£17 sB&B⌐£22 dB&B⌐£36 ⊟
12P ❄ CFA *xmas*
V ⚡ Bar Lunch £3.80-£7.20alc Dinner £7&alc Last dinner 8pm
Credit Cards 1 2 3 5

SENNEN Cornwall & Isles of Scilly Map **02** SW32

★★★**66% The State House** TR19 7AA
☎Penzance(0736)871844 FAX (0736) 871812
34⇌3⊞ CTV in all bedrooms ® T ✗ (ex guide dogs)
sB&B⇌£40-£60 dB&B⇌£60-£100 ⊟
☾ 50P *xmas*
☋ English & French V ♈ ☗ Lunch £8-£12 High tea £5-£8.50 Dinner £12.50-£18 Last dinner 9.30pm
Credit Cards 1 2 3 £

★★**Old Success Inn** Sennen Cove TR19 7DG ☎(0736)871232
Set in an enviable beach-side position against the panoramic backdrop of Sennen Cove, this busy, fully licensed little holiday hotel, with its character bars, provides a popular venue for both tourists and the locals. Cosy bedrooms are spotlessly clean, well decorated and appointed, many of them offering good views across the cove, while the equally bright and comfortable public rooms include a restaurant serving skilfully cooked meals which make effective use of fresh ingredients. Personally managed, the hotel provides a pleasant retreat or an ideal base from which to explore the tip of Cornwall.
11rm(9⇌)2⊞ CTV in all bedrooms ® ✗ sB&B⇌£25-£30 dB&B⇌£50-£60 ⊟
CTV 30P
♈ ☗
Credit Cards 3 £

SETTLE North Yorkshire Map **07** SD86

★★★**62% *Falcon Manor*** Skipton Rd BD24 9BD (Consort)
☎(07292)3814 FAX (07292) 2087
This family-run hotel stands in the busy Dales town that is the starting point of the famous Settle to Carlisle railway and the gateway to Ribblesdale and the Yorkshire Dales National Park. Its two bars and comfortable lounge provide an ideal setting in which to relax after enjoying the well-prepared food – including some typical local specialities – served in the elegant restaurant.
16rm(15⇌1⌐)(2fb)4⊞ CTV in all bedrooms ® T
85P ❄ solarium bowling green
☋ English & Continental V ♈ ☗ Last dinner 9.30pm
Credit Cards 1 3 5

★★**Royal Oak** Market Place BD24 9ED ☎(07292)2561
Closed Xmas day night
This owner-run, town-centre pub, originally built in 1684, offers good bedrooms and an attractive restaurant serving good food.
6rm(5⇌1⌐) CTV in all bedrooms ® T ✗ (ex guide dogs)
20P 2🚗
☋ English & French V ♈ ☗ Last dinner 10pm

SEVENOAKS Kent Map **05** TQ55

★★***Royal Oak*** Upper High St TN14 5PG ☎(0732)451109
FAX (0732) 740187
A popular hotel with a good deal of character, informally run, features a range of individually styled bedrooms equipped to modern standards. The bar's blackboard menu offers a good range of dishes as an alternative to the more elegant cuisine of the formal restaurant.
21rm(19⇌2⌐) CTV in all bedrooms ® T
☾ 30P
☋ English & French V ♈ ☗ ⚡ Last dinner 9.30pm
Credit Cards 1 2 3 5

★★**Sevenoaks Park** Seal Hollow Rd TN13 3SH ☎(0732)454245
Telex no 95571 FAX (0732) 457468
The efficient, family-run hotel provides above-average public areas, friendly service and good standards of cooking.
16rm(3⇌3⌐)Annexe10⇌⌐(3fb) CTV in all bedrooms ® T
✗ sB&B£30-£45 sB&B⇌⌐£40-£45 dB&B£45-£55
dB&B⇌⌐£45-£55
33P 🚗 ❄ ⇒(heated)
☋ English & French Lunch fr£8.95 Dinner £8.50-£10.50 Last dinner 9pm
Credit Cards 1 2 3 5

SHAFTESBURY Dorset Map **03** ST82

★★★**50% The Grosvenor** The Commons SP7 8JA (Trusthouse Forte) ☎(0747)52282
A former coaching inn with a friendly, informal atmosphere and nicely equipped bedrooms which have been upgraded.
47rm(41⇌1⌐)(2fb)2⊞⚡in 4 bedrooms CTV in all bedrooms ® ✱ sB⇌⌐£53 dB£59 dB⇌⌐£69 (room only) ⊟
P xmas
V ♈ ☗ ⚡ Lunch £6.50-£8.50 High tea £4.50-£6.50 Dinner £10-£15alc Last dinner 9pm
Credit Cards 1 2 3 4 5

★★★**64% Royal Chase** Royal Chase Roundabout SP7 8DB (Best Western) ☎(0747)53355 Telex no 418414
FAX (0747) 51969
A hotel of some character with well-equipped bedrooms and a new restaurant. Personally supervised by the proprietor it has a warm and friendly atmosphere and good leisure facilities.
31rm(27⇌4⌐)(15fb) CTV in all bedrooms ® T S%
sB&B⇌⌐£52-£56 dB&B⇌⌐£62-£70 ⊟
CTV 100P ❄ ⊡(heated) solarium croquet putting *xmas*
V ♈ ☗ ⚡ S% Lunch £7-£16alc Last high tea 6.30pm
Credit Cards 1 2 3 5

SHALDON

See **Teignmouth**

SHANKLIN

See **Wight, Isle of**

SHAP Cumbria Map **12** NY51

★★**Shap Wells** CA10 3QU (situated 3m SW of Shap Village off A6) ☎(09316)628 744
Closed 2 Jan-14 Feb
Set in its own extensive grounds in a quiet location, the large hotel stands close to the M6 and provides a convenient base from which to explore many interesting areas, notably the Lake District.
90rm(80⇌3⌐)(11fb) CTV in 26bedrooms ® T
sB&B£16.50-£18 sB&B⇌⌐£27.50-£45 dB&B£30-£32.50
dB&B⇌⌐£44-£65 ⊟
CTV 200P ❄ 🎾 (hard) snooker ♫
☋ English & French V ♈ Lunch fr£5.50 Dinner £10.50-£12&alc Last dinner 8.30pm
Credit Cards 1 2 3 5

See advertisement under KENDAL

All hotels awarded three or more stars are now also given a percentage grading for the quality of their facilities. Please see p 16 for a detailed explanation.

SHAPWICK Somerset Map **03** ST43

★★🏨Shapwick House
Monks Dr TA7 9NL
☎Ashcott(0458)210321

This historic country house near the Polden Hills offers a relaxing, casual atmosphere, good fresh food and spacious bedrooms. The Hendersons make a special point of giving guests a warm welcome.
16rm(9⇌7🚿)1⊟ CTV in all bedrooms ® **T** ✱ S10% sB&B⇌🚿£36-£40.50 dB&B⇌🚿£66-£76 ⊟
60P 3🚗 (£1.50 per night) ⊕ ❊ sauna gymnasium croquet *xmas*
♁ French **V** ♁ ♁ S10% Lunch £1.50-£5.50&alc High tea £2.50&alc Dinner £10.50&alc Last dinner 8.30pm
Credit Cards 1 2 3 5 £

SHARDLOW Derbyshire Map **08** SK43

★★The Lady In Grey Wilne Ln DE7 2HA ☎Derby(0332)792331
This fully restored old house offers comfortable accommodation in modern, well-equipped bedrooms. The restaurant, which overlooks attractive gardens, emphasises Spanish cuisine and offers a good, reasonably-priced wine list.
9rm(1⇌8🚿)2⊟ CTV in all bedrooms ® **T** ✗ ✱ sB&B⇌🚿£35-£55 dB&B⇌🚿£50-£75 ⊟
35P ⊕ ❊ ♫
♁ English & Continental **V** ♁ Lunch £5-£6.75&alc Dinner £9.75-£12.75&alc Last dinner 10pm
Credit Cards 1 2 3 5

SHEFFIELD South Yorkshire Map **08** SK38

★★★★ 53% Grosvenor House Charter Square S1 3EH (Trusthouse Forte) ☎(0742)720041 Telex no 54312 FAX (0742) 757199
Modern, fourteen-storey hotel in the town centre.
103⇌⊬in 14 bedrooms CTV in all bedrooms ® **T** sB⇌fr£70 dB⇌fr£86 (room only) ⊟
Lift ☾ 82🚗 CFA *xmas*
♁ International **V** ♁ ♁ ⊬ Lunch fr£9 Dinner fr£14 Last dinner 10pm
Credit Cards 1 2 3 4 5

★★★★ 53% Hallam Tower Post House Manchester Rd, Broomhill S10 5DX (Trusthouse Forte) ☎(0742)670067 Telex no 547293 FAX (0742) 682620
Twelve-storey, modern tower block hotel, overlooking the city.
136⇌⊬in 18 bedrooms CTV in all bedrooms ® **T** ✱ S% sB⇌£67 dB⇌£78-£86 (room only) ⊟
Lift ☾ 120P ❊ CFA ⊡(heated) sauna solarium gymnasium Health & Fitness Centre ♫ *xmas*
V ♁ ♁ ⊬ S% Lunch £9.70&alc High tea fr£4&alc Dinner £14&alc Last dinner 10.15pm
Credit Cards 1 2 3 4 5

★★★ 65% Beauchief 161 Abbeydale Rd S7 2QW (Lansbury) ☎(0742)620500 Telex no 54164 FAX (0742) 350197
An original coaching inn, pleasantly set amongst trees, has been extended and modernised to provide a good standard of well appointed accommodation; its restaurant is complemented by the popular Michel's Cellar Bar, and pleasant staff create a lively, friendly atmosphere throughout.
41⇌🚿(2fb)2⊟⊬in 10 bedrooms CTV in all bedrooms ® **T** ✗ (ex guide dogs) sB&B⇌🚿fr£58 dB&B⇌🚿fr£68 ⊟
☾ 200P ❊ sauna solarium gymnasium
♁ English & Continental **V** ♁ ⊬ Lunch fr£7.95alc Dinner £13.50-£16alc Last dinner 10pm
Credit Cards 1 2 3 5

★★★ 71% Charnwood 10 Sharrow Ln S11 8AA ☎(0742)589411 FAX (0742) 555107
Though set in urban surroundings, this charming Georgian mansion has been restored to its former elegance – stylishly decorated and tastefully appointed – in such a way as to capture the relaxed air and welcoming atmosphere of a country house. The restaurant offers both table d'hôte and à la carte menus, featuring such exotic dishes as whole quail stuffed with pistachios, baked in puff pastry and served on creamed eggs, or fillets of brill roasted with lobster and served with a herb scented veal stock.
21⇌ CTV in all bedrooms ® **T** ✗ (ex guide dogs) ✱ sB&B⇌£54-£64 dB&B⇌£70-£80
☾ 22P ⊕ ♫
V ♁ ♁ ⊬ Lunch fr£9.25&alc Dinner fr£13.95&alc Last dinner 10pm
Credit Cards 1 2 3 5 £

★★★ 67% Dinnington Hall Hotel Falcon Way S31 3NY ☎Worksop(0909)569661 FAX (0909)563411
(For full entry see Dinnington)

★★★ 65% Mosborough Hall High St, Mosborough S19 5AE (7m SE A616) (Consort) ☎(0742)484353
A peaceful country house-style hotel offering friendly service and good restaurant menus.
24rm(21⇌3🚿)(1fb)5⊟ CTV in all bedrooms ® **T** ✱ sB&B⇌🚿£30-£45 dB&B⇌🚿£45-£55 ⊟
☾ CTV 100P ❊ 🎾 (hard)

▶

English & French V Lunch £2-£3.50 Dinner £12-£13&alc Last dinner 9.30pm
Credit Cards 1 2 3

★★★61% **Royal Victoria** Victoria Station Rd S4 7YE ☎(0742)768822 Telex no 547539 FAX (0742) 724519
Closed 25-26 Dec & 1 Jan
Large four-storey Victorian hotel near the former railway station in the town centre.
93⇌↑2 CTV in all bedrooms ® T sB&B⇌↑£56-£69.50 dB&B⇌↑£67-£80.50
Lift ☾ 250P CFA
English & French V Lunch £7.50-£9.50 Dinner fr£9.50 Last dinner 10pm
Credit Cards 1 2 3 5

★★★62% **Hotel St George** Kenwood Rd S7 1NQ (Swallow) ☎(0742)583811 Telex no 547030 FAX (0742) 500138
Modern hotel situated in own grounds and gardens, close to city centre. Recently updated public rooms offer comfort and relaxation in pleasant surroundings.
141rm(140⇌1↑) CTV in all bedrooms ® T S% sB&B⇌↑fr£54 dB&B⇌↑fr£70
Lift ☾ 200P ❋ CFA (heated) sauna solarium gymnasium Spa bath
English & French V Lunch fr£9.25&alc Dinner fr£12&alc Last dinner 10pm
Credit Cards 1 2 3 5

★★★50% **St James** George St S1 2PF ☎(0742)739939 Telex no 54361 FAX (0742) 768332
A gentleman's club situated in the heart of the city has been converted to provide modern, well-equipped bedrooms ideal for the business person. A small downstairs bar is popular for lunchtime snacks and conference/meeting facilities are also available.
32rm(25⇌7↑)(2fb) CTV in all bedrooms ® T ✱ sB&B⇌↑£35-£49 dB&B⇌↑£45-£61
Lift ☾ P̸
Credit Cards 1 2 3 5 £

★★★70% **Sheffield Moat House** Chesterfield Rd South S8 8BW (Queens Moat) ☎(0742)375376 Telex no 547890 FAX (0742) 378140
Close to the junction of the A61/A6102 ring road, a brand new hotel offers attractive bedrooms, a well-equipped leisure centre and extensive facilities for meetings. Efficient room service is provided by friendly staff.
95⇌(9fb) in 20 bedrooms TV available ® T sB⇌fr£58 dB⇌fr£68 (room only)
Lift ☾ 260P ❋ (heated) sauna solarium gymnasium Health & beauty treatment room ♫
French V Lunch fr£10.25&alc Dinner fr£11.95&alc Last dinner 10pm
Credit Cards 1 2 3 5

★★★64% **Staindrop Lodge** S30 4UH ☎(0742)846727
(For full entry see Chapeltown)

★★**Roslyn Court** 178-180 Psalter Ln, Brincliffe S11 8US ☎(0742)666188
Three-storey building in a residential area.
31rm(21⇌10↑)(2fb) CTV in all bedrooms ® T ✱ sB&B⇌↑£21-£35 dB&B⇌↑£39.50-£52
☾ CTV 25P
V Lunch £5 Dinner £7-£8.55&alc Last dinner 9pm
Credit Cards 1 2 3 5

★★**Rutland** 452 Glossop Rd, Broomhill S10 2PY (Exec Hotel) ☎(0742)664411 Telex no 547500 FAX (0742) 670348
Seven detached stone houses, interconnected by walkways, form a modern hotel which is popular with businessmen. Public rooms include a spacious reception lounge with separate public lounge, writing room and small, intimate restaurant with adjoining cocktail bar. An extremely good bedroom annexe stands close by.
73rm(68⇌1↑)Annexe17rm(15⇌2↑)(9fb) CTV in all bedrooms ® T sB&B£33-£36 sB&B⇌↑£36-£50 dB&B⇌↑£56-£66
Lift ☾ CTV 80P CFA *xmas*
V Lunch fr£4.95&alc Dinner fr£8.50&alc Last dinner 9.30pm
Credit Cards 1 2 3 5

★***Montgomery*** Montgomery Rd, Netheredge S7 1LN ☎(0742)553454 553224 Telex no 54662
Situated in an attractive residential suburb close to the city centre, the hotel has well-fitted, compact bedrooms and a relaxed atmosphere.
24rm(1⇌4↑)(2fb) CTV in all bedrooms ® T
☾ CTV 1P snooker sauna solarium gymnasium
Mainly grills V Last dinner 9.30pm
Credit Cards 1 2 3 5

○***Granada Lodge*** 340 Prince of Wales Rd S2 1FF (Granada) ☎(0742)530935
61⇌

SHEPPERTON Surrey

See LONDON plan 5*A1*(page 412)

★★★57% **Shepperton Moat House** Felix Ln TW17 8NP (Queens Moat) ☎Walton-on-Thames(0932)241404 Telex no 928170 FAX (0932) 245231
Closed 26-30 Dec
Quietly situated in 11 acres of grounds next to River Thames, this busy modern conference and commercial hotel has well equipped bedrooms, compact bathrooms and some leisure activities.
156⇌↑(4fb) CTV in all bedrooms ® T sB&B⇌↑£36-£65 dB&B⇌↑£50-£83.50
Lift ☾ 225P ❋ CFA snooker sauna solarium gymnasium ♫
English & French V Lunch £11.75 Dinner £11.75 Last dinner 9.30pm
Credit Cards 1 2 3 5

SHEPTON MALLET Somerset Map **03** ST64

✕✕**Bowlish House** Wells Rd, Bowlish BA4 5JD (on the Wells road A371) ☎(0749)2022 due to change to (0749) 342022
Closed 24-27 Dec
Lunch not served
International V 26 seats Dinner fr£16 Last dinner 10pm 10P
Credit Cards 1 3

✕**Blostin's** 29 Waterloo Rd BA4 5HH ☎(0749)3648
Small, country town restaurant where blackboard menus offer simple, inexpensive 2 or 3 course meals using good quality fresh produce.
Closed Sun, Mon, 3-19 Jan, 1-8 Jun & 1 wk Etr
Lunch not served
French 30 seats Dinner £10.95-£11.95&alc Last dinner 9.30pm P̸
Credit Cards 1 3 5

SHERBORNE Dorset Map **03** ST61

★★★75% **Eastbury** Long St DT9 3BY ☎(0935)813131 Telex no 46644
An 18th-century town house tastefully restored to provide comfortable, well-appointed accommodation. The attractive conservatory restaurant provides excellent, traditional English dishes and service is friendly and attentive.
12⇌↑(1fb)1 CTV in all bedrooms ® T (ex guide dogs) sB&B⇌↑fr£52.50 dB&B⇌↑fr£75
24P ❋ *xmas*

🍷 English & French V ♿ 🍴 Lunch fr£10.50 Dinner fr£17.50
Last dinner 9.30pm
Credit Cards [1] [3]

See advertisement on page 601

★★★62% **Post House** Horsecastles Ln DT9 6BB (Trusthouse Forte) ☎(0935)813191 Telex no 46522 FAX (0935) 816493
Many of the rooms of this hospitable modern hotel have been upgraded to a high standard and all are well-equipped, whilst lounge facilities are comfortable though limited and friendly staff provide helpful service.
60🛁🚿🚭in 10 bedrooms CTV in all bedrooms ® T S%
sB🛁🚿£60-£68 dB🛁🚿£70 (room only) 🅱
☾ 100P ✲ CFA croquet putting *xmas*
V ♿ 🍴 🚭 S% Lunch £7.50-£7.95 High tea £3-£6 Dinner £12.50&alc Last dinner 10pm
Credit Cards [1] [2] [3] [4] [5]

★★**Half Moon Toby** Half Moon St DT9 3LN (Toby) ☎(0935)812017
Bars and a carvery restaurant make up the ground floor area of this town-centre hotel; bedrooms have been refurbished fairly recently and are comfortable and well equipped.
15🛁🚿(2fb)🚭in 4 bedrooms CTV in all bedrooms ® T
sB&B🛁🚿£31.50-£41.50 dB&B🛁🚿£41.50-£51.50 🅱
44P (charged) 🐾 pool table & skittles
V ♿ 🚭 Lunch £6.45-£11 Dinner £6.45-£11 Last dinner 10pm
Credit Cards [1] [2] [3]

✕**Pheasant's** 24 Greenhill DT9 4EW ☎(0935)815252
Housed in an old stone cottage this small, intimate restaurant specialises in English and French cuisine. Well-prepared dishes are complemented by an equally well-balenced wine list.
Closed Mon & Jan
Dinner not served Sun

▶

S

English & French V 30 seats Lunch £6.75-£9.50&alc Dinner £12-£17alc Last lunch 2.15pm Last dinner 10.30pm 10P
Credit Cards 1 3

SHERINGHAM Norfolk Map **09** TG14

★★***Beaumaris*** South St NR26 8LL (0263)822370
Closed 19 Dec-31 Jan
25rm(18⇌3)(5fb) CTV in all bedrooms ®
CTV 25P
Last dinner 8.30pm
Credit Cards 1 2 3

★★**Southlands** South St NR26 8LL (0263)822679
Closed 0ct-Etr
A small, comfortable hotel run in an informal manner by the Beasy family. Situated close to the town and sea front it has light, clean bedrooms, a cosy bar and a large lounge overlooking the garden.
18rm(13⇌1)(2fb) CTV in all bedrooms ® sB&B£22 sB&B⇌£25 dB&B£44 dB&B⇌£50
22P
Dinner £10-£11.50 Last dinner 7.45pm

SHETLAND Map **16**

BRAE Map **16** HU36

★★★67% **Busta House**
ZE2 9QN (Consort)
(080622)506
Telex no 9312100

An eighteenth century mansion house is situated on the western shores of Busta Voe with a private road leading down to its own little harbour. It offers compact but well-equippped bedrooms, two comfortable lounges and a cosy country bar ; the restaurant features a short, carefully chosen dinner menu of good quality which uses only local produce.
21rm(13⇌8)1 CTV in all bedrooms ® T ✱
sB&B⇌£28.50-£43 dB&B⇌£37-£56
35P sea fishing & water sports
International V Lunch £8.50 Dinner £15.50 Last dinner 9.30pm
Credit Cards 1 2 3 5

LERWICK Map **16** HU44

★★★56% **Kveldsro House** ZE1 0AN (0595)2195
Standing in a quiet area of the town, this small business hotel offers functional but thoughtfully equipped bedrooms, sound menus which combine quality with quantity, and limited lounge facilities.
14rm(9⇌) CTV in all bedrooms ® T (ex guide dogs)
sB&Bfr£33.35 sB&B⇌fr£44.85 dB&B⇌fr£54.62
28P
V Lunch fr£5.50alc Dinner £8.50&alc Last dinner 8.30pm

★★★***Lerwick*** South Rd ZE1 0RB (0595)2166 Telex no 75128 FAX (0595) 4419
31rm(22⇌9)(1fb) CTV in all bedrooms ® T
22P sauna solarium
English & French V Last dinner 9pm
Credit Cards 1 2 3 £

★★★66% **Shetland** Holmsgarth Rd ZE1 0PW (0595)5515 Telex no 75432 FAX (0595) 5828
Standing opposite the car ferry terminal, this purpose-built, modern hotel provides spacious bedrooms and the services of friendly staff.
64⇌(4fb) CTV in all bedrooms ® T sB&B⇌£52-£54 dB&B⇌£59-£62
Lift 150P (heated) sauna solarium gymnasium
International V Lunch £5.50-£7.50 Dinner £11.50&alc Last dinner 9.30pm
Credit Cards 1 2 3 4 5

VIRKIE Map **16** HU31

★***Meadowvale*** Sumburgh(0950)60240
11rm(3)(1fb) T
CTV 20P snooker
V

SHIELDAIG Highland *Ross & Cromarty* Map **14** NG85

★★***Tigh an Eilean*** IV54 8XN (05205)251
Closed Nov-Etr
A small family-run hotel, beautifully situated on the shores of Loch Torridon.
13rm(4⇌1)(2fb) ®
CTV 15P
Last dinner 8.30pm
Credit Cards 1 3

SHIFNAL Shropshire Map **07** SJ70

★★★★54% **Park House** Silvermere Park, Park St TF11 9BA (Associated Leisure) Telford(0952)460128 Telex no 35438 FAX (0952) 461658
This extensive complex of leisure accommodation is located on the Wolverhampton side of the town. Formed by linking 2 country houses and their grounds the hotel has built a well-deserved reputation for high standards of comfort and friendly caring staff. Recent conversion of a cottage-style annexe adds further accommodation.
54⇌(2fb) in 2 bedrooms CTV in all bedrooms ® T sB&B⇌fr£66 dB&B⇌fr£77
Lift 160P (heated) sauna solarium jacuzzi *xmas*
French V Lunch £9.50-£12.50&alc Dinner £11.95-£18.95&alc Last dinner 10.30pm
Credit Cards 1 2 3 5

SHINFIELD Berkshire Map **04** SU76

✕✕✕**L'Ortolan** Church Ln RG2 9BY
Reading(0734)883783 FAX (0734) 885391
John Burton-Race continues to impress at this delightful country restaurant on the outskirts of Reading. His menus are elaborate, lengthy and by no means understated – faults or virtues, depending on your point of view – and dishes tend to be at their most successful when least complex. A delightful pink-roasted squab, for instance, simply served with a shiny 'jus' and a mousse of the birds livers, sandwiched in a potato galette, could hardly be bettered. Service is correct and polite, and the extensive cellar includes a good range of half bottles.
Closed Mon, last 2 wks Feb & last 2 wks Aug
Dinner not served Sun
French V 55 seats ✱ Lunch fr£22 Dinner fr£37 Last lunch 2.15pm Last dinner 10.15pm 30P
Credit Cards 1 2 3

SHIPDHAM Norfolk Map **05** TF90

★★**Shipdham Place** Church Close IP25 7LX
☎Dereham(0362)820303
The peaceful surroundings of what was once Shipdham Rectory, dating back to the seventeenth century, provide the ideal opportunity for escape and relaxation. Its charming bedrooms are individually decorated, comfortable lounge areas are tastefully furnished, a table d'hôte menu makes good use of quality fresh ingredients and personal service is rendered by resident owners.
8rm(7⇌)(1fb)2 T
CTV 25P ❊
English & French V Last dinner 9.30pm
Credit Cards 1 3 £

See advertisement on page 603

SHIPHAM Somerset Map **03** ST45

★★**Daneswood House**
Cuck Hill BS25 1RD
☎Winscombe
(093484)3145 & 3945
FAX (093484) 3824
RS 24Dec-Jan

From its quiet woodland setting in the Mendip Hills, this friendly, personally-run hotel commands rural views across its terraced gardens and the valley beyond. The Edwardian house has recently been upgraded to offer spacious, comfortable bedrooms which retain their original character while providing modern facilities – the three garden ▶

S

suites with their own lounges andpatio doors on to the terrace are particularly well designed to offer additional comfort and a degree of independence – and good use has been made of pleasing soft decor and complementary fabrics throughout. Food standards are worthy of note for their imaginative treatment of quality ingredients and local produce. The hotel's site makes it an ideal tourist base and easy access to Bristol and its airport is an attraction for businessmen.

9⇌🚿Annexe3⇌🚿(6fb) CTV in all bedrooms ® **T** ✗ (ex guide dogs) ✱ sB&B⇌🚿£35-£49.50 dB&B⇌🚿£52.50-£75 ⊟

☾25P 2🚗 ✿

🍷 English & Continental **V** ♡ ☕ ⚡ Lunch £12.95-£14.95alc Dinner £14.95-£17.95alc Last dinner 9pm

Credit Cards 1 2 3 5 £

See advertisement under BRISTOL

★**Penscot Farmhouse** The Square BS25 1TW (Minotels) ☎Winscombe(093484)2659

RS Dec-Jan

Small village hotel popular with ramblers and tourists, with a comfortable lounge bar.

18rm(12🚿)(2fb)1⊟ ® **T** sB&B£22.50-£26 sB&B🚿£26 dB&B£35 dB&B🚿£42 ⊟

CTV 40P ✿

V ♡ ☕ ⚡ Lunch £8.25-£12.75alc Dinner £6.50-£12.75&alc Last dinner 9pm

Credit Cards 1 2 3 5 £

SHIPLEY West Yorkshire Map **07** SE13

✗**Aagrah** 27 Westgate BD18 3QX ☎Bradford(0274)594660

The menu at this small Indian restaurant offers authentic dishes, including a number of house specialities, using fresh, quality produce.

Closed 23 Aug & 25 Dec

Lunch not served

🍷 Asian **V** 50 seats ✱ Dinner £4.40-£10.75 Last dinner 12.45am 20P ⚡

Credit Cards 1 2 3 5

See advertisement under BRADFORD

SHIPTON-UNDER-WYCHWOOD Oxfordshire Map **04** SP21

★★**Shaven Crown** OX7 6BA ☎(0993)830330

Formerly a 14th-century hospice to Bruern Abbey, and retaining many of its original features, this small family-run hotel and restaurant offers individually styled bedrooms with modern facilities, an intimate candle-lit restaurant and a good range of buffet and bar food.

9rm(5⇌3🚿)(1fb) CTV in all bedrooms ® ✗ (ex guide dogs) sB&B£24-£26 dB&B⇌🚿£56-£60 ⊟

15P ✿ bowling green *xmas*

🍷 Continental **V** ♡ ☕ Lunch £9.75 Dinner £13.75-£20 Last dinner 9.30pm

Credit Cards 1 3

✗***Lamb Inn*** High St OX7 6DQ ☎(0993)830465

This character Cotswold inn features a small restaurant with bright, cosy surroundings where service is friendly and informal. Although the menu is short, its limited range of dishes is prepared with a degree of imagination and flair, making good use of quality produce.

Closed 25 Dec-1 Jan

Lunch not served Mon-Sat

Dinner not served Sun

30 seats Last dinner 9pm 25P nc14yrs

Credit Cards 1 2 3 5

SHORNE Kent Map **05** TQ67

★★★62% **Inn on the Lake** Watling St (A2) DA12 3HB ☎(047482)3333 Telex no 966356 FAX (047482) 3175

Busy hotel in attractive, well-kept gardens with a delightful lake. The accommodation is comfortable and well-maintained and service is pleasant.

78⇌ CTV in all bedrooms ® **T** ✗ (ex guide dogs) sB&B⇌£60-£70 dB&B⇌£75-£85

☾250P ✿ CFA ⛳ ♫

🍷 English & French ♡ ☕ Lunch £9.50-£10 Dinner fr£12alc Last dinner 9.45pm

Credit Cards 1 2 3 5

SHRAWLEY Hereford & Worcester Map **07** SO86

★★★63% **Lenchford** WR6 6TB ☎Worcester(0905)620229

Closed 24, 25 & 26 Dec

Set in beautiful and peaceful surroundings beside the River Severn, the hotel is nevertheless only about seven miles west of Droitwich and the M5 motorway. Several of its spacious bedrooms have balconies with river views, and relaxed, informal service adds to the quality of your visit.

16rm(14⇌1🚿)(1fb) CTV in all bedrooms ® **T** ✗ ✱ sB&B£29.50 sB&B⇌🚿£39.50-£42.50 dB&B⇌🚿£55.50-£59.50 ⊟

50P ✿ ⛱(heated) ⛳

🍷 English & French **V** ♡ Lunch £10.95 Dinner £12.95-£14.95 Last dinner 9.30pm

Credit Cards 1 2 3 5 £

See advertisement under WORCESTER

SHREWSBURY Shropshire Map **07** SJ41

★★★★61% **Albrighton Hall** Albrighton SY4 3AG (2.5m N on A528) (Associated Leisure) ☎Bomere Heath(0939)291000 Telex no 35726 FAX 0939 291123

Beautifully preserved 17th-century house, set in 14 acres of gardens and grounds, providing high standards of accommodation and facilities for conferences and functions.

33⇌🚿(2fb)6⊟ CTV in all bedrooms ® **T** ✗ (ex guide dogs) ✱ S% sB&B⇌🚿£47-£64 dB&B⇌🚿£57-£70 ⊟

☾120P 🚗 ✿ ⛱(heated) squash snooker sauna solarium gymnasium *xmas*

🍷 International **V** ♡ ☕ Lunch £9 Dinner £15-£27alc Last dinner 10.30pm

Credit Cards 1 2 3 5

★★★63% **The Lion** Wyle Cop SY1 1UY (Trusthouse Forte) ☎(0743)53107 FAX (0743) 52744

Centrally located traditional hotel popular with businessmen, tourists and locals. Elegant function rooms, including the Adam ballroom are an example of the hotel's amenities.

59⇌(1fb)1⊟⚡in 5 bedrooms CTV in all bedrooms ® **T** ✱ S% sB⇌fr£56 dB⇌fr£72 (room only) ⊟

Lift ☾72P CFA *xmas*

🍷 English **V** ♡ ☕ ⚡ S% Lunch £8-£9&alc Dinner fr£13.50&alc Last dinner 10pm

Credit Cards 1 2 3 4 5

★★★58% ***Lord Hill*** Abbey Foregate SY2 6AX ☎(0743)232601 Telex no 35104 FAX (0743) 69734

Near the Lord Hill column, just on the outskirts of the town, the hotel offers well-equipped bedrooms (most of which are contained in a modern annexe), good food and the use of a large function room.

22rm(9⇌13🚿)Annexe24⇌🚿(2fb) CTV in all bedrooms ® **T** ☾P CFA

🍷 English & Continental **V** ♡ ☕ Last dinner 9.30pm

Credit Cards 1 2 3 5

★★★62% Prince Rupert Butcher Row SY1 1UQ (Queens Moat)
☎(0743)236000 Telex no 35100 FAX (0743) 57306
Dating back to the 15th century, the hotel is named after James I's grandson and was Prince Rupert's Civil War headquarters. It is privately owned and managed.
65⇔(4fb)2⊞ CTV in all bedrooms ® T ✱ sB&B⇔£51-£54 dB&B⇔£66-£69 ⊟
Lift ☾ CTV 60P CFA games room
♀ English, French & Italian V ♡ ☕ Lunch £8.50-£9 Dinner £12-£12.50 Last dinner 10.45pm
Credit Cards 1 2 3 5 £

★★★61% Radbrook Hall Radbrook Rd SY3 9BQ (Berni/Chef & Brewer) ☎(0743)236676
This extended hotel offers guests well-equipped bedrooms, a grill-style restaurant and a leisure and health centre.
28rm(20⇔8↱)(3fb)1⊞ CTV in all bedrooms ® T ✗ (ex guide dogs) ✱ sB&B⇔↱fr£44.50 dB&B⇔↱fr£57 ⊟
☾ CTV 250P ✲ squash sauna solarium gymnasium games room
V ♡ ☕ ⊁ Lunch fr£8 Dinner fr£9 Last dinner 10.30pm
Credit Cards 1 2 3 5

★★Lion & Pheasant 49-50 Wyle Cop SY1 1XJ (Consort)
☎(0743)236288
Closed 25 & 26 Dec
Popular with visitors and locals, this old coaching inn is situated on the edge of the shopping area. The first floor, split-level restaurant serves a filling evening meal and there is a comprehensive bar snack menu at lunchtime.
19rm(4⇔8↱)(1fb) CTV in all bedrooms ® T sB&B£17-£25 sB&B⇔↱£20-£35 dB&B£34-£38 dB&B⇔↱£40-£48 ⊟
CTV 30P
V ♡ ☕ Lunch £4.95-£6.95 High tea £5-£7.50 Dinner £6.95-£9.50&alc Last dinner 9.30pm
Credit Cards 1 2 3 5 £

S

★★Shelton Hall Shelton SY3 8BH (2m NW A5) ☎(0743)3982
Closed Xmas
Situated adjacent to the A5 the hotel is found at the end of a private drive in 2 acres of well-kept grounds. Popular for small functions and wedding parties.
11rm(2⇨6↱)(1fb) CTV in all bedrooms ® **T** ✗ ✳ sB&Bfr£30 sB&B⇨↱fr£40 dB&B⇨↱fr£50
CTV 50P ⊞ ✲
♉ English & Continental **V** ♂ Lunch £8-£10 Dinner fr£12 Last dinner 8.30pm
Credit Cards [1] [3]

★★The Shrewsbury Bridge Place, Mardol SY1 1TU ☎(0743)231246
A family-run hotel standing near the Welsh Bridge and the town centre has recently undergone complete refurbishment to provide a choice of bars, a small but comfortable first floor lounge and compact bedrooms which are well furnished and equipped.
26rm(19⇨)(3fb) CTV in all bedrooms ® **T** ✳ sB&B£25 sB&B⇨£35 dB&B£40 dB&B⇨£45 ⊟
☾ 34P
♂ Lunch £5.50-£8.95alc Dinner fr£7.95&alc Last dinner 9pm
Credit Cards [1] [2] [3] [5]

SIBSON Leicestershire Map **04** SK30

★★Millers Hotel & Restaurant Main Rd CV13 6LB (6m N of Nuneaton on A444 Rd to Burton) ☎Tamworth(0827)880223 FAX (0827) 880223
A bakery and watermill have been beautifully reconstructed to create a privately owned hotel where the original waterwheel, still working, features in the bar and the millstone is used as a table. Bedrooms with en suite facilities provide well-equipped accommodation, and guests enjoy traditional English food in the large dining room.
40rm(38⇨2↱)(1fb)2⊟ CTV in all bedrooms ® **T** sB&B⇨↱£45-£50 dB&B⇨↱£53-£60 ⊟
☾ CTV 100P 2⌂ (£3 per night) *xmas*
♉ English & ContinentaL **V** ♂ ⊈ Lunch £7.50-£10.50&alc Dinner £11.95-£12.50&alc Last dinner 9.45pm
Credit Cards [1] [2] [3] [5]

SIDMOUTH Devon Map **03** SY18

★★★★69% Belmont The Esplanade EX10 8RX (Brend) ☎(0395)512555 Telex no 42551 FAX (0395) 579154
A totally refurbished hotel with fine sea views stands at the quieter end of the promenade; bedrooms and public areas alike are comfortable and well-equipped, while friendly, efficient service is provided in all areas.
54⇨(10fb) CTV in all bedrooms ® **T** ✗ (ex guide dogs) sB&B⇨£45-£63.50 dB&B⇨£75-£105 ⊟
Lift ☾ CTV 30P ⊞ ✲ putting green ♫ *xmas*
♉ English & French **V** ♂ ⊈ Lunch £9&alc Dinner £14&alc Last dinner 9pm
Credit Cards [1] [2] [3] [5]

★★★★66% Victoria Esplanade EX10 8RY (Brend) ☎(0395)512651 Telex no 42551 FAX (0395) 579154
Set in a prime position overlooking the sea, this fine Victorian hotel complements spaciously comfortable public rooms with a range of leisure activities that includes a hairdressing salon and both indoor and outdoor swimming pools.
61⇨(18fb) CTV in all bedrooms ® **T** ✗ (ex guide dogs) sB&B⇨£57-£64 dB&B⇨£80-£142 ⊟
Lift ☾ CTV 100P 4⌂ (£4.00 per day) ⊞ ✲ CFA ⊡(heated) ⩳(heated) ℘ (hard) snooker sauna solarium spa bath putting green ♫ *xmas*
♉ English & French **V** ♂ ⊈ Lunch £9.25&alc Dinner £16-£17&alc Last dinner 9pm
Credit Cards [1] [2] [3] [5]

S

Sidmouth

★★★64% ***Bedford*** Esplanade EX10 8NR ☏(03955)3047
Closed Nov-mid Mar
Large traditional hotel on a corner of the promenade. There are fine sea views.
39rm(22⇌5↑)(6fb) CTV in all bedrooms ® T
Lift windsurfing sailing
V Last dinner 8.15pm
Credit Cards 1 2 3 5

★★★63% **Fortfield** Station Rd EX10 8NU ☏(0395)512403
A privately owned country house style hotel run on cosily traditional lines offers spaciously comfortable, elegant lounges containing many antiques and fine pieces of furniture; bedrooms have received varying degrees of upgrading, but all are well equipped though some are smaller than others. There is a small leisure centre in the extensive grounds that overlook the sea. Prompt, friendly service is provided in all areas by experienced, capable staff.
52rm(43⇌9↑)(7fb) CTV in all bedrooms ® T
sB&B⇌↑£30-£43 dB&B⇌↑£60-£86
Lift CTV 60P CFA (heated) sauna solarium games room putting green *xmas*
Bar Lunch £2.50-£6.50 Dinner £9-£10&alc Last dinner 8.30pm
Credit Cards 1 2 3

★★★78% **Riviera** The Esplanade EX10 8AY ☏(0395)515201
Telex no 42551 FAX 0395 577775
Situated in a prime position off the seafront, this fine, bow-fronted Georgian hotel has been totally refurbished to provide tasteful, comfortable public areas and particularly well-equipped quality bedrooms. Staff are friendly and efficient, and a good room service menu is available.
34rm(25⇌4↑)(3fb) CTV in all bedrooms T
sB&B⇌↑£42.55-£57.50
dB&B⇌↑£85.10-£115.30 (incl dinner)
Lift 12P 9 (£2 per 24hrs) *xmas*
English & French V Lunch £9.78&alc Dinner £14.95&alc Last dinner 9pm
Credit Cards 1 2 3 5

★★★62% ***Royal Glen*** Glen Rd EX10 8RW ☏(03955)3221
During the last century, members of the Royal Family (including Princess Victoria, later to become Queen Empress) visited this country house hotel with its old world charm.
36rm(20⇌10↑)(6fb) CTV in all bedrooms T
CTV 16P 8 (£1 per night) (heated) nc8yrs
Last dinner 8pm
Credit Cards 1 2 3

★★★57% **Salcombe Hill House** Beatlands Rd EX10 8JQ ☏(0395)514697
Closed Nov-Feb
A coastal hotel situated about half a mile from the sea front achieves a countryhouse feeling under the management of proprietors of 35 years' standing; guests have the use of a well-tended garden and swimming pool.
33rm(24⇌4↑)(5fb) CTV in all bedrooms ® T sB&B£19-£28 sB&B⇌↑£21-£32 dB&B£38-£56 dB&B⇌↑£42-£64
Lift 35P 4 (£2.20 daily) (heated) (grass) pool table putting games room nc3yrs
V Lunch £7-£8.50&alc Dinner £10-£12&alc Last dinner 8.30pm
Credit Cards 1 3 5

★★★68% **Westcliff** Manor Rd EX10 8RU ☏(0395)513252
Closed 21 Dec-Mar RS 30 Oct-20 Dec & 2 Feb-1 Apr
Traditionally hospitable standards of service are offered by this popular, family-owned and personally run hotel, which commands good sea views from a setting amid 2 acres of lawns and gardens – its position directly opposite Connaught Gardens providing a pleasant and picturesque gateway to Jacob's Ladder and the Western Beach. Recent upgrading of the public rooms has brought them to a commendable standard, with the addition of a pleasing new cocktail bar, while many of the spotlessly clean bedrooms boast balconies.
40rm(35⇌5↑)(15fb) CTV in all bedrooms ® T
sB&B⇌↑£36.50-£51.15
dB&B⇌↑£73-£106.96 (incl dinner)
Lift CTV 40P (heated) solarium gymnasium croquet, games room, jacuzzi, pool table
English & Continental V Sunday Lunch £8.50 Dinner £14.50-£20 Last dinner 8.30pm
Credit Cards 1 3

★★**Abbeydale** Manor Rd EX10 8RP ☏(0395)512060
Closed Jan-Feb
Comfortable friendly holiday hotel offering good service and cuisine.
18rm(17⇌1↑)(2fb) CTV in all bedrooms ® T
sB&B⇌↑£15-£30 dB&B⇌↑£30-£60
Lift 24P nc4yrs *xmas*
English & French Bar Lunch £3.75-£6alc Dinner fr£11 Last dinner 8pm

★★**Applegarth** Church St, Sidford EX10 9QP (2m N B3175) ☏(0395)513174
A charming little 16th-century hotel, conveniently located for tourists and businessmen alike, stands in its own grounds just off the Sidford road, about a mile from the sea. Its cosy bedrooms are spotlessly clean, charmingly decorated and provided with modern facilities, while the equally well decorated public areas – though not very large – provide a choice of beamed lounges and the delightul Cottage Restaurant where fresh, quality home cooking is complemented by friendly personal service under the direction of the hotel's new owners.
8rm(3⇌1↑) CTV in all bedrooms ®
CTV 12P
English & French
Credit Cards 1 3

★★**Brownlands** Sid Rd
EX10 9AG
☏(0395)513053
Closed Nov, Jan & Feb RS Dec & Mar

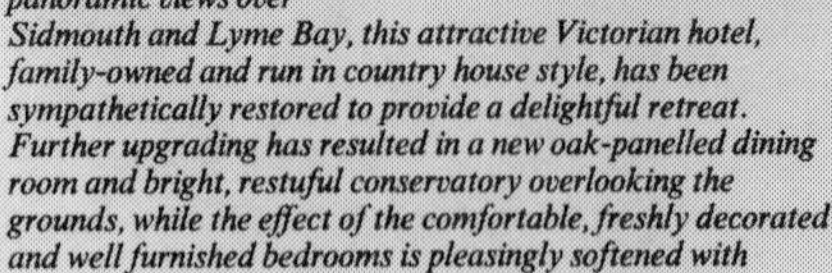

Set amid trees in 7 acres on the wooded slopes of Salcombe Hill, enjoying panoramic views over Sidmouth and Lyme Bay, this attractive Victorian hotel, family-owned and run in country house style, has been sympathetically restored to provide a delightful retreat. Further upgrading has resulted in a new oak-panelled dining room and bright, restful conservatory overlooking the grounds, while the effect of the comfortable, freshly decorated and well furnished bedrooms is pleasingly softened with

Entries for rosetted restaurants, red-star and country-house hotels are highlighted by a tinted panel. For a full list of these establishments, consult the Contents page.

attractive fabrics. Public rooms are luxuriously furnished and, like the bedrooms, spotlessly clean.
15rm(9⇌6🚿)(1fb) CTV in all bedrooms ®
sB&B⇌🚿£30.80-£34
dB&B⇌🚿£61.60-£82.50 (incl dinner) ⊟
CTV 25P ✿ (hard) putting nc8 yrs *xmas*
International V Sunday Lunch £7.50-£8.25 Dinner £13.95-£15&alc Last dinner 8, 00pm

See advertisement on page 609

★★***Kingswood*** Esplanade EX10 8AX ☎(0395)516367
Closed Nov-Mar
A gabled, terraced hotel on the sea front with fine sea and beach views from several rooms. Accommodation is comfortable and the owners are attentive.
26rm(6⇌15🚿)(7fb) CTV in all bedrooms ® T
Lift CTV 7P 2🚗

See advertisement on page 609

★★**Littlecourt** Seafield Rd EX10 8HF ☎(0395)515279
Regency house with its own garden, in a quiet position only a short distance from the shops and the sea.
21rm(12⇌6🚿)(3fb)1⊟ CTV in all bedrooms ®
sB&B£19.90-£26.50 sB&B⇌🚿£22.50-£33.50
dB&B⇌🚿£39.80-£69 (incl dinner) ⊟
CTV 17P ✿ (heated) *xmas*
English & French V Lunch £4.50 Dinner fr£8.80
Last dinner 8pm
Credit Cards 1 3

For key to symbols see the inside front cover.

★★Mount Pleasant Salcombe Rd EX12 8JA ☎(03955)4694
Closed Oct-Apr
Comfortable and friendly hotel in a quiet position, yet close to the sea and shops.
16rm(5⇨11↱)(1fb)1⊞ CTV in all bedrooms ® S14%
sB&B⇨↱£28-£33 dB&B⇨↱£56-£66 (incl dinner) ⊟
22P 1🚗 ⊞ ✲ ▶9 nc6 yrs
V ✧ ⊒ ⅍

★★Royal York & Faulkner Esplanade EX10 8AZ
☎(0395)513043 FAX 0395 577472
Closed Nov-mid Mar
Regency-style building, personally-run, on the sea front close to shopping facilities.
69rm(33⇨22↱)(8fb) CTV in all bedrooms ® S10%
sB&B£24.60-£30.35 sB&B⇨↱£27.70-£37.90
dB&B£49.20-£60.70 dB&B⇨↱£55.40-£75.80 (incl dinner) ⊟
Lift CTV 7P sauna solarium gymnasium jacuzzi spa pool
☋ English & French V ✧ ⊒ Lunch £4.50-£5.50&alc Dinner £7.50-£9&alc Last dinner 8pm
Credit Cards 1 2 3

★★*Westbourne* Manor Rd EX10 8RR ☎(03955)3774
Closed Nov-Feb
This Victorian house in its own grounds, with award-winning garden, has an intimate bar and a gracious dining room.
14rm(9⇨1↱)(2fb) CTV in all bedrooms ®
16P ⊞
V ✧ ⊒ Last dinner 7.30pm

★★*Woodlands* Station Rd EX10 8HG ☎(03955)3120
A Regency house on the approach road to the sea front, offering a quiet atmosphere and lovely garden.
30rm(14⇨4↱)(1fb) CTV in 4bedrooms ®
CTV 22P ⊞ ✲ putting nc3 yrs
✧ ⊒ Last dinner 8pm
Credit Cards 1 3

SILLOTH Cumbria Map **11** NY15

★★★70% The Skinburness Hotel Skinburness CA5 4QY
☎(06973)32332
A traditional hotel, tastefully restored in 1988, will appeal to business guests and tourists with its well appointed bedrooms, comfortable lounge, spacious lounge bar and attractive restaurant.
25rm(24⇨1↱) CTV in all bedrooms ® **T** ✳ sB&B⇨↱fr£37
dB&B⇨↱£65-£75 ⊟
70P ✲ snooker sauna solarium gymnasium ♫ *xmas*
☋ English & French V ✧ ⊒ Lunch fr£7.95 Dinner £11.95 Last dinner 9pm
Credit Cards 1 2 3 5

★★Golf Criffel St CA5 4AB ☎(06973)31438
Closed 25 Dec
Steadily improving commercial hotel with some nice bedrooms.
22rm(14⇨8↱)(4fb)1⊞ CTV in all bedrooms ® **T**
sB&B⇨↱£30-£35 dB&B⇨↱£45-£55 ⊟
P
☋ English & Continental ✧ ⊒ Lunch £6.75-£8.75&alc Dinner £11.50-£13.50&alc Last dinner 9.30pm
Credit Cards 1 2 3 5

SILVERDALE Lancashire Map **07** SD47

★Silverdale Shore Rd LA5 0TP ☎(0524)701206
10rm(1⇨1↱)(2fb) **T** ✳ sB&Bfr£16.50 sB&B⇨↱fr£21.50
dB&Bfr£27.50 dB&B⇨↱fr£32.50
CTV 30P ⌂
V ✧ ⊒ Last high tea 9.30pm
Credit Cards 1 3

SIMONSBATH Somerset Map **03** SS73

★★Simonsbath House
TA24 7SH
☎Exford(064383)259
Closed Dec-Jan
Set in the natural beauty of Exmoor this fine 17th-century house provides a high degree of comfort and hospitality augmented by freshly prepared food selected from a balanced menu. Bedrooms are well appointed and furnished in keeping with the style of the house, yet have the modern-day facilities; most also have fine countryside views. The owners, Mr & Mrs Burns, extend a very warm welcome – the offer of a tea-tray in front of the log fire in the cooler evenings is most welcome.
7⇨3⊞ CTV in all bedrooms ® **T** ✗ sB&B⇨£38-£43
dB&B⇨£72-£82 ⊟
40P 2🚗 ⊞ ✲ nc10yrs
✧ ⊒ ⅍
Credit Cards 1 2 3 5 £

SIX MILE BOTTOM Cambridgeshire Map **05** TL55

★★★70% Swynford Paddocks CB8 0UE ☎(063870)234
FAX (063870) 283
Closed 1 & 2 Jan RS Sat lunch-closed
Peaceful country house with spacious, elegant rooms.
15⇨↱2⊞ CTV in all bedrooms ® **T** S% sB&B⇨↱£55-£60
dB&B⇨↱£80-£120 ⊟
60P ⊞ ✲ 🎾(hard) croquet putting outdoor chess *xmas*
☋ English & French V ✧ ⊒ Lunch fr£12.50&alc Dinner fr£17&alc Last dinner 9.30pm
Credit Cards 1 2 3 5

SKEABOST BRIDGE

See Skye, Isle of

SKEGNESS Lincolnshire Map **09** TF56

★★*County* North Pde PE25 2UB ☎(0754)2461
Large, four-storey sea front hotel to the north of the town centre.
44rm(33⇨11↱)(2fb) CTV in all bedrooms ® **T**
Lift ☾ 40P 4🚗 sauna
V ✧ ⊒ Last dinner 9.30pm
Credit Cards 1 3 5

★★Vine Vine Rd PE25 3DB (Exec Hotel) ☎(0754)3018 & 610611
Closed Xmas
Tennyson reputedly wrote 'Come Into the Garden, Maud' at this hotel, which dates back to 1660. Standing in pleasant grounds, half a mile south of the town centre, it provides comfortable accommodation.
20⇨↱(4fb) CTV in all bedrooms **T** ✳ sB&B⇨↱fr£34
dB&B⇨↱fr£48 ⊟
100P ✲
V ✧ ⊒ Lunch fr£5.50 Dinner fr£8.50 Last dinner 9pm
Credit Cards 1 2 3 5 £

SKELMORLIE Strathclyde *Ayrshire* Map **10** NS16

★★★ 63% Manor Park
PA17 5HE

☎Wemyss Bay
(0475)520832

Closed 4 Jan-2 Mar

This delightfully situated small hotel, personally run by resident proprietors, offers fine views over its beautiful, immaculate gardens to the mountains beyond the Clyde. The house features attractive plasterwork, the domed ceiling of the entrance foyer being particularly striking; bedrooms vary in size but are generally spacious and, like the public rooms, traditionally furnished.

7rm(5⇌1🚿) CTV in all bedrooms ® T ✱
sB&B⇌🚿fr£49 dB&B⇌🚿fr£96

150P ✿ *xmas*

Scottish & Continental V ♦ Lunch fr£10&alc Dinner fr£18.50&alc Last dinner 9.30pm

SKIPTON North Yorkshire Map **07** SD95

★★*Tarn House* Stirton BD23 3LQ (1m N of A59/A65/A629 rbt)
☎(0756)4891

This is a stone-built house in its own grounds in open countryside yet close to the town. Personally owned and run, it offers pleasant accommodation.

8rm(6⇌1🚿)(2fb) CTV in all bedrooms ® T

▶

S

40P ⇌ ✽ ⌂
♔ ♕
Credit Cards 1 3 4

★*Midland* Broughton Rd BD23 1RT ☎(0756)2781
Stone-built hotel, situated opposite the station.
11rm(2fb) ®
CTV 30P ♫
♔ Last dinner 9pm
Credit Cards 3

★*Unicorn* Keighley Rd BD23 2LP ☎(0756)4146
A well-furnished, comfortable small hotel, family owned and run, is located in the centre of the town.
10rm(9⇌1♠)(5fb) CTV in all bedrooms ® T
P̸ ⇌
V ♔ ♕ Last dinner 8.30pm
Credit Cards 1 2 3

○*TraveLodge* Gargrave Rd BD23 1 (A65/A59 roundabout) (Trusthouse Forte) ☎(0756)68091
32⇌

✕✕✕*Oats* Chapel Hill BD23 1NL ☎(0756)68118
Comfortable and elegant, the restaurant offers courteously attentive service and an interesting menu featuring such freshly-cooked dishes as seafood casserole, chicken, oyster and mushroom pie and a mouthwatering range of puddings.
Closed Sun & 25-29 Dec
V 45 seats Last lunch 1.45pm Last dinner 9.45pm 20P 5 bedrooms available
Credit Cards 1 2 3 4 5

SKYE, ISLE OF Highland *Inverness-shire* Map 13

ARDVASAR Map 13 NG62

★★**Ardvasar** IV45 8RS ☎(04714)223
Closed 24-25 Dec & 1-3 Jan RS Nov-Mar
Justifiably popular, the hotel enjoys an attractive setting on the southern tip of the island, conveniently situated for users of the Armadale/Mallaig ferry. The owners provide high standards of housekeeping, hospitality and cuisine, the latter making good use of fresh local produce generally and seafood in particular.
11rm(8⇌)(1fb) CTV in 1bedroom ®
CTV 30P ⇌
♙ Scottish & French V ♔ Last dinner 8.30pm
Credit Cards 3

BROADFORD Map 13 NG62

★★**Broadford** IV49 9AB ☎(04712)204/5 & 414
The compact but well-equipped bedrooms of this modest hotel have recently been refurbished to include modern en suite facilities, and improvements continue.
20rm(10⇌10♠)Annexe9rm(2⇌7♠)(3fb) CTV in all bedrooms ® T ✱ sB&B⇌♠£25 dB&B⇌♠£50 ⊟
100P ✽ ♩ snooker gymnasium
V ♔ ♕ Bar Lunch fr£2.50 Dinner fr£10&alc Last dinner 9pm
Credit Cards 1 3

COLBOST Map 13 NG24

✕*Three Chimneys* IV55 8ZT ☎Glendale(047081)258
In a remote but beautiful corner of Skye, overlooking Loch Dunvegan, a sympathetically converted crofter's cottage features a beamed ceiling, exposed stone walls and candle-lit tables, these cosy, atmospheric surroundings provide a perfect background to the enjoyment of well-cooked food based on good local ingredients. Menus are à la carte, the simpler lunchtime range offering such dishes as Partan Pie or Stovies, whilst in the evening – when booking is essential – you may enjoy wild Skye salmon, scallops or steak; delicious home-made bread and puddings may accompany either meal.
Closed Nov-Mar
Lunch not served Sun
V 35 seats Last lunch 2pm Last dinner 9pm 30P nc5yrs
Credit Cards 1 3

CULNACNOC Map 13 NG56

❀ ★**Glenview Inn** IV51 9JH ☎Staffin(047062)248
Closed Nov-Feb
Linda Thompson and her family offer friendly and informal hospitality at this small country inn, which has attractive bedrooms and a lively bar. The high point of any visit must be the food – Scottish country cooking at its very best. A typical dinner could be Boudin of Monkfish and Lobster, served in a pool of dill butter, Highland Kidney Pudding (the lambs kidneys are cooked in Drambuie and cream), followed by the tallest chocolate gateau our inspector had ever seen. Breakfasts are no less impressive.
6rm(3♠) CTV in all bedrooms ® ✱ sB&Bfr£21 dB&Bfr£42 dB&B♠fr£46
15P ⇌ ✽
♔ ♕ Bar Lunch £1.25-£6.50alc Dinner fr£15.50alc Last dinner 9.30pm
Credit Cards 1

DUNVEGAN Map 13 NG24

★*Atholl House* IV55 8WA ☎(047022)219
Closed 3 weeks Nov
Enjoying a fine view of Macleods Tables from its village setting, this small, family-run hotel offers relaxed, friendly service, well-equipped bedrooms, and home-cooked meals that make use of fresh produce whenever available.
9rm(6♠)(2fb) CTV in all bedrooms ® T
CTV 12P ⇌
V ♔ ♕ ⊁ Last dinner 9.30pm
Credit Cards 1 3

HARLOSH Map 13 NG24

★**Harlosh** IV51 5AB ☎Dunvegan(047022)367
Closed Nov-Apr 12
Situated on a isolated coastal loop road, this charming small family-run hotel offers magnificent views across Barcadale Bay to the Cuillin Hills. Mr and Mrs Bates, aided by their friendly staff, have established a reputation for providing good food and hospitality.
7rm(2⇌)(2fb) TV available ® ✗ (ex guide dogs) sB&B£20.50-£21.50 dB&B£41-£45 dB&B⇌£46-£51
10P ⇌ ✽
♔ ♕ ⊁ S% Dinner £11-£25alc Last dinner 9pm
Credit Cards 1 3

ISLE ORNSAY Map 13 NG61

★★**Duisdale** IV43 8QW ☎(04713)202
RS Nov-Mar
From its own grounds just north of the village, a former hunting lodge commands magnificent views of the Sound of Sleat and the mainland beyond. Bedrooms are generally spacious and comfortable, some now having small modern bathrooms.
21rm(7⇌3♠)(2fb) ® sB&B£20-£24 dB&B£40-£48 dB&B⇌♠£48-£64 ⊟

Entries for rosetted restaurants, red-star and country-house hotels are highlighted by a tinted panel. For a full list of these establishments, consult the Contents page.

CTV 20P ❋ croquet putting ⌂ *xmas*
V ✆ ☕ High tea fr£7.50 Dinner £12-£15 Last dinner 8.30pm
Credit Cards [1] [3] £

❀★★ **Kinloch Lodge**
IV43 8QY
☎(04713)214 & 333
FAX (04713) 277
Closed Dec-14 Mar
(Rosette awarded for dinner only)

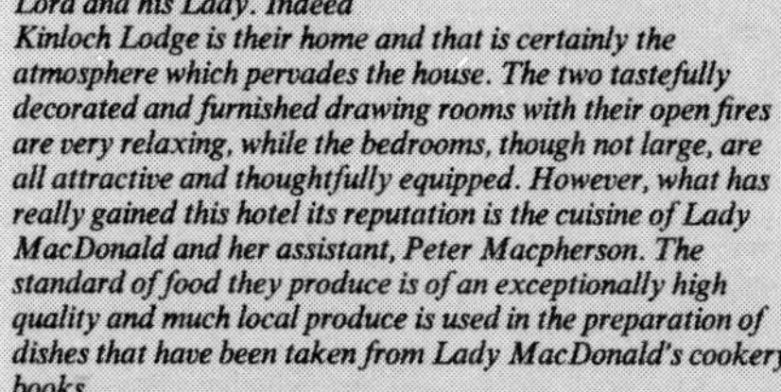

Idyllically situated at the head of a loch, Kinloch Lodge is run by a real life Highland Lord and his Lady. Indeed Kinloch Lodge is their home and that is certainly the atmosphere which pervades the house. The two tastefully decorated and furnished drawing rooms with their open fires are very relaxing, while the bedrooms, though not large, are all attractive and thoughtfully equipped. However, what has really gained this hotel its reputation is the cuisine of Lady MacDonald and her assistant, Peter Macpherson. The standard of food they produce is of an exceptionally high quality and much local produce is used in the preparation of dishes that have been taken from Lady MacDonald's cookery books.
10rm(8⇌) ® sB&B£50-£60 sB&B⇌£50-£60
dB&B£100-£120 dB&B⇌£100-£120
CTV 18P ⛟ ❋ ✓ stalking
✆ ☕ ⍻ Dinner £26 Last dinner 8pm
Credit Cards [1] [3]

★ ***Hotel Eilean Iarmain*** Camuscross, Sleat IV43 8QR
☎(04713)332 Telex no 75252 FAX (04713) 260
6rm(2⇌)Annexe6⇌(2fb)1 ▣ ® T
20P ❋ ✓ ♫ ⌂
V ✆ ☕ Last dinner 9pm
Credit Cards [1] [3]

PORTREE Map 13 NG44

★★★ 61% **Coolin Hills** IV51 9LU ☎(0478)2003
Set in its own grounds high above the bay, this traditional resort/family hotel offers well-equipped bedrooms, comfortable lounges and honest home cooking.
17rm(14⇌3♠)Annexe9rm(5⇌4♠)(5fb) CTV in all bedrooms ® T S% sB&B⇌♠£28-£40 dB&B⇌♠£50-£76 ⊟
☾ CTV 40P ⛟ ❋ snooker ⌂ *xmas*
V ✆ ☕ S12% Lunch £4.75-£6.75 Dinner £13.50-£17.50 Last dinner 8.30pm
Credit Cards [1] [3] £

★★ **Rosedale** IV51 9DB ☎(0478)3131
Closed Oct-mid May
Friendly, helpful service and good honest meals are notable features of this comfortable holiday hotel overlooking the harbour. Bedrooms are modestly equipped but well maintained and clean, whilst public rooms display a good deal of character.
20rm(13⇌7♠)Annexe3⇌(1fb) CTV in all bedrooms ® T
sB&B⇌♠£26-£30 dB&B⇌♠£48-£56 ⊟
18P ⛟
✆ Dinner £13.50-£14 Last dinner 8pm

★★ ***Royal*** ☎(0478)2525
This traditional tourist and business hotel in the town centre provides some accommodation in a 1970's extension.
25rm(20⇌5♠)(6fb) CTV in all bedrooms ®
CTV ₱ ⛟
V ✆ ☕ ⍻ Last dinner 9.30pm

★ **Isles** Somerled Square IV51 9EH ☎(0478)2129
Closed Nov-Mar
This attractively appointed small hotel, set at the centre of the harbour town, offers bright, comfortable bedroom accommodation of a standard higher than its classification would lead one to expect.
10rm(5♠) CTV in all bedrooms ® sB&B£19-£20.50
dB&B♠£44-£48
CTV ₱ ❋
Bar Lunch fr£1.10alc Dinner £5.25-£10.50alc Last dinner 8.30pm

SKEABOST BRIDGE Map 13 NG44

★★★ 66% **Skeabost House** IV51 9NR
☎(047032)202
Closed mid Oct-Apr

Peacefully situated in attractive, well-kept gardens which include a 9-hole golf course, and surrounded by twelve acres of woodland, this whitewashed former hunting lodge enjoys fine views over Loch Snizort. The well decorated bedrooms, though for the most part compact, offer modern amenities, service is provided by the resident proprietors aided by a friendly young staff – and the availability of eight miles of fishing on the River Snizort makes it a popular choice with anglers.
▶

21rm(14⇌6↱)Annexe5⇌(4fb)2⊟ CTV in all bedrooms ® T sB&B£26-£31 sB&B⇌↱£27 dB&B£48 dB&B⇌↱£56-£69
☾CTV 40P ✲ ⛳9 ↙ snooker
♁ ⅅ Bar Lunch £3.55-£6.30 Dinner £14.50 Last dinner 8.30pm

TEANGUE Map **13** NG60

★★**Toravaig House** Knock Bay IV44 8RJ (Inter)
☎Isle Ornsay(04713)231
Closed Nov-Feb
Operated by friendly owners in the style of a country house, the hotel is pleasantly set in its own wooded grounds.
9rm(6⇌3↱) CTV in all bedrooms ® dB&B⇌↱£44-£52 ⊨
20P ⇎ ✲ ↙
♁ ⅅ ⁄ Bar Lunch £3-£5 Dinner £13-£15 Last dinner 8pm
Credit Cards 2 3 5 £

UIG Map **13** NG36

★★**Uig** IV51 9YE ☎(047042)205 FAX (047042) 308
Closed 8 Oct-mid Apr
Well appointed family run hotel overlooking Uig Bay.
11rm(6⇌5↱)Annexe6rm(3⇌3↱)(1fb) CTV in all bedrooms ® T ✻ sB&B⇌↱£28-£30 dB&B⇌↱£56-£60 ⊨
20P ⇎ ✲ U nc12yrs
♁ ⅅ ⁄ Bar Lunch fr£2.50 Dinner fr£12 Last dinner 8pm
Credit Cards 1 2 3 4 5

★**Ferry Inn** IV51 9XP ☎(047042)242
Closed Xmas day & 1-2 Jan RS All year
As its name suggests, this friendly Highland inn is conveniently situated for those using the ferries to the Outer Hebrides, and an ongoing programme of improvement has resulted in a smartly appointed dining room and comfortable public bar; bedroom accommodation is modest but, like the rest of the hotel, spotlessly clean.
6rm(2⇌4↱)(2fb) TV in all bedrooms ® dB&B⇌↱£30-£36 ⊨
CTV 12P ⇎
V ♁ ⅅ Bar Lunch fr80p&alc Dinner £6-£12alc Last dinner 8.30pm
Credit Cards 1 3 £

SLOUGH Berkshire Map **04** SU97

★★★★ 64% **Holiday Inn** Ditton Road, Langley SL3 8PT (Holiday Inns) ☎(0753)44244 Telex no 848646
FAX (0753) 40272
A modern hotel conveniently located for direct access to the M4 and London. Facilities include large conference rooms, a leisure club and an à la carte restaurant. Lounge service for drinks is enhanced by live music in the evenings.
302⇌↱(132fb)⁄in 26 bedrooms CTV in all bedrooms T sB⇌↱fr£85 dB⇌↱fr£105 (room only) ⊨
Lift ☾ ⊞ 385P ✲ CFA ⊡(heated) ℘ (hard) sauna solarium gymnasium table tennis golf net ♫ *xmas*
☋ International V ♁ ⅅ ⁄ Lunch fr£16 Dinner fr£16 Last dinner 11pm
Credit Cards 1 2 3 4 5

SMALLWAYS North Yorkshire Map **12** NZ11

★*A66 Motel* DL11 7QW ☎Teesdale(0833)27334
6rm(1⇌) CTV in all bedrooms
30P ✲
V ♁ Last dinner 11pm
Credit Cards 1 3 5

SNAINTON North Yorkshire Map **08** SE98

★★*Coachman Inn* YO13 9PL ☎Scarborough(0723)85231
A small village inn with a cosy bar and unpretentious accommodation. Good home-cooked dinners are served.
10rm(5⇌3↱)Annexe2↱ CTV in 7bedrooms ®
CTV 50P ✲
♁ Last dinner 9pm
Credit Cards 1 2 3 5

SOLIHULL West Midlands Map **07** SP17

★★★64% **George** High St B91 3RF (Embassy) ☎021-7112121
Telex no 334134 FAX 021-711 3374
An old coaching inn with modern extensions overlooking a medieval bowling green.
74⇌↱(5fb)1⊟⁄in 20 bedrooms CTV in all bedrooms ® T sB⇌↱£23-£76 dB⇌↱£48-£94 (room only) ⊨
Lift ☾ 120P 2⛟(£10) *xmas*
☋ English & French V ♁ ⅅ ⁄ Lunch £12-£14 Dinner £16.50-£19&alc Last dinner 9.45pm
Credit Cards 1 2 3 4 5

★★★69% ***Regency*** Stratford Rd, Shirley B90 4EB (Crown & Raven) ☎021-745-6119 Telex no 334400
Imposing Regency-style hotel completely redesigned and refurbished to a high standard offering high quality bedrooms, good food and conference facilities. Friendly staff make guests welcome throughout the complex.
59⇌↱(10fb)⁄in all bedrooms CTV in all bedrooms ® T
Lift ☾ 275P ⇎
☋ French V ♁ ⅅ ⁄ Last dinner 10pm
Credit Cards 1 2 3

★★★65% **St John's Swallow** 651 Warwick Rd B91 1AT (Swallow) ☎021-7113000 Telex no 339352 FAX 021 705 6629
Set in a leafy residential area at the edge of the town centre, within easy reach of the major business and tourist areas, the large, modern hotel offers specialist conference facilities.
206⇌↱(6fb) CTV in all bedrooms ® T ✻ S12.5% sB&B⇌↱£65 dB&B⇌↱£80 ⊨
Lift ☾ CTV 380P ✲ CFA ⊡(heated) sauna solarium gymnasium ♫ *xmas*
V ♁ ⅅ S12.5% Lunch fr£10&alc Dinner fr£13.75&alc Last dinner 9.45pm
Credit Cards 1 2 3 4 5

★★**Flemings** 141 Warwick Rd, Olton B92 7HW ☎021-7060371
Telex no 94014189 FAX 021 706 4494
Closed 4 days Xmas
Situated midway between the NEC and Birmingham this hotel with well-equipped bedrooms has been vastly extended as adjoining premises are acquired.
84rm(35⇌49↱)(4fb) CTV in all bedrooms ® T ✻ S% sB&B⇌↱£26-£35 dB&B⇌↱£36.50-£45 ⊨
☾ CTV 85P ✲ snooker
☋ Asian & European V ♁ ⅅ Lunch £6.50-£8.50 High tea £5 Dinner £9.50&alc Last dinner 9.30pm
Credit Cards 1 2 3

★★***Saracens Head*** Stratford Road, Shirley B90 3AG (Porterhouse) ☎021-744 1016
A tastefully-styled modern hotel in a busy shopping area provides well-equipped bedrooms and is conveniently located for the NEC and Airport; it also makes an ideal base for touring.
34↱ CTV in all bedrooms ® T ✗
☾ 100P ⇎
☋ International V ♁
Credit Cards 1 2 3 5

○***Brookes*** Homer Rd ☎(0905)26489
Due to open May 1990
118⇌

❀✕✕ ***Liaison French Cuisine*** 761 Old Lode Ln B92-8JE
☎021-743 3993
(Rosette awarded for dinner only)
Set on the edge of Solihull, the Liaison continues to be celebrated for fine modern French cuisine. Meticulous preparation and subtle combinations of delicate flavours, drawn from the best fresh ingredients, make the dishes here a feast for both eye and palate. Owner Ank Van der Tuin and chef Patricia Plunkett are to be congratulated on achieving such high standards.
Closed Sun, Mon, 1 wk Xmas & Aug
Lunch not served
♁ French **V** 32 seats Last dinner 10pm 10P
Credit Cards [1] [2] [3] [5]

SOMERTON Somerset Map **03** ST42

★★**The Lynch Country House** Behind Berry TA11 7PD
☎(0458)72316
Enjoying lovely views over the Somerset countryside, this charming 18th-century hotel stands in well-kept gardens that make a delightful setting. The well-proportioned rooms are furnished in keeping with the period and standards of comfort are exceptionally high. The owner, Mr Copeland, is very much involved with the day-to-day management of the hotel and guests are sure of a warm welcome and personal attention.
6rm(5⇌1↱)1⊟ CTV in all bedrooms **T** ✱ sB&B⇌↱£35-£45 dB&B⇌↱£45-£80 ⊟
15P ⊞ ✲ hot air ballooning
♁ English & Continental **V** ♧ ⊻ Dinner £16 Last dinner 9.30pm
Credit Cards [1] [2] [3] [5]

SOURTON Devon Map **02** SX59

★★♔**Collaven Manor**
EX20 4HH
☎Bridestowe
(083786)217 522
A delightful stone manor, dating back to 1485 and set in five acres of grounds, offers well-equipped bedrooms, charming public rooms and meals cooked with imagination and flair.

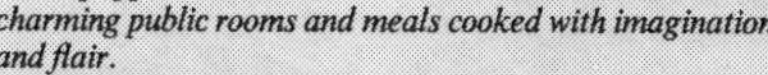

9⇌↱1⊟ CTV in all bedrooms ® **T** ✕ ✱
sB&B⇌↱£35-£45 dB&B⇌↱£55-£90 ⊟
20P ⊞ ✲ croquet, clay pigeon shooting, putting nc12yrs *xmas*
♁ Mainly grills **V** ♧ Lunch £7.95-£13.95 Dinner £13.95-£18.95 Last dinner 9.30pm
Credit Cards [1] [3]

SOUTHAMPTON Hampshire Map **04** SU41

See **Town Plan Section**

★★★53% **The Dolphin** High St SO9 2DS (Trusthouse Forte)
☎(0703)339955 Telex no 477735 FAX (0703) 333650
A traditionally-styled town centre hotel with characterful public areas and a variety of bedrooms currently undergoing much needed refurbishment.
73rm(71⇌2↱)⊬in 12 bedrooms CTV in all bedrooms ® **T** ✱
sB⇌↱£60-£65 dB⇌↱£77-£85 (room only) ⊟
▶

S

Lift ☾ 70P CFA health & fitness facilities *xmas*
🍷 English V ♔ 🍸 ⁄ Lunch £6.95-£9.50&alc Dinner fr£12.50&alc Last dinner 9.45pm
Credit Cards 1 2 3 4 5

★★★50% **The Polygon** Cumberland Place SO9 4DG (Trusthouse Forte) ☎(0703)330055 Telex no 47175 FAX (0703) 332435
This city centre commercial hotel is in process of upgrading its bedrooms to modern standards comparable with those of its fine conference facilities and the spacious restaurant with its choice of table d'hôte and à la carte menus.
109⇌(1fb)⁄in 14 bedrooms CTV in all bedrooms ® T S% sB⇌£67-£79 dB⇌£83-£91 (room only) ⊟
Lift ☾ 120P CFA *xmas*
🍷 International V ♔ 🍸 ⁄ Lunch £7.50-£9.50&alc Dinner £12.95&alc Last dinner 10pm
Credit Cards 1 2 3 4 5

★★★53% **Post House** Herbert Walker Av SO1 0HJ (Trusthouse Forte) ☎(0703)330777 Telex no 477368 FAX (0703) 3322510
Well-positioned 10 storey hotel with spacious well-equipped bedrooms, some withinteresting dockland views. The "no smoking" Liner Restaurant offers traditional dishes and the recently opened health and fitness centre is adjacent to the hotel.
132⇌(2fb)⁄in 15 bedrooms CTV in all bedrooms ® T S% sB⇌fr£70 dB⇌fr£80 (room only) ⊟
Lift ☾ 250P ✲ CFA ⊡(heated) sauna solarium gymnasium spa bath *xmas*
🍷 English & Continental V ♔ 🍸 ⁄ S% Lunch £9-£10.50&alc High tea £4.25 Dinner £14-£15.25&alc Last dinner 9.45pm
Credit Cards 1 2 3 4 5

★★★62% **Southampton Park** Cumberland Place SO9 4NY (Forestdale) ☎(0703)223467 Telex no 47439 FAX 0703 332538
Closed 25 & 26 Dec nights
Formerly the Royal, this hotel offers a choice of restaurants and a new leisure facility. The well-equipped bedrooms are double glazed.
72⇌2⊞⁄in 5 bedrooms CTV in all bedrooms ® T
Lift ☾ ⁄P CFA ⊡(heated) sauna solarium gymnasium
V ♔ 🍸 ⁄ Last dinner 11pm
Credit Cards 1 2 3 5 £

★★**Elizabeth House** 43-44 The Avenue SO1 2SX ☎(0703)224327
A small, family owned and run hotel with a friendly atmosphere offers bedrooms that are furnished in a utilitarian manner but provided with modern facilities, a smart dining room and a cellar bar – the whole constituting good commercial accommodation.
24rm(9⇌11♠) CTV in all bedrooms ® T ✱ sB&B£26 sB&B⇌♠£36 dB&B⇌♠£46 ⊟
CTV 20P ⊞
🍷 English V ♔ Lunch £6.85-£13.40alc Dinner £6.85-£13.40alc Last dinner 9.15pm
Credit Cards 1 2 3 5

★★**Star** High St SO9 4ZA ☎(0703)339939 FAX (0703) 335291
Closed 24 Dec-3 Jan
This centrally-situated, family-run hotel provides well-equipped bedrooms, with some recently built "no smoking" rooms, and a choice of carvery and à la carte menus in the dinning room. Standards of service are friendly.
45rm(14⇌21♠)⁄in 7 bedrooms CTV in all bedrooms ® T ✱ sB&B£15-£30 sB&B⇌♠£25-£55 dB&B⇌♠£35-£65 ⊟
Lift ☾ 20P 10🚗
V ♔ Lunch £5-£12 Dinner £8.50-£11.95alc Last dinner 9.00pm
Credit Cards 1 2 3 5

✕✕✕**Geddes** Town Quay SO1 0AR ☎(0703)221159
A former warehouse adjacent to Ocean Village, this ground-floor restaurant – entered through the Cellar Bar – offers carefully prepared French cuisine, presented in the modern style and served by a small team of young, formally-attired staff. The lunchtime table d'hôte menu represents particularly good value for money, while a speciality of the evening's à la carte menu is itsgood choice of fresh fish. A typical meal might include Parfaite de Foie de Volaille, then Côtelette d'Agneau au Sauce d'Ail and finally Marquise de Chocolat Armagnac, with coffee and delicious petits fours to round it off.
Closed Sun & BH's
Lunch not served Sat
🍷 French V 60 seats ✱ Lunch £12.50 Dinner £18-£22&alc Last lunch 2.30pm Last dinner 10.30pm ⁄P ⁄
Credit Cards 1 2 3 5

✕✕**Kohinoor Tandoori** 2 The Broadway, Portswood SO2 1WE ☎(0703)582770 & 584339
The cosiness of this intimate restaurant is emphasised by the high-backed seats that enclose the tables, and the cheerfully informal atmosphere is enhanced by the native costumes of the staff. Outstandingly fresh and well-flavoured food includes some interesting Tandoori dishes.
Closed 25 & 26 Dec
🍷 Indian & Continental V 40 seats Lunch £6-£10alc Dinner £9.80-£15alc Last lunch 2pm Last dinner 11.30pm 20P ♫
Credit Cards 1 2 3

❀✕✕***Kuti's*** 70 London Rd SO1 2AJ
☎(0703)221585
A very smart, modern North Indian restaurant comfortably appointed and gaily decorated with Indian murals. In its warm friendly atmosphere you can enjoy dishes superbly prepared with spices and herbs, delicately blended to ensure excellent flavour and served by pleasant, willing staff.
🍷 Indian 80 seats Last lunch 2.30pm Last dinner 11.45pm 20P
Credit Cards 1 2 3

❀✕**Golden Palace** 17A Above Bar St SO1 0DQ
☎(0703)226636
A colourful, modern first floor Chinese restaurant decorated and furnished in the traditional style. Friendly, attentive staff offer extensive à la carte and set menus of Cantonese cuisine, portions are generous.
🍷 English & Chinese V 87 seats Last dinner 11.45pm ⁄P
Credit Cards 1 2 3 5

SOUTH BRENT Devon Map 03 SX66

★★🏛***Glazebrook House Hotel & Restaurant*** TQ10 9SE
☎(03647)3322

Substantial Victorian house with good food, imaginative dècor and friendly owners.

11rm(8⇌3♠)3⊞⁄in 1 bedroom CTV in all bedrooms ® T ✗
CTV 50P ⊞ ✲
🍷 English & French V ♔ 🍸 ⁄ Last dinner 9pm
Credit Cards 1 2 3 4

See advertisement under PLYMOUTH

SOUTHEND-ON-SEA Essex Map **05** TQ88

★**Balmoral** 34 Valkyrie Rd, Westcliffe-on-Sea SS0 8BU
☎(0702)342947 FAX 0702 337828
A quiet, traditional, family-run hotel in a residential area providing small well-equipped bedrooms, friendly services and good home cooking.
22rm(15⇨7↱)(4fb) CTV in all bedrooms ® **T**
sB&B⇨↱£32-£35 dB&B⇨↱£46-£48 ⊟
CTV 19P ⊞
☋ English & French ✿ ⊻ Lunch £3-£7&alc Dinner fr£7.50&alc Last dinner 7.30pm
Credit Cards [1] [3]

SOUTH GODSTONE Surrey Map **05** TQ34

✕✕**La Bonne Auberge** Tilburstow Hill RH9 8JY
☎(0342)892318 FAX (0342) 893435
Closed Mon
Dinner not served Sun
☋ French **V** 75 seats ✻ Lunch £16-£21&alc Dinner £25-£26&alc Last lunch 2pm Last dinner 10pm 50P nc6yrs ♫
Credit Cards [1] [2] [3]

SOUTH MIMMS Hertfordshire Map **04** TL20

★★★60% **Crest** Bignells Corner EN6 3NH (junc A1/A6) (Crest)
☎Potters Bar(0707)43311 Telex no 299162 FAX (0707) 46728
RS Xmas
A large, modern, commercial hotel with a busy atmosphere offers well-equipped accommodation and a leisure complex; its open-plan lounge provides a popular meeting place, whilst restaurant and bar are also well frequented.
115⇨(6fb)⅟in 20 bedrooms CTV in all bedrooms ® **T** ✻
sB⇨fr£68.50 dB⇨fr£80.50 (room only) ⊟
☾ 150P ✿ CFA ⊡(heated) sauna solarium gymnasium outdoor childrens play area
☋ International **V** ✿ ⊻ ⅟ Lunch £12.50&alc Dinner £14.50&alc Last dinner 10pm
Credit Cards [1] [2] [3] [4] [5]

SOUTH MOLTON Devon Map **03** SS72

★★♣**Marsh Hall** EX36 3HQ
(1.25m N towards North Molton)
☎(07695)2666
Elegant Victorian house set in peaceful grounds with terraced lawns. The well appointed bedrooms have magnificent views and the menus are carefully prepared.
7rm(5⇨2↱)1⊟ CTV in all bedrooms ® **T**
sB&B⇨↱£28-£35 dB&B⇨↱£56-£64 ⊟
15P ⊞ ✿ ∪ nc12yrs *xmas*
☋ Continental **V** ✿ Bar Lunch £3-£6 Dinner fr£14.95 Last dinner 8.45pm
Credit Cards [3]

SOUTH NORMANTON Derbyshire Map **08** SK45

★★★50% **Swallow** Carter Ln East DE55 2EH (junc 28 M1 Motorway) (Swallow) ☎Ripley(0773)812000 Telex no 377264 FAX (0733) 580032
Large, modern hotel, conveniently situated next to the M1.
123⇨↱(6fb)⅟in 61 bedrooms CTV in all bedrooms ® **T** S%
sB&B⇨↱fr£69 dB&B⇨↱fr£85 ⊟
▶

S

☾ 200P ✲ CFA ⊡(heated) sauna solarium gymnasium jacuzzi steam room *xmas*
♉ International V ✥ ♊ ⚡ S% Lunch fr£10.50 Dinner fr£15 Last dinner 10.30pm
Credit Cards [1] [2] [3] [4] [5]

SOUTHPORT Merseyside Map **07** SD31

★★★★54% Prince of Wales Lord St PR8 1JS (Trusthouse Forte) ☏(0704)36688 Telex no 67415 FAX (0704) 43488
This large hotel in Southport's famous Lord Street, set conveniently close to both seafront and main shopping areas, provides comfortable public rooms and a choice of restaurants.
104rm(90⇌14↱)(7fb)1⊞ CTV in all bedrooms ® T
sB⇌↱£64-£69 dB⇌↱£80-£85 (room only) ⊟
Lift ☾ 95P ✲ CFA *xmas*
♉ English & French V ✥ ♊ ⚡ S% Lunch £6.95-£12.50&alc Dinner £9.95-£11.50&alc Last dinner 10pm
Credit Cards [1] [2] [3] [5]

★★★62% Royal Clifton Promenade PR8 1RB (Best Western) ☏(0704)33771 Telex no 677191 FAX 0704 500657
Large seaside hotel overlooking promenade and gardens.
114rm(98⇌8↱)(2fb)2⊞⚡in 2 bedrooms CTV in all bedrooms ® T ✳ ⊟
Lift ☾ 95P CFA ⊡(heated) sauna solarium gymnasium sunbed, jacuzzi ♫ *xmas*
♉ English & French ✥ ♊
Credit Cards [1] [2] [3] [5] £

★★★60% *Scarisbrick* Lord St PR8 1NZ ☏(0704)43000 Telex no 67107 FAX (0704) 33335
Situated in famous Lord Street this modernised former coaching inn still retains some of its original character with Victorian-style furnishing and décor and some four poster bedrooms.
60rm(56⇌4↱)(5fb)6⊞ CTV in all bedrooms ® T
Lift ☾ CTV 40P 12🚗 ♫
V ✥ ♊ Last dinner 9.30pm
Credit Cards [1] [2] [3] [5]

★★Balmoral Lodge 41 Queens Rd PR9 9EX ☏(0704)544298 & 530751
Friendly hotel with well equipped bedrooms. Home cooking.
15rm(13⇌2↱)(1fb)1⊞ CTV in all bedrooms ® T ✗ ✳
sB&B⇌↱£21-£30 dB&B⇌↱£42-£46 ⊟
CTV 10P ⊞ sauna *xmas*
Bar Lunch £1.20-£3.50 Dinner fr£9&alc Last dinner 8.30pm
Credit Cards [1] [2] [3] [5]

★★*Bold* Lord St PR9 0BE ☏(0704)32578 FAX (0704) 32528
A Victorian hotel at the northern end of Lord Street has been completely refurbished to give attractive bedrooms and public areas. The elegant restaurant offers many tantalising dishes from a creative menu and a competitively priced wine list complements the delicious food.
22rm(15⇌6↱)(4fb) CTV in all bedrooms ® T ✗ (ex guide dogs)
☾ 8P
♉ English & French V ✥ ♊ Last dinner 9.45pm
Credit Cards [1] [2] [3] [4] [5]

★★Lockerbie House 11 Trafalgar Rd, Birkdale PR8 2EA ☏(0704)65298
A friendly family-fun hotel, standing in a residential area close to Birkdale station and the famous golf course, features an attractively comfortable ground floor lounge and bedrooms which are steadily being improved and are, for the most part, spacious.
14rm(4⇌7↱)(3fb) CTV in all bedrooms ® sB&Bfr£18.50 sB&B⇌↱£21.50-£23 dB&B£36-£38 dB&B⇌↱£40-£44 ⊟
CTV 14P 2🚗 ✲ snooker ⌂
V ✥ ♊ Lunch £4.50-£6.50 Dinner fr£8.50 Last dinner 8pm
Credit Cards [1] [2] [3] [5]

★★Metropole Portland St PR8 1LL ☏(0704)36836
Pleasant, family-run hotel.
26rm(9⇌9↱)(2fb) CTV in all bedrooms ® T S%
sB&B£1800-£20 sB&B⇌↱£25-£27.50 dB&B£31-£36 dB&B⇌↱£43-£48.50 ⊟
CTV 12P ⊞ snooker *xmas*
✥ S% Lunch fr£4.50 Dinner fr£8 Last dinner 8.30pm
Credit Cards [1] [2] [3]

★★Stutelea Hotel & Leisure Club Alexandra Rd PR9 0NB ☏(0704)44220 FAX 0704 500232
The family-run hotel enjoys a quiet location, with a garden in which guests can relax; accommodation is provided in well-appointed bedrooms.
21rm(15⇌6↱)(5fb)2⊞ CTV in all bedrooms ® T ✗
sB&B⇌↱fr£30 dB&B⇌↱fr£50 ⊟
CTV 18P ⊞ ✲ ⊡(heated) sauna solarium gymnasium games room jacuzzi
V ✥ ♊ Lunch £8.50-£10.50 High tea £1.10-£1.95 Dinner £8.50-£10.50 Last dinner 8pm
Credit Cards [1] [2] [3] [5] £

SOUTH QUEENSFERRY Lothian *West Lothian* Map **11** NT17

★★★60% Forth Bridges Moat House Forth Bridge EH30 9SF (Queens Moat) ☏031-3311199 Telex no 727430 FAX 031-319 1733
A popular business and tourist hotel, overlooking the Firth from its convenient situation at the south side of the Forth road bridge, has been substantially refurbished to provide comfortable modern accommodation.
108⇌↱(30fb)⚡in 5 bedrooms CTV in all bedrooms ® T ✳
sB⇌↱£60-£65 dB⇌↱fr£76 (room only) ⊟
Lift ☾ 200P ✲ ⊡(heated) squash snooker sauna solarium gymnasium *xmas*
♉ English & French V ✥ ♊
Credit Cards [1] [2] [3] [5] £

SOUTHSEA

See **Portsmouth & Southsea**

SOUTH SHIELDS Tyne & Wear Map **12** NZ36

★★★51% *Sea* Sea Rd NE33 2LD ☏091-427 0999 Telex no 53533 FAX 091-454 2053
The majority of bedrooms still have to be refurbished at this commercial hotel, but it offers two bars in contrasting style and a spacious, popular restaurant which serves good value meals. The amusements and side-shows of the pier are within easy reach of its sea-front position.
33⇌(2fb) CTV in all bedrooms ® T
☾ 40P (charged)
♉ English & French V ✥ ♊ Last dinner 9.30pm
Credit Cards [1] [2] [3] [5]

★★New Crown Mowbray Rd NE33 3NG ☏Tyneside091-455 3472
Large pub with comfortable bars, attractive dining rooms and modest bedrooms.
11rm(6⇌1↱)(1fb) CTV in all bedrooms ® T ✳ sB&B£26-£28 sB&B⇌↱£29-£31 dB&B£43-£46 dB&B⇌↱£47-£50
50P ♫
♉ English & Continental V ✥ Sunday Lunch £4.95-£5.95 Dinner £6.45-£7.95 Last dinner 9.30pm
Credit Cards [1] [2] [3] [5]

Book as early as possible for busy holiday periods.

S

SOUTH UIST, ISLE OF Western Isles *Inverness-shire* Map **13**

LOCHBOISDALE Map **13** NF71

★★Lochboisdale PA81 5TH ☎(08784)332
20rm(10⇌)(1fb) ® sB&B£20-£25 sB&B⇌£25-£30 dB&B£38-£43 dB&B⇌£47.50-£52.50 ⊟
CTV 25P ✿ ⌐ snooker birdwatching trips ♫
French Bar Lunch 90p-£8alc High tea 90p-£8alc Dinner £12.50-£15 Last dinner 9.30pm
Credit Cards [1] [3]

SOUTHWAITE SERVICE AREA (M6) Cumbria

Granada Lodge M6 Motorway, Broadfield Site CA4 0NT (Granada) ☎Southwaite(06974)73476 FAX (06974) 73669
39⇌(10fb)⊁in 6 bedrooms CTV in all bedrooms ® ✖ (ex guide dogs) S% sB⇌£23-£26 dB⇌£26-£28 (room only)
40P
Credit Cards [1] [2] [3] [5]

SOUTHWELL Nottinghamshire Map **08** SK75

★★★ 62% Saracen's Head Market Place NG25 0HE (Trusthouse Forte) ☎(0636)812701 Telex no 377201 FAX (0636) 815408
Ancient coaching inn where in years past many English monarchs have stayed.
27⇌↱1⊟⊁in 6 bedrooms CTV in all bedrooms ® T ✱
sB⇌↱£57-£67 dB⇌↱£73-£83 (room only) ⊟
☾ 80P CFA *xmas*
V ⊁ Lunch £8.95-£16.95&alc Dinner £12.50-£16.95&alc
Last dinner 10pm
Credit Cards [1] [2] [3] [4] [5]

SOUTHWOLD Suffolk Map **05** TM57

★★★65% **Swan** Market Place IP18 6EG ☎(0502)722186
Telex no 97223 FAX 0502 724800
A particularly well-managed, traditional hotel at the heart of this charming town features comfortable, relaxing public areas which have recently been refurbished; bedrooms in the main house (which are currently undergoing refurbishment) promote the country house image and are more spacious than those in the garden annexe.
27rm(25⇌2♪)Annexe18⇌(2fb) CTV in all bedrooms **T** ✱
sB&B£35-£40 sB&B⇌♪£37-£42 dB&B⇌♪£55-£72
Lift ☾ 50P ⛟
♡ ☑ Lunch £12-£18alc Dinner £13.95-£21.50alc Last dinner 9.30pm
Credit Cards 1 2 3

★★*Crown Southwold* 90 High St IP18 6DP ☎(0502)722275
Telex no 97223
Originally a Georgian coaching inn, the Crown is now both a small hotel and the headquarters of Adnams Wine Merchants. Bedroom accommodation is simple but comfortable; public areas – in particular the front bar – are full of character, and the restaurant features appetising menus accompanied by an extensive choice of wines available both by the bottle and the glass.
12rm(8⇌1♪)(1fb) CTV in all bedrooms **T** ✗ (ex guide dogs)
15P 8⌂ ⛟
♡ ☑ Last dinner 9.45pm
Credit Cards 1 2 3

★★**Pier Avenue** Pier Av IP18 6AY ☎(0502)722632
13rm(5⇌4♪)(1fb)1⊟ CTV in all bedrooms ®
sB&B£23.50-£26 sB&B⇌♪£26.50-£30.50 dB&B£35-£40
dB&B⇌♪£45-£51 ⊟
CTV 10P
♡ Lunch fr£6.75&alc Dinner fr£9.75&alc Last dinner 9.30pm
Credit Cards 1 2 3 £

SOUTH ZEAL Devon Map **03** SX69

★★**Oxenham Arms** EX20 2JT
☎Okehampton(0837)840244 & 840577
A 12th-century inn of great character located in the village centre.
8rm(6⇌) CTV in all bedrooms ® **T** sB&B£32-£36
sB&B⇌£36-£38.50 dB&B£36-£40 dB&B⇌£45-£50
CTV 8P ⛟ ✻ *xmas*
♡ International **V** ♡ ☑ Lunch £6.50-£9.50 Dinner £12.50-£14 Last dinner 9pm
Credit Cards 1 2 3 5 £

SOWERBY BRIDGE West Yorkshire Map **07** SE02

★★**The Hobbit** Hob Ln, Norlands HX6 3QL
☎Halifax(0422)832202
A charming stone built hotel in a rural location high above the town. Service is friendly, accommodation comfortable, and the menus offer a good selection of dishes at very reasonable prices.
16rm(4⇌12♪)(2fb)1⊟ CTV in all bedrooms ® **T** ✗
sB&B⇌♪£27-£44 dB&B⇌♪£39-£54 ⊟
100P *xmas*
♡ English, French & Italian **V** Lunch £7.50-£10 Dinner fr£12.50alc Last dinner 10.30pm
Credit Cards 1 2 3 5

SPALDING Lincolnshire Map **08** TF22

★★**Woodlands** 80 Pinchbeck Rd PE11 1QF ☎(0775)69933
Standing just north of the town centre, an Edwardian house has been tastefully converted to provide modern, well-equipped accommodation.
18rm(1⇌17♪)(1fb)⊬in 2 bedrooms CTV in all bedrooms ® **T**
✱ sBfr£42.50 dB⇌♪fr£55 (room only) ⊟
CTV 60P ✻ ⌂
♡ English & French **V** ♡ ☑ ⊬ Lunch £2.50-£7.50&alc Dinner £2.50-£10.50&alc Last dinner 10pm
Credit Cards 1 2 3 5 £

SPEAN BRIDGE Highland *Inverness-shire* Map **14** NN28

See also **Letterfinlay and Roy Bridge**
★★**Spean Bridge** PH34 4ES ☎(039781)250
Originally a coaching inn, log fires still provide a welcome.
7⇌Annexe19rm(14⇌3♪)(4fb) CTV in 16bedrooms ® ✱
sB&B£23-£25 sB&B⇌♪£25-£27 dB&B⇌♪£50-£53 ⊟
CTV 50P ⛟ ▶9 ✓
V ♡ ☑ Bar Lunch 95p-£5.25 Dinner fr£11.50 Last dinner 9pm
Credit Cards 1 2 3 5

SPRATTON Northamptonshire Map **04** SP77

★★★56% ***Broomhill*** Holdenby Rd NN6 8LD
☎Northampton(0604)845959 FAX (0604) 845834
Closed Xmas eve & Xmas day
A friendly, Victorian country hotel in extensive grounds overlooking the countryside of the Pytchley Hunt. Bedrooms are comfortable and there is a cosy lounge with an open fire.
13rm(11⇌2♪)(1fb) CTV in all bedrooms ® **T**
CTV 100P ✻ ⌒(heated) ℘ (hard) squash
♡ English & French ♡ ☑ Last dinner 10pm
Credit Cards 1 2 3 5

STADDLE BRIDGE North Yorkshire Map **08** SE49

✕✕**McCoys (Tontine Inn)** DL6 3JB ☎East Harsley(060982)671
A 1920's atmosphere will greet diners arriving at this unusual restaurant – large plants, enormous, comfortable old-fashioned sofas and armchairs and music from the '20's combine to create a realistic atmosphere. The dining room has large parasols and intimate lighting. The main feature of this restaurant, and rightly so, is the carefully prepared menu which offers individual cooking throughout. The excellent food is complemented by an extensive wine list.
Closed Sun, Xmas & Public hols
Lunch not served
♡ International **V** 60 seats ✱ Lunch £4.95-£22alc Dinner £4.95-£22alc Last lunch 2pm Last dinner 11pm 80P
Credit Cards 1 2 3 5

STAFFORD Staffordshire Map **07** SJ92

★★★63% **Tillington Hall** Eccleshall Rd ST16 1JJ (De Vere)
☎(0785)53531 Telex no 36566 FAX (0785) 59223
RS Xmas & New Year
Conveniently sited on the northern outskirts of town, only half a mile from Junction 14 of the M6, this is an extended Victorian house with a popular restaurant, well-equipped bedrooms and a new leisure complex.
90rm(88⇌2♪)(3fb)1⊟ CTV in all bedrooms ® **T** ✱
sB&B⇌♪£40-£60 dB&B⇌♪£60-£70 ⊟
Lift ☾ 150P CFA ⌒(heated) ℘ (hard) snooker gymnasium table tennis jacuzzi ♫ *xmas*
♡ French **V** ♡ ☑ Lunch fr£7&alc Dinner fr£8&alc Last dinner 9.45pm
Credit Cards 1 2 3 5 £

★★**Abbey** 65-68 Lichfield Rd ST17 4LW ☎(0785)58531
Closed 23 Dec- 7 Jan
A row of terraced houses has been converted to offer comfortable accommodation at a very reasonable price.
21rm(1⇌6♪)(1fb) CTV in all bedrooms ® ✗ ✱
21P ⛟
♡ English & French **V** ♡ Bar Lunch £2-£5alc Dinner £5.50-£7&alc Last dinner 8.30pm
Credit Cards 1 3

★★Albridge 73 Wolverhampton Rd ST17 4AW ☎(0785)54100
Closed Xmas Day RS 26-31Dec
Commercial hotel, a quarter of a mile from the town centre, with a Victorian terrace frontage, offering value for money accommodation.
11rm(1⇨8⌒)Annexe8rm(2fb) CTV in 12bedrooms ® T
sB&B£11-£24.95 sB&B⇨⌒£21.95-£28.95 dB&B£19-£28.95
dB&B⇨⌒£28.95-£34.95 ⊟
CTV 20P
V ✿ ⊻ ⚔ Lunch £2.95-£3.50 Dinner fr£5.95&alc Last dinner 9.45pm
Credit Cards [1] [2] [3] [5] (£)

★★*Garth* Wolverhampton Rd, Moss Pit ST17 9JR (Crown & Raven) ☎(0785)56124 Telex no 36479
RS 25-26 Dec
An attractive house with modern extensions set in its own grounds on the southern edge of town close to Junction 13 of the M6. The modern bedrooms suit both business and holidaymakers and the hotel is popular for lunchtime snacks.
60⇨⌒⚔in 12 bedrooms CTV in all bedrooms ® T
☾175P ❊
☋ English & French V ✿ ⊻ Last dinner 10pm
Credit Cards [1] [2] [3]

★★Swan Greengate St ST16 2JA (Berni/Chef & Brewer)
☎(0785)58142
Sixteenth century inn with grill restaurant and extensive menu.
32rm(30⇨2⌒)(5fb)2⊞ CTV in all bedrooms ® T ✗ (ex guide dogs) sB&B⇨⌒fr£37.50 dB&B⇨⌒fr£55.50 ⊟
☾50P CFA
☋ Mainly grills V ✿ ⊻ ⚔ Lunch fr£8 Dinner fr£9 Last dinner 10pm
Credit Cards [1] [2] [3] [5]

S

★★ ***Vine*** Salter St ST16 2JU (Crown & Raven)
☎(0785)51071 44112 Telex no 36479
Reputedly the oldest licensed establishment in Staffordshire, the Vine has been tastefully restored to retain its original beams and exposed brickwork. Bedrooms are also full of character and have all modern amenities.
27rm(10⇨17⌐)(1fb) CTV in all bedrooms ® **T**
30P
English & French **V** Last dinner 10pm
Credit Cards 1 2 3

STAINES Surrey Map **04** TQ07

★★★57% **The Thames Lodge** Thames St TW18 4SF (Trusthouse Forte) ☎(0784)464433 Telex no 8812552 FAX (0784) 454858
Very pleasantly located by the river, the hotel offers well-appointed bedrooms (some with small balconies), a popular Pizza and Pitcher bar which incorporates a charming conservatory area, and a comfortable bar/lounge for the use of residents and diners in the à la carte restaurant.
47⇨(2fb) in 6 bedrooms CTV in all bedrooms ® **T** ✱
sB⇨fr£78 dB⇨fr£88 (room only)
☾ 32P *xmas*
French **V** Lunch £10.50-£12.50&alc Dinner fr£13.50&alc Last dinner 9.45pm
Credit Cards 1 2 3 4 5

STAMFORD Lincolnshire Map **04** TF00

★★★63% **Garden House** St Martin's PE9 2LP ☎(0780)63359
Telex no 329230
The charming, 18th-century house has been sympathetically improved to provide modern comforts with the conservatory lounge making an effective link with the walled gardens and lawns. Staff are friendly and helpful.
21rm(20⇨)(2fb) CTV in all bedrooms **T** S% sB&B⇨fr£54.75 dB&B⇨fr£67.50
25P 5 ✲
English & French **V** Lunch fr£8.50 Dinner fr£15 Last dinner 9.30pm
Credit Cards 1 2 3 £

★★★71% **George of Stamford** St Martins PE9 2LB
☎(0780)55171 Telex no 32578 FAX (0780) 57070
Originally a 16th-century inn, this beautiful hotel combines historic charm and atmosphere with the provision of comfort and good service. Public areas include the lounge with its open log fire, a garden lounge featuring exotic plants and trees, and an oak-panelled restaurant where interesting food and good wine are served; comfortable bedrooms are well furnished, and demand for them has been increased by the provision of a modern business centre. The delightful courtyard is particularly popular in summer, as diners enjoy substantial meals from the Garden Lounge menu.
47rm(44⇨3⌐)(2fb)4 CTV in all bedrooms **T**
sB&B⇨⌐£59.50-£80 dB&B⇨⌐£86-£130
☾ 120P ✲ CFA croquet *xmas*
English, French & Italian **V** Lunch £15-£25alc Dinner £17.50-£25alc Last dinner 10pm
Credit Cards 1 2 3

★★**Crown** All Saints Place PE9 2AG ☎(0780)63136
Closed Xmas day night
An old two-storey, stone-built hotel in the town centre.
18rm(5⇨10⌐)(2fb)1 CTV in all bedrooms ® ✱ sB&Bfr£30 sB&B⇨⌐fr£35 dB&Bfr£40 dB&B⇨⌐fr£45
40P
European **V** Lunch fr£6.95 Dinner fr£6.95&alc Last dinner 9.30pm
Credit Cards 1 2 3 5

★★**Lady Anne's** 37-38 High Street, St Martins PE9 2BB
☎(0780)53175 Telex no 32376
An 18th century stone built house in 3.5 acres of grounds on the B1081.
28rm(15⇨10⌐)(6fb)2 CTV in all bedrooms ® **T** ✱
sB&B£35 sB&B⇨⌐£39.50 dB&B⇨⌐£57-£70
CTV 150P ✲ (hard) *xmas*
V Lunch £8.50&alc Dinner £9.50-£12.50&alc Last dinner 9.45pm
Credit Cards 1 2 3 4 5

STANDISH Greater Manchester Map **07** SD51

★★★64% **Kilhey Court Hotel** WN1 2XN (on A5106 1.5m N of A49/A5106 junction) (Best Western)
☎(0257)423083 & 422040 Telex no 67460 FAX 0257 423083
Situated in 10 acres of grounds and gardens with a lake, this extended Victorian mansion provides comfortable accommodation and excellent cuisine.
20⇨⌐(2fb)1 CTV in all bedrooms ® **T** sB&B⇨⌐£45-£55 dB&B⇨⌐£65-£75
☾ 180P ✲
French **V** Lunch £8.75-£9.75&alc Dinner £14.50-£18.50&alc Last dinner 9.30pm
Credit Cards 1 2 3 5

✕✕**Beeches** School Ln WN6 0TD ☎(0257)426432
Set in its own grounds beside the A5209 to the west of the town, a detached house offers comfortable lounges and a well-appointed, attractive restaurant which provides an ideal setting for its excellent meals. Cuisine is modern in style and uses only the finest fresh ingredients – a delectable main course might be Scallops in Pastry with a cream and white wine sauce, or Supreme of Chicken in a port wine sauce – while lounge bar meals are also popular.
Lunch not served Sat
Dinner not served Sun
French **V** 60 seats ✱ S% Lunch £5-£9&alc Dinner £12-£18alc Last lunch 2pm Last dinner 9.45pm 110P 11 bedrooms available
Credit Cards 1 2 3 5

STAVERTON Devon Map **03** SX76

★**Sea Trout Inn** TQ9 6PA ☎(080426)274
A comfortable village inn in a peaceful situation offering attentive service from the resident owners.
6rm(1⇨)(1fb) ® sB&B£20-£30 sB&B⇨£25-£30 dB&B⇨£35-£50
CTV 70P
English & French **V** Sunday Lunch £6.25-£6.95 Dinner £11.50&alc Last dinner 10pm
Credit Cards 1 2 3 £

STEEPLE ASTON Oxfordshire Map **04** SP42

★★★67% **Hopcrofts Holt** OX5 3QQ ☎(0869)40259
FAX 0869 40865
This 15th-century, character, highwayman's inn has been comfortably appointed to provide modern accommodation. The dining room offers a carvery selection at lunchtime and an à la carte menu in the evening.
88rm(71⇨15⌐)(2fb) CTV in 60bedrooms ® **T**
sB&B⇨⌐fr£54.95 dB&B⇨⌐fr£69.90
☾ CTV 200P ✲ games room *xmas*
English & French **V** S% Lunch £8.50-£9.50&alc Dinner fr£12&alc Last dinner 9.30pm
Credit Cards 1 2 3 5 £

See advertisement under BANBURY

Book as early as possible for busy holiday periods.

S

STEPPS Strathclyde *Lanarkshire* Map **11** NS66

★★Garfield House Cumbernauld Rd G33 6HW ☎041-779 2111 FAX 041-779 2111
An extended and modernised Victorian house where the majority of bedrooms have been upgraded to provide modern facilities for the businessman. The restaurant offers a choice of menus. Extensive car parking facilities.
27⇌↱(2fb) CTV in all bedrooms ® **T** ✱ sB&B⇌↱£35-£45 dB&B⇌↱£45-£55 ⊟
(80P *xmas*
V ♁ ⊻ Lunch £5.95&alc Dinner fr£8.50alc Last dinner 9.30pm
Credit Cards [1] [2] [3] [5] £

STEVENAGE Hertfordshire Map **04** TL22

★★★55% Blakemore Little Wymondley SG4 7JJ (2m W A602) (Thistle) ☎(0438)355821 Telex no 825479 FAX (0438) 742114
(For full entry see Hitchin)

★★★57% The Roebuck Old London Rd, Broadwater SG2 8DS (Trusthouse Forte) ☎(0438)365444 Telex no 825505 FAX (0438) 741308
Charming 15th century inn with modern bedrooms.
54⇌⊬in 6 bedrooms CTV in all bedrooms ® **T** S% sB⇌fr£62 dB⇌fr£72 (room only) ⊟
(80P ✿ CFA *xmas*
♉ English & French **V** ♁ ⊻ ⊬ S% Lunch £8.90-£8.95 Dinner £14.25 Last dinner 9.45pm
Credit Cards [1] [2] [3] [4] [5]

★★★56% *Stevenage Moat House* High St, Old Town SG1 3AZ (Queens Moat) ☎(0438)359111 Telex no 8950511
Historically interesting old world hotel with modern, well-equipped bedrooms.
60⇌(4fb) CTV in all bedrooms ®
(100P ✿
♉ English & French **V** ♁ ⊻
Credit Cards [1] [2] [3] [4] [5]

STEWARTON Strathclyde *Ayrshire* Map **10** NS44

★★★ 75% Chapeltoun House KA3 3ED
☎(0560)82696
FAX (0560) 85100
This charming mansion, set in 20 acres of grounds and gardens in delightful countryside, offers style and seclusion combined with character and comfort. Public rooms with their wood panelling, ornate plasterwork and elaborate stone work are tastefully decorated and furnished whilst the bedrooms vary in size, are individually decorated and equipped with many thoughtful extras. The menus feature traditional dishes using local produce and the food is complemented by an extensive wine list.
8rm(6⇌2↱)1⊟ CTV in all bedrooms T sB&B⇌↱£60-£70 dB&B⇌↱£89-£115 ⊟
50P 4 ✿ nc12yrs
♉ French V ♁ ⊻ ⊬ Lunch fr£15.50&alc Dinner fr£23.50 Last dinner 9pm
Credit Cards [1] [2] [3] £

S

STIRLING Central *Stirlingshire* Map **11** NS79

★★***King Robert*** Glasgow Rd, Bannockburn FK7 0LT ☎Bannockburn(0786)811666
Standing beside the famous Bannockburn battlefield, this modern, privately-owned hotel combines practical commercial standards with modest, yet well-equipped bedrooms.
24rm(21⇨)(1fb) CTV in 21bedrooms ® **T** ✗
CTV 100P ✽
V ♉ ⊻
Credit Cards [1][2][3][5]

★★**Terraces** 4 Melville Ter FK8 2ND (Consort) ☎(0786)72268 Telex no 778025 FAX 0786 50314
A small, Georgian town house, set in an elevated terrace close to the shopping centre, has been converted to create a hotel which is popular with businessmen.
15rm(7⇨8↟)(2fb) CTV in all bedrooms ® **T**
sB&B⇨↟£37-£39.95 dB&B⇨↟£53 ⊟
☾25P ♫ *xmas*
☋ International **V** ♉ ⊘ Lunch £9.30-£16alc Dinner £9.75&alc Last dinner 9pm
Credit Cards [1][2][3][5]

⌂**Granada Lodge** Pirnhall Roundabout, Snabhead FK7 8EU (junc M9/M80) (Granada) ☎(0786)815033 FAX 0786 813614
Meals can be obtained from the adjacent Country Kitchen restaurant.
37⇨(10fb)⊘in 5 bedrooms CTV in all bedrooms ® ✗ (ex guide dogs) S% sB⇨£23-£26 dB⇨£26-£28 (room only)
CTV 100P
V ♉ ⊻ ⊘
Credit Cards [1][2][3][5]

STOCKBRIDGE Hampshire Map **04** SU33

★★★61% **Grosvenor** High St SO20 6EU (Lansbury) ☎Andover(0264)810606 Telex no 477677 FAX (0264) 810606
Set at the heart of an attractive old market village in the Test Valley, the hotel is home to the Houghton Fishing Club. Bedrooms are particularly well equipped, and the standard of cuisine is high, under the close personal supervision of the resident manager.
25⇨↟1⊞⊘in 5 bedrooms CTV in all bedrooms ® **T** ✗ (ex guide dogs) ✱ sB&B⇨↟£30-£58 dB&B⇨↟£60-£68 ⊟
☾45P ⇛ ✽ sauna
☋ Continental **V** ♉ ⊻ Lunch fr£8.50 Dinner fr£12.50 Last dinner 10.30pm
Credit Cards [1][2][3][5]

STOCKPORT Greater Manchester Map **07** SJ88

★★★62% **Alma Lodge** 149 Buxton Rd SK2 6EL (Embassy) ☎061-483 4431 Telex no 665026 FAX 061-483 1983
RS Xmas
Set on the A6 Buxton road, one and a half miles from both the town centre and junction 12 of the M63 motorway, a converted Victorian hotel with modern extensions provides sound accommodation in well-appointed rooms.
58rm(52⇨)(2fb)⊘in 4 bedrooms CTV in all bedrooms ® **T**
sBfr£29.50 sB⇨£55-£65 dB⇨£67.50-£77.50 (room only) ⊟
☾200P CFA
☋ English & French **V** ♉ ⊻ Lunch fr£10.50&alc Dinner fr£10.50&alc Last dinner 9.30pm
Credit Cards [1][2][3][4][5]

★★★62% **Bramhall Moat House** SK7 2EB (Queens Moat) ☎061-439 8116 Telex no 668464 FAX 061-440 8071
(For full entry see Bramhall)

★★**Rudyard Toby** 271 Wellington Rd North, Heaton Chapel SK4 5BP (1.5m N off A6) (Toby) ☎061-432 2753
Telex no 668594
An attractive Victorian building with modern bedrooms and comfortable bars reached by a flower-bedecked, colonial-style veranda.
21⇨↟(2fb)⊘in 8 bedrooms CTV in all bedrooms ® **T** ✱
sB&B⇨↟£35.50-£45.50 dB&B⇨↟£45.50-£55.50 ⊟
☾82P Golf
V ♉ ⊻ ⊘ Lunch £6.35-£11.30 Dinner £6.35-£11.30 Last dinner 10.00pm
Credit Cards [1][2][3][4][5]

★★***Wycliffe Villa*** 74 Edgeley Rd, Edgeley SK3 9NQ ☎061-477 5395
RS Sun & BH's
Small, family-run hotel with a friendly atmosphere. The villa restaurant offers an extensive menu of mostly Italian dishes at reasonable prices.
12rm(2⇨10↟) CTV in all bedrooms ® ✗
CTV 20P ⇛ nc5yrs
☋ English, French & Italian **V** Last dinner 9.30pm
Credit Cards [1][2][3][5] £

★**Acton Court** Buxton Rd SK2 7AB ☎061-483 6172 FAX 061-483 0147
Closed Boxing Day, New Year & Bank Hols
A gabled and extended building on the A6 about 2 miles south east of the town centre. Recent improvements have considerably enhanced the well-equipped bedrooms and attractive restaurant provides a good standard of cooking.
37rm(13⇨15↟) CTV in all bedrooms ® **T** ✱ sB&B£24-£26 sB&B⇨↟£31-£36 dB&B£34-£39 dB&B⇨↟£42-£49 ⊟
☾CTV 200P ⇛ ✽ ♫
☋ French **V** Lunch £6&alc Dinner £8&alc Last dinner 10pm
Credit Cards [1][2][3][5]

STOCKTON-ON-TEES Cleveland Map **08** NZ41

★★★★50% **Swallow** 10 John Walker Square TS18 1QZ (Swallow) ☎(0642)679721 Telex no 587895
Modern multi-storey town centre hotel.
122⇨↟⊘in 25 bedrooms CTV in all bedrooms ® **T** S%
sB&B⇨↟£59-£65 dB&B⇨↟£75-£82 ⊟
Lift ☾400P CFA *xmas*
☋ English & French **V** ♉ ⊻ S%
Credit Cards [1][2][3][4][5]

★★★54% **Billingham Arms** The Causeway, Billingham TS23 2HD (3m NE A19) ☎(0642)553661 Telex no 587746 FAX 0642 552104
A town centre commercial hotel offers bedrooms which are for the most part compact, several bars and extensive function facilities.
64rm(43⇨12↟)(1fb)1⊞⊘in 4 bedrooms CTV in all bedrooms ® **T** ✱ sBfr£18 sB⇨↟£31-£43 dBfr£38 dB⇨↟£46-£54 (room only) ⊟
Lift ☾ ⊞ CTV 150P 2⌂ CFA solarium pool table *xmas*
☋ International **V** ♉ ⊻ Lunch £6.95-£7.25&alc Dinner fr£9.95&alc Last dinner 11pm
Credit Cards [1][2][3][4][5] £
See advertisement under BILLINGHAM

★★★57% ***Golden Eagle*** Trenchard Av, Thornaby-on-Tees TS17 0DA (1m E A174) ☎(0642)766511 Telex no 587565
Large, modern hotel in a residential and shopping area.
57⇨↟(1fb)⊘in 5 bedrooms CTV in all bedrooms ® **T** ✗
Lift ☾ CTV 80P CFA
☋ English & French **V** ♉ Last dinner 9.30pm
Credit Cards [1][3]

★★★64% **Parkmore** 636 Yarm Rd, Eaglescliffe TS16 0DH (3m S A19) (Best Western) ☎(0642)786815 Telex no 58298 FAX (0642) 790485
This constantly improving hotel offers good value for money with some very smart executive rooms and a new leisure suite.
55rm(51⇨4↟)(3fb)4⊞ CTV in all bedrooms ® **T**
sB&B⇨↟£42-£50 dB&B⇨↟£54-£64 ⊟
☾ CTV 140P ✽ ⊡(heated) snooker sauna solarium gymnasium jacuzzi steam room beauty salon

English & French V Lunch £7.95-£8.95 Dinner £12.45-£12.95&alc Last dinner 9.30pm
Credit Cards 1 2 3 5

★★★61% **Post House** Low Ln, Thornaby-on-Tees TS17 9LW (Trusthouse Forte) ☎Middlesbrough(0642)591213 Telex no 58426 FAX (0642) 594989
Situated one mile east on the A1044 this is a busy hotel with friendly staff, an à la carte restaurant and a coffee shop.
135⇌(17fb) in 20 bedrooms CTV in all bedrooms ® T ✱ S% sB⇌£64 dB⇌£75 (room only)
250P CFA sauna solarium
V S% Lunch £6.75&alc High tea £8.40-£13.45alc Dinner £8.40-£26.80alc Last dinner 10.15pm
Credit Cards 1 2 3 4 5

★***Claireville*** 519 Yarm Rd, Eaglescliffe TS16 9BG (3m S A135) ☎(0642)780378
RS Xmas & New Year
This modestly-furnished, family-run hotel is set in an acre of gardens.
19rm(3⇌)(1fb) CTV in 18bedrooms ®
CTV 20P
V Last dinner 7.30pm
Credit Cards 1 3 5

★***Stonyroyd*** 187 Oxbridge Ln TS18 4JB ☎(0642)607734
A pleasant, homely, comfortable hotel where guests are made welcome by the resident proprietor. Good standards are maintained throughout.
13rm(8)(1fb) CTV in all bedrooms ®
CTV 6P solarium
International V Last dinner 8pm
Credit Cards 1 3

STOKE CANON Devon Map 03 SX99

★★★72% **Barton Cross Hotel & Restaurant** Huxham EX5 4EJ ☎Exeter(0392)841245 & 841584 Telex no 42603 FAX (0392) 50402
Conveniently situated for Exeter, this small owner-managed hotel offers character public rooms in the original thatched building and very comfortable, well-equipped bedrooms in a new wing. Efficient, friendly service complements the imaginative food in the intimate, galleried restaurant.
6rm(5⇌1) CTV in all bedrooms ® T sB&B⇌£35-£57.75 dB&B⇌£55-£70
24P shooting, windsurfing instruction *xmas*
V Lunch £11.50-£20.65&alc Dinner £15.50-£19.50alc Last dinner 9.30pm
Credit Cards 1 2 3 4 5

See advertisement under EXETER

STOKE GABRIEL Devon Map 03 SX85

★★★ 65% **Gabriel Court**
TQ9 6SF
☎(080428)206 & 267
Closed Feb

Situated on the edge of this character village, a pleasantly proportioned Georgian house offers well-equipped bedrooms and comfortable public areas with some good paintings and antiques. Atmosphere is friendly and service relaxed yet attentive.

21rm(14⇌5) CTV in all bedrooms ® T
sB&B⇌£30-£44 dB&B⇌£60-£70
CTV 13P 7 (heated) croquet *xmas*
S% Lunch £9-£15 Dinner £16.50-£25 Last dinner 8.30pm
Credit Cards 1 2 3 5

STOKE-ON-TRENT Staffordshire Map 07 SJ84

See also Newcastle-under-Lyme

★★★★50% **The North Stafford** Station Rd ST4 2AE ☎(0782)744477 Telex no 36287 FAX (0782) 744477
Located opposite the railway station entrance, the attractive, ornamented, brick-faced hotel offers comfortable accommodation and friendly service. The work of local potters is on display.
70rm(48⇌21)(2fb) CTV in 69bedrooms ® T ✱ S% sB⇌£64-£69.50 dB⇌£77-£83 (room only)
Lift 120P CFA *xmas*
V S% Lunch £6.95-£9.75&alc Dinner £15.50&alc Last dinner 10.15pm
Credit Cards 1 2 3 4 5

★★★62% ***Clayton Lodge*** Clayton Rd ST5 4AF (Embassy) ☎Newcastle-Under-Lyme(0782)613093
(For full entry see Newcastle-under-Lyme)

★★★69% ***Haydon House*** 1-13 Haydon St, Basford ST4 6JD ☎(0782)711311 Telex no 36600
Attentive service is a feature of this fully extended and modernised Victorian house. The Glebe Mews annexe offers superior bedrooms, many with private lounges, and imaginative food is served in the restaurant.
18rm(10⇌8) CTV in 26bedrooms ® T

▶

S

52P
English & French V Last dinner 10.30pm
Credit Cards 1 2 3 5

★★★63% **Stakis Grand** 66 Trinity St, Hanley ST1 5NB (Stakis) (0782)202361 Telex no 367264 FAX (0782) 286464
This city centre hotel has undergone major refurbishment to provide good quality accommodation which includes bedrooms for the disabled, a leisure complex with heated swimming pool, and both carvery and à la carte restaurants.
86(5fb) in 30 bedrooms CTV in all bedrooms ® T (ex guide dogs) S% sB£58-£68 dB£71-£81 (room only)
Lift 175P (heated) sauna solarium gymnasium whirlpool spa *xmas*
V S% Lunch £6.50-£9&alc Dinner fr£12.50&alc Last dinner 10.00pm
Credit Cards 1 2 3 5

★★**George** Swan Square, Burslem ST6 2AE (0782)577544
A busy, commercial hotel with comfortable bedrooms and a restaurant which offers à la carte and carvery menus. Functions are a speciality here.
41rm(20 20)(1fb) CTV in all bedrooms ® T (ex guide dogs) sB&B£19.50-£25.50 sB&B£25.50-£34 dB&B£31-£37 dB&B£37-£45
Lift 14P sauna solarium
International V Lunch fr£6.75&alc Dinner fr£8.25&alc Last dinner 10.30pm
Credit Cards 1 2 3 5

STONE Staffordshire Map **07** SJ93

★★★56% **Crown Toby** High St ST15 8AS (Toby) (0785)813535
A traditional hotel in the centre of town with oak panelling and a glass domed restaurant offering a choice of menus.
13 Annexe16(4fb) CTV in 30bedrooms ® (ex guide dogs) sB&B£22.50-£33 dB&B£32.50-£42.50
200P *xmas*
English & Continental V Lunch £5.25-£6.50&alc Dinner £7.50&alc Last dinner 9.30pm
Credit Cards 1 2 3

★★★62% **Stone House** ST15 0BQ (Lansbury) (0785)815531 FAX (0785) 814764
An Edwardian house, one mile south of the town, has recently been extended to include extra bedrooms and a leisure and conference complex.
50rm(41 9)(2fb) CTV in all bedrooms ® T sB&Bfr£65 dB&Bfr£75
100P (heated) (hard) sauna solarium gymnasium croquet, putting green *xmas*
International V Lunch fr£9&alc Dinner fr£11.50&alc Last dinner 10pm
Credit Cards 1 2 3 5

All hotels awarded three or more stars are now also given a percentage grading for the quality of their facilities. Please see p 16 for a detailed explanation.

STON EASTON Somerset Map **03** ST65

★★★ **STON EASTON PARK** BA3 4DF (Pride of Britain)
Chewton Mendip (076121)631
Telex no 444738
FAX (076121) 377

Waterfalls and a folly in grounds landscaped by Humphry Repton, combined with Palladian architecture and some of the finest Georgian decorations in the west of England would make a stay at Ston Easton memorable enough – but it is also special for its particularly pleasant atmosphere. Taking the lead from proprietors Peter and Christine Smedley (who are continually improving the houseand grounds), manager Kevin Marchant has built up a friendly and capable team who make this very much the welcoming country house. It is easy to forget one is in a hotel, an effect which is more often sought than achieved in places such as this. Inside, the grandest room is the magnificently decorated formal saloon, but the intimate library and light, fresh dining room both have charm as well. Bedrooms are furnished with antiques and are available in varying degrees of splendour, while all are extremely comfortable. The park's own vegetable garden and greenhouses provide much of the produce for the skills of Mark Harrington, and a new refinement is descernible in dishes such as medallions of venison marinated with apricot brandy and fresh apricots, and terrine of duck livers and foie gras with toasted brioche.
20rm(19)6 CTV in all bedrooms T sB&B£60 dB&B£105-£260 Continental breakfast
CTV 40P 2 snooker croquet hot air ballooning nc12yrs *xmas*
English & French V Lunch £19.50 Dinner £29.50 Last dinner 9.30pm
Credit Cards 1 2 3 5

STONEHAVEN Grampian *Kincardineshire* Map **15** NO88

★★**County** Arduthie Rd AB3 2EH (0569)64386
Closed 1 Jan
Friendly commercial hotel in north-east coastal town.
14rm(12 2)(4fb) CTV in all bedrooms ® T S% sB&B£25-£30 dB&B£42-£44
CTV 40P squash sauna solarium gymnasium
Scottish, English & Italian V Dinner £8&alc Last dinner 8.45pm
Credit Cards 1 2 3

STONEHOUSE Gloucestershire Map **04** SO80

★★★66% **Stonehouse Court** Bristol Rd GL10 3RA (045382)5155 Telex no 437244 FAX (045382) 4611
Set in six acres of attractive grounds, an hotel dating from the early seventeenth century offers pleasant accommodation, for the most part in a modern garden wing; refurbishment of the rooms in the main house is planned.
10 Annexe27 1 CTV in all bedrooms ® T (ex guide dogs) sB&Bfr£60 dB&Bfr£75
200P croquet bowls mini golf *xmas*
English & French V Lunch fr£10.50 Dinner fr£17.50 Last dinner 9.30pm
Credit Cards 1 3

S

STONOR Oxfordshire Map **04** SU78

❀ ✕✕**Stonor Arms** RG9 6HE
☎Turville Heath(049163)345
Stephen Frost keeps up the good work at this convivial restaurant converted from an 18th-century inn at the heart of the village. The stylish, intimate rooms are all richly furnished and service is professional and discreet. The menu changes with the season, but always illustrates Stephen's originality and finesse. Dishes which have attracted praise from our inspectors include morel mushrooms in light flaky pastry with a rich truffle sauce, terrine of Gressingham duck with smoked quail, and rack of lamb with an onion and marmalade sauce. Equally tempting desserts include a white chocolate steamed pudding with white chocolate sauce and juniper berries, and fresh lime tart with strawberry sauce, while good, plentiful coffee and delicious home-made petits fours make a fitting finish.
Lunch not served Mon-Sat
Dinner not served Sun
40 seats Sunday Lunch £17.95-£21.95 Dinner £24.75-£25.75&alc Last lunch 1.45pm Last dinner 9.30pm 30P
Credit Cards [1] [2] [3]

STORNOWAY
See **Lewis, Isle of**

STORRINGTON West Sussex Map **04** TQ01

❀ ✕✕✕**Manleys** Manleys Hill RH20 4BT
☎(0903)742331
This immaculately presented restaurant offers a choice of prix fixe and à la carte menus featuring some original cooking; superbly constructed dishes are accompanied by a selection of fine wines and complemented by service which is well supervised though sometimes uneven.
Closed Mon, 1st 2 wks Jan, last wk Aug & 1st wk Sep
Dinner not served Sun
🍷 Austrian & French **V** 45 seats ✱ Sunday Lunch fr£14.55&alc Last lunch 2pm Last dinner 9.30pm 25P
Credit Cards [1] [2] [3] [5]

STOURBRIDGE West Midlands Map **07** SO88

★★***Talbot*** High St DY8 1DW (Crown & Raven) ☎(0384)394350 Telex no 335464
The busy, town-centre hotel, said to be over 500 years old, is a popular meeting place for shoppers and business people.
25rm(13⇌7↱)(4fb)1⊟ CTV in all bedrooms ® **T**
☾ 25P
🍷 English & French **V** ✧ ☕ Last dinner 10pm
Credit Cards [1] [2] [3]

STOURPORT-ON-SEVERN Hereford & Worcester Map **07** SO87

★★★63% **Stourport Moat House** 35 Hartlebury Rd DY13 9LT (Queens Moat) ☎(0299)827733 Telex no 333676 FAX (02993) 78520
Modernised hotel with sports and conference facilities.
68⇌↱2⊟ CTV in all bedrooms ® **T** sB&B⇌↱£52-£60 dB&B⇌↱£60-£65 ⊟
☾ 400P ✲ CFA ⇌ ▶ ♪ (hard) squash snooker sauna gymnasium clay pigeon shooting ♫
🍷 English & French **V** ✧ ☕ Lunch fr£9&alc Dinner fr£11.25&alc Last dinner 9.55pm
Credit Cards [1] [2] [3] [5]

★★**Swan** High St DY13 8BX (Porterhouse) ☎(02993)71661
This town-centre hotel has comfortable, refurbished bedrooms and a popular, value-for-money restaurant.
32⇌↱(2fb) CTV in all bedrooms ® **T** ✱ sB&B⇌↱fr£31 dB&B⇌↱fr£52 ⊟
CTV 60P ⌂
🍷 English, French & Spanish **V** ✧ Sunday Lunch fr£6.75alc Dinner £7.95-£15alc Last dinner 9.45pm,
Credit Cards [1] [2] [3] [5] £

STOW CUM QUY Cambridgeshire Map **05** TL56

★**Quy Mill** CB5 9AG ☎Cambridge(0223)853383
FAX (0223) 853770
Family-run hotel, adjacent to the A45, which is being developed from several former mill buildings. The newer bedrooms are well equipped and standards are being raised throughout. Popular for bar lunches.
26rm(1⇌19↱)1⊟ ⚟in 10 bedrooms CTV in all bedrooms ® **T** sB&B£35-£39 sB&B⇌↱£45-£49 dB&B£44-£49 dB&B⇌↱£55-£59 Continental breakfast ⊟
☾ CTV 100P ✲ ⌡
🍷 English, French & Italian **V** ✧ ☕ Lunch £9-£12&alc Dinner £9-£12&alc Last dinner 9.15pm
Credit Cards [1] [3] [5] £

STOWMARKET Suffolk Map **05** TM05

★★**Cedars** Needham Rd IP14 2AJ ☎(0449)612668
FAX (0449) 674704
Closed Xmas-New Year
Built in the 16th-century as a farmhouse, the Cedars retains many of its original fine timbers and exposed studwork. The popular bar has an extensive snack menu and a traditional à la carte menu is served in the attractive restaurant. Service is friendly and helpful.
21rm(13⇌8↱)(2fb) CTV in all bedrooms ® **T** ✱ sB&B⇌↱fr£35 dB&B⇌↱fr£45 ⊟
60P ✲
🍷 English & French ✧ ☕ Lunch £8-£15alc Dinner £8-£15alc Last dinner 9pm
Credit Cards [1] [3] £

See advertisement under IPSWICH

○***Travelodge*** A45 IP14 3PY (Trusthouse Forte)
☎Central reservations 01-567 3444
Due to have opened summer 1989
40⇌
P

STOW-ON-THE-WOLD Gloucestershire Map **04** SP12

★★★60% **Unicorn Crest** Sheep St GL54 1HQ (Crest)
☎Cotswold(0451)30257 Telex no 437186 FAX (0451) 31090
A delightful Cotswold stone building dating back to the 17th century with well-furnished bedrooms equipped to modern standards. The bar and lounge have open fires which add to the charm of this friendly hotel.
20rm(17⇌3↱)2⊟ ⚟in 3 bedrooms CTV in all bedrooms ® **T** ✱ sB⇌↱£53-£65 dB⇌↱£65-£77 (room only) ⊟
CTV 45P *xmas*
🍷 English & French **V** ✧ ☕ ⚟ Sunday Lunch fr£8.95 Dinner fr£14.50 Last dinner 9.30pm
Credit Cards [1] [2] [3] [4] [5]

A rosette is the AA's highest award for quality of food and service in a restaurant.

★★★🏅75% **Wyck Hill House** Wyck Hill GL54 1HY
☎Cotswold(0451)31936
Telex no 43611
FAX (0451) 32243

Standing in 100 acres of grounds and overlooking the Windrush Valley, this hotel offers well-equipped bedrooms both in the main house and in the carefully converted stable block. Public rooms are comfortable and pleasingly furnished, in keeping with the character of the building; a spacious, recently refurbished restaurant serves interesting dishes which are carefully prepared from the best produce available, and a hard working, friendly staff creates a warm, hospitable atmosphere throughout.
16rm(13⇌3🚿)Annexe10⇌(30fb)3⊟ CTV in all bedrooms T ✗ ✻ sB&B⇌🚿£65-£120 dB&B⇌🚿£80-£150
Lift ☾ 100P ✿ croquet clay pigeon shooting nc6yrs *xmas*
☋ International V ♈ Lunch £13.50&alc Dinner £23.50&alc Last dinner 9.30pm
Credit Cards [1] [2] [3] ⓔ

★★**Fosse Manor** GL54 1JX (Consort) ☎Cotswold(0451)30354
FAX (0451) 32486
Closed 1 wk Xmas
Comfortable, well-equipped, hotel with friendly atmosphere. Restaurant provides consistently good cooking.
14rm(10⇌4🚿)Annexe6rm(2⇌)(6fb)1⊟ CTV in all bedrooms ® T ✻ sB&B⇌🚿fr£38 dB&B⇌🚿£68-£80 ⊟
CTV 20P ⊞ ✿ solarium croquet ⌂
☋ English & Continental V ♈ ☕ Lunch £10.95-£12.95&alc Dinner fr£12.95&alc Last dinner 9.30pm
Credit Cards [1] [2] [3] [5]

★★**Grapevine** Sheep St GL54 1AU (Best Western)
☎Cotswold(0451)30344 Telex no 43423 FAX (0451) 32278
11 Jan-24 Dec
Whether you visit 'The Grapevine' just for a meal, or to stay, you can be assured of a memorable visit and a warm welcome from owner Sandra Elliot and her charming staff. An attractive feature of the dining room, is a very old vine, and here, as in the separate bar where lighter meals can be enjoyed, the cooking is sound and honest. The main reception lounge is comfortable, and even more peaceful is the quiet writing room with French windows leading onto the terrace. The use of high-quality soft furnishings, combined with modern facilities, make the bedrooms delightful. The atmosphere here is relaxed and informal and nothing seems too much trouble.
13rm(10⇌3🚿)Annexe4⇌(3fb)1⊟ CTV in all bedrooms ® T ✗ sB&B⇌🚿£48-£59 dB&B⇌🚿£66-£88 ⊟
17P ⊞
☋ English, French & Italian V ♈ ☕ ⊁ Lunch fr£5.50alc Dinner £15.95-£20.95 Last dinner 9.30pm
Credit Cards [1] [2] [3] [5] ⓔ

★★**Old Farmhouse** Lower Swell GL54 1LF (1m W B4068)
☎Cotswold(0451)30232
Closed 26 Dec RS 24-25 & 27-28 Dec
Small, personally-run hotel offering imaginative food and comfortable bedrooms, some of which are in the old Stable House a former, part 16th-century barn.
7⇌🚿Annexe6⇌🚿(1fb)2⊟ CTV in all bedrooms ® S% dB&B⇌🚿£39-£64.50 ⊟
25P ✿ board games ⌂ *xmas*
☋ International V ♈ ☕ ⊁ S% Lunch £9.95 High tea £3.95-£5 Dinner £11.25&alc Last dinner 9pm
Credit Cards [1] [3]

See advertisement on page 629

★★**Old Stocks** The Square GL54 1AF ☎Cotswold(0451)30666
Closed 21-30 Dec
Hospitable small hotel with well-appointed bedrooms.
17rm(15⇌2🚿)(3fb) CTV in all bedrooms ® T sB&B⇌🚿£22-£28.50 dB&B⇌🚿£44-£57 ⊟
CTV 12P 2🚗 ✿ ⌂
V ♈ ☕ Lunch £7.50 Dinner £7.50-£12.50 Last dinner 9.30pm
Credit Cards [1] [2] [3]

★★**Royalist** Digbeth St GL54 1BN ☎Cotswold(0451)30670
A proprietor supervised hotel. The building retains some of the features of its historic past.
14rm(8⇌6🚿)1⊟ CTV in all bedrooms ® T ✗ sB&B⇌🚿£25-£38 dB&B⇌🚿£40-£62
12P ⊞ CFA
V ♈ ☕ Bar Lunch £1.25-£6.95alc Dinner £11-£15alc Last dinner 9pm
Credit Cards [1] [2] [3] ⓔ

★★**Stow Lodge** The Square GL54 1AB ☎Cotswold(0451)30485
Closed 20 Dec-mid Jan
Country house style hotel set back from the market square and in its own grounds. Family owned and personally run, offering warm, caring services and an informal atmosphere. Bedrooms in the main house and annexe are well furnished and comfortable as are the public areas.
11rm(10⇌)Annexe10⇌(2fb)1⊟⊁in 1 bedroom CTV in all bedrooms ® ✗ ✻ sB&B⇌£30-£36.50 dB&B⇌£40-£56 ⊟
☾ 30P ⊞ ✿ nc5yrs
▶

Bar Lunch £7.20-£12alc Dinner fr£10&alc Last dinner 9pm
Credit Cards 2 5

STRACHUR Strathclyde *Argyllshire* Map **10** NN00

★★★61% **Creggans Inn** PA27 8BX (036986)279
Telex no 778425
Extensively and tastefully modernised, this seventeenth-century inn on the shores of Loch Fyne offers compact but cheerful, attractively decorated bedrooms. In the restful split-level restaurant good food is served by friendly, courteous staff.
22rm(15 2) CTV in all bedrooms **T** sB&Bfr£35 sB&B fr£40 dB&Bfr£60 dB&B fr£76
CTV 80P xmas
French **V** Lunch £8.15-£12alc Dinner £17-£23alc Last dinner 9.30pm
Credit Cards 1 2 3 5

STRANRAER Dumfries & Galloway *Wigtownshire* Map **10** NX06

★★★69% **North West Castle** DG9 8EH (Exec Hotel) (0776)4413 Telex no 777088 FAX (0776) 2646
Family owned and managed this spacious, elegant hotel has been sympathetically modernised and extended to provide a wide range of leisure and recreational facilities. Many of the comfortable, well-equipped bedrooms enjoy fine views of Loch Ryan.
74 (12fb)1 CTV in all bedrooms ® **T** (ex guide dogs) sB&B £34-£38 dB&B £52-£56
Lift 100P CFA (heated) snooker sauna solarium curling (Oct-Apr) games room *xmas*
V Dinner fr£14.50 Last dinner 9.30pm

STRATFORD-UPON-AVON Warwickshire Map **04** SP25

See **Town Plan Section**
See also **Charlecote**
★★★★ ***Moat House International*** Bridgefoot CV37 6YR (Queens Moat) (0789)414411 Telex no 311127 FAX (0789) 298589
Very busy, large modern hotel on banks of River Avon.
249 (20fb) CTV in all bedrooms ® **T**
Lift CTV 350P
British & French **V** Last dinner 10.30pm
Credit Cards 1 2 3 5

★★★★57% **The Shakespeare** Chapel St CV37 6ER (Trusthouse Forte) (0789)294771 Telex no 311181 FAX (0789) 415411
Situated in the heart of town this magnificent timbered building dates back to at least 1637. The hotel offers comfortable public areas, with good levels of service. Bedrooms are continually being sympathetically upgraded to offer modern accommodation, but some of the older rooms are still awaiting attention.
70 2 in 5 bedrooms CTV in all bedrooms ® **T** sB £70-£78 dB £97-£116 (room only)
Lift 45P CFA *xmas*
English & Continental **V** Lunch £12-£13&alc Dinner £15&alc Last dinner 10pm
Credit Cards 1 2 3 4 5

★★★★73% **Welcombe** Warwick Rd CV37 0NR (0789)295252
Telex no 31347 FAX (0789) 414666
Closed 29 Dec-4 Jan
Standing on the outskirts of Stratford in a parkland estate which offers an 18-hole golf course and two all-weather floodlit tennis courts, this Jacobean mansion features truly traditional service rendered by a charming and efficient staff. Public rooms are comfortable, and a major refurbishment programme is upgrading most bedrooms to a luxurious standard – including many suites and fourposter rooms – though the older, garden wing accommodation remains simple.
76 (2fb)7 CTV in all bedrooms **T** S% sB&B fr£80 dB&B £115-£300
100P 6 CFA 18 snooker croquet putting table-tennis *xmas*
English & French **V** Lunch fr£13.50&alc Dinner fr£22.50 Last dinner 9.30pm
Credit Cards 1 2 3 5

★★★59% **Alveston Manor** Clopton Bridge CV37 7HP (Trusthouse Forte) (0789)204581 Telex no 31324
FAX (0789) 414095
An attractive hotel with well-kept gardens just across the river from the theatre and town centre. Afternoon tea can be enjoyed in the cocktail bar which has 16th-century oak panelling.
108 (6fb)1 in 10 bedrooms CTV in all bedrooms ® **T** sB fr£67 dB £89-£141 (room only)
200P CFA pitch & putt *xmas*
French **V** Lunch £10.50-£12&alc High tea £2-£3 Dinner £15-£16&alc Last dinner 9.30pm
Credit Cards 1 2 3 4 5

★★★50% ***Arden*** Waterside CV37 6BA (Mount Charlotte) (0789)294949 Telex no 311726
The building dates from the Regency period and is situated opposite the Royal Shakespeare Theatre.
65 (7fb) CTV in all bedrooms ® **T**
CTV 55P
V Last dinner 9pm
Credit Cards 1 2 3 4 5

★★★76% **Billesley Manor Hotel** B49 6NF (3m W off A422) (Norfolk Capital)(Prestige) (0789)400888 Telex no 312599
FAX (0789) 764145
(For full entry see Billesley)

★★★61% **Charlecote Pheasant Country** CV35 9EW (3m E off B4086) (Queens Moat) (0789)470333 Telex no 31688
(For full entry see Charlecote)

★★★60% **Dukes** Payton St CV37 6UA (0789)69300
Telex no 31430 FAX (0789) 414700
Closed 2 days Xmas
The hotel offers attractive accommodation in cosy bedrooms which are compact yet well furnished with good facilities. Public rooms are beautifully appointed, the comfortable, spacious lounge and elegant restaurant being of a particularly high standard, as is also the lovingly-tended garden, enjoyed by guests and visitors alike.
22rm(15 7)2 CTV in all bedrooms ® **T** sB&B fr£37.50 dB&B fr£59
30P nc12 yrs
European **V** Lunch fr£12.50alc Dinner fr£16.50alc Last dinner 9.45pm
Credit Cards 1 2 3 5 £

★★★54% **Falcon** Chapel St CV37 6HA (Queens Moat) (0789)205777 Telex no 312522 FAX (0789) 414260
Located close to the town centre, this busy conference hotel dating back to 1640 offers well-equipped bedrooms in various styles and sizes together with an extensive range of conference/meeting rooms.
73 (13fb)1 CTV in all bedrooms ® **T** S% sB&B £55-£70 dB&B £74-£82
Lift 100P 24 CFA *xmas*
French **V** S% Lunch £8.95-£14&alc High tea £4.50-£7.50 Dinner £14-£16&alc Last dinner 9pm
Credit Cards 1 2 3 4 5

★★★50% **Grosvenor House** Warwick Rd CV37 6YT (Best Western) (0789)269213 Telex no 311699 FAX (0789) 66087
Closed Xmas
This family-run hotel is particularly hospitable, and a friendly atmosphere prevails; the well-equipped health centre is now an added attraction.
52rm(34 18)(8fb)2 CTV in all bedrooms ® **T** sB&B £45-£55 dB&B £64-£90

S

☾ CTV 40P CFA sauna solarium gymnasium beauty salon
♔ Lunch £7-£10 Dinner £10-£12&alc Last dinner 8.45pm
Credit Cards [1] [2] [3] [5] (£)

★★★The Swan's Nest Bridgefoot CV37 7LT (Trusthouse Forte)
☎(0789)66761 FAX (0789) 414547
Standing beside the River Avon, the hotel is conveniently placed for both town and theatre. It offers guests comfortable bedrooms and a choice of menus.
60⇨(1fb)⅟in 7 bedrooms CTV in all bedrooms ® **T**
sB⇨£65-£105 dB⇨£81-£115 (room only) ⊟
☾ 100P ✲ CFA ♫ *xmas*
V ♔ ♕ ⅟ S% Lunch fr£9.50&alc Dinner fr£14.25&alc Last dinner 9.30pm
Credit Cards [1] [2] [3] [4] [5]

★★★53% The White Swan Rother St CV37 6NH (Trusthouse Forte) ☎(0789)297022
Traditional 15th-century inn situated in the town centre.
42⇨(4fb)1⊟⅟in 5 bedrooms CTV in all bedrooms ® **T** ✱
sB⇨£67 dB⇨£83 (room only) ⊟
☾ 8P CFA *xmas*
V ♔ ♕ ⅟ Lunch fr£6.50&alc Dinner £9.85-£25.40alc Last dinner 9pm
Credit Cards [1] [2] [3] [4] [5]

★★Stratford House Sheep St CV37 6EF ☎(0789)68288
Telex no 311612
Closed Xmas
This highly individual small hotel at the very heart of the town has comfortable, well-decorated bedrooms, a lovely sitting room overlooking the bustle of Sheep Street and an oasis of quiet in its flower-filled walled courtyard. It also houses Shepherds Restaurant, where chef Nigel Lambert bases superb English and French dishes in the light modern style on the best fresh ingredients available each day, presenting them most attractively.
10rm(6⇨3↾)(1fb) CTV in all bedrooms ® **T** ✗
sB&B⇨↾£45-£55 dB&B⇨↾£70-£80 ⊟
P̸ ⊞ nc2 yrs
♔ ♕ Lunch £12.50-£13.50&alc Dinner £14-£18alc Last dinner 9.30pm
Credit Cards [1] [2] [3] [5]

★★Swan House The Green CV37 9XJ (3m N off A34)
☎(0789)67030
(For full entry see Wilmcote)

STRATHBLANE Central *Stirlingshire* Map **11** NS57

★★★61% Country Club Milngavie Rd G63 9AH
☎Blanefield(0360)70491
Set in 15 acres of grounds this former country mansion is now a comfortable hotel with special appeal for the businessman. Bedrooms are individually decorated and well-equipped and a good standard of cuisine is served in the restaurant. Lounge facilities are limited.
10rm(8⇨2↾)⅟in 2 bedrooms CTV in all bedrooms ® **T**
sB&B⇨↾£40 dB&B⇨↾£65 ⊟
60P ⊞ ✲
♖ European **V** ♔ Lunch £8.50-£10.50&alc Dinner £14.50-£15.40&alc Last dinner 9.30pm
Credit Cards [1] [2] [3] [4] [5] (£)

★★Kirkhouse Inn G63 9AA ☎Blanefield(0360)70621
Hotel with good standards throughout, situated in a lovely village.
15⇨(2fb)1⊟ CTV in all bedrooms ® **T** ✱ S%
☾ 350P
♖ Scottish & French **V** ♔ ♕ S% Lunch fr£9&alc High tea £4-£7 Dinner fr£13.50&alc Last dinner 10pm
Credit Cards [1] [2] [3] [5]
See advertisement under GLASGOW

STRATHPEFFER Highland *Ross & Cromarty* Map **14** NH45

★★Holly Lodge IV14 9AR ☎(0997)21254
This attractive stone-built hotel stands in its own grounds overlooking the Victorian spa resort of Strathpeffer. It offers warm hospitality and good food influenced by a hint of the orient. The public rooms – in particular the charming residents' lounge area and the comfortable bedrooms also have an oriental feel about them.
7rm(3⇨3↾) CTV in all bedrooms ® sB&B⇨↾fr£19
dB&B⇨↾fr£38 ⊟
CTV 15P 2⌂ ⊞ ✲ shooting ♫
♖ Scottish & Oriental ♔ ♕ Dinner £11-£13.50 Last dinner 9.00
(£)

★★McKay's The Square IV14 9DL ☎(0997)21542
A painted stone Victorian hotel with attractive gardens situated in the centre of this popular Highland spa village. Bedrooms are pleasantly appointed and the menu offers a range of home-cooked Scottish dishes.
18rm(5⇨5↾)(1fb) CTV in all bedrooms ® ✗ (ex guide dogs)
sB&B£15-£18 sB&B⇨↾£17.50-£20.50 dB&B£28-£36
dB&B⇨↾£33-£42 ⊟
CTV 30P ✲
♔ ♕ Bar Lunch fr£4.50alc Dinner £9.50&alc Last dinner 8.30pm
Credit Cards [1] [3] (£)

★Brunstane Lodge IV14 9AT ☎(0997)21261
RS mid Oct-Apr
A small family run hotel offering warm and friendly service and good facilities. In an elevated position overlooking the village and hills.
6rm(2⇨2↾)(1fb) ® sB&B£15-£18.50 dB&B⇨↾£37-£40 ⊟
CTV 12P ✲ ⌂

▸

S

V ♔ ⊡ ⅙ Bar Lunch £2.50-£5 Dinner £10-£12.50 Last dinner 9pm
Ⓛ

STRATHTUMMEL Tayside *Perthshire* Map **14** NN86

★★⛨Port-an-Eilean
PH16 5RU
☎Tummel Bridge (08824)233
Closed mid Oct-late Apr

Comfortable hotel in a splendid location by the Loch side, personally supervised by the proprietors.
9⇌(2fb) Ⓡ sB&B⇌£28 dB&B⇌£46
20P 2🚗 ⚘ ✲ ♩
♔ ⊡ Dinner fr£12 Last dinner 8.45pm

STRATHYRE Central *Perthshire* Map **11** NN51

★***The Inn*** Main St FK18 8NA ☎(08774)224
This small, friendly family-run inn stands by the side of the main road at the eastern end of the village. Accommodation is modest but comfortable.
6rm(4⇌) Ⓡ
CTV 30P
☋ Mainly grills ♔ ⊡ Last dinner 8.30pm

STRATTON Cornwall & Isles of Scilly Map **02** SS20

★***Stamford Hill*** EX23 9AY ☎Bude(0288)2709
Closed Oct-Etr
This quietly situated Georgian manor house , built on the site of the Battle of Stamford Hill (1643), is now a small, family holiday hotel.
15rm(5⇌4♪)(9fb)1⛫ Ⓡ ✗
CTV 17P ✲ ⌒(heated) ♪ (grass) sauna badminton putting green ⌂
☋ English, French & Italian V ⊡ Last dinner 7.30pm
Credit Cards 1 3

STREATLEY Berkshire Map **04** SU58

★★★ 69% ***Swan Diplomat*** High St RG8 9HR ☎Goring-on-Thames(0491)873737 Telex no 848259 Gultel G
FAX (0491) 872554
Nestling beneath the ancient ridgeway in a fold of hills beside the River Thames, this tastefully renovated hotel offers spacious bedrooms, individually decorated and furnished in traditional mahogany, with river or hill views. Otherfacilities include the riverside restaurant with its candlelit atmosphere, a cocktail bar and the Magdalen Barge, which is popular for meetings and private functions, weather permitting. More recently a boathouse bar and leisure complex have been added to the hotel's attractions.
46⇌♪1⛫ CTV in all bedrooms Ⓡ
☾ CTV 146P ✲ ⌒(heated) sauna solarium gymnasium
☋ French V ♔ ⊡ Last dinner 9.30pm
Credit Cards 1 2 3 5

STREET Somerset Map **03** ST43

★★★ 64% **Bear** 53 High St BA16 OEF ☎(0458)42021
Recently refurbished town centre hotel with well-appointed bedrooms and a smart restaurant offering ambitious dishes. Service is by cheerful staff.
10rm(8⇌2♪)Annexe5⇌(3fb)⅙in 5 bedrooms CTV in all bedrooms Ⓡ T S% sB&B⇌♪£36-£39 dB&B⇌♪£49-£52 ⊟
36P ✲ *xmas*
☋ French & English V ♔ ⊡ ⅙ Lunch £4.50-£8 Dinner £9.95-£10.95&alc Last dinner 10pm
Credit Cards 1 2 3 5 Ⓛ

★★★ 55% **Wessex** High St BA16 0EF (Consort) ☎(0458)43383 Telex no 57515 ATTN 75 FAX (0458) 46589
Situated in the centre of Street, this hotel built in the 1970's, a popular stopping place for coaches, offers comfortable bedrooms and open-plan public areas.
50⇌♪(4fb) CTV in all bedrooms Ⓡ T
sB&B⇌♪£34.50-£50.50 dB&B⇌♪£50.50-£67.50 ⊟
Lift ☾ 60P 30🚗 CFA *xmas*
☋ English & French V ♔ ⊡ ⅙ Lunch £1.20-£6.50 Dinner £10.50-£11.50 Last dinner 9.15
Credit Cards 1 2 3 5 Ⓛ

STREETLY West Midlands Map **07** SP09

★★**Parson & Clerk Motel** Chester Rd B73 6SP (junc A452/ B4138) (Porterhouse) ☎021-353 1747
RS Xmas Day
A motel overlooking Sutton Park consists of an accommodation block with residents' bar and breakfast room plus a grill-type restaurant some 75 yards away. Staff are friendly and efficient.
30rm(1⇌29♪) CTV in all bedrooms Ⓡ T ✗ (ex guide dogs) ✳
sB&B⇌♪£29-£36 dB&B⇌♪£35-£43 ⊟
CTV P
V ♔ ⊡
Credit Cards 1 2 3 5

STRETTON Cheshire Map **07** SJ68

★★**Old Vicarage** WA4 4NS (Best Western)
☎Norcott Brook(092573)706 FAX (092573) 740
Situated just off the A49 near junction 10 of the M56, a friendly hotel is convenient for business person and tourist alike – whilst its location close to the church and its secluded gardens make it ideal for wedding receptions. Improvements continue within the hotel.
28rm(16⇌7♪)(2fb) CTV in 35bedrooms Ⓡ T sB&B£25-£45 sB&B⇌♪£45 dB&B£55 dB&B⇌♪£60 ⊟
Lift ☾ CTV 150P 8🚗 ✲ ♪ (hard) ♫ *xmas*
V ♔ ⊡ Lunch £8.25 High tea £2.50-£5 Dinner £11&alc Last dinner 10pm
Credit Cards 1 2 3 Ⓛ

STRETTON Leicestershire Map **04** SK91

★★**Ram Jam Inn** Great North Rd LE15 7QX
☎Castle Bytham(0780)410776 Telex no 342888
This beautifully refurbished inn is a welcome new addition for motorists on the A1. High quality 'fast food' from snacks to full meals is available from 7am – 11pm to motorists and residents alike. Bedrooms are well-equipped and there are comfortable lounge and bar facilities.
Annexe8⇌(2fb) CTV in all bedrooms Ⓡ T sB⇌£35-£37.50 dB⇌£45-£50 (room only)
100P ✲
♔ ⊡ Lunch £10-£15alc Dinner £10-£10alc Last dinner 11pm
Credit Cards 1 2 3

STRONTIAN Highland *Argyllshire* Map **14** NM86

★★**Kilcamb Lodge** PH36 4HY ☎(0967)2257
Closed Nov-Mar
Situated on the outskirts of the village with grounds stretching down to Loch Sunart.
9rm(2⇌6♪)(1fb) Ⓡ ✗ ✳ sB&B⇌♪£41.50-£46 dB&B⇌♪£83-£92 (incl dinner) ⊟
CTV 50P ⚘ ✲
☋ Scottish & French V ♔ ⅙ Bar Lunch £1-£10alc Dinner fr£16.50 Last dinner 7.00pm

★★**Loch Sunart** PH36 4HZ ☎(0967)2471
Closed Nov-Etr
A relaxing atmosphere and good food is provided at this family run traditional Highland hotel overlooking the loch.
11rm(4⇌2⩡)(1fb) ® sB&B£19 sB&B⇌⩡£21 dB&B£38 dB&B⇌⩡£42 ⊟
CTV 30P ⁂ ✲
V ✧ ☕ ✗ Bar Lunch 80p-£8 High tea £1.15-£3.30 Dinner £15 Last dinner 7.30pm

STROUD Gloucestershire Map **03** SO80

See also **Amberley and Painswick**
★★★ **58% The Bear of Rodborough** Rodborough Common GL5 5DE (.5m SW) (Trusthouse Forte) ☎(0453)878522
Telex no 437130 FAX (0453) 872523
Character Cotswold stone hotel giving fine views over its extensive grounds and 900 acres of adjoining National Trust land.
47rm(44⇌3⩡)1 ⊟ ✗in 5 bedrooms CTV in all bedrooms ® sB⇌⩡£68-£75 dB⇌⩡£83-£95 (room only) ⊟
☾ 200P *xmas*
♉ European **V** ✧ ☕ ✗ Lunch £8-£10&alc Dinner £13.50&alc Last dinner 9.30pm
Credit Cards [1] [2] [3] [4] [5]

Entries for rosetted restaurants, red-star and country-house hotels are highlighted by a tinted panel. For a full list of these establishments, consult the Contents page.

★★★ **64% Burleigh Court** Brimscombe GL5 2PF (2.5m SE off A419)
☎Brimscombe (0453)883804
FAX (0453) 886870
Closed 25 Dec-10 Jan

Hospitable country house hotel with comfortable bedrooms.
11rm(9⇌2⩡)Annexe6⇌(1fb) CTV in all bedrooms ® T ✗ ✲ sB&B⇌⩡£49 dB&B⇌⩡£64-£75 ⊟
40P 1⛟ ⁂ ✲ ⇌(heated) putting green
♉ English & French V ✧ ☕ ✗ S% Lunch £8-£11&alc Dinner £15-£24&alc Last dinner 8.45pm
Credit Cards [1] [2] [3] [5]

★★**Alpine Lodge** Stratford Rd GL5 4AJ
☎(04536)4949 due to change to 764949
RS Sundays
A privately-owned hotel with popular bars.
10rm(8⇌)(4fb) CTV in all bedrooms ® **T** sB&B£18-£20 sB&B⇌£24-£26 dB&B⇌£32-£34
CTV 50P 2⛟
♉ Mainly grills V ✧ ☕ Lunch £3.50-£5&alc Dinner £6&alc Last dinner 9pm
Credit Cards [1] [3] [5]

S

★★**Imperial** Station Rd GL5 3AP (Berni/Chef & Brewer) ☎(04536)4077
Conveniently situated opposite the railway station, a Georgian coaching inn clad in colourful creeping ivy offers well-equipped bedrooms, refurbished and with en suite bathrooms, complemented by a ground floor restaurant featuring the popular 'new look' Berni menu.
25⇌♠(2fb)2⊞ CTV in all bedrooms ® T ✗ (ex guide dogs) sB&B⇌♠fr£37.50 dB&B⇌♠fr£51 ⊟
15P
♀ Mainly grills V ✿ ⅟ Lunch £8 Dinner £9 Last dinner 10.30pm
Credit Cards 1 2 3 5

★★**London** 30-31 London Rd GL5 2AJ ☎(0453)759992
The hotel has a comfortable, attractive lounge bar and restaurant, and well-equipped if rather compact accommodation.
12rm(2⇌6♠) CTV in all bedrooms ® T ✗ ✻ sB&B£22-£25 sB&B⇌♠£28.50-£39 dB&B£34 dB&B⇌♠£40-£52 ⊟
10P ⇏ nc2 yrs
♀ Continental V ✿ ⊈ Lunch £4.67-£9.85alc Dinner £10.95&alc Last dinner 9.30pm
Credit Cards 1 2 3 4 5 £

❀✗**Oakes** 169 Slad Rd GL5 1RG
☎(0453)759950
Chef Chris Oakes and his family run this impressive restaurant – spotlessly clean with polished wooden floor, sparkling table settings and crisp napery. Each of the 3 menus offers two dishes for every course, but diners are not restricted to one menu and can make a 'mix and match' meal from all three. If your ideal is a meal oozing with calories and plates piled high, then Oakes is not for you – here portions are fairly small, but flavours are exquisite The warm onion tart melts away to leave its creamy filling of onion puree and tomato sauce – just the natural ingredients with a hint of garlic ; and the breast of duck with roast baby vegetables is served with an intense sauce made from its own carcase. The wine list is not extensive, but carries many modest prices and wines to match the superb cooking.
Closed Mon & end Dec-end Feb
Dinner not served Sun
♀ English & French V 30 seats ✻ Lunch £12.50-£28 Dinner £24-£28 Last lunch 1.45pm Last dinner 9.30pm 12P
Credit Cards 1 3

STRUY Highland *Inverness-shire* Map **14** NH43

★★**Cnoc** Erchless Castle Estate IV4 7JU ☎(046376)264 & 219
This friendly little hotel, ideal for anglers, offers good, home-made cooking.
8rm(6⇌2♠)(2fb) ® T sB&B⇌♠£25-£28 dB&B⇌♠£40-£50 ⊟
CTV 40P ⇏ ✿ shooting
V ✿ ⊈ Lunch £6-£7.50alc Dinner £10-£15.50alc Last dinner 8.30pm
Credit Cards 1 3 £

STUDLAND Dorset Map **04** SZ08

★★★63% **Knoll House** Ferry Rd BH19 3AH ☎(092944)251
Apr-Oct
Set in National Trust land this hotel is constantly improving its facilities. Children are well-catered for here, they have their own restaurant, a playroom and a playground. It is a hotel for all ages with fine leisure facilities, good food, friendly staff and caring owners.
57rm(42⇌)Annexe22rm(15⇌)(30fb) T sB&B£40-£50 sB&B⇌£50-£60 dB&B£80-£100 dB&B⇌£92-£120 (incl dinner)
☾ CTV 100P ⇏ ✿ ⛆(heated) ⚑ 9 ⚲ (hard) sauna solarium gymnasium jacuzzi & leisure centre ⌂
✿ ⊈ Lunch fr£11 Dinner fr£13 Last dinner 8.30pm

★★⌂**Manor House**
BH19 3AU
☎(092944)288
Closed 21 Dec-3 Feb
Gothic-style manor house with secluded gardens and grounds overlooking the sea and cliffs.
20rm(14⇌6♠)(9fb)4⊞ CTV in all bedrooms ® sB&B⇌♠£47.50-£57.50 dB&B⇌♠£77-£97 (incl dinner) ⊟
40P ⇏ ✿ ⚲ (hard) nc5 yrs
♀ English & French V ✿ ⊈ Bar Lunch £2.50-£5 High tea fr£2.50 Dinner fr£13.50 Last dinner 8.30pm
Credit Cards 1 3

STURMINSTER NEWTON Dorset Map **03** ST71

❀✗✗**Plumber Manor** DT10 2AF (2m SW on Hazlebury Brian rd) (Pride of Britain)
☎(0258)72507
(Rosette awarded for dinner only)
A long drive leads to this impressive Jacobean country house which is tastefully and comfortably furnished and has some well-appointed bedrooms available. The small, but elegant restaurant has a relaxing, intimate atmosphere and chef Brian Prideaux-Brune combines his skill and imagination with the best fresh produce to provide some interesting dishes. The Mousseline of Crab is well worth recommending and the Aylesbury Duckling in a flavoursome raspberry vinegar sauce should be tried. The cooking is enhanced by a well-balanced wine list with some good wines available at reasonable prices. Service is friendly and informal with proprietor Richard Prideaux-Brune supervising the proceedings.
Closed 1st 2 wks Feb
Lunch not served
♀ English & French V 60 seats ✻ Dinner £17-£21 Last dinner 9.30pm 25P nc12yrs
Credit Cards 1 3

SUDBURY Suffolk Map **05** TL84

✗**Mabey's Brasserie** 47 Gainsborough St CO10 7SS
☎(0787)74298
In this simple brasserie the skill of one of England's most accomplished chefs is brought to the production of interesting country dishes from top quality ingredients. Interested customers can watch Robert Mabey at work – either duringthe daily routine or in one of his periodic demonstrations – as his cooking area is in full view of diners. An extensive blackboard menu offers such traditional savoury fare as saddle of hare, haunch of wild rabbit, rack of lamb and salmon, all matched with compatible vegetables, and you can complete your meal with an individual bread and butter pudding, a roast apple dessert or rich parfaits.
♀ International V 38 seats ✻ Lunch fr£2.95alc Last lunch 2pm Last dinner 10pm Ᵽ
Credit Cards 1 3

SUNDERLAND Tyne & Wear Map **12** NZ35

★★★63% **Seaburn** Queen's Pde, Seaburn SR6 8DB (Swallow) ☎091-529 2041 Telex no 53168 FAX 091-529 4227
A well-managed hotel built in the 1930's is pleasantly situated two miles north of the town centre, overlooking the sandy beaches of Whitburn. All bedrooms are well-equipped, though those in the new part of the building are more comfortable and up-to-date; there are plans for further extensive modernisation.
82rm(79⇌3↱)(4fb)⊁in 20 bedrooms CTV in all bedrooms ® T S% sB&B⇌↱£30-£65 dB&B⇌↱£45-£80 ⊟
Lift ☾ CTV 110P CFA ♫
⊕ English & French V ✪ ☕
Credit Cards 1 2 3 5

★★***Mowbray Park*** Toward Rd SR1 1PR ☎091-567 8221 Telex no 587746
This town centre, commercial hotel provides a range of bars and good-value menus.
52rm(33⇌2↱)(5fb) CTV in all bedrooms ® T
Lift ☾ CTV 400P (charged) 20⌂ (charged)
⊕ French V ✪ ☕ ⊁
Credit Cards 1 2 3 4 5

★★**Roker** Roker Ter SR6 0PH (Berni/Chef & Brewer) ☎091-567 1786
A well-furnished hotel, with good modern bedrooms, occupying a pleasant position overlooking the North Sea.
45rm(44⇌1↱)(5fb) CTV in all bedrooms ® T ✗ (ex guide dogs) sB&B⇌↱fr£38 dB&B⇌↱fr£49.50 ⊟
☾ 200P
⊕ Mainly grills V ✪ ☕ ⊁ Lunch fr£8 Dinner fr£9 Last dinner 10.30pm
Credit Cards 1 2 3 5

★**Gelt House** 23 St Bede's Ter SR2 8HS (Exec Hotel) ☎091-567 2990
A small, friendly hotel is situated in a tree-lined private road close to the town centre and offers simple, clean and comfortable accommodation.
14rm(3⇌6↱)Annexe8rm(2fb) CTV in all bedrooms ® T ✻ sB&B£21.50 sB&B⇌↱£27.50 dB&B£32 dB&B⇌↱£38 ⊟
☾ 14P ⛟
⊁ Dinner £7.50 Last dinner 9pm
Credit Cards 1 2 3 5

SURBITON Greater London

See **LONDON plan 5*B1***(page 412) **Telephone codes are due to change on 6th May 1990. See page 421.**
✕✕**Chez Max** 85 Maple Rd KT6 4AW ☎01-399 2365
Chef/patron Max Markarian offers a well-balanced fixed-price menu at this cosy restaurant, using seasonal produce to advantage and making good use of sauces. Service is supervised by Mrs Markaman who has a team of charming French waitresses. The wine list remains well-balanced.
Closed Sun, Mon, 25-26 Dec, 1-2 Jan & Good Fri
Lunch not served Sat
⊕ French V 30 seats ✻ Lunch £17.50 Dinner £20-£23alc Last lunch 2pm Last dinner 10.30pm ₱ nc7yrs
Credit Cards 1 2 3 5

SUTTON Greater London

See **LONDON plan 5*B1***(page 412) **Telephone codes are due to change on 6th May 1990. See page 421.**
○***Crest*** Cheam Rd(Crest) ☎Central reservations 0800-123234
Due to have opened Sep 1989
115⇌

For key to symbols see the inside front cover.

S

✕Partners 23 23 Stonecot Hill SM3 9HB ☎01-644 7743
Tim McEntire provides the culinary expertise while his partner Andrew Thompson warmly welcomes diners at this popular, bright restaurant in a residential shopping area. Short but imaginative set price menus feature dishes such as escalope of salmon and turbot with a crab and chive sauce or glazed veal loin steak; seasonal vegetables are nicely cooked and simply presented and the sweets are tempting.
Closed Sun, Mon & 25 Dec-4 Jan
Lunch not served Sat
English & French 30 seats Lunch £14.25-£17.75 Dinner fr£25.95 Last lunch 2pm Last dinner 9.30pm nc10yrs
Credit Cards 1 2 3 5

SUTTON BENGER Wiltshire Map **03** ST97

★★★60% Bell House SN15 4RH ☎Seagry(0249)720401
Set in formal gardens in a pretty village this hotel has ornate bedrooms and a formal well-managed restaurant offering a continental menu.
12⇌Annexe2⇌(2fb)1 CTV in all bedrooms ® T ✱
sB&B⇌£40.50-£43.50
dB&B⇌£65.50-£72.50 Continental breakfast
40P
International V Lunch £9.25-£11.95&alc Dinner £11-£18alc Last dinner 10.30pm
Credit Cards 1 2 3 5

See advertisement under CHIPPENHAM

SUTTON COLDFIELD West Midlands Map **07** SP19

★★★★51% Penns Hall Penns Ln, Walmley B76 8LH (Embassy) ☎021-351 3111 Telex no 335789 FAX 021-313 1297
Popular with business and conference delegates this large hotel in extensive grounds is well-placed for Birmingham city centre, the NEC and the M6 motorway. The new leisure complex provide facilities for weekend leisure breaks.
115⇌in 20 bedrooms CTV in all bedrooms ® T S%
sB⇌£82-£92 dB⇌£92-£102 (room only)
Lift (500P CFA (heated) squash snooker sauna solarium gymnasium *xmas*
French & Italian V Lunch £11-£18&alc High tea fr£2alc Dinner £15-£18&alc Last dinner 10pm
Credit Cards 1 2 3 4 5

★★★66% Moor Hall Moor Hall Dr, Four Oaks B75 6LN (Best Western) ☎021-308 3751 Telex no 335127 FAX 021-308 8974
Situated in peaceful parkland and overlooking a golf course this hotel has been extensively modernised and improved to provide good quality, well-equipped accommodation. A self contained banquetting hall and a choice of restaurants are additional features.
75⇌(3fb)3 in 5 bedrooms CTV in all bedrooms ® T ✱
sB&B⇌£60-£85 dB&B⇌£70-£95
Lift (180P CFA sauna solarium gymnasium *xmas*
International V Lunch fr£8.50 Dinner £12.50-£14.50&alc Last dinner 10.30pm
Credit Cards 1 2 3 4 5

★★★76% New Hall Walmley Rd B76 8QX (Thistle) ☎021-378 2442 Telex no 333580 FAX 021-378 4637
Dating from the 12th-century New Hall has the reputation of being the oldest inhabited manor house in England. Suites and bedrooms in the main building are generally large with high quality fittings and furnishings, including many antiques, whilst those in the courtyard extension are equally comfortable, and well-equipped. In the restaurant, an important venue for both business and private diners, Chef Allan Garth provides mainly British cuisine prepared in the light, modern, international style that is now so popular. Managers Ian and Caroline Parkes and their excellent team of staff ensure the quality of service and hospitality throughout.
64⇌2 CTV in all bedrooms T ✱ sB⇌£75-£90
dB⇌£90-£150 (room only)
(80P croquet clay pigeon shooting archery
V Lunch £12.50-£15.20 Dinner £19.50-£21.20&alc Last dinner 10pm
Credit Cards 1 2 3 4 5 £

★★★63% Sutton Court 60-66 Lichfield Rd B74 2NA (Consort) ☎021-355 6071 Telex no 334175 FAX 021-355 0083
56rm(47⇌9)(9fb)1 in 13 bedrooms CTV in all bedrooms ® T S% sB&B⇌£60-£65 dB&B⇌£76-£84
(90P *xmas*
International V S% Lunch fr£5.95&alc Dinner fr£13.95&alc Last dinner 9pm
Credit Cards 1 2 3 4 5 £

See advertisement under BIRMINGHAM (NATIONAL EXHIBITION CENTRE)

★★Berni Royal High St B72 1UD (Berni/Chef & Brewer) ☎021-355 8222
Once the home of photography pioneer William Morris Grundy, this handsome Georgian hotel has been completely modernised to offer pretty, well-equipped bedrooms and comfortable public areas which include attractive bars and a restaurant offering mainly grilled food.
22⇌ CTV in all bedrooms ® T (ex guide dogs) sB&B⇌£42
dB&B⇌£53
(80P *xmas*
V Lunch fr£8 Dinner fr£9 Last dinner 11pm
Credit Cards 1 2 3 5

★★Cloverley 17 Anchorage Rd B74 2PJ ☎021-354 5181
A hotel situated close to the town centre and railway station provides rooms with basic furnishings and limited modern facilities, some single accommodation being very compact.
26rm(6⇌20)(2fb)2 CTV in all bedrooms ® T ✱
sB&B⇌£31.45-£45.83 dB&B⇌£50.63-£54.08
CTV 26P *xmas*
Continental V Lunch fr£8&alc Dinner £8.50-£8.35&alc Last dinner 10pm
Credit Cards 1 2 3

SUTTON-ON-SEA Lincolnshire Map **09** TF58

★★*Bacchus* High St ☎(0521)41204
A predominantly holiday hotel with large grounds, close to the sea front.
22rm(6⇌)(1fb) CTV in 6bedrooms ®
CTV 60P 10 putting, bowls
V Last dinner 8pm
Credit Cards 1 2 3

★★Grange & Links Sea Ln, Sandilands LN12 2RA ☎(0521)41334
14rm(11⇌3)Annexe3(1fb) CTV in all bedrooms ® T
sB&B⇌fr£41.40 dB&B⇌fr£55.20
(CTV 60P 18 (hard) snooker *xmas*
French V Sunday Lunch £8.50-£8 Dinner fr£11.50&alc Last dinner 8.30pm
Credit Cards 1 2 3 5

Entries for rosetted restaurants, red-star and country-house hotels are highlighted by a tinted panel. For a full list of these establishments, consult the Contents page.

SUTTON SCOTNEY Hampshire Map **04** SU43

⌂**TraveLodge** A34 Trunk Rd Southside SO21 3JY (on A34) (Trusthouse Forte) ☎Winchester(0962)760779
Bedrooms, all at ground floor level, offer flexible and well-equipped accommodation. Close to service station and Little Chef restaurant.
Annexe40⇨⌒(40fb) CTV in all bedrooms Ⓡ sB⇨⌒£21.50 dB⇨⌒£27 (room only)
☾ 40P 🚗
🍷 Mainly grills
Credit Cards 1 2 3

○*Travelodge* A34 Trunk Rd Northside, Sutton Scotney SO21 3JY (Trusthouse Forte) ☎Central reservations 01-567 3444
Due to have opened summer 1989
31⇨
P

SUTTON UPON DERWENT Humberside Map **08** SE74

★★**Old Rectory** YO4 5BX ☎Elvington(090485)548
A former rectory offering tranquility, comfortable accommodation and friendly service from resident proprietors.
6rm(2⌒)(2fb) CTV in all bedrooms Ⓡ S% sB&B£22-£27 dB&B£36-£38 dB&B⌒£40-£42 Ⓑ
50P 🚗 ✲
🍷 Dinner £10-£12 Last dinner 7pm
Credit Cards 1 £

SWAFFHAM Norfolk Map **05** TF80

★★**George** Station Rd PE37 7LJ (Consort) ☎(0760)721238
Tastefully restored Georgian building in the centre of town. Bedrooms, both those in the main building and the adjoining modern block, are comfortable and well-equipped and the cosy bar is popular with residents and locals alike. Recent improvements include a new reception area and lounge.
27rm(24⇨1⌒) CTV in all bedrooms Ⓡ sB&B⇨⌒£39-£49 dB&B⇨⌒£49-£59 Ⓑ
☾ 100P CFA *xmas*
🍷 English & French V 🍷 ☕ Lunch £6.95-£16 High tea £4-£7 Dinner £9.95-£16 Last dinner 9.30pm
Credit Cards 1 2 3 4 5 £

★★**Grady's Country House** Norwich Rd PE37 7QS ☎(0760)23355
The recently refurbished hotel offers comfortable accommodation with a good range of facilities and service.
12rm(2⇨10⌒)(1fb)1🛏 CTV in all bedrooms Ⓡ T sB&B⇨⌒£35.50-£39.50 dB&B⇨⌒£45-£49 Ⓑ
☾ 70P *xmas*
V 🍷 ☕ Lunch £10-£11.50 Dinner £11.50-£20alc Last dinner 9.30pm
Credit Cards 1 2 3 £

SWALLOWFIELD Berkshire Map **04** SU76

★★**The Mill House** RG7 1PY ☎Reading(0734)883124 Telex no 847423
This attractive Georgian property, tastefully converted and with well-equipped bedrooms, is now under a pleasant husband and wife management team with friendly staff. There is room for improvement in the standard of cooking.
10rm(4⇨6⌒)(2fb)1🛏 CTV in all bedrooms Ⓡ T sB&B⇨⌒£59 dB&B⇨⌒£70 Ⓑ
40P 🚗 ✲ ♪
🍷 French V 🍷 ☕ S10% Lunch £9.75-£13.95&alc Dinner £16.50&alc Last dinner 10pm
Credit Cards 1 2 3 5

S

SWANAGE Dorset Map **04** SZ07

★★★61% Grand Burlington Rd BH19 1LU (Best Western) ☎(0929)423353 Telex no 9401694 FAX (0929) 427068
Occupying an excellent cliff-top position, this family resort hotel has been upgraded to provide comfortable accommodation in well-equipped bedrooms and relaxing lounges. Other facilities include an unusual and attractively appointed restaurant offering both à la carte and table d'hôte menus, and good leisure amenities which are also open to non residents. Friendly staff offer attentive and efficient services in all areas.
30rm(22⇨8♠)(5fb)1⊟ CTV in all bedrooms ® **T**
sB&B⇨♠fr£32 dB&B⇨♠fr£64 ⊟
Lift ☾ 15P ✻ ⊠(heated) ♪ sauna solarium gymnasium spa bath table tennis *xmas*
☋ English & French **V** ♤ ⌂ Lunch fr£6.50 High tea £4.50-£5.50 Dinner fr£11.95 Last dinner 10pm
Credit Cards [1] [2] [3] [5]

★★★55% The Pines Burlington Rd BH19 1LT ☎(0929)425211 Telex no 418297
A family-run resort hotel with an excellent cliff-top location offers spacious, comfortable lounges, well-equipped bedrooms and the services of a friendly, attentive staff.
51rm(46⇨3♠)(26fb) CTV in all bedrooms **T** ✱
Lift ☾ 60P ⊞ ✻ CFA
☋ Continental **V** ♤ ⌂ Last high tea 6pm
Credit Cards [1] [3] £

★*Suncliffe* Burlington Rd BH19 2NZ ☎(0929)423299
Small, family-run hotel with a warm, friendly atmosphere. Bedrooms, though rather basic, are of a good size and public rooms are comfortable.
14rm(1⇨7♠)(5fb) ⋈
CTV 14P 4⌂ ⊞ ⌂
♤

SWANICK

See **Alfreton**

SWANSEA West Glamorgan Map **03** SS69

See also **Langland Bay and Mumbles**

★★★51% Dolphin Whitewalls SA1 3AB (Inter) ☎(0792)650011 Telex no 48128 FAX (0792) 642871
This popular, businessman's hotel in the centre of Swansea features recently upgraded bedrooms and a new coffee shop on the ground floor.
65⇨(5fb) CTV in all bedrooms ® **T** ✱ sB⇨fr£42.50 dB⇨fr£52.50 (room only) ⊟
Lift ☾ Ᵽ *xmas*
☋ English & Continental **V** ♤ ⌂ Lunch fr£6.50 Dinner fr£10.50 Last dinner 9.30pm
Credit Cards [1] [2] [3] [5] £

★★★61% Fforest Pontardulais Rd, Fforestfach SA5 4BA (on A483 1.5m S of M4 junc 47) (Lansbury) ☎(0792)588711 Telex no 48105 FAX (0792) 586219
Conveniently situated just off junction 47 of the M4, this modern hotel provides comfortable well-equipped bedrooms. Other facilities comprise a pine-furnished restaurant offering a good choice of food, sound conference amenities and a small gymnasium with sauna.
34⇨(1fb)1⊟ ⅟in 4 bedrooms CTV in all bedrooms ® **T**
sB&B⇨fr£55 dB&B⇨fr£65 ⊟
☾ CTV 200P sauna solarium
☋ English **V** ♤ ⌂ ⅟ Lunch £8.15-£14.95alc Dinner £8.15-£14.95alc Last dinner 10.30pm
Credit Cards [1] [2] [3] [5]

Book as early as possible for busy holiday periods.

★★★64% Hilton National Phoenix Way, Swansea Enterprise Park SA7 9EH (1m S M4, jct 44 & 45, SW of Llansamlet) (Hilton) ☎(0792)310330 Telex no 48589 FAX (0792) 797535
A modern hotel set in the heart of the Enterprise Park just off junction 45 of the M4 offers good accommodation in well-equipped bedrooms which include three specially designed for the disabled. An open-plan public area and fine conference facilities are also available.
114⇨♠(18fb)⅟in 10 bedrooms CTV in all bedrooms ® **T** ✱
sB⇨♠£65-£80 dB⇨♠£83-£98 (room only) ⊟
☾ 200P ✻ ⊠(heated) sauna gymnasium *xmas*
☋ English & French **V** ♤ ⌂ ⅟ Lunch £7.50-£9.50&alc Dinner £12.50-£14.25&alc Last dinner 9.45pm
Credit Cards [1] [2] [3] [5]

★★Beaumont 72 Walter Rd SA1 4QA ☎(0792)643956 FAX (0792) 643044
This small, personally owned and managed hotel has undergone commendable upgrading recently. It offers comfortable bedrooms, quality, character lounges and hospitable service from proprietors and staff.
17rm(4⇨13♠)2⊟⅟in 1 bedroom CTV in all bedrooms ® **T** ✱ sB&B⇨♠£36-£44 dB&B⇨♠£50-£60 ⊟
10P ⊞
☋ Welsh, French & Italian **V** ♤ ⌂ Lunch £7.50-£12.50 High tea fr£3.50 Dinner fr£10.50 Last dinner 9pm
Credit Cards [1] [2] [3] [5]

See advertisement on page 641

★★Nicholaston House Nicholaston SA3 2HL ☎(0792)371317
(For full entry see Penmaen)

★★Oak Tree Parc SA7 9JR ☎Skewen(0792)817781
(For full entry see Birchgrove)

S

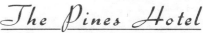

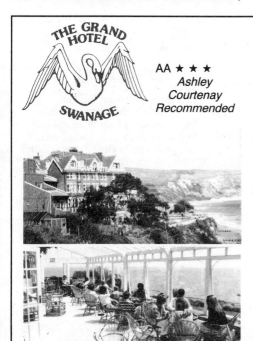

★Windsor Lodge Mount Pleasant SA1 6EG
☎(0792)642158 & 652744
Closed 25-26 Dec
Situated on rising ground close to the town centre, this pleasant Georgian house has been carefully restored and enlarged to provide well-appointed public areas. Bedrooms though compact are brightly decorated and equipped with modern facilities. The dining room serves good, well-prepared dishes supported by a comprehensive wine list; the self-service breakfast buffet is particularly noteworthy. The hotel is very popular with business people.
19rm(11⇌4↱) CTV in all bedrooms ® **T** ✱ sB&Bfr£25.30 sB&B⇌↱fr£32.20 dB&Bfr£37.50 dB&B⇌↱fr£46 ⊟
25P 1🚗 ⛟ sauna
🍷 English & French **V** ✿ Lunch fr£10 High tea fr£2 Dinner fr£12 Last dinner 9.30pm
Credit Cards [1] [2] [3] [5] £

○***Campanile*** St Thomas Station, Pentra Guinea Rd(Campanile) ☎Central reservation 01-569 5757
Due to have opened September 1989
50⇌

○**The Dragon** Kingsway Circle SA1 5LS (Trusthouse Forte)
☎(0792)651074 Telex no 48309 FAX (0792) 456044
Previously awarded 4 stars, this hotel has been closed for extensive refurbishment and is due to reopen in March 1990.
118⇌

SWAY Hampshire Map **04** SZ29

★★White Rose Station Rd SO41 6BA (Exec Hotel)
☎Lymington(0590)682754
Substantial red brick house standing in 6 acres of grounds with well-equipped, if plainly-appointed bedrooms, and an attractive bar serving good value imaginative bar meals.
12rm(9⇌)(2fb) CTV in all bedrooms ® **T** S10% sB&Bfr£27 sB&B⇌£35 dB&Bfr£48 dB&B⇌£60 ⊟
Lift 50P ⛟ ✲ ⛱ *xmas*
V ✿ ☕ S10% Lunch £7-£9&alc Dinner £8-£10&alc Last dinner 9pm
Credit Cards [1] [3]

SWINDON Wiltshire Map **04** SU18

★★★★ 68% **Blunsdon House Hotel & Leisure Club** Blunsdon SN2 4AD (3m N off A419) (Best Western) ☎(0793)721701
Telex no 444491 FAX (0793) 721056
Family owned and run hotel where the proprietors take a personal interest in their guests' well being. Bedrooms are comfortable and well-equipped and there is a formal restaurant and a separate carvery. Supervised creche for younger guests.
89⇌↱(11fb)5⊠ CTV in all bedrooms ® **T** ✗ (ex guide dogs) ✱ sB&B⇌↱£67.50-£75 dB&B⇌↱£75-£82.50 ⊟
Lift ☾ 250P ✲ CFA ⊡(heated) ℘ (hard) squash snooker sauna solarium gymnasium spa pool skittles beauty therapy ♫ *xmas*
🍷 English & French **V** ✿ ☕ Lunch £8.50-£12&alc Dinner £9.50-£15&alc Last dinner 10pm
Credit Cards [1] [2] [3] [5]

Entries for rosetted restaurants, red-star and country-house hotels are highlighted by a tinted panel. For a full list of these establishments, consult the Contents page.

★★★66% Crest Oxford Rd, Stratton St Margaret SN3 4TL (3m NE A420) (Crest) ☎(0793)831333 Telex no 444456
FAX (0793) 831401
Purpose built hotel on the edge of town with comfortable bedrooms, an attractive restaurant and pleasant staff.
94⇌↱(20fb)⊬in 25 bedrooms CTV in all bedrooms ® **T** sB⇌↱£72-£75 dB⇌↱£84-£87 (room only) ⊟
☾ 150P ✲ pool ♫ *xmas*
🍷 English & French **V** ✿ ☕ ⊬ Lunch £10.50-£12.50&alc Dinner £13.95-£15.95&alc Last dinner 9.45pm
Credit Cards [1] [2] [3] [4] [5]

★★★55% Goddard Arms High St, Old Town SN1 3EW (Trusthouse Forte) ☎(0793)692313 Telex no 444764
FAX (0793) 512984
Built in 1750 of warm Cotswold stone, with ivy clinging to the walls, this hotel is well-situated in the tranquil part of the old town. The inn also has motel-style rooms in the grounds.
18⇌Annexe47⇌⊬in 12 bedrooms CTV in all bedrooms ® **T** S% sB⇌£21-£67 dB⇌£35-£78 (room only) ⊟
☾ 120P CFA
V ✿ ☕ ⊬ Lunch £9.95-£12.50&alc Dinner £12.50&alc Last dinner 9.30pm
Credit Cards [1] [2] [3] [4] [5]

★★★64% Post House Marlborough Rd SN3 6AQ (Trusthouse Forte) ☎(0793)24601 Telex no 444464 FAX (0793) 512887
Modern, purpose-built hotel near the town centre and motorway interchange. It has a new leisure centre and a popular restaurant with a choice of menus.
104⇌(26fb)⊬in 10 bedrooms CTV in all bedrooms ® **T** S% sB⇌£70-£81 dB⇌£81-£90 (room only) ⊟
☾ 200P ✲ CFA ⊡(heated) sauna solarium gymnasium jacuzzi *xmas*

▶

♈ English & French V ♈ ♈ ⅟ Lunch £9-£11&alc High tea £4.50-£8alc Dinner £13&alc Last dinner 10pm
Credit Cards 1 2 3 4 5

★★★57% South Marston Hotel & Country Club Sandy Ln, South Marston SN3 4SL ☎(0793)827777 Telex no 444634 FAX (0793) 827879
Located half a mile from the A420 Swindon/Oxford road this hotel has extensive indoor and outdoor sports facilities, many conference rooms and modern, spacious bedrooms. Discos and live entertainment are sometimes a feature of the sports bar/coffee shop/lounge area.
40⇌(4fb) CTV in all bedrooms ® T S8% sB&B⇌£75 dB&B⇌£85 ⊟
☾ CTV 200P 1🚗 ✲ ⊡(heated) ⌂(heated) squash snooker sauna solarium gymnasium badminton spa bath table tennis pool ⌂ *xmas*
♈ English & French V ⅟ S8% Lunch £5-£13.75 High tea 50p-£3.75 Dinner £1375-£23.75&alc Last dinner 9.45pm
Credit Cards 1 2 3 5 ⓔ

★★★62% *Wiltshire* Fleming Way SN1 1TN (Mount Charlotte) ☎(0793)28282 Telex no 444250
A purpose-built hotel close to the town centre with parking facilities in a nearby, multi-storey car park. Bedrooms have been completely renovated to provide a high standard of comfort and facilities.
93⇌♠ CTV in all bedrooms ® T
Lift ☾ ⅌ CFA
♈ English & French V ♈ ♈ Last high tea 6pm
Credit Cards 1 2 3 5

★★Salthrop House Basset Down SN4 9QP ☎(0793)812990 FAX (0793) 814380
Set in 16 acres of grounds and lovingly restored to its former glory, this classical Georgian stone house has only recently been opened as a country hotel. Its ideal situation combines with pleasant accommodation in stylish bedrooms, elegant public areas and a small cellar restaurant to make this hotel perfect for a quiet business seminar or country weekend.
10rm(9⇌1♠)2⊟ CTV in all bedrooms ® T ✈ ✳
sB&B⇌♠£65-£75 dB&B⇌♠£80-£90 ⊟
CTV 100P ⊞ ✲ nc14yrs
♈ French Lunch £16.50-£20 Dinner £16.50-£24 Last dinner 9.15pm
Credit Cards 1 3 5

SYMONDS YAT (EAST) Hereford & Worcester Map **03** SO51

★★Royal HR9 6JL ☎(0600)890238
Closed 3-30 Jan
Popular with both holidaymakers and businessmen this former Victorian hunting lodge, on the banks of the River Wye, has been extended in recent times to provide comfortable, well-equipped accommodation.
20rm(12⇌8♠)4⊟ ® T sB&B⇌♠£27.50-£35.50 dB&B⇌♠£55-£65 ⊟
60P ⊞ ✲ ♩ sauna solarium abseiling canoeing clay pigeon shooting nc12yrs *xmas*
♈ British, French & Italian V ♈ ♈ Lunch £8.25&alc Dinner fr£17.50&alc Last dinner 9.30pm
Credit Cards 1 2 3

SYMONDS YAT (WEST) (near Ross-on-Wye) Hereford & Worcester Map **03** SO51

★★Paddocks HR9 6BL ☎(0600)890246 FAX (0600) 890964
Situated in extensive grounds and gardens, which extend to the River Wye, this friendly family-run hotel though particularly popular with tourists is equally suitable for travelling business people. Bedrooms are well-equipped.
26rm(20⇌4♠)(1fb) CTV in all bedrooms ® T
sB&B⇌♠£36.50 dB&B⇌♠£53 ⊟
150P ✲ ♀ (hard)
♈ English & French V ♈ ♈
Credit Cards 1 2 3 5 ⓔ

TAIN Highland *Ross & Cromarty* Map **14** NH88

★★★65% Morangie House Morangie Rd IV19 1PY ☎(0862)2281
An imposing Victorian mansion standing in three acres of grounds to the north of Tain with uninterrupted views to Dornoch Firth. Bedrooms offer a high standard of comfort whatever their size, and décor is in keeping with the period. Public rooms retain their Victorian stained-glass windows.
11rm(9⇌2♠)(1fb)1⊟ CTV in all bedrooms ® T
sB&B⇌♠£28-£35 dB&B⇌♠£42 ⊟
30P ✲
♈ Scottish & Continental V ♈ ♈ Lunch £5.50-£12.50&alc Dinner £12.50-£12.50&alc Last dinner 10pm
Credit Cards 1 2 3 5

★★★62% *Royal* High St IV19 1AB (Minotels) ☎(0862)2013 FAX (0862) 3450
Nicely appointed and comfortable hotel catering for business people and holiday-makers.
25rm(9⇌13♠) CTV in all bedrooms ® T
10P 6🚗 (£2.00)
V ♈ ♈ Last dinner 9pm
Credit Cards 1 2 3 5

TALKE Staffordshire Map **07** SJ85

○***Granada Lodge*** North Links(Granada) ☎Stoke-on-Trent(0782)777162
Due to open Apr 1990
70⇌

TALLAND BAY Cornwall & Isles of Scilly Map **02** SX25

★★★⚑73% Talland Bay
PL13 2JB (Inter)
☎Polperro(0503)72667
FAX (0503) 72940
Closed 2 Jan-10 Feb
Lovely gardens surround this charming hotel whose rooms have excellent sea views, are tastefully appointed and well equipped. The food is good, the staff helpful, and the hotel has access to the beach.
16⇌Annexe2⇌(4fb)1⊟ CTV in all bedrooms T
sB&B⇌£40-£63 dB&B⇌£80-£126 (incl dinner) ⊟
25P ⊞ ✲ ⌂(heated) sauna solarium croquet games room putting *xmas*
♈ English & French V ♈ ♈ Lunch £7.50 High tea £5&alc Dinner £14.50&alc Last dinner 9pm
Credit Cards 1 2 3 5

TALSARNAU Gwynedd Map **06** SH63

★★Maes y Neuadd
LL47 6YA (2m SE on unclass rd off B4573)

☎Harlech(0766)780200
FAX (0766) 780211
Closed 3-31 Jan

A most beautiful old Welsh granite house with distant views of mountains and sea. Under the personal attention of the Horsfall and Slatter families, it also offers a wonderful tranquility in which the pressures of modern life seem very far away. Trevor Pharoah's cooking is very good, there is a luxurious lounge bar with leather chesterfields in front of open fires, and the comfortable bedrooms also do much to induce a relaxed frame of mind. This hotel continues to improve and we hope it will not be too long before Red Stars can be awarded.

13rm(12⇌1⛆)Annexe2rm(1⇌1⛆)1 CTV in all bedrooms T sB&B⇌⛆£38-£55 dB&B⇌⛆£75-£116
50P ✽ nc7 yrs *xmas*
V Lunch £10.50-£13.50alc
Credit Cards 1 2 3 5

★★Tregwylan LL47 6YG ☎Penrhyndeudraeth(0766)770424
Originally a farmhouse, the hotel has been considerably extended to provide good, modern bedrooms. There is a cosy lounge and bar, and the varied menu offers a choice of good food. Family-owned and run, Tregwylan is a friendly place to stay, set in its own grounds overlooking sea and mountains.
10rm(3⇌3⛆)(3fb) CTV in all bedrooms ® (ex guide dogs) sB&B£15-£16.50 sB&B⇌⛆£18.50-£21 dB&B£28-£31 dB&B⇌⛆£34-£37.50
CTV 20P ✽
V Bar Lunch £1.50-£3.80 Dinner £9.50-£10.50 Last dinner 8.30pm
Credit Cards 1 £

TAL-Y-BONT (near Conwy) Gwynedd Map **06** SH76

★★Lodge LL32 8YX ☎Dolgarrog(049269)766
Resident owners offer a friendly reception to guests at this small, village hotel in the beautiful Conwy Valley. Bedrooms are in a modern, single-storey block at the back of the main building and have good facilities. The standard of food is good.
Annexe10⇌⛆ CTV in all bedrooms ® T ✱ sB&B⇌⛆£25 dB&B⇌⛆£40
50P ✽ *xmas*
British & French V Lunch £3.50-£10.50 Dinner £9.50-£9.95&alc Last dinner 9.30pm
Credit Cards 1 3 £

TALYBONT-ON-USK Powys Map **03** SO12

★★Aberclydach House Aber LD3 7YS (2m SW) ☎(087487)361
A renovated country house one mile from the village provides accommodation in well-equipped bedrooms; service is friendly, and there are good facilities for small conferences.
11rm(6⇌5⛆) in 4 bedrooms CTV in all bedrooms ® T sB&B⇌⛆£31.50 dB&B⇌⛆£53
CTV 14P ✽
V Lunch £5.50-£7.50 High tea fr£3.95 Dinner £13.95 Last dinner 8.30pm
Credit Cards 1 2 3 5

TAL-Y-LLYN Gwynedd Map **06** SH70

★★*Tyn-y-Cornel* LL36 9AJ ☎Abergynolwyn(065477)282
Closed Jan & Feb RS Nov & Dec
Delightful lakeside hotel where most rooms have beautiful views.
4rm(2⇌)Annexe12rm(11⇌1⛆)(3fb) CTV in 15bedrooms ® T 60P 3 ✽ (heated) sauna solarium sailing canoeing windsurfing
English & Continental V Last dinner 9.30pm
Credit Cards 1 2 3 5

★ MINFFORDD
LL36 9AJ

☎Corris(065473)665
Closed Jan-Feb RS Nov-Dec & Mar

Although situated on the main road between Dolgellau and Machynlleth, it is easy to miss this small stone and slate house. Also in spite of its main road location, its setting is delightful with hills on both sides. The bedrooms are mostly small, yet all but one have en suite facilities. There are two comfortable lounges, a cosy bar and an unusual dining room which has a central staircase. Services are limited and bedrooms lack television, but it is the policy of owner, Mr Pickles, that people stay at Minffordd to get away from television and newspapers – he and his cheerful wife actively encourage guests to talk to each other instead. Naturally, some respond to this approach more readily than others. Son, Jonathan, produces food of a sound standard from a limited choice menu, and overall prices remain modest. ▶

T

Essentially, this is a place to relax, unwind and rediscover some lost pleasures in life.

7rm(5⇌2↱)(1fb) ® **T** ✕ sB&B⇌↱£38-£48 dB&B⇌↱£66-£86 (incl dinner) ⊟

12P ⌂ ✲ nc3yrs *xmas*

☋ English ♔ ⊁ Dinner £14-£14 Last dinner 8.30pm

Credit Cards 1 3 5

TAMWORTH Staffordshire Map **07** SK20

○***Granada Lodge*** M42/A5(Granada)
☎Central reservation 05255-5555
Due to have opened Jul 1989
62⇌

TANGUSDALE

See **Barra, Isle of**

TAPLOW Buckinghamshire Map **04** SU98

★★★★★ 73% Cliveden
SL6 0JF (Prestige)

☎Maidenhead (0628)668561
Telex no 846562
FAX (0628) 661837

This unique and splendid hotel makes the most of its glittering history. Formerly the home of the Astors, the château, set in 400 acres of National Trust land, was the setting for many glamorous and distinguished house parties, and this is the atmosphere the hotel seeks, for the most part successfully, to recreate. The panelled Great Hall and Library are furnished with antiques, and paintings, photographs and other mementos of the Astor family are much in evidence. Lady Nancy Astor's boudoir is transformed into a very pretty sitting room and the Astor's ornate French dining room is reserved for breakfast and for private parties. Bedrooms are luxurious and the bathrooms magnificent. Added to this, the fine team of professional staff, ably led by the General Manager the Hon. John Sinclair, provide a style of service in keeping with the surroundings. Chef John Webber is in charge of the kitchens, and both the à la carte and table d'hôte menus offer a high standard of cooking, with a wine list to match. Recreational facilities include squash, tennis, swimming and croquet, while indoors are a card room, billiard room and health club.

25rm(24⇌1↱)1⊟ CTV in all bedrooms **T** ✱ S% sB&B⇌↱fr£130 dB&B⇌↱£170-£375

Lift ☾ 30P 3⌂ ⌂ ✲ ▭(heated) ⌓(heated) ▶4 ℘ (hard) ♪ squash ∪ snooker sauna solarium gymnasium indoor tennis turkish bath ♫ *xmas*

☋ English S% Lunch fr£25&alc Dinner fr£39 Last dinner 9.30pm

Credit Cards 1 2 3 4 5

TARBERT

See **Harris, Isle of**

All the information in the guide is annually updated, but details of prices and facilities may change during the currency of this guide.

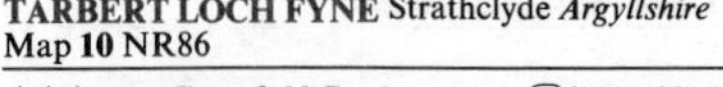

TARBERT LOCH FYNE Strathclyde *Argyllshire*
Map **10** NR86

★★★55% *Stonefield Castle* PA29 6YJ ☎(08802)836
Telex no 776321
In a quiet, secluded position, surrounded by fifty acres of beautiful grounds, the hotel combines the charm and character of a previous age with modern comforts.

33rm(30⇌2↱)(4fb) CTV in all bedrooms ® **T**
Lift ☾ CTV 50P ⌂ ✲ ⌓(heated) ℘ (hard) snooker sauna solarium gymnasium
♔ ♖ ⊁
Credit Cards 1 2 3 5

★West Loch PA29 6YF ☎Tarbert(08802)283
The small, roadside, family-run hotel has a reputation for producing fine, imaginative food. The style of cooking is international and the intentionally limited dinner menu, which is changed daily, features fresh local sea-food and game in season.
6rm(2fb) ✱ sB&B£16 dB&B£32-£45 Continental breakfast ⊟
CTV 20P ⌂ ✲
☋ International **V** ♔ ♖ ⊁ Lunch £1-£20alc Dinner £14.50-£25alc Last dinner 8.30pm

TARPORLEY Cheshire Map **07** SJ56

★★★ 69% The Wild Boar Whitchurch Rd, Beeston CW6 9NW (two and a half miles S off A49) (Associated Leisure)
☎Bunbury(0829)260309 Telex no 61222 FAX (0829) 261081
Located on the A49 about 3 miles south of Tarporley. A new building with good bedroom accommodation has been constructed looking out over the beautiful rolling countryside and blending perfectly with the striking mock-Tudor style of the elegant restaurant which adjoins. The restaurant itself is quickly earning favour for its high standard of cuisine.
37⇌↱ CTV in all bedrooms ® **T** ✕ (ex guide dogs) ✱ S% sB&B⇌↱£38-£65 dB&B⇌↱£60-£70 ⊟
☾ 70P ✲ *xmas*
V ♔ ♖ Lunch £11.50-£12&alc Dinner £16.50&alc Last dinner 10pm
Credit Cards 1 2 3 5

★★ *The Willington Hall*
Willington CW6 0NB (3m NW off unclass rd linking A51 & A54)

☎Kelsall(0829)52321
Closed Xmas Day

This mock Elizabethan house, built in 1825, is set in delightful parkland with fine countryside views. The bedrooms are modern and particularly comfortable.

10⇌(1fb) CTV in all bedrooms ® **T**

60P 1⌂ ⌂ ✲ ℘ (hard) nc5yrs

V

Credit Cards 1 2 3 5

TAUNTON Somerset Map **03** ST22

★★★ 51% The County East St TA1 3LT (Trusthouse Forte)
☎(0823)337651 Telex no 46484 FAX (0823) 334517
Conference and banqueting facilities have made this town-centre hotel popular with a business clientele. Bedrooms vary from the sumptuous to the modest. The dining room offers a limited menu of mostly English dishes.
67⇌⊁in 6 bedrooms CTV in all bedrooms ® **T** sB⇌£60-£69 dB⇌£76-£83 (room only) ⊟
Lift ☾ CTV 100P CFA *xmas*

V ♔ ⊡ ⅄ Lunch £7.50-£8.95 Dinner fr£12.95 Last dinner 9.30pm
Credit Cards [1] [2] [3] [4] [5]

★★★67% Crest Hotel Deane Gate Av TA1 2UA (Crest)
☎(0823)332222 Telex no 46703 FAX (0823) 332266
A modern purpose-built hotel with extensive conference facilities, near to junction 25 of the M5. For eating there is a choice of formal restaurant or coffee shop. Bedrooms are uniformly well equipped.
101⇨♠(85fb)⅄in 8 bedrooms CTV in all bedrooms ® T S% sB⇨♠fr£62 dB⇨♠fr£74 (room only) 🗐
Lift ☾ 250P sauna gymnasium ♫ *xmas*
♔ International V ♔ ⊡ ⅄ S% Lunch £11.50-£12.50&alc Dinner £14.50-£17.50&alc Last dinner 10pm
Credit Cards [1] [2] [3] [5] £

★★Corner House Park St TA1 4DQ ☎(0823)284683 & 272665 Telex no 46288 FAX (0823) 332276
Conveniently situated in the town centre, the hotel is privately owned and run, has some modern, spacious bedrooms, a formal dining room and is popular with both business people and tourists.
33rm(23⇨4♠)(4fb) CTV in all bedrooms ® T ✗ (ex guide dogs) sB&B£35-£49 dB&B⇨♠£50-£60
CTV 40P 2🚗 ⛟
♔ English & French V ♔ ⊡ Lunch fr£6.50&alc
Credit Cards [1] [3]

★★Falcon Henlade TA3 5DH (3m E A358) (Exec Hotel)
☎(0823)442502
Closed Xmas day
Small, informal hotel with comfortable, well-appointed bedrooms with easy access to the motorway.
11rm(9⇨2♠)(1fb)1🗐⅄in 3 bedrooms CTV in all bedrooms ® T ✗ sB&B⇨♠£39.50 dB&B⇨♠£55 🗐
25P ⛟ ✲ ⌂ *xmas*

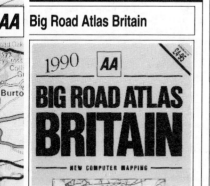

▶

T

🍽 International V ♘ ⅅ ⅀ Lunch £5-£9.50&alc High tea £1.50-£2.50 Dinner fr£9.50&alc Last dinner 9.30pm
Credit Cards [1] [3]

★★Rumwell Manor Rumwell TA4 1EL ☎(0823)254861
10rm(5⇨)(3fb) CTV in all bedrooms ® ✱ sB&B£17-£23.50 sB&B⇨£27.50-£32.50 dB&B£34 dB&B⇨£39-£43 ⊟
CTV 30P ⇎ ✽ ⇋ *xmas*
🍽 English & French V ♘ ⅅ ⅀ Lunch £5.50-£7.50alc High tea £1.75 Dinner £11.50&alc Last dinner 8.30pm
Credit Cards [1] [2] [3] [5]

○ ***The Mount Somerset*** Lower Henlade TA3 5NB
☎(0823)442500 FAX (0823) 442900
Due to have opened Sep 1989
14⇨

TAUNTON DEANE MOTORWAY SERVICE AREA (M5) Somerset Map 03 ST12

○ ***Roadchef Lodge*** M5 Southbound TA1 4BA ☎(0823)332228 FAX (0823) 338131
Due to have opened July 1989
39rm

TAVISTOCK Devon Map 02 SX47

★★★60% The Bedford Plymouth Rd PL19 8BB (Trusthouse Forte) ☎(0822)613221
A stone-built hotel, on the original site of Tavistock Abbey, the hotel combines traditional character and modern facilities.
30⇨⅀in 4 bedrooms CTV in all bedrooms ® ✱ sB⇨fr£61 dB⇨fr£71 (room only) ⊟
24P 5🚗 (£2 per night) ✽ *xmas*
V ♘ ⅅ ⅀ Lunch £7-£9&alc High tea fr£3 Dinner fr£12&alc Last dinner 9pm
Credit Cards [1] [2] [3] [4] [5]

TAYNUILT Strathclyde *Argyllshire* Map 10 NN03

★★Brander Lodge Bridge of Awe PA35 1HT (Consort)
☎(08662)243 & 225
Small, comfortable family run Highland hotel with relaxing, friendly atmosphere.
20rm(19⇨1♠)(2fb) CTV in all bedrooms ® T sB&B⇨♠£21.50-£30 dB&B⇨♠£43-£48 ⊟
100P ✽ pool table ⌂ *xmas*
🍽 Scottish & International V ♘ ⅅ Lunch 95p-£10.45&alc High tea fr95p Dinner £12.50&alc Last dinner 9pm
Credit Cards [1] [2] [3] [5] [£]

★★Polfearn PA35 1JQ (Consort) ☎(08662)251
Family-run, small granite hotel with gardens and a grazing field at the front.
16rm(2⇨12♠)(2fb) ® ✱ sB&B£18-£22 sB&B⇨♠£22-£26 dB&B⇨♠£36-£44
CTV 20P *xmas*
V ♘ ⅅ ⅀ Bar Lunch £2.50-£7alc Dinner £10-£11.50 Last dinner 9pm
Credit Cards [1] [3] [£]

TEANGUE

See Skye, Isle of

TEDBURN ST MARY Devon Map 03 SX89

★★*King's Arms Inn* EX6 6EG ☎(0647)61224
Pleasant village-centre inn with a congenial atmosphere and a popular bar. It is conveniently located for the A30.
7rm(1⇨) CTV in all bedrooms ®
50P 2🚗
🍽 English & French V ♘ Last dinner 9.30pm
Credit Cards [1] [2] [3] [5]

TEES-SIDE AIRPORT Co Durham Map 08 NZ31

★★★62% *St George* Middleton St George DL2 1RH (Mount Charlotte) ☎Darlington(0325)332631 Telex no 587623
Modern hotel within airport complex.
59⇨♠(2fb)1⊠ CTV in all bedrooms ® T
☾ 200P 20🚗 (£2.50 per day) ✽ CFA squash sauna solarium
🍽 English & French V ♘ ⅅ Last high tea 5pm
Credit Cards [1] [2] [3] [5]

TEIGNMOUTH Devon Map 03 SX97

★★Ness House Marine Dr, Shaldon TQ14 0HP
☎Shaldon(0626)873480 FAX (0626) 873486
A comfortable Regency hotel with good sea views and modern accommodation. The attractive restaurant offers a commendable standard of cooking.
7⇨♠(2fb)1⊠ CTV in all bedrooms ® T ✈ (ex guide dogs) sB&B⇨♠£24.50-£42.50 dB&B⇨♠£49-£65 ⊟
20P ⇎ ✽
🍽 French V ♘ ⅅ Lunch £8-£12.95alc Dinner £8-£12.95alc Last dinner 10pm
Credit Cards [1] [2] [3] [£]

★Bay 15 Powerham Terrace, Sea Front TQ14 8BL
☎(0626)774123
Closed Nov-Mar (ex Xmas)
Hotel features comfortable lounge bar overlooking seafront lawns and tennis courts.
20rm(5⇨5♠)(5fb) CTV in all bedrooms ® ✱ sB&B£14-£15.50 sB&B⇨♠£17-£19.50 dB&B£28-£31 dB&B⇨♠£34-£39
☾ CTV 16P *xmas*
🍽 English & Continental V ♘ ⅅ Dinner £5.50-£5.50&alc Last dinner 7pm
Credit Cards [1] [2] [3] [5] [£]

★Belvedere Barnpark Rd TQ14 8PJ ☎(0626)774561
This friendly, family-run hotel is set back from the town but is convenient for the shopping centre and railway station. Bedrooms are modestly appointed and there are comfortable public rooms.
13rm(3⇨6♠)(4fb) CTV in 4bedrooms ® ✈ ✱ sB&B£15.50-£16.50 sB&B⇨♠£17.50-£18.50 dB&B£31-£33 dB&B⇨♠£35-£37
CTV 10P 1🚗 ✽ *xmas*
V ♘ ⅅ
Credit Cards [1] [3] [£]

★Coombe Bank Landscore Rd TQ14 9JL ☎(0626)772369
Central holiday hotel with warm welcome from young owners.
11rm(1⇨3♠)(2fb) CTV in 9bedrooms ® ✱ sB&B£14.25-£16 dB&B£28.50-£32 dB&B⇨♠£32.50-£36 ⊟
CTV 12P *xmas*
🍽 English & French V ⅀ Bar Lunch £1.50-£1.85 Dinner £6.50 Last dinner 7.30pm
Credit Cards [1] [3] [£]

★Drakes 33 Northumberland Place TQ14 8UG ☎(0626)772777
RS 24 Sept – 12 Oct
The running of this small, tastefully appointed and comfortable hotel is personally supervised by the resident owners. An interesting choice of well-cooked food is available throughout the day in the Bistro Coffee Shop, and candlelit suppers are served in the exquisite restaurant.
6rm(1⇨4♠)(1fb) CTV in all bedrooms ® T sB&B£15.50-£20 dB&B⇨♠£31-£42 ⊟
CTV ℙ ⇎ *xmas*
🍽 English & Continental V ♘ ⅅ Lunch £3.50-£5.50&alc High tea £1.50-£3.50 Dinner £4.50-£7.50&alc Last dinner 9.30pm
Credit Cards [1] [3] [£]

Book as early as possible for busy holiday periods.

★**Glenside** Ringmoor Rd, Shaldon TQ14 0EP (1m S off A379) ☎Shaldon(0626)872448
Closed Nov & 3-4 weeks during Feb or Mar
On the south bank of the Teign Estuary stands a cottage-style hotel which was built as a private residence in about 1820. Tastefully appointed in keeping with its style and character, it offers a warm welcome and provides a high standard of home cooking.
10rm(1⇨6↱)(1fb) CTV in all bedrooms ® sB&B£14.40-£17.50 sB&B⇨↱£16-£19.75 dB&B£28-£35 dB&B⇨↱£32-£39.50 ⊟
10P ⚘ *xmas*
V Bar Lunch £3-£4 Dinner £7.70-£8.80 Last dinner 6.30pm

TELFORD Shropshire Map **07** SJ60

★★★60% **Buckatree Hall** Ercall Ln, Wellington TF6 5AL (Best Western) ☎(0952)641821 Telex no 35701
Nine acres of woodland surround this modern hotel at the foot of the Wrekin and a mile from junction 7 of the M54. Buckatree has established a flourishing conference trade and has a popular international-style restaurant.
37⇨↱(1fb)4⊞ CTV in all bedrooms ® **T** sB&B⇨↱fr£52 dB&B⇨↱fr£63 ⊟
☾ 120P ✲ *xmas*
International **V** Lunch fr£8.50 Dinner fr£9.75&alc Last dinner 10pm
Credit Cards 1 2 3 5 £

★★★63% ***Telford Hotel Golf & Country Club*** Great Hay, Sutton Hill TF7 4DT (Queens Moat) ☎(0952)585642
Telex no 35481 FAX (0952) 586602
Golf and other good sporting facilities are the principal attractions of this country-club hotel. The restaurant has superb views over the Ironbridge Gorge and there are some superior bedrooms in the Darby wing which was once the home of Abraham Darby III, ▶

Ironmaster of Coalbrookdale and a major figure of the Industrial Revolution.
59⇌↱(4fb) CTV in all bedrooms ® T
(200P ✲ ▭(heated) ▶9 squash snooker sauna ⌂
♡ International V ♡ ⊡ Last dinner 10pm
Credit Cards 1 2 3 4 5

★★★ 65% **Telford Moat House** Forgegate, Telford Centre TF3 4NA (Queens Moat) ☎(0952)291291 Telex no 35588
FAX (0952) 292012
Closed 26-30 Dec
Opened in 1986 to cater for the business and conference trade, an extension has already had to be built to increase bedroom and restaurant capacity. Diners can choose between a carvery-style meal or the à la carte menu which offers a variety of dishes to suit all tastes.
148⇌↱(8fb) CTV in all bedrooms ® T sB&B⇌↱£56-£63 dB&B⇌↱£61-£74 ⊟
Lift (300P ▭(heated) sauna solarium gymnasium games room mini-gym ♫
♡ English & French V ♡ ⊡ Lunch £12.50&alc High tea £6 Dinner £12.50&alc Last dinner 9.30pm
Credit Cards 1 2 3 4 5

★★**Charlton Arms** Wellington TF1 1DG ☎(0952)51351
FAX (0952) 222077
The old coaching inn has retained many of its original characteristics. The lounge bar is a popular meeting place for local residents, and the hotel boasts a large ballroom suitable for private parties of up to 200 people.
26rm(22⇌1↱)(1fb)1⊟ CTV in all bedrooms ® T sB&B£35-£37 sB&B⇌↱£45-£47 dB&B£45-£48 dB&B⇌↱£57-£60 ⊟
(75P *xmas*
♡ European V ♡ ⊡ Lunch £7.50-£8&alc Dinner £7.50-£8&alc Last dinner 10pm
Credit Cards 1 2 3 5

★★**Falcon** Hoylhead Road, Wellington TF1 2DD
☎(0952)255011
Closed Xmas RS Closed Sunday lunchtimes
13rm(2⇌3↱)(1fb) CTV in all bedrooms ✗ sB&Bfr£30 sB&B⇌↱fr£35 dB&Bfr£38 dB&B⇌↱fr£45 ⊟
CTV 30P ⊞ nc2yrs
♡ English & Continental V ♡ Bar Lunch 85p-£6.50alc Dinner £7.50-£14.50alc Last dinner 9pm
Credit Cards 1 3

★★**White House** Wellington Rd, Muxton TF2 8NG (off A518)
☎(0952)604276
Originally a farmhouse, the hotel has recently undergone alterations which included the addition of a new wing of bedrooms, so that comfortable accommodation can now be provided in 23 modern, well-equipped rooms, most of which have en suite facilities. Similarly high standards have been maintained in the pleasant, popular restaurant and bar. Guests will find themselves conveniently placed for access to Telford New Town and the M54 motorway.
26rm(17⇌2↱)(4fb) CTV in all bedrooms ® T S% sB&B£31.50-£41.50 sB&B⇌↱£41.50 dB&B£45 dB&B⇌↱£55 ⊟
100P ✲
♡ English & French V ♡ ⊡ S% Lunch £6.50&alc Dinner £9.50&alc Last dinner 9.30pm
Credit Cards 1 2 3 £

○***Crest*** The St Quentin Roundabout(Crest)
☎Central reservations 0800-123234
Due to have opened Sep 1989
100⇌

TEMPLECOMBE Somerset Map **03** ST72

★★**Horsington House** Horsington BA8 0EG (1m N A357)
☎(0963)70721
23rm(19⇌4↱)(2fb) CTV in all bedrooms ® T ✱
sB&B⇌↱£39-£46 ⊟
55P ✲ ♪ (hard) croquet putting ⌂ *xmas*
♡ English & Continental V ♡ ⊡ Lunch £6-£10 High tea fr£5 Dinner fr£12.50&alc Last dinner 9.30pm
Credit Cards 1 2 3 £

TEMPLE SOWERBY Cumbria Map **12** NY62

★★**Temple Sowerby House** CA10 1RZ
☎Kirkby Thore(07683)61578
Back in the early 1600s Temple Sowerby House was a farmhouse. Additions from the Georgian period have heightened its charm and style and the modern amenities, installed during its conversion to a hotel, render it a beautiful yet practical place to stay. The building has immense character throughout; it features a comfortable library/lounge, a cosy lounge bar and a delightful restaurant with oak beams and tasteful décor. The bedrooms retain many old features with good paintings and furnishings. A glass conservatory faces the walled garden of lawns and flower-beds – a delight in the sunshine. The staff evidently devote care and attention to providing a friendly service and the proprietors, Mr and Mrs Edwards, show an interest and concern for their guests.
8⇌Annexe4⇌(2fb)2⊟ CTV in all bedrooms ® T sB&B£37-£40 dB&B£52-£60 ⊟
30P ⊞ ✲ croquet badmington ⌂ *xmas*
♡ International V ♡ ⊡ ⊁ Lunch fr£14 Dinner fr£18 Last dinner 9pm
Credit Cards 1 2 3 £

TENBY Dyfed Map **02** SN10

★★**Albany** The Norton SA70 8AB ☎(0834)2698
22rm(17⇌5↱)(2fb) CTV in all bedrooms ® ✱
sB&B⇌↱£20.50-£25.50 dB&B⇌↱£39-£49 ⊟
♫ *xmas*
♡ French V ♡ ⊡ ⊁ Lunch fr£5.50 Dinner fr£7.75&alc Last dinner 9.30pm
Credit Cards 1 2 3

★★**Atlantic** Esplanade SA70 7DU ☎(0834)2881 & 4176
Superbly situated Victorian hotel with caring service, well-equipped bedrooms and comfortable public areas.
40rm(25⇌15↱)(8fb)1⊟ CTV in all bedrooms ® T
sB&B⇌↱£30-£33 ⊟
30P ✲ CFA ▭(heated) solarium spa bath
♡ French V ⊁ Bar Lunch £1.20-£4.50 Dinner fr£11 Last dinner 8.30pm
Credit Cards 1 3

★★**Esplanade** The Esplanade SA70 7DU ☎(0834)3333
A well modernised hotel on the sea front and near the centre of this charming town. Bedrooms are well equipped, there is a small but comfortable lounge and, in the season, an all-day coffee lounge for refreshments.
15rm(9⇌6↱)Annexe3rm(1⇌2↱)(5fb) CTV in all bedrooms ® T sB&B⇌↱£15.50-£21 dB&B⇌↱£25-£65 ⊟
𝑷 ⊞
♡ French ♡ ⊡ Lunch £11.50 High tea £4.50 Dinner £11.50-£14.50 Last dinner 9.30pm
Credit Cards 1 2 3 5 £

★★**Fourcroft** The Croft SA70 8AP ☎(0834)2886
Closed Nov-Etr
A hand-painted Roman scene is an interesting feature of the new, attractive, outdoor swimming pool of this hotel overlooking the harbour. Friendly service and a relaxed atmosphere will make your stay here a pleasant one.
38rm(36⇌2↱)(6fb) CTV in all bedrooms ® T ✱
sB&B⇌↱£27.50-£31.50 dB&B⇌↱£50-£58 ⊟

▶

T

Lift ☾ 5P (£1 per night) ❊ ⛆(heated) sauna gymnasium games room spa pool
☋ International V ♉ ⚡ Dinner fr£10 Last dinner 8.30pm
Credit Cards 1 3 £

★★**Harbour Heights** 11 The Croft SA70 8AP ☎(0834)2132
Overlooking the sands of the North Beach, this small, family-run hotel is comfortable and well equipped. Fresh produce is used in the kitchens and the food is good, although the choice of dishes is necessarily fairly small.
8⇌⎡(4fb) CTV in all bedrooms ® ✗ sB&B⇌⎡£36.50-£40 dB&B⇌⎡£66-£72 (incl dinner) ⊟
𝒫 ⛟ nc8yrs *xmas*
☋ English & Continental Dinner £14.50-£17 Last dinner 9.30pm
Credit Cards 1 2 3 5 £

★★***Royal Lion*** High St SA70 7ES ☎(0834)2127
Closed Nov-Feb
This Victorian hotel occupies a fine seafront position with views over the harbour; the comfortable bedrooms are well equipped, and service is friendly.
36rm(14⇌1⎡)(8fb) CTV in all bedrooms ®
Lift ☾ CTV 40P
♉ ⚞
Credit Cards 1 3 5

★**Buckingham** Esplanade SA70 7DU ☎(0834)2622
Closed Dec-Feb
Friendly holiday hotel overlooking the beach and Caldey Island.
8rm(4⇌2⎡)(2fb) CTV in all bedrooms ® sB&B£15-£16 sB&B⇌⎡£18-£22 dB&B⇌⎡£30-£40
𝒫 ⛟
☋ English V ♉ Lunch £5-£6 Dinner £8-£8 Last dinner 7.45pm
Credit Cards 1 3 £

TETBURY Gloucestershire Map 03 ST89

❀★★★ ♔ CALCOT MANOR

Calcot GL8 8YJ (3 m W at junc A4135/A46) (Pride of Britain)
☎Leighterton(066689)391
Telex no 437105
FAX (066689) 394

A cluster of farm buildings hides the approach to this lovely Cotswolds hotel. Some of these buildings have been restored and converted into beautiful bedrooms or apartments whilst others, including a 14th-century tithe barn, are awaiting the loving attention of owners Barbara and Brian Ball who have plans to breathe life back into their mellow golden framework. Their son has now joined the team of young staff, whose caring and concerned manner has earned the hotel its high reputation for hospitality and warmth. In the candle-lit dining room, chef Ramon Farthing's highly imaginative and carefully prepared food has continued to earn praise from our inspectors, who recommend the moderately light crab mousse accompanied by succulent slices of monkfish and the local lamb, trimmed and lightly cooked. Vegetables include an excellent ratatouille encased in slices of carrot and courgette. Final courses are of colour photograph perfection, with taste to match, and the excellent cheeseboard is earning deserved attention.
7⇌Annexe6⇌1⊞ CTV in all bedrooms T ✗ (ex guide dogs) sB&B⇌£70-£90 dB&B⇌£95-£120 ⊟
30P 3⛍ ⛟ ❊ CFA ⛆(heated) croquet lawn ♫ nc12yrs *xmas*
☋ English & French ♉ ⚞ ⚡ Lunch £16-£25 Dinner £30-£38 Last dinner 9.30pm
Credit Cards 1 2 3 5

★★★77% **Close** 8 Long St GL8 8AQ ☎(0666)502272
FAX (0666) 504401
Closed 1-16 Jan
15rm(12⇌3⎡)3⊞ CTV in all bedrooms T ✗ (ex guide dogs) sB&B⇌⎡£80-£115 dB&B⇌⎡£100-£160 ⊟
20P ⛟ nc10yrs *xmas*
V ♉ ⚞ ⚡ Lunch £14.95-£16.95&alc Dinner £27.50 Last dinner 9.45pm
Credit Cards 1 2 3 5

★★★55% **Hare & Hounds** Westonbirt GL8 8QL (Best Western)
☎Westonbirt(066688)233 Telex no 94012242
FAX (066688) 241
A traditional country hotel in 9 acres of grounds.
21⇌Annexe8⇌(3fb)5⊞ CTV in all bedrooms ® T ✳
sB&B⇌£48-£58 dB&B⇌£66-£72 ⊟
80P 6⛍(£2) ❊ 𝓅 (hard) squash croquet table tennis *xmas*
☋ English & French V ♉ ⚞ S% Lunch £9.50-£10.50&alc Dinner £15-£17.50&alc Last dinner 9pm
Credit Cards 1 2 3

★★★71% **Snooty Fox** Market Place GL8 8DD 1300
☎(0666)52436 Telex no 437334 FAX (0666) 53479
Honey coloured Cotswold stone building facing the old Market Hall, this popular hotel has been ambitiously refurbished to a high standard. The bedrooms are individually designed while the oak panelled restaurant provides a delightful setting for the excellent food.
12rm(11⇌1⎡)(1fb)1⊞ CTV in all bedrooms T ✗ (ex guide dogs) sB&B⇌⎡£66-£72 dB&B⇌⎡£84-£88 ⊟
𝒫 *xmas*
☋ English & French V ♉ ⚞ Lunch £12&alc Dinner fr£16.50&alc Last dinner 10pm
Credit Cards 1 2 3 5

TEWKESBURY Gloucestershire Map 03 SO83

★★★50% **Bell** Church St GL20 5SA (Best Western)
☎(0684)293293 Telex no 43535
Dating back to Victorian times, the inn is full of character. Its bedrooms have modern facilities but the size of rooms varies greatly.
25rm(23⇌2⎡)(2fb)3⊞⚡in 1 bedroom CTV in all bedrooms ® T sB&B⇌⎡£49.50-£65 dB&B⇌⎡£59.50-£85 ⊟
☾ 55P CFA *xmas*
☋ English & French V ♉ ⚞ Lunch £8.95-£11.95 Dinner £12.95-£15.95&alc Last dinner 9.30pm
Credit Cards 1 2 3 5 £

★★★68% **Royal Hop Pole Crest** Church St GL20 5RT (Crest)
☎(0684)293236 Telex no 437176 FAX (0684) 296680
Great efforts have been made to preserve the character of this half-timbered building at the heart of the old market town, and the overall effect both of bedrooms and of public areas is most welcoming. The car park at the rear of the hotel is a distinct advantage in such a crowded town.
29rm(27⇌2⎡)(2fb)1⊞⚡in 6 bedrooms CTV in all bedrooms ® T ✳ sB⇌⎡£63-£66 dB⇌⎡£75-£78.50 (room only) ⊟
☾ 30P ❊ CFA *xmas*
☋ English & French V ♉ ⚞ ⚡ Lunch £7-£10&alc Dinner £15-£16.50&alc Last dinner 9.45pm
Credit Cards 1 2 3 4 5

T

★★★ 66% **Tewkesbury Hall** Puckrup GL20 6EL (3m N A38) (Select) ☎(0684)296200 FAX (0684) 850788
Forty acres of grounds surround this country-house-style hotel which is within easy reach of the M5/M50 junction. The interior has been refurbished to a high standard and the bedrooms are well equipped.
16⇌2⊞ CTV in all bedrooms **T**
☾ 80P ⊞ ✲ ♩ snooker
English & French **V** Last dinner 9.30pm
Credit Cards 1 2 3 5

★★★ 66% **Tewkesbury Park Golf & Country Club** Lincoln Green Ln GL20 7DN ☎(0684)295405 Telex no 43563 FAX (0684) 292386
An attractive rambling old mansion forms the core of this hotel, set in 176 acres of parkland, with a mature golf course and a comprehensive leisure complex. A modern wing provides accommodation with the full range of facilities you would expect from a development of this style.
78⇌↱(10fb) CTV in all bedrooms ® **T** (ex guide dogs) ✳ sB&B⇌↱£75-£85 dB&B⇌↱£85-£100
☾ CTV 180P ✲ CFA (heated) 18 (hard) squash snooker sauna solarium gymnasium steam room whirlpool *xmas*
English & French **V** Lunch fr£9.50 Dinner fr£14&alc Last dinner 10pm
Credit Cards 1 2 3 4 5

★★ **Tudor House** High St GL20 5BH ☎(0684)297755
Character hotel of historic interest sensitively upgraded to offer modern facilities.
16rm(8⇌4↱)(1fb)1⊞ CTV in all bedrooms ® **T** ✳ sB&B£30 sB&B⇌↱£46 dB&B£45 dB&B⇌↱£54-£75
22P ⊞
English & French **V** Lunch £6.95 Dinner £11.75-£12.85&alc Last dinner 9pm
Credit Cards 1 2 3 5

T

THAKEHAM (near Storrington) West Sussex Map **04** TQ11

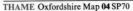

⊛★★★⚜74% **Abingworth Hall** Storrington Rd RH20 3EF
☎West Chiltington (07983)3636 Telex no 877835
The tranquillity of the setting is reflected in the elegant style captured by the drawing room and the individually decorated bedrooms of this charming hotel. Chef Peter Cannon cooks in the nouvelle style, using only fresh and home-made produce, and meals are served in the candlelit restaurant. The menu changes weekly.
21rm(20⇨1↱)⊁in 1 bedroom CTV in all bedrooms **T** ✈
sB&B⇨↱£55 dB&B⇨↱£76 ⊟
50P ⊞ ✲ ⇒(heated) ▶9 ℘(hard) croquet lawn nc10yrs *xmas*
♡ English & French **V** Lunch fr£14.50&alc Dinner fr£24&alc Last dinner 9pm
Credit Cards 1 2 3 4 5

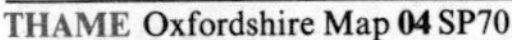

THAME Oxfordshire Map **04** SP70

★★★66% **Spread Eagle** Cornmarket OX9 2BW ☎(084421)3661 Telex no 83343
Closed 28-30 Dec
A very special hotel with warm hospitality and modern bedrooms.
22⇨(1fb) CTV in all bedrooms **T** ✈ (ex guide dogs) S%
sB&B⇨£61.55-£72.55
dB&B⇨£72.55-£80.25 Continental breakfast ⊟
☾80P CFA *xmas*
♡ English & French **V** ♉ S% Lunch fr£12.35&alc Dinner fr£14.55&alc Last dinner 10pm
Credit Cards 1 2 3 5 £

THAXTED Essex Map **05** TL63

★★**Four Seasons** Walden Rd CM6 2RE ☎(0371)830129
There has been a inn on this pleasant country site since the 16th century. The hotel has naturally undergone extensive modernization since that time. A good selection of bar foods is available in the spacious and comfortable bar lounge, while the tastefully-decorated restaurant offers a choice of freshly-prepared, popular dishes. Bedrooms offer some modern facilities and are comfortable. The proprietors, Mr and Mrs Murfitt, personally supervise the hotel service and a pleasant, hospitable welcome is made at all times.
9↱ CTV in all bedrooms ® **T** ✈ ✱ sB&B↱fr£40
dB&B↱fr£55 Continental breakfast ⊟
CTV 100P ⊞ ✲ nc12yrs
V ♉ ⊁ Lunch £9.95 Dinner £12.50&alc Last dinner 9.30pm
Credit Cards 1 2 3

THETFORD Norfolk Map **05** TL88

★★★62% **The Bell** King St IP24 2AZ (Trusthouse Forte) ☎(0842)754455 FAX (0842) 755552
This 15th-century coaching house has been carefully converted to an elegant, comfortable hotel.
47⇨(4fb)1⊟⊁in 11 bedrooms CTV in all bedrooms ® **T**
sB⇨£57-£61 dB⇨£70-£82 (room only) ⊟
☾50P ✲ *xmas*
V ♉ ⊻ ⊁ Lunch fr£7.50 Dinner £11.75&alc Last dinner 10pm
Credit Cards 1 2 3 4 5

★★**Anchor** Bridge St IP24 3AE (Berni/Chef & Brewer) ☎(0842)763925
Close to the town centre, on the banks of the Little Ouse River, this typical coaching inn offers comfortable accommodation with a good range of facilities; meals can be obtained in Barnaby's Carvery.
17rm(12⇨3↱) CTV in all bedrooms ® **T** ✈ (ex guide dogs)
sB&B⇨↱fr£35.50 dB&B⇨↱fr£47.50 ⊟
60P
V ♉ ⊻ ⊁ Lunch £8 Dinner £9 Last dinner 10pm
Credit Cards 1 2 3 5

★★**Historical Thomas Paine** White Hart St IP24 1AA (Best Western) ☎(0842)755631 Telex no 58298
Partly Georgian hotel, reputed to be the birthplace of Thomas Paine, a famous son of Thetford.
14rm(7⇨7↱)(1fb)1⊟ CTV in all bedrooms ® **T** S%
sB&B⇨↱£38-£45 dB&B⇨↱£50-£55 ⊟
30P ⊞
V ♉ ⊻ S% Lunch £7.50-£10&alc Dinner £9.95-£12&alc Last dinner 9.30pm
Credit Cards 1 2 3 5

THIRLSPOT Cumbria Map **11** NY31

★★***Kings Head*** CA12 4TN ☎Keswick(07687)72393
RS Nov-Mar
Attractively situated at the foot of Helvellyn, on the A591, the 17th-century coaching inn retains many of its characteristics, despite modernisation.
13rm(6⇨)(3fb) CTV in all bedrooms ® **T**
60P ⊞
V ♉ Last dinner 9pm

THIRSK North Yorkshire Map **08** SE48

★★**The Golden Fleece** Market Place YO7 1LL (Trusthouse Forte) ☎(0845)23108
A historic coaching inn in the market square of this old Yorkshire town. Bedrooms are comfortable and well furnished.
22rm(6⇨)2⊟⊁in 3 bedrooms CTV in all bedrooms ® **T** ✱
sBfr£45 sB⇨fr£55 dBfr£58 dB⇨fr£67 (room only) ⊟
50P *xmas*
V ♉ ⊻ ⊁ Lunch fr£7 Dinner fr£11.50&alc Last dinner 9.15pm
Credit Cards 1 2 3 4 5

★★**Sheppard's** Church Farm, Front St, Sowerby YO7 1JF (Guestaccom) ☎(0845)23655
Closed 1st week Jan
A charming conversion of old farm buildings has created a hotel set round a cobbled courtyard in a quiet village. The restaurant in the former stables offers a good choice of mainly English dishes.
3⇨Annexe4rm(2↱)(2fb) CTV in all bedrooms ® ✈
sB&Bfr£30 sB&B⇨↱fr£40 dB&Bfr£38 dB&B⇨↱fr£48 ⊟
35P ⊞ nc8yrs
♡ International Lunch fr£12 Dinner £14.50-£19.80alc Last dinner 9.30pm
Credit Cards 1 3

★★ ***Three Tuns*** Market Place YO7 1LH ☎(0845)23124
A three-storey coaching inn situated in the market square.
12rm(7⇨1↱)(2fb) CTV in all bedrooms ®
80P 2🚗
♡ English & Continental **V** ♉ Last dinner 9.30pm
Credit Cards 1 2 3 5

★**Old Red House** Station Rd YO7 4LT ☎(0845)24383
6rm(1⇨5↱)(1fb) CTV in all bedrooms ® **T** ✱ sB&B£15
sB&B⇨↱£15 dB&B£22 dB&B⇨↱£22 ⊟
30P *xmas*

V S% Sunday Lunch £3.75-£6&alc High tea £3-£4.50&alc Dinner £5.50-£7&alc Last dinner 10pm
Credit Cards [2] [3] [5]

THORNBURY Avon Map **03** ST69

★★★ **THORNBURY CASTLE**

BS12 1HH (Pride of Britain)
☎(0454)418511
Telex no 449986
FAX (0454) 416188

Closed 2-12 Jan RS 24-29 Dec

This beautiful old castle is encircled by its vineyard, gardens and high walls, and cannot have changed very much in appearance since Henry VIII and Anne Boleyn visited in the 16th century. Sensitively converted into a hotel, it makes a wonderful setting for a relaxing stay. The ornate oriel windows and wood panelling of the rooms are enhanced by antique furnishings, heraldic shields and paintings. Big open fires are lit in winter, and the two dining rooms have a baronial grandeur which is matched by the pleasurably sumptuous comfort of the lounge and library. Bedrooms have been individually styled to retain the original character and features of the castle, but are also well equipped for today's guest. Some have fireplaces, and some overlook the castle's walled gardens. The cooking is a reliable blend of British and ▶

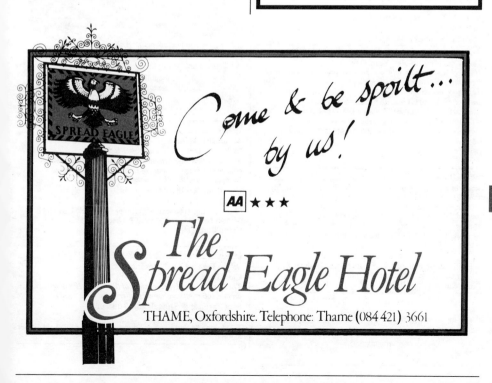

T

French styles, and the wine list includes a variety of good vintages.
18⇌8 CTV in all bedrooms T sB&B⇌£64-£75 dB&B⇌£80-£180 Continental breakfast
40P croquet nc12yrs *xmas*
English & French V Lunch £13.75-£15.50 Dinner £24 Last dinner 9.30pm
Credit Cards 1 2 3 4 5

See advertisement under BRISTOL

THORNE South Yorkshire Map **08** SE61

★★Belmont Horsefair Green DN8 5EE ☎(0405)812320
Telex no 54480
A friendly hotel near the town centre offering good value for money.
23rm(17⇌6)(3fb)1 CTV in all bedrooms ® T S% sB&B⇌£33.50-£35.50 dB&B⇌£46.50-£48.50
25P *xmas*
English & French V S% Lunch £4.55-£8.50&alc Dinner £10.50-£15alc Last dinner 9.30pm
Credit Cards 1 3 £

THORNHILL Dumfries & Galloway *Dumfriesshire* Map **11** NX89

★★*Trigony House* Closeburn DG3 5EZ (2m S off A76)
☎(0848)31211
An attractive, ivy-clad country house, set close to the A76 just south of Thornhill, offers bedrooms which are, in the main, recently refurbished and thoughtfully appointed. Public areas are well-maintained and comfortable, the straightforward cuisine is enjoyable, and good service is provided by the proprietor's family and a cheerful staff.
9rm(2⇌6)Annexe3rm(1fb) ®
CTV 40P
V Last dinner 8.45pm

★George Hotel Drumlanrig St DG3 5LU ☎(0848)30326
Closed Xmas Day & New Years Day
The hotel has been carefully modernised to preserve its 'village inn' atmosphereand the comfortable lounge bar is now proving popular for its good bar meals.
8rm(2⇌4)(1fb) CTV in all bedrooms ® T ✳ sB&B⇌£22.50 dB&B£27.50 dB&B⇌£32.50-£37.50
CTV 10P Indoor bowling carpet
V Bar Lunch £1-£7.45 Dinner £6.50-£15alc Last dinner 8.55pm
Credit Cards 1 3

THORNLEY Durham Map **08** NZ33

★★Crossways Dunelm Rd DH6 3HT (5m SE of Durham City)
☎Wellfield(0429)821248 FAX (0429) 820034
Popular with business travellers, this modern, family-run hotel has compact but well equipped bedrooms. There is a choice of bars and an attractive, small dining room serving good-value meals.
12rm(4⇌8)(6fb) CTV in all bedrooms ® sB&B⇌£29-£45 dB&B⇌£40-£55
CTV 150P solarium *xmas*
English & French V Lunch £8.50 High tea £4.50 Dinner £8.50&alc Last dinner 9.45pm
Credit Cards 1 2 3 5 £

All AA-appointed establishments are inspected regularly to ensure that required standards are maintained.

THORNTHWAITE Cumbria Map **11** NY22

★★Ladstock Country House CA12 5RZ
☎Braithwaite(059682)210
Closed Jan
Situated 2.5 miles north-west of Keswick, this period house sits in its own attractive gardens with a backdrop of wooded hillside. There are good views across the valley to the peaks of Skiddaw.
23rm(11⇌7)(2fb)3 CTV in 16bedrooms ® sB&B£20-£25 sB&B⇌£30-£50 dB&B£40-£60 dB&B⇌£50-£70
CTV 50P bowling shooting *xmas*
Lunch £8-£10alc Dinner £12-£14alc Last dinner 8.30pm
Credit Cards 1 3

★★Swan CA12 5SQ ☎Braithwaite(059682)256 due to change to (07687) 78256
Closed Nov-Etr
A 17th-century inn amid the mountain scenery overlooking Lake Bassenthwaite with Skiddaw in the background.
14rm(3⇌5) CTV in 13bedrooms S10% sB&B£26.30-£28.85 dB&B£52.60-£57.70 dB&B⇌£59.30-£64.90 (incl dinner)
CTV 60P 3 (£1.75)
English & Continental Bar Lunch £1-£9alc
Credit Cards 1 3

★★Thwaite Howe
CA12 5SA
☎Braithwaite(059682)281
Closed Nov-Feb
Peacefully situated hotel with a friendly atmosphere. Bedrooms are large and comfortable.
8⇌ CTV in all bedrooms ® sB&B⇌£45 dB&B⇌£70 (incl dinner)
12P nc12yrs
English & Continental V Dinner fr£12.50 Last dinner 7pm
£

THORNTON CLEVELEYS Lancashire Map **07** SD34

✕The River House Skippool Creek FY5 5LF (2m E A585)
☎Poulton-Le-Fylde(0253)883497 & 883307
Elegantly furnished, friendly restaurant beside River Wyre, renowned for high standard of cooking. All meals cooked individually and must be ordered in advance.
Closed Sun & 6-18 Aug
Lunch not served Sat
International 40 seats S% Dinner £30-£60alc Last lunch 2.30pm Last dinner 9.30pm 20P 4 bedrooms available
Credit Cards 1 2

THORNTON DALE North Yorkshire Map **08** SE88

★New Inn YO18 7LF ☎Pickering(0751)74226
Closed Nov-Feb
The New Inn stands at the centre of the village. It is dated at around 1600. Although small it offers good home comfort.
6rm(1fb) ® ✳ S10% sB&B£19 dB&B£28
CTV 9P 1
V Lunch £4.90-£12.65alc Dinner £4.90-£12.65alc Last dinner 8.30pm

THORNTON HOUGH Merseyside Map **07** SJ38

★★★ 61% ***Thornton Hall*** Neston Rd L63 1JF ☎051-336 3938 Telex no 628678
A large private house has been sympathetically converted into an attractive hotel, retaining features such as the fine panelling and wood carving of the entrance hall and staircase. A separate modern wing houses most of the bedrooms and those in the hall itself have recently been upgraded. Much emphasis is placed on the high standard of cuisine provided in the elegant restaurant.
9⇌⋒Annexe28⇌⋒(24fb) CTV in all bedrooms ® **T** ✗ (ex guide dogs)
☾100P ✽
English, French & Italian **V** Last dinner 9.30pm
Credit Cards 1 2 3 4 5

THORNTON WATLASS North Yorkshire Map **08** SE28

★**Buck Inn** HG4 4AH ☎Bedale(0677)22461
A small, friendly village inn overlooking the green. Accommodation is simple but comfortable and good value meals are served in the bar and restaurant.
6rm(1fb) ® sB&Bfr£15 dB&Bfr£26
CTV 10P ✽ quoits pool table childrens play area ♫
English & Continental **V** Lunch £6-£12alc Dinner £7-£14alc Last dinner 9.30pm
Credit Cards 1 3

THORPE (DOVEDALE) Derbyshire Map **07** SK15

★★★ 62% ***Izaak Walton*** DE6 2AY (1m W on Ilam rd) ☎Thorpe Cloud(033529)555 Telex no 378406
A much extended 18th-century farmhouse enjoying excellent views of Dovedale.
33⇌(2fb)2 CTV in all bedrooms **T**
☾80P ✽
English & French **V** Last dinner 9pm
Credit Cards 1 2 3 5

★★★ 65% **Peveril of the Peak** DE6 2AW (Trusthouse Forte) ☎Thorpe Cloud(033529)333 FAX (033529) 507
Eleven acres of grounds surround this hotel nestling at the foot of Thorpe Cloud. This is an ideal base for touring the Peak District and has warm, comfortable lounges to welcome you back from your day out.
47⇌in 4 bedrooms CTV in all bedrooms ® **T** S% sB⇌£56-£76 dB⇌£75-£95 (room only)
☾60P ✽ CFA (hard) *xmas*
V Lunch £7.75-£11.25&alc Dinner fr£12.50&alc Last dinner 9.30pm
Credit Cards 1 2 3 4 5

THORPE BAY

See Southend-on-Sea

THORPE-LE-SOKEN Essex Map **05** TM12

✕✕**Thorpe Lodge** Landermere Rd CO16 0NG ☎Clacton-on-Sea(0255)861509
A converted country vicarage with two dining rooms, where freshly prepared dishes such as crab soufflé and goulash can feature on the menu.
Lunch by arrangement
English & French **V** 75 seats ✱ Lunch £15-£20alc Dinner £15-£20alc Last lunch 2pm Last dinner 9.15pm 25P
Credit Cards 1 3 5

See advertisement under HARWICH

THREE COCKS Powys Map **03** SO13

★★**Three Cocks** LS3 0SL ☎Glasbury(04974)215
Closed Dec & Jan
(Rosette awarded for dinner only)
The attractive, stone-built hotel stands near the small village of Three Cocks, providing a good standard of cuisine and courteous, friendly service by the proprietor and his wife. Food is imaginatively prepared, using fresh ingredients wherever possible; vegetables are particularly good, being fresh and attractively presented. Your meal may be chosen from the fixed-price menu, four-course menu, or from an à la carte selection which changes monthly to include seasonal produce where possible.
7rm(5⇌1⋒)(2fb) ✗ ✱ dB&B⇌⋒£48
CTV 40P ✽
Continental **V** Lunch fr£17alc Dinner fr£17alc Last dinner 9pm
Credit Cards 1 3

THRESHFIELD North Yorkshire Map **07** SD96

★★★ 66% **Wilson Arms** Station Rd BD23 5EL ☎Grassington(0756)752666
A pleasant, friendly hotel with comfortable lounges, where the high standard of cooking is to be particularly recommended.
14⇌(1fb) CTV in all bedrooms ® **T** ✱ sB&B⇌£40-£46.50 dB&B⇌£80-£83 (incl dinner)
Lift ☾ CTV 40P ✽ (grass) *xmas*
English & French **V** Lunch £7.50-£8.50 Dinner £12.50 Last dinner 9.30pm
Credit Cards 1 2 3 £

THRUSSINGTON Leicestershire Map **08** SK61

○***TraveLodge*** Green Acres Filling Station LE7 8TE (A46) (Trusthouse Forte) ☎Rearsby(066474)525
32⇌

THURLASTON Warwickshire Map **04** SP47

○***Travelodge*** A45 London Rd, Thurlaston CV23 9LG (Trusthouse Forte) ☎Dunchurch(0788)521538
40⇌

THURLESTONE Devon Map **03** SX64

★★★★ 68% **Thurlestone** TQ7 3NN ☎Kingsbridge(0548)560382 Telex no 42513 FAX (0548) 560382
Spacious hotel, built, owned and managed by the Grose family for 90 years, which has fine country and sea views.
68rm(65⇌3⋒)(13fb) CTV in all bedrooms **T** sB&B⇌⋒£47-£75 dB&B⇌⋒£94-£150 (incl dinner)
Lift ☾ 100P 25 ✽ CFA (heated) (heated) ▶9 (hard) squash snooker sauna solarium gymnasium games room badminton spa bath *xmas*
English & French **V** Lunch £1.50-£7.50&alc Dinner £18.50&alc Last dinner 9pm
Credit Cards 1 2 3 5

See advertisement on page 657

THURSO Highland *Caithness* Map **15** ND16

★★**Pentland** Princes St KW14 7AA ☎(0847)63202
Popular commercial and tourist hotel near town centre.
55rm(20⇌14⋒)(4fb) CTV in all bedrooms **T** sB&B£15 sB&B⇌⋒fr£20 dB&B£30 dB&B⇌⋒£36
☾

▶

V ♔ ⩍ Lunch fr£2.75alc High tea fr£4.75alc Dinner fr£6alc Last dinner 8.30pm
Credit Cards 1 3

TINTAGEL Cornwall & Isles of Scilly Map **02** SX08

★★**Atlantic View** Treknow PL34 0EJ ☎Camelford(0840)770221
Small, comfortable, hotel in a prominent position with good sea views.
14rm(10⇨2♠)(2fb)4⊞⁄in all bedrooms CTV in all bedrooms ® ✱ sB&B⇨♠£21-£26.50 dB&B⇨♠£30-£41 ⊟
CTV 20P ✲ ⊡(heated) solarium nc4yrs
♔ European V ♔ ⩍ ⁄ Lunch £7.50-£12.50 High tea £2.50 Dinner £10 Last dinner 7pm
Credit Cards 1 3 £

★★**Bossiney House** PL34 OAX ☎Camelford(0840)770240
Closed end Oct-Etr
Modern holiday hotel in its own grounds with sea views.
19⇨♠ ® ✱ sB&B⇨♠£24-£28 dB&B⇨♠£38-£42 ⊟
CTV 15P putting green
V ♔ ⩍ Dinner £9.50 Last dinner 8pm
Credit Cards 1 2 3 5

TINTERN Gwent Map **03** SO50

★★★61% **The Beaufort** NP6 6SF (Embassy) ☎(0291)689777 FAX (0291) 689727
The hotel stands opposite the Abbey and the views are magnificent. Standards of comfort are good and the staff helpful.
24rm(17⇨7♠)(2fb) CTV in all bedrooms ® T sB&B⇨♠£55-£60 dB&B⇨♠£75-£80 ⊟
60P ✲ games room *xmas*
♔ English & French V ♔ ⩍ Lunch £8.95-£9.50 Dinner £12.95-£13.95&alc Last dinner 9pm
Credit Cards 1 2 3 4 5

★★***Royal George*** NP6 6SF ☎(0291)689205 Telex no 498280
2rm(1⇨)Annexe14⇨(14fb)1⊞ CTV in all bedrooms ® T
30P ✲
♔ English & French V ♔ ⩍ Last dinner 9.30pm
Credit Cards 1 2 3 5

TISBURY Wiltshire Map **03** ST92

✕***Garden Room*** 2-3 High St SP3 6PS ☎(0747)870907
This 'little gem' of a restaurant, has a bright garden style décor and an equally bright atmosphere. It is owned and personally run by Jonathan Ford and Paul Firmin. The restaurant is open for both lunch and dinner, with an à la carte menu available at both meals, while a well priced table d'hôte menu is also available at lunch time. The menus are changed frequently, thereby offering seasonal meats, game, fish, and vegetables. Paul Firmin's cuisine is modern in style, creating interesting dishes which are cooked with care, and with appealing presentation but without being fussy. The wine list is well chosen, and you are assured of a warm welcome and attentive service from Jonathan Ford.
Closed Mon, 2 wks late Feb & 1 wk Sep/Oct
Lunch not served Tue-Sat
Dinner not served Sun
♔ English & Continental V 32 seats Last dinner 10pm P̸
Credit Cards 1 2 3

TITCHWELL Norfolk Map **09** TF74

★★**Titchwell Manor** PE31 8BB (Best Western)
☎Brancaster(0485)210221 & 210284 Telex no 32376
Comfortable and friendly family hotel facing the bird-watching area of the salt marshes.
7rm(4⇨1♠)Annexe3⇨(2fb) CTV in all bedrooms ® ✱ sB&B£27-£35.50 sB&B⇨♠£31.50-£35.50 dB&B£54-£62 dB&B⇨♠£54-£62 ⊟
50P ⊞ ✲
♔ European V ♔ ⩍ ⁄ Lunch £6.95 High tea £2-£5 Dinner £13-£15 Last dinner 9.30pm
Credit Cards 1 2 3 5

TIVERTON Devon Map **03** SS91

★★★64% **Tiverton** Blundells Rd EX16 4DB ☎(0884)256120 Telex no 42551 FAX (0884) 258101
Attracting both business people and tourists, the hotel has been recently refurbished, creating spacious, well furnished bedrooms. There is an attractive, open-plan public area.
75⇨♠(75fb) CTV in all bedrooms ® T ✱ sB&B⇨♠£29-£39 dB&B⇨♠£48-£68 (incl dinner) ⊟
☾ 130P CFA ♫ *xmas*
♔ English, French & Italian V ♔ ⩍ ⁄ Lunch £1.50-£7.50
Credit Cards 1 2 3 5 £

★★**Hartnoll Country House** Bolham EX16 7RA (1.5m N on A396) ☎(0884)252777
Georgian house in its own lawned grounds, near to Tiverton. The owners and their pleasant staff give a personal touch and help lend the hotel a friendly, informal atmosphere. There are pleasant bedrooms in the main house, and an attractive cottage annexe consisting of five rooms.
11rm(9⇨2♠)Annexe5♠(3fb)1⊞ CTV in all bedrooms ® T sB&B⇨♠£25-£40 dB&B⇨♠£35-£50 ⊟
100P ✲ *xmas*
♔ English & Continental V ♔ ⩍ Lunch £8.50-£10.50&alc High tea £2.50-£3.15 Dinner £8.50-£12.95&alc Last dinner 10pm
Credit Cards 1 2 3 5 £

For key to symbols see the inside front cover.

Near Tiverton, BOLHAM

The Hartnoll Country House Hotel

★★

Tel./FAX:
Tiverton (0884) 252777

The Hartnoll offers a chance to relax, whether on business or exploring the unspoilt Exe Valley.

Set in its own lawns, surrounded by rolling farmland, The Hartnoll has an excellent restaurant, open to non-residents, serving fresh local produce and fine wines. Comfortable en suite rooms with colour TV, radio, telephone and beverage tray.

Open all year.

MELVICH HOTEL ★★

Melvich, Sutherland KW14 7YJ
Telephone: (064 13) 206

Privately owned country hotel with superb view over Melvich Bay across the Pentland Firth to the Orkney Islands. All bedrooms have en suite facilities which include tea making facilities and colour television. Trout and salmon fishing is available as well as sea angling, pony trekking and hill walking. The hotel provides a high standard of Highland cooking and hospitality. Children welcome.

"It is remarkable how many return year after year. There must clearly be an explanation and I venture to suggest that it is not only the beauty of the countryside and the speciality of the hotel's location that attracts, but in great measure the quality of service and the friendly atmosphere in the hotel".

Richard Thompson J.P.,
Guest at the Thurlestone Hotel 1987.

Thurlestone Hotel

Thurlestone, near Kingsbridge, South Devon, TQ7 3NN
Telephone: Kingsbridge: (0548) 560382
Fax: (0548) 560382

T

✕✕**Henderson's** 18 Newport St EX16 6NL ☎(0884)254256
FAX (0884) 258803
An attractive, double-fronted restaurant near the market features a welcoming lounge area where aperitifs are served with home-made pastry appetisers. At lunch time a good-value limited menu is available, but dinner can be chosen from a more comprehensive à la carte selection of carefully cooked, attractively presented dishes. The bright dining room, overlooking a walled terrace, provides a pleasant atmosphere, the wine list is well chosen, and service is friendly and attentive.
Closed Sun, Mon, 1 wk Xmas & 1-7 Jan
♡ English & French V 32 seats ✱ Lunch £8-£10&alc Dinner £13-£18alc Last lunch 1.45pm Last dinner 9.30pm ⅊ ⅍
Credit Cards 1 2 3 5

TOBERMORY

See **Mull, Isle of**

TODDINGTON SERVICE AREA (M1) Bedfordshire Map 04 SP92

○ ***Granada Lodge*** M1 Motorway LU5 6HR (Granada)
☎(05255)3881
43🛁

TODMORDEN Lancashire Map 07 SD92

★★★ 70% **Scaitcliffe Hall** Burnley Rd OL14 7DQ
☎(0706)818888
FAX (0706) 818825

13🛁🚿(2fb)1⊞ CTV in all bedrooms ® T ✱
sB🛁🚿£27.75-£35.75 dB🛁🚿£42.75-£52.75 (room only) ⊟
☾ 200P ✲ *xmas*
V ♤ ⊡ Lunch £5.95&alc Dinner £12.95&alc Last dinner 10pm
Credit Cards 1 2 3 5

TODWICK South Yorkshire Map 08 SK48

★★★ 67% **Red Lion** Worksop Rd S31 0DJ (Lansbury)
☎Worksop(0909)771654 Telex no 54120 FAX (0909) 773704
A roadside inn extended and cleverly converted in the style of a period coaching inn. It offers comfortable accommodation just a short distance from junction 31 of the M1.
29🛁🚿1⊞⅍in 7 bedrooms CTV in all bedrooms ® T ✗ (ex guide dogs) sB&B🛁🚿fr£55 dB&B🛁🚿fr£65 ⊟
☾ 90P
♡ English & French V ♤ Lunch fr£8.95&alc Dinner fr£12&alc Last dinner 10pm
Credit Cards 1 2 3 5

TONBRIDGE Kent Map 05 TQ54

★★**The Rose & Crown** High St TN9 1DD (Trusthouse Forte)
☎(0732)357966
An historic posting and coaching house, with modern well-equipped bedrooms, particularly in the original building.
51🛁(1fb)1⊞⅍in 6 bedrooms CTV in all bedrooms ® T ✱
sB🛁£60 dB🛁£71 (room only) ⊟
☾ 62P CFA *xmas*
♡ English V ♤ ⊡ ⅍ S% Lunch £7.95-£9.50&alc Dinner fr£11.50&alc Last dinner 10pm
Credit Cards 1 2 3 4 5

TONGUE Highland *Sutherland* Map 14 NC55

★★**Ben Loyal** IV27 4XE ☎(084755)216
RS Nov-28 Feb
Small, friendly family run tourist hotel.
13rm(6🛁) ✱
CTV 19P
♤ ⊡ Bar Lunch £1.80-£5.50 Dinner £9.50 Last dinner 8.45pm
Credit Cards 1 3 5

★★***Tongue*** IV27 4XD (Inter) ☎(084755)206
The friendly, family-run hotel provides specific facilities for fishing and offers a good selection of well-prepared local products in its comfortable dining room.
21rm(14🛁)(1fb) TV available ®
CTV 60P ✲ ⅃ ⌂
♡ Scottish & French V ♤ ⊡ Last dinner 8.45pm
Credit Cards 1 3

TOPSHAM Devon Map 03 SX98

★★**Ebford House** Exmouth Rd EX3 0QH (1m E on A376)
☎(0392)877658 FAX (0392) 874424
Conveniently situated for Exeter and the coastal resorts, this well restored Georgian house offers comfortable bedrooms with excellent en-suite bathrooms. For meals, there is a choice of either a bistro or a formal restaurant.
9rm(8🛁1🚿)1⊞⅍in 4 bedrooms CTV in 10bedrooms ® T ✗
sB&B🛁🚿£36-£40 dB&B🛁🚿£52-£65
45P ⊞ ✲ sauna solarium gymnasium multi-gym
♡ English & French ♤ ⅍ Lunch £14&alc Dinner £14&alc Last dinner 9.30pm
Credit Cards 1 2 3

See advertisement under EXETER

TORBAY

See under **Brixham, Paignton & Torquay**

TORCROSS Devon Map 03 SX84

★**Grey Homes** TQ7 2TH ☎Kingsbridge(0548)580220
Closed Nov-Mar
Overlooking Slapton Sands, this colonial-style house offers genuine hospitality, a good standard of accommodation and home-cooked food.
7🛁(1fb) CTV in all bedrooms ® ✱ sB&B🛁£22-£25
dB&B🛁£44-£50 ⊟
CTV 15P 3🚗 (charged) ⊞ ✲ nc5yrs
♤ ⊡ Dinner £8.70-£9.10 Last dinner 7.30pm
Credit Cards 3

TORMARTON Avon Map 03 ST77

★★**Compass Inn** GL9 1JB (Inter)
☎Badminton(045421)242 & 577 FAX (045421) 741
Closed Xmas
Old, family-run inn offering modern facilities.
19rm(17🛁2🚿)(7fb) CTV in all bedrooms ® T
sB&B🛁🚿£47.95-£49.95 dB&B🛁🚿£59.95-£64.95 ⊟
160P ✲
V ♤ ⊡ Bar Lunch £7.25-£9.50alc Dinner £13-£15.50alc Last dinner 9.30pm
Credit Cards 1 2 3 5 £

Book as early as possible for busy holiday periods.

TORQUAY Devon Map **03** SX96

See **Town Plan Section** Some telephone numbers may change during the currency of this guide.

★★★★★63% **The Imperial** Park Hill Rd TQ1 2DG (Trusthouse Forte) ☎(0803)294301 Telex no 42849 FAX (0803) 298293
The spacious hotel, overlooking the town from its elevated position, provides a well-appointed restaurant and public rooms, together with an excellent new healt h and beauty centre. Most of the bedrooms have been refurbished to a very high standard, and service is pleasant and courteous.
167⇨(7fb)⅟in 45 bedrooms CTV in all bedrooms **T** ✱ sB&B⇨£79-£91 dB&B⇨£138-£162 ⊟
Lift ☾ 200P 60🚗 (£3.50 per day) ✱ CFA ▭(heated) ⇨(heated) ℘ (hard) squash snooker sauna solarium gymnasium health fitness centre croquet putting ♫ *xmas*
V ♦ ☐ ⅟ Lunch £12.50-£13&alc Dinner fr£24&alc Last dinner 9.30pm
Credit Cards [1] [2] [3] [4] [5]

See advertisement on page 661

★★★★52% **Grand** Sea Front TQ2 6NT ☎(0803)296677 Telex no 42891 FAX (0803) 213462
This large, sea-front, family hotel offers friendly service and features the comfortable Boaters bar and lounges.
112⇨🚿(30fb) CTV in all bedrooms ® **T** sB&B⇨🚿£38-£50 dB&B⇨🚿£76-£100 ⊟
Lift ☾ 35🚗 ✱ CFA ▭(heated) ⇨(heated) ℘ (hard) sauna solarium gymnasium jacuzzi hairdressers *xmas*
☐ English & French **V** ♦ ☐ Lunch £8-£12&alc High tea fr£5.50 Dinner £13-£15&alc Last dinner 9.30pm
Credit Cards [1] [2] [3] [5]

For key to symbols see the inside front cover.

T

★★★★66% **Palace** Babbacombe Rd TQ1 3TG ☎(0803)200200 Telex no 42606 FAX (0803) 299899
Standing in more than 20 acres of landscaped grounds, this spacious hotel has excellent indoor and outdoor leisure and sports facilities. The well trained staff are efficient, and recent refurbishment of the bedrooms has created six suites of a very high standard.
141rm(112⇌29↱)(10fb)6⊟ CTV in all bedrooms ® **T** ✗ (ex guide dogs)
Lift ☾ CTV 100P 40🚗 (charged) ✻ CFA ⊡(heated) ⇌(heated) ▶9 ♪ (hard) squash snooker sauna croquet putting table tennis ♫ ⌂
V ♡ ☕ ⚡ Last dinner 9.15pm
Credit Cards 1 2 3 5

★★★69% **Abbey Lawn Hotel** Scarborough Rd TQ2 5UQ ☎(0803)295791 Telex no 299670 FAX (0803) 291460
70rm(66⇌4↱) CTV in all bedrooms ® **T** S%
sB&B⇌↱£41-£56 dB&B⇌↱£82-£92 ▤
Lift ☾ 50P ⇌(heated) ♪ (hard) ♫ nc8yrs *xmas*
☥ English & French **V** ♡ ☕ S% Lunch £8.50&alc Dinner £12.50&alc Last dinner 8.30pm
Credit Cards 1 2 3 5 £

★★★60% **Belgrave** Seafront TQ2 5HE ☎(0803)296666 FAX (0803) 211308
Situated in a good position overlooking the bay, the hotel offers bright, modern public rooms, attractive bars and well furnished bedrooms.
68rm(66⇌2↱)(16fb) CTV in all bedrooms ® **T**
sB&B⇌↱£29-£37 dB&B⇌↱£58-£76 ▤
Lift ☾ 80P 6🚗 (£1.50) ⊟ ✻ CFA ⇌(heated) ♫ ⌂ *xmas*
☥ English & French ♡ ☕ Bar Lunch £4-£7 Dinner £9-£9 Last dinner 8.30pm
Credit Cards 1 2 3 5

★★★73% **Corbyn Head** Torquay Rd, Sea Front, Livermead TQ2 6RH ☎(0803)213611 FAX (0803) 296152
The hotel has a commanding position with good sea views. All the rooms are attractive and well furnished, and there is a choice of restaurants.
51rm(47⇌4↱)(1fb)3⊟ CTV in all bedrooms ® **T**
sB&B⇌↱£28-£42 dB&B⇌↱£56-£84 ▤
☾ 50P CFA ⇌(heated) *xmas*
☥ English **V** ♡ ☕ Bar Lunch £1.50-£6 Dinner £11.50&alc Last dinner 9pm
Credit Cards 1 2 3 5

★★★51% ***Devonshire*** Parkhill Rd TQ1 2DY ☎(0803)291123 Telex no 42988 FAX (0803) 291710
Large detached hotel with pleasant garden, set in a quiet position.
47rm(35⇌11↱)Annexe12rm(10⇌2↱)(9fb) CTV in all bedrooms ® **T**
☾ ▦ CTV 50P ✻ CFA ⇌(heated) ♪ (hard) snooker horse riding surfing ♫ ⌂
☥ English, French, Italian & German ♡ ☕ Last dinner 8.30pm
Credit Cards 1 2 3 4 5

See advertisement on page 663

★★★67% **Homers** Warren Rd TQ2 5TN ☎(0803)213456 FAX (0803) 213458
Closed 2 Jan-8 Feb
Occupying one of the best positions, overlooking the bay, Homers retains many of the features of the original house, including fine, ornate ceilings in its well proportioned rooms. In the pleasant restaurant you will not only enjoy the imaginative cooking but also the panoramic views.
15rm(12⇌2↱)(2fb)1⊟ CTV in all bedrooms **T**
sB&B⇌↱fr£45 dB&B⇌↱fr£60 ▤
CTV 5P ⊟ ✻ nc7yrs *xmas*
☥ European **V** ♡ ☕ ⚡ Lunch fr£8.50 Dinner fr£19 Last dinner 9.30pm
Credit Cards 1 2 3 5

See advertisement on page 663

★★★61% **Kistor** Belgrave Rd TQ2 5HF ☎(0803)212632 FAX (0803) 293219
Commercial and tourist hotel close to the beach, affording personal attention.
59⇌(17fb) CTV in all bedrooms ® **T**
Lift CTV 45P ✻ CFA ⊡(heated) sauna solarium gymnasium spa pool games room ♫
☥ English & Continental **V** ♡ ☕ Last dinner 8.30pm
Credit Cards 1 2 3 5

★★★54% **Lincombe Hall** Meadfoot Rd TQ1 2JX ☎(0803)213361 FAX (0803) 211485
Large detached Victorian-style building, quarter of a mile from the beach and the town centre.
43rm(41⇌2↱)(6fb)3⊟ CTV in all bedrooms ® **T**
☾ 60P ✻ CFA ⇌(heated) ♪ (hard) sauna solarium putting spa bath
V ♡ ☕ Last dinner 8.30pm
Credit Cards 1 2 3 5 £

★★★56% **Livermead Cliff** Sea Front TQ2 6RQ (Best Western) ☎(0803)299666 & 292881 Telex no 42424 FAX (0803) 294496
Castellated three-storey red stone building whose grounds are enclosed by a sea wall. (Sports facilities at nearby hotel, 'Livermead House', available to guests).
64rm(54⇌10↱)(21fb) CTV in all bedrooms ® **T**
sB&B⇌↱£26.50-£42.50 dB&B⇌↱£52-£82 ▤
Lift ☾ CTV 60P 12🚗 ✻ CFA ⇌(heated) ♩ solarium ⌂ *xmas*

▶

Belgrave Hotel

Torquay

- ★ Superb Seafront location. Easy level walk to theatre, harbour and main shopping areas.
- ★ Seventy bedrooms with private bathrooms, colour television, radios, tea and coffee making facilities.
- ★ Spacious, modern, restaurant, bars, sun lounge and heated outdoor swimming pool.

Large car park and lock-up garages.
Open all year. "Torquay Weekend Away" special terms from October to April.
Residential conference facilities.

Sea Front Torquay **Telephone: 0803 296666** **Fax: 0803 211308**

The Imperial

★★★★★

TORQUAY

The Imperial, the only 5 star hotel in the South West, has been England's foremost exclusive resort hotel ever since it was opened in 1866. Situated on a cliff-top with a perfect panoramic view over the whole of Torbay, surrounded by 5 acres of beautiful gardens, it commands a unique position.

The hotel has 150 luxurious bedrooms and 17 superbly appointed suites, most of which have sea views and private balconies. Guests have the use of the fully equipped Health and Leisure Club.

The Imperial is world famous for its special events; Gastronomic, Art & Antique and Gardening. The superb Banqueting and Conference facilities can cater for up to 350 people.

★★★★★

The Imperial, Torquay, England

[0803] 294301

🍷 English & Continental V ♆ ☕ Lunch £6.75-£7.50&alc Dinner £11-£11.50&alc Last dinner 8.30pm
Credit Cards [1] [2] [3] [5]

★★★53% **Livermead House** Torbay Rd TQ2 6QJ (Best Western) ☎(0803)294361 Telex no 42918
Attractive hotel facing the sea with bright public rooms, good sporting facilities and friendly staff.
66rm(56⇌10♒)Annexe2rm(1⇌1♒)(11fb) CTV in 66bedrooms Ⓡ **T**
Lift ☾ CTV 90P ✲ ⛆(heated) 🎾(hard) ⛳ squash snooker sauna solarium gymnasium games room
🍷 English & French V ♆ ☕ Last dinner 8.30pm
Credit Cards [1] [2] [3] [5] Ⓔ

★★★58% ***Hotel Nepaul*** 27 Croft Rd TQ2 5UD
☎(0803)28457 28458
Soundly-appointed hotel in a good position with fine views.
37rm(31⇌6♒)(7fb)2⊞ CTV in all bedrooms Ⓡ **T**
Lift ☾ 14P 5🚗 ✲ ⛆(heated) ♫ 🏠
🍷 English & French V ♆ ☕ ✂
Credit Cards [1] [2] [3] [5]

★★★🏠70% ***Orestone Manor House*** Rockhouse Lane, Maidencombe TQ1 4SX
☎(0803)38098
FAX (0803) 38336
Closed Jan-Feb

Peacefully set in a quiet valley with good sea views, the pretty Georgian house offers hospitable service from owners and staff. Its charm and character are complemented by the more tangible advantages of modern, cosy bedrooms and commendable food standards.
20rm(13⇌7♒)(4fb) CTV in all bedrooms Ⓡ **T**
CTV 30P ✲ ⛆(heated) putting green games room 🏠
🍷 English & French V ♆ ☕ ✂ Last dinner 9pm
Credit Cards [1] [2] [3] [5]

See advertisement on page 665

★★★50% ***Oswald's*** Palermo Road, Babbacombe TQ1 3NW
☎(0803)39292
The many spacious rooms of this hotel and its proximity to the downs and beaches make it ideal for family holidays.
52rm(28⇌24♒)(3fb) CTV in all bedrooms Ⓡ
Lift ☾ 30P ✲
♆ ☕
Credit Cards [1] [3]

See advertisement on page 665

★★★64% ***Overmead*** Daddyhole Rd TQ1 2EF (Consort)
☎(0803)295666 & 297633 FAX (0803) 211175
Stone-built, split level hotel with a modern wing extension set in a quiet position.
55rm(38⇌17♒)(7fb) CTV in all bedrooms Ⓡ **T**
Lift ☾ 11P ✲ ⛆(heated) snooker sauna solarium gymnasium ♫
🍷 International V ♆ ☕ Last dinner 9pm
Credit Cards [1] [2] [3] Ⓔ

See advertisement on page 665

Red-star hotels offer the highest standards of hospitality, comfort and food.

T

★★★ 50% **Rainbow House** Belgrave Rd TQ2 5HJ
☎(0803)213232 Telex no 42551 FAX (0803) 212925
Modern soundly appointed hotel near the sea front.
100rm(92⇌8♠)(20fb) CTV in all bedrooms ® T ✱
sB&B⇌♠£32-£40 dB&B⇌♠£60-£75
Lift ☾ ▦ CTV 70P ✲ CFA ▭(heated) ⛱(heated) squash snooker sauna solarium gymnasium *xmas*
☋ International V ♆ ⅅ ⅟ Lunch £4-£6 Dinner £9.50-£11.50&alc Last dinner 8.45pm
Credit Cards 1 2 3 5

See advertisement on page 667

★★★ 62% **Sefton** Babbacombe Downs Rd, Babbacombe TQ1 3LH ☎(0803)38728 & 36591
The Powell family, assisted by a young, friendly staff, have made this Babbacombe hotel popular. All the bedrooms are attractive and there is a large entertainments room, a cocktail bar and a relaxing restaurant.
47rm(43⇌4♠)(11fb)1⊟ CTV in all bedrooms ® T ✱
sB&B⇌♠£27.50-£35 dB&B⇌♠£55-£74 ⊨
Lift 40P snooker ♫ *xmas*
V ♆ ⅅ Lunch fr£6&alc High tea 60p-£2.50 Dinner fr£9.95&alc Last dinner 9pm
Credit Cards 1 2 3 £

★★★ 60% ***Toorak*** Chestnut Av TQ2 5JS ☎(0803)291444
Telex no 42885 FAX (0803) 291666
This imposing Victorian hotel, close to the centre, is currently (1989) being totally refurbished, but until work is complete, guests can enjoy a wide range of leisure facilities in adjacent hotels under the same management.
59rm(55⇌)(24fb) CTV in all bedrooms ® T
☾ CTV 60P ⛟ ✲ CFA ⛱(heated) ⅌ (hard) snooker ♫
☋ English & French V ♆ ⅅ Last dinner 8.30pm
Credit Cards 1 2 3

★★ ***Albaston*** 27 St Marychurch Rd TQ1 3JF ☎(0803)26758
Closed Dec
Small family-run hotel, occupying a main road position, half a mile from the town centre.
13rm(1⇌6♠)(4fb) CTV in 12bedrooms ®
CTV 12⌂ ⛟ ⌂
☋ English & French V ♆ ⅅ Last dinner 9pm
Credit Cards 1 3

★★ **Ansteys Lea** Babbacombe Rd, Wellswood TQ1 2QJ
☎(0803)294843
A tastefully restored, large Victorian villa, situated close to Babbacombe beach. Rooms are spacious and comfortable, the staff friendly, and the attractive gardens contain a small, secluded swimming pool.
25rm(7⇌8♠)(7fb) CTV in all bedrooms ® sB&B£14-£19.50
sB&B⇌♠£16-£21.50 dB&B£26-£36.50
dB&B⇌♠£30.25-£41 ⊨
CTV 18P ✲ ⛱(heated) solarium games room *xmas*
☋ English & French ♆ ⅅ Lunch £4.50-£7 High tea £2.25-£2.75 Dinner £7-£9 Last dinner 7.30pm
£

★★ ***Hotel Balmoral*** Meadfoot Sea Rd TQ1 2LQ
☎(0803)23381 & 299224
Closed Feb
This large, Victorian house is close to Meadfoot beach. Bedrooms, though small, are well equipped and the public rooms are spacious.
23rm(21♠)(6fb) CTV in all bedrooms T
CTV 18P ✲ pool table games room ⌂
☋ English & French V ♆ ⅅ Last dinner 8pm
Credit Cards 1 2 3

Book as early as possible for busy holiday periods.

★★ **Bancourt** Avenue Rd TQ2 5LG ☎(0803)295077
Modern hotel complex a short distance from the shops and sea front.
49rm(20⇌4♠)(8fb) CTV in all bedrooms ® T
☾ CTV 50P ✲ ▭(heated) snooker
☋ English & French ♆ ⅅ Last dinner 8pm
Credit Cards 1 2 3

★★ **Belvedere House** Braddons Hill Rd West TQ1 1BG
☎(0803)293313
Built in 1832, this hotel was once the home of the Mountbattens, (then the Battenburgs). The current owners have restored it and it now provides a cosy retreat in the heart of Torquay. Standing in an elevated position a little way above and behind the harbour, the hotel looks out over Tor Bay.
10rm(2⇌8♠)(1fb) CTV in all bedrooms ®
sB&B⇌♠£27-£39.50 dB&B⇌♠£54-£69 (incl dinner) ⊨
CTV 9P ⛟ nc10yrs *xmas*
☋ English & Continental ♆ ⅅ ⅟ Lunch £5.95-£7.95 Dinner £8.95-£11.95 Last dinner 7.30pm
Credit Cards 1 3 £

★★ **Bowden Close** Teignmouth Rd, Maidencombe TQ1 4TJ
☎(0803)38029
Personally run hotel with well appointed rooms, offering a warm welcome.
19rm(2⇌14♠)(2fb) CTV in all bedrooms ® sB&B£17-£23
sB&B⇌♠£23-£25 dB&B£34-£46
dB&B⇌♠£46-£50 (incl dinner) ⊨
CTV 25P 2⌂ ✲ pool table
♆ ⅅ ⅟ Lunch £5.50-£7.50 Dinner £7 Last dinner 8pm
Credit Cards 1 3 £

★★ **Burlington** 462-466 Babbacombe Rd TQ1 1HN
☎(0803)294374 FAX (0803) 200189
RS 1Jan-31Jan 1990 for development
A tourist hotel situated on a main road about quarter of a mile from beach and town centre.
44rm(21⇌23♠)(7fb)1⊟ CTV in all bedrooms ® T ✱
sB&B⇌♠£19-£25 dB&B⇌♠£38-£50 ⊨
☾ CTV 20P ✲ ▭(heated) sauna solarium pool table spa bath ♫ *xmas*
☋ English, French & Italian V ♆ ⅅ S% Bar Lunch £1-£5 Dinner £8&alc Last dinner 8pm
Credit Cards 1 3 £

★★ **Bute Court** Belgrave Rd TQ2 5HQ (Minotels) ☎(0803)23771
White-painted Victorian building whose spacious and modernised rooms have good sea views.
46rm(35⇌7♠)(10fb) CTV in all bedrooms ® T S%
sB&B£17-£22.50 sB&B⇌♠£19-£28 dB&B£31-£42
dB&B⇌♠£37-£53 ⊨
Lift ☾ CTV 37P ✲ ⛱(heated) snooker ⌂ *xmas*
☋ English & Continental ♆ ⅅ S% Bar Lunch £1-£3.25alc Dinner £7-£9 Last dinner 8pm
Credit Cards 1 2 3 5 £

See advertisement on page 667

★★ ***Carlton*** Falkland Rd TQ2 5JJ ☎(0803)291166
Closed 29 Dec-1 Feb
A popular, family hotel offers friendly service under the personal direction of the proprietor. A range of lounges and facilities has much to offer to all age groups.
32rm(25⇌4♠)(17fb) CTV in all bedrooms ® T
Lift ☾ CTV 26P ✲ ⛱(heated) ♫ ⌂
V ♆ ⅅ Last dinner 7.30pm
Credit Cards 1 3

★★ **Chelston Tower** Rawlyn Rd TQ2 6PQ ☎(0803)607351
Closed Jan
Well proportioned villa with central tower, this friendly hotel offers good food and service. It is set in well kept gardens with good sea views.
▶

★★★

The New Sefton Hotel

**THE SEA FRONT,
BABBACOMBE DOWNS ROAD,
BABBACOMBE, TORQUAY,
DEVON**

TEL: 0803 38728/36591

Situated on the picturesque Babbacombe Downs, overlooking Lyme Bay and the surrounding countryside, this family run hotel is now open all year. All 47 rooms have bath or shower, toilet, colour TV, telephone and tea making facilities with the added comfort of full central heating. Free entertainment most nights or if you prefer a quiet evening relax in our intimate residents bar. You can be assured of excellent service and cuisine in the Chandelier Restaurant whilst enjoying the spectacular views.

The Oswalds Hotel

★★★ **BABBACOMBE** **AA**

The hotel offers the perfect retreat for a marvellous holiday. The chef takes pride in offering an excellent choice of menus with at least 4 choices of main course, at lunch and dinner. With full central heating, radio/intercom, tea making facilities. Colour TV in all rooms (most with private facilities). Spacious lounges, live entertainment nightly, cocktail bar, secluded gardens, etc. Oswalds Hotel must be your first choice.

Write or telephone for a colour brochure of the hotel – "Where the Customer is always King"

**Telephone:
TORQUAY (0803) 39292**

Torquay's Premier Victorian Country House Hotel.

Set amongst Torbay's finest scenery ★ Extensively refurbished resulting in 4 suites and 51 ★ Luxurious rooms.

Excellent Leisure facilities. We offer first class hospitality and friendly service.

★★★

**Daddyhole Road,
Meadfoot, Devon
Telephone 0803 297633**

Speak to us soon. You won't be disappointed.

***AA Country House Award B.T.A. Commended
Country House Hotel & Restaurant***

Orestone Manor House

Rockhouse Lane, MAIDENCOMBE, Nr Torquay
★★★ **Telephone: (0803) 328098/328099**

"Orestone is a warm, inviting Georgian Manor House set in lovely peaceful countryside – by the sea. Secluded grounds, beautiful gardens and heated pool – relax and enjoy the fine English cuisine in delightful surroundings. 20 en-suite bedrooms, all with tea/coffee makers, colour TV and direct dial telephones, some with sea views . . . run by people who care for people – well worth finding!"

Member of Inter Hotels **ExecHotels 33**

24rm(9⇌2↱)(11fb) sB&B£16.50-£25.50 sB&B⇌↱£19-£28 dB&B£33-£51 dB&B⇌↱£38-£56
CTV 40P ✽ ≈(heated) games room *xmas*
☙ ☕ Dinner £11-£11 Last dinner 7.30pm
(£)

★★***Clevedon*** Meadfoot Sea Rd TQ1 2LQ ☎(0803)294260
Closed Oct – Mar
Friendly hotel with spacious sun lounge and good home cooking.
14rm(4⇌6↱)(4fb) CTV in all bedrooms ®
CTV 8P ⛟ ✽ CFA table tennis nc2yrs
♀ English & Continental ☙ ☕ Last dinner 7.15pm
Credit Cards [3]

★★**Conway Court** Warren Rd TQ2 5TS ☎(0803)299699
Friendly holiday hotel with spectacular views across Tor Bay.
38rm(16⇌19↱)(3fb)4⛫ CTV in all bedrooms ® **T**
sB&B⇌↱£26-£32 dB&B⇌↱£52-£64 (incl dinner) ⊟
CTV ⱣP heated spa pool *xmas*
☙ ☕ ⊬ Bar Lunch 90p-£5 Dinner £9.50-£12.50 Last dinner 8pm
Credit Cards [1] [2] [3] [5]

★★**Coppice** Barrington Rd TQ1 2QJ ☎(0803)297786
Closed Nov-Apr
The pleasant, family, holiday hotel, under personal supervision, is out of the town centre yet conveniently near to amenities. It is attractively set amid sub-tropical gardens, complete with pool.
34rm(29⇌3↱)(10fb) CTV in all bedrooms ® **T**
sB&B£14-£17.60 sB&B⇌↱£16-£19.60 dB&B£28-£35.20 dB&B⇌↱£32-£39.20 ⊟
☾ CTV 26P ✽ ≈(heated) solarium ♫ *xmas*
☙

★★***Frognel Hall*** Higher Woodfield Rd TQ1 2LD ☎(0803)28339
Closed Jan & Feb RS Dec
Once a private house, secluded in its own grounds, Frognel Hall was originally converted into a hotel in about 1860. It has now been restored to provide a charming little retreat, peacefully located yet within easy reach of both town and beaches, featuring generous public areas and comfortable, modern bedrooms.
27rm(12⇌9↱)(3fb) CTV in 7bedrooms ®
Lift CTV 25P ✽ sauna solarium croquet games room ♫
♀ English & French ☙ ☕ Last dinner 7.30pm
Credit Cards [3]

★★**Gresham Court** Babbacombe Rd TQ1 1HG ☎(0803)293007
Closed Dec-Feb
Sited on a corner, and within easy walking distance of harbour and town centre, this family-operated hotel continues to be popular for its friendly, informal atmosphere.
30rm(15⇌15↱)(6fb) ® sB&B⇌↱£15.75-£21 dB&B⇌↱£31.50-£42
Lift CTV 4P ♫
♀ English **V** Bar Lunch £1-£3 Dinner £6 Last dinner 8pm
Credit Cards [1] [3]

★★**Howden Court** 23 Croft Rd TQ2 5UD ☎(0803)294844
Closed Nov-Mar
Large villa in its own grounds.
32rm(12⇌20↱)(10fb) CTV in 20bedrooms ®
sB&B⇌↱£19.50-£23 dB&B⇌↱£32-£39 ⊟
CTV 25P ✽ ♫ *xmas*
♀ English & French & Italian **V** ☙ ☕ Bar Lunch 90p-£3.50 Dinner fr£8.50 Last dinner 8pm
(£)

★★***Hunsdon Lea*** Hunsdon Rd TQ1 1QB ☎(0803)26538
Closed Nov-Etr
This friendly, family, holiday hotel enjoys the personal attention of its proprietors and a quiet setting which is nevertheless conveniently close to central shopping area, harbour and amenities.
16rm(8⇌3↱)(5fb) CTV in all bedrooms ✘
12P ⛟ ≈(heated) solarium pool table & table tennis
V ☙ ☕ ⊬

★★**Lansdowne** Babbacombe Rd TQ1 1PW ☎(0803)299599
Closed 17 Oct-Etr
Hotel with a modern exterior in a quiet position, quarter of a mile from the town centre.
30rm(2↱)(7fb) CTV in all bedrooms ® **T**
CTV 30P ✽ ≈(heated) pool table & table-tennis
♀ English, French & Italian **V** ☙ ☕ ⊬ Last dinner 8.30pm
Credit Cards [1] (£)

★★**Meadfoot Bay** Meadfoot Sea Rd TQ1 2LQ ☎(0803)294722
Closed Nov-Feb
Double-fronted villa standing in its own grounds in the Meadfoot Bay area.
25rm(13⇌7↱)(6fb) CTV in all bedrooms ® sB&B£15-£21 sB&B⇌↱£18-£25 dB&B£30-£42 dB&B⇌↱£36-£50 ⊟
CTV 15P games room *xmas*
♀ English & French **V** ☙ ☕ Bar Lunch £1.50-£5 Dinner £8.95 Last dinner 7.30pm
Credit Cards [1] [2] [3]

★★***Morningside*** Babbacombe Downs TQ1 3LF ☎(0803)327025
On Babbacombe Downs with panoramic views towards Lyme Bay.

14rm(10⇌4↱) CTV in all bedrooms ® **T** ✘
CTV 16P nc10yrs
V ☙ ☕
Credit Cards [1] [3]

★★***Nethway*** Falkland Rd TQ2 5JR ☎(0803)27630
Closed Jan-Feb RS Nov-Dec
Hotel is in elevated position near Abbey gardens.
27rm(12⇌12↱)(4fb) CTV in 12bedrooms TV in 15bedrooms ®
☾ CTV 26P ✽ ≈(heated) ℘ (grass) games room pool table jacuzzi ♫ nc5yrs
☙ ☕
Credit Cards [1] [3]

★★**Norcliffe** 7 Babbacombe Downs Rd, Babbacombe TQ1 3LF ☎(0803)38456 due to change to 328456
Imposing villa on Babbacombe sea front, offering fine views and near to the shops.
20rm(10⇌10↱)(2fb)1⛫ CTV in all bedrooms ® **T** ✱
sB&B⇌↱£14-£28 dB&B⇌↱£28-£56 (incl dinner)
Lift 16P *xmas*
☙ ☕ Lunch £5.25 Dinner £8 Last dinner 7.30pm
Credit Cards [3] (£)

See advertisement on page 669

★★**Oscar's Hotel & Restaurant** 56 Belgrave Rd TQ2 5HY ☎(0803)293563
Closed 12 Nov-17 Dec
A tall, Victorian, terraced house, tastefully converted, Oscars is in the Belgravia area of Torquay. Bedrooms are comfortable and the intimate bistro is open from March to October.
12rm(1⇌4↱)(2fb) CTV in all bedrooms ® ✘ (ex guide dogs)
✱ sB&B£13-£18.50 dB&B£26-£36 dB&B⇌↱£28-£39 ⊟
CTV 8P ⛟
♀ International **V** ☙ ⊬ Dinner £6.50-£8.50&alc Last dinner 8.30pm
Credit Cards [1] [2] [3] [4] [5] (£)

★★**Red House** Rousdown Rd, Chelston TQ2 6PB ☎(0803)607811
A red stone house in a quiet residential area has been tastefully modernised and equipped with good leisure and health facilities. Compact bedrooms are furnished in the modern style, whilst comprehensive catering facilities are amalgamated with a pleasant bar area.
▶

T

10rm(9⇌1⚑)(3fb) CTV in all bedrooms ® S%
sB&B⇌⚑£18-£29 dB&B⇌⚑£28-£50 ⊟
10P ✿ ✲ ▭(heated) ⌂(heated) sauna solarium gymnasium games room spa pool *xmas*
☋ English & French V ✧ ⊥ ⊬ S% Lunch fr£4alc High tea £1-£2.50alc Dinner £7.50-£8.50&alc Last dinner 8pm
Credit Cards 1 3

★★Sunray Aveland Rd, Babbacombe TQ1 3PT ☎(0803)38285
RS Nov-Apr (ex Xmas)
This modern, friendly hotel, under family ownership, is efficiently run by experienced staff. Conveniently situated a short distance from Cary Park, it is also within easy reach of the Downs.
21rm(10⇌11⚑)(3fb) CTV in all bedrooms ® ✱
sB&B⇌⚑£17-£23 dB&B⇌⚑£34-£46 (incl dinner) ⊟
CTV 15P 1⌂ *xmas*
☋ English, French & Italian ⊬
Credit Cards 1 3 £

★★Hotel Sydore Meadfoot Rd TQ1 2JP ☎(0803)294758
This villa in its own grounds is near town centre and harbour.
13rm(6⇌6⚑)(5fb)1⊟ CTV in all bedrooms ® ✱
sB&B⇌⚑£20 dB&B⇌⚑£40 ⊟
CTV 17P ✲ pool table games room croquet *xmas*
☋ English & French V ✧ ⊥ S% Lunch fr£5.50 Dinner fr£7 Last dinner 8.45pm
Credit Cards 1 3 £

★★Templestowe Tor Church Rd TQ2 5UU ☎(0803)299499
FAX (0803) 295101
Holiday hotel personally supervised by the resident owners, close to the beach and the town centre.
87rm(56⇌31⚑)(28fb) CTV in all bedrooms ® T
sB&B⇌⚑£19.65-£35 dB&B⇌⚑£39.30-£70
Lift ☾ CTV 60P ⌂(heated) ℘ (hard) solarium crazy golf table tennis pool table ♫ *xmas*
☋ French ✧ ⊥ Lunch £5-£5 Dinner £7-£7&alc Last dinner 8.30pm
Credit Cards 1 3

★★*Vernon Court* Warren Rd TQ2 5TR ☎(0803)292676
Closed Nov-Feb (except Xmas)
In superb, commanding position offering panoramic views over Tor Bay and the sea.
21rm(14⇌3⚑)(6fb) CTV in all bedrooms ®
CTV 9P
☋ English & Continental V ✧ ⊥ Last dinner 8pm
Credit Cards 1 2 3 5 £

★Ashley Rise 18 Babbacombe Rd, Babbacombe TQ1 3SJ
☎(0803)37282 due to change to 327282
Closed Dec-Mar except xmas
Detached modern hotel on the main Babbacombe road into Torquay, near the sea front and the shops.
29rm(3⇌7⚑)(5fb) ® sB&B£15-£18 sB&B⇌⚑£16-£19 dB&B£28-£32 dB&B⇌⚑£32-£36
CTV 14P ⌂ ♫ *xmas*
✧ Dinner fr£6.50 Last dinner 7pm
£

★Fairmount House Herbert Road, Chelston TQ2 6RW
(Guestaccom) ☎(0803)605446
Closed 6 Nov-Feb
Set in secluded gardens this small, personally-run hotel offers cosy bedrooms and commendable standards of cooking.
7rm(2⇌5⚑)(3fb) ® sB&B⇌⚑£17-£20 dB&B⇌⚑£34-£40 ⊟
CTV 8P
☋ English & Continental ✧ ⊥ ⊬ Lunch £8.50-£8.50 Dinner £8.50-£8.50 Last dinner 7.30pm
Credit Cards 1 2 3 £

★*Shelley Court* Croft Rd TQ2 5UD ☎(0803)295642
Attractive detached hotel in secluded private grounds, facing south with panoramic views of Tor Bay.
29rm(3⇌19⚑)(3fb) ® ✈
CTV 20P ✲ ♫
✧ Last dinner 7.30pm
Credit Cards 1

★Sunleigh Livermead Hill TQ2 6QY ☎(0803)607137
RS Jan-Etr
Set in its own grounds only a few hundred yards from Livermead beach, the hotel has sea views from its slightly elevated position. Bedrooms have recently been refurbished, the lounge bar has modern fittings, and the comfortably equipped lounge is furnished with delightful antiques.
22⚑(3fb) CTV in all bedrooms ® sB&B⚑£21-£26
dB&B⚑£42-£52 (incl dinner) ⊟
CTV 18P ♫ *xmas*
Dinner £7.95 Last dinner 7pm

★*Windsurfer* St Agnes Ln TQ2 6QE ☎(0803)606550
Closed 27 Nov-22 Dec & 29 Dec-13 Jan
The semi-detached villa stands in a quiet location near Abbey lawns and Torbay station. Bedrooms are well-equipped and public rooms tastefully and comfortably appointed.
10rm(5⇌5⚑)(5fb) CTV in all bedrooms ® ✈
CTV 14P ✲
Last dinner 8pm
Credit Cards 2

❀ ✕✕The Table 135 Babbacombe Rd TQ1 3SR
☎(0803)34292
A cosy, intimate restaurant in the centre of Babbacombe, converted from a shop by Jane and Trevor Brooks. Jane is the charming and attentive hostess, while Trevor is the innovative chef, preparing local produce with fresh herbs and robust sauces. His background as a patissier in some of Britain's finest restaurants reveals itself throughout, from the light home-made rolls to the delicious desserts. The wine list is young but carefully compiled, and offers good value for money.
Closed Mon, 1-16 Feb & 1-10 Sep
Lunch not served
☋ British & French 20 seats ✱ Dinner £18.50-£20.50 Last dinner 10pm ⁄P nc10yrs

✕Remy's Restaurant Francais 3 Croft Rd TQ2 5UF
☎(0803)292359
A small restaurant, set in a terraced house, creates a very French atmosphere, patron/chef Remy Bopp producing three-course meals at three price levels, with a predominance of commendable cuisine from the Alsace region. Typical dishes on offer are foie gras, saddle of venison with cranberry sauce and breast of pheasant with madeira and truffle sauce, whilst some interesting Alsatian wines are available as well as the more classic varieties.
Closed Sun, Mon & 2 wks Aug
Lunch not served
☋ French 33 seats Dinner £15.85 Last dinner 9.30pm ⁄P nc7yrs
Credit Cards 2 3

TOTLAND BAY

See Wight, Isle of

See the preliminary section 'Hotel and Restaurant Classification' for an explanation of the AA's appointment and award scheme.

TOTNES Devon Map **03** SX86

See also **Harbertford & Staverton**

★★Royal Seven Stars TQ9 5DD ☎(0803)862125 & 863241

This town-centre hotel, originally a coaching inn dating back to 1660, offers character bars and public rooms. Bedrooms, though modest, have modern facilities and the small, covered courtyard is both interesting and attractive.

18rm(12⇌)(5fb) CTV in all bedrooms ® **T** sB&Bfr£32 sB&B⇌fr£42 dB&Bfr£44 dB&B⇌fr£52

CTV 25P ♫ *xmas*

English & Continental **V** Lunch £7-£8&alc Dinner £13.50-£15&alc Last dinner 9.30pm

Credit Cards 1 3 5

See advertisement on page 671

TOWCESTER Northamptonshire Map **04** SP64

○ ***Travelodge*** A43 East Towcester by pass NN12 0DD (Trusthouse Forte) ☎(0327)359105

33⇌

P

✕✕ ***Vine House*** 100 High St, Paulerspury NN12 7NA (3m S A5) ☎Paulerspury(032733)267

This small restaurant, attached to a cottage-style hotel in the picturesque village centre, is fast achieving a high reputation in the country. The young chefs use first-class produce and have a lovely, light touch with dishes such as Pithiviers of Duck with a Port Wine and pink peppercorn sauce, tartlet of wild mushrooms with a cream and chive sauce, the tomato butter sauce accompanying the pan-fried fillet of salmon showed real depth of flavour, and to conclude the meal there is a small selection of tempting desserts or carefully-chosen selection of cheeses.

Closed Sun

▶

Lunch not served Sat & Mon
45 seats Last dinner 9.30pm 20P 5 bedrooms available
Credit Cards 1 3

TREARDDUR BAY Gwynedd Map **06** SH27

★★★58% **Beach** LL65 2YT (Best Western) ☎(0407)860332
Telex no 61529
This is an imposing hotel, enjoying a prominent position close to the beach. Its extensive leisure facilities include a nightclub and there are two separate dining rooms, each with a different style.
26rm(22⇨4⬈)(2fb) CTV in all bedrooms ® **T** ✱
sB&B⇨⬈£33-£38
dB&B⇨⬈£43-£50 Continental breakfast ⊟
☾ CTV 150P squash snooker sauna solarium gymnasium spa *xmas*
♡ English & French **V** ♨ ⚲ Lunch £5.50-£7.50&alc Dinner fr£10.50&alc Last dinner 9.30pm
Credit Cards 1 2 3 5 £

★★★60% ***Trearddur Bay*** LL68 2UN ☎(0407)860301
Telex no 61609
This large, seaside hotel stands in its own grounds and has fine views of the Anglesey coast. Refurbishment carried out in 1989 adds to the hotel's amenities.
27rm(20⇨)(7fb) CTV in all bedrooms ® **T**
☾ CTV 300P ✲ ⊡(heated)
V ♨ ⚲
Credit Cards 1 2 3 4 5

★★***Seacroft*** Ravenspoint Rd LL65 2YU ☎(0407)860348
Two-storey hotel near the beach.
6rm(1⇨2⬈)(3fb) CTV in all bedrooms ® ✗
CTV 30P ✲
♡ French **V** ♨ Last dinner 9pm

TREBETHERICK Cornwall & Isles of Scilly Map **02** SW97

★★***St Moritz*** PL27 6SD (Inter) ☎(020886)2242
Closed 5 Nov-17 Mar
Comfortable, family hotel near the beach with well-equipped bedrooms. The two restaurants, recently upgraded, are popular locally.
50⇨(3fb) CTV in all bedrooms ® **T**
⊞ CTV 80P ✲ solarium
♡ English & Continental **V** ♨ ⚲
Credit Cards 1 2 3 5

TREFRIW Gwynedd Map **06** SH76

★★**Hafod House** LL27 0RQ (Inter) ☎Llanrwst(0492)640029
FAX (0492) 641351
This 17th-century farmhouse has been carefully restored and extended to provide very comfortable bedrooms and large public areas. It is family run, and the chef/proprietor offers good food based on local produce.
7rm(6⇨1⬈)1⊞ CTV in all bedrooms ® **T** ✗ (ex guide dogs)
sB&B⇨⬈£19.50-£28.50 dB&B⇨⬈£35-£49 ⊟
20P ✲ nc11yrs *xmas*
♡ English & French ♨ ⚲ Lunch fr£7.95 Dinner £12.50-£14.50 Last dinner 9.45pm
Credit Cards 1 2 3 5 £

TRELIGHTS Cornwall & Isles of Scilly Map **02** SW97

★★**Long Cross** PL29 3TF ☎Bodmin(0208)880243 & 880560
Closed Nov-Etr
Set amongst well tended Victorian gardens, the hotel has a friendly atmosphere, good bedrooms and bathrooms, and a pleasant, period atmosphere in its public rooms. Its separate bars open directly onto the gardens.
12⇨1⊞ CTV in all bedrooms ® ✱ sB&B⇨fr£28.50
dB&B⇨fr£52.90 (incl dinner) ⊟
CTV 20P ⊞ ✲ nc14yrs
V ♨ ⚲ Bar Lunch fr£1.75alc Dinner fr£7.50alc Last dinner 9pm
Credit Cards 1 3 £

TREMADOG Gwynedd Map **06** SH54

★★**Madoc** LL49 9RB ☎Porthmadog(0766)512021
Stone-built, and dating back to the early 19th century, the hotel stands in the market square. Furnishings are comfortable, and the dining room serves good, honest food.
21rm(1⇨3⬈)(3fb) ® ✱ sB&B£16.50-£18.50
sB&B⇨⬈£18.50-£25 dB&B£32-£37 dB&B⇨⬈fr£37 ⊟
12P 4⌂
V ♨ ⚲ Lunch £4.50-£6 Dinner £6.95-£14 Last dinner 9.30pm
Credit Cards 1 3 £

TRESCO

See **Scilly, Isles of**

TREYARNON BAY Cornwall & Isles of Scilly Map **02** SW87

★★***Waterbeach*** PL28 8JW ☎Padstow(0841)520292
Closed Nov-Feb
Comfortable, personally-run, family holiday hotel in a peaceful setting, 200 yards from the beach.
16rm(7⇨2⬈)(2fb) ® **T** ✗
CTV 20P ⊞ ✲ ⚲ (hard) putting
V ♨ ⚲ Last dinner 8.15pm
Credit Cards 1 2 3

TRING Hertfordshire Map **04** SP91

★★**Rose & Crown** High St HP23 5AH (Lansbury)
☎(044282)4071 Telex no 826538 FAX (044282) 890735
A former coaching inn in the town's High Street, the Rose and Crown is run by cheerful and friendly staff. Bedrooms are well decorated and modernised and there is an attractive restaurant.
28rm(26⇨2⬈)(1fb)2⊞ ⚞in 5 bedrooms CTV in all bedrooms ® **T** ✗ (ex guide dogs) sB&B⇨⬈fr£58 dB&B⇨⬈fr£68 ⊟
☾ 60P ✲ ⌂ *xmas*
♡ Mainly grills **V** ♨ ⚞ Lunch fr£8alc Dinner fr£15alc Last dinner 10pm
Credit Cards 1 2 3 5

⌂**Crows Nest Travel Inn** Tring Hill HP23 4LD ☎(044282)4819
30⇨⬈ CTV in all bedrooms ® ✗ (ex guide dogs)
sB⇨⬈fr£22.50 dB⇨⬈fr£27.50 (room only)
140P
V ♨ ⚞ Lunch fr£5.50 Dinner fr£7 Last dinner 10.30pm
Credit Cards 1 2 3 5

TRINITY

See **Jersey under Channel Islands**

TROON Strathclyde *Ayrshire* Map **10** NS33

★★★★63% **Marine Highland** KA10 6HE (Scottish Highland)
☎(0292)314444 Telex no 777595 FAX (0292) 316922
This comfortable hotel is delightfully situated beside the Championship Golf Course overlooking the Firth of Clyde. It has been completely refurbished to a high standard and additional facilities include a Sports and Leisure Club and a smart new Conference and Banqueting Centre. The hotel has a lot to commend it.
72⇨(7fb)1⊞ CTV in all bedrooms ® **T** sB&B⇨£62-£67
dB&B⇨£92-£99 ⊟
Lift ☾ 100P ✲ CFA ⊡(heated) squash snooker sauna solarium gymnasium shooting fishing golf ♫ *xmas*

T

☺ International V ♔ ☐ Lunch £7.95-£8.95&alc Dinner £16.95-£17.95&alc Last dinner 11pm
Credit Cards [1] [2] [3] [5]

★★★67% **Piersland House** Craigend Rd KA10 6HD (Consort) ☎(0292)314747 FAX (0292) 315613
15rm(10⇌5♠)Annexe2⇌(2fb)1 ▣ CTV in all bedrooms ® T sB&B⇌♠£44-£59 dB&B⇌♠£66-£95 ▤
☾ 150P ✲ croquet putting *xmas*
☺ Scottish, English & Contininental V ♔ ☐ Lunch £14-£22alc High tea £4.50-£8 Dinner fr£16.50&alc Last dinner 9.30pm
Credit Cards [1] [2] [3] [5]

★★**Ardneil** 51 St Meddans St KA10 6NU ☎(0292)311611
A privately-owned, well supervised and friendly hotel close to the town centre and railway station. Bedrooms are compact but comfortable and mealtimes are very busy.
9rm(3⇌4♠)(2fb) CTV in all bedrooms ® sB&B£21.50-£24 sB&B⇌♠£25-£27 dB&Bfr£37 dB&B⇌♠fr£47
100P ✲ snooker
V ♔ ☐ Lunch £4-£6alc High tea £5-£8alc Dinner £6-£10alc Last dinner 9pm
Credit Cards [1] [2]

★★**Craiglea** South Beach KA10 6EG ☎(0292)311366
Family run resort hotel on seafront.
20rm(10⇌1♠)(2fb) CTV in all bedrooms ® T sB&B£26-£33 sB&B⇌♠£29-£36 dB&B£40-£46 dB&B⇌♠£44-£50 ▤
CTV 14P ⌂ *xmas*
☺ English V ♔ ☐ Lunch £6-£7.50&alc Dinner £9.50-£10.50&alc Last dinner 8.45pm
Credit Cards [1] [2] [3] [5]

For key to symbols see the inside front cover.

★★**South Beach** South Beach Rd KA10 6EG ☎(0292)312033
Close to the seafront, the hotel is popular with families and has recently completed a new leisure centre.
29rm(6⇌9♠)(4fb) CTV in all bedrooms ® T
CTV 50P ♩ sauna solarium gymnasium jacuzzi ♫
French ♈ Ⓓ Last dinner 8.30pm
Credit Cards 1 2 3 £

✕✕**Highgrove House** Old Loans Rd KA10 7HL ☎(0292)312511
Set on a hilside east of Troon the restaurant is owned and run by chef Bill Costley, whose cooking has impressed our inspectors for a number of years. We feel sure that, now that he is his own master, there will soon be further accolades, especially as he is keen to extend his modern-style cooking. He has ambitious plans for Highgrove which will be interesting to see. At the moment, the bedrooms attached to the restaurant are somewhat spartan, but nonetheless adequate.
V 70 seats ✱ Lunch £9.50 Dinner £13-£19alc Last lunch 3pm Last dinner 10pm 80P 6 bedrooms available
Credit Cards 1 2 3

✕**Campbell's Kitchen** 3 South Beach KA10 6EF ☎(0292)314421
This popular little bistro restaurant enjoys a good local reputation. The cosy interior is delightfully simple, with subdued lighting and a friendly relaxed atmosphere. The short, imaginative menu reflects a French influence, and service is unobtrusively efficient.
Closed Sun, Mon, 25-26 Dec & 2 wks Jan
Scottish & French 36 seats ✱ Lunch £2.95-£10.50 Dinner £14.95-£22.50&alc Last lunch 2.30pm Last dinner 9.30pm
Credit Cards 1 2 3

TROTTON West Sussex Map **04** SU82

★★★72% **Southdowns** GU31 5JN (Exec Hotel)
☎Rogate(073080)521 & 763 Telex no 86658
FAX (073080) 790
Quietly situated in rural countryside four miles south-west of Midhurst off the A272, this well-managed hotel is the ideal base for business and leisure, offering good levels of service and very good facilities, including the Kingfisher Club. The Country Restaurant features an extensive choice of dishes, professionally cooked and using fresh local ingredients.
22⇌(3fb)1 CTV in all bedrooms ® T ✗ sB&B⇌£45-£60 dB&B⇌£60-£80
CTV 70P ✲ (heated) ♩ sauna solarium *xmas*
V ♈ Ⓓ Lunch £8.50-£15&alc High tea £2.50-£8.50 Dinner £15-£20&alc Last dinner 10pm
Credit Cards 1 2 3

See advertisement under MIDHURST

TROUTBECK (near Windermere) Cumbria Map **11** NY32

★★***Mortal Man*** LA23 1PL ☎Ambleside(05394)33193
Closed mid Nov-mid Feb
An old lakeland inn, built in 1689, features oak beams in its cosy lounge and bars; family-run, it offers reliably good service.
12rm(11⇌1♠) CTV in 10bedrooms ®
CTV 20P ✲ nc5yrs
♈ Ⓓ Last dinner 8pm

TROWBRIDGE Wiltshire Map **03** ST85

★★***Polebarn House*** Polebarn Gardens, Polebarn Rd BA14 7EW ☎(0225)777006
Refurbished hotel in Grade II listed building.
13rm(2⇌11♠)(1fb) CTV in all bedrooms ® T ✗
10P nc3yrs
V ♈ Ⓓ
Credit Cards 1 3

Book as early as possible for busy holiday periods.

★**Hilbury Court** Hilperton Rd BA14 7JW ☎(0225)752949
Closed 24-31 Dec
This attractive, late-Georgian house stands in its own grounds on the outskirts of Trowbridge. The public rooms are comfortable and the bedrooms, some with en suite facilities, are tastefully decorated and very well equipped. The owner's wife is in charge of the dining room, and the food is good, unfussy and freshly prepared.
13rm(4⇌3♠)(2fb) CTV in all bedrooms ® T ✗ (ex guide dogs) ✱ sB&B£30-£33 sB&B⇌♠£35 dB&B£40 dB&B⇌♠£46
CTV 14P ✲
V ♈ Ⓓ Lunch £3.50-£7.50 High tea £4-£7 Dinner £8-£10 Last dinner 7.30pm
Credit Cards 1 3

TRURO Cornwall & Isles of Scilly Map **02** SW84

★★★76% ***Alverton Manor*** Tregolls Rd TR1 1XQ ☎(0872)76633
25rm(23⇌2♠)

★★★56% **Brookdale** Tregolls Rd TR1 1JZ (Inter)
☎(0872)73513 & 79305
Closed Xmas wk
A small and well-managed hotel, pleasantly situated in the centre of Truro. The restaurant offers an imaginative menu and dishes are carefully prepared.
21rm(17⇌4♠) CTV in all bedrooms ® T S10% sB&B⇌♠£41 dB&B⇌♠£56
50P 10
English, French & Italian ♈ Ⓓ S% Bar Lunch 90p-£6.85 Dinner £13 Last dinner 8.45pm
Credit Cards 1 2 3 5

★★**Carlton** Falmouth Rd TR1 2HL ☎(0872)72450
Closed 21 Dec-5 Jan
Detached Victorian mansion with extension. Family run by Chef proprietor. Quiet situation but close to city centre.
30rm(5⇌22♠)(4fb) CTV in all bedrooms ® T ✱
sB&B£22.50-£31.90 sB&B⇌♠£27.50-£31.90 dB&Bfr£35.20 dB&B⇌♠fr£43.50
32P ✲ sauna solarium gymnasium spa bath
V ♈ Ⓓ Lunch £6 Dinner £7.30&alc Last dinner 8pm
Credit Cards 1 3 £

TUNBRIDGE WELLS (ROYAL) Kent Map **05** TQ53

★★★71% **Spa** TN4 8XJ (Best Western) ☎(0892)20331
Telex no 957188 FAX (0892) 510575
This well established hotel retains a gracious air, suited to its good standards of hospitality and service. The lounge is spacious and comfortable, the dining room attractive and high-ceilinged, and there is also a very well equipped leisure complex to cater for present-day expectations. Bedrooms vary in size but are well equipped and nicely furnished.
76rm(75⇌1♠)(9fb) CTV in all bedrooms ® T ✗ (ex guide dogs) ✱ S10% sB⇌♠£55-£60 dB⇌♠£68-£73 (room only)
Lift ☾ 120P ✲ CFA (heated) (hard) sauna solarium gymnasium *xmas*
English & French V ♈ Ⓓ S10% Lunch £15 Dinner £18 Last dinner 9.30pm
Credit Cards 1 2 3 4 5

★★**Calverley** TN1 2LY ☎Tunbridge Wells(0892)26455
Telex no 957565 FAX (0892) 512044
The good, well-run, old-fashioned hotel provides spacious bedrooms and friendly service.
43rm(23⇌9♠)(2fb)1 CTV in all bedrooms ® T sB&Bfr£37 sB&B⇌♠fr£41 dB&Bfr£55 dB&B⇌♠fr£62
Lift ☾ CTV 34P ✲ *xmas*
English V ♈ Ⓓ Lunch fr£9alc Dinner fr£11alc Last dinner 8.30pm
Credit Cards 1 2 3 5 £

★★**Royal Wells Inn** TN4 8BE (Consort)
☎Tunbridge Wells(0892)511188 FAX (0892) 511908
Closed 25-26 Dec RS 1 Jan & BH Mons
This comfortable, old-fashioned hotel is popular for its elegant first-floor restaurant and for its more casual bar meals. Bedrooms have been refurbished to offer nicely appointed accommodation with individual character. Staff are friendly and helpful.
25rm(21⇌4♠)2⊞ CTV in all bedrooms ® T S10%
sB&B⇌♠£47-£50 dB&B⇌♠£62-£67 ⊟
Lift 28P 4⌂ ⊞
♀ English & French V ♉ S10% Lunch £10.75-£12.25&alc Dinner £13.75-£25&alc Last dinner 10pm
Credit Cards 1 2 3 5 £

★★**Russell** TN1 1DZ (Inter) ☎Tunbridge Wells(0892)544833
Telex no 95177 FAX (0892) 515846
A friendly, comforable hotel, personally supervised by the owners, Mr and Mrs Wilkinson, assisted by staff who are enthusiastic and very willing to please. The dinner menu offers plenty of choice of mostly traditional dishes and the bedrooms are spacious and well appointed.
21rm(16⇌5♠)(3fb)⊬in 4 bedrooms CTV in all bedrooms ® T
✗ (ex guide dogs) sB&B⇌♠£48-£54 dB&B⇌♠£60-£66 ⊟
(20P
♀ English & French V ♉ ⊈ Bar Lunch fr£3 Dinner fr£13 Last dinner 9.30pm
Credit Cards 1 2 3 5

✕✕**Eglantine** High St ☎(0892)24957
Closed Sun & Mon, 1-14 Jan, 16-30 Sep
♀ French V 35 seats ✱ S10% Lunch £10 Dinner £17 Last lunch 1.45pm Last dinner 9.30pm ₱ ⊬
Credit Cards 1 2 3

⊛✕✕**Thackeray's House** TN1 1EA
☎(0892)511921
A consistently high standard of French cuisine is offered at this pleasant town house, once the home of the novelist William Makepeace Thackeray. The interesting range of dishes changes to make the most of seasonal produce, and the fixed-price menus are reasonably priced, with a wine list to match.
Closed Sun, Mon & Xmas
♀ English & French V 35 seats S% Lunch £13.90-£15.75 Dinner £26.50-£32 Last lunch 2.30pm Last dinner 10pm ₱
Credit Cards 1 3

✕**Cheevers** 56 High St TN1 1XF ☎(0892)545524
This small restaurant, run by active young proprietors, charms by its simplicity and the well-balanced selection of interesting, professionally prepared dishes. The influence is predominantly, but not exclusively French. Our Inspector particularly recommended the duckling with ginger and spring onions and the home-made bread as something out of the ordinary. The wine list is small but in keeping with the style of the restaurant.
Closed Sun, Mon 1 wk Xmas, 2 wks Etr & 2 wks Summer
34 seats Lunch £10-£18alc Dinner £18 Last lunch 2pm Last dinner 10.30pm ₱
Credit Cards 1 3

TURNBERRY Strathclyde *Ayrshire* Map 10 NS20

★★★★77% **Turnberry** KA26 9LT ☎(0655)31000
Telex no 777779 FAX (0655) 31706
A fine hotel for sport, looking out over the championship golf courses and the sea towards Arran and Ailsa Craig. The standard of service cannot be faulted in any aspect, not least in the restaurant where they serve excellent cuisine. An ambitious programme of upgrading to highest international standards has been set into motion and results are already evident in luxurious public areas and some splendid bedrooms.
115⇌♠(7fb)2⊞ CTV in all bedrooms T S%
sB&B⇌♠£105-£130 dB&B⇌♠£140-£170 ⊟
Lift (CTV 200P ⊞ ✽ CFA ⊡(heated) ▶18 ℘ (hard) U snooker sauna solarium gymnasium pitch & putt putting table tennis ♫ *xmas*
♀ Scottish & French V ♉ ⊈ ⊬ S% Lunch £13.75&alc High tea £7.50&alc Dinner £24.50&alc Last dinner 9.30pm
Credit Cards 1 2 3 5

TUTBURY Staffordshire Map 08 SK22

★★★55% **Ye Olde Dog & Partridge** High St DE13 9LS
☎Burton-on-Trent(0283)813030 Telex no 347220
FAX (0283) 813178
Closed 25-26 Dec & 1 Jan
A half-timbered building in the town centre, the Dog and Partridge has been maintained in an excellent state of preservation, considering that parts date back to the 15th century. All the bedrooms are comfortable and well equipped and there is a carvery restaurant. From Tuesday to Saturday, a more formal restaurant is available, housed in a separate building close to the hotel.
3⇌Annexe14rm(12⇌2♠)(1fb)3⊞ CTV in all bedrooms ® T
✱ sB&B⇌♠fr£50 dB&B⇌♠fr£62 ⊟
(120P ✽ ♫
♀ English & French V ♉ ⊬ Lunch £8.75&alc Dinner £10.75&alc Last dinner 9.45pm
Credit Cards 1 2 3

TUXFORD Nottinghamshire Map 08 SK77

★★**Newcastle Arms** Market Place NG22 0LA
☎Retford(0777)870208
11rm(7⇌4♠)(1fb)1⊞ CTV in all bedrooms ® T ✱
sB&B⇌♠£30-£35 dB&B⇌♠£35-£45 Continental breakfast
50P 2⌂ snooker
♀ French V ♉ ⊈ Lunch £6.25-£11.95&alc Dinner £11.95&alc Last dinner 9.30pm
Credit Cards 1 2 3 5

TWICKENHAM Greater London

See **LONDON plan 5*B2*(page 412) Telephone codes are due to change on 6th May 1990. See page 421.**

✕**Cezanne** 68 Richmond Rd TW1 3BE ☎01-892 3526
A pretty little restaurant situated close to the town centre, with an un-assuming entrance from the street. The sensible, à la carte menus offer an interesting choice of freshly prepared food, with dishes such as sole and smoked trout terrine with a sweet red-pepper sauce, or roast quail with cassis sauce. The puddings are good, too, and the wine list is keenly priced. Service is friendly and informal.
Closed Sun, 1 wk Xmas & BH's
Lunch not served Sat
♀ French V 38 seats ✱ Lunch £12.95-£18.95alc Last lunch 2pm Last dinner 10.30pm ₱
Credit Cards 1 2 3

✕**McClements** 12 The Green TW2 5AA ☎01-755 0176
Lunch not served Sat
♀ French V 30 seats ✱ Lunch fr£15&alc Dinner fr£21alc Last lunch 2.15pm Last dinner 10.30pm ₱ ⊬
Credit Cards 1 2 3 4

TWO BRIDGES Devon Map 02 SX67

★★**Two Bridges** PL20 6SW ☎Princetown(082289)206
Closed Xmas day
A coaching inn which dates from the 18th century is centrally situated on Dartmoor, with the West Dart River running through the grounds. Llamas and other rare breeds of animal are kept here.

20rm(7⇌8♠)(2fb)1⊞⊬in all bedrooms CTV in all bedrooms T sB&B£19-£33 sB&B⇌♠fr£30 dB&B£33-£50 dB&B⇌♠£46-£50 ⊟

CTV 150P ✻ ♪ U snooker
English & French V ✿ ⚡ Bar Lunch £5.20-£9alc Dinner £6.50-£15alc Last dinner 8.45pm
Credit Cards [1] [2] [3] [5]

See advertisement on page 677

TYNEMOUTH Tyne & Wear Map **12** NZ36

★★★61% **Park** Grand Pde NE30 4JQ ☎091-257 1406
FAX 091-257 1716
RS Xmas & New Year
A modern functional hotel situated in a prominent position on sea front.
49rm(41⇨2↑)(4fb)⚡in 10 bedrooms CTV in all bedrooms ® T sB&B£24-£34 sB&B⇨↑£24-£52 dB&B⇨↑£48-£58 ⊟
☾ 400P solarium gymnasium ♫
English & French V ✿ ⚡ Lunch £6.50-£9.50&alc Dinner £7-£11&alc Last dinner 9.30pm
Credit Cards [1] [2] [3] [5]

TYNET Grampian *Banffshire* Map **15** NJ36

★★***Mill Motel*** AB5 2HJ ☎Clochan(05427)215 & 233
Closed 1-2 Jan
Converted mill whose modern facilities blend well with the original features.
16rm(12⇨3↑)(2fb) CTV in all bedrooms ® T
CTV 100P ♫
V ✿ ☕ Last dinner 9pm
Credit Cards [1] [2] [3] [5]

For key to symbols see the inside front cover.

TYWYN Gwynedd Map **06** SH50

★**Greenfield** High St LL36 9AD ☎(0654)710354
Closed Nov RS Dec-Feb
Small family-run hotel with separate restaurant serving good, inexpensive meals.
14rm(2⇌)(3fb) ® ✗ (ex guide dogs) sB&B£12.50 sB&B⇌£15 dB&B£25 dB&B⇌£30
CTV P̸ ⛟
V Lunch £4.95 Dinner £5.95&alc Last dinner 8pm

UCKFIELD East Sussex Map **05** TQ42

★★★ **HORSTED PLACE**

Little Horsted TN22 5TS (2m S A26) (Prestige)
☎Isfield(082575)581
Telex no 95548
FAX (0825) 75459
Closed 1st wks Jan

This elegant country house in the grand manner was built in Victorian times and has, in its day, welcomed members of our Royal family. The superb Pugin interior centres on a beautifully carved staircase, the grand gallery and the luxurious main lounge. A complete change of management and staff has taken place recently and, although there has been a shift in emphasis, General Manager, Julian Hook, and his enthusiastic team have maintained the high levels of service and attention which have always been the strength of this hotel. Chef Paul Bingham has introduced a new à la carte menu and a professional style of cooking, and the restaurant service is well supervised throughout. Bedrooms, some of which are quite magnificent, offer refined comfort, every modern facility and lots of luxurious little extras.
17⇌↱ CTV in all bedrooms ® T ✗ (ex guide dogs) sB&B⇌↱£110-£280 dB&B⇌↱£150-£280 ⊟
Lift 30P 6🚗 ✲ ⊡(heated) ℘ (hard) croquet nc7yrs *xmas*
♀ English & French V Lunch £15&alc Dinner £25&alc Last dinner 9.15pm
Credit Cards 1 2 3 5 £

UDDINGSTON Strathclyde *Lanarkshire* Map **11** NS66

★★**Redstones** 8-10 Glasgow Rd G71 7AS ☎(0698)813774
Closed 1-2 Jan
A well-decorated, privately owned business hotel.
18rm(13⇌3↱) CTV in all bedrooms ® T ✗ ✱ sB&B£38 sB&B⇌↱£48 dB&B⇌↱£65 ⊟
☾ 33P ⛟ ✲
♀ Scottish & French V ♆ ☐ Lunch £3-£10 High tea £5.75-£6.75&alc Dinner £11.95&alc Last dinner 9.30pm
Credit Cards 1 2 3 5

UIG

See **Skye, Isle of**

UIST (SOUTH), ISLE OF

See **South Uist, Isle of**

Places with AA hotels and restaurants are identified on the location atlas at the back of the book.

ULLAPOOL Highland *Ross & Cromarty* Map **14** NH14

See also **Leckmelm**

★★**Ceilidh Place** West Argyle St IV26 2TV ☎(0854)2103
A friendly and informal hotel with varied entertainment and a popular restaurant where the emphasis is on seafood and vegetarian dishes.
15rm(8⇌)(7fb) ✱ sB&B£15-£30 sB&B⇌£25-£35 dB&B£40-£50 dB&B⇌£48-£60 ⊟
30P ✲ *xmas*
♀ International V ♆ ☐ ⅟ Bar Lunch £4-£9alc High tea fr£5.50 Dinner fr£13.25&alc Last dinner 9pm
Credit Cards 1 2 3 5

★★**Four Seasons** Garve Rd IV26 2SX ☎(0854)2905
Closed 15 Nov-1 Mar
Set in its own grounds on the edge of Loch Broom, this is a family-run modern hotel with open plan public rooms and a restaurant specialising in seafood.
16↱(3fb) CTV in all bedrooms ® sB&B↱£19-£24 dB&B↱£38-£46
30P ✲
♀ English & French ♆ Lunch £5-£20alc Dinner fr£10.50&alc Last dinner 8.30pm
Credit Cards 1 2 3

★***Ferry Boat Inn*** Shore St IV26 2UJ ☎(0854)2366
A small, friendly, family run hotel in pleasant shore location.
11rm(2⇌)(1fb) ®
CTV P̸ ⛟
♆ ☐ ⅟
Credit Cards 1 3 5

❀✗✗ ***Altnaharrie Inn*** IV26 2SS
☎Dundonnell(085483)230
(Rosette awarded for dinner only)
Perhaps one of our most inaccessible restaurants, but well worth the effort for the excellence of Gunn Eriksen's table. Its dramatic location, on the south shore of Loch Broom, is best reached by telephoning for the restaurant's own ferry for the ten-minute crossing. Cooking is best described as modern/natural and five-course dinners may begin with a crab bisque, light and full of flavour, with home-made bread. A main course of fillet of lamb with sweetbreads was perfectly cooked and served with its own juices. Puddings also excel and we can heartily recommend this restaurant which we believe serves some of the best food in Scotland.
Closed late Oct-Etr
Lunch not served (except to residents)
14 seats Last dinner 7.45pm P̸ nc12yrs 6 bedrooms available ⅟

ULLSWATER

See **Glenridding, Patterdale, Pooley Bridge & Watermillock**

ULVERSTON Cumbria Map **07** SD27

★★**Sefton House** Queen St LA12 7AF ☎(0229)52190
Situated near the centre of the town, this very pleasant commercial hotel offers good accommodation and a warm, friendly welcome.
11rm(2⇌5↱) CTV in all bedrooms ® T ✗ (ex guide dogs) ✱ sB&B£24.50-£29.50 sB&B⇌↱£30-£36 dB&B£39-£44 dB&B⇌↱£48-£55 ⊟
CTV 15P 3🚗 ⛟
V ♆ ☐ Lunch £3.50-£7 Dinner £7.50-£10.50&alc Last dinner 8.30pm
Credit Cards 1 3

★★Virginia House Queen St LA12 7AF ☎(0229)54844
The newly-furnished hotel provides good all-round facilities; set in a delightful Georgian house, family owned and run, it offers good meals in a pleasant restaurant.
7⌐(1fb) CTV in all bedrooms ® T ✱ sB&B⌐£31 dB&B⌐£44
V Dinner £10.95&alc Last dinner 9pm
Credit Cards 1 2 3 5 £

✕Bay Horse Inn & Bistro LA12 9EL
☎(0229)53972
The restaurant here is housed in a newly built conservatory offering diners wonderful views over the Leven estuary. This is chef Robert Lyons' first independent venture after many years with John Tovey at the famous Miller Howe Hotel. At the Bay Horse he has developed his own style of cooking and the à la carte menu changes weekly and offers five choices at each meal, plus daily specials, for each course. Portions are generous and our Inspector particularly enjoyed his medallions of venison, pan-fried with strips of bacon, garlic and chestnuts in a rich red-wine sauce. Service is friendly and informal, as well as being professional.
Dinner not served Sun
V 32 seats ✱ S10% Lunch £10.50&alc Last lunch 1.15pm Last dinner 9pm nc12yrs
Credit Cards 1

UMBERLEIGH Devon Map **02** SS62

★★Rising Sun Inn EX37 9DU (Berni/Chef & Brewer)
☎High Bickington(0769)60447
A small, friendly village inn on the main road provides attractive, upgraded bedroom accommodation which meets all modern requirements. Public areas include cosy bars, a lounge and a dining room offering a short table d'hote menu of home-cooked dishes.
6rm(4⇌2⌐) CTV in all bedrooms ® T (ex guide dogs) sB&B⇌⌐fr£31.50 dB&B⇌⌐fr£45.50
CTV 20P 2
V Lunch £8 Dinner £9 Last dinner 9pm
Credit Cards 1 2 3 5

UNDERBARROW Cumbria Map **07** SD49

★★Greenriggs Country House LA8 8HF
☎Crosthwaite(04488)387
Closed Jan-Feb RS Nov-Dec & Mar
An 18th-century house has been tastefully converted into a hotel of charm and character which offers a warm welcome and a comfortable stay.
12rm(8⇌2⌐)(4fb) ® S% sB&B⇌⌐£20-£25 dB&B⇌⌐£45-£55
CTV 25P croquet *xmas*
S% Dinner £15 Last dinner 8pm
Credit Cards 1 3

Book as early as possible for busy holiday periods.

UPHALL Lothian *West Lothian* Map **11** NT07

★★★65% Houstoun House EH52 6JS
☎Broxburn(0506)853831
Telex no 727148
FAX (0506) 854220
Closed 1-3 Jan
An historic, baronial country hotel with splendid period bedrooms supplemented by a modern extension. The vaulted cellar bar is a popular feature and cuisine enterprising and enjoyable.
28rm(27⇌1⌐)Annexe2⇌10 CTV in all bedrooms ® T sB&B⇌⌐£66-£80 dB&B⇌⌐£88-£105
100P
V Lunch £14-£15 Dinner £23-£25 Last dinner 9.30pm
Credit Cards 1 2 3 4 5

UPHOLLAND Lancashire Map **07** SD50

★★Holland Hall 6 Lafford Ln WN8 0QZ ☎(0695)624426
FAX (0695) 622433
RS Xmas Day & 2 Jan
Overlooking the golf course, this well-furnished and comfortable hotel is popular for its delightful restaurant.
29rm(22⇌7⌐)Annexe5rm(3⇌2⌐)(2fb)1 CTV in all bedrooms ® T S10% sB&B⇌⌐£39-£49 dB&B⇌⌐£46-£60

U

☾200P ☼
🍷 English, American & French V ♁ ⚑ Lunch £7.50 Dinner £13.75-£14.75 Last dinner 10pm
Credit Cards ▭1 ▭2 ▭3 ▭5 ▭£

UPLYME Devon Map **03** SY39

See also Lyme Regis
★★★50% Devon Lyme Rd DT7 3TQ (Best Western)
☎Lyme Regis(02974)3231 Telex no 42513
Closed 6 Nov-9 Mar
Former 16th-century monastery which has been converted into a relaxing hotel.
21rm(18⇌3⌒)(4fb) CTV in all bedrooms ® **T** ✻
sB&B⇌⌒£34.50-£39.50 dB&B⇌⌒£69-£79 ⊟
30P ⊞ ☼ (heated) games room putting green
🍷 English & French ♁ ⚑ Bar Lunch £3.50-£6.50 Dinner fr£10&alc Last dinner 8.15pm
Credit Cards ▭1 ▭2 ▭3 ▭5 ▭£

UPPER SLAUGHTER Gloucestershire Map **04** SP12

⊛★★★ 74% Lords of the Manor GL54 2JD
☎Cotswold(0451)20243
Telex no 83147
FAX (0451) 20696
This attractive 17th-century manor with later additions, is a stylish country-house hotel, exuding character and charm. A high level of traditional service is promoted under the personal direction of Richard Young. Originality and expertise are evident in the cuisine.
15rm(14⇌1⌒)2⊞ CTV in all bedrooms **T** ✗ (ex guide dogs) sB&B⇌⌒fr£60 dB&B⇌⌒£85-£120 ⊟
20P ⊞ ☼ ♩ croquet *xmas*
♁ ⚑ Lunch fr£12.95 Dinner fr£27 Last dinner 9.30pm
Credit Cards ▭1 ▭2 ▭3 ▭5

UPPINGHAM Leicestershire Map **04** SP89

★★★67% Falcon High St LE15 9PY (Inter) ☎(0572)823535
FAX (0572) 821620
Former coaching inn situated in the attractive town centre.
19⇌⌒Annexe6rm(2fb)1⊞ CTV in all bedrooms **T** ✻
sB&B⇌⌒£47 dB&B⇌⌒£85 ⊟
☾15P 3🚗 *xmas*
🍷 English & French V ♁ ⚑ Lunch £11.50-£13.05&alc Dinner £11.50-£13.05&alc Last dinner 9.45pm
Credit Cards ▭1 ▭2 ▭3 ▭5 ▭£

★★Garden 16 High St West LE15 9QD ☎(0572)822352
FAX (0572) 821156
Very friendly family run hotel with cosy, attractively decorated bedrooms, many of them overlooking the walled gardens.
12rm(7⇌3⌒)(1fb) CTV in all bedrooms ® **T** sB&B£21
sB&B⇌⌒£35-£40 dB&B⇌⌒£45-£50
CTV ₽
🍷 English V ♁ ⚑ Lunch £11 High tea £4 Dinner £12.25 Last dinner 9pm
Credit Cards ▭1 ▭2 ▭3

★★Lake Isle High St East LE15 9PZ ☎(0572)822951
Once a barber's shop known as Sweeny Todd's, this quaint and unusual town house hotel has been cleverly converted from an 18th-century house by Claire and David Whitfield. Tucked away down a narrow passageway, it has a peaceful little walled garden behind. The small bar and country-style restaurant are full of character, nd the modern bedrooms are extremely well equipped. A short menu of 3 to 5 courses is complemented by a list of some 300 bins.
10rm(7⇌3⌒)(1fb) CTV in all bedrooms ® **T** S%
sB&B⇌⌒£34-£45 dB&B⇌⌒£51-£65 ⊟
4P ⊞
🍷 English & French V Lunch £10-£11.25 Dinner £16.50-£20 Last dinner 10pm
Credit Cards ▭1 ▭2 ▭3 ▭5 ▭£

UPTON ON SEVERN Hereford & Worcester Map **03** SO84

★★★60% White Lion High St WR8 0HJ (Exec Hotel)
☎(06846)2551
Closed Xmas Day RS 26 Dec
Recently improved family-run town centre hotel with a popular restaurant serving traditional English dishes.
10rm(8⇌2⌒)1⊞ CTV in all bedrooms ® **T** sB&B⇌⌒fr£42
dB&B⇌⌒£57-£62 ⊟
18P 1🚗
🍷 English & French V ♁ ⚑ Lunch fr£13.25&alc Dinner fr£13.25&alc Last dinner 9.15pm
Credit Cards ▭1 ▭2 ▭3 ▭5 ▭£

★★Star High St WR8 0HQ
☎Upton upon Severn(06846)2300 & 4601 FAX (06846) 2929
17rm(12⇌5⌒)(2fb)1⊞ CTV in all bedrooms ® **T** ✻
sB&B⇌⌒£30 dB&B⇌⌒£42 ⊟
9P ♫
V ♁ ⚑ Lunch £3.95-£6.95&alc Dinner fr£8alc Last dinner 9.30pm
Credit Cards ▭1 ▭3

USK Gwent Map **03** SO30

★★Glen-yr-Afon Pontypool Rd ☎(02913)2302
Elegant country house style hotel with attractive library. Good home cooked food.
17rm(11⇌6⌒)(2fb) CTV in all bedrooms **T** ✻ sB&B£31.05
sB&B⇌⌒£34.50 dB&B⇌⌒£46 ⊟
☾CTV 42P 1🚗 ⊞ ☼ croquet ⌂ *xmas*
V ♁ ⚑ ⅟ Lunch £9-£10.50 High tea £2.50-£7 Dinner £10-£14 Last dinner 9.30pm
Credit Cards ▭1 ▭3

★★*Three Salmons* Bridge St NP5 1BQ ☎(02913)2133
Closed 24-26 Dec
A one-time coaching inn, The Three Salmons is well-known as a retreat for anglers, having assumed the role of character hotel.
12rm(10⇌2⌒)Annexe17rm(14⇌2⌒)(1fb)2⊞ CTV in 28bedrooms ® **T**
40P
♁
Credit Cards ▭1 ▭2 ▭3 ▭4 ▭5

UTTOXETER Staffordshire Map **07** SK03

★★Bank House Church St ST14 8AG ☎(0889)566922
FAX (0889) 567565
Pleasant public areas and comfortable, well-equipped bedrooms are provided by this late 18th-century country house on the outskirts of the town centre, once Uttoxeter's first bank. The unsupported spiral staircase is worthy of note, being one of the best examples of its kind in the country.
16rm(6⇌10⌒)(2fb)1⊞ CTV in all bedrooms ® **T**
sB&B⇌⌒£42-£46 dB&B⇌⌒£55-£65 ⊟
CTV 16P *xmas*
V ♁ ⚑ Lunch fr£8.50alc Dinner £10.50-£18.50alc Last dinner 9.45pm
Credit Cards ▭1 ▭2 ▭3 ▭5

○**TraveLodge** Ashbourne Rd ST14 5AA (A50) (Trusthouse Forte) ☎(0889)562043
32⇨

UXBRIDGE Greater London Map **04** TQ08

★★★61% **Master Brewer Motel** UB10 9NX ☎(0895)51199
Telex no 946589 FAX (0895) 810330
(For full entry see Hillingdon)

VALE

See **Guernsey, under Channel Islands**

VENTNOR

See **Wight, Isle of**

VERYAN Cornwall & Isles of Scilly Map **02** SW93

★★★69% **Nare** Carne Beach TR2 5PF ☎Truro(0872)501279
FAX (0872) 501856
Attractive hotel, personally run, in magnificent situation commanding extensive views. Fine gardens and good amenities.
36rm(30⇨6↱)Annexe2⇨(6fb) CTV in all bedrooms ® T
sB&B⇨↱£32-£42 dB&B⇨↱£64-£106
80P ✱ ⛆(heated) ♟ (hard) snooker sauna solarium gymnasium boating windsurfing ⌂ *xmas*
English & French V ♿ Sunday Lunch £10&alc Dinner £16&alc Last dinner 9.15pm
Credit Cards [1] [3]

See advertisement on page 681

A rosette is the AA's highest award for quality of food and service in a restaurant.

★★★★

Tredunnock, Nr Usk, Gwent, S Wales NP5 1PG
Telephone: (063349) 521
Fax: (063349) 220

17th century manor house resting serenely in 17 acres of grounds and gardens. All bedrooms en suite and with TV, radio, and video. Period 4 poster suites available. Intimate restaurant offering French influenced cuisine, fine wines and attentive service. Extensive leisure and health club including swimming pool, sauna, squash, tennis, gym, solaria, steam room and perimeter jogging track. Weekend and Xmas packages available.

Glen-yr-Afon House Hotel ★★

Pontypool Road, Usk, Gwent NP5 1SY
Telephone: Usk 2302 & 3202

An elegant country house, providing gracious service and fine home-cooked food in a warm, friendly atmosphere. Situated in mature, secluded grounds, five minutes walk from the historic village of Usk. It has tastefully decorated rooms (most with private bath), three comfortable lounges (one with colour TV, the other containing a fully stocked bar). Under the personal supervision of the proprietors.

THE FALCON HOTEL ★★★

High Street East, Uppingham
Leicestershire LE15 9PY
Tel: 0572 823535 Fax: 0572 821620

A renowned coaching Inn where the old entrance arch and cobbled yard through which the coaches used to pass is now the main lounge and reception area. Situated in the beautiful small market town of Uppingham the hotel's aim is to provide a relaxed atmosphere where every possible requirement is attended to by friendly, caring and efficient staff. Elegant period surroundings complimented by superb table d'hôte and à la carte menus with carefully chosen wine list make for a perfect stay.

Weekend breaks available.

V

★★*Elerkey House* TR2 5QA ☎Truro(0872)501261
Closed Nov-Etr
Small country hotel in this picturesque old Cornish village. Peaceful atmosphere and pleasant garden.
7rm(3⇔2♠)⊁in all bedrooms CTV in all bedrooms ® ✗
CTV 12P ⊞ ✲ nc10 yrs
♔ ☐ ⊁ Last dinner 8.30pm
Credit Cards 1 3

✗ *Treverbyn House* Pendower Rd TR2 5QL
☎Truro(0872)501201
This tiny, unsophisticated restaurant with letting rooms provides home cooking at its best. There is a good wine list.
Lunch not served
20 seats Last dinner 8.30pm 9P nc7yrs

VIRKIE

See Shetland

WADEBRIDGE Cornwall & Isles of Scilly Map 02 SW97

★★**Molesworth Arms** Molesworth St PL27 7DP ☎(020881)2055
Original 16th-century inn, comfortably furnished and offering a relaxed atmosphere.
18rm(14⇔)(2fb) CTV in all bedrooms ® ✻ sB&B⇔£21 dB&B⇔£36
CTV 14P
V ♔ ☐ Bar Lunch £4.05-£5.70alc High tea fr£1.25alc Dinner £5.70-£14.15alc Last dinner 9.30pm
Credit Cards 1 3

WADHURST East Sussex Map 05 TQ63

★★**Spindlewood Country House Hotel & Restaurant** Wallcrouch TN5 7JG (2.25m SE of Wadhurst on B2099) (Inter)
☎Ticehurst(0580)200430
Closed 4 days Xmas
The small, relaxing, family-run hotel is peacefully situated and furnished with antiques. Imaginative country cooking is complemented by good, personal service and attention to detail.
9rm(8⇔1♠)(1fb) CTV in all bedrooms ® T ✗ (ex guide dogs) ✻ sB&B⇔♠£42-£45 dB&B⇔♠£35-£40 ⊟
60P ⊞ ✲
☐ English & French V ♔ Lunch £10.50-£16&alc Dinner £12-£13&alc Last dinner 9pm
Credit Cards 1 2 3

WAKEFIELD West Yorkshire Map 08 SE32

★★★ 65% **Cedar Court** Denby Dale Road, Calder Grove WF4 3QZ ☎(0924)276310 Telex no 557647 FAX (0924) 280221
This large modern hotel, situated close to the M1 at junction 39, offers a choice of restaurants with English, French and Italian cuisine. The public areas are stylish, and bedrooms are spacious and well appointed.
151⇔♠(18fb)⊁in 64 bedrooms CTV in all bedrooms ® T sB&B⇔♠£43-£80 dB&B⇔♠£59-£98 ⊟
Lift ☾ ⊞ 240P ✲
☐ English, French & Italian V ♔ ☐ Lunch fr£9&alc Dinner fr£10&alc Last dinner 11pm
Credit Cards 1 2 3 5 £

★★★ 61% **Post House** Queen's Dr, Ossett WF5 9BE (Trusthouse Forte) ☎(0924)276388 Telex no 55407 FAX (0924) 280277
A modern, purpose-built hotel, conveniently situated near junction 40 of the M1. The restaurant offers a good-value dinner menu.
99⇔⊁in 20 bedrooms CTV in all bedrooms ® T S10% sB⇔£67-£78 dB⇔£78-£86 (room only) ⊟
Lift ☾ 140P ✲ CFA *xmas*
V ♔ ☐ ⊁ S% Lunch £10-£10&alc High tea fr£6 Dinner £15-£15&alc Last dinner 10pm
Credit Cards 1 2 3 4 5

★★★ 50% *Stoneleigh* 211-223 Doncaster Rd WF1 5HA (Inter) ☎(0924)369461 Telex no 51458
Stone built Victorian terrace stylishly converted into a well-equipped hotel which offers attractive cocktail and lounge bars, a very good restaurant and services of high standard.
36rm(29⇔7♠)(1fb) CTV in all bedrooms ® T ✗ (ex guide dogs)
Lift ☾ 80P ⊞
☐ English & Italian ♔ ☐
Credit Cards 1 2 3 5

★★★ 62% **Swallow** Queens St WF1 1JV (Swallow) ☎(0924)372111 Telex no 557464 FAX (0924) 383648
Well-appointed bedrooms and friendly service are features which make this city-centre hotel popular.
64rm(56⇔8♠)(4fb) CTV in all bedrooms ® T sB&B⇔♠£52-£59 dB&B⇔♠£70-£76 ⊟
Lift ☾ 40P CFA *xmas*
☐ English & French V ♔ ☐ Lunch fr£7.50 Dinner fr£11.50 Last dinner 9.15pm
Credit Cards 1 2 3 5

★★★ 60% *Waterton Park* Walton Hall, The Balk Walton WF2 6PW (3m SE off B6378) (Consort) ☎(0924)257911
A Georgian mansion, set on the island of a picturesque lake, provides an attractive setting for this up-to-date hotel with good conference and leisure facilities. Bedrooms, like public rooms, are fitted and furnished to a high standard, whilst the cuisine is designed to please perceptive palates.
31rm(30⇔1♠)(4fb)2⊟ CTV in all bedrooms ® T ✗
☾ 150P ⊞ ✲ ⊡(heated) squash snooker sauna solarium gymnasium boating putting
☐ English & French V ♔ ☐ Last dinner 10pm
Credit Cards 1 2 3 5

⌂**Granada Lodge** M1 Service Area, West Bretton WF4 4LQ (Granada) ☎(0924)850371 FAX (0924) 830609
(For full entry see Woolley Edge)

WALBERSWICK Suffolk Map 05 TM47

★★*Anchor* IP18 6UA ☎Southwold(0502)722112 Telex no 97223
The gabled, mock-Tudor exterior of this hotel gives way to the Scandinavian-style lounge and dining room while there are also chalets in a garden setting.
6rm(2⇔)Annexe8⇔(2fb) CTV in all bedrooms ®
30P ⊞
♔ ☐
Credit Cards 1 2 3 5

All AA-appointed establishments are inspected regularly to ensure that required standards are maintained.

WALKERBURN Borders *Peeblesshire* Map **11** NT33

★★Tweed Valley
Galashiels Rd EH43 6AA
(Inter)
☎(089687)636
Telex no 9401334

The privately owned and managed hotel, which has an attractive wood-panelled dining room, was recently refurbished.

15rm(11⇌4↱)(2fb)1⊞ CTV in all bedrooms ® T
sB&B⇌↱£29-£36.50 dB&B⇌↱£58-£63 ⊟
35P ⊞ ✲ ♩ sauna solarium gymnasium shooting stalking
xmas
♀ Scottish & French V ♁ ☐ ⚟ Lunch £6.75-£14.50alc
High tea £6.75-£12.50alc Dinner £12.50-£15.75alc Last dinner 9.30pm
Credit Cards 1 2 3 5 £

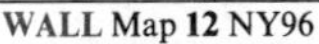

WALL Map **12** NY96

★★Hadrian Humshaugh ☎(043481)232 & 236
9rm(1⇌2↱) 2⊞ CTV in all bedrooms ® T ⊟
40P 3⌂ ✲
♁ ☐ Last dinner 10pm
Credit Cards 1 4

WALLASEY Merseyside Map **07** SJ29

★*Grove House* Grove Rd L45 3HF ☎051-630 4558
RS Sun evenings & BH's
Conveniently situated within easy reach of Wallasey station and Liverpool, this friendly hotel offers good standards of service.
13rm(3⇌5↱)(1fb) CTV in all bedrooms ® T
14P ⊞ ✲
♀ English & French V ♁ Last dinner 9pm
Credit Cards 1 3 5

WALLINGFORD Oxfordshire Map **04** SU68

★★★67% ***George*** High St OX10 0BS (Mount Charlotte)
☎(0491)36665 Telex no 847468
At the heart of the town, the timbered George Hotel dates from Tudor times and provides a high standard of accommodation in pleasant surroundings. The beamed public bar is a popular rendezvous, and in the restaurant, imaginative dishes are served.
39⇌(1fb)⚟in 9 bedrooms CTV in all bedrooms ® T
☾ 60P
♀ English & French V ♁ ☐
Credit Cards 1 2 3 5

★★★59% **Shillingford Bridge** Shillingford OX10 8LZ (2m N A329) ☎Warborough(086732)8567 Telex no 837763
Closed Xmas wk
The hotel stands on the banks of the River Thames, between Oxford and Henley-on-Thames, with superb views along the river. Dinner-dances are frequently held in the pleasant restaurant.
25⇌2⊞ CTV in all bedrooms ® T
100P ✲ ⌇(heated) ♩ squash ♫
V ♁ ☐ Last dinner 10pm
Credit Cards 1 2 3 5

See advertisement on page 683

W

WALLSEND Tyne & Wear Map **12** NZ26

★★★59% **Newcastle Moat House** Coast Rd NE28 9HP (Queens Moat) ☎091-262 8989 & 091-262 7044 Telex no 53583
FAX 091-263 4172
Closed 24-26 Dec
Spacious modern hotel with comfortable bedrooms.
150⇨↱(8fb)⊁in 10 bedrooms CTV in all bedrooms ® T S%
sB&B⇨↱£45-£60 dB&B⇨↱£55-£70 ⊟
Lift ☾ 500P sauna solarium gymnasium
☋ English & Continental V ♤ ☊ ⊁ S10% Lunch £6.95-£10.50&alc Dinner £10.50&alc Last dinner 9.45pm
Credit Cards [1] [2] [3] [5] [£]

WALSALL West Midlands Map **07** SP09

See also **Barr, Great**

★★★61% **Barons Court** Walsall Road, Walsall Wood WS9 9AH (3m NE A461) (Best Western) ☎Brownhills(0543)452020
Telex no 333061 FAX (0543) 361276
This busy commercial hotel built in a mock Tudor style stands on the outskirts of the town. It has some particularly well-appointed bedrooms and popular leisure facilities.
100⇨(5fb)23⊡⊁in 6 bedrooms CTV in all bedrooms ® T
sB&B⇨£54-£58 dB&B£62-£69 ⊟
Lift ☾ 180P CFA ⊟(heated) sauna solarium gymnasium health hydro whirlpool ♫ *xmas*
☋ English & French V ♤ ☊ Lunch £7.95&alc Dinner £12.95&alc Last dinner 9.45pm
Credit Cards [1] [2] [3] [4] [5] [£]

★★★54% **Crest Hotel-Birmingham/Walsall** Birmingham Rd WS5 3AB (Crest) ☎(0922)33555 Telex no 335479
FAX (0922) 612034
A modern hotel, conveniently situated on the ring road and just two miles from junction 9 of the M6. It has three bars and the very popular Orangery Restaurant.
101⇨↱(3fb)⊁in 21 bedrooms CTV in all bedrooms ® T
sB⇨↱£69 dB⇨↱£81 (room only) ⊟
Lift ☾ 250P CFA 2 pool tables ♫
☋ Continental V ♤ ☊ ⊁ Lunch £8.95&alc Dinner £12.95&alc Last dinner 9.45pm
Credit Cards [1] [2] [3] [4] [5]

★★★65% **Fairlawns** 178 Little Aston Road, Aldridge WS9 0NU (3m NE off A454) (Consort) ☎Aldridge(0922)55122
Telex no 339873 FAX (0922) 743120
RS 24 Dec-2 Jan
On the A454, between Aldridge and the A452 Chester Road, stands a modern, comfortable hotel where the owners take an active role in providing service to guests.
36rm(25⇨11↱)(2fb) CTV in all bedrooms ® T
sB&B⇨↱£39.50-£59.50 dB&B⇨↱£67.50-£75 ⊟
☾ 80P ✲
☋ English & French V ♤ ☊ Lunch fr£15&alc Dinner fr£16.50&alc Last dinner 10pm
Credit Cards [1] [2] [3] [4] [5] [£]

★★★68% **Friendly Hotel** 20 Wolverhampton Rd West, Bentley WS2 0BS (junction 10, M6) (Consort) ☎(0922)724444
Telex no 334854 FAX (0922) 723148
Situated at junction 10 of the M6 motorway, and near to both Walsall and Wolverhampton, the modern hotel offers a wide range of well-equipped and comfortably furnished accommodation which includes some premier and non-smoking rooms as well as one designed for the disabled; an open-plan ground floor provides a bar, lounge area and a carvery.
120⇨↱(20fb)2⊡⊁in 30 bedrooms CTV in all bedrooms ® T
✳ sB&B⇨↱£49.50-£59.50
dB&B⇨↱£65-£69.50 Continental breakfast ⊟
☾ 140P ✲ ⊟(heated) sauna solarium gymnasium jacuzzi
☋ English & French V ♤ ☊ ⊁ Lunch £9.25-£10.50&alc Dinner £10.50-£11.75&alc Last dinner 10pm
Credit Cards [1] [2] [3] [5] [£]

★★**Bescot** Bescot Rd WS2 9DG ☎(0922)22447
The friendly hotel, with its Victorian frontage and well-equipped bedrooms, stands only a few moments' drive away from junction 9 of the M6.
13rm(10⇨3↱)(1fb) CTV in all bedrooms ® T ✖ (ex guide dogs) sB&B⇨↱£32.20 dB&B⇨↱£46 ⊟
☾ CTV 30P
☋ International V ♤ ☊ Lunch £8.50-£12.50&alc High tea fr£7 Dinner fr£8.50 Last dinner 9.30pm
Credit Cards [1] [2] [3] [5] [£]

★★**Beverley** 58 Lichfield Rd WS4 2DJ ☎(0922)614967 & 22999
FAX (0922) 724187
A converted house on the outskirts of the town offers facilities for small conferences and private functions.
31rm(16⇨5↱)Annexe2⇨(2fb)1⊡⊁in 2 bedrooms CTV in all bedrooms ® T ✖ (ex guide dogs) sB&B£23-£28
sB&B⇨↱£23-£38.50 dB&B£29-£46.50
dB&B⇨↱£29-£46.50 ⊟
☾ CTV 60P sauna solarium gymnasium
☋ English & French V ♤ ☊ ⊁ Lunch £6.95&alc High tea £4.50 Dinner £9.95&alc Last dinner 9.30pm
Credit Cards [1] [3] [£]

★**Abberley** 29 Bescot Rd WS2 9AD ☎(0922)27413
FAX (0922) 720933
Comfortable small hotel, personally run by the proprietors, which offers value for money accommodation and food; it is popular with businessmen.
29rm(21⇨3↱)(4fb)1⊡⊁in 4 bedrooms CTV in all bedrooms ® T ✳ sB&B£19.55-£34.50 sB&B⇨↱£34.50 dB&B£32
dB&B⇨↱£46 ⊟
☾ 29P
☋ English, Asian, Chinese & Vietnamese V ♤ ☊ Lunch £5.50-£10&alc High tea £3.50-£3.50 Dinner £7.50-£7.50&alc Last dinner 8.30pm
Credit Cards [1] [3] [£]

WALTHAM ABBEY Essex Map **05** TL30

★★★71% **Swallow Hotel** Old Shire Ln EN9 3LX (Swallow)
☎Lea Valley(0992)717170 Telex no 916596
FAX (0992) 711841
This hotel and leisure club is particularly well situated for the business traveller, close to junction 26 of the M25. Well-appointed bedrooms include honeymoon and executive suites and some have been especially adapted for disabled guests. Public areas are all air-conditioned, and include a brasserie and formal restaurant.
163⇨(10fb)4⊡⊁in 60 bedrooms CTV in all bedrooms ® T ✳
S10% sB&B⇨fr£76 dB&B⇨fr£86 ⊟
☾ ⊞ 240P ⊟(heated) sauna solarium gymnasium steam room ♫ *xmas*
☋ English & Continental V ♤ ☊
Credit Cards [1] [2] [3] [5]

WALTON ON THE HILL Surrey Map **04** TQ25

✕✕**Ebenezer Cottage** 36 Walton St KT20 7RT
☎Tadworth(0737)813166
Early 16th-century cottage restaurant offering traditional English food in a number of period styled dining rooms.
Closed Mon
Dinner not served Sun
☋ English & French 65 seats ✳ Lunch £12.75-£14.50&alc Dinner £22.95 Last lunch 1.45pm Last dinner 9.30pm 40P ⊁
Credit Cards [1] [2] [3] [5]

WALTON UPON THAMES

See **Shepperton & Weybridge**

W

WANSFORD Cambridgeshire Map **04** TL09

★★ ***The Haycock*** PE8 6JA ☎Stamford(0780)782223 Telex no 32710 FAX (0780) 783031
At the centre of the quiet village, this 17th-century, stone-built coaching inn stands on the banks of the River Nene in an award-winning garden. The very popular restaurant features English food, with a daily roast, local game and fresh fish. An extensive building programme undertaken during 1988-9 will add new bedrooms and a business centre as well as improving existing rooms.
25rm(16⇔9↖)4⊞ CTV in all bedrooms **T**
☾ 300P ✲ ♩ petanque outdoor chess
V ♁ ⊻ Last dinner 10.15pm
Credit Cards [1] [3] [5]

★**Sibson House** PE8 6ND (Berni/Chef & Brewer) ☎Stamford(0780)782227
This attractive, stone-built inn complex alongside the A1 provides accommodation in comfortable bedrooms, some of which are built round a courtyard at the rear of the hotel.
19rm(16⇔3↖)Annexe14⇔(1fb)2⊞ CTV in all bedrooms ® **T**
✗ (ex guide dogs) sB&B⇔↖fr£46 dB&B⇔↖fr£54.50 ⊟
55P ✲
♀ Ehglish **V** ♁ ⊻ ⁄ Lunch £8 Dinner £9 Last dinner 9.30pm
Credit Cards [1] [2] [3] [5]

WANTAGE Oxfordshire Map **04** SU48

★★ ***Bear*** Market Place OX12 8AB (Consort) ☎(02357)66366 Telex no 41363
A comfortable hotel in the heart of this bustling market town, the Bear has compact modern bedrooms. The King Alfred Restaurant, on the first floor and overlooking the market place has a good standard of cooking and friendly service.
33rm(26⇔7↖)(3fb) CTV in all bedrooms ® **T**
Lift ₱
♀ French **V** ♁ ⊻ ⁄
Credit Cards [1] [2] [3] [5]

See advertisement under OXFORD

WARE Hertfordshire Map **05** TL31

★★★63% **Ware Moat House** Baldock St SG12 9DR (Queens Moat) ☎(0920)465011 Telex no 817417 FAX (0920) 468016
Closed 25-31 Dec
Modern, two-storey brick hotel with good car parking.
50rm(43⇔6↖)(1fb)⁄ in 6 bedrooms CTV in all bedrooms ® **T**
✱ sB&B⇔↖fr£65 dB&B⇔↖fr£75 ⊟
Lift ☾ 100P
V ♁ ⊻
Credit Cards [1] [2] [3] [4] [5]

WAREHAM Dorset Map **03** SY98

★★★74% **Priory** Church Green BH20 4ND ☎(09295)2772 Due to change to (0929) 552772 Telex no 41143 FAX (0929) 554519
An attractive 16th-century converted priory, the hotel stands in a tranquil setting with two acres of gardens leading to the river. Tastefully furnished bedrooms combine modern facilities with fine antiques, and some of the bathrooms have whirlpool baths. Public rooms are elegant, with breakfast and lunch taken in the Greenwood Room and dinner served in the intimate Cellar Restaurant.
15rm(11⇔4↖)Annexe4⇔2⊞ CTV in all bedrooms **T** ✗ (ex guide dogs) ✱ sB&B⇔↖£45-£75 dB&B⇔↖£60-£150 ⊟
☾ 25P ⊞ ✲ ♩ croquet sailing ♫
V ♁ ⊻ Lunch £11-£13&alc High tea £10-£12.50 Dinner £18.50-£21&alc Last dinner 10pm
Credit Cards [1] [2] [3] [5]

W

★★★ 67% ***Springfield Country*** Grange Road, Stoborough BH20 5AL (1.5m S off A351) ☎(09295)2177 & 51785
A family-run hotel set in attractive gardens has been upgraded to provide comfortable accommodation in well equipped bedrooms; two restaurants offer skilfully prepared dishes.
32⇌(7fb) CTV in all bedrooms ® T
Lift ☾ 100P ✽ (heated) (hard) snooker solarium table tennis pool table nc2yrs
English & Continental Last dinner 9pm
Credit Cards 1 2 3

★★**Kemps Country House** East Stoke BH20 6AL ☎Bindon Abbey(0929)462563
Guests are offered friendly attention at this pleasant hotel with its comfortable lounges and attractive, well-appointed restaurant.
5rm(1⇌3)Annexe4⇌(3fb) CTV in all bedrooms ® T sB&B⇌£37-£47 dB&B⇌£57-£87
50P ✽
French V Lunch £7.50&alc Dinner £12.95&alc Last dinner 9.30pm
Credit Cards 1 2 3 4 5 £

★★**Red Lion** Towncross BH20 4AB ☎(09295)2843
A character inn at the heart of the town features popular bars and a small, informal restaurant.
20rm(5⇌)(5fb) CTV in all bedrooms ® sB&B£20 sB&B⇌£22 dB&B£37 dB&B⇌£48 Continental breakfast
15P snooker skittle alley
V Lunch £7.95&alc Dinner £11.95&alc Last dinner 9.30pm
Credit Cards 1 2 3

★★**Worgret Manor** BH20 6AB ☎(09295)2957
Quiet Georgian hotel with modern extension.
9rm(4)(3fb) CTV in all bedrooms ® sB&B£26 sB&B£35 dB&B£42 dB&B£50
CTV 40P ✽
English & French V Lunch £8-£8&alc Dinner £11-£12&alc Last dinner 9.15pm
Credit Cards 1 2 3 5

★***Black Bear*** 14 South St BH20 4LT ☎(09295)3280
An 18th-century coaching inn with simple bedrooms.
15rm(2⇌)(3fb) CTV in all bedrooms ® T
4P
French V
Credit Cards 1 3 4

WARK Northumberland Map 12 NY87

★***Battlesteads*** NE48 3LS ☎Bellingham(0660)30209
A pleasant village inn with charm and character.
6rm(1fb)
CTV 50P ✽
Mainly grills V

WARMINSTER Wiltshire Map 03 ST84

★★★★ **Bishopstrow House** BA12 9HH
☎(0985)212312
Telex 444829
FAX (0985) 216769

A gracious Georgian country house offering high standards of comfort and service. Sumptuously decorated bedrooms often have jacuzzis as well as bathrooms. The restaurant has recently been enlarged.

15⇌ Annexe 13⇌1 CTV in all bedrooms T ☾ 25P ✽ (heated) sauna solarium
nc 3yrs *xmas* V Last dinner 9pm
Credit Cards 1 2 3 5

★★**Old Bell** Market Place BA12 9AN ☎(0985)216611 FAX (0985) 217111
Contrasting colour-washed brick building in the centre of Warminster with a colonnaded arcade front.
16rm(9⇌1)(2fb) CTV in all bedrooms ® T ✱ sB&B£32 sB&B⇌£36 dB&B£44 dB&B⇌£50
21P
V Lunch £7-£15alc Dinner £7-£15alc Last dinner 10.30pm
Credit Cards 1 2 3 5 £

Granada Lodge A36 Bath Rd BA12 7RU (Granada) ☎(0985)219639 FAX (0985) 214380
Closed 24 & 25 Dec evenings
32⇌(10fb) in 7 bedrooms CTV in all bedrooms ® (ex guide dogs) sB⇌£24.50 dB⇌£27.50 (room only)
70P
V
Credit Cards 1 2 3 5

WARRINGTON Cheshire Map 07 SJ68

★★★ 59% ***Fir Grove*** Knutsford Old Rd WA4 2LD ☎(0925)67471 Telex no 628117 FAX (0925) 67471 ext 246
Situated just off the A50 on the south-eastern approach to the town, the hotel offers compact bedrooms with every modern facility.
39rm(19⇌20) CTV in all bedrooms ® T
☾ CTV 100P ♫
French V Last dinner 10pm
Credit Cards 1 2 3 5

★★**Old Vicarage Hotel** WA4 4NS (Best Western) ☎Norcott Brook(092573)706 FAX (092573) 740
(For full entry see Stretton (Cheshire))

★★**Paddington House** 514 Old Manchester Rd WA1 3TZ (Exec Hotel) ☎(0925)816767
Conveniently situated off the A57 and a mile from the M6 at junction 21, this hotel has function and converence rooms.
37rm(17⇌20)(1fb)1 CTV in all bedrooms ® T ✱ S10% sB&B⇌£38.50 dB&B⇌£50
Lift ☾ 100P 2 (£5) ✽ *xmas*
French V S10% Lunch fr£12 Dinner fr£12 Last dinner 9pm
Credit Cards 1 3 £

★★**Patten Arms** Parker St WA1 1LS ☎(0925)36602
Closed Xmas
Tall brick-built hotel with a modern extension, close to the railway station and the town centre.
43rm(30⇌13)(1fb) CTV in all bedrooms ® T sB&B⇌£47.50 dB&B⇌£57.50
☾ CTV 18P ♫
V
Credit Cards 1 2 3 5

★★**Rockfield** 3 Alexandra Rd, Grappenhall WA4 2EL (1.75m SE off A50) ☎(0925)62898 & 63343
Closed Xmas Day & Boxing Day
A charming Edwardian building, with immaculate bedrooms, the hotel is in a quiet residential area to the south-east of the town, off the A50 and near to junction20 of the M6.
7rm(3⇌)Annexe7rm(2⇌2) CTV in all bedrooms ® T sB&Bfr£30 sB&B⇌fr£35 dB&Bfr£40 dB&B⇌fr£50
CTV 30P ✽ ♫
English, French & Italian V High tea fr£3 Dinner fr£10&alc Last dinner 9pm
Credit Cards 1 3 5

★**Ribblesdale** Balmoral Rd, Grappenhall WA4 2EB
☎(0925)601197
Small, quiet, friendly hotel, supervised by resident owners.
15rm(12⇨) CTV in all bedrooms ® T ✱ sB&B£26 sB&B⇨£32 dB&B£37 dB&B⇨£43
20P ✲
French V Lunch £7.95-£10.25alc Dinner £9&alc Last dinner 9pm
Credit Cards 1 2 3

WARSASH Hampshire Map **04** SU40

✕**Nook and Cranny** Hook Ln, Hook Village SO3 6HH
☎Locks Heath(0489)584129
An 18th-century cottage in the village of Hook has been converted to an attractive restaurant where chef/proprietor Colin Wood and his team serve interesting French dishes.
Closed Sun, Mon, 1 wk Nov, 25-30 Dec & BH's
Dinner not served Sat
French 50 seats ✱ S10% Lunch £8.95 Dinner £14-£18alc
Last lunch 2pm Last dinner 9.45pm 15P
Credit Cards 1 3

WARWICK Warwickshire Map **04** SP26

See also **Barford and Leamington Spa**
★★★ 58% **Hilton National** Longbridge Roundabout CV34 6RE (Junc A41/A46/A429) (Hilton) ☎(0926)499555
Telex no 312468 FAX (0926) 410020
A popular hotel for both leisure and buisness guests, with modern conference facilities. Bedrooms are well furnished.
150rm(149⇨1)(8fb) in 37 bedrooms CTV in all bedrooms ® T
Lift 220P ✲ (heated) pool table
V Last dinner 10pm
Credit Cards 1 2 3 5

See advertisement on page 687

W

★★★60% ***Westgate*** Bowling Green St CV34 4DD
☎(0926)492362 Telex no 311928
Luxurious bedrooms, attentive service and fine food are the main attractions of this comfortable hotel in the centre of Warwick. Classic French and English style dishes are served in the well-appointed restaurant which overlooks the gardens and Warwick racecourse.
10⇌♠ CTV in all bedrooms ® T ✗
☾ ⊞ 45P ✤ ❖
♔ ⊡ Last dinner 10.30pm
Credit Cards 1 2 3 5

★★**Lord Leycester** Jury St CV34 4EJ (Consort) ☎(0926)491481 Telex no 41363 FAX (0202) 299182
Central hotel near Warwick Castle on a busy road through Warwick.
52rm(42⇌10♠)(4fb)1⊟ CTV in all bedrooms ® T S%
sB&B⇌♠fr£39 dB&B⇌♠fr£54 ⊨
Lift ☾ 40P *xmas*
♀ English & French V ♔ ⊡ S% Lunch £6.50-£10&alc Dinner £7-£10&alc Last dinner 8.30pm
Credit Cards 1 2 3 5 £

★★**Warwick Arms** High St CV34 4AJ (Minotels)
☎(0926)492759 FAX (0926) 410587
A busy hotel dating back to 1591, in the centre of Warwick.
35rm(13⇌22♠)(4fb) CTV in all bedrooms ® T ✳
sB&B⇌♠£37.50-£42.50 dB&B⇌♠£52-£58 ⊨
21P *xmas*
♀ English & French V ♔ ⊡ Lunch fr£7.95 High tea £1.75-£3.60alc Dinner fr£11.95&alc Last dinner 9.30pm
Credit Cards 1 2 3 5 £

★***Penderrick*** 36 Coten End CV34 4NP ☎(0926)499399
The large, Victorian house stands close to St Nicholas Park and only a few moments' walk from the town centre and castle. It provides accommodation that is ideal for holiday-makers and business clients alike, with well-equipped bedrooms and willing service from the friendly family who own it.
7rm(4♠)(2fb) CTV in all bedrooms ® T
CTV 9P 2⌂ ✤ ⌂
♔ ⊡ ⚟ Last dinner 9pm
Credit Cards 1 2 3 5

✕✕**Randolph's** Coten End CV34 4NT ☎(0926)491292
Mr R. J. Prymaka has taken over this tiny restaurant, and with it a very high reputation for good food: it is much to be hoped that the consistently high standards which have earned Randolphs its reputation will be maintained. The menu is predominantly French and service is friendly and relaxed.
Closed Sun & 25-30 Dec
Lunch not served Sat-Tue
Dinner not served Mon
♀ French V 30 seats Dinner £22-£27alc Last lunch 1.30pm
Last dinner 9.30pm ⚟ nc9yrs
Credit Cards 1 2 3

WASDALE HEAD Cumbria Map **11** NY10

★★***Wasdale Head Inn*** CA20 1EX ☎Wasdale(09406)229
Closed mid Nov-mid Mar
Situated at the head of the spectacular Wasdale Valley, the hotel is the perfect centre for those who simply want a peaceful holiday in lovely surroundings. Both the accommodation and food are very good, and a warm welcome is extended by the staff.
10rm(8⇌2♠)(3fb) ® T
50P ✤ ❖
Last dinner 7.30pm
Credit Cards 1 3

WASHINGTON Tyne & Wear Map **12** NZ35

★★★70% **Washington Moat House** Stone Cellar Rd NE37 1PH
☎091-417 2626 Telex no 537143 FAX 091-415 1166
Set in extensive grounds, this modern hotel combines a wide range of leisure facilities with well-equipped bedrooms and public rooms – equally suitable for business use or for families.
106rm(104⇌2♠)(9fb)2⊟⚟in 16 bedrooms CTV in all bedrooms ® T ✳ sB⇌♠£35.50-£75
dB⇌♠£57-£75 (room only) ⊨
☾ CTV 200P ❖ CFA ▭(heated) ⚑ 18 squash snooker sauna solarium gymnasium golf driving range hair-dressing salon *xmas*
♀ English & French V ♔ ⊡ ⚟ Bar Lunch fr£2.85 Dinner fr£11.95&alc Last dinner 9.30pm
Credit Cards 1 2 3 5

★★★61% **Post House** Emerson Distrist 5 NE37 1LB
(Trusthouse Forte) ☎091-416 2264 Telex no 537574
This large, modern and well furnished hotel stands close to the A1(M) on the south side of Newcastle.
138⇌(52fb)⚟in 30 bedrooms CTV in all bedrooms ® ✳
sB⇌£64-£75 dB⇌£75-£84 (room only) ⊨
Lift ☾ 198P ❖ CFA pitch & putt ⌂ *xmas*
♀ English & Continental V ♔ ⊡ ⚟ Lunch fr£7.50&alc Dinner £10.50-£14.10&alc Last dinner 10pm
Credit Cards 1 2 3 4 5

WASHINGTON SERVICE AREA Tyne & Wear
Map **12** NZ25

⌂**Granada Lodge** A1M, Portobello DH3 2SJ (Granada) ☎091-410 0076 FAX 091-410 9899
35⇌(10fb)⚟in 6 bedrooms CTV in all bedrooms ® ✗ (ex guide dogs) S% sB⇌£23-£26 dB⇌£26-£28 (room only)
40P
Credit Cards 1 2 3 5

WATCHET Somerset Map **03** ST04

★★**Downfield** 16 St Decuman's Rd TA23 0HR ☎(0984)31267
A pleasant, detached Victorian house in well-tended gardens overlooking the harbour.
6rm(2⇌4♠)(2fb) CTV in all bedrooms ® T ✳
sB&B⇌♠£28.75-£35 dB&B⇌♠£35-£50
22P ❖ ⌂ *xmas*
♀ English, French & German V ♔ ⊡ Lunch £8-£10alc Dinner £8-£10alc Last dinner 9.30pm
Credit Cards 1 2 3 5 £

WATERGATE BAY Cornwall & Isles of Scilly Map **02** SW86

★★**Tregurrian** TR8 4AB ☎St Mawgan(0637)860280
Closed Nov-Feb
A family-run hotel, close to the beach.
27rm(1⇌20♠)(8fb) TV available ® ✳ sB&B£12.65-£16.88
sB&B⇌♠£17.25-£21.28 dB&B£25.30-£33.95
dB&B⇌♠£29.90-£37.95 ⊨
CTV 26P ❖ ⌂(heated) solarium games room ♫ ⌂
♔ ⊡ S% Bar Lunch £1.80-£5alc Dinner £5.50-£7alc Last dinner 7.30pm
Credit Cards 1 3

WATERHOUSES Staffordshire Map **07** SK05

⊛✕✕**Old Beams Restaurant** Leek Rd ST10 3HW
☎(0538)308254
Continuous improvements made to this lovely 18th-century stone cottage have transformed it into a comfortable restaurant, where oak beams, fresh flowers and sparkling glass make a welcoming sight. Ann Wallis and her friendly
▶

W

waitresses provide attentive service in the dining room and large conservatory area, but the main attraction is undoubtedly the cooking of chef Nigel Wallis. The lightest of pastry, and well-flavoured but never overpowering sauces, feature throughout the menu, which is complemented by a wine list which also continues to improve. The addition of two delightful double bedrooms with en suite bathrooms makes this a perfect base for a relaxed tour of the Peak District.

Closed Mon, 1st 2 wks Jan

Lunch not served Sat

Dinner not served Sun

English & French 50 seats ✱ Lunch fr£11 Dinner fr£18.90&alc Last lunch 2pm Last dinner 10pm 22P nc4yrs 6 bedrooms available

Credit Cards 1 2 3 5

WATERINGBURY Kent Map **05** TQ65

★★★59% Wateringbury Tonbridge Rd ME18 5NS (Lansbury) ☎Maidstone(0622)812632 Telex no 96265 FAX (0622) 812720

This busy hotel provides comfortable and well-equipped accommodation with a cosy bar and lively restaurant. The menu offers a variety of popular dishes including some for vegetarians.

28⇌1 in 3 bedrooms CTV in all bedrooms ® T ✱ sB&B⇌£30-£65 dB&B⇌£60-£75

85P sauna *xmas*

European Lunch fr£8.50 Dinner fr£12.50 Last dinner 10.30pm

Credit Cards 1 2 3 5

WATERMILLOCK Cumbria Map **12** NY42

★★★ 75% Leeming House Ullswater CA11 0JJ (Trusthouse Forte)

☎Pooley Bridge(08536)622 due to change to (07684) 86622 Telex no 64111 FAX (08536) 443

Standing in extensive landscaped gardens, with woodland reaching down to the lakeside, this peaceful and civilised hotel retains much of its original character. Elegant public rooms with blazing fires are comfortably furnished, while the bedrooms, though compact, are thoughtfully equipped and enjoy fine views of the lake and fells. An imaginative 6-course dinner menu, changed daily, offers fine food based on local produce, as do the good breakfasts and the afternoon teas with their homemade preserves. Service of a high standard is provided by a charming young staff under the supervision of a professional manager.

18rm(14⇌2)in 2 bedrooms CTV in all bedrooms T S% sB⇌£60-£80 dB⇌£70-£103 (room only)

CTV 35P *xmas*

V S% Lunch £13.50&alc Dinner £27 Last dinner 8.45pm

Credit Cards 1 2 3 4 5

W

All hotels awarded three or more stars are now also given a percentage grading for the quality of their facilities. Please see p 16 for a detailed explanation.

★★ OLD CHURCH HOTEL CA11 0JN

☎Pooley Bridge(08536)204 due to change to (07684) 86204

Closed Dec-Feb RS Nov & Mar

A wonderful setting in leafy grounds on the shores of Lake Ullswater is only part of the charm of this delightful small hotel. Bedrooms are smart and well appointed, and though they lack radios and televisions (a conscious decision of the owners, to ensure peace and quiet) they all have en suite bathrooms. There are no fewer than 3 separate lounges – one with a television, one with a bar and the third overlooking the lake. The dining room is smart and spacious and sound English cooking is provided from a sensibly restricted menu. Outside the kitchen, all the staff are smart and cheerful young girls, with the owners, Kevin and Maureen Whitemoor, keeping a watchful eye on events. Here at the Old Church guests will find space, comfort, peace and hospitality – all in an unforgettable location.

10⇌ T (ex guide dogs) ✱ sB&B⇌£65 dB&B⇌£130 (incl dinner)

CTV 30P boat hire

English & French Dinner £19.50 Last dinner 8pm

★★Rampsbeck Country House CA11 0LP ☎Pooley Bridge(08536)442 & 688

Closed 4 Jan-Feb

(Rosette awarded for dinner only)

Perched right beside Lake Ullswater, this welcoming hotel boasts spacious, elegantly furnished public rooms and a superb table d'hôte menu. Delicate dishes like millefeuille foie gras or supreme of duck in a rich cherry sauce are matched by delectable puddings, of which strawberry and kirsch souffle with hot strawberry sauce and truffle biscuit is particularly memorable. Good food, hospitable service and the setting make the Rampsbeck an enticing retreat indeed.

19rm(17⇌2)(2fb) CTV in all bedrooms ® T ✱ sB&B⇌£30-£36 dB&B⇌£50-£70

30P nc5yrs *xmas*

English & French Lunch £15-£25alc Dinner £22.50-£27.50 Last dinner 9pm

Credit Cards 1 3

WATFORD Hertfordshire Map **04** TQ19

★★★56% Hilton National Elton Way WD2 8HA (Hilton) ☎(0923)35881 Telex no 923422 FAX (0923) 220836

(For full entry see Bushey)

WATTON Norfolk Map **05** TF90

★★Clarence House 78 High St IP25 6AH (Exec Hotel) ☎(0953)884252 & 884487 FAX (0953) 881323

The small, family-managed hotel provides value-for-money accommodation in comfortable surroundings and a friendly atmosphere.

6rm(1⇌5)(1fb) CTV in all bedrooms ® T S% sB&B⇌£32 dB&B⇌£45

7P ⊞ *xmas*
☋ English & French V ♆ ⊥ S% Lunch £6.95-£11.95&alc Dinner £13.95-£14.65&alc Last dinner 9pm
Credit Cards 1 2 3 5 ⓔ

WEEDON Northamptonshire Map **04** SP65

★★★70% Crossroads NN7 4PX (Best Western) ☎(0327)40354 Telex no 312311 FAX (0327) 40849
Closed 25-26 Dec RS 24 Dec
At the junction of the A5 and A45 and close to the M1, this hotel has been modernised and extended to include an attractive Garden Wing annexe with individually designed bedrooms. Service in the restaurant is attentive and friendly, beneath the ticking of several interesting clocks which are a feature of the decor.
10⇌Annexe40⇌(3fb)3⊞ CTV in all bedrooms ® **T** ✖ (ex guide dogs) sB&B⇌£60-£65 dB&B⇌£70-£80 ⊟
100P ✲ ℘ (hard)
V ♆ ⊥ S% Lunch £15-£20 High tea £6-£8 Dinner £10-£15 Last dinner 10.15pm
Credit Cards 1 2 3 5

See advertisement under NORTHAMPTON

★★Heart Of England Daventry Rd NN7 4QD (Berni/Chef & Brewer) ☎(0327)40335
An 18th-century hotel stands on the banks of the Grand Union Canal, with easy access to the A5/A45. Its bedrooms are particularly well equipped and comfortable, providing ideal accommodation for the businessman or holiday-maker.
12rm(1⇌1↱)1⊞ CTV in all bedrooms ® **T** ✖ (ex guide dogs) sB&B⇌↱£33-£37.50 dB&B⇌↱£47-£51
70P ⊞ ✲
V ♆ ⊥ Lunch fr£8 Dinner fr£9 Last dinner 10pm
Credit Cards 1 2 3 5

★Globe High St NN7 4QD (Inter) ☎(0327)40336 FAX (0327) 349058
Once an 18th-century coaching inn, this comfortable, small hotel stands conveniently near to the junction of the A5 and A45. Its public rooms are full of character and the bedrooms are well-equipped.
14rm(5⇌9↱)(1fb) CTV in all bedrooms ® **T** ✳
sB&B⇌↱£32-£37.50 dB&B⇌↱£37-£48 ⊟
40P ♫
☋ Mainly grills V ♆ ⊥ Lunch £5.50-£10 Dinner fr£8.95&alc Last dinner 9.30pm
Credit Cards 1 2 3 5 ⓔ

WELLINGBOROUGH Northamptonshire Map **04** SP86

★★★57% Hind Sheep St NN8 1BY (Queens Moat) ☎(0933)222827 FAX (0933) 441921
Standing in the centre of the town, the Hind dates back to the 17th century and offers modern, well-equipped accommodation in rooms which retain their old character.
34⇌↱(1fb)1⊞ CTV in all bedrooms ® **T** S%
sB&B⇌↱£53-£60 dB&B⇌↱£68-£80 ⊟
☾ 13P 3⌂ CFA
☋ English & Continental V ♆ ⊥ ⚟ S% Lunch fr£7.95&alc Dinner fr£9.95&alc Last dinner 10pm
Credit Cards 1 2 3 4 5

★★Columbia 19 Northampton Rd NN8 3HG (Consort) ☎(0933)229333
Closed 24-27 Dec
Commercial hotel close to the town centre with comfortable accommodation ideal for the business clientele.
29rm(21⇌8↱)(1fb) CTV in all bedrooms ® **T** ✖ (ex guide dogs) sB&B⇌↱£26-£40 dB&B⇌↱£38-£50 ⊟
CTV 18P
☋ English & French V ♆ ⊥ Lunch £5.50-£6.50&alc Dinner £8.50-£8.50&alc Last dinner 9.30pm
Credit Cards 1 2 3

★★High View 156 Midland Rd NN8 1NG ☎(0933)78733 due to change to 278733 FAX (0933) 225948
Friendly, mainly commercial, family-run hotel close to the town centre.
14⇌↱(1fb) CTV in all bedrooms ® **T** sB&B⇌↱£23-£38 dB&B⇌↱£32-£44 ⊟
CTV 8P 1⌂ ✲ games room
V ♆ ⚟ Lunch fr£7.20&alc Dinner fr£7.20&alc Last dinner 8.30pm
Credit Cards 1 2 3 5 ⓔ

WELLINGTON

See **Telford**

WELLS Somerset Map **03** ST54

★★★54% Swan Sadler St BA5 2RX (Best Western) ☎(0749)78877 Telex no 449658 FAX (0749) 77647
Overlooking the West Front of the cathedral, this 16th-century and Victorian hotel offers spacious and well equipped bedrooms, many with antique furnishings. Other amenities include a bar and lounge with log fires and a cosy dining room whose range of good English food includes traditional roasts.
32rm(27⇌5↱)(2fb)9⊞ CTV in all bedrooms **T**
sB&B⇌↱fr£48.75 dB&B⇌↱£68.50-£75 ⊟
30P CFA squash *xmas*
☋ English V ♆ ⊥ Lunch fr£9.25&alc Dinner fr£14.50 Last dinner 9.30pm
Credit Cards 1 2 3 5

See advertisement on page 691

The AA's star-rating scheme is the market leader in hotel classification.

W

★★*Crown* Market Place BA5 2RP ☎(0749)73457
Standing opposite the Bishop's Palace, this pleasant old coaching-house hotel retains many original features. An attractive restaurant serves well-prepared dishes and the bar serves light meals and afternoon teas.
21rm(14⇨7♠)4 CTV in all bedrooms ® T
15P squash
V Last dinner 10pm
Credit Cards 1 2 3 4 5

★**Ancient Gate House** Sadler St BA5 2RR ☎(0749)72029
Enthusiastically run hotel of great character backing onto Cathedral green.
10rm(1⇨2♠)(1fb)6 CTV in all bedrooms ✱ sB&B£23-£25 sB&B⇨♠£29-£32 dB&B£35-£38 dB&B⇨♠£42-£44
4P
English & Italian V Lunch £4.25-£8.45&alc Dinner £12.75-£13.75&alc Last dinner 10.30pm
Credit Cards 1 2 3 5

WELLS-NEXT-THE-SEA Norfolk Map 09 TF94

★**Crown** The Buttlands NR23 1EX (Minotels)
☎Fakenham(0328)710209
Dating from Tudor times, this attractive coaching inn has a Georgian façade and stands in a quiet, tree-lined square close to the harbour. Fresh fish, caught locally, is a speciality.
16rm(3⇨5♠)(3fb) CTV in all bedrooms ® sB&Bfr£28 sB&B⇨♠fr£38 dB&Bfr£43 dB&B⇨♠fr£48
10P *xmas*
English & Continental V Lunch fr£8.50&alc Dinner fr£12.50&alc Last dinner 9.30pm
Credit Cards 1 2 3 5

✕**Moorings** 6 Freeman St NR23 1BA ☎Fakenham(0328)710949
Locally caught seafood is a speciality of this charming little restaurant that stands close to the harbour of this small Norfolk fishing town. Dishes are predominantly provincial French – mussels, oysters, sea-trout and dogfish are well-flavoured, with a lavish use of herbs. Vegetarians are particularly well catered for, with dishes such as eggs and broccoli with mustard and cheese sauce or Chinese vegetables with beancurd. The wine list is extensive and modestly priced.
Closed Wed, 2 wks early Jun & late Nov-mid Dec
Lunch not served Thu
Dinner not served Tue
English & French V 40 seats ✱ Lunch fr£10.45 Dinner fr£12.25 Last lunch 1.45pm Last dinner 8.45pm

WELSH HOOK Dyfed Map 02 SM92

✕✕**Stone Hall** SA62 5NS ☎Letterston(0348)840212
Stone Hall stand near the hamlet of Welsh Hook between Haverfordwest and Fishguard. The charming restaurant in the 600-year-old part of the house serves imaginative food prepared by a talented young chef whose experience was gained in Nice and Brittany.
Closed Mon (Nov-Mar only) & 6-18 Nov
Lunch not served ex by prior arrangement
French V 34 seats ✱ Lunch £11-£12.50 Dinner £11-£12.50&alc Last dinner 9.30pm 50P 5 bedrooms available
Credit Cards 1 2 3

WELSHPOOL Powys Map 07 SJ20

★★**Royal Oak** SY21 7DG (Consort) ☎(0938)2217 due to change to 552217 Telex no 57515
Situated in the heart of the small market town, this hotel has comfortable bedrooms and an attractive, part-timbered dining room.
25rm(19⇨6♠)(1fb)1 CTV in all bedrooms ® T (ex guide dogs) sB&B⇨♠£26.50-£30 dB&B⇨♠£49-£54
CTV 60P 2 (charged)
English, French & Italian V Lunch £7-£8&alc Dinner £9-£10&alc Last dinner 9pm
Credit Cards 1 2 3 £

★*Garth Derwen* Buttington SY21 8SU (2.5m NE A458)
☎Trewern(093874)238
Small, personally-run, comfortable hotel with good home cooking.
8rm(5♠)(4fb)1 CTV in all bedrooms ® (ex guide dogs)
20P
International V Last dinner 9.45pm
Credit Cards 1 3

WELWYN GARDEN CITY Hertfordshire Map 04 TL21

★★★57% **Crest** Homestead Ln AL7 4LX (Crest)
☎(0707)324336 Telex no 261523 FAX (0707) 326447
A small, lively hotel attracting a busy commercial trade, the hotel is located in a residential area.
58rm(51⇨7♠)in 12 bedrooms CTV in all bedrooms ® T sB⇨♠£68 dB⇨♠£68-£80 (room only)
Lift 80P CFA *xmas*
International V Lunch £10-£11 Dinner £12.95-£13.95&alc Last dinner 10pm
Credit Cards 1 2 3 4 5

WEMBLEY Greater London

See LONDON plan 5*B4*(page 412) Telephone codes are due to change on 6th May 1990. See page 421.
✕✕*Moghul Brasserie* 525 High Rd HA0 4AG ☎01-903 6967 & 01-902 8665
Intimate and tastefully appointed, this town-centre restaurant offers authentic dishes based on good fresh produce, well marinated prior to cooking. Of particular interest are the succulent King Prawn Bhuna and a fine selection of breads which includes an excellent Spinach Paratha.
Closed 25-26 Dec
Indian V 60 seats Last dinner 11.15pm 20P
Credit Cards 1 2 3 5

✕**Woodlands** 402A High Rd HA9 7AB ☎01-902 9869 FAX 01-908 0253
A friendly, intimate atmosphere prevails in this South Indian vegetarian restaurant.
Closed Xmas Day
South Indian V 55 seats ✱ Lunch £8.50&alc Dinner £8.50&alc Last lunch 2.30pm Last dinner 10.30pm 2P
Credit Cards 1 2 3 5

WENTBRIDGE (near Pontefract) West Yorkshire Map 08 SE41

★★★67% **Wentbridge House** WF8 3JJ (Select)
☎Pontefract(0977)620444
FAX (0977) 620148
Closed Xmas night

A building dating from 1700, and set in about fifteen acres of attractive grounds near the A1, has been converted into a comfortable, family-run hotel; despite its unspoiled village location it is ideally placed for access to all parts of Yorkshire. The Fleur de Lys Restaurant, under the close personal supervision of the proprietors, serves excellent French and International cuisine, making good use of fresh ingredients and providing consistently high standards of service. The wine list itemises 333 wines, ranging from the modest to the more expensive.

12⇔🚿1 ⊞ CTV in all bedrooms T ✗ (ex guide dogs) ✱ S10% sB&B⇔🚿fr£55 dB&B⇔🚿£65-£90 ⊟
100P ⊞ ❖
♀ French V ♡ Lunch fr£12 Dinner fr£21alc Last dinner 9.30pm
Credit Cards [1] [2] [3] [5]

WEST BAY

See **Bridport**

WEST BEXINGTON Dorset Map **03** SY58

★★Manor Beach Rd DT6 9DF
☎Burton Bradstock(0308)897616
This charming stone manor house standing in pleasant grounds is particularly popular with families. It has well-equipped bedrooms and serves good-quality meals.
10rm(6⇔4🚿)(1fb) CTV in all bedrooms ® ✗
sB&B⇔🚿£29.95-£33.50 dB&B⇔🚿£49-£55.90 ⊟
28P ❖
V ♡ Lunch £12.50-£10 Dinner £15.45-£16.45 Last dinner 10pm
Credit Cards [1] [2] [3]

See advertisement under BRIDPORT

WEST BROMWICH West Midlands Map **07** SP09

See also **Barr, Great**
★★★58% ***Great Barr Hotel & Conference Centre*** Pear Tree Dr, off Newton Rd B43 6HS ☎021-357 1141 Telex no 336406 FAX 021-357 7557
(For full entry see Barr, Great)

★★

Country Ways

Marsh Lane, Farrington Gurney, Bristol.
Telephone: Temple Cloud (0761) 52449

Spend some time relaxing in the warm, informal atmosphere of our country hotel situated halfway between Bath and Wells. Enjoy a drink in front of the fire in winter or on the terrace when the sun shines, followed by good food and wine served with a smile.
Six delightful bedrooms all with bathrooms, telephone, colour television, radio and welcome tray.
See gazetteer entry under Farrington Gurney.

★★

Market Place, Wells, Somerset BA 5 2RP
Telephone: (0749) 73457

A mediaeval building and subsequent coaching Inn close to the cathedral and nestling at the foot of the Mendip Hills. All bedrooms are en-suite, some with four poster beds and rooms available for non-smokers. The Crown Restaurant is non-smoking with a selection of tables also available in the Penn Bar. The Cheese Shop, a speciality of the hotel, offers 150 varieties of local/English and Continental cheese. Restricted parking within the grounds.

SWAN HOTEL

— WELLS —

SOMERSET

TEL WELLS 78877

A 15th-century coaching Inn with original four-poster beds and cheerful log fires. Enjoy our panelled Restaurant with joint of the day from the Silver trolley. With a superb view of the West Front of Wells Cathedral it's just the place if you wish to tour the West Country.

Please write or telephone the Manager for further details.

A MEMBER OF
BEST WESTERN HOTELS

AA ★ ★ ★

W

★★★60% ***West Bromwich Moat House*** Birmingham Rd B70 6RS (Queens Moat) ☎021-553 6111 Telex no 336232 FAX 021-525 7403
A popular, modern hotel with good conference facilities, the Moat House is closeto junction 1 of the M5.
170⇌⌐ ⅟in 17 bedrooms CTV in all bedrooms ® T
Lift ☾ ▦ 200P CFA
☋ English & French V ♉ ☡
Credit Cards 1 2 3 5

WEST CHILTINGTON West Sussex Map 04 TQ01

★★★57% **Roundabout** Monkmead Ln RH20 2PF (1.75m S) (Best Western) ☎(07983)3838 Telex no 94013840
Quiet Tudor style hotel with compact well furnished bedrooms.
20⇌(4fb)4⊟ CTV in all bedrooms ® T S10%
sB&B⇌£49.95-£53.95 dB&B⇌£68.25-£77.25 ⊟
46P ❖ nc3yrs *xmas*
☋ English & French V ♉ ☡ S10% Lunch £10.25-£12.25&alc Dinner £14.95-£15.50&alc Last dinner 9pm
Credit Cards 1 2 3 4 5

WESTCLIFFE-ON-SEA

See **Southend-on-Sea**

WESTERHAM Kent Map 05 TQ45

★★★ 61% ***Kings Arms*** Market Square TN16 1AN ☎(0959)62990
This family-owned hotel, a 200-year-old building, has been attractively decorated and tastefully furnished. It provides spacious bedrooms, a comfortable bar lounge and a charming restaurant offering à la carte and, during the week, carvery menus.
13⇌(2fb) CTV in all bedrooms ® T
35P ⊟
☋ International ♉
Credit Cards 1 2 3 5

WESTGATE-ON-SEA Kent Map 05 TR37

★★***Ivyside*** 25 Sea Rd CT8 8SB ☎Thanet(0843)31082
Generally acceptable bedrooms, mainly designed and furnished for families with children.
51rm(31⇌18⌐)(44fb) CTV in all bedrooms ® T ✗
☾ CTV 30P ❖ CFA ▭(heated) ⌂(heated) squash snooker sauna solarium gymnasium ⌂
☋ English & French V ♉ ☡ Last dinner 6pm
Credit Cards 1 3

WESTHILL Grampian *Aberdeenshire* Map 15 NJ80

★★★ 61% ***Westhill*** AB3 6TT (Consort)
☎Aberdeen(0224)740388 Telex no 739925
Six miles west of Aberdeen, this modern hotel is set in a rural development area, just off the A944 and offers well-appointed public rooms and extensive car-parking facilities.
38⇌Annexe14rm(6⇌8⌐) CTV in all bedrooms ® T
Lift ☾ ▦ 350P CFA sauna solarium gymnasium ♫
V ♉ Last dinner 10pm
Credit Cards 1 2 3 5

See advertisement under ABERDEEN

WESTLETON Suffolk Map 05 TM46

★★***The Crown at Westleton*** IP17 3AD ☎(072873)273
Closed 25-26 Dec
Small, friendly village inn, ideally situated for visits to the RSPB Minsmere Bird Reserve and the coast.
7rm(3⇌)Annexe7rm(5⇌2⌐)(3fb)3⊟ CTV in all bedrooms ® T
30P
V ♉ ⅟ Last dinner 9.30pm
Credit Cards 1 2 3 5

WEST LULWORTH Dorset

★**Bishop's Cottage** BH20 5RQ ☎(092941)261
Closed Nov-Feb
Guests can enjoy a friendly, informal atmosphere and comfortable accommodation at this family-run hotel, set into the hillside on the edge of Lulworth Cove.
11rm(6⇌1⌐)Annexe3rm(2⇌)(3fb) ® S10%
sB&B£17.60-£19.80 dB&B£35.20-£39.60
dB&B⇌⌐£37.40-£41.80 ⊟
CTV 6P ❖ ⌂(heated) ⌂
☋ English V ♉ ☡ Sunday Lunch £4.95-£10&alc Last high tea 7pm
Credit Cards 1 3

★**Shirley** Main Rd BH20 5RL ☎(092941)358
Closed early Nov-Feb
This small, friendly, personally-run hotel provides easy parking and good food. There is also a heated swimming pool and giant chess in the garden.
17rm(10⇌7⌐)(2fb) CTV in all bedrooms ® T
sB&B⇌⌐£16-£19.80 dB&B⇌⌐£32-£39.60 ⊟
20P ⊟ ⌂(heated)
V ⅟ Bar Lunch £2.90-£4.40 Dinner £6.55-£7.20 Last dinner 8pm
Credit Cards 1 3

WEST MERSEA Essex Map 05 TM01

✕**Le Champenois (Blackwater Hotel)** 20-22 Church Rd CO5 8QH ☎Colchester(0206)383338 & 383038
Fresh seafood, veal and duck feature in the enjoyable, simple dishes presented in this attractive French restaurant which forms part of the Blackwater Hotel on Mersea Island. Charming and efficient staff provide attentive service and a high standard of hospitality.
Closed 5-28 Jan
Lunch not served Tue
Dinner not served Sun
☋ English & French V 42 seats ✳ Lunch £8.50-£11&alc Dinner £12-£20alc Last lunch 2pm Last dinner 9.45pm 15P 7 bedrooms available
Credit Cards 1 2

WESTON-ON-THE-GREEN Oxfordshire Map 04 SP51

★★★ 65% **Weston Manor** OX6 8QL (Best Western)
☎Bletchington(0869)50621 Telex no 83409 FAX (0869) 50901
In the past this 14th-century manor house has been the ancestral home of earls, then a monastery, and has now been restored to make a stylish hotel featuring a unique, oak-panelled restaurant with minstrels' gallery. The bedrooms combine comfort with character, and there are extensive leisure facilities.
17⇌⌐Annexe7rm(6⇌1⌐)(3fb)2⊟ CTV in all bedrooms ® T ✗ (ex guide dogs) ✳ sB&B⇌⌐fr£75 dB&B⇌⌐fr£95 ⊟
☾ 150P ❖ ⌂(heated) ⌐ squash croquet *xmas*
☋ English & French V ♉ ☡ Lunch fr£13.50 Dinner fr£18.50 Last dinner 9.30pm
Credit Cards 1 2 3 5 £

WESTON-SUPER-MARE Avon Map 03 ST36

★★★ 59% **Commodore** Beach Rd, Sand Bay, Kewstoke BS22 9UZ ☎(0934)415778 FAX (0934) 636483
Located only a couple of miles from the resort, with panoramic views of the coast and across to Wales, this popular hotel offers comfortable, simply furnished accommodation and, at mealtimes, the choice of a formal restaurant or the carvery.
12rm(9⇌3⌐)Annexe4rm(2⇌)(1fb) CTV in all bedrooms ® T ✗ (ex guide dogs) sB&B£36 sB&B⇌⌐£38 dB&B£50 dB&B⇌⌐£54 ⊟
85P ❖ ♫ ⌂

☋ English & Continental V ♈ ☡ ⅟ Lunch fr£6.25&alc High tea £4.50-£6 Dinner £10-£15alc Last dinner 10pm
Credit Cards 1 2 3 5 £

★★★ 65% **The Grand Atlantic** Beach Rd BS23 1BA (Trusthouse Forte) ☎(0934)626543 FAX (0934) 415048
A high level of hospitality is the hallmark of this large, traditional, sea-front hotel where refurbishment continues. Many of the bedrooms enjoy impressive sea views.
76⇌⅟in 15 bedrooms CTV in all bedrooms ® T S%
sB⇌fr£56 dB⇌fr£78 (room only) ⊟
Lift ☾ 150P ✲ CFA ⇌(heated) ℘ (hard) ♧ *xmas*
☋ English & French V ♈ ☡ ⅟ S% Lunch fr£8.50&alc Dinner fr£11.50&alc Last dinner 9.30pm
Credit Cards 1 2 3 4 5

★★★ 56% **Royal Pier** Birnbeck Rd BS23 2EJ (Best Western) ☎(0934)626644
Comfortable hotel with good sized lounges, looking across Weston Bay.
40rm(33⇌3♠)(4fb) CTV in all bedrooms ® T ✗ ✳
sB&B£42-£49.50 sB&B⇌♠£42-£49.50 dB&B⇌♠£65-£69 ⊟
Lift ☾ CTV 70P ⇎ pool table & table tennis *xmas*
☋ European V ♈ ☡ Lunch fr£8.25&alc Dinner fr£12.50&alc Last dinner 9.15pm
Credit Cards 1 2 3 5 £

See advertisement on page 695

★★ **Beachlands** 17 Uphill Rd North BS23 4NG ☎(0934)621401
A small, warm, personally-run hotel stands close to the coast, offering good-value accommodation with sound home cooking and useful parking facilities.
18rm(8⇌10♠)(5fb) CTV in all bedrooms ® T ✳
sB&B⇌♠£23.75-£25.75 dB&B⇌♠£47.50-£51.50 ⊟
CTV 15P ⇎ *xmas*

▶

W

🍽 English & French ☕ 🍸 Bar Lunch 60p-£6 Dinner £7.95-£8.95 Last dinner 8pm
Credit Cards 1 2 3 5

★★Berni Royal South Pde BS23 1JN (Berni/Chef & Brewer) ☎(0934)623601
An impressive Georgian-style building, in its own grounds, the hotel is near to the Central Pier and the beach.
37rm(35⇌2🚿)2🛏 CTV in all bedrooms ® **T** 🐕 (ex guide dogs) sB&B⇌🚿fr£36 dB&B⇌🚿fr£59.50 🅱
Lift ☾ 150P ❃
🍽 Mainly grills **V** ☕ 🚭 Lunch fr£8 Dinner fr£9 Last dinner 10.30pm
Credit Cards 1 2 3 5

★★Rozel Madeira Cove BS23 2BU (Inter) ☎(0934)415268
Large, traditional family-owned and run holiday and business hotel on the seafront.
49rm(36⇌10🚿)(15fb) CTV in all bedrooms ® **T** ✱ sB&B⇌🚿£35-£45 dB&B⇌🚿£58-£68 🅱
Lift ☾ 30P 50🚗 ❃ CFA ⛆(heated) ♫ *xmas*
🍽 English & French **V** ☕ 🍸 Lunch £7.50-£9.50 Dinner £9.90 Last dinner 8.30pm
Credit Cards 1 2 3 5 £

WESTON-UNDER-REDCASTLE Shropshire Map **07** SJ52

★★★53% **Hawkstone Park** SY4 5UY (1m E of A49 between Shrewsbury & Whitchurch) (Best Western)
☎Lee Brockhurst(093924)611 Telex no 35793
FAX (093924) 311
Much extended and modernised former country house with excellent golfing facilities.
43⇌🚿Annexe16⇌(10fb) CTV in all bedrooms ® **T** 🐕 (ex guide dogs) ✱ S10% sB&B⇌🚿£46-£52 dB&B⇌🚿£72-£100 🅱
☾ CTV 250P ❃ CFA ⛆ ⛳ 18 🎾 (grass) ✔ snooker sauna solarium gymnasium croquet games room *xmas*
☕ 🍸 S10% Lunch £4.99-£10.20&alc High tea £3.50-£5.95 Dinner £10.75 Last dinner 9pm
Credit Cards 1 2 3 5

WEST RUNTON Norfolk Map **09** TG14

★★★63% **Links Country Park Hotel & Golf Club** Sandy Ln NR27 9QH ☎(026375)691 FAX (026375) 8264
Standing in 35 acres of grounds above the village and commanding superb views across the Norfolk coastline, this hotel has its own nine-hole golf course as well as a popular leisure centre. Bedrooms are comfortable and include the new 'Garden Room' extension.
22rm(20⇌2🚿)Annexe10⇌ CTV in all bedrooms ® **T** sB&B⇌🚿£39-£53 dB&B⇌🚿£78-£100 (incl dinner) 🅱
Lift ☾ 150P ❃ CFA ⛆(heated) ⛳ 9 🎾 (hard) sauna solarium *xmas*
🍽 English & French **V** ☕ 🍸 Lunch £11.50-£12.50&alc High tea £2.50-£5 Dinner £13.50-£14.50&alc Last dinner 9.30pm
Credit Cards 1 3

WESTWARD HO! Devon Map **02** SS42

★★Culloden House Fosketh Hill EX39 1JA
☎Bideford(02372)79421
Closed Nov-Feb
The friendly, relaxed hotel specialises in cricket and golfing holidays.
9rm(2⇌5🚿)(2fb) CTV in all bedrooms sB&B£24-£30 sB&B⇌🚿£26-£32 dB&B£36-£44 dB&B⇌🚿£38-£48
CTV 9P 🚸 ❃
V ☕ 🍸 Lunch £9-£12 Dinner £11-£14 Last dinner 8.45pm
Credit Cards 1 2 3 5

WEST WITTON North Yorkshire Map **07** SE08

★★Wensleydale Heifer Inn DL8 4LS (Consort)
☎Wensleydale(0969)22322 Telex no 57515
A 17th-century village inn on the main road through this Dales village.
9rm(8⇌1🚿)Annexe10rm(5⇌5🚿)(1fb)3🛏 CTV in all bedrooms ® **T** ✱ sB&B⇌🚿fr£35 dB&B⇌🚿£50-£70 🅱
25P *xmas*
V ☕ 🍸 Lunch fr£7.50 Dinner fr£14.50 Last dinner 9.30pm
Credit Cards 1 2 3 5 £

See advertisement under LEYBURN

WETHERAL Cumbria Map **12** NY45

★★★66% **Crown** CA4 8ES (Shire)(Consort) ☎(0228)61888
Telex no 64175 FAX (0228) 61637
Situated in a charming village, this former 18th-century fishing inn has been extended and carefully modernised to provide comfortable and well-appointed accommodation with conference facilities and a leisure complex. The young staff are friendly and attentive and the conservatory restaurant is an attractive setting for enjoyable meals.
49⇌(6fb)1🛏🚭in 8 bedrooms CTV in all bedrooms ® **T** ✱ sB&B⇌fr£66.50 dB&B⇌fr£85 🅱
☾ CTV 80P ❃ CFA ⛆(heated) squash snooker sauna solarium gymnasium 🏠 *xmas*
🍽 English & French **V** ☕ 🍸 🚭 Lunch £8.50-£9.25&alc Dinner £14-£19&alc Last dinner 9.30pm
Credit Cards 1 2 3 5

★Killoran The Green CA4 8ET ☎(0228)60200
Set in its own gardens in an attractive village, this period mansion looks out over the priory to the River Eden. The hotel provides modest bedrooms, limited lounge facilities and a cosy bar and restaurant offering a good range of good food.
10rm(2fb) CTV in 4bedrooms TV in 6bedrooms ®
sB&Bfr£21.25 dB&B£37
CTV 70P ❃ 🏠
🍽 English & Continental **V** ☕ 🍸 Lunch £2-£7&alc Dinner £8.50-£10&alc Last dinner 9.30pm
Credit Cards 1 3

✕Fantails The Green CA4 8ET ☎(0228)60239
Set in a building which dates back to the 17th-century, the charming restaurant features oak beams, leaded windows and open fires. Food, chosen from a short but interesting à la carte menu, is of a very high standard.
🍽 International **V** 50 seats ✱ Lunch £12-£18.50alc Dinner £12-£18.50alc Last lunch 2pm Last dinner 9.30pm 25P 🚭
Credit Cards 1 2 3 5

WETHERBY West Yorkshire Map **08** SE44

★★★57% **Penguin** Leeds Rd LS22 5HE (junc A1/A58)
☎(0937)63881 Telex no 556428 FAX (0937) 580062
A modern hotel with good facilities, bars and restaurants, the Penguin is conveniently situated near to the A1.
72⇌🚿(2fb)🚭in 8 bedrooms CTV in all bedrooms ® **T** ✱ sB⇌🚿£60 dB⇌🚿£75 (room only) 🅱
☾ 150P ❃ *xmas*
V ☕ 🍸 🚭 Lunch £6.50-£8.50 High tea fr£5 Dinner fr£12.50&alc Last dinner 9.45pm
Credit Cards 1 2 3 5 £

Entries for rosetted restaurants, red-star and country-house hotels are highlighted by a tinted panel. For a full list of these establishments, consult the Contents page.

W

★★★ WOOD HALL
Trip Ln, Linton LS22 4JA
(Select) ☎(0937)67271

This lovely part Jacobean and part Georgian house, surrounded by 100 acres of park and woodland, has been successfully converted into a peaceful and spacious country house hotel. It provides not only a high standard of comfort, but also a caring and friendly staff, ably led by General Manager, Clive Schreiber. No less a personality is chef Andrew Mitchell, who places quality above all in producing his interesting à la carte and speciality table d'hôte menus. The bedrooms are all individually furnished and decorated, and have been equipped with many of those thoughtful extras which make a stay at Wood Hall such a treat. Some of the bedrooms are housed in the Jacobean part of the building, with external access only, and, though more compact, they provide the same standard of accommodation as those in the main building. There are lovely views across open farmland and guests can enjoy walks along the various bridle paths which cross the estate.

22⇨ Annexe6⇨ 1 in 4 bedrooms CTV in 22bedrooms ® T
CTV 70P ✽ (heated) snooker sauna solarium
Last dinner 9.30pm
Credit Cards 1 2 3 4 5

BATCH FARM COUNTRY HOTEL

AA ★★

LYMPSHAM, Nr WESTON-SUPER-MARE SOMERSET (0934) 750371

Proprietors: Mr & Mrs D. J. Brown

A family run hotel with a long reputation for friendly atmosphere and excellent traditional English food, à la carte menus also available. Delightfully situated in own grounds, panoramic views from all rooms. 5 miles Weston-super-Mare. 5 miles Burnham-on-Sea. Fishing in river. Fully licensed lounge bar. All bedrooms are en suite and have colour TV and tea making facilities. Ample parking, games room. Egon Ronay/Ashley Courtenay recommended.

Fantails ×

The Green, Wetheral, Carlisle, Cumbria CA4 8ET
Telephone: (0228) 60239

Open 6 days a week for lunch and dinner.

The building dates back to the 18th century when it was a simple barn and hayloft and later a stable 'cum' blacksmiths. Then in 1953 it was converted into an eating house, with many of the old beams and other interesting features still retained. Central heating was installed but an open fire provdes a friendly welcome. The Dove Room, a small private function room, is available for seminars, conferences and dinner parties with special meals arranged.

AA ★★★

THE Royal Pier HOTEL

Birnbeck Road, Weston-Super-Mare
Avon BS23 2EJ Telephone (0934) 626644

WE LOOK FORWARD TO THE PLEASURE OF YOUR COMPANY!

The Royal Pier Hotel is a three star hotel, open all year, managed by resident proprietors. In an unrivalled position on the water's edge, most bedrooms and public rooms have magnificent views of the Bay and Channel. An ongoing programme of refurbishment has produced a high standard of comfort, service and decor, with the majority of bedrooms en suite, and all with colour TV, radio and telephone.

Fully licensed, there are two bars – the renamed luxurious 'Kennedys' or the more informal Prince Consort Bar which also serves a wide selection of bar food. The excellent restaurant offers a choice of food and menus, complemented by a well stocked cellar. Two function rooms are available and ample parking is adjacent. Tariffs including Winter Weekends, Christmas etc., are available.

W

✕✕✕*Linton Spring* Sicklinghall Rd LS22 9XX ☎(0937)65353
Despite its rural location, this comfortable country house restaurant lies only a few minutes' drive from the town. The menu offers an imaginative range of freshly prepared dishes, with Aberdeen Angus beef a speciality, and game, chicken, sole and crab used to interesting effect.
Closed Mon & 1st wk Jan
Lunch not served Sat
Dinner not served Sun
English & Continental V 80 seats Last lunch 2.30pm Last dinner 10pm 50P ♫
Credit Cards 1 2 3 4 5

WEYBOURNE Norfolk Map **09** TG14

★★**Maltings** NR25 7SY (Consort) ☎(026370)731
Telex no 57515 ATTN 129
Formerly a manor, malting house and dairy, this original Norfolk flintstone house dates from the 16th century.
11rm(6⇌5♠)Annexe11rm(7⇌2♠)(3fb)2 CTV in all bedrooms T ✳ sB&B⇌♠fr£35 dB&B⇌♠fr£54
150P ✽ *xmas*
International V ♥ Sunday Lunch £8.50&alc Dinner £14-£15&alc Last dinner 9pm
Credit Cards 1 2 3 5

WEYBRIDGE Surrey

See LONDON plan 5*A1*(page 412.)
★★★69% **Ship Thistle** Monument Green KT13 8BQ (Thistle)
☎(0932)848364 Telex no 894271 FAX (0932) 857153
Relaxing and comfortable, the hotel has attractive and spacious bedrooms. Recently, a cocktail bar has been opened, in addition to the lounge bar, and there is a pleasant restaurant, offering a good standard of cooking, mainly in the French tradition.
39⇌♠ CTV in all bedrooms ® T ✳ sB⇌♠£75-£85 dB⇌♠£85-£95 (room only)
(50P 20 ✽ ♫
International ♥ Lunch fr£9.95&alc Dinner fr£13.75&alc Last dinner 10pm
Credit Cards 1 2 3 4 5

WEYMOUTH Dorset Map **03** ST68

★★*Crown* 51-52 St Thomas St DT4 8EQ ☎(0305)760800
Closed 25-26 Dec
Centrally situated on the town's complicated one-way system, a busy coaching hotel of imposing appearance offers good value accommodation with comfortable bedrooms and simple fare.
79rm(43⇌10♠)(12fb) ® (ex guide dogs)
Lift (CTV 8 (£1) CFA ♫
V ♥ Last dinner 8pm
Credit Cards 1 3

★★**Glenburn** 42 Preston Rd DT3 6PZ (3m NE A353)
☎Preston(0305)832353
Closed 25 Dec-1 Jan
This family-run hotel has a warm and friendly atmosphere. All bedrooms are attractive and all have en suite facilities.
13rm(5⇌7♠)(1fb) CTV in all bedrooms ® ✳
sB&B⇌♠fr£27 dB&B⇌♠fr£52
30P ✽ ♫ nc3 yrs
V ♥ Lunch fr£6.50 Dinner fr£11 Last dinner 8.30pm
Credit Cards 1 3

★★**Hotel Prince Regent** 139 The Esplanade DT4 7NR (Consort)
☎(0305)771313 Telex no 94011219
Closed 24 Dec-3 Jan
Standing directly on the sea front, the Prince Regent has a popular bar and restaurant. All the bedrooms are well furnished and some command excellent views across the bay.
50rm(37⇌8♠)(25fb) CTV in all bedrooms ® T sB&Bfr£35 sB&B⇌♠fr£45 dB&Bfr£47.50 dB&B⇌♠fr£60
Lift (5P 14 CFA
English & French V ♥ Bar Lunch £1.50-£7alc Dinner £9.75-£10.75&alc Last dinner 8.30pm
Credit Cards 1 2 3 5

★★**Rembrandt** 12-16 Dorchester Rd DT4 7JU ☎(0305)780384
Telex no 418154 FAX (0305) 760807
This is a good holiday hotel, with well-equipped bedrooms, a good restaurant and leisure facilities.
70rm(49⇌12♠)(34fb) CTV in all bedrooms ® T
sB&B£30.50-£45 sB&B⇌♠£39.50-£49.50 dB&B£44-£55 dB&B⇌♠£52-£75
Lift (CTV 80P (heated) sauna solarium jacuzzi steam room ♫
V ♥ Bar Lunch £1.50-£6 High tea £1.50-£5 Dinner £7-£15 Last dinner 10pm
Credit Cards 1 2 3 4 5

★★**Hotel Rex** 29 The Esplanade DT4 8DN ☎(0305)760400
Closed Xmas
The hotel has a terraced Georgian façade and offers views across Weymouth Bay.
31rm(17⇌14♠)(5fb) CTV in all bedrooms ® T ✳
sB&B⇌♠£25-£32 dB&B⇌♠£46-£62
Lift (CTV 6 (£1 per night)
International V ♥ Dinner £6.50-£6.50&alc Last dinner 10.30pm
Credit Cards 1 2 3 £

★★**Streamside** 29 Preston Rd DT3 6PX ☎Preston(0305)833121
This privately owned mock Tudor hotel has a friendly, informal atmosphere and offers small but well-appointed bedrooms and comfortable public rooms.
15rm(10⇌1♠)(4fb) CTV in all bedrooms ® T sB&B£27-£32 sB&B⇌♠£29-£36 dB&B£40-£48 dB&B⇌♠£47-£58
35P ✽ games room
English & French V ♥ Sunday Lunch £9.25 Dinner £9.75&alc Last dinner 9.30pm
Credit Cards 1 2 3 5 £

WHEDDON CROSS Somerset Map **03** SS93

★★**Raleigh Manor**
TA4 7BB
☎Timberscombe (064384)484 due to change to (0643) 841484
Closed Nov-Feb

The pleasant detached property, built a hundred years ago and offering fine views of surrounding countryside, is comfortable and well-appointed throughout. Friendly owners offer attentive service, and well-prepared meals based on fresh ingredients are attractively served.
7rm(5⇌2♠)1 CTV in all bedrooms ®
sB&B⇌♠£32-£38 dB&B⇌♠£64-£76 (incl dinner)
8P ✽ nc8yrs
♥ Dinner fr£12.50 Last dinner 8pm
Credit Cards 3

The AA's star-rating scheme is the market leader in hotel classification.

WHIDDON DOWN Devon Map **03** SX69

○***Granada Lodge*** (Granada) ☎Central reservation 05255-5555
Due to have opened autumn 1989
32⇔

WHIMPLE Devon Map **03** SY09

★★Woodhayes EX5 2TD
☎(0404)822237

Conveniently situated between Exeter and Honiton near the cider apple village ofWhimple, this fine Georgian house is managed by the friendly and enthusiastic Rendle family. The charming public rooms include two comfortable lounges and a pretty dining room with polished mahogany tables. Bedrooms are, in general, spacious and comfortably furnished, offering modern facilities whilst still retaining much of their original character.
6rm(5⇔) CTV in all bedrooms T ✱ sB&B⇔fr£55 dB&B⇔fr£75
20P 2 ✱ croquet nc12yrs *xmas*
English & French V Lunch fr£14 High tea fr£8 Dinner fr£15
Credit Cards 1 2 3 5

WHITBY North Yorkshire Map **08** NZ81

★★Royal West Cliff YO21 3HA (Consort) ☎(0947)602234
FAX (0947) 820355
An imposing building overlooking the harbour and the Abbey.
134rm(23⇔44♠)(20fb) CTV in 4bedrooms ®
Lift (CTV ♫
English & Continental **V**
Credit Cards 1 2 3 5

★★Saxonville Ladysmith Av, (Off Argyle Road) YO21 3HX
☎(0947)602631
Closed mid Oct-mid May
A pleasant and friendly family-run hotel, offering good food and value for money.
24rm(9⇔12♠)(3fb) CTV in all bedrooms ® S%
sB&Bfr£21.50 sB&B⇔♠fr£23.50 dB&Bfr£43 dB&B⇔♠fr£47
20P
S% Bar Lunch 85p-£8.60alc Dinner fr£10.50&alc Last dinner 8.30pm
Credit Cards 1 2 3 £

★★*Sneaton Hall* Beacon Way, Sneaton YO22 5HP (3m S B1416)
☎(0947)605929
Situated in a peaceful village, just south of Whitby, this is a friendly family-run hotel in an elegant Georgian house.
8rm(4⇔4♠)(2fb) CTV in all bedrooms ®
16P
Last dinner 8.30pm

★★Stakesby Manor High Stakesby YO21 1HL ☎(0947)602773
A comfortable, converted old manor house where good value dinners are especially recommended.
8rm(6⇔2♠) CTV in all bedrooms ® T (ex guide dogs)
sB&B⇔♠£30.50 dB&B⇔♠£44-£46
40P

▶

☺ International V ✿ ☐ Lunch £9.90&alc Dinner £9.90&alc
Last dinner 9.30pm
Credit Cards [1] [3] (£)

★White House Upgang Lane, West Cliff YO21 3JJ
☎(0947)600469 & 602098
This Victorian farmhouse was converted into the present hotel in the 1920's.
12rm(6⇌4↱)(3fb) CTV in all bedrooms ® sB&B£17-£20 sB&B⇌↱£20-£23 dB&B£34-£40 dB&B⇌↱£40-£44 ⊟
CTV 50P ✽ *xmas*
☺ English & French V ✿ Sunday Lunch £5.50 Dinner £8.50-£9.50&alc Last dinner 10pm
Credit Cards [1] [2] [3]

WHITCHURCH Shropshire Map 07 SJ54

★★★62% Dodington Lodge Dodington SY13 1JP (Inter)
☎(0948)2539
A tastefully modernised Georgian house standing at the junction of the A41 and A49, particularly popular for receptions and private functions.
9rm(5⇌2↱)(1fb)1⊠ CTV in all bedrooms ® T ✱ sB&B£32.50-£35 sB&B⇌↱£32.50-£35 dB&B⇌↱£45-£55 ⊟
☾ CTV 70P ✽
V ✿ ☐ Lunch £5.95-£9.50&alc Dinner fr£9.50alc Last dinner 9.30pm
Credit Cards [1] [3] [5]

★★★62% Terrick Hall Country Hill Valley SY13 4JZ (off A49 NE of town centre) (Minotels) ☎(0948)3031
A busy, country house-style hotel, almost surrounded by the local golf course and with well-maintained gardens, an ornamental pool and hard tennis courts.
10⇌(7fb) CTV in all bedrooms ® T ✱ sB&B⇌£26-£29.50 dB&B⇌£41-£45
CTV 50P ✽ ▶9 ♀ (hard) squash snooker sauna
☺ International V ✿ ☐ S% Lunch £3.90-£6.95&alc Dinner £8.95&alc Last dinner 9pm
Credit Cards [1] [2] [3] [5]

★★Redbrook Hunting Lodge Wrexham Rd SY13 3ET (Inter)
☎Redbrook Maelor(094873)204 & 533
(For full entry see Redbrook, Clwyd)

WHITEBRIDGE Highland *Inverness-shire* Map 14 NH41

★★♣ KNOCKIE LODGE
IV1 2UP (Pride of Britain)
☎Gorthleck(04563)276
Closed 30 Oct-29 Apr

Set high above Loch Ness, with magnificent views across rugged slopes, this unique, 200-year-old hotel offers cosy accommodation in well-proportioned, low-ceilinged rooms. The drawing room, with its large open fireplace and well-filled bookcase (with small bar built in) invites relaxation, and a billiard room with full-sized table has now been added for those of a more competitive inclination. A gracious, candle-lit dining room with polished antique tables provides the perfect background against which to enjoy a 5-course dinner for which the menu is changed daily. The wild, unspoiled nature of the surrounding countryside gives rise to a host of outdoor activities, ranging from bird-watching, shooting, painting and photography to sailing and deer-stalking. Fishermen are particularly well catered for with brown trout fishing from a variety of surrounding lochs and salmon fishing from the hotel's boat on Loch Ness.
10⇌ sB&B⇌fr£65 dB&B⇌£100-£138 (incl dinner)
20P ⇟ ✽ ↲ snooker sailing nc10yrs
Lunch fr£10 Dinner fr£18 Last dinner 8pm
Credit Cards [1] [2] [3] [5]

★★Whitebridge IV1 2UN (Exec Hotel) ☎Gorthleck(04563)226
A family-run traditional Highland hotel.
12rm(3⇌5↱)(2fb) CTV in all bedrooms ® sB&B£13-£17 sB&B⇌↱£15-£19 dB&B£26-£34 dB&B⇌↱£30-£38
30P (50p) 2⌂ ⇟ ✽ ↲
✿ ☐ Bar Lunch £5-£10alc Dinner £10-£12 Last dinner 9pm
Credit Cards [1] [2] [3] [5] (£)

WHITEBROOK Gwent Map 03 SO50

★★Crown at Whitebrook NP5 4TX (Exec Hotel)
☎Monmouth(0600)860254 Telex no 498280
This pleasant "restaurant with rooms" stands in a quiet wooded valley, yet conveniently near major roads, and offers small comfortable bedrooms and an attractive restaurant and bar.
12⇌1⊠ CTV in all bedrooms ® T sB&B⇌£49.50-£55 dB&B⇌£89-£100 (incl dinner) ⊟
40P ⇟ ✽
☺ French V ✿ ☐ ⚟ Lunch £10.95-£10.95 Dinner £19.50-£19.50 Last dinner 9.30pm
Credit Cards [1] [2] [3] [4] [5]

WHITLAND Dyfed Map 02 SN21

★★★♣62% *Waungron Country Mansion* SA34 0QX (off B4328)
☎(0994)240232

Standing in an elevated position above the village in several acres of attractive grounds, this small family-run hotel offers friendly service and well-equipped comfortable bedrooms.
9rm(7⇌2↱) CTV in all bedrooms T
50P 10⌂ ✽ ↲ ⌂
V ✿ ☐
Credit Cards [1] [3]

★*Waungron Farm* Waungron Isaf SA34 0QX (1m SW off B4328)
☎(0994)240682
Closed Xmas wk
14rm(8⇌6↱)(3fb)1⊠ CTV in all bedrooms ®
CTV 100P ✽ ↲
V ✿ Last dinner 9pm
Credit Cards [1] [3]

WHITLEY BAY Tyne & Wear Map 12 NZ37

★★Holmedale 106 Park Av NE26 1DN ☎091-251 3903 & 091-253 1162 FAX 091-297 0278
Friendly, unpretentious hotel, managed by resident proprietors.
18rm(7⇌9↱)(3fb)1⊠ CTV in 20bedrooms ® T ✱ sB&B£15.50-£25 sB&B⇌↱£21-£35 dB&B£23-£45 dB&B⇌↱£28-£50 ⊟

W

CTV 10P
♀ English & Continental Dinner £6.95-£8.50&alc Last dinner 8pm
Credit Cards 1 2 3 5

★★Windsor South Pde NE25 8UT ☎091-252 3317
Telex no 537388 FAX 091-297 0272
Closed Xmas day
A recently extended and modernised hotel, offering well-equipped bedrooms designed for the business traveller, and tastefully appointed public rooms.
55rm(38⇌5♠)(14fb) CTV in all bedrooms ® T ✱ sB&B£26 sB&B⇌♠£29-£44 dB&B£33-£48 dB&B⇌♠£33-£48 ⊟
Lift ☾ CTV 25P 2♠ *xmas*
♀ European V ♦ ☕
Credit Cards 1 2 3 5 £

★Cavendish 51 Esplanade NE26 2AS ☎091-253 3010
Simple seaside hotel managed by proprietors and his family.
11rm(5⇌1♠)(2fb) CTV in 9bedrooms ® ✱ sB&B£14-£20 sB&B⇌♠£20 dB&B⇌♠£35
CTV 12P
V Sunday Lunch £5.25 Dinner £7.25&alc Last dinner 9.30pm
Credit Cards 1 3

★Downton South Pde NE26 2RE ☎091-252 5941 091-253 0830
A small, family-run hotel, offering comfortable accommodation and friendly service, caters for both the businessman and the family on holiday.
24rm(1⇌8♠)(3fb) CTV in all bedrooms ® T ✱ sB&B£16 sB&B⇌♠£22 dB&B£25 dB&B⇌♠£30
♫
V Dinner £5-£8 Last dinner 8pm
Credit Cards 1 3

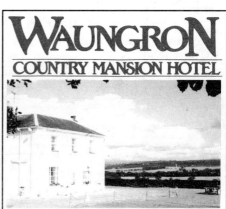

W

★***Park Lodge Hotel*** 160-164 Park Av NE26 1AO ☎091-253 0288
A small, friendly hotel managed by the resident proprietress and offering good value, home cooked dinners.
16rm(2⇨4↱)(4fb) CTV in 11bedrooms ® **T** ✖
CTV 5P ⛟ snooker solarium gymnasium nc
Credit Cards 1 3

WHITTINGTON Shropshire Map **07** SJ33

★**Ye Olde Boot Inn** SY11 4DG (Frederic Robinson)
☎Oswestry(0691)662250
A modernised old inn set in rural surroundings.
6⇨↱(2fb) CTV in all bedrooms ® ✖ (ex guide dogs) ✱
sB&B⇨fr£19 dB&B⇨fr£34.50 ₽
100P
V ♔ ♕ Lunch £4.50

WHITWELL-ON-THE-HILL North Yorkshire Map **08** SE76

★★★ 63% **Whitwell Hall Country House** YO6 7JJ
☎(065381)551
Telex no 57697
FAX (065381) 554
An impressive country house hotel with furnishings which reflect the character of the house. The extensive gardens provide splendid views and tranquility, which together with good dinner menus will ensure an enjoyable visit.
12rm(9⇨3↱)Annexe11rm(8⇨3↱)2⊟ CTV in all bedrooms ® **T** ✖ (ex guide dogs) sB&B⇨↱£45-£56 dB&B⇨↱£63-£95 ₽
40P 4⛟ ✲ ▭(heated) ♪ (hard) sauna croquet putting nc18yrs *xmas*
V ♔ ♕ ⅟ Lunch £10 Dinner £17-£22 Last dinner 8.30pm
Credit Cards 1 2 3

See advertisement under YORK

WICK Highland *Caithness* Map **15** ND35

★★**Mackay's** Union St KW1 5ED ☎(0955)2323
Closed 1-2 Jan
Housed in a Victorian building, the friendly commercial and tourist hotel stands by the River Wick in the town centre. Owners of many years' standing have modernised the interior of the premises to provide up-to-date facilities. Free squash and golf available.
26rm(23⇨1↱)(4fb) CTV in all bedrooms ® **T** ✱
sB&B⇨↱£28 dB&B⇨↱£44 ₽
Lift ☾ CTV 12P ⛟
V ♔ ⅟ Bar Lunch £2.50-£5
Credit Cards 1 3

WICKHAM Hampshire Map **04** SU51

❀★★**Old House** The Square PO17 5JG
☎(0329)833049 FAX (0329) 833672
Closed 10 days Xmas, 2 wks Etr & 2 wks Jul/Aug
A charming small hotel standing in the square at the heart of this conservation village. The restaurant is of particular note where chef Nick Harman cooks in the French Regional style using fresh produce, simply presented, with dishes including terrine de volaille et ris de veau à la pistache, Saumon frais

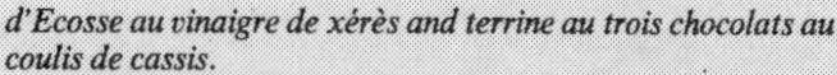

d'Ecosse au vinaigre de xérès and terrine au trois chocolats au coulis de cassis.
9rm(8⇨)(1fb) CTV in all bedrooms **T** ✖ S10%
sB&B⇨£60-£65 dB&B⇨£80-£90
12P ⛟
♕ French **V** S10% Lunch £20.50-£30alc Dinner £20.50-£30alc Last dinner 9.30pm
Credit Cards 1 2 3 5

WICKHAM MARKET Suffolk Map **05** TM35

✕***Bears*** 56 Market Hill ☎(0728)747395
Standing in the middle of the town's market place, this attractive restaurant emphasises the teddy bear theme in a profusion of paintings and prints. Its simple menu features good hearty food – a starter of meat balls in tomato sauce or rich lentil and bacon soup may be followed by chicken with pecan nut and stilton or pork, apple and cider pie, with good old Spotted Dick to follow.
Lunch not served
V 50 seats
Credit Cards 1 3

WIDNES Cheshire Map **07** SJ58

★★**Hill Crest** 75 Cronton Ln WA8 9AR ☎ Liverpool051-424 1616 Telex no 627098 FAX 051-495-1348
57rm(39⇨18↱)(1fb) CTV in all bedrooms ® **T**
sB&B⇨↱£35-£55 dB&B⇨↱£40-£70
Lift ☾ 200P ⛟ ♫ *xmas*
♕ Continental ♔ ♕ Lunch £8.75-£17.50alc Dinner fr£9.25&alc Last dinner 10pm
Credit Cards 1 2 3 5

WIGAN Greater Manchester Map **07** SD50

★★★ 59% ***Brocket Arms*** Mesnes Rd WN1 2DD ☎(0924)46283
Telex no 628117
Close to the town centre and convenient for the M6 motorway, this hotel offers comfortable bars and well-equipped bedrooms. Suites for banquets and conferences are popular with business and leisure users alike.
27rm(25⇨2↱) CTV in all bedrooms ® **T** ✖
☾ 60P
V ♔ Last dinner 9.30pm
Credit Cards 1 2 3 5

★★★ 64% **Kilhey Court Hotel** WN1 2XN (Best Western)
☎Standish(0257)423083 422040 Telex no 67460
FAX 0257 423083
(For full entry see Standish)

★★**Bel-Air** 236 Wigan Ln WM1 2NU ☎(0942)41410
FAX (0942) 43967
Conveniently located a mile north of the town centre and close to the A49, this small, friendly hotel, personally run by the proprietors, offers a pleasant bar and lounge facilities as well as its compact but well appointed bedrooms.
12rm(10⇨2↱)(3fb)1⊟ CTV in all bedrooms ® **T** ✱
sB&B⇨↱fr£28 dB&B⇨↱fr£38 ₽
CTV 12P
♕ English & Continental **V** ♔ ♕ Lunch £4-£6
Credit Cards 1 3

★★**Bellingham** Wigan Ln WN1 2NB ☎(0942)43893
A commercial hotel, off the A49 on the north side of town.
30⇨↱(4fb)2⊟⅟in 4 bedrooms CTV in all bedrooms ® **T** ✖ (ex guide dogs) ✱ sB&B⇨↱£25-£36 dB&B⇨↱£37-£48 ₽
Lift ☾ CTV 35P
♕ English & French **V** ♔ ♕ ⅟
Credit Cards 1 2 3 £

WIGHT, ISLE OF Map 04

BEMBRIDGE Map 04 SZ68

★★Birdham 1 Steyne Rd PO35 5UH
☎Isle of Wight(0983)872875
Small comfortable inn with good cuisine.
14rm(12⇌)(5fb)⊬in 4 bedrooms CTV in all bedrooms ® ✱
sB&B£15 sB&B⇌£18 dB&B£30 dB&B⇌£36
☾ CTV 100P ✼ pool table petanque ⌂
♉ Continental **V** ✪ ⊬ Lunch £10-£20alc Dinner £8.50-£25alc
Last dinner 10pm

BONCHURCH See Bembridge

CHALE Map 04 SZ47

★Clarendon Hotel & Wight Mouse Inn PO38 2HA
☎Isle of Wight(0983)730431
Built in or around 1845 to bridge the gap between Casey's Cottage and the historic White Mouse, the hotel now offers a choice of comfortable, family-style bedrooms, extensive bar meals and popular live entertainment, which, coupled with friendly service, ensures a pleasant and lively atmosphere. A link with the past is provided by the panelling in the bar, which was rescued from the wreck of the Varvassi.
13rm(2⇌7↱)(9fb) CTV in all bedrooms ® sB&B£19.50
sB&B⇌↱£21.85 dB&B£39 dB&B⇌↱£43.70
CTV 200P ✼ boule pool ♫ ⌂
V ✪ ⊻ Lunch £4-£8 Dinner £6-£14 Last dinner 10pm
Ⓔ

COWES Map 04 SZ49

See also **Whippingham**

★★Cowes 260 Artic Rd PO31 7PJ ☎Isle of Wight(0983)291541
Telex no 86284
Closed 27 Dec-1 Jan
Modernised former public house with comfortably appointed bedrooms and friendly atmosphere.
18rm(11⇌7↱)(1fb) CTV in 15bedrooms ✱
sB&B⇌↱fr£34.50 dB&B⇌↱fr£48.30 ⊟
☾ 24P ⛟ sauna
♉ English & French **V** ✪ ⊻ Lunch £11.95-£14.45alc High tea fr£1.70 Dinner £11.95-£14.45alc Last dinner 9.30pm
Credit Cards [1] [2] [3] [5]

See advertisement on page 703

★★*Fountain* High St PO31 7AN ☎Isle of Wight(0983)292397
Located in West Cowes, alongside the Cowes Ferry and Hydrofoil Terminal and the Quay, this popular coaching inn is ideally placed for business travellers. Accommodation comprises well-equipped, modern bedrooms, the popular Henekey Restaurant and the lively Quayside Bar. Car parking can be difficult.
20⇌ CTV in all bedrooms ® **T** ✖ (ex guide dogs)
Ᵽ ⛟
♉ European **V** ✪ ⊻ Last dinner 10.30pm
Credit Cards [1] [2] [3] [4] [5]

✕Sullivan's 10 Bath Rd, The Parade PO31 7QN
☎Isle of Wight(0983)297021
Small cottage-style restaurant run by chef/patron, Michael Sullivan, formerly of the Café des Amis du Vin in Covent Garden, and his wife. The short menu features both new style and classical dishes. Fresh ingredients are prepared with care and flavours and clear and well defined.
♉ French 42 seats ✱ Lunch £12-£15.50alc Dinner
£12-£15.50alc Last lunch 3pm Last dinner 11.30pm Ᵽ
Credit Cards [1] [2] [3]

For key to symbols see the inside front cover.

FRESHWATER Map 04 SZ38

★★★ 50% Albion PO40 9RA ☎Isle of Wight(0983)753631
FAX (0983) 755295
This developing hotel stands in a unique sea-shore position, most of its bedroomhaving a balcony or terrace facing the sea; a new cocktail lounge has recently been added, and bedroom refurbishment is planned. Good standards of cooking are complemented by acceptable service, though management can be uneven.
43⇌↱(28fb) CTV in all bedrooms ® **T** sB&B£21-£23
sB&B⇌↱£26.50-£29.50 dB&B£42-£46 dB&B⇌↱£51-£56 ⊟
☾ CTV 75P ⛟ *xmas*
♉ International **V** ✪ ⊻ Lunch £9-£10.50&alc Dinner £12-£13
Last dinner 9pm
Credit Cards [1] [2] [3] [5]

NEWPORT Map 04 SZ48

★★*Bugle* High St PO30 1TP ☎(0983)522800 Telex no 86479
This hotel with royal connections and an historic background, a popular meeting place for 300 years, offers a variety of well-equipped bedrooms complemented by the Henekey Restaurant and a comfortably furnished bar; friendly service is provided throughout.
26rm(25⇌1↱)1⊞ CTV in all bedrooms ® **T** ✖ (ex guide dogs)
☾ 35P ⛟
♉ European **V** ✪ Last dinner 10.30pm
Credit Cards [1] [2] [3] [5]

RYDE Map 04 SZ59

★★★ 61% Hotel Ryde Castle The Esplanade PO33 1JA
☎Isle of Wight(0983)63755 Telex no 869466
FAX (0983) 616436
An unusual castle-style building offering excellent sea views and an informal, relaxed atmosphere. Many of the comfortable bedrooms have four poster beds and are well-equipped with modern facilities. The restaurant, decorated to resemble the interior of a galleon, offers an interesting menu featuring French and English cuisine of a good standard.
17rm(10⇌7↱)7⊞⊬in 1 bedroom CTV in all bedrooms ® **T**
sB&B⇌↱£34.50-£60 dB&B⇌↱£69-£100 ⊟
75P ⛟ ♫
♉ English & French **V** ✪ ⊻ Lunch £2.50-£6.50&alc Dinner fr£11.45&alc Last dinner 9.45pm
Credit Cards [1] [3]

★★Biskra House Beach 17 St Thomas's St PO33 2OL
☎Isle of Wight(0983)67913
This charming small family-run hotel has a friendly atmosphere and a choice of bedrooms equipped to the highest standards. There are two restaurants, one offering an international menu, the other fondues, both of a high standard, alsoa beachside patio, small bar and cosy lounge.
9rm(4⇌5↱) CTV in all bedrooms **T** ✖ ✱ S% sB&B⇌↱fr£28
dB&B⇌↱£46-£56 ⊟
14P ⛟
♉ French & Italian ✪ ⊻ Lunch £3.95-£10&alc Dinner fr£12.95&alc Last dinner 10.30pm
Credit Cards [1] [3] Ⓔ

See advertisement on page 703

★★Yelf's Union St PO33 2LG (Trusthouse Forte) ☎(0983)64062
Conveniently located in the town centre, with parking facilities nearby, this former coaching inn dates from the early 19th century. Bedrooms are well equipped, and guests can enjoy a meal in the relaxing, friendly restaurant or try the popular lunchtime bar buffet.
21⇌(2fb)⊬in 2 bedrooms CTV in all bedrooms ® ✱
sB⇌fr£50 dB⇌fr£67 (room only) ⊟
Ᵽ *xmas*

▶

☋ English V ♔ ⚐ ⅟ Lunch £7.60-£7.60 Dinner £10-£10&alc
Last dinner 9pm
Credit Cards 1 2 3 4 5

ST LAWRENCE Map **04** SZ57

★★***Rocklands*** PO38 1XH ☎Ventnor(0983)852964
Closed Nov-Apr
A very friendly family hotel with many facilities for children.
16rm(10⇌6♠)Annexe5rm(1⇌)(9fb)1⊞ CTV in all bedrooms ⅟
CTV 18P ❖ ⇌(heated) snooker sauna solarium ⌂
☋ English & Continental V ♔ ⚐ Last dinner 8.15pm

★**The Lawyers Rest** Undercliff Dr PO38 1XF
☎Isle of Wight(0983)852610
RS Oct-Mar
Looking across gardens to the sea from its fine position on a terraced hillside, this impressive and elegantly furnished house, built in 1840, boasts a relaxing drawing room and separate cocktail bar, complemented by a modern restaurant serving fine, freshly produced food and excellent wines. Bedrooms are individually furnished, some enjoying sea views, and friendly service is supervised by the proprietor.
8rm(4⇌4♠) sB&B⇌♠£28-£29.50
dB&B⇌♠£56-£59 (incl dinner)
13P nc10 *xmas*
☋ English/International V ♔ ⚐ Bar Lunch £1.50-£4alc
Credit Cards 2 3

SANDOWN Map **04** SZ58

★★★55% **Melville Hall** Melville St PO36 9DH
☎Isle of Wight(0983)406526
Melville Hall is quietly situated within its own mature grounds, yet is within easy reach of the shops and the seafront. There has been extensive renovation in recent years, amd public rooms are attractive and bedrooms are well-equipped. The coffee shop and restaurant offer a varied choice, and the service is friendly and well-managed.
33rm(29⇌4♠)(11fb) CTV in all bedrooms ® T ⅟ (ex guide dogs) sB&B⇌♠£30-£40 dB&B⇌♠£60-£80 (incl dinner) ⊟
30P ❖ ⇌(heated) games room 9 hole putting *xmas*
☋ English & Continental V ♔ ⚐ Lunch £6.50 Dinner fr£11.95&alc Last dinner 9.30pm
Credit Cards 1 3 £

SEAVIEW Map **04** SZ69

❀★★**Seaview** High St PO34 5EX
☎Isle of Wight(0983)612711
The heart of this seaside hotel must be the dining room, where young chef Charles Bartlett produces unpretentious, but innovative cuisine, using mostly local produce and seafood. The rest of the hotel has charm too, however Bedrooms are individually styled and thoughtfully provided with many extras, and a drawing room, coffee lounge and ward room are also available. The owners are Nicholas and Nicola Hayward, who personally supervise the extensive services.
16rm(14⇌2♠)(2fb) CTV in all bedrooms
sB&B⇌♠£33-£48 dB&B⇌♠£55-£64 ⊟
12P ⊞ *xmas*
☋ English & French V ♔ ⚐ ⅟ Lunch £9.90-£16.85alc
Dinner £9.90-£16.85alc Last dinner 9.30pm
Credit Cards 1 2 3

Book as early as possible for busy holiday periods.

SHANKLIN Map **04** SZ58

★★★58% **Cliff Tops** Park Rd PO37 6BB (Best Western)
☎Isle of Wight(0983)863262 Telex no 869441
FAX (0983) 867139
Cliff Tops boasts a superb position with glorious sea views from the front bedrooms and balconies. There is a direct lift access to the beach below, and recent refurbishment has improved the accommodation and leisure facilities. There is a popular carvery restaurant and live bar entertainment most evenings.
88⇌♠(8fb) CTV in all bedrooms ® T ✱ sB&B⇌♠£45-£49
dB&B⇌♠£65-£69 ⊟
Lift (40P CFA ⊡(heated) snooker sauna solarium gymnasium steam room beautician hairdresser ♫ *xmas*
V ♔ ⚐ Lunch £5.50-£7.50 Dinner £11.50-£12&alc Last dinner 10pm
Credit Cards 1 2 3 5

★★★57% **Holliers** Church Rd, Old Village PO37 6NU
☎Isle of Wight(0983)862764
Conveniently situated for the town centre and all local amenities, Holliers offers comfortable well-equipped bedrooms, several bars, pleasant restaurant and good indoor leisure facilities.
37rm(30⇌7♠)(7fb)3⊞ CTV in all bedrooms ® T ⅟ ✱
sB&B⇌♠£27-£29 dB&B⇌♠£54-£58
40P ⊡(heated) ⇌(heated) sauna solarium ♫ *xmas*
♔ ⚐ Bar Lunch fr£2.50 Dinner fr£9.75 Last dinner 8.30pm
Credit Cards 1 2 3

★★**Fernbank** Highfield Rd PO37 6PP
☎Isle of Wight(0983)862790
Closed Jan
Located in a peaceful setting there are good views of the countryside, and guests can relax in the hotel's sheltered garden. There is a comfortable lobby lounge, bar and good leisure facilities, and friendly attentive service is supervised by the resident proprietors, Mr. and Mrs. Sladden.
20rm(8⇌9♠)Annexe3rm(6fb)1⊞ CTV in all bedrooms ® T
sB&B⇌♠£26.30-£32 dB&B⇌♠£52.60-£64 (incl dinner) ⊟
20P ❖ ⊡(heated) sauna solarium pool table whirlpool bath nc7yrs
V ♔ ⚐ ⅟ Bar Lunch £2-£4 Dinner £8.50 Last dinner 8pm
Credit Cards 1 3

★★**Luccombe Hall** Luccombe Rd PO37 6RL (Exec Hotel)
☎Isle of Wight(0983)862719 FAX (0983) 867482
RS Jan
Overlooking the sea and Culver Down, Luccombe Hall is set in a quiet residential area. The comfortable bedrooms are complemented by excellent leisure facilities.
31rm(27⇌3♠)(15fb) CTV in all bedrooms ® T
sB&B⇌♠£28-£35 dB&B⇌♠£46-£60 ⊟
CTV 30P ❖ ⊡(heated) ⇌(heated) ℘ (grass) squash sauna solarium gymnasium games room *xmas*
☋ English & Continental ♔ ⚐ ⅟ Bar Lunch £1-£3.50 Dinner fr£12.75 Last dinner 8pm
Credit Cards 1 3

See advertisement on page 705

★★**Melbourne Ardenlea** Queen's Rd PO37 6AP
☎Isle of Wight(0983)862283
Closed Dec-Feb RS Mar & late Oct
An ideal family hotel, there is a good choice of family bedrooms, and good leisure facilities. Excellent value for money.
51rm(44⇌7♠)(9fb) CTV in all bedrooms ® ✱
sB&B⇌♠£17-£23 dB&B⇌♠£34-£46
Lift CTV 28P ❖ ⊡(heated) sauna solarium games room spa bath ♫
☋ English & French V Lunch £5-£7 Dinner £7-£9&alc Last dinner 8pm
Credit Cards 1 3 £

Wight, Isle of

★★*Shanklin Manor House* Church Rd, Old Village PO37 6QX
☎Isle of Wight(0983)862777
Closed mid Nov-mid Jan
This is a Victorian hotel, situated away from the seafront in semi-rural surroundings, with spacious bedrooms and good leisure facilities.
38rm(21⇨12↱)(12fb) CTV in all bedrooms ® ✗
50P ❋ ⛀(heated) ⚲ (hard) sauna solarium gymnasium spa bath putting croquet ♫ nc6mths
☋ English & French ✪ ⚞

✕**La Petite Maison** 34 High St PO37 6JY
☎Isle of Wight(0983)863205
A small French restaurant combines interesting à la carte French-style cuisine with some fresh fish and Italian dishes. Popular, value for money choices include the smoked trout mousse, fish bisque, Supreme of Chicken and Beef Wellington; all dishes are freshly cooked and well presented.
☋ Continental V 23 seats ✱ Lunch £10-£15alc Dinner £15-£25alc Last lunch 2.30pm Last dinner 10.30pm ⚑
Credit Cards 1 2 3 5

TOTLAND BAY Map 04 SZ38

★★*Country Garden* Church Hill PO39 0ET (Inter)
☎Isle of Wight(0983)754521 Telex no 94017218
Quietly situated in 2 acres of mature grounds, this hotel offers spacious modern bedrooms, cosy lounge, bar and a popular restaurant with good standards of cooking. The service is friendly and professional.
16⇨↱Annexe2rm CTV in all bedrooms ® T
☾ 30P 2🚗 ❋ nc14
☋ English & French V ✪ ⚞ Last dinner 9.30pm
Credit Cards 1 2 3 5

★★*Sentry Mead* Madeira Rd PO39 0BJ
☎Isle of Wight(0983)753212
This is a pleasant, cosy, personally-run hotel. The comfortable lounges are a feature here, and the newly-furnished bedrooms have modern facilities.
12rm(8⇨2↱)(4fb) CTV in all bedrooms ®
CTV 10P ⛟ ❋ putting
☋ European ✪ ⚞ Last dinner 8pm
Credit Cards 2

VENTNOR Map 04 SZ57

★★★50% **Royal** Belgrave Rd PO38 1JJ (Trusthouse Forte)
☎Isle of Wight(0983)852186
Well-appointed hotel overlooking the sea, with many other facilities.
54⇨(6fb)⚟in 4 bedrooms CTV in all bedrooms ® ✱
sB⇨fr£55 dB⇨fr£77 (room only) ⛿
Lift 56P ❋ CFA ⛀(heated) snooker *xmas*
V ✪ ⚞ ⚟ Bar Lunch fr£4 Dinner fr£11.50&alc Last dinner 9pm
Credit Cards 1 2 3 4 5

★★★62% ***Ventnor Towers*** Madeira Rd PO38 1QT (Consort)
☎Isle of Wight(0983)852277 Telex no 8951182
FAX (0983) 855536
Commanding fine sea views from its cliff-top location, this upgraded, family-run hotel offers comfortable accommodation, a warm, friendly atmosphere and excellent outdoor sporting facilities.
27rm(17⇨5↱)(4fb) CTV in 30bedrooms ® T
☾ 40P 1🚗 ❋ ⛀(heated) ⚑ 9 ⚲ (hard) croquet games room
☋ English & French V ✪ ⚞ ⚟ Last dinner 8.30pm
Credit Cards 1 2 3 5

For key to symbols see the inside front cover.

★🏰**Madeira Hall** Trinity Rd PO38 1NS
☎Isle of Wight (0983)852624
Closed Nov-mid Mar
A charming, tranquil hotel, beautifully situated in peaceful surroundings, offers charmingly decorated, spacious bedrooms, comfortable lounges with carved oak fireplaces and an informal, homely atmosphere.
12rm(6⇨2↱)(4fb) CTV in all bedrooms ® ✱ S5%
sB&B£20 sB&B⇨↱£22.50 dB&B£40 dB&B⇨↱£45
CTV 12P ⛟ ❋ ⛀(heated) putting
✪ S5% Lunch fr£6.50&alc Dinner fr£6.50&alc Last dinner 7.30pm
Credit Cards 1 2 3

WOOTTON Map 04 SZ58

✕**Lugley's** Staplers Rd PO33 4RW ☎Isle of Wight(0983)882202
Chef/proprietor Angela Hewitt's individual style and attention to detail is very evident – the short menu here includes local game, homemade breads and some of her own specialities, and portions are generous. Reservations are carefully timed to allow for everything being cooked 'à la minute'. The good food is complemented by the quiet country setting of this Edwardian house.
Closed Sun 2 wks Nov & 2 wks Apr
Lunch not served in winter (ex prior arrangement)
16 seats ✱ Lunch fr£12.95 Dinner £16-£23alc Last lunch 2pm Last dinner 9.30pm 10P nc12yrs 2 bedrooms available

WIGTON Cumbria Map 11 NY24

★★**Greenhill Lodge** Red Dial CA7 8LS (2m S off A595)
☎(0965)43304
A converted 17th-century manor house, standing off the A595, serves extensive, good-quality, home-made bar meals and dinners.
7rm(6⇨1↱)2⛟ CTV in all bedrooms ® T ✱
sB&B⇨↱£27.50 dB&B⇨↱£40 ⛿
100P ❋ *xmas*
☋ International V ✪ Lunch £5.50-£13.50 Dinner £13.50 Last dinner 9pm
Credit Cards 1 3 £

★★***Wheyrigg Hall*** CA7 0DH (4m NW on B5302)
☎Abbeytown(09656)242
Conveniently situated on B5302 between Silloth and Wigton, the family-run hotel is a converted farmhouse. In addition to its very busy and popular restaurant, it offers six comfortable and well-appointed bedrooms.
6rm(2⇨)(2fb) CTV in all bedrooms ® ✗
⊞ 60P ❋ ♫
V ✪ ⚞
Credit Cards 1 2 3 4 5

Entries for rosetted restaurants, red-star and country-house hotels are highlighted by a tinted panel. For a full list of these establishments, consult the Contents page.

WILLERBY Humberside Map **08** TA03

★★★75% **Grange Park** Main St HU10 6EA (Best Western)
☎Hull(0482)656488 Telex no 592773 FAX (0482) 655848
Extensive leisure facilities are a feature at this very comfortable hotel. There are two restaurants – French and Italian – both offering interesting and extensive menus.
50rm(45⇨5↱)1⊟ CTV in all bedrooms ® T sB&B⇨↱£58 dB&B⇨↱£71 ⊟
Lift ☾ ⊞ 300P ✲ ⊡(heated) sauna solarium gymnasium hairdressing ♫ *xmas*
☋ English, French & Italian ♱ ⊻
Credit Cards 1 2 3 5 £

★★★69% **Willerby Manor** Well Ln HU10 6ER
☎Hull(0482)652616 Telex no 592629 FAX (0482) 653901
This attractive old manor house has had two bedroom wings added, providing comfortable well-equipped rooms. Two restaurants offer good value for money.
34rm(31⇨3↱)(1fb) CTV in all bedrooms ® **T** ✗ (ex guide dogs) sB⇨↱£37.50-£51 dB⇨↱£49-£62 (room only) ⊟
☾ 250P ✲ CFA *xmas*
☋ French **V** ♱ ⊻ Lunch £7.95-£9&alc Dinner £10&alc Last dinner 9.45pm
Credit Cards 1 2 3 £

See advertisement under HULL

WILLITON Somerset Map **03** ST04

❀★★ ***White House*** Long St TA4 4QW
☎(0984)32306
Closed Nov-16 May
(Rosette awarded for dinner only)
Kay and Dick Smith are in their 22nd year at this Georgian house, and have made a name for good cooking and accommodation. Their pleasantly uncomplicated dishes are prepared from quality ingredients, including good, fresh fish. Comfortable bedrooms range from country style to more modern in the courtyard rooms.
8rm(5⇨)Annexe5rm(4⇨)(1fb) CTV in all bedrooms
15P ✗
☋ English & French Last dinner 8.30pm

WILMCOTE Warwickshire Map **04** SP15

★★**Swan House** The Green CV37 9XJ ☎Stratford-upon-Avon(0789)67030
RS 24-28 Dec
Recent refurbishment has resulted in light, fresh bedrooms, all with good modern bathrooms. New public areas offer spacious comfort, but the character of this village inn has been retained – the well in the bar is an attractive feature.
12rm(6⇨6↱)(1fb)1⊟ CTV in all bedrooms ® ✗ (ex guide dogs) sB&B⇨↱£30-£38 dB&B⇨↱£48-£60 ⊟
40P ✲ snooker ♫
☋ English & French **V** ♱ ⊻ S% Sunday Lunch £7.50-£8 Dinner £6-£12alc Last dinner 9.30pm
Credit Cards 1 2 3 £

See advertisement under STRATFORD-UPON-AVON

WILMSLOW Cheshire Map **07** SJ88

See also **Manchester Airport**

❀★★★71% **Stanneylands** Stanneylands Rd SK9 4EY
☎(0625)525225 Telex no 8950511 FAX (0625)537282
RS 1 Jan & Good Fri
▶

W

Set in its own well-kept grounds and surrounded by farmland, yet not far from Manchester Airport, this attractive, family-managed hotel features a classical interior. The fine, oak-panelled dining room provides an ideal environment in which to enjoy your choice from the innovative short à la carte menu, the 'market special' or a table d'hôte 5-course dinner, dishes such as fillet of seabass cooked with ginger and roast Gressingham duck in a patchwork of puréed vegetables being backed up by an impressive wine list. All bedrooms are comfortable, well equipped and pleasantly decorated, though some are more compact than others.

33⇌↱2⊞ CTV in all bedrooms **T** ✗ sB⇌↱£68-£85 dB⇌↱£78-£85 (room only) ⊟

☾80P ⊞ ✲

V ♧ ⊡ Lunch fr£9 Dinner fr£20 Last dinner 10pm

Credit Cards 1 2 3 5

WIMBORNE MINSTER Dorset Map **04** SZ09

★★★57% **The King's Head** The Square BH21 1JA (Trusthouse Forte) ☎(0202)880101

This busy, country town hotel offers comfortable well-appointed public areas, an attractive restaurant with table d'hote and a la carte menus, and well-equipped bedrooms of good size. Service is provided by friendly, willing staff.

27⇌(1fb)⊬in 3 bedrooms CTV in all bedrooms ® sB⇌£58-£63 dB⇌£74-£79 (room only) ⊟

Lift CTV 25P *xmas*

V ♧ ⊡ ⊬ Lunch £10.50&alc Dinner £12.50&alc Last dinner 9pm

Credit Cards 1 2 3 4 5

★★**Coach House Inn** Tricketts Cross BH22 9NW (Consort) ☎Ferndown(0202)861222 Telex no 265871 FAX (0202) 894130

(For full entry see Ferndown)

WINCANTON Somerset Map **03** ST72

★★**Holbrook House** Holbrook BA9 8BS

☎(0963)32377

Closed New Year's Eve

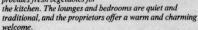

This comfortable country-house hotel stands in 15 acres of grounds. A walled garden provides fresh vegetables for the kitchen. The lounges and bedrooms are quiet and traditional, and the proprietors offer a warm and charming welcome.

20rm(8⇌6↱)(2fb) ® **T** ✗ sB&B⇌↱£35-£43 dB&B£60 dB&B⇌↱£65 ⊟

CTV 30P 4⊞ ⊞ ✲ ⇌(heated) ℘ (hard & grass) squash croquet table tennis *xmas*

V ♧ Lunch £5.50-£10&alc Dinner £14&alc Last dinner 8.30pm

Credit Cards 1 2 3

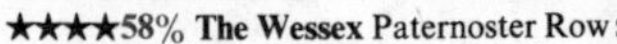

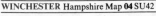

WINCHESTER Hampshire Map **04** SU42

★★★★58% **The Wessex** Paternoster Row SO23 9LQ (Trusthouse Forte) ☎(0962)61611 Telex no 47419 FAX (0962) 841503

Conveniently located next to the Cathedral precinct, this modern hotel offers a varied selection of bedrooms, equipped and furnished to several different standards. For meals, guests can choose between the coffee shop and Waltons Restaurant, and there is also a popular cocktail lounge.

94rm(92⇌2↱)⊬in 9 bedrooms CTV in all bedrooms ® **T** S% sB⇌↱fr£74.50 dB⇌↱fr£91 (room only) ⊟

Lift ☾ 25P 40⊞ CFA *xmas*

♕ French **V** ♧ ⊡ ⊬ S% Lunch fr£11.50&alc High tea fr£5 Dinner fr£17 Last dinner 10pm

Credit Cards 1 2 3 4 5

❀75% ★★★**Lainston House** Sparsholt SO21 2LT (3m NW off A272) (Prestige)

☎(0962)63588

Telex no 477375

FAX (0962) 72672

(Rosette awarded for dinner only)

Gracious luxury is a feature in this charming William and Mary house, set in 63 acres of parkland. The public rooms are elegantly furnished and the attractive, well-kept bedrooms are individually designed – the hotel has a reputation for quality modern British cuisine, coupled with traditional sauces, flavours and portions. Fine fresh ingredients are used, including local game and fish from Cornwall.

32rm(30⇌1↱)(1fb) CTV in all bedrooms **T** sB⇌↱fr£75 dB⇌↱fr£90 (room only) ⊟

☾ 150P ⊞ ✲ ⌡ riding croquet clay pigeon shoot ♫ ⌂ *xmas*

♕ English & French **V** ♧ ⊡ Lunch £14-£20alc Dinner £23-£34alc Last dinner 10pm

Credit Cards 1 2 3 4 5

See advertisement on page 709

★★★63% **Royal** St Peter St SO23 8BS (Best Western) ☎(0962)840840 Telex no 477071 FAX (0962) 841582

Once a convent, this well-managed hotel is a peaceful haven in the centre of the city. A modern bedroom extension, overlooking the colourful gardens, provides particularly comfortable, modern bedrooms. There is an attractive conservatory style restaurant.

59⇌↱(4fb)1⊞ CTV in all bedrooms ® **T** sB⇌↱£64.50-£75 dB⇌↱£78.50-£91 (room only) ⊟

☾ 60P ✲ fly fishing *xmas*

♕ English & French ♧ ⊡ S10% Lunch £9 Dinner £15&alc Last dinner 9.30pm

Credit Cards 1 2 3 5

★★★61% **Saxon Court** Worthy Ln SO23 7AB (Consort) ☎(0962)68102 Telex no 47383 FAX (0962) 840862

Sited on the former coach station, near to a car park, this purpose-built hotel offers well-equipped bedrooms and a restaurant featuring table d'hôte menus.

70⇌↱(6fb)⊬in 20 bedrooms CTV in all bedrooms ® **T** sB⇌↱£62.50-£75 dB⇌↱£75-£85 (room only) ⊟

☾ CTV 65P ⊡(heated) sauna solarium gymnasium *xmas*

♕ English & French **V** ♧ ⊡ Lunch £9.50-£12.50&alc Dinner £13.50-£15&alc Last dinner 9.45pm

Credit Cards 1 2 3 5

W

WINDERMERE Cumbria Map **07** SD49

See **Town Plan Section**

★★★★ 57% **The Old England** Church St, Bowness LA23 3DF (Trusthouse Forte) ☎(09662)2444 Telex no 65194 FAX (09662) 3432

Set in a stunning Lakeside position with views of the fells, this rambling, 4-storey Georgian hotel provides a wide range of bedrooms and an elegant, spaciously comfortable lounge. The traditional menus offered in its restaurant are complemented by service of a high standard.

82⇌(8fb)⊬in 6 bedrooms CTV in all bedrooms ® **T** S% sB⇌£57-£67 dB⇌£90-£105 (room only) ⊟

Lift ☾ 80P ✲ CFA ⛆(heated) croquet golf driving net ♫ *xmas*

V ♡ ⊈ ⊬ S% Lunch £6.95-£8.50 Dinner £12.95 Last dinner 9.30pm

Credit Cards 1 2 3 4 5

★★★ 56% **Beech Hill** Newby Bridge Rd, Cartmel Fell LA23 3LR (Trusthouse Forte) ☎(09662)2137 Telex no 65156 FAX (09962) 3745

Leisure facilities are a feature of this hotel.

47rm(37⇌10↱)(4fb)⊬in 11 bedrooms CTV in all bedrooms ® **T** ✱ sB⇌↱fr£49 dB⇌↱fr£64 (room only) ⊟

☾ 50P ✲ CFA ⛆(heated) sauna solarium *xmas*

♡ British & French **V** ♡ ⊈ ⊬ Lunch £3.95-£6.95 High tea £3.95-£5.75 Dinner £11.50-£12.50&alc Last dinner 9.30pm

Credit Cards 1 2 3 4 5

★★★ 58% **The Belsfield** Kendal Rd, Bowness LA23 3EL (Trusthouse Forte) ☎(09662)2448 Telex no 65238 FAX (09662) 6397

This popular holiday and business hotel is attractively set in 6 acres of gardens overlooking the lake. There is a good range of leisure and conference facilities.

66rm(48⇌18↱)2⊞⊬in 6 bedrooms CTV in all bedrooms ® **T** sB⇌↱£54-£65 dB⇌↱£72-£82 (room only) ⊟

Lift ☾ 80P ✲ CFA ⛆(heated) ℛ (grass) sauna solarium mini golf putting green ♫ *xmas*

♡ French **V** ♡ ⊈ ⊬ Sunday Lunch £8.50-£9.50 High tea £4-£6 Dinner £13-£15&alc Last dinner 9.30pm

Credit Cards 1 2 3 4 5

★★★ 62% **Burn How Garden House Hotel, Motel & Rest** Back Belsfield Rd, Bowness LA23 3HH ☎(09662)6226

This hotel is delightfully situated in a slightly elevated position above Lake Windermere. Accommodation is available in family chalets, a recently modernised Victorian house, or in a purpose-built wing offering sun balconies and four-poster beds. The attractive restaurant specialises in English and French cuisine.

Annexe26⇌↱(10fb)4⊞ CTV in all bedrooms ® **T** ✈ sB&B⇌↱£35-£50 dB&B⇌↱£50-£65 ⊟

30P ⊞ ✲ sauna solarium gymnasium water sports ⌂ *xmas*

♡ English & French **V** ♡ ⊬ Bar Lunch £2.50-£10alc Dinner £13.50-£15&alc Last dinner 9pm

Credit Cards 1 2 3 5

★★★ 63% **Burnside** Kendal Road, Bowness LA23 3EP ☎(09662)2211 Telex no 65430 FAX (09662) 3824

This large Victorian house in an elevated position, is steadily being enlarged and improved to provide spacious, comfortable and well-equipped bedrooms. It boasts new leisure facilities which are also part of a time-share complex situated within the hotel grounds.

45⇌(11fb)4⊞ CTV in all bedrooms ® **T** ✱ sB&B⇌£38-£50 dB&B⇌£68-£100 ⊟

Lift 80P ✲ ⛆(heated) squash snooker sauna solarium gymnasium watersports steam room badminton ♫ *xmas*

V ♡ ⊈ Sunday Lunch £6.50-£8.50 High tea £1.95-£5.50 Dinner £12.50-£14&alc Last dinner 9pm

Credit Cards 1 2 3 5 ⓔ

W

★★★*Hydro* Helm Rd, Bowness LA23 3BA (Mount Charlotte) ☎(09662)4455 Telex no 65196
Modernised Victorian hotel overlooking Lake Windermere, with views of the Langdale Pikes.
96⇨↱(9fb) CTV in all bedrooms ®
Lift ☾ 140P
V ♧ Last high tea 6pm
Credit Cards [1] [2] [3] [5]

★★★♛64% Langdale Chase LA23 1LW
☎Ambleside(05394)32201 FAX (05394) 32604

Despite its proximity to the A591, this old hotel retains the air of a country house, with an impressive oak-panelled interior and well-kept gardens running down to Lake Windermere. Bedrooms, though traditional in style, are equipped with modern amenities, some commanding the same lake views as are enjoyed by the terrace and comfortable public areas. For those with a real desire to be close to the water, a boathouse has been converted into a particularly restful bedroom, served as efficiently and caringly as the rest of the hotel.
28rm(18⇨6↱)Annexe7⇨(3fb)2▣ CTV in all bedrooms ® T S% sB&Bfr£33 sB&B⇨↱fr£36 dB&Bfr£66 dB&B⇨↱fr£72 ▤
☾ 36P ⇼ ✲ ♪ (grass) croquet rowing boats putting *xmas*
♉ English & French ♧ ⊈ S% Lunch fr£9 Dinner fr£18 Last dinner 8.45pm
Credit Cards [1] [2] [3] [5]

★★★58% Low Wood LA23 1LP (3m N A591) (Best Western) ☎Ambleside(05394)33338 Telex no 65273 FAX (05394)34072
This large rambling hotel, full of character, stands in spacious gardens and lawns on the northern bank of Lake Windermere.
98rm(92⇨6↱)(10fb)3▣ CTV in all bedrooms ® T S% sB&B⇨↱£49-£99 dB&B⇨↱£98-£145 ▤
Lift ☾ CTV 200P ✲ CFA ⌡ water skiing sub aqua diving ⌂ *xmas*
♉ International V ♧ ⊈ ⊁ S% Sunday Lunch £8-£12 Dinner £15.50&alc Last dinner 9pm
Credit Cards [1] [2] [3] [5] Ⓔ

★★★69% Wild Boar Crook LA23 3NF (2.5m S of Windermere on B5284 Crook road) (Best Western) ☎(09662)5225 Telex no 65464 FAX (09662) 2498
This 18th-century country hotel, in a secluded setting of woodland and fell, hasa good atmosphere and personal attention and service. Low beamed ceilings in the public rooms contribute to the character, and bedrooms offer traditional country-syle comfort and appointments with modern facilities.
36rm(32⇨4↱)(3fb)4▣ CTV in all bedrooms ® T sB&B⇨↱£37-£45 dB&B⇨↱£74-£90 ▤
60P ⇼ ✲ CFA free boat launching facilities ♫ *xmas*
♉ English & French V ♧ ⊈ ⊁ Lunch £4.25-£8.80&alc Dinner £17&alc Last dinner 8.45pm
Credit Cards [1] [2] [3] [4] [5]

★★Applegarth College Rd LA23 1BU ☎(09662)3206
An elegant and individual mansion, built in 1890 and quietly situated within easy reach of all amenities.
15rm(1⇨14↱)(5fb)4▣ CTV in all bedrooms ® T sB&B⇨↱£24-£31 dB&B⇨↱£42-£64 ▤
20P ⇼ *xmas*
V ♧ Bar Lunch £3-£8 Dinner fr£12.50 Last dinner 9pm
Credit Cards [1] [2] [3]

★★Bordriggs Country House Longtail Hill, Bowness LA23 3LD ☎(09662)3567 FAX (09662) 6949
Closed Dec & Jan
Delightfully run by enthusiastic proprietors, this is a comfortable and relaxing hotel with excellent standards. The bedrooms are well-appointed, and there is a comfortable well-furnished lounge and attractive gardens.
9⇨↱Annexe2⇨↱(2fb)1▣⊁in all bedrooms CTV in all bedrooms T ✈ (ex guide dogs) sB&B⇨↱fr£30 dB&B⇨↱fr£55 ▤
☾ 20P ⇼ ✲ ⌓(heated) croquet badminton nc10yrs
♉ English & Continental V

★★Cedar Manor Hotel & Restaurant Ambleside Rd LA23 1AX (Exec Hotel) ☎(09662)3192
This charming and peaceful hotel takes its name from the magnificent 200-year-old cedar tree in the garden. Carefully decorated and furnished by the friendly proprietors, the bedrooms are spacious and well-appointed. There is a cosy bar, and well-prepared food is served in the attractive dining room.
10rm(8⇨2↱) Annexe 2 ⇨(4fb)1▣ CTV in all bedrooms ® T sB&B⇨↱£30-£46.50 dB&B⇨↱£60-£79 (incl dinner) ▤
15P ⇼ ✲ *xmas*
♉ English & French V ♧ ⊈ ⊁ High tea £2.50-£3 Dinner £12.50-£16 Last dinner 8.30pm
Credit Cards [1] [3]

★★Craig Foot Country House Lake Rd, Bowness LA23 3AR ☎(09662)3902
Closed Nov-Feb
The elegant and very comfortable house has magnificent lake views and a lovely restaurant serving good food.
9rm(4⇨5↱)Annexe1rm(1fb) CTV in all bedrooms ® ✈ dB&B⇨↱£64-£78 (incl dinner) ▤
20P ⇼ ✲ nc12yrs
V ⊁
Credit Cards [3]

★★Ellerthwaite Lodge New Rd LA22 3LA ☎(09662)5115
Closed Dec-Jan
This charming, detached house in the centre of Windermere features an attractive new coffee shop in its basement.
12rm(10⇨2↱)(1fb) CTV in all bedrooms ® T ✈ (ex guide dogs) ✱ sB&B⇨↱£17.50-£23.50 dB&B⇨↱£35-£47
CTV 20P
♧ ⊈ Last high tea 6.30pm
Credit Cards [1] [3]

★★Hideaway Phoenix Way LA23 1DB ☎(09662)3070
This traditional Westmoreland stone-built Victorian house is peacefully set on the west side of the village. There are attractive and comfortable public rooms and the bedrooms are prettily decorated.
12rm(6⇨6↱)Annexe5rm(2fb)6▣ CTV in all bedrooms ® sB&B⇨↱£25-£40 dB&B⇨↱£50-£80 ▤
16P ⇼ ✲ *xmas*
♉ English & Continental V ♧ ⊈ ⊁ Bar Lunch fr£1 Dinner fr£12 Last dinner 7.30pm

★★*Hillthwaite House* Thornbarrow Rd LA23 2DF ☎(09662)3636 & 6691
Set on a hill, the hotel has magnificent views of Lake Windermere and the surrounding fells. Accommodation is comfortable, with a particularly pleasant lounge and lounge bar.
25rm(23⇨2↱)(2fb)8▣ CTV in all bedrooms ® T
26P ⇼ ✲ ⊡(heated) sauna solarium
♉ English & French V ♧ ⊈ Last dinner 9pm
Credit Cards [1] [2] [3]

★★Holbeck Ghyll Country House Holbeck Ln LA23 1LU
☎Ambleside(05394)32375
Closed Jan

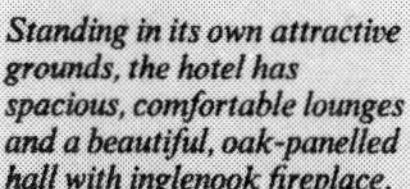

Standing in its own attractive grounds, the hotel has spacious, comfortable lounges and a beautiful, oak-panelled hall with inglenook fireplace.

14rm(13⇌1♠)(1fb)1 CTV in all bedrooms ® T sB&B⇌♠£47.50 dB&B⇌♠£76-£100 (incl dinner)
20P snooker putting green *xmas*
English & French V Sunday Lunch £8.50 Dinner fr£16.50 Last dinner 8.45pm
Credit Cards 1 3

See advertisement under AMBLESIDE

★★The Knoll Bowness LA23 2JF ☎(09662)3756
Closed Dec-Feb
A peaceful old house affording lovely views of the lake and adjacent fells is personally managed by the resident proprietor to provide informal, friendly service.
12rm(6⇌3♠)(4fb) CTV in all bedrooms ® S10%
CTV 20P nc3yrs
V Last dinner 7.30pm
Credit Cards 1 3 £

★★Lindeth Fell Upper Storrs Park Rd, Bowness LA23 3JP
☎(09662)3286 & 4287
Closed Dec-Feb

Beautifully located and standing in fine gardens, this Lakeland country house hotel enjoys impressive views across the lake to the Cumbrian mountains. Run very much as an extension of the owner's private home, the hotel offers high levels of décor, comfort and catering, the 5-course dinner and its accompanying wine list representing particularly good value for money.

14rm(9⇌5♠)(2fb) CTV in all bedrooms ® T
sB&B⇌♠£39-£45 dB&B⇌♠£70-£80 (incl dinner)
20P (grass) croquet putting nc7yrs
S% Sunday Lunch fr£8 Dinner fr£16.50 Last dinner 8.15pm
Credit Cards 1 2 3 5

See the preliminary section 'Hotel and Restaurant Classification' for an explanation of the AA's appointment and award scheme.

★★Linthwaite Bowness LA23 3JA
☏(09662)3688
Closed Dec-mid Apr

In a charming hillside location above Lake Windermere within a small rural community, this converted private residence possesses its own splendid gardens, complete with woodland and tarn. The friendly proprietors are happy to impart their knowledge of the locality and promote a welcoming atmosphere. The 5 course table d'hôte menu offers good food at excellent value. The bedrooms, whilst being simple in terms of décor, are exceptionally clean and bright and lack nothing in terms of guests' comfort.

11⇨ CTV in all bedrooms ® T S% sB&B⇨fr£43.50 dB&B⇨£80-£88 (incl dinner)
25P putting green nc8yrs
English & French
Credit Cards 1 2 3

★★

❀★★ **MILLER HOWE** Rayrigg Rd LA23 1EY
☏(09662)2536
FAX (09662) 5664
Closed mid Dec-mid Feb
(Rosette awarded for dinner only)

After years of running this lakeland hotel and earning world renown in the process, John Tovey is no longer so actively involved, but the standards he has set are ably maintained by the caring manager and keen young staff. Our inspectors have reported very favourably on the cuisine, and they believe that the food is now more honest, with less reliance on over-garniture. Young chef, Gaulton Blackerston, is not afraid to come into the restaurant after dinner to discuss the work of his team in interesting detail. In other respects, Miller Howe remains the cherishable place it has always been. Fine porcelain collections and interesting objets d'art still decorate the attractive lounges; the lounges still have their chunky Chesterfields, and the comfortable bedrooms are as well supplied as ever with thoughtful touches. Not all bedrooms have colour televisions or telephones, nor en suite facilities. Reassuringly, Miller Howe resists modern pressures and rests its reputation on the attentiveness of the staff, who, together with the beauty of the building and surrounding scenery make a visit here a unique experience.

13rm(11⇨2⌐)1⊟ TV available T ✱ sB&B⇨⌐fr£85 dB&B⇨⌐£60-£105 (incl dinner)
40P nc12yrs
V Dinner £26 Last dinner 8.30pm
Credit Cards 1 2 3 5

Book as early as possible for busy holiday periods.

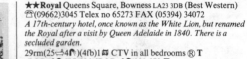

★★Royal Queens Square, Bowness LA23 3DB (Best Western)
☏(09662)3045 Telex no 65273 FAX (05394) 34072
A 17th-century hotel, once known as the White Lion, but renamed the Royal after a visit by Queen Adelaide in 1840. There is a secluded garden.
29rm(25⇨4⌐)(4fb)1⊟ CTV in all bedrooms ® T
sB&B⇨⌐£27-£36 dB&B⇨⌐£54-£72
16P 5 (£1.50) sub-aqua diving water skiing pool table *xmas*
English & French V S% Lunch £5-£7.50 High tea £4.50-£6 Dinner £12-£14&alc Last dinner 9pm
Credit Cards 1 2 3 4 5

★★*Sun* Troutbeck Bridge LA23 1HH (3m N) ☏(09662)3274
A roadside inn by the A591, on the outskirts of Windermere.
10rm(2⇨2⌐)(2fb) CTV in all bedrooms ®
CTV 30P
Last dinner 8.30pm
Credit Cards 1 2 3 5

★Quarry Garth Country House Troutbeck Bridge LA23 1LF
☏(09662)3761
FAX (09662) 6584

Small family run hotel in spacious grounds, serving good home cooking and having attractive bedrooms.

11rm(6⇨5⌐)(2fb) CTV in all bedrooms ® T ✱
sB&B⇨⌐£35-£50 dB&B⇨⌐£59-£80 (incl dinner)
30P *xmas*
English & French V Lunch £4-£10alc Dinner £15 Last dinner 9.15pm
Credit Cards 1 2 3 5 £

★Ravensworth Ambleside Rd LA23 1BA ☏(09662)3747
Small, comfortably furnished hotel near village centre. Warm, friendly atmosphere.
13rm(10⇨3⌐)(2fb)3⊟ CTV in all bedrooms ® ✱
sB&B⇨⌐£24-£28 dB&B⇨⌐£44-£48
15P *xmas*
French V Dinner fr£10alc Last dinner 7pm
Credit Cards 1 3

★Willowsmere Ambleside Rd LA23 1ES ☏(09662)3575
Closed Dec-Etr
A very genuine family-run hotel provides a friendly atmosphere and enjoyable, imaginative home cooking.
13rm(12⇨1⌐)(7fb) ®
CTV 20P
English & Austrian
Credit Cards 1 2 3 5

❀✕ **Porthole Eating House** 3 Ash St, Bowness LA23 3EB
☏(09662)2793
(Rosette awarded for dinner only)
Booking is strongly advised at this hugely popular restaurant in a quiet street near the lakeside. The Porthole is somewhat cramped, but its cheerful atmosphere and friendly, attentive staff more than compensate. A range of English and Italian dishes can be ordered à la carte, but many opt for the daily speciality menus, featuring such Italian delights as fettuchini al pesto or perhaps English lamb in a style created by one of

the chefs. The wine list is truly outstanding, with many unusual wines at competitive prices.
Closed Tue & mid Dec-mid Feb
Lunch not served not served
English, French & Italian V 36 seats ✱ Dinner £15.50-£22alc Last dinner 11pm
Credit Cards [1] [2] [3] [5]

✕**Rogers** 4 High St LA23 1AF ☎(09662)4954
The warm atmosphere, attractive décor and quality napery of this delightful little restaurant on the edge of town help to make it the ideal setting in which to enjoy a very good meal. The menu offers a range of French and English dishes, all based on fresh produce, and features specially set meals in winter. Reservations are necessary.
Closed Sun (ex BH's) & 2 wks in Jan, Feb & Mar
Lunch not served (ex by prior arrangement)
English & French 42 seats ✱ Lunch £12-£18alc Dinner £18-£20alc Last lunch 1.30pm Last dinner 9.45pm
Credit Cards [1] [2] [3] [5]

WINDSOR Berkshire Map **04** SU97

See also **Datchet**

★★★★73% **Oakley Court** Windsor Road, Water Oakley SL4 5UR (2m W A308) (Norfolk Capital)(Prestige)
☎Maidenhead(0628)74141 Telex no 849958
FAX (0628) 37011
Set in acres of landscaped gardens sloping gently to the Thames, this is an ideal venue for business meetings and conferences. The spacious public rooms are comfortable and beautifully appointed – some with splendid river views. The Mansion House suites are being restored, and an additional accommodation block has been skilfully blended with the main house and gardens. The restaurant offers imaginative menus, and recreational facilities include croquet lawn, pitch and putt course and exclusive fishing rights on the river.
65 Annexe27 (19fb)5 CTV in all bedrooms T (ex guide dogs) sB £97.50-£125
dB £120-£200 (room only)
120P 9 snooker croquet *xmas*
English & French V Lunch fr£17.50&alc Dinner fr£27.50&alc Last dinner 10pm
Credit Cards [1] [2] [3] [5]

★★★68% **The Castle** High St SL4 1LJ (Trusthouse Forte)
☎(0753)851011 Telex no 849220 FAX (0753) 830244
Modernised Georgian hotel with large bedrooms, comfortable bar and restaurant.
85 (40fb)1 in 6 bedrooms CTV in all bedrooms ® T ✱
S% sB £75-£85 dB £95-£105 (room only)
Lift 90P CFA *xmas*
V S% Lunch £13.50-£16&alc Dinner £18&alc Last dinner 9.45pm
Credit Cards [1] [2] [3] [4] [5]

★★***Aurora Garden*** 14 Bolton Av SL4 3JF ☎(0753)868686
Telex no 849462 FAX (0753) 74928
Situated in a quiet, tree-lined avenue only a short distance from the town centre, this hotel offers attractive, comfortable and well-equipped bedrooms, a cosy bar/lounge area and conference and banquetting facilities. The terrace at the rear of the hotel overlooks a delightful, well-tended water garden.
14rm(3 11)(1fb) CTV in all bedrooms ® T
20P
V Last dinner 9pm
Credit Cards [1] [2] [3] [5]

W

★★Royal Adelaide 46 Kings Rd SL4 2AG ☎(0753)863916 Telex no 848522 FAX (0628) 773625
A converted Victorian house with newly refurbished and attractive foyer, bar and restaurant. Bedrooms vary in size but all offer good facilities.
39rm(9⇌30⬈)(1fb) CTV in all bedrooms ® T ✻ sB&B⇌⬈£55-£67 dB&B⇌⬈£65-£80 ⊟
(30P *xmas*
English & French V ⅄ Dinner fr£12.25 Last dinner 9pm
Credit Cards 1 2 3 5

★★Ye Harte & Garter High St SL4 1PH (Berni/Chef & Brewer) ☎(0753)863426
This hotel is characteristic of hotels built in the 1890s in the Victorian red-brick style. In addition to the bars and grill restaurants, there is a ballroom. Bedrooms are well-equipped.
50rm(36⇌7⬈)(8fb) CTV in all bedrooms ® T ✕ (ex guide dogs) sB&B⇌⬈£39.50-£47 dB&B⇌⬈fr£69.50 ⊟
Lift (
Mainly grills V ⅄ Lunch fr£8 Dinner fr£9 Last dinner 10.30pm
Credit Cards 1 2 3 5

WINSFORD Somerset Map 03 SS93

★★Royal Oak Inn Exmoor National Park TA24 7JE ☎(064385)455 Telex no 46529
This old thatched hotel is full of character – there are three comfortable lounges, two small bars, and a contry-style restaurant serving freshly-prepared English dishes. The pretty bedrooms are well-equipped, and staff are friendly and helpful.
8⇌Annexe5⇌(1fb) CTV in all bedrooms T ✕ sB⇌fr£49.50 dB⇌fr£59 (room only) ⊟
20P 3 hunting shooting *xmas*
V Lunch fr£10.50 Dinner fr£20 Last dinner 9.30pm
Credit Cards 1 2 3 5 £

WINTERBOURNE ABBAS Dorset Map 03 SY69

★★Whitefriars Copyhold Ln DT2 9LT ☎Martinstown(0305)889206
A well-maintained Victorian building, decorated and furnished to a high standard and achieving a friendly, informal atmosphere under the personal supervision of its owner, provides well equipped and thoughtfully appointed bedrooms. The attractive restaurant offers an interesting menu of dishes which are well prepared from fresh produce.
7rm(6⇌1⬈) CTV in all bedrooms ® T ✻ sB&B⇌⬈£32.50-£40 dB&B⇌⬈£55-£60 ⊟
16P ✻ nc12yrs *xmas*
V Lunch £5-£7&alc Dinner fr£10&alc Last dinner 9.30pm
Credit Cards 1 2 3 5 £

WISBECH Cambridgeshire Map 05 TF40

★★Queens South Brink PE13 1JJ ☎(0945)583933 Telex no 329197
Situated close to the centre of the market town, this family-managed hotel offers a welcome to tourists and commercial guests alike.
12rm(11⇌1⬈)Annexe6⇌(3fb)2 CTV in all bedrooms ® T sB&B⇌⬈£35-£37.50 dB&B⇌⬈£45-£60 ⊟
40P ✻ *xmas*
English & French V Lunch fr£8.95&alc High tea fr£3.75 Dinner fr£8.95&alc Last dinner 10pm
Credit Cards 1 3 5

★★White Lion 5 South Brink PE13 1JD (Consort) ☎(0945)584813
Situated close to the town centre and the River Nene, this coaching inn offers varying standards of accommodation, some single bedrooms being rather compact. Guests have a choice of 2 bars, and good parking facilities are provided.
18rm(11⇌5⬈)(1fb) CTV in all bedrooms ® T sB&B£30.80 sB&B⇌⬈£36.30-£41.25 dB&B£44 dB&B⇌⬈£49.50-£54.45 ⊟
25P
English & French V Lunch £9.75&alc Dinner £9.75-£10.75&alc Last dinner 9pm
Credit Cards 1 2 3 5 £

WISHAW West Midlands Map 07 SP19

★★★★65% The Belfry Lichfield Rd B76 9PR (A446) (De Vere) ☎Curdworth(0675)70301 Telex no 338848 FAX (0675) 70178
A busy hotel with fine leisure facilities, linked with national golf centre.
219⇌(34fb)2 CTV in all bedrooms ® T ✕ (ex guide dogs) sB&B⇌£90-£135 dB&B⇌£115-£135 ⊟
Lift (1500P ✻ CFA (heated) 18 (hard) squash snooker sauna solarium gymnasium archery clay pigeon shooting
xmas
French V Lunch £14.50&alc Dinner £14.50&alc Last dinner 10pm
Credit Cards 1 2 3 5

★★★50% Moxhull Hall Holly Ln B76 9PE (Exec Hotel) ☎021-329 2056 Telex no 333779
This fine, red-brick house, standing in eight acres of garden and woodland just off the A446, is popular with local families for its leisurely atmosphere and French-style bistro.
21rm(16⇌5⬈)(2fb)1 CTV in all bedrooms ® T sB&B⇌⬈fr£42.50 dB&B⇌⬈fr£50 ⊟
60P ✻ croquet ♫
English & French V Lunch fr£8.95&alc Dinner fr£8.95&alc Last dinner 10pm
Credit Cards 1 2 3 5

See advertisement under SUTTON COLDFIELD

WITCHINGHAM, GREAT (Lenwade) Norfolk Map 09 TG01

★★*Lenwade House*
NR9 5QP
☎Norwich(0603)872288

A comfortable hotel, in an attractive setting, with warm and friendly atmosphere.

14rm(9⇌5⬈)(2fb)1 CTV in all bedrooms ® T
CTV 40P ✻ (heated) (grass) squash
solarium putting croquet nc5 yrs
English & French V Last dinner 9pm
Credit Cards 1 2 3 5

WITHAM Essex Map 05 TL81

★★White Hart Newland St CM8 2AF (Berni/Chef & Brewer) ☎(0376)512245
18rm(12⇌6⬈)(1fb)1 CTV in all bedrooms ® T ✕ (ex guide dogs) sB&B⇌⬈fr£35.50 dB&B⇌⬈fr£47.50 ⊟
43P
V ⅄ Lunch £8 Dinner £9 Last dinner 10pm
Credit Cards 1 2 3 5

For key to symbols see the inside front cover.

WITHERSLACK Cumbria Map **07** SD48

★ **OLD VICARAGE COUNTRY HOUSE**
LA11 6RS (Exec Hotel)

☎(044852)381
Telex no 668230
FAX (044852) 373

Closed Xmas wk

Peace and tranquility prevail in this wooded valley in the southern Lake District, and the Old Vicarage at its heart makes an idyllic place in which to stay. It has been run for 10 years by two families – Jill and Roger Burrington-Brown and Irene and Stanley Reeve – who provide guests with an utterly relaxing haven of comfort. The hotel is a Georgian house set in neat gardens with a wild garden area to one side and an all-weather tennis court (due for completion by the time we go to print). Bedrooms are individually decorated and supplied with all sorts of little luxuries, including canned orange juice, mineral water and Kendal mint cake. A set dinner served at 8 o'clock is prepared in traditional style from fresh ingredients with an emphasis on local produce, complemented by a wine list of some 200 bins (Roger Burrington-Brown is a wine enthusiast). There is a choice of two puddings, one of them hot, and indecisive guests may be encouraged to have both. The English cheeseboard is noteworthy for its range of several local cheeses, but perhaps most memorable are the breakfasts. Fresh orange juice, excellent bread and rolls, Cumberland sausage, black pudding and home-produced eggs should keep walkers on their feet all day.

13rm(5⇌5↖) CTV in all bedrooms ® **T** ✳
sB&B⇌↖£45.50-£65 dB&B⇌↖£65-£85 ⊟

2P ✲ (hard) nc10yrs

Dinner fr£19.50 Last dinner 6pm

Credit Cards 1 2 3 5 £

See advertisement under GRANGE-OVER-SANDS

WITHYPOOL Somerset Map **03** SS83

★★**Royal Oak Inn** TA24 7QP ☎Exford(064383)506
Telex no 46529
Closed 25 & 26 Dec
This is a small, but well-appointed and comfortable country inn. The restaurant is very popular with the locals for its good freshly-prepared food. Bedrooms are nicely decorated and well-equipped, and staff are cheerful and friendly.
8rm(3⇌3↖)(1fb)1 CTV in all bedrooms ® **T** ✳
sB&B£25-£40 sB&B⇌↖£40 dB&B£40-£56 dB&B⇌↖£54-£56
20P ✲ shooting nc10yrs *xmas*
English & French **V** Bar Lunch £5-£15.60 Dinner £14.50-£19.50&alc Last dinner 9.30pm
Credit Cards 1 2 3 5

Places with AA hotels and restaurants are identified on the location atlas at the back of the book.

★★ **Westerclose Country House** TA24 7QR

☎Exford(064383)302

Closed Jan-23 Mar & 6 Nov-31 Dec

Small, privately owned and run hotel in extensive grounds which includes stabling for guests' horses.

11rm(9⇌)Annexe1⇌(3fb)1 CTV in all bedrooms ®
sB&B⇌£25 dB&B⇌£50-£56

12P ✲ hunting

English & French Bar Lunch fr£3 Dinner fr£13&alc Last dinner 8.30pm

Credit Cards 1 2 3

WITNEY Oxfordshire Map **04** SP30

★★**Witney Lodge** Ducklington Ln OX8 7TS (Consort)
☎(0993)779777 Telex no 83459
RS 25 & 26 Dec
Conveniently located just outside the town, this attractive, recently opened, Cotswold-style hotel is ideally positioned for both business travellers and tourists. Bedrooms are particularly good, their furnishings combining with an extensive range of facilities including tiled, bright bathrooms, and a restaurant in homely style offers good, value-for-money food and friendly service.
34⇌ CTV in all bedrooms ® **T** (ex guide dogs) ✳ sB⇌£57 dB⇌£62 (room only) ⊟
85P

V ✿ ☡ S% Lunch £7.25-£8.95&alc Dinner £7.25-£8.95&alc
Last dinner 10pm
Credit Cards [1] [2] [3] [4] [5]

WIVELISCOMBE Somerset Map **03** ST02

❀★ LANGLEY HOUSE
Langley Marsh TA4 2UF (1m N on unclass rd)
☎(0984)23318
Telex no 46648
(Rosette awarded for dinner only)
An attractive, family-run hotel dating from the 16th-century is set in beautifully kept grounds on the edge of this small country town at the foot of the Brendon Hills. Warm and welcoming, it provides accommodation in 8 individually decorated and furnished bedrooms with private facilities and thoughtful touches like fresh flowers, boxed soap and a glass of sherry on arrival. The bright but well chosen colour schemes of the two sitting rooms create an atmosphere of modern elegance and charm in keeping with the general ambience of the building; the dining room serves a set 5-course dinner, skilfully prepared from the freshest of local produce to maintain the reputationfor excellent cuisine that the hotel enjoys. A successful blend of professionalism and genuine friendliness on the part of the proprietors, Peter and Anne Wilson, and their staff, contribute much to the success of the hotel.
9rm(6⇨2↱)(1fb)1⊞ CTV in all bedrooms **T** ✱ S%
sB&B⇨↱£50-£52.50 dB&B⇨↱£57-£85 ⊟
16P 4⌂ (£2.50) ⊞ ✲ croquet nc7yrs ⌂ *xmas*
✿ ☡ ⊁ S% Dinner £18.50-£21 Last dinner 9pm
Credit Cards [1] [2]

WOBURN Bedfordshire Map **04** SP93

✕✕✕ *Paris House* Woburn Park MK17 9QP ☎(0525)290692
Originally constructed for the Paris Exhibition of 1878, this impressive folly has been rebuilt in Woburn Park, off the A4012 and two miles south-east of the village. The immense creativity of chef Peter Chandler is displayed in his Prix Fixe de la Semaine.
Closed Mon & Feb
Dinner not served Sun
☋ French **V** 50 seats Last lunch 2pm Last dinner 10pm 20P
Credit Cards [1] [2] [3] [5]

WOKINGHAM Berkshire Map **04** SU86

★★★★66% Reading Moat House Mill Ln, Sindlesham RG11 5DF (Queens Moat) ☎Reading(0734)351035
Telex no 846360 FAX (0734) 666530
Closed 26-28 Dec
The River Loddon gently flows through the 19th-century Mill House, now the backdrop of this new, modern hotel, with well-equipped bedrooms and a la carte restaurant. Facilities include a conference and leisure centre, The Poachers pub, coffee shop and The Mill nightclub.
96⇨(10fb) CTV in all bedrooms ® **T** ✱ sB⇨£85
dB⇨£90 (room only) ⊟
Lift ☾ 350P ✲ sauna solarium gymnasium
☋ International **V** ✿ ☡ Lunch £12.45-£24.45&alc High tea £5.25 Dinner £12.45-£24.45&alc Last dinner 10.30pm
Credit Cards [1] [2] [3] [5]

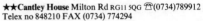

★★Cantley House Milton Rd RG11 5QG ☎(0734)789912
Telex no 848210 FAX (0734) 774294
Set 600 yards back from the road in its own grounds, a converted, late-Victorian, private house offers sound food and friendly, informal service.
29⇨↱(2fb)1⊞ CTV in all bedrooms ® **T** ✱
sB&B⇨↱£35-£56 dB&B⇨↱£45-£68 ⊟
☾ 70P ✲ ♪ (hard) croquet pool ♫
☋ English & French **V** ✿ Lunch £13.50&alc Dinner £12-£20alc
Last dinner 9.30pm
Credit Cards [1] [2] [3] [5]

WOLVERHAMPTON West Midlands Map **07** SO99

See also **Himley**

★★★59% Connaught Tettenhall Rd WV1 4SW ☎(0902)24433
Telex no 338490 FAX (0902) 710353
This is a modern, well furnished and comfortable hotel, and is particularly suitable for conferences and conventions. The bedrooms are modern, and the menus in the restaurant are extensive.
61rm(51⇨10↱)(2fb) CTV in all bedrooms ® **T** S10%
sB&B⇨↱£45-£50 dB&B⇨↱£67.50
Lift ☾ 100P sauna solarium health & beauty centre *xmas*
☋ English & French **V** ✿ ☡ ⊁ S10% Lunch fr£9.50 Dinner fr£9.50&alc Last dinner 10pm
Credit Cards [1] [2] [3] [5]

★★★59% *Goldthorn* Penn Rd WV3 0DX ☎(0902)29216
Telex no 339516 FAX (0902) 710419
Closed 25-26 Dec
The original hotel has been extended to provide further accommodation in the lodge and business centre. After refurbishment of some rooms, standards vary throughout the hotel, some single rooms being compact. Two bars include the Captains Table, which is a popular lunchtime venue, while the restaurant offers hearty meals served by friendly staff.
70rm(59⇨3↱)Annexe27rm(17⇨5↱)(1fb)6⊞ CTV in all bedrooms ® **T**
☾ 150P
☋ English & French **V** ✿ ☡ Last dinner 9.30pm
Credit Cards [1] [2] [3] [5]

★★★63% Mount Mount Road, Tettenhall Wood WV6 8HL (2.5m W off A454) (Embassy) ☎(0902)752055 Telex no 333546
FAX (0902) 745263
Set in four and a half acres of landscaped gardens and located in a rural area, the hotel is nevertheless near enough to the centre of Wolverhampton to be popular with business people.
49⇨↱(11fb)⊁in 4 bedrooms CTV in all bedrooms ® **T**
sB⇨↱fr£63 dB⇨↱fr£73 (room only) ⊟
☾ 250P ✲ CFA ♫ *xmas*
☋ English & French **V** ✿ ☡ S% Lunch fr£9 Dinner fr£11.50&alc Last dinner 9.45pm
Credit Cards [1] [2] [3] [4] [5]

★★★61% Park Hall Park Drive, Goldthorn Park WV4 5AJ (2m S off A459) (Embassy) ☎(0902)331121 Telex no 333546
FAX (0902) 344760
Formerly the home of the Earl of Dudley, an extended and modernised hotel stands just 3 miles from the centre of the town. It features up-to-date accommodation, 2 bars and a restaurant offering a choice between its à la carte menu and a selection from the carvery.
57⇨↱⊁in 6 bedrooms CTV in all bedrooms ® **T** ✱
sB⇨↱fr£56 dB⇨↱fr£64 (room only) ⊟
☾ 408P ✲ CFA ♫ *xmas*
☋ English & French **V** ✿ ☡ Lunch fr£10.50&alc High tea fr£6 Dinner fr£10.50&alc Last dinner 9.45pm
Credit Cards [1] [2] [3] [4] [5]

W

★★Castlecroft Castlecroft Rd WV3 8NA ☎(0902)764040
RS Xmas
The hotel, popular with a business clientele, stands in a residential area of the town, surrounded by well-kept gardens and local sports grounds.
20rm(6⇌11⌐)(1fb) CTV in all bedrooms ® **T**
sB&B⇌⌐£35-£45 dB&B⇌⌐£48-£55 ⊟
100P 6🚗 ❊ solarium
☋ English & French **V** ♧ ☕ Sunday Lunch £8.50 Dinner £9.50&alc Last dinner 9pm
Credit Cards 1 2 3

★★York 138-140 Tettenhall Rd WV6 0BQ (Exec Hotel)
☎(0902)758211
Closed 24 Dec-1 Jan
This is a small but very popular personally-run hotel, offering a good standard of comfort and well-prepared meals.
16rm(11⇌5⌐)(2fb) CTV in all bedrooms ® **T** S%
sB&B⇌⌐£32.50-£42.50 dB&B⇌⌐£45-£55 ⊟
CTV 20P
☋ English & French **V** ♧ ☕ Lunch fr£7.50 Dinner fr£10 Last dinner 9.30pm
Credit Cards 1 2 3 5 £

WOOBURN COMMON Buckinghamshire Map **04** SU98

★★Chequers Inn HP10 0JQ (1m W unclass towards Bourne End)
☎Bourne End(06285)29575 Telex no 849832
This busy 17th-century inn has been thoughtfully modernised to provide comfortable and well-equipped accommodation. The service is friendly and helpful, under the personal supervision of the proprietors.
17rm(16⇌1⌐)(1fb)1⊞ CTV in all bedrooms ® **T** ✗ (ex guide dogs) sB&B⇌⌐fr£64 dB&B⇌⌐£70.40-£82.50 ⊟
50P
☋ English & French **V** ♧ ☕ Lunch £11-£13&alc Dinner £14-£15&alc Last dinner 9pm
Credit Cards 1 2 3

See advertisement under BEACONSFIELD

WOODBRIDGE Suffolk Map **05** TM24

★★★♛72% Seckford Hall
IP13 6NU
☎(0394)385678
Telex no 987446
FAX (0394) 380610
Closed 25 Dec

Picturesque Elizabethan manor house, set amid gardens, parkland and lake.

24⇌⌐4⊞ CTV in all bedrooms ® **T** ✱ S10%
sB&B⇌⌐£55-£65 dB&B⇌⌐£65-£70 ⊟
☾ 200P ❊ ▭(heated) ♩ gymnasium spa bath
☋ International **V** ♧ S10% Lunch £9.50&alc Dinner £15-£20alc Last dinner 9.30pm
Credit Cards 1 2 3 5

★★The Crown Thoro'fare IP12 1AD (Trusthouse Forte)
☎(03943)4242 FAX (03943) 7192
Centrally situated, fully modernised old coaching inn, with parts dating from 1532.
10⇌Annexe10⇌(2fb)⊬in 3 bedrooms CTV in all bedrooms ® **T** ✱ sB⇌fr£57 dB⇌fr£70 (room only) ⊟
30P *xmas*
V ♧ ☕ ⊬ Lunch fr£8.50&alc Dinner fr£12.95 Last dinner 9pm
Credit Cards 1 2 3 4 5

WOODFORD Greater Manchester Map **07** SJ88

✗3 Gates 547 Chester Rd SK7 1PR ☎061-440 8715 & 061 439 7824
This attractive restaurant (formerly a bistro) close to the village church offers a varied menu in a warm and friendly atmosphere.
Closed Sun
Lunch not served Sat
☋ English & French 46 seats ✱ Lunch £10.95&alc Dinner £19-£25alc Last lunch 2pm Last dinner 10pm 16P
Credit Cards 1 2 3 5

WOODFORD BRIDGE Devon Map **02** SS31

★★★64% Woodford Bridge EX22 7LL
☎Milton Damerel(040926)481 FAX (040926) 328
This impressive thatched building, originally a 15th century inn, has been converted to a comfortable, high quality hotel. The bedrooms are comfortably furnished, and there is a pleasing dining room. Nine luxury cottages are situated in the grounds, and there is also a good leisure complex.
12⇌(1fb) CTV in all bedrooms ® **T** ✱ sB&B⇌£41 dB&B⇌£64 ⊟
☾ 100P ❊ ▭(heated) ♪ (hard) ♩ squash snooker sauna solarium gymnasium ⌂
☋ English & French **V** ♧ ☕ Last high tea 7pm
Credit Cards 1 2 3 5 £

Book as early as possible for busy holiday periods.

W

WOODFORD GREEN Greater London

See **LONDON plan 5***F5*(page 412) **Telephone codes are due to change on 6th May 1990. See page 421.**

★★★66% **Woodford Moat House** Oak Hill IG8 9NY (Queens Moat) ☎01-505 4511 Telex no 264428 FAX 01-506 0941

In an ideal position on the edge of Epping Forest, there are comprehensive facilities here for both business and pleasure. Bedrooms are comfortable and vey well-equipped, and the attractive wood-panelled Churchill Restaurant offers tempting set and à la carte menus. Young staff provide friendly and attentive service.

99rm(69⇌30♠) CTV in all bedrooms ® **T** sB&B⇌♠£70-£74 dB&B⇌♠£82-£86 ⊟

Lift ☾ 150P CFA

English & French **V** Lunch £12.50-£13.50&alc Dinner £12.50-£13.50&alc Last dinner 10.15pm

Credit Cards [1] [2] [3] [5]

WOODHALL SPA Lincolnshire Map **08** TF16

★★★58% **Petwood** Stixwould Rd LN10 6QF (Best Western) ☎(0526)52411 Telex no 56402 FAX (0526) 53473

Set in 30 acres of secluded gardens and mature woodlands, this lovely building was once the country house of Sir Archibald Weigall. The hotel is presently being refurbished to offer good accommodation and comfort in public areas, while still keeping the charm and atmosphere of this period house. During World War II the "Dambusters", 617 Squadron, had its officers' mess here, and the bar has an interesting display of memorabilia.

46⇌♠(3fb)3 CTV in all bedrooms ® **T** ✱ sB⇌♠£57-£67 dB⇌♠£67-£110 (room only) ⊟

Lift ☾ 80P ✿

English & French **V** Sunday Lunch fr£7.50 Dinner fr£10.95&alc Last dinner 9.30pm

Credit Cards [1] [2] [3] [5]

WOODLANDS Hampshire Map **04** SU31

★★**Busketts Lawn** 174 Woodlands Rd SO4 2GL ☎Ashurst(042129)2272 & 2077/3417

Set in a rural residential area, this old brick-built house is a pleasant family hotel with happy and friendly staff, and the hotel is a popular venue for functions and receptions. The gardens are well-tended and attractive.

14rm(7⇌7♠)(3fb) CTV in all bedrooms ® **T** S% sB&B⇌♠£30-£56 dB&B⇌♠£54-£70 ⊟

CTV 50P ✿ (heated) putting croquet football *xmas*

English & Continental **V** S% Lunch £7.50-£8.50 High tea £3.50-£5.50 Dinner £10.50-£12.50&alc Last dinner 8.30pm

Credit Cards [1] [2] [3] [5]

WOODSTOCK Oxfordshire Map **04** SP41

★★★67% **Bear** Park St OX7 1SZ (Trusthouse Forte) ☎(0993)811511 Telex no 837921 FAX (0993) 813380

This ancient coaching inn retains parts of the original 16th-century structure and a staircase of that date. Bedrooms are particularly comfortable and well-equipped, the lounge bar, with traditional features and log fire, is characteristic of an old English inn and the comfortably-appointed beamed restaurant offers à la carte and table d'hôte menus.

33⇌Annexe12⇌(1fb)5 in 6 bedrooms CTV in all bedrooms ® **T** ✱ sB⇌£69-£75 dB⇌£99-£150 (room only) ⊟

☾ 40P CFA *xmas*

V Lunch £12.50-£16.50&alc Dinner fr£16.95&alc Last dinner 10pm

Credit Cards [1] [2] [3] [4] [5]

★★**Feathers** Market St OX7 1SX ☎(0993)812291 Telex no 83147 FAX (0993) 813158

Dating from the 17th century, this delightful hotel has been restored by its owner Gordon Campbell-Grey, with the help of Jane Spencer-Churchill. The superb colour schemes, antique furniture and old prints certainly combine to set off the flag-stoned hall, wainscoted library, drawing room and smart green bar to the best advantage. The open fires which burn in the public rooms in season and lovely flowers perfect the scene. A cobbled courtyard where guests can sit out in fine weather and take refreshment is another feature of this hotel not to be missed. As you might imagine, bedrooms in an old building like this vary in size, but all are beautifully decorated and well equipped as well as having many nice little extras. The candle-lit dining room is very elegantly decorated and appointed with high-backed chairs. Here Stanley Matthews is the talented chef who prepares the excellent dishes for the fixed price and à la carte lunch and dinner menus. Cuisine at the Feathers, which is classically based, has gained such a high reputation that it is advisable to book your table in advance.

15rm(13⇌2♠) CTV in all bedrooms **T** ✱ sB&B⇌♠fr£50 dB&B⇌♠£72-£105 ⊟

xmas

V Lunch £12.50-£13.50 Dinner £19.50-£25alc Last dinner 9.45pm

Credit Cards [1] [2] [3] [5]

★★**King's** Market St OX7 1ST (Trusthouse Forte) ☎(0993)811592 & 812073 Telex no 837921 FAX (0993) 813380

This historic hotel was one of the properties given to the town by Queen Elizabeth I on her accession. Today the hotel features a comfortable interior, with compact but very well-equipped bedrooms, and public rooms with much character. The renowned Wheelers Fish Restaurant offers an extensive and commendable menu; the alternative is Mario and Franco's, which provides a variety of fresh pasta dishes accompanied by numerous meat and vegetable sauces.

9rm(5⇌4♠)2 CTV in all bedrooms ® **T** ✱ sB⇌♠£50 dB⇌♠£66-£76 (room only) ⊟

xmas

V Lunch £10-£14&alc Dinner £17&alc Last dinner 10.15pm

Credit Cards [1] [2] [3] [4] [5]

WOODY BAY Devon Map **03** SS64

★★**Woody Bay** EX31 4QX ☎Parracombe(05983)264

Closed early Jan-mid Feb RS mid Feb-mid Mar & Nov-Dec

Set in a magnificent spot overlooking the bay on the edge of Exmoor National Park, this spacious Victorian house offers comfortable bedrooms – many with sea views, a cosy chintzy lounge and imaginative cooking. An interesting feature here is a small sanctuary for injured owls.

14rm(11⇌2♠)(1fb)2 ® sB&B£20-£30 dB&B⇌♠£40-£60 ⊟

CTV 15P ✿ nc8yrs *xmas*

English & French **V** Bar Lunch £4.50-£11alc Dinner £12&alc Last dinner 8.30pm

Credit Cards [1] [3]

WOOLACOMBE Devon Map **02** SS44

★★★68% **Watersmeet** Mortehoe EX34 7EB ☎(0271)870333 FAX (0271) 870890

Closed Jan-mid Feb

Beautifully situated on the headland of Morthoe, this hotel has undergone extensive refurbishment to provide individually designed bedrooms which offer a good combination of quality and comfort. Relaxing public areas include a restaurant with fine panoramic views.

24rm(23⇌1♠)(4fb)1 CTV in all bedrooms **T** ✱ S% sB&B⇌♠£47-£54.50 dB&B⇌♠£89-£104 (incl dinner) ⊟

CTV 20P 10 ✿ (heated) (grass) clay pigeon shooting *xmas*

For key to symbols see the inside front cover.

☋ English & French V ♔ ☲ S% Lunch fr£5 Dinner fr£18.50
Last dinner 9pm
Credit Cards 1 2 3 5

See advertisement on page 721

★★★63% **Woolacombe Bay** South St EX34 7BN (Best Western)
☎(0271)870388 Telex no 46761
Closed Jan
This comfortable family-run hotel overlooks the bay, and has a good range of public rooms, well-equipped bedrooms and an excellent range of indoor and outdoor facilities.
48⇌♠(26fb)1⊞ CTV in all bedrooms ® T ✗ (ex guide dogs)
sB&B⇌♠£43-£81 dB&B⇌♠£86-£162 (incl dinner) ⊟
Lift ☾ CTV 100P ✲ ⊡(heated) ⌂(heated) ▶9 ℘ (hard)
squash snooker sauna solarium gymnasium spa bath ♫ *xmas*
☋ English & French V ♔ ☲ Lunch £6.50 High tea £4.50
Dinner £13 Last dinner 9.45pm
Credit Cards 1 2 3 5

★★***Atlantic*** Sunnyside Rd EX34 7DG ☎(0271)870469
Closed Oct-Feb
Comfortable, friendly, privately owned holiday hotel, overlooking village and bay.
14rm(9⇌1♠)(8fb) ®
CTV 14P table tennis & pool table
♔ ☲

★★**Devon Beach** The Esplanade EX34 7DJ ☎(0271)870449
Closed Oct-Etr
This friendly, personally-run hotel overlooking the sea offers bright bedrooms (some of the sea-facing ones having balconies) and quite spacious public areas which include a lounge for non-smokers.
36rm(24⇌)(21fb) CTV in all bedrooms ® ✻ sB&B£20-£35
sB&B⇌£22-£36 dB&B£42-£70 dB&B⇌£44-£72 (incl dinner)
▶

28P 2⌂ (£3.50 per day) ⊡(heated) solarium ♫
♡ English & French ♱ ⊥ ⚡ Lunch £1-£3.50 Dinner £6.50-£10
Last dinner 8.15pm

★★Little Beach The Esplanade EX34 7DJ
☎Barnstaple(0271)870398
Closed Nov-Jan
An Edwardian gentleman's residence by the sea features a relaxed atmosphere and imaginative, carefully-prepared food.
10rm(4⇨4↱)(1fb) CTV in all bedrooms sB&B£19.25-£21.50
dB&B⇨↱£33-£49 ⊟
8P ⌘ sauna nc7yrs
♡ English & Continental Dinner £9.50-£10.50 Last dinner 8pm
Credit Cards 1 3

★★Whin Bay Bay View Rd EX34 7DQ ☎(0271)870475
Situated in a fine position overlooking the bay, this friendly family hotel has well-equipped bedrooms – many with balconies, and the comfortable public rooms include a sun lounge with panoramic views.
18rm(4⇨11↱)(5fb) CTV in all bedrooms ® **T**
sB&B£18-£25 ⊟
CTV 16P *xmas*
V ♱ ⊥
Credit Cards 1 2 3

★Crossways The Esplanade EX34 7DJ ☎(0271)870395
Closed Nov-Feb
Bright, attractive hotel, personally run by the proprietors, provides accommodation in compact bedrooms which are attractively decorated and spotlessly clean. Lounge and dining room are comfortable, and residents can obtain lunchtime snacks in the feature bar.
9rm(5↱)(5fb) CTV in all bedrooms ® S10%
sB&B£13.50-£16.50 sB&B↱£15-£18 dB&B£27-£33
dB&B↱£30-£36 ⊟
9P ⌘
♱ ⚡ Bar Lunch £1-£2.50 Dinner fr£6.50 Last dinner 6.30pm

★Headlands Beach Rd EX34 7BT ☎(0271)870320
Family-run small hotel, specialising in family holidays.
14rm(4⇨6↱)(3fb)1⊞⚡in 2 bedrooms CTV in all bedrooms
® ✱ sB&B£20-£26 sB&B⇨↱£22-£28 dB&B£40-£52
dB&B⇨↱£44-£56 (incl dinner) ⊟
CTV 14P games room hang gliding *xmas*
♡ English & Continental **V** ♱ ⊥ ⚡ Bar Lunch £1.50-£3.50
Dinner fr£6.50 Last dinner 7.30pm
Credit Cards 1 3 £

★Sunnyside Sunnyside Rd EX34 7DG ☎(0271)870267
Closed Nov-Mar
Pleasant family holiday hotel in a quiet position.
16rm(2⇨)(5fb) ® ✱ sB&B£20-£22 sB&B⇨£22.50-£24.50
dB&B£40-£44 dB&B⇨£42.50-£46.50 (incl dinner) ⊟
CTV 12P ✲ ♫ ⌂
V ♱ Dinner fr£7 Last dinner 7.15pm

WOOLER Northumberland Map **12** NT92

★★Tankerville Arms Cottage Rd NE71 6AD (Minotels)
☎(0668)81581
Closed 22 Dec-28 Dec
This large, comfortable inn is managed by resident proprietors who maintain a high level of service.
14rm(6⇨3↱)(1fb) CTV in 9bedrooms ® sB&B£18.75-£21.50
sB&B⇨↱£26.50 dB&B£37.50
dB&B⇨↱£43-£49.50 Continental breakfast ⊟
CTV 100P ✲ ⌂
V ♱ ⚡ Sunday Lunch £5.95-£7.45 High tea £4.25-£6 Dinner £11.50-£15 Last dinner 9pm
Credit Cards 1 3 5 £

WOOLLEY EDGE MOTORWAY SERVICE AREA (M1)
West Yorkshire Map **08** SE31

⌂Granada Lodge M1 Service Area, West Bretton WF4 4LQ
(between junct 38/39, adj to service area) (Granada)
☎Wakefield(0924)850371 FAX (0924) 830609
31⇨(4fb)⚡in 7 bedrooms CTV in all bedrooms ® S%
sB⇨£23-£26 dB⇨£26-£28 (room only)
☾ 40P
V ♱ ⊥ ⚡
Credit Cards 1 2 3 5
See advertisement under WAKEFIELD

WOOLVERTON Somerset Map **03** ST75

★★*Woolverton House* BA3 6QS ☎Frome(0373)830415
Closed 2 wks Xmas
Set in its own attractive grounds, this is a pretty stone-built manor house witha friendly, relaxed atmosphere. The public rooms are splendid – with panelling and attractive soft furnishings. Bedrooms are neat and cosy.
10⇨↱(1fb)⚡in 4 bedrooms CTV in all bedrooms ® **T** ✗
☾ 100P ⌘ ✲ nc14yrs
♡ French **V** ♱ ⊥ ⚡ Last dinner 9.30pm
Credit Cards 1 2 3 4 5

WOOTTON

See **Wight, Isle of**

WORCESTER Hereford & Worcester Map **03** SO85

★★★75% Fownes City Walls Rd WR1 2AP ☎(0905)613151
Telex no 335021 FAX (0905) 23742
This 200-year-old former glove factory has been cleverly converted into a large luxurious hotel which offers a choice of restaurants, pleasant public areas and modern well-equipped accommodation. Convenient for the city centre, Fownes has good conference and function facilities.
61⇨↱(4fb) CTV in all bedrooms ® **T** ✗ (ex guide dogs)
sB⇨↱£70-£80 dB⇨↱£82-£88 (room only) ⊟
Lift ☾ 94P sauna gymnasium ♫ *xmas*
♡ English & French **V** ♱ ⊥ ⚡ Lunch £8.95-£11.95&alc
Dinner fr£15.95&alc Last dinner 9.45pm
Credit Cards 1 2 3 5 £

★★★55% The Giffard High St WR1 2QR (Trusthouse Forte)
☎(0905)726262 Telex no 336689 FAX (0905) 723458
Busy, modern hotel in the centre of Worcester, offering a wide range of conference and banqueting facilities.
103⇨⚡in 10 bedrooms CTV in all bedrooms ® **T** sB⇨£58
dB⇨£80 (room only) ⊟
Lift ☾ ℱ CFA snooker ♫ *xmas*
♡ English & International **V** ♱ ⊥ ⚡ Lunch fr£7.50&alc
Dinner £14-£20 Last dinner 10pm
Credit Cards 1 2 3 4 5

★★Diglis Hotel Riverside, Severn St WR1 2NF ☎(0905)353518
RS Xmas day night
Situated on the banks of the River Severn, close to the cathedral and the county cricket ground, a charming old house with terraced gardens has recently been refurbished to provide simple, comfortable accommodation with informal service.
14rm(3⇨)(1fb) CTV in all bedrooms ® ✱ sB&B£23.50-£32.50
sB&B⇨fr£32.50 dB&B£39.50-£47.50 dB&B⇨fr£47.50 ⊟
CTV ✲ ♪
♡ English & French **V** ♱ ⊥ Sunday Lunch fr£7.95 High tea fr£1.50alc Dinner £9.95 Last dinner 9.45pm
Credit Cards 1 3

Book as early as possible for busy holiday periods.

W

★★**Loch Ryan Hotel** 119 Sidbury Rd WR5 2DH ☎(0905)351143
Situated just south of the city centre on the A44, this Grade II listed Georgian building close to the cathedral was once the house of the Bishop of Worcester. The well maintained, comfortable accommodation and friendly, informal service provides good value for money and is equally suitable for tourists and business people.
12rm(2⇨)Annexe1⌐(1fb) CTV in all bedrooms ✗ (ex guide dogs) ✱ sB&Bfr£20 sB&B⇨⌐fr£25 dB&Bfr£34 dB&B⇨⌐fr£44 ⊟
P̸ ✿ ⌂
V ♧ ☕ ⚟ Lunch £2.50-£10.50alc Dinner £2.50-£10.30alc Last dinner 8.30pm

★★***Star*** Foregate St WR1 1EA (Crown & Raven) ☎(0905)24308 Telex no 335075
Town-centre hotel popular with business people.
46⇨(2fb) CTV in all bedrooms ® **T**
Lift ☾ 55P
♡ English & French **V** ♧ ☕ Last dinner 10pm
Credit Cards [1] [2] [3]

★★**Ye Olde Talbot** Friar St WR1 2NA (Lansbury) ☎(0905)23573 Telex no 333315 FAX (0905) 612760
A warm and pleasant atmosphere pervades this old 13th-century coaching inn. The bedrooms and public rooms are sympathetically furnished, comfortable and well-equipped, and the staff are particularly caring and friendly.
29⇨(6fb)1⊞ ⚟in 3 bedrooms CTV in all bedrooms ® **T** ✗ (ex guide dogs) sB&B⇨fr£52 dB&B⇨fr£62 ⊟
☾ 8P
♡ Mainly grills **V** ♧ ☕ Lunch £7.75&alc High tea 75p-£3 Dinner £8.90-£14.95alc Last dinner 10pm
Credit Cards [1] [2] [3] [5]

★**Park House** 12 Droitwich Rd WR3 7LJ (Guestaccom) ☎(0905)21816
Located north of the city centre, on the A38 close to its junction with the A449, this small family-run hotel provides simple, but comfortable bedrooms and informal service.
7rm(3⌐)(1fb) CTV in all bedrooms ® ✱ sB£17-£25 sB⌐£25-£32 dB£28-£32 dB⌐£32-£35 (room only)
CTV 10P ⛟
V ♧ ☕ Lunch £7-£9 High tea £5-£7 Dinner £9 Last dinner 8pm

✕✕**Brown's** The Old Cornmill, South Quay WR1 2JN ☎(0905)26263
Situated within a cleverly converted corn mill overlooking the River Severn, close to the cathedral and city centre, this smart restaurant features art nouveau furnishings and a galleried lounge area. The good value fixed price menu offers a good selection of meat dishes which are given a distinctive flavour by charcoal grilling, and fish is always available.
Closed Xmas wk & BH Mon's
Lunch not served Sat
Dinner not served Sun
♡ English & French 70 seats ✱ Lunch fr£16.95 Dinner fr£23 Last lunch 1.45pm Last dinner 9.45pm P̸ nc10yrs
Credit Cards [1] [2] [3] [5]

Entries for rosetted restaurants, red-star and country-house hotels are highlighted by a tinted panel. For a full list of these establishments, consult the Contents page.

W

WORFIELD Shropshire Map **07** SJ40

★★Old Vicarage WV15 5JZ
☎(07464)497
Telex no 35438
FAX (07464) 552
RS 24-27 & 29 Dec

The quiet location of this hotel offers guests peaceful tranquility complementedby hospitable elegance. The public rooms include a most attractive Edwardian-style conservatory lounge. The restaurant offers imaginative traditional dishes, with fresh ingredients carefully prepared by the resident chef.
11rm(9⇒2↑)(1fb)1 ⊠ ⊬in 1 bedroom CTV in all bedrooms ® **T** sB&B⇒↑£42.50 dB&B⇒↑£62.50-£68.50 ⊟
CTV 30P ⊞ ✲ croquet *xmas*
V ✧ ⊻ ⊬ Lunch £16.50 Dinner £17.50-£23.50 Last dinner 9pm
Credit Cards [1] [2] [3] [5]

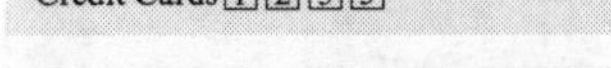

WORKINGTON Cumbria Map **11** NX92

★★★59% ***Cumberland Arms*** Belle Isle St CA14 2XQ ☎(0900)64401
Closed Xmas Day
Fully modernised hotel opposite the railway station.
29rm(26⇒3↑)(1fb) CTV in all bedrooms ® **T**
Lift ☾ CTV 60P pool table
♁ English & French ✧ ⊻
Credit Cards [1] [2] [3] [5]

★★★67% **Washington Central** Washington St CA14 3AW ☎(0900)65772 FAX (0900) 68770
This modern town-centre hotel is built around a small enclosed courtyard. The bedrooms are pleasant and cosy, there is an attractive cocktail bar, peaceful lounge and a restaurant where well-prepared dishes are served by young and friendly staff. Good home-baking is offered in the all-day coffee shop.
40rm(36⇒4↑)(4fb) CTV in all bedrooms ® **T** ✕ (ex guide dogs) sB&B⇒↑£36.50 dB&B⇒↑£57.50 ⊟
Lift ☾ 50P ♫ ⌂
V ✧ ⊻ ⊬ Bar Lunch £1-£5.50&alc High tea £3-£6 Dinner £11.95-£11.95&alc Last dinner 9.30pm
Credit Cards [1] [2] [3]

★★★62% ***Westland*** Braithwaite Rd CA14 4TD ☎(0900)4544
Telex no 64229
Located 2 miles south-east of Workington, this modern hotel is next to Workington Golf Course. The lounge and bar area is attractive and spacious, and bedrooms are comfortable and well-equipped.
50rm(47⇒) CTV in all bedrooms ® **T**
☾ 200P ✲ ⌂
♁ English & French ✧ ⊻ Last dinner 9.30pm
Credit Cards [1] [2] [3] [5]

★★*Crossbarrow Motel* Little Clifton CA14 1XS (3m E on A595)
☎(0900)61443
A purpose-built complex with modern functional bedrooms.
37rm(29⇒8↑)(3fb) CTV in all bedrooms ®
50P ⊞ ✲
V ✧ Last dinner 9.30pm
Credit Cards [1] [3]

WORKSOP Nottinghamshire Map **08** SK57

★★Regancy Carlton Rd S80 1PS ☎(0909)474108
Comfortable accommodation and value for money are provided at this hotel, conveniently situated near the town centre and next to the railway station. Good food is provided and the staff are friendly and helpful.
13rm(7↑)(1fb) CTV in 12bedrooms TV in 1bedroom ® sB&B£15-£20 sB&B↑£20-£20 dB&B£25-£35 dB&B↑£35-£35
CTV 25P 5⌂ ⊞
♁ English Lunch £3.40-£3.40&alc Dinner £6-£7&alc Last dinner 8pm
Credit Cards [1] [2] [3] [5]

WORMIT Fife Map **11** NO32

★★Sandford Hill DD6 8RG ☎Newport-on-Tay(0382)541802
Closed 1-2 Jan
Located 3 miles south of the Tay Road Bridge, this well-established hotel is popular with both businessmen and tourists. The public rooms have a homely atmosphere and the practical modern bedrooms are well-equipped.
15rm(13⇒)(3fb) CTV in all bedrooms ® **T** sB&B⇒£33-£39 dB&B£40-£44 dB&B⇒£50-£60 ⊟
CTV 50P ⊞ ✲ ℛ (hard)
♁ Scottish & Continental **V** ✧ ⊻ Lunch £9-£11 High tea £5-£7 Dinner £15-£17 Last dinner 9pm
Credit Cards [1] [2] [3] [5] (£)

WORSLEY Greater Manchester Map **07** SD70

★★★60% **Novotel Manchester West** Worsley Brow M28 4YA (adjacent to M62 junc 13) (Novotel) ☎061-799 3535
Telex no 669586 FAX 061-703 8207
Just off junction 13 of the M62, this modern hotel provides functional and well-equipped accommodation. Ideal for families and business travellers, this hotel is convenient for Manchester airport.
119⇒↑(119fb)⊬in 20 bedrooms CTV in all bedrooms ® **T** sB⇒↑£49-£53 dB⇒↑£53-£58 (room only) ⊟
Lift 133P ✲ ⇒(heated) ♫
♁ English & French **V** ✧ ⊻ ⊬ Lunch £8-£10.50&alc Dinner £12.50-£14.50&alc Last dinner mdnt
Credit Cards [1] [2] [3] [5]

See advertisement under MANCHESTER

WORTHING West Sussex Map **04** TQ10

★★★71% ***Beach*** Marine Pde BN11 3QJ ☎(0903)34001
With its enviable postion facing the sea, this traditional and efficiently-run hotel features extensive helpful service, excellent lounge facilities, cocktail bar, well-managed restaurant and well-equipped bedrooms. Good conference facilities are available, as well as a self-contained rear car park.
91rm(72⇒9↑)(3fb) CTV in all bedrooms **T** ✕
Lift ☾ 55P ⊞ CFA nc8yrs
V ✧ ⊻ Last dinner 8.45pm
Credit Cards [1] [2] [3] [4] [5]

★★★62% **Chatsworth** Steyne BN11 3DU ☎(0903)36103
Telex no 877046 FAX (0903) 823726
The hotel has an attractive Georgian frontage and overlooks Steyne Gardens and the sea.
105rm(83⇒17↑)(5fb) CTV in all bedrooms ® **T** sB&B⇒↑£43-£53 dB&B⇒↑£65-£69 ⊟
Lift ☾ ⨍ CFA snooker sauna solarium gymnasium games room *xmas*
♁ English & Continental **V** ⊬ Lunch £9.95 Dinner £12.50 Last dinner 8.30pm
Credit Cards [1] [2] [3] [5]

★★★ 50% **Eardley** 3-10 Marine Pde BN11 3PW ☎(0903)34444 Telex no 877046 FAX (0903) 823726

Modernised Victorian terraced house in quiet position overlooking the sea.

77rm(64⇔13↱) CTV in all bedrooms ® **T** sB&B⇔↱£39-£50 dB&B⇔↱£59-£75 ⊟

Lift ☾ 20P CFA *xmas*

V ♦ ☕ Lunch £8.95-£10 Dinner £10.95-£12&alc Last dinner 9.30pm

Credit Cards [1] [2] [3] [5]

★★ **Ardington** Steyne Gardens BN11 3DZ (Best Western) ☎(0903)30451

Closed Xmas

This established family-run commercial hotel is conveniently situated overlooking Steyne Gardens. The bedrooms are well-equipped, and the resident proprietors' personal service and supervision complement the friendly and informal atmosphere.

55rm(22⇔22↱)(4fb) CTV in all bedrooms ® **T** ✱ sB&Bfr£27 sB&B⇔↱£35-£45 dB&Bfr£46 dB&B⇔↱£53-£57 ⊟

☾ P̸

☋ International ♦ ☕ Dinner £9.50 Last dinner 8.15pm

Credit Cards [1] [2] [3] [5]

★★ **Kingsway** Marine Pde BN11 3QQ ☎(0903)37542 & 37543 FAX (0903) 204173

This is a very popular seafront hotel, with very friendly and helpful service and hospitality provided by the proprietors and their loyal team of staff. The bedrooms are modern and comfortable (some with sea views), there are good lounge and bar facilities and a carvery restaurant.

28rm(20⇔8↱)(1fb) CTV in 30bedrooms ® **T** sB&B⇔↱£36-£40 dB&B⇔↱£46-£60 ⊟

Lift ☾ 12P ⊞ *xmas*

V ♦ ☕ ⁄ Lunch £8.50&alc Dinner £12.90&alc Last dinner 9pm

Credit Cards [1] [2] [3] [5] (£)

★★ **Windsor House** 14/20 Windsor Rd BN11 2LX ☎(0903)39655

33rm(12⇔11↱)(9fb) CTV in all bedrooms ® **T** ✗ (ex guide dogs) ✱ sB&B£18.50-£20.50 sB&B⇔↱£28.50-£32.50 dB&B£37-£41 dB&B⇔↱£49-£55 ⊟

CTV 18P ♫ *xmas*

☋ English & French **V** ♦ ☕ Lunch £2-£9.50&alc High tea £2-£5.50 Dinner £7.75-£8.75 Last dinner 9.30pm

(£)

WREXHAM Clwyd Map **07** SJ34

See also **Marchwiel and Marford**

★★★ 72% ***Llwyn Onn Hall*** Cefn Rd LL13 0NY

☎(0978)261225

Built around 1700 this lovely old mansion has been sympathetically restored and retains much of the original character. Bedrooms are furnished with antiques, and there is a panelled and beamed lounge bar. In the dining room you can rely on varied and interesting meals.

13rm(10⇔3↱)1⊞ CTV in all bedrooms **T**

70P nc8yrs

♦ ☕

Credit Cards [1] [2] [3] [5]

★★★ 61% **Wynnstay Arms** High Street/Yorke St LL13 8LP (Consort) ☎(0978)291010 Telex no 61674 FAX (0978) 362138

Modern hotel, situated in the town centre.

75⇔↱(8fb)⁄in 4 bedrooms CTV in all bedrooms ® **T** sB⇔↱£38.50-£45.50 dB⇔↱£48.50-£55 (room only) ⊟

Lift ☾ CTV 50P 20🚗 *xmas*

V ♦ ☕ ⁄ Lunch £5.25-£8.75 High tea fr£3.50 Dinner fr£9.85&alc Last dinner 9.45pm

Credit Cards [1] [2] [3] [5] (£)

○ ***Travelodge*** Ruadon LL14 4EJ (A483 Wrexham rbt) (Trusthouse Forte) ☎(0978)365705

31⇔

WRIGHTINGTON Lancashire Map **07** SD51

✽✗✗✗ **High Moor** Highmoor Ln WN6 9QA junct 27 off M6, take B5239

☎Appley Bridge(02575)2364

Perched on a hillside, looking across Lancashire towards Cheshire, this charming country restaurant is not easy to find, though it is within easy reach of junction 27 of the M6. The meals served here are designed to satisfy the heartiest Lancashire appetite, though they are surprisingly untraditional in style, offering tagliatelli of smoked salmon for example, as a starter. A list of daily specials supplements the à la carte menu, the range and quality of food available making this a popular lunchtime venue much used for business entertaining, specially tailored lunch menus being available if the meal is booked in advance.

Closed Mon

Lunch not served Sat

Dinner not served Sun

▶

🍷 English & French **V** 80 seats ✱ Lunch £8-£16&alc Dinner £17-£23alc Last lunch 1.45pm Last dinner 9.45pm 35P
Credit Cards [1] [2] [3] [5]

WROTHAM HEATH Kent Map **05** TQ65

★★★★54% Post House London Rd TN15 7RS (Trusthouse Forte) ☎Borough Green(0732)883311 Telex no 957309 FAX (0732) 885850
After a meal in the carvery restaurant of this modern, very well equipped hotel, guests can visit the leisure complex or relax in comfortable lounges or on the patio; bedrooms are spacious, tastefully appointed and well equipped.
119⇨↱⅟in 24 bedrooms CTV in all bedrooms ® **T** S%
sB⇨↱£75-£85 dB⇨↱£93-£120 (room only) ⊟
(138P ⊡(heated) sauna solarium gymnasium health & fitness centre ♫ ⌂ *xmas*
V ♁ ⊈ ⅟ Lunch £8.50-£12.50&alc Dinner £14.70-£24.20alc Last dinner 11pm
Credit Cards [1] [2] [3] [4] [5]

See advertisement under MAIDSTONE

WROXHAM Norfolk Map **09** TG31

★★Broads Station Rd NR12 8UR ☎Norwich(0603)782869
A hard-working family team will do their utmost to make your stay in this small hotel a comfortable one, offering friendly, attentive service, and the premises stand conveniently close to the Wroxham boating centre.
19rm(12⇨1↱)(2fb) CTV in all bedrooms ® **T** ✱ sB&B£20 sB&B⇨↱£26-£30 dB&B⇨↱£36-£48 ⊟
40P ♫ *xmas*
🍷 English & French **V** ♁ ⊈ Last high tea 5.30pm
Credit Cards [1] [2] [3] [5]

★★Hotel Wroxham Broads Centre, Hoveton NR12 8AJ ☎(0603)782061 FAX (0603) 784279
This hotel's low, modern building forms part of a shopping complex in the centre of this Broads town. Many of its bedrooms have balconies overlooking the river and the bars and restaurant are popular with visitors.
18⇨↱(2fb) CTV in all bedrooms ® **T** ✱ sB&Bfr£26 sB&B⇨↱£34-£37 dB&Bfr£38 dB&B⇨↱£46-£49 ⊟
CTV 60P ✓ riverside patio area ♫ *xmas*
V ♁ ⊈ Lunch £7-£12&alc High tea £2.50 Dinner fr£8.50&alc Last dinner 9.30pm
Credit Cards [1] [2] [3] [5]

★Kings Head Station Rd NR12 8UR (Berni/Chef & Brewer) ☎(0603)782429
6rm(3⇨3↱)(2fb) CTV in all bedrooms ® **T** ✗ (ex guide dogs) sB&B⇨↱£35.50 dB&B⇨↱£47.50 ⊟
50P
V ♁ ⊈ ⅟ Lunch £8 Dinner £9 Last dinner 9.30pm
Credit Cards [1] [2] [3] [5]

WYE Kent Map **05** TR04

✕✕Wife of Bath 4 Upper Bridge St TN25 5EW ☎(0233)812540
Small cottage restaurant with low-ceilinged rooms.
Closed Sun, Mon & 25 Dec-2 Jan
🍷 French 50 seats ✱ Lunch fr£15.90 Dinner fr£15.90 Last lunch 1.45pm Last dinner 9.45pm 15P
Credit Cards [1]

Red-star hotels offer the highest standards of hospitality, comfort and food.

WYKEHAM (near Scarborough) North Yorkshire Map **08** SE98

★★Downe Arms YO13 9QB ☎Scarborough(0723)862471 Telex no 527192 FAX (0723) 864688
This popular old 18th-century coaching inn offers very good value for money. The lounge bar and dining room are very attractive, and there are good facilities for functions and receptions.
10rm(3⇨7↱)(1fb) CTV in all bedrooms ® **T** ✱
sB&B⇨↱£19.50-£21.50 ⊟
Lift CTV 150P 2⌂ ❈ shooting *xmas*
🍷 English & French **V** ♁ ⊈ Lunch fr£6.75 Dinner fr£9.50&alc Last dinner 9pm
Credit Cards [1] [2] [3] [5]

WYMONDHAM Norfolk Map **05** TG10

★★★58% Sinclair 28 Market St NR18 0BB ☎(0953)606721 FAX (0953) 601361
A family-run hotel offering a warm welcome in this newly converted Victorian building occupying a central position in a historic market town.
20rm(10⇨10↱)(2fb)2⊞⅟in 12 bedrooms CTV in all bedrooms ® **T** ✗ sB&B⇨↱£36-£40 dB&B⇨↱£46-£51 ⊟
8P ❈ sauna *xmas*
V ♁ ⊈ Lunch £8-£10 Dinner £8.50-£10&alc Last dinner 9.30pm
Credit Cards [1] [2] [3]

★★Abbey Church St NR18 0PH ☎(0953)602148 Telex no 975711 FAX (060545) 8224
This hotel overlooking Wymondham Abbey has been sympathetically modernised to retain traces of its 16th-century origin and Victorian development. Lounge and separate bar are cosy and comfortable, and the excellent sports facilities of Barnham Broom Leisure Centre, 5 miles away, are available for guests.
29rm(22⇨)(4fb) CTV in all bedrooms ® **T** ✱ S%
sB&B⇨£33-£35 dB&B⇨£47-£50 ⊟
Lift (25P *xmas*
V ♁ ⊈ S% Lunch £4.50-£7.50 Dinner £10.50-£11.50 Last dinner 9.15pm
Credit Cards [1] [2] [3]

✕Jennings 16 Damgate St NR18 0BQ ☎(0953)603533
A former butcher's shop, set in a row of cottages just off the High Street, this betrays its origins only by the row of hooks in the ceiling and an old quarry tile floor. An almost Victorian atmosphere has now been achieved by the use of natural wood, hand-stencilled walls and attractive prints and paintings; against this charming background the proprietors present a short menu with a choice of some Continental dishes, though the emphasis is on English fare, light cooking and the subtle use of herbs retaining the natural flavours of fresh local produce.
Closed Sun & Mon
Lunch not served
Lunch by arrangement
V 30 seats ✱ Lunch £9.50&alc Dinner £9.50&alc Last dinner 10.30pm ⅌ ⅟
Credit Cards [1] [2] [3]

YARCOMBE Devon Map **03** ST20

★★The Belfry Hotel EX14 9BD (Minotels)
☎Upottery(040486)234 & 588 FAX (040486) 579
Closed 11-25 Feb
6rm(5⇨1↱)(1fb) CTV in all bedrooms ® **T** ✗ (ex guide dogs)
sB&B⇨↱£35 dB&B⇨↱£53 ⊟
10P ⊞ nc12yrs *xmas*
🍷 English & French **V** ♁ ⊈ Lunch £6.05-£7.75 Dinner £12.95&alc Last dinner 9.30pm
Credit Cards [1] [2] [3] [5]

YARM Cleveland Map **08** NZ41

✕✕**Santoro** 47 High St TS15 9BH ☎Eaglescliffe(0642)781305
This modern, first-floor restaurant in the High Street features a spacious, open-plan area which includes an attractive dining room, small bar and comfortable lounge. The interesting menu shows both French and Italian influences and offers very good value.
Closed Sun & BH's
Lunch not served Sat
English, French & Italian **V** 45 seats ✱ Lunch £5.70-£11.20alc Dinner £11.20-£17alc Last lunch 2pm Last dinner 10.15pm 20P
Credit Cards 1 2 3 5

YARMOUTH, GREAT Norfolk Map **05** TG50

★★★69% **Cliff** Gorleston NR31 6DH (2m S A12) (Best Western) ☎Great Yarmouth(0493)662179 Telex no 975608 FAX (0493) 653617
30rm(24⇌6↑)(5fb)1 in 2 bedrooms CTV in all bedrooms **T** sB&B⇌↑£42-£58 dB&B⇌↑£60-£68
70P xmas
V Lunch £8.50-£9&alc High tea £2 Dinner £11-£12&alc Last dinner 9.30pm
Credit Cards 1 2 3 5 £

★★★56% ***Dolphin*** Albert Square NR30 3JH ☎(0493)855070 Telex no 975037 FAX (0493) 853798
A commercial-style hotel in a tourist area, the Dolphin offers many amenities, including two restaurants. One of these, the Porthole, specialises in fresh fish dishes.
49⇌(1fb) CTV in all bedrooms ® **T**
CTV 12P 12 (heated) sauna solarium gymnasium pool table spa bath
V Last dinner 10pm
Credit Cards 1 2 3 5

★★**Burlington** 11 North Dr NR30 1EG
☎Great Yarmouth(0493)844568 & 842095
Closed Jan-Feb RS Dec
The family hotel is situated on the quieter North Drive, having views of the sea, gardens and tennis courts.
32rm(16⇌7↑)(9fb) CTV in all bedrooms ® **T** (ex guide dogs) sB&B£27.50-£38.50 sB&B⇌↑fr£29.50 dB&B£34-£46 dB&B⇌↑£40-£52
Lift CTV 40P CFA (heated) sauna solarium gymnasium jacuzzi turkish steamroom ♫ *xmas*
English & French **V** Lunch £7-£10.50 High tea £5 Dinner £8.50 Last dinner 8pm
Credit Cards 1 3

★★**Imperial** North Dr NR30 1EQ
☎Great Yarmouth(0493)851113 FAX (0493) 852229
Family run seafront hotel with modern, comfortable accommodation.
41rm(32⇌9↑)(8fb) CTV in all bedrooms ® **T** sB&B⇌↑fr£42 dB&B⇌↑fr£56
Lift CTV 50P CFA *xmas*
English & French **V** Lunch £6.50-£9.50 Dinner £13.50 Last dinner 10.30pm
Credit Cards 1 2 3 4 5

★★**Two Bears** South Town Rd NR31 0HV (Berni/Chef & Brewer) ☎Great Yarmouth(0493)603198
11⇌ CTV in all bedrooms ® **T** (ex guide dogs) sB&B⇌£35.50 dB&B⇌£47.50
120P
V Lunch £8 Dinner £9 Last dinner 9.30pm
Credit Cards 1 2 3 5

For key to symbols see the inside front cover.

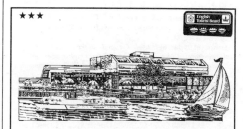

★***Dukes Head*** Hall Quay NR30 1HP ☎(0493)859184
Former coaching inn overlooking the Haven Bridge on the River Yare.
9rm CTV in all bedrooms ®
8P
♉ ☐
Credit Cards [1] [2] [3]

YATTENDON Berkshire Map **04** SU57

★★**Royal Oak** The Square RG16 0UF
☎Hermitage(0635)201325
A charming and welcoming 16th-century roadside inn offering pretty bedrooms and well prepared food.
5rm(3⇌) CTV in all bedrooms **T** sB&Bfr£50 sB&B⇌fr£60 dB&Bfr£(0 dB&B⇌fr£70 ⊟
30P
☋ English & French **V** ♉ ☐ Lunch fr£25alc Dinner fr£25alc Last dinner 10pm
Credit Cards [1] [2] [3]

YELDHAM, GREAT Essex Map **05** TL73

✕✕**White Hart** ☎(0787)237250
A black and white, timbered building dating from the 15th-century is set in three acres of garden bordered by the River Colne. Both à la carte and table d'hôte menus make skilful use of fresh, local products in creating interesting dishes, and a young staff provides courteous, friendly service.
Lunch not served Sat
Dinner not served Sun
☋ English & French **V** 60 seats ✱ Lunch fr£9&alc Last lunch 2pm Last dinner 9pm 50P
Credit Cards [1] [3]

See advertisement under HALSTEAD

YELVERTON Devon Map **02** SX56

★★★70% **Moorland Links** PL20 6DA (Forestdale)
☎(0822)852245 Telex no 45616 FAX (0822) 855004
Closed 24Dec-2Jan
Standing in its own well-tended grounds on the edge of Dartmoor, this two-storey, Colonial-style hotel features stylish bedrooms and public areas. A 'Look After Your Heart' healthy eating campaign has made an addition to the already good choice of menus, and the hotel is popular with business people.
30⇌⅍in 5 bedrooms CTV in all bedrooms ® **T** ✱
sB&B⇌£51.75-£62.75 dB&B⇌£71.50-£78.50 ⊟
(120P ✲ CFA ℘ (hard)
V ♉ ☐ ⅍ Lunch £9.50-£22.50alc Dinner £12.20-£25alc Last dinner 10pm
Credit Cards [1] [2] [3] [5] £

YEOVIL Somerset Map **03** ST51

★★★57% ***Four Acres*** West Coker BA22 9AJ (3m W A30)
☎West Coker(093586)2555 Telex no 46666
Set back off the A30 Yeovil – Crewkerne Road this stone-built property has a modern wing of bedrooms and an attractive restaurant.
20rm(16⇌3♨)Annexe5⇌ CTV in 24bedrooms ® **T** ✗ (ex guide dogs)
40P 5⛟ ⊕ ✲ pool table
☋ French **V** ♉ ☐ Last dinner 9.30pm
Credit Cards [1] [2] [3] [5]

★★★63% **Manor Crest** Hendford BA20 1TG (Crest)
☎(0935)23116 Telex no 46580 FAX (0935) 706607
Well-appointed hotel in city centre. Bedrooms are particularly well-equipped. The standard of food and service are especially worthy of mention.
20rm(19⇌1♨)Annexe21rm(20⇌1♨)1⊞⅍in 9 bedrooms CTV in all bedrooms ® **T** ✱ sB⇌♨fr£56
dB⇌♨fr£68 (room only) ⊟
(50P CFA *xmas*
V ♉ ☐ ⅍ Lunch fr£8.95&alc Dinner fr£13.45 Last dinner 10pm
Credit Cards [1] [2] [3] [4] [5] £

★★★65% **Yeovil Court** West Coker Rd BA20 2NE
☎(093586)3746 FAX (093586) 3990
An attractive hotel, pleasantly decorated inside and out, stands on the A30 road to West Coker; friendly staff are attentive to guests' needs.
15⇌Annexe3⇌(4fb)1⊞ CTV in all bedrooms ® **T** ✱
sB&B⇌£40-£49 dB&B⇌£49-£85 ⊟
75P ✲
☋ French **V** ♉ ☐ Lunch £7.50-£9.50 High tea £1-£1.50 Dinner £10.50&alc Last dinner 10pm
Credit Cards [1] [2] [3] [5] £

★**Preston** 64 Preston Rd BA20 2DL ☎(0935)74400
A small, convivial hotel, family-owned and run, is situated on the Taunton Road at the edge of the town and offers good parking.
7rm(2⇌3♨)(1fb) CTV in all bedrooms ® sB&Bfr£20
sB&B⇌♨£26-£30 dB&Bfr£33 dB&B⇌♨fr£40
19P ⊕
☋ English & French **V** ♉ ☐ ⅍
Credit Cards [1] [3]

YORK North Yorkshire Map **08** SE65

During the currency of this guide some telephone numbers are liable to change.

★★★★62% **Crest** Clifford Tower, Tower St YO1 1SB (Crest)
☎(0904)648111 Telex no 57566 FAX (0904) 610317
An elegant hotel with a striking red-brick façade. Additional comforts include spa bathrooms and luxury suites. International cuisine can be sampled in the restaurant and the informal brasserie offers a good choice of popular dishes.
128⇌♨(10fb)⅍in 26 bedrooms CTV in all bedrooms ® **T**
sB⇌♨fr£73 dB⇌♨fr£85 (room only) ⊟
Lift (40⛟ golf riding
☋ English & French **V** ♉ ☐ ⅍ Lunch fr£9.50 Dinner fr£15 Last dinner 10.30pm
Credit Cards [1] [2] [3] [4] [5] £

★★★★63% **Viking** North St YO1 1JF (Queens Moat)
☎(0904)659822 Telex no 57937 FAX (0904) 641793
The large, modern hotel is situated beside the River Ouse, in the heart of the city. With a choice of three restaurants, it caters for business people and for tourists.
188rm(174⇌14♨)(7fb) CTV in all bedrooms ® **T** ✗ (ex guide dogs) ✱ S% sB&B⇌♨£62.50-£66 dB&B⇌♨£82.50-£87 ⊟
Lift (15P 90⛟ sauna solarium gymnasium spa bath ♫ *xmas*
☋ English & French **V** ♉ ☐ Lunch £6.75-£9.50 High tea £4.75-£5.75 Dinner £11.95-£12.95&alc Last dinner 9.45pm
Credit Cards [1] [2] [3] [5] £

★★★65% **Dean Court** Duncombe Place YO1 2EF (Best Western) ☎(0904)625082 Telex no 57584 FAX (0904) 620305
Situated opposite the Minster, this hotel can be especially commended for its warm and friendly service. At the time of our inspection, total refurbishment was under way.
41rm(37⇌4♨) CTV in all bedrooms ® **T** ✗
sB&B⇌♨£45-£50 dB&B⇌♨£85-£110 ⊟
Lift (25P ⊕ *xmas*
☋ English & French **V** ♉ ☐ Lunch £6.50-£9&alc High tea £5-£10&alc Dinner fr£13.50 Last dinner 9.30pm
Credit Cards [1] [2] [3] [4] [5]

Y

★★★62% **Fairfield Manor** Shipton Road, Skelton YO3 6XW (Consort) ☎(0904)625621 Telex no 57476 FAX (0904) 612725
An early Georgian mansion, with extensive lawns and gardens, lies three miles north of the city on the A19.
25rm(22⇌3🚿)(1fb)2 CTV in all bedrooms ® T
sB&B⇌🚿£45-£49 dB&B⇌🚿£65-£69
50P ✱ 9 hole pitch & putt *xmas*
English & French V Lunch £6.25-£7.25&alc Dinner £9.75-£10.50&alc Last dinner 9.15pm
Credit Cards 1 2 3 5

★★★76% **Middlethorpe Hall** Bishopthorpe Rd YO2 1QB (Prestige) ☎(0904)641241 Telex no 57802 FAX (0904) 620176
This fine old country house hotel dates back to 1699 and has been enthusiastically restored, whilst providing for the needs of the 20th-century traveller. Conveniently located just outside the city and overlooking the racecourse, the hotel is an easily distinguishable landmark. There are several lounge areas and an attractive panelled dining room. At the time of our visit the new chef, Kevin Francksen, had not quite filled the shoes of his predecessor, some of the sauces being a little disappointing, but the menus are innovative and we will continue to watch his progress with interest.
31⇌🚿1 CTV in all bedrooms ® T S10% sB⇌🚿£80-£90 dB⇌🚿£105-£175 (room only)
Lift ☾ 70P ✱ croquet nc8yrs *xmas*
V S10% Lunch £13.50-£15.90 Dinner £20.90-£25.90&alc Last dinner 9.45pm
Credit Cards 1 2 3 5

★★★62% **Novotel** Fishergate YO1 4AD (Novotel) ☎(0904)611660 Telex no 57556 FAX (0904) 610925
124⇌🚿(124fb) in 14 bedrooms CTV in all bedrooms ® T ✱
sB⇌🚿fr£48 dB⇌🚿fr£56 (room only)
Lift ☾ 150P (heated) *xmas*
English & French V Lunch £7.95&alc High tea £4 Dinner £10.95&alc Last dinner mdnt
Credit Cards 1 2 3 5

★★★63% **Post House** Tadcaster Rd YO2 2QF (Trusthouse Forte) ☎(0904)707921 Telex no 57798 FAX (0904) 702804
This multi-storey hotel near the race course has spacious, attractive lounges, a dining room with a garden patio and well-fitted bedrooms.
147⇌(28fb) in 32 bedrooms CTV in all bedrooms ® T S%
sB⇌fr£67 dB⇌fr£81 (room only)
Lift ☾ 180P ✱ CFA *xmas*
International V Lunch £7.50&alc High tea £4.50 Dinner £13.50&alc Last dinner 10pm
Credit Cards 1 2 3 4 5

★★★67% **Swallow Chase** Tadcaster Rd YP2 2QQ (Swallow) ☎(0904)701000 Telex no 57582 FAX (0904) 702308
116⇌🚿 CTV in all bedrooms ® T S10% sB&B⇌🚿£60-£80 dB&B⇌🚿£80-£100
Lift ☾ CTV 200P 5 ✱ CFA (heated) sauna solarium gymnasium putting green golf practise net ♫ *xmas*
English & French V S10% Lunch £8.50-£10 Dinner £14-£16 Last dinner 10pm
Credit Cards 1 2 3 5

★★★64% **York Pavilion** 45 Main St, Fulford YO1 4PJ (Best Western) ☎(0904)622099 Telex no 57305 FAX (0904) 626939
11⇌Annexe10rm(8⇌2🚿)(3fb) CTV in all bedrooms ® T (ex guide dogs) sB&B⇌🚿£57.50 dB&B⇌🚿£75
46P *xmas*
V Lunch fr£7.50alc Dinner £11.50-£13.95&alc Last dinner 9.30pm
Credit Cards 1 2 3 5

Y

A rosette is the AA's highest award for quality of food and service in a restaurant.

★★*Abbots' Mews* 6 Marygate Ln, Bootham YO3 7DE ☎(0904)34866 due to change 634866 Telex no 5777
This hotel near the city centre was converted from a coachman's cottage and stables.
12🚿Annexe31rm(16⇌14🚿)(8fb) CTV in 42bedrooms ® T
30P ✱
International V Last dinner 9.30pm
Credit Cards 1 2 3 5

See advertisement on page 731

★★**Alhambra Court** 31 St Mary's, Bootham YO3 7DD ☎(0904)628474
A pair of tall, impressive town houses has been combined to create this well-equipped hotel within walking distance of the Minster. Public areas include a cosy lounge of character (with satellite TV) and a well-appointed lower-ground floor à la carte restaurant with adjacent matching lounge bar. Well-designed bedrooms combine modern facilities with the charm of the houses' original period.
25⇌🚿(5fb)1 CTV in all bedrooms ® T ✱
sB&B⇌🚿£26.50-£29 dB&B⇌🚿£40-£48
Lift CTV 25P *xmas*
French & Italian Dinner £8.50-£10&alc Last dinner 10pm
Credit Cards 1 3

★★**Ashcroft** 294 Bishopthorpe Rd YO2 1LH (Minotels) ☎(0904)659286
Closed Xmas & New Year
Large but quiet house with restful atmosphere and good home cooking.
11rm(10⇌1🚿)Annexe4rm(3⇌1🚿)(3fb) CTV in all bedrooms ® T ✱ sB&B⇌🚿fr£27 dB&B⇌🚿fr£49.50
CTV 40P ✱
V Lunch fr£4.95alc High tea fr£4.95alc Dinner fr£8.75&alc Last dinner 8pm
Credit Cards 1 2 3 5 £

★★**Beechwood Close** 19 Shipton Rd, Clifton YO3 6RE (Minotels) ☎(0904)658378 FAX (0904) 647124
Closed 25 Dec
A converted country house with its own gardens stands in a surburban area to the north of the city. It provides homely public areas, an attractive restaurant and the attention of friendly proprietors.
14rm(8⇨6↱)(2fb) CTV in all bedrooms ® **T** ✗ sB&B⇨↱£28.50-£31.50 dB&B⇨↱£49-£54 ⊟
CTV 36P ⇌
V ♡ ⊻ Lunch £5.95-£6.50 Dinner £9.95-£10.90 Last dinner 9pm
Credit Cards 1 2 3 £

★★**Cottage** 3 Clifton Green YO3 6LH ☎(0904)643711
Closed 24-26 Dec
A pair of town houses overlooking the Green in the village of Clifton has been converted into a cosy, cottage-style hotel, featuring exposed brickwork and beams and furnished in compatibly antique fashion. Traditional English and Yorkshire dishes are served in the dining room by friendly staff.
18rm(14⇨4↱)(3fb) CTV in all bedrooms ® **T** ✗ (ex guide dogs) ✱ sB&B⇨↱£30-£35 dB&B⇨↱£55-£60 ⊟
12P
♡ Dinner £9-£10&alc Last dinner 9pm
Credit Cards 1 2 3 5 £

★★**Disraeli's** 140 Acomb Rd YO2 4HA ☎(0904)781181
Closed 25 Dec-1 Jan
The gabled, brick-built hotel stands in its own grounds in the suburb of Acomb. It offers well-proportioned bedrooms, tastefully appointed, and an elegant restaurant.
9⇨↱(3fb) CTV in all bedrooms ® **T** ✗ sB&B⇨↱£33-£47 dB&B⇨↱£56-£64 ⊟
CTV 40P ⇌ ❊
♡ Cosmopolitan V ♡ ⊻ Lunch £5.85-£7.50 Dinner £10.75-£11.50&alc Last dinner 9.30pm
Credit Cards 1 2 3

★★**Heworth Court** 76-78 Heworth Green YO3 7TQ ☎(0904)425156 & 425126 Telex no 57571 FAX (0904) 415290
Comfortable hotel with modern facilities and pleasant dining area.
7rm(3⇨4↱)Annexe9rm(3⇨6↱) CTV in all bedrooms ® **T** ✗ ✱ sB&B⇨↱£33-£35 dB&B⇨↱£52-£54 ⊟
CTV 16P 1⌂ ⇌ *xmas*
V ♡ ⊻ Lunch fr£8.50&alc Dinner fr£12.50&alc Last dinner 9.30pm
Credit Cards 1 2 3 5 £

★★**The Hill** 60 York Rd, Acomb YO2 5LW (Exec Hotel) ☎(0904)790777 Telex no 57567
Closed mid Dec-mid Jan
A modernised Georgian residence, suitably restored and renovated, lies in three-quarters of an acre of walled garden about two miles from the city centre. Well-appointed bedrooms and public rooms retain some original features, while modern bedrooms in the new wing are well equipped.
10⇨(1fb)2⊟ CTV in all bedrooms ® **T** ✗ sB&B⇨£33 dB&B⇨£56 ⊟
12P ⇌ ❊ *xmas*
V ⅟
Credit Cards 1 2 3 5 £

See advertisement on page 733

★★**Hudsons** 60 Bootham YO3 7BZ ☎(0904)621267
Large Victorian hotel of character, with modern facilities and new wing.
28rm(26⇨2↱)(3fb)1⊟ CTV in all bedrooms ® **T** ✗ (ex guide dogs) ✱ sB&B⇨↱£35-£40 dB&B⇨↱£59-£70 ⊟
Lift ⊞ 34P pool table ♫ *xmas*

►

Y

🍷 English & French V ♔ 🍽 Sunday Lunch £8.95 Dinner £11-£12&alc Last dinner 9.30pm
Credit Cards [1] [2] [3] [5]

★★Kilima 129 Holgate Rd YO2 4DE (Inter)
☎(0904)658844 & 625787 Telex no 57928
This carefully restored and upgraded Victorian rectory stands about a mile outside the city walls and has its own car park. Victorian accessories add to the charm of the lower ground floor restaurant and lounge bar, whilst bedrooms are well equipped.
15rm(11⇒4⌐)(1fb)1⊞ CTV in all bedrooms ® T ✱ sB&B⇒⌐£35-£40 dB&B⇒⌐£52-£56 ⊟
20P ⊞ *xmas*
🍷 English & French V ♔ 🍽 ⊁ Lunch fr£10.50&alc Dinner fr£13.75&alc Last dinner 9.30pm
Credit Cards [1] [2] [3] [5]

★★Knavesmire Manor 302 Tadcaster Rd YO2 2HE
☎(0904)702941 FAX (0904) 430313
13rm(8⇒1⌐)Annexe9⌐(2fb)1⊞ CTV in all bedrooms ® T sB&B£22.50-£32 sB&B⇒⌐£32-£45 dB&B£32-£38 dB&B⇒⌐£35-£56 ⊟
Lift 26P 1🚗 ⊡(heated) sauna *xmas*
V ♔ 🍽 High tea £3-£7 Dinner £11.75-£18 Last dinner 9pm
Credit Cards [1] [2] [3] [5]

★★Lady Anne Middletons Hotel Skeldergate YO1 1DS
☎(0904)32257/30456 Telex no 57577
Closed 24 Dec-27 Dec
40rm(38⌐)Annexe10⌐(2fb) CTV in all bedrooms ® T ✗ (ex guide dogs) S% sB&B⌐£42 dB&B⌐£55 ⊟
☾ CTV 50P ✲ sauna jacuzzi
V ♔ 🍽 Sunday Lunch fr£6.75 Dinner fr£11.95 Last dinner 9pm
Credit Cards [1] [2] [3]

★★Railway King George Hudson St YO1 1JL ☎(0904)645161
Closed Xmas
Standing in a central position, the hotel provides a convenient base from which to explore all the facilities of the ancient city. It offers well-equipped bedrooms, a smart lounge bar and a popular restaurant.
22rm(6⇒16⌐)(2fb) CTV in all bedrooms ® T ✗ (ex guide dogs) sB&B⇒⌐£25-£32.50 dB&B⇒⌐£35-£45
☾ 6P ⊞
🍷 International ♔ Bar Lunch 90p-£5.25alc
Credit Cards [1] [2] [3] [5]

★★Savages 15 St Peters Grove YO3 6AQ ☎(0904)610818
Closed Xmas Day
An interesting Victorian house in a quiet, tree-lined avenue has been enlarged and pleasingly converted into a very comfortable small hotel. Nicely equipped bedrooms are complemented by a well-appointed lounge, bar and restaurant complex.
18rm(7⇒8⌐)(4fb) CTV in 17bedrooms ® T ✗ (ex guide dogs) sB&B£24-£32 sB&B⇒⌐£26-£34 dB&B£48-£56 dB&B⇒⌐£52-£60 ⊟
CTV 16P solarium gymnasium
♔ 🍽 ⊁ Lunch £5.50-£10.50 Dinner fr£10.50 Last dinner 8pm
Credit Cards [1] [2] [3] [5] Ⓔ

★★*The Sheppard* 63 Blossom St YO2 2AP ☎(0904)643716
Telex no 57950
Four-storey town hotel, dating from 1834, on the A64.
20rm(16⇒)(3fb)1⊞⊁in 6 bedrooms CTV in all bedrooms ® T ✗ (ex guide dogs)
CTV 10P 6🚗(£1.25) ♩
🍷 English & French V 🍽 Last dinner 9.30pm
Credit Cards [1] [3]

Book as early as possible for busy holiday periods.

★★Town House 100-104 Holgate Rd YO2 4BB ☎(0904)626171
FAX (0904) 623044
Closed 24-31 Dec
Friendly, hospitable hotel with well appointed accommodation.
23rm(12⇒6⌐)(5fb) CTV in all bedrooms T ✱ sB&Bfr£22 sB&B⇒⌐fr£33 dB&B⇒⌐fr£45 ⊟
25P ⌂
🍷 European V ♔ 🍽 Last high tea 6.30pm
Credit Cards [1] [2] [3] [5]

★Clifton Bridge Waterend, Clifton YO3 6LL ☎(0904)610510
A neat and tidy hotel with a modern bedroom extension, a snug lounge bar and friendly, helpful service.
11rm(7⇒4⌐)(1fb) CTV in all bedrooms ® T
sB&B⇒⌐£25-£30 dB&B⇒⌐£36-£46 ⊟
12P ⊞
V ♔ 🍽 Dinner £6.50-£9.75&alc Last dinner 7.45pm
Credit Cards [1] [3] Ⓔ
See advertisement on page 735

★Fairmount 230 Tadcaster Road, Mount Vale YO2 2ES
☎(0904)38298
This small, comfortable, quietly elegant hotel overlooking the race-course is under the personal management of a resident proprietor who looks after her guests attentively. It provides a cosy lounge bar, a separate main lounge, and a restaurant which concentrates on a short list of English dishes and a few good value wines.
10rm(4⇒4⌐)(4fb) CTV in all bedrooms ® ✱ sB&B⇒⌐fr£25 dB&B⇒⌐£39-£42 ⊟
7P 3🚗
🍷 International V ♔ 🍽 Last high tea 6pm
Credit Cards [1] [3] Ⓔ
See advertisement on page 735

★Holgate Bridge 106-108 Holgate Rd YO2 4BB ☎(0904)635971
Closed 24-26 Dec
A pair of town houses has been combined and modified to create this friendly hotel. The accommodation is equipped to modern standards with a charm and character enhanced by the conservatory-style entrance lounge and cosy basement dining room.
14rm(5⇌6⋔)(4fb)1⊟ CTV in all bedrooms ® sB&B£18-£28 sB&B⇌⋔£25-£30 dB&B£30-£32 dB&B⇌⋔£35-£50 ⊟
16P
V Bar Lunch £1.50-£11.75alc Dinner fr£7.95&alc Last dinner 9pm
Credit Cards [1] [3] ⓔ

★Newington 147 Mount Vale YO2 2DJ (1.5m S of Burnley, off A646) ☎(0904)625173 Telex no 65430
Four town houses have been suitably converted to form this hotel on the A1036 (south) approach road into the city.
25rm(7⇌18⋔)Annexe15rm(1⇌14⋔)(3fb)2⊟ CTV in all bedrooms ® **T** ✗ sB&B⇌⋔£30-£35 dB&B⇌⋔£48-£54 ⊟
Lift 40P ⊡(heated) sauna solarium *xmas*
V ♡ Lunch £5.95-£6.95 Dinner £10.50-£10.95 Last dinner 9.30pm
Credit Cards [1] [2] [3] [5] ⓔ

✗19 Grape Lane 19 Grape Ln YO1 2HU ☎(0904)636366
This charming little restaurant occupies two floors in its city-centre location. Short, but interesting menus are based on contemporary English cookery. Dishes such as a tasty fish mousse with a tomato and brandy mayonnaise might be followed by a rich salmis of pigeon or roast duck with a black cherry sauce, all carefully prepared and served with good vegetables. Service is competent and there is a decent wine list.
Closed Sun & Mon, last two wks Jan, 23 Sep-6 Oct
V 34 seats Lunch £8.50&alc Dinner £16.50&alc Last lunch 2pm Last dinner 10.30pm ₱

Country House Hotels

Identified in the gazetteer by the symbol 🌲, country house hotels are often secluded and though they are not always rurally situated, you will be assured of peaceful surroundings and a restful night. The atmosphere will be relaxed and informal and you will receive a personal welcome. Some of the facilities may differ from those to be found in purpose-built urban hotels of the same star rating. Full details can be found in the gazetteer entries.

ENGLAND

AVON

Freshford
★★★Homewood Park
Rangeworthy
★★64% Rangeworthy Court Hotel
Thornbury
★★★77% Thornbury Castle

BEDFORDSHIRE

Flitwick
★★★76% Flitwick Manor

BUCKINGHAMSHIRE

Taplow
★★★★★73% Cliveden

CHESHIRE

Chester
★★★71% Crabwall Manor
Nantwich
★★★75% Rookery Hall
Sandiway
★★★75% Nunsmere Hall Country House
Tarporley
★★ The Willington Hall

CLEVELAND

Easington
★★★72% Grinkle Park

CORNWALL

Falmouth
★★★72% Penmere Manor
Helston
★★ Nanslee Manor
Lamorna Cove
★★★59% Lamorna Cove
Liskeard
★★ Country Castle
❀★★ Well House
Mawnan Smith
★★★73% Meudon
Penzance
★★★62% Higher Faugan
Portscatho
★★ Roseland House
St Wenn
★ Wenn Manor
Talland Bay
★★★73% Talland Bay

CUMBRIA

Alston
★★ Lovelady Shield Country House
Appleby-in-Westmorland
★★★65% Appleby Manor
Bassenthwaite
★★★★51% Armathwaite Hall
★★ Overwater Hall
Blawith
★★ Highfield Country
Brampton
❀★★ Farlam Hall
Crosby-on-Eden
★★★69% Crosby Lodge Country House
Grasmere
❀★★★ Michael's Nook
Hawkshead
★★★53% Tarn Hows
★ Highfield House
Howtown
❀❀★★★ Sharrow Bay Country House
Keswick
★★ Lyzzick Hall Country House
★★ Red House
Loweswater
★★ Scale Hill
Thornthwaite
★★ Thwaite Howe
Underbarrow
★★ Greenriggs Country House
Watermillock
★★★75% Leeming House
★★ Old Church
Windermere
★★★64% Langdale Chase
★★ Holbeck Ghyll Country House
★★ Lindeth Fell
★★ Linthwaite
Witherslack
★ Old Vicarage Country House

DERBYSHIRE

Ashbourne
★★ Callow Hall
Ashford-in-the-Water
★★ Riverside Country House
Bakewell
★★ Croft Country House
Matlock
★★★70% Riber Hall
★★ Red House
Rowsley
★★ East Lodge Country House

DEVON

Ashburton
★★ Holne Chase
Barnstaple
★★★57% Roborough House
★★ Downrew House
★ Halmpstone Manor
Bideford
★★ Yeoldon House
Burrington
★★★67% Northcote Manor
Chagford
★★★ Gidleigh Park
★★★75% Mill End
★★★75% Teignworthy
Chittlehamholt
★★★74% Highbullen
Clawton
★★ Court Barn Country House
Fairy Cross
★★★71% Portledge
Gittisham
★★★67% Combe House
Hawkchurch
★★★71% Fairwater Head
Haytor
★★★70% The Bel Alp House
Holbeton
★★★65% Alston Hall
Honiton
★★★67% Deer Park
Horn's Cross
★★★67% Foxdown Manor
Kingsbridge
★★★78% Buckland-Tout-Saints
Lee
★★ Lee Manor Country House
Lewdown
★★ Lewtrenchard Manor
Lynton
★★ Hewitts
Mary Tavy
★★ Moorland Hall
Moretonhampstead
★★ Glebe House
Newton Ferrers
★★ Court House
North Huish
★★ Brookdale House
Sidmouth
★★ Brownlands
Sourton
★★ Collaven Manor
South Brent
★★ Glazebrook House
South Molton
★★ Marsh Hall
Stoke Gabriel
★★★65% Gabriel Court
Torquay
★★★70% Orestone Manor House
Whimple
★★ Woodhayes

DORSET

Gillingham
★★ Stock Hill House
Milton Abbas
★★ Milton Manor
Studland
★★ Manor House

EAST SUSSEX

Battle
★★★ Netherfield Place

Uckfield
★★★Horsted Place
Wadhurst
★★ Spindlewood Country House

ESSEX

Dedham
★★★Maison Talbooth

GLOUCESTERSHIRE

Bibury
★★ Bibury Court
Buckland
★★★ Buckland Manor
Charingworth
★★★80% Charingworth Manor
Cheltenham
★★★Greenway
Lower Slaughter
★★★ Lower Slaughter Manor
Stow-on-the-Wold
★★★75% Wyck Hill Park
Stroud
★★★64% Burleigh Court
Tetbury
★★★ Calcot Manor
Upper Slaughter
★★★74% Lords of the Manor

HAMPSHIRE

Brockenhurst
★★ Whitley Ridge Country House
Hurstbourne Tarrant
★★ Esseborne Manor
Lymington
★★★73% Passford House
Lyndhurst
★★★66% Parkhill
New Milton
★★★★ Chewton Glen
Rotherwick
★★★★79% Tylney Hall
Winchester
❀★★★75% Lainston House

HEREFORD & WORCESTER

Abberley
★★★77% Elms
Broadway
★★ Collin House
Chaddesley Corbett
★★★74% Brockencote Hall Country House
Hereford
★★ Netherwood
Ledbury
★★ Hope End Country House
Lugwardine
★★ Longworth Hall
Malvern
★★★63% Cottage in the Wood
★★ Holdfast Cottage
Pencraig
★★ Pencraig Court
Ross-on-Wye
★★★61% Pengethley Manor
★★ Glewstone Court

HUMBERSIDE

Great Driffield
★★ Wold House Country
Little Weighton
★★★66% Rowley Manor

ISLE OF WIGHT

Ventnor
★ Madeira Hall

KENT

Ashford
★★★★ Eastwell Manor
Cranbrook
★★ Kennel Holt Country House

LANCASHIRE

Garstang
★★ The Pickerings

LEICESTERSHIRE

Melton Mowbray
★★★★73% Stapleford Park
Normanton
★★★75% Normanton Park
Oakham
★★★ Hambleton Hall

LINCOLNSHIRE

Lincoln
★★★62% Washingborough Hall Country House

NORFOLK

Bunwell
★★ Bunwell Manor
Grimston
❀★★★ Congham Hall Country House

NORTH YORKSHIRE

Appleton-le-Moors
★★ Dweldapilton Hall
Arncliffe
★★ Amerdale House
Bilbrough
★★★ Bilbrough Manor Country House
Crathorne
★★★★57% Crathorne Hall
Great Ayton
★★★70% Ayton Hall
Hackness
★★★66% Hackness Grange Country
Hawes
★★ Stone House
Kirkby Fleetham
★★★72% Kirkby Fleetham Hall
Lastingham
★★ Lastingham Grange
Markington
★★★74% Hob Green
Monk Fryston
★★★68% Monk Fryston Hall
Scarborough
★★★64% Wrea Head Country
Whitwell-on-the-Hill
★★★63% Whitwell Hall Country House

NORTHUMBERLAND

Allendale
★★ Bishopfield Country House
Belford
★★ Warren House
Cornhill-on-Tweed
★★★58% Tillmouth Park
Powburn
★★ Breamish House

OXFORDSHIRE

Chadlington
★★ The Manor
Great Milton
❀❀❀★★★ Le Manoir Aux Quat' Saisons
Horton-cum-Studley
❀★★★ Studley Priory

SHROPSHIRE

Oswestry
★★ Sweeney Hall
Worfield
★★ Old Vicarage

SOMERSET

Dulverton
★★★72% Carnarvon Arms
★★ Ashwick House
Hawkridge
★★ Tarr Steps
Shapwick
★★ Shapwick House
Ston Easton
★★★ Ston Easton Park

SUFFOLK

Brome
★★ Oaksmere Hotel & Country Club
Bury St Edmunds
★★★75% Ravenwood Hall
Hintlesham
❀★★★ Hintlesham Hall
Woodbridge
★★★72% Seckford Hall

SURREY

Bagshot
★★★★69% Pennyhill Park

WARWICKSHIRE

Billesley
❀★★★76% Billesley Manor
Ettington
★★ The Chase Hotel at Ettington
Leamington Spa (Royal)
❀★★★ Mallory Court
Hockley Heath
❀★★★ Nuthurst Grange Country House

WEST SUSSEX

Amberley
★★★79% Amberley Castle
Arundel
★ Burpham Country
Climping
★★★72% Bailiffscourt
Cuckfield
★★ Hilton Park
East Grinstead
❀★★★ Gravetye Manor
Lower Beeding
★★★74% South Lodge
Thakeham
❀★★★74% Abingworth Hall

WEST YORKSHIRE

Todmorden
★★★70% Scaitcliffe Hall
Wentbridge
★★★67% Wentbridge House

Wetherby
★★★ Wood Hall

WILTSHIRE

Bradford on Avon
★★★73% Woolley Grange
Castle Combe
★★★75% Manor House
Limpley Stoke
★★★59% Cliffe
Malmesbury
★★★72% Whatley Manor
Melksham
★★★74% Beechfield House
Warminster
★★★★70% Bishopstrow House

CHANNEL ISLANDS

JERSEY

Rozel Bay
★★★76% Château la Chaire
St Saviour
★★★★ Longueville Manor

SCOTLAND

BORDERS

Dryburgh
★★★56% Dryburgh Abbey
Kelso
★★★75% Sunlaws House
Peebles
★★ Cringletie House
★★ Venlaw Castle

CENTRAL

Callander
★★★68% Roman Camp
Dunblane
❀★★★ Cromlix House

DUMFRIES & GALLOWAY

Auchencairn
★★★69% Balcary Bay
Crossmichael
★★ Culgruff House
Newton Stewart
★★★★61% Kirroughtree
Portpatrick
❀❀★★ Knockinaam Lodge
Port William
★★★63% Corsemalzie House
Rockcliffe
★★★68% Baron's Craig

FIFE

Letham
★★★63% Fernie Castle

GRAMPIAN

Banchory
★★★★71% Invery House
★★★ Banchory Lodge
Kildrummy
★★★75% Kildrummy Castle
Rothes
★★★64% Rothes Glen

HIGHLAND

Achnasheen
★★ Ledgowan Lodge
Arisaig
★★★ Arisaig House
Drumnadrochit
❀★★ Polmaily House
Fort William
❀❀★★★★ Inverlochy Castle
Invergarry
★★ Glengarry Castle
Inverness
★★★71% Bunchrew House
Isle Ornsay
❀★★ Kinloch Lodge
Kentallen
❀★★ Ardsheal House
Skeabost Bridge
★★★66% Skeabost House
Whitebridge
★★ Knockie Lodge

LOTHIAN

Aberlady
★★ Greencraig Country House
Gullane
★★★75% Greywalls
Humbie
★★★66% Johnstounburn House
Uphall
★★★65% Houstoun House

SHETLAND

Brae
★★★67% Busta House

STRATHCLYDE

Appin
★★ Invercreran Country House
Barrhill
❀★★★77% Kildonan
Dolphinton
★★★64% Dolphinton House
Eriska
★★★ Isle of Eriska
Kilchrenan
❀★★★ Ardanaiseig
★★★66% Taychreggan
Kilwinning
★★★67% Montgreenan Mansion House
Langbank
❀★★★ Gleddoch House
Skelmorlie
★★★63% Manor Park
Stewarton
★★★75% Chapletoun House

TAYSIDE

Auchterarder
★★★69% Auchterarder House
Auchterhouse
★★★68% Old Mansion House
Blairbowrie
★★★71% Kinloch House
Cleish
★★★68% Nivingston House
Kinclaven
★★★75% Ballathie House
Letham
★★★63% Idvies House
New Scone
❀★★★72% Murrayshall Country House
Pitlochry
★★★68% Pine Trees

WESTERN ISLES

Scarista
★★ Scarista House

WALES

CLWYD

Llangollen
★★★65% Bryn Howel
Northop
★★★75% Soughton Hall
Rossett
★★★73% Llyndir Hall
Wrexham
★★★72% Llwyn Onn Hall

DYFED

Aberystwyth
★★★61% Conrah
Eglwysfach
★★★55% Ynyshir Hall
Lamphey
★★★64% Court
Llechryd
★★★52% Gwesty Castell Maelgwyn
St Davids
★★★62% Warpool Court
Whitland
★★★62% Waungron Country Mansion

GWYNEDD

Aberdovey
★★★64% Hotel Plas Penhelig
Abersoch
★★★68% Porth Tocyn
Beddgelert
★ Bryn Eglwys Country House
Betws-y-Coed
★★★ Craig-y-Dderwyn Country House
★★★66% Plas Hall
Criccieth
★★★69% Bron Eifion Country House
Llanbedr
★★ Cae Nest Hall
Llandudno
★★★ Bodysgallen Hall
Llanrug
★★★79% Seiont Manor
Llanrwst
★★★63% Plas Maenan Country House
Rowen
★ Tir-y-Coed Country House
Talsarnau
★★ Maes y Neuadd

POWYS

Llangammarch Wells
❀★★★76% Lake
Llanwddyn
★★★68% Lake Vyrnwy

WEST GLAMORGAN

Reynoldston
★★ Fairyhill Country House

AA Lodges

LOCATION	NAME	COMPANY
Alrewas	○ Travelodge	THF
Alwalton	⇧ Travelodge	THF
Amesbury	○ Travelodge	THF
Aust Motorway Service Area	○ Rank Motor Lodge	Rank
Baldock	○ Travelodge	THF
Barnsdale Bar	○ Travelodge	THF
Barton Mills	○ Travelodge	THF
Barton Stacey	⇧ Travelodge	THF
Barton under Needwood	⇧ Travelodge	THF
Basildon (Essex)	⇧ Campanile	Campanile
Basildon (Essex)	⇧ Watermill Travel Inn	Whitbread
Basingstoke	○ Travelodge	THF
Bebington	⇧ Travelodge	THF
Birch Service Area	⇧ Granada Lodge	Granada
Birmingham	⇧ Campanile	Campanile
Blyth (Nottinghamshire)	⇧ Granada Lodge	Granada
Bothwell Motorway Service Area	○ Roadchef Lodge	Roadchef
Burnley	○ Travelodge	THF
Cannock	⇧ Longford House Travel Inn	Whitbread
Cardiff	⇧ Campanile	Campanile
Cardiff	○ Rank Motor Lodge	Rank
Colsterworth	○ Granada Lodge	Granada
Colsterworth	○ Travelodge	THF
Coventry	○ Travelodge	THF
Coventry	⇧ Campanile	Campanile
Coventry	○ Campanile Hotel	Campanile
Cross Hands	○ Travelodge	THF
Doncaster	○ Campanile Hotel	Campanile
Dorking	○ Travelodge	THF
Droitwich	○ Travelodge	THF
Dumbarton	○ Travelodge	THF
East Horndon	⇧ Travelodge	THF
Edinburgh	○ Travelodge	THF

LOCATION	NAME	COMPANY
Farthing Corner Service Area	⇧ Rank Motor Lodge	Rank
Felling	○ Travelodge	THF
Fenstanton	○ Travelodge	THF
Ferrybridge Service Area	○ Granada Lodge	Granada
Five Oaks	○ Travelodge	THF
Fontwell	○ Travelodge	THF
Forton Motorway Service Area	○ Rank Motor Lodge	Rank
Four Marks	○ Travelodge	THF
Frankley Motorway Service Area	⇧ Granada Lodge	Granada
Gordano Motorway Service Area	○ Travelodge	THF
Grantham	○ Travelodge	THF
Gretna	⇧ Travelodge	THF
Halkyn	○ Travelodge	THF
Hamilton Motorway Service Area	○ Roadchef Lodge	Roadchef
Heston Motorway Service Area	⇧ Granada Lodge	Granada
Hilton Park Services	⇧ Rank Motor Lodge	Rank
Hull	⇧ Campanile	Campanile
Kinross	⇧ Granada Lodge	Granada
Knutsford	○ Travelodge	THF
Leigh Delamere Service Area	⇧ Granada Lodge	Granada
Liverpool	○ Campanile	Campanile
Llandegai	○ Rank Motor Lodge	Rank
Lolworth	○ Travelodge	THF
Markfield	○ Granada Lodge	Granada
Markham Moor	○ Travelodge	THF
Marston Moretaine	○ Travelodge	THF
Musselburgh	○ Granada Lodge	Granada
Newark-on-Trent	⇧ Travelodge	THF
North Muskham	○ Travelodge	THF
Northampton	○ Travelodge	THF
Nuneaton	⇧ Griff House Travel Inn	Whitbread
Oldbury	○ Travelodge	THF
Oswestry	⇧ Travelodge	THF
Pencoed	○ Travelodge	THF
Penrith	○ Travelodge	THF

LOCATION	NAME	COMPANY
Peterborough	⇧ Travelodge	THF
Plymouth	⇧ Hotel Campanile	Campanile
Podimore	○ Travelodge	THF
Reading	○ Travelodge	THF
Redditch	⇧ Campanile	Campanile
Rownhams Motorway Service Area	○ Roadchef Lodge	Roadchef
Rugeley	○ Travelodge	THF
Saltash	⇧ Granada Lodge	Granada
Sampford Peverell	⇧ Travelodge	THF
Sarn Park Service Area	⇧ Travelodge	THF
Scotch Corner	○ Travelodge	THF
Scotch Corner	○ Rank Motor Lodge	Rank
Sedgemoor Motorway Service Area	○ Roadchef Lodge	Roadchef
Sedgemoor Motorway Service Area	○ Travelodge	THF
Skipton	○ Travelodge	THF
Sourton	○ Travelodge	THF
Southwaite Service Area	⇧ Granada Lodge	Granada
Stirling	⇧ Granada Lodge	Granada
Stowmarket	○ Travelodge	THF
Sutton Scotney	⇧ Travelodge	THF
Sutton Scotney	○ Travelodge	THF
Swansea	○ Campanile Hotel	Campanile
Tamworth	○ Granada Lodge	Granada
Taunton Deane Motorway Service Area	○ Roadchef Lodge	Roadchef
Thrussington	○ Travelodge	THF
Thurlaston	○ Travelodge	THF
Toddington Service Area	○ Granada Lodge	Granada
Towcester	○ Travelodge	THF
Tring	⇧ Crows Nest Travel Inn	Whitbread
Uttoxeter	○ Travelodge	THF
Warminster	⇧ Granada Lodge	Granada
Washington Service Area	⇧ Granada Lodge	Granada
Whiddon Down	○ Granada Lodge	Granada
Woolley Edge	⇧ Granada Lodge	Granada
Wrexham	○ Travelodge	THF

Hotel Groups

Key to abbreviations and central reservation telephone numbers (where applicable)

Special corporate rates are available at hotel companies marked with an *, to those business travellers who have a company account with the AA Business Travel Service.

Bookings may be made via the AA Travel Agencies listed below

Company	Abbreviations	Telephone
Associated Leisure Hotels Ltd	Associated Leisure	061-941 6848
Berni Chef & Brewer	Berni and Chef & Brewer	
*Best Western	Best Western	01-541 0033
Brend Hotels Ltd	Brend	Barnstaple (0271) 44496
*Consort Hotels Ltd	Consort	York (0904) 643151
*Commonwealth Holiday Inns of Canada Ltd	Holiday Inns	01-722 7755
*Crest Hotels Ltd	Crest	Banbury (0295) 267722
Crown & Raven	Crown & Raven	
De Vere Hotels Ltd	De Vere	Warrington (0925) 65050
*Embassy Hotels	Embassy	01-581 3466
Exec Hotels	Exec Hotel	
Forestdale Hotels Ltd	Forestdale	
Frederic Robinson Ltd	Frederic Robinson	
Granada Motorway Services Ltd	Granada	05255-5555
Greenall Whitley Hotels Ltd	GW Hotels	Warrington (0925) 65050
Guestaccom	Guestaccom	
*Hilton National & Associated Hotels Ltd	Hilton	01-734 6000
Leading Hotels of the World for Berkeley, Claridges, Connaught, Savoy, Hyde Park, London; Royal Crescent, Bath, Avon; Lygon Arms, Broadway, Worcs; Grosvenor, Chester; Chewton Glen, New Milton, Hants		Freephone 0800 181123
Inter-Hotels	Inter-Hotels	01-373 3241
Minotels	Minotels	Blackpool (0253) 594185
*Mount Charlotte Hotels Ltd	Mount Charlotte	Freephone (0800) 700400
*Norfolk Capital Hotels Ltd	Norfolk Capital	01-589 7000
*Novotel International	Novotel	01-724 1000
Porterhouse Restaurants Ltd	Porterhouse	
Prestige Hotels	Prestige	01-439 2365
Pride of Britain Ltd	Pride of Britain	Andover (026476) 444
*Queens Moat House Ltd	Queens Moat	Harrogate (0423) 52644
*Rank Organisation Ltd	Rank	01-262 2893
Relais et Châteaux Hotels	Relais et Châteaux	
Scottish Highland Hotels	Scottish Highland	041-332 6538
Shire Inns Ltd	Shire	
*Stakis Hotels & Inns	Stakis	041-332 4343
*Swallow Hotels Ltd	Swallow	091-529 4666
*Thistle Hotels (Scottish & Newcastle Breweries)	Thistle	01-937 8033
Toby Restaurants Ltd	Toby	
*Trusthouse Forte Hotels Ltd	Trusthouse Forte	01-567 3444
*Whitbread/Lansbury		

Automobile Association

Bookings for hotels belonging to groups marked * can only be made if your company has an account with AA Business Travel Service. Business Travel Centres are located throughout the UK and are listed below with telephone numbers.

Aberdeen	(0224) 645138	Guildford	(0483) 574070	Twickenham	01-891 6211
Basingstoke	(0256) 492434	Halesowen	021-501 7779	Manchester	061-488 7499
Bristol	(0272) 308373	Leeds	(0532) 448981	Northampton	(0604) 22700
Edinburgh	031-225 7677	Leicester Sq.	01-930 6854	Reading	(0734) 580663
Glasgow	041-221 4373	Stanmore	01-954 6718		

Overseas Offices of the British Tourist Authority

Australia
British Tourist Authority
Midland House
171 Clarence St
Sydney
N.S.W. 2000
☎ (02) 29-8627

Belgium
British Tourist Authority
Rue de la Montagne 52
Bergstraat B2
1000 Brussels
☎ 02/511 4390

Brazil
British Tourist Authority
Avenida Ipiranga 318–A
12° Andar, conj 1201
Edificio Vila Normanda
01046 Sâo Paulo =SP
☎ 257-1834

Canada
British Tourist Authority
94 Cumberland Street
Suite 600
Toronto
Ontario
M5R 3N3
☎ (416) 925-6326

Denmark
British Tourist Authority
Møntergade 3
DK-1116 København K
☎ (01) 120793

France
British Tourist Authority
63 Rue Pierre Charron
75008 Paris
☎ (1) 42 89 11 11

Germany
British Tourist Authority
Neue Mainzer Str 22
6000 Frankfurt am Main 1
☎ (069) 23 80707

Ireland
British Tourist Authority
123 Lower Baggot Street
Dublin 2
☎ 614188

Italy
British Tourist Authority
Corso Vittorio Emanuele 11
No 337
00186 Rome
☎ 654 0821

Japan
British Tourist Authority
246 Tokyo Club Building
3-2-6 Kasumigaseki,
Chiyoda-ku
Tokyo 100
☎ (03) 581-3603

Mexico
British Tourist Authority
Edificio Alber
Paseo de la Reforma 332-5 Piso
06600 Mexico DF
☎ 5336375

Netherlands
British Tourist Authority
Aurora Gebour (5c)
Stadhouderskade 2
1054 ES Amsterdam
☎ (020) 855051

New Zealand
British Tourist Authority
8th Floor
Norwich Insurance House
Corner, Queen & Durham Streets
Auckland 1
☎ (09) 31 446

Norway
Postboks 1554 Vika
0117 Oslo 1
☎ (02) 41 18 49

Singapore
British Tourist Authority
14 Collyer Quay 05-03
Singapore Rubber House
Singapore 0104
☎ 535 2966

South Africa
British Tourist Authority
PO Box 6256
Johannesburg 2000
☎ (011) 296770

Spain
British Tourist Authority
Torre de Madrid 6/4
Plaza de Espana
Madrid 28008
☎ (91) 241 1396

Sweden
British Tourist Authority
For visitors:
Malmskillnadsgatan 42
1st Floor
For Mail: Box 7293
S-10390 Stockholm
☎ 08 212444

Switzerland
British Tourist Authority
Limmatquai 78, 8001 Zurich
☎ 01/47 4277 or 474297

USA Chicago
British Tourist Authority
John Hancock Centre Suite 3320
875 N. Michigan Avenue
Chicago Illinois 60611
☎ (312) 787-0490

USA Dallas
British Tourist Authority
Cedar Maple Plaza
2305 Cedar Springs Road
Dallas Texas 75201-1814
☎ (214) 720 4040

USA Los Angeles
British Tourist Authority
World Trade Center
350 South Figueroa Street
Suite 450
Los Angeles, CA90071
☎ (213) 628-3525

USA New York
British Tourist Authority
40 West 57th Street
New York N.Y. 10019
☎ (212) 581-4700

Index of Town Plans

Plan	Page No.
Aberdeen	2
Bath	4
Birmingham (Central)	6
Birmingham & District	8
Bournemouth & District	10
Central	11
Boscombe & Southbourne	12
Westbourne & Branksome	12
Brighton	5
Bristol	14
Cardiff	16
Eastbourne	17
Edinburgh	18
Exeter	20
Falmouth	21
Gatwick Airport & District	29
Glasgow	22
Heathrow Airport	30
Inverness	24
Keswick	25
Liverpool	26
Llandudno	28
London—London plans precede the London section of the gazetteer	
London Airports: Gatwick & District	29
Heathrow	30
Manchester	32
Newcastle-upon-Tyne	34
Newquay	36
Nottingham	38
Oxford	40
Perth	44
Plymouth	42
Scarborough	45
Southampton	46
Stratford-upon-Avon	47
Torquay	48
Westbourne & Branksome	12
Windermere & Bowness	49

Key to Town Plans

- - -	Roads with restricted access
†	Churches
i	Tourist Information centre
AA	AA Centre
P	Car parking
3	Hotel and restaurant
★ 9	Red Star hotel
	Distance to hotels from edge of plan
4 2m	Mileage to town from edge of plan

Aberdeen

1 Amatola ★★★
2 Atlantis ✕
3 Bucksburn Moat House ★★★★
4 Caledonian Thistle ★★★
4A Copthorne ★★★
7 New Marcliffe ★★★
8 Skean Dhu Altens ★★★★
9 Stakis Treetops ★★★
10 Swallow Imperial ★★★

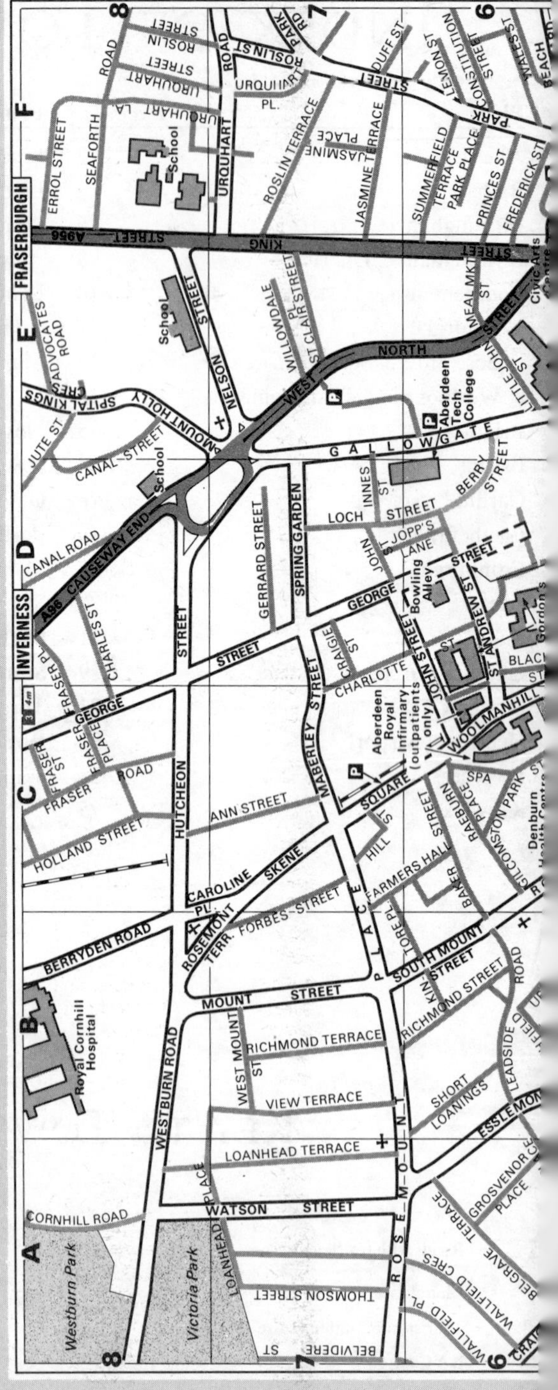

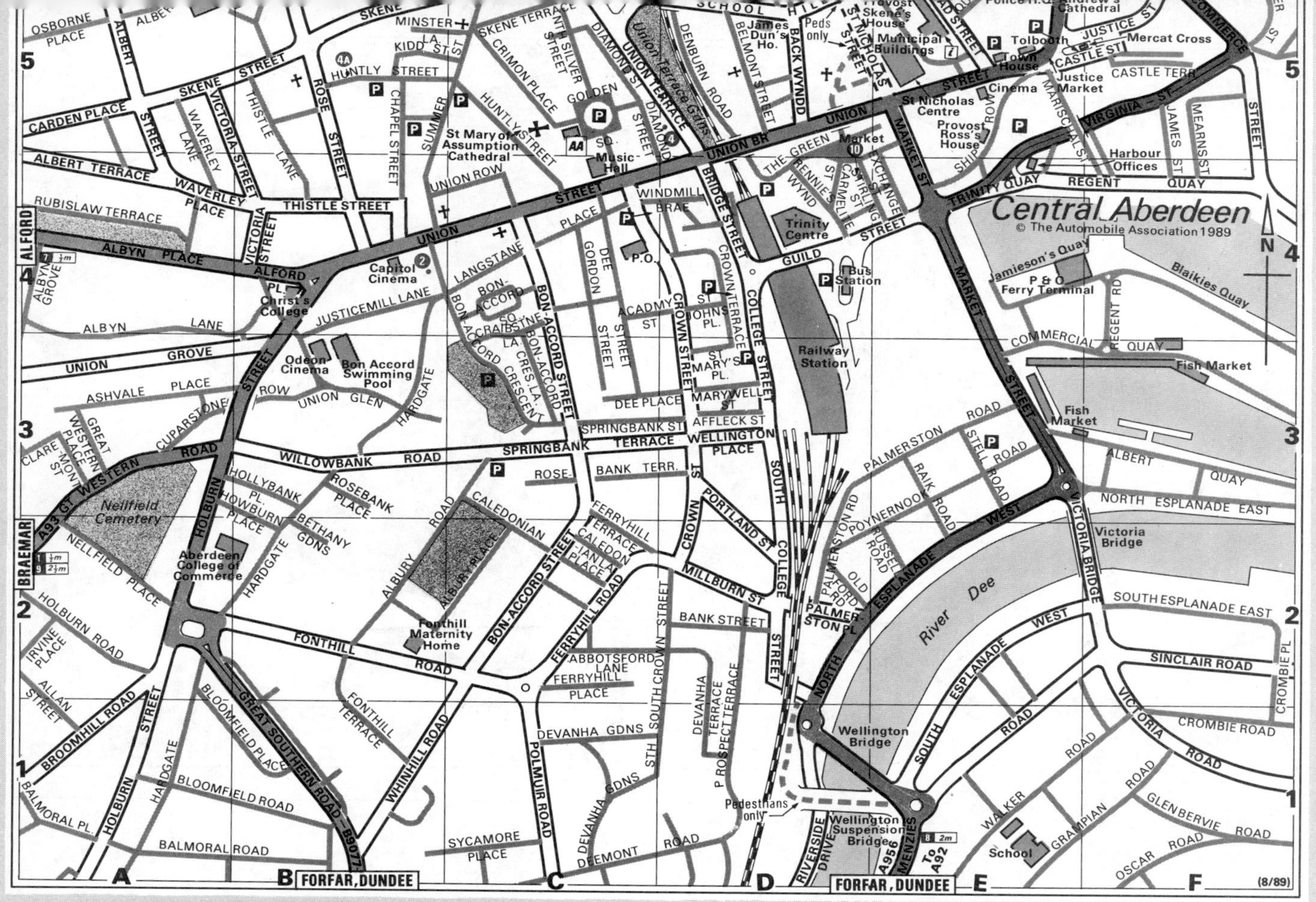

Central Aberdeen
© The Automobile Association 1989
(8/89)
N
UNION STREET
UNION TERRACE
Union Terrace Gdns
ALBYN PLACE
ALFORD
BRAEMAR
FORFAR, DUNDEE
A956
B9077
A93 GT WESTERN ROAD
To A92
HOLBURN STREET
GREAT SOUTHERN ROAD
BON-ACCORD STREET
BON-ACCORD CRESCENT
CROWN STREET
SOUTH CROWN STREET
COLLEGE STREET
SOUTH COLLEGE STREET
BRIDGE STREET
GUILD STREET
MARKET STREET
VICTORIA BRIDGE
Wellington Bridge
Wellington Suspension Bridge
River Dee
NORTH ESPLANADE WEST
NORTH ESPLANADE EAST
SOUTH ESPLANADE WEST
SOUTH ESPLANADE EAST
RIVERSIDE DRIVE
MENZIES
VICTORIA ROAD
SINCLAIR ROAD
CROMBIE ROAD
CROMBIE PL
GLENBERVIE ROAD
GRAMPIAN ROAD
WALKER ROAD
OSCAR ROAD
School
Railway Station
Bus Station
Trinity Centre
St Nicholas Centre
Provost Ross's House
Provost Skene's House
Municipal Buildings
Town House
Tolbooth
Mercat Cross
Justice Market
Harbour Offices
P & O Ferry Terminal
Jamieson's Quay
Blaikies Quay
Fish Market
ALBERT QUAY
REGENT QUAY
TRINITY QUAY
COMMERCIAL QUAY
REGENT RD
VIRGINIA ST
CASTLE ST
CASTLE TERR
JUSTICE ST
JAMES ST
MEARNS ST
MARISCHAL ST
SHIPROW
EXCHANGE ST
STIRLING ST
CARMELITE ST
RENNIE'S WYND
THE GREEN
BACK WYND
SCHOOL HILL
BELMONT STREET
DENBURN ROAD
James Dun's Ho.
ST NICHOLAS STREET
Peds only
UNION BR
WINDMILL BRAE
DIAMOND ST
DIAMOND STREET
GOLDEN SQ.
Music Hall
SILVER STREET
CRIMON PLACE
SKENE TERRACE
HUNTLY STREET
St Mary of Assumption Cathedral
UNION ROW
SUMMER ST
CHAPEL STREET
KIDD ST
MINSTER LA
SKENE STREET
ROSE STREET
THISTLE STREET
THISTLE LANE
VICTORIA STREET
WAVERLEY LANE
WAVERLEY PLACE
ALBERT STREET
ALBERT TERRACE
CARDEN PLACE
OSBORNE PLACE
RUBISLAW TERRACE
ALBYN GROVE
ALBYN LANE
UNION GROVE
ASHVALE PLACE
GREAT WESTERN PLACE
CLAREMONT ST
CUPARSTONE ROW
Christ's College
Capitol Cinema
Odeon Cinema
Bon Accord Swimming Pool
UNION GLEN
JUSTICEMILL LANE
LANGSTANE PLACE
HARDGATE
DEE STREET
GORDON STREET
ACADMY ST
DEE PLACE
P.O.
CROWN TERRACE
ST JOHNS PL.
ST MARY'S PL.
MARYWELL ST
AFFLECK ST
WELLINGTON PLACE
SPRINGBANK TERRACE
SPRINGBANK ST
BANK TERR.
ROSE ST
WILLOWBANK ROAD
ROSEBANK PLACE
HOLLYBANK PL.
HOWBURN PLACE
BETHANY GDNS
Aberdeen College of Commerce
Nellfield Cemetery
NELLFIELD PLACE
HOLBURN ROAD
IRVINE PLACE
ALLAN STREET
BROOMHILL ROAD
BALMORAL PL.
BALMORAL ROAD
BLOOMFIELD ROAD
BLOOMFIELD PLACE
FONTHILL ROAD
FONTHILL TERRACE
Fonthill Maternity Home
ALBURY ROAD
ALBURY PLACE
CALEDONIAN PLACE
CALEDONIAN TERRACE
FERRYHILL TERRACE
FERRYHILL ROAD
FERRYHILL PLACE
ABBOTSFORD LANE
WHINHILL ROAD
POLMUIR ROAD
SYCAMORE PLACE
DEEMONT ROAD
DEVANHA GDNS
DEVANHA TERRACE
PROSPECT TERRACE
BANK STREET
MILLBURN ST
PORTLAND ST
PALMERSTON PL
PALMERSTON RD
PALMERSTON ROAD
OLD FORD RD
RUSSELL ROAD
POYNERNOOK ROAD
RAIK ROAD
STELL ROAD
Pedestrians only

Bath

1 Bath ★★★
2 Berni Royal ★
3 Garlands ✕
4 Dukes' ★★
6 Flowers ✕
7 Francis ★★★★
8 Gainsborough ★
9 Hole in the Wall ✕✕
10 Lansdown Grove ★★★
11 Popjoys ✕✕✕
12 Pratts ★★★
13 The Priory ★★★
14 Rajpoot Tandoori ✕✕
15 Redcar ★★★
16 Royal Crescent ★★★★

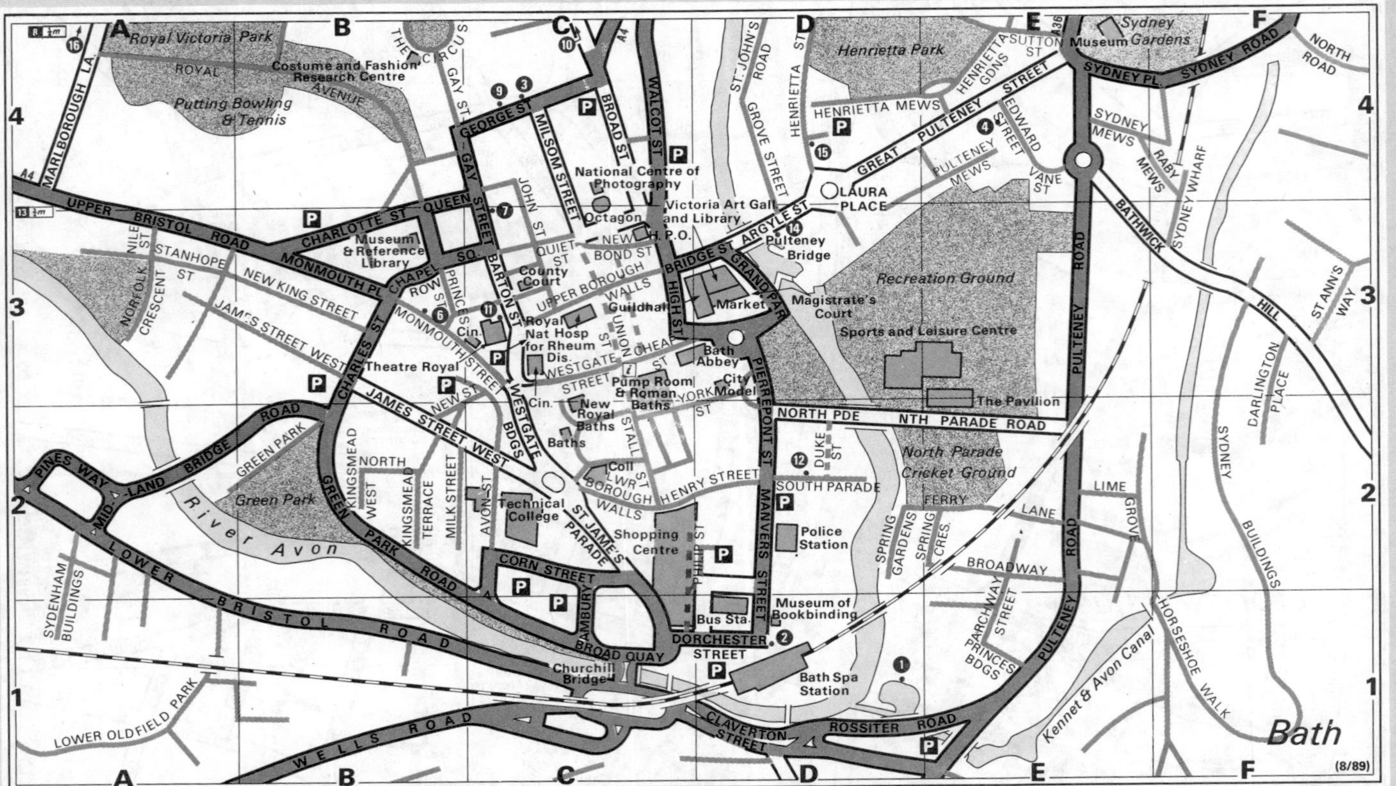

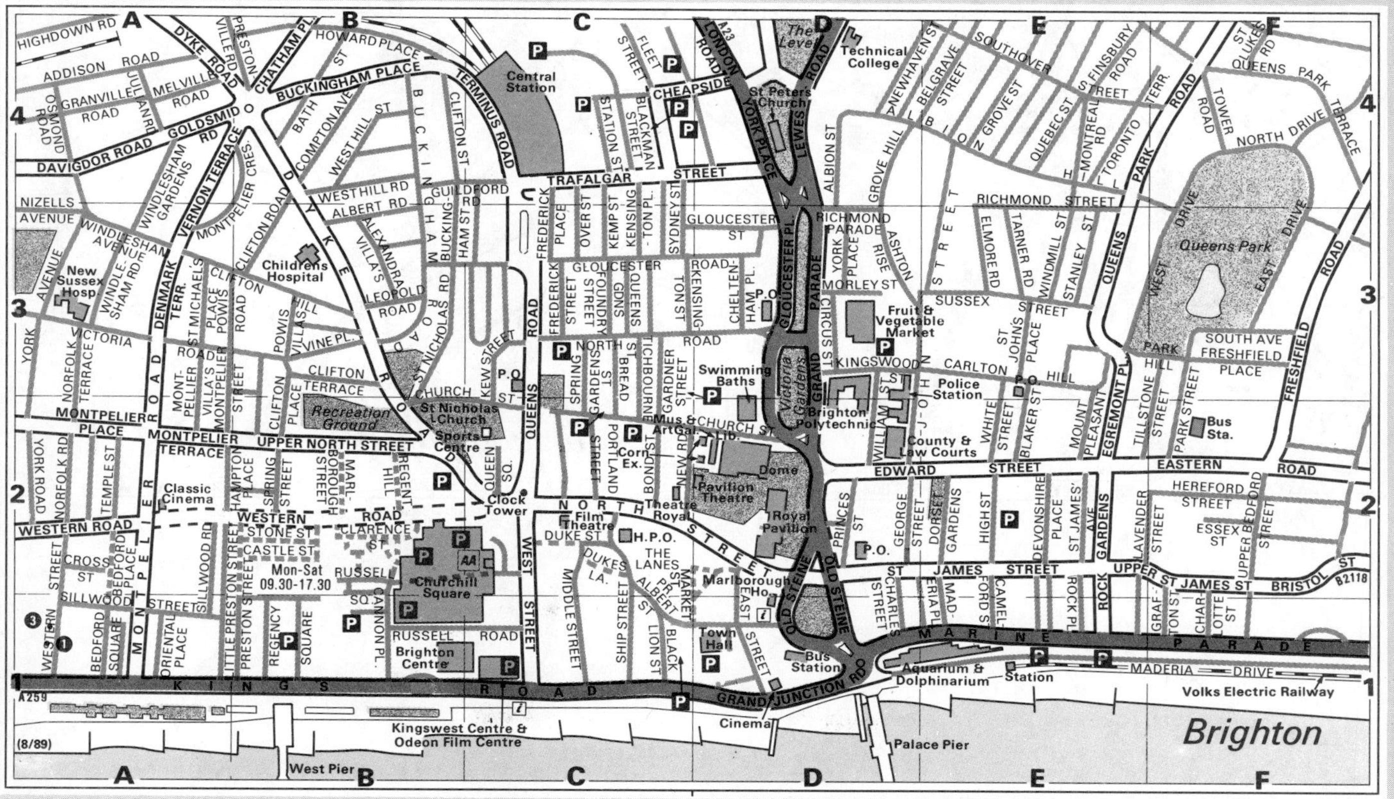

Brighton

1 Le Grandgousier ✕
3 Whyte's ✕

Birmingham Central

1 Albany ★★★★
2 Biarritz ✕✕
3 Chung Ying ✕✕
7 Grand ★★★
8 Henry's ✕✕
10 Holiday Inn ★★★★
14 Rajdoot ✕✕
15 Royal Angus Thistle ★★★

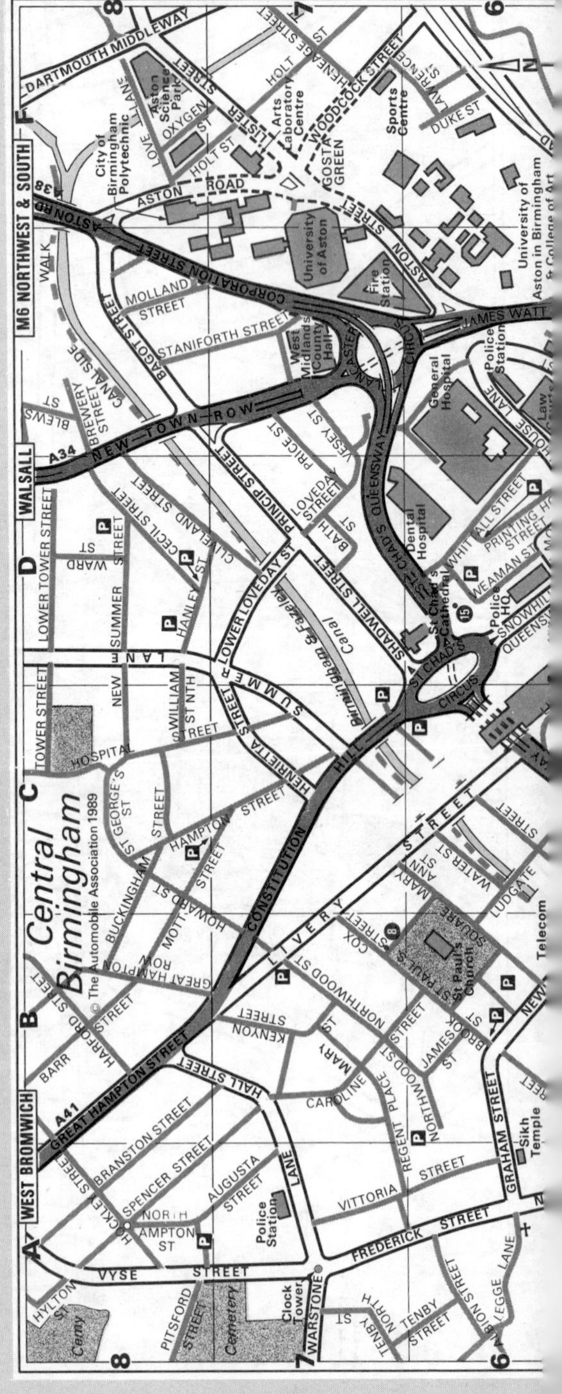

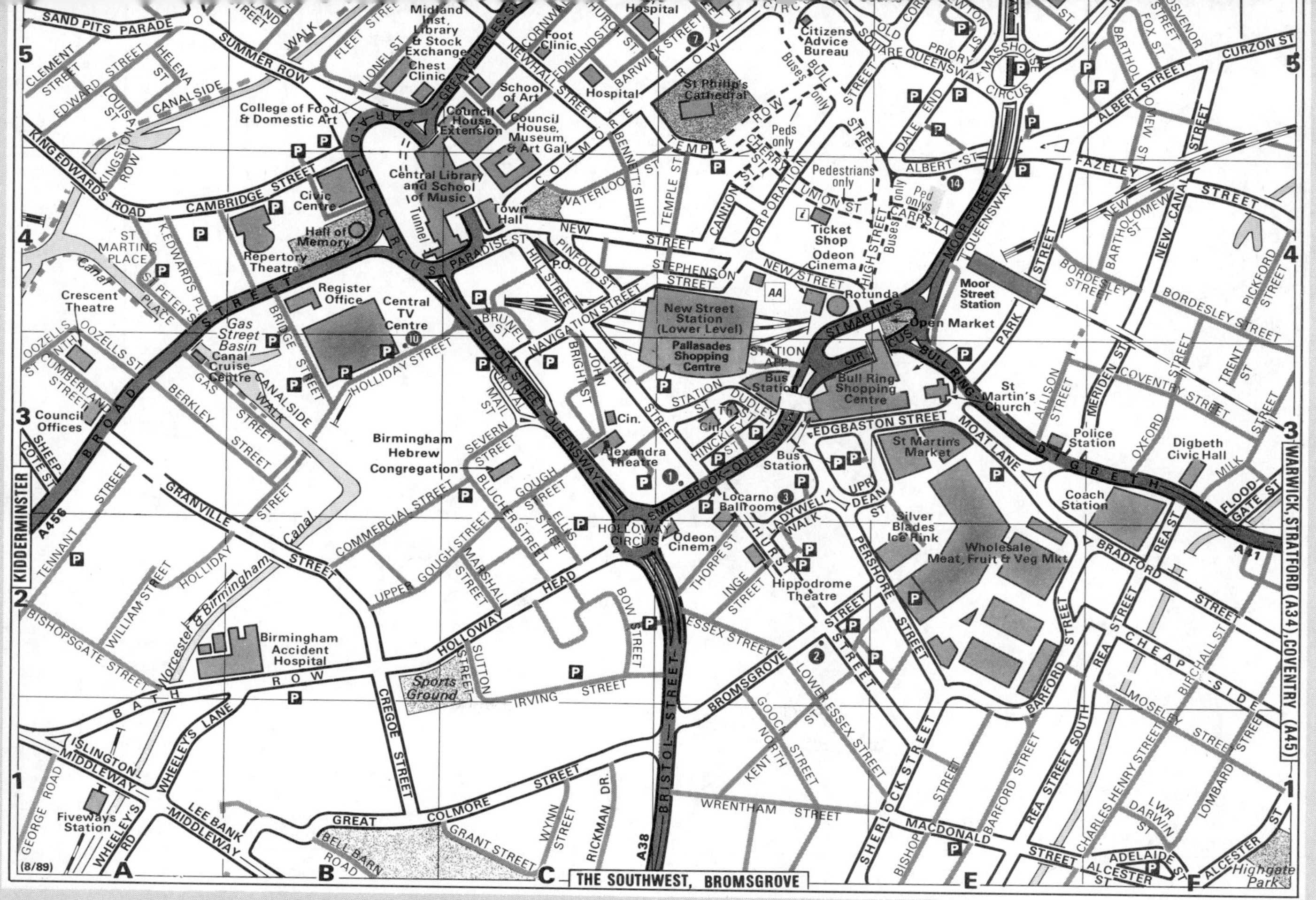

WARWICK, STRATFORD (A34), COVENTRY (A45)
KIDDERMINSTER
THE SOUTHWEST, BROMSGROVE
A38
A41
A456
(8/89)
Digbeth Civic Hall
Police Station
Coach Station
Moor Street Station
Open Market
St Martin's Church
St Martin's Market
Wholesale Meat, Fruit & Veg Mkt
Silver Blades Ice Rink
Bull Ring Shopping Centre
Rotunda
Odeon Cinema
Ticket Shop
Citizens Advice Bureau
St Philip's Cathedral
New Street Station (Lower Level)
Pallasades Shopping Centre
Bus Station
Locarno Ballroom
Hippodrome Theatre
Alexandra Theatre
Town Hall
Council House, Museum, & Art Gall.
Council House Extension
Central Library and School of Music
School of Art
Foot Clinic
Chest Clinic
Midland Inst. Library & Stock Exchange
Hospital
Central TV Centre
Register Office
Birmingham Hebrew Congregation
Hall of Memory
Civic Centre
Repertory Theatre
College of Food & Domestic Art
Gas Street Basin
Canal Cruise Centre
Crescent Theatre
Council Offices
Birmingham Accident Hospital
Sports Ground
Fiveways Station
Highgate Park
DIGBETH
BULL RING
MOOR STREET
QUEENSWAY
SMALLBROOK QUEENSWAY
SUFFOLK STREET QUEENSWAY
HOLLOWAY CIRCUS
HOLLOWAY HEAD
BRISTOL STREET
BROMSGROVE STREET
PERSHORE STREET
SHERLOCK STREET
CHEAPSIDE
MOSELEY STREET
REA STREET
REA STREET SOUTH
BARFORD STREET
BRADFORD STREET
EDGBASTON STREET
MOAT LANE
CORPORATION STREET
NEW STREET
COLMORE ROW
PARADISE CIRCUS
BROAD STREET
GREAT CHARLES ST.
CAMBRIDGE STREET
KING EDWARDS ROAD
SAND PITS PARADE
SUMMER ROW
GRANVILLE STREET
BATH ROW
ISLINGTON MIDDLEWAY
LEE BANK MIDDLEWAY
WHEELEYS LANE
WHEELEY'S RD
GEORGE ROAD
BELL BARN ROAD
CREGOE STREET
GREAT COLMORE STREET
IRVING STREET
SUTTON STREET
BOW STREET
RICKMAN DR.
WYNN STREET
GRANT STREET
WRENTHAM STREET
KENT STREET
GOOCH STREET NORTH
LOWER ESSEX STREET
ESSEX STREET
INGE STREET
THORPE ST
HURST ST
LADYWELL WALK
UPPER DEAN ST
HINCKLEY ST
DUDLEY ST
STATION ST
HILL STREET
JOHN BRIGHT ST
NAVIGATION STREET
PINFOLD ST
STEPHENSON STREET
TEMPLE ST
BENNETT'S HILL
WATERLOO ST
CANNON ST
CHERRY ST
UNION ST
HIGH STREET
CARRS LA
ALBERT ST
DALE END
PRIORY QUEENSWAY
MASSHOUSE CIRCUS
SQUARE
NEWHALL STREET
EDMUND ST
BARWICK ST
FLEET STREET
GOUGH STREET
UPPER GOUGH STREET
COMMERCIAL STREET
SEVERN STREET
BLUCHER STREET
MARSHALL STREET
ELLIS STREET
MAIL ST
ROYAL
BRUNEL ST
HOLLIDAY STREET
BRIDGE STREET
CANALSIDE WALK
BERKLEY STREET
GAS STREET
WILLIAM STREET
BISHOPSGATE STREET
TENNANT STREET
OOZELLS ST
CUMBERLAND STREET
SHEEPCOTE ST
ST PETER'S PLACE
ST MARTINS PLACE
K. EDWARDS PL
KINGSTON ROW
HELENA ST
LOUISA ST
CLEMENT STREET
EDWARD STREET
CANALSIDE
MACDONALD STREET
BISHOP STREET
ADELAIDE ST
ALCESTER ST
LWR DARWIN ST
CHARLES HENRY STREET
BIRCHALL ST
LOMBARD STREET
GATE ST
FLOOD ST
MILK ST
OXFORD
ALLISON STREET
PARK STREET
MERIDEN ST
COVENTRY STREET
BORDESLEY STREET
TRENT ST
PICKFORD STREET
NEW CANAL STREET
NEW BARTHOLOMEW ST
BARTHOLOMEW ST
FAZELEY STREET
ALBERT STREET
CURZON ST
FOX ST
Worcester & Birmingham Canal

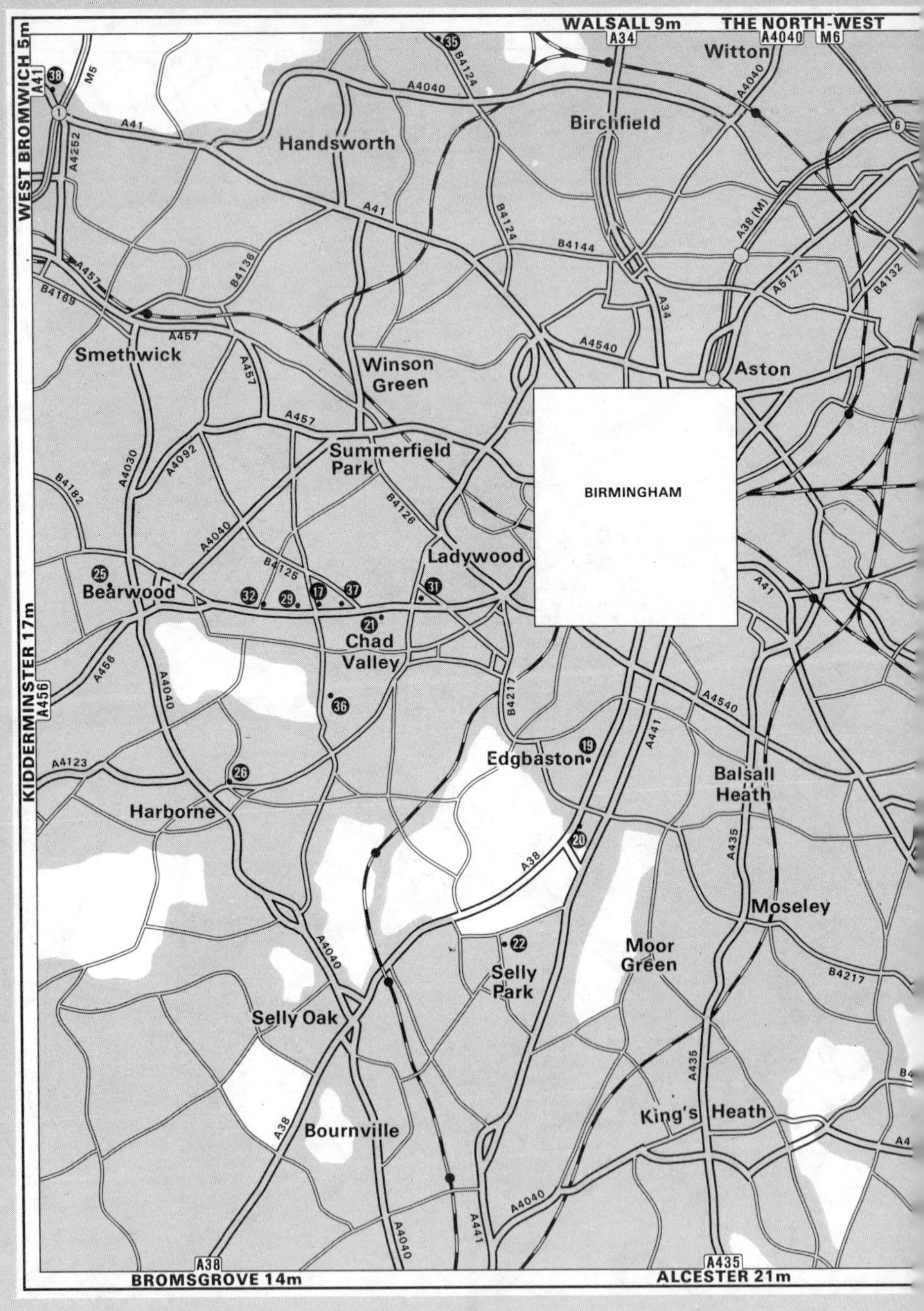

Birmingham District

17 Apollo ★★★
18 Arden ★★★
(Listed under Birmingham National Exhibition Centre)
19 Beechwood ★★
20 Bristol Court ★★
21 Cobden ★★
22 Copperfield House ★★
23 Excelsior ★★★
(Listed under Birmingham Airpo
24 Flemings ★★ (Listed under Solih
25 Franzl's ✕

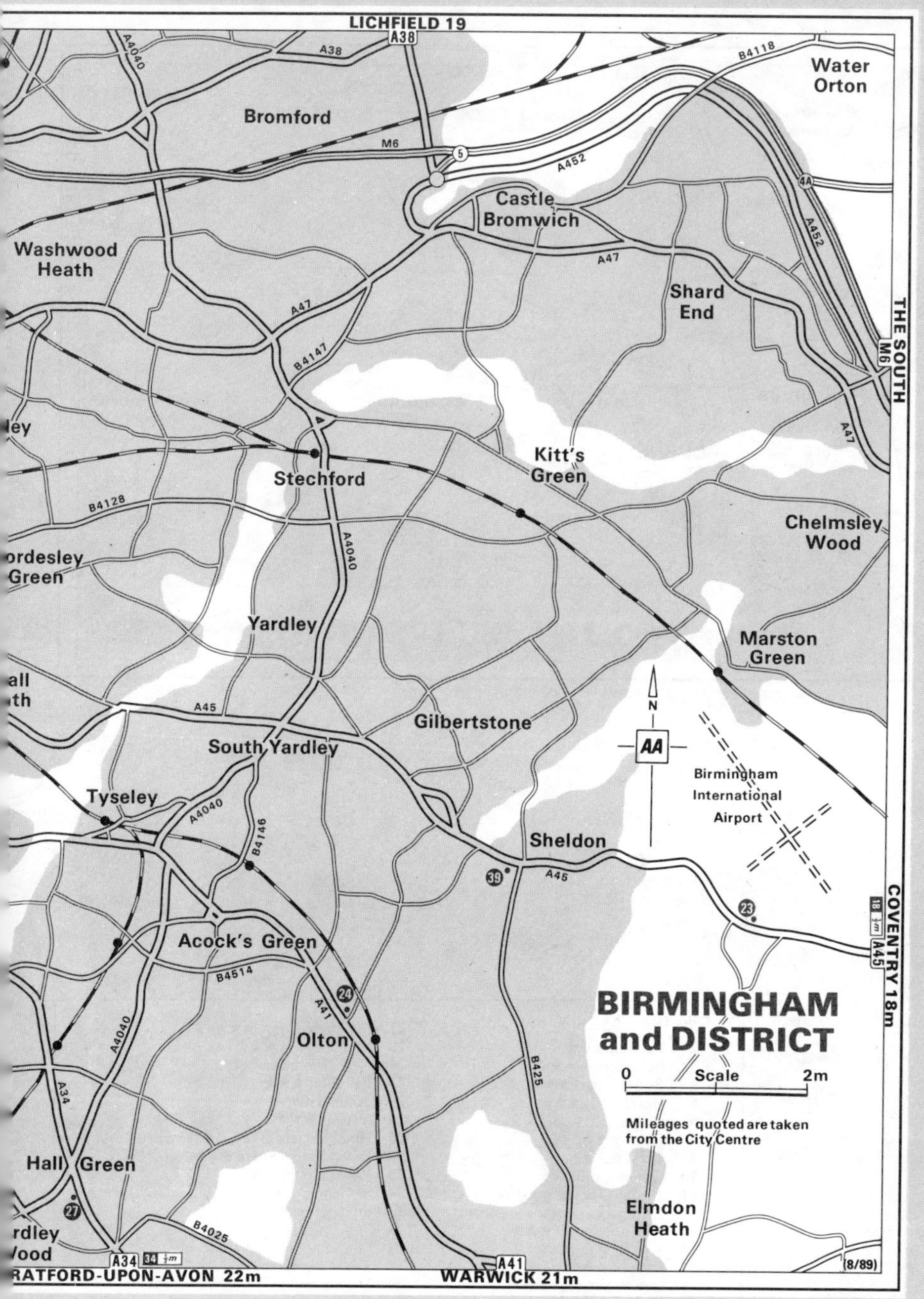

Henry Wong ✕
Jays ✕
Norfolk ★★
Plough & Harrow ★★★★
32 Portland ★★
34 Saracens Head ★★ (See under Solihull)
35 Sheriden House ★★
36 Sloan's ✕✕✕
37 Strathallan Thistle ★★★
38 West Bromwich Moat House ★★★ (See under West Bromwich)
39 Wheatsheaf ★★

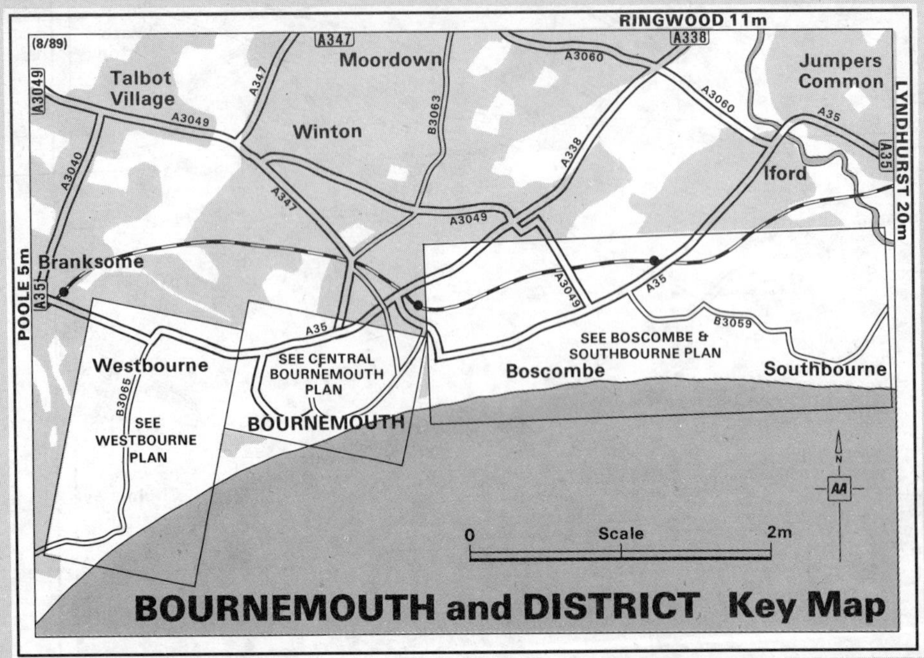

Bournemouth Central

2 Arlington ★★
3 Belvedere ★★★
4 Burley Court ★★★
5 Hotel Cecil ★★★
6 Connaught Court ★★
7 County ★★
8 Crest ★★★
10 Durley Chine ★★
11 Durley Grange ★★
12 Durley Hall ★★★
13 Durlston Court ★★★
14 East Anglia ★★★
15 Embassy ★★★
16 Gresham Court ★★
17 Grosvenor ★★★
18 Heathlands ★★★
19 Highcliff ★★★★
20 Lynden Court ★
21 Mansfield ★★
22 Marsham Court ★★★
23 Melford Hall ★★★
26 New Dorchester ★
27 Pavillion ★★★
28 Pinehurst ★★
29 Queens ★★★
30 Hotel Riviera (West Cliff Gardens) ★★
31 Royal Bath ★★★★★
32 Royal Exeter ★★
34 St George ★★
35 Silver How ★
36 Sophisticats ✕✕
37 Sun Court ★★
38 Trouville ★★★
40 Wessex ★★★
41 West Cliff Hall ★★
42 Whitehall ★★
43 White Hermitage ★★★
44 Winterbourne ★★
46 Woodcroft Tower ★★

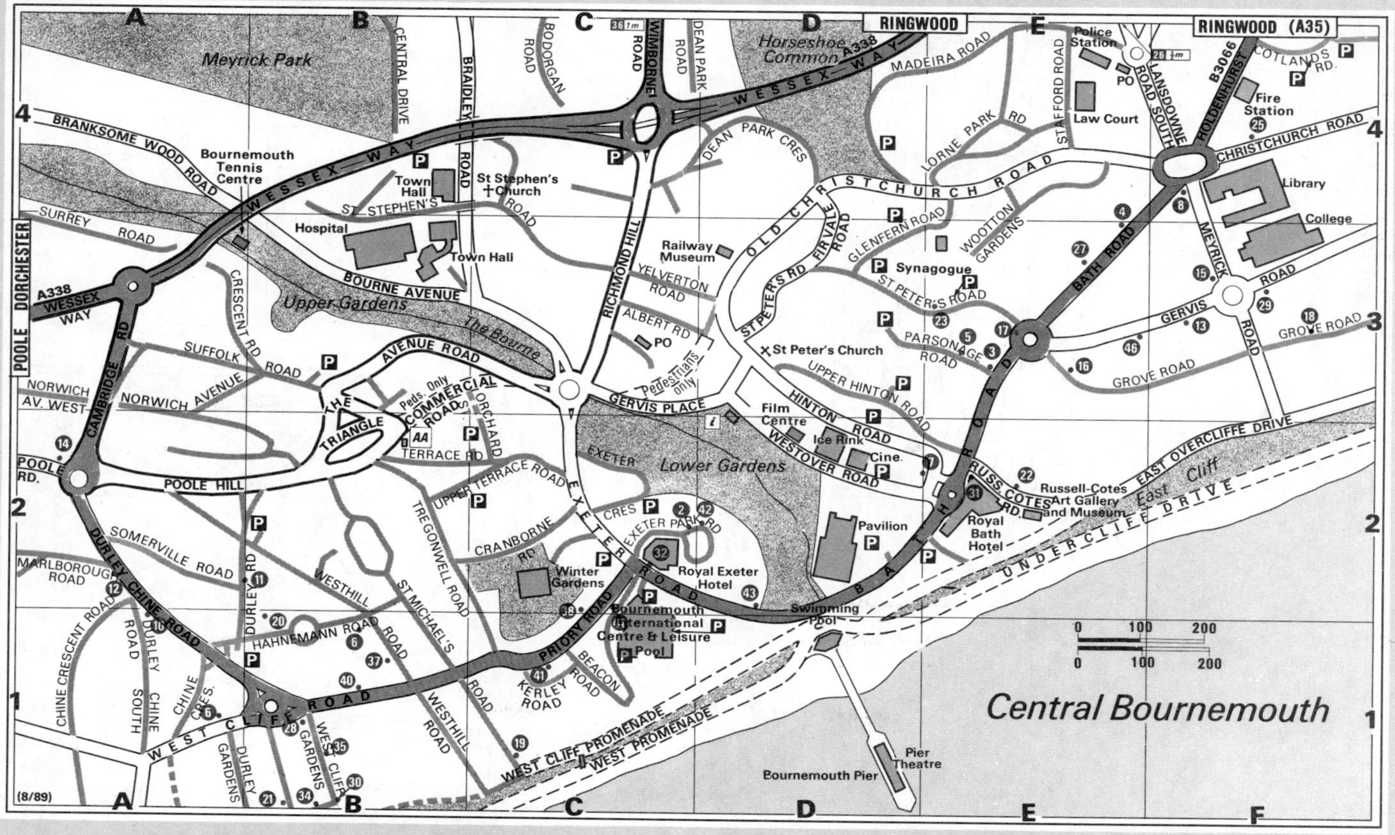
Central Bournemouth
RINGWOOD
RINGWOOD (A35)
POOLE DORCHESTER
Meyrick Park
Horseshoe Common
A338
WESSEX WAY
WIMBORNE ROAD
BODORGAN ROAD
DEAN PARK ROAD
DEAN PARK CRES
CENTRAL DRIVE
BRAIDLEY ROAD
BRANKSOME WOOD ROAD
Bournemouth Tennis Centre
SURREY ROAD
Town Hall
St Stephen's Church
ST STEPHEN'S ROAD
Hospital
BOURNE AVENUE
Upper Gardens
The Bourne
RICHMOND HILL
Railway Museum
YELVERTON ROAD
ALBERT RD
PO
Pedestrians only
GERVIS PLACE
CAMBRIDGE RD
CRESCENT RD
SUFFOLK ROAD
AVENUE ROAD
NORWICH AV. WEST
NORWICH AVENUE
THE TRIANGLE
Peds. Only
COMMERCIAL ROAD
ORCHARD ST
AA
TERRACE RD
UPPER TERRACE ROAD
POOLE RD.
POOLE HILL
EXETER CRES
Lower Gardens
EXETER PARK RD
EXETER ROAD
Royal Exeter Hotel
CRANBORNE RD
Winter Gardens
TREGONWELL ROAD
ST MICHAEL'S ROAD
WESTHILL ROAD
SOMERVILLE ROAD
MARLBOROUGH ROAD
DURLEY RD
HAHNEMANN ROAD
DURLEY CHINE ROAD
CHINE CRESCENT ROAD
DURLEY CHINE ROAD SOUTH
CHINE CRES.
WEST CLIFF ROAD
WEST CLIFF GARDENS
DURLEY GARDENS
PRIORY ROAD
Bournemouth International Centre & Leisure Pool
BEACON ROAD
KERLEY ROAD
WEST CLIFF PROMENADE
WEST PROMENADE
Swimming Pool
Bournemouth Pier
Pier Theatre
OLD CHRISTCHURCH ROAD
ST PETER'S RD
FIRVALE ROAD
GLENFERN ROAD
WOOTTON GARDENS
Synagogue
ST PETER'S ROAD
St Peter's Church
PARSONAGE ROAD
UPPER HINTON ROAD
HINTON ROAD
Film Centre
Ice Rink
Cine.
WESTOVER ROAD
Pavilion
BATH ROAD
RUSS COTES RD.
Russell-Cotes Art Gallery and Museum
Royal Bath Hotel
East Cliff
EAST OVERCLIFFE DRIVE
East Drive
UNDERCLIFF DRIVE
MADEIRA ROAD
LORNE PARK RD
STAFFORD ROAD
Police Station
PO
Law Court
LANSDOWNE ROAD SOUTH
B3066
HOLDENHURST
COTLANDS RD.
Fire Station
CHRISTCHURCH ROAD
Library
College
MEYRICK ROAD
GERVIS ROAD
GROVE ROAD
(8/89)

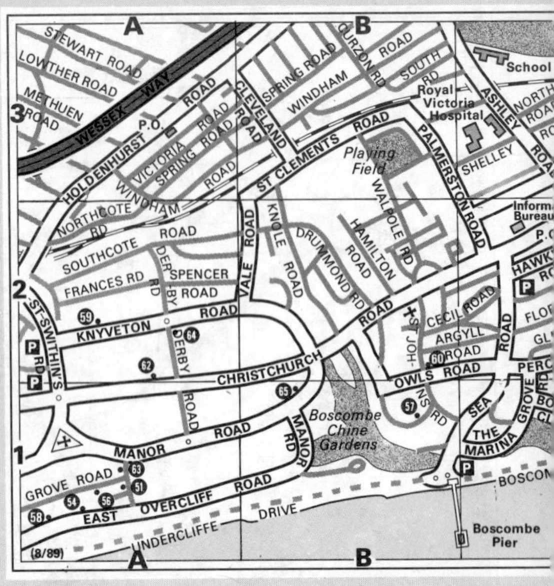

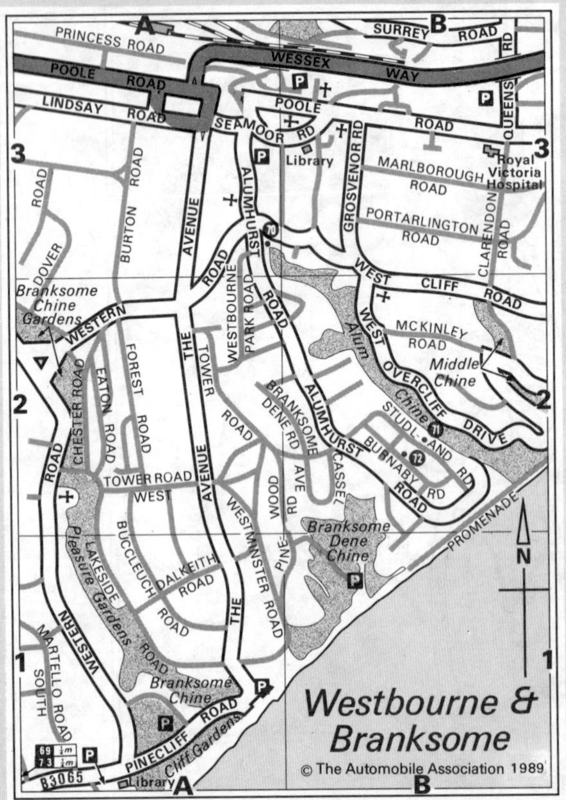

Westbourne & Branksome

69 Le Chateau ✕✕ (Listed under Poole)
70 Chinehead ★★
71 Chinehurst ★★
72 Riviera (Burnaby Rd) ★★
73 Seawitch ★★ (Listed under Poole)

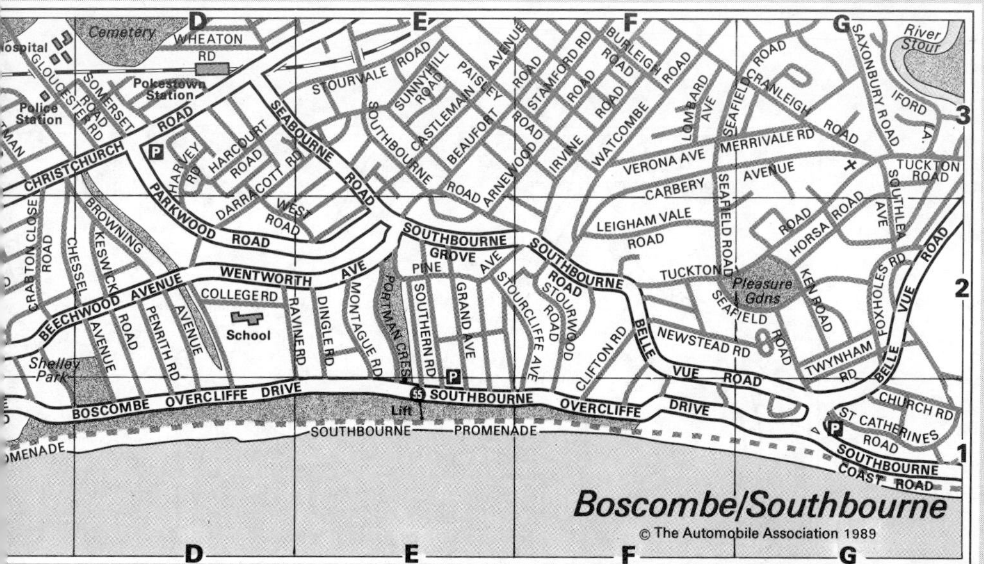

Boscombe & Southbourne

51 Chesterwood ★★★
54 Cliffeside ★★★
55 Commodore ★
56 Cottonwood ★★
57 Hotel Courtlands ★★★
58 Cumberland ★★★
59 Elstead ★★★
60 Fircroft ★★
62 Hartford Court ★
63 Hinton Firs ★★
64 Langtry Manor ★★★
65 Manor House ★★

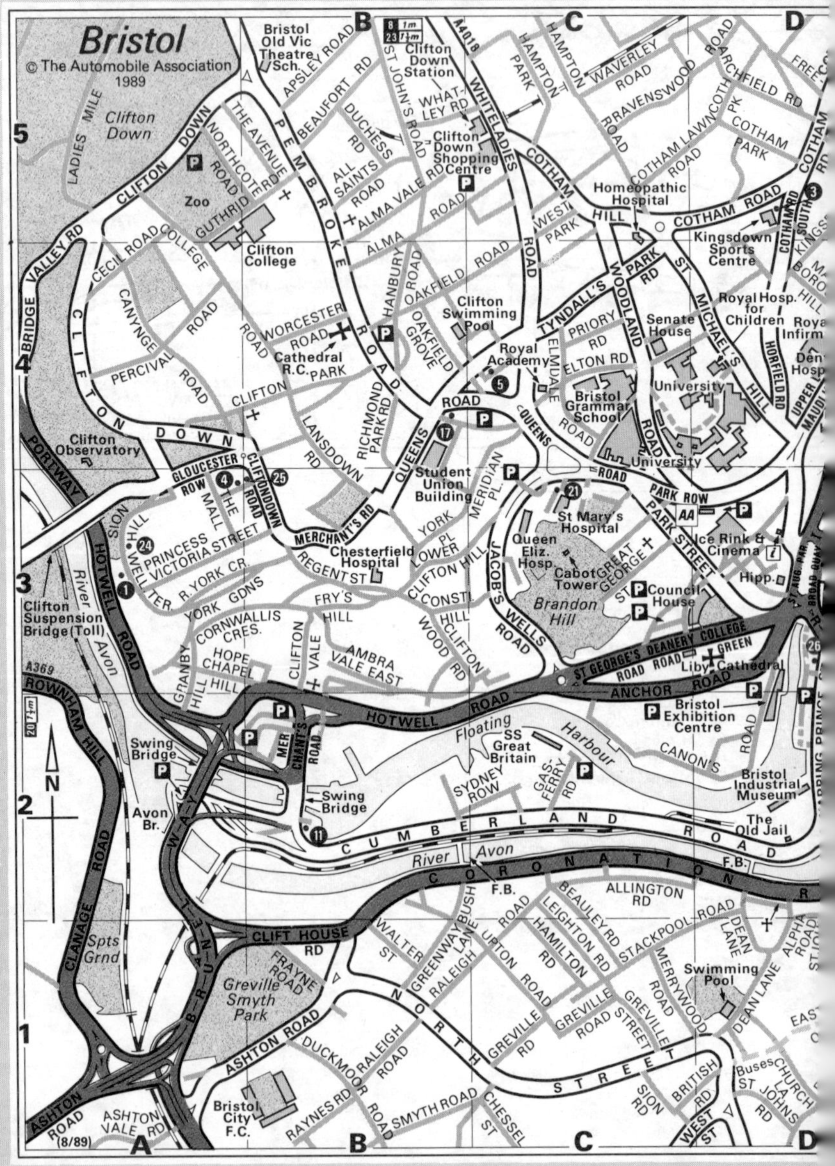
Bristol
© The Automobile Association 1989
Clifton Down
Zoo
Clifton College
Clifton Observatory
Clifton Suspension Bridge (Toll)
Cathedral R.C.
Chesterfield Hospital
Student Union Building
St Mary's Hospital
Queen Eliz. Hosp.
Cabot Tower
Brandon Hill
Council House
Bristol Grammar School
University
Senate House
Royal Academy
Clifton Swimming Pool
Homeopathic Hospital
Kingsdown Sports Centre
Royal Hosp. for Children
Ice Rink & Cinema
Bristol Exhibition Centre
SS Great Britain
Floating Harbour
Bristol Industrial Museum
The Old Jail
Swing Bridge
Avon Br.
River Avon
Greville Smyth Park
Bristol City F.C.
Swimming Pool
Spts Grnd
Clifton Down Station
Clifton Down Shopping Centre
Bristol Old Vic Theatre Sch.
CUMBERLAND ROAD
CORONATION
HOTWELL ROAD
NORTH STREET
(8/89)

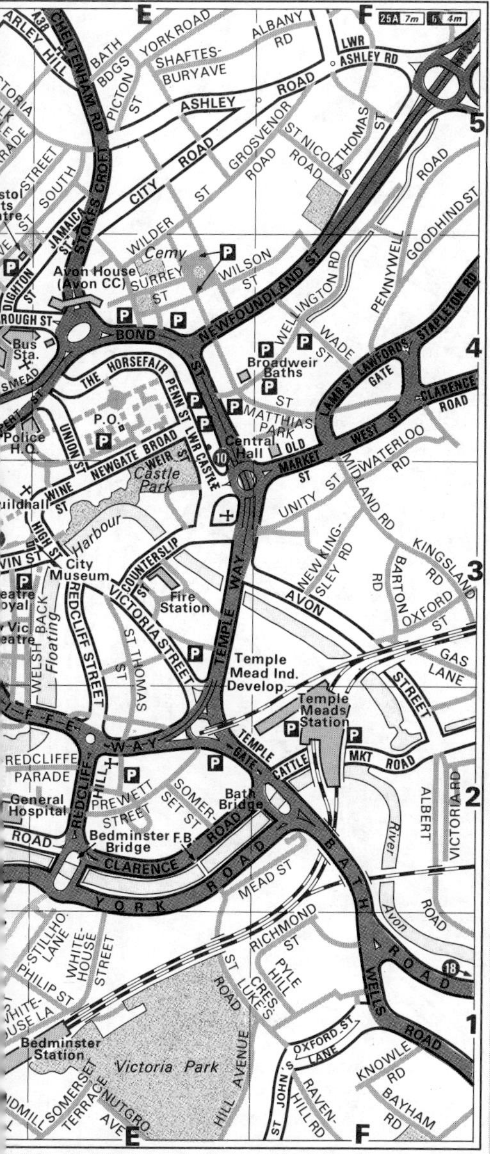

Bristol

1	Avon Gorge ★★★
2	Barbizon ✕✕
3	Bistro Twenty One ✕
4	Bouboulina's ✕
5	Clifton ★★
6	Crest ★★★
8	Henbury Lodge ★★★
10	Holiday Inn ★★★★
11	Howards ✕
17	Orient Rendezvous ✕✕
18	Parkside ★★
19	Raj Tandoori ✕
20	Redwood Lodge & Country Club ★★★
21	Restaurant Danton ✕✕
23	Restaurant Lettonie ✕✕
24	St Vincent's Rocks ★★★
25	Rodney ★★
25A	Stakis Leisure Lodge ★★★
26	Unicorn ★★★

Cardiff

1 La Chaumiere ✕
2 Crest ★★★
3 Gibsons ✕
4 Holiday Inn ★★★★
5 Lincoln ★★
6 Park ★★★★
7 Post House ★★★
8 Riverside ✕
9 Royal ★★★

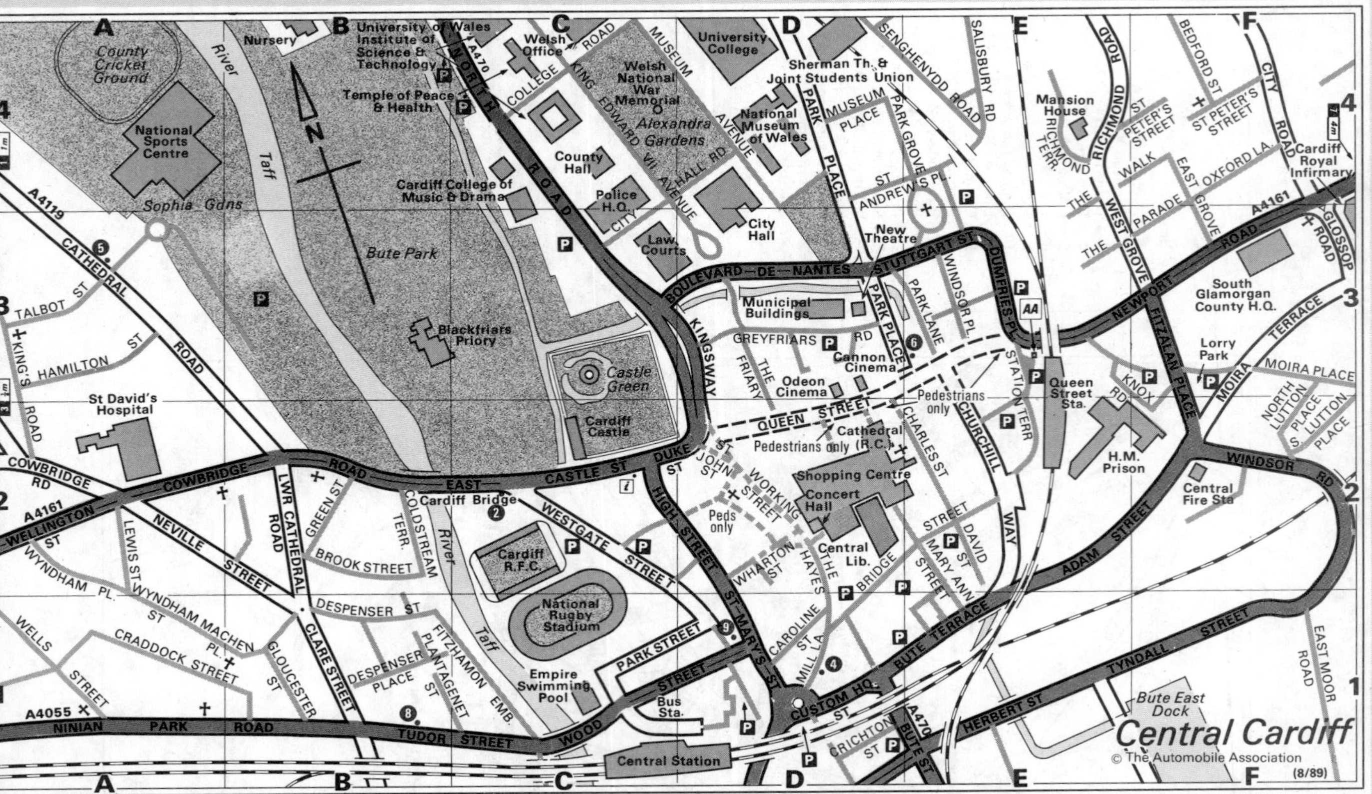

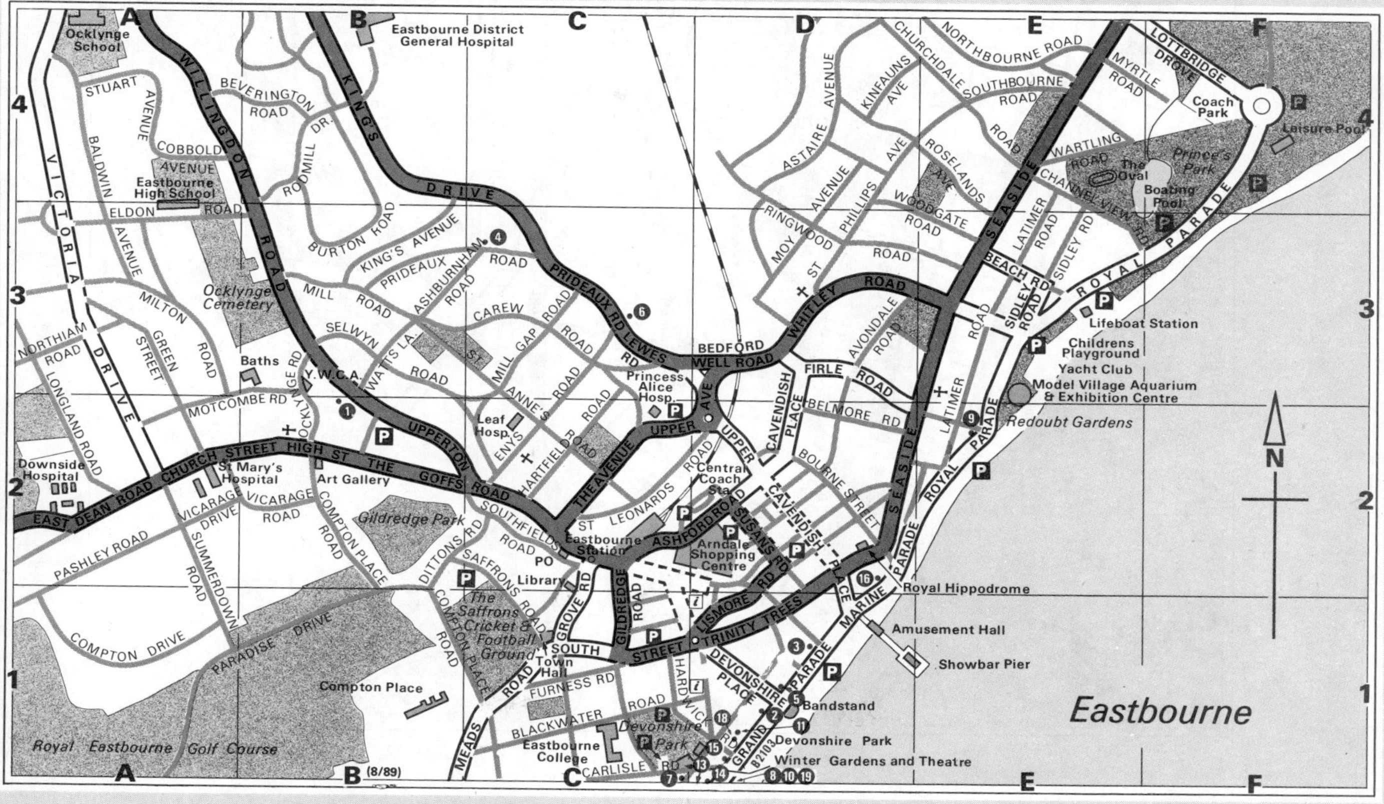

Eastbourne

		5	Cumberland ★★★				
1	Byrons ✕	6	Downland ★	10	Lansdowne ★★★	15	Princes ★★★
2	Cavendish ★★★★	7	Farrar's ★★	11	Lathom ★	16	Queens ★★★★
3	Chatsworth ★★★	8	Grand ★★★★★	13	New Wilmington ★★	18	West Rocks ★★
4	Croft ★★	9	Langham ★★	14	Oban ★	19	Wish Tower ★★★

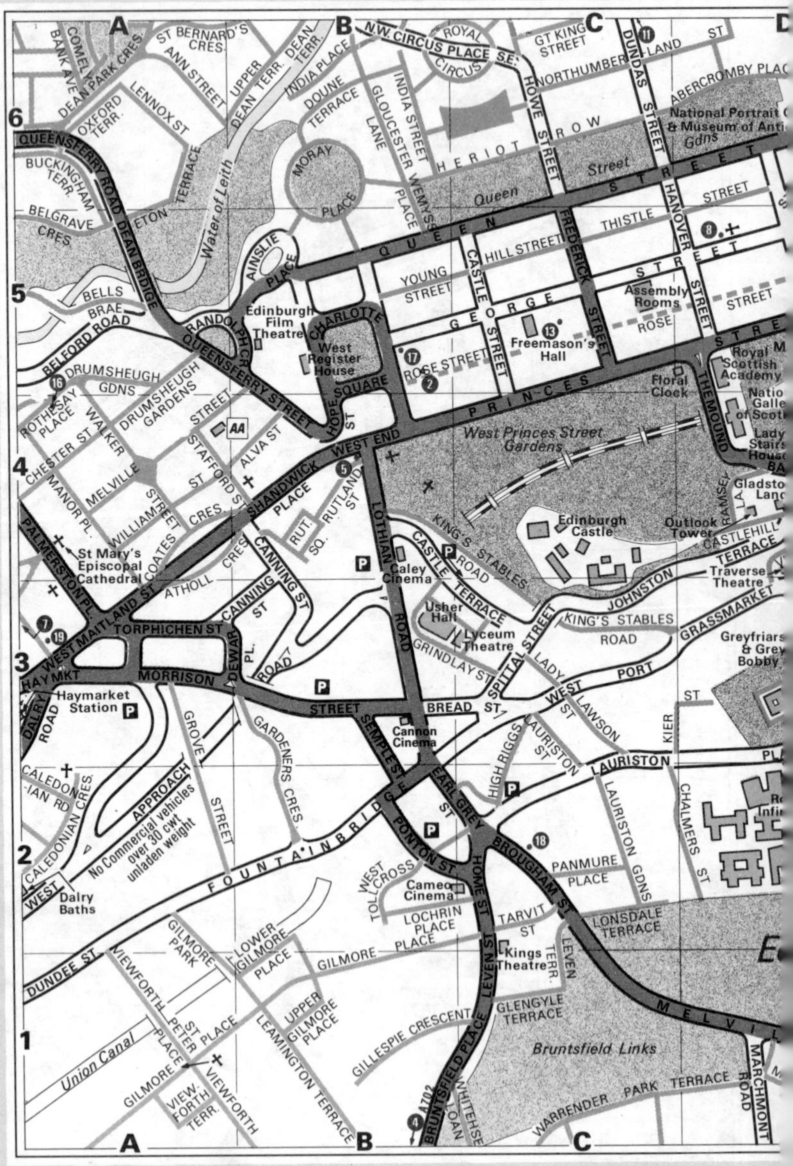

A
B
C
D
1
2
3
4
5
6
COMELY BANK AVE
DEAN PARK CRES
ST BERNARD'S CRES.
ANN STREET
UPPER DEAN TERR.
DEAN TERR.
INDIA PLACE
N.W. CIRCUS PLACE
ROYAL CIRCUS
GT KING STREET
DUNDAS STREET
LAND
ST
NORTHUMBER
HOWE STREET
OXFORD TERR.
LENNOX ST
ETON TERRACE
DOUNE TERRACE
GLOUCESTER LANE
INDIA STREET
WEMYSS PLACE
HERIOT ROW
Queen Street Gdns
National Portrait
& Museum of Anti
QUEENSFERRY ROAD
BUCKINGHAM TERR.
BELGRAVE CRES
DEAN BRIDGE
Water of Leith
MORAY PLACE
AINSLIE PLACE
QUEEN STREET
YOUNG STREET
CASTLE STREET
HILL STREET
FREDERICK STREET
THISTLE STREET
HANOVER STREET
GEORGE STREET
Assembly Rooms
ROSE STREET
BELLS BRAE
BELFORD ROAD
RANDOLPH CR.
Edinburgh Film Theatre
CHARLOTTE SQUARE
West Register House
Freemason's Hall
Royal Scottish Academy
QUEENSFERRY STREET
DRUMSHEUGH GDNS
DRUMSHEUGH GARDENS
ROTHESAY PLACE
WALKER STREET
HOPE ST
PRINCES STREET
Floral Clock
THE MOUND
AA
STAFFORD ST
ALVA ST
WEST END
West Princes Street Gardens
CHESTER ST
MANOR PL.
MELVILLE STREET
WILLIAM ST
SHANDWICK PLACE
RUTLAND ST
RUT. SQ.
COATES CRES.
LOTHIAN ROAD
KING'S STABLES ROAD
Edinburgh Castle
RAMSEY LA.
Outlook Tower
CASTLEHILL
PALMERSTON PL.
St Mary's Episcopal Cathedral
ATHOLL CRES
CANNING ST
Caley Cinema
CASTLE TERRACE
JOHNSTON TERRACE
Traverse Theatre
WEST MAITLAND ST
TORPHICHEN ST
Usher Hall
Lyceum Theatre
KING'S STABLES ROAD
GRASSMARKET
Greyfriars & Grey Bobby
HAYMKT
MORRISON STREET
DEWAR PL.
CANNING ST
GRINDLAY ST
SPITTAL STREET
LADY LAWSON ST
WEST PORT
Haymarket Station
DALRY ROAD
GROVE STREET
GARDENERS CRES.
BREAD ST
Cannon Cinema
SEMPLE ST
HIGH RIGGS
LAURISTON ST
LAURISTON PL
KIER ST
CALEDONIAN RD
CALEDONIAN CRES.
APPROACH
No Commercial vehicles over 30 cwt unladen weight
EARL GREY ST
LAURISTON GDNS
CHALMERS ST
WEST APPROACH
FOUNTAINBRIDGE
PONTON ST
HOME ST
BROUGHAM ST
PANMURE PLACE
Dalry Baths
WEST TOLLCROSS
Cameo Cinema
LOCHRIN PLACE
TARVIT ST
LONSDALE TERRACE
DUNDEE ST.
VIEWFORTH
GILMORE PARK
LOWER GILMORE PLACE
GILMORE PLACE
Kings Theatre
LEVEN TERR.
LEVEN ST
UPPER GILMORE PLACE
GLENGYLE TERRACE
MELVILLE
PETER PLACE
LEAMINGTON TERRACE
GILLESPIE CRESCENT
Union Canal
Bruntsfield Links
MARCHMONT ROAD
GILMORE PLACE
VIEWFORTH TERR.
BRUNTSFIELD PLACE
A702
WHITEHSE LOAN
WARRENDER PARK TERRACE

Edinburgh

1	Albany ★★★
2	Alp-Horn ✕✕
3	L'Auberge ✕✕
4	Bruntsfield ★★★
5	Caledonian ★★★★★
6	Carlton Highland ★★★★
7	Clarendon ★★
8	George ★★★★
11	Howard ★★★
12	King James Thistle ★★★
13	Martins ✕✕
15	Old Waverley ★★★
16	Rothesay ★★
17	Roxburghe ★★★
18	Shamiana ✕
19	Stakis Grosvenor ★★★

Exeter

1	Buckerell Lodge Crest ★★★	3	Exeter Arms Toby ★★★	7	Red House ★★	10	St Andrews ★★
2	Countess Wear Lodge ★★★	4	Gipsy Hill ★★★	8	Rougemont ★★★	11	St Olaves Court ★★★
		6	Imperial ★★★	9	Royal Clarence ★★★	12	White Hart ★★★

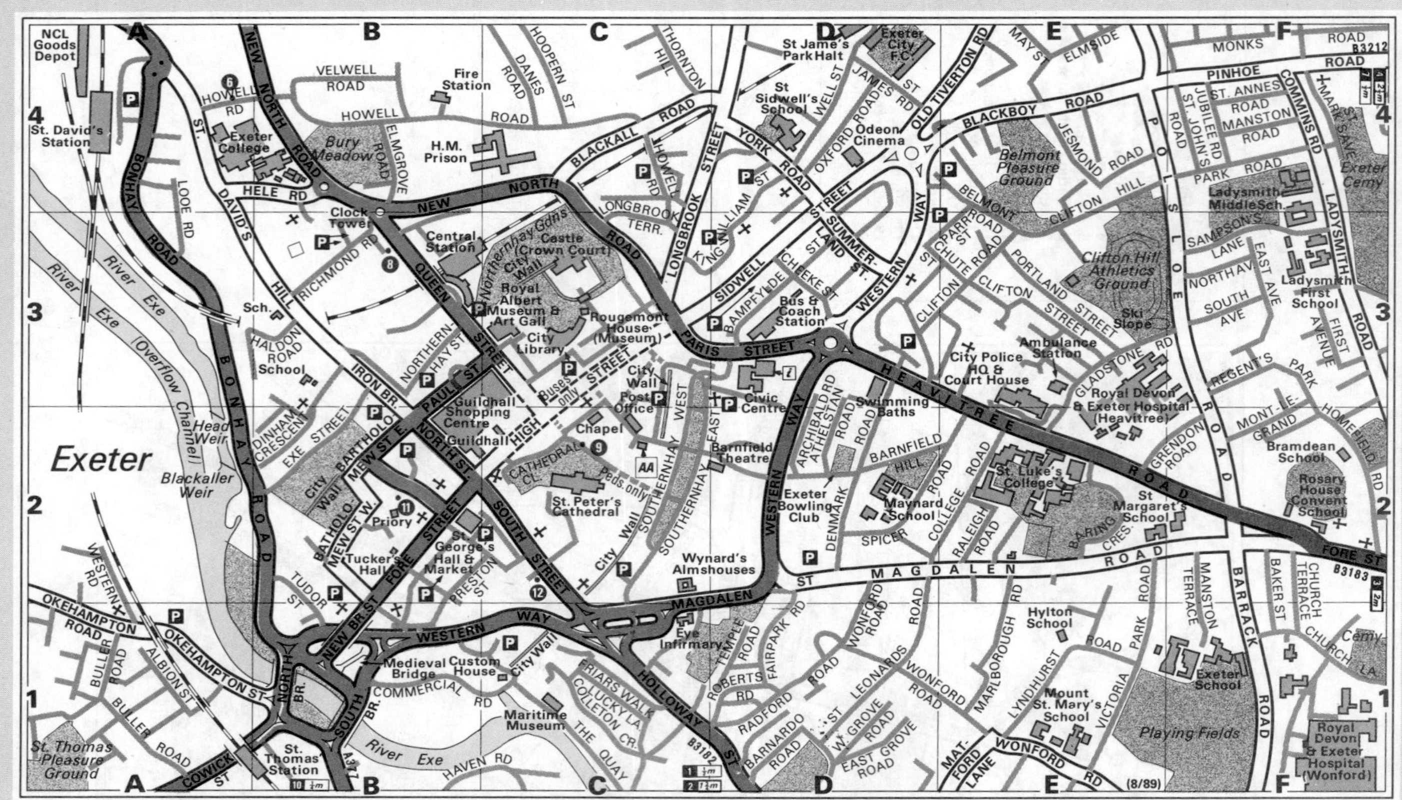

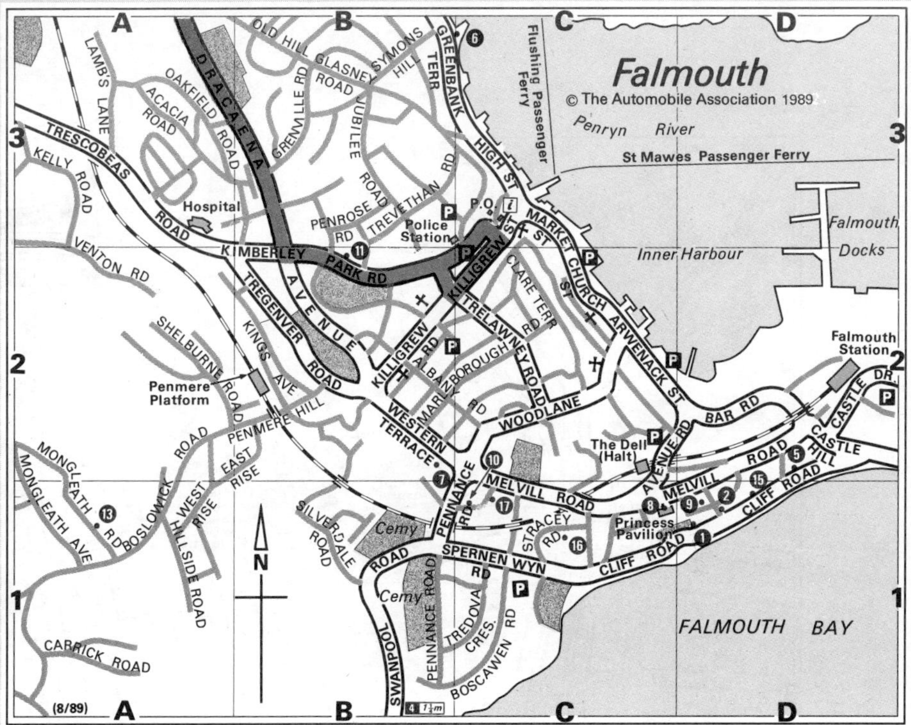

Falmouth

1	Bay ★★★
2	Carthion ★★
4	Crill House ★★
5	Falmouth ★★★
6	Greenbank ★★★
7	Green Lawns ★★★
8	Gyllyngdune ★★★
9	Lerryn ★★
10	Melville ★★
11	Park Grove ★★
13	Penmere Manor ★★★
15	Royal Duchy ★★★
16	Hotel St Michaels ★★★
17	Somerdale ★★

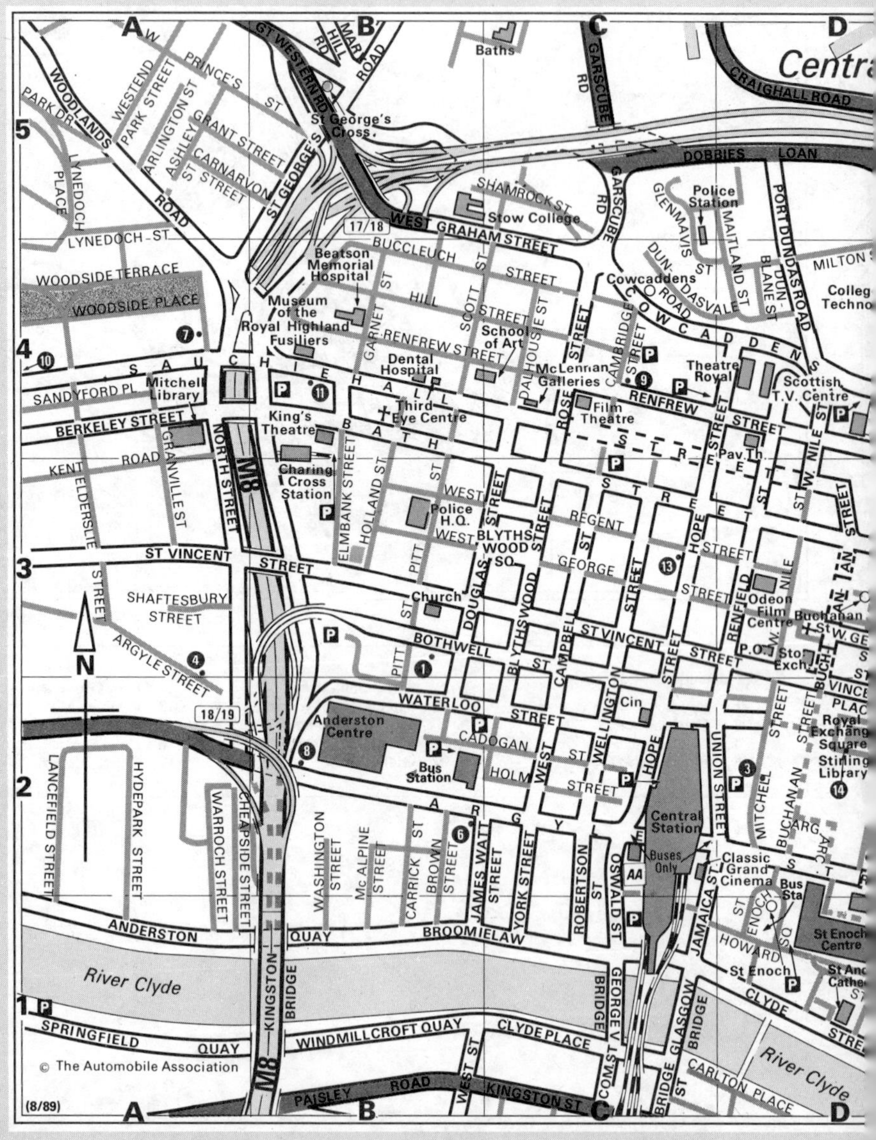
A
B
C
D
Central
CRAIGHALL ROAD
WOODLANDS ROAD
PARK DR
WESTEND PARK STREET
PRINCE'S ST
ARLINGTON ST
ASHLEY ST
GRANT STREET
CARNARVON STREET
ST GEORGE'S RD
GT WESTERN RD
HILL
MARY
RD
ROAD
St George's Cross
Baths
GARSCUBE RD
DOBBIES LOAN
LYNEDOCH PLACE
LYNEDOCH ST
17/18
SHAMROCK ST
Stow College
WEST GRAHAM STREET
Police Station
GLENMAVIS ST
MAITLAND ST
PORT DUNDAS ROAD
DUNBLANE ST
MILTON S
BUCCLEUCH
STREET
Beatson Memorial Hospital
DUNDASVALE RD
Cowcaddens
COWCADDENS
College Techno
WOODSIDE TERRACE
WOODSIDE PLACE
Museum of the Royal Highland Fusiliers
GARNET ST
HILL
SCOTT ST
DALHOUSIE ST
STREET
School of Art
RENFREW STREET
Dental Hospital
McLennan Galleries
ROSE STREET
CAMBRIDGE STREET
Theatre Royal
Scottish T.V. Centre
SAUCHIEHALL
SANDYFORD PL
Mitchell Library
Third Eye Centre
Film Theatre
RENFREW STREET
BERKELEY STREET
King's Theatre
BATH
GRANVILLE ST
NORTH STREET
M8
STREET
KENT ROAD
ELDERSLIE STREET
Charing Cross Station
ELMBANK STREET
HOLLAND ST
PITT ST
WEST
Police H.Q.
WEST
BLYTHSWOOD SQ
Pav.Th.
W. NILE ST
ST VINCENT
STREET
REGENT
GEORGE
HOPE STREET
STREET
DOUGLAS STREET
WELLINGTON
SHAFTESBURY STREET
Church
BLYTHSWOOD ST
CAMPBELL ST
ST VINCENT STREET
RENFIELD ST
Odeon Film Centre
Buchanan St
NILE
ARGYLE STREET
N
BOTHWELL
P.O.
Sto Exch
PITT
WATERLOO STREET
Cin
Royal Exchange Square
18/19
Anderston Centre
CADOGAN ST
Stirling Library
Bus Station
HOLM STREET
WEST
HOPE
UNION STREET
MITCHELL
BUCHANAN ST
LANCEFIELD STREET
HYDEPARK STREET
WARROCH STREET
CHEAPSIDE STREET
WASHINGTON STREET
McALPINE STREET
CARRICK ST
BROWN STREET
JAMES WATT STREET
YORK STREET
ROBERTSON ST
OSWALD ST
ARGYLE
Central Station
Buses Only
AA
Classic Grand Cinema
JAMAICA ST
ENOCH
SQ
Bus Sta
St Enoch Centre
ANDERSTON QUAY
BROOMIELAW
HOWARD
St Enoch
KINGSTON BRIDGE
GEORGE V BRIDGE
River Clyde
GLASGOW BRIDGE
St And Cathe
CLYDE STREET
SPRINGFIELD QUAY
WINDMILLCROFT QUAY
CLYDE PLACE
© The Automobile Association
M8
WEST ST
COM.ST
BRIDGE ST
CARLTON PLACE
River Clyde
(8/89)
PAISLEY ROAD
KINGSTON ST
1
2
3
4
5

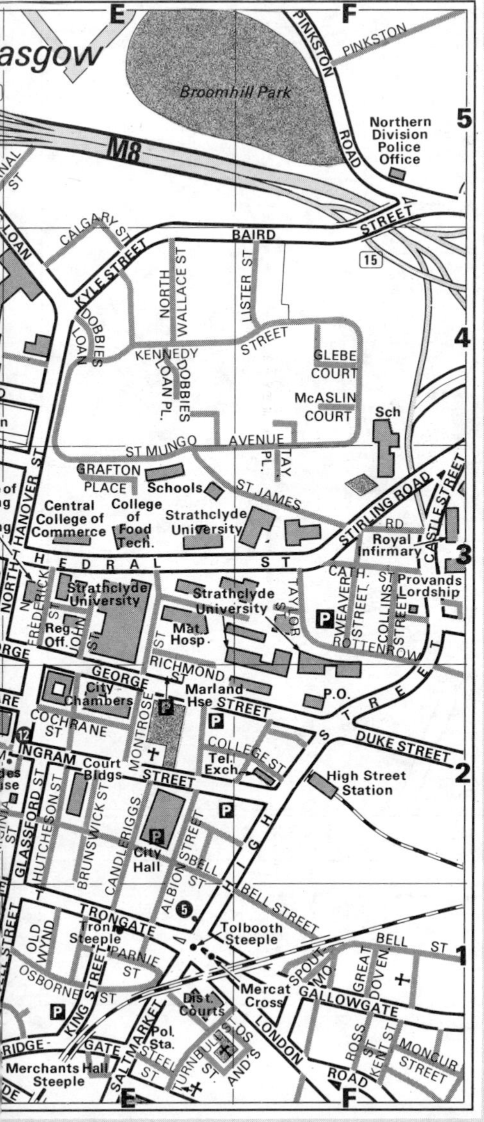

Glasgow

1	Albany ★★★★
3	L'Ariosto Ristorante ✕✕
4	Buttery ✕✕
5	Colonial ✕✕
6	Crest Hotel Glasgow-City ★★★
7	Fountain ✕✕✕
8	Holiday Inn Glasgow ★★★★
9	Hospitality Inn ★★★★
10	Kelvin Park Lorne ★★★
11	Loon Fung ✕
12	Stakis Ingram ★★★
13	Peking Inn ✕
14	Rogano ✕✕

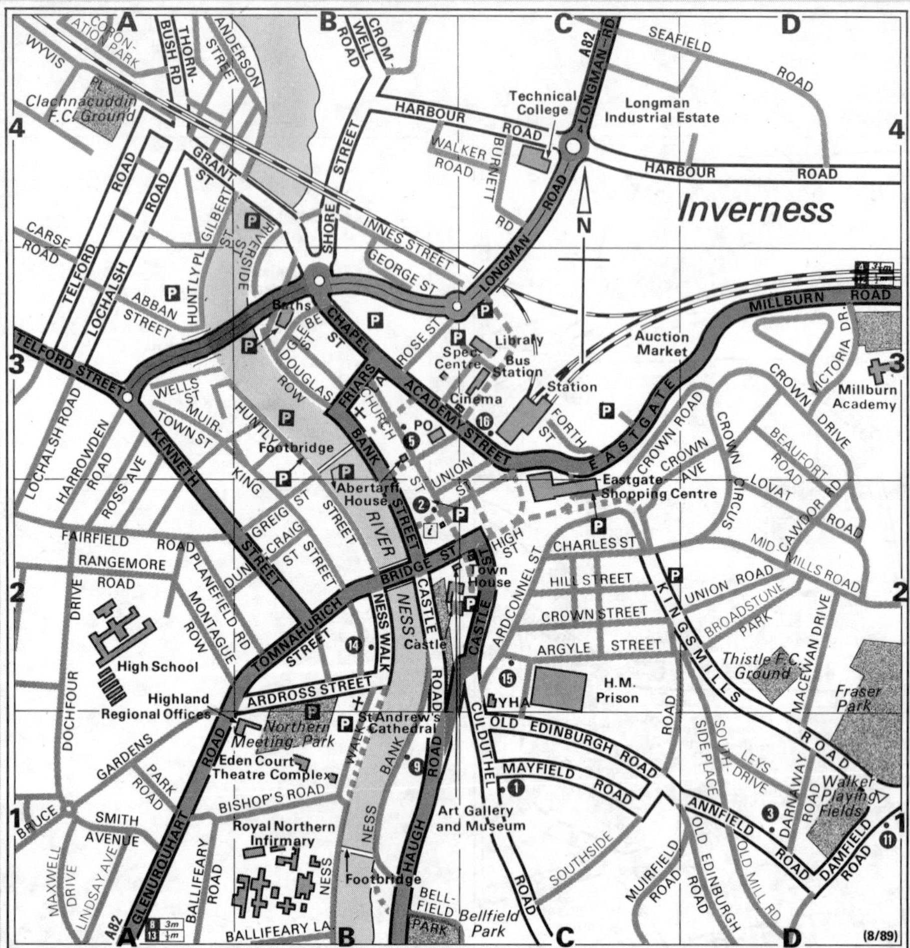

Inverness

1	Beaufort ★★	4	Culloden House ★★★★	12	Mercury ★★★
2	Caledonian ★★★	5	Cummings ★★	13	Loch Ness House ★★
3	Craigmonie ★★★	8	Dunain Park ★★	14	Palace ★★★
		9	Glen Mhor ★★	15	Redcliffe ★
		11	Kingsmills ★★★	16	Station ★★★

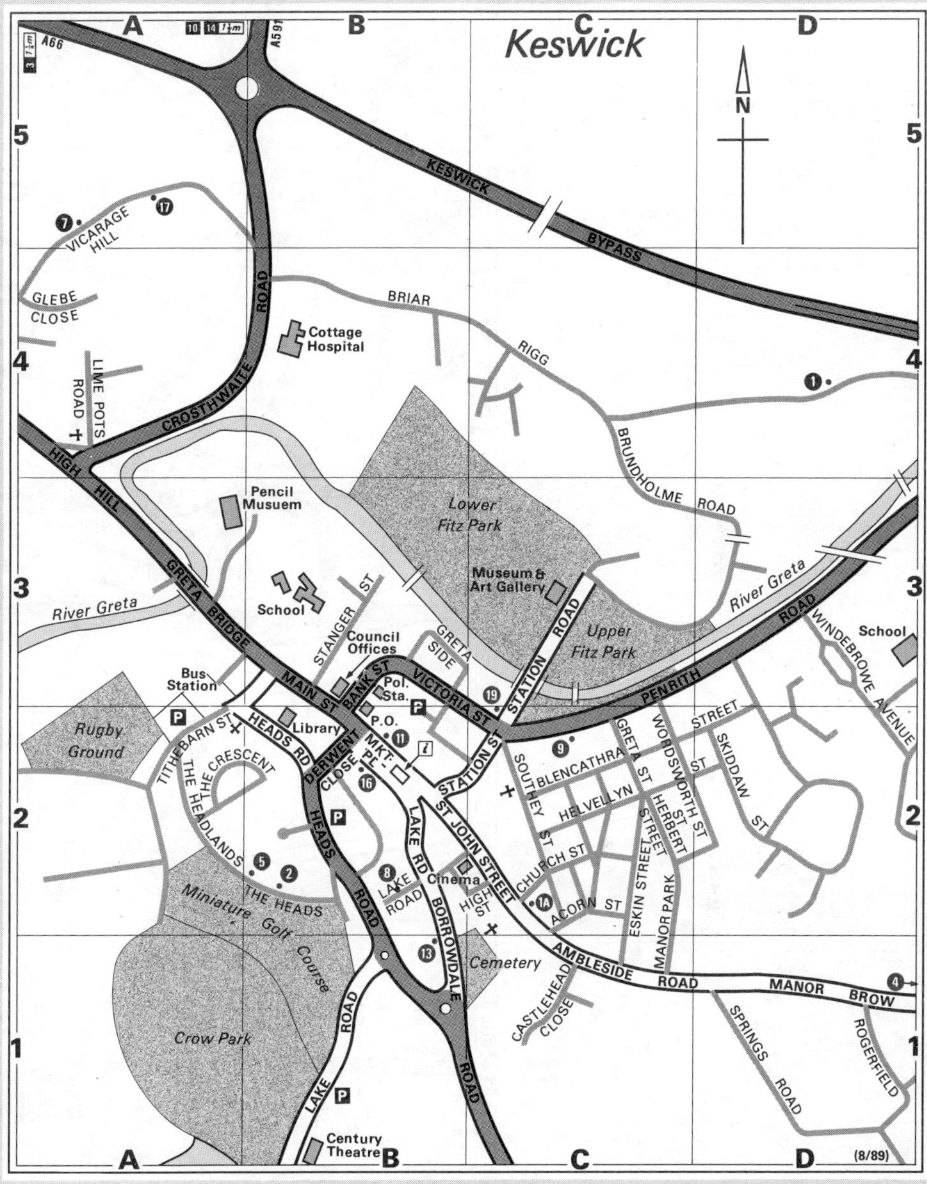

Keswick

1 Brundholme Country House ★★★
1A Chaucer House ★★
2 Crow Park ★★
3 Derwentwater ★★★
4 Grange Country House ★★
5 Highfield ★
7 Lairbeck ★★
8 Latrigg Lodge ★
9 Linnett Hall ★
10 Lyzzick Hill ★★
11 Queen's ★★
13 Priorholm ★
14 Red House ★★
16 Skiddaw ★★
17 Skiddaw Grove ★
19 Walpole ★★

Liverpool

1 Atlantic Tower ★★★★
2 Blundellsands ★★★
(See under Blundellsands)
4 Crest Hotel Liverpool-City ★★★
4A Far East ✕✕
6 Grange ★★
7 Green Park ★★
9 Liverpool Moat House ★★★★
11 Park ★★★ (See under Bootle)
12 St George's ★★★
13 Trials ★★★

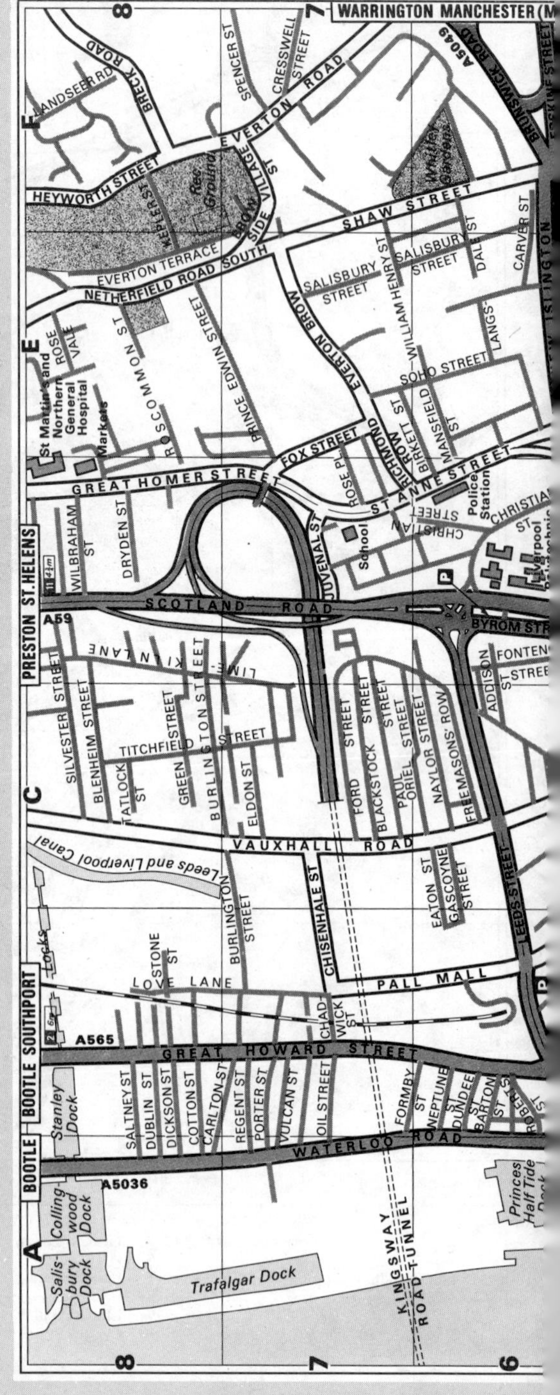

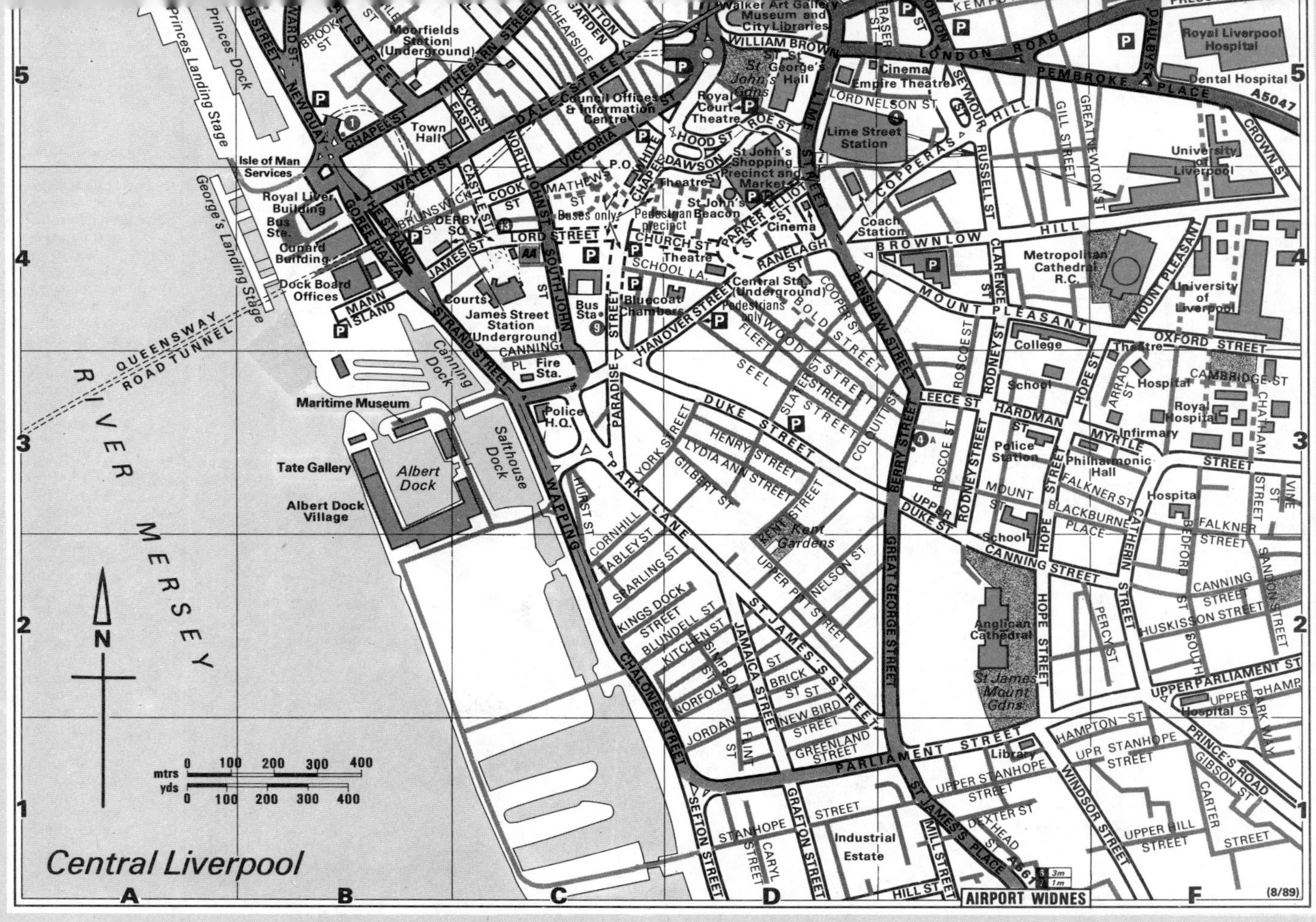
Central Liverpool
(8/89)
RIVER MERSEY
QUEENSWAY ROAD TUNNEL
Princes Dock
Princes Landing Stage
George's Landing Stage
Isle of Man Services
Royal Liver Building
Cunard Building
Dock Board Offices
Bus Ste.
Maritime Museum
Tate Gallery
Albert Dock Village
Albert Dock
Canning Dock
Salthouse Dock
Town Hall
Moorfields Station (Underground)
James Street Station (Underground)
Courts
Police H.Q.
Fire Sta.
Bus Sta.
Bluecoat Chambers
Central Sta. (Underground)
Pedestrians only
Pedestrian precinct
Buses only
Lime Street Station
St. George's Hall
Walker Art Gallery Museum and City Libraries
St John's Gdns
Royal Court Theatre
Empire Theatre
Cinema
Coach Station
St John's Shopping Precinct and Market
St John's Beacon
Council Offices & Information Centre
Metropolitan Cathedral R.C.
University of Liverpool
Royal Liverpool Hospital
Dental Hospital
Royal Hospital
Infirmary
College
School
Police Station
Philharmonic Hall
Anglican Cathedral
St James Mount Gdns
Library
Industrial Estate
Kent Gardens
STRAND STREET
WAPPING
CHALONER STREET
PARK LANE
DUKE STREET
HANOVER STREET
RENSHAW STREET
LIME STREET
LONDON ROAD
PEMBROKE PLACE
MOUNT PLEASANT
HOPE STREET
RODNEY STREET
GREAT GEORGE STREET
ST JAMES'S PLACE
PARLIAMENT STREET
UPPER PARLIAMENT ST
PRINCE'S ROAD
CATHERIN STREET
CANNING STREET
WINDSOR STREET
SEFTON STREET
GRAFTON STREET
JAMAICA STREET
ST JAMES'S STREET
BERRY STREET
BOLD STREET
SEEL ST
WOOD ST
FLEET ST
SLATER STREET
COLQUITT ST
NELSON ST
UPPER PITT STREET
HENRY STREET
LYDIA ANN STREET
YORK STREET
PARADISE STREET
CHURCH ST
LORD STREET
SOUTH JOHN ST
NORTH JOHN ST
CASTLE ST
WATER ST
DALE STREET
VICTORIA ST
TITHEBARN STREET
THE STRAND
GOREE PIAZZA
MANN ISLAND
NEW QUAY
CHAPEL ST
CANNING PL
KINGS DOCK STREET
CORNHILL
HURST ST
A5047
AIRPORT WIDNES
mtrs 0 100 200 300 400
yds 0 100 200 300 400
N
A B C D F
1 2 3 4 5

Llandudno

1 Bedford ★★
2 Belle Vue ★★
3 Bodysgallen Hall ★★★★
4 Branksome ★
5 Bromwell Court ★★
6 Bron Orme ★
7 Bryn-y-Bia Lodge ★★
8 Chatsworth House ★★★
9 Clontarf ★
10 Cornerways ★
12 Dunoon ★★
13 Empire ★★★
14 Esplanade ★★
16 Floral ✕✕
17 Four Oaks ★★
18 Gogarth Abbey ★★★
19 Gwesty Leamore ★
20 Headlands ★★
21 Hilbre Court ★
22 Imperial ★★★
23 Lanterns ✕✕
24 Merrion ★★
25 Min-y-Don ★
26 Oak Alyn ★
27 Ormescliffe ★★
27A Plas Fron Deg ★★
28 Quinton ★
29 Ravenhurst ★
31 Risboro ★★★
33 Royal ★★
34 St Tudno ★★
35 Sandringham ★★
36 Sefton Court ★★
37 Somerset ★★
38 Sunnymede ★
39 Tan-Lan ★★

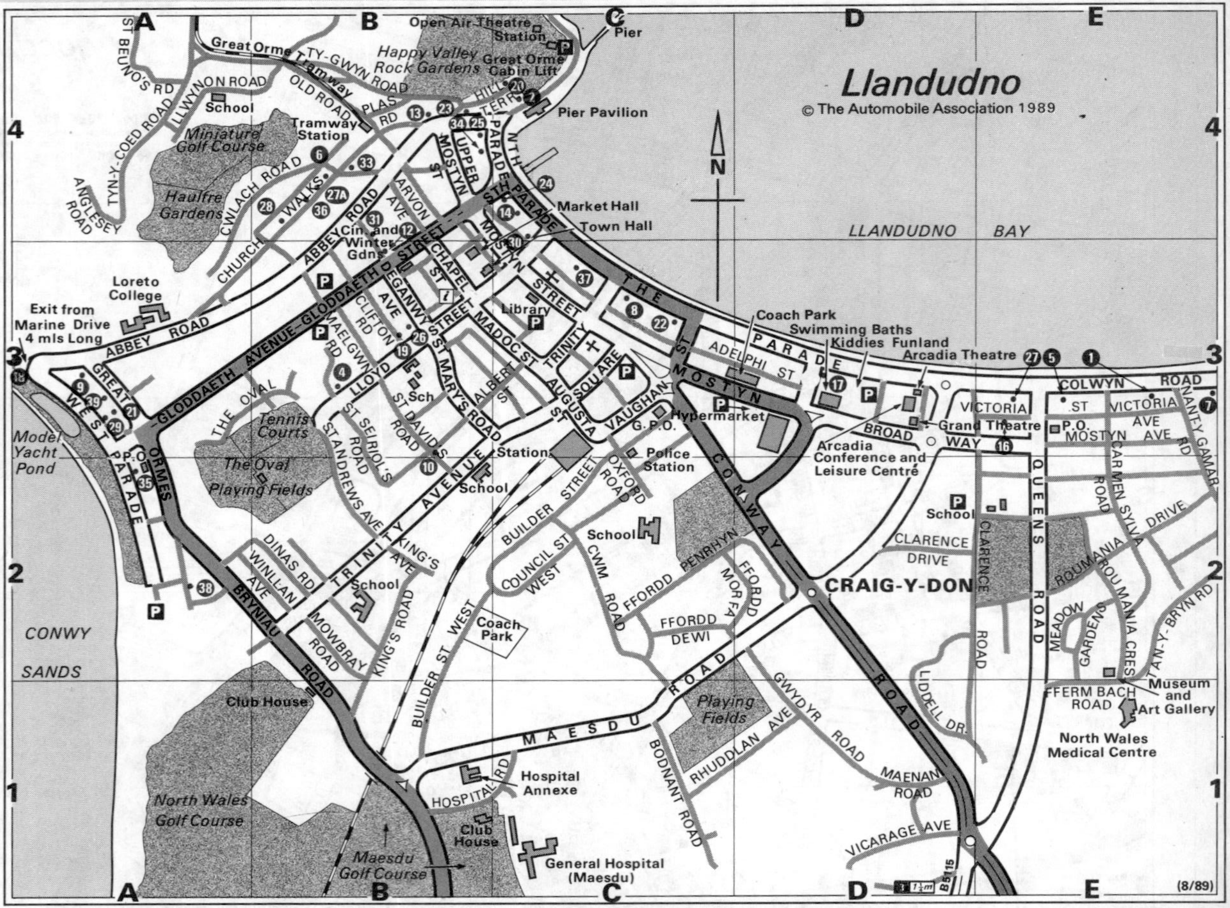

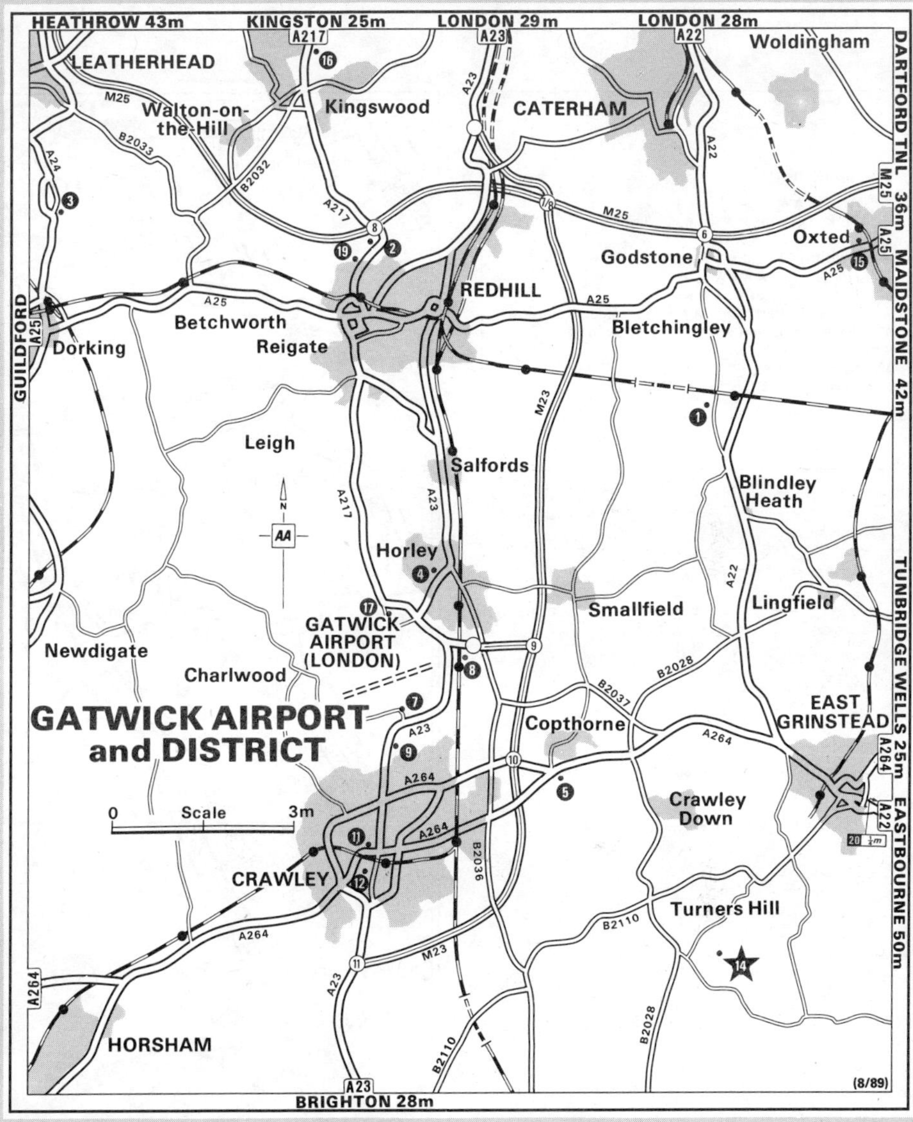

Gatwick Airport & District

1 La Bonne Auberge ✕✕ (See under South Godstone)
2 Bridge House ★★★ (See under Reigate)
3 Burford Bridge ★★★★ (See under Dorking)
4 Chequers Thistle ★★★
5 Copthorne ★★★★
7 Gatwick Concorde ★★★
8 Gatwick Hilton International ★★★★
9 Gatwick Manor ★★
11 George ★★★
12 Goffs Park ★★★
14 Gravetye Manor ★★★ (See under East Grinstead)
15 Hoskins ★★ (See under Oxted)
16 Heathside ★★ (See under Burgh Heath)
17 Post House ★★★
19 Reigate Manor ★★★ (See under Reigate)
20 Woodbury House ★★ (See under East Grinstead)

Heathrow Airport

1 Ariel ★★★
2 Berkeley Arms ★★★
3 Excelsior ★★★★
4 Heathrow Penta ★★★★
5 Holiday Inn ★★★★
6 Hotel Ibis Heathrow ★★
7 Master Robert Motel ★★★ (See under Hounslow)
8 Thames Lodge ★★★ (See under Staines)
9 Post House ★★★
12 Skyway ★★★
13 Terrazza ✕✕ (See under Ashford)

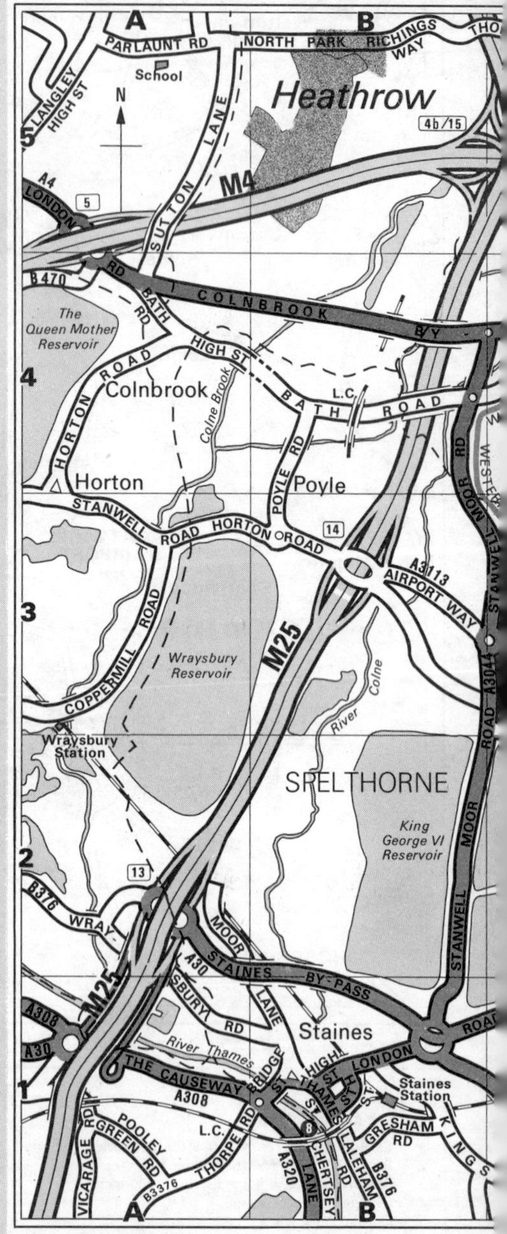

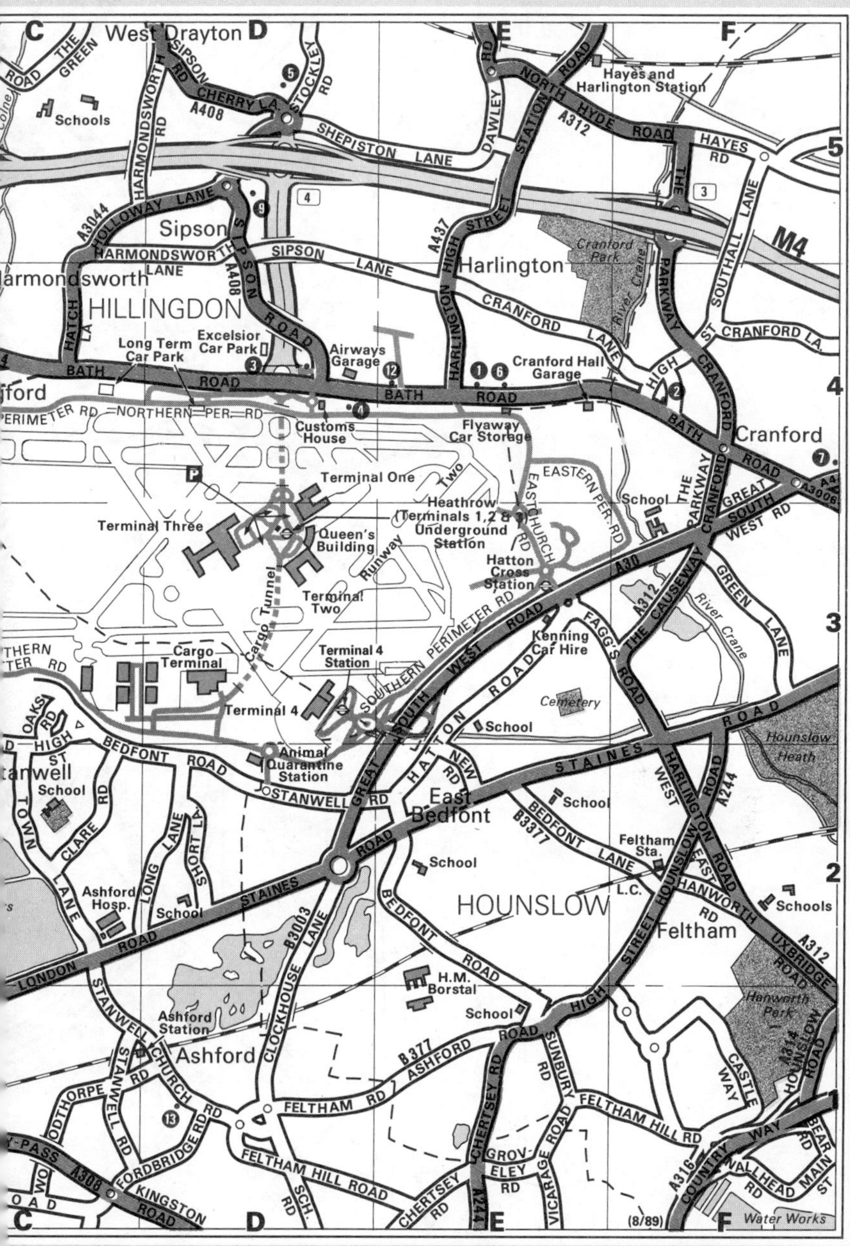

West Drayton
Sipson
Harmondsworth
HILLINGDON
Harlington
Hayes and Harlington Station
Cranford
Cranford Park
Long Term Car Park
Excelsior Car Park
Airways Garage
Cranford Hall Garage
Customs House
Flyaway Car Storage
Terminal One
Terminal Three
Terminal Two
Queen's Building
Heathrow (Terminals 1,2 & 3) Underground Station
Hatton Cross Station
Cargo Terminal
Terminal 4 Station
Terminal 4
Animal Quarantine Station
Kenning Car Hire
Cemetery
Hounslow Heath
East Bedfont
Stanwell
Ashford Hosp.
HOUNSLOW
Feltham
Feltham Sta.
H.M. Borstal
Ashford Station
Ashford
Hanworth Park
Water Works
M4
(8/89)

Manchester

1 Brasserie St Pierre ✕✕
2 Gaylord ✕✕
4 Holiday Inn Crowne Plaza ★★★★
5 Hopewell City ✕
7 The Koreana ✕
8 Kosmos Taverna ✕
9 Lime Tree ✕
10 Market ✕
11 Hotel Piccadilly ★★★★
12 Portland Thistle ★★★★
13 Post House ★★★
14 Mina-Japan ✕
15 Mitre ★★
16 Rajdoot ✕✕
17 Willow Bank ★★★
18 Woodlands ✕✕
19 Woo Sang ✕✕

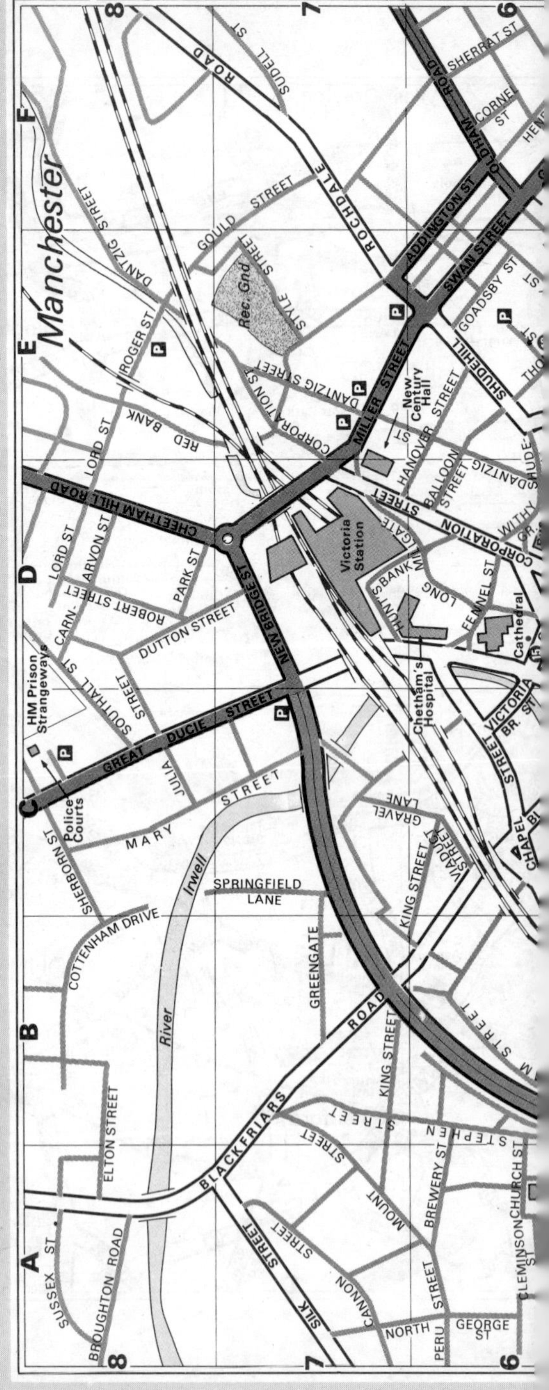

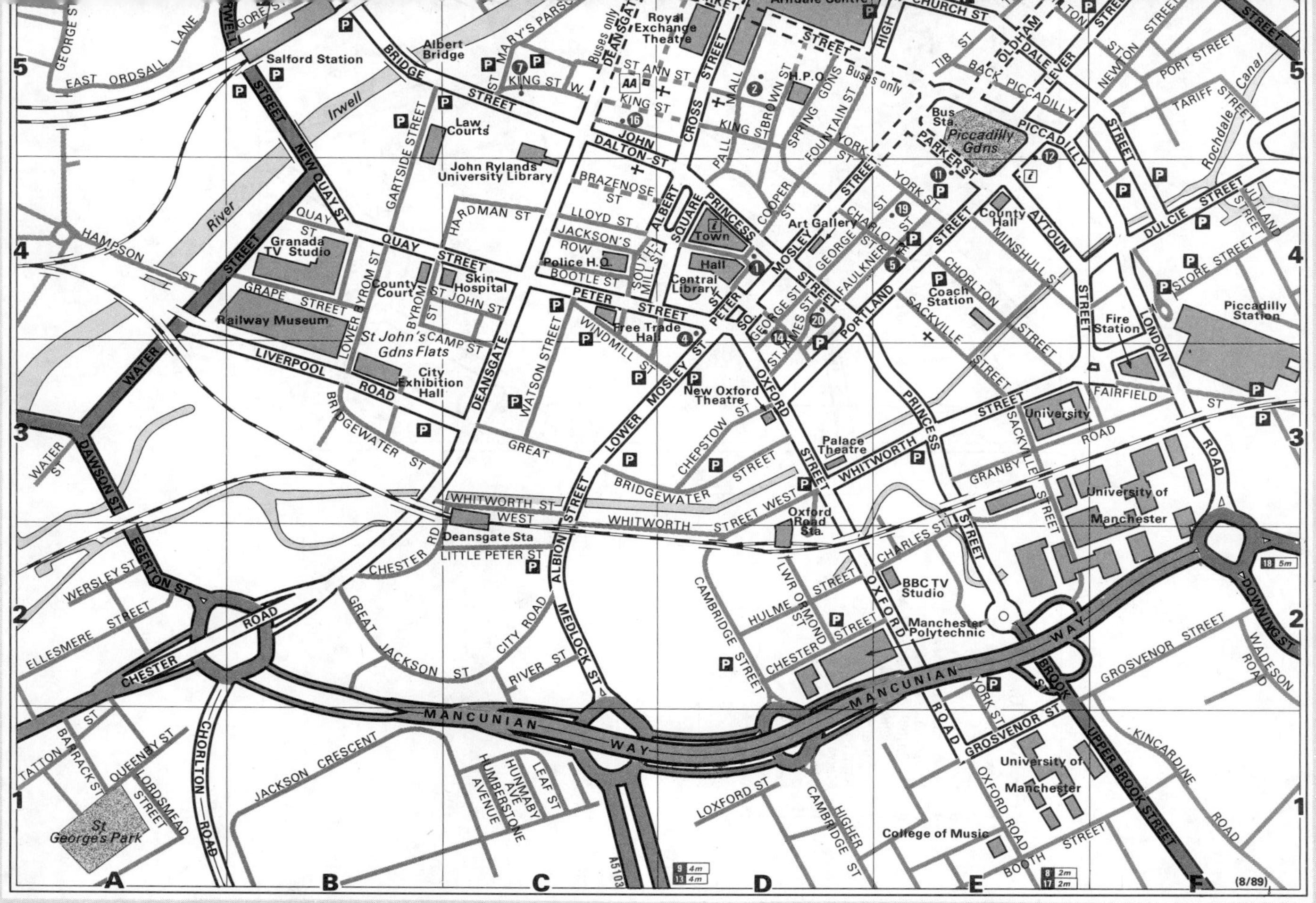

Salford Station
Albert Bridge
Royal Exchange Theatre
Law Courts
John Rylands University Library
Granada TV Studio
Railway Museum
County Court
Skin Hospital
St John's Gdns Flats
City Exhibition Hall
Police H.Q.
Town Hall
Central Library
Free Trade Hall
Art Gallery
Bus Sta.
Piccadilly Gdns
County Hall
Coach Station
Fire Station
Piccadilly Station
New Oxford Theatre
Palace Theatre
Oxford Road Sta.
Deansgate Sta
University
University of Manchester
BBC TV Studio
Manchester Polytechnic
College of Music
St George's Park
MANCUNIAN WAY
OXFORD STREET
OXFORD ROAD
DEANSGATE
QUAY STREET
NEW QUAY ST
WATER STREET
LIVERPOOL ROAD
PRINCESS STREET
PORTLAND STREET
MOSLEY STREET
LOWER MOSLEY ST
WHITWORTH STREET WEST
ALBION STREET
MEDLOCK ST
LONDON ROAD
UPPER BROOK STREET
CHORLTON ROAD
CHESTER ROAD
DOWNING ST
River Irwell
Rochdale Canal
A5103
(8/89)

Newcastle Upon Tyne

1 Hospitality Inn ★★★
2 Cairn ★★
3 County Thistle ★★★
4 Newcastle Crest ★★★
5 Fishermans Lodge ✕✕✕
6 Gosforth Park Thistle ★★★★
8 Holiday Inn ★★★★
9 Imperial ★★★
10 King Neptune ✕✕
12 Morrach ★★
14 Northumbria ★★★
15 Osborne ★
16 Le Roussillon ✕✕
17 Swallow ★★★
18 Whites ★★

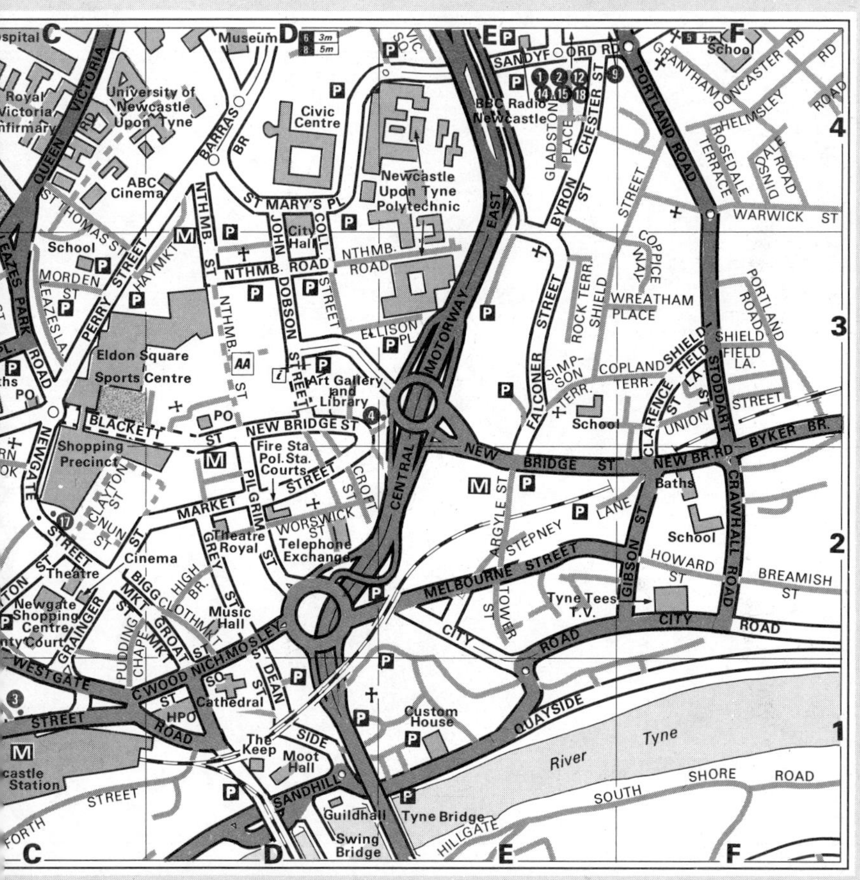
Museum
University of Newcastle Upon Tyne
Royal Victoria Infirmary
Civic Centre
Newcastle Upon Tyne Polytechnic
BBC Radio Newcastle
ABC Cinema
City Hall
School
Eldon Square Sports Centre
Art Gallery and Library
Shopping Precinct
Fire Sta. Pol. Sta. Courts
Theatre Royal
Telephone Exchange
Cinema
Theatre
Newgate Shopping Centre
Music Hall
Cathedral
The Keep
Moot Hall
Custom House
Guildhall
Tyne Bridge
Swing Bridge
Tyne Tees T.V.
Baths
School
WREATHAM PLACE
River Tyne
QUAYSIDE
CITY ROAD
MELBOURNE STREET
NEW BRIDGE ST
BYKER BR.
PORTLAND ROAD
CRAWHALL ROAD
CENTRAL MOTORWAY EAST
SOUTH SHORE ROAD
HILLGATE
SANDHILL
WESTGATE
FORTH STREET
NEWGATE
BLACKETT ST
PERCY STREET
HAYMKT
BARRAS BR
ST MARY'S PL
NTHMB. ROAD
JOHN DOBSON STREET
PILGRIM STREET
MARKET ST
GREY ST
MOSLEY ST
DEAN ST
GRAINGER ST
STODDART ST
WARWICK ST
BREAMISH ST
HOWARD ST
GIBSON ST
FALCONER STREET
ARGYLE ST
STEPNEY LANE
BYRON ST
GLADSTONE PLACE
CHESTER ST
COPPICE WAY
ROCK TERR.
COPLAND TERR.
SHIELD FIELD LA.
UNION STREET
CLARENCE ST
GRANTHAM RD
DONCASTER RD
HELMSLEY RD
ROSEDALE TERRACE
DINSDALE ROAD
C D E F
1 2 3 4

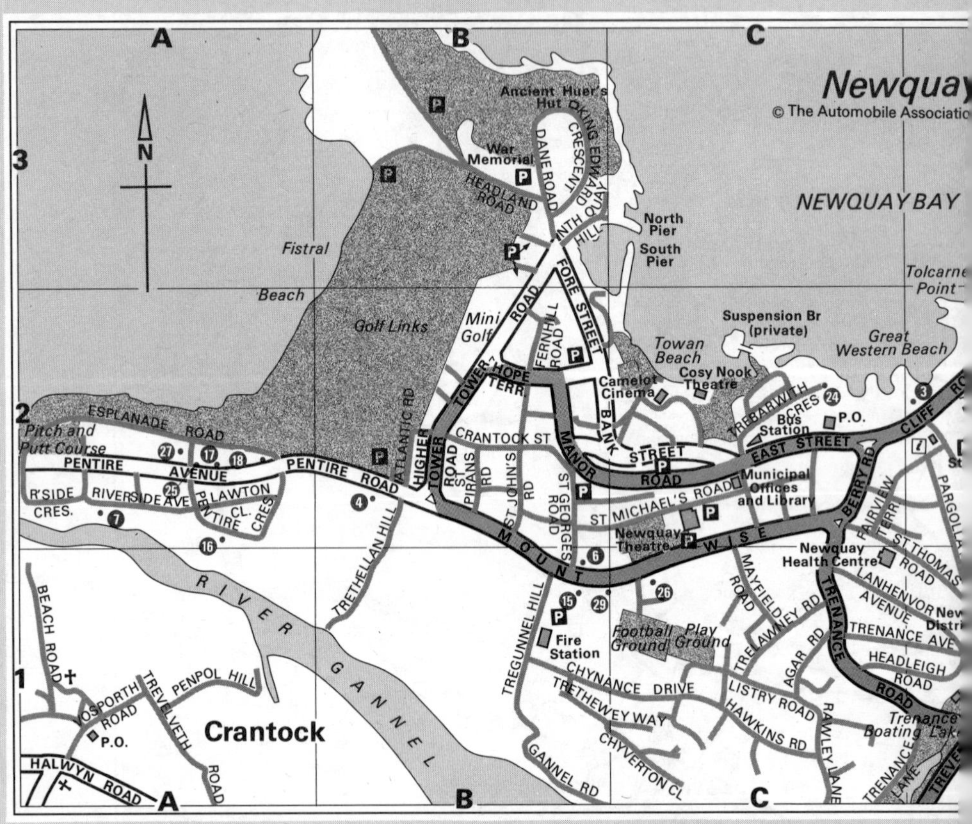

Newquay
© The Automobile Association
NEWQUAY BAY
Ancient Huer's Hut
War Memorial
North Pier
South Pier
Fistral Beach
Golf Links
Mini Golf
Towan Beach
Cosy Nook Theatre
Camelot Cinema
Suspension Br (private)
Great Western Beach
Tolcarne Point
Bus Station
P.O.
Municipal Offices and Library
Newquay Theatre
Newquay Health Centre
Fire Station
Football Ground
Play Ground
Pitch and Putt Course
RIVER GANNEL
Crantock
Trenance Boating Lake
ESPLANADE ROAD
PENTIRE AVENUE
PENTIRE ROAD
R'SIDE CRES.
RIVERSIDE AVE
LAWTON CRES
PENTIRE CL.
HEADLAND ROAD
DANE ROAD
KING EDWARD CRESCENT
FORE STREET
TOWER ROAD
HIGHER TOWER ROAD
FERNHILL ROAD
HOPE TERR
ATLANTIC RD
TRETHELLAN HILL
CRANTOCK ST
ST PIRANS RD
ST JOHN'S RD
ST GEORGES ROAD
MANOR ROAD
BANK STREET
EAST STREET
CLIFF RD
TREBARWITH CRES
ST MICHAEL'S ROAD
MOUNT WISE
BERRY RD
FAIRVIEW TERR
ST THOMAS ROAD
LANHENVOR AVENUE
TRENANCE AVE
HEADLEIGH ROAD
TRENANCE ROAD
TRENANCE LANE
MAYFIELD ROAD
TRELAWNEY RD
AGAR RD
LISTRY ROAD
HAWKINS RD
RAWLEY LANE
TREGUNNEL HILL
CHYNANCE DRIVE
TRETHEWEY WAY
CHYVERTON CL
GANNEL RD
BEACH ROAD
VOSPORTH ROAD
TREVELVETH ROAD
PENPOL HILL
HALWYN ROAD
A
B
C
1
2
3
N

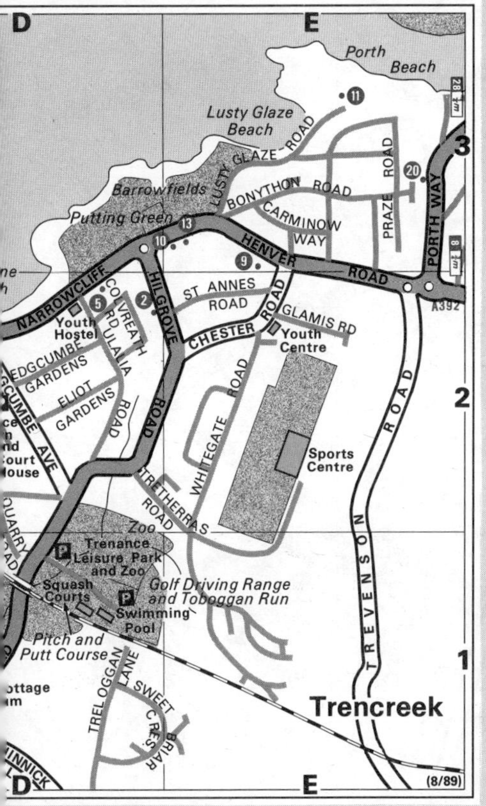

Newquay

2 Barrowfield ★★★
3 Beachcroft ★★
4 Bewdley ★★
5 Hotel Bristol ★★★
6 Cedars ★★
7 Corisande Manor ★★
8 Cross Mount ★★
9 Cumberland ★★
10 Edgcumbe ★★★
11 Glendorgal ★★★
13 Kilbirnie ★★★
15 Hotel Lowenva ★
16 Minto House ★★
17 Hotel Mordros ★★★
18 Philema ★★
20 Porth Veor Manor House ★★
24 Trebarwith ★★★
25 Tremont ★★
26 Trevone ★
27 Water's Edge ★★
28 Whipsiderry ★★
29 Windsor ★★★

Nottingham

1 Albany ★★★★
2 Les Artistes Gourmands ✕✕
7 Priory ★★
9 Royal Moat House International ★★★★
10 Rufford ★★
11 Savoy ★★★★
12 Shôgun ✕
14 Strathdon Thistle ★★★
16 Stakis Victoria ★★★
17 Waltons ★★★

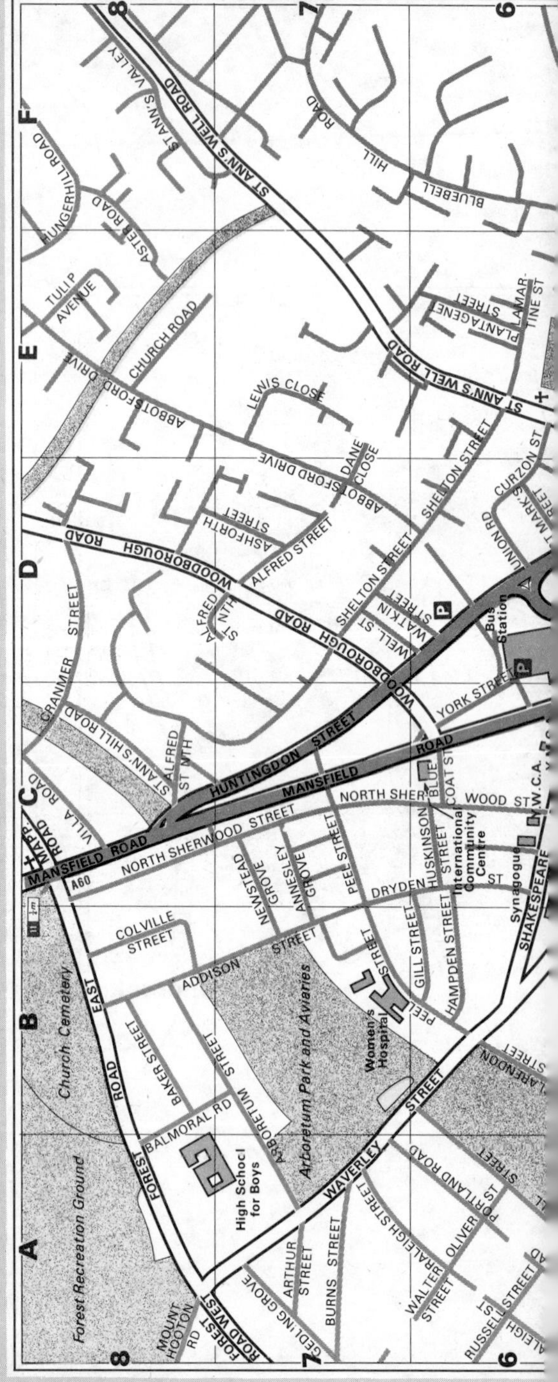

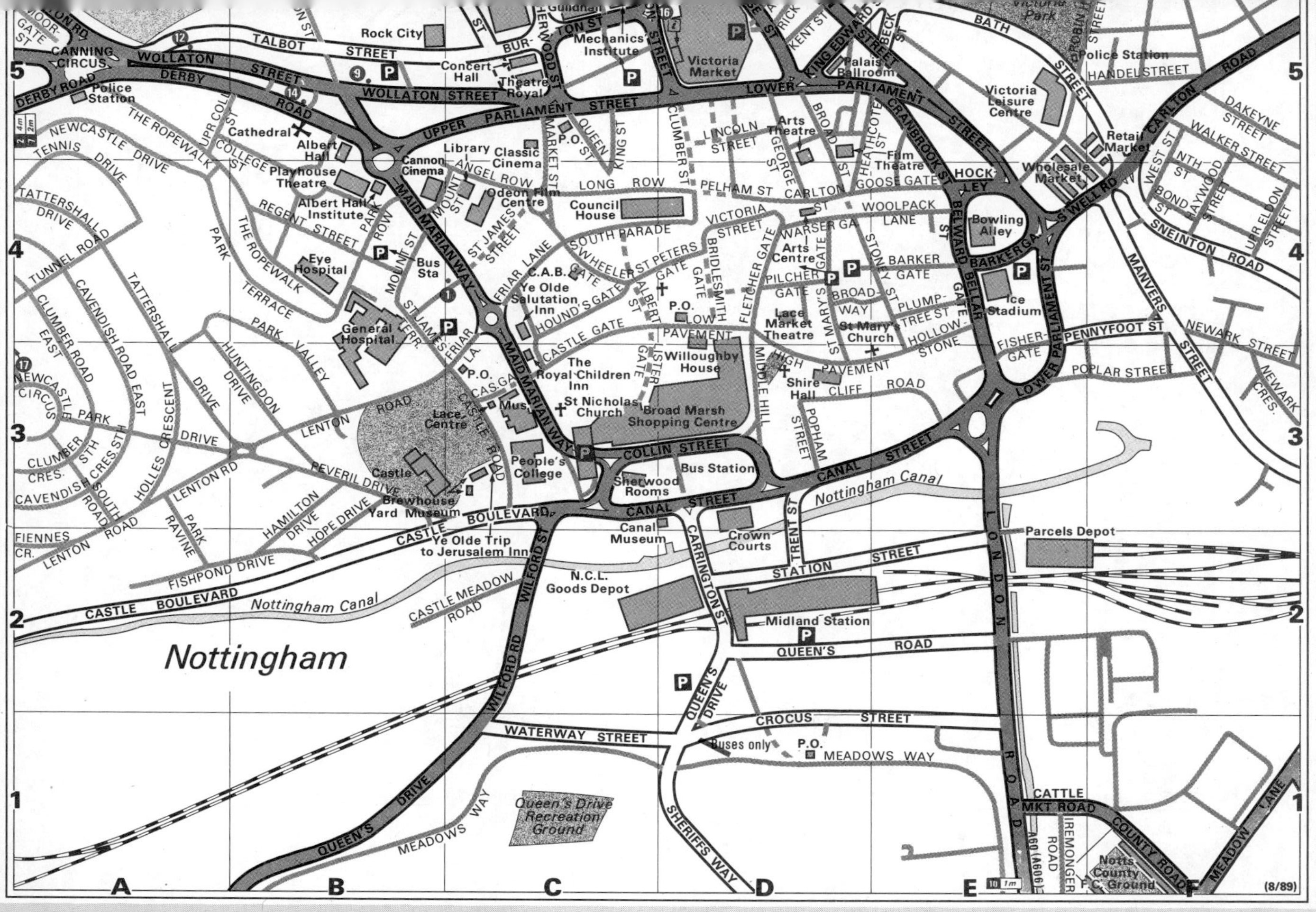

Nottingham
Nottingham Canal
Midland Station
Parcels Depot
N.C.L. Goods Depot
Crown Courts
Canal Museum
Castle
Brewhouse Yard Museum
Ye Olde Trip to Jerusalem Inn
Lace Centre
General Hospital
Eye Hospital
Albert Hall
Albert Hall Institute
Playhouse Theatre
Cathedral
Rock City
Concert Hall
Theatre Royal
Council House
Victoria Market
Victoria Leisure Centre
Ice Stadium
Bowling Alley
Wholesale Market
Retail Market
Police Station
Broad Marsh Shopping Centre
Bus Station
Sherwood Rooms
St Nicholas Church
St Mary's Church
Lace Market Theatre
Shire Hall
Arts Theatre
Film Theatre
Palais Ballroom
Willoughby House
People's College
Notts County F.C. Ground
Queen's Drive Recreation Ground
Mechanics' Institute
Library
Cannon Cinema
Odeon Film Centre
Classic Cinema
Ye Olde Salutation Inn
The Royal Children Inn
MAID MARIAN WAY
LONDON ROAD
CANAL STREET
WILFORD RD
QUEEN'S DRIVE
CASTLE BOULEVARD
UPPER PARLIAMENT STREET
LOWER PARLIAMENT STREET
WOLLATON STREET
DERBY ROAD
CANNING CIRCUS
CARRINGTON ST
STATION STREET
QUEEN'S ROAD
SHERIFFS WAY
MEADOWS WAY
WATERWAY STREET
CROCUS STREET
MANVERS STREET
SNEINTON ROAD
CARLTON ROAD
COUNTY ROAD
MEADOW LANE
IREMONGER ROAD
CATTLE MKT ROAD
A60 (A606)
(8/89)

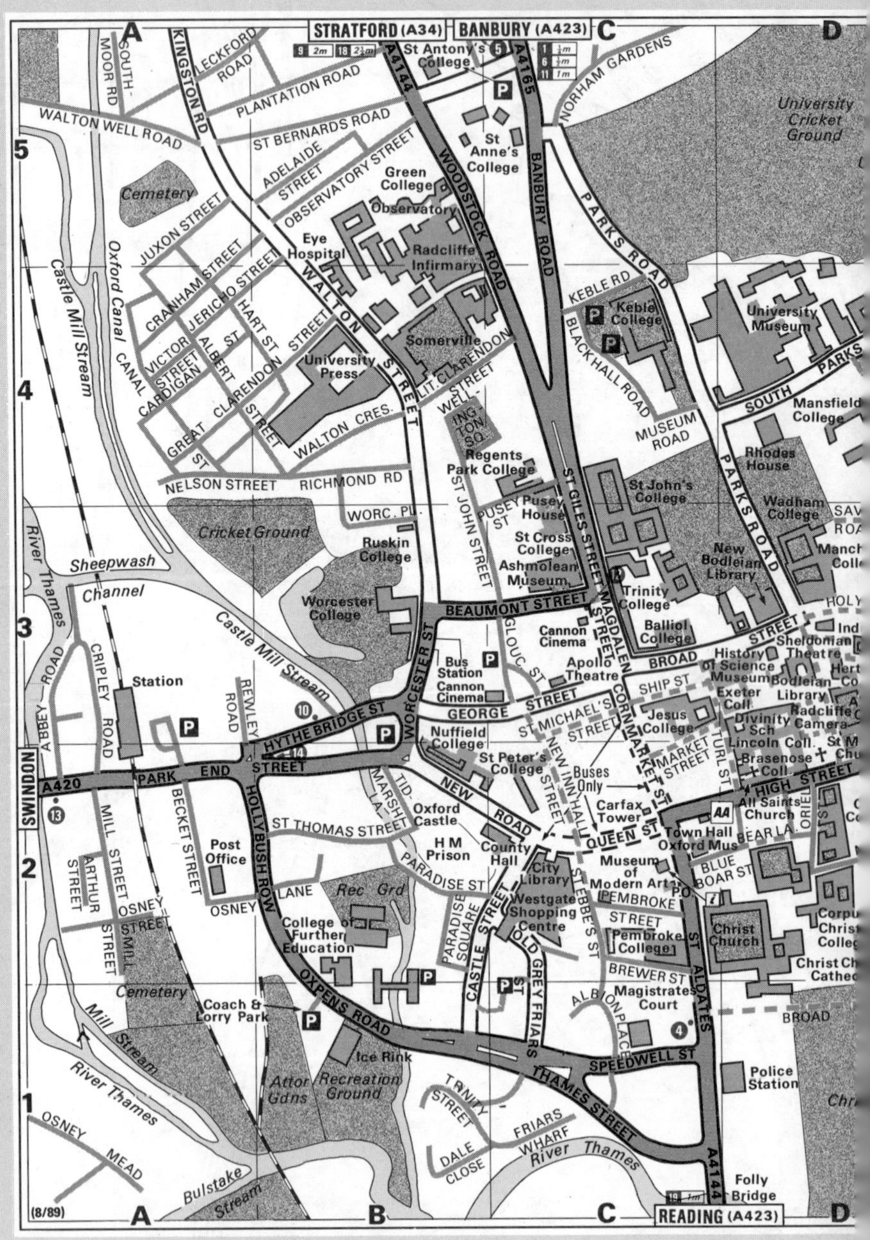

STRATFORD (A34)
BANBURY (A423)
A
B
C
D
1
2
3
4
5
9 2m
18 2½m
1 ¼m
6 ½m
11 1m
St Antony's College
A4144
A4165
NORHAM GARDENS
University Cricket Ground
SOUTH-MOOR RD
KINGSTON RD
LECKFORD ROAD
PLANTATION ROAD
WALTON WELL ROAD
ST BERNARDS ROAD
ADELAIDE STREET
OBSERVATORY STREET
Green College
Observatory
St Anne's College
WOODSTOCK ROAD
BANBURY ROAD
PARKS ROAD
Cemetery
JUXON STREET
Oxford Canal
Castle Mill Stream
CRANHAM STREET
JERICHO STREET
HART ST
Eye Hospital
Radcliffe Infirmary
WALTON STREET
KEBLE RD
Keble College
BLACKHALL ROAD
University Museum
VICTOR STREET
ALBERT ST
CANAL STREET
CARDIGAN ST
CLARENDON STREET
University Press
Somerville
LIT. CLARENDON STREET
SOUTH PARKS
Mansfield College
GREAT CLARENDON ST
WALTON CRES.
WELLINGTON SQ.
MUSEUM ROAD
Rhodes House
Regents Park College
NELSON STREET
RICHMOND RD
WORC. PL.
ST GILES STREET
St John's College
Wadham College
PUSEY ST
Pusey House
ST JOHN STREET
St Cross College
Cricket Ground
Ruskin College
Ashmolean Museum
New Bodleian Library
River Thames
Sheepwash Channel
Trinity College
Worcester College
BEAUMONT STREET
MAGDALEN STREET
Cannon Cinema
Balliol College
Castle Mill Stream
Bus Station
Cannon Cinema
GLOUC. ST
Apollo Theatre
BROAD STREET
History of Science Museum
Sheldonian Theatre
Bodleian Library
ABBEY ROAD
CRIPLEY ROAD
Station
REWLEY ROAD
SHIP ST
Exeter Coll.
GEORGE STREET
Jesus College
Divinity Sch
Radcliffe Camera
HYTHE BRIDGE ST
WORCESTER ST
Nuffield College
ST MICHAEL'S STREET
CORNMARKET ST
MARKET STREET
TURL ST
Lincoln Coll.
Brasenose Coll.
SWINDON
A420
PARK END STREET
St Peter's College
NEW INN HALL STREET
Buses Only
HIGH STREET
All Saints Church
MILL STREET
BECKET STREET
HOLLYBUSH ROW
TIDMARSH LA.
NEW ROAD
Oxford Castle
Carfax Tower
AA
Town Hall
Oxford Mus
BEAR LA.
ORIEL ST
ST THOMAS STREET
QUEEN ST
Post Office
H M Prison
County Hall
Museum of Modern Art
BLUE BOAR ST
ARTHUR STREET
PARADISE ST
City Library
P.O.
OSNEY STREET
OSNEY LANE
Rec Grd
Westgate Shopping Centre
ST EBBE'S ST
PEMBROKE STREET
Christ Church
College of Further Education
PARADISE SQUARE
CASTLE STREET
OLD GREYFRIARS ST
Pembroke College
ST ALDATES
Christ Church Cathedral
Cemetery
Coach & Lorry Park
OXPENS ROAD
BREWER ST
ALBION PLACE
Magistrates Court
BROAD
Mill Stream
Ice Rink
SPEEDWELL ST
River Thames
Attor Gdns
Recreation Ground
THAMES STREET
Police Station
TRINITY STREET
OSNEY MEAD
DALE CLOSE
FRIARS WHARF
River Thames
A4144
Folly Bridge
Bulstake Stream
(8/89)
READING (A423)

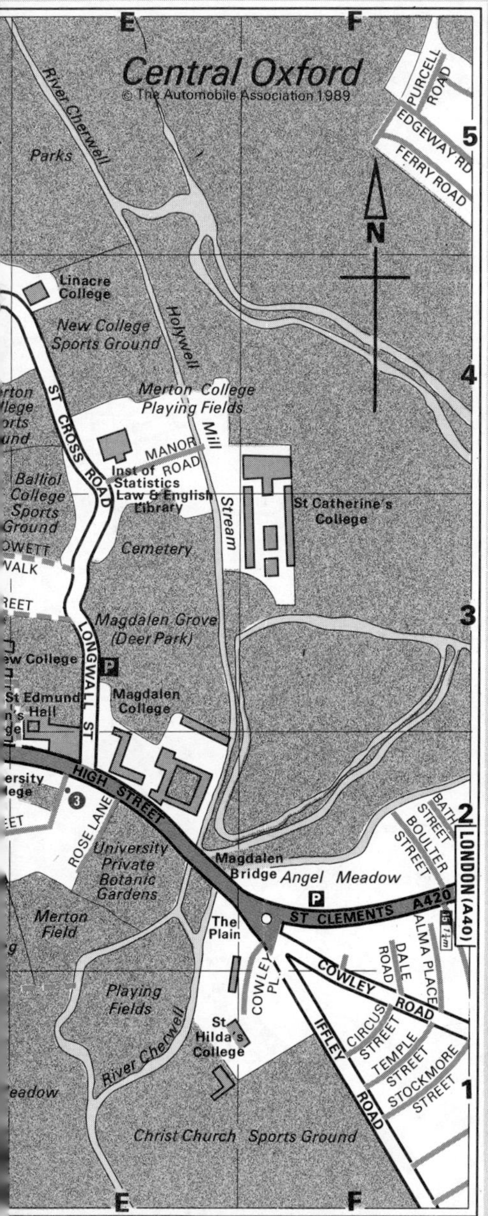

Oxford

1 Cotswold Lodge ★★★
3 Eastgate ★★★
4 Restaurant Elizabeth ✕✕✕
5 15 North Parade ✕
6 Linton Lodge ★★★
9 Oxford Moat House ★★★
10 Paddyfield ✕✕
11 Gees ✕✕
12 Randolph ★★★★
13 River ★
14 Royal Oxford ★★
18 Welcome Lodge ★★
19 Victoria ★★

Plymouth

1 Astor ★★★
3 Chez Nous ✕
5 New Continental ★★★
6 Copthorne ★★★★
7 Drake ★
9 Grosvenor ★★
11 Plymouth Moat House ★★★★
12 Imperial ★
13 Invicta ★★
14 Mayflower Post House ★★★
16 Novotel Plymouth ★★★
17 Strathmore ★★

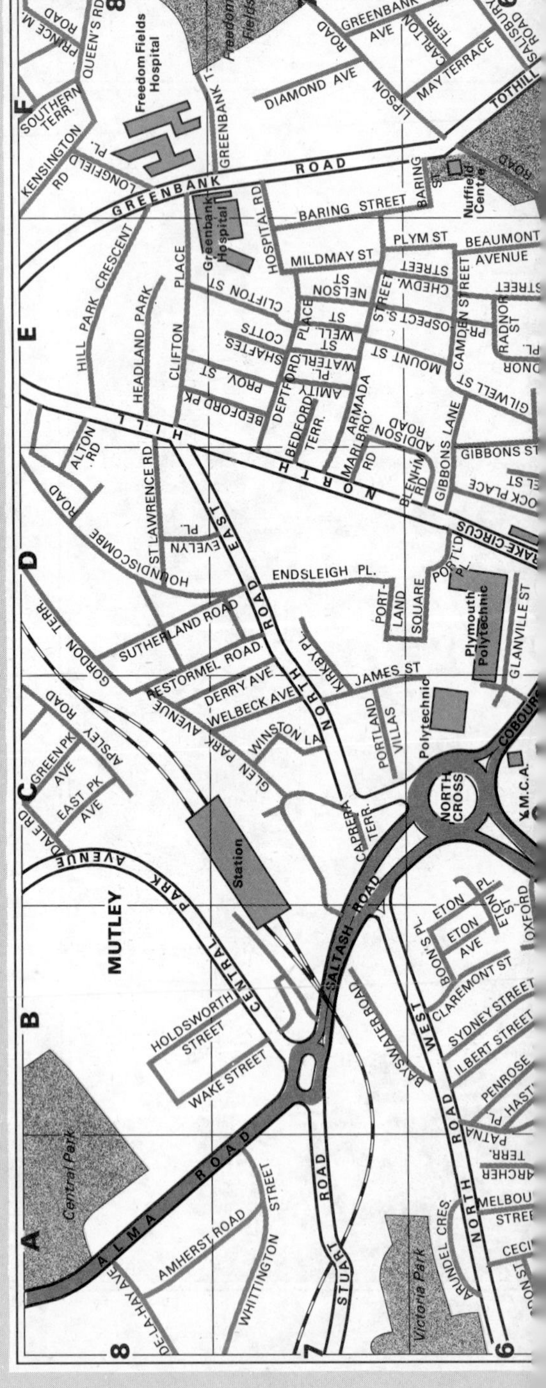

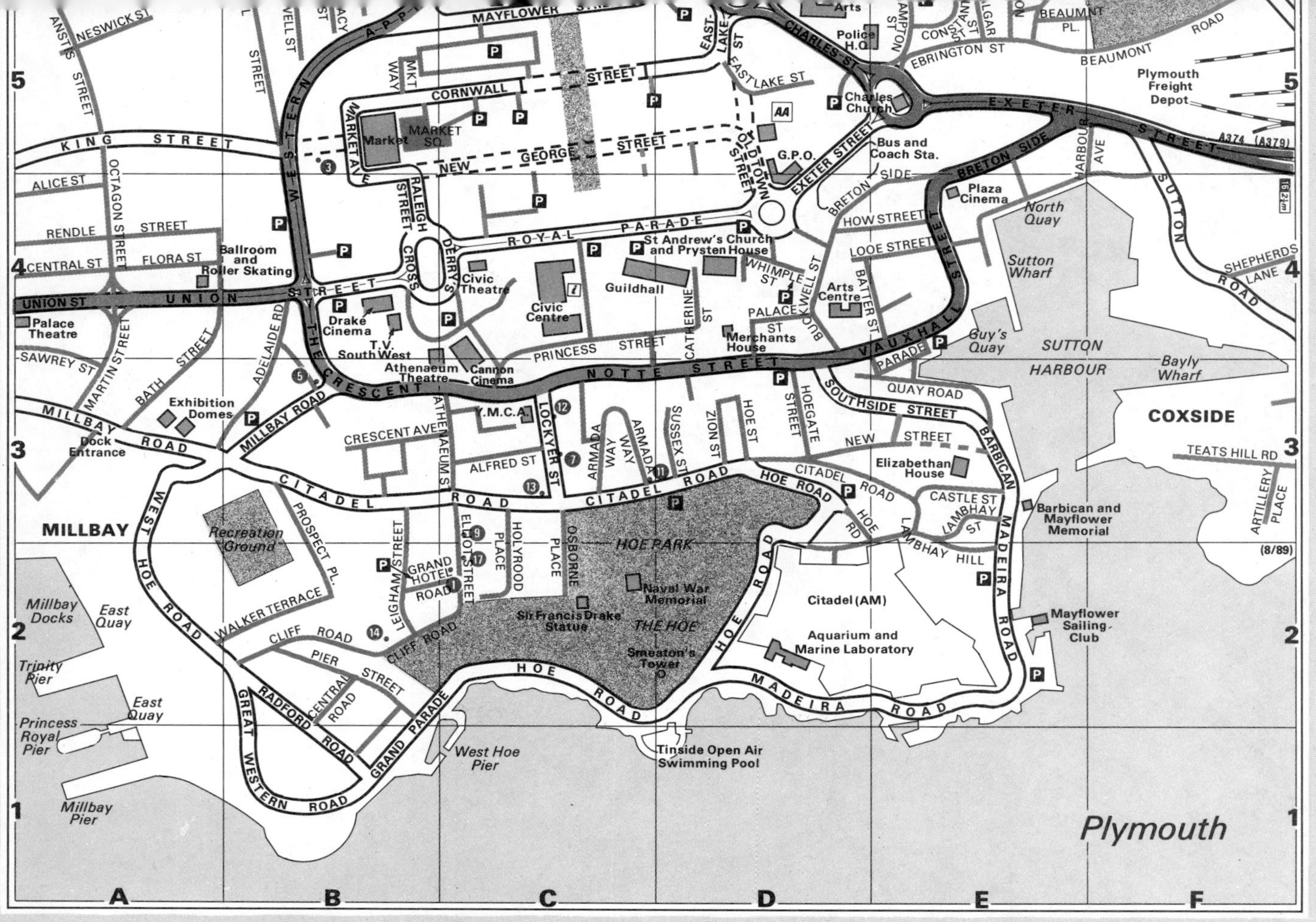
Plymouth
COXSIDE
SUTTON HARBOUR
Sutton Wharf
North Quay
Guy's Quay
Bayly Wharf
MILLBAY
Millbay Docks
East Quay
Trinity Pier
Princess Royal Pier
Millbay Pier
West Hoe Pier
Plymouth Freight Depot
Police H.Q.
Arts
Charles Church
Bus and Coach Sta.
Plaza Cinema
G.P.O.
Arts Centre
Merchants House
St Andrew's Church and Prysten House
Guildhall
Civic Centre
Civic Theatre
Cannon Cinema
Athenaeum Theatre
T.V. South West
Drake Cinema
Market
MARKET SQ.
Y.M.C.A.
Elizabethan House
Barbican and Mayflower Memorial
Mayflower Sailing Club
Citadel (AM)
Aquarium and Marine Laboratory
Tinside Open Air Swimming Pool
HOE PARK
THE HOE
Naval War Memorial
Smeaton's Tower
Sir Francis Drake Statue
Recreation Ground
Exhibition Domes
Ballroom and Roller Skating
Palace Theatre
Dock Entrance
EXETER STREET
SUTTON ROAD
SHEPHERDS LANE
TEATS HILL RD
ARTILLERY PLACE
HARBOUR AVE
BRETON SIDE
VAUXHALL STREET
SOUTHSIDE STREET
QUAY ROAD
PARADE
BARBICAN
MADEIRA ROAD
LAMBHAY HILL
LAMBHAY ST
CASTLE ST
NEW STREET
CITADEL ROAD
HOE ROAD
HOE RD
HOEGATE STREET
HOE ST
ZION ST
SUSSEX ST
ARMADA WAY
LOCKYER ST
ALFRED ST
OSBORNE PLACE
HOLYROOD PLACE
ELLIOT STREET
GRAND HOTEL ROAD
ATHENAEUM ST
CRESCENT AVE
LEIGHAM STREET
CLIFF ROAD
PIER STREET
CENTRAL ROAD
RADFORD ROAD
GRAND PARADE
GREAT WESTERN ROAD
WEST HOE ROAD
PROSPECT PL.
WALKER TERRACE
NOTTE STREET
THE CRESCENT
PRINCESS STREET
CATHERINE ST
PALACE ST
WHIMPLE ST
BUCKWELL ST
BATTER ST
LOOE STREET
HOW STREET
OLD TOWN STREET
ROYAL PARADE
DERRY'S CROSS
RALEIGH STREET
NEW GEORGE STREET
CORNWALL STREET
MARKET AVE
MKT WAY
MAYFLOWER ST
EAST-LAKE ST
EASTLAKE ST
CHARLES ST
EBRINGTON ST
BEAUMONT ROAD
BEAUMONT PL.
WESTERN APPROACH
UNION STREET
UNION ST
MILLBAY ROAD
ADELAIDE RD
BATH STREET
MARTIN STREET
SAWREY ST
KING STREET
OCTAGON STREET
FLORA ST
RENDLE STREET
CENTRAL ST
ALICE ST
ANSTIS STREET
NESWICK ST
A374 (A379)
(8/89)
1
2
3
4
5
A
B
C
D
E
F

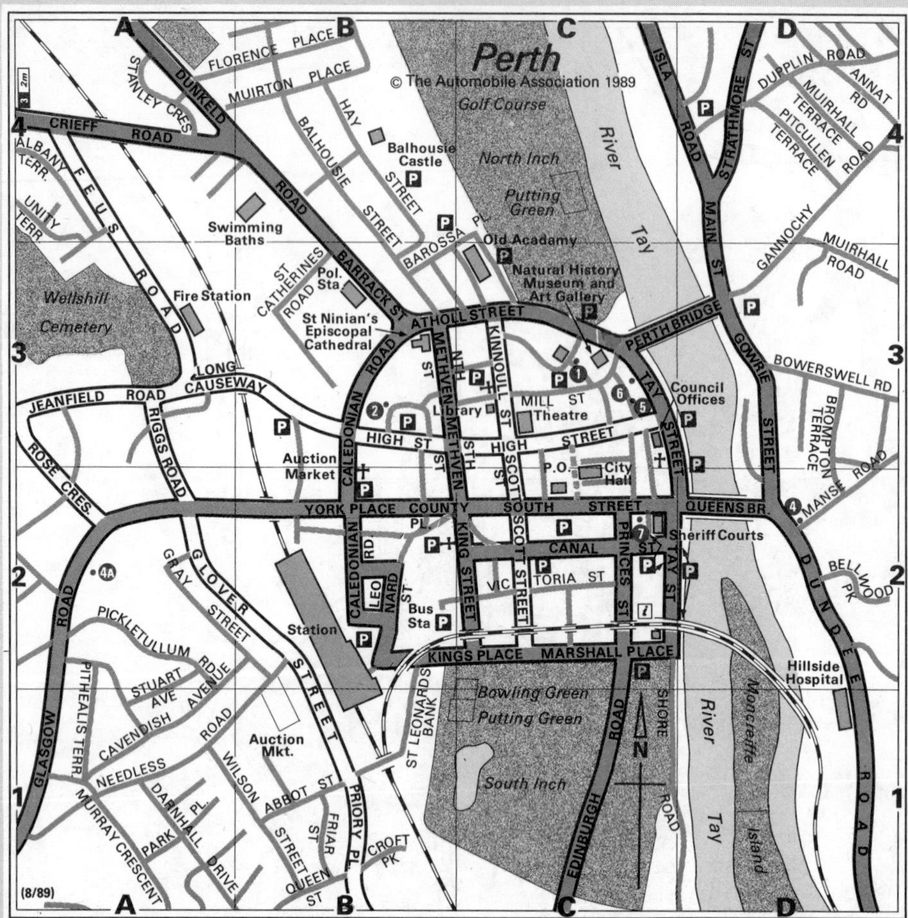

Perth

1 Coach House ✕✕
2 Stakis City Mills ★★★
3 Huntingtower ★★★
4 Isle of Skye Toby ★★★
4A Lovat ★★★
5 Number Thirty Three ✕✕
6 Royal George ★★★
7 Salutation ★★

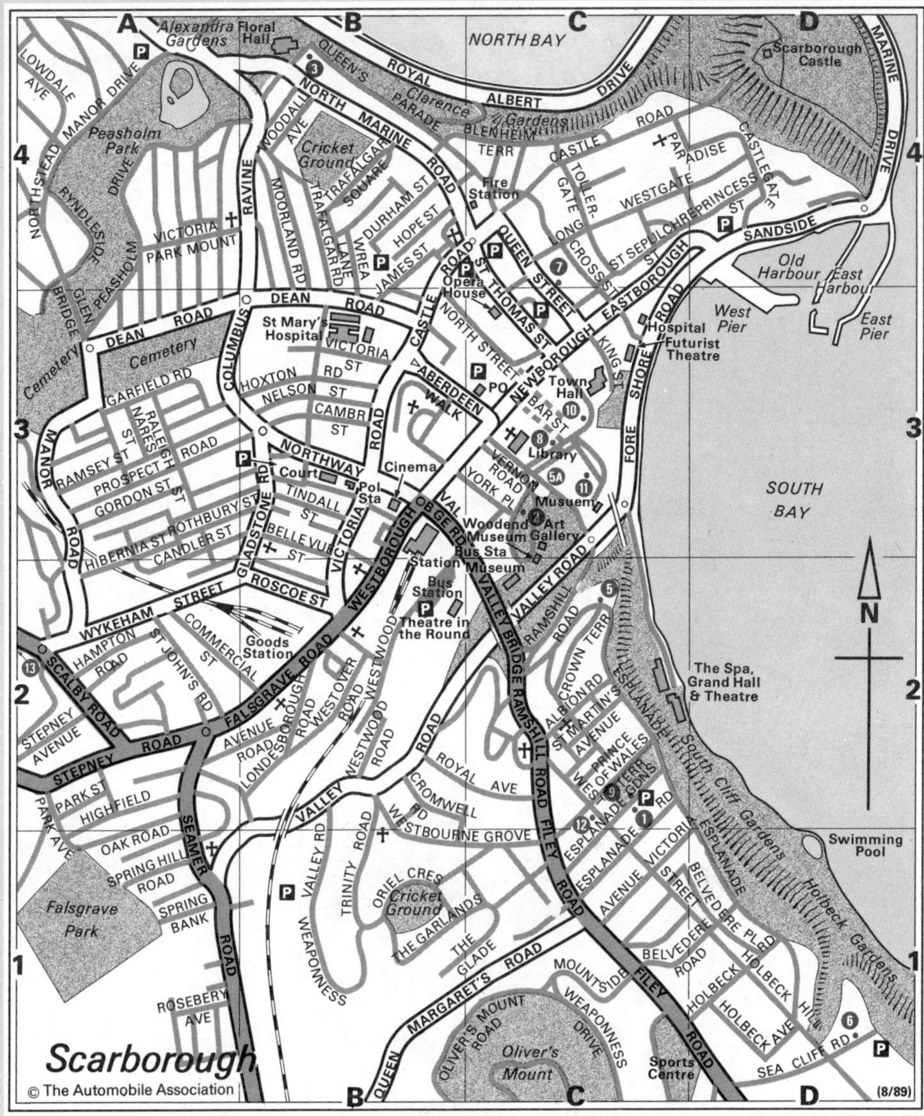

Scarborough

1 Brooklands ★★
2 Central ★★
3 Clifton ★★★
5 Esplanade ★★★
5A Gridley's Crescent ★★
6 Holbeck Hall ★★★★
7 Lanterna Ristorante ✕✕
8 Palm Court ★★★
9 Red Lea ★★
10 Royal ★★★★
11 Hotel St Nicholas ★★★
12 Southlands ★★
13 Wrea Head Country ★★★

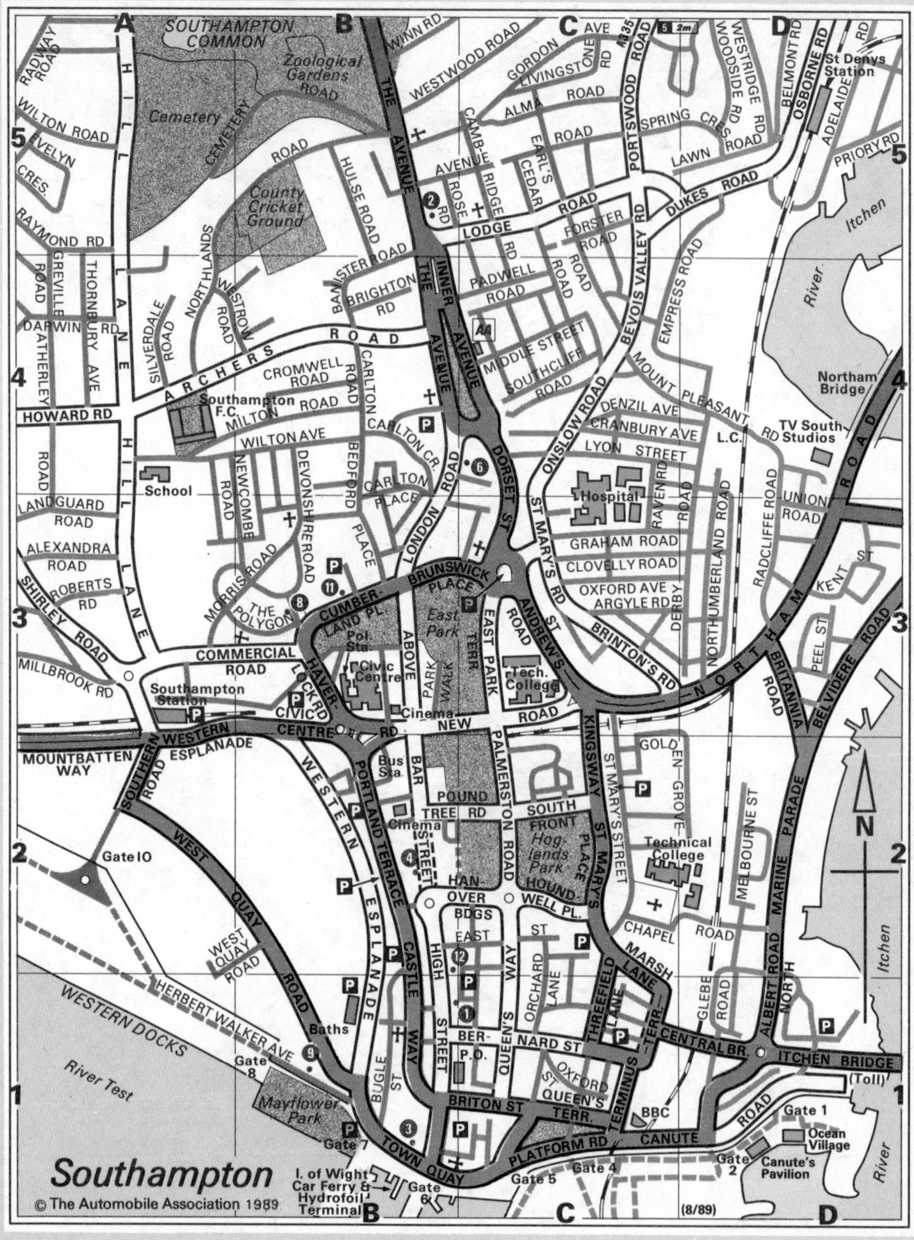

Southampton

		3	Geddes ✕✕✕	8	Polygon ★★★
		4	Golden Palace ✕	9	Post House ★★★
1	Dolphin ★★★	5	Kohinoor Tandoori ✕✕	11	Southampton Park ★★★
2	Elizabeth House ★★	6	Kuti's ✕✕	12	Star ★★

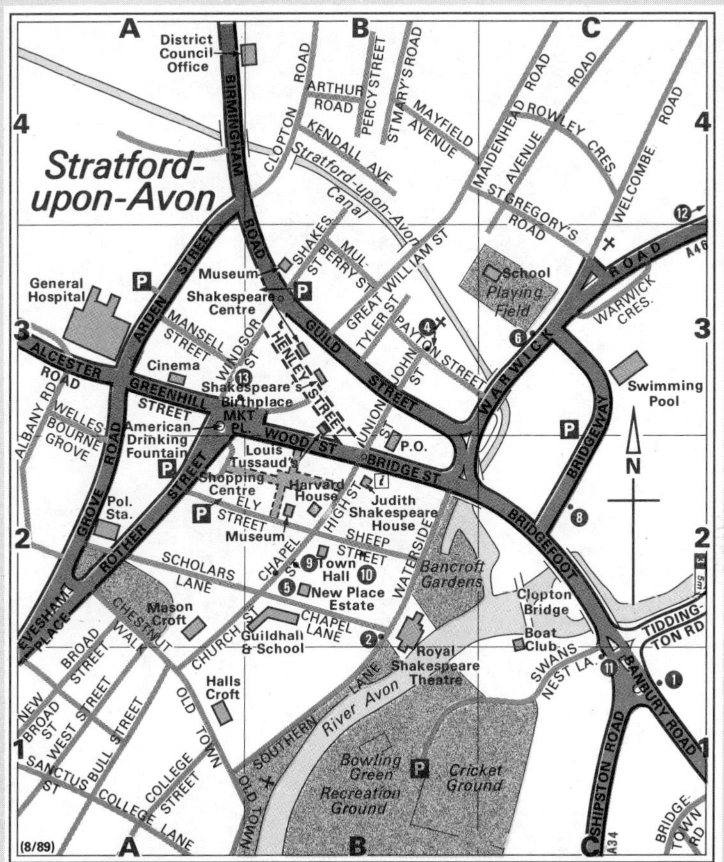

Stratford-upon-Avon

1 Alveston Manor ★★★
2 Arden ★★★
3 Charlecote Pheasant ★★★ (listed under Charlecote)
4 Dukes ★★★
5 Falcon ★★★
6 Grosvenor House ★★★
8 Moat House International ★★★★
9 Shakespeare ★★★★
10 Stratford House ★★
11 Swan's Nest ★★★
12 Welcombe ★★★★
13 White Swan ★★★

Torquay

1	Albaston ★★	9	Chelston Towers ★★	18	Imperial ★★★★★	27	Rainbow House ★★★
2	Bancourt ★★	10	Conway Court ★★	19	Kistor ★★★	28	Red House ★★
3	Belgrave ★★★	11	Devonshire ★★★	20	Lansdowne ★★	29	Remy's Restaurant Francais ✕
4	Belvedere House ★★	12	Frognel Hall ★★	21	Lincombe Hall ★★★	32	Shelley Court ★
5	Burlington ★★	13	Grand ★★★★	22	Livermead Cliff ★★★	33	Sydore ★★
6	Bute Court ★★	14	Gresham Court ★★	23	Livermead House ★★★	34	Templestowe ★★
7	Carlton ★★	15	Homers ★★★	24	Hotel Nepaul ★★★	35	Toorak ★★★
		16	Howden Court ★★	25	Nethway ★★	36	Vernon Court ★★
		17	Hunsdon Lea ★★	26	Oscar's ★★	37	Windsurfer ★

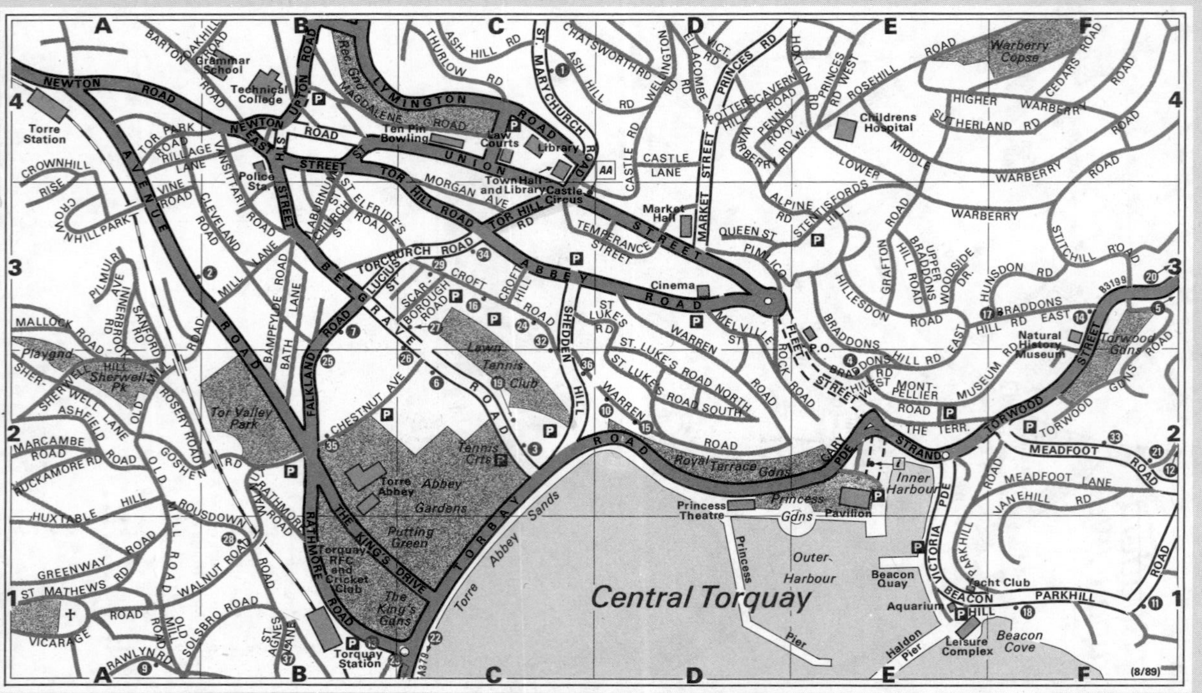

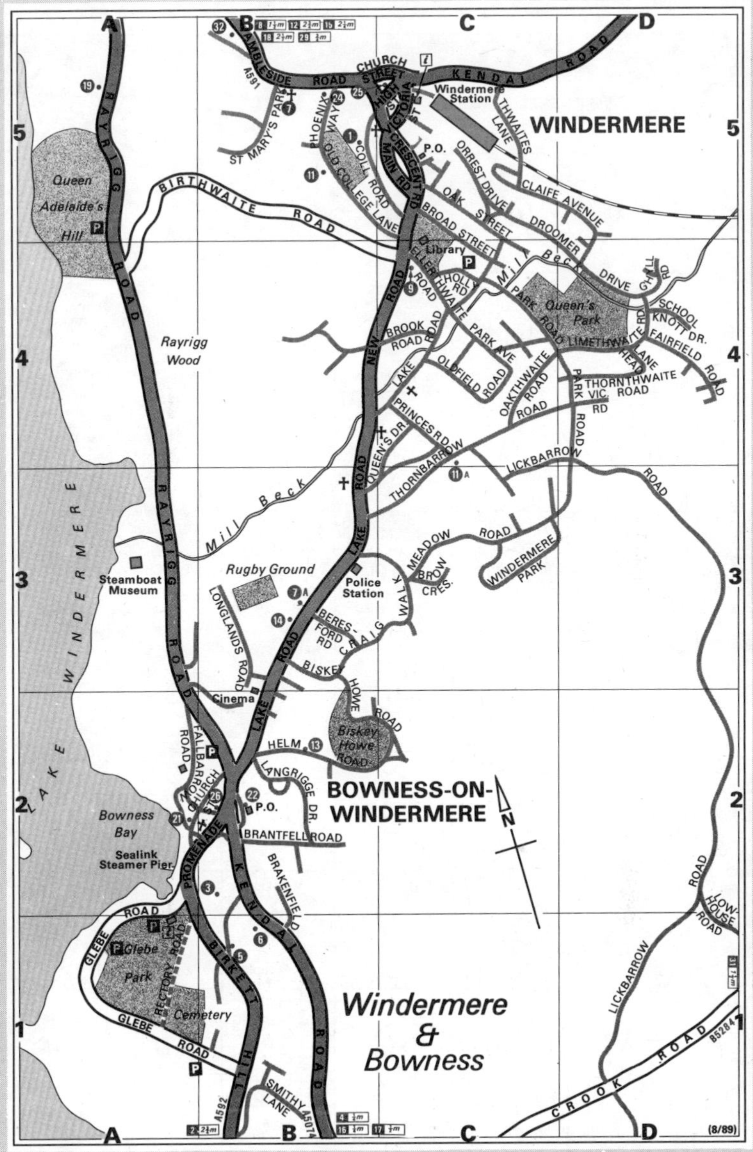

Windermere		8	Quarry Garth Country House ★	18	Low Wood ★★★
1	Applegarth ★★	9	Ellerthwaite Lodge ★★	19	Miller Howe ★★
2	Beech Hill ★★★	11	Hideaway ★★	21	The Old England ★★★★
3	Belsfield ★★★	11A	Hillthwaite House ★★	22	Porthole Eating House ✕
4	Bordriggs Country House ★★	12	Holbeck Ghyll ★★	24	Ravensworth ★
5	Burn How Garden House Hotel, Motel and Rest ★★★	13	Hydro ★★★	25	Rogers ✕
6	Burnside ★★★	14	Knoll ★★	26	Royal ★★
7	Cedar Manor ★★	15	Langdale Chase ★★★	29	Sun ★★
7A	Craig Foot Country House ★★	16	Lindeth Fell ★★	31	Wild Boar ★★★
		17	Linithwaite ★★	32	Willowsmere ★

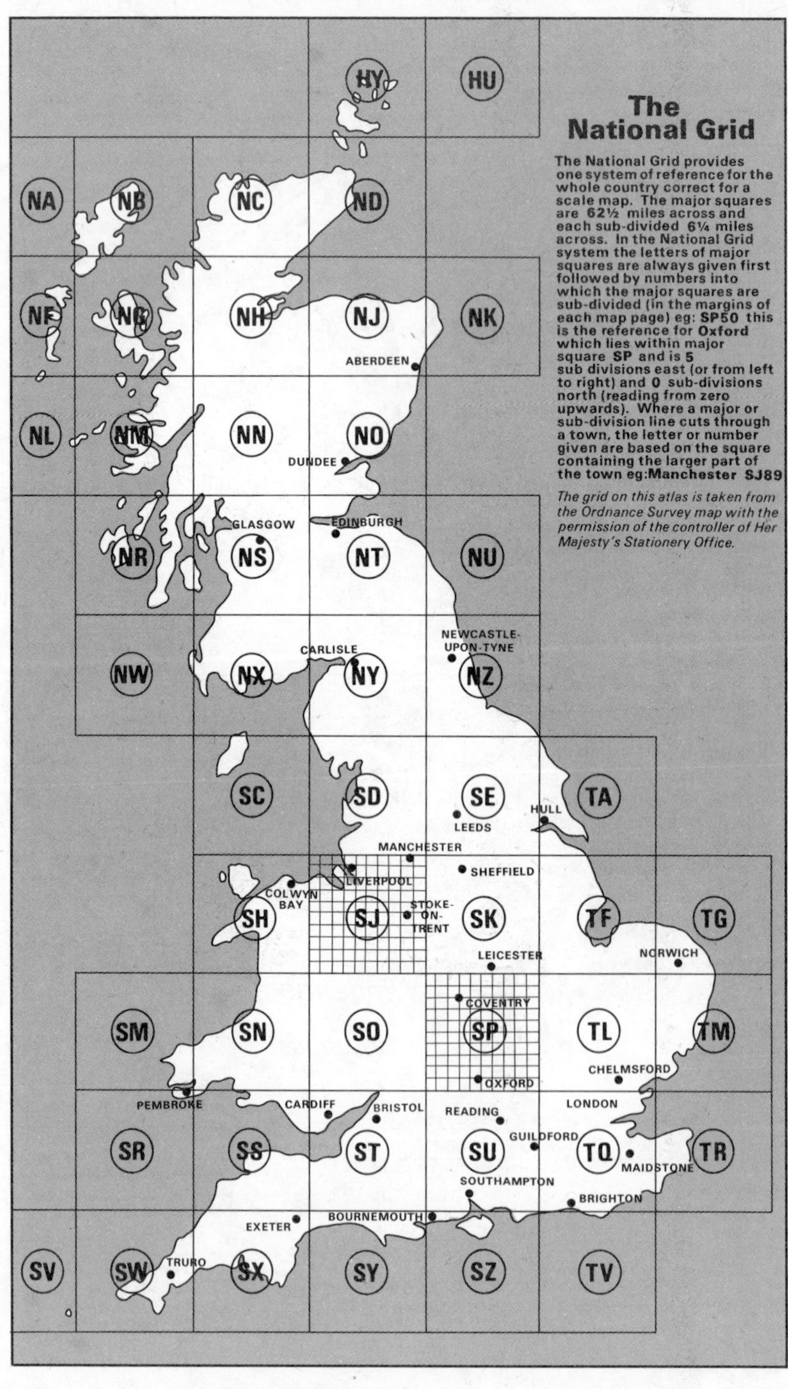

The National Grid
The National Grid provides one system of reference for the whole country correct for a scale map. The major squares are 62½ miles across and each sub-divided 6¼ miles across. In the National Grid system the letters of major squares are always given first followed by numbers into which the major squares are sub-divided (in the margins of each map page) eg: SP50 this is the reference for Oxford which lies within major square SP and is 5 sub divisions east (or from left to right) and 0 sub-divisions north (reading from zero upwards). Where a major or sub-division line cuts through a town, the letter or number given are based on the square containing the larger part of the town eg: Manchester SJ89
The grid on this atlas is taken from the Ordnance Survey map with the permission of the controller of Her Majesty's Stationery Office.
HY
HU
NA
NB
NC
ND
NF
NG
NH
NJ
NK
ABERDEEN
NL
NM
NN
NO
DUNDEE
GLASGOW
EDINBURGH
NR
NS
NT
NU
NEWCASTLE-UPON-TYNE
CARLISLE
NW
NX
NY
NZ
SC
SD
SE
TA
HULL
LEEDS
MANCHESTER
LIVERPOOL
SHEFFIELD
COLWYN BAY
SH
SJ
STOKE-ON-TRENT
SK
TF
TG
LEICESTER
NORWICH
COVENTRY
SM
SN
SO
SP
TL
TM
CHELMSFORD
OXFORD
PEMBROKE
CARDIFF
BRISTOL
READING
LONDON
GUILDFORD
SR
SS
ST
SU
TQ
TR
MAIDSTONE
SOUTHAMPTON
BRIGHTON
EXETER
BOURNEMOUTH
TRURO
SV
SW
SX
SY
SZ
TV

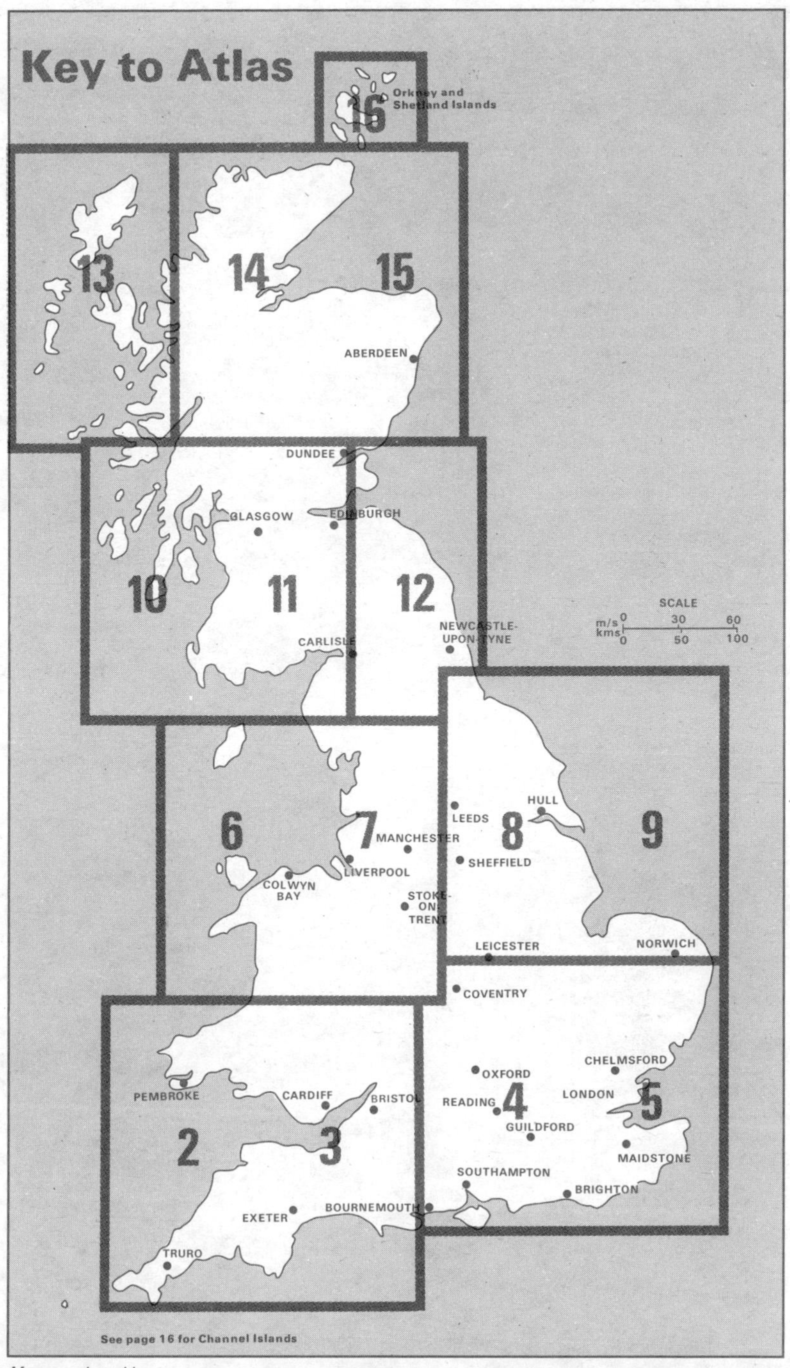

Maps produced by

The Automobile Association from the Automaps database.

This atlas is for location purposes only: see Members Handbook for current road and AA road services information.

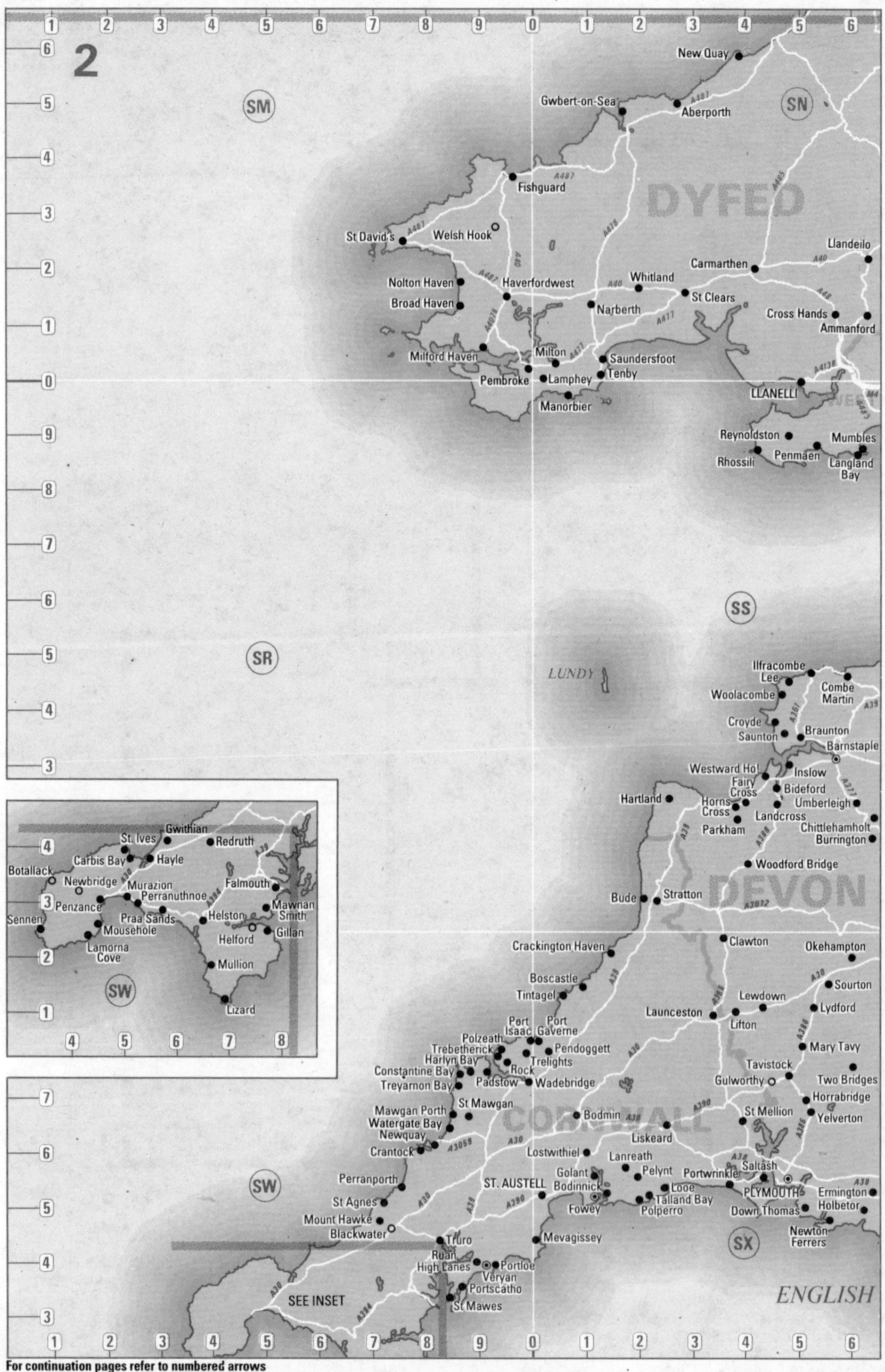

For continuation pages refer to numbered arrows

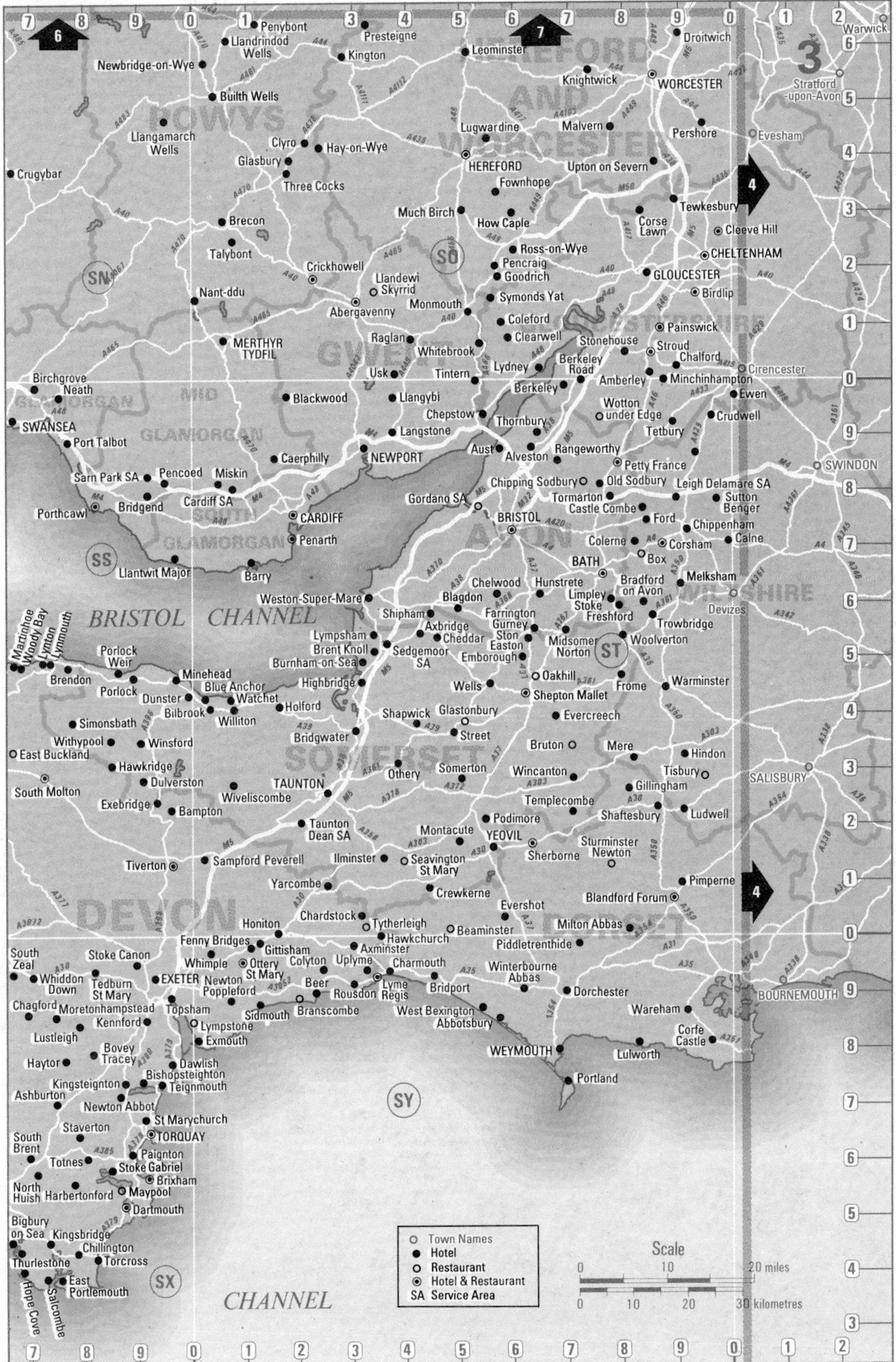

6
7
3
4
Penybont
Llandrindod Wells
Presteigne
Kington
Leominster
Droitwich
Warwick
Newbridge-on-Wye
Builth Wells
HEREFORD AND WORCESTER
Knightwick
WORCESTER
Stratford -upon-Avon
POWYS
Llangamarch Wells
Clyro
Hay-on-Wye
Glasbury
Three Cocks
Lugwardine
Malvern
Pershore
Evesham
HEREFORD
Upton on Severn
Crugybar
Fownhope
Much Birch
How Caple
Tewkesbury
Corse Lawn
Cleeve Hill
Brecon
Talybont
Ross-on-Wye
CHELTENHAM
Crickhowell
Llandewi Skyrrid
Pencraig
Goodrich
GLOUCESTER
Nant-ddu
Abergavenny
Monmouth
Symonds Yat
Birdlip
Coleford
Clearwell
GLOUCESTERSHIRE
Painswick
MERTHYR TYDFIL
Raglan
Whitebrook
GWENT
Stonehouse
Stroud
Chalford
Tintern
Lydney
Berkeley Road
Minchinhampton
Cirencester
Usk
Amberley
Birchgrove
Neath
WEST GLAMORGAN
MID GLAMORGAN
Blackwood
Llangybi
Berkeley
Ewen
SWANSEA
Chepstow
Thornbury
Wotton under Edge
Crudwell
Port Talbot
Langstone
Tetbury
Aust
Alveston
Rangeworthy
Caerphilly
NEWPORT
Petty France
SWINDON
Sarn Park SA
Pencoed
Miskin
Chipping Sodbury
Old Sodbury
Leigh Delamare SA
Sutton Benger
Bridgend
Cardiff SA
Gordano SA
Tormarton
Castle Combe
Porthcawl
SOUTH GLAMORGAN
CARDIFF
BRISTOL
Ford
Chippenham
AVON
Penarth
Colerne
Corsham
Calne
Box
Llantwit Major
Barry
BATH
Melksham
Chelwood
Hunstrete
Bradford on Avon
WILTSHIRE
Weston-Super-Mare
Blagdon
Limpley Stoke
Freshford
Devizes
BRISTOL CHANNEL
Shipham
Farrington Gurney
Trowbridge
Martinhoe
Woody Bay
Lynton
Lynmouth
Axbridge
Cheddar
Ston Easton
Midsomer Norton
Woolverton
Lympsham
Brent Knoll
Sedgemoor SA
Emborough
Porlock Weir
Burnham-on-Sea
Brendon
Minehead
Oakhill
Frome
Warminster
Highbridge
Porlock
Dunster
Blue Anchor
Watchet
Wells
Shepton Mallet
Bilbrook
Williton
Holford
Simonsbath
Shapwick
Glastonbury
Evercreech
Street
Withypool
Winsford
Bridgwater
Bruton
Mere
Hindon
East Buckland
SOMERSET
Hawkridge
Othery
Somerton
Wincanton
Tisbury
SALISBURY
Dulverston
TAUNTON
Gillingham
South Molton
Wiveliscombe
Templecombe
Exebridge
Bampton
Podimore
Shaftesbury
Ludwell
Taunton Dean SA
Montacute
YEOVIL
Sturminster Newton
Sherborne
Tiverton
Sampford Peverell
Ilminster
Seavington St Mary
Pimperne
Yarcombe
Crewkerne
DEVON
Evershot
Blandford Forum
Chardstock
Tytherleigh
Beaminster
Milton Abbas
DORSET
Honiton
Hawkchurch
Fenny Bridges
Gittisham
Axminster
Piddletrenthide
South Zeal
Stoke Canon
Whimple
Ottery St Mary
Colyton
Uplyme
Charmouth
Winterbourne Abbas
Whiddon Down
Tedburn St Mary
EXETER
Newton Poppleford
Beer
Lyme Regis
Bridport
Dorchester
BOURNEMOUTH
Chagford
Moretonhampstead
Topsham
Sidmouth
Branscombe
Rousdon
West Bexington
Abbotsbury
Wareham
Kennford
Lympstone
Corfe Castle
Lustleigh
Exmouth
WEYMOUTH
Lulworth
Haytor
Bovey Tracey
Dawlish
Bishopsteighton
Portland
Kingsteignton
Teignmouth
Ashburton
Newton Abbot
St Marychurch
Staverton
TORQUAY
South Brent
Paignton
Totnes
Stoke Gabriel
North Huish
Harbertonford
Brixham
Maypool
Dartmouth
Bigbury on Sea
Kingsbridge
Chillington
Thurlestone
Torcross
Hope Cove
Salcombe
East Portlemouth
CHANNEL
SN
SO
SS
ST
SY
SX
Town Names
Hotel
Restaurant
Hotel & Restaurant
SA Service Area
Scale
0
10
20 miles
0
10
20
30 kilometres

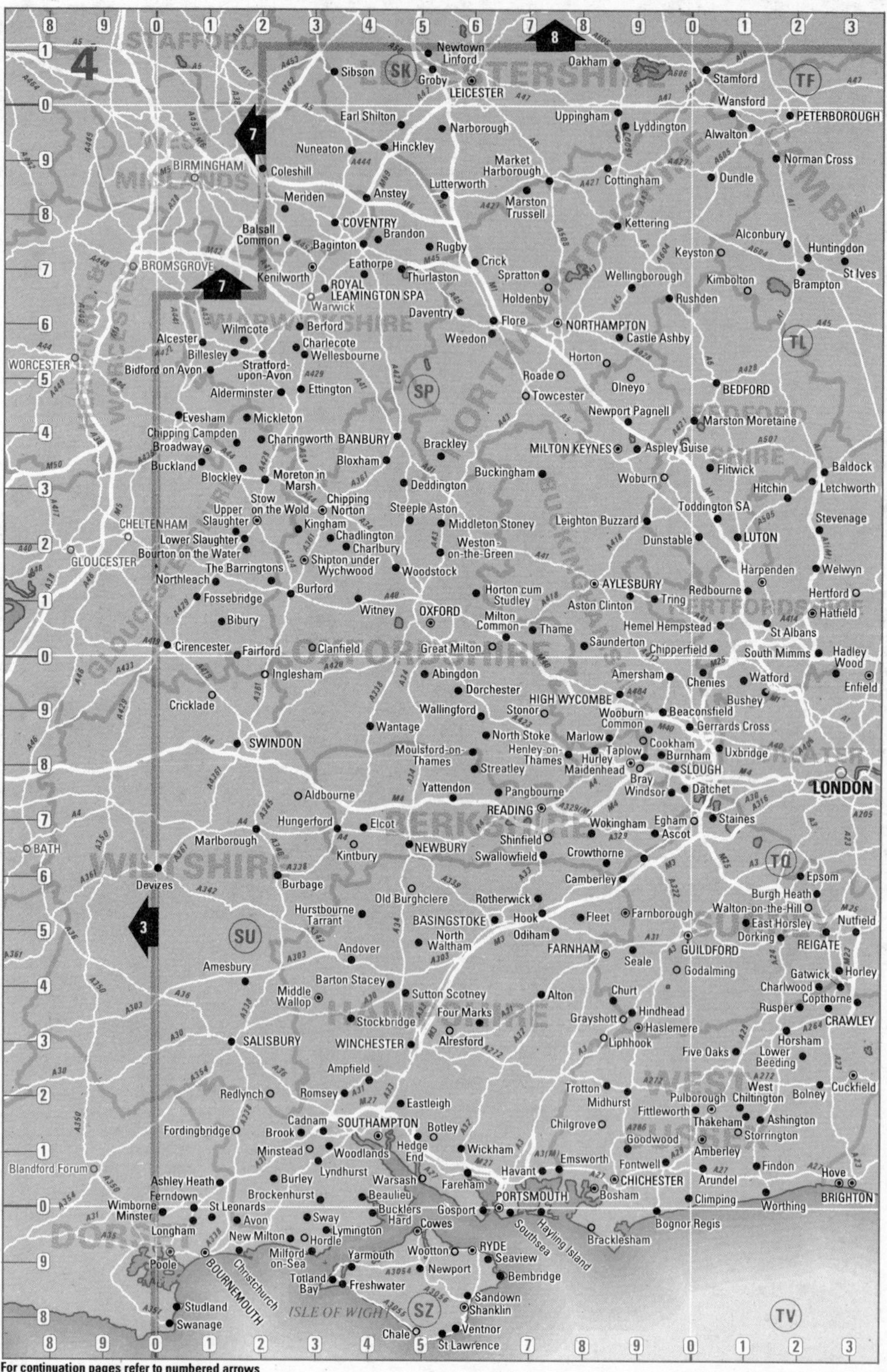

For continuation pages refer to numbered arrows

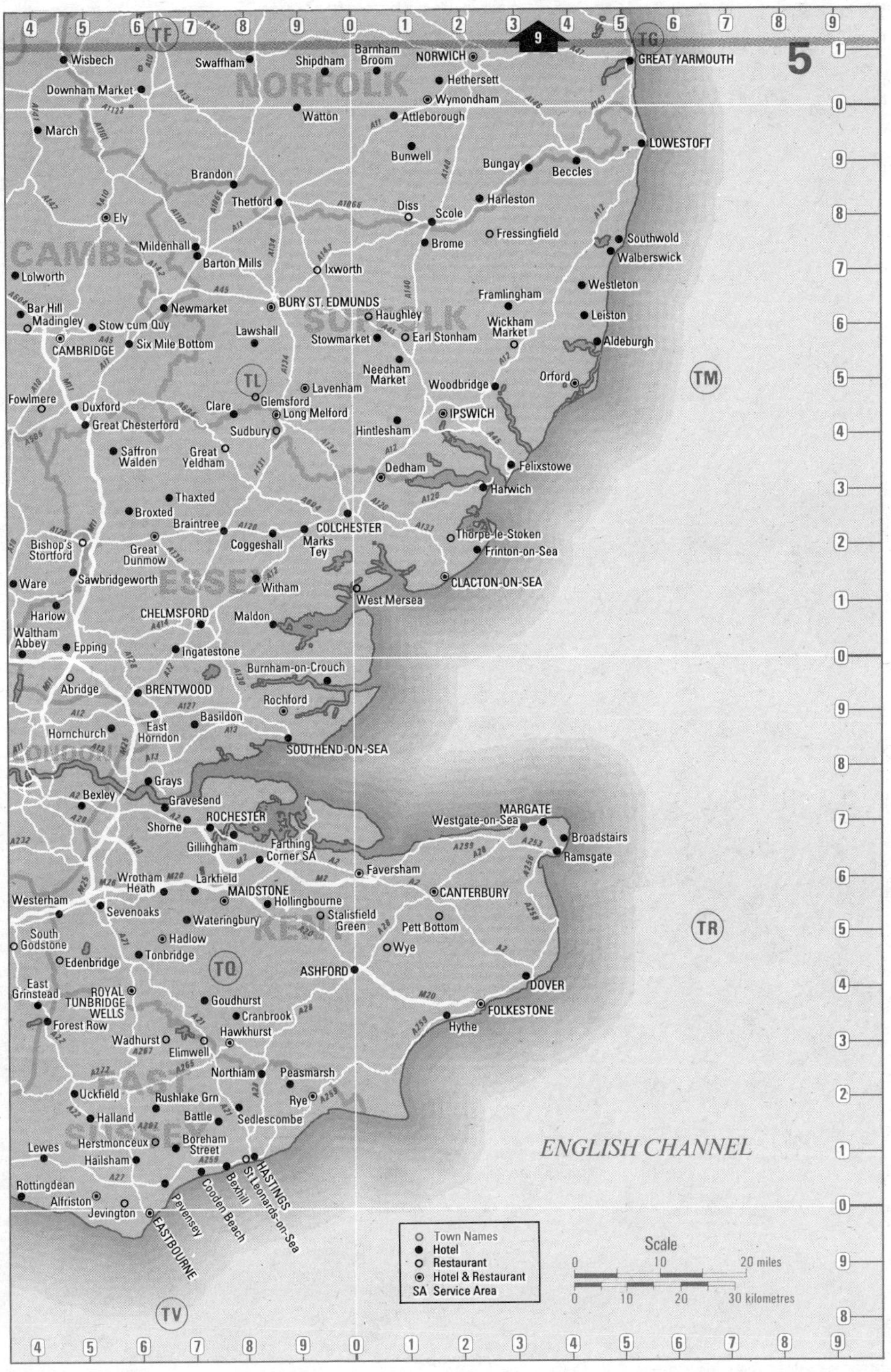

5
9
TF
TG
TL
TM
TQ
TR
TV
NORFOLK
CAMBS
SUFFOLK
ESSEX
LONDON
KENT
EAST
SUSSEX
Wisbech
Swaffham
Shipdham
Barnham Broom
NORWICH
GREAT YARMOUTH
Hethersett
Downham Market
Wymondham
Watton
Attleborough
March
LOWESTOFT
Bunwell
Bungay
Beccles
Brandon
Thetford
Harleston
Diss
Scole
Ely
Fressingfield
Southwold
Mildenhall
Brome
Walberswick
Barton Mills
Ixworth
Lolworth
Westleton
Framlingham
Bar Hill
Newmarket
BURY ST. EDMUNDS
Haughley
Leiston
Madingley
Stow cum Quy
Wickham Market
Lawshall
Stowmarket
Earl Stonham
Aldeburgh
CAMBRIDGE
Six Mile Bottom
Needham Market
Orford
Woodbridge
Lavenham
Glemsford
Fowlmere
Duxford
Clare
Long Melford
IPSWICH
Great Chesterford
Sudbury
Hintlesham
Saffron Walden
Great Yeldham
Felixstowe
Dedham
Harwich
Thaxted
Broxted
COLCHESTER
Braintree
Thorpe-le-Stoken
Coggeshall
Marks Tey
Bishop's Stortford
Great Dunmow
Frinton-on-Sea
CLACTON-ON-SEA
Ware
Sawbridgeworth
Witham
West Mersea
Harlow
CHELMSFORD
Maldon
Waltham Abbey
Epping
Ingatestone
Burnham-on-Crouch
Abridge
BRENTWOOD
Rochford
Basildon
Hornchurch
East Horndon
SOUTHEND-ON-SEA
Grays
Bexley
Gravesend
MARGATE
Westgate-on-Sea
ROCHESTER
Shorne
Broadstairs
Gillingham
Farthing Corner SA
Ramsgate
Faversham
Wrotham Heath
Larkfield
MAIDSTONE
CANTERBURY
Westerham
Hollingbourne
Sevenoaks
Wateringbury
Stalisfield Green
Pett Bottom
South Godstone
Hadlow
Wye
Edenbridge
Tonbridge
ASHFORD
East Grinstead
ROYAL TUNBRIDGE WELLS
DOVER
Goudhurst
FOLKESTONE
Forest Row
Cranbrook
Hythe
Wadhurst
Hawkhurst
Elimwell
Northiam
Peasmarsh
Uckfield
Rye
Rushlake Grn
Halland
Battle
Sedlescombe
Lewes
Herstmonceux
Boreham Street
ENGLISH CHANNEL
Hailsham
HASTINGS
St Leonards-on-Sea
Bexhill
Cooden Beach
Pevensey
Rottingdean
Alfriston
Jevington
EASTBOURNE
Town Names
Hotel
Restaurant
Hotel & Restaurant
SA Service Area
Scale
0
10
20 miles
0
10
20
30 kilometres

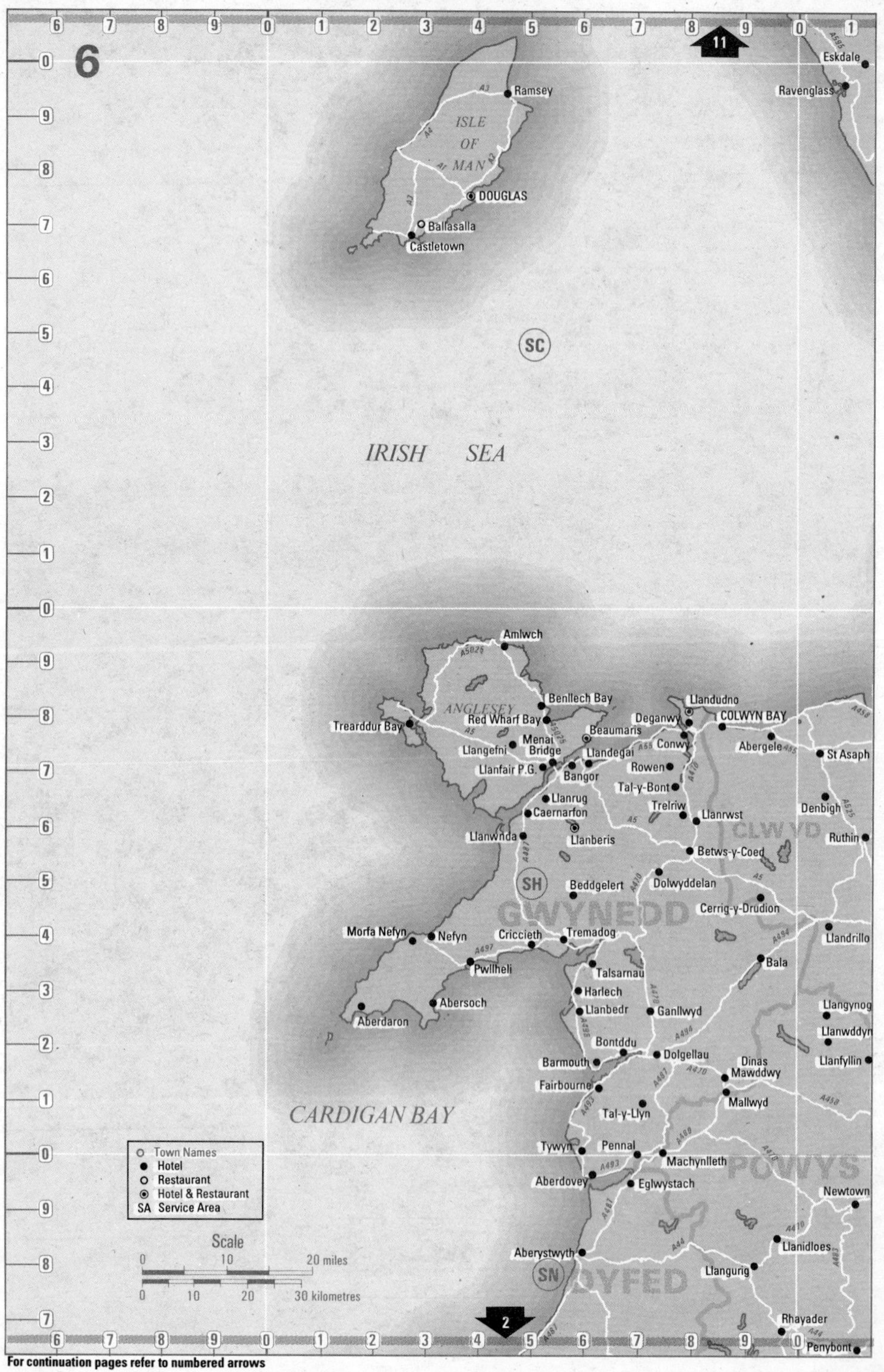

For continuation pages refer to numbered arrows

7
12
NY
NZ
SD
SE
SJ
SK
SO
SP
8
8
4
3
NORTH
YORKSHIRE
LANCASHIRE
WEST
YORKSHIRE
SOUTH
YORKSHIRE
CHESHIRE
DERBYSHIRE
NOTTINGHAMSHIRE
LEICESTERSHIRE
SHROPSHIRE
STAFFORDSHIRE
CLWYD
HEREFORD AND WORCESTER
WARWICKSHIRE
Tebay West SA
Elterwater
Ambleside
Little Langdale
Troutbeck
Hawkshead
Windermere
Coniston
Bowness-on-Windermere
Grizedale
Kendal
Broughton-in-Furness
Blawith
Underbarrow
Newby Bridge
Witherslack
Crooklands
Cartmel
Heversham
Ulverston
Grange-over-Sands
Beetham
Casterton
Kirkby Lonsdale
Silverdale
Carnforth
Melling
BARROW-IN-FURNESS
Rampside
Hornby
MORECAMBE
LANCASTER
Hampson Green
Forton S.A.
Fleetwood
Garstang
Thornton Cleveleys
Ravenstonedale
Richmond
Reeth
Northallerton
Askrigg
Carperby
Leyburn
Hawes
Bainbridge
West Witton
Middleham
Buckden
Arncliffe
Kettlewell
Kilnsey
Austwick
Settle
Threshfield
Grassington
Burnsall
Bolton Abbey
Pateley Bridge
Ripon
Malton
HARROGATE
YORK
Skipton
Gisburn
Ilkley
Kildwick
Keighley
Bingley
Shipley
Haworth
BRADFORD
LEEDS
Hurst Green
Barton
Longridge
Nelson
BLACKPOOL
Bartle
PRESTON
Langho
Burnley
Lytham St Anne's
Blackburn
Accrington
Hebden Bridge
Halifax
Todmorden
Darwen
Hawtenstall
Sowerby Bridge
Brighouse
Holywell Green
HUDDERSFIELD
Leyland
SOUTHPORT
Chorley
Charnock Richard
Ramsbottom
Ripponden
Wrightington
Adlington
Rochdale
Parbold
Horwich
Bury
Birch S.A.
Standish
Bolton
Upholland
Wigan
Oldham
Leigh
Worsley
Ashton-under-Lyne
DONCASTER
Blundellsands
Haydock
Salford
MANCHESTER
Glossop
Bootle
St Helens
Newton-le-Willows
Wallasey
LIVERPOOL
BIRKENHEAD
Romiley
Stockport
Altrincham
Widnes
Warrington
Lymm
Marple
SHEFFIELD
Manchester Airport
Bramhall
Disley
Bebington
Runcorn
Bromborough
Handforth
Woodford
Heswall
Stretton
Daresbury
Bucklow Hill
Wilmslow
St Andrew
Parkgate
Thornton Hough
Mottram
Pott Shrigley
Holywell
Sandiway
Knutsford
Prestbury
Bollington
Puddington
Northwich
Chalford
MACCLESFIELD
Buxton
Halkyn
Holmes Chapel
Normanton
Northop Hall
CHESTER
Longnor
Tarporley
Sandbach
CREWE
Hartington
MANSFIELD
Matlock
Rossett
Marford
Alsager
Talke
Leek
Broxton
Bottomhouse
WREXHAM
Marchwiel
Nantwich
Thorpe
Fenny Bentley
STOKE-ON-TRENT
Waterhouses
Ashbourne
Newcastle-under-Lyme
Ruabon
Redbrook
Alton
Whitchurch
NOTTINGHAM
Llangollen
Erbistock
Hanchurch
Glyn Ceiriog
DERBY
Ellesmere
Uttoxeter
Market Drayton
Stone
LLanarmon Dyffryn Ceiriog
Whittington
Oswestry
Eccleshall
Weston-under-Redcastle
Hodnet
Bretby
Rangemore
STAFFORD
LOUGHBOROUGH
Newport
Rugeley
Barton under Needwood
Donnington
SHREWSBURY
TELFORD
Alrewas
Cannock
Wellington
Lichfield
Welshpool
Shifnal
Hilton Park S.A.
LEICESTER
Tamworth
Norton
Wolverhampton
Walsall
Much Wenlock
Pattingham
Streetly
Sutton Coldfield
Great Barr
Montgomery
Worfield
Himley
Wishaw
Church Stretton
Bishop's Castle
Bridgnorth
Dudley
West Bromwich
Coleshill
Oldbury
BIRMINGHAM
Alveley
Birmingham Airport
Stourbridge
National Exhibition Centre
Frankley
Clun
Solihull
Cleobury Mortimer
COVENTRY
Ludlow
Bewdley
Kidderminster
Dorridge
Chaddesley Corbett
Kington
BROMSGROVE
Stourport-on-Severn
Crossway Green
Brinfield
Abberley
Redditch
Henley in Arden
ROYAL LEAMINGTON SPA
Shrawley
Warwick

For continuation pages refer to numbered arrows

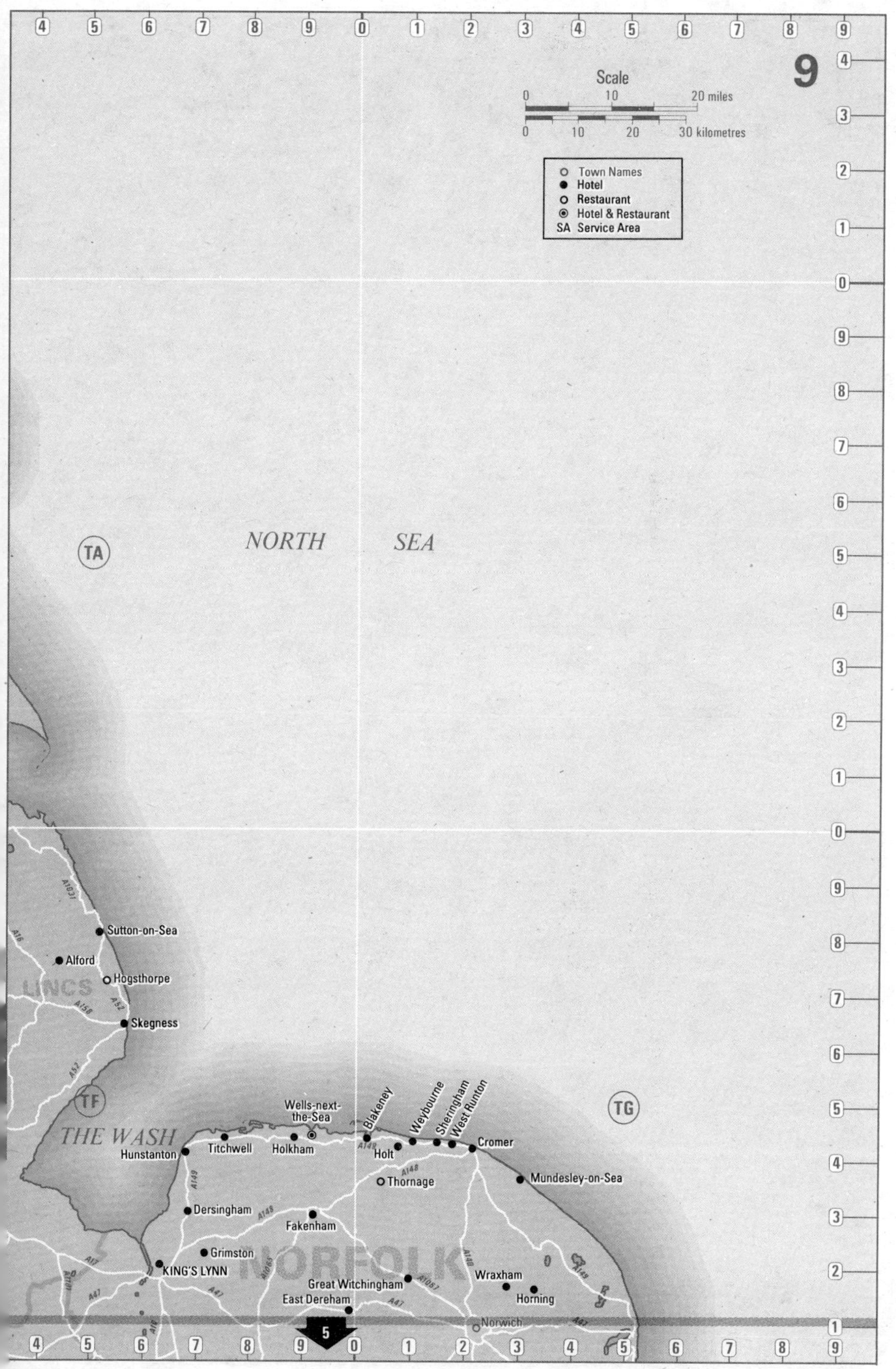
9
Scale
0 10 20 miles
0 10 20 30 kilometres
Town Names
Hotel
Restaurant
Hotel & Restaurant
SA Service Area
NORTH SEA
TA
TF
TG
LINCS
NORFOLK
THE WASH
Sutton-on-Sea
Alford
Hogsthorpe
Skegness
Hunstanton
Titchwell
Holkham
Wells-next-the-Sea
Blakeney
Weybourne
Sheringham
West Runton
Cromer
Holt
Thornage
Mundesley-on-Sea
Dersingham
Fakenham
Grimston
KING'S LYNN
Great Witchingham
East Dereham
Wraxham
Horning
Norwich
5

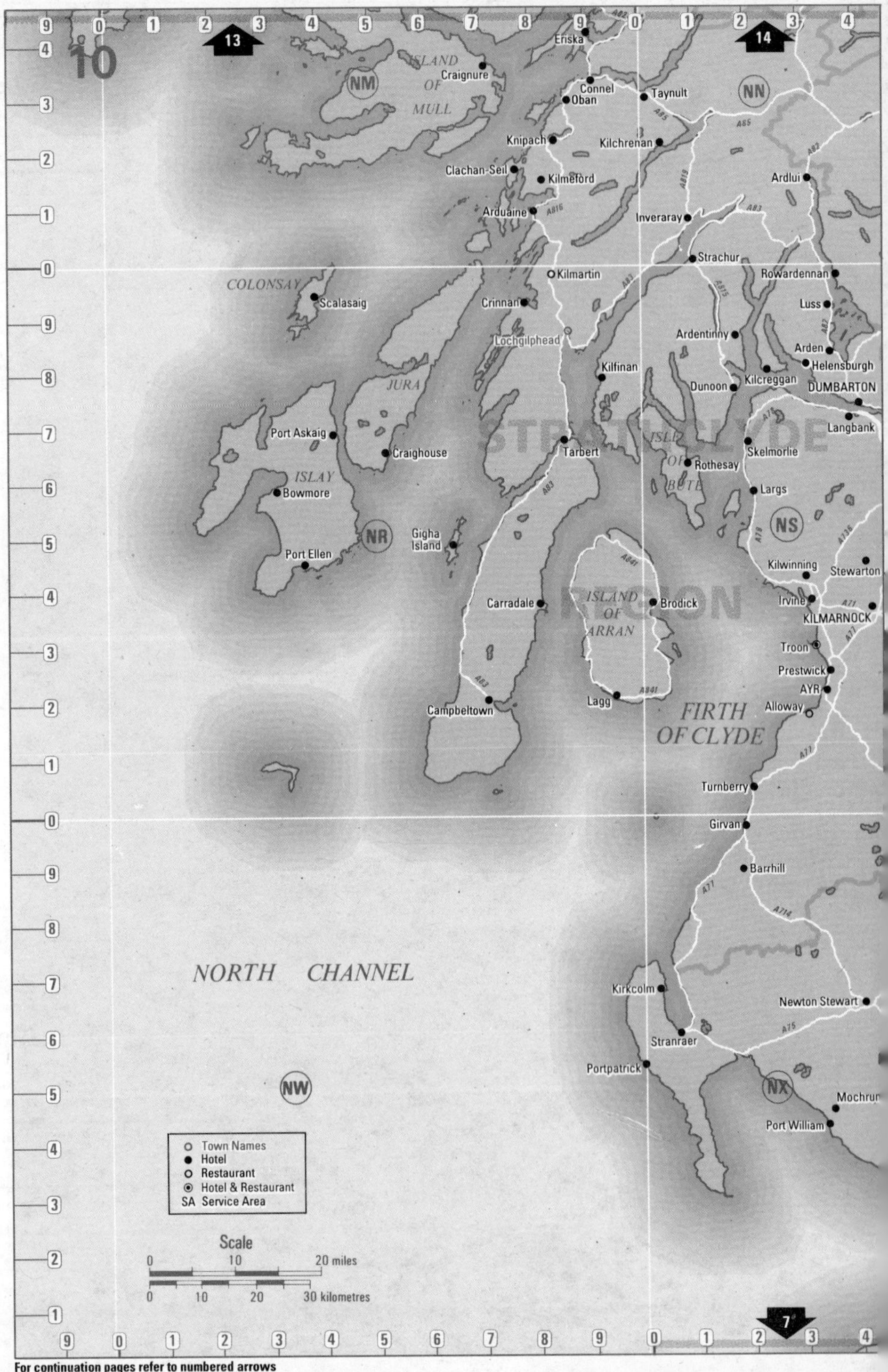

For continuation pages refer to numbered arrows

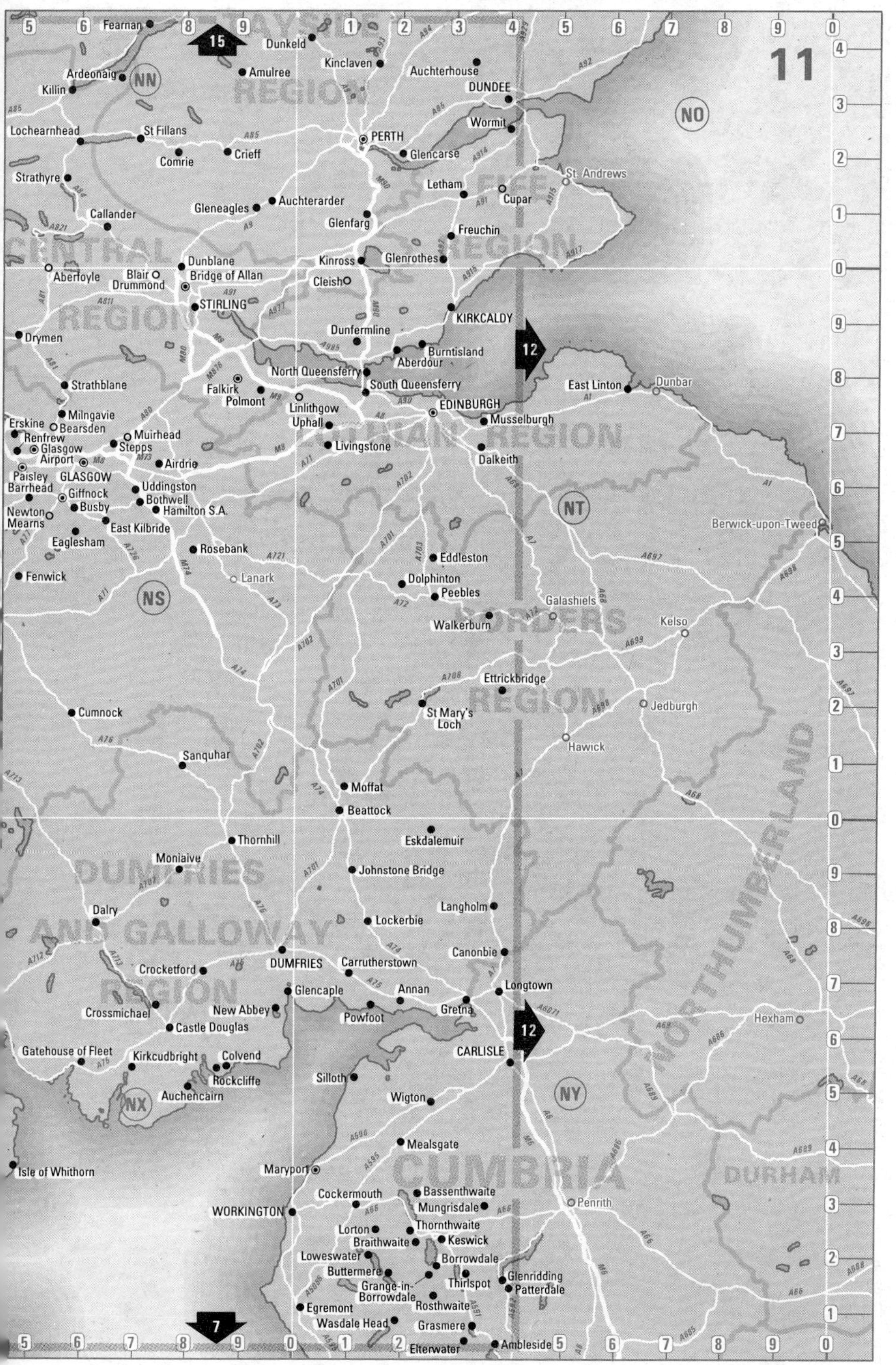

11
15
12
12
7
NN
NO
NT
NS
NX
NY
TAYSIDE REGION
FIFE REGION
CENTRAL REGION
LOTHIAN REGION
BORDERS REGION
DUMFRIES AND GALLOWAY REGION
CUMBRIA
NORTHUMBERLAND
DURHAM
Fearnan
Dunkeld
Kinclaven
Auchterhouse
DUNDEE
Ardeonaig
Killin
Amulree
Wormit
Lochearnhead
St Fillans
PERTH
Glencarse
Comrie
Crieff
Strathyre
St. Andrews
Letham
Cupar
Gleneagles
Auchterarder
Callander
Glenfarg
Freuchin
Kinross
Glenrothes
Dunblane
Aberfoyle
Blair Drummond
Bridge of Allan
Cleish
STIRLING
KIRKCALDY
Drymen
Dunfermline
Burntisland
Aberdour
North Queensferry
South Queensferry
Strathblane
Falkirk
Polmont
Linlithgow
East Linton
Dunbar
EDINBURGH
Milngavie
Uphall
Musselburgh
Erskine
Bearsden
Renfrew
Muirhead
Glasgow Airport
Stepps
Livingstone
Dalkeith
Paisley
GLASGOW
Airdrie
Barrhead
Giffnock
Uddingston
Bothwell
Newton Mearns
Busby
Hamilton S.A.
East Kilbride
Berwick-upon-Tweed
Eaglesham
Rosebank
Eddleston
Fenwick
Lanark
Dolphinton
Peebles
Galashiels
Kelso
Walkerburn
Ettrickbridge
Jedburgh
St Mary's Loch
Cumnock
Hawick
Sanquhar
Moffat
Beattock
Eskdalemuir
Thornhill
Moniaive
Johnstone Bridge
Langholm
Dalry
Lockerbie
Canonbie
DUMFRIES
Carrutherstown
Crocketford
Annan
Longtown
Glencaple
Gretna
New Abbey
Powfoot
Hexham
Crossmichael
Castle Douglas
CARLISLE
Gatehouse of Fleet
Kirkcudbright
Colvend
Rockcliffe
Silloth
Auchencairn
Wigton
Mealsgate
Isle of Whithorn
Maryport
Cockermouth
Bassenthwaite
Penrith
WORKINGTON
Mungrisdale
Lorton
Thornthwaite
Braithwaite
Keswick
Loweswater
Borrowdale
Buttermere
Glenridding
Grange-in-Borrowdale
Thirlspot
Patterdale
Egremont
Rosthwaite
Wasdale Head
Grasmere
Elterwater
Ambleside

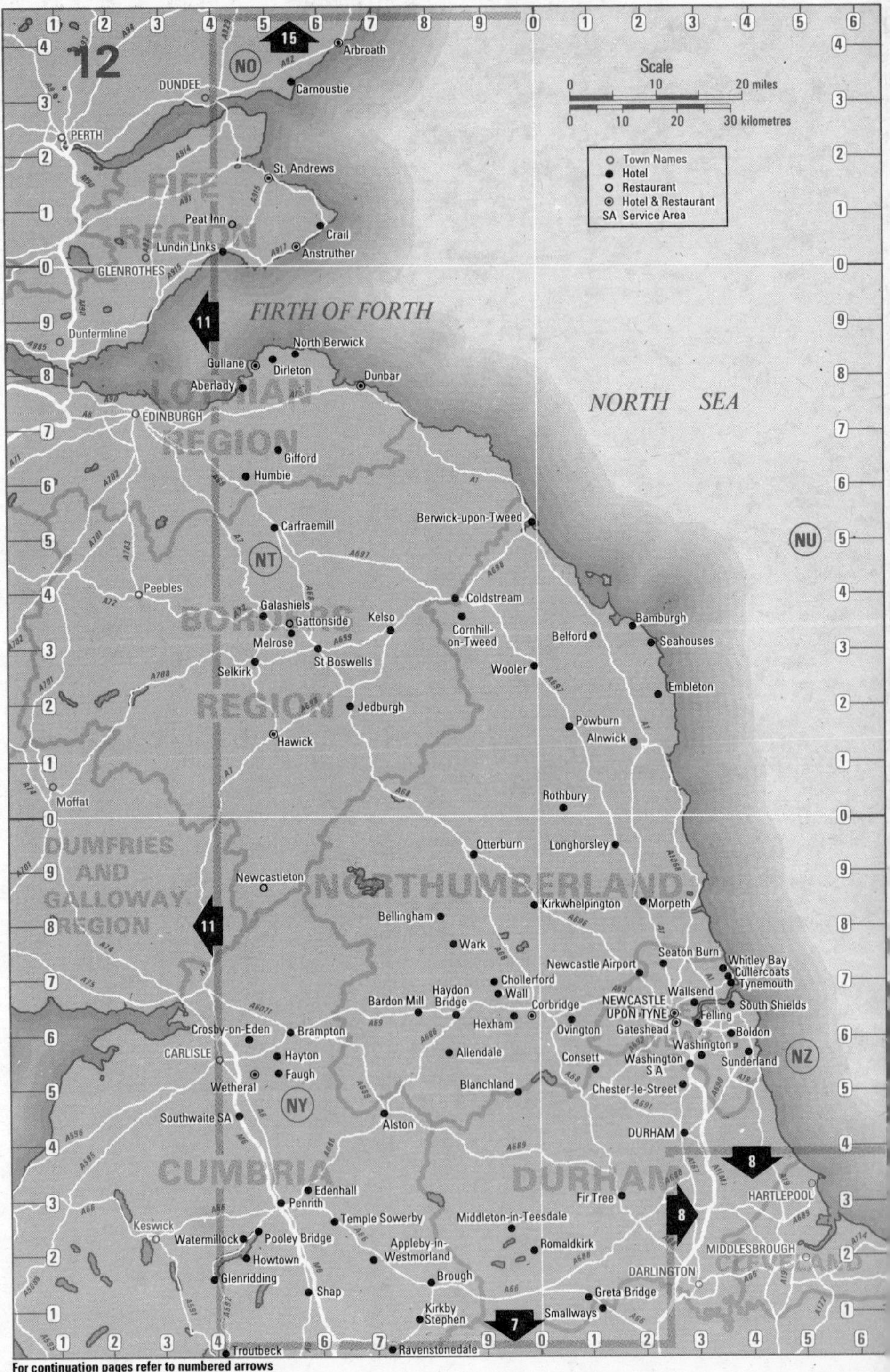

For continuation pages refer to numbered arrows

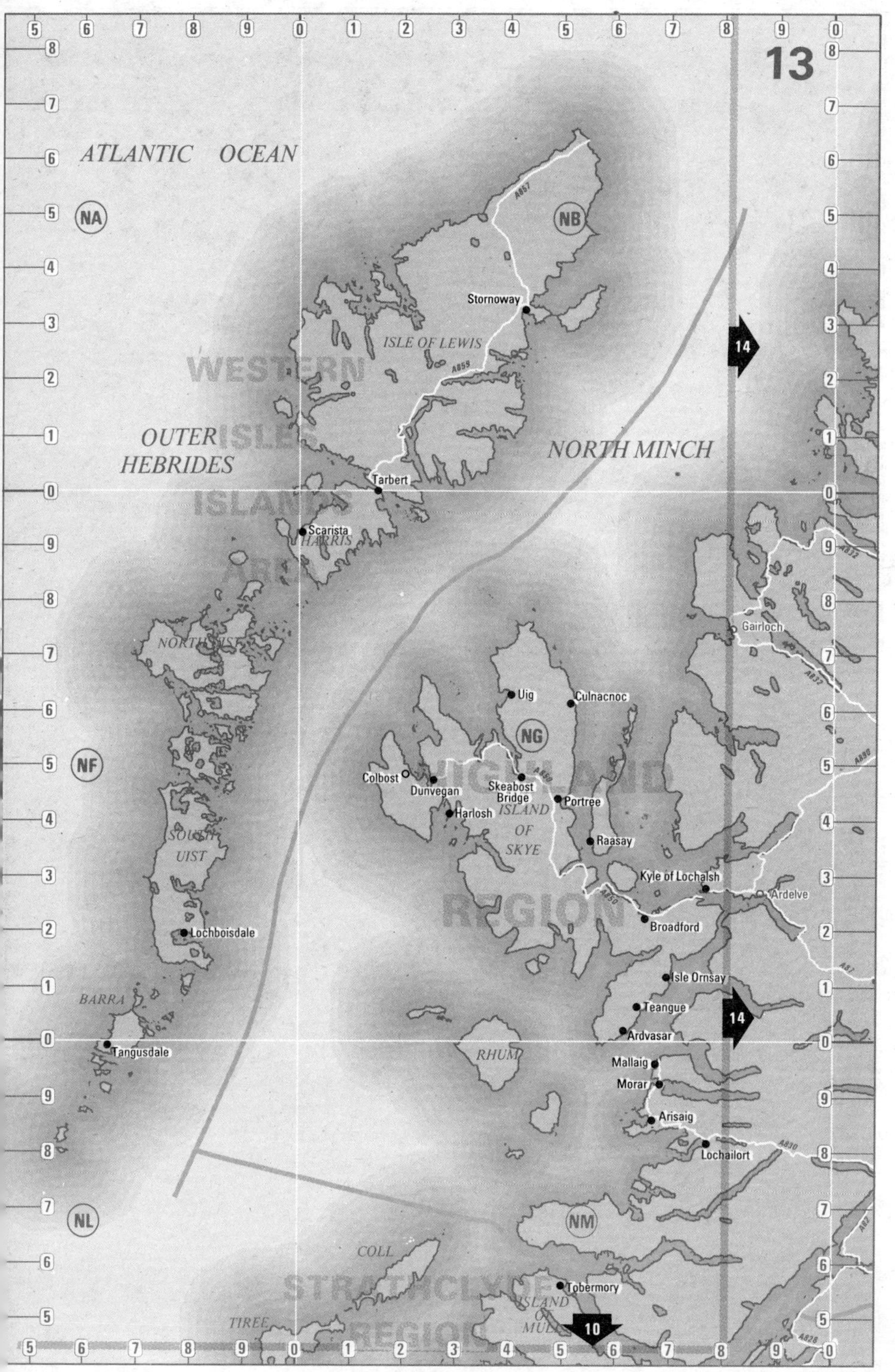

13
ATLANTIC OCEAN
NA
NB
Stornoway
ISLE OF LEWIS
A857
A859
WESTERN
OUTER
HEBRIDES
ISLES
ISLANDS
AREA
NORTH MINCH
Tarbert
Scarista
HARRIS
NORTH UIST
14
Gairloch
Uig
Culnacnoc
NG
NF
Colbost
Dunvegan
Skeabost Bridge
Portree
HIGHLAND
Harlosh
ISLAND OF SKYE
Raasay
SOUTH UIST
Kyle of Lochalsh
Ardelve
REGION
Broadford
Lochboisdale
Isle Ornsay
Teangue
BARRA
Ardvasar
Tangusdale
RHUM
Mallaig
Morar
Arisaig
Lochailort
NL
NM
COLL
STRATHCLYDE
Tobermory
ISLAND OF MULL
TIREE
REGION
10

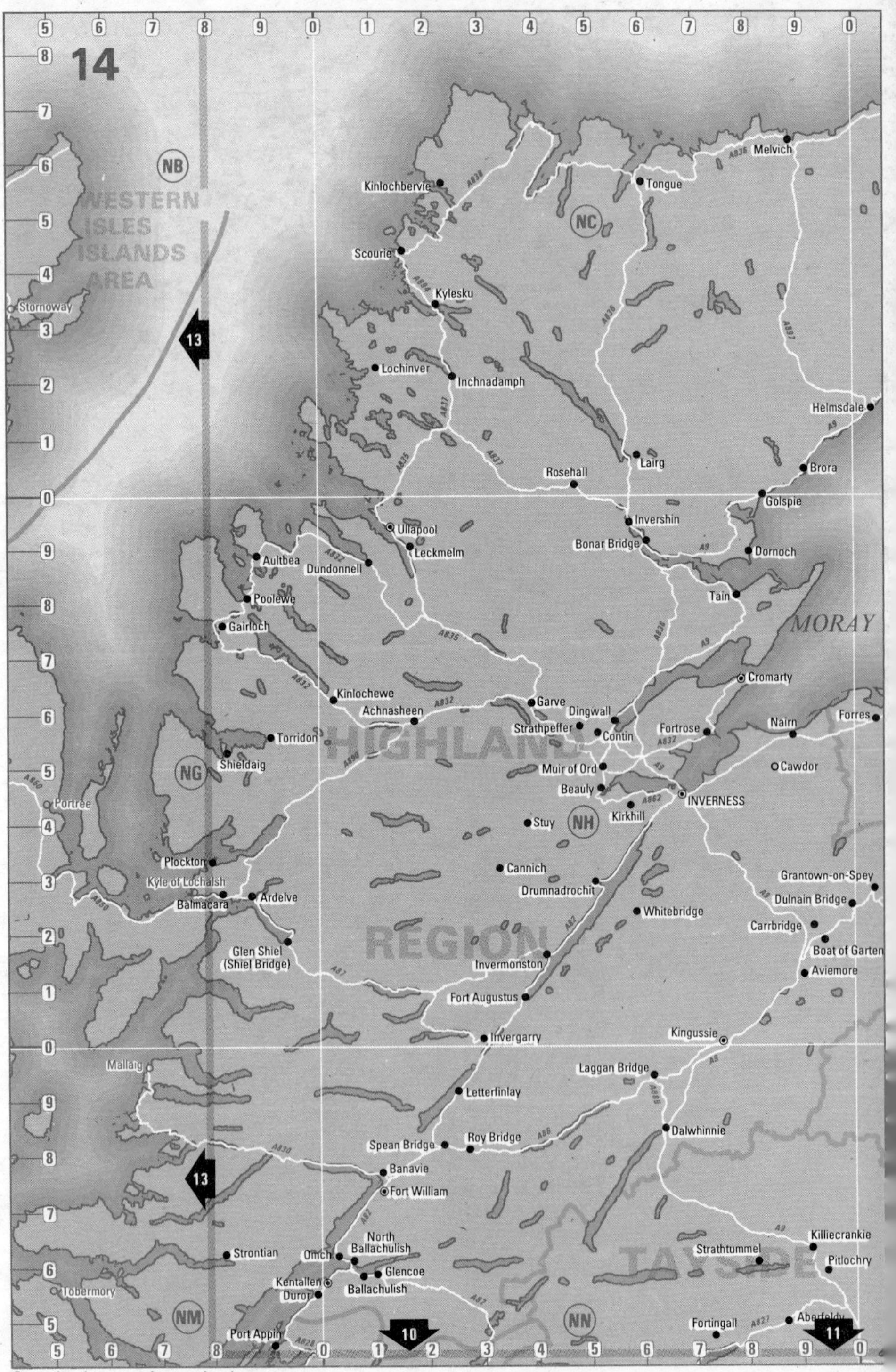

For continuation pages refer to numbered arrows

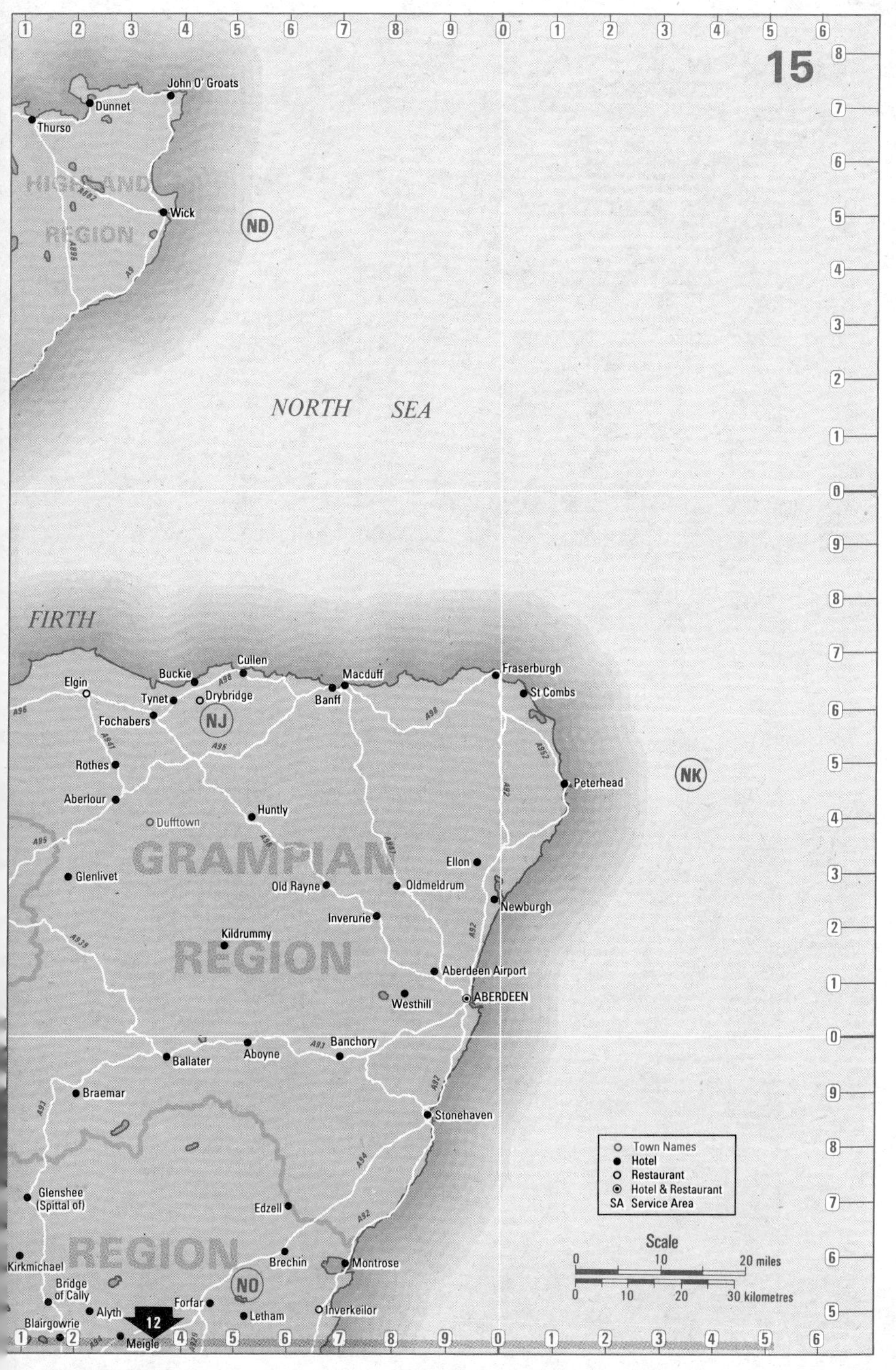
15
John O' Groats
Dunnet
Thurso
HIGHLAND
REGION
Wick
ND
NORTH SEA
FIRTH
Cullen
Buckie
Macduff
Fraserburgh
Elgin
Tynet
Drybridge
Banff
St Combs
Fochabers
NJ
Rothes
Peterhead
NK
Aberlour
Huntly
Dufftown
GRAMPIAN
REGION
Ellon
Glenlivet
Old Rayne
Oldmeldrum
Newburgh
Inverurie
Kildrummy
Aberdeen Airport
Westhill
ABERDEEN
Banchory
Aboyne
Ballater
Braemar
Stonehaven
Town Names
Hotel
Restaurant
Hotel & Restaurant
SA Service Area
Glenshee (Spittal of)
Edzell
Scale
0
10
20 miles
0
10
20
30 kilometres
REGION
Kirkmichael
Brechin
Montrose
Bridge of Cally
NO
Forfar
Alyth
Letham
Inverkeilor
Blairgowrie
12
Meigle

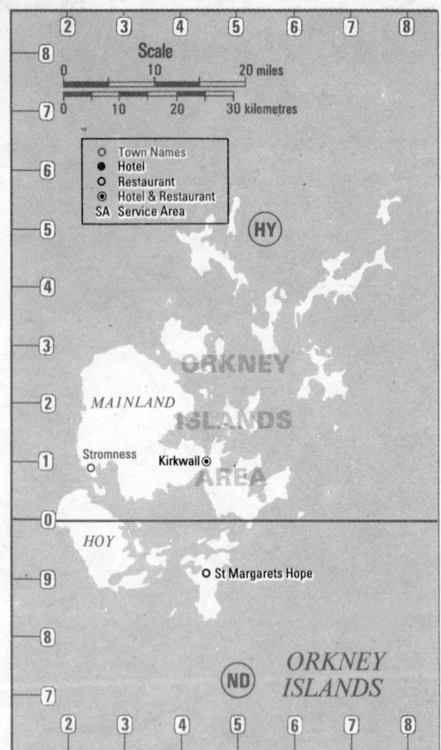

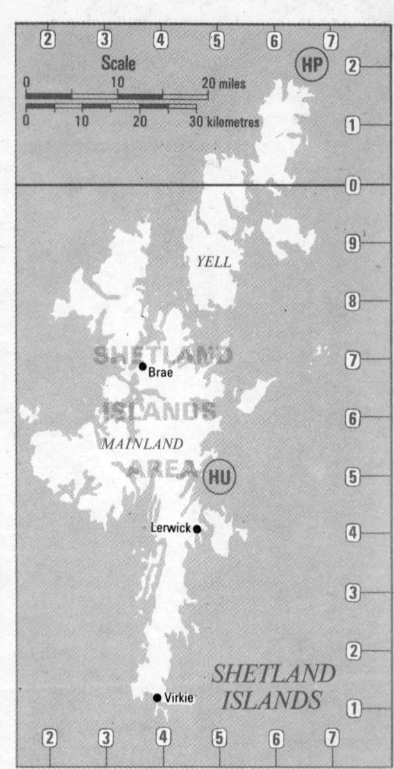

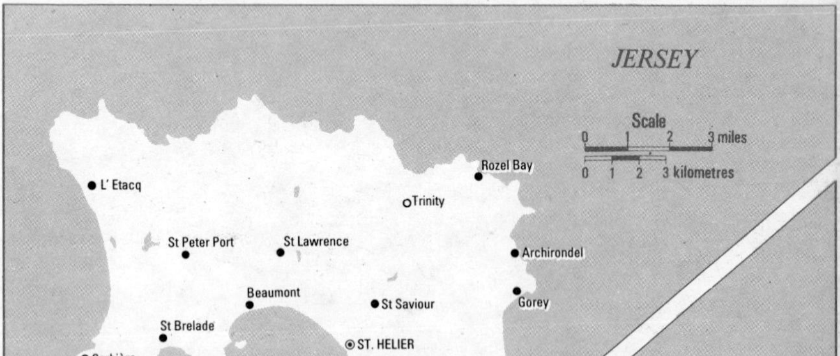

JERSEY

Scale
0 1 2 3 miles
0 1 2 3 kilometres

Rozel Bay
L' Etacq
Trinity
St Peter Port
St Lawrence
Archirondel
Beaumont
St Saviour
Gorey
St Brelade
ST. HELIER
Corbière

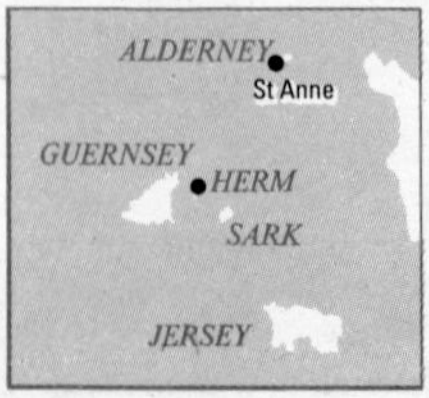

ALDERNEY
St Anne
GUERNSEY
HERM
SARK
JERSEY

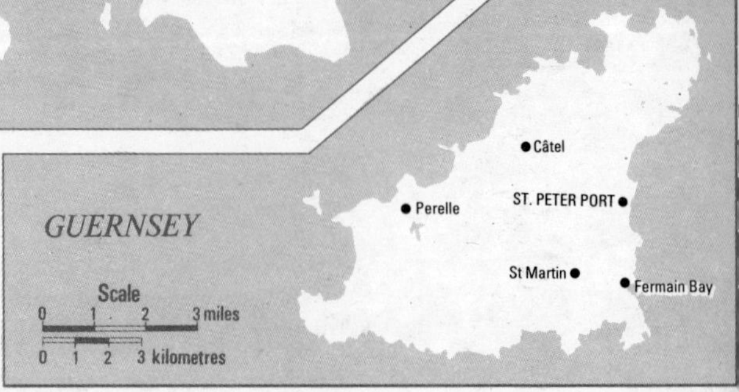

GUERNSEY

Scale
0 1 2 3 miles
0 1 2 3 kilometres

Câtel
Perelle
ST. PETER PORT
St Martin
Fermain Bay